SOUTH
AFRICA
YEARBOOK
2005/06

Foreword

South Africa has entered the second year of the Second Decade of Freedom, fully geared to meet the popular mandate to halve unemployment and poverty by 2014.

Government has adopted a detailed programme of action, encompassing attention to improving the capacity of the State; building a growing economy that benefits all; expanding social services; and entrenching peace, security and democratic governance in our region and continent.

This programme outlines detailed steps that need to be taken in each area of social endeavour and, where appropriate, allocates timelines for each project.

It is in part a measure of the encouraging possibilities that our country faces that what is now the longest recorded upward economic trend in our history, gathered further momentum in the past year.

However, rather than merely celebrate this positive environment, government has joined hands with social partners to develop a comprehensive initiative that will raise the range of growth to higher levels, and do so in a manner that benefits all South Africans. The Accelerated and Shared Growth Initiative for South Africa is centred on higher rates of public and private investments as well as expanding work opportunities.

As the *South Africa Yearbook 2005/06* goes to print, the initiative is being developed in further detail and government is consulting with social partners to ensure that the final product unites us all in pursuit of common development and growth objectives.

The *South Africa Yearbook* highlights the policies and programmes that have brought our country to the point at which we can proclaim with confidence that tomorrow looks much brighter than yesterday.

Together we can and shall indeed do the many more things that need to be done to build a South Africa that truly belongs to all.

President Thabo Mbeki
November 2005

South Africa Yearbook 2005/06
Thirteenth edition
Originally published as *South Africa Official Yearbook*
ISSN 0302-0681

Editor: Delien Burger

Assistant editors: Elias Tibane and Louise van Niekerk

Photographs supplied by the Government Communication and Information System (GCIS), Department of Water Affairs and Forestry, Department of Foreign Affairs, Department of Housing, PictureNet Africa, Satour, Rand Water.

Proofreader: Kathleen Bartels for Wordsmiths

Design and layout: Adam Rumball of STE Publishers

Indexer: Mirié van Rooyen

Suggested reading lists: Prof Reuben Musiker

Compiled, edited and published by GCIS
Private Bag X745, Pretoria, 0001
Telephone: (012) 314 2911, Fax: (012) 323 0557
Website: *www.gcis.gov.za*

Co-published by STE Publishers, PO Box 93446, Yeoville 2143 Tel: +27 11 484 7824

Publishing consultant: Zann Hoad – Sharp Sharp Media +27 11 442-8707

Printed and bound in the Republic of South Africa by Formeset Printers

ISBN 1-919855-70-X
ISSN 1022-9515
Library of Congress Catalogue Card Number: 57-40609

The *South Africa Yearbook* is compiled and edited by the GCIS. The editorial staff has taken all reasonable care to ensure correctness of facts and statistics. However, any person requiring formal confirmation of any data in the *Yearbook*, or more detailed specific information, should consult the contributors. The information is also available on Government Online *[ww.gov.za]*.

Unless otherwise specified, the information contained in this book was the latest available in October 2005.

Contents

The land and its people

The combination of South Africa's landscape, people, history and culture makes it one of the most enchanting countries in the world.

The country boasts some of the world's most breathtaking scenery, and features an extraordinary variety of bird and wildlife species, including the Big Five (lion, leopard, elephant, buffalo and rhino), as well as a spectacular variety of plants with some 10% of the world's flowering species found within its borders.

South Africa is often called the Cradle of Humankind, for this is where archaeologists discovered 2,5-million-year-old fossils of our earliest ancestors, as well as 100 000-year-old remains of modern man.

The people

The results of the second democratic Census (Census 2001) were released in July 2003. On the night of 10 October 2001, there were 44 819 778 people in South Africa. Of these, 79% classified themselves as African; 9,6% as white; 8,9% as coloured; and 2,5% as Indian/Asian.

According to Statistics South Africa (Stats SA), the mid-2005 population was estimated at about 46,9 million. Africans were in the majority (about 37,2 million) and constituted about 79% of the total South African population. The white population was estimated at 4,4 million, the coloured population at 4,1 million and the Indian/Asian population at 1,1 million.

The provincial estimates show that KwaZulu-Natal has 20,6% of the population, followed by Gauteng with 19,2% and the Eastern Cape with 15%. The Northern Cape has the smallest share of the population, namely 1,9%.

The South African population consists of the following groups: the Nguni (consisting of the Zulu, Xhosa, Ndebele and Swazi people); the Sotho-Tswana, who include the Southern, Northern and Western Sotho (Tswana people); the Tsonga; Venda; Afrikaners; English; coloureds; Indians; and those who have immigrated to South Africa from the rest of Africa, Europe and Asia and maintain a strong cultural identity. A few remaining members of the Khoi and the San also live in South Africa.

Languages

According to the Constitution of the Republic of South Africa, 1996 (Act 108 of 1996), everyone has the right to use the language and to participate in the cultural life of their choice, but no one may do so in a manner inconsistent with any provision of the Bill of Rights. Each person also has the right to instruction in their language of choice where this is reasonably practicable.

Official languages
The Constitution recognises 11 official languages, namely Afrikaans, English, isiNdebele, isiXhosa, isiZulu, Sesotho sa Leboa, Sesotho, Setswana, siSwati, Tshivenda and Xitsonga.

Recognising the historically diminished use and status of the indigenous languages, the Constitution expects government to implement positive measures to elevate the status and advance the use of these languages.

According to Census 2001, isiZulu is the mother tongue of 23,8% of the population, followed by isiXhosa (17,6%), Afrikaans (13,3%), Sesotho sa Leboa (9,4%), and English and Setswana (8,2% each).

The least-spoken indigenous language in South Africa is isiNdebele, which is spoken by 1,6% of the population.

Although English is the mother tongue of only 8,2% of the population, it is the language most widely understood, and the second language of the majority of South Africans. However, government is committed to promoting all the official languages.

South Africa has 12 public holidays:
New Year's Day – 1 January
Human Rights Day – 21 March
Good Friday – Friday before Easter Sunday
Family Day – Monday after Easter Sunday
Freedom Day – 27 April
Workers' Day – 1 May
Youth Day – 16 June
National Women's Day – 9 August
Heritage Day – 24 September
Day of Reconciliation – 16 December
Christmas Day – 25 December
Day of Goodwill – 26 December
If any of these days falls on a Sunday, the following Monday becomes a public holiday.

Language policy
The National Language Service (NLS) provides a range of language services for official documentation, develops and promotes national language policy, and advises on standardising and disseminating information on a range of terminology. The NLS is responsible for implementing the National Language Policy Framework (NLPF).

The NLS functions as government's professional language support system by translating official documents in all official languages. Its terminology service assists with the development and modernisation of the technical vocabularies of the official languages. The language-planning functions include advising government on the development of language policy and implementation strategies.

National Language Policy Framework
In 2003, Cabinet approved the NLPF, which is guided by the following principles:
• promoting and protecting linguistic and cultural diversity
• supporting democracy through the entrenchment of language equity and language rights
• asserting the view that multilingualism is a resource
• encouraging the learning of other South African languages.

Where government is required to communicate comprehensive information, documents will be published in all 11 official languages; otherwise national government departments will publish documents simultaneously in at least six languages on a rotational basis. Provinces will formulate their own policies according to regional circumstances. The NLPF will be phased in progressively.

The NLS received a once-off amount of R11,9 million in 2004/05 to implement the NLPF.

The implementation of the NLPF will increase the demand for translation and editing work and interpreting services, especially in the African languages.

The language research and development centres are the implementation agencies of South Africa's National Language Policy. In 2004/05, the Department of Arts and Culture spent R9 million to establish nine centres, hosted mainly at tertiary education institutions, to develop South Africa's indigenous languages.

Telephone Interpreting Service of South Africa (TISSA)

A permanent TISSA was launched on 9 May 2005 to promote and develop the previously marginalised indigenous languages. TISSA, the first of its kind in Africa, aims to bridge the communication gap between government and the people. Initiated by the Department of Arts and Culture, TISSA makes South Africa a truly functional multilingual country.

By mid-2005, the project employed more than 60 full-time personnel, including interpreters, project managers and call-centre operators.

Pan South African Language Board (PanSALB)

PanSALB was created in terms of Section 6 of the Constitution and defined by the PanSALB Act, 1995 (Act 59 of 1995). Section 4 sets out the organisation's independence and impartiality, and also provides that no organ of state or any other person is allowed to interfere with the board or its staff's activities.

The board promotes the recognition, implementation and promotion of multilingualism in South Africa, and the development of previously marginalised languages.

PanSALB's vision is to achieve equal status and use of all official languages, including Khoi, Nama, San and South African Sign Language.

The board promotes multilingualism in South Africa by:
- creating conditions for the development and equal use of all official languages
- fostering respect for and encouraging the use of other languages in the country
- encouraging the best use of the country's linguistic resources to enable South Africans to free themselves from all forms of linguistic discrimination, domination and division.

The board may also make recommendations on language legislation, practice and policy, and render advice on the co-ordination of language planning in South Africa.

PanSALB may investigate the alleged violation of any language right, policy or practice. It may also summon any person, body or state organ to give evidence. PanSALB is furthermore empowered to negotiate or mediate in cases of language conflict and attempts to achieve conciliation.

The PanSALB Amendment Act, 1999 (Act 10 of 1999), provided the board with a progressive shift from being a watchdog state organ to addressing the country's language development needs.

The Amendment Act also provided for the establishment of national lexicography units (NLUs) for all official languages. The purpose of these units is to compile monolingual explanatory and other dictionaries to satisfy the needs of the different linguistic communities.

PanSALB received R26,2 million in 2005/06.

National lexicography units

Eleven NLUs have been established and registered as section 21 companies since 2000. They are:
- Afrikaans: Buro van die Woordeboek van die Afrikaanse Taal
- English: Dictionary Unit for South African English
- isiNdebele: IsiHlathululi-Mezwi SesiNdebele
- isiXhosa: isiXhosa NLU
- isiZulu: Isikhungo Sesichazamazwi SesiZulu
- siSwati: Silulu SesiSwati NLU
- Setswana: Setswana NLU
- Sesotho: Sesiu sa Sesotho NLU
- Sesotho sa Lebowa: Sesotho sa Lebowa Dictionary Unit
- Tshivenda: Tshivenda NLU
- Xitsonga: Xitsonga NLU.

The NLUs are financed on a monthly basis by PanSALB.

The Department of Arts and Culture allocated more than R3 million towards its Language Bursary Scheme. In 2004, 26 graduates received funding to complete their postgraduate programmes. This scheme will improve the pool of indigenous language professionals and will encourage South Africans to take up the study of languages as a career.

National language bodies

National language bodies have been established for all 11 official languages.

The Khoi and San national language bodies were officially launched in October 1999 in Upington, Northern Cape, to promote and develop these languages. These language bodies conduct surveys in communities where the Khoi and San languages are spoken, to record and standardise new terminology and words. They liaise closely with other professional bodies that can help to enrich and expand the Khoi and San languages.

These advisory bodies assist PanSALB in its endeavours to promote multilingualism as a national resource, and to take meaningful decisions regarding the standardisation, orthography, terminology and literature issues of each language.

Commission for the Promotion and Protection of the Rights of Cultural, Religious and Linguistic Communities

In 2002, the Commission for the Promotion and Protection of the Rights of Cultural, Religious and Linguistic Communities Act, 2002 (Act 19 of 2002), was passed. The 18-member commission aims to contribute meaningfully and constructively to social transformation and nation-building. Its mission is to promote and develop peace, friendship, humanity, tolerance and national unity among linguistic communities. To achieve this, the commission will:

- be a channel of communication between the State and communities

In a first for South Africa, the Western Cape Language Policy was launched in February 2005 to ensure the linguistic rights of its citizens. Following a five-year consultation process by the Western Cape Language Committee, the policy will ensure equal status and use of the province's three official languages, namely Afrikaans, English and isiXhosa. It also provides for the development and promotion of other national official languages, as well as South African Sign Language and the Khoi and San languages.

- monitor compliance by the State and civil society
- mediate in intercommunity conflict situations and facilitate harmonious co-existence
- facilitate the development of programmes that foster sensitivity, respect and understanding for cultural, religious and linguistic diversity
- lobby government departments and legislative authorities to identify and recommend amending, repealing or enacting laws undermining or supporting those rights, respectively.

Religion

Religious groups

Almost 76% of South Africa's population follows the Christian faith. Other major religious groups are the Hindus, Muslims, Jews and Buddhists. A minority of South Africa's population do not belong to any of the major religions, but regard themselves as traditionalists or of no specific religious affiliation.

Freedom of worship is guaranteed by the Constitution, and the official policy is one of non-interference in religious practices.

Christian churches

There are many official and unofficial ecumenical relations between the various churches. One of the most important of these links is the South African Council of Churches (SACC), although it is not representative of the full spectrum of churches.

The major African indigenous churches, most of the Afrikaans churches, and the Pentecostal and charismatic churches are, as a rule, not members of the SACC, and usually have their own co-ordinating liaison bodies.

Church attendance in South Africa is favourable in both rural and urban areas, and churches are well served by a large number of clerics and officials.

On the whole, training for the church ministry is thorough and intensive, and based on a variety of models, due to the variety of church denominations.

Apart from the work of the churches, a number of Christian organisations (para-church organisations) operate in South Africa, doing missionary and evangelical work and providing aid and training.

Regular religious programmes on radio and television, as well as the abundance of places of worship, reflect the importance of religion in South Africa. Many newspapers carry a daily scriptural message, and various religious magazines, newspapers and books are produced and sold in religious bookshops.

African independent churches (AICs)

The largest grouping of Christian churches is the AICs, and one of the most dramatic aspects of religious affiliation has been the rise of this movement.

Although these churches originally resulted from a number of breakaways from various mission churches (the so-called 'Ethiopian' churches), the AICs have developed their own dynamics and momentum, and continue to flourish. The majority are no longer regarded as Ethiopian churches, but rather Zionist or Apostolic churches. The Pentecostal movement also has its independent offshoots in this group.

The Zion Christian Church (ZCC) is the largest of these churches in South Africa and the largest church overall. The teaching is a syncretism between Christianity and African traditional religion. More than a million members gather twice a year at Zion City, Moria, north-west of Polokwane in Limpopo, at Easter and for the September festival. Traditionally, Easter is the religious highlight of the year. ZCC members, estimated to be over four million, are not obliged to make the pilgrimage, but have loyally observed the tradition for more than 80 years.

The 4 000 or more independent churches have a membership of more than 10 million people, making this movement the single most important religious group in South Africa.

The independent churches attract people from both rural and urban areas. There are, for example, hundreds of separate churches in rural KwaZulu-Natal, and at least 900 from all ethnic groups in the urban complex of Soweto alone. In the northern KwaZulu-Natal and Mpumalanga areas, these churches serve more than half the population.

Afrikaans churches

The Afrikaans churches are predominantly Protestant. Of these churches, the Dutch Reformed Church family of churches in South Africa is the largest and represents some 3,5 million people. The Dutch Reformed Church, also known as the *Nederduitse Gereformeerde Kerk*, is the largest with a total of about 1 200 congregations countrywide.

The other churches are the Uniting Reformed Church in Southern Africa, the Dutch Reformed Church in Africa and the smaller Reformed Church in Africa, with predominantly Indian members. The *Nederduitsch Hervormde Kerk* and the *Gereformeerde Kerk* are regarded as sister churches of the Dutch Reformed Church.

There are several other churches with Afrikaans-speaking adherents, some with very large memberships, such as the Apostolic Faith Mission and the *Afrikaanse Protestantse Kerk*.

The Dutch Reformed Church also has six fully fledged English-language congregations, one congregation for Dutch-speaking people, and four for Portuguese-speaking people. In total, there are about 2 000 members in each of these congregations.

Roman Catholic Church

Although South Africa is predominantly Protestant, the Roman Catholic Church has grown significantly in number and influence in recent years. It works closely with other churches on the socio-political front.

The Southern African Catholic Bishops' Conference, founded more than 50 years ago, is the representative body of this church in southern Africa.

Other Christian churches

Other established churches in South Africa include the Church of the Province of Southern Africa (Anglican Church), the Methodist Church, various Lutheran and Presbyterian churches, and the Congregational Church.

Although the different Baptist groups are not large, they represent a strong church tradition. Together, they form the nucleus of the SACC.

The largest traditional Pentecostal churches are the Apostolic Faith Mission, the Assemblies of God and the Full Gospel Church, but there are numerous others. Many of them enjoy fellowship in groups such as the Church Alliance of South Africa, and operate in all communities.

Hundreds of independent charismatic churches have mushroomed across the country. The largest of these groups is the International Fellowship of Christian Churches (IFCC). Rhema Church, with its 32 000-member congregation, spearheads the movement. The IFCC, representing over 400 churches, is also a member of the SACC.

Also active in South Africa, among the smaller groups, are the Greek Orthodox Church, the Seventh Day Adventist churches, the Church of the Nazarenes and the Salvation Army.

African traditionalists

Because the traditional religion of the African people has a strong cultural base, the various groups have different rituals, but there are certain common features.

A supreme being is generally recognised, but ancestors are of far greater importance, being the deceased elders of the group. They are regarded as part of the community; indispensable links with the spirit world and the powers that control everyday affairs. These ancestors are not gods, but because they play a key part in bringing about either good or ill fortune, maintaining good relations with them is vital; and they have to be appeased regularly through a variety of ritual offerings.

While an intimate knowledge of herbs and other therapeutic techniques, as well as the use of super-

natural powers, can be applied for the benefit of the individual and the community, some practitioners are masters of black magic, creating fear among people. As a result of close contact with Christianity, many people find themselves in a transitional phase somewhere between traditional African religion and Christianity.

Other religions

The majority of Indians who originally came to South Africa were Hindu. They retained their Hindu religion and today, some two-thirds of South Africa's Indians are Hindus. The rest are Muslims and a minority are Christians.

The Muslim community in South Africa is small, but is growing rapidly. The major components of this community are the Cape Malays, who are mainly descendants of Indonesian slaves, and 20% of people of Indian descent.

The Jewish population is less than 100 000. Of these, the majority are Orthodox Jews.

Buddhism is barely organised in South Africa. However, the Nan Hua Buddhist temple has been built at Bronkhorstspruit near Pretoria. The number of Parsees has decreased, while there is a small group of Jains in Durban. Followers of the Baha'i Faith are establishing groups and temples in various parts of the country.

The land

South Africa occupies the southernmost part of the African continent, stretching latitudinally from 22° to 35° S and longitudinally from 17° to 33° E. Its surface area is 1 219 090 km².

The country has common boundaries with Namibia, Botswana and Zimbabwe, while Mozambique and Swaziland lie to the north-east. Completely enclosed by South African territory in the south-east is the mountain kingdom of Lesotho.

To the west, south and east, South Africa borders on the Atlantic and Indian oceans. Isolated, 1 920 km south-east of Cape Town in the Atlantic, lie the Prince Edward and Marion islands, annexed by South Africa in 1947.

Number of individuals by religion (Census 2001)	
Religion	**%**
Christian	79,8%
African traditional	0,3%
Judaism	0,2%
Hinduism	1,2%
Islam	1,5%
Other	0,6%
No religion	15,1%
Undetermined	1,4%
Total	**100%**

The oceans

South Africa is surrounded by the ocean on three sides – to the west, south and east – and has a coastline of about 3 000 km. The coastline is swept by two major ocean currents – the warm south-flowing Mozambique-Agulhas and the cold Benguela. The former skirts the east and south coasts as far as Cape Agulhas, while the Benguela current flows northwards along the west coast as far as southern Angola.

The contrast in temperature between these two currents partly accounts for important differences in climate and vegetation between the east and west coasts of South Africa. It also accounts for the differences in marine life. The cold waters of the west coast are much richer in oxygen, nitrates, phosphates and plankton than those of the east coast. Consequently, the South African fishing industry is centred on the west coast.

The coasts

The coastline itself is an even, closed one with few bays or indentations naturally suitable for harbours. The only ideal natural harbour along the coastline is Saldanha Bay on the west coast. However, the area lacks fresh water and offers no natural lines of penetration to the interior.

Most river-mouths are unsuitable as harbours because large sandbars block entry for most of the year. These bars are formed by the action of waves and currents, and by the intermittent flow, heavy sediment load and steep gradients of most South African rivers. Only the largest rivers, such as the Orange and Limpopo, maintain narrow permanent channels through the bars. For these reasons, the country has no navigable rivers.

Relief features

South Africa's surface area falls into two major physiographic categories: the interior plateau, and the land between the plateau and the coast. Forming the boundary between these two areas is the Great Escarpment, the most prominent and continuous relief feature of the country. Its height above sea level varies from about 1 500 m in the dolerite-capped Roggeveld scarp in the south-west, to a height of 3 482 m in the KwaZulu-Natal Drakensberg.

Inland from the escarpment lies the interior plateau, which is the southern continuation of the great African plateau stretching north to the Sahara Desert.

The plateau itself is characterised by wide plains with an average height of 1 200 m above sea level.

The dissected Lesotho plateau, which is more than 3 000 m above sea level, is the most prominent. In general, the escarpment forms the highest parts of the plateau.

Between the Great Escarpment and the coast lies an area which varies in width from 80 to 240 km in the east and south, and a mere 60 to 80 km in the west. At least three major subdivisions are recognised: the eastern plateau slopes, the Cape folded belt and adjacent regions, and the western plateau slopes.

Climatic features

The subtropical location, on either side of 30° S, accounts for the warm temperate conditions so typical of South Africa, making it a popular destination for foreign tourists.

The country also falls squarely within the subtropical belt of high pressure, making it dry, with an abundance of sunshine.

The wide expanses of ocean on three sides of South Africa have a moderating influence on its climate. More apparent, however, are the effects of the warm Agulhas and the cold Benguela currents along the east and west coasts respectively. While Durban (east coast) and Port Nolloth (west coast) lie more or less on the same latitude, there is a difference of at least 6° C in their mean annual temperatures.

Gale-force winds are frequent on the coasts, especially in the south-western and southern coastal areas.

Rainfall

South Africa has an average annual rainfall of 450 mm, compared with a world average of 860 mm.

Sixty-five percent of the country receives less than 500 mm per year, which is generally accepted as the minimum amount required for successful dry-land farming. Twenty-one percent of the country, mainly the arid west, receives less than 200 mm per year.

In Cape Town, the capital city of the Western Cape, the average rainfall is highest in the winter months, while in the capital cities of the other eight provinces, the average rainfall is highest during summer.

South Africa's rainfall is unreliable and unpredictable. Large fluctuations in the average annual rainfall are the rule rather than the exception in most areas of the country. Below-average annual rainfall is more commonly recorded than above-average total annual rainfall. South Africa is periodically afflicted by drastic and prolonged droughts, which often end in severe floods.

Temperatures

Temperature conditions in South Africa are characterised by three main features. Firstly, temperatures tend to be lower than in other regions at similar latitudes, for example, Australia. This is due primarily to the greater elevation of the subcontinent above sea level.

Secondly, despite a latitudinal span of 13 degrees, average annual temperatures are remarkably uniform throughout the country. Owing to the increase in the height of the plateau towards the north-east, there is hardly any increase in temperature from south to north as might be expected.

The third feature is the striking contrast between temperatures on the east and west coasts.

Temperatures above 32° C are fairly common in summer, and frequently exceed 38° C in the lower Orange River Valley and the Mpumalanga Lowveld.

Frost, humidity and fog

Frost often occurs on the interior plateau during cold, clear, winter nights, with ice forming on still pools and in water pipes. The frost season (April to October), is longest over the eastern and southern plateau areas bordering on the escarpment. Frost decreases to the north, while the coast is virtually frost-free. Average annual relative humidity readings show that, in general, the air is driest over the west-

ern interior and the plateau. Along the coast, the humidity is much higher, and at times may rise to 85%. Low stratus clouds and fog frequently occur over the cool west coast, particularly during summer. The only other area that commonly experiences fog is the 'mist belt' along the eastern foothills of the escarpment.

Sunshine

South Africa is famous for its sunshine. Generally speaking, April and May are the most pleasant months when the rainy season over the summer-rainfall region has ended, and before the rainy season in the winter-rainfall area has begun. At this time of year, the hot summer weather has abated and the winds are lighter than during the rest of the year.

In certain areas, however, notably the hot, humid KwaZulu-Natal coast, Mpumalanga and Limpopo, June and July are the ideal holiday months.

The provinces

In terms of South Africa's Constitution, the country is divided into nine provinces, each with its own legislature, premier and executive councils. The provinces, with their own distinctive landscapes, vegetation and climate, are the Western Cape, the Eastern Cape, KwaZulu-Natal, the Northern Cape, Free State, North West, Gauteng, Mpumalanga and Limpopo. (See chapter 21: *Tourism.*)

Western Cape

The Western Cape is situated on the southernmost tip of the African continent. It is a region of majestic mountains; beautiful valleys; wide, sandy beaches; and breathtaking scenery, which makes it one of the South Africa's prime tourist destinations.

The cold Atlantic Ocean along the west coast is a rich fishing area, while the warmer Indian Ocean skirts the province's southern beaches.

Visitors to the Western Cape can disembark at Cape Town International Airport, George Airport or at the ports of Cape Town, Mossel Bay or Saldanha. A network of roads also leads to Cape Town, the capital, fondly known as the Mother City.

Other important towns in the province include Saldanha, a notable harbour for iron exports and the fishing industry; Worcester and Stellenbosch in the heart of the winelands; George, renowned for its indigenous timber and vegetable produce; Oudtshoorn, known for its ostrich products and the world-famous Cango caves; and Beaufort West on the dry, sheep-farming plains of the Great Karoo.

The Western Cape boasts one of the world's six accepted floral kingdoms. Although it is the smallest of them all, the Cape Floral Kingdom, which is characterised by fynbos, contains more plant species than the whole of Europe. These include the famous proteas and heathers.

In 2004, the World Heritage Committee officially recognised the Cape Floristic Region as South Africa's sixth World Heritage Site. Covering an area of more than 553 000 hectares (ha), the Cape Floristic Region World Heritage Site comprises eight separate protected areas stretching from the Cape Peninsula into the Eastern Cape. The Kirstenbosch National Botanical Garden is included in this area, which makes it a world first for South Africa, since no other World Heritage Site includes a botanical garden.

The Knysna-Tsitsikamma region has the country's biggest indigenous forests; a fairyland of ancient forest giants, ferns and colourful birdlife. Products of the forests include sought-after furniture made from the indigenous yellowwood, stinkwood and white pear trees.

Tourism
The Western Cape's natural beauty, complemented by its famous hospitality, cultural diversity, excellent wine and colourful cuisine, makes the province one of the world's greatest tourist attractions.

The tourism industry in the Western Cape contributes 14% to the total Gross Domestic Product (GDP) of the province and is the most important growth force in the province.

The people
More than 4,6 million people live in the Western Cape on 129 370 km² of land (*Mid-Year Estimates, 2005*). Afrikaans is spoken by the majority, with isiXhosa and English being the other main

languages. The Western Cape has the highest adult-education level in the country, with only 5,7% of people aged 20 years or older having undergone no schooling (Census 2001). The province has a strong network of Higher Education (HE) institutions, including the University of Cape Town, Stellenbosch University, the University of the Western Cape and the Cape Peninsula University of Technology.

A potpourri of diverse cultural backgrounds gives the province a cosmopolitan ambiance, resulting in a demographic profile quite different from that of the national pattern. The profile draws on elements from different parts of Europe, south-east Asia, India and Africa, which are richly reflected in the diversity of the area.

The official unemployment figure for the province is 17,6% (*Labour Force Survey, March 2005*). This was somewhat lower than the national unemployment rate of 26,5% in March 2005.

Agriculture and marine fishery
The Western Cape is rich in agriculture and fisheries.

Primary industries, i.e. agriculture, forestry and fishing, and mining and quarrying, contributed 5,1% to the GDP of the province in 2003, which translated to R9 299 million (gross domestic product per region [GDPR], 2003).

The sheltered valleys between the mountains provide ideal conditions for the cultivation of top-grade fruits, such as apples, table grapes, olives, peaches and oranges. In the eastern part of the Western Cape, a great variety of vegetables is cultivated.

Western Cape

Capital: Cape Town
Principal languages: Afrikaans 55,3%
                           isiXhosa 23,7%
                           English 19,3%
Population: 4 645 600 (*Mid-Year Estimates, 2005*)
Area (km²): 129 370
% of total area: 10,6%
GDPR* at current prices (2003): R181 069 million
% of total GDP**: 14,5%
* GDPR (Gross Product per Region)
** GDP (Gross Domestic Product)

The province can be divided into three climatic regions. The area around the Cape Peninsula and the Boland, further inland, is a winter-rainfall region with sunny, dry summers.

Towards George, along the south coast, the climate gradually changes to year-round rainfall, while inland, towards the more arid Great Karoo, the climate changes to summer rainfall.

The Western Cape is known as one of the world's finest grape-growing regions. Many of its wines have received the highest accolades at international shows.

The wheat-growing Swartland district around Malmesbury, and the Overberg around Caledon, form the bread basket of the country.

The inland Karoo region (around Beaufort West), and the Overberg district (around Bredasdorp), produce wool and mutton, as well as pedigree Merino breeding stock.

Other animal products include broiler chickens, eggs, dairy products, beef and pork. The Western Cape is the only province with an outlet for the export of horses. This earns the country millions of rand in foreign revenue.

The province has also established itself as the leading facilitator in the export of ostrich meat to Europe. It boasts the most export abbatoirs in the country, from which products to the value of about R1 billion are exported per year. In addition to meat, fine leatherware and ostrich feathers are also exported to destinations all over the world.

More than 70% of registered export farms are situated in the Western Cape, centred mainly in the Klein Karoo region around Oudtshoorn. The industry is not only an important contributor to the provincial economy, but the ostrich has become a significant part of Western Cape culture, branding and identity. The number of ostriches slaughtered in South Africa increased from 152 000 in 1993 to 340 000 in 2004 at a value of more than R560 million, creating about 20 000 jobs nationwide.

The provincial Department of Agriculture's ostrich-breeding herd at Oudtshoorn is the only one in the world for which production data for several generations of ostriches can be connected to their pedigrees.

The plankton-rich cold Benguela current flows along the west coast of the province and is considered to be one of the world's richest fishing grounds. This resource is protected from overfishing by foreign vessels by means of a 200-km commercial fishing zone and a strict quota system.

Snoek, Cape lobster, abalone, calamari, octopus, oysters and mussels are among the most sought-after piscatorial delights.

Industry

The Western Cape economy contributed 14,5% (at current prices) to South Africa's GDP in 2003 and grows at an average of 3,2%, which is higher than the national average. The tertiary sector, which involves finance, real estate, retail and tourism, has shown substantial growth and is the main contributor to the GDPR. The value of residential property has increased significantly.

Many of South Africa's major insurance companies and banks are based in the Western Cape. The majority of the country's petroleum companies and the largest segment of the printing and publishing industry are located in Cape Town.

Information and communications technology is one of the fastest growing sectors in the province and operations are being expanded to other countries.

After Gauteng and KwaZulu-Natal, the Western Cape's manufacturing sector is the third-largest contributor to the national manufacturing sector. The clothing and textile industry remains the most significant industrial source of employment in the province.

Cape Town remains the economic hub of the province, encompassing industrial areas such as Epping, Montagu Gardens, Parow and Retreat. Along the west coast, the Saldanha Steel Project has led to increased economic activity.

Eastern Cape

The Eastern Cape, a land of undulating hills, expansive sandy beaches, majestic mountain ranges and emerald green forests, is in surface area the second-largest of the nine provinces.

The region boasts a remarkable natural diversity, ranging from the dry, desolate Great Karoo; to the lush forests of the Wild Coast and the Keiskamma Valley; the fertile Langkloof, renowned for its rich apple harvests; and the mountainous southern Drakensberg region at Elliot.

The Eastern Cape's main feature is its spectacular coastline lapped by the Indian Ocean. With its long stretches of pristine sandy beaches, rocky coves, secluded lagoons and towering cliffs, the coastline provides the province with an unsurpassed natural tourist attraction.

The graceful curve of Algoa Bay provides an ideal setting for the port of Port Elizabeth. East London offers equally favourable harbour facilities. The province is serviced by three airports situated in Port Elizabeth, East London and Umtata.

The architecture of many of its cities and towns reflects the rich heritage of its people. Important towns in the province include Bisho, the capital; Uitenhage, which has important motor vehicle-manufacturing and related industries; King William's Town, rich in early settler and military history; Grahamstown, also known as the City of Saints because of its more than 40 churches; Graaff-Reinet, with its interesting collection of historic buildings; Cradock, the hub of the Central Karoo; Stutterheim, the forestry centre of the province; Aliwal North, famous for its hot sulphur springs; and Port St Johns, the largest town on the Wild Coast.

In the Eastern Cape, various floral habitats meet. Along the coast, the northern tropical forests intermingle with the more temperate woods of the south. This makes for an interesting forest habitat of various species endemic to this region.

Age-old forests occur at Keiskammahoek, Dwesa, Port St Johns and Bathurst; dune forests are found at Alexandria; and mangroves along the Wild Coast.

Rolling grasslands dominate the eastern interior of the province, while the western central plateau is savanna bushveld. The northern inland is home to the aromatic, succulent-rich Karoo.

The people

The Eastern Cape has more than seven million people living on 169 580 km² of land. The majority of the people speak isiXhosa, followed by Afrikaans and English.

The province has a number of HE institutions, including the Nelson Mandela Metropolitan University, the University of Fort Hare and the Walter Sisulu University of Technology. Despite the high quality of education facilities, 22,8% of the population aged 20 years or older have never received any schooling, while 6,3% have completed some form of HE (Census 2001).

In 2005, the unemployment rate of the province stood at 27,1% (*Labour Force Survey, March 2005*).

The dominant productive sectors in the province at current prices are manufacturing (17,3% of GDPR), finance/real estate/business services (18,6% of GDPR), and wholesale/retail/trade/hotels and restaurants (13,11% of GDPR).

The province's GDPR in 2003 represented just over 8,1% of national GDP, while the province's share of the national population was around 15,5%.

Agriculture, fishing and forestry

The Eastern Cape has excellent agricultural and forestry potential. The fertile Langkloof Valley in the south-west has enormous deciduous fruit orchards, while the Karoo interior is an important sheep-farming area. Angora wool is also produced here.

The Alexandria-Grahamstown area produces pineapples, chicory and dairy products, while coffee and tea are cultivated at Magwa. People in the former Transkei region are dependent on cattle, maize and sorghum-farming. An olive nursery has been developed in collaboration with the University of Fort Hare to form a nucleus of olive production in the Eastern Cape.

Eastern Cape

Capital: Bisho
Principal languages: isiXhosa 83,4%
Afrikaans 9,3%
English 3,6%
Population: 7 039 300 (*Mid-Year Estimates, 2005*)
Area (km²): 169 580
% of total area: 13,9%
GDPR at current prices (2003): R88 032 million
% of total GDP: 8,1%

Extensive exotic forestry plantations in the high rainfall areas of Keiskammahoek provide employment for large numbers of the population. The province is a summer-rainfall region with high rainfall along the coast, becoming gradually drier behind the mountain ranges into the Great Karoo.

The basis of the province's fishing industry is squid, some recreational and commercial fishing for line fish, the collection of marine resources, and access to line-catches of hake.

Ostrich exports are flourishing and the provincial Department of Agriculture has been hailed for the support it is giving this industry. Each ostrich-export establishment has a resident official veterinarian, which is a requirement for exporting ostrich products to the European Union.

The game industry is enjoying unprecedented demand in the international market due to health-conscious consumers increasingly demanding lean organic game meat.

Industry

The metropolitan economies of Port Elizabeth and East London are based primarily on manufacturing, the most important being motor manufacturing. The province is the hub of South Africa's automotive industry.

Several of the world's biggest motor manufacturers, such as Volkswagen, Ford (Samcor), General Motors (Delta) and Daimler Chrysler, have plants in the Eastern Cape.

With two harbours and three airports offering direct flights to the main centres, and an excellent road and rail infrastructure, the province has been earmarked as a key area for growth and economic development. Environmentally friendly projects include the Fish River Spatial Development Initiative (SDI), the Wild Coast SDI, and two industrial development zones (IDZs), namely the West Bank (East London) and the Coega IDZs. The latter, 20 km east of the Port Elizabeth-Uitenhage metropoles, was the first IDZ to be earmarked and is one of the biggest initiatives ever undertaken in South Africa. Plans for the development of the area as an export-orientated zone include the building of the Port of Ngqura.

The French investment and industrial company Pechiney invested R18,6 billion in an aluminium smelter at Coega. The R40-million contract for building the IDZ village was awarded largely to emerging small, medium and micro enterprises, and includes female contractors.

The forestry developments and the construction of the N1 toll road as part of the Wild Coast SDI is expected to create more than 20 000 jobs. An additional 5 000 jobs are expected to be created in the mining sector through upstream and downstream investment.

The Kei Rail Project, undertaken at a cost of R663 million over the next three years, is expected to ensure integration of the former Transkei economy with the IDZs. The project will also serve to stimulate the agricultural, agro-forestry and furniture industry in the area, including the development of a chipping plant at Langeni.

KwaZulu-Natal

Aptly called South Africa's garden province, KwaZulu-Natal is one of the country's most popular holiday destinations. This verdant region includes South Africa's lush subtropical east coast. Washed by the warm Indian Ocean, it stretches from Port Edward in the south, and northwards to the Mozambique boundary. In addition to the magnificent coastline, the province also boasts sweeping savanna in the east, and the majestic Drakensberg mountain range in the west.

Visitors to KwaZulu-Natal can either disembark at Durban International Airport or at Durban Harbour. Alternatively, they can make use of the extensive national road network.

Durban is one of the fastest-growing urban areas in the world. Its port is the busiest in South Africa and is one of the 10-largest in the world. The Port of Durban handles over 30 million tons (t) of cargo annually with a value of more than R100 billion. The Port of Richards Bay handles about 1 000 containers per month. Combined, these two ports handle about 78% of South Africa's cargo tonnage.

KwaZulu-Natal is the only province with a monarchy specifically provided for in the Constitution.

Pietermaritzburg is KwaZulu-Natal's capital and Richards Bay is an important coal-export harbour. The province has several popular coastal holiday resorts, such as Port Shepstone, Umhlanga Rocks and Margate. In the interior, Newcastle is well-known for steel production and coal-mining, Estcourt for meat processing, and Ladysmith and Richmond for mixed agriculture. The KwaZulu-Natal coastal belt yields sugar cane, wood, oranges, bananas, mangoes and other tropical fruit.

The province is also well known for its active conservation activities. The Royal Natal National Park has more than 1 000 plant species, 12 species of antelope and three of the world's seven species of crane. There are several other reserves such as Giant's Castle and the Kamberg Nature Reserve. Some of South Africa's best-protected indigenous coastal forests are found along the subtropical coastline of KwaZulu-Natal, for example, at Dukuduku and Kosi Bay. It is also along this coast that the magnificent St Lucia Estuary and Kosi Bay lakes are located. In 1999, the Greater St Lucia Wetlands Park was declared a World Heritage Site.

Separating KwaZulu-Natal from Lesotho, the Drakensberg runs 200 km along the western boundary of the province.

The northern part of the province, south of the Swaziland border, is typical African savanna, providing a natural backdrop for its rich wildlife, protected in several game parks.

The people

KwaZulu-Natal has more than 9,6 million people living on 92 100 km² of land (*Mid-Year Estimates, 2005*). The principal language spoken is isiZulu, followed by English and Afrikaans. Remnants of British colonialism, together with Zulu, Indian and Afrikaans traditions make for an interesting cultural mix in the province.

The province boasts several universities, universities of technology and other educational institutions, including the University of KwaZulu-Natal and the Durban Institute of Technology.

A total of 21,9% of the province's population of the province aged 20 and above have received no form of education (Census 2001).

KwaZulu-Natal was the second-highest contributor to the South African economy during 2003, at 16,5% (at current prices) of GDP.

The key strength of this province's economy is its trade and transport infrastructure.

The province's unemployment rate of 31,7% is the second-highest of the provinces after Limpopo (*Labour Force Survey, March 2005*).

Agriculture and industry

Richards Bay is the centre of operations for South Africa's aluminium industry. The Richards Bay Coal Terminal is instrumental in securing the country's position as the second-largest exporter of steam coal in the world. Richards Bay Minerals is the largest sand-mining and mineral-processing operation in the world.

The motor vehicle-manufacturing industry has created a considerable multiplier effect in component- and service-providers. The automotive leather industry has grown rapidly, with exports significantly increasing foreign exchange earnings. In recent times, the province has undergone rapid industrialisation owing to its abundant water supply and labour resources. Industries are found at Newcastle, Ladysmith, Dundee, Richards Bay, Durban, Hammarsdale, Richmond, Pietermaritzburg and Mandeni.

The sugar-cane plantations along the Indian Ocean coastal belt form the mainstay of the economy and agriculture of the region. The coastal belt is also a large producer of subtropical fruit, while the farmers in the hinterland concentrate on vegetable, dairy and stock-farming. Another major source of

KwaZulu-Natal

Capital: Pietermaritzburg
Principal languages: isiZulu   80,9%
                   English   73,6%
                   Afrikaans   1,5%
Population: 9 651 100 (*Mid-Year Estimates, 2005*)
Area (km²): 92 100
% of total area: 7,6%
GDPR at current prices (2003): R206 766 million
% of total GDP: 16,5%

income is forestry, in the areas around Vryheid, Eshowe, Richmond, Harding and Ngome. Ngome also has tea plantations.

The summer-rainfall coastal regions of this province are hot and humid with a subtropical climate. The KwaZulu-Natal Midlands between the coastal strip and the southern Drakensberg Escarpment are drier, with extremely cold conditions in winter and snow on the high-lying ground. In the north, the subtropical strip extends further around Swaziland to the edge of the escarpment.

During 2004/05, substantial progress was made to advance the Dube Trade Port and King Shaka International Airport project at La Mercy. It is estimated that redevelopment of the current airport site could lead to the creation of 269 200 jobs at national level over a 25-year period. The airport is expected to be operational by 2010, in time for the Soccer World Cup. In 2005, R100 million was allocated for the acquisition of the La Mercy land and necessary road interchanges.

Northern Cape

The Northern Cape lies to the south of its most important asset, the mighty Orange River, which provides the basis for a healthy agricultural industry. The landscape is characterised by vast arid plains with outcroppings of haphazard rock piles. The cold Atlantic Ocean forms the western boundary.

This region covers the largest area of all the provinces and has the smallest population. Its major airports are situated at Kimberley, the capital, and Upington. The Northern Cape has an excellent road

Northern Cape

Capital: Kimberley
Principal languages: Afrikaans 68%
　　　　　　　　　Setswana 20,8%
　　　　　　　　　English 2,5%
Population: 902 300 (*Mid-Year Estimates, 2005*)
Area (km²): 361 830
% of total area: 29,7%
GDPR at current prices (2003): R29 659 million
% of total GDP: 2,4%

network, which makes its interior easily accessible from South Africa's major cities, harbours and airports.

Important towns are Upington, centre of the karakul sheep and dried-fruit industries, and the most northerly wine-making region of South Africa; Springbok, in the heart of the Namaqualand spring-flower country; Kuruman, founded by the Scottish missionary Robert Moffat; and De Aar, hub of the South African railway network. Sutherland is host to the southern hemisphere's largest astronomical observatory, the multinational-sponsored Southern African Large Telescope.

Other important Northern Cape towns include the sheep-farming towns of Carnarvon, Colesberg, Kenhardt and Prieska.

Apart from a narrow strip of winter-rainfall area along the coast, the Northern Cape is a semi-arid region with little rainfall in summer. The weather conditions are extreme – cold and frosty in winter, with extremely high temperatures in summer.

The largest part of the province falls within the Nama-Karoo biome, with a vegetation of low shrub-land and grass, and trees limited to water courses. The area is known worldwide for its spectacular display of spring flowers which, for a short period every year, attracts thousands of tourists.

This biome is home to many wonderful plant species, such as the elephant's trunk (halfmens), tree aloe (kokerboom) and a variety of succulents.

The province has several national parks and conservation areas. The Kalahari Gemsbok National Park, together with the Gemsbok National Park in Botswana, is Africa's first transfrontier game park, known as the Kgalagadi Transfrontier Park. It is one of the largest nature-conservation areas in southern Africa and one of the largest remaining protected natural ecosystems in the world. The park provides unfenced access to a variety of game between South Africa and Botswana, and has a surface area of more than 3,6 ha.

The Ai-Ais-Richtersveld Transfrontier Conservation Park spans some of the most spectacular scenery of the arid and desert environments in southern Africa. Bisected by the Orange River, which forms the border between South Africa and

Namibia, it comprises the Ai-Ais Hot Springs Game Park in Namibia, and the Richtersveld National Park in South Africa. Some of the distinctive features in the area include the Fish River Canyon (often likened to the Grand Canyon in the United States of America) and the Ai-Ais hot springs. This arid zone is further characterised by a unique and impressive variety of succulent plant species.

Nowhere is the Orange River more impressive than at the Augrabies Falls, which ranks among the world's greatest cataracts on a major river. The Augrabies Falls National Park was established to preserve this natural wonder.

The people

The Northern Cape is sparsely populated and houses some 902 300 people on 361 830 km^2 of land (*Mid-Year Estimates, 2005*). About 68% of the population speak Afrikaans. Other languages spoken are Setswana, isiXhosa and English.

The official unemployment rate of the Northern Cape is 29,4% (*Labour Force Survey,* March 2005).

The last remaining true San (Bushman) people live in the Kalahari area of the Northern Cape. The area, especially along the Orange and Vaal rivers, is rich in San rock engravings. A good collection can be seen at the McGregor Museum in Kimberley. The province is also rich in fossils.

Agriculture and industry

The Northern Cape is enjoying a tremendous growth in value-added activities, including game-farming.

Food production and processing for the local and export market is also growing significantly.

Underpinning the growth and development plan of the province are the investment projects that link up with the existing plans of the Namaqua Development Corridor. The focus is on the beneficiation and export of sea products.

The economy of a large part of the Northern Cape, the interior Karoo, depends on sheep-farming, while the karakul-pelt industry is one of the most important in the Gordonia district of Upington.

The province has fertile agricultural land. In the Orange River Valley, especially at Upington, Kakamas and Keimoes, grapes and fruit are culti-vated intensively. Wheat, fruit, peanuts, maize and cotton are produced at the Vaalharts Irrigation Scheme near Warrenton.

Mining

The Northern Cape is rich in minerals. The country's chief diamond pipes are found in the Kimberley district. In 1888, the diamond industry was formally established with the creation of De Beers Consolidated Mines. Alluvial diamonds are also extracted from the beaches and the sea between Alexander Bay and Port Nolloth.

The Sishen Mine near Kathu is the biggest source of iron ore in South Africa, while the copper mine at Okiep is one of the oldest mines in the country. Copper is also mined at Springbok and Aggenys. The province is rich in asbestos, manganese, fluorspar, semi-precious stones and marble.

Until recently, the majority of small- to medium-scale alluvial operations were concentrated along or near the Vaal River system. With the rapidly depleting deposits available for mining, there has been a gradual shift towards the Orange River system. Two recent larger-scale investments also show continued prospects in this sector.

Free State

The Free State lies in the heart of South Africa, with Lesotho nestling in the hollow of its bean-like shape. Between the Vaal River in the north and the Orange River in the south, this immense rolling prairie stretches as far as the eye can see.

The capital, Bloemfontein, has a well-established institutional, educational and administrative infrastructure and houses the Supreme Court of Appeal. The city is also home to some of the province's many tertiary educational institutions, including the University of the Free State and the Central University of Technology.

Important towns include Welkom, the heart of the goldfields and one of the few completely pre-planned cities in the world; Odendaalsrus, another gold-mining town; Sasolburg, which owes its existence to the petrol-from-coal installation established there; Kroonstad, an important agricultural, administrative and educational centre; Parys, on the banks of the Vaal River; Phuthaditjhaba, well-known for the beautiful handcrafted items produced by the local people; and Bethlehem, gateway to the Eastern Highlands of the Free State.

Nestled in the rolling foothills of the Maluti mountains in the north-eastern Free State, the Golden Gate Highlands National Park is the province's prime tourist attraction. The park derives its name from the brilliant shades of gold cast by the sun on the spectacular sandstone cliffs, especially the imposing Brandwag rock, which keeps vigil over the park.

The national road, which is the artery between Gauteng and the Western and Eastern Cape, passes through the middle of the Free State.

The people

The Free State houses more than 2,9 million people on about 129 480 km² of land (*Mid-Year Estimates, 2005*). The main languages spoken are Sesotho and Afrikaans. Some 16% of people aged 20 years or older have received no schooling (Census 2001).

According to the *Labour Force Survey* of March 2005, the official unemployment rate is 30,6%.

Many of the towns display a cultural mix clearly evident in street names, public buildings, monuments and museums. Dressed-sandstone buildings abound on the Eastern Highlands, while beautifully decorated Sotho houses dot the grasslands. Some of South Africa's most valued San rock art is found in the Free State. The districts of Bethlehem, Ficksburg, Ladybrand and Wepener have remarkable collections of this art form.

Free State

Capital: Bloemfontein
Principal languages: Sesotho   64,4%
                        Afrikaans 11,9%
                        isiXhosa   9,1%
Population: 2 953 100 (*Mid-Year Estimates, 2005*)
Area (km²): 129 480
% of total area: 10,6%
GDPR at current prices (2003): R69 094 million
% of total GDP: 5,5%

Agriculture

This summer-rainfall region can be extremely cold during the winter months, especially towards the eastern mountainous regions where temperatures drop to as low as 9,5° C. The western and southern areas are semi-desert.

Known as the Granary of The Country, the Free State has cultivated land covering 3,2 million ha, while natural veld and grazing cover 8,7 million ha.

Field crops yield almost two-thirds of the gross agricultural income of the province. Animal products contribute a further 30%, with the balance generated by horticulture.

Ninety percent of the country's cherry crop is produced in the Ficksburg district, while the two largest asparagus canning factories are also situated in this district. Soya, sorghum, sunflowers and wheat are cultivated, especially in the eastern Free State, where farmers specialise in seed production. About 40% of the country's potato yield comes from the high-lying areas of the Free State.

The province produces about 100 000 t of vegetables and 40 000 t of fruit each year. The main vegetable crop is asparagus, both white and green varieties. The industry is expanding and becoming increasingly export-orientated. However, most produce leaves the province unprocessed (*Provincial Economies, 2003*).

In terms of floriculture, the Free State has an advantage due to the opposing seasons of the southern and northern hemispheres. The province exports about 1,2 million t of cut flowers per year.

Mining

The mining industry is the major employer in the Free State. Investment opportunities are substantial in productivity-improvement areas for mining and related products and services.

South Africa is the world's largest producer of gold. A gold reef of over 400 km long, known as the Goldfields, stretches across Gauteng and the Free State; the largest gold-mining complex being Free State Consolidated Goldfields, with a mining area of 32 918 ha.

Some 82% of the region's mineral production value is derived from this activity, primarily in the goldfields region, which comprises the districts of Odendaalsrus, Virginia and Welkom. Twelve gold mines operate in the province. Roughly 30% of South Africa's gold is obtained from this region, and the province qualifies for fifth position as a global producer. The Harmony Gold Refinery is the only refinery authorised to sell gold directly to jewellery manufacturers.

Harmony Gold Refinery and Rand Refinery are the only two gold refineries in South Africa.

Gold mines in the Free State also supply a substantial portion of the total silver produced in the country, while considerable concentrations of uranium occurring in the gold-bearing conglomerates of the goldfields are extracted as a by-product.

Bituminous coal is mined in the province and converted to petrochemicals at Sasolburg.

Diamonds from this region, extracted from kimberlite pipes and fissures, are of a high quality.

The largest deposit of bentonite in the country occurs in the Koppies district.

Manufacturing and industry

Since 1989, the Free State economy has changed from being dependent on the primary sector to being a manufacturing, export-orientated economy. The Free State GDPR amounted to about R69 094 million in 2003, which represented a 5,5% contribution to the South African economy.

In 2003, the manufacturing industry contributed 12,7% at current prices to the total value added at basic prices (GDPR, 2003). Some 14% of the province's manufacturing is classified as being in high-technology industries, which is the highest percentage of all the provincial economies.

An important manufacturing industry in the province can be found in the northern Free State, which is one of the most important chemical hubs in the southern hemisphere. The province has competitive advantages in the production of certain fuels, waxes, chemicals and low-cost feedstock from coal.

The growth in high-tech industries is significant in the context of the changing contribution of the gold-mining industry to gross geographic product (GGP).

The province's three-tier development strategy centres on competitiveness, empowerment, capacity-building and beneficiation.

North West

North West is centrally located in the sub-continent with direct road and rail links to all the southern African countries, and to its own airport situated near the capital city, Mafikeng. The province borders on Botswana and is fringed by the Kalahari desert in the west and the Witwatersrand area in the east.

Due to its significant platinum production, North West is sometimes referred to as the Platinum Province.

The province is divided into five regions, namely the Central, Bophirima (towards the west), Southern, Rustenburg and Eastern regions. Most economic activity is concentrated in the Southern Region (between Potchefstroom and Klerksdorp), Rustenburg, and the Eastern Region, where more than 83,3% of GDPR of the province is produced.

The province offers several tourist attractions including the internationally renowned Sun City, the popular Pilanesberg National Park, the Madikwe Game Reserve and the Rustenburg Nature Reserve.

The people

Of the 3 823 900 people living in the North West, 65% live in the rural areas (*Mid-Year Estimates, 2005*). The official unemployment rate is 28,8% (*Labour Force Survey*, March 2005).

The province has the lowest number of people aged 20 years and older (5,9%) who have received HE. The literacy rate is in the region of 57%.

Mining

Mining contributes 23,3% to the economy at current prices and 17,8% of total employment in the North West. It makes up 22,51% of the mining GDP in South Africa. North West is also the dominant province in mineral sales with a contribution of 17,8% to the South African mining sector (*Provincial Economies, 2003*).

18

Diamonds are mined at Lichtenburg, Koster, Christiana and Bloemhof, while Orkney and Klerksdorp have gold mines.

The area surrounding Rustenburg and Brits boasts the largest single platinum-production area in the world. Marble is also mined here. Fluorspar is exploited at Zeerust.

Manufacturing

Manufacturing contributes 6,9% of the province's GDP and 9% of its employment opportunities. It provides 2,61% of the South African manufacturing sector's contribution to GDP.

Manufacturing is almost exclusively dependent on the performance of a few sectors in which the province enjoys a competitive advantage. These are fabricated metals (51%), the food sector (18%) and non-metallic metals (21%) (*Provincial Economies, 2003*).

Industrial activity is centred around the towns of Brits, Klerksdorp, Vryburg and Rustenburg.

The Brits industries concentrate mostly on manufacturing and construction, while those at Klerksdorp are geared towards the mining industry, and those at Vryburg and Rustenburg towards agriculture.

The Platinum SDI will unlock further development. It is situated on the Coast-to-Coast highway that links the Port of Maputo in Mozambique to Walvis Bay in Namibia.

About 200 potential project opportunities in tourism, manufacturing, agriculture and mining have been identified.

North West

Capital: Mafikeng
Principal languages: Setswana 65,4%
Afrikaans 7,5%
isiXhosa 5,8%
Population: 3 823 900 (*Mid-Year Estimates, 2005*)
Area (km²): 116 320
% of total area: 9,5%
GDPR at current prices (2003): R81 442 million
% of total GDP: 6,5%

Five anchor projects within the Platinum SDI have been identified with an estimated R4,3-billion capital investment component, around which there are dozens of other development and investment opportunities. Employment along the Platinum Corridor, from Pretoria to eastern Botswana, accounts for over a third of total employment in North West. The aim of the Mafikeng IDZ is to create jobs and enhance the economic potential of the Central Region, the entire North West and the Southern African Development Community (SADC) region.

Agriculture

Agriculture is of extreme importance to the North West. It contributes about 6,2% of the total GDPR and 19% of formal employment.

Some 5,6% of the South African GDP in agriculture and 16,96% of total labour in agriculture are based in the North West (*Provincial Economies, 2003*).

The province is an important food basket in South Africa. Maize and sunflowers are the most important crops and the North West is the major producer of white maize in the country.

Some of the largest cattle herds in the world are found at Stellaland near Vryburg, which explains why this area is often referred to as the Texas of South Africa. Marico is also cattle-country. The areas around Rustenburg and Brits are fertile, mixed-crop farming land.

Gauteng

Although the smallest of the nine provinces, Gauteng is the powerhouse of South Africa and the heart of its commercial business and industrial sectors.

Gauteng's economy has grown at an impressive rate over the past five years.

According to figures released by Stats SA, the province recorded a real economic growth rate of 2,9% in 2003. The GDPR grew at an average of 3,1% between 1996 and 2002. Gauteng's contribution to South Africa's GDP during 2003 was 33% (at current prices), the largest of all the provinces.

The province is not only an important contributor to the country's GDP, it also plays a critical role in the regional SADC and Africa economies. It generates about 9% and 25% of the total African continent and SADC gross national products, respectively.

Gauteng represents the highest per capita income level in the country.

It is also the financial services capital of Africa. More than 70 foreign banks have their head offices here, as do at least the same number of South African banks, stockbrokers and insurance giants.

The three most important sectors contributing to GDPR are financial and business services, logistics and communications, and mining.

The growth and development plans for the province are underpinned by the Blue IQ projects. These consist of 11 mega projects in economic-infrastructure development, in the areas of technology, tourism, transport and high-value-added manufacturing.

The aim is to attract some R100 billion in direct investment over the next 10 years. Gauteng's main cities are Johannesburg, the largest city in southern Africa; and Pretoria, the administrative capital of the country.

The province blends cultures, colours and first- and third-world traditions in a spirited mix that is flavoured by many foreign influences.

Gauteng's primary attraction is business opportunity, but there is more to this province. A wealth of culture is to be found in the museums, galleries, art routes and historical battlefields.

Most overseas visitors enter South Africa via Johannesburg International Airport.

Johannesburg, nicknamed *Egoli* (Place of Gold), is the capital of the province and is a city of contrasts. Mine-dumps and headgear stand proud as symbols of its rich past, while modern architecture rubs shoulders with examples of 19th-century engineering prowess. Gleaming skyscrapers contrast with Indian bazaars and African muti (medicine) shops, where traditional healers dispense advice and traditional medicine.

The busy streets ring out with the calls of fruit-sellers and street vendors. An exciting blend of ethnic and western art and cultural activities is reflected in theatres and open-air arenas throughout the city.

South of Johannesburg is Soweto, developed as a township for black people under the apartheid system. Most of the struggle against apartheid was fought in and from Soweto, which is estimated to be inhabited by over two million people. Soweto is a city of enterprise and cultural interaction. It is a popular tourist destination with sites such as Kliptown, where the Freedom Charter was drawn up; the home of former President Nelson Mandela; the Hector Petersen Memorial site; and restaurants and shopping malls. It boasts one of the largest hospitals on the continent, the Chris Hani-Baragwanath Hospital.

Some 50 km north of Johannesburg lies Pretoria, dominated by government services and the diplomatic corps of foreign representatives in the country.

Pretoria, also known as the Jacaranda City, is renowned for its colourful gardens, shrubs and trees, particularly beautiful in spring when some 50 000 jacaranda trees envelop the avenues in mauve. The city developed at a more sedate pace than Johannesburg, and town planners had the foresight to include an abundance of open space. Pretoria has more than 100 parks, including bird sanctuaries and nature reserves.

An air of history pervades much of central Pretoria, especially Church Square, around which the city has grown. Many buildings of historical and architectural importance have been retained or restored to their former splendour.

The industrial area of Rosslyn and the townships of Soshanguve and GaRankuwa are situated north of Pretoria. Cullinan, known for its diamonds, lies to the east.

Other important Gauteng towns include Krugersdorp and Roodepoort on the West Rand, and Germiston, Springs, Boksburg, Benoni, Brakpan and Kempton Park on the East Rand. The hominid sites at Swartkrans, Sterkfontein and Kromdraai (also known as the Cradle of Humankind) are a World Heritage Site.

Vanderbijlpark and Vereeniging in the south of the province are major industrial centres, while Heidelberg, Nigel and Bronkhorstspruit to the east are important agricultural areas.

Although the province is highly urbanised and industrialised, it contains wetlands of international importance, such as Blesbokspruit near Springs.

The people

Gauteng is the most densely populated province in South Africa. It houses more than nine million of the country's people (*Mid-Year Estimates, 2005*). The level of urbanisation is 97%.

Gauteng recorded an unemployment rate of 26,7% in the *Labour Force Survey,* released in March 2005.

It has the most important educational and health centres in the country. Pretoria boasts the largest residential university in South Africa, the University of Pretoria, and what is believed to be the largest correspondence university in the world, the University of South Africa (UNISA).

According to the recent Biotechnology Audit (*www.egolibio.co.za*), Gauteng hosts 41% of core biotechnology companies in South Africa. In addition, Gauteng is home to leading research institutions such as the Council for Scientific and Industrial Research, the Agricultural Research Council, Onderstepoort Veterinary Institute and various universities. More than 60% of South Africa's research and development takes place in Gauteng.

According to the 2001 Census findings, only 8,4% of adults in the province have no formal education.

Johannesburg has two residential universities, namely the University of the Witwatersrand and the University of Johannesburg. There are also several teacher-training colleges, technical colleges and universities of technology in the province.

Manufacturing

The manufacturing sector in Gauteng includes over 9 300 firms, employing more than 600 000 people. Industries that have contributed significantly to this output are basic iron and steel; fabricated and metal products; food; machinery, electrical machinery, appliances and electrical supplies; vehicle parts and accessories; and chemical products.

The automotive parts and components industry in Gauteng, with its 200 firms, employs about 38 000 workers and contributes an estimated 4,3% to the province's GGP. This equates to an industry worth about R13 billion per year.

Technology

The province's economy is being realigned to move away from traditional heavy industry markets and low value-added production towards sophisticated high value-added production, particularly in information technology, telecommunications and other high-tech industries.

In an international survey in 2000, Gauteng was identified as one of 46 global hubs of technological innovation. The burgeoning 'high-tech' corridor in Midrand (halfway between Pretoria and Johannesburg) is the fastest developing area in the country.

Agriculture and industry

Gauteng's agricultural sector is geared to provide the cities and towns of the province with daily fresh produce, including dairy products, vegetables, fruit, meat, eggs and flowers.

A large area of the province falls within the so-called Maize Triangle. The districts of Bronkhorstspruit, Cullinan and Heidelberg hold important agricultural land, where ground-nuts, sunflowers, cotton and sorghum are produced.

This summer-rainfall area has hot summers and cold winters with frost. Hail is common during the summer thunderstorms.

Gauteng is an integrated industrial complex with major areas of economic activity in three sub-regional areas, namely the Vaal Triangle; the East,

Gauteng

Capital: Johannesburg
Principal languages: isiZulu 21,5%
Afrikaans 14,4%
Sesotho 13,1%
English 12,5%
Population: 9 415 231 (*Mid-Year Estimates, 2005*)
Area (km²): 17 010
% of total area: 1,4%
GDPR at current prices (2003): R413 554 million
% of total GDP: 33%

West and Central Rand; and Pretoria. The Vaal Triangle has a strong manufacturing sector; the West Rand concentrates on primary mining; and the Central Witwatersrand is dominated by the manufacturing and finance sectors, with mining capital playing a major role. All sectors rely heavily on the Vaal Dam (on the Vaal River), from where water is piped across the province.

Agriculture made up a small share of the provincial economy and accounted for R2,1 billion of the GDPR (at current prices) in 2002. Important agricultural products include selected grain crops, certain vegetables, herbs and flowers.

Food, food processing and beverages make up around R9,9 billion of GGP. There are about 4 000 food-processing companies operating in South Africa, of which roughly half are based in Gauteng. These companies employ around 50 000 of the estimated 183 000 people working in the sector.

The competitive trade areas which are being explored include: organics, essential oils, packaging, floriculture, medicinal plants, natural remedies and health foods. High-value niche crops include the nutritious njugo bean, morogo and cowpeas.

Most steel in South Africa is produced and consumed in Gauteng.

South Africa is also one of the top 10 primary producers of aluminium in the world. The value of this industry in Gauteng is worth about US$20 million.

Johannesburg houses the JSE Limited, the largest securities exchange in Africa.

Mpumalanga

Mpumalanga means Place Where The Sun Rises. Due to the province's spectacular scenic beauty and abundance of wildlife, it is one of South Africa's major tourist destinations.

Bordered by Mozambique and Swaziland in the east, and Gauteng in the west, it is situated mainly on the high plateau grasslands of the Middleveld, which roll eastwards for hundreds of kilometres. In the north-east, it rises towards mountain peaks and terminates in an immense escarpment. In some places, this escarpment plunges hundreds of metres down to the low-lying area known as the Lowveld.

The area has a network of excellent roads and railway connections, making it highly accessible. Because of its popularity as a tourist destination, Mpumalanga is also served by a number of small airports. The Kruger Mpumalanga International Airport became operational in 2002.

Nelspruit is the capital of the province and the administrative and business centre of the Lowveld. Witbank is the centre of the local coal-mining industry; Standerton, in the south, is renowned for its large dairy industry; and Piet Retief in the south-east is a production area for tropical fruit and sugar. A large sugar industry is also found at Malelane in the east; Ermelo is the district in South Africa that produces the most wool; Barberton is one of the oldest gold-mining towns in South Africa; and Sabie is situated in the forestry heartland of the country.

The Maputo Corridor, which links the province with Gauteng and Maputo in Mozambique, heralds a new era in terms of economic development and growth for the region.

As the first international toll road in Africa, the Maputo Corridor is set to attract investment and release the local economic potential of the landlocked parts of the country. It will thus generate sustainable economic growth that will lead to sustainable high-quality jobs.

Mpumalanga produces about 80% of the country's coal and remains the largest production region for forestry and agriculture. Mining, manufacturing and electricity contribute about 41,4% of the province's GDP, while the remainder comes from government services, agriculture, forestry and related industries. Mpumalanga is the fourth-biggest contributor to the country's GDP.

The best-performing sectors in the province include mining, manufacturing and services. Tourism and agroprocessing are potential growth sectors in the province.

Mpumalanga falls mainly within the grassland biome. The escarpment and the Lowveld form a transitional zone between this grassland area and the savanna biome. Long sweeps of undulating grasslands change abruptly into thickly forested ravines and thundering waterfalls of the escarpment, only to change again into the subtropical wildlife splendour of the Lowveld.

Sabie and Graskop provide a large part of the country's total requirement for forestry products. These forestry plantations are an ideal backdrop for ecotourism opportunities, with a variety of popular hiking trails, a myriad waterfalls, patches of indigenous forest and many nature reserves.

Lake Chrissie is the largest natural freshwater lake in South Africa and is famous for its variety of aquatic birds, especially flamingos.

The people

Even though it is one of the smaller provinces (79 490 km² in surface area), Mpumalanga has a population of more than 3,2 million (*Mid-Year Estimates, 2005*). According to the 2001 Census results, some 27,5% of those aged 20 years or older have not undergone any schooling, while the population growth rate is higher than the national average.

Mpumalanga's official unemployment rate is 27,4% (*Labour Force Survey*, March 2005).

Agriculture and forestry

The province is a summer-rainfall area divided by the escarpment into the Highveld region with cold frosty winters, and the Lowveld region with mild winters and a subtropical climate.

The escarpment area sometimes experiences snow on high ground. Thick mist is common during the hot, humid summers.

Mpumalanga

Capital: Nelspruit
Principal languages: siSwati   30,8%
                 isiZulu   26,4%
                 isiNdebele 12,1%
Population: 3 219 900 (*Mid-Year Estimates, 2005*)
Area (km²): 79 490
% of total area: 6,5%
GDPR at current prices (2003): R87 461 million
% of total GDP: 7,0%

An abundance of citrus fruit and many other subtropical fruits – mangoes, avocados, litchis, bananas, pawpaws, granadillas, guavas – as well as nuts and a variety of vegetables are produced here.

Nelspruit is the second-largest citrus-producing area in South Africa and is responsible for one-third of the country's export in oranges. The Institute for Tropical and Subtropical Crops is situated here.

Groblersdal is an important irrigation area, which yields a wide variety of products such as citrus fruit, cotton, tobacco, wheat and vegetables.

Carolina-Bethal-Ermelo is mainly a sheep-farming area, but potatoes, sunflowers, maize and peanuts are also produced in this region.

Industry

Mpumalanga is very rich in coal reserves. The country's major power stations, three of which are the biggest in the southern hemisphere, are situated here. Unfortunately, these cause the highest levels of air pollution in the country. Secunda, where South Africa's second petroleum-from-coal installation is situated, is also located in this province.

One of the country's largest paper mills is situated at Ngodwana, close to its timber source. Middelburg produces steel and vanadium, while Witbank is the biggest coal producer in Africa.

Limpopo

Limpopo, South Africa's northernmost province, lies within the great elbow of the Limpopo River and is a province of dramatic contrasts – from true bushveld country to majestic mountains, primeval indigenous forests, latter-day plantations, unspoilt wilderness areas and a patchwork of farming land.

Limpopo has a strong rural basis. Its growth strategy centres on addressing infrastructure backlogs, the alleviation of poverty, and social development.

Limpopo is the gateway to the rest of Africa. It is favourably situated for economic co-operation with other parts of southern Africa as it shares borders with Botswana, Zimbabwe and Mozambique.

The province is linked to the Maputo Development Corridor through the Phalaborwa SDI, a network of rail and road corridors connecting to the major seaports, which will open up Limpopo for trade and investment. This is complemented by the presence of smaller airports in centres such as Phalaborwa and Musina, as well as the Gateway International Airport in Polokwane. The airport carries about 38 000 passengers a year.

The Maputo Corridor will link the province directly with the Port of Maputo, creating development and trade opportunities, particularly in the south-eastern part of the province.

The highest average real-economic-growth rate recorded in South Africa between 1995 and 2003 was that of Limpopo at 3,5% (GDPR).

The provincial economy more than doubled in size from R31 065 billion (at current prices) in 1995 to R81 295 billion (at current prices) in 2003. In 1995, the provincial economy was 5,7% of national GDP. It reached 6,5% in 2003.

Investments totalling some R24 billion occurred in the province between 1998 and 2003.

Substantially, these investments were in the mining sector, which was a dominant sector at 24,9% of the GDPR (2002).

Polokwane is the capital city and lies strategically in the centre of the province.

The Great North Road running through the centre of the province strings together a series of interesting towns. Bela-Bela, with its popular mineral spa, is near the southern border of the province.

Further north lie Modimolle, with its table-grape industry and beautiful Waterberg range; Mokopane; Polokwane; Makhado at the foot of the Soutpansberg mountain range; and Musina, with its thick-set baobab trees.

The crossing into Zimbabwe is at Beit Bridge, where the South African section of this important route north into Africa ends.

Other important Limpopo towns include the major mining centres of Phalaborwa and Thabazimbi, and Tzaneen, producer of tea, forestry products and tropical fruits.

This province is in the savanna biome, an area of mixed grassland and trees, which is generally known as bushveld. A trip through this summer-rainfall area soon convinces one that this is tree country.

Rich in natural beauty, culture and wildlife, Limpopo is the ideal break-away destination for tourists. The province's natural resources include 54 provincial reserves, as well as several private game reserves. The largest section of the Kruger National Park is situated along the eastern boundary of Limpopo with Mozambique.

The people

In Limpopo, more than 5,6 million people live on about 123 910 km^2 of land (*Mid-Year Estimates, 2005*).

According to the Census 2001 results, more than a third of those in Limpopo aged 20 years and older have not received any form of education or schooling.

The official unemployment rate for Limpopo is 32,4%, the highest in the country (*Labour Force Survey*, March 2005).

Several museums and national monuments bear testimony to ancient peoples and fearless pioneers who braved the unknown. Living museums include the Bakone Malapa Museum near Polokwane, where Bapedi tribesmen practise age-old skills for the benefit of visitors, and the Tsonga Open-Air Museum near Tzaneen. Mapungubwe (Place of The Jackal) Hill, some 75 km from Musina, used to be a natural fortress for its inhabitants from about AD 950 to 1200. It was declared a World Heritage Site in 2003.

Valuable archaeological artefacts, including many golden objects, have been discovered in this area, as well as in the northern part of the Kruger National Park.

Limpopo

Capital: Polokwane
Principal languages: Sesotho sa Leboa   52,1%
                              Xitsonga   22,4%
                              Tshivenda   15,9%
Population: 5 635 000 (*Mid-Year Estimates, 2005*)
Area (km^2): 123 910
% of total area: 10,2%
GDPR at current prices (2003): R81 295 million
% of total GDP: 6,5%

24

Agriculture

The bushveld is cattle country, where controlled hunting is often combined with ranching. About 80% of South Africa's hunting takes place in this province.

Sunflowers, cotton, maize and peanuts are cultivated in the Bela-Bela-Modimolle area. Modimolle is also known for its table-grape crops.

Tropical fruit, such as bananas, litchis, pineapples, mangoes and pawpaws, as well as a variety of nuts, are grown in the Tzaneen and Makhado areas. Extensive tea and coffee plantations create many employment opportunities in the Tzaneen area.

The province produces about 75% of the country's mangoes; 65% of its papaya; 36% of its tea; 25% of its citrus, bananas, and litchis; 60% of its avocados; 60% of its tomatoes; 285 000 t of potatoes, 70% of its mangoes and 35% of its oranges (*Provincial Economies, 2003*).

More than 45% of the R2-billion annual turnover of the Johannesburg Fresh Produce Market is from the province.

The largest tomato farm in South Africa lies between Tzaneen and Makhado. Extensive forestry plantations are also found here. Plantations of hard woods for furniture manufacturing have also been established.

Many of the rural people practise subsistence farming.

The northern and eastern parts of this summer-rainfall region are subtropical with hot, humid summers and mist in the mountainous parts. Winter throughout the province is mild and mostly frost-free.

Industry

Mining is a significant economic activity in the province. According to figures released by the Minerals Bureau in 2002, the mining sector employed about 49 000 people in Limpopo.

Limpopo is rich in mineral deposits including platinum, group metals, iron ore, chromium high- and middle-grading coking coal, diamonds, antimony, phosphate and copper, as well as mineral reserves like gold, emeralds, scheelite, magnetite, vermiculite, silicon and mica. Base commodities such as black granite, corundum and feldspar are also found in the province.

Mining's contribution to GDPR at current prices increased from 16,5% in 1995 to 21,9% in 2003.

The province is a typical developing area, exporting primary products and importing manufactured goods and services. It has a high potential and capacity with appropriate economic development, and is an attractive location for investors. Resources such as tourism, rain-fed agriculture, minerals and an abundant labour force offer excellent investment opportunities.

The manufacturing sector's contribution to GDPR improved slightly in 2003 to 3,7%, from 3,6% in 2002.

Acknowledgements

Original text by Theuns and Heila van Rensburg

Bulletin of Statistics (March 2004), published by Statistics South Africa

Department of Water Affairs and Forestry

Labour Force Survey (March 2005), published by Statistics South Africa

Northern Cape Provincial Government

Provincial Economies (May 2003), published by the Department of Trade and Industry

Statistics South Africa

Western Cape Provincial Government

www.fs.gov.za

www.geda.co.za

www.gov.za

www.limpopo.gov.za

www.southafrica.info

Suggested reading

Absalom, E. *'Previously Called' Coloured People – Past and Present: 350 Years*. Rehoboth (Namibia): CBH Publishers, 2001.

Atlas of Southern Africa and the World. Halfway House: Southern Book Publishing, 1992.

Beall, J., Crankshaw, O. and Parnell, S. *Uniting a Divided City: Governance and Social Exclusion in Johannesburg*. London: Earthscan Publications, 2002.

Bekker, S. *et al. Shifting African Identities*. Pretoria: Human Sciences Research Council (HSRC), 2001.

Bowes, B. and Pennington, S. eds. *South Africa: The Good News*. Johannesburg: Good News, 2002.

Bowes, B. and Pennington, S. eds. *South Africa: More Good News*. Johannesburg: Good News, 2003.

Burger, D. ed. *Pocket Guide to South Africa*. Cape Town: STE Publishers on behalf of Government Communications, 2004.

Contemporary South Africa. Basingstoke: Palgrave Macmillan, 2004.

Deacon, H.H. and Deacon, J. *Human Beginnings in South Africa. Uncovering the Secrets of the Stone Age*. Cape Town: David Philip, 1999.

De Gruchy, J.W. *Christianity and Democracy*. Cape Town: David Philip, 1995.

De Gruchy, J.W. *The Church Struggle in South Africa*. Cape Town: David Philip, 1992.

De Klerk, W. *Afrikaners, Kroes, Kras, Kordaat*. Cape Town: Human and Rousseau, 1999.

Du Toit, Z.B. *Die Nuwe Toekoms: 'n Perspektief op die Afrikaner by die Eeuwisseling*. Pretoria: JP van der Walt, 1999.

Earle, J. *Sasol First Guide to Weather in Southern Africa*. Cape Town: Struik, 2004.

Elphick, R. and Davenport R. eds. *Christianity in South Africa: A Political, Social and Cultural History*. Cape Town: David Philip, 1997.

Erasmus, Z. *Coloured by History, Shaped by Place: New Perspectives on Coloured Identity in Cape Town*. Cape Town: Kwela Books, 2001.

Fodor's South Africa: The Complete Guide to the Cities, Winelands and Game Parks, with Zimbabwe and Botswana. 2nd new edition. Compiler: A. Barbour. New York: Fodor's Travel Publications, 1998.

Fox, R. and Rowntree K. eds. *The Geography of South Africa in a Changing World*. Cape Town: Oxford University Press Southern Africa, 2000.

Free State, The Winning Province. Johannesburg: Chris van Rensburg Publications, 1997.

Freund, B. and Padayachee, V. *Durban Vortex: South African City in Transition*. Pietermaritzburg: University of Natal Press, 2002.

Friend, J.F.C. *Environmental Management in South Africa: The Blue Model*. Pretoria: Impact Books, 2003.

Gall, S. *The Bushmen of Southern Africa: Slaughter of the Innocent*. London: Pimlico, 2002.

Germond, P. and de Gruchy, S. *Homosexuality and Christian Faith in South Africa*. Cape Town: David Philip, 1997.

Giliomee, H. *The Afrikaners: Biography of a People*. Cape Town: Tafelberg, 2003.

Haldenwang, B.B. *A Socio-Demographic Profile of the Southern African Development Community Region*. Stellenbosch: Institute for Futures Research, University of Stellenbosch, 1997.

Hendriks, H.J. *Studying Congregations in Africa.* Wellington (Cape): Lux Verbi, 2004.

Hollman, J. ed. *Customs and Beliefs of the !Xam Bushmen.* Johannesburg: Wits University Press, Philadelphia: Ringing Rocks Press, 2004.

Illustrated Guide to the Game Parks and Nature Reserves of Southern Africa. 3rd ed. Cape Town: Reader's Digest Association, 1997.

James, W., Caliquire, D. and Cullinan, K., eds. *Now That We Are Free: Coloured Communities in Democratic South Africa.* Cape Town: Institute for Democracy in South Africa, 1996.

Jenkins, E.R., Raper, P.E. and Moller, L.A. *Changing Place Names.* Durban: Indicator Press, 1996.

Johannesburg: Africa's World City. Johannesburg: Centre for Development and Enterprise, 2002.

Katz, R. *et al. Healing Makes Our Hearts Happy: Spirituality and Cultural Transformation Among the Kalahari Jul'hoansi.* Rochester, Vermont: Inner Traditions International, 1997.

Knobel, J. *The Magnificent Natural Heritage of South Africa.* Llandudno, South Africa: Sunbird Publishing, 1999.

Kobo, J. *After Mandela: The Road Ahead.* Umtata: the author, 2003.

Kok, P. *et al. Post-Apartheid Internal Migration in South Africa.* Cape Town: HSRC, 2003.

Kollenberg, A. *et al.* eds. *Jewish Life in the South African Communities. Vol 1. The Northern Great Escarpment, The Lowveld, The Northern Highveld, The Bushveld.* Johannesburg: South African Friends of Beth Hatefutsoth, 2002.

Le Roux, M. *The Lemba: A Lost Tribe of Israel in Southern Africa?* Pretoria: University of South Africa (UNISA), 2003.

Lee, P. *Compromise and Courage: Anglicans in Johannesburg 1864 – 1999.* Pietermaritzburg: Cluster Publications, 2005.

Lively, A. *Masks: Bleakness, Race and the Imagination.* Oxford: Oxford University Press, 2000.

Magubane, P. *Vanishing Cultures of South Africa: Changing Customs in a Changing World.* Cape Town: Struik, 1998.

Majodina, Z. ed. *The Challenge of Forced Migration in Southern Africa.* Pretoria: Africa Institute of South Africa, 2001.

Meckel, D. and Ole, K. *Straight Talk: Voices from the New South Africa.* Cape Town: Struik, 2004.

Mitchley. C. ed. *South African Heritage: A Guide to Our Land, Our People, History and Culture.* Caledon: Mill Street Publications, 2005.

Moon, B.P. and Dardis, C.F. *Geomorphology of Southern Africa.* Halfway House: Southern Book Publishers, 1992.

Morrell, R. ed. *Changing Man in Southern Africa.* Pietermaritzburg: University of Natal Press, 2001.

Mountain, A. *First People of the Cape.* Cape Town: David Philip, 2003.

Preston-Whyte, R.A. and Tyson, P.D. *Atmosphere and Weather of Southern Africa.* Cape Town: Oxford University Press, 1989.

Rogerson, C. and McCarthy, J. eds. *Geography in a Changing South Africa: Progress and Prospects.* Cape Town: Oxford University Press, 1992.

Schadeberg, J. *Soweto Today.* Pretoria: Protea Book House, 2002.

Schadeberg, J. *The San of the Kalahari.* Pretoria: Protea Book House, 2002.

Schoeman, K. *The Early Mission in South Africa/Die Vroeë Sending in Suid-Afrika 1799 – 1819.* Pretoria: Protea Book House, 2005.

Smith, A. *et al. The Bushmen of Southern Africa: A Foraging Society in Transition.* Cape Town: David Philip, 2000.

Smith, A. *et al. The Cape Herders: A History of the Khoikhoi of Southern Africa.* Cape Town: David Philip, 2000.

Shain, M. and Mendelsohn, R. eds. *Memories, Dreams and Realities: Aspects of the South African Jewish Experience.* Johannesburg: Jonathan Ball, 2002.

Shimoni, G. *Community and Conscience: The Jews in Apartheid South Africa.* Johannesburg: David Philip, 2003.

Simon, D. ed. *South Africa in Southern Africa: Reconfiguring the Region.* Oxford: James Currey; Cape Town: David Philip, 1998.

Tyson, P.D. *Climatic Change and Variability in Southern Africa.* Cape Town: Oxford University Press, 1986.

Tyson, P.D. and Preston-Whyte, R.A. *Weather and Climate of Southern Africa; 2nd ed.* Cape Town: Oxford University Press Southern Africa, 2004.

Van Rooyen, J. *The New Great Trek: The Story of South Africa's White Exodus.* Pretoria: UNISA, 2000.

Van Zyl Slabbert, F. *Afrikaner, Afrikaan.* Cape Town: Tafelberg, 1999.

Venter, L. *In the Shadow of the Rainbow.* Sandton: Heinemann, 2001.

Villa-Vicencio, C. *Civil Disobedience and Beyond: Law, Resistance and Religion in South Africa.* Cape Town: David Philip, 1990.

History

The early inhabitants

There seems to be general agreement among scholars that humankind had its earliest origins in Africa. South Africa is rich in fossil evidence of the evolutionary history of the human family, going back several million years. The discovery of the skull of a Taung child in 1924; recent discoveries of hominid fossils at Sterkfontein caves, recently declared a World Heritage Site; and the ground-breaking work done at Blombos Cave in the southern Cape, have all put South Africa at the forefront of palaeontological research into the origins of humanity. Modern humans have lived in the region for over 100 000 years.

The small, mobile bands of Stone Age hunter-gatherers, who created a wealth of rock art, were the ancestors of the Khoekhoe and San of historical times. The Khoekhoen and San (the 'Hottentots' and 'Bushmen' of early European terminology), although collectively known as the Khoisan, are often thought of as distinct peoples.

The former were those who, some 2 000 years ago, adopted a pastoralist lifestyle herding sheep and, later, cattle. Whereas the hunter-gatherers adapted to local environments and were scattered across the subcontinent, the herders sought out the pasturelands between modern-day Namibia and the Eastern Cape, which, generally, are near the coast.

At around the same time, Bantu-speaking agropastoralists began arriving in southern Africa, bringing with them an iron age culture and domesticated crops. After establishing themselves in the well-watered eastern coastal region of southern Africa, these farmers spread out across the interior plateau, or 'highveld', where they adopted a more extensive cattle-farming culture.

Chiefdoms arose, based on control over cattle, which gave rise to systems of patronage and hence hierarchies of authority within communities. Cattle exchanges formed the basis of polygamous marriage arrangements, facilitating the accumulation of social power through control over the labour of kin groups and dependants.

Metallurgical skills, developed in the mining and processing of iron, copper, tin and gold, promoted regional trade and craft specialisation. At several archaeological sites, such as Mapungubwe and Thulamela in the Limpopo Valley, there is evidence of sophisticated political and material cultures, based in part on contact with the East African trading economy. These cultures, which were part of a broader African civilisation, predate European encroachment by several centuries. Settlement patterns varied from the dispersed homesteads of the fertile coastal regions in the east, to the concentrated towns of the desert fringes in the west.

The farmers did not, however, extend their settlement into the western desert or the winter-rainfall region in the south-west. These regions remained the preserve of the Khoisan until Europeans put down roots at the Cape of Good Hope. This meant that the farmers were little affected by the white presence for the first century during which European settlement expanded from the Western Cape.

Currently, aided by modern science in uncovering the continent's past, which forms part of the African Renaissance, South Africa is gaining a greater understanding of its rich precolonial past and African polities and achievements that were to be disrupted and all but hidden from sight in the period that followed.

The early colonial period

Portuguese seafarers, who pioneered the sea route to India in the late 15th century, were regular visitors to the South African coast during the early 1500s. Other Europeans followed from the late 16th century.

In 1652, the Dutch East India Company (VOC) set up a station in Table Bay (Cape Town) to provision passing ships. Trade with the Khoekhoe(n) for slaughter stock soon degenerated into raiding and warfare. Beginning in 1657, European settlers were allotted farms by the colonial authorities in the arable regions around Cape Town, where wine and wheat became the major products. In response to the colonists' demand for labour, the VOC imported slaves from East Africa, Madagascar, and its possessions from the East Indies.

By the early 1700s, the colonists had begun to spread into the hinterland beyond the nearest mountain ranges. These relatively independent and mobile farmers (*trekboers*), who lived as pastoralists and hunters, were largely free from supervision by the Dutch authorities.

As they intruded further upon the land and water sources, and stepped up their demands for livestock and labour, more and more of the indigenous inhabitants were dispossessed and incorporated into the colonial economy as servants. Diseases such as smallpox, which was introduced by the Europeans in 1713, decimated the Khoisan, contributing to the decline of their cultures. Unions across the colour line took place and a new multiracial social order evolved, based on the supremacy of European colonists. The slave population steadily increased since more labour was needed.

By the mid-1700s, there were more slaves in the Cape than there were 'free burghers' (European colonists). The Asian slaves were concentrated in the towns, where they formed an artisan class. They brought with them the Islam religion, which gained adherents and significantly shaped the working-class culture of the Western Cape. Slaves of African descent were found more often on the farms of outlying districts.

In the late 1700s, the Khoisan offered far more determined resistance to colonial encroachment across the length of the colonial frontier. From the 1770s, colonists also came into contact and conflict with Bantu-speaking chiefdoms some 700 km east of Cape Town. A century of intermittent warfare ensued during which the colonists gained ascendancy, first over the Khoisan and then over the Xhosa-speaking chiefdoms to the east. It was only in the late 1800s that the subjugation of these settled African societies became feasible. For some time their relatively sophisticated social structure and economic systems fended off decisive disruption by incoming colonists, who lacked the necessary military superiority.

At the same time, a process of cultural change was set in motion, not least by commercial and missionary activity. In contrast to the Khoisan, the black farmers were by and large immune to European diseases. For this and other reasons, they were to greatly outnumber the whites in the population of white-ruled South Africa, and were able to preserve important features of their culture. A spate of state-building was launched beyond the frontiers of European settlement.

Perhaps because of population pressures, combined with the actions of slave traders in Portuguese territory on the east coast, the old order was upset and the Zulu kingdom emerged as a highly centralised state. In the 1820s, the innovative leader Shaka established sway over a considerable area of south-east Africa and brought many chiefdoms under his dominion.

As splinter groups conquered and absorbed communities in their path, the disruption was felt as far north as central Africa. Substantial states, such as Moshoeshoe's Lesotho and other Sotho-Tswana chiefdoms, were established, partly for reasons of defence. The *mfecane* or *difaqane*, as this period of disruption and state formation became known, remains the subject of much speculative debate. But the temporary disruption of life on the Highveld served to facilitate Boer expansion northwards from the 1830s, and provided a myth of the 'empty land' which whites employed to justify their domination over the subcontinent in the 20th century.

The British colonial era

In 1795, the British occupied the Cape as a strategic base against the French, controlling the sea route to the East.

After a brief reversion to the Dutch in the course of the Napoleonic wars, it was retaken in 1806 and kept by Britain in the post-war settlement of territorial claims. The closed and regulated economic system of the Dutch period was swept away as the Cape Colony was integrated into the dynamic international trading empire of industrialising Britain.

A crucial new element was evangelicalism, brought to the Cape by Protestant missionaries. The evangelicals believed in the liberating effect of 'free' labour and in the 'civilising mission' of British imperialism. They were convinced that indigenous peoples could be fully assimilated into European Christian culture once the shackles of oppression had been removed.

The most important representative of the mission movement in South Africa was Dr John Philip, who arrived as superintendent of the London Missionary Society in 1819. His campaign on behalf of the oppressed Khoisan coincided with a high point in official sympathy for philanthropic concerns.

One result was Ordinance 50 of 1828, which guaranteed equal civil rights for 'people of colour'

within the colony and freed them from legal discrimination. At the same time, a powerful anti-slavery movement in Britain promoted a series of ameliorative measures, imposed on the colonies in the 1820s, and the proclamation of emancipation, which came into force in 1834. The slaves were subject to a four-year period of 'apprenticeship' with their former owners, on the grounds that they must be prepared for freedom, which came on 1 December 1838.

Although slavery had become less profitable because of a depression in the wine industry, Cape slave-owners rallied to oppose emancipation. The compensation money, which the British treasury paid out to sweeten the pill, injected unprecedented liquidity into the stagnant local economy. This brought a spurt of company formation, such as banks and insurance companies, as well as a surge of investment in land and wool sheep in the drier regions of the colony, in the late 1830s. Wool became a staple export on which the Cape economy depended for its further development in the middle decades of the century.

For the ex-slaves, as for the Khoisan servants, the reality of freedom was very different from the promise. As a wage-based economy developed, they remained a dispossessed and exploited element in the population, with little opportunity to escape their servile lot.

Increasingly, they were lumped together as the 'coloured' people, a group which included the descendants of unions between indigenous and European peoples and a substantial Muslim minority who became known as the 'Cape Malays' (misleadingly, as they mostly came from the Indonesian archipelago).

The coloured people were discriminated against on account of their working-class status as well as their racial identity. Among the poor, especially in and around Cape Town, there continued to be a great deal of racial mixing and intermarriage throughout the 1800s.

In 1820, several thousand British settlers, who were swept up by a scheme to relieve Britain of its unemployed, were placed in the eastern Cape frontier zone as a buffer against the Xhosa chiefdoms.

The vision of a dense settlement of small farmers was, however, ill-conceived and many of the settlers became artisans and traders. The more successful became an entrepreneurial class of merchants, large-scale sheep farmers and speculators with an insatiable demand for land.

Some became fierce warmongers who pressed for the military dispossession of the chiefdoms. They coveted Xhosa land and welcomed the prospect of war involving large-scale military expenditure by the imperial authorities. The Xhosa engaged in raiding as a means of asserting their prior claims to the land. Racial paranoia became integral to white frontier politics. The result was that frontier warfare became endemic through much of the 19th century, during which Xhosa war leaders such as Chief Maqoma became heroic figures to their people.

By the mid-1800s, British settlers of similar persuasion were to be found in Natal. They too called for imperial expansion in support of their land claims and trading enterprises.

Meanwhile, large numbers of the original colonists, the Boers, were greatly extending white occupation beyond the Cape's borders to the north, in the movement that became known as the Great Trek, in the mid-1830s. Alienated by British liberalism, and with their economic enterprise usurped by British settlers, several thousand Boers from the interior districts, accompanied by a number of Khoisan servants, began a series of migrations northwards. They moved to the Highveld and Natal, skirting the great concentrations of black farmers on the way by taking advantage of the areas disrupted during the *mfecane*.

When the British, who were concerned about controlling the traffic through Port Natal (Durban), annexed the territory of Natal in 1843, those emigrant Boers who had hoped to settle there returned inland. The Voortrekkers (as they were later called) coalesced in two land-locked republics, the South African Republic (Transvaal) and the Orange Free State. There, the principles of racially exclusive citizenship were absolute, despite the trekkers' reliance on black labour.

With limited coercive power, the Boer communities had to establish relations and develop alliances with some black chiefdoms, neutralising those who obstructed their intrusion or who posed a threat to their security.

Only after the mineral discoveries of the late 1800s did the balance of power swing decisively towards the colonists. The Boer republics then took on the trappings of real statehood and imposed their authority within the territorial borders that they had notionally claimed for themselves.

The Colony of Natal, situated to the south of the mighty Zulu State, developed along very different lines from the original colony of settlement, the Cape. The size of the black population left no room for the assimilationist vision of race domination embraced in the Cape. Chiefdoms consisting mainly of refugee groups in the aftermath of the *mfecane* were persuaded to accept colonial protection in return for reserved land and the freedom to govern themselves in accordance with their own customs. These chiefdoms were established in the heart of an expanding colonial territory.

Natal developed a system of political and legal dualism, whereby chiefly rule was entrenched and customary law was codified. Although exemptions from customary law could be granted to the educated products of the missions, in practice they were rare. Urban residence was strictly controlled and political rights outside the reserves were effectively limited to whites. Natal's system is widely regarded as having provided a model for the segregationism of the 20th century.

Natal's economy was boosted by the development of sugar plantations in the subtropical coastal lowlands. Indian-indentured labourers were imported from 1860 to work the plantations, and many Indian traders and market gardeners followed.

These Indians, who were segregated and discriminated against from the start, became a further important element in South Africa's population. It was in South Africa that Mohandas Gandhi refined, from the mid-1890s, the techniques of passive resistance, which he later effectively practised in India. Although Indians gradually moved into the Transvaal and elsewhere, they remain concentrated in Natal.

In 1853, the Cape Colony was granted a representative legislature in keeping with British policy, followed in 1872 by self-government. The franchise was formally non-racial, but also based on income and property qualifications. The result was that Africans and coloured people formed a minority – although in certain places a substantial one – of voters.

What became known as the 'liberal tradition' in the Cape depended on the fact that the great mass of Bantu-speaking farmers remained outside its colonial borders until late in the 19th century. Non-racialism could thus be embraced without posing a threat to white supremacy.

Numbers of Africans within the Cape colony had had sufficient formal education or owned enough property to qualify for the franchise. Political alliances across racial lines were common in the eastern Cape constituencies. It is therefore not surprising that the eastern Cape became a seedbed of African nationalism, once the ideal and promise of inclusion in the common society had been so starkly violated by later racial policies.

The mineral revolution

By the late 19th century, the limitations of the Cape's liberal tradition were becoming apparent. The hardening of racial attitudes that accompanied the rise of a more militant imperialist spirit coincided locally with the watershed discovery of mineral riches in the interior of southern Africa. In a developing economy, cheap labour was at a premium, and the claims of educated Africans for equality met with increasingly fierce resistance.

At the same time, the large numbers of Africans in the chiefdoms beyond the Kei River and north of the Gariep (Orange River), then being incorporated into the Cape Colony, posed new threats to racial supremacy and white security, increasing segregationist pressures.

Alluvial diamonds were discovered on the Vaal River in the late 1860s. The subsequent discovery of dry deposits at what became the city of Kimberley drew tens of thousands of people, black and white, to the first great industrial hub in Africa, and the largest diamond deposit in the world. In 1871, the British, who ousted several rival claimants, annexed the diamond fields, which fell in sparsely populated territory to the west of the main corridors of northward migration.

The Colony of Griqualand West thus created was incorporated into the Cape Colony in 1880. By 1888, the consolidation of diamond claims had led to the creation of the huge De Beers monopoly under the control of Cecil Rhodes. He used his power and wealth to become prime minister of the Cape Colony (1890 – 1896) and, through his chartered British South Africa Company, conqueror and ruler of modern-day Zambia and Zimbabwe.

The mineral discoveries had a major impact on the subcontinent as a whole. A railway network linking the interior to the coastal ports revolutionised transportation and energised agriculture. Coastal cities such as Cape Town, Port Elizabeth, East London and Durban experienced an economic boom as port facilities were upgraded.

The fact that the mineral discoveries coincided with a new era of imperialism and the scramble for Africa, brought imperial power and influence to bear in southern Africa as never before.

Independent African chiefdoms were systematically subjugated and incorporated by their white-ruled neighbours. The most dramatic example was the Anglo-Zulu War of 1879, which saw the Zulu State brought under imperial control, during which King Cetshwayo's impis inflicted a celebrated defeat on British forces at Isandlwana. In 1897, Zululand was incorporated into Natal.

The South African Republic (Transvaal) was annexed by Britain in 1877. Boer resistance led to British withdrawal in 1881, but not before the Pedi (northern Sotho) State, which fell within the republic's borders, had been subjugated. The indications were that, having once been asserted, British hegemony was likely to be reasserted. The southern Sotho and Swazi territories were also brought under British rule but maintained their status as imperial dependencies, so that both the current Lesotho and Swaziland escaped the rule of local white regimes.

The discovery of the Witwatersrand goldfields in 1886 was a turning point in the history of South Africa. It presaged the emergence of the modern South African industrial State.

Once the extent of the reefs had been established, and deep-level mining had proved to be a viable investment, it was only a matter of time before Britain and its local representatives again found a pretext for war against the Boer republics of Transvaal and the Orange Free State.

The demand for franchise rights for English-speaking immigrants on the goldfields (uitlanders) provided a lever for applying pressure on the Government of President Paul Kruger. Egged on by the deep-level mining magnates, to whom the Boer Government seemed obstructive and inefficient, and by the expectation of an uitlander uprising, Rhodes launched a raid into the Transvaal in late December 1895. The raid's failure saw the end of Rhodes' political career, but Sir Alfred Milner, British High Commissioner in South Africa from 1897, was determined to overthrow Kruger's government and establish British rule throughout the subcontinent. The Boer Government was eventually forced into a declaration of war in October 1899.

The mineral discoveries had a radical impact on every sphere of society. Labour was required on a massive scale and could only be provided by Africans, who had to be drawn away from the land.

Many Africans did respond with alacrity to the opportunities presented by wage labour, travelling long distances to earn money to supplement rural enterprise in the homestead economy.

In response to the expansion of internal markets, Africans exploited their farming skills and family labour to good effect to increase production for sale. A substantial black peasantry arose, often by means of share-cropping or labour tenantry on white-owned farms.

For the white authorities, however, the chief consideration was ensuring a labour supply and undermining black competition on the land. Conquest, land dispossession, taxation and pass laws were designed to force black men off the land and channel them into labour markets, especially to meet the needs of the mines.

Gradually, the alternatives available to them were closed, and the decline of the homestead economy made wage labour increasingly essential for survival. The integration of Africans into the emerging urban and industrial society of South Africa should have followed these developments, but short-term, recurrent labour migrancy suited employers and the authorities, which sought to entrench the system.

The closed compounds pioneered on the diamond fields, as a means of migrant labour control, were replicated at the gold mines. The preservation of communal areas from which migrants could be drawn had the effect of lowering wages, by denying Africans rights within the urban areas and keeping their families and dependants on subsistence plots in the reserves.

Africans could be denied basic rights if the fiction could be maintained that they did not belong in 'white South Africa' but to 'tribal societies' from which they came to service the 'white man's needs'. Where black families secured a toehold in the urban areas, local authorities confined them to segregated 'locations'. This set of assumptions and policies informed the development of segregationist ideology and, later (from 1948), apartheid.

The Anglo-Boer/South African War (October 1899 – May 1902) and its aftermath

The war that followed the mineral revolution was mainly a white man's war. In its first phase, the Boer forces took the initiative, besieging the frontier towns of Mafeking (Mafikeng) and Kimberley in the northern Cape, and Ladysmith in northern Natal. Some colonial Boers rebelled, however, in sympathy with the republics. But, after a large expeditionary force under lords Roberts and Kitchener arrived, the British advance was rapid. Kruger fled the Transvaal shortly before Pretoria fell in June 1900.

The formal conquest of the two Boer republics was followed by a prolonged guerrilla campaign. Small, mobile groups of Boers denied the imperial forces their victory, by disrupting rail links and supply lines.

Commandos swept deep into colonial territory, rousing rebellion wherever they went. The British were at a disadvantage owing to their lack of familiarity with the terrain and the Boers' superior skills as horsemen and sharpshooters. The British responded with a scorched-earth policy.

This included farm burnings, looting and the setting-up of concentration camps for non-combatants, in which some 26 000 Boer women and children died from disease. The incarceration of black (including coloured) people in the path of the war in racially segregated camps has been absent in conventional accounts of the war and has only recently been acknowledged.

They too suffered appalling conditions and some 14 000 (perhaps many more) are estimated to have died. At the same time, many black farmers were in a position to meet the demand for produce created by the military, or avail themselves of employment opportunities at good wages. Some 10 000 black servants accompanied the Boer commandos, and the British used Africans as labourers, scouts, dispatch riders, drivers and guards.

The war also taught many Africans that the forces of dispossession could be rolled back if the circumstances were right. It gave black communities the opportunity to recolonise land lost in conquest, which enabled them to withhold their labour after the war. Most supported the British in the belief that Britain was committed to extending civil and political rights to black people. In this they were to be disappointed, as in the Treaty of Vereeniging that ended the war, the British agreed to leave the issue of rights for Africans to be decided by a future self-governing (white) authority. All in all, the Anglo-Boer/South African War was a radicalising experience for Africans.

Britain's reconstruction regime set about creating a white-ruled dominion by uniting the former Boer republics (both by then British colonies) with Natal and the Cape.

The most important priority was to re-establish white control over the land and force the Africans back to wage labour. The labour-recruiting system was improved, both internally and externally. Recruiting agreements were reached with the Portuguese authorities in Mozambique, from where much mine labour came.

When, by 1904, African sources still proved inadequate to get the mines working at pre-war levels, over 60 000 indentured Chinese were brought in. This precipitated a vociferous outcry from proponents of white supremacy in South Africa and liberals in Britain.

By 1910, all had been repatriated, a step made easier when a surge of Africans came forward from areas such as the Transkeian territories and the northern Transvaal, which had not previously been large-scale suppliers of migrants. This was the heyday of the private recruiters, who exploited families' indebtedness to procure young men to labour in the mines. The Africans' post-war ability to withhold their labour had been undercut by government action, abetted by drought and stock disease.

The impact of the Anglo-Boer/South African War as a seminal influence on the development of Afrikaner nationalist politics became apparent in subsequent years.

The Boer leaders – most notably Louis Botha, Jan Smuts and J.B.M. Hertzog – played a dominant role in the country's politics for the next half century. After initial plans for anglicisation of the defeated Afrikaners through the education system and numerical swamping through British immigration were abandoned as impractical, the British looked to the Afrikaners as collaborators in securing imperial political and economic interests.

During 1907 and 1908, the two former Boer republics were granted self-government but, crucially, with a whites-only franchise. Despite promises to the contrary, black interests were sacrificed in the interest of white nation-building across the white language divide. The National Convention drew up a constitution and the four colonies became an independent dominion called the Union of South Africa on 31 May 1910.

The 19th-century formally non-racial franchise was retained in the Cape but was not extended elsewhere, where rights of citizenship were confined to whites alone.

It was clear from the start that segregation was the conventional wisdom of the new rulers. Black people were defined as outsiders, without rights or claims on the common society that their labour had helped to create.

Segregation

Government policy in the Union of South Africa did not develop in isolation, but against the backdrop of black political initiatives. Segregation and apartheid assumed their shape, in part, as a white response to Africans' increasing participation in the country's economic life and their assertion of political rights. Despite the Government's efforts to shore up traditionalism and retribalise them, black people became more fully integrated into the urban and industrial society of 20th-century South Africa than happened elsewhere on the continent. An educated élite of clerics, teachers, business people, journalists and professionals grew to be a major force in black politics.

Mission Christianity and its associated educational institutions exerted a profound influence on African political life, and separatist churches were early vehicles for African political assertion. The experiences of studying abroad, and in particular, interaction with black people struggling for their rights elsewhere in Africa, the United States of America and the Caribbean, played an important part. A vigorous black press, associated in its early years with such pioneer editors as J.T. Jabavu, Pixley Seme, Dr Abdullah Abdurahman, Sol Plaatje and John Dube, served the black reading public.

At the same time, African communal struggles to maintain access to the land in rural areas posed a powerful challenge to the white State. Traditional authorities often led popular struggles against intrusive and manipulative policies. Government attempts to control and co-opt the chiefs often failed.

Steps towards the formation of a national political organisation of coloureds began around the turn of the century, with the formation of the African Political Organisation in 1902 by Dr Abdurahman, mainly in the Cape Province.

The African National Congress (ANC), founded in 1912, became, however, the most important black organisation drawing together traditional authorities and the educated African élite in common causes.

In its early years, the ANC was concerned mainly with constitutional protest.

Worker militancy emerged in the wake of the First World War, and continued through the 1920s. It included strikes and an anti-pass campaign given impetus by women, particularly in the Free State, resisting extension of the pass laws to them. The Industrial and Commercial Workers' Union, under the leadership of Clements Kadalie, was (despite its name) the first populist, nationwide organisation representing blacks in rural as well as urban areas. But it was short-lived.

The Communist Party, formed in 1921 and since then a force for both non-racialism and worker organisation, was to prove far longer-lasting. In other sections of the black population too, the turn of the century saw organised opposition emerging. Gandhi's leadership of protest against discriminatory laws gave impetus to the formation of provincial Indian congresses, including the Natal Indian Congress formed by Gandhi in 1894.

The principles of segregationist thinking were laid down in a 1905 report by the South African Native Affairs Commission and continued to evolve in response to these economic, social and political pressures. In keeping with its recommendations, the first Union Government enacted the seminal Natives Land Act in 1913.

This defined the remnants of their ancestral lands after conquest for African occupation, and declared illegal all land purchases or rent tenancy outside these reserves. The reserves ('homelands' as they were subsequently called) eventually comprised about 13% of South Africa's land surface. Administrative and legal dualism reinforced the division between white citizen and black non-citizen, a dispensation personified by the Governor-General who, as 'supreme chief' over the country's African majority, was empowered to rule them by administrative fiat and decree.

The Government also regularised the job colour bar, reserving skilled work for whites and denying African workers the right to organise. Legislation, which was consolidated in the Natives (Urban Areas) Act, 1923, entrenched urban segregation and controlled African mobility by means of pass laws. The pass laws were intended to enmesh Africans in a web of coercion designed to force them into labour and keep them there under conditions and at wage levels that suited white employers, and to deny them any bargaining power.

In these and other ways, the foundations of apartheid were laid by successive governments representing the compromises hammered out by the National Convention of 1908 to 1909 to effect the union of English- and Afrikaans-speaking whites.

Divisions within the white community remained significant, however. Afrikaner nationalism grew as a factor in the years after union. It was given impetus in 1914, both by the formation of the National Party (NP), in a breakaway from the ruling South African Party, and by a rebellion of Afrikaners who could not reconcile themselves with the decision to join the First World War against Germany. In part, the NP spoke for Afrikaners impoverished by the Anglo-Boer/South African War and dislodged from the land by the development of capitalist farming.

An Afrikaner underclass was emerging in the towns, which found itself uncompetitive in the labour market, as white workers demanded higher wages than those paid to blacks.

Soon, labour issues came to the fore. In 1920, some 71 000 black mineworkers went on strike in protest against the spiralling cost of living, but the strike was quickly put down by isolating the compounds where the migrant workers were housed.

Another threat to government came from white workers. Immigrant white workers with mining experience abroad performed much of the skilled and semi-skilled work on the mines. As mine owners tried to cut costs by using lower-wage black labour in semi-skilled jobs, white labour became increasingly militant. These tensions culminated in a bloody and dramatic rebellion on the goldfields in 1922, which the Smuts Government put down with military force. In 1924, a pact government under Hertzog, comprising Afrikaner nationalists and representatives of immigrant labour, ousted the Smuts regime.

The pact was based on a common suspicion of the dominance of mining capital, and a determination to protect the interests of white labour by inten-

sifying discrimination against blacks. The commitment to white labour policies in government employment such as the railways and postal service was intensified, and the job colour bar was reinforced, with one of its main objectives to address what was known as a 'poor-white problem'.

In 1934, the main white parties fused to combat the local effects of a worldwide depression.

This was followed by a new Afrikaner nationalist breakaway under Dr D.F. Malan. In 1936, white supremacy was further entrenched by the United Party with the removal of the Africans of the Cape Province who qualified, from the common voters' roll. Meanwhile, Malan's breakaway NP was greatly augmented by an Afrikaner cultural revival spearheaded by the secret white male Afrikaner Broederbond and other cultural organisations during the year of the Voortrekker centenary celebrations (1938), as well as by anti-war sentiment from 1939.

Apartheid

After the Second World War in 1948, the NP, with its ideology of apartheid that brought an even more rigorous and authoritarian approach than the segregationist policies of previous governments, won the general election. It did so against the background of a revival of mass militancy during the 1940s, after a period of relative quiescence in the 1930s when black groups attempted to foster unity among themselves.

The change was marked by the formation of the ANC Youth League in 1943, fostering the leadership of figures such as Anton Lembede, A.P. Mda, Nelson Mandela, Oliver Tambo and Walter Sisulu, who were to inspire the struggle for decades to come.

In the 1940s, squatter movements in peri-urban areas brought mass politics back to the urban centres. The 1946 mineworkers' strike was a turning point in the emergence of a politics of mass mobilisation.

As was the case with the First World War, the experience of the Second World War and post-war economic difficulties enhanced discontent. For those who supported the NP, its primary appeal lay in its determination to maintain white domination in the face of rising mass resistance; uplift poor Afrikaners; challenge the pre-eminence of English-speaking whites in public life, the professions and business; and abolish the remaining imperial ties. The State became an engine of patronage for Afrikaner employment. The Afrikaner Broederbond co-ordinated the party's programme, ensuring that Afrikaner nationalist interests and policies attained ascendancy throughout civil society.

In 1961, the NP Government under Prime Minister H.F. Verwoerd declared South Africa a republic, after winning a whites-only referendum on the issue.

A new currency, the Rand, new flag, anthem and coat of arms were formally introduced. South Africa, having become a republic, had to apply for continued membership of the Commonwealth. In the face of demands for an end to apartheid, South Africa withdrew its application and a figurehead president replaced the Queen (represented locally by the Governor-General) as head of state.

In most respects, apartheid was a continuation, in more systematic and brutal form, of the segregationist policies of previous governments.

A new concern with racial purity was apparent in laws prohibiting interracial sex and provisions for population registration requiring that every South African be assigned to one discrete racial category or another.

For the first time, the coloured people, who had always been subjected to informal discrimination, were brought within the ambit of discriminatory laws. In the mid-1950s, government took the drastic step of overriding an entrenched clause in the 1910 Constitution of the Union so as to be able to remove coloured voters from the common voters' roll. It also enforced residential segregation, expropriating homes where necessary and policing massive forced removals into coloured 'group areas'.

Until the 1940s, South Africa's racial policies had not been entirely out of step with those to be found in the colonial world. But by the 1950s, which saw decolonisation and a global backlash against racism gather pace, the country was dramatically opposed to world opinion on questions of human rights. The architects of apartheid, among whom Dr Verwoerd

was pre-eminent, responded by elaborating a theory of multinationalism.

Their policy, which they termed 'separate development', divided the African population into artificial ethnic 'nations', each with its own 'homeland' and the prospect of 'independence', supposedly in keeping with trends elsewhere on the continent. This divide-and-rule strategy was designed to disguise the racial basis of official policy-making by the substitution of the language of ethnicity. This was accompanied by much ethnographic engineering as efforts were made to resurrect tribal structures. In the process, the Government sought to create a significant collaborating class.

The truth was that the rural reserves were by this time thoroughly degraded by overpopulation and soil erosion. This did not prevent four of the 'homeland' structures (Transkei, Bophuthatswana, Venda and Ciskei) being declared 'independent', a status which the vast majority of South Africans, and therefore also the international community, declined to recognise. In each case, the process involved the repression of opposition and the use by the Government of the power to nominate and thereby pad elected assemblies with a quota of compliant figures.

Forced removals from 'white' areas affected some 3,5 million people and vast rural slums were created in the homelands, which were used as dumping grounds. The pass laws and influx control were extended and harshly enforced, and labour bureaux were set up to channel labour to where it was needed. Hundreds of thousands of people were arrested or prosecuted under the pass laws each year, reaching over half a million a year from the mid-1960s to the mid-1970s. Industrial decentralisation to growth points on the borders of (but not inside) the homelands was promoted as a means of keeping blacks out of 'white' South Africa.

In virtually every sphere, from housing to education to healthcare, central government took control over black people's lives with a view to reinforcing their allotted role as 'temporary sojourners', welcome in 'white' South Africa solely to serve the needs of the employers of labour. But these same programmes of control became the focus of resistance. In particular, the campaign against the pass laws formed a cornerstone of the struggle.

The end of apartheid

The introduction of apartheid policies coincided with the adoption by the ANC in 1949 of its programme of action, expressing the renewed militancy of the 1940s. The programme embodied the rejection of white domination and a call for action in the form of protests, strikes and demonstrations. There followed a decade of turbulent mass action in resistance to the imposition of still harsher forms of segregation and oppression.

The Defiance Campaign of 1952 carried mass mobilisation to new heights under the banner of non-violent resistance to the pass laws. These actions were influenced in part by the philosophy of Mohandas Gandhi.

A critical step in the emergence of non-racialism was the formation of the Congress Alliance, including the ANC; South African Indian Congress; the Coloured People's Congress; a small white congress organisation (the Congress of Democrats); and the South African Congress of Trade Unions.

The alliance gave formal expression to an emerging unity across racial and class lines that was manifested in the Defiance Campaign and other mass protests, including against Bantu education, of this period which also saw women's resistance take a more organised character with the formation of the Federation of South African Women.

In 1955, the Freedom Charter was drawn up at the Congress of the People in Soweto. The charter enunciated the principles of the struggle, binding the movement to a culture of human rights and non-racialism. Over the next few decades, the Freedom Charter was elevated to an important symbol of the freedom struggle.

The Pan-Africanist Congress (PAC), founded by Robert Sobukwe and based on the philosophies of 'Africanism' and anti-communism, broke away from the Congress Alliance in 1959.

The State's initial response, harsh as it was, was not yet as draconian as it was to become. Its attempt to prosecute more than 150 anti-apartheid leaders for treason, in a trial that began in 1956, ended in acquittals in 1961. But by that time, mass organised opposition had been banned.

Matters came to a head at Sharpeville in March 1960, when 69 anti-pass demonstrators were killed when police fired on a demonstration called by the PAC. A state of emergency was imposed and detention without trial was introduced.

The black political organisations were banned and their leaders went into exile or were arrested. In this climate, the ANC and PAC abandoned their long-standing commitment to non-violent resistance and turned to armed struggle, combined with underground organisation and mobilisation as well as mobilisation of international solidarity. Top leaders, including members of the newly formed military wing Umkhonto we Sizwe (MK) (Spear of the Nation), were arrested in 1963. In the 'Rivonia trial', eight ANC leaders, including Nelson Mandela, were convicted of sabotage (instead of treason, the original charge) and sentenced to life imprisonment.

In this period, leaders of other organisations, including the PAC and the New Unity Movement, were also sentenced to long terms of imprisonment and/or banned.

The 1960s was a decade of overwhelming repression and relative political disarray among blacks in the country. Armed action was contained by the State.

State repression played a central role in containing internal resistance, and the leadership of the struggle shifted increasingly to the missions in exile. At the same time, the ANC leadership decided to embark on a campaign to infiltrate the country through what was then Rhodesia. In August 1967, a joint force of MK and the Zimbabwean People's Revolutionary Army (ZIPRA) of the Zimbabwe African People's Union (ZAPU) entered Zimbabwe, and over a two-month period engaged the joint Rhodesian and South African security forces. Although the joint MK-ZIPRA force failed to reach South Africa, this was the first military confrontation between the military forces of the ANC-led alliance and white security forces.

The resurgence of resistance politics from the early 1970s was dramatic. The Black Consciousness Movement, led by Steve Biko (who was killed in detention in 1977), reawakened a sense of pride and self-esteem in black people. News of the brutal death of Biko reverberated around the globe and led to unprecedented outrage.

As capitalist economies sputtered with the oil crisis of 1973, black trade unions revived. A wave of strikes reflected a new militancy that involved better organisation and was drawing new sectors, in particular intellectuals and the student movement, into mass struggle and debate over the principles informing it. Rallies at black universities in support of Frelimo, the Mozambican liberation movement, also gave expression to the growing militancy.

The year 1976 marked the beginning of a sustained anti-apartheid revolt. In June, school pupils of Soweto rose up against apartheid education, followed by youth uprisings all around the country. Despite the harsh repression that followed, students continued to organise, with the formation in 1979 of organisations for school students (Congress of South African Students) and college and university students (Azanian Students Organisation).

By the 1980s, the different forms of struggle – armed struggle, mass mobilisation and international solidarity – were beginning to integrate and coalesce.

The United Democratic Front and the informal umbrella, the Mass Democratic Movement, emerged as legal vehicles of democratic forces struggling for liberation. Clerics played a prominent public role in these movements. The involvement of workers in resistance took on a new dimension with the formation of the Congress of South African Trade Unions and the National Council of Trade Unions.

Popular anger was directed against all those who were deemed to be collaborating with the Government in the pursuit of its objectives, and the black townships became virtually ungovernable. From the mid-1980s, regional and national states of emergency were enforced.

Developments in neighbouring states, where mass resistance to white minority and colonial rule led to Portuguese decolonisation in the mid-1970s and the abdication of Zimbabwe's minority regime in 1980, left South Africa exposed as the last bastion of white supremacy.

Under growing pressure and increasingly isolated internationally, the Government embarked on a dual strategy, introducing limited reform coupled with intensifying repression and militarisation of society, with the objective of containing the pressures and increasing its support base while crushing organised resistance.

An early example of reform was the recognition of black trade unions to try to stabilise labour relations. In 1983, the Constitution was reformed to allow the coloured and Indian minorities limited participation in separate and subordinate houses of Parliament. The vast majority of these groups demonstrated their rejection of the tricameral dispensation through massive boycotts of elections, but it was kept in place by the apartheid regime despite its visible lack of legitimacy. Attempts to legitimise community councils as vehicles for participation of Africans outside the Bantustans in local government met a similar fate.

Militarisation included the ascendancy of the State Security Council, which usurped the role of the executive in crucial respects, and a succession of states of emergency as part of the implementation of a comprehensive counter-insurgency strategy to combat what, by the mid-1980s, was an endemic insurrectionary spirit in the land.

However, by the late 1980s, popular resistance was taking the form of mass defiance campaigns, while struggles over more localised issues saw broad sections of communities mobilised in united action. Popular support for released political prisoners and for the armed struggle was being openly expressed.

In response to the rising tide of resistance, the international community strengthened its support for the anti-apartheid cause. A range of sanctions and boycotts was instituted, both unilaterally by countries across the world and through the United Nations (UN). These sanctions were called for in a co-ordinated strategy by the internal and external anti-apartheid movement in South Africa.

F.W. de Klerk, who replaced P.W. Botha as state president in 1989, announced at the opening of Parliament in February 1990 the unbanning of the liberation movements and release of political prisoners, notably Nelson Mandela. A number of factors led to this step. International financial, trade, sport and cultural sanctions were clearly biting.

Above all, even if South Africa were nowhere near collapse, either militarily or economically, several years of emergency rule and ruthless repression had clearly neither destroyed the structures of organised resistance, nor helped establish legitimacy for the apartheid regime or its collaborators. Instead, popular resistance, including mass and armed action, was intensifying.

The ANC, enjoying popular recognition and legitimacy as the foremost liberation organisation, was increasingly regarded as a government-in-waiting. International support for the liberation movement came from various countries around the globe, particularly from former socialist countries and Nordic countries as well as the Non-Aligned Movement (NAM). The other liberation organisations increasingly experienced various internal and external pressures and did not enjoy much popular support. It was obvious that Botha's strategy of reform initiatives combined with repression had failed to stabilise the internal situation.

To outside observers, and also in the eyes of growing numbers of white South Africans, apartheid stood exposed as morally bankrupt, indefensible and impervious to reforms. The collapse of global communism, the negotiated withdrawal of Cuban forces from Angola, and the culmination of the South-West African People's Organisation's liberation struggle in the negotiated independence of Namibia – formerly South-West Africa, administered by South Africa as a League of Nations mandate since 1919 – did much to change the mindset of whites. No longer could whites demonise the ANC and PAC as fronts for international communism.

White South Africa had also changed in deeper ways. Afrikaner nationalism had lost much of its *raison d'être*. Many Afrikaners had become urban, middle class and relatively prosperous. Their ethnic grievances and attachment to ethnic causes and symbols had diminished. A large part of the NP's core constituency was ready to explore larger national identities, even across racial divides, and yearned for international respectability. Apartheid

increasingly seemed more like a straitjacket than a safeguard. In 1982, disenchanted hardliners split from the NP to form the Conservative Party, leaving the NP open to more flexible and modernising influences. After this split, factions within the Afrikaner élite openly started to pronounce in favour of a more inclusive society, causing more friction with the NP Government, which increasingly became militaristic and authoritarian.

A number of business, student and academic Afrikaners held meetings publicly and privately with the ANC in exile. Secret talks were held between the imprisoned Mandela and government ministers about a new dispensation for South Africa, with blacks forming a major part of it.

Inside the country, mass action became the order of the day. Petty apartheid laws and symbols were openly challenged and removed. Together with a sliding economy and increasing international pressure, these developments made historic changes inevitable.

The First Decade of Freedom

After a long negotiation process, sustained despite much opportunistic violence from the right wing and its surrogates, and in some instances sanctioned by elements of the State, South Africa's first democratic election was held in April 1994 under an interim Constitution.

The interim Constitution divided South Africa into nine new provinces in place of the previous four provinces and 10 'homelands', and provided for the Government of National Unity to be constituted by all parties with at least 20 seats in the National Assembly.

The ANC emerged from the election with a 62% majority. The main opposition came from the NP, which gained 20% of the vote nationally, and a majority in the Western Cape. The Inkatha Freedom Party (IFP) received 10% of the vote, mainly in its KwaZulu-Natal base. The NP and the IFP formed part of the Government of National Unity until 1996, when the NP withdrew. The ANC-led Government embarked on a programme to promote the reconstruction and development of the country and its institutions.

This called for the simultaneous pursuit of democratisation and socio-economic change, as well as reconciliation and the building of consensus founded on the commitment to improve the lives of all South Africans, in particular the poor. It required the integration of South Africa into a rapidly changing global environment.

Pursuit of these objectives has been a consistent focus of government during the First Decade of Freedom, seeking the unity of a previously divided society in working together to overcome the legacy of a history of division, exclusion and neglect.

Converting democratic ideals into practice required, among other things, initiating a radical overhaul of the machinery of government at every level, working towards service delivery, openness, and a culture of human rights. It has required a more integrated approach to planning and implementation to ensure that the many different aspects of transformation and socio-economic upliftment cohere with maximum impact.

A significant milestone in the democratisation of South Africa was the exemplary Constitution-making process, which in 1996 delivered a document that has evoked worldwide admiration. So too have been the elections subsequent to 1994 – all conducted peacefully, with high levels of participation compared with the norm in most democracies, and accepted by all as free and fair in their conduct and results.

Local government elections during 1995 and 1996, and then again in 2000 after the transformation of the municipal system, gave the country its first democratically elected non-racial municipal authorities.

Since 2001, participatory democracy and interactive governance have been strengthened through the practice of imbizo, in which members of the executive, in all three spheres of government, including The Presidency, regularly engage directly with the public around implementation of programmes of reconstruction and development.

The second democratic national election in 1999 saw the ANC majority increase to just short of two-thirds and the election of Mr Thabo Mbeki as president in succession to Mr Nelson Mandela. It saw a sharp decline of the NP (then the New National Party [NNP]) and its replacement by the Democratic Party, led by Mr Tony Leon, as the official opposition in Parliament. These two parties formed the Democratic Alliance, which the NNP left in 2001.

Although the new Constitution does not provide for a government of national unity, the Government continued to include representatives of opposition parties, namely the IFP, later the Azanian People's Organisation, and the NNP.

The Truth and Reconciliation Commission (TRC), under the leadership of Archbishop Desmond Tutu, helped inculcate a commitment to accountability and transparency in South Africa's public life, at the same time helping to heal wounds inflicted by the inhumanities of the apartheid era.

During 2003, Parliament accepted the Government's response to the final report of the TRC. Out of 22 000 individuals or surviving families appearing before the commission, 19 000 were identified as needing urgent reparation assistance – virtually all, where the necessary information was available, received interim reparations. As final reparations, government is providing a once-off grant of R30 000 to individuals or survivors who appeared before, and were designated by, the TRC, over and above the programmes for material assistance. There will also be systematic programmes to project the symbolism of the struggle and the ideal of freedom. These include the Freedom Park Monument and other symbols and monuments, and such matters as records of history, remaking of cultural and art forms, and geographical and place names.

The ethos of partnership informed the establishment of the National Economic Development and Labour Council. It brings together government, business, organised labour and development organisations to confront the challenges of growth and development for South Africa in a turbulent and globalising international economy.

The Presidential Jobs Summit in 1998 and the Growth and Development Summit (GDS) in June 2003 brought these sectors together to collectively take advantage of the conditions in South Africa for faster growth and development. At the GDS, a comprehensive set of agreements was concluded to address urgent challenges in a practical way and speed up job-creating growth and development.

Partnership between government and civil society has been further strengthened by the creation of a number of working groups through which sectors of society – business, organised labour, Higher Education, religious leaders, youth and women – engage regularly with the President.

From the start, government placed emphasis on meeting basic needs through programmes for socio-economic development such as the provision of housing, piped water, electricity, education and healthcare, as well as social grants for those in need.

The impact of these programmes is seen in the increased proportion of South Africans who now have access to these basic services. This has been achieved despite a social revolution reflected in smaller household sizes (with the number of households growing almost three times faster than the population) and therefore many more households needing basic services.

Another priority has been the safety and security of citizens, requiring both transforming the police into a service working with the community, and overcoming grave problems of criminality and a culture of violence posed by the social dislocations inherited from the past. By the end of the first decade of democracy, crime levels had been stabilised and many categories were beginning to decrease.

On the economic front, the key objectives have been job creation, poverty eradication, reduction of inequality and overall growth. There has been progress in rebuilding the economy, in particular with the achievement of macro-economic stability and the initiation of programmes of micro-economic reform. But unemployment remains a major challenge – the number of jobs created has not been enough, as the economically active population has grown faster, and the economy needs more skilled workers. By the end of 2004, growth was accelerating and there were signs of the beginnings of a reduction in unemployment.

The integration of South Africa into the global political, economic and social system has been a priority for democratic South Africa. As a country isolated during the apartheid period; an African country; a developing country; and a country whose liberation was achieved with the support of the international community, it has been of critical importance to build political and economic links with the countries and regions of the world, and to work with others for an international environment more favourable to development across the world, and in Africa and South Africa in particular.

The South African Government is committed to the African Renaissance, which is based on the consolidation of democracy, economic development and a co-operative approach to resolving the challenges the continent faces.

South Africa hosted the launch in 2002 of the African Union (AU), a step towards further unification of Africa in pursuit of socio-economic development, the Organisation of African Unity having fulfilled its mandate to liberate Africa. President Mbeki chaired the AU for its founding year, handing over the chair to President Joaquim Chissano of Mozambique in July 2003. In 2004, the AU decided that South Africa should host the Pan-African Parliament and it met for its second session in South Africa, the first time on South African soil, in September of that year.

By participating in UN and AU initiatives to resolve conflicts and promote peace and security on the continent – in among other countries, the Democratic Republic of Congo, Burundi and Sudan – South Africa has been contributing to the achievement of conditions conducive to the entrenchment of stability, democracy and faster development.

Through the New Partnership for Africa's Development (NEPAD), the development programme of the AU, South Africa works with the rest of the continent and its partners in the industrialised world for the development and regeneration of the African continent.

Democratic South Africa has sought to play an active role in international and multilateral organisations. During the First Decade of Freedom, it acted at various times as chair of the Southern African Development Community, NAM, AU and the

Commonwealth Heads of Government meeting. It has played host to several international conferences, including the UN Conference on Trade and Development in 1996, the 2000 World AIDS Congress, World Conference Against Racism in 2001, World Summit on Sustainable Development in 2002, and the World Parks Congress in 2003.

South Africa is playing an increasing role in multilateral institutions – for example the Minister of Finance has been a member of the International Monetary Fund's Development Committee since 2002, and the National Commissioner of the South African Police Service was elected president of Interpol in 2004.

South Africa has proved itself too as a venue for the world's major sporting events, and is busy as a nation preparing to host the 2010 Soccer World Cup Tournament.

Into the Second Decade of Freedom

During 2004, South Africa celebrated 10 years of freedom. There were also celebrations across the world, in countries whose peoples had helped bring freedom to South Africa through their solidarity, and are today partners in reconstruction and development.

The *Towards a Ten-Year Review* initiated by government during 2003, documented the great progress that South Africans have made in pursuit of their goals, as well as the challenges that face the nation as it begins the second decade of its freedom, at the beginning of the 21st century. Some of these challenges are shared with the rest of the world, especially developing countries.

Globalisation, the digital divide, poverty, HIV and AIDS, and creating conditions conducive to sustainable development are some of the critical issues for which the nation is seeking solutions in partnership with others.

Other challenges are specific to South Africa. Among them are the further strengthening of social partnerships for the development of South African society, the eradication of poverty, improving the performance of the State, addressing the consequences of the social transition that has followed the end of apartheid, and improving the regional environment and implementing NEPAD.

Meeting these challenges, the *Ten-Year Review* concluded, is essential to taking the country to a path of faster growth and development that is needed to sustain and even surpass the progress of the First Decade.

By the end of 2005, all indicators pointed to conditions conducive to meeting these challenges.

In its third democratic elections, in April 2004, the country gave an increased mandate to the Government's programme for reconstruction and development and for the entrenchment of the rights inscribed in the Constitution. In this context, the Programme of Action of the new Government placed emphasis on the effective implementation of agreed policies, with particular focus on creating work opportunities and fighting poverty.

Better economic performance which began in late 1999 – resulting in the longest business cycle upswing on record – gathered further momentum in 2004 and the first half of 2005. The pace of economic growth was expected to be just above 4% during 2006, and to reach between 4,5% and 5% a year in 2007 and 2008.

The sense of national unity among South Africans and confidence in the direction of the country were at levels not seen since the dawn of freedom in 1994.

In this context of an unprecedented confluence of encouraging possibilities, and working with its social partners, the Government has developed the Accelerated and Shared Growth Initiative for South Africa, systematically to raise the trajectory of growth to an average of 6% between 2010 and 2014. Such rates of growth, combined with improved labour absorption, would ensure that South Africa is able to halve unemployment and poverty in the Second Decade of Freedom.

The fabric of South African society is continually changing, creating not only new challenges but also greater stability and peace, and laying the foundation for a society in which the individual and collective human potential of the nation can come to full fruition.

Acknowledgement

This History chapter has evolved year by year, based on initial text from the Institute for Historical Research, University of the Western Cape.

Suggested reading

Alexander, P. *Workers, War and the Origins of Apartheid: Labour and Politics in South Africa, 1939 – 1948*. Cape Town: David Philip, 2001.

An Extraordinary 20th Century. Johannesburg: Star Independent Newspapers, 1999.

Barber, J. *Mandela's World: The International Dimension of South Africa's Political Revolution*. Cape Town: David Philip, 2004.

Beinart, W. *Twentieth Century South Africa*. 2nd ed. Cape Town: Oxford University Press, 2001.

Bell, T. and Ntsebeza, D.B. *Unfinished Business: South Africa's Apartheid and Truth*. Observatory: Redworks on behalf of Understanding Our Past, 2001.

Berger, L.R. *In the Footsteps of Eve: The Mystery of Human Origins*. Washington: National Geographic Society, 2000.

Bergh, J.S. and Morton, F. *To Make Them Serve: The 1871 Transvaal Commission on African Labour*. Pretoria: Protea Book House, 2003.

Between Anger and Hope: South Africa's Youth and the Truth and Reconciliation Commission, edited by K. Chubb and L. van Dijk. Johannesburg: Witwatersrand University Press, 2004.

Bickford-Smith, V. *Ethnic Pride and Racial Prejudice in Victorian Cape Town*. Johannesburg: Witwatersrand University Press, 1995.

Bond, P. *Elite Transition: From Apartheid to Neoliberalism in South Africa*. Pietermaritzburg: University of Natal Press, 2000.

Bonner, P. and Segal, L. *Soweto: A History*. Cape Town: Maskew Miller Longman, 1998.

Bozzoli, B. *Theatre of Struggle and the End of Apartheid*. Johannesburg: Witwatersrand University Press, 2004.

Brink, E. *et al. Soweto: 16 June 1976*. Cape Town: Kwela Books, 2001.

Bulbulia, F. and Isiakpere, F. eds. *Council of the Elders: A Tribute to the Veterans of the South African Liberation Struggle*. Lagos: Minaj Publishers, 1997.

Callinicos, L. *People's History of South Africa*. Johannesburg: Ravan Press, 1981 – 1993. 3 vols.

Coleman, M. ed. *A Crime Against Humanity: Analysing the Repression of the Apartheid State*. Bellville: Mayibuye Books, University of the Western Cape, 1998.

Commissioning the Past: Understanding South Africa's Truth and Reconciliation Commission, edited by D. Posel and G. Simpson. Johannesburg: Witwatersrand University Press, 2004.

Coombes, A.E. *History after Apartheid: Visual Culture and Public Memory in a Democratic South Africa*. Johannesburg: Witwatersrand University Press, 2003.

Couzens, T. *Battles of South Africa*. Cape Town: David Philip, 2004.

Davenport, T.R.H. *The Transfer of Power in South Africa*. Cape Town: David Philip, 1998.

Davenport, T.R.H. and Saunders, C. *South Africa: A Modern History*. 5th ed. London: Macmillan, 2000.

De Gruchy, J. ed. *The London Missionary Society in Southern Africa: Historical Essays*. Cape Town: David Philip, 1999.

Drew, A. *Discordant Comrades: Identities and Loyalties of the South African Left*. Pretoria: University of South Africa, 2002.

Driver, C.J. *Patrick Duncan: South African and Pan-African*. Cape Town: David Philip, 2000.

Du Pre, R.H. *Separate But Unequal: The Coloured People of South Africa: A Political History*. Johannesburg: Jonathan Ball, 1994.

Dubow, S. *The African National Congress*. Johannesburg: Jonathan Ball, 2000.

Ebrahim H. *The Soul of a Nation: Constitution-Making in South Africa*. Cape Town: Oxford University Press, 1998.

Evans, M.M. *Encyclopaedia of the Boer War*. Oxford: ABC – Clio, 2000.

Every Step of the Way: The Journey to Freedom in South Africa, edited by J. Linnegar. Cape Town: Human Sciences Research Council (HSRC), 2004.

Field, S. ed. *Lost Communities, Living Memories*. Cape Town: David Philip, 2001.

Fitt, J.K. *Beyond Fear*. Cape Town: Pretext Publishers, 2003.

Foster, D., Haupt, P and De Beer, M. *The Theatre of Violence: Narratives of Protagonists in the South African Conflict*. Cape Town: HSRC Press, 2005.

Frankel, G. *Rivonia's Children: Three Families and the Price of Freedom in South Africa*. Johannesburg: Jonathan Ball, 1999.

Frankel, P. *An Ordinary Atrocity: Sharpeville and its Massacre*. Johannesburg: Witwatersrand University Press, 2001.
Freund, B. *The Making of Contemporary Africa: The Development of African Society Since 1800*. 2nd ed. London: Macmillan, 1998.
Hadland, A. and Rantao, J. *Life and Times of Thabo Mbeki*. Rivonia, Johannesburg: Zebra Press, 1997.
Hamilton, C. *Terrific Majesty: The Powers of Shaka Zulu and the Limits of Historical Intervention*. Cape Town: David Philip, 1998.
Hammond-Tooke, D. *The Roots of Black South Africa: An Introduction to the Traditional Culture of the Black People of South Africa*. Johannesburg: Jonathan Ball, 1993.
Harris, J.E. *Africans and their History*. 2nd ed. New York: Meridian, 1998.
Harvey, R. *The Fall of Apartheid: The Inside Story from Smuts to Mbeki*. Basingstoke: Palgrave Macmillan, 2002.
Honikman, A. *In the Shadow of Apartheid*. Johannesburg: Quartz Press, 1998.
Hopkins, P. and Grange, H. *The Rocky Rioter Teargas Show: The Inside Story of the 1976 Soweto Uprising*. Cape Town: Zebra, 2001.
Images of Defiance. Johannesburg: STE Publishers, 2004. 2nd ed.
Isichei, E.A. *History of African Societies to 1870*. Cambridge: University Press, 1997. (Southern Africa discussed in Chapter 22, pp. 409 – 430.)
Johnson, R.W. and Schlemmer L. *Launching Democracy in South Africa. The First Open Election, 1994 – 1996*. New Haven: Yale University Press, 1996.
Johnson, R.W. and Welsh, D. *Ironic History: Liberalism in Post-Liberation South Africa*. Cape Town: Oxford University Press, 1998.
Joyce, P. *Concise Dictionary of South African Biography*. Cape Town: Francolin, 1999.
Kathrada, A. *Letters from Robben Island: A Selection of Ahmed Kathrada's Prison Correspondence*. 2nd ed. Zebra Press, 2000.
Keegan, T. *Colonial South Africa and the Origins of the Racial Order*. Cape Town: David Philip, 1996.
Laband, J.P.C. *Rope of Sand: The Rise and Fall of the Zulu Kingdom in the Nineteenth Century*. Johannesburg: Jonathan Ball, 1995.
Le May, G.H.L. *The Afrikaners: A Historical Interpretation*. Oxford: Blackwell Publishers, 1995.
Limits to Liberation in South Africa: The Unfinished Business of Democratic Consolidation, edited by H. Melber. Cape Town: HSRC, 2003.
Lodge, T. *Bus Stop for Everyone*. Cape Town: David Philip, 2002. 2nd ed.
Loos, J. *Echoes of Slavery: Voices from South Africa's Past*. Cape Town: David Philip, 2004.
Louw, P.E. *The Rise, Fall and Legacy of Apartheid*. Westport, CT: Praeger, 2004.
Marks, S.C. *Conflict Resolution during South Africa's Transition to Democracy*. Washington: United States Institute of Peace Press, 2000.
Mathebula, M. *800 Years of Tsonga History*. Polokwane: Sharp-Shoot Publishing, 2002.
Matshikiza, T. and Matshikiza, J. *With the Lid Off: South African Insights from Home and Abroad, 1959 – 2000*. Johannesburg: M & G Books, 2000.
Maylam, P. *A History of the African People of South Africa: From the Early Iron Age to the 1970s*. Cape Town: David Philip, 1995.
Mbeki, G. *The Struggle for Liberation in South Africa: A Short History*. Cape Town: David Philip, 1997.
Mbeki, T. *Letters from the President: Articles from the first 100 editions of ANC Today*. Johannesburg: ANC Communications Unit, 2003.
McKinley, D.T. *The ANC and the Liberation Struggle: A Critical Political Biography*. London: Pluto Press, 1997.
Meiring, P. *Chronicle of the Truth Commission: A Journey through the Past and Present into the Future of South Africa*. Vanderbijlpark: Carpe Diem Books, 1999.
Meredith, M. *The State of Africa: A History of Fifty Years of Independence*. Johannesburg: Jonathan Ball, 2005.
Mitchell, P. *The Archaeology of Southern Africa*. Cape Town: Cambridge University Press, 2002.
Morris, M. *Every Step of the Way: The Journey to Freedom in South Africa*. Cape Town: HSRC Press, 2004.
Mostert, N. *Frontiers: The Epic of South Africa's Creation and the Tragedy of the Xhosa People*. London: Jonathan Cape, 1992.
Moving in Time: Images of Life in a Democratic South Africa, edited by G. Hallett. Johannesburg: KMM Review Publishing, 2004.
Musiker, N. and Musiker, R. *A Concise Historical Dictionary of Greater Johannesburg*. Cape Town: Francolin, 2000.
Naidoo, I. *Island in Chains: Ten Years on Robben Island*. London: Penguin, 2000.
Ndlovu, S.M. *The Soweto Uprisings: Counter-Memories of June 1976*. Randburg: Ravan Press, 1998.
New Dictionary of South African Biography: Volume 2. Editor: N.E. Sonderling. Pretoria: HSRC, 1999.

Noonan, P. *They're Burning the Churches.* Johannesburg: Jacana, 2003.

Nuttall, S. and Coetzee, C. eds. *Negotiating the Past: The Making of Memory in South Africa.* Cape Town: Oxford University Press, 1998.

O'Meara, D. *Forty Lost Years: The Apartheid State and the Politics of the National Party.* Johannesburg: Ravan Press, 1996.

Omer-Cooper, J.D. *History of Southern Africa.* 2nd ed. Cape Town: David Philip, 1994.

Pakenham, T. *The Scramble for Africa 1876 – 1912.* Johannesburg: Jonathan Ball, 1991.

Peires, J. *The Dead will Arise: Nongqawuse and the Great Xhosa Cattle-killing of 1856-57.* Cape Town: Jonathan Ball, 2004.

Peires, J. *The House of Phalo.* Cape Town: Jonathan Ball, 2004.

Penn, N. *Rogues, Rebels and Runaways: Eighteenth Century Cape Characters.* Cape Town: David Philip, 2000.

Prah, K.K. *Beyond the Colour Line: Pan-Africanist Disputations.* Florida: Vivlia, 1997.

Rantete, J.M. *The African National Congress and the Negotiated Settlement in South Africa.* Pretoria: Van Schaik, 1998.

Reader's Digest Illustrated History of South Africa. 3rd ed. Cape Town: Reader's Digest, 1994.

Reynolds, A. ed. *Election '99: South Africa from Mandela to Mbeki.* Cape Town: David Philip, 1999.

Road to Democracy in South Africa. South African Democracy Education Trust. Vol. 1: 1960 – 1970. Cape Town: Zebra Press, 2004.

Ross, R. *Concise Cambridge History of South Africa.* Cambridge: 1999.

Sachs, A. *The Soft Vengeance of a Freedom Fighter.* 2nd ed. Cape Town: David Philip, 2000.

Sampson, A. *Mandela: The Authorised Biography.* Johannesburg: Jonathan Ball, 1999.

Saunders, C. and Southey, N. *A Dictionary of South African History.* 2nd ed. Cape Town: David Philip, 2001.

Schoeman, K. *The Griqua Captaincy of Philippolis, 1826 – 1861.* Pretoria: Protea Book House, 2002.

Seekings, J. *The UDF: A History of the United Democratic Front in South Africa, 1983 – 1991.* Cape Town: David Philip, 2000.

Sideropoulos, E. *Apartheid Past, Renaissance Future.* Johannesburg: South African Institute of International Affairs, 2004.

South Africa's 1940s: Worlds of Possibilities; edited by S. Dubow and A. Jeeves. Cape Town: Double Storey, 2005.

South Africa's Nobel Laureates; edited by K. Asmal, D. Chidester, W. James. Johannesburg: Jonathan Ball, 2004

Smith, C. *Mandela.* Cape Town: Struik, 1999.

Spies, S.B. *Methods of Barbarism: Roberts, Kitchener and the Civilians of the Boer Republics: January 1900 – May 1902.* Johannesburg: Jonathan Ball, 2001.

State-Building Democracy in Southern Africa: Comparative Study of Botswana, South Africa and Zimbabwe. Pretoria: HSRC Publishers, 1995.

State of the Nation: South Africa 2003 – 2004, edited by J. Daniel, A. Habib and R. Southall. Cape Town: HSRC Press, 2003.

'Stidy' (A. Stidolph). *Over the Rainbow: the First Ten Years of South Africa's Democracy in Cartoons.* Pietermaritzburg: The Witness, 2003.

Suttner, R. *Inside Apartheid's Prison: Notes and Letters of Struggle.* Pietermaritzburg: University of Natal Press, 2001.

Suttner, R. ed. *All My Life and All My Strength: Ray Alexander Simons.* Johannesburg: STE Publishers, 2004.

Terreblanche, S. *A History of Inequality in South Africa, 1652 – 2002.* Pietermaritzburg: University of Natal Press, 2002.

Thompson, D. and Watson, B. *They are Africans Who Worked Toward the Liberation, Unity and Solidarity of Africa and African People Throughout the World.* Cape Town: Kwela Books, 2000.

Truth and Reconciliation Commission. Final Report. 5 vols. Distributors: Cape Town: Juta, 1998.

Turok, B. *Nothing but the Truth: Behind the ANC's Struggle Politics.* Johannesburg: Jonathan Ball, 2003.

Van der Merwe, H.W. *Peacemaking in South Africa: A Life in Conflict Resolution.* Cape Town: Tafelberg, 2000.

Voices of the Transition: The Politics, Poetics and Practices of Social Change in South Africa, edited by E. Pieterse and F. Meintjies. Sandown: Heinemann, 2004.

Wadley, L. ed. *Our Gendered Past: Archaeological Studies of Gender in Southern Africa.* Johannesburg: Witwatersrand University Press, 1997.

Waldmeir, P. *Anatomy of a Miracle: The End of Apartheid and the Birth of the New South Africa.* London: Penguin Books, 1998.

Webster, R. *At the Fireside: True South African Stories.* Cape Town: Spearhead, 2002.

Welsh, F. *History of South Africa.* London: Harper Collins, 1998.

Wilson, M. and Thompson L.M. eds. *Oxford History of South Africa.* Oxford: Clarendon Press, 1969 – 1971. 2 vols.

Witz, L. *Apartheid's Festival: Contesting South Africa's National Pasts.* Cape Town: David Philip, 2003.

Worden, N. *Concise Dictionary of South African History.* Cape Town: Francolin, 1998.

Overview

Introduction

Democracy presented government with twin challenges:
- institutional transformation and the introduction of new policies in line with the democratic Constitution
- dealing with the legacy of apartheid in South Africa while integrating the country in a rapidly changing global environment.

From 1994, the State has set out to dismantle apartheid social relations and create a democratic society based on equity, non-racialism and non-sexism. New policies and programmes have been put in place to dramatically improve the quality of life of all South Africans.

This process, defined in the Reconstruction and Development Programme (RDP), has been elaborated in all post-1994 policies. The RDP identifies the following key objectives:
- meeting basic needs
- building the economy
- democratising the State and society
- developing human resources
- nation-building.

The RDP objectives were elaborated to include more specific priorities of different government clusters and departments. In 2003, government conducted the *Towards a Ten Year Review* to see how it had met these objectives through the work of its five clusters, and to assess the challenges of the Second Decade of Freedom.

Governance and Administration Cluster

The first years of democracy saw a new constitutional and legislative framework introduced. The Constitution was adopted in 1996 and an average of 90 Acts of new legislation were introduced per year in the first 10 years.

New global standards of governance are emerging. These include governance reforms and performance areas. Citizens of developing countries are demanding better performance on the part of their governments, and they are increasingly aware of the costs of poor management, corruption and lack of delivery in certain areas. South Africa is no exception. A compendium of development indicators has been identified for government-wide monitoring and evaluation (M&E) to measure the performance of the South African Government both in the medium and long term, using indicators for:

- governance and institutional quality
- social development and poverty alleviation
- economic development and growth indicators
- justice, peace and security
- international relations.

These indicators are deemed most appropriate to South Africa's particular needs and will be refined over time.

Achievements

The integration of Bantustan and central government civil services into an integrated public service has been a great success. Plans to create an integrated public service including local government are underway.

Integration increased the number of personnel and amount of expenditure and resulted in the implementation of Resolution 7 of the Public Service Co-ordinating Bargaining Council Agreement to address the restructuring of the Public Service. This involved the identification of skills with job descriptions and the retraining of staff. The Public Service has also come close to meeting its targets of representivity – previously disadvantaged people, mainly Africans, now make up the majority of the Public Service.

The introduction of a senior management service improved conditions with the aim of retaining and attracting skilled personnel in the Public Service. There is more stability in the top echelons although

a general lack of technically skilled personnel at all levels is a matter of concern. This is particularly acute in provincial and local government. Career-pathing, especially at the highest levels of the Public Service, is not yet fully developed, and skilled and experienced personnel developed since 1994 are being lost to the private sector.

In the 11 years of democracy, government has established public entities to allow flexibility in conditions of service, to retain income from revenue raised, to expedite systems such as procurement, to ensure operational autonomy and to implement commercial principles and practices. They receive considerable state funding and employ more than 288 980 people. The challenges facing them, which government is addressing, relate to performance, corporate governance and in some cases orientation to the Government's overall development objectives. A policy framework for the administration and governance of public-sector institutions has been developed to address these challenges. By April 2005, there were 280 registered public entities. This figure can be broken down as follows, using the classification in the Public Finance Management Act (PFMA), 1999 (Act 1 of 1999):

- major public entities: 18
- national public entities: 138
- national government business enterprises: 30
- provincial public entities: 81
- provincial government business enterprises: 13.

This total figure excludes constitutional institutions of which there are nine and which are not regarded

Level of representativity in the Public Service

	African		Asian		Coloured		White		Female	Male
	Female	Male	Female	Male	Female	Male	Female	Male	Head Cnt	Head Cnt
Eastern Cape	57,1%	30,1%	0,2%	0,3%	4,3%	2,6%	3,4%	1,8%	65,2%	34,8%
Free State	47,1%	33,1%	0,1%	0,1%	2,2%	1,3%	11,0%	5,3%	60,3%	39,7%
Gauteng	49,1%	24,5%	1,6%	0,9%	2,6%	1,2%	14,5%	5,5%	67,9%	32,1%
KwaZulu-Natal	53,4%	27,8%	6,7%	4,7%	1,4%	0,6%	3,7%	1,8%	65,2%	34,8%
Limpopo	52,7%	44,8%	0,1%	0,1%	0,1%	0,1%	1,5%	0,8%	54,3%	45,7%
Mpumalanga	54,7%	34,6%	0,2%	0,2%	0,5%	0,2%	6,5%	3,0%	62,0%	38,0%
North West	56,3%	34,2%	0,2%	0,3%	0,9%	0,5%	5,3%	2,4%	62,7%	37,3%
Northern Cape	19,0%	13,1%	0,2%	0,2%	31,3%	20,4%	11,2%	4,6%	61,7%	38,3%
Western Cape	9,7%	5,6%	0,4%	0,3%	40,9%	22,9%	12,8%	7,4%	63,7%	36,3%
National departments	17,6%	46,4%	1,4%	3,8%	2,8%	5,8%	8,8%	13,3%	30,6%	69,4%
Total	**39,1%**	**34,6%**	**1,7%**	**2,0%**	**4,9%**	**4,0%**	**7,4%**	**6,3%**	**53,0%**	**47,0%**

as public entities. It also excludes any subsidiary entity or entity under the ownership control of any other entity.

The introduction of the PFMA, 1999 improved accountability in government and to Parliament. Implementation of the PFMA, 1999 and the change to a medium-term budget cycle have improved budgeting and national and provincial financial management. The challenge remains to include local government within government's budgeting and planning cycles. The national planning framework is a government tool that ensures that the strategic priorities of government are held in view by all three spheres and public entities. The review of the national planning framework was presented to the Cabinet Lekgotla in July 2005. The Policy Co-ordination and Advisory Services unit in The Presidency is updating the national planning framework and will publish the documents for all three spheres of government. The reviewed national planning framework clarifies the alignment of fiscal, strategic and political cycles of government as indicated below.

The National Spatial Development Perspective (NSDP) was developed to facilitate dialogue between and within spheres about the country's spatial priorities for infrastructure investment and development spending. The introduction of integrated development plans (IDPs), as well as the Cluster approach, the Forum of South African Directors-General (FOSAD), the Presidential Co-ordinating Council and the restructured Cabinet committees have all contributed to better co-ordination of policy-making and implementation. The Presidency is leading the alignment of the NSDP, provincial growth and development strategies (PGDS) and IDPs. Guidelines for the formulation and implementation of PGDS are being used to assess all PGDS through a self and peer review mechanism. Through this process, municipalities should have clearer direction in respect of economic development and spatial restructuring of their areas. The review and update of the NSDP are underway.

In an effort to improve service delivery, multi-purpose community centres (MPCCs) have been set up to provide information and services to the public.

The aim was to establish one per district/metro by the end of 2005 and then expand them to each municipality in the next decade. Phase I of the MPCC programme – an MPCC in every district – is nearly completed and Phase II has begun. By September 2005, there were 66 operational MPCCs while only four districts still lacked MPCCs – Eastern Cape (three) and Northern Cape (one).

The Batho Pele Gateway is making comprehensive information about government services instantly available through government offices, MPCCs, citizen post offices (CPOs) and intermediaries such as community development workers (CDWs) and community and development organisations. Phase One of the Batho Pele e-Government Gateway was launched in August 2004, with a portal at *www.gov.za*. The Batho Pele Gateway call centre's number is 1020. By October 2005, nine MPCCs and 55 CPOs had been linked to the Gateway Portal.

This is being complemented by the decision taken in 2003 to introduce CDWs to enhance access to government's socio-economic programmes. The key function of these multiskilled CDWs is to maintain direct contact with the public. By September 2005, 2 238 full-time CDWs and CDW learners had been recruited and were active in the programme. Of this number, 1 329 had completed their yearlong learnership programme. Provinces were recruiting a further 920 CDW learners, which will bring the total of CDWs to 3 158. Progress made by September 2005 indicated that the initial target of 2 840 CDWs countrywide would be exceeded by March 2006.

CDWs have been recruited particularly in Urban Renewal and Integrated Sustainable Rural Development Programme nodes.

Public reaction to high-profile government's commitment to fight corruption has been positive. Since 1994, government has initiated various anti-corruption programmes and projects. In March 1997, the departments responsible for the South African National Crime Prevention Strategy (NCPS) initiated a programme to work on corruption in the criminal justice system (CJS). In June 1997, the Code of Conduct for the Public Service became part of the regulations for every public servant.

The National Anti-Corruption Forum is a national structure that brings the public, business and civil-society sectors together to further national consensus against corruption. The second National Anti-Corruption Summit was held in March 2005. The summit adopted 27 resolutions as the basis of a national strategy to fight corruption and involved representatives from all sectors of the society including government; Parliament; national, provincial and local administrations; unions; business; non-governmental organisations (NGOs); community-based organisations (CBOs); academia; research institutions; and CDWs. The National Anti-Corruption Programme was developed on the basis of the 27 resolutions that were agreed to at the summit. An implementation committee has commenced with its first project on the Prevention and Combating of Corrupt Activities Act, 2004 (Act 12 of 2004).

Programme of Action

Each year, government defines a programme of action for the year to advance implementation of its electoral mandate. The programme is defined by the January Cabinet Lekgotla, attended by ministers, deputy ministers and now also premiers of provinces, as well as senior officials.

The President announces the programme in the State of the Nation Address at the beginning of the parliamentary year and it is further elaborated in a week of media briefings at that time by the ministerial clusters.

Reflecting the emphasis in the Second Decade of Freedom on implementation, an M&E system was initiated by the Government elected in 2004. Clusters report every two months to Cabinet on progress in implementing the programme, and identify challenges and problems as well as remedial measures. A mid-year lekgotla in July reviews implementation and identifies emerging priorities.

The Programme of Action and the results of the two monthly cycle of reporting are communicated to the public in various ways – through the government website; regular ministerial media briefings; and mass multimedia communication via print and broadcast media as well as information products produced by government. Communication is struc-

tured to promote the widest dissemination, including to people with the least access to media.

These activities are part of the first phase of the development of a government-wide system (GWM&ES), introduced to promote implementation and facilitate public involvement in M&E and in partnering government in implementation.

The first phase of the implementation of the GWM&ES has included formulating minimum standards and improving contributory systems. The initial draft report on reporting norms and standards was expected to be completed by year-end 2005. A draft proposal to enhance and align the Electronic Information Management System and the Programme of Action System is under discussion.

Challenges

A major challenge arising from the *Ten Year Review* is improved performance by the State to achieve policy objectives that are largely correct.

During the first 10 years, a major new architecture of institutions was created for the State, spanning the three spheres of government. Many procedures and practices have been revised in line with international best practice. Significant personnel mobility has brought in new skills and motivated people, though it has also led to the loss of experience and institutional memory, especially regarding civil servants recruited after 1994. The combined impact of these changes has meant that state institutions are still undergoing significant growing pains and face the danger of a permanent and debilitating state of flux.

Government is working on proposals for the establishment of a single public service to allow for skills and human resources allocation across the three spheres of government. This work will also enhance implementation of the Intergovernmental Relations Act, 2005 (Act 13 of 2005).

The *Ten Year Review* suggested that the capacity and performance of all spheres of the State need to be more critically assessed, and that national or provincial government may need to intervene much more quickly where there is evidence of poor performance. The national Government may have to show its strong commitment to improving performance where institutions persistently demonstrate weaknesses of governance. This should happen as an evolutionary process of creating a uniform public service across all three spheres unfolds.

FOSAD is working on a review of the capacity and organisation of the State. The July 2005 Cabinet Lekgotla considered the results of a study into the capacity constraints and needs of the housing sector, with a specific focus on the implementation of the Sustainable Human Settlement Plan, and decided that further sectoral reviews should be conducted on the capacity to implement government's social and economic developmental objectives.

The State has made significant progress in recent years in improving policy co-ordination within and across spheres of government, but these efforts need to be further consolidated with greater attention to implementation, now that the basic policy frameworks of the democratic dispensation have been created.

Research commissioned for the *Ten Year Review* suggests that the needs of local government are most critical, with most municipalities not having the requisite capacity to perform their service-delivery functions. This means that while government should make every effort to work within the current framework of institutions and practices, where serious capacity constraints persist, government may need to consider changing responsibilities and structures, as is being done with the introduction of the National Social Security Agency.

Two challenges arise from this. Firstly, how to ensure realisation of a national vision in actual practice, given the relative autonomy of each sphere of government in critical areas of social delivery. Secondly, whether there is a case for differential or asymmetric allocation of responsibility, assigning more responsibility where there is capacity to undertake functions beyond the provisions of the Constitution, and inversely to effect necessary interventions where such capacity does not exist, even if matters have not reached the stage requiring invocation of Section 100 of the Constitution.

In this context, Project Consolidate, initiated in 2004, is a national two-year programme of hands-on support and capacity-building, which has identified 136 municipalities in need of assistance.

Government also needs to further promote the participation and interaction of the people with the State. Since 1994, the State has provided many new opportunities for ordinary people to become involved in governance, ranging from ward committees, the IDP process, chapter 9 institutions, the National Economic Development and Labour Council, and the management of pension funds and workplace fora. Yet, actual participation in such structures and/or the capacity to take advantage of their existence has been limited mainly to interest groups, or hindered by considerations of short-term self-interest. Government promotes new ways of encouraging ordinary people to utilise their freedom. Related to this are the initiatives pertaining to CDWs, M&E, massive expansion of the MPCC project and the Batho Pele Gateway.

Conclusion

The policies for Governance and Administration in the First Decade of Freedom were largely the required interventions. Most institutions are operating effectively, although the stabilisation of the intergovernmental system needs improvement. More flexibility in the Public Service will make it more responsive to public needs. Government must continue with what it has started, only more diligently and more vigorously. Improved capacity of the State to deliver social services requires greater capacity in national departments and attention to some provincial and local weaknesses. Compliance with regulations is high, but there are some weaknesses with regard to government's capacity to involve the informal sector in adhering to their civic obligations. Success in fighting corruption is slow but notable.

The key challenges for the next decade include:
- improving service delivery by building the necessary institutions and initiatives
- using the NSDP to focus government's attention on localities with the greatest potential for development, and poverty alleviation while rebuilding other areas
- organisation and capacity of government with special emphasis on the local government system

- improving accountability to, and contact with, citizens by all levels of government
- developing and maintaining partnerships with civil society, with the emphasis on practical programmes
- providing leadership to social partners through the articulation of an encompassing framework for South Africa's development in the next decade and beyond
- developing and implementing the GWM&ES.

In line with the principles of deepened democracy and participatory governance, government has promoted the integration of platforms of interactive governance with municipal processes. This includes the alignment of izimbizo with Project Consolidate, in the form of a municipal imbizo programme that was launched by President Thabo Mbeki in May 2005.

Social Cluster

The central programme of the social sector focuses on poverty alleviation through a range of programmes that address income, human capital and asset poverty. It is in this intersection between access to services, income and assets that the issue of overall poverty trends since 1994 should be examined.

Inequality, as measured at household level before and after factoring in social spending by the State, shows that the impact of social spending (including the tax effect) reduced the degree of inequality massively due to a redirection of spending to the poor since 1994 (see *Towards a Ten Year Review*).

Income poverty alleviation

According to Statistics South Africa, it is estimated that in 1995 about 28% of households and 48% of the population were living below the estimated poverty line – calculated on the basis of expenditure, thus excluding access to services and assets. In 1999, there were 3,7 million such households out of 11,4 million (just under 33%) living below the poverty line. Part of this increase in household income poverty would be due to large-sized poor households unbundling into smaller households.

The unbundling has the effect of removing additional income earners from the household and would therefore reflect an increasing number of households being classified as poor.

According to a report of the UNISA Bureau of Market Research, *National Personal Income of South Africans by Population Group, Income Group, Life Stage and Lifeplane 1960 – 2007*, in 2001, 4,1 million out of 11,2 million households in South Africa lived on an income of R9 600 and less per year. This decreased to 3,6 million households in 2004, even after taking the negative effect of price increases on spending power into account. On the other hand, the number of households receiving a real income of R153 601 and more per year rose from 721 000 in 1998 to more than 1,2 million in 2004.

At least two major government programmes address income poverty in the form of direct transfers and public works programmes. This excludes the social wage, which was estimated at R88 billion in 2003.

Income grants

Social grants are no longer allocated on a racial basis as they were under apartheid. Grants are targeted at pensioners, poor families with children, war veterans, foster care and grants in aid for families taking care of children and people in need. Beneficiaries of social grants increased from 2,6 million in 1994 to more than 10 million in September 2005.

By September 2005, more than 6,2 million children were receiving the Child Support Grant (CSG), 286 131 the Foster Care Grant, and 87 093 the Care Dependency Grant. About R6,9 billion and an additional R19 billion were allocated for the 2005/06 period for the further extension of the CSG to children under the age of 14 years.

Government aims to register an additional 1,2 million children between the ages of 11 and 14 for CSG in 2005/06. This will bring the total number of grant beneficiaries to 11 million and expenditure to over R55 billion. By February 2005, the target of registering 1,8 million children under the age of 11 for the CSG was exceeded when 1,9 million eligible children were registered.

There are almost 1,3 million beneficiaries of the Disability Grant while more than two million people receive the Old-Age Grant.

Social assistance grant transfers grew from around 2% of gross domestic product (GDP) in 2000/01 to more than 3% of GDP in 2004/05. They were expected to reach 3,4% of GDP in 2005/06.

Public works programmes

One of the key programmes launched by government is the Expanded Public Works Programme (EPWP), which is operational in all provinces.

The EPWP is on course to reach its target of one million job opportunities in five years. By September 2005, some 223 400 gross work opportunities had been created from 3 400 EPWP projects nationwide in the first year of the EPWP, yielding at least R823 million in total wages paid. Of those who benefited from these projects in the first year of the programme, 38% were women, 41% youth, and 0,5% disabled people.

The EPWP focuses on ensuring that labour-intensive methods are used in government service-delivery programmes in the infrastructure, environmental and culture, social and economic sectors.

It provides on-the-job training to those participating so that they will be better equipped to find permanent employment afterwards.

Asset poverty alleviation

Housing and shelter

Between 1994 and 2005, about 2 686 907 subsidies were approved for an expenditure of R44 736 billion in the same period. As a result of the housing programme, housing beneficiaries increased from 325 086 to 1,6 million beneficiaries in 2005.

Land

By the end of June 2005, government had settled 62 127 out of the 68 000 restitution claims launched. However, during validation the actual figure of the launched claims came to 79 000. The resolved claims where land restoration had been an option contributed to 916 470 ha.

The redistribution programme had delivered 3,1 million ha of land, benefiting rural and urban communities through the Extension of Tenure Programme, labour tenants, emerging farmers through Land Reform for Agricultural Development and commonage programmes.

Water and sanitation

By the end of March 2005:
- 44,5 million people had access to an improved water supply
- basic water infrastructure had been supplied to 15 million people (over 10 million people were supplied by the Department of Water Affairs and Forestry)
- 31,9 million South Africans (66,3%) had access to free basic water
- basic sanitation infrastructure had been provided to over 8,2 million people
- it was estimated that by 2008, the entire water supply backlog will have been eradicated and by 2010, so will that of sanitation.

Electrification

A key objective is the electrification of all households, and the provision of free basic electricity to poor households. The electrification programme has seen 3,5 million homes electrified since 1994. This translates into over 435 000 homes per year on average. By May 2005, access to electricity was estimated at 71%.

Human capital poverty alleviation

Healthcare

To make the health system more equitable, efficient and effective, the Department of Health embarked on a complete transformation of the health delivery system.
- Primary healthcare (PHC)

  By 1996, the proportion of public health spending devoted to PHC had increased from an estimated 11% in 1992 to 21%. Expenditure on non-hospital-based PHC grew from R58 per person in 1992/93 to R141 per person in 2002/03, and increased to R183 in 2005/06.

- Clinic-building and Upgrading
  Government's Clinic-building and Upgrading Programme resulted in the building and upgrading of more than 1 300 clinics between 1994 and February 2005.
- Hospital revitalisation
  The Hospital Revitalisation Grant increased by 12,7% from R911 million in 2004/05 to R1 027 billion in 2005/06. Government completed the revitalisation of four hospitals in 2004 with another 37 in various stages of completion.
- Free healthcare
  The Free Healthcare Policy started in 1994 with free healthcare for pregnant and lactating mothers and children under six years, and was extended in 1996 to cover all PHC services for everyone in the public health system.
- Expanded Programme on Immunisation
  In South Africa it is recommended that children under the age of five be immunised against the most common childhood diseases. Immunisation should be administered at birth, six weeks, 10 weeks, 14 weeks, nine months, 18 months and five years of age. Childhood immunisations are given to prevent polio, tuberculosis (TB), diphtheria, pertussis, tetanus, haemophilus influenzae type B, hepatitis B and measles.

The set routine immunisation coverage target for fully immunised children under one year is 90%. In 2005, the overall routine immunisation coverage for South Africa stood at 82% but some districts were still lagging behind with less than 60% immunisation coverage.

- Integrated Food Security and Nutrition
  Since the start of the National Food Emergency Scheme in 2004, a total of 245 000 households have benefited from the programme. Agricultural starter packs to the value of R31 million have been delivered to some 18 575 households in all provinces as a measure of encouraging the development of sustainable food gardens.

A number of schools participating in the National School Nutrition Programme have established vegetable gardens to enrich the nutritional value of the meals served in schools.

- HIV and AIDS
  The response to HIV, AIDS and sexually transmitted infections was fairly limited before 1994, and focused predominantly on the provision of condoms and information, education and communication. Dedicated expenditure on HIV and AIDS programmes across national departments increased from about R30 million in 1994 to R342 million in 2001/02. This excludes allocations from provincial equitable share. Expenditure was further set to increase to R3,6 billion in 2005/06. This increased expenditure funds a comprehensive prevention, care and treatment programme.

Antenatal surveys showed HIV prevalence rates, which increased rapidly to 1998 (22,8%) from 0,7% in 1990, stabilising around 22,4% in 1999, 24,5% in 2000 and 24,8% in 2001. The same research showed the prevalence of syphilis among pregnant women decreasing from 6,5% in 1999 to 2,8% in 2001. Behavioural studies indicate extended abstinence, increase in condom use and a drop in the number of sexual partners in younger age categories. Based on its sample of more than 16 000 women attending antenatal clinics across all nine provinces, the Department of Health estimated that 29,5% of pregnant women were living with HIV in 2004. The provinces which recorded the highest HIV rates were KwaZulu-Natal, Gauteng and Mpumalanga.

The Government's Comprehensive Plan for the Management, Care and Treatment of HIV and AIDS centres around preventing the spread of HIV-infection and improving the health system to enable it to provide a series of interventions aimed at improving the lives of those infected and affected by HIV and AIDS.

By September 2005, there were 178 service sites spread across all the 53 districts and in about 60% of the subdistricts. Some 62 00 patients had been enrolled for antiretroviral treatment.

- National TB Control Programme
  South Africa has 188 000 new TB cases a year. Free testing is available at public clinics countrywide.

Government is strengthening the TB Control Programme by:
- appointing TB co-ordinators in each health district
- enhancing the laboratory system
- strengthening the implementation of the Directly Observed Treatment Strategy
- mobilising communities to ensure that patients complete their treatment.

The challenges posed by TB emphasise the need to address the weaknesses that still exist in the national health system and the importance of a comprehensive approach to the management of diseases in the country.

- Malaria control

  The prevalence of malaria has been decreased significantly and substantially over the past five years from prevalence levels above 80% in some areas to current levels, which are below 10%. This can be attributed to the success of in-door residual spraying using DDT and the partnership with Mozambique and Swaziland. The total number of malaria cases reported from January to May 2005 was 4 539, representing a 44,5% decrease from the 8 173 cases reported during the same period in 2004. During the same period, 35 deaths were reported compared with 55 in 2004, representing a 36,4% decrease in malaria-related deaths.

Education

In 2005/06, the total allocation for the Department of Education was R12,397 billion. Included were transfer payments to Higher Education (HE) institutions (79,85%) and to the National Student Financial Aid Scheme (6,97%), transfer payments to public and other entities (0,54%), conditional grants to provincial education departments (8,46%), funds earmarked in support of conditional grants to provinces (0,10%) and contributions to commonwealth of learning (0,01%). The balance of 4% was for operational expenditure.

With regard to Early Childhood Development (ECD) participation in the reception year, enrolment increased from about 150 000 to 280 000 between 1999 and 2002. The target of enrolling 300 000 Grade R learners was met in 2004.

Access to educational opportunities has been significantly expanded. Thousands of young people who are first-generation entrants to HE enjoy state-funded support for study at this level and positive growth has begun in increasing graduation rates in critical fields of study.

Enrolment of female learners in HE has increased from 44% in 1994 to 53% in 2003. Black students account for over 72% of enrolments in HE. In Further Education and Training (FET), institutional reform has been achieved with the formation of 50 FET colleges from 152 technical colleges, and 21 HE institutions from 36 universities and universities of technology, some of which bring together historically black and historically white institutions.

Education interventions over the past decade have contributed towards a respectable matric pass rate of over 70%. This was a significant achievement to round off the first 10 years of freedom and democracy. Results in 2004 achieved an increase in the number of matric exemptions, more Mathematics and Science Higher Grade passes, and increased participation of girl learners.

Literacy rate measurement is based on the subjective opinion of people, regarding whether they are able to read or write in at least one language. Using this criteria, the literacy rate among 15- to 24-year olds has exhibited an upward trend since 1996. Literacy in this age group increased from 95% in 1996 to 98% in 2004.

Conclusion

The social-sector programmes have helped address the apartheid legacy of poverty and inequality. However, the challenge of eradicating poverty and other social ills is compounded by societal dynamics set in motion in part by the transition itself. Among these are the decrease in the average size of households and the corresponding increase in the number of households, rapid labour force growth and an increase in rural-urban migration. These trends sharpen the challenges for the social sector and government as a whole in the coming period.

To take the interventions in the Second Economy forward, the following additional programmes will be introduced or further strengthened, as part of the

EPWP, and focused on providing training, work experience and temporary income, especially to women and youth. These are:
- The ECD programme, based on community participation, having ensured a common approach among all three spheres of government. The necessary additional funding will be provided.
- Increasing the numbers of community health workers, having harmonised training standards and increased resources allocated to the programme.

To better understand the dynamics of the Second Economy and ensure effective targeted interventions, a socio-economic survey of these communities will be carried out in three-year intervals.

In addition, campaigns to reduce non-communicable and communicable diseases as well as non-natural causes of death continue, through the promotion of healthy lifestyles and increased focus on TB, AIDS, malaria, cholera and other water-borne diseases, and generally increasing the standard of living of the poorest.

Broad trends in mortality confirm the need to continue to pay particular attention to the health of the nation. With regard to HIV and AIDS in particular, government's comprehensive plan, among the best in the world, combining awareness, treatment and home-based care, is being implemented with greater vigour.

With regard to the social sector, government has continued to allocate more resources and put in more effort to provide services to society at large and a safety net for the indigent. Project Consolidate will further increase the capacity of municipalities to improve performance in these areas.

More resources have been allocated for the various interventions in the area of education and training, including the merger of institutions of higher learning, improved teaching and learning especially in Mathematics and Natural Sciences, the provision of additional support to schools in poor areas, and allocations already announced for the salaries of educators.

Government's social-sector programme for 2005/06 includes the intensification of existing programmes to meet long-term objectives such as the provision of clean running water to all households by 2008, decent and safe sanitation by 2010 and electricity for all by 2012.

During the course of 2005, government committed itself to:
- update the Schools Register of Needs and iron out the creases among the implementing agents within and across the spheres of government to ensure that it meets the objective of safe classrooms and healthy environments in schools in as short a time as possible
- allocate additional resources over the next three years to cover outstanding claims in the land restitution programme
- complete discussions with Eskom, provincial governments and local municipalities to ensure that free basic electricity is provided to all with minimum delay
- improve the capacity of municipalities to ensure that the target of providing sanitation to 300 000 households per year is met as from 2007
- continue the effort to ensure that all citizens have access to affordable medicines
- intensify the programme to refurbish hospitals and provide more professionals, especially in rural areas.

During 2005, government launched the National Social Security Agency and implemented systematic plans against corruption, including with regard to definitions of disability and allocations to the Foster Care Grant.

As part of better understanding societal dynamics, especially at household and community levels, plans are underway to undertake a systematic tracking of households' decision-making through a panel household study. The Social Sector Cluster is developing the Macro-Social Development Strategic Framework, as a response to the findings of the Macro-Social Report and its policy implications.

Economic Cluster

Policy framework
The RDP has framed government's social and economic development programme since the first democratic election in 1994. Its main elements were to:

build the economy, meet basic needs, democratise the State and society, develop human resources, and build the nation.

In 1996, the Growth Employment and Redistribution (GEAR) programme was introduced to provide a clearer macro-economic framework for stable and accelerated growth.

In 2001, the National Treasury shifted towards a more expansionary stance, having won credibility from financial markets for conservative and predictable macro-economic policies. In the same year, elements of the Micro-Economic Reform Strategy (MERS) were introduced, and formalised in Cabinet in early 2002.

Macro-economic stability

Economic growth, employment and government's social programmes have improved the well-being of millions. Between 1998 and 2004, more than two million people moved out of the poorer end of the scale of living standards measures according to the South African Advertising Research Foundation and many are entering the ranks of the middle strata.

South Africa achieved a level of macro-economic stability it had not seen for 40 years. These advances create opportunities for real increases in expenditure on social services, reduce the costs and risks for all investors, and therefore lay the foundation for increased investment and growth.

Investment

Investment currently averages around 16% of GDP, much lower than the over 25% of GDP recorded in the early 1980s and in previous decades. Private-sector investment fell from 17% of GDP to as low as 12%, and broad public-sector investment decreased from around 12% of GDP to 4%. Private investment fell due to great uncertainties and economic isolation before 1994, and due to a lack of confidence in the new Government's ability to turn the economy around after 1994.

However, since 1999, both private- and public-sector investment have entered a rising trend, supported by strong inflows of foreign capital, mostly in portfolio investment, but increasingly in foreign direct investment (FDI) as confidence in the Government's economic and broader policies grows.

Growth and wealth

On average, per-capita growth was negative in the decade before 1994. The economy has grown at a rate of 2,94% per year, on average, since then. If the Asian crisis years of 1998 and 1999 are ignored, the average growth rate was 3,3%. Either number is a considerable improvement on the two decades before 1994. Real per-capita growth has been about 1% per year since the beginning of 1994. In other words, on average, South Africans grew wealthier at about 1% per year since 1994. In comparison with strong growing economies, this is a mediocre performance, although it is a steady but unspectacular performance compared with most developing economies.

Employment

Drawing on official surveys between 1995 and 2004, the number of people employed in South Africa appears to have grown from 9 557 185 to 11 984 000. This suggests over 2,4 million net new jobs. However, during the same period, the number of unemployed people grew from 1 909 468 to 4 532 000, an increase of about 2 623 000 according to the strict definition. This reflects a considerable increase in the numbers of those seeking work, which now includes a greater proportion of women from rural areas. Figures show that in 2002, out of a total of 8,9 million employees, 1 115 000 were temporary (12,5%), 567 000 were casual workers (6,4%), 365 000 had fixed-term contracts (4,1%) and 62 000 were seasonal (0,7%).

However since the early 2000s, in spite of the phenomenal growth in the economically active population, unemployment has actually fallen. Most new employment since then has been in the formal sector.

Government is discussing with its social partners ways of assisting the sectors hard hit by current trends.

Despite progress, unemployment is unacceptably high for historical reasons. While there is overall growth, restructuring sees some sectors shrinking with severe impact on many workers. The creation of jobs and other economic opportunities is the primary concern of government and was the core of the mandate on which government was elected in the 2004 election.

Since then, the economy has shown signs of lift-off to the higher growth path that is required to achieve government's social objectives, but various constraints have put limits on this and its sustainability.

In this context, the President announced in July 2005 that the Deputy President had been asked to lead the Accelerated and Shared Growth Initiative, tasked with dealing with challenges of ensuring that South Africa raises the trajectory of growth to average at least 4,5% in the next five years and about 6% between 2010 and 2014.

Combined with focus on improving labour absorption, such growth rates would ensure meeting the mandate of government to halve unemployment and poverty in the Second Decade of Freedom.

The task team reported in October 2005 to Cabinet that the approach being followed is to identify the constraints to higher rates of growth and job creation and to select a set of projects that would deal with these issues.

Proceeding from the premise that the current macro-economic environment brings the opportunity to pursue higher and shared growth, the main issues under consideration include: infrastructure development, sector investment strategies, education and skills development, Second Economy interventions, and improving the capacity of the State to provide economic services.

The report to Cabinet was to be followed by further detailed work and consultations with social partners to ensure that the final product was one that unites all South Africans in pursuit of common objectives.

Trade reform, industrial restructuring and industrial policy

The reform of trade and industrial policies is reflected in an improved balance of trade and a shift from primary exports to higher value-added secondary and tertiary exports. This is due to government's success in promoting trade liberalisation within a multilateral rules-based global trading regime, and its use of supply-side measures.

Key initiatives included the renegotiation of the Southern African Customs Union (SACU) Agreement; the negotiation of a Southern African Development Community (SADC) free trade agreement (FTA); and the negotiation of a bilateral trade and development agreement with the European Union (EU). The unilateral American Africa Growth and Opportunity Act provision has also aided South Africa's exports. These agreements contribute to new trade activity and to new FDI into South Africa. South Africa is a leading developing country participant in the Doha Round of the World Trade Organisation (WTO); has entered free trade talks with the United States of America (USA); signed an FTA in December 2004 with the Latin American members of the MERCOSUR; and is discussing possible bilateral trade agreements with India and China. It has had a framework discussion with China and is planning negotiations with India.

In the late 1990s, government's emphasis shifted in two main respects: firstly, incentive programmes were extended beyond traditional manufacturing sectors; and secondly, key industries were targeted for special attention. These include growth sectors like autos and tourism, and cross-cutting sectors like Information and Communications Technology. The sectors are now becoming a focus for the allocation of supply-side support, including funds for technology and human research development (HRD).

State enterprise restructuring

Policy on state-owned enterprises (SOEs) focuses primarily on the key economic sectors of telecommunications, energy, defence supplies and transport. Reforming the SOEs aimed at improving the access of the historically disadvantaged to services such as telecommunications and electricity; increasing efficiencies and hence reducing costs; and using the revenues earned through the disposal of state assets to reduce public debt. One major concern was that restructuring had to be carefully managed as the SOEs employed tens of thousands of workers. Another was that in restructuring corporations, Black Economic Empowerment (BEE) should be encouraged.

An objective achieved unambiguously was the reduction of public debt by R24 billion. Other consequences include the creation of a more entrepreneurial class of those interested in restructuring activities, the advancement of regulation, the opening up of some industries to competition, and the widening of share-ownership. Commercialisation and/or partial privatisation led to the reduction in public debt by raising funds from the private sector, thereby reducing pressure on the fiscus, and creating an environment for competition. Within the policy framework, greater competition and further improvements to the regulatory environment should ensure that nationally strategic services such as energy, transportation and telecommunications are provided at low cost and high quality. As in the rest of the economy, there has been a shift of jobs mainly from sunset to sunrise sectors (e.g. cellphones) due to the improvement of business processes and the introduction of new technology. In recent years, oversight over financial, economic and socio-developmental activities of SOEs has been tightened to ensure that SOEs are aligned to the objectives of the developmental State.

Regulatory quality, labour legislation and taxation
In restructuring state assets and liberalising previously monopolised markets, new systems of regulation have been established. These include new regulators in the transport, telecommunications and energy sectors. Though South African regulators are relatively well endowed by developing country standards, they are poorer than the corporations they regulate. Relations between the regulators, their boards/councils, and government vary considerably; even regulators that have similar functions.

South Africa has progressed in introducing and amending labour laws that give employers and employees certainty and security in the employment contract. A huge fall in person-strike-days per year

bears testimony to the success of the policy. The balance between the degree of job security and the kind of labour market flexibility that encourages employers to take on new employees is still being fine-tuned.

Company taxation meets South Africa's needs and is consistent with international practice. However, there are some concerns. On the one hand, there are concerns that 'creeping' forms of taxation are clouding the clarity of the basic system, for example, the skills levy on wages, the obligations of empowerment programmes and municipal rates and levies. On the other hand, further qualitative reductions in corporate tax in the current period may generate further social polarisation. There is also the question of whether there is scope for the design of the tax system to further support developmental objectives.

Competition
New competition authorities, established under the Competition Act, 1998 (Act 89 of 1998), delivered a stronger performance than their predecessors. The competition authorities have not yet been as effective in the field of combating prohibited practices, except where those practices are specifically outlawed, compared with their merger control function. Industry concentration remains high in some sectors in South Africa, with conglomerates of the 1980s having given way to industry-focused powerhouses.

Small, micro and medium business sector development
The Small Business Council, Khula Enterprise Finance Corporation and Ntsika Enterprise Promotion Agency have made modest impact, though the National Manufacturing Advisory Centre (NAMAC) programme is considered world-class. The contribution of the small, medium and micro enterprise (SMME) sector to GDP and employment indicates the limited role that this sector is playing in the South African economy. Small and medium enterprises contribute less than half of total employment, 30% of total GDP and one out of five units exported.

To address some of the problems with SMME development, it was decided to merge Ntsika and NAMAC into the Small Enterprise Development Agency (SEDA). By October 2005, the merger was progressing smoothly with the CEO and executive level for SEDA being appointed and the National Small Business Act, 1996 (Act 102 of 1996), amended as a legal framework for SEDA establishment. SEDA is engaging with the provinces to establish a joint working relationship. SEDA is also fast-tracking implementation strategies and systems.

Skills development

Large numbers of unskilled workers are unemployed, but employers cite a shortage of semi-skilled and skilled workers as a constraint on expansion. Substantial resources have been directed towards both general education and skills training, and government has restructured institutions that deliver education and skills. Both public- and private-sector employers have been slow in taking advantage of the training opportunities available despite the skills shortage being cited as one of their major constraints. However, performance is improving, and the focus on the performance of the sector education and training authorities should yield better results. The target of 72 000 completed learnerships for the unemployed was exceeded in 2004.

There are many young unemployed matriculants and even graduates of universities of technology and universities. The percentage of unemployed graduates of tertiary institutions grew from 6% in 1995 to 15% in 2002. For Africans, the percentage of unemployed graduates rose from 10% in 1995 to 26% in 2002. School, university of technology and university programmes need to be effectively geared towards employability and school-goers and school-leavers need more guidance regarding practical study and career paths.

Empowerment

The proportion of black top managers grew from 12% to 13% between 2000 and 2001, while the number of senior managers grew from 15% to 16%. The proportion of skilled professionals and middle managers grew even more slowly, by 0,2%. Empowerment in the workplace is continuing, but slowly. Progress was slow in extending black ownership, with an estimate of black equity in public companies indicating 9,4% in 2002, compared with 3,9% in 1997, from being virtually non-existent before 1994. The number of previously disadvantaged individual (PDI) directors of public companies grew from 14 (1,2%) in 1992 to 397 (15,6%) in 2002, but the proportion of PDI executive directors remains very small. These trends are expected to improve with the implementation of government's Broad-Based BEE programme. By September 2004, of a total of 2 701 board positions within JSE-listed companies, 435 or 16,1% were held by black people. In 2003, there were 432 black people on JSE boards, representing just over 17% of total directors.

As far as women are concerned, their progress in the workplace has been equally slow. Just 13% of top managers in 2001 were women, only 1% more than in 2000. Women in senior management grew a little faster, by 1,7% to 17,7%. Only 74 (3%) of directors of public companies are black women. Black women make up 3,2% of all directorships on the JSE, and only 0,8% of executive director positions.

Evidence from the Census suggests that the proportion of black managers and professionals has increased relative to their white counterparts although the rate of change is still very slow, with the proportion of black managers, senior officials and legislators rising from 42,5% in 1996 to 44,3% in 2001. Progress in professional, associated professional and technical positions shows that blacks comprised 61,4% of these groupings in 2001, up from 57,6% in 1996.

Innovation and research and development (R&D)

The progress in industrial policy has not yet had major pay-offs in the form of greater levels of domestic innovation and R&D. Expenditure on R&D fell to 0,69% of GDP in the 1990s, but has since risen to about 0,75%. Government has set up an effective system of national innovation with a number of imaginative innovation-support programmes. Innovation levels would have fallen further had these measures not been introduced. The 2002 R&D Strategy established new, relevant missions for the National System of Innovation, which include the Biotechnology Strategy, the Advanced Manufacturing Technology Strategy and the Astronomy Geographical Advantage Programme.

Country economic competitiveness

By most international benchmarking measures, the competitiveness of the South African economy has improved since the early 1990s. Two key indicators are the improvement and diversification of exports, and the significant improvement in labour productivity. However, most measures still indicate that the availability of skilled labour remains a key weakness. Other concerns are the cost of transport and telecommunications, which are key factors in an economy at such great distance from major world markets. Hence the focus of the MERS on input costs and skills.

Conclusion

Government has been successful in ensuring macro-economic stability, improving the trade regime, and taking advantage of the country's natural resources and financial and physical infrastructure. The country's skills base, the volatility of the exchange rate, the cost of input such as transport and telecommunications, lack of competition in the domestic market, and poor perceptions of Africa and southern Africa held back higher rates of investment. While competition from Asia, slow improvements in skills and input costs, and weaknesses in implementation have held back progress, investment trends have turned strongly positive since 1999.

Justice, Crime Prevention and Security (JCPS) Cluster

The departments in the JCPS Cluster, like others, were affected by the apartheid legacy. They lacked integrity and legitimacy. Their main functions were vague and ambiguous and largely directed at maintaining apartheid.

Government was therefore faced with enormous challenges of amalgamating, rationalising and transforming these departments to protect the new Constitution, including redirecting mandates and functions to focus on combating and preventing crime and improving national security.

This included new legislation and mechanisms to create constitutionally mandated bodies such as the Constitutional Court and other judicial commissions, and to establish civilian oversight and monitoring structures.

Upholding the rule of law has been greatly improved by the transformation of the judiciary, particularly through the following activities:

- affirming the supremacy of the Constitution in South Africa
- establishing the Judicial Services Commission
- integrating the judiciary into a single entity with rationalised jurisdictions
- demographic changes in relation to race and gender of the judiciary.

Reducing crime

The NCPS emphasised that crime was not purely a security or law-enforcement issue but that it was also a social issue. Consequently, it gave equal importance to preventing crime on the one hand and combating it on the other.

In respect of social crime prevention, government has implemented several interventions, particularly in development nodes, which have resulted in significant reductions in the levels of crime in those areas in particular.

The cluster has identified and prioritised 169 police stations that register highest levels of contact crime. Working and acting in consultation with the provincial administrations, the cluster has developed socio-graphic profiles of these priority police-station areas. On the basis of these area profiles, relevant developmental projects aimed at preventing crime are being developed.

The responsibility to implement such projects rests with the social and economic clusters, the provincial administrations and local government authorities.

The National Crime Combating Strategy (NCCS) evolved as an operational element of the NCPS that focused on reducing crime in the select and priority crime spots that accounted for 50% of all crime – particularly violent crime – in the country.

The NCCS has stabilised levels of crime, particularly in the 169 police-station areas that accounted for most crime. Furthermore, law-enforcement agencies, in co-operation with other departments, were able to identify and neutralise several organised-crime syndicates.

Government faces the twin challenges of sustaining the NCCS and vigorously implementing social crime-prevention initiatives in a more co-ordinated and structured manner. This requires integrated implementation in all spheres of government. Furthermore, for the cluster to effectively implement social crime prevention, new programmes have to be developed and sustained in partnership with organs of civil society.

Crime trends, 2003/04 – 2004/05

Crimes recorded by the South African Police Service (SAPS) over the past 10 years show crime to be decreasing and/or stabilising. The total of all crimes recorded by the SAPS increased slowly from 1994/95 and then began to decrease from 2001/02. Contact crime and property crime follow a similar trend.

From 2003/04 to 2004/05, trends for most contact crime decreased. Murder decreased by 5,6%, attempted murder by 18,8%, and common assault and assault with grievous bodily harm by 5,1% and 4,5% respectively.

Common robberies decreased by 5,3% from 2002/03 to 2004/05. Between 2003/04 and 2004/05, aggravated robbery decreased by 5,5%. The high levels of robbery correlate with a high number of street robberies and muggings recorded by the police in socially depressed areas. Car hijackings decreased by 9,9% between 2003/04 and 2004/05.

However, robbery of cash in transit increased by 14,6% between 2003/04 and 2004/05. In the same period rape increased by 4% and indecent assault by 8%.

Key areas of intervention

Government has prioritised interventions to deal with some specific crimes. These include sexual offences, domestic violence, organised crime and corruption, cross-border crime, taxi violence and regulating the ownership and possession of firearms. The Victim-Empowerment Programme has also been a priority of government in addressing the needs of victims.

Sexual offences and domestic violence

The Criminal Law (Sexual Offences Amendment Bill) and Domestic Violence Act, 1998 (Act 116 of 1998), seek to improve services for victims of these crimes and increase conviction of offenders. Government has introduced the Anti-Rape Strategy, which saw the establishment of Thuthuzela care centres to reduce secondary victimisation. Sexual offences courts have been set up.

A major challenge pertaining to sexual offences is the high case-withdrawal rate – some 53% of cases referred to court in 2000 were withdrawn.

Dealing with illegal firearms

Reducing the number of illegal firearms in circulation and restricting the issuing of firearms are among key government priorities. Over the past 11 years, government has destroyed over 80 000 illegal firearms. More were destroyed in Operation Rachel (a joint operation with the Mozambican law-enforcement authorities) and in the case of firearms declared redundant by the South African National Defence Force (SANDF) and other state departments.

To further regulate legal firearms in circulation, government passed the Firearms Control Act, 2000 (Act 60 of 2000), to provide a framework to regulate ownership and the possession of firearms.

The impact of firearms on crime, particularly serious and violent crime, suggests that more interventions are needed to control and reduce the number of both legal and illegal firearms in circulation.

From January to June 2005, amnesty for the possession of illegal firearms was introduced. Government called on people with illegal firearms to voluntary hand their guns to the SAPS without facing prosecution for the offence. The amnesty was limited only to the possession of illegal firearms and not to crimes committed with them. The table below shows the number of firearms and amount of ammunition that was surrendered and destroyed during the amnesty period.

Organised crime

The fight against organised crime was enhanced by the establishment of the Directorate: Special Operations (DSO), which emphasised closer integration between all the law-enforcement agencies, the prosecution service and the intelligence structures, which include the Financial Intelligence Centre. These initiatives and ongoing SAPS operations have yielded some good results. Between 2001/02 and 2003/04, SAPS identified and infiltrated 341 organised-crime groups. Some 977 syndicate leaders and 5 034 syndicate members were arrested. In the same period, the DSO finalised 505 investigations into organised crime, financial crime and corruption. Some 481 prosecutions were finalised, with a 92% average conviction rate.

In 2004, government identified and targeted the 200 top criminals responsible for organised crime and corruption. By April 2005, the 200 individuals identified had been apprehended. The cluster has broadened the criteria for top criminals to include multiple offenders for murder, rape, robbery and burglary.

The specialised commercial crime courts yielded an average conviction rate of 95% between April 2003 and March 2004. About 129 forfeiture orders amounting to R76 million were executed and assets worth R500 million frozen.

Effectiveness of the criminal justice system

To improve the effectiveness of the CJS, the cluster has introduced programmes and projects to fast-track case flow and reduce the number of awaiting-trial prisoners and prison overcrowding. These interventions include:
* integrated justice system court centres
* additional and Saturday courts
* specialised commercial crime courts
* community courts.

These interventions reduced the average case preparation time from 152 days in 2002 to 79 days by April 2004. District and regional courts have improved sitting time from an average 3,5 hours to over four hours. Conviction rates in these courts have increased from 64% to 74% since their inception in 2001.

Additional and Saturday courts reduced the backlog of cases pending trial by 53 055 cases.

Notwithstanding these gains, the cluster still faces a challenge in the backlog of cases, coupled with a large number of awaiting-trial detainees and consequent overcrowding in correctional facilities.

In terms of overcrowding, there were 187 446 offenders in correctional service facilities in January 2005, whereas the approved accommodation space was for 113 825 inmates. Of the total inmate population, 52 326 were unsentenced.

The number of sentenced prisoners started stabilising from 2003 due to programmes such as correctional supervision as well as a review of parole policies. The number of unsentenced inmates

Number of firearms and ammunition surrendered and destroyed during amnesty

	Firearms	Rounds of ammunition
Legal firearms voluntarily handed over	44 343	795 226
Illegal firearms voluntarily handed over	31 043	558 291
Illegal firearms confiscated by the South African Police Service	17 343	364 469
Firearms destroyed	14 786	

declined from 2000 and stabilised in part due to programmes such as the IJS court centres and additional and Saturday courts.

The number of children and juveniles in prisons remains a concern. By the end of July 2005, there were about 1 244 unsentenced children detainees and 1 001 sentenced children detainees aged between seven and 17 years. In the same period, there were 8 932 unsentenced and 9 275 sentenced detainees aged between 18 and 25 years.

In accordance with the Constitution and the *White Paper on Corrections*, the department has granted pardon, reprieve, amnesty and special remission to certain detainees. The process was initiated on 30 May 2005 and completed on 9 August 2005. A total of 65 837 offenders benefited from the special remission. A total of 157 offenders who benefited from the special remission had been admitted to correctional centres as awaiting-trial detainees.

National security

National security is protected, in part, in the context of transforming the notion of national security and the departments that carry out this function.

National security departments continue to play a critical role in peace-support operations in the region and on the continent. Important examples include Lesotho, the Democratic Republic of Congo (DRC), the Comoros, Burundi and Ethiopia. They have also taken part in disaster-relief operations, notably in Mozambique.

South Africa's territorial integrity is rendered vulnerable by the limited capability of the SANDF, the absence of a national security strategy and a commonly understood national security management system.

However, government has done much with regard to border control, both at ports of entry and in respect of borderline security.

While government has enacted the Regulation of Foreign Military Assistance Act (FMAA) 1998 (Act 15 of 1998), its provisions are vague with respect to South Africans who join the national defence forces of foreign countries. Of necessity, such citizens potentially pose a counter-intelligence threat. The

amendments to FMAA, 1998, rectifying vague and ambiguous provisions, were approved by Cabinet in August 2005.

Government has attended to several priorities within the realm of national security, including terrorism; the security of government information and systems; and political violence.

Regarding terrorism, it has dealt decisively with urban terror as was carried out by the People Against Gangsterism and Drugs; and the right-wing terror wave of the *Boeremag*; and continues to give attention to international terrorism.

Government further needs to enhance the capacity, co-ordination and readiness of the National Disaster Management System.

Continuing attention is needed to improve the security of government information and systems, among other things, through resolute implementation of the Minimum Information Security Standards policy document. There is also a need to tighten regulations that govern the activities and movements of diplomats accredited to South Africa.

Government has substantially reduced the level of political violence. Sporadic attacks continue, but without the degree of organisation present in earlier violence. Government is giving priority to instituting community rehabilitation interventions, particularly in areas that were ravaged by violence.

Among the priorities for the next 10 years is the need to entrench the rule of law and enhance national security, with specific attention to:
- further reducing levels of crime, both organised and serious and violent crime
- enhancing co-ordination with the social and economic clusters and organs of civil society to vigorously implement social crime-prevention initiatives
- continued improvement of the CJS and its operations
- improving border control
- monitoring extremism and terrorism
- improving the capacity of the security and intelligence departments, including the development of a national security strategy and an effective national security management system.

International Relations, Peace and Security (IRPS) Cluster

Democracy opened a remarkable new chapter in South Africa's international relations. Over the first 11 years, South Africa has established itself as a respected partner and force for good within the community of nations, and has become a leading voice in the developing world for a more progressive, people-centred and multilateral rules-based global system. Given the apartheid State's isolated and ignominious past, the country's achievements in and contributions to international, continental and regional affairs during the First Decade of Freedom have been truly spectacular.

Since 1994, several strategic objectives have informed the work of the IRPS Cluster of departments. Importantly, South Africa's foreign policy revolves around the international pursuit of the country's domestic policies and priorities, particularly as they relate to nation-building, reducing poverty, and creating economic opportunities and a better life for all. To this end, government has pursued the following objectives:

- to normalise, expand and strengthen South Africa's diplomatic relations with the international community
- to protect and promote the country's national interests and values through bilateral and multilateral interaction
- to promote economic development in an interdependent and globalised world through diversified and deepened trade relations, inflows of FDI and regional integration
- to promote and deepen international co-operation in science and technology (S&T)
- to promote international respect for human rights and democracy
- to contribute towards and support initiatives for international peace, security and stability as well as post-conflict reconstruction (including international crime prevention and management)
- to prioritise the interests and development of Africa in international affairs
- to promote the agenda of the South through South-South co-operation and North-South partnerships
- to support a strong, effective and equitable multilateral rules-based global order that promotes and protects the interests of developing countries.

International normalisation

South Africa has successfully normalised its diplomatic relations with the world and rejoined all significant regional, continental and multilateral institutions. By July 2005, South Africa had 83 embassies/high commissions, 16 consulates and 46 honorary consulates abroad. Foreign representation in South Africa by July 2005 included 113 diplomatic missions, 53 consulates, 22 multilateral organisations and non-residential accreditation from 16 countries. This represents a dramatic increase in diplomatic activity from the days of the isolated and ostracised apartheid State.

Over the past decade, the country was honoured to host a number of important multilateral conferences, including the United Nations (UN) Conference on Trade and Development IX (1996), Non-Aligned Movement (1998), Commonwealth (1999), World Conference Against Racism (2001), African Union (AU) (2002) and World Summit on Sustainable Development (2002). In these fora, South Africa has consistently worked to promote agendas and outcomes that address poverty and the underdevelopment of the South. South Africa also hosted several international sports tournaments and preparations are well underway to host the FIFA Soccer World Cup in 2010.

These conferences and events have raised the country's international profile, generally had a positive impact on the economy, and have favourably maintained South Africa in the global media. The hosting of these events has supported the campaigns of South African Tourism and the initiatives of the International Marketing Council to image, brand and market the country, particularly for attracting an ever-increasing number of tourists.

South Africa recorded its highest-ever number of foreign tourism arrivals during 2004/05 – more than 6,6 million visitors, a 2,7% increase over the previous year. Visitors spent R47,8 billion in South Africa during this period. For the first time in South Africa's history, tourism eclipsed gold as an earner of foreign exchange.

Economic development and co-operation in a globalising world

Government has diversified and deepened the country's trading networks, export markets and sources of FDI. Apart from its traditional trading partners, South Africa has developed more extensive relations with South America, Asia and Africa, thereby enhancing South-South economic co-operation. As part of its global trade strategy, government has identified strategic partner countries with which to develop economic relations through bilateral FTAs, although it is not seeking FTA negotiations with all of them at this stage.

Over the past decade, South Africa has concluded, or is currently engaged in, a number of trade negotiations:

- WTO: South Africa played an important role in the launch of the new Doha Round (which emerged with a developmental agenda) in 2001, and continues to participate in this round of negotiations through the G20, Africa and Cairns groups.
- Trade, Development and Co-operation Agreement (TDCA) with the EU: This came into effect on 1 January 2000 and the agenda for its review was finalised at the end of 2004.
- SADC Trade Protocol: This was signed in 1996 and there were subsequently negotiations around revised rules of origin.
- New SACU Agreement: This was concluded in October 2002.
- SACU: The union is finalising, negotiating or exploring FTAs with the European Free Trade Area (EFTA), the USA, China, India and MERCOSUR.

South Africa's investment climate, regime and credit ratings have greatly improved. This is reflected in the net positive FDI inflows that the country has attracted since 1994, although these capital inflows remain low relative to other emerging markets with broadly similar profiles.

South Africa has, over the past decade, signed a number of co-operation agreements in S&T, and established a number of important S&T projects with strong international participation.

Promotion of international respect for human rights and democracy

Democratic South Africa has sought to promote international respect for human rights, democracy and good governance. In particular, government has placed a strong premium on the rights of women, children and the disabled. Government has broadly approached the issue of human rights in concert with its African partners and through multilateral mechanisms such as the UN, Organisation of African Unity (OAU)/AU and SADC.

Commitment to peace, stability and development in Africa

The area where South Africa has arguably made the greatest strides in its foreign policy over the past decade, is in its contribution to the development of the African continent. South Africa played a leading role in reconstituting the former OAU into the AU as a more effective pan-African continental body, and in crafting and promoting what became the New Partnership for Africa's Development (NEPAD). NEPAD was launched as the socio-economic programme of the AU at the Durban AU Summit in July 2002. Most of the critical organs of the AU are now established and operational. In 2004, South Africa was accorded the great honour of permanently hosting the Pan-African Parliament (PAP). It hosted the fourth session of the PAP in November 2005.

As part of the NEPAD process, the African Peer Review Mechanism has been established as a voluntary mechanism with the mandate to ensure that the policies and practices of participating states conform to agreed political, economic and corporate governance values, codes and standards. It is envisaged as a system of self-assessment, constructive peer dialogue, and persuasion, and for sharing experiences and best practices among members. South Africa is among the first countries to be peer re-viewed, with its review having commenced in 2005.

At regional level, South Africa has promoted integration within the context of the SADC, the SACU and the Common Monetary Area. South Africa has actively supported the restructuring of the SADC and the development of the Regional Indicative Strategic Development Programme, as well as protocols on particular areas of functional co-operation.

Development can, however, only take place within the context of a stable, secure and peaceful Africa. For this reason, South Africa has invested substantial human and financial resources to support regional and continent-wide initiatives to promote peace, stability and security.

Over the past decade, South Africa has made a number of interventions that have contributed to peace, stability and security in several countries on the continent and beyond. South Africa also played an important role in the diplomatic resolution of the Lockerbie case. It has assisted in various humanitarian and relief operations in southern Africa, as well as in post-conflict reconstruction.

On the multilateral front, South Africa was involved in the formulation and drafting of the SADC Protocol on Politics, Defence and Security Co-operation and the SADC Mutual Defence Pact. Police co-operation agreements have been concluded with several countries in southern Africa and beyond, facilitating cross-border operations and the combating of crime domestically, regionally and internationally. At continental level, South Africa made significant contributions to the drafting of the framework for the Common African Defence and Security Policy, and participated in drafting the AU Convention on the Prevention and Combating of Terrorism. On a global level, South Africa played a role in the establishment of the International Criminal Court.

South Africa is a relative newcomer to peace-support operations, but has quickly developed a reputation for its positive contribution in support of UN- and AU-mandated peace-support operations. Members of the SANDF are performing exemplary duties in the name of peace and stability as part of the UN and AU missions in the DRC, Burundi and Ethiopia/Eritrea, and more recently in Liberia and Sudan. South Africa continues to play a role as mediator in the conflict among the warring factions in the Côte d'Ivoire. South African peace initiatives have seen the adoption of a constitution in the DRC while two largely peaceful and successful elections were held in Burundi.

South-South co-operation and transformation of North-South relations

South Africa has sought the transformation of North-South relations (particularly with respect to debt relief, market access and fairer terms of trade) while consolidating South-South relations. The latter includes a new alignment of co-operation between India, Brazil and South Africa. A trilateral commission and co-operation agenda between these three countries has been established and is being implemented. The country's strategy in transforming North-South relations has included an ongoing and meaningful dialogue with the North through bilateral meetings, engagement with the G8 countries, and a series of conferences examining mutual issues of concern such as sustainable development, HIV and AIDS and racism. The engagement of South Africa alongside some of its counterparts in Africa, Asia and South America with the G8 has resulted in these countries committing themselves to the writing-off of 100% of the debt of 18 highly indebted and poor countries, 14 of whom are in Africa. This is complemented by the commitment to increase aid to the developing world to annual sums of US$50 billion (half of this amount pledged to Africa) by 2010.

Commitment to multilateralism and international law

Over the past decade, South Africa has consistently emphasised the need to strengthen and deepen multilateralism to meet the global challenges of poverty, insecurity and underdevelopment. Multilateralism has provided South Africa with a vehicle through which to advance a number of foreign policy priorities, including human rights, democracy, debt relief, peace and stability, an equitable global trading system, sustainable development, and an enhanced international response to issues of poverty and health. South Africa has also actively advocated for the democratisation and reform of the UN, in particular its Security Council.

Key findings and lessons of the First Decade of Freedom

The challenges of the next decade arise from lessons of the First Decade of Freedom and from new challenges created by the process of change and transformation itself.

Influence of the Government's successes have often, though not always, been where it has had significant control, and less so where its influence has been indirect.

There has been great progress in building a new constitutional democracy, three spheres of government and a more integrated administration – but in many areas of service delivery there is a need for better performance by the Public Service.

There has been a major extension of social services, with striking impact on women's rights. However, many of those entitled to grants are still unregistered or poorly serviced. There are still many people who have not been reached by services they need.

Very good progress has been made in economic areas under government control, but it has not been matched in areas where new agencies or partnerships are involved – such as small business, HRD, restructuring of SOEs and empowerment. Govern-ment has had even less success in matters that depend on the private sector and civil society – including investment and employment creation.

National security has been enhanced, the rule of law established and institutions transformed. But, owing to challenges of the social transition, insufficient civil-society involvement, and new forms of organised crime, the gains in crime prevention could have been better.

Internationally, government has made progress beyond its limited resources as the country re-integrated in the global arena.

The social transition
Four major social trends of the First Decade of Freedom shape the challenges ahead:

More and smaller households
From 1996 to 2001, the South African population grew 11% from 40,4 million to 44,8 million. But the number of households grew by 30% from 9,7 million to 11,8 million, as households became smaller. The average household size has dropped from 4,5 to 3,8 persons. So, government has to provide additional housing and services for instance, to almost three million instead of one million households.

Bigger economically active population
The population has grown about 2% a year since 1995, but the economically active population grew over 4% a year (from 11,5 million to 16,8 million). The number of jobs grew by 20% (after accounting for jobs lost) but the economically active population has grown by over 40%. New job seekers are not only young adults but also older people who, under apartheid, did not consider themselves part of the labour market. Many of them are African women from rural areas.

Two economies in one country
While all main economic sectors grew between 1995 and 2002, there was a shift from public services, construction and mining to financial and business service sectors (where employment doubled). This is consolidating 'two economies' in one country. One is advanced and skilled, becoming more globally competitive. The second is mainly informal, marginalised and unskilled. Despite impressive gains in the First Economy, the benefits have yet to reach the Second Economy, which could fall even further behind without decisive government intervention.

Increased rural migration
There has been a shift from rural to big urban areas.

Twenty percent of people in the main urban areas are new migrants. This puts pressure on urban service delivery and economic opportunities, and causes loss of people and opportunities in rural areas.

These trends, added to the apartheid backlog, help explain the scale of the past decade's challenges and some of the limitations in progress, for example in unemployment, poverty alleviation and the fight against crime.

The global setting

As we enter the Second Decade of Freedom, the global environment is uncertain, with increasing tension, unilateralism and unresolved international trade issues.

But there are also new opportunities for developing countries to assert their interests. While many developments could marginalise Africa, there are opportunities for the continent to mobilise itself for a more humane approach to its plight and that of other poor regions. Among governments and citizens of developed countries there is potential to focus attention on the common objectives of humanity contained in the UN Millennium Declaration. South Africa is equipped to play a critical role in this regard due to its location, the size of its economy on the continent, and its current endeavours and outlook.

Challenges and opportunities in the Second Decade of Freedom

If South Africans are to make continued and faster progress towards a united, non-racial, non-sexist and democratic society in the Second Decade of Freedom, then they should move to a higher growth and development path. To achieve this, South Africa needs a major intervention: to reinforce the consolidation of democracy with measures aimed at integrating all of society into a growing economy from which they can benefit. This will require:

- an encompassing framework and vision defining a shared approach by all sectors of society in partnership around common development objectives
- better performance by the State, with focus on efficient implementation and decisive intervention to unlock any delivery logjams
- addressing consequences of the social transition, by improving access to work opportunities and sustainable livelihoods in urban and rural areas, and ensuring that, when people migrate, they have the skills and information to take advantage of opportunities
- improving the regional environment and implementing NEPAD, so that South Africa can weld together a number of southern African countries into a locomotive for faster growth in sub-Saharan Africa.

Agriculture and land affairs

The Department of Agriculture aims to lead and support sustainable agriculture and promote rural development by:
- ensuring access to sufficient, safe and nutritious food
- eliminating skewed participation and inequity in the sector
- maximising growth, employment and income in agriculture
- improving the sustainable management of natural agricultural resources and ecological systems
- ensuring effective and efficient governance
- ensuring knowledge and information management.

The department's budget increased from R871,1 million in 2001/02 to R1,4 billion in 2004/05.

For 2005/06, expenditure was expected to continue to increase rapidly, rising to R1 194 701 billion in 2007/08. These increases are allocated to the new Comprehensive Agricultural Support Programme (CASP), agricultural disaster-relief programmes, the LandCare Programme, and regulatory services to contain animal and plant-disease outbreaks.

Strategic Plan for South African Agriculture

The department, through its socio-economic development initiatives, is committed to reducing poverty in South Africa and on the continent, broadening access to agriculture and increasing productivity and profitability within the agriculture sector.

The Strategic Plan for South African Agriculture, adopted in 2001, consists of three core objectives:
- equitable access and participation
- global competitiveness and profitability
- sustainable resource management.

The plan is the result of collaboration between government, Agri SA and the National African Farmers' Union (NAFU).

74

Agricultural economy

South Africa has a dual agricultural economy, comprising a well-developed commercial sector and a predominantly subsistence-oriented sector in the rural areas. About 13% of South Africa's surface area can be used for crop production. High-potential arable land comprises only 22% of total arable land. Some 1,3 million hectares (ha) are under irrigation.

The most important factor limiting agricultural production is the availability of water. Rainfall is distributed unevenly across the country. Almost 50% of South Africa's water is used for agricultural purposes.

The country can be subdivided into a number of farming regions according to climate, natural vegetation, types of soil and the type of farming practised. Agricultural activities in these regions range from intensive crop production and mixed farming in winter-rainfall and high summer-rainfall areas, to cattle-ranching in the bushveld, and sheep-farming in the more arid regions. Owing to its geographical location, some parts of South Africa are prone to drought.

Primary commercial agriculture contributes about 3,3% to South Africa's gross domestic product (GDP) and about 7,2% to formal employment. However, there are strong backward and forward linkages into the economy, so that the agro-industrial sector is estimated to comprise 15% of GDP.

Today, South Africa is not only self-sufficient in virtually all major agricultural products, but in a normal year it is also a net food exporter. However, major import products include wheat, rice and vegetable oils.

Despite the farming industry's declining share of GDP, it remains vitally important to the economy, and the development and stability of the southern African region.

For the past five years, agricultural exports have contributed on average about 8% (7,6% in 2004) of total South African exports.

Normally, South Africa is a net exporter of agricultural products in rand value. The largest export groups are wine; citrus; sugar; grapes; maize; fruit juice; wool; and deciduous fruit such as apples, pears, peaches and apricots. Other important export products are non-alcoholic beverages, food preparations, meat, avocados, pineapples, ground-nuts, preserved fruit and nuts, hides and skins, and dairy products.

During 2004, the United Kingdom (UK), The Netherlands, Germany, the United States of America (USA) and Mozambique were the five largest trading partners of South Africa in terms of export destination.

Genetically modified organisms (GMOs)

South Africa does not have ideal conditions for crop production. Less than 12% of its land is arable, and serious climatic constraints, such as periodic droughts, hinder agricultural production.

Despite these circumstances, productivity must increase to meet the population's growing food requirements. Recent developments in biotechnology have brought hope to the challenge of increasing food production. Genetic modification provides a way of meeting the growing demand for food

Exports						
	2000	**2001**	**2002**	**2003**	**2004**	**Average: five years**
Total South African products ('000 000)	210 022	245 448	314 927	274 640	292 261	267 460
Total agricultural products ('000 000)	15 820	20 075	25 460	23 001	22 187	21 309
Agriculture as % of total exports	7,5	8,2	8,1	8,4	7,6	8,0

Source: Directorate: Agricultural Statistics, Department of Agriculture

without placing even greater pressure on scarce resources.

The GMO Act, 1997 (Act 15 of 1997), that was implemented on 1 December 1999 provides for the regulation of GMOs in South Africa, particularly new biosafety assessments.

In terms of the Act, permits are issued for trials and the commercial release of any GMO crops in the country, to ensure contained cultivation and reduced environmental impact.

The objectives of the Act are to increase crop yield while protecting biodiversity. In 2001, the Department of Agriculture approved the planting of three commercial genetically modified (GM) crops: insect-resistant cotton, herbicide-resistant cotton and insect-resistant maize.

There are no GM crops planted for human consumption in South Africa. Neither are there fresh GM fruit and vegetables on sale in the country. Imported engineered soya is used in processed meat and other locally produced food.

In terms of the GMO Act, 1997, the advisory committee, comprising scientific experts, conducts risk assessments to determine if a particular GMO is safe for humans, animals and the environment. The Foodstuffs, Cosmetics and Disinfectants Act, 1972 (Act 54 of 1972), oversees the safety of food in South Africa.

Sustainable resource management and use

South Africa, at most times, is able to meet its own food requirements with considerable food exportation. However, improved information about the potential and limitations of the natural resource base is essential for good management decisions.

An inventory of soils, terrain forms and climate (land types) was undertaken by the Agricultural Research Council's (ARC) Institute for Soil, Climate and Water. The National Land Type Survey, completed in 2001, assists land-use planning and decision-making. Data from this and other more detailed soil and climate surveys are integrated into the comprehensive Agricultural Geo-Referenced Information

System (GIS), which provides access to information, via the Internet, on agricultural potential and land suitability.

Although it is generally recognised that soil degradation is a problem, little reliable data has been collected systematically over time. Soil degradation is largely related to the decline in soil organic matter. Monoculture cereal production, intensive tillage, short-to-no fallow, and limited crop rotation have contributed to this in the commercial sector.

Excessive fuel-wood collection, inappropriate land-use, population density and overgrazing are the main causes of soil degradation in communal areas. In addition, it is estimated that about 60% of the cropland area is moderately to severely acidic, and probably at least 15% is affected by subsoil acidity.

Physical degradation

Physical degradation of South Africa's agricultural land results in soil erosion by both water and wind. It has been estimated that water erosion affects about 6,1 million ha of cultivated soil in South Africa, and wind erosion about 10,9 million ha. Another degradation problem is compaction within the soil profile, especially with fine sandy soils where, for example, maize yields can be adversely affected by some 30% to 40%.

Urban spread, industrialisation and mining (such as opencast coal-mining in Mpumalanga) also affect the sustainable use of agricultural land.

In accordance with the Conservation of Agricultural Resources Act, 1983 (Act 43 of 1983), the Department of Agriculture exercises control over the use of South Africa's natural agricultural resources. The Act provides for the conservation of these resources by maintaining the land's production potential, eliminating and preventing erosion and bush encroachment, protecting vegetation, and combating weeds and invader plants. The Act generally applies to agricultural land in South Africa, except for the sections dealing with weeds and invader plants, which also apply to urban areas.

To promote natural agricultural resource conservation, policies, norms, standards and guidelines have been developed, as has a national agricultural resource audit division and a conservation GIS. National long-term grazing capacity norms were derived from national oceanic and atmospheric administration satellite data, as well as seasonal norms, taking into account the impact of climate on biomass production. At farmer level, conservation committees can be appointed to promote the conservation of natural agricultural resources in the area concerned.

Production

The prices of agricultural products increased by 2,3% from 2003 to 2004. During 2004, the estimated total volume of agricultural production was 0,1% higher than during 2003. Producer prices of agricultural products decreased, on average, by 6,8% from 2003 to 2004, compared with an increase of 6,9% during the previous year.

In 2004, producer prices of horticultural products decreased by 3,4% compared with 2003. During the same period, the prices of fresh vegetables decreased significantly by 14,1%, while the prices of fruit fell by 8,2%.

The producer prices of animal products were only 1,7% higher in 2004 than in 2003. Prices received for slaughtered stock increased by 8,8%. However, prices received for pastoral products decreased by 15,6%. The price farmers received for milk was 3,6% lower. Prices received by poultry farmers showed almost no change compared with 2003.

During 2004, the producer price of field crops was 18,1% higher than during 2003.

According to the results of the Census of Agriculture, there were 45 818 active commercial farming units in South Africa in 2002. The number of paid workers employed by the formal agricultural sector decreased by 152 445 (13,9%) from 1 093 265 in 1993 to 940 820 in 2002. Nearly half of the employees in 2002 were casual and seasonal workers.

According to the Labour Force Survey, released by Statistics South Africa in March 2005, 1 170 000 people were employed in agriculture.

The total gross value of agricultural production (total production during a production season valued at the average basic prices received by producers) for 2004 was estimated at R71 211 million (R70 855 million in 2003) – an increase of 0,5%.

Farm income

The gross income of producers (the value of sales and production for other uses plus the value of changes in inventories) for 2004 amounted to R68 805 million compared with R68 717 million in 2003 – an increase of only 0,1%.

In 2004, the gross income from field crops decreased by 8% to R17 284 million compared with R18 780 million in 2003. This was mainly because of lower wheat production, as well as the downward trend in the prices that farmers received for summer crops during 2004.

Gross income from horticultural products increased by 2,1%, from R20 023 in 2003, to R20 451 million in 2004.

Income from deciduous and other summer fruit increased by 17,6% to R5 498 million, while that of citrus fruit increased by only 1,1% to R3 671 million. The increase in deciduous fruit and other summer fruit can be attributed to both an increase in production and in domestic prices received.

The income from vegetables amounted to R6 235 million – a decrease of 6,6%. Income from potatoes, which maintained a contribution of about 38% to the gross income from vegetables, decreased by 10% from R2 627 million in 2003 to R2 364 million in 2004.

Gross income from animal products was 3,9% higher and amounted to R31 070 million. Producers earned R6 992 million from the slaughtering of cattle and calves – an increase of 20,4%.

The price of beef increased by 10,8%. Income from slaughtered sheep grew by 3,5% and amounted to R1 689 million. Income from poultry and egg production amounted to R13 390 million – an increase of 0,8%. Income from ostrich feathers and products, however, dropped by 7,7% to R275 million, mainly as a result of the decrease in the number of ostriches slaughtered.

Field crops and horticulture

The largest area of farmland is planted with maize, followed by wheat and, to a lesser extent, sugar cane and sunflowers.

The grain industry is one of the largest in South Africa and is also a very strategic one.

This industry produces between 25% and 33% of the total gross value of agricultural production. The gross value of grain production is usually around R12 billion, but in the 2001/02 season, it increased to R22 billion as a result of, among other things, higher prices.

Grain South Africa represents a total of 17 000 grain producers, of whom 11 000 are from disadvantaged communities. These farmers represent roughly 90% of all grain produced in South Africa.

Other major role-players include the silo, milling, baking and animal-feed industries.

Maize

Maize is the largest locally produced field crop, and the most important source of carbohydrates in the Southern African Development Community (SADC) for animal and human consumption.

South Africa is the main maize producer in the SADC, with an average production of about 9,2 million tons (mt) a year over the past 10 years.

It is estimated that more than 8 000 commercial maize producers are responsible for the major part of the South African crop, while the rest is produced by thousands of small-scale producers.

Maize is produced mainly in North West; the north-western, northern and eastern Free State; the Mpumalanga Highveld; and the KwaZulu-Natal Midlands. Local commercial consumption of maize amounts to about 8 mt, and surplus maize is usually exported.

A total of 9,7 mt of maize was produced in 2003/04 on 3,2 million ha of land (developing agriculture included). An estimated 3 mt surplus of maize was carried over to 2004/05. This carry-over contributed to the slump in maize prices to four-year lows in the first quarter of 2005.

Maize prices plunged from more than R1 000 per ton in November 2004 to less than R600 during the first quarter of 2005. It is expected that the price of maize will remain low. Better than expected rains also contributed to the maize price slide.

Wheat

Wheat is produced mainly in the winter-rainfall areas of the Western Cape and the eastern parts of the Free State. Production in the Free State is the highest, but there are considerable annual fluctuations. The price of wheat increased by 9,2% in 2003/04, compared with the previous marketing season.

Wheat is imported to meet local requirements.

Barley

Barley is produced mainly on the southern coastal plains of the Western Cape. The area where barley is planted totalled 82 650 ha in the 2004/05 production season. Production totalled 189 365 tons (t).

Ground-nuts

Ground-nuts are grown mainly in the Free State, North West and the Northern Cape. Ground-nut planting decreased by 40% from 71 500 ha in 2003/04 to 42 800 ha in 2004/05.

Sunflower seed

South Africa is the world's 11th-largest producer of sunflower seed. Sunflower seed is produced in the Free State, North West and on the Mpumalanga Highveld, as well as in Limpopo.

An area of 530 000 ha was planted in 2003/04, producing 648 000 t.

Lucerne seed

For many years, Oudtshoorn, De Rust and Douglas were the only areas in South Africa in which lucerne seed was produced in reasonable quantity. Today, the Oudtshoorn district is responsible for about 8,5% of the lucerne seed produced in South Africa.

Sorghum

Sorghum is cultivated mostly in the drier parts of the summer-rainfall areas such as Mpumalanga, the Free State, Limpopo, North West and Gauteng.

In 2003/04, production of sorghum totalled 373 000 t on 130 000 ha of land.

Sugar

South Africa is ranked as the world's 13th-largest sugar producer. The South African sugar industry is one of the world's leading cost-competitive producers of high-quality sugar.

Sugar cane is grown in 14 cane-producing areas extending from northern Pondoland in the Eastern Cape, through the coastal belt and Midlands of KwaZulu-Natal, to the Mpumalanga Lowveld.

There are more than 50 000 registered cane growers.

Gross value of agricultural production, 2004 (R'000)	
Field crops	
Maize	8 318 266
Wheat	2 000 529
Hay	2 257 501
Grain sorghum	404 228
Sugar cane	2 730 628
Ground-nuts	367 307
Tobacco	581 999
Sunflower seed	1 235 948
Cotton	215 102
Other	1 318 057
Total	19 428 565
Horticulture	
Viticulture	2 623 417
Citrus fruit	3 670 562
Subtropical fruit	1 336 969
Deciduous and other fruit	5 743 251
Vegetables	3 870 485
Potatoes	2 364 441
Other	1 171 116
Total	20 780 241
Animal products	
Wool	936 607
Poultry and poultry products	13 389 903
Cattle and cattle slaughtered	6 991 676
Sheep and goats slaughtered	1 760 828
Pigs slaughtered	1 276 595
Fresh milk	3 776 064
Milk for dairy products	1 171 814
Other	1 766 442
Total	31 069 939
Grand total	**71 279 745**

Preliminary source: Directorate: Agricultural Statistics, Department of Agriculture

It is a diverse industry combining the agricultural activities of sugar-cane cultivation with the industrial factory production of raw and refined sugar, syrups, specialised sugars and a range of by-products.

An estimated average of 2,5 mt of sugar is produced per season. About 50% of this sugar is marketed in southern Africa. The remainder is exported to numerous markets in Africa, the Middle East, North America and Asia.

Employment within the sugar industry totals about 85 000 jobs, with direct and indirect employment estimated at 350 000 people. About one million people depend on the sugar industry. Based on actual sales and selling prices in 2004/05, it is estimated that the South African sugar industry contributed R2,38 billion to South Africa's foreign exchange earnings.

The South African sugar industry makes an important contribution to the national economy, given its agricultural and industrial investments, foreign exchange earnings, its high employment, and linkages with major suppliers, support industries and customers.

The established sugar industry aims to redistribute at least 78 000 ha of sugar-producing land to black farmers by 2015, as part of its contribution to the 30% national target of the redistribution of agricultural land. In 2004/05, government committed R6 million towards the first phase of the programme.

Deciduous fruit

Deciduous fruit is grown mainly in the Western Cape and in the Langkloof Valley in the Eastern Cape. Smaller production areas are found along the Orange River and in the Free State, Mpumalanga and Gauteng. This industry's export earnings represent 12% of the country's total earnings from agricultural exports. In 2003/04, apples made up the largest percentage of the crop (43%), while pears totalled 20% and grapes 19%. About 75% of the total crop was produced in the Western Cape, 14% in the Northern Cape, 8% in the Eastern Cape and 3% in Limpopo.

In 2002/03, the producer price of horticultural products increased by 19%. During 2003, South

Africa was the largest exporter in the southern hemisphere of table grapes to Europe. Horticulture represented 77% of the total value of agricultural exports, while deciduous fruit made up 60% of horticultural products.

In 2003/04, income from deciduous fruit increased by 18% from R4 478 million in 2002/03 to R5 266 million in 2003/04.

Wine

South Africa is the eighth-largest wine producer in the world.

About 110 200 ha of land are under cultivation with about 322 million vines. About 80% of wines are produced by co-operatives. Some 4 401 primary wine producers employ about 67 000 people. According to the South African Wine and Spirits Export Association, the export of white wine increased from 20 million litres (ML) in 1992 to 119 ML in 2004.

In 2004, South Africa harvested 312 184 t of grapes, which resulted in the production of 1 016 ML of wine, compared with 1 233 689 t and about 956 ML of wine in 2003. This represented an increase of 60 ML compared with the 2003 vintage.

In 2004, South Africa exported 266,5 ML of wine worldwide, which was a 12% volume increase from 2003, despite the robust Rand and aggressive competition prompted by a global oversupply. In addition to the USA, other high-growth destinations were the Netherlands, which grew by 18%, Germany (34%), Sweden (31%) and Canada (40%).

The Wine and Spirits Agreement between South Africa and the European Union (EU) was signed on 28 January 2002.

The agreement improves access for South African wine and spirits to the large European market. Applying an annual duty-free tariff quota of 42 ML ensures better access for South African wines. In addition, the EU makes available an amount of 15 million euro for restructuring the South African wine and spirits industry.

Part of the agreement involves phasing out names traditionally used in South Africa for specific types of wines. The names 'port' and 'sherry' were to be phased out over five years for exports to non-

SADC markets, starting from 1 January 2000. They must be phased out of all markets after 12 years. South Africa also has to phase out the names *grappa, ouzo, korn/kornbrand, jägertee* and *pacharan* within five years of signing the agreement.

Citrus and subtropical fruit

Citrus production is largely limited to the irrigation areas of Limpopo, Mpumalanga, the Eastern and Western Cape, and KwaZulu-Natal.

A total of 2 mt of citrus was produced in 2003/04, an increase of 4% from 2002/03.

Pineapples are grown in the Eastern Cape and northern KwaZulu-Natal. Other subtropical crops such as avocados, mangoes, bananas, litchis, guavas, papayas, granadillas and macadamia and pecan nuts are produced mainly in Mpumalanga and Limpopo at Levubu and Letaba, and in the subtropical coastal areas of KwaZulu-Natal and the Eastern Cape.

In 2003/04, South Africa produced over 595 000 t of subtropical fruit.

Potatoes

About 40% of the country's potato crop is grown in the high-lying areas of the Free State and Mpumalanga. Limpopo, the Eastern, Western and Northern Cape, and the high-lying areas of

The estimated value of imports during 2004 amounted to about R15 847 million, compared with R13 921 million in 2003.

The estimated value of exports decreased from R23 453 million in 2003 to about R22 662 million in 2004. According to the 2004 export values, citrus fruit, wine, grapes, apples, pears and quinces, as well as sugar, were the most important export products.

Rice, wheat, oil cake, undenatured ethyl alcohol and palm oil were the most important import products. During 2004, the United Kingdom, the Netherlands, Germany, Mozambique and the United States of America (USA) were South Africa's five largest trading partners in terms of export destinations.

The five largest trading partners from whom South Africa imported agricultural products during 2004 were Argentina, Brazil, the USA, Thailand and Australia.

KwaZulu-Natal are also important production areas. About two-thirds of the country's total potato crop is produced under irrigation.

Of the total crop, 52% is delivered to fresh-produce markets and a further 20% is processed. The South African potato-processing industry has grown tremendously over the past few years. This growth took place primarily in the three main disciplines of the processing industry, namely crisps, chips and French fries. Frozen French fries comprise 45% of total processed potato products in South Africa.

In terms of gross income to the grower (apart from potatoes, which contribute 38%), tomatoes, onions, green mealies and sweetcorn are probably the most important vegetable crops.

These crops contribute 40% to the income derived from vegetables.

Income from potatoes decreased by 7%, from R2 933 million in 2002/03, to R2 540 million in 2003/04.

Tomatoes

Tomatoes are produced countrywide, but mainly in Limpopo, the Mpumalanga Lowveld and Middleveld, the Pongola area of KwaZulu-Natal, the southern parts of the Eastern Cape and the Western Cape.

Onions

Onions are grown in Mpumalanga; in the districts of Caledon, Ceres and Worcester in the Western Cape;

Production of important field crops and horticultural products, 2004 ('000 t)

Maize	9 737
Wheat	1 738
Sugar cane	19 095
Grain sorghum	449
Ground-nuts	128
Sunflower seed	677
Deciduous and other soft fruit	1 901
Citrus fruit	1 802
Subtropical fruit	619
Vegetables	2 015
Potatoes	1 656

Preliminary source: Directorate: Agricultural Statistics, Department of Agriculture

and at Venterstad and adjoining areas in the southern Free State.

Cabbages

Cabbages are also grown countrywide, but are concentrated in Mpumalanga and the Camperdown and Greytown districts of KwaZulu-Natal.

Cotton

Cotton is cultivated in Mpumalanga, Limpopo, Northern Cape, KwaZulu-Natal and North West. It constitutes 74% of natural fibre and 42% of all fibre processed in South Africa. Cotton is grown under irrigation as well as in dry-land conditions.

Cotton under irrigation usually contributes almost as much to the national crop as that grown in dry-land conditions, although the number of hectares under dry-land conditions exceeds those under irrigation. About 75% of local production is harvested by hand. In 2002/03, the price of cotton increased by 10,5%.

Black farmers are being assisted to grow cotton on 9 000 ha of land in four provinces.

The Strategic Plan for the South African Cotton Sector has been developed to:

- grow farm output to a stable 370 000 lint bales by 2007
- broaden participation to enable emerging farmers to deliver an average of 100 000 lint bales annually by 2007
- raise productivity by training at least 60% of small growers by 2007
- improve research, extension services and technology transfer; expand exports by value, diversity, country of destination and client base; and accelerate the elimination of unfair competition by promoting regional and international co-operation, and through more effective lobbying in international trade fora.

Tobacco

Virginia tobacco is produced mainly in Mpumalanga, Limpopo and North West. The production of Oriental tobacco ceased in 2001. There are 630 growers in South Africa who produce an annual average of 37 million kilograms (kg) on about 13 800 ha of land.

The industry employs 23 580 workers. About 50% to 60% of leaf tobacco is exported annually. Excise duties and value-added tax on tobacco amount to R6 billion annually.

Tea

Honeybush tea grows mainly in the coastal and mountainous areas of the Western Cape, but also in certain areas of the Eastern Cape. Honeybush has grown into a commercial crop, with the production of more than 120 t of processed tea per year. The industry has seen an improvement in the quality of tea and the establishment of export standards, the construction of a large processing and packaging facility in Mossel Bay, increased consumer awareness, the appearance of several brand names on supermarket shelves, and a growing overseas market.

Rooibos tea is an indigenous herb produced mainly in the Cedarberg area of the Western Cape. In 2004, the demand for rooibos was estimated to be 9 800 t compared with 6 200 t exported in 2001. The active producers of rooibos tea are estimated at 320, ranging from small to large farming enterprises.

Ornamental plants

Ornamental plants are produced throughout the country, but production aimed particularly at the export market is concentrated in the central parts of Limpopo, Mpumalanga and Gauteng. Ornamental-plant production includes nursery plants, cut flowers and pot plants. The country's most important plant export products are gladioli, proteas, bulbs, chrysanthemum cuttings and roses.

Amaryllis bulbs are a lucrative export product to the USA. The ARC is involved in several ongoing research activities in support of the protea and fynbos industry. Dried flowers form an important component of this industry. A large variety of proteas, conebushes and other products are well-established in the marketplace.

Ornamental plants are produced throughout the country, with greenhouse and open-field production concentrated mainly in Limpopo, Mpumalanga and Gauteng. The protea industry is mainly concentrated in the Western Cape.

Flowers

South Africa's indigenous flowers, such as, gladioli, nerine, freesia and gerbera, have undergone many years of extensive research in Europe, and have become major crops throughout the world.

South Africa is the leading exporter of protea cut flowers, which account for more than half of proteas sold on the world market. South African proteas and so-called Cape greens (fynbos) are mainly marketed in Europe.

Livestock

Livestock is farmed in most parts of South Africa. Numbers vary according to weather conditions. Stock-breeders concentrate mainly on the development of breeds that are well-adapted to diverse climatic and environmental conditions. The latest estimates for cattle and sheep are 13,8 million and 25,5 million, respectively. South Africa normally produces 85% of its meat requirements, while 15% is imported from Namibia, Botswana, Swaziland, Australia, New Zealand and Europe.

The livestock industry is the largest national agricultural sector. The local demand for products, which generally outstrips production, creates a dependence on imports, even though there are untapped production reserves in the communal farming sector.

Dairy-farming

Dairy-farming is practised throughout South Africa, with the highest concentration of dairy farms in the

A protracted R6-million rights- and licence-fee dispute over the right to use the term 'rooibos' ended in June 2005. Rooibos Limited, the Western Cape Government, the Department of Trade and Industry and the international trademark holder reached a final agreement that worldwide registration of the name would be cancelled.

The plant is believed to have been introduced to botanists for the first time by the Khoi people in 1772.

In terms of the settlement, worldwide registration of the word 'rooibos' will be cancelled and the name will be regarded as generic – without a brand name.

eastern and northern Free State, North West, the KwaZulu-Natal Midlands, the Eastern and Western Cape, the Gauteng metropolitan area and the southern parts of Mpumalanga.

The ARC participates fully in the Multiple Across-Country Evaluation for all four major dairy breeds in South Africa, namely Holstein, Jersey, Guernsey and Ayrshire. A new rye grass cultivar developed by the ARC Range and Forage Institute can improve the milk production of a Jersey herd by 0,9 litres (l) per cow per day, and the production of a Holstein herd by 1,5 l per cow per day.

Milk SA co-ordinates industry matters, including the information and research functions, and is financed by means of voluntary contributions. Market forces determine prices. The dairy industry is an important employer as some 4 300 milk producers employ about 60 000 farm workers and indirectly provide jobs to some 40 000 people. Milk production for 2004 was estimated at 2 000 ML.

Stock-farming

Cattle ranches are found mainly in the Eastern Cape, parts of the Free State and KwaZulu-Natal, Limpopo and the Northern Cape. The indigenous Afrikaner and Nguni, and the locally developed Bonsmara and Drakensberger, are popular beef breeds. British, European and American breeds, such as Charolais, Hereford, Angus, Simmentaler, Sussex, Brahman and Santa Gertrudis are maintained as pure breeds or used in cross-breeding.

The Taurus Livestock Improvement Co-operative (in Irene, Gauteng) is one of the companies providing the country's beef farmers with an annual average of some 110 000 units of semen, and the dairy industry with 580 000 units of semen, for use in artificial insemination.

Livestock numbers, 2003 – 2004 (million)		
	2003	2004
Cattle	13,84	13,82
Sheep	25,84	25,51
Pigs	1,65	1,67
Goats	6,42	6,44
Source: Agricultural Statistics, Department of Agriculture		

Sheep-farming is concentrated mainly in the arid and extensive grazing areas of the country. As a result, most of the 25,5 million sheep in South Africa are found in the Eastern Cape (30%), followed by the Northern Cape (26%), Free State (20%), Western Cape (10%) and Mpumalanga (7%). Most sheep (18 million) are woolled or dual-purpose sheep.

The sheep breed with the highest wool production per head in South Africa is the pure-bred Merino, followed by other dual-purpose Merino strains, of which the Dohne Merino, the South African Mutton Merino, the Afrino and the Letelle are the most popular. Dual-purpose breeds are bred with the specific aim of maximising wool and mutton income, because these breeds have a better body conformation than the Merino, but produce slightly less wool per kilogram of body weight.

Average Merino fleece weights vary from 4 kg to 5 kg per year in the semi-arid regions, to up to 8 kg per year from sheep grazing on cultivated pastures. The total wool production for the 2003/04 season was 46,4 million kg per year and was sold for R1 004 million. Mutton sheep are mostly found in the semi-desert areas of the Northern and Western Cape.

The most popular mutton breed is the locally developed Dorper, which is a hardy and highly reproductive breed. Limited numbers of indigenous fat-tailed sheep and Karakul sheep are still found. The Merino and Dorper account for most of the 5,5 million sheep slaughtered annually in South Africa.

A large proportion of the 6,4 million goats in South Africa occur in communal grazing areas. The Eastern Cape has the most goats (40%), followed by Limpopo (16%).

Karakul sheep are farmed in the more arid areas. Only 5 876 Karakul pelts were produced during 2004. The gross value of pelts is estimated at R2,4 million.

The indigenous meat-producing Boer goat accounts for about 40% of all goats in South Africa. Almost all of South Africa's Angora goat (mohair) farmers are located in the Eastern Cape, where they farm with about one million head of Angora goats.

The South African mohair clip of four million kg accounts for 60% of the world's mohair production.

About 63% of all goats in South Africa are the so-called indigenous goats. The gross income from animal products increased by 3,9%, from R29 915 million in 2003 to R31 070 million in 2004. Slaughtered cattle and calves earned producers R6 992 million in 2004, compared with R5 808 million in 2003 – an increase of 20,4%. The average price of beef increased by 10,8% during 2004.

Poultry and pig-farming

The poultry and pig industries are more intensive than the sheep and cattle industries and are located on farms near metropolitan areas such as Gauteng, Durban, Pietermaritzburg, Cape Town and Port Elizabeth. The predominant pig breeds are the South African Landrace, the Large White, the Duroc and the Pietrain.

South Africa's annual poultry meat production is estimated at 895 000 t. Broiler production contributes about 80% to total poultry-meat production, with the rest made up of mature chicken slaughter (culls), small-scale and backyard poultry production, ducks, geese, turkeys and other specialised white-meat products.

Income from poultry and egg production amounted to R13 389 million in 2004. Commercial producers slaughtered an estimated 558 million broilers during 2004.

South Africa accounts for 68% of world sales of ostrich products, namely leather, meat and feathers. The income from ostrich products is derived as follows: leather (50% – 70%), meat (20% – 30%) and feathers (20% – 30%).

The gross value for ostrich products during 2004 was estimated at R299,6 million.

In 2003/04, some 292 000 ostriches were slaughtered compared with 307 000 in 2002/03.

Game-farming, aquaculture and bee-keeping

South Africa has more game and a wider variety of game species than most countries. Game-farming has grown over the years, and today it is a viable industry with great economic potential. The main game areas are in Limpopo, North West, Mpumalanga, the Free State, the Eastern Cape, the Karoo, the Kalahari in the Northern Cape, and the thorn scrub of KwaZulu-Natal.

Despite periodic droughts in the past, game numbers have consistently increased.

The aquaculture industry in South Africa continues to make meaningful progress in cultivation technology, marketing strategy, marketing practice and scientific innovation. Mussels, trout, tilapia, catfish, oysters and waterblommetjies (Cape pondweed) are the major aquaculture species. Mussel-farming occurs mainly at Saldanha Bay.

The South African honey industry, which is still relatively small, is worth some R56 million annually.

Veterinary services

State Veterinary Services constantly guards against the introduction of animal diseases from outside South Africa. Existing animal diseases, which may be detrimental to South Africa's economy and to human and animal health, are also controlled and combated. Stock in the high-risk areas is inspected at short intervals.

The Directorate: Animal Health of the national Department of Agriculture sets norms and standards for the delivery of veterinary services in South Africa.

Legislation provides the necessary powers to control diseases such as foot-and-mouth disease (FMD), swine fever, rabies and anthrax. South Africa,

In June 2005, reigning world champion sheep-shearer Elliot Ntsombo retained his World Blade Shearing title at the World Shearers Championship held in Toowoomba, Australia.

The championship has showcased the best sheep-shearers in the world for more than two decades. South African shearers have dominated the event since 1996.

Bongani Joel of Alwynskop in Lesotho took second place, and Zokezele Doba and Zweliwile Hans, both from Sterkspruit in the Eastern Cape, took third and fifth place respectively.

excluding the Kruger National Park and surrounding game reserves, is recognised as an FMD-free zone by the *Office International des Épizooties* (OIE), the world animal health organisation.

Animal-disease control is an important factor in ensuring the productivity of the livestock sector and promoting international trade in agricultural products.

Surveillance systems are in place to ensure that all agricultural products entering and leaving the country are disease-free and thus safe for human consumption. All ports are thoroughly monitored, making sure that imported and exported goods are disease-free.

Particular emphasis is placed on the control of borders with neighbouring countries to prevent the introduction of FMD.

National and provincial governments spent more than R38 million in 2004/05 to successfully contain the outbreak of Avian flu in the Eastern Cape and FMD in Limpopo.

Animal health and disease

The Department of Agriculture delivers a number of critical regulatory and control services aimed at ensuring that the country's animals are disease-free.

In 2004, the department introduced *sedupe* – sniffer dogs – to detect illegal food items in airport luggage. By April 2005, the dogs had detected 307 illegal food consignments in the baggage carousel areas.

In January 2005, government allocated R100 million for drought relief in eight provinces to assist farmers in purchasing fodder, and for transportation to save livestock that were severely affected by drought. The money was also expected to be used for boreholes, the purchasing of fodder and transportation thereof.

Eastern Cape was allocated R8 million; Free State R17 million; KwaZulu-Natal R18 million; Limpopo R2 million; Mpumalanga R2 million; North West R18 million; Western Cape R9 million and Northern Cape R26 million.

Following the signing of the Ministerial Treaty between South Africa, Zimbabwe and Mozambique, continuous state veterinary input through the Joint Management Board ensures that no undue animal-disease risks emanate from the Great Limpopo Transfrontier Park.

Onderstepoort Biological Products (OBP)

The OBP is a state-owned public company. It has the capacity and technology to produce veterinary vaccines and related biological products for local and international markets.

The OBP is the sole or main producer of at least 15 vaccines for African animal diseases, and eight vaccines for world tropical diseases. The OBP provides vaccines to fight major outbreaks of diseases such as CBPP (lung-sickness in cattle), lumpy-skin disease, Rift Valley fever, horse sickness and anthrax.

The OBP has also joined the Pan-African Vaccine Network to supply rinderpest and lung-sickness vaccines for Africa, and is involved in projects of the OIE, the World Health Organisation (WHO) and the EU to supply vaccines to African countries.

In the cutting-edge area of biotechnology, the research and development work by the OBP has led to the successful creation of new and innovative vaccines, such as the Doublesure vaccine, which is a combination treatment of the anthrax and blackwater diseases.

A key achievement has been the successful transformation of the organisation, with 50% of executive management being from previously disadvantaged groups, and 40% being women. Some 75% of the scientists are from previously disadvantaged groups, and 40% are women. The company is entirely self-financing and derives its revenue from the sale of vaccines and related biological products. Since its inception in 2000, the company has consistently shown a positive growth in sales. The contribution of export sales has increased from 25% to 50% of total sales, while the growth in profit has increased three-fold.

Pest control

Most countries have established maximum residue limits (MRLs) for pesticides used in the control of agricultural pests and diseases, not only to safeguard consumer health, but also to minimise the presence of residue in the environment.

As a condition of market access, products exported must comply with these residue standards. To ensure compliance with legislation, monitoring samples are drawn for analysis during quality inspections.

Exporters and producers are obliged to:
- comply with the requirements of the correct, approved use and application of pesticide remedies
- keep records of the chemical remedies used in spray programmes and as a post-harvest treatment, and provide this information on request to the responsible authorities
- verify the MRLs with their importer or agent in the relevant country
- keep up with the registration and re-registration processes of pesticides within South Africa as well as in importing countries
- inform the Directorate: Plant Health and South African Agricultural Food and Quarantine Inspection Services (SAAFQIS) of any rejections by importing country authorities due to residues.

Migratory pest control

In terms of the Agricultural Pests Act, 1983 (Act 36 of 1983), the Department of Agriculture is continuously involved in the control of migratory pests such as the quelea, locust and blackfly.

Quelea is controlled by aerial chemical spraying and explosives.

Locust outbreaks are controlled by knapsack sprayers, sprayers mounted on bakkies and by aerial chemical sprayers if the outbreak is very high.

Blackfly is controlled by aerial and boat chemical spraying, depending on the water level of the river.

Research conducted by the ARC contributes towards maximising South Africa's ability to provide timely and reliable forecasts of brown locust outbreaks, both for its own food-security needs and those of neighbouring countries in the brown locust invasion area.

The South African Pest Control Association (SAPCA) is the official representative of the pest-, termite- and woodborer-control industries. All SAPCA-qualified inspectors have to register with the Department of Agriculture.

South Africa liaises with other countries and international organisations to ensure technology transfer on pest control.

In 2004, South Africa provided advice, logistical support and material resources against the outbreak of locusts in the Sahel region countries of Morocco, The Gambia, Niger, Senegal, Cape Verde, Chad, Burkina Faso and Tunisia.

Guided by the New Partnership for Africa's Development's (NEPAD) African Agricultural Development Programme (AADP), the Department of Agriculture, under the leadership of the Department of Foreign Affairs, provided spraying aircraft, pilots and chemicals to a total value of R10 million to cover 12 000 ha in Mali alone.

The four pillars of the AADP are land and water infrastructure, market access, food security, and research and development.

Marketing

South Africa's agricultural marketing has undergone transformation since 1994 through the introduction of the Marketing of Agricultural Products Act, 1996 (Act 47 of 1996).

This Act has changed agricultural marketing policy and practice dramatically to ensure that it occurs in a free environment. The deregulation process was aimed at ensuring that farmers and agribusinesses position themselves as players in the globally competitive environment.

The deregulation process entailed the closing of agricultural marketing boards, phasing out import- and export-control measures, eliminating subsidies, and introducing tariffs to protect the domestic agricultural industry value chains against unfair international competition.

Since deregulation, the sector has begun to adjust to the high levels of competitiveness across most value chains. Deregulation has further created many opportunities and has resulted in an increase in the number of new entrepreneurs participating in different nodes of agricultural marketing value chains. These include producers, processors, traders and providers of other supplementary services to ensure efficiency in the operation of the overall marketing value chains.

The phasing out of controls and the closure of marketing boards resulted in a shortage of essential services that were formerly provided by co-operatives and marketing boards, ranging from storage, grading, deliveries, and value adding, to information dissemination, research, etc.

Subsequent to the setting up of the National Marketing Council (NAMC) in 1997, a need arose for the establishment of the Directorate: Marketing in the Department of Agriculture. The directorate was established in 2002 to work closely with the NAMC on agricultural marketing matters. The purpose of the directorate is to develop, implement and promote policies, programmes and measures aimed at supporting equitable access to competitive and profitable agricultural markets on a sustainable basis. This broad mandate is achieved through the following:

- administrating trade and market access measures in the form of trade (import and exports)
- facilitating the growth of fair, open, efficient and competitive domestic markets
- developing policies and strategies and implementing programmes and measures to facilitate equitable access to mainstream the domestic market
- liaising with other government departments and

Ncera Farms (Pty) Ltd is a public company with the Department of Agriculture as the sole shareholder.
It is situated in the Eastern Cape on about 3 102 hectares of state-owned land and is dedicated to assisting small and emerging farmers through providing various services to the surrounding rural communities in the form of advice, extension services and training.

other relevant parties to enhance the efficiency of the agricultural marketing value chains.

The directorate comprises three subdirectorates, namely Marketing Administration, Commodity Marketing, and Marketing Development and Support.

The Subdirectorate: Marketing Administration administers the issuing of import and export permits to enhance trade and market access. At the same time, it facilitates the participation of new entrants in the trading environment.

The Subdirectorate: Commodity Marketing profiles key agricultural commodity marketing value chains and undertakes further analysis of market structures to determine market access qualifiers. It further investigates the behaviour of commodity and non-commodity markets to recommend policy options, thus ensuring equitable access to mainstream markets by all.

The Subdirectorate: Market Development and Support implements programmes and measures to enhance the development of a vibrant domestic market. The following initiatives are being undertaken:

- establishing a real-time agricultural marketing information system
- facilitating agricultural marketing capacity-building (training) for resource-poor farmers and extension officers
- facilitating the development of norms and standards for the establishment of agricultural marketing infrastructure.

National Agricultural Marketing Council

The NAMC was established in terms of the Marketing of Agricultural Products Act, 1996, as amended by Act 59 of 1997 and Act 34 of 2001.

The mandate of the NAMC is, when requested by the Minister of Agriculture or of its own accord, to investigate the establishment, continuation, amendment or revocation of statutory measures and other regulatory measures affecting the marketing of agricultural products.

The NAMC continues to do important work, monitoring the agricultural marketing environment to promote the existence of a more diverse and competitive sector. Attendance at agricultural shows, farmers' days, conferences and workshops offers the NAMC the opportunity to disseminate information to farmers.

The NAMC provides marketing-assistance programmes for new entrants in the various commodity sectors in collaboration with the private sector and government as part of transformation and empowerment imperatives.

Funding to the NAMC in 2005/06 amounted to R13,1 million.

Land administration

The Department of Agriculture, through the Directorate: Farmer Settlement and Development, controls and administers 686 916 ha of state agricultural land.

State agricultural land is divided as follows:
- some 105 052 ha of land expropriated by the South African Development Trust
- some 91 388 ha of commercial land purchased from insolvent estates and properties transferred by the Department of Public Works in terms of Section 7 of the Disposal Act, 1961 (Act 48 of 1961).

The primary goal of the directorate is the internal administration of state agricultural land, with the aim of farmer settlement and ownership reform.

Food security

Cabinet approved the Integrated Food Security and Nutrition Programme in July 2002 as one of the key programmes of the Social Cluster. The programme aims to achieve physical, social and economic access to safe and nutritious food for all South Africans.

Its goal is to eradicate hunger, malnutrition and food insecurity by 2015.

Between the start of the National Food Emergency Scheme in 2004 and June 2005, 245 000 households benefited. Agricultural starter packs to the value of R31 million were delivered to

18 575 households in all provinces as a measure of encouraging the development of sustainable food gardens.

By June 2005, business plans and a financial model for financing the Farmer Support Programme had been finalised and the Department of Agriculture was in the process of finalising a memorandum of agreement with key partner institutions in preparation for the implementation of the programme.

Agricultural state and state-supported community schemes have seen a significant increase in the number of viable projects.

The Department of Agriculture also joined forces with its neighbouring SADC countries and adopted an action plan for food security. This includes the establishment of domestic support measures for vulnerable small-holder farmers, to ensure access to key agricultural input, and to encourage research and the development of affordable farming equipment.

The directorates: plant health and SAAFQIS drafted the Draft Food Security Bill to ensure not only food safety, but also the quality of agricultural products, including fresh fruit and vegetables, exported within the current control system. By implementing the prevention-is-better-than-cure rule, control is transferred from end-product testing to the design and manufacture of such products.

In any international exchange of plants and plant products, there is a risk of pests and diseases being introduced into the territory of the importing country. In view of this, the South African Government is a signatory member of various multinational agreements.

The most important, in terms of safeguarding the country's agricultural resources and natural environment, are the International Plant Protection Convention (IPPC) and the World Trade Organisation (WTO) Agreement on the Application of Sanitary and Phytosanitary Measures (WTO-SPS).

The Human Rights Commission and United Nations (UN) Council for Human Rights officials have hailed the Draft Bill as the first of its kind to comprehensively address all pertinent food-related issues. The document will be used as a basis for discussions in Africa and at the UN. Normal procedures on new legislation and policy guidelines will follow when discussions are finalised.

Regional issues

South Africa participates in the Regional Advisory Committee (RAC) of the Regional Food Security Training Programme (RFSTP).

The RFSTP has been developed over a five-year period as endorsed by the RAC. The activities of the RFSTP focus on three main areas: strengthening the supply of food-security training services, strengthening the effective demand for training and development, and sustaining regional markets for food-security-related training services.

The SADC has instituted the Subcommittee for Plant Protection, tasked with harmonising phytosanitary requirements in southern Africa. South Africa is also a member of the Inter-African Phytosanitary Council, which was established in 1954. Regional plant-protection organisations such as these are able to provide valuable co-ordination for the activities and objectives of the IPPC at local level.

International issues

As a signatory to the Rome Declaration, South Africa has committed itself to the implementation of the World Food Summit Plan of Action. For this purpose, South Africa reports annually to the World Committee for Food Security. South Africa is also collaborating with the Food and Agricultural Organisation (FAO) on the implementation of the Special Programme for Food Security, within the context of the Integrated Sustainable Rural Development Programme (ISRDP).

South Africa is an active participant in other international standard-setting bodies vital to its global market share, such as the IPPC and Codex Alimentarius.

Risk management

Government is moving forward with the development of an agricultural risk-management programme that includes agricultural risk insurance as one of the major tools for managing agricultural production risk.

The Directorate: Agricultural Risk Management delivers early warning monthly climate advisories to farmers to enable them to anticipate possible natural disasters.

The Department of Agriculture is working on the Disaster Management Plan that aims to minimise the impact of natural disasters in South Africa. The document emanated from the mandate of the Disaster Management Act, 2002 (Act 57 of 2002), which prescribes the formulation of such plans. The plan will be aligned to the disaster-management framework guidelines provided by the Department of Provincial and Local Government.

Early warning information can be accessed through the *www.agis.agric.za* website.

Drought management

The Drought Management Plan has been discussed internally and consultations with provincial departments and organised agriculture completed. The core principles emphasise proactive measures such as mitigation, preparedness, training and education as well as research. The document will be gazetted and workshops conducted for public input and comments.

Some R100 million was allocated in 2004/05 for drought-relief programmes in the nine provincial departments of agriculture. Some R15 million was budgeted for drilling and the maintenance of boreholes for livestock, while R85 million was allocated for the purchase and transportation of fodder. An additional allocation of R120 million will be used to augment the R100 million.

Long-term interventions by the department include improved research, a fully functional early warning system and agricultural sector strategies to address disaster-management issues.

Credit and assistance

The agricultural sector has, to date, been a net borrower, in that it borrows more than it saves. In fact, the total debt of South African farmers has increased by about 10% a year since 1995 – reaching R33 286 million by the end of 2004, compared with R9 495 million at the end of 1984.

The six major sources of credit for farmers are banks (50%), agricultural co-operatives and agribusinesses (12%), the Land Bank (21%), private creditors (8%), other creditors and financial institutions (9%), and the State (1%).

Business and Entrepreneurial Development (BED)

The Directorate: BED of the Department of Agriculture is responsible for promoting and providing strategic support in the development of viable and empowered businesses to stimulate growth and promote unity through partnerships and niches.

The ultimate aims are to:
- unlock the economic potential of idle to underutilised resources of emergent groups through empowerment efforts
- facilitate restructuring and the expansion of existing farming/agribusinesses to enhance their competitiveness and contribution to the sector and the economy at large.

The directorate has three units. The Business Development Unit works closely with industries/commodity groups to develop inclusive, enhanced and harmonised commodity strategies and joint action plans.

Through the directorate, the department has contributed towards the development of the National Emergent Red Meat Producers' Organisation's database, the Fruit Industry Plan and the implementation of the Cotton Industries Strategy.

The focus has been on working with NAFU and emerging farmer leaders to mobilise increased participation of emerging farmers into commodity groups. Together with the Co-operative Development Initiative (CDI), the directorate has initiated a programme of incorporating mentorship and linking emerging farmers/agribusinesses with established businesses in nodal areas.

The Entrepreneurial Development Unit encourages and supports entrepreneurs in the agricultural sector.

A process adapting the Small, Medium and Micro Enterprise Excellence Model for agriculture has been completed. Eleven potential nodal projects have been identified jointly with the CDI. These projects were selected based on their potential for being linked with local established businesses. The excellence models aim to improve management capability for enhanced competitiveness.

The Black Economic Empowerment (BEE) Policy Unit is concerned with harnessing and unlocking idle and underutilised economic potential for growth and wealth creation in the agricultural sector.

The unit has been working closely with organised agriculture and related business, facilitating the development of policy guidelines for empowerment in the sector. In July 2004, the Minister of Agriculture and Land Affairs, Ms Thoko Didiza, launched the AgriBEE Framework for public comment.

The framework is the department's response to improving equitable access to and participation in agricultural opportunities, deracialising land and enterprise ownership, and unlocking the full entrepreneurial potential in the sector. The framework was developed in collaboration with agriculture stakeholders, and the process was expected to culminate in an AgriBEE charter before the end of 2005.

LandCare Programme

The LandCare Programme is a community-based and government-supported approach to the sustainable management and use of agricultural natural resources.

The vision of the LandCare Programme is for communities and individuals to adopt an ecologically sustainable approach to the management of South Africa's environment and natural resources, while improving their quality of life. It implies that cultivation, livestock grazing and the harvesting of natural resources should be managed in such a manner that no further degradation (such as soil erosion, nutrient loss, loss of components of the vegetation, and increased run-off) occurs.

The overall goal of the LandCare Programme is to optimise productivity and sustainability of natural resources, resulting in greater productivity, food security, job creation and better quality of life for all.

The LandCare Programme has been expanded into additional rural nodes. The department's new policy on the expanded LandCare Programme will enable provincial departments of agriculture and other stakeholders to facilitate the sound management of agricultural resources through awareness campaigns and capacity-building.

LandCare themes are grouped into two areas, namely, focused investment (WaterCare, VeldCare, SoilCare, Eco-Agriculture, Agri-Tourism and JuniorCare) and small community grants.

Projects are underway countrywide.

The LandCare Implementation Framework serves as a guideline to empower resource-poor communities to develop LandCare groups and activities through awareness, training and education. This includes communication strategies directed towards rural community groups and young people. The framework formulates policy and legislation to develop incentives for natural-resource management.

It also serves as a tool to establish and implement a monitoring system to evaluate progress, assess contemporary issues and provide a basis for planning and research.

The department also aims to promote its National Policy on Agricultural Land and Resource Management in all spheres of government and among other stakeholders.

In 2005/06, government set aside about R64 million for the LandCare Programme. Government envisages that 6 000 ha will be cultivated over the next year, benefiting about 3 000 households. The implementation of this project will be jointly conducted by the provincial departments of agriculture, district and local municipalities, as well as the Department of Provincial and Local Government.

In 2004/05, as a direct response to persistent drought conditions, the Department of Agriculture facilitated the drilling and rehabilitation of 427 boreholes in rural areas and built 267 structures to combat the effects of soil erosion. The departments of agriculture and of water affairs and forestry drafted a drilling policy, which was being further developed to include water quality, particularly where underground water is used for human consumption and livestock.

The ARC's water-harvesting research team has implemented a water-harvesting project in the Free State. It is also promoting the in-field rainwater-harvesting technique at two new projects in the Eastern Cape, focusing on five villages in the vicinity of Alice.

By May 2005, negotiations were underway for further support to ensure that LandCare training would be accredited and that every province would develop its long-term LandCare strategic plan.

Focused investment

The WaterCare theme targets Limpopo in particular, because of water shortages and the importance of water for irrigation. This theme establishes a framework for managing land and preventing the silt-up of dams for irrigation. WaterCare works in partnership with the community to develop action plans for managing and restoring irrigation schemes. The rehabilitation of irrigation schemes increases water supply and household food security. WaterCare promotes the development of techniques for water-resource management and encourages opportunities for training in this field.

Under the WaterCare project, 28 schemes had been revived and 60 schemes were in progress by April 2005. There are 138 smallholder schemes, predominantly in Limpopo. A business plan for the revitalisation of smallholder irrigation schemes has been developed. It aims to revive the remaining schemes over a six-year period from 2003 to 2009.

VeldCare promotes best-grazing systems and erosion-prevention practices to improve production. It develops and maintains agricultural activities in accordance with the principles of ecologically sustainable development. Economic and social development opportunities are realised by improving grazing areas and maintaining viable grazing areas throughout rural communities.

SoilCare encourages rural farmers in KwaZulu-Natal, the Eastern Cape and Mpumalanga to build innovative structures to combat soil erosion. This includes reducing the depletion of soil fertility and acidity. Through SoilCare, sustainable agricultural production systems such as diversification, management of input and conservation tillage are introduced.

The Eco-Agriculture Extended LandCare Programme was introduced in 2004/05 to complement the Expanded Public Works Programme. The Department of Agriculture is contributing R42,9 million to job creation and training.

The objectives of JuniorCare are to empower previously disadvantaged youth by providing training in facilitation and leadership skills.

This includes the promotion of food security at home and at schools, awareness of sustainable agriculture, and stimulating the formation of youth clubs and projects that aim to promote other components of LandCare. JuniorCare addresses the needs of young people in an integrated way and involves interdisciplinary approaches.

Land and Agricultural Development Bank of South Africa (Land Bank)

The Land Bank operates as a development-finance institution within the agricultural and agribusiness sectors, and is regulated by the Land and Agricultural Development Bank Act, 2002 (Act 15 of 2002). It provides a range of finance options to a broad spectrum of clients in the agricultural sector, including rural entrepreneurs, women and youth, through its network of 27 branches and 37 satellite offices, supplemented by mobile branches, which are primarily located in rural areas.

The bank's mission is to:
- develop and provide appropriate products for commercial and development clients
- leverage private-sector investment in the agricultural sector
- develop techniques for financing high-risk agriculture and new business areas
- support programmes of the Ministry of Agriculture and Land Affairs by aligning the bank's products with these programmes
- contribute to rural development by linking up with government structures and activities.

These programmes and structures include Land Redistribution for Agricultural Development (LRAD), the Agricultural Strategic Plan and the ISRDP.

The Land Bank offers various strategies to support historically disadvantaged individuals (HDIs). These include easy access to loans, equity finance, loans for land-reform beneficiaries, a special loan for HDIs buying farms for the first time (Special Mortgage Bond), incentives (a lower interest rate for farmers who show commitment), and micro-loans for people starting an enterprise or a small farming business. The 'We Come to You' programme makes banking more accessible through its branches nationally, its rural satellite offices and partner organisations such as development, finance and government institutions.

Micro-Agricultural Financial Institutions Scheme of South Africa (MAFISA)

MAFISA, the first State-owned scheme to provide micro and retail agricultural financial services on a large, accessible, cost-effective and sustainable basis in rural areas, was approved in principle by Cabinet in January 2005, with an initial budget of R1 billion.

This followed the announcement by President Thabo Mbeki in his State of the Nation Address on 21 May 2004, that government would re-establish the agricultural credit scheme in the Department of Agriculture. On 30 May 2005, the Minister of Agriculture and Land Affairs launched MAFISA at the Ga-Mabintane Sports Grounds near Nebo in Limpopo.

MAFISA will see the poor and many of the emerging farmers who were previously turned down by financial institutions obtaining loans of up to R100 000 at an affordable rate.

The 10 million potential beneficiaries include farm and non-farm entrepreneurs such as farm workers, tenants, household producers, landless people, small landholders, food-garden producers, and rural and micro entrepreneurs.

MAFISA's four products and services for the rural working poor and enterprises are credit, savings, insurance and payment facilities. It provides basic short- and medium-term loans, with a number of permutations that would be available to the poor at the rural district councils of the poorest provinces in terms of the Human Development Index, as determined by Statistics South Africa.

MAFISA will work with financial institutions to implement the provisions of the Financial Services Charter relevant to the development of small and medium farming enterprises.

Agri SA

Agri SA is a federation of agricultural organisations comprising nine provincial unions, 28 national commodity organisations and the Agricultural Business Chamber (ABC).

It is a member of Business Unity South Africa, the International Federation of Agricultural Producers, the Southern African Federation of Agricultural Unions and the Cairns Group Farm Leaders.

Agri SA participates in a presidential working group dealing with policy matters specifically in terms of the Strategic Plan for Agriculture.

The mission and vision of Agri SA is to promote the economic opportunities and social well-being of commercial and commercially oriented farmers, by positively influencing agricultural policy and rendering support services.

Agri SA's policy advocacy includes work on trade negotiations, industrial policy, labour laws, training, taxation, financing, land reform, farmer development, environmental affairs, water rights, farm safety, law and order, infrastructure, technology development and transfer, statistical information and local government matters.

It publishes a bimonthly magazine, a weekly electronic newsletter and runs a regular radio programme in collaboration with the SABC.

Agricultural Business Chamber

The ABC is a sectoral body representing an important component of South Africa's business sector. ABC's members represent total assets of almost R30 billion and an annual agricultural business turnover of about R50 billion.

ABC members operate more than 2 000 service centres countrywide with more than 100 000 employees. In many rural areas, members of the ABC are the business hub of the community and make a key contribution towards maintaining rural infrastructure.

The ABC is an integral part of the Agri SA Group, and is associated with Business South Africa and international bodies such as the International Federation of Agricultural Producers, the International Chamber of Commerce and the International Agribusiness Management Association.

The chamber represents agricultural companies, agricultural co-operatives, companies which arose out of the conversion of agricultural co-operatives, and other agricultural business enterprises and organisations.

Agricultural businesses play a significant role in the economy of South Africa as handlers, processors and marketers of agricultural products, and as suppliers of production input and services.

Transvaal Agricultural Union (TAU)

TAU SA was established in 1897 as the Transvaal Agricultural Union. In 2002, the union reorganised to become a national agricultural union serving commercial farmers. It also renders unique services to its members in terms of:
- property rights
- economic issues
- safety and security.

TAU SA conducts a variety of projects to enhance the concept of successful agriculture. The various farmers' markets and the marketing of effective micro-organisms contribute to alternative options available to members and the public.

Agribusiness as an economic sector

Agribusiness can be divided into two categories: non-co-operative business ventures and co-operatives or transformed co-operatives.

Non-co-operative business ventures, also known as profit companies, are involved in the production and distribution of agricultural equipment and production requisites, and the marketing of agricultural products.

Co-operatives dominate the distribution of intermediate requisites and the handling, processing and marketing of agricultural products.

Agricultural co-operatives or agribusinesses are regarded as the farmers' own independent business organisations. There are close to 1 000 primary agricultural co-operatives and agribusinesses throughout the country. They supply their members with production input such as seed, fertiliser, fuel and repair services. They also provide credit and extension services, and handle a large percentage of their members' produce.

There are more than 15 central co-operatives in the country, which aim to supply the primary co-operatives with specific services such as the processing and marketing of agricultural products, insurance services for crops, short-term cover and farming requisites.

The structure of agribusiness has changed substantially since the deregulation of the agricultural sector into a free-market economy in 1994. Many co-operatives transformed into private companies, consolidations and mergers occurred, international groups entered South Africa, and agribusinesses listed on the JSE Limited.

Agribusinesses are involved in the production and distribution of agricultural equipment and production requisites, and in the marketing and processing of agricultural products.

The co-operative movement in South African agriculture is expected to grow. The Co-operative Bill is under consideration and it is envisaged that this enabling legislation will make co-operatives accessible to all communities through outgrower projects, contracting and share-equity schemes. Its administration was transferred to the Department of Trade and Industry.

The Co-operative Development Initiative is one of many efforts to facilitate such linkages, and support a 'growth-with-equity' development path for South African agriculture.

National African Farmers' Union

NAFU strives to promote the interests of the disadvantaged farming sector by lobbying for access to support services and empowering its members through effective communication and capacity-building programmes.

Institutional capacity-building

The Department of Agriculture has developed a databank for South Africa's agricultural human resource capacity.

In collaboration with the Economic Development Institute of the World Bank, the department has designed and developed training courses for rural restructuring and development. The Youth Entrepreneurship Programme was launched in 1999.

Comprehensive Agriculture Support Programme

On 18 August 2004, the Minister of Agriculture and Land Affairs launched the CASP in Boston, KwaZulu-Natal.

The CASP focuses on on-and-off farm infrastructure, information and knowledge management, financial assistance, technical and advisory services, training and capacity-building, and marketing and business development.

The multiphase CASP specifically targets emerging farmers, including women, in rural areas.

The Department of Agriculture committed R210 million in 2004/05 for the initial roll-out of the CASP.

MAFISA is intended to complement the CASP and provide further assistance to emerging farmers and land-reform beneficiaries.

During 2005/06, government planned to spend R250 million on CASP to reach over 50 000 beneficiaries in the rural areas, particularly in the rural development nodes serviced by the department.

Training and research

South African agriculture has a strong research component. Many of the people involved are world leaders in their respective fields. The ARC, an autonomous statutory body set up in terms of the Agricultural Research Act, 1990 (Act 86 of 1990), is the largest agricultural research organisation in Africa.

The ARC provides research support to the Department of Agriculture and the nine provincial departments of agriculture. ARC scientific expertise supports most of the Department of Agriculture's regulatory directorates, such as the Directorate: Public Veterinary Health, the Directorate: Animal Health, the Directorate: Plant Health and Quality, the Directorate: Agricultural Resource Conservation and the Directorate: Agricultural Production Input. The ARC also supports other agricultural institutions such as the Registrar of Livestock Improvement and Identification, the Registrar of Brands, the South African Veterinary Council and the Perishable Products Export Control Board.

South Africa has a number of specialised agricultural high schools and regular schools offering a comprehensive range of agricultural subjects. Prospective farmers are trained at 11 agricultural colleges: Cape Institute for Agricultural Training (Western Cape), Cedara and Owen Sithole (KwaZulu-Natal), Grootfontein Agricultural College at the Grootfontein Agricultural Development Institute (run by the Department of Agriculture), Glen (Free State), Potchefstroom (North West), Lowveld (Mpumalanga), Fort Cox and Tsolo (Eastern Cape), and Tompi Seleka and Madzi-vhandila (Limpopo). Diploma courses are also offered at various universities of technology. Degree courses are offered by the faculties of agriculture at various universities.

Veterinary surgeons are trained at the University of Pretoria's Faculty of Veterinary Sciences at Onderstepoort. The former Faculty of Veterinary

Government keeps track of price trends and initiates further detailed investigation when necessary.

Overall, the increase in food prices slowed down quite dramatically, with many products decreasing in price for the period January to December 2004. The good performers were flour (-9,0%), cauliflower (-11,6%), cabbage (-18,7%), onions (-17,8%), tomatoes (-9,8%), canned pilchards (-15,6%), oranges (-9,4%), picnic ham (-9,7%) and cooking oil (-29,4%).

Prices increased for hubbard squash (+43,1%), beef products, which increased on average by 19,5%, lamb chops (+15,9%), pork chops (+12,7%), boerewors (+10,6%) and bread (+9,2%).

However, having taken 75 different products into account, food prices increased overall by 1% for the period January to December 2004.

Sciences at the Medical University of South Africa (now University of Limpopo) has amalgamated with the University of Pretoria. State veterinarians are assisted countrywide by qualified animal health technicians.

Qualified meat inspectors in the provincial Directorate: Veterinary Services assist state veterinarians with meat inspections at abattoirs.

International relations

The Department of Agriculture's Directorate: International Relations facilitates and co-ordinates international activities on both multilateral and bilateral bases.

The department is a member of the FAO; the Consultative Group on International Agricultural Research; the Food, Agriculture and Natural Resources Sector of the SADC; the International Seed-Testing Association; the Organisation for Economic Co-operation and Development's Seed Schemes; and the Union for the Protection of New Varieties of Plants.

Contributing to the political, social and economic development of Africa is a key international priority for the department. Agriculture continues to be the mainstay of African economies and is an important driver for socio-economic growth.

South Africa's agricultural engagement in Africa is guided by a clear sense of the enormous potential for agricultural trade, training, research and technical co-operation opportunities that exist within the rest of Africa. South Africa has much to benefit through co-operation with Africa.

The Directorate: International Relations co-ordinates, facilitates and supports the promotion of South Africa's agricultural interests internationally through bilateral and multilateral relations.

The directorate developed the International Agricultural Strategy, which sets priorities for international engagement in the medium term. The strategy is guided by South Africa's foreign policy and economic development objectives. The priorities are:

- consolidation of the African agenda
- active participation in the African Union (AU)

- active participation in and efficient implementation of the programme of the SADC food, agriculture and natural resources and trade, finance and investment directorates
- sustainable development and poverty alleviation through NEPAD
- implementation of the Southern African Customs Union (SACU).

The ARC participates in various co-operative research agreements, international organisations and networks.

The ARC also supports various government departments in deliberations regarding international agreements and disputes, for example the Convention on Biodiversity, the Kyoto Protocol on Global Change, the Montreal Protocol, GMO policy and indigenous knowledge systems issues.

International trade relations

The Department of Agriculture's Directorate: International Trade analyses international trade and related policies, advises on multilateral and bilateral agricultural trade policy, and promotes trade initiatives. The directorate is responsible for dealing with matters concerning agricultural trade relations with other countries and organisations, such as the SACU, the SADC, the WTO and the International Grains Convention.

South Africa maintains bilateral trade agreements with countries in Africa, and is involved in negotiations as part of SACU with the USA, South American Common Market (MERCOSUR), and the European Free Trade Area. It is also involved in the WTO negotiations individually, and as a member of the G20 of the Cairns Group and the Africa Group.

Work relating to agricultural relations in the field of trade is done by the directorate, in co-operation with the departments of trade and industry and of foreign affairs.

The Directorate: International Trade is responsible for implementing South Africa's commitments in terms of the WTO Marrakech Agreement. These commitments include the reduction of tariffs, export subsidies, and domestic support given to agriculture.

In addition, the department is creating market-access opportunities by implementing the minimum market-access commitments contained in the agreement.

South Africa's objectives in the agricultural negotiations, as part of the Doha Development Agenda, are to achieve a substantial reduction in domestic support and the elimination of export subsidies, mainly from developed countries. Other objectives are to achieve a substantial improvement of market access for South African agricultural exports; and to ensure that South Africa's commitment, in terms of domestic support, fully covers the development needs of the country.

South Africa is developing trade relations with other countries. This includes the implementation of the agricultural aspects of the SACU Agreement that came into effect in July 2004; the SADC Protocol on Trade; and the SA-EU Trade, Development and Co-operation Agreement (TDCA).

The SA-EU TDCA was implemented on 1 January 2000. The department has introduced a system whereby market opportunities under the agreement can be fully utilised. This includes providing information to potential exporters, as well as the administration of export quotas granted to South Africa under the agreement. Since 1 January 2000, the department has been issuing export permits for various products such as wine, canned fruit, fruit juice, cut flowers, proteas, cheese and frozen strawberries to be exported to the EU at reduced levels of duty.

The South African Government signed the Fixed Preferences Agreement with MERCOSUR (a treaty establishing a common market between Argentina, Brazil, Paraguay and Uruguay) in December 2004.

With the enlargement of the EU, the agreement was extended to include the new members. It provides for reciprocal preferential access for the agreed list of products (including agriculture).

The directorate participates in exploring possible new trade relations in collaboration with the Department of Trade and Industry.

The department is investigating and evaluating export opportunities for agricultural products on world markets. A subdirectorate was formed to deal specifically with issues related to the strategic repositioning of the agricultural export sector. Strategic market research and the formulation of new industry strategies for exports are priorities. Export-led development projects are also being considered as a means to alleviate poverty.

The Directorate: International Trade Relations facilitates the training of role-players in the use of trade tools.

International agreements and conventions

South Africa is a signatory to a number of international agreements and conventions requiring that the matter of sustainable resource-use and management be addressed in a responsible way.

Agenda 21 is an action plan and blueprint for sustainable development, and was one of five documents adopted by more than 178 governments at the UN Conference on Environment and Development (UNCED) in Rio de Janeiro in 1992. Specific to sustainable resource-use is Chapter 14, which addresses the promotion of agriculture and rural development.

International conventions that apply to aspects of sustainable resource-use include the Convention on Biological Diversity, the UN Framework Convention on Climate Change, and the Convention to Combat Desertification (CCD). The CCD requires that South Africa draws up a national action programme, which will be integrated into a regional programme for the SADC region. All these activities are receiving attention under the leadership of the Department of Environmental Affairs and Tourism, involving all stakeholders, including the national and provincial departments of agriculture.

Import and export control

The aim of the Import Export Policy Unit of the Department of Agriculture's Directorate: Animal Health is to formulate and support policies to reduce sanitary (health) risks in the import and export of animals and animal products.

Import requirements vary according to the product and the animal-health situation in individual countries.

South Africa is an active member of the OIE. Disease reports are received from the OIE and through direct contact with the veterinary administrations in exporting countries.

Trade in animals and animal products is based on a series of requirements considered appropriate by the importing country to prevent the entry of diseases.

The department is one of the key regulatory State departments with the authority to enforce laws enacted by Parliament to protect the South African consumer, the environment and other national interests. The department's regulatory activities, with regard to plants and plant products, are primarily enforced by the directorates: plant health, SAAFQIS and genetic resources. In addition, South Africa's Customs Service participates in this effort by detaining imported goods when requirements are not met.

The directorates: plant health and SAAFQIS promote and regulate the availability of healthy and productive plant material and the quality of agricultural products in South Africa. Import control is vital to prevent the introduction of potentially harmful foreign pests. Prospective importers of plants and plant products have to apply for an import permit for those controlled goods not published in the *Government Gazette R1013* of 1989.

A pest-risk analysis, based on scientific data, is conducted, and specific phytosanitary requirements are set out according to the phytosanitary risk(s) involved. These conditions are then stipulated in the permit issued to the importer. Importers are obliged to present the material to the executive officer of the Act or the official representative for inspection.

Should any potentially harmful pest be introduced into and become established in South Africa, the Directorate: Plant Health and Quality will conduct a survey to determine the distribution of the organism, draft an eradication programme, liaise with other relevant parties, and possibly co-ordinate and participate in the eradication programme.

Despite strict precautions in the past, several harmful alien organisms have become established in specific production areas in South Africa, causing substantial losses to agriculture. Control measures are published to prevent or combat the spread of these organisms to other areas in the country. Quarantine services ensure imported plant material and biological control agents are appropriately handled to guarantee that harmful alien organisms do not enter and become established in the country.

In export control, South Africa has to comply with the import conditions of the specific country or group of countries it is exporting to, by issuing phytosanitary certificates. The directorate furthermore maintains a database of the import conditions and procedures of various countries, and the occurrence of harmful organisms within South Africa. It renders advisory and identification services, carries out field inspections, and conducts laboratory tests as requested by the importing country.

All consignments of plants and plant products intended for export are inspected, evaluated and certified by the directorate.

Food safety and quality assurance

Food safety has become an international public health issue, which is considered a top priority by the WHO.

The Department of Agriculture's Directorate: Food Safety and Quality Assurance was created in 2002 to develop policy and set norms and standards for agricultural food products of plant and animal origin, as well as to regulate agricultural production input such as fertilisers, farm feeds, pesticides and stock remedies.

As a result of its diverse agroclimate, South Africa cannot remain competitive without the use of certain chemicals. To address this matter, the department, the agricultural industry and the EU have embarked on the South African Pesticide Initiative Programme (SAPIP).

The objective of SAPIP is to assist the local industry to adopt good agricultural practices, and find alternatives or do away with the affected agrochemicals. A financing agreement between the EU and South Africa was signed to faciltate the programme.

To ensure the safety of exported products, the directorate has also drafted food-safety regulations with regard to products of plant origin.

Before the registration of agricultural products, an appropriate risk and value assessment is conducted. The value assessment considers whether using the product has merit and whether the application rates will be effective.

Fertilisers, farm feeds, agricultural and stock remedies will be registered if the data requirements of efficacy, safety and quality have been adequately addressed, and the human and environmental risks associated with their proposed use are acceptable. The household remedies, swimming pool remedies and pest-control operators are also regulated in terms of the Fertilisers, Farm Feeds, Agricultural Remedies and Stock Remedies Act, 1947 (Act 36 of 1947).

The inspection service ensures compliance with regulations. It investigates complaints about a specific product registered in terms of the Act and can take administrative and/or legal action against offenders when necessary.

In terms of the Meat Safety Act, 2000 (Act 40 of 2000), no person may sell or provide meat for human or animal consumption unless the animal from which the meat is sourced has been slaughtered at a registered abattoir. The directorate is responsible for inspecting and auditing export abattoirs.

The Pathogen Reduction Programme is due for implementation in high capacity red-meat abattoirs.

It is envisaged that a national residue-monitoring programme will be introduced within the next three years to ensure that South African consumers enjoy the same level of protection as consumers in export markets.

Land Affairs

The Department of Land Affairs aims to provide an equitable and sustainable land dispensation that promotes social and economic development.

The department's key focus is to provide access to land and extend land rights, with particular emphasis on historically disadvantaged communities, within a well-planned environment.

The department is responsible for:
- deeds registration
- cadastral surveys
- surveys and mapping
- spatial planning and information (SPI)
- land reform, implementation management and co-ordination
- land-reform systems and support services.

Deeds registration

The aim of the Department of Land Affairs' Chief Directorate: Deeds Registration is to maintain a public register of land, as well as an efficient system of registration, aimed at affording security of title to land and rights to land.

During 2004/05, the chief directorate played an important role in supporting the department's land-reform initiatives. Land-registration information supplied from the Deeds Registration System database plays a vital role during the preliminary investigative stages of any land-delivery initiative, while the final step in the process, the registration of the relevant title deeds, is handled by the nine deeds registries.

These are situated in Pretoria, Cape Town, Johannesburg, Pietermaritzburg, Bloemfontein, Kimberley, King William's Town, Vryburg and Umtata. Despite an increase in their workload over the past year, deeds registries have been able to

The Communal Land Rights Act (CLaRA), 2004 (Act 11 of 2004), provides for legal security of tenure by transferring communal land, including KwaZulu-Natal Ingomnyama land, to communities, or by awarding comparable redress.
It also provides for the:
- conduct of a land-rights inquiry to determine the transition from old order rights to new order rights
- democratic administration of communal land by communities
- co-operative performance of municipal functions on communal land
- creation of land rights boards.
The CLaRA was expected to be implemented in KwaZulu-Natal in 2005/06 as a pilot and rolled out countrywide from 2006/07.

maintain a turnaround time of their vital registration function of 10 working days from lodgement.

Deeds registries are responsible for the:
- registration of real rights in land
- maintenance of a public-land register
- provision of land-registration information
- maintenance of an archive of registration records.

Deeds and documents lodged with deeds registries are examined by deeds controllers for accuracy regarding the content, as well as for compliance with common, case and statutory law, and attachments against the property.

Holders of a title deed registered in the deeds registries are therefore assured of the security of their title to the property.

Deeds offices supply registration information in support of all units in the Department of Land Affairs conducting research for land-reform purposes.

Cadastral surveys

The Department's Chief Directorate: Cadastral Surveys aims to ensure accurate cadastral surveys and promote cadastral information services in support of land reform and orderly development.

The Directorate: Cadastral Spatial Information and Professional Support is responsible for, among other things, preparing and updating cadastral maps in both paper and digital form, and examining and approving diagrams and general plans prior to them being registered by the Deeds Registry.

The website of the Chief Surveyor-General contains information and links to a number of related sites.

Service delivery has improved and good turnaround times have been maintained in the offices of the Surveyor-General.

In 2004/05, the Directorate: Cadastral Spatial Information continued to update and develop the Cadastral Information System, which is an essential tool for spatial planning and orderly development.

Two client-service centres have been established at the Pretoria and Cape Town surveyor-general offices.

The centres serve 100 to 150 clients a day and supply a legal registration help-desk function to attorneys, land surveyors and other professionals in the property industry.

Services provided to government include the preparation of documentation relating to the awarding of tenders to private land-survey firms for the survey of state land. Assistance is given to the Land and Tenure Reform Branch and land claims commissions (regional and provincial) in the form of surveys, the provision of cadastral information, the undertaking of field inspections and investigations to determine magisterial boundaries, and the upgrading of data on the former Transkei, Bophuthatswana, Venda and Ciskei. A tendering process is administered by the surveyor-general offices for the appointment of land surveyors on request from either unit.

The formal and informal cadastral spatial data has proved invaluable in providing assistance to components dealing with land reform and restitution.

To transform the survey profession, which is still largely white-male-dominated, the Surveying Profession Bill, aimed at addressing residual discrimination and employment-equity barriers, is being drafted.

Surveys and mapping

The Department of Land Affairs' Chief Directorate: Surveys and Mapping is responsible for the official, definitive, national topographic mapping and control network system of South Africa. It provides a range of maps, aerial photography, survey services and computer data products for government departments, commerce, planning, administrative, educational, management and leisure use.

National mapping

Mapping is a crucial resource for decision-making and development, and one of the most important deliverables of the chief directorate to support orderly development planning and sustainable land use.

All the maps of the national mapping series are continuously revised to reflect the change in landscape and other geospatial features. The 1:50 000 topographical map series is the largest scale map series, providing full coverage of South Africa. Small-scale maps of 1:250 000 and 1:500 000 are produced from the 1:50 000 map series.

The popular large-scale 1:10 000 orthophoto map series provides coverage of predominantly built-up areas, areas of economic importance and areas experiencing rapid development.

The chief directorate is a full member of the National Air Space Committee and produces aeronautical charts for the southern African region that are vital to the interests of air safety. The chief directorate provides up-to-date charts that reflect changes to airspace with respect to the Future Airspace Management Efficiency Programme.

Topographical information system

The maintenance and continuous updating of the Digital Topographic Information System is a key activity of the chief directorate. This system contains major features such as roads, railways, built-up areas, contours and rivers of the entire 1:50 000 national map series in digital format. A digital elevation model is available in horizontal intervals of 400 m and 200 m in mountainous areas, and 50 m for the major metropolitan and development areas.

Individuals and organisations, both public and private, use these data sets for planning, engineering, social and scientific purposes. The database serves as a fundamental data set for the country and is used, among many others, by Statistics South Africa for census planning and by the Independent Electoral Commission for the delineation of voting areas.

The map awareness and map literacy campaign of the Chief Directorate: Surveys and Mapping adds to the general drive to promote map literacy. MapAware workshops, offered to both public and private organisations, strive to develop and enhance the map skills of people who use spatial information in the workplace.

National Control Survey System

The National Control Survey System will facilitate the advance towards a uniform geodetic network for the continent.

This network plays a leading role in the African Reference Framework project aimed at harmonising and linking spatial reference systems across Africa, in support of NEPAD. The National Control Survey System consists of a network of about 62 000 control points distributed throughout the country. The network is made up of about 28 000 trigonometric beacons, 24 000 town survey marks and 10 000 elevation benchmarks.

The co-ordinates of these marks are referenced to the Hartebeesthoek 94 Datum, which, in turn, is referenced to the International Terrestrial Reference Frame. Cadastral, engineering and mapping surveys are referenced to this datum, which facilitates the exchange of data, uniform standards of accuracy and reduced costs of survey and spatial data to the public.

In 2001, the chief directorate embarked on a five-year plan to move away from passive networks (trigonometric beacons and town survey marks) and to adopt active global positioning system (GPS) networks.

This will entail the installation of 38 active GPS base stations, known as 'Trignet'. A total of 34 base stations has already been established and operationalised. The remaining four base stations are expected to be established during 2006.

The National Land Summit was held in July 2005 in Johannesburg to:
- inform the South African public about progress made in the land and agrarian reform process
- acknowledge challenges facing this process
- affirm commitment to this process
- invite South Africans to actively participate in land and agrarian reform.

National aerial photography and imagery

The national aerial photography and imagery archive is of national importance, providing coverage of the whole country (1,2 million km²).

This archive of aerial photography, dating back to 1934, is increased annually with the acquisition of new photography.

In 2004/05, new coverage of about 32% of the country was attained. Aerial-photography programmes and priorities are determined in co-operation with local, provincial and national government departments, and are focused on the nodal areas defined by the ISRDP and the Urban Renewal Programme (URP).

The archive is used for mapping, land-resource planning, infrastructure development, and legal and land restitution matters.

Spatial planning and information

The mandate of the Department of Land Affairs' Chief Directorate: SPI is to support land development and reform by ensuring an effective and efficient system of spatial planning, land-use management and the National Spatial Information Framework (NSIF) in the country.

Core functional areas of the chief directorate include:
- supporting the land reform process
- adopting an ISRDP and URP
- finalising policy, legislation and regulations with regard to spatial planning
- improving access to spatial information
- providing planning support for the formulation of local spatial plans
- supporting the formulation of spatial development frameworks (SDFs) at provincial level
- initiating the formulation of the National Spatial Development Framework
- improving stakeholder relations.

The SPI programme comprises the following sub-programmes:
- NSIF
- Land Development.

The NSIF is responsible for developing and maintaining a national data and policy framework to ensure accessibility and effective utilisation of spatially related information that supports municipalities in preparing their SDFs.

The Land Development Programme aims to facilitate and support integrated spatial and environmental planning, as well as land-use planning and management systems in all spheres of government.

Land-reform implementation management, and co-ordination

The Department of Land Affairs' Chief Directorate: Land-Reform Implementation Management, and Co-ordination is located in the Branch: Land and Tenure Reform.

The chief directorate's aim is the actual delivery of land and tenure reform. This is primarily done through nine provincial land reform offices (PLROs) and 36 operational regions.

The main objective of the LRAD Programme, in line with the department's mission, is to provide access to land, and to extend land rights to previously disadvantaged communities.

Launched in 2001, the LRAD provides financial support to emerging farmers through a match-funding arrangement in which the beneficiary has to make a contribution in the form of money, labour (sweat equity) or capital equipment.

Depending on the size of the contribution, the beneficiary qualifies for a grant of between R20 000 and R100 000. The LRAD's target is to redistribute 30% of all agricultural land to previously disadvantaged farmers by 2014.

To achieve this, about 2% has to be redistributed each year. By February 2005, about 13% had been distributed. Of the 23 520 LRAD beneficiaries, 19% were youths and 34,7% women.

Some 209 000 ha of agricultural land have been transferred to emergent farmers or communities since 1994. By April 2005, 30 400 ha of land had been leased out with an option to purchase.

Land-reform systems and support services

The Department of Land Affairs' Chief Directorate: Land-Reform Systems and Support Services forms part of the Branch: Land and Tenure Reform, and consists of three directorates, namely Public Land Support Services, Tenure Reform Implementation Systems and Redistribution Implementation Systems.

The chief directorate aims to develop and refine legislation, systems and procedures to enable PLROs to deliver at scale to land-reform participants. The chief directorate also lends a support service function in terms of capacity-building and information management and communication to the PLROs.

The Chief Directorate: Land-Reform Systems and Support Services has proactively engaged with the private sector to increase their involvement in land reform to improve the scale of delivery. Positive engagements were initiated with the South African Banking Council. An existing service level agreement with the Land Reform Empowerment Facility (LREF) has been maintained.

The LREF is a wholesale credit facility hosted and administered by Khula Enterprise Finance, which was created by the department to assist in the establishment of commercially viable land-reform projects.

Commission on the Restitution of Land Rights (CRLR)

In 1995, the CRLR was established in terms of the Restitution of Land Rights Act, 1994 (Act 22 of 1994), which aims to:

- provide equitable redress to victims of racial land dispossession
- provide access to rights in land, including land ownership and sustainable development
- foster national reconciliation and stability
- improve household welfare, underpin economic growth and contribute to poverty alleviation.

The original budget allocated to the commission for the 2004/05 financial year was R933 million, but this had to be increased to R1,13 billion, in line with the increased number of claims settled.

Actual expenditure for the year was R1,18 billion including both capital and recurrent expenditure. An additional six million euro (about R49 million) was made available by the Belgian Government for the claimant verification process.

The total number of claims settled increased from 48 825 in March 2004 to 59 345 in March 2005. The increase was 13% lower than in 2004, but was still on an upward trend. This phenomenon is expected to continue because the commission is dealing largely with rural community claims. These represent a small number on its database although they account for a very large number of beneficiaries as well as hectares of land.

The number of beneficiaries increased from 662 307 in 2004 to 869 506 in 2005. The number of hectares delivered increased from 810 292 ha in 2004 to 887 093 ha in 2005.

About 80% of the total number of claims lodged were urban while 20% were rural. Most of the urban claimants opted for financial compensation for their lost land rights while most rural claimants have opted for land restoration.

The total number of rural claims settled by mid-2005 was 6 536, while that of urban claims was 52 809.

Some R2 454 billion was committed to financial compensation for all urban claims settled by mid-2005. A typical rural claim involves 300 to 4 000 households for 300 to 15 000 ha of land. Most of these rural communities did not have registered rights to the land, because of the inequitable practices of the past, but had beneficial occupation rights.

Their land was not surveyed at the time of dispossession as they had no title deeds. This demands that the department conducts detailed research, documents and authenticates oral evidence, maps out the land parcels claimed and links the rightful claimants to the claimed land, resolves boundary disputes and facilitates land acquisition for claimants. An amount of R1 729 billion was committed to land acquisition for all claims settled by mid-2005 for those who had opted for land restoration. Over R459 million was committed to grants for development support.

The target for 2005 was to settle all outstanding urban claims by December 2005 and about 2 800 rural claims by the end of the 2005/06 financial year. This will leave the commission with about 5 000 rural claims to settle over the next two financial years ending March 2008. The budgetary allocation for 2005/06 was R2,7 million.

Acknowledgements

Agricultural Research Council
BuaNews
Commission for the Restitution of Land Rights
Department of Agriculture
Department of Land Affairs
Estimates of National Expenditure 2005, published by National Treasury
http://land.pwv.gov.za
www.landbank.co.za
www.gov.za
www.news24.com

Suggested reading

Abstract of Agricultural Statistics. Pretoria: Department of Agriculture, Directorate: Agricultural Information Services, annually.

African Farm Management Conference (1998: Stellenbosch, South Africa) *Farm and Farmer Organisation for Sustainable Agriculture in Africa*, 26 – 30 January 1998, Stellenbosch, South Africa.

AgriBEE: Broad-Based Black Economic Empowerment Framework for Agriculture. Pretoria: Department of Agriculture, 2004.

Agriculture in South Africa. 5th ed. Johannesburg: Chris van Rensburg, 1994.

Agricultural Land Reform in South Africa: Policies, Markets and Mechanisms. Cape Town: Oxford University Press,1996.

Department of Agriculture, Directorate: Agricultural Information Services. Pretoria: Government Printing Works.

Auerbach, R.M.B. *Design for Participation in Ecologically Sound Management of South Africa's Mlazi River Catchment*. Wageningen: *Landbouwuniversiteit*, 1999.

Bonti-Ankomah, S. ed. *Audit of Research on Land, Agriculture, Food, Security and Rural Development: The Issues and Gaps*. Johannesburg: National Institute of Economic Policy, 2000.

Bundy, C. *Rise and Fall of the South African Peasantry*. 2nd ed. Cape Town: David Philip, 1988.

Cross, C.R. and Haines, R.J. eds. *Towards Freehold: Options for Land Development in South Africa's Black Rural Areas*. Cape Town: Juta, 1988.

De Klerk, M. ed. *Harvest of Discontent: The Land Question in South Africa*. Cape Town: Institute for a Democratic South Africa, 1991.

De Villiers, B. ed. *Land Claims and National Parks*. Pretoria: Human Sciences Research Council (HSRC), 1999.

Devereux, S. and Maxwell, S. eds. *Food Security in Sub-Saharan Africa*. Pietermaritzburg: University of Natal Press, 2003.

Dreyer, A. *Weather Derivatives in the South African Agriculture Sector*. Stellenbosch: University of Stellenbosch, 2002.

Economic Review of South African Agriculture. Pretoria: Department of Agriculture, annually.

Employment Trends in Agriculture in South Africa/Statistics South Africa and National Department of Agriculture. Pretoria: Statistics South Africa (Stats SA), 2000.

Environmental Development Agency. *People's Farming Workbook*. 3rd revised ed. Cape Town: David Philip, 1999.

Investment, Farming and Agribusiness South Africa. Johannesburg: Trade Edge, annually.

Jeeves, A.H. and Crush, J. eds. *White Farms, Black Labour: The State and Agrarian Change in Southern Africa, 1910 – 1950*. Pietermaritzburg: University of Natal Press, 1997.

Jiggins, J. *Breaking New Ground: Options for Agricultural Extension and Development in South Africa*. Johannesburg, South Africa: Land and Agriculture Policy Centre, 1997.

Johnson, R.W. and Schlemmer, L. *Farmers and Farm Workers in KwaZulu-Natal: Employment Conditions, Labour Tenancy, Land Reform, Attitudes and Relationships*. Johannesburg: Helen Suzman Foundation, 1998.

Johnson, R.W. and Schlemmer, L. *Attitudes and Relationships*. Johannesburg: Helen Suzman Foundation, 1998.

Keegan, T.J. *Facing the Storm: Portraits of Black Lives in Rural South Africa*. Cape Town: David Philip, 1988.

Kirsten, J., Van Zyl, J. and Vink, N. *The Agricultural Democratisation of South Africa*. Project co-ordinators: Cape Town: Published for Africa Institute for Policy Analysis and Economic Integration by Francolin Publishers, 1998.

Kleinhans, T.E. *et al. SADC Agricultural Potential Assessment: The Spatial Organisation of Resources for Policy-Making*. Halfway House, Development Bank of South Africa, 2001.

Kok, P. and Pietersen, J. *Agriculture and Agroprocessing*. Pretoria: HSRC, 2000.

Kruger, E. *Farmer to Farmer: A Story of Innovation and Solidarity*. Scottsville: Farmer Support Group, University of Natal, 1998.

Land Redistribution for Agricultural Development: A Subprogramme of the Land Redistribution Programme: Operational Manual: Guidelines for Applicants, Sellers and Government Officials. Pretoria: Ministry of Agriculture and Land Affairs, 2001.

Land Reform and Agrarian Change in Southern Africa: An occasional paper series. Bellville, RSA: University of the Western Cape. No. 10, 12 (1999).

Le Roux, R. *Agricultural Workers: A Historical and Contemporary Perspective*. Cape Town: Institute of Development and Labour Law, University of Cape Town, 2002.

Lee, M. and Colvard, K. eds. *Unfinished Business: The Land Crisis in Southern Africa*. Pretoria: AISA, 2004.

Letsoabo, E.M. *Land Reform in South Africa: A Black Perspective*. Johannesburg: Skotaville, 1987.

Levin, R. and Weiner, D. eds. *Community Perspectives on Land and Agrarian Reform in South Africa*. Chicago: MacArthur Foundation, 1994.

Marcus, T. *Commercial Agriculture in South Africa: Modernising Super Exploitation*. London: Zed Books, 1989.

Marcus, T., Eales, K. and Wildschut, A. *Land Demand in the New South Africa*. University of Natal: Indicator Press, 1996

Maswikaneng, M.J. *Urban Agriculture in the Informal Settlements of Atteridgeville*, Pretoria. Technikon Pretoria, 2003.

Meer, S. ed. *Women, Land and Authority: Perspectives from South Africa*. Cape Town: David Philip in association with the National Land Committee, 1997.

Moyo, S. and Yeros, P. eds. *Reclaiming the Land: The Resurgence of Rural Movements in Africa, Asia and Latin America*. London: Zed Books; Cape Town: David Philip, 2005.

Nemutanzhela, T. *Ploughing Amongst the Stones: The Story of 'Betterment' in the Zoutpansberg 1939 – 1944*. Johannesburg: Ravan Press, 1999.

Nieuwoudt, L. and Groenewald, J. eds. *The Challenge of Change: Agriculture, Land and the South African Economy*. Pietermaritzburg: University of Natal Press, 2003.

Ntsekhe, W.P. and Farrell, J. *The Conservation Ideal: The Fourth Decade: Being the SARCCUS Record for the Period 1981 to 1990*. Pretoria: SARCCUS, 1998.

Palmer, R. *Contested Land in Southern and Eastern Africa: A Literature Survey*. London: Oxfam, 1997.

People's Farming Workbook. 2nd ed. Cape Town: Environmental and Development Agency Trust, 1998.

People's Farming Workbook. Cape Town: David Philip, 1995.

People's Farming Workbook. 2nd ed. Cape Town: David Philip for Environmental Development Agency Trust, 1998.

Perret, S. and Mercoiret, M.R. eds. *Supporting Small-Scale Farmers and Rural Organisations: Learning from Experiences in West Africa: A Handbook for Development Operators and Local Managers*. Pretoria: Protea Book House, 2003.

Shabalala, N. *Report on the Survey of Large and Small-Scale Agriculture*. Pretoria: Stats SA, 2002.

Sombalo, L.L. *Urban Livelihood Strategies and Agricultural Activities in Khayelitsha Communities, Western Cape*. Pretoria: University of Pretoria, 2003.

Southey, J. *Footprints in the Karoo: A Story of Farming Life*. Johannesburg: Jonathan Ball, 1990.

Strategic Plan for South African Agriculture, Pretoria: Department of Agriculture, 2001.

Strategic Plan for the Agricultural Research Council, Pretoria, ARC: 2001.

Strategic Plan for the Department of Agriculture 2004. Pretoria: Department of Agriculture, 2004.

Tainton, N, ed. *Pasture Management in South Africa*. Pietermaritzburg: University of Natal Press, 2000.

The Dynamics of the South African Export Basket. Compiled by the Department of Economic Research and Development, Industrial Development Corporation of South Africa, Ltd. Sandton, RSA, 1996.

The Nutritional Content of South African Beef. Compiled by H.C. Schönfeldt *et al*. Pretoria: South African Meat Board, 1996.

Thirtle, C., Van Zyl, J. and Vink, N. *South African Agriculture at the Crossroads: An Empirical Analysis of Efficiency, Technology and Productivity*. New York: St. Martin's Press, 2000.

Thomson, J. *Genes for Africa*. Cape Town: UCT Press, 2002.

Van der Walt, A.J. *Land Reform and the Future of Land Ownership in South Africa*. Cape Town: Juta, 1991.

Van Onselen, C. *The Seed is Mine: The Life of Kas Maine: A South African Sharecropper, 1894 – 1985*. Cape Town: David Philip, 1996.

Van Rooyen, J., Groenewald J. and Kirsten, J. eds. *Agricultural Policy Reform in South Africa*. Pretoria: University of Pretoria, 1998.

Vink, N. and Kirsten, J. *Deregulation of Agricultural Marketing in South Africa: Lessons Learned*. Sandton: Free Market Foundation, 2000.

Wethli, E. *The South African Chicken Book: How to Start a Small Business Keeping Chickens*. Berold, R. ed; Illustrator: Gilbert, L. Kenwyn, RSA: Juta, 1999.

Winburg, M. *Back to the Land*. Johannesburg: Porcupine Press, 1996.

Arts and culture

The Department of Arts and Culture aims to develop and preserve South African culture to ensure social cohesion and nation-building. It is the custodian of South Africa's diverse cultural, artistic and linguistic heritage.

Funding

A large portion of the department's budget is dedicated to supporting and developing institutional infrastructure to showcase, restore and preserve South Africa's heritage for future generations.

The Arts and Culture in Society Programme develops and promotes arts and culture in South Africa and mainstreams their role in social development. It funds performing arts institutions, orchestras, the National Arts Council (NAC) and the Promotion of Arts and Culture in South Africa Subprogramme. During 2004/05, the department funded the establishment of two large instrumental ensembles – one in Cape Town and the other in Johannesburg. A music training programme directed at township youth in Gauteng also received a grant.

The department funds six playhouses. In 2004/05, it contributed over R89 million towards the running of these institutions.

In 2005/06, the performing arts institutions received just over R97,7 million. The combined budget for the declared cultural institutions was over R237 million.

The NAC received an increased budget of R47,9 million in 2005/06. The Pan South African Language Board (PanSALB) received R26,2 million and the National Film and Video Foundation (NFVF) R24,6 million. The National Heritage Council (NHC) received R17,4 million and the South African Heritage Resources Agency (SAHRA) R24,298 million.

National symbols

National anthem

South Africa's national anthem is a combined version of *Nkosi Sikelel' iAfrika* and *The Call of South Africa (Die Stem van Suid-Afrika)*. *The Call of South Africa* was written by C.J. Langenhoven in May 1918. The music was composed by the Rev. M.L. de Villiers in 1921. *Nkosi Sikelel' iAfrika* was composed in 1897 by Enoch Sontonga, a Methodist mission school teacher.

The words of the first stanza were originally written in isiXhosa as a hymn. Seven additional stanzas in isiXhosa were later added by the poet Samuel Mqhayi. It has been translated into most of South Africa's official languages.

National flag

South Africa's national flag was launched and used for the first time on Freedom Day, 27 April 1994. The design and colours are a synopsis of the principal elements of the country's flag history.

The central design of the flag, beginning at the flag-pole in a 'V' form and flowing into a single horizontal band to the outer edge of the fly, can be interpreted as the convergence of diverse elements within South African society, taking the road ahead in unity. The flag was designed by the State Herald.

When the flag is displayed vertically against a wall, the red band should be to the left of the viewer, with the hoist or the cord seam at the top. When it is displayed horizontally, the hoist should be to the left of the viewer and the red band at the top. When the flag is displayed next to or behind the speaker at a meeting, it must be placed to the speaker's right. When it is placed elsewhere in the meeting place, it should be to the right of the audience.

National coat of arms

South Africa's coat of arms was launched on Freedom Day, 27 April 2000.

A focal point of the coat of arms is the indigenous secretary bird with its uplifted wings, crowned with an image of the rising sun. The sun not only symbolises a life-giving force, but represents the flight of darkness and the triumph of discovery, knowledge and understanding of things that have been hidden. It also illuminates the new life that is coming into being. An indigenous South African flower, the protea, is placed below the bird. It represents beauty, the aesthetic harmony of the different cultures, and South Africa flowering as a nation. The ears of wheat symbolise the fertility of the land, while the tusks of the African elephant, depicted in pairs to represent men and women, also represent wisdom, steadfastness and strength.

The shield, placed in the centre, signifies the protection of South Africans from one generation to the next. The spear and a knobkierie above it are representative of the defence of peace rather than the pursuit of war. This shield of peace, which also brings to mind an African drum, conveys the message of a people imbued with a love of culture. Its upper part is a shield imaginatively represented by the protea.

Contained within the shield are some of the earliest representations of humanity in the world. Those depicted were the very first inhabitants of the land, namely the Khoisan people. These figures are derived from images on the Linton Stone, a world-famous example of South African rock art. The motto on the coat of arms, *!ke e:/xarra//ke*, written in the Khoisan language of the /Xam people, means 'diverse people unite' or 'people who are different joining together'.

National orders

National orders are the highest awards that the country can bestow on individual South Africans and eminent foreign leaders and personalities.

The Order of Mapungubwe is awarded to South African citizens for excellence and exceptional achievement.

The Order of the Baobab is awarded to South African citizens for distinguished service in the fields of business and the economy; science, medicine and technological innovation; and community service.

The Order of the Companions of O.R. Tambo is awarded to heads of state and other dignitaries for promoting peace, co-operation and friendship towards South Africa.

The Order of Luthuli is awarded to South Africans who have made a meaningful contribution to the struggle for democracy, human rights, nation-building, justice and peace, and conflict resolution.

The Order of Ikhamanga is awarded to South African citizens who have excelled in the fields of arts, culture, literature, music, journalism and sport.

The Order of the Mendi Decoration for Bravery is awarded to South African citizens who have performed extraordinary acts of bravery.

National symbols and orders

National bird: Blue Crane

National fish: Galjoen

National animal: Springbok

National tree: Real Yellowwood

National flower: King Protea

The Order of the Baobab

The Order of Mapungubwe

The Order of the
Companions of O.R. Tambo

The Order of Luthuli

The Order of the
Mendi Decoration
for Bravery

The Order of Ikhamanga

National symbols

South Africa's national symbols are:

- National animal: Springbok
- National bird: Blue Crane
- National fish: Galjoen
- National flower: King Protea
- National tree: Real Yellowwood.

Arts and culture organisations

National Heritage Council

The NHC, a statutory body that aims to bring equity to heritage promotion and conservation, was launched in February 2004.

The 23-member council was appointed by the Minister of Arts and Culture in terms of the NHC Act, 1999 (Act 25 of 1999), to:

- develop, promote and protect the national heritage for present and future generations
- co-ordinate heritage management
- protect, preserve and promote the content and heritage that reside in oration to make it accessible and dynamic
- integrate living heritage with the functions and activities of the council and all other heritage authorities and institutions at national, provincial and local level
- promote and protect indigenous knowledge systems
- intensify support for promoting the history and culture of all South Africans, and particularly support for research and publications on enslavement in South Africa.

Transfers to the NHC started at R16,7 million in 2004/05, rose to R17,4 million in 2005/06 and are expected to reach R19,6 million in 2007/08.

South African Heritage Resources Agency

The National Heritage Resources Act, 1999 (Act 25 of 1999), established the SAHRA to manage the heritage resources of the country in co-operation with similar provincial agencies.

The SAHRA has established the National Heritage Resources Fund to provide financial assistance, in the form of a grant or a loan, to an approved body or individual, for any project which contributes to the conservation and protection of South Africa's national heritage resources.

Conservation categories include:

- national heritage sites, registers, areas and objects
- protected areas
- structures over 60 years old
- burial grounds and graves
- fossils (palaeontology) and archaeology
- rock art
- historical shipwrecks.

South African Geographical Names Council (SAGNC)

The SAGNC is an advisory body appointed by the Minister of Arts and Culture in terms of the SAGNC Act, 1998 (Act 118 of 1998). The council advises the minister on the transformation and standardisation of official geographical names in South Africa.

The council has jurisdiction over all names of geographical features and entities falling within the territories over which the South African Government has sovereignty or jurisdiction acquired by treaty.

The following principles are adhered to:

- each individual feature or entity should have only one official name
- the following types of geographical names should generally be avoided:
  - approved names of places elsewhere in South Africa
  - names of places in other countries, and names of countries
  - names that are blasphemous, indecent, offensive, vulgar, unaesthetic or embarrassing
  - names that are discriminatory or derogatory
  - names that may be regarded as an advertisement for a particular product, service or firm
  - names of living persons.

Geographical names committees have been established in all nine provinces. These provincial committees play an important role in the standardisation of geographical names.

The national anthem

Nkosi sikelel' iAfrika
Maluphakanyisw' uphondo lwayo,
Yizwa imithandazo yethu,
Nkosi sikelela, thina lusapho lwayo.

Morena boloka setjhaba sa heso,
O fedise dintwa le matshwenyeho,
O se boloke, O se boloke setjhaba
sa heso,
Setjhaba sa South Afrika –
South Afrika.

Uit die blou van onse hemel,
Uit die diepte van ons see,
Oor ons ewige gebergtes,
Waar die kranse antwoord gee.

Sounds the call to come together,
And united we shall stand,
Let us live and strive for freedom,
In South Africa our land.

National Arts Council of South Africa

The NAC took over the structures and responsibilities of the Foundation of the Creative Arts on 29 October 1997.

The NAC aims to:

- support arts practice by creating and providing opportunities to achieve excellence in the arts, within a climate of freedom
- achieve equity by redressing imbalances in the allocation of resources
- promote and develop appreciation, understanding and enjoyment of the arts through strategies that include education, information and marketing
- enhance support for and recognition of the arts by promoting and facilitating national and international liaison between individuals and institutions
- establish and recommend policy in the development, practice and funding of the arts.

The NAC supports several genres, such as music and opera, literature, the visual arts, crafts, theatre and musical theatre, dance and choreography, and multidisciplinary arts. It supports and funds a range of individuals and groups.

It also offers block bursaries to tertiary institutions for undergraduate students. Individual bursaries are offered for studies towards a postgraduate qualification in South Africa and abroad.

During 2004/05, the council made grants available to 500 projects and 60 performing arts companies in the disciplines of theatre, dance and music. The number of projects benefiting during 2005/06 was expected to increase to 800.

Mmino

Mmino, a South Africa-Norwegian education and music programme, hosted by the NAC in close co-operation with the Norwegian Concert Institute, is the only funding programme in South Africa that funds music projects exclusively.

Since the inception of the Mmino Programme in August 2000, 176 projects have been funded. Funds are allocated twice a year.

Mmino aims to support projects with national impact in the areas of music education, documentation, research and exchange, choral music and festivals. The goal of Mmino is to strengthen South Africa's musical cultures.

Living Treasures

The Living Treasures Project aims to create a living treasure of artists who are still alive and who have contributed to a democratic South Africa. Award recipients include Mr Jackson Hlongwane, Ms Matshidiso Motimele, Prof. Es'kia Mphahlele, Mr Winston Ntshona, Ms Maria Zulu, Mr Abner Mahlaba, Mr Alfred Nokwe and Ms Thandi Zulu.

Arts institutions

The following arts institutions assist in creating a sustainable performing arts industry based on access, excellence, diversity and redress, and encourage the development of the full range of performing arts:

- State Theatre
- Playhouse Company
- ArtsCape
- Market Theatre
- Performing Arts Centre of the Free State
- Windybrow Theatre
- KwaZulu-Natal Philharmonic Orchestra
- Cape Philharmonic Orchestra
- Gauteng Orchestra.

The institutions receive annual transfers from the Department of Arts and Culture, but also generate revenue through entrance fees, donor assistance and sponsorships.

Business Arts South Africa (BASA)

BASA was launched in 1997 as a joint initiative between the Government, through the Department

In March 2005, the Department of Arts and Culture launched the *Arts in Prisons* Campaign. It uses the arts to rehabilitate offenders, thereby contributing to social cohesion and social justice.

of Arts and Culture, and the business sector. It promotes and encourages sustainable partnerships between the business and the arts sectors, to their mutual benefit and that of the community at large. With funding from government, BASA has introduced the supporting grant scheme, whereby additional funds are made available to sponsor arts organisations or events.

BASA is a member of the International Network of Business Arts Associations, linking with similar organisations internationally.

Business Day continues to partner BASA in its annual awards, which acknowledge the importance of private sponsorships in the development of the arts.

BASA offers corporate membership to major companies and receives funding by way of subscriptions paid by these companies. In March 2004, membership stood at 101 corporate members and plans were to increase its membership to 200 paid-up corporate members by the end of 2005. It further intended to increase the number of regional representatives and to leverage the interest in itself and art through media partnerships.

BASA made grants to to the value of R2,5 million during the 2003/04 financial year.

Arts and Culture Trust (ACT)

ACT was launched in October 1994 to finance and manage funding for the arts in South Africa. The trust, with former President Nelson Mandela as its chief patron, has Nedbank, Sun International, the Ministry of Arts and Culture, Vodacom and the Dutch Government as its major funders. The trust also seeks to build a better arts and culture dispensation through proactive initiatives such as:

- fora, conferences and campaigns around strategic issues, such as support for the arts through the National Lottery
- the annual ACT Awards, which recognise the important contributions of role-players such as administrators, journalists and educators
- establishing mutually beneficial relationships between the trust and the arts and culture community.

ACT is the oldest independent body established to fund arts and culture in post-apartheid South Africa.

It has disbursed almost R10 million to more than 400 projects in all disciplines since 1996 including, but not limited to, arts administration, arts education, community art, festivals, heritage art, crafts, fine art, dance, music, theatre, film and video, literature, multidisciplinary art and new media. With renewed support from all of the founding trustees, ACT was expected to disburse a further R1,5 million during the 2005 funding cycle. A portion of these funds were expected to be made available for bursaries to formal and non-formal educational institutions specialising in arts and culture.

Other cultural organisations

Non-governmental organisations (NGOs), community-based organisations and other cultural projects that were previously not considered for funding are now being funded.

Community art centres are positioned to be the leading centres for poverty-alleviation programmes in both rural and urban communities.

Successful local projects take place in many community arts centres. For example, in 2004/05, the Department of Arts and Culture provided funds for equipment at the Mdantsane Music School.

A community arts centre was established in Jagersfontein, an impoverished Free State rural town. Support also included the purchasing of industrial sewing machines for a women's group in the Queenstown Arts Centre in an Integrated Sustainable Rural Development Programme (ISRDP) node; a women's sewing project in Sekhukhuneland, also in an ISDRP node; a women's weaving project at Ingwe; and the Mtubatuba Craft Project in KwaZulu-Natal. These projects have the potential to grow into small businesses.

Arts and culture initiatives

Legacy projects

Monuments, museums, plaques, outdoor art, heritage trails and other symbolic representations create visible reminders of, and commemorate, the many aspects of South Africa's past.

Several national legacy projects were initiated by government to establish commemorative symbols of South Africa's history and celebrate its heritage.

The legacy projects include the:

- Women's Monument: On 9 August 2000, President Thabo Mbeki unveiled a monument to commemorate the contribution of the women of South Africa to the struggle for freedom. The ceremony marked the day, in 1956, when 20 000 women marched to the Union Buildings in Pretoria to protest against government's pass laws.
- Chief Albert Luthuli's house in KwaDukuza, KwaZulu-Natal, has been restored by the Department of Arts and Culture as a museum with a visitors' interpretative centre. The project also involved the unveiling of Chief Luthuli's sculpture at the KwaDukuza municipal grounds. On 21 March 2004, the first of the Annual Chief Albert Luthuli lectures was held at the University of KwaZulu-Natal. A posthumous doctoral degree was conferred on Chief Luthuli. President Mbeki launched the legacy project on 21 August 2004.
- Battle of Blood River/Ncome Project: Following the unveiling of the Ncome Monument and Wall of Remembrance on 16 December 1998, the Ncome Museum was opened on 26 November 1999. The structures honour the role played by the Zulu nation in the battle.
- Samora Machel Project: The Samora Machel Monument in Mbuzini, Mpumalanga, was unveiled on 19 October 1998.
- Nelson Mandela Museum: The museum was opened on 11 February 2000. It is being developed as a single component comprising three elements, namely a museum in Umtata, a youth centre at Qunu, and a visitors' centre in Mvezo, where the former President was born.
- Constitution Hill Project: The Old Fort Prison in Hillbrow, Johannesburg, was developed into a multidimensional and multipurpose precinct that houses the Constitutional Court (CC) and accommodates various constitutional commissions. As part of the 10 Years of Freedom celebrations, the new CC building was officially opened in March 2004. The Constitution Hill project involved the development of the Constitutional Hill precinct to accommodate the CC, the Constitution Museum, the Nelson Mandela Library and a commercial precinct.

- Khoisan Project: Consultation with relevant role-players at national, provincial and local level has been initiated to promote and protect the Khoisan heritage. It was decided to develop a heritage trail that will showcase the heritage of the Khoisan people.
- Freedom Park Project: Construction of the Freedom Park Project, a memorial to the anti-apartheid struggle at Salvokop in Pretoria, began in 2002.

The first phase of the R560-million memorial site was handed over to government in March 2004. This phase, costing R45 million, involved the design and construction of the Garden of Remembrance for the country's departed freedom fighters. The second phase was expected to commence in October 2005, with the building of a museum and interpretation centre.

Additional legacy projects were expected to be announced in 2005/06.

Education and training

Training is critical for the development of arts and culture, to achieve both the developmental and economic potential of the sector.

The creative industries form part of the Media, Advertising, Publishing, Printing and Packaging Sector Education and Training Authority (MAPPP-SETA).

Recognising the challenges facing this sector, the MAPPP-SETA, in partnership with the departments of arts and culture and of labour, the NAC and the NFVF, initiated the CREATE SA (Creative Research Education and Training Enterprise South Africa) Strategic Project to develop a comprehensive on-the-job training framework for the creative industries. The project is funded by the National Skills Fund and the Department of Arts and Culture, and focuses on people who otherwise might not have had access to training opportunities.

Through CREATE SA, learnerships driven by industry demand have been awarded in a wide range of areas, including music, design, crafts, arts management, heritage and the performing arts.

The Cultural Development and International Co-operation Programme is responsible for the Investing in Culture Programme. It focuses on the crafts, music, heritage and cultural tourism sectors. Investing in Culture identifies and uses existing skills within communities and among individuals. It is the single most significant intervention the department is making in the Second Economy.

It has sites located in all the urban and rural nodes in most provinces of South Africa. Currently, these projects are funded in three-yearly cycles. The nodes include Alexandra, Mdantsane, Motherwell, O.R. Tambo region, Ukhahlamba district, Khayelitsha, Mitchell's Plain, Galeshewe and Kalahari-Kgalagadi. There are others in Inanda, KwaMashu, Indonsa, Umkhanyakude in the Lubombo Corridor, Ugu district, Sekhukhune cross-border district and Thabo Mofutsanyane district. They were started in response to demands from the poor living in these areas.

Since 2001, the Department of Arts and Culture has recast what used to be a poverty-alleviation programme into Investing in Culture. With the projects it has initiated, the department hopes to make a meaningful impact in these targeted areas:

- in music, 2 000 jobs can be created both directly and indirectly through small and medium enterprises and Black Economic Empowerment projects
- its intervention in craft and design will see the creation of 4 000 jobs
- in books and publishing, an estimated 500 jobs will be created
- in film and video, 2 000 jobs will be created
- in the heritage sector, 1 000 jobs will be created
- in the archives and libraries division, 200 jobs will be created
- through the Directorate: Arts and Culture in Society, 500 jobs will be created
- in a language development programme, 100 jobs will be created through learnerships
- within the area of heraldry, 200 jobs will be created
- within the performing arts, 1 500 jobs can be created by boosting the technical services pro-

gramme to stimulate transformation and facilitate human resource development.

The department aims to create 10 000 job opportunities in designated poverty nodes.

The majority of the beneficiaries of these projects will be women and young people, who constitute the majority of the poverty-stricken and unemployed.

The department committed R249 million to be spent between 2004/05 and 2006/07 towards these projects. These funds will be spread over all nine provinces, but with a focus on the poorest ones.

More information is available at *www.createsa.org.za.*

Cultural tourism

Cultural tourism is one of the most rapidly growing sectors of the multibillion-Rand international tourism industry, and is an area in which South Africa is well-placed to compete. Professional and innovative museums, galleries and theatres are key attractions for cultural tourists.

Cultural villages

Most tourists visiting South Africa are eager to explore the country's cultural diversity. At the same time, an increasing number of local tourists want to learn more about the people they were separated from under apartheid. (See chapter 21: *Tourism.*)

In February 2005, former President Nelson Mandela formally donated more than 2 000 gifts and awards he received during his tenure as the first democratically elected President of South Africa (1994 – 1999) to the nation. The event coincided with the Nelson Mandela Museum's fifth anniversary celebrations.

Awards include honorary fellowships, freedom of the city awards, honorary citizenships, honorary degrees, peace and human rights awards, literary awards, media awards and orders of merit from more than 50 countries around the world. Among these is the Official Presidential Medallion commemorating Mr Mandela's Presidential inauguration in 1994.

Various projects around the country offer insight into South Africa's cultural wealth, ranging from traditional dances and rituals in rural areas, to excursions into the urban and township milieux that give South Africa its defining features. These include Khaya Lendaba near Port Elizabeth; the Basotho Cultural Village situated in the QwaQwa Nature Reserve near Harrismith, Free State; the Makhosini Cultural Village and Tourism Initiative in the Valley of Kings at Umgungundlovu in KwaZulu-Natal; Lesedi Cultural Village near Johannesburg; Tlholego in Magaliesburg; the KoMjekejeke Cultural Village north of Pretoria; the Mapoch Ndebele Village in Winterveld, north-west of Pretoria; the Gaabo Motho Cultural Village in Mabopane; the Rainbow Cultural Village west of the Hartbeespoort Dam, North West; Botshabelo in Middelburg, Mpumalanga; and Shangana in Hazyview, Mpumalanga.

Cultural Industries Growth Strategy

The Cultural Industries Growth Strategy capitalises on the economic potential of the craft, music, film, publishing and design industries. The Department of Arts and Culture provides support in the form of financing, management capacity, advocacy and networking, and developing public-private partnerships and other initiatives that use culture as a tool for urban regeneration.

Through financial support to the NFVF, the department encourages and ensures the growth of the film industry. The music industry task team set up by the minister has outlined 37 recommendations, which include the development of enabling legislation and the economic growth of the industry. The department continues to support industry initiatives that are consistent with the objectives of job creation and economic development. To this end, it is also focusing on the design, craft and publishing sectors.

International relations

The Department of Arts and Culture's participation in various activities in the international cultural arena helps to identify, promote and exploit mutually beneficial partnerships for social and economic development in South Africa.

Collaborations involve about 39 countries, including Mexico, Tunisia, France and Brazil, as well as the United Nations Educational, Scientific and Cultural Organisation and the Southern African Development Community. Overseas development aid programmes and international agreements or partnerships have been established with a number of countries.

Together with the African Union (AU) and New Partnership for Africa's Development, South Africa has embarked on the road to restore, preserve and protect African heritage. In 2004, South Africa was elected chair of the 29th session of the World Heritage Committee.

In July 2005, South Africa hosted the conference in Durban. Some 180 countries are signatories to the World Heritage Convention. This was the first time the World Heritage Committee met in sub-Saharan Africa since the convention was adopted in 1972. With other African countries, and with the support of the AU, South Africa drafted an African position paper, outlining the 10-year strategy for the preservation of Africa's heritage.

Arts festivals

The range of arts festivals around South Africa offers visitors the opportunity to combine their pursuit of culture with sightseeing, wine tasting, beach visits, wildlife viewing, history, palaeoanthropology and relaxing in some of South Africa's most beautiful spots.

The National Arts Festival, held annually in July in Grahamstown, Eastern Cape, is one of the largest and most diverse arts gatherings of its kind staged in Africa, rating favourably with similar international festivals. It showcases southern African talent in all arts disciplines.

There is also growing interest and participation from artists in other African countries and from the rest of the world.

The *Klein Karoo Nasionale Kunstefees* is a vibrant festival for the performing arts, presented mainly, but not exclusively, in Afrikaans. It is held annually in

Oudtshoorn in the first quarter of the year. Disciplines include drama, cabaret and contemporary and classical music.

The Arts Alive International Festival, held in Johannesburg, is an annual festival of music, dance, theatre and performance-poetry.

Heritage reclamation festivals are also emerging at local level in communities destroyed by apartheid such as Vrededorp (Fietas) in Johannesburg.

The Mangaung Cultural Festival (Macufe) is gaining status as one of the biggest cultural tourism events in southern Africa.

Aardklop, held annually in Potchefstroom, is inherently Afrikaans, but universal in character. The festival provides a platform for the creativity and talent of local artists.

Other festivals that attract visitors at both national and international level are the Joy of Jazz International Festival; Oppikoppi; Calabash; The One City Festival in Taung, North West; the Awesome Africa Music Festival in Durban; the Spier Summer Festival at Spier Estate in the Western Cape; and the Windybrow Theatre Festival in Johannesburg.

The Department of Arts and Culture and the NAC support numerous festivals throughout South Africa, including the Cape Town International Jazz Festival (formerly the North Sea Jazz Festival), Port St Johns Festival, Splashy Fen Music Festival in Durban and the National Arts Festival in Grahamstown.

The departments of arts and culture and of environmental affairs and tourism have established a forum of festival directors to maximise tourism opportunities.

Theatre

The theatre scene in South Africa is vibrant, with many active spaces across the country offering everything from indigenous drama, music, dance, cabaret and satire, to West End and Broadway hits, classical music, opera and ballet.

Apart from early productions, notably the groundbreaking musical *King Kong* in the 1960s, theatre created in South Africa by South Africans only began to make an impact with the advent of Johannesburg's innovative Market Theatre in the mid-1970s,

just as the cultural, sporting and academic boycott was taking hold.

The performing arts marketed South Africa to overseas audiences most effectively during the 1980s, specifically through theatre and musical productions.

South African theatre is internationally acclaimed as unique and top-class.

Music

South African music is characterised by its fusion of diverse musical forms. It generates R900 million a year and employs over 12 000 people.

South Africa has nurtured the development of an array of distinctive styles of music, and it has contributed significantly to music heard on the continent.

These styles range from South African jazz, which describes a range of music from early marabi-

The South African Music Awards ceremony was held in April 2005. The winners were:
- Best African Gospel Album – Deborah for *Ngixolele*
- Best Contemporary Gospel Album – Joyous Celebration for *Joyous Celebration 8*
- Best South African Traditional Jazz – McCoy Mrubata for *Livumile Icamagu*
- Best Contemporary Jazz Album – Tlala Makhene
- Best Adult Contemporary Album – Thandiswa Mazwai for *Zabalaza*
- Best Adult Contemporary Album Afrikaans – Coenie de Villiers
- Best Adult Contemporary Album English – Nianell
- Best Music Video – Supervillain for *Indoda* by Mandoza
- Best Pop Album – Mandoza and Danny K for *Same Difference*
- Best Rock Album – Sugardrive
- Best Dance Album – Lebo Mathosa for *Drama Queen*
- Best Rap Album – Mr Selwyn
- Best Afro Pop – Mafikizolo
- Best Newcomer – Simphiwe Dana
- Best Duo or Group – Revolution
- Best Kwaito Album – Brown Dash
- Best Female Artist – Thandiswa Mazwai
- Best Male Artist – Themba Mkhize
- Song of the Year – Brown Dash for *Phansi Komthunzi Welanga*

118

inspired sounds in the late-1930s and 1940s by bands like the Merry Blackbirds Orchestra, to current performers such as trumpeter Hugh Masekela and others.

Kwaito music is very popular. It combines elements of rap, reggae, hip-hop and other musical styles into a distinctly South African style. Popular kwaito musicians include Arthur Mafokate, Mzekezeke, Bongo Maffin, Zola, Skwatta Kamp, Mandoza and Mdu.

Music is one of the key cultural industries identified in the *Cultural Industrial Growth Strategy Report,* and government has committed itself to harnessing its potential. In addition to its cultural value, music plays an important economic role in the country, generating significant copyright revenue.

In music, the department has solid foundations to build on. These include the annual South African

The Department of Arts and Culture is involved in the South African Presidential Initiative of South African and Malian Co-operation on the Timbuktu Manuscripts. This has been adopted as a New Partnership for Africa's Development Cultural Project.

The historically important West African town of Timbuktu was once a regional centre of commerce and scholarship.

The Timbuktu manuscripts cover a range of subjects, including astronomy, optics, chemistry, mathematics, botany, traditional medicines, law, philosophy, conflict resolution and musicology. The immediate challenge is to preserve and conserve this wealth of knowledge.

South Africa has been involved in the training of Malian conservators working at the Ahmed Baba Centre, Timbuktu. Hosted by the National Archives of South Africa, five conservators were trained at the Conservation Studios, Pretoria, and at the National Library, Cape Town.

The project also aims to raise funds in South Africa to rebuild and restore the Ahmed Baba Centre. A team of South African architects, engineers and builders have visited Mali to initiate the construction programme.

This forms part of reclaiming and embracing Africa's rich cultural heritage. South African and Malian leaders believe that the manuscripts will stimulate academic study and research in a range of subjects.

Music Week, the in-school education programme run in conjunction with the Department of Education, and the Music in Public Spaces Initiative.

The department's three-year plan for music includes establishing a legal aid facility for musicians, setting up a benevolent fund for artists, establishing a music industry export council, and implementing a levy on blank tapes. It also aimed to introduce a regulatory framework in 2005 to standardise contracts and work permits for musicians.

The Cape Town International Jazz Festival secured South Africa's position on the international jazz circuit when it was hosted on African soil for the first time in March 2001.

Indigenous music

The department funds the annual National Traditional Dance and Music Festival called *Zindala Zombili,* under the auspices of the African Cultural Heritage Trust. This platform showcases and promotes the rich and diverse indigenous traditional dance and music of South Africa.

The festival consists of 22 regional and eight provincial competitions, culminating in a national festival.

Dance

South African dance is unique in its vitality and energy. More and more South African dance companies, individual dancers and choreographers are being invited to perform at festivals throughout Europe, Australia and the United States of America (USA).

Contemporary work ranges from normal preconceptions of movement and performance art or performance theatre, to the completely unconventional.

Added to this is the African experience, which includes traditional dance inspired by wedding ceremonies, battles, rituals and the trifles of everyday life.

An informal but highly versatile performance venue in Johannesburg, The Dance Factory, provides a permanent platform for a variety of dance and movement groups.

The Wits Theatre (part of the University of the Witwatersrand) is also a popular dance venue. It is home to the annual First National Bank (FNB) Dance Umbrella.

This annual festival of contemporary choreography and dance offers a free platform for original new work, to promote the development of creative talent on every level.

The FNB Dance Umbrella hosts community and youth groups, young up-and-coming choreographers and established South African and international dance companies.

The FNB Dance Umbrella 2005, held in February and March, featured 19 programmes of work that was representative of all forms of contemporary South African choreography and dance − including 10 commissioned new works.

The Cape Town City Ballet, started in 1934 as the University of Cape Town Ballet Company, is the oldest ballet company in the country.

Visual arts

Art galleries in South Africa's major cities, such as the Durban Art Gallery in KwaZulu-Natal; the Johannesburg Art Gallery in Gauteng; the South African National Gallery in Cape Town; and the King George VI Gallery in Port Elizabeth in the Eastern Cape, showcase collections of indigenous, historical and contemporary works.

Universities also play an important role in acquiring artwork of national interest. These include, among others, collections housed in the Gertrude Posel Gallery of the University of the Witwatersrand, the University of South Africa (UNISA) gallery in Pretoria, the Edoardo Villa Museum and other galleries at the University of Pretoria, a collection of contemporary Indian art at the University of Durban-Westville and a collection of medieval and early Renaissance wood sculptures, as well as some fine examples of German expressionist graphic art, at the University of Stellenbosch. There are also several corporate collections of national interest, including those of Standard Bank, Absa Bank and the MTN cellular phone network.

The Department of Arts and Culture supports a number of projects that promote the visual arts. These range from arts publications and women-empowerment programmes to national and international exhibitions and infrastructure funding.

Photography

With its scenic beauty, abundant wildlife, diversity of cultures and rich historical heritage, South Africa is a photographers' paradise. Many South African photographers have been acclaimed for their work, which feature in coffee-table books, documentaries, local and overseas exhibitions, magazines and newspapers.

National and international photographic exhibitions and competitions are held in South Africa annually, and various national awards are bestowed on local photographers. South Africa is especially well-known for its excellent wildlife photography. The Agfa Wildlife & Environment Photographic Awards, presented for the first time in 1981, has become one of Africa's most prestigious wildlife photographic competitions, attracting entries from top wildlife photographers, not only from Africa, but throughout the world.

Architecture

South Africa has a rich architectural heritage to which all the cultural groups in the country have contributed. Through the centuries, a trend in South

The 2005 New Music Indaba, held during the National Arts Festival in July, in Grahamstown, examined the music of Africa under the theme *Reimagining Africa*.

The annual indaba is held under the auspices of New Music SA, the South African section of the International Society for Contemporary Music.

The 2005 indaba took participants on a virtual tour of the African continent, examining how composers construct their African identities.

The work of some 40 composers and improvisers, mostly African, but also from Europe and North America, featured in the course of 13 concerts.

The indaba marked the Enoch Sontonga centenary with the performance of different versions of his well-known *Nkosi Sikelel' iAfrika* throughout the event.

Africa's architectural style has developed, which has been referred to as an innovative marrying of traditions. Today, this is evident in the variety of architectural structures found all over the country, ranging from humble dwellings, historical homesteads and public buildings, to modern commercial buildings reflecting state-of-the-art technology and designs that are on a par with the best in the world. Schools of architecture exist within various South African universities, including the universities of Pretoria, Stellenbosch, Natal, Cape Town and the Witwatersrand.

The SAHRA conserves buildings of historical or architectural value. More than 4 000 buildings, sites and other objects (including trees) have been declared national monuments.

Heritage South Africa is a non-profit private organisation that conserves South Africa's variety of architectural gems.

Rock art

There are many traces of ancient cultures that existed in the country in the distant past. The San people left a priceless and unique collection of Stone Age paintings and engravings in South Africa, which is also the largest in the world. The mountains, especially the Drakensberg range and those in the Cape, are home to fascinating rock art panels.

Rock engravings are scattered on flat rock surfaces and boulders throughout the interior. The artworks mainly depict hunter-gatherers and their relationship with the animal world and historical events, as well as interaction with and observation of new-

In 2006, the Publisher's Association of South Africa will team up with the Frankfurt Book Fair to host the first Cape Town Book Fair.

In 2004, the Frankfurt Book Fair attracted 270 413 visitors and 6 691 exhibitors from 110 countries.

The Cape Town Book Fair, to be held in June 2006, is expected to attract similar numbers of visitors.

comers encroaching upon their living space. Indigenous people with spears and Nguni cattle, Khoikhoin fat-tailed sheep, European settlers on horseback with rifles and wagons, and ships and soldiers in uniform were captured in surprising detail.

Immortalised visions of the artists' spiritual world are found on the sandstone canvases. These depict complex symbols and metaphors to illustrate the supernatural powers and potency they received from nature.

The oldest dated rock art in South Africa, an engraved stone, was discovered in a living floor some 10 200 years old at the Wonderwerk Cave near Kuruman in the Northern Cape.

The oldest painted stones (6 400 years) were recovered at Boomplaas Cave in the Cango Valley near Oudtshoorn.

Three painted stones were also found at the Klasies River caves, which yielded the second-oldest painted stone, dating back 3 900 years.

The Department of Arts and Culture supports a number of projects, including a rock heritage project in Clanwilliam in the Western Cape.

Crafts

The crafts industry in South Africa employs over 1,2 million people and generates an income of R3,5 billion a year. The crafts they produce are exported all over the world.

The development of South Africa's crafts industry is an ongoing priority for government, through the Department of Arts and Culture. Numerous stakeholders are involved in various initiatives to develop this sector.

The National Crafts Development Initiative, spearheaded by the NAC and supported by several national bodies, is one such example, providing a platform for developing the local market by staging craft fairs at various levels.

As a joint venture with the Department of Trade and Industry, the Department of Arts and Culture is developing a craft marketing strategy geared at enhancing export opportunities to curb the exploitation of crafters.

Examples of successful craft projects include the rural development projects in Limpopo, where the Council for Scientific and Industrial Research (CSIR) linked with various rural craft projects to develop new products. In Thohoyandou, in Limpopo, the Ifa textile project is producing fashionable handbags in traditional Venda designs. Crafters of the Lubombo Spatial Development Initiative in northern KwaZulu-Natal have incorporated minimal interventions in their designs to produce butter dishes, thus creating new marketing opportunities.

The department has 115 craft projects in all nine provinces. The products of these and other projects can be viewed at a number of venues, including two state-assisted outlets at the Bus Factory in Newtown, Johannesburg and the Boardwalk in Port Elizabeth.

Design

The Department of Arts and Culture has launched a number of initiatives aimed at creating centres of expertise. These have promoted collaborative ventures between the private and public sectors in areas of product design and the use of computer-aided design engineering. The initiatives involve the following:

- The launch of the National Product Development Centre at the CSIR. This initiative operates within a national framework, optimising the contributions of service-providers throughout the country in the area of design technology.
- The launch of the computer-aided design initiative at the CSIR, which is linked to the technology station at the Free State University of Technology, as well as similar institutions in KwaZulu-Natal and the Eastern Cape.
- The establishment of the Cape Craft and Design Institute.
- The award of design learnerships through CREATE SA to help emerging designers.
- The annual Design Indaba Conference and Expo held in Cape Town in February. The indaba is regarded as one of the premier design events in the world. The expo is a gallery, a marketplace, a school and a theatre showcasing the finest

In March 2005, the Minister of Arts and Culture, Dr Pallo Jordan, paid tribute to Prof. Mazisi Kunene in Durban, the winner of the South African National Laureate Prize, for his role in the preservation of African literature and history through poetry.

original South African design, covering everything from homeware and jewellery to architecture, fashion, film, multimedia and graphic design.

Literature

South Africa has a vibrant and rich oral tradition. This form of expression goes back many centuries, and has been passed down from generation to generation as an important way of sharing advice, remembering history, telling stories and reflecting on contemporary society.

The African Languages Literary Museum at UNISA caters for all indigenous languages. Featured authors include Prof. Maja Serudu, E.M. Ramaila, O.K. Matsepe and Semakaleng Monyaise. The museum also features books, manuscripts, old typewriters used by certain African writers, antiques, and authors' portraits.

There is an English literary museum in Grahamstown and an Afrikaans museum in Bloemfontein.

The Print Industries Cluster Council established a writer's network in 2000.

In February 2005, Ladysmith Black Mambazo won the award for Best Traditional World Music Album at the 47th annual Grammy Awards in Los Angeles, United States of America. The group sold over six million albums, making it the number-one record seller in Africa.

In a career spanning 30 years, the group has been nominated for nine Grammys. Its previous Grammy win was in 1987 for the album *Shaka Zulu*.

The National Language Service of the Department of Arts and Culture is encouraging the emergence of new literary magazines in English, Afrikaans and all the African languages. The department plans on consulting with publishers about the development of a national strategy to promote a reading culture in South Africa.

The department will also be addressing the challenge of preserving indigenous language writings dating from the mid-19th century. To achieve this, it will embark on initiatives to reproduce these old works in various African languages.

A comprehensive study on the print industry, funded by the Print Industries Cluster Council, established that the industry has an estimated annual turnover of R1,5 billion, pays royalties to some 8 309 authors/other parties, and employs more than 3 000 people.

In an effort to promote the craft of writing, particularly in indigenous languages, the Department of Arts and Culture is collaborating with Skotaville Media to establish a project that focuses on publishing emerging writers in all languages and across all genres. The key objective of this project is to assist previously marginalised writers, to begin a process of engaging publishers countrywide in addressing key social issues beyond profit, and to help develop indigenous languages.

The project kicked off in January 2005 and by April 2005, 60 manuscripts had been received. Thirty manuscripts in indigenous languages were being considered for publication.

The department has endorsed the concept of a literary heroes campaign, a project that will give recognition to writers who have made a significant

In March 2005, South African films won several awards at the Fespaco Film Festival. *Drum*, by Zola Maseko, won the Best Feature Film Award. *Zulu Love Letter* won the Award for Best Actress (Pamela Nomvete), as well as the European Union Award. *Max and Mona*, created by Teddy Mattera, won the Award for Best First Feature Film.

contribution to the development of South African literature in all the languages recognised by the Constitution of the Republic of South Africa, 1996 (Act 108 of 1996).

The Department of Arts and Culture commissioned the Print Industries Cluster Council to conduct research on intellectual property rights in the print industries sector. This forms part of a broader initiative to identify policy and development needs in the cultural industries.

This initiative will be followed by the development of a national book policy, which will serve as a legal instrument providing a comprehensive framework to guide activities in the book and publishing industry. Such a policy will help to create the foundation necessary for establishing, developing and sustaining a viable national publishing industry that encourages the development of indigenous African languages.

Government established PanSALB to help promote the recognition, use and development of all official languages, with the emphasis on the previously disadvantaged indigenous languages.

The department has established language research and development centres for each official indigenous language. These centres focus, among other things, on the promotion of reading and writing in African languages. The department has budgeted R250 000 for each of these centres.

They work in collaboration with writers' associations and any other NGOs actively involved with writers' associations or individual authors. Workshops and seminars will be conducted to help those who are interested in indigenous languages.

Some R2 million has been dedicated to a pilot project aimed at developing literature in indigenous African languages. The department aims to identify and nurture new talent by creating an annual literary prize for new creative work in the indigenous languages, and will also offer an annual prize for established writers in indigenous languages.

About R1 million was set aside for the National Literature Exhibition, which was opened in May 2005.

In May 2005, the Minister of Arts and Culture, Dr Pallo Jordan, launched and presented the Literary Awards in Johannesburg, a first for Africa.

The awards, which recognise all official languages, promote the writing and reading of South African literature. Some of the lifetime achievers who received the first awards are:

- Prof. B. Breytenbach in Afrikaans
- Ms M. Poland in English
- Mr O.K. Matsepe, posthumously in Sesotho sa Leboa (Sepedi)
- Mr M.J. Ntsime in Setswana
- Mr K.P.D. Maphalla in Sesotho
- Prof. P.T. Mtuze in isiXhosa
- Prof. D.B.Z. Ntuli in isiZulu
- Mr B.D. Masango in isiNdebele
- Mr T.N. Maumela in Tshivenda
- Dr G.A. Malindzisa in siSwati
- Mr B.K.M. Ntombeni in Xitsonga.

Film

The South African film industry, which is centred mainly in Cape Town and Johannesburg, generates some R518 million a year. The industry has a strong skills base, boasting more than 1 000 registered producers. Outstanding production and post-production facilities are also in place. The cost of film production in South Africa is 30% to 40% lower than in the USA, and 20% lower than in Australia.

The NFVF was established in terms of the NFVF Act, 1997 (Act 73 of 1997), to develop and promote the film and video industry in South Africa. It provides and promotes opportunities for people from disadvantaged communities to participate in the industry. The NFVF also promotes local film and video productions, supports the development of and access to the industry, and addresses historical imbalances in infrastructure, skills and resources in the industry.

During 2004, the NFVF allocated R36,9 million for the production of films and the development of the film industry. It was also involved in the development of projects that appeal to targeted audiences and have greater commercial returns. It ensured a South African presence at international film markets, festivals, trade fairs and exhibitions.

The foundation aims to attract more foreign and local investment in the film industry by making available and managing training and development

grants, establishing a national strategy for film education and training, and ensuring that research is conducted into audience appeal.

During 2004/05, the foundation received R34,7 million, including a once-off payment of R11,9 million to implement the Film Fund to support the local film industry.

The NFVF also participated in the Independent Communications Authority of South Africa's inquiry into local content targets for broadcasting and other initiatives throughout the country that aim to boost the film and video industry.

Strategic initiatives undertaken by the NFVF include the establishment of the Sectoral Information System, Demand Simulation and Audience Development and the development of local content.

The industry received a major boost with the launch of the Film and Television Production Rebate by the Department of Trade and Industry in June 2004.

The rebate complements existing support measures. It aims to provide for the production of both foreign and local large-budget films made in South Africa or under co-production agreements.

For a company to be eligible for the rebate, it must be a South African resident company, or a non-South African resident company with a South African business registration that is operating with a permanent establishment in the country.

A number of large South African media companies have acquired production companies to increase their capabilities in the media and entertainment sector. The increase in the number of television channels available to South African viewers has resulted in an increased demand for local programming, due to local-content quotas. In South Africa, locally produced television productions are extremely popular with viewers.

South African broadcasters are exploring opportunities to distribute local productions in the rest of Africa through direct sales and a form of bartering, where content is exchanged for advertising airtime. This is expected to increase the demand for locally produced television content.

The three largest film distributors in South Africa are Ster-Kinekor, United International Pictures and

Nu-Metro. Ster-Kinekor has a specialised art circuit called Cinema Nouveau with theatres in Johannesburg, Cape Town, Durban and Pretoria.

Film festivals include the Sithengi Film and Video Festival and Market in Cape Town; the Durban Film Festival; the North West Film Festival; the Apollo Film Festival in Victoria West; the Three Continents Film Festival (specialising in African, South American and Asian films); the Soweto Film Festival, established in 2004; and the Encounters Documentary Festival, which alternates between Cape Town and Johannesburg.

Film and Publication Board

The Films and Publications Act, 1996 (Act 65 of 1996), as amended by the Films and Publications Amendment Act, 1999 (Act 34 of 1999), provides for the regulation of films and publications intended for distribution and/or exhibition in South Africa.

The Act recognises the right of all South Africans to freely choose what they wish to watch or read. It encroaches on constitutional rights and freedom only where there is a risk of harm. The Act allows for the invasion of privacy only where child pornography is concerned. The implementation of the Act has been entrusted to the Film and Publication Board, which consists of members appointed through a process of public nominations.

The Film and Publication Board no longer censors, but instead classifies movies for age appropriateness. Its main focus is to protect children from harmful and disturbing material, while allowing

The National Conference Against Child Pornography under the guiding theme *United Against Child Pornography*, was held in June 2005 at Coega Conference Centre, Eastern Cape.

The 300 delegates attending the conference adopted a declaration and committed all organs of civil society, government and the private sector to take radical steps to combat the scourge of child pornography in all its manifestations.

adults to make informed decisions about what they do and do not want to watch, or allow their children to watch or not to watch. There is no pre-classification of magazines. Publications are classified only when a valid complaint about a certain publication is lodged with the board.

In terms of legislation, the board may ban the distribution of visual material containing:
• sexual acts involving persons under the age of 18 years or who appear to be under the age of 18 years
• bestiality
• explicit violent acts that promote violence
• material that promotes religious hatred
• explicit violent acts coupled with sexual conduct.

Although such material, classified as XX, is only banned from distribution, the possession of child pornography is a criminal offence. People found guilty of possessing child pornography face up to five years in prison for each item found. The Act has been amended to include the regulation and control of child pornography on the Internet, and a more precise definition of what constitutes child porno-graphy. The Act also provides for the regulation of trade in previously banned, sexually explicit material. Adult shops that do not comply with the pro-visions of the Act may be closed for up to a year.

The Films and Publications Amendment Act, 2004 (Act 18 of 2004), provides for the prohibition of child pornography and for more effective investigation and prosecution of child pornography offenders.

The Act also seeks to:
• amend the definition of child pornography, as the current definition is limited to images and the display of genitals
• bring Internet service-providers within its jurisdiction insofar as child pornography is concerned
• impose an obligation on persons who have material which is potentially disturbing and harmful to children, to take reasonable steps to prevent access to such material by children
• increase the maximum prison sentence for offences involving child pornography from five to 10 years.

During 2003/04, the board classified 3 424 films and interactive computer games. As part of its efforts to protect children from being used in child pornography, the board has established a hotline for members of the public to report child pornography.

Compliance inspectors have been appointed in the major cities to monitor distributors on site to ensure that films are distributed in compliance with the provisions of the Act.

Inspectors have been appointed in Cape Town, Port Elizabeth, Durban and Johannesburg. This will be extended to other areas in the country during the next financial year. The board is funded by an annual transfer: R6,8 million in 2005/06; R7,2 million in 2006/07; and R7,7 million in 2007/08.

Museums

Museums are the windows to the natural and cultural heritage of a country. South Africa can justifiably be called the museum country of Africa, with the earliest of its museums dating back to the first half of the 19th century.

Today, more than 300 of the approximately 1 000 museums in Africa are situated in South Africa. They range from museums of geology, history, the biological sciences and the arts, to mining, agriculture, forestry and many other disciplines.

Most of the country's national museums are declared cultural institutions (national museums that have framework autonomy and are managed by their own councils), and fall under the overall jurisdiction of the Department of Arts and Culture. They receive an annual subsidy from the department, but are otherwise autonomous.

In terms of the Cultural Institutions Act, 1998 (Act 119 of 1998), the declared museum institutions in Gauteng and Cape Town have been grouped together into two new organisations, known as flagship institutions. While the components of these two museum flagships (the museums from which they have been constituted) continue to operate as semi-independent museums regarding their core functions (collection, preservation, research and education), other functions, particularly administration,

financing and human resource management, have been centralised.

The following museums report to the Minister of Arts and Culture in terms of the Act:
• Northern Flagship Institution, Pretoria
• Iziko museums, Cape Town
• Natal Museum, Pietermaritzburg
• National Museum, Bloemfontein
• Afrikaanse Taalmuseum, Paarl
• National English Literary Museum, Grahamstown
• Voortrekker Museum, Pietermaritzburg
• War Museum of the Boer Republics, Bloemfontein
• Robben Island Museum, Cape Town
• William Humphreys Art Gallery, Kimberley
• Engelenburg House Art Collection, Pretoria
• Nelson Mandela Museum, Umtata.

The Northern Flagship consists of the National Cultural History Museum (NCHM) and its former satellite museums (Kruger House, Tswaing Crater Museum, Willem Prinsloo Agricultural Museum, Pioneer Museum, Sammy Marks Museum and the Coert Steynberg Museum), the Transvaal Museum of Natural History in Pretoria, and the South African

In February 2005, *U-Carmen eKhayelitsha*, the acclaimed version of Bizet's opera, *Carmen*, set in the context of Cape Town's Khayelitsha township, won the prestigious Golden Bear Award at the 55th Berlin Film Festival in Germany.

The South African film *Yesterday* was nominated for an Academy Award in the category Best Foreign Film in 2005. *Yesterday* was funded by various South African bodies, including the National Film and Video Foundation.

Hotel Rwanda, a co-production partnership involving South Africa, Italy and the United Kingdom, was also nominated for an Oscar award.

Cecelia Bobak was nominated for an Oscar for set-design for the film *Phantom of the Opera*.

Later in 2005, *Tsotsi*, directed by Gavin Woods, won the Standard Life Award and the Michael Powel Award for Best Film at the Edinburgh Festival and the People's Choice Award at the Toronto Film Festival, respectively. It is South Africa's official submission for the 2006 Academy Awards for Best Foreign Film.

National Museum of Military History in Johannesburg.

The Southern Flagship (renamed Iziko museums of Cape Town) consists of the South African Museum, South African Cultural History Museum and its satellite museums, the South African National Gallery, the William Fehr Collection and the Michaelis Collection.

In terms of the Cultural Institutions Act, 1998, the declared museums in other provinces continue to operate as before. These include the National Museum and the Anglo-Boer War Museum (Bloemfontein); the William Humphreys Art Gallery (Kimberley); the Natal Museum and the Voortrekker Museum (Pietermaritzburg); and the South African Institute for Aquatic Biodiversity in Grahamstown.

The Act also provides for the National Museums Division, comprising the flagship museums and other declared museums.

The Robben Island Museum was established as a national monument and museum, and declared South Africa's first World Heritage Site in 1999. Guided tours are offered to historical sites on the island, including the cell in which former President Mandela was imprisoned. The Robben Island Museum has its own council and is a separate declared institution, independent of Iziko.

Apart from the declared museums that fall under the department, there are also a number of other national museums, which are administered by central government departments or research councils. Notable examples are the Museum of the Council for Geoscience (Pretoria); the Theiler Veterinary Science Museum at Onderstepoort (Pretoria); the South African Air Force Museum at Air Force Base Zwartkop (Pretoria) with its satellites in Cape Town, Port Elizabeth and Durban; the Museum of the Department of Correctional Services (Pretoria); and the Porcinarium (the world's first pig museum) outside Pretoria on the Irene Campus of the Agricultural Research Council.

A number of museums fall directly or indirectly under the provincial government departments responsible for arts and culture. In some provinces, these museums render museum-support services at provincial level, while other provinces, notably Gauteng, KwaZulu-Natal, Western Cape and the Free State, have separate museum-service organisations.

However, many museum and heritage services are also rendered by the declared national museums on a consultancy basis. Many municipalities also manage museums. Other museums fall under universities and university departments, or are owned and managed by private-sector companies, NGOs and individuals.

The largest museums are situated in Johannesburg, Pretoria, Cape Town, Durban, Pietermaritzburg and Bloemfontein. The best-known natural history collections in South Africa are housed in the Iziko museums and the Northern Flagship Institution, as well as in the following:

• Natal Museum, Pietermaritzburg
• National Museum, Bloemfontein
• McGregor Museum, Kimberley
• East London Museum
• South African Institute for Aquatic Biodiversity, Grahamstown
• Port Elizabeth Museum
• Durban Museum of Natural History.

The best-known cultural-history collections are housed in the Iziko museums and the Northern Flagship Institution, as well as in the following:

• National Museum, Bloemfontein
• Natal Museum, Pietermaritzburg
• Durban Local History Museum
• Museum Africa, Johannesburg.

Among the art museums are the following:

• South African National Gallery, Cape Town
• Johannesburg Art Gallery
• Pretoria Art Museum
• William Humphreys Art Gallery, Kimberley.

The South African Cultural History Museum in Cape Town houses the oldest cultural history collection in the country.

The South African Museum (Cape Town) showcases the natural history of South Africa, as well as relics of the early human inhabitants of the subcontinent. The huge Whale Hall houses possibly the most impressive of all its exhibitions. This is the only collection in South Africa with a planetarium attached to it.

The Transvaal Museum in Pretoria houses the skull of Mr Ples (until recently believed to be Mrs Ples), a 2,5-million-year-old hominid fossil, and depicts the origin and development of life in South Africa, from the most primitive unicellular form of life to the emergence of mammals and the first human beings. It has a collection of early human fossils.

The Tswaing Meteorite Crater is situated to the north-west of Pretoria. It supports the Presidential imperatives by combining a museum with a cultural-development initiative.

The NCHM (former African Window) in Pretoria is a centre for the preservation and promotion of the culture and heritage of all South Africans. It explores cultural diversity and commonalities, links the present and the past to offer a better understanding of both, and nurtures the living culture of all South Africans.

Mining is best represented by the De Beers Museum at the Big Hole in Kimberley, where visitors can view the biggest hole ever made by man with pick and shovel. It includes an open-air museum, which houses many buildings dating back to the era of the diamond diggings.

Another important mining museum is at Pilgrim's Rest, Mpumalanga, where the first economically viable goldfield was discovered. The entire village has been conserved and restored.

Agriculture in South Africa is depicted mainly at two museums. These are Kleinplasie in Worcester, Western Cape, which showcases the wine culture and the characteristic architecture of the winelands; and the Willem Prinsloo Agricultural Museum between Pretoria and Bronkhorstspruit in Gauteng. This museum comprises two 'house' museums, and runs educational programmes based on their extensive collection of early farming implements, vehicles of yesteryear, and indigenous farm animals.

The Absa Museum and Archives in Johannesburg, which belongs to Amalgamated Banks of South Africa (Absa), aims to preserve the banking group's more than 110 years of history. It also houses a unique and very valuable coin and banknote collection.

The Apartheid Museum in Johannesburg offers a realistic view of the political situation in South Africa during the 1970s and 1980s. Exhibitions in the museum feature, among other things, audio-visual footage recorded during the apartheid era.

One of the most common types of museum in South Africa is the 'house' museum. Examples include an entire village nucleus in Stellenbosch; an example of the lifestyle of the wealthy wine farmer in Groot Constantia in the Western Cape; the mansion of the millionaire industrialist Sammy Marks, outside Pretoria; the Victorian affluence mirrored in Melrose House, Pretoria; and the Kruger House Museum in Pretoria, former residence of President Paul Kruger.

Simpler architectural variations have not been neglected, for instance the pioneer-dwelling in Silverton, Pretoria, and the humble farmhouse at Suikerbosrand near Heidelberg in Gauteng. There are several open-air museums, which showcase the black cultures of the country, for example Tsongakraal near Letsitele, Limpopo; the Ndebele Museum in Middelburg, Mpumalanga; the Bakone Malapa Museum in Polokwane, Limpopo; and the South Sotho Museum in Witsieshoek, Free State.

South Africa has two national military history museums. The South African Museum for Military History in Johannesburg reflects the military history of the country, while the War Museum in Bloemfontein depicts the Anglo-Boer/South African War in particular. The famous battlefields of KwaZulu-Natal, the Northern Cape and North West are also worth a visit.

The work of the War-Graves Division of the SAHRA includes the upkeep of the graves of victims of the struggle for South Africa's liberation.

Archives and heraldry

Archives of governmental bodies are transferred to archive repositories after a period of 20 years, and are accessible to the public and the office of origin. National Archives functions in terms of the National Archives and Records Service of South Africa Act, 1996 (Act 43 of 1996).

The National Archives in Pretoria includes the National Film, Video and Sound Archives (NAFVSA). Its primary functions are to obtain and preserve films, videotapes and sound recordings of archival value, and to make these available for research and reference purposes.

The archives of central government are preserved in the National Archives' repository in Pretoria. Provincial archive repositories in Pretoria, Cape Town, Pietermaritzburg, Durban, Ulundi, Umtata, Port Elizabeth and Bloemfontein house archives dating from before 1910, as well as the relevant provincial archives. Record centres for archives younger than 20 years exist in Pretoria, Bloemfontein and Cape Town.

The retrieval of information from archives is facilitated by the national automated archival information system (*www.national.archives.gov.za*), which includes national registers of manuscripts, photographs and audio-visual material. National Archives also renders a comprehensive record-management service for current records, aimed at promoting efficient administration.

During 2004, National Archives collaborated with the South African Bureau of Standards to adopt a national standard for records management.

National Archives is responsible for collecting non-public records with enduring value of national significance. In so doing, it is obliged to pay special attention to aspects of the nation's experience neglected by archives of the past.

The Oral History Project seeks to build the National Archives' capacity to document the spoken word, and to develop a national oral history programme. The automated National Register of Oral Sources is an important element of the project.

The Act also provides government with a measure of control over private collections. Archives are taken to the people through co-ordinated national and provincial archive services. At the same time, National Archives is responsible for ensuring effective, transparent and accountable management of all public records as far as possible.

The Bureau of Heraldry is responsible for the registration of coats of arms; badges and other emblems such as flags, seals, medals and insignia of rank and offices of order; as well as the registration of names and uniforms (colours) of associations and organisations, such as universities.

Library and Information Services (LIS) sector

South African libraries have developed over a period of more than 150 years. The world's first free public library service was established here by Lord Charles Somerset in 1820, by levying a tax on the sale of wine. When he returned to England, tax reforms by the new governor spelt the end of the free library; but it formed the basis of what is today the National Library of South Africa (NLSA) in Cape Town.

By 1900, subscription libraries were operating in most towns and cities, financed by annual membership fees and, in most cases, grants from local authorities. An investigation in the 1930s by the Carnegie Corporation of New York found that most of these libraries were inadequate and poorly funded. The necessity for government support to ensure free public libraries was recognised.

By the 1950s, all four provinces of the Union of South Africa had ordinances that set out the functions of local and provincial government, and public library development gathered momentum.

In 1985, librarians commissioned UNISA to investigate the role that libraries could and should play in developing South Africa. The result was that greater emphasis was placed on providing material that would support formal and informal education. Outreach programmes to schools and pre-schools received priority. Many libraries also started presenting literacy classes for adults.

South Africa's growing LIS sector includes a national library, public/community libraries, special libraries, government libraries and Higher Education (HE) libraries. By mid-2003, South Africa had more than 11 373 libraries, with 77 HE libraries, 9 416 school libraries, 79 government departmental libraries, one national library with two branches, and 1 800 public libraries provided by provincial and local government (library services and metro libraries). Less than 10% of secondary schools had school libraries.

Provincial library services

The nine provincial library authorities provide, in

partnership with local governments, extensive public library services. Public libraries, among other services, increasingly render community and general information services, and provide study material and facilities for school and tertiary students.

The approximately 1 800 public libraries in the country have to provide services to a total population of about 44,8 million. According to Census 2001 figures, this translates into one library service point for every 25 000 people.

Library services at national level

Meta-information
The Subdirectorate: Meta-Information of the Department of Arts and Culture is the national focal point within national government that handles certain policy matters pertaining to LIS at national level. Meta-information means information about information.

The subdirectorate is located within the National Archives, Records, Meta-Information, and Heraldic Services Chief Directorate of the Department of Arts and Culture and reports to the National Archivist.

The vision of the subdirectorate is to create and maintain an effective meta-information system that promotes access to information, ensuring that all communities participate in the information society, thereby contributing to the development of the country.

Its mission is to advise the Minister of Arts and Culture on the development, co-ordination and maintenance of the national meta-information policy and infrastructure.

The national meta-information system in South Africa consists of various types of libraries and other information organisations and is enabled by a legislative framework. The subdirectorate's remit, within this framework, pertains specifically to:
- the National Council for Library and Information Services (NCLIS)
- the NLSA
- the South African Library for the Blind (Blindlib)
- the Legal Deposit Committee and those libraries and archives that function as places of legal deposit and/or official publication depositories

- Blind SA (formerly the South African Blind Workers' Organisation) and the Braille Services Trust, as well as the South African National Council for the Blind regarding Braille projects.

National Council for Library and Information Services
The NCLIS was established in terms of the NCLIS Act, 2001 (Act 6 of 2001) (Annexure A). The NCLIS advises the ministers of arts and culture and of education on matters relating to LIS in order to support and stimulate the socio-economic, educational, cultural, recreational, scientific research, technological and information development of all communities in the country. The functions of the council are to develop and co-ordinate LIS in the country.

National Library of South Africa
The NLSA was formed on 1 November 1999 through the NLSA Act, 1998 (Act 92 of 1998), with the amalgamation of the State Library in Pretoria and the South African Library in Cape Town.

The functions of the NLSA are to build a complete collection of published documents emanating from or relating to South Africa, to maintain and preserve the collections and to provide access to them through bibliographic, reference, information and interlibrary-lending services; and to promote information awareness and information literacy. The Centre for the Book in Cape Town, a specialised unit, promotes the culture of reading, writing and publishing in all South Africa's official languages.

In terms of the Legal Deposit Act, 1997 (Act 54 of 1997), the NLSA, as one of five legal deposit libraries, receives two copies of each book, periodical, newspaper, map, manuscript material or other publication that is published in South Africa in any medium, print or electronic, for its campuses in Pretoria and Cape Town.

South African Library for the Blind
Blindlib is a statutory organisation located in Grahamstown. Its object is to provide, free of charge as far as is reasonably possible, a national LIS to serve blind and print-handicapped readers in South

Africa. It is partly state-funded and depends for the remainder of its financial needs on soliciting funds from the private sector and the general public.

Blindlib also produces documents in special media such as Braille and audio formats. It develops standards for the production of such documents and researches production methods and technology in the appropriate fields. It also acquires, manufactures and disseminates the technology needed by people with print disabilities to read.

The vision of Blindlib is based on five broad objectives, namely to significantly contribute to:

- helping build a nation of readers
- assisting the organised blind community
- improving the lives of individuals with print disabilities by meeting their information needs
- helping the State to discharge its cultural mandate and its obligations to blind people
- Africa's development by providing advice, expertise and documents in accessible formats for blind persons and the institutions that serve their information needs.

The Department of Arts and Culture is erecting a R160-million building to house the National Library of South Africa in Pretoria. The project will be executed by the Department of Public Works.

There will be about 33 000 usable square metres of space for its book collections, reading rooms and other facilities currently scattered in various premises around Pretoria.

The building will provide about 1 800 seats for library users, a marked improvement on the 130 seats available now.

The site will become part of the Government Boulevard, linking the city centre with the Union Buildings. Its central location will benefit the many users who rely on public transport.

Blind SA

Blind SA is an organisation of the blind governed by the blind and is located in Johannesburg. One of its prime objectives is to provide services for blind and partially sighted individuals to uplift and empower them by publishing books, magazines and other documents in Braille. Blind SA provides:

- study bursaries for blind and partially-sighted students
- interest-free loans (for adaptive equipment)
- information (free Braille magazines)
- assistance to find sustainable employment
- advocacy (to act as a pressure group for disability rights)
- Braille publications at affordable prices in all official languages.

Braille is the only accessible format of reading for a blind person. The Braille Services Department of Blind SA produced 2,8 million pages during 2004 and subsidies exceeded R1 million.

Legal Deposit Act, 1997

The purpose of the Legal Deposit Act, 1997 is to:

- provide for the preservation of the national documentary heritage through legal deposit of published documents
- ensure the preservation and cataloguing of, and access to, published documents emanating from, or adapted for, South Africa
- provide for access to government information
- provide for a legal deposit committee
- provide for matters connected with it.

The places of legal deposit are: NLSA, Pretoria Campus; NLSA, Cape Town component; Mangaung Library Services; Msunduzi Municipal Library; Library of Parliament; and NAFVSA.

(See chapter 8: *Education*.)

Acknowledgements

BuaNews
Department of Arts and Culture
Department of Home Affairs
Estimates of National Expenditure 2005, published by the National Treasury
Film and Publication Board
National Cultural History Museum
Sunday Times
www.artsculturetrust.co.za
www.basa.co.za
www.createsa.org.za
www.gov.za
www.nac.org.za
www.sapa.org.za
www.southafrica.info

Suggested reading

African Compass: New Writing from Southern Africa. Compiled by J.M. Coetzee. Kenilworth: Spearhead, 2005.
African Posters: A Catalogue of the Basler Afrika Bibliographien. Compiled by G. Miescher and D. Henrichsen. Basel: Basler Afrika Bibliographien, 2004.
Agordoh, A.A. *Studies in African Music*. Ghana: New Age Publications, 1994.
Ansell, G. *Soweto Blues: Jazz, Popular Music and Politics in South Africa*. New York: Continuum, 2004.
Arnold, M. *Women and Art in South Africa*. Cape Town: David Philip, 1996.
Barry, S. *et al* (eds). *Ink and Boiling Point: A Selection of 21st Century Black Women's Writing from the Southern Tip of Africa*. Cape Town: Weave, 2002.
Bassett, S.T. *Rock Paintings of South Africa*. Cape Town: David Philip, 2001.
Becker, R. and Keene, R. *Art Routes: A Guide to South African Art Collections*. Johannesburg: Witwatersrand University Press, 2000.
Bedford, E. ed. *Decade of Democracy: South African Art 1994 – 2004*. Cape Town: Double Storey, 2004.
Berman, E. *Art and Artists of South Africa*. 3rd ed. Halfway House: Southern Book Publishers, 1992.
Berman, E. *Painting in South Africa*. Halfway House: Southern Book Publishers, 1993.
Blignaut, J. and Botha, M. *Movies, Moguls and Mavericks: South African Cinema, 1979 – 1991*. Cape Town: Vlaeberg, 1992.
Botha, M. and Van Aswegen, A.H. *Images of South Africa: The Rise of the Alternative Film*. Pretoria: Human Sciences Research Council (HSRC), 1992.
Breakey, B. and Gordon, S. *Beyond the Blues: Township Jazz in the '60s and '70s*. Cape Town: David Philip, 1997.
Brink, A. *Reinventing a Continent: Writing and Politics in South Africa, 1982 – 1995*. London: Secker and Warburg, 1996.
Brown, D. *Voicing the Text: South African Oral Poetry and Performance*. Cape Town: Oxford University Press Southern Africa, 2004.
Campbell, J. ed. *Directory of South African Contemporary Art Practices*. Cape Town: Contemporary Art Publishers, 1999.
Caplan, D. *In the Township Tonight: South Africa's Black City Music and Theatre in South Africa*. Johannesburg: Ravan, 1985.
Chapman, M. *Southern African Literatures*. Pietermaritzburg: University of Natal Press, 2003.
Cole, M. *Collectables*. Johannesburg: South African Antique Dealers Association and BDFM Publishers, 2003.
Contemporary South African Art: The Gencor Collection. Johannesburg: Jonathan Ball, 1997.
Crwys-Williams, J. *Penguin Dictionary of South African Quotations*. 2nd ed. Sandton: Penguin Books, 1999.
Daymond, M.J. *et al.* eds. *Women Writing Africa: The Southern Region*. Johannesburg: Witwatersrand University Press, 2004.
De Gruchy, J. ed. *London Missionary Society in Southern Africa: Historical Essays in Celebration of the Bicentenary of the LMS in Southern Africa, 1799 – 1999*. Cape Town: David Philip, 1999.

Deacon, H. *et al. The Subtle Power of Intangible Heritage: Legal and Financial Instruments for Safeguarding Intangible Heritage.* Cape Town: HSRC, 2004.

Diawara, M. *African Cinema: Politics and Culture.* Johannesburg: Witwatersrand University Press, 1992.

Dikeni, S. *Soul Fire: Writing the Transition.* Pietermaritzburg: University of Natal Press, 2002.

Directory of South African Contemporary Art. Vol. 1. (Painting, 1997/98). Stanford, Western Cape: Contemporary Arts Publishers, 1997.

Dissel, P. *Zebra Register of South African Artists and Galleries, Vol. 3.* Clarens: Derrick Dissel, 2003.

Du Preez, M. *Of Warriors, Lovers and Poets: Unusual Stories From South Africa's Past.* Cape Town: Zebra Press, 2004.

Fisher, R.C., le Roux, S. and Marè, E. eds. *Architecture of the Transvaal.* Pretoria: University of South Africa (UNISA), 1998.

Fletcher, J. *Story of Theatre in South Africa: A Guide to its History from 1780 – 1930.* Cape Town: Vlaeberg, 1994.

Fransen, H. *The Old Buildings of the Cape.* Cape Town: Jonathan Ball, 2004.

Goldblatt, D. *South Africa: The Structure of Things Then.* Cape Town: Oxford University Press, 1998.

Gray, S. *Indaba: Interviews with African Writers.* Pretoria: Protea Book House, 2005.

Gray, S. ed. *Modern South African Stories: Revised Selection.* Johannesburg: Jonathan Ball, 2002.

Grundlingh, K. ed. *Line of Sight.* Cape Town: South African National Gallery, 2001.

Gunner, L. ed. *Politics and Performance: Theatre, Poetry and Song in Southern Africa.* Johannesburg: Witwatersrand University Press, 1993.

Harris, V. *Exploring Archives: An Introduction to Archival Ideas and Practice in South Africa.* National Archives of South Africa, Pretoria, 2000.

Hauptfleisch, T. *Theatre and Society in South Africa: Some Reflections in a Fractured Mirror.* Pretoria: Van Schaik, 1997.

Helgesson, S. *Writing in Crisis: Ethics and History in Gordimer, Ndebele and Coetzee.* Pietermaritzburg: University of KwaZulu-Natal Press, 2004.

Herreman, F. ed. *Liberated Voices: Contemporary Art from South Africa.* New York: Museum for African Art, 1999.

Images of Defiance: South Africa Resistance Posters of the 1980s. Johannesburg: STE Publishers, 2004.

Jackson, G.S. *Outside Insights: Quotations for Contemporary South Africa.* Cape Town: Human and Rousseau, 1997.

Kalu, A.C. *Women, Literature and Development in Africa.* Trenton, New Jersey, Africa World Press, 2001.

Kaschula, R. *The Bones of the Ancestors are Shaking.* Cape Town: Juta, 2002.

Kaschula, R. ed. *African Oral Literature: Functions in Contemporary Contexts.* Claremont: New Africa Books, 2001.

Kavanagh, R.M. *Theatre and Cultural Struggle in South Africa.* London: ZED Books, 1985.

Kavanagh, R.M. *Making People's Theatre.* Johannesburg: Witwatersrand University Press, 1997.

Kearney, J. A. *Representing Dissension: Riot, Rebellion and Resistance in the South African English Novel.* Pretoria: UNISA, 2004.

Kivnick, H.Q. *Where is the Way: Song and Struggle in South Africa.* New York: Viking Penguin, 1990.

Kourie, C. and Kretzschmar, L. eds. *Christian Spirituality in South Africa.* Pietermaritzburg: Cluster Publications, 2000.

Krige, R. and Zegeye, A. eds. *Culture in the New South Africa After Apartheid.* Cape Town: Kwela Books, 2001.

Larlham, P. *Black Theatre, Dance and Ritual in South Africa.* Ann Arbor, Michigan (USA): UMI Research Press, 1985.

Layiwold, D. ed. *Rethinking African Arts and Culture.* Cape Town: CASAS, 2000.

Levine, L. *The Drum Cafe's Traditional Music of South Africa.* Johannesburg: Jacana, 2005.

Levinsohn, R.R. *Art and Craft of Southern Africa.* Johannesburg: Delta Books, 1984.

Lewis-Williams, D. *Images of Mystery: Rock Art of the Drakensberg.* Cape Town: Double Storey Books, 2003.

Lewis-Williams, D. ed. *Stories that Float from Afar: Ancestral Folklore of the San of Southern Africa.* Cape Town: David Philip, 2000.

Lewis-Williams, D. and Blunt, G. *Fragile Heritage: A Rock Art Fieldguide.* Johannesburg: Witwatersrand University Press, 1998.

Lewis-Williams, D. and Dowson, T. *Discovering Southern African Rock Art.* Cape Town: David Philip, 2000.

Losambe, L. and Sarinjeive, D. eds. *Pre-Colonial and Post-Colonial Drama and Theatre in Africa.* Cape Town: New Africa Books, 2001.

Magubane, P. and Klopper, S. *African Heritage: Arts and Crafts; African Heritage: Ceremonies; African Heritage: Dress and Adornment.* Cape Town: Struik, 2002.

Makeba, M. and Mwamuka, N. *Makeba: The Miriam Makeba Story.* Johannesburg: STE Publishers, 2004.

Marschall, S. *Community Mural Art in South Africa.* Pretoria: UNISA, 2002.

Masekela, H and Cheers, M. *Still Grazing: The Musical Journey of Hugh Masekela.* New York: Crown Publishers, 2004.

Mbatha, A. *Within Loving Memory of the Century.* Pietermaritzburg: University of Kwazulu-Natal Press, 2005.

Meiring, H. *My Country in Line and Colour.* Cape Town: Fernwood Press, 2004.

Miles, E. *Land and Lives: A Story of Early Black Artists.* Cape Town: Human and Rousseau, 1997.

Moffett, H. and Mphahlele, E. eds. *Seasons Come to Pass.* Cape Town: Oxford University Press, 2002.

133

Molefe, Z.B. and Mzileni, M. *A Common Hunger to Sing: A Tribute to South Africa's Black Women of Song, 1950 to 1990*. Text by Z.B. Molefe; photographs by M. Mzileni. Cape Town: Kwela Books, 1997.

Morris, J. *Speaking with Beads: Zulu Beads from Southern Africa*. Text by E. Preston Whyte. London: Thames and Hudson,1994.

Music Africa Directory, 1997. Sandton: Sun Circle, 1997 – Annual.

Muwanga, C. *South Africa: A Guide to Recent Architecture*. London: Ellipsis, 1998.

Nettleton, A. and Hammond-Tooke, W.D. *African Art in South Africa: From Tradition to Township*. Johannesburg: Donker, 1989.

New Century of South African Short Stories. Compiled by M. Chapman. Johannesburg: Donker, 2004.

Nuttall, S. and Michael, C. eds. *Senses of Culture: South African Culture Studies*. Cape Town: Oxford University Press, 2001.

Okurè, T. ed. *To Cast Fire Upon the Earth: Bible and Mission Collaborating in Today's Multicultural Global Context*. Pietermaritzburg: Cluster Publications, 2000.

Opland, J. *The Dassie and the Hunter: A South African Meeting*. Pietermaritzburg: University of Natal Press, 2005.

Orkin, M. *Drama and the South African State*. Johannesburg: Witwatersrand University Press, 1991.

Over the Rainbow: An Anthology of African Verse. Scottburgh: Poetry Institute of Africa, 1997.

Petersen, B. *Monarchs, Missionaries and African Intellectuals: African Theatre and the Unmasking of Colonial Marginality*. Johannesburg: Witwatersrand University Press, 2000.

Phelps, A. ed. *Sunshine and Shadows: A Collection of South African Short Stories*. Empangeni: Echoing Green Press, 2004.

Picton-Seymour, D. *Victorian Buildings in South Africa*. Cape Town: Balkema, 1977.

Plastow, J. ed. *African Theatre: Women*. Johannesburg: Witwatersrand University Press, 2002.

Radford, D. *A Guide to the Architecture of Durban and Pietermaritzburg*. Cape Town: David Philip, 2002.

Rasebotsa, N. *et al.* eds. *Nobody Ever Said AIDS: Stories and Poems from Southern Africa*. Cape Town: Kwela, 2004.

Rogosin, L. *Come Back Africa*. Johannesburg: STE Publishers, 2004.

Saron, G. *The Jews of South Africa: An Illustrated History to 1953*, edited by N. Musiker. Johannesburg: South African Jewish Board of Deputies, 2001.

Schadeberg, J. *The Black and White Fifties: Jurgen Schadeberg's South Africa*. Pretoria: Protea Book House, 2001.

South Africa's Visual Culture. Edited by J. van Eeden and A. du Preez. Pretoria: Van Schaik, 2005.

Strauss, P. *Africa Style in South Africa*. Johannesburg: Jonathan Ball, 1994.

Tales from Southern Africa: translated and retold by A.C. Jordan; foreword by Z. Pallo Jordan; introduction and commentaries by H. Scheub. Johannesburg: Ad Donker, 2004.

Tomaselli, K. ed. *Cinema of Apartheid: Race and Class in South African Film*. Bergvlei: Random Century, 1989.

Urban 03: Collected New South African Short Stories, edited by D. Chislett. Cape Town: Spearhead, 2003.

Van Graan, M. and Ballantyne, T. *The South African Handbook on Arts and Culture, 2002 – 2003*. Cape Town: David Philip, 2002.

Van Rensburg, J.J. *The Paradigm Shift: An Introduction to Post-Modern Thought and its Implications for Theology*. Pretoria: Van Schaik, 2000.

Wasserman, H. and Jacobs, S. eds. *Shifting Selves: Post-Apartheid Essays on Mass Media, Culture and Identity*. Cape Town: Kwela Books, 2004.

Williamson, S. and Jamal, A. *Art in South Africa: The Future Present*. Cape Town: David Philip, 1996.

Winburg, M. *My Eland Heart. The Art of the !Xu and Khwe*. Cape Town: David Philip, 2001.

Woodhouse, H.C. *Bushman Art of Southern Africa*. Durban: Art Publishers, 2003.

Zegeye, A. and Kriger, R. *Culture in the New South Africa – After Apartheid*. Cape Town: Kwela Books, 2003.

10 years 100 artists: Art in a Democratic South Africa; edited by S. Perryer. Cape Town: Bell Roberts, 2004.

Communications

The Department of Communications is the centre of policy-making and policy review for the postal, telecommunications and broadcasting sectors in the country. This includes policy-making that affects state-owned enterprises (SOEs) such as Telkom SA Ltd, the South African Post Office (SAPO) (Pty) Ltd, Sentech, the South African Broadcasting Corporation (SABC), the National Electronic Media Institute of South Africa (NEMISA), as well as the regulator, the Independent Communications Authority of South Africa (ICASA).

Policy

The Department of Communications is at the forefront of government initiatives to bridge the digital divide and provide universal access to Information and Communications Technology (ICT) for all South Africans. In addition, policy development since 1998/99 has sought to restructure SOEs, introduce competition, accelerate the penetration of services into underserviced communities and streamline the regulatory framework.

Developing a stable and predictable regulatory regime on e-commerce is central to the department's vision of moving South Africa into the knowledge economy.

The Electronic Communications and Transactions Act, 2002 (Act 25 of 2002), paved the way for a secure environment for e-commerce transactions. The DOT ZA Domain Name Authority was established and incorporated as a section 21 company in accordance with the Act. A representative board was appointed, reflecting cultural and linguistic diversity.

The Convergence Bill is aimed at removing policies that hinder the development of cross-sector applications, services and businesses. The legislation is expected to reflect the integration of telecommunications with Information Technology (IT), broadcasting and broadcasting signal distribution.

It will also ensure citizens are empowered with better access to knowledge and information.

The Telecommunications Amendment Act, 2001 (Act 64 of 2001), gives effect to the policy of managed liberalisation of the South African telecommunications market. Increased competition in the sector is expected to bring down the cost of telecommunications and remove growth constraints. Liberation of the sector became effective on 1 February 2005.

It also provides for the licensing of operators in underserviced areas with a teledensity of less than 5%. The majority of these are situated in the Integrated Sustainable Rural Development Programme's (ISRDP) nodal points. This process will bring about the most significant ownership and involvement in the communications sector by women and black people in South Africa. The amendments provide for a new public emergency telephone service and an emergency number, 112. A pilot project has been established in the Western Cape to test the technology to be rolled out across the country.

Section 40 of the Telecommunications Amendment Act, 2001 requires underserviced area licences (USALs) to provide telecommunications services, including voice-over Internet protocol, fixed mobile services and public pay telephones.

The Minister of Communications, Dr Ivy Matsepe-Casaburri, granted USALs to six successful companies in 2004. The companies are Bokone Telecommunications from Limpopo, Thinta Thinta Telecommunications and Kingdom Communications from KwaZulu-Natal, Ilizwi Telecommunications from the Eastern Cape, Karabo from North West and Bokamoso from the Free State.

In keeping with its mandate of bridging the digital divide, the Universal Service Agency (USA) is subsidising the USALs with R15 million each over the next three years.

In May 2005, seven more USALs were announced to assist in accelerating the development of the economy and the building of the information society in KwaZulu-Natal, Eastern Cape, Limpopo, Free State and North West. Some of these licences are 60% to 70% owned by women and ordinary communities. Fourteen more licences were expected to be applied for in 2005 in these and other provinces. These licences are expected to improve not only access to ICTs by citizens, but also to expand services by government such as health, education, safety, security, welfare, etc.

On 17 September 2004, a licence to provide public switched telecommunications services in South Africa was granted to the Second National Operator (SNO) comprising Nexus Connexion (Pty), Transtel, Esitel, WIP Investments Nine (Pty) Ltd trading as CommuniTel, Two Telecom Consortium (Pty) Ltd, and a remaining unallocated equity shareholder. The licence was subject to the following conditions:

- acceptance of the shareholding and control structure of the SNO
- finalisation of and agreement on the business plan
- finalisation of the shareholders' and subscription agreements.

According to the structure of the SNO:

- a new company, SepCo, will be incorporated, and will hold 51% of the equity share capital of the SNO
- control of SepCo will be held by a new financial investor, which will have a 51% shareholding in SepCo, while CommuniTel and Two Telecom Consortium (Pty) Ltd will each hold 24,5% of SepCo
- Transtel and Esitel will together hold 30% of the equity share capital of the SNO
- Nexus will hold 19% of the equity share capital of the SNO
- a new financial investor will control the board of SepCo
- SepCo will, in turn, control the board of the SNO.

ICASA will manage the integration of the SNO company and the finalisation of the licensing process.

In May 2005, the Information and Communications Technology (ICT) Steering Committee presented the final Draft ICT Black Economic Empowerment (BEE) Charter to the Minister of Communications, Dr Ivy Matsepe-Casaburri.

The handover brought to an end a process that had taken over two years to reach consensus on the development of a charter that would guide BEE activities in the broadcasting, electronics, information technology and telecommunications industries.

The draft charter drew extensively from the draft codes of good practice being finalised by the Department of Trade and Industry.

The steering committee expected that the final charter (published as a code of good practice) would be in operation by the end of 2005.

In February 2005, VSNL, as part of the TATA Group and represented in South Africa by TATA Africa Holdings (SA) Pty Limited, was allocated the 26% equity stake in the SNO with immediate effect.

By mid-June 2005, the stakeholders were about to finalise the integration process. The business plan was ready and the shareholders' agreement was expected to be completed.

Telecommunications

By October 2003, South Africa's ICT industry was the 20th-largest in the world, contributing 0,5% to worldwide ICT revenue.

In the last 10 years, investment in the telecommunications sector has exceeded R60 billion.

The telecommunications sector has witnessed an accelerated growth of data communications. The rate of connections of mobile subscribers, in particular, has surpassed that of fixed line services.

Regulators and licensing

Independent Communications Authority of South Africa

ICASA was established in terms of the ICASA Act, 2000 (Act 13 of 2000). Before ICASA was established, two separate authorities regulated broadcasting and telecommunications. These were the Independent Broadcasting Authority (IBA) and the South African Telecommunications Regulatory Authority.

ICASA's tasks include:
- licensing broadcasters and telecommunications operators
- formulating rules, policies and regulations that govern the two sectors
- monitoring the activities of the licensees and enforcing compliance
- planning the broadcast frequency spectrum
- receiving, hearing and adjudicating complaints
- regulating the broadcasting and telecommunications industry as a whole.

ICASA's vision is to be a strong, service-orientated and responsive communications regulator in South Africa.

Its mission is to increase access to communications services, through the promotion of a competitive and socially responsive communications industry.

Universal Service Agency

The USA was launched in May 1997. It is a statutory body created in terms of the Telecommunications Act, 1996 (Act 103 of 1996), and its objectives include advising the minister on ways to bring about universal access and service, and co-ordinating initiatives by service-providers such as Telkom, Vodacom, Mobile Telephone Network (MTN) and Cell C.

It extends access to telecommunications by working with community-based organisations (CBOs), non-governmental organisations (NGOs), donor organisations and businesses. The Universal Service Fund is used to reinforce the development of infrastructure in underserviced communities. In addition, support is given to schools procuring IT equipment.

The USA and the Department of Communications launched the Community ICT Tele-Container on 4 June 2005 in Polokwane, Limpopo. It aims to improve universal access to ICTs by communities in the underserviced areas of South Africa.

In May 2005, the Meraka Institute, also known as the African Advanced Institute for Information and Communications Technology (AAIICT), was launched in Pretoria.

The AAIICT will contribute towards stimulating the development of the local Information and Communications Technology (ICT) industry through the provision of intellectual human capital.

Meraka is a Sesotho word meaning 'common grazing', denoting sharing, mutual benefit and the potential for prosperity.

The Meraka Institute will also support regional initiatives under the New Partnership for Africa's Development and collaborate with ICT organisations through staff and student exchanges.

It will focus on the development of people and the application of their knowledge in ICT.

It incorporates some elements of the Institute for Space and Software Applications and the National Electronic Media Institute.

The tele-container is equipped with six computers with Internet access, a photocopying machine, fax machine and printer.

The united action for equitable access provided by the tele-container involves public and private partners such as MTN, Telkom, Sentech, Vodacom, Cell C, Fundisa and Bokgoni Projects.

Information Technology

Knowledge Management Unit

The Knowledge Management Unit of the Department of Communications promotes awareness of knowledge management among stakeholders, particularly within government, focusing on local government.

The unit aims to:

- take advantage of the convergence of communications technologies in the areas of telecommunications, broadcasting, IT and multimedia
- increase the human resource capability of the communications sector
- make South Africa globally competitive by becoming a hub of multimedia development, particularly through opening up opportunities for historically disadvantaged communities

South Africa ranks 34th out of 104 countries surveyed in the World Economic Forum's *Global Information Technology Report 2004/05* – up from 37th place overall in 2003/04 and ahead of such countries as China, Greece, Hungary, Italy and India.

The report, in its fourth year, assessed countries' readiness to participate in and benefit from global developments in Information and Communications Technology (ICT).

Variables taken into account included the quality of technical infrastructure, government prioritisation and procurement of ICT, and the quality of Mathematics and Science education, as well as of scientific research institutions and business schools.

Countries are also ranked according to affordability of telephone connections and Internet access, availability of training opportunities for the labour force and the existence of a well-developed venture capital market.

- contribute towards an African communications strategy that will help build an information backbone to ensure the success of Africa's renewal.

State Information Technology Agency (SITA)

On 29 January 1999, SITA was incorporated as a private company, with the State as sole shareholder, to provide IT-related services exclusively to the Public Service. (See chapter 12: *Government system*.)

arivia.kom

arivia.kom is a leading South African IT solutions company and service-provider. The group has offices in Nigeria, Ghana and Botswana.

Its shareholders are Denel (22,98%), Transnet Ltd (31,96%) and Eskom Enterprises (45,06%).

It is rated one of the four-largest IT professional service-providers in South Africa.

The group focuses on high-end business technology solutions that support the public sector and large private-sector corporates, primarily within the Africa client base.

arivia.kom supports Black Economic Empowerment (BEE) through shareholder equity, employment equity, procurement and corporate social investment.

Presidential International Advisory Council on Information Society and Development

The Presidential International Advisory Council on Information Society and Development aims to assist government in narrowing the digital divide between South Africa and the rest of the world. The council consists of chief executive officers (CEOs) from major international ICT corporations, and industry experts. The council meets once a year to exchange ideas.

Presidential National Commission on Information Society and Development

The Presidential National Commission on Information Society and Development mobilises national knowledge and builds common approaches. The commission recommends strategies to bridge the digital divide and helps to develop an ICT policy framework.

Internet

A World Wide Worx survey, entitled *The Goldstuck Report: Internet Access in South Africa 2004*, estimated that 3,28 million South Africans had access to the Internet at the end of 2003.

The Telecommunications Business Unit in the Department of Communications has established a specialist unit to develop a national strategy and to develop and expand the Internet. The unit is required to fulfil the following obligations under the Electronic Communications and Transactions Act, 2002:

- develop the National E-Strategy for submission to the Cabinet
- co-ordinate and monitor the implementation of the National E-Strategy
- conduct research into and keep abreast of developments relevant to electronic communications and transactions.

The unit is responsible for establishing the foundations for the requisite technical regulatory structures, including the:

- Domain Name Authority
- authentication of service-providers
- cryptography-providers
- accreditation authority
- listing of critical databases
- establishment of the Cyber Inspectorate
- alternative dispute-resolution regulations.

The unit has, in collaboration with the Department of Education, implemented a programme of connectivity in schools across the country, providing access to the Internet and e-mail.

Readership of South African Internet sites has increased by 25% since August 2004, according to the Online Publishers Association (OPA). The South African web attracted a combined local and overseas audience of 4,38 million readers or unique browsers in April 2005, generating 111,6 million page impressions.

Independently audited by Nielsen//Netratings, an Internet media and research company, the OPA's April 2005 statistics showed an increase of 900 000 online readers over August 2004.

International co-operation

As part of the New Partnership for Africa's Development (NEPAD) ICT programme, the departments of communications and of education launched the NEPAD e-schools project, which is managed under the NEPAD e-Africa Commission. Six schools from each country were selected for the demonstration project.

The project garnered a nomination for an award from the Intelligent Community Forum in recognition of its visionary outlook.

South Africa has been active in the reform of the International Telecommunications Union, chairing its Restructuring Committee. The country also chaired the Ministerial Oversight Committee of the African Telecoms Union for four years.

The African Network Information Service, which is responsible for the management and allocation of Internet addresses, has started its technical operations in South Africa with the assistance of the Department of Communications and the Council for Scientific and Industrial Research.

Telkom

On 7 May 2002, the South African telecommunications landscape faced the end of Telkom's period of exclusivity, which opened the door to competition. During this time, Telkom transformed itself into a competitive player, providing total communications solutions in the ICT sector.

During its five-year period of exclusivity, the company was required to comply with a number of conditions and obligations relating to milestone targets, as set out in its licence.

The public switched telecommunications services licence included service and fixed-line roll-out targets. Telkom substantially met all of these, with the exception of the residential fault-rate target, targets relating to service provision in underserviced villages and the replacement of analogue lines with digital ones. The company narrowly missed the aggregate fixed-line roll-out target as it decided to refrain from rolling out lines in areas that were not economically viable.

On 4 March 2003, Telkom listed on the JSE Securities Exchange (JSE) and the New York Stock Exchange.

At 30 September 2004, the South African Government owned 38,3% of Telkom's issued share-capital, Thintana Communications LLC 15,1%, and the public 46,6%. Thintana Communications LLC sold its entire stake to the South African business community in 2005.

Telkom's listing created meaningful value for BEE shareholders. Over 100 000 South African retail investors subscribed during Telkom's initial public offering, specifically targeted at historically disadvantaged individuals. In its first year as a listed company, the estimated value created for retail shareholders amounted to about R560 million.

Telkom maintains market leadership in the mobile sector through its 50% ownership of the Vodacom Group.

Highlights for 2005 included:
• growth in the number of Internet subscribers to 225 280, repesenting a 49% increase
• growth of 188% in the number of asymmetric digital subscriber line customers to 58 532
• growth of 9,8% in the Integrated Services Digital Network
• growth in fixed-line revenue of 15,6%
• growth in managed data network sites of 32%
• mobile gross connections of 6,2 million, 56% market share and total mobile traffic of 15 014 million minutes.

Telkom has a socially responsible retrenchment programme, the efficiency of which has been greatly assisted by the Agency for Career Opportunities. This is an initiative to help employees, often through reskilling, to become re-employed either internally or externally.

Telkom Foundation

The Telkom Foundation, founded in 1998, enables Telkom to play an active role in South Africa's socio-economic development.

On 1 July 2002, the foundation became an autonomous legal entity of Telkom SA Ltd and a non-profit organisation. It is now registered as a trust, with a board of trustees and its own CEO.

Despite its autonomy, the foundation remains Telkom's sole corporate social-investment arm tasked with co-ordinating the company's social-investment activities.

The foundation continues to pursue a philosophy of empowerment and sustainable development by focusing on:
• Mathematics, Science and Technology
• the empowerment of women, children and people with disabilities
• education and training.

Establishing partnerships with national and provincial role-players in government and NGOs, ensuring full community involvement and building relationships with stakeholders and structures in historically disadvantaged communities, form the core of its philosophy.

Economic empowerment

By March 2005, BEE procurement spending had increased from the previous year's amount of R4,6 million to R5,2 billion, representing 61,9% of Telkom's total procurement spend. The amount spent on black small, medium and micro enterprises (SMMEs) to provide core and non-core services totalled R901 million.

In 2004, for the second successive year, Empowerdex and *Financial Mail* voted Telkom the company that had made the most progress in terms of BEE.

By 2005, Telkom had spent R29 billion to achieve its empowerment goals since 1997 and had commissioned an independent study into the impact of its BEE programme on the sustainability of businesses that it supports.

Telkom was the first company in South Africa to launch the Enterprise Development and Affirmative Procurement Programme, which enables new black-owned companies to grow their businesses into more profitable ventures. Through Telkom's Centre for Learning, SMMEs are trained in Building Entrepreneurial Capacity – a programme provided with the support of the National African Federated Chamber of Commerce.

Representivity

By March 2005, nine of the 11 board members were black, including three women. This amounted to 82% black representation. Top management comprised 19 black people, including five black women, representing 69% black representation.

At the lower level of supervisors in the company, 41% were black compared with just 4% in 1994 – while at operational level, black representation was 62% compared with 21% in 1994.

Women represented 26,7% of the total workforce, while the technical development programme was aimed at women and black people.

Training and development spending totalled R390 million in 2004 – more than 1% of company revenue.

Centres of excellence (CoEs)

This is a collaborative programme between Telkom, the telecommunications industry and the Department of Trade and Industry to promote postgraduate research in ICT and allied social sciences. It also provides facilities that encourage young scientists and engineers to pursue their interests in South Africa.

Launched in 1997, the programme improves local telecommunications and IT skills, yielding substantial benefits for the academic institutions involved. It has helped Telkom and its local technology partners to solve technical problems and cut costs. Telkom's corporate partners are also reaping rewards, as the work undertaken at the CoEs is relevant to their areas of business.

By mid-2004, there were 15 centres located at tertiary institutions around the country. About 350 students conducted postgraduate telecommunications research through the CoE programme. Seventy-three of these received support from Telkom to conduct full-time research.

Mobile communications

Over the years, South Africa has witnessed tremendous growth in the cellular industry. Restrictions that entrenched Telkom's monopoly have been removed and the process of facilitating the reduction in the cost of telecommunications by giving service-providers and consumers more choice has started.

South Africa has three operators, namely Vodacom, MTN and Cell C.

Cell C (Pty) Ltd is wholly owned by 3C Telecommunications (Pty) Ltd, which in turn is 60% owned by Oger; Telecom South Africa, a division of Saudi Oger; and 40% by CellSAF. It also brought in Verizon Communications, the biggest cellular operator in the United States of America, as its operating partner.

Cell C has six active roaming agreements in Namibia, Mozambique, Spain, the Ivory Coast, Mauritius and Swaziland, and has entered into roaming agreements with an additional 49 international operators.

Vodacom is a Pan-African cellular communications company and provides a service to millions of customers in South Africa, Tanzania, Lesotho, the Democratic Republic of Congo and Mozambique.

Vodacom's commitment to rolling out subsidised community telephones in South Africa's underserviced areas has significantly boosted the company's coverage in rural areas.

Vodacom's shareholders include Telkom SA (Ltd) (50%), Venfin Ltd (15%) and Vodafone Group plc (35%).

At the end of June 2005, Vodacom had 17,2 million and the MTN Group 17 million subscribers on its networks across the African continent.

MTN International offers cellular network access and associated services through its subsidiaries and joint ventures in Nigeria, Cameroon, Uganda, Rwanda and Swaziland.

The Telecommunications Act, 1996 provides for 1 800 MHz spectrum (as well as 2,4 GHz – 3G spectrum) to be issued to existing operators, the SNO and underserviced area operators. A key element in this process is the determination of access fees and universal service obligations (USOs) for the allocation of the frequency spectrum.

The Department of Communications negotiated these issues, including new service fees and additional USOs, with the industry. The proposed obligations will include:

- the supply of 250 000 free phones and numbers to public emergency services over a period of five years

- the provision of Internet access, phone links and computers to schools
- public payphones in accessible places in rural areas and multi-purpose community centres (MPCCs)
- the issue of some four million free SIM cards over five years.

The postal sector

Policy and legislation

The cornerstone of national policy for the postal sector is the provision of a universal service at an affordable price and acceptable standard of service for all citizens. To ensure this, a USO is placed on SAPO. To offset the cost of providing a basic service in low-density, rural or uneconomical areas, it has also been common practice to confer exclusive rights and privileges, i.e. a monopoly on the provision of the basic letter service.

A USO is an obligation to provide specified services to the whole community, even though these services may not be commercially viable in their own right. The universal postal service implies that all citizens have equal access to a basic letter service:

- that is reasonably accessible to all people
- at a single uniform rate of postage
- at the lowest price consistent with meeting all its obligations, financial and otherwise
- to places outside the country
- at a standard of performance which reasonably meets the needs of the population.

On 26 May 2005, Anelisa Balfour, a 10th grader at Byletts Combined School in rural Centane village, Eastern Cape, accompanied President Thabo Mbeki for a day as part of The Presidency's participation in the *Take a Girl Child to Work* Campaign.

Cell C seeks to provide girl learners in grades 10, 11 and 12 with workplace experience to deepen their thinking and aspirations about their roles in society. About 200 000 girl learners were expected to converge on workplaces around the country on the day.

In terms of the Post Office Act, 1958 (Act 4 of 1958), SAPO enjoyed exclusive rights and privileges, including a monopoly on letter mail up to 2 kg. According to the Postal Services Act, 1998 (Act 124 of 1998), SAPO continues to enjoy certain exclusive rights and privileges. The monopoly is on letter mail up to 1 kg.

In addition, SAPO is obliged to operate under a 25-year licence, with explicit universal service targets and other terms and conditions. The monopoly and compliance with the terms and conditions of the licence will be reviewed and monitored by the Postal Regulator.

New projects of the postal policy section include the establishment of a postal training institute for the industry and postal-security improvements, both local and regional.

Postal services regulatory framework

The Postal Regulator, established in terms of the Postal Services Act, 1998, is responsible for exercising regulatory functions in relation to reserved and unreserved postal services. The regulator encourages the expansion of postal services and promotes the interests of postal-service users in terms of the cost of reserved services. The regulator is also responsible for issuing postal licences and monitoring compliance with licence conditions by the operators.

South African Post Office

SAPO's 2004/05 financial year was the most significant in the history of the organisation. SAPO increased its operating profit before post-retirement medical benefits from R36,3 million in 2003 to R266,1 million in 2004.

The 2004/05 results were achieved through a voluntary retrenchment programme that resulted in a 21% decrease in staff, a R569-million increase in the Postbank depositor base, a 35% decrease in the fleet, improved controls and streamlined decision-making processes.

The Government subsidy to SAPO (which was terminated in 2000) was reintroduced in 2002/03 at a level of R300 million a year. The subsidy is allocated to fund postal outlets, especially in rural areas. A further R750 million was provided in 2004/05 to reimburse the Postbank for depositors' funds that SAPO utilised to fund its operations during its loss-making years.

Operations

The Post Office delivers some eight million mail items to almost 6,5 million addresses. Of these, 3,4 million are street addresses and three million are postboxes.

Speed Services Couriers move 37 tons of mail each night. To move mail in South Africa, 70 50-ton container vehicles ply the nation's major routes, together covering 19 million km a year. The area to which SAPO delivers exceeds 1,2 million km^2. With over 2 000 outlets and 5 500 service points, the Post Office is one of the largest business undertakings in the country. Business mail comprises 85% of the mail items moved daily.

SAPO reaches more than two million people a year with its life skills programme, which teaches people (who in many cases have never been in a post office) what services the Post Office offers, how to use these and basic skills such as addressing a letter correctly. Money gained by selling SAPO property (such as the old head office in Pretoria) has been used to build better mail-handling facilities such as the Cape Town, Johannesburg and Durban mail-sorting centres.

In 2004, SAPO started a project to upgrade and customise post offices to provide financial and business services, such as stationery, facsimiles and access to the Internet. Thirty-four new-look post offices were completed by mid-2005. There were also plans to upgrade and customise more post offices throughout the country.

Bridging the digital divide

The partnership between the Department of Communications and SAPO in addressing ICT disparities has provided a solid base for eventually bridging the digital divide. A number of projects have been earmarked in this regard, including public Internet terminals (PITs) and citizens' post offices (CPOs).

Public Internet terminals

The main objective of the PIT project is to create a communications infrastructure through which the public has access to information from government/business/SAPO, as well as to empower citizens to communicate via e-mail or the Internet.

PITs offer five basic categories of services. These are government information and forms, an e-mail service, Internet browsing, a business section, and educational services.

A PIT-customised truck houses computer terminals, which have access to the Internet and all the back-end services available to other terminals currently housed in post offices. This is made possible by the satellite link between the truck and the servers. The satellite-link technology is provided by Sentech. This has helped to broaden the PIT project's services to any place in the country.

During 2004, 600 PITs were installed throughout the country, bringing the total number of PITs rolled out to 700. Some 575 of the newly installed PITs were operational by mid-2005.

Citizens' post offices

This project provides electronic-based services as a one-stop shop in the Internet café mode. By July 2004, 17 CPOs had been launched. A further roll-out of 200 sites was planned for 2005.

The main target market for the CPOs is SMMEs. The services on offer include Internet browsing and e-mail; government services and information; Microsoft Office products like Word, Excel and PowerPoint; faxing; photocopying; binding; and all related stationery.

National Address Database

In 2005, SAPO, Statistics South Africa and the Department of Communications established a task team to launch the National Address Database and Registry aimed at ensuring that every household in the country has access to mail delivery, and that every citizen in the country has a physical address. SAPO has been providing addresses through boxes and street addresses. The target, as set out and confirmed in the licence agreement, is 4 018 100.

By July 2004, some 3 641 540 new addresses had been rolled out.

A pilot project was completed in the village of Garasai in North West. The entire community received street addresses. Early in 2005, another project was implemented in rural Eastern Cape.

Postbank

The Postbank is responsible for:

- providing banking services to lower-income groups and rural areas underserved by financial institutions
- fulfilling the need for a countrywide network of financial services
- mobilising savings and therefore contributing to domestic investment
- developing values of thrift and savings
- treasury and investment (to be the empowerment vehicle for SMMEs)
- being a deposit facility for welfare and maintenance payments.

Postbank's net contribution for the financial year to 31 March 2004 was R84,3 million (R69,5 million in 2003).

After repositioning itself, the participation of the Postbank in the Mzanzi Account has been very successful. By May 2005, the Postbank had already overtaken the four major banks with 152 000 accounts opened, which was 29% of the total market share.

The number of new Postbank accounts increased at an average of 51 000 a month compared with 47 000 a month in 2003/04. The number of Postbank accounts totalled 3,2 million at the end of November 2004, an increase of 22,2% from November 2003.

Social investment

This includes:

- supporting the fight against HIV, AIDS and cancer
- awarding scholarships and bursaries
- supporting choral development
- contributing towards poverty alleviation
- promoting the recognition of South Africa's legends and heritage through philately
- promoting the culture of writing, through letter-writing contests.

International and regional co-operation

South Africa is a member of the Universal Postal Union (UPU). The country participates in technical assistance programmes within the UPU, and uses its international accounting facility. It also participates in other international bodies such as the Pan-African Postal Union (PAPU), Council of Commonwealth Postal Administrations and the Southern African Transport and Communications Commission.

South Africa, through the Department of Communications, is a signatory to international treaties, conventions and agreements. It co-operates and works in partnership with other postal administrations through either bilateral or multilateral agreements relating to letters, parcels and financial postal services.

In February 2005, more than 190 postal services representatives from Africa attended the regional conference of PAPU in Johannesburg to discuss better ways of improving global postal services.

PAPU is a specialised agency of the African Union (AU) devoted to the development of postal services on the continent.

The media

Media freedom

According to the Bill of Rights, as contained in the Constitution of the Republic of South Africa, 1996 (Act 108 of 1996), everyone has the right to freedom of expression, which includes:

- freedom of the press and other media
- freedom to receive or impart information or ideas
- freedom of artistic creativity
- academic freedom and freedom of scientific research.

Several laws, policies and organisations act to protect and promote press freedom in South Africa.

The third Press Freedom Index by Reporters Without Barriers, released on World Press Freedom Day on 3 May 2005, ranked press freedom in South Africa as 26th in the world – beating such countries as the United Kingdom (28th), Greece (33rd), Italy and Spain (tied at 39th), Australia (41st) and Japan (42nd).

The only developing countries to earn a better score than South Africa were the Caribbean states of Trinidad and Tobago (tied at 11th with Estonia, Germany and Sweden) and Jamaica (24th).

Broadcasting

South Africa has an extremely diverse broadcast media sector catering for the unique demands of the local market.

Policy and legislation

The Broadcasting Act, 1999 (Act 4 of 1999), and the IBA Act, 1993 (Act 153 of 1993), are aimed at establishing and developing a broadcasting policy to regulate and control all broadcasting, to:

- contribute to democracy, nation-building, the provision of education, and strengthening the moral fibre of society
- encourage ownership and control of broadcasting services by people from historically disadvantaged communities
- ensure fair competition in the sector
- provide for a three-tier system of public, commercial and community broadcasting services
- establish a strong and committed public broadcaster to service the needs of all South Africans.

The Broadcasting Act, 1999 defines the objectives of the South African broadcasting system, the structure of the SABC and the role of the various sectors in meeting these objectives. It also guarantees the independence of the SABC as public broadcaster. Section 8 of the Act sets out the objectives of the SABC. The SABC is being corporatised and restructured to better fulfil its mandate of meeting its audiences' needs.

These include broadcasting accurate and credible news and current affairs programmes; South African content programming in languages reflecting the country's cultural diversity; educational programming to advance lifelong learning; and programming targeted at children, women and people with disabilities.

The Act deals with the restructuring of the SABC to fit into the changing broadcasting environment. It requires that the SABC Board establish two man-agement boards to focus on the public and commercial services. Under the new dispensation, the public broadcasting wing will execute and meet its public-service mandate free from commercial interests. The commercial wing will be allowed to generate profit to be self-sustainable.

Editorial policy

The Broadcasting Amendment Act, 2002 (Act 64 of 2002), brings into effect, among other things, the new Code of Conduct for Broadcasters. Implementation of the Act will result in a better definition of public and commercial broadcasting services.

The SABC has developed, for the first time, editorial policies for news and other programming that cover current affairs, including content accuracy and impartiality. These policies are open to public comment.

The Broadcasting Amendment Act, 2002 provides for the establishment of two regional television licences: the first for the northern region, to cater for those speaking the Sesotho, Xitsonga, Tshivenda and Sesotho sa Leboa languages; and the second for the southern region, to cater for those speaking the isiXhosa, Siswati, isiZulu and isiNdebele languages.

In March 2004, the SABC submitted an application for the amendment of its broadcasting licences, in terms of Section 22 of the Broadcasting Act, 1999.

By mid-2005, the SABC had made applications to ICASA for two regional broadcasting services to meet provincial and language needs.

Cross-media control and South African content

ICASA released a position paper requiring local radio and television stations to increase their quotas of locally produced content as of August 2003. Quotas for public and community radio stations were doubled to 40%, while quotas for private and public commercial stations were raised to 25%. Quotas for television were increased to 55% for public broadcasters; 35% for commercial, private and public free-to-air stations; and 8% for pay stations.

Broadcasting role-players

Radio

The first radio broadcasts in South Africa took place under the auspices of a broadcasting committee of the South African Railways. The first experimental broadcast was undertaken in Johannesburg on 18 December 1923 by the Western Electric Company.

During 1924, the Associated Scientific and Technical Association of South Africa began regular broadcasts in Johannesburg. The Cape Peninsula Publicity Broadcasting Association began a similar service, and the Durban Municipality followed suit with its own regular broadcasts.

The first radio station, JB Calling, went on air in July 1924.

By 1926, all radio transmission and reception was placed under the control of the Postmaster-General, under the Radio Act, 1926 (Act 20 of 1926).

Following the contribution made by Sir John Reith, the then Director-General of the British Broadcasting Corporation, the SABC was established on 1 August 1936.

The SABC is the country's public broadcaster. It introduced its own national news service on 17 July 1950, with daily news bulletins on the English service, the Afrikaans service and Springbok Radio.

Radio Zulu, Radio Xhosa and Radio Sesotho were established on 1 June 1960.

In 2005, the SABC's national radio network comprised 15 public broadcast service radio stations, and three commercial radio stations broadcasting in 11 languages, and an external radio service in four languages that reached an average daily adult audience of 19 million.

For its internal coverage, Radio News uses about 13 editorial offices, a countrywide network of 1 300 correspondents and more than 2 000 news contacts.

World news is provided by international news agencies and strategically situated foreign correspondents.

Copy supplied to Radio News amounts to almost a million words a day, and is compiled around the clock into 300 news bulletins and 27 current affairs programmes broadcast daily on the SABC's radio services. There is a public broadcasting service radio station for each language group.

Channel Africa Network comprises four language services that reach millions of listeners throughout Africa. Broadcasts are in English, French, Kiswahili and Portuguese. It is targeted at audiences in Africa and the Indian Ocean islands, and concentrates on providing programmes with a specific African content.

Commercial radio stations

The following private radio stations have been granted licences by ICASA:

- Radio Algoa (ex-SABC)
- Classic FM (greenfield)
- Kaya FM (greenfield)
- YFM (greenfield)
- Highveld Stereo (ex-SABC)
- Radio 702
- Radio Jacaranda (ex-SABC)
- Radio Oranje (ex-SABC)
- East Coast Radio (ex-SABC)
- P4 (greenfield)
- Cape Talk MW (greenfield)
- Radio KFM (ex-SABC).

Stations such as Radio Jacaranda, Highveld Stereo, Radio Oranje, Radio Algoa and East Coast Radio were initially SABC stations, but were sold to private owners to diversify radio ownership in South Africa as part of the transformation of the public broadcaster.

On 13 January 2004, ICASA released the *Position Paper on the Ownership and Control of Broadcasting Services and Existing Commercial Sound Broadcasting Licences*. According to the position paper, at least seven new commercial sound broadcasters will be licensed over the next two years.

At least four of these licences will be granted in secondary markets, and at least three will be granted in primary markets. By March 2006, this should increase the current number of commercial sound broadcasting licensees from 13 to 23, taking into account the sale and licensing of Capital Radio in the short-term, as well as the relicensing of the medium wave (MW) frequencies forfeited by Punt Geselsradio.

Community radio stations
Community radio stations have a huge potential for the support of, among other things, cultural and educational information exchange. These radio stations all use indigenous languages, thus ensuring that people receive information in languages they understand.

By February 2005, 92 licences had been issued. ICASA had called for applications for a further 18 in the nodal points in KwaZulu-Natal, Limpopo and Mpumalanga, Eastern Cape, Western Cape, Northern Cape, North West and Gauteng.

Satellite Communications Network
The Satellite Communications Network makes it possible for grassroots communities, through their community radio stations, to access parliamentary proceedings, general news, and government information and services.

The Department of Communications is responsible for rolling out infrastructure to radio stations.

Initially, 30 radio stations were linked. The network will, on completion, link 90 stations.

Low Power Sound Broadcasting Licences
In October 2003, ICASA published the *Position Paper for Low Power Sound Broadcasting Services*. Low power sound broadcasting is defined in the Broadcasting Act, 1999 as broadcasting services operating with the maximum of one ERP. According to the position paper, low power broadcasting is divided into commercial sound broadcasting and community sound broadcasting. On 8 February 2005, the authority published guidelines for low power sound broadcasting licence applications. By May 2005, two applications had been received, from Kriel Info Radio and Voice of Wits.

Television

SABC
A one-channel television service was introduced on 5 January 1976.

Today, the SABC's national television network comprises three full-spectrum free-to-air channels and one satellite pay-TV channel aimed at audiences in Africa. Combined, the free-to-air sound broadcasting stations broadcast in 11 languages and reach a daily adult audience of almost 18 million people via the terrestrial signal distribution network and a satellite signal.

There are more than four million licensed television households in South Africa. South Africa has the largest television audience in Africa.

About 50% of all programmes transmitted are produced in South Africa. Locally produced television programmes are augmented by programmes purchased abroad, and by co-productions undertaken with other television programming organisations. Television news is fed by SABC news teams reporting from all parts of the country, using modern portable electronic cameras and line-feed equipment via more than 220 television transmitters. Ad hoc satellite feeds are arranged from wherever news events occur.

News bulletins are broadcast in all 11 official languages.

The SABC's terrestrial television channels devote about 17% of their airtime during prime time to news and news-related programmes.

NewsBreak 082 152, a news-by-telephone service, is one of the country's most popular audio news/information lines. This joint venture with Vodacom and Marketel gives the latest news in English and isiZulu, with regular sports and weather updates.

South Africa's top online publisher is Media24, which includes News24 and Finance24, with a unique readership of over 1,7 million and almost 27 million page impressions in April 2005.

Independent Online was in second place, with a unique readership of 1,3 million and 13 million page impressions.

Third was M-Web, followed by SuperSport Zone, Ananzi, iafrica, Mail & Guardian Online, Johnnic Communications, CareerJunction and Moneyweb.

M-Net

M-Net, South Africa's first private subscription television service, was launched in 1986. Today, M-Net broadcasts its array of general entertainment and niche channels to more than 1,3 million subscribers in more than 50 countries across the African continent and adjacent Indian Ocean islands.

M-Net's television channels are delivered to subscribers through analogue terrestrial and digital satellite distribution.

The main M-Net channel, which is available as a terrestrial and satellite service, offers movies, sport, children's programmes, international and local series and local reality shows.

The second terrestrial channel, CSN (Community Services Network), offers sport as well as programming aimed at a variety of South African communities.

Development of the local film and television industries is a priority for M-Net and is supported by various projects such as New Directions, which identifies and mentors emerging film-makers; the learner initiative; and EDIT, which gives final-year film and television students the opportunity to produce programmes for broadcast on M-Net.

In 2003, M-Net commissioned seven full-length films to boost the South African film industry. Among them was the Oscar-nominated drama *Yesterday*.

Satellite broadcasting

MultiChoice Africa (MCA) was formed in 1995 to manage the subscriber services of its sister company, M-Net. It became the first African company on the continent to offer digital satellite broadcasting.

Operations include subscriber-management services and digital satellite television platforms broadcasting 55 video and 48 audio channels, 24 hours a day. Included are six data channels, which were the first interactive television offerings on the continent.

Multichoice's digital bouquet is the home of several M-Net channels: M-Net Movies 1 and 2, DStv subscribers' all-day movie ticket; The Series channel; the Afrikaans channel kykNET; Channel O, the first TV music channel playing back-to-back music aimed at Africa's youth; Action X, the home of high-adrenaline movies and series; AfricaMagic, a channel featuring movies and programmes made on the African continent; and various SuperSport channels.

MCA is owned by the MIH Group, which is listed on the JSE, NASDAQ in New York, and AEX in Amsterdam.

Free-to-air television

The *White Paper on Broadcasting Policy*, released in June 1998, provided for the extension of free-to-air, pay and regional television services. On 30 March 1998, the consortium Midi Television was awarded the first privately owned free-to-air television licence.

The station they operate, e.tv, is a commercial service dependent on advertising. It does not charge subscription fees.

Since its launch in 1998, e.tv has shown phenomenal audience growth. News broadcasts and a 24-hour service were introduced early in 1999.

e.tv appeals to all race, age and income groups and is the most watched English language channel. By mid-2005, viewership totalled 11 461 000 according to the All Media Products Survey 2004A.

Signal distribution

Sentech began operating in 1992 under the auspices of the SABC as a signal distributor for all transmissions related to the public broadcaster. This mandate included services provided to M-Net, Radio 702, Radio Ciskei, Radio Transkei and the Bophuthatswana Broadcasting Corporation.

After an inquiry was launched and the subsequent report approved by Parliament in March 1996, Sentech started operating as a commercial SOE with its own board of directors.

Sentech owns and operates about 210 terrestrial transmitter sites where short-wave, MW, Frequency Modulation (FM), television and multichannel multipoint distribution service transmitters (more than 1 200) are accommodated to serve the various broadcasters in the country.

In May 2002, Sentech was granted two telecommunications licences, thus allowing the company to move into international telephony and multimedia communications. The International Telecommunications Gateway licence allows Sentech to carry international traffic on behalf of other licensed operators. The multimedia services licence enables the company to deliver e-commerce, Internet, broadband and value-added telecommunications services directly to consumers and businesses.

Sentech has assisted in connecting over 50 MPCCs and expanding television coverage. The AU has asked it to provide secure telecommunications infrastructure to its headquarters and contribute to the Pan-African Radio and Television Network. Sentech is working with SITA, the Medical Research Council and the USA to provide bandwidth for underserviced areas in the Bohlabela/Sekhukhune nodal points for tele-medicine tests.

Orbicom (Pty) Ltd was registered in 1993, and grew to become a leading-edge satellite communications company, which was acquired by MTN Group Holdings, formerly known as MCell Limited, in September 1999. It provides wireless communications solutions and services.

Print

Technical handling of the print media in South Africa rates among the best in the world. On the editorial side, concerns have been raised about the general quality of content from a journalistic point of view. Research has shown that journalists lack certain basic skills, and the juniorisation of newsrooms has affected most of the major publications negatively.

Over the last two years, the industry has held strategic planning sessions and implemented special training programmes in an attempt to improve the quality of newspapers' editorial content.

The roots of the print media in South Africa can be traced back to the 19th century, when the first issue of a government newspaper, the *Cape Town Gazette and African Advertiser/Kaapsche Stads Courant and Afrikaansche Berigter*, was published in 1800.

The first independent publication, *The South African Commercial Advertiser*, was published in 1824 by Thomas Pringle and John Fairbairn. It was banned 18 months later and reappeared only after various representations had been made to the authorities in London.

South African newspapers and magazines are mainly organised into press groups, which have burgeoned over the years as a result of take-overs.

The major press groups are Independent Newspapers (Pty) Ltd, Media24 Ltd, CTP/Caxton Publishers and Printers Ltd, and Johnnic Communi-cations.

Other important media players include Primedia; M&G Media; Associated Magazines; Ramsay, Son & Parker; NAIL (New Africa Investments Limited); and Kagiso Media. NAIL has unbundled into a commercial company (New Africa Capital) and a media company (New Africa Media).

Johnnic Communications clinched a deal with NAIL in which it acquired NAIL's shares in New Africa Publications, the owners of *Sowetan* and *Sunday World*.

Since 1994, the major press groups have embarked on programmes to boost BEE in media ownerships.

Newspapers

Most South African newspapers are based on the British model. Management and editorial departments are controlled separately.

The size of the country – 1 400 km separating the main centres of Cape Town and Johannesburg – still precludes national dailies in the true sense of the word.

In 2003, an attempt to break into the daily market by *ThisDay* failed and the newspaper ceased to exist in October 2004.

Some of the bigger titles and specialist newspapers such as Business Day are distributed in metropolitan areas. The only truly national newspapers are the *Sunday Times, Rapport, Sunday Independent, Sunday Sun, City Press* and *Sowetan Sunday World*.

All are published simultaneously in various cities, using the printing facilities of related dailies. A number of newspapers have introduced separate weekend editions of their daily newspapers, e.g. *Saturday Dispatch* and *Weekend Witness. The Post Weekend* and the Saturday edition of the *Herald* in Port Elizabeth ceased trading.

Sunday World, launched in March 1999, soon lost its initial popularity. It was relaunched in 2000 as *Sowetan Sunday World* and almost doubled its circulation.

150

The ongoing biggest success story of the South African newspaper scene is that of *Daily Sun,* with a daily circulation of more than 300 000.

This Gauteng newspaper, launched by Media24 in July 2002, has become the biggest daily in South Africa. Imitating the tabloid format and the controversial content line that appears in its British namesake, *The Sun*, it took the South African daily market by storm.

Tabloid journalism was the new trend in 2004/05 with another English title *The Daily Voice* being launched in the Western Cape. It is published by Independent Newspapers. An Afrikaans version, *Die Son*, launched on 28 March 2003, initially focused its distribution within the Western Cape, but has extended its circulation to Gauteng with the launch of its North edition in November 2003.

By mid-2005, there were 21 dailies and eight Sunday papers in South Africa. Almost 150 regional or country newspapers, most of which are weekly tabloids, serve particular towns or districts in the country, by covering local affairs and carrying local advertising. Most are published in English and Afrikaans. The most popular publication day is Thursday.

Newspapers appearing only in certain neighbourhoods are also part of this section. They are known as knock-and-drops, free-sheets or freebies, as they are distributed free of charge. They have a guaranteed readership with advertising being their only source of income. More than 4,5 million newspapers in this sector are distributed weekly.

In 2004, there were more than 200 such papers listed. They are distributed mainly in urban areas, and number in the hundreds when unlisted ones are considered. Press groups such as Media24 and CTP/Caxton are major players in this field.

Since 1996, local newspapers, freebies and corporate newspapers have ventured into reporting in indigenous languages as well. In Durban, Independent Newspapers started the isiZulu newspaper *Isolezwe*, which is steadily growing.

With 11 official languages, it can be expected that more home-language publications will emerge. Separate newspapers for different cultural groups are still preferred, with English being the popular language of choice.

Circulation

Community newspapers
Paid-for community newspapers showed significant growth in circulation from 268 000 in 2003 to 393 000 in the latter half of 2004 (July to December). The free-sheet newspapers showed a huge increase in circulation from 3,1 million per week in 2000 to 4,5 million per week in 2004.

Winners of major annual press trophies

	Frewin*	McCall**	Cronwright***	Hultzer****	Joel Mervis*****
2001	The Star	The Mercury	Chronicle	Herald Potchefstroom	Rapport
2002	Beeld	Natal Witness	Paarl Post	Herald	Rapport
2003	Beeld	Business Day	South Coast Herald	Springs and Brakpan Advertiser	Mail & Guardian
2004	Beeld	Witness	Paarl Post	Eikestadnuus	Naweek-Beeld
2005	The Witness	The Witness	–	–	Weekend Witness

*	Best daily newspaper
**	Best daily with a circulation under 50 000
***	Best community newspaper with a circulation exceeding 10 000
****	Best community newspaper with a circulation below 10 000
*****	Best urban weekly
–	Not available by time of going to press

Source: Print Media South Africa

Daily newspapers

Daily Sun still remains the biggest selling daily newspaper in South Africa and showed an increase in circulation from 235 386 (July to December) in 2003 to 364 356 for the same period in 2004. *Isolezwe* also showed an increase from 55 195 to 65 109 in 2004.

The Star remains South Africa's second-biggest newspaper, with a circulation of 166 461 compared with 165 948 in 2003.

Sowetan saw a slight decrease from 123 590 to 122 825 in 2004. *The Citizen* also saw a decline from 98 228 in 2003 to 76 183 in 2004.

Weekly newspapers

South Africa's biggest weekly Sunday newspaper, *Sunday Times*, saw a slight decrease in circulation from 505 717 to 505 402 in 2004. *Rapport*, the second-largest Sunday newspaper, showed a similar decrease from 324 882 to 322 731 in 2004, while *City Press* increased from 167 885 to 173 992 in 2004.

Soccer Laduma increased from 217 594 to 244 509 in 2004, and *Die Son* increased from 90 015 to 199 959 in 2004 (ABC July to December 2003 versus the same period in 2004).

Newspaper readership

Daily newspapers showed an upward trend in readership from 20,2% in 2003 to 21% in 2004 with 6,357 million readers. Weekly newspapers remained stable at 31,2% or 9,422 million readers. In general, newspapers saw a decline in readership among 16- to 24-year-olds.

Magazines circulation and readership

The magazine industry in South Africa is a fiercely competitive environment in which new titles appear all the time, despite the worldwide challenge from electronic and interactive media. It seems that many readers are still attracted to print, considering the proliferation of titles on the shelves in supermarkets and bookstores. However, there is evidence to suggest that the overall magazine reading population in South Africa is shrinking, which is a concern for the industry.

A positive development has been the segmentation of the market into niched publications that provide opportunities for advertisers to reach target markets.

Because of rising printing and paper costs, prices have increased accordingly and magazines have had to offer readers value for their money to retain their loyalty. Weeklies *Huisgenoot* and *You* are the two biggest money-making magazines in South Africa and gossip and celebrity titles are the biggest over-the-counter sellers. *FHM* and *Heat* are in the top five.

Women's magazines

In the women's magazine sector, publications have had to market themselves aggressively to survive. Consumers are now spoilt for choice and if a magazine is to be sustainable it has to compete, especially with new entries such as *Glamour*, *Heat* and *Seventeen* being launched against the established brands.

Overall, there was a general decline in readership in this sector. *Cosmopolitan* dropped from 119 562 to 117 255. *Glamour's* sales declined from 121 591 to 92 552. *Elle's* figures went down from 38 215 to 37 267, *Essentials* from 78 448 to 76 295 and *Fairlady* from 93 607 to 88 123. *Femina* dropped from 48 932 to 44 883 and *Marie Claire* from 51 923 to 43 110. *Oprah's* sales remained more or less steady at 62 754.

In the Afrikaans market, the same trend was apparent. *Rooi Rose* declined from 127 271 to 119 994 and so did the weekly *Vroue Keur* from

The Audit Bureau of Circulations' calculated figures for the period January to June 2005, released on 16 August 2005, showed continued growth over the past five years in magazine and newspaper circulation.

The youth consumer and customer magazine categories showed marked growth in circulation – also due to new entrants to the market.

Other growth categories included the home (consumer), woman's special interest (consumer), parenting (consumer), and travel, tourism and hospitality (business-to-business).

119 994 to 100 121. *Sarie* remains a leader in the sector, but its figures also decreased. *True Love* saw similar decreases, but *Dit* gained from 70 994 to 77 811.

General interest titles

Sales of the weeklies, *You* and *Huisgenoot*, 222 845 and 340 570 respectively, declined by about 2 500 and 1 500 each. *Drum*'s figures went down alarmingly and *Bona* declined from 103 599 to 96 584. *People's* figures decreased too, but *TV Plus* gained about 30 000 readers.

Décor

Décor magazines, on the other hand, proved to be a major growth area.

However, not all titles are doing well. *House and Garden*, *House & Leisure* and *Habitat* all declined while *Elle Decoration*'s figures remained stable. *Visi* continued to be popular and *SA Home Owner* increased its sales by about 10 000.

Parenting

This category is also booming. *Baba en Kleuter*, *Parents* and *Your Baby* all remained fairly stable, while *Healthy Pregnancy* gained readership and *Living and Loving*'s figures declined slightly.

Youth

There has been a proliferation of magazines in the youth sector in the last few years. *Wicked* increased from 20 609 to 25 311 and *Saltwater Girl* maintained its position as the top-selling female teen magazine in South Africa. New entry *Blunt* grew from 16 936 to 18 329 and *Seventeen* from 28 097 to 30 741. *Teenzone*'s sales declined slightly, as did figures for *Barbie*.

Male interest

GQ's figures dropped, while *FHM* increased from 105 194 to 118 428. *Men's Health*, too, showed an upward trend.

Motoring

Car declined from 108 693 to 105 934, *Leisure Wheels* was consistent at 14 000 and *Speed and Sound* increased from 29 295 to 44 644. *Topcar's* figures also grew, while *Wiel* declined to 7 648.

Lifestyle

Judging by the most recent circulation figures, *Weg* has cornered the Afrikaans outdoor lifestyle market while *Getaway* remained constant. *Style*'s figures declined dramatically, while Woolworth's *Taste* became increasingly popular, attaining sales of 20 075. *SA Country Life* and *Caravan and Outdoor Life* are extremely niched publications that have a consistent readership.

Sport

Amakhosi dropped from 40 051 to 37 772, *Bicycling SA* remained fairly steady and *Bike SA* declined slightly. *Compleat Golfer* remained at 24 115 while *Golf Digest* grew from 19 382 to 21 479. Football magazines, *Kick Off* (60 893), *Soccer Laduma* and *Full Time* continued to attract loyal readers, although *Soccer Life*'s sales figures went down from 30 662 to 17 163. *Runners' World* remained steady at 17 000, while *Sports Illustrated* grew from 38 000 to 42 145. Niche publications such as *SA Rugby*, *Complete Fly Fisherman* and *Stywe Lyne/Tight Lines* remained stable.

The 29-year-old surfing magazine, *Zigzag*, declined slightly.

Special interest

Finance Week/Finansies en Tegniek both grew by about 5 000 and 6 000 in sales, but the *Financial Mail* decreased slightly from 26 691 to 25 612. Targeted publications *Popular Mechanics*, *Threads and Crafts* and *Wine* continued to attract a loyal readership.

Distribution

In cities, newspapers rely heavily on street sales and door-to-door delivery. Cafés, spaza shops and general stores provide additional selling points. In rural areas, newspapers are distributed mainly by special truck deliveries, often covering hundreds of kilometres in a single run. The cost of bulk transport by air is very high.

Newspaper Circulation Services and Magazine Circulation Services handle all Johnnic Communications' circulation. The Afrikaans press group, Media24 (*Nasionale Nuusdistribueerders*), handles most of its distribution itself. Allied Publishing handles Independent Newspapers and RNA Distributors handles distribution for Caxton/CTP.

Online media
South African websites attract more than 3,5 million highly educated users.

Johannesburg has the largest audience with 24% users, followed by Cape Town (15%), Pretoria (10%) and Durban (6%).

Media organisations and role-players
Several organisations and associations play an important role in the media field.

Print Media South Africa (PMSA), formed in 1996, is an umbrella organisation administering individual bodies, namely the Newspaper Association of South Africa (the oldest communication organisation, established in 1882), Magazine Publishers Association of South Africa, and the Association of Independent Publishers (AIP). The AIP was formed in September 2004 after the major publishing groups withdrew from the Community Press Association (CPA) to give independent publishers an opportunity to transform the CPA into an association that would serve their own specific needs. The AIP represents the interests of more than 200 independent publishers in southern Africa.

The purpose of the PMSA is to represent, promote, interact and intervene in all matters concerning the collective industry and matters of common interest. It represents some 617 newspaper and magazine titles in South Africa. PMSA is a member of a number of international bodies such as the World Association of Newspapers and Federation of Periodical Press. Allied to PMSA, but not a constituent member, is the Audit Bureau of Circulation, responsible for auditing and verifying print-media circulation and cinema attendance figures.

The South African National Editors' Forum (SANEF) was conceived at a meeting of the Black Editors' Forum, the Conference of Editors, and senior journalism educators and trainers in October 1996.

SANEF's membership includes editors and senior journalists from the print, broadcast and online/Internet media, as well as journalism educators from all the major training institutions in South Africa.

SANEF has facilitated the mobilisation of the media in the *Partnership Against AIDS* Campaign, and in campaigns to end violence against women and children.

Various seminars and debates are held on media freedom and transformation, especially in relation to gender and technology. SANEF is involved in train-

Sold magazines with the largest circulation, July – December 2004

Name	Frequency	Language	Audited circulation
Huisgenoot	W	A	340 570
You	W	E	222 845
Sarie	M	A	137 970
TV Plus	F	B	135 563
AA Traveller	Q	E	133 593
Rooi Rose	M	A	119 994
FHM	M	E	118 428
Cosmopolitan	M	E	117 255
True Love	M	E	114 793
Car	M	E	105 934

The abbreviations used are the following: W (weekly), F (fortnightly), E (English), M (monthly), Q (quarterly), A (Afrikaans), B (bilingual).

Source: Audit Bureau of Circulation

Daily and weekly papers

Name	Publisher	Contact information	Frequency	Language	Audited circulation Jul – Dec 2004
Beeld (Daily)	Media 24	PO Box 333, Auckland Park, 2006 T. 011 713-9000 / F. 011 713-9960 E-mail: beeld@beeld.com	MD, M-F	A	102 070
Beeld (Saturday)	Media 24	PO Box 333, Auckland Park, 2006	W, Sat	A	88 402
Burger, Die (Daily)	Media 24	PO Box 692, Cape Town, 8000	MD, M-F	A	104 102
Burger, Die (Saturday)	Media 24	PO Box 692, Cape Town, 8000 T. 021 406-2214 / F. 021 406-3211	W, Sat	A	117 092
Business Day	BDFM Publishers (Pty) Ltd	PO Box 1742, Saxonwold, 2132 T. 011 280-3000 / F. 011 280-5505 E-mail: bday@tml.co.za	MD, M-F	E	40 541
Cape Argus, The	Independent Newspapers Cape Ltd	PO Box 56, Cape Town, 8000 T. 021 488-4911 / F. 021 488-4173 E-mail: josepha@ctn.independent.co.za	AD, M-F	E	73 230
Cape Times	Independent Newspapers Cape Ltd	PO Box 56, Cape Town, 8000 T. 021 488-4911 / F. 021 488-4173 E-mail: chriswh@independent.co.za	MD, M-F	E	49 526
Citizen, The (Daily)	Caxton Publishers & Printers Ltd	PO Box 43069, Industria, 2042 T. 011 248 6000 / F. 011 248 6222 E-mail: news@citizen.co.za	MD, M-F	E	76 183
Citizen, The (Saturday)	Caxton Publishers & Printers Ltd	PO Box 43069, Industria, 2042	W, Sat	E	57 935
City Press	RCP Media Bpk	PO Box 3413, Johannesburg, 2000 T. 011 713-9002 / F. 011 713-9977 E-mail: news@citypress.co.za	W, Sun	E	173 992
Daily Dispatch	Dispatch Media (Pty) Ltd	PO Box 131, East London, 5200 T. 043 702 2000 / F. 011 702 2968	AD, M-F	E	33 338
Daily News	Independent Newspapers KZN	PO Box 47397, Greyville, 4023 T. 031 308-2472 / F. 013 308-2662 E-mail: tbruce@nn.independent.co.za	AD, M-F	E	51 194
Daily Sun	Media 24	PO Box 333, Auckland Park, 2006 T. 011 713 9000 / F 011 713 9960	MD, M-F	E	364 356
Diamond Fields Advertiser	Independent Newspapers Gauteng Ltd	PO Box 610, Kimberley, 8300 T. 053 832-6261 / F. 053 832-8902 E-mail: pbe@independent.co.za	MD, M-F	E	8 948
Herald (Daily)	Johnnic Pub. Eastern Cape	PO Box 1117, Port Elizabeth, 6000 T. 041 504-7911 / F. 041 585 3947 E-mail: epherald@tmecl.co.za	MD, M-F	E	29 719
Ilanga	Mandla Matla Publishing Co (Pty) Ltd	PO Box 2159, Durban, 4000 T. 031 309-4350 / F. 031 309-3489	BW, Th, Mo	Z	103 597
Isolezwe	Independent Newspapers KZN	PO Box 47549, Greyville, 4023 T. 031 308 2878 / F. 031 308 2885	MD, M-F	Z	65 109
Independent on Saturday, The	Independent Newspapers KZN	PO Box 47397, Greyville, 4023 T. 031 308-2472 / F. 013 308-2662	W, Sat	E	56 216
Mail and Guardian	M&G Media (Pty) Ltd	PO Box 91667, Aucklandpark, 2006 T. 011 727-7000 / F. 011 727-7110 E-mail: newsroom@mg.co.za	W, Fr	E	40 162
Mercury, The	Independent Newspapers KZN	PO Box 47397, Greyville, 4023 T. 031 308 2472 / F. 031 308 2662	MD, M-F	E	39 343
Witness	Natal Witness Pr & Pub Co (Pty) Ltd	PO Box 362, Pietermaritzburg, 3200 T. 033 355-1111 / F. 033 355-1377 E-mail: news@witness.co.za	MD, M-S	E	23 514
Post	Independent Newspapers KZN	PO Box 47397, Greyville, 4023 T. 031 308-2472 / F. 031 308-2662 E-mail: khalil@independent.co.za	W, Wed	E	42 626

Daily and weekly papers

Name	Publisher	Contact information	Frequency	Language	Audited circulation Jul – Dec 2004
Pretoria News (Daily)	Independent Newspapers Gauteng Ltd	PO Box 439, Pretoria, 0001 T. 012 300-2000 / F. 012 325 7300 E-mail: tle@pretorianews.co.za	AD, M-F	E	28 690
Pretoria News (Saturday)	Independent Newspapers Gauteng Ltd	PO Box 439, Pretoria, 0001 T. 012 300-2000 / F. 012 325 7300	W, Sat	E	17 406
Rapport	RCP Media	PO Box 333, Auckland Park, 2006 T. 011 713-9002 / F. 012 713 9977 E-mail: aleroux@rapport.co.za	W, Sun	A	322 731
Saturday Dispatch	Dispatch Media (Pty) Ltd	PO Box 131, East London, 5200 T. 043 702 2000 / F. 043 743 2968	W, Sat	E	27 927
Saturday Star, The	Independent Newspapers Gauteng Ltd	PO Box 1014, Johannesburg, 2000 T. 011 633-9111 / F. 011 834-3918 E-mail: starnews@star.co.za	W, Sat	E	137 385
Soccer-Laduma	CT Media Proprietor	PO Box 787, Sea Point, 8060 T. 021 439 8080 / F. 021 439 7434	W, Thu	E	244 509
Son, Die	Media 24	PO Box 692, Cape Town, 8000 T. 021 406 2075 / F. 021 406 3221	W, Fri	A	199 959
Southern Cross, The	Catholic News-papers & Pub Co Ltd	PO Box 2372, Cape Town, 8000 T. 021 465 5007 / F. 021 465 3850	W, Sun	E	9 931
Sowetan	New Africa Publications (NAP) Ltd	PO Box 6663, Johannesburg, 2000 T. 011 471-4000 / F. 011 474-2074 E-mail: editor@sowetan.co.za	MD, M-F	E	122 825
Sowetan Sunday World	NAP Ltd	PO Box 6663, Johannesburg, 2000 T. 011 471-4200 / F. 011 471-4163 E-mail: newsed@sundayworld.co.za	W, Sun	E	143 208
Star, The	Independent Newspapers Gauteng Ltd	PO Box 1014, Johannesburg, 2000 T. 011 633-9111 / F. 011 834-3918 E-mail: starnews@star.co.za	MD, M-F	E	166 461
Sunday Independent, The	Independent Newspapers Gauteng, Ltd	PO Box 1014, Johannesburg, 2000 T. 011 633-9111 / F. 011 834-7520 E-mail: newstips@independent.co.za	W, Sun	E	41 464
Sunday Sun	RCP Media Ltd	PO Box 8422, Johannesburg, 2000 T. 011 713-9465 / F. 011 713-9731	W, Sun	E	173 738
Sunday Times	Johnnic Pub.	PO Box 1742, Saxonwold, 2132 T. 011 280-5101 / F. 011 280-5111 E-mail: suntimes@tml.co.za	W, Sun	E	505 402
Sunday Tribune	Independent Newspapers KZN	PO Box 47549, Greyville, 4023 T. 031 308-2911 / F. 011 308-2662 E-mail: clarke@independent.co.za	W, Sun	E	109 774
Volksblad, Die (Daily)	Media24	PO Box 267, Bloemfontein, 9300 T. 051 404-7600 / F. 051 447-7034 E-mail: mvanrooyen@volksblad.com	MD, M-F	A	29 018
Volksblad, Die (Saturday)	Media24	PO Box 267, Bloemfontein, 9300 T. 051 404-7600 / F. 051 430-7034	W, Sat	A	24 431
Weekend Argus	Independent Newspapers Cape Ltd	PO Box 56, Cape Town, 8000 T. 021 488-4528 / F. 021 488-4229	W, Sat & Sun	E	103 953
Weekend Post	Johnnic Pub. Eastern Cape	PO Box 1121, Port Elizabeth, 6000 T. 041 504-7911 / F. 041 585-3947	Sat	E	33 372
Weekend Witness	Natal Witness Pr & Pub Co Pty Ltd	PO Box 362, Pietermaritzburg, 3200 T. 033 355-1377 / F. 033 355-1377	W, Sat	E	31 073

The abbreviations used are the following: MD (morning daily), AD (afternoon daily), BW (biweekly), M-F (Monday to Friday), Mo (Monday), Tu (Tuesday), W (Wednesday), Th (Thursday), Fri (Friday), Sat (Saturday), Sun (Sunday), A (Afrikaans), E (English), Z (Zulu), n/a (not available)

Source: Audit Bureau of Circulation

ing initiatives and in setting practical standards in journalism education.

Against the backdrop of positive political developments on the African continent, SANEF spearheaded the formation of the All Africa Editor's Conference.

The Southern African Editors' Forum was subsequently formed in 2003. South Africa is its first chairperson, while the secretariat is held by Swaziland. The Central, Eastern, Western and Northern African Forum bodies are in various stages of being formed.

The Forum of Black Journalists, consisting only of black journalists, tackles issues that directly affect its members.

Members of the public who have complaints or concerns about reports in newspapers and magazines can submit their grievances to the Office of the Press Ombudsman.

Should they not be satisfied with the resultant ruling, they can lodge an appeal with an independent appeal panel. The Office of the Press Ombudsman was set up by the PMSA, SANEF, the Media Workers' Association of South Africa, and the South African Union of Journalists (SAUJ).

As self-regulating mechanisms of the media industry, the Press Ombudsman and the appeal panel act in accordance with the South African Constitution, 1996 and embrace the spirit of transformation in South Africa.

The Freedom of Expression Institute (FXI) was established in 1994 to protect and foster the rights to freedom of expression and access to information, and to oppose censorship.

The FXI undertakes a wide range of activities in support of its objectives, including lobbying, educating, monitoring, research, publicity, litigation and the funding of legal cases that advance these rights.

In the process, it networks and collaborates with a wide range of local and international organisations.

Another body that protects freedom of speech is the Freedom of Commercial Speech Trust. Backed by the marketing communication industry and supported by organised business and consumer organisations, the trust focuses on transparent negotiations with legislators.

The SAUJ has fought consistently and primarily for a free and independent media, and for acceptable working conditions for its members. To this end, the SAUJ has signed formal agreements with most employer groupings, and participates in structures aimed at fostering and enhancing media freedom.

In September 2004, the Forum of Community Journalists (FCJ) relaunched the organisation as an independent body to serve the interests of all community newspaper journalists in southern Africa. The FCJ was originally set up as a substructure of the CPA and only represented journalists employed at member organisations.

The decision to become an independent body followed the restructuring of the CPA into the AIP. The restructuring was triggered after the major groups withdrew from the CPA to create a platform for independent publishers to transform the association into a body that will better serve and address their specific interests.

The FCJ's launch as an independent body allows it to represent all journalists, including independent community press journalists, and assists in meeting its objective of becoming a more diverse and representative body for the community press industry.

The Broadcasting Complaints Commission of South Africa is an independent self-regulatory body, which serves as a voluntary watchdog to adjudicate complaints from the public about programmes flighted by members subscribing to its code of conduct. It is empowered by its members, which include, among others, the SABC, M-Net, Radio 702 and Trinity Broadcasting Network. However, the commission does not deal with X-rated material which, under criminal law, is prohibited.

The Broadcasting Monitoring Complaints Committee (BMCC) was established under sections 21 and 22 of the IBA Act, 1993.

It monitors broadcasting licensees for their compliance with, or adherence to, the terms, conditions and obligations of:
• their broadcasting licences
• the Code of Conduct for Broadcasting Services
• the Code of Advertising Practice.

The BMCC receives and adjudicates complaints from the public with regard to licence conditions, and is also entitled to initiate its own investigations into suspected non-compliance by a broadcaster.

If a member of the public is concerned that a broadcaster is not observing its licence conditions, that person may lodge a complaint with ICASA. If a broadcaster is found to be guilty of contravening its licence conditions, the BMCC makes recommendations to ICASA about action that should be taken.

Material that could be considered X-rated must be submitted to the Film and Publication Board prior to being shown. (See chapter 5: *Arts and culture.*)

The mission of the National Association of Broadcasters is to protect the interests of broadcasting as a whole, at the same time interfacing with ICASA on matters such as freedom of speech.

Other press organisations operating in the country are the Foreign Correspondents' Association of South Africa, the Printing Industries Federation of South Africa, the South African Typographical Union, the Specialist Press Association, the South African Guild of Motoring Journalists, Professional Photographers of South Africa, the Media Institute of Southern Africa, and press clubs in major centres.

The mission of the OPA is to provide a non-profit forum in which South African online publishers can address issues of common interest, and which can represent these publishers before advertising agencies and the advertising community, the press, government and the public.

News agencies

The South African Press Association, which is a national news agency, is a co-operative, non-profit news-gathering and distribution organisation operating in the interests of its members and the public. SAPA's foreign news is received from Associated Press (AP) and its representatives in London.

The main foreign news agencies operating in South Africa are *Agence France-Presse*, AP, *Deutsche Presse Agentur*, Reuters and United Press International.

Other agencies are the Eastern Cape News Agency and African Eye News Service in Mpumalanga.

Training centres

Over 40 institutions offer media training in South Africa.

Tertiary institutions include various universities of technology and universities such as Tshwane University of Technology, and Rhodes, Potchefstroom, Stellenbosch and Witwatersrand universities; and organisations such as the Cape Town Film and Television School; the SABC's Television Training Centre; the Radio Freedom Institute; the Institute for the Advancement of Journalism; Cross Media Training Centre; and NEMISA, a government-funded training institute specialising in broadcasting, news media and multimedia skills.

The Media, Advertising, Publishing, Printing and Packaging Sector Education and Training Authority (MAPPP-SETA) was gazetted on 15 March 2000.

It has six advisory committees, comprising representatives from labour, business and government, which advise on:

- print media
- advertising
- publishing
- printing
- packaging
- film and electronic media.

The MAPPP-SETA is responsible for co-ordinating a sector training plan across the media industry, and assesses the quality of training courses that are run by the industry.

Parallel to this, the South African Qualifications Authority has approved the establishment of several standards-generating bodies for the media industry.

Similar bodies were implemented for journalism training and communication studies. These bodies are substructures of the National Standards Body (language and communication), which co-ordinates standard-setting in the communication and language sectors.

Journalism awards

The most important awards include the:

- Mondi Shanduka Newspaper Awards
- Nat Nakasa Award for Courageous Journalism
- SAPPI Magazine Publishers Association of South Africa PICA Awards

- Sanlam Community Press Awards
- Vodacom Awards for Journalism Across All Mediums
- South African Breweries (SAB) Journalism Awards
- Sanlam's Financial Journalist of the Year Award, which was won by Tim Cohen, *Business Day's* editor-at-large, in May 2005.

The winner of the 2005 Nat Nakasa Award for Courageous Journalism was veteran photographer Alf Kumalo.

In April 2005, the Mondi Shanduka Newspaper Lifetime Achiever Award was given posthumously to Dr Aggrey Klaaste.

In 2005, the Sanlam Community Press Journalist of the Year was Annelien Dean from *The People's Post.*

Media diversity

Media diversity in any country is regarded as a sign of the status of its democracy. South Africa is on its way to achieving wide diversity and, apart from the public broadcaster and an array of major commercial newspapers and broadcasting services, it has established the Media Development and Diversity Agency (MDDA), which is tasked with providing financial and other support to community and small commercial media projects.

Media Development and Diversity Agency

The MDDA was established in terms of the MDDA Act, 2002 (Act 14 of 2002), which provides for the establishment of an independent, statutory body, jointly funded by government, the media industry and other donors.

The MDDA Act, 2002 was developed after extensive discussion with major media players who agreed to jointly fund such an agency with government to develop media diversity. The MDDA is tasked with creating an enabling environment for media diversity and development by providing support to media projects, and research into media development and diversity issues.

The agency functions independently and at arm's length from all of its funders and from political party and commercial interests. This arrangement enables government, the media industry and donors to work together towards addressing the legacy of imbalances in access to the media.

The MDDA awarded its first grants to community and small commercial media projects in January 2004.

By the end of March 2005, the MDDA had provided support to close to 60 different media and research projects around South Africa.

In addition, the MDDA has provided workshops and training opportunities to a wide range of media projects and has set aside support to assist up to 15 new community radio initiatives to prepare for the licence application process.

Apart from providing financial support, the MDDA is further working together with a range of media-sector and other related organisations to leverage resources for the sector to create an enabling environment for media development. For example, the agency has established partnerships with advertising and marketing organisations to run workshops that deal with securing advertising across the country.

Advertising

Since 2004, two publications have recognised excellence and achievement in South African advertising, namely *AdFocus* as published in *Financial Mail,* and *AdReview* as published in *Finance Week* and *Finansies en Tegniek.* Their 2005 acknowledgements are summarised below:

AdFocus 2005 winners:
- Agency of the Year – Net#work BBDO
- Media Agency of the Year – Nota Bene
- Agency Leader of the Year – Keith Shipley
- Media Owner of the Year – Primedia
- Newcomer of the year – Wingwing Mdlulwa
- Lifetime Achievement – Nkwenkwe Nkomo.

AdReview winners:
- Agency of the Year and Medium-sized Agency of the Year – Net#work BBDO
- Large Agency of the Year – Ogilvy SA
- Small Agency of the Year – MorrisJones
- Newcomer of the Year – 9November
- Marketing Services Company of the Year – KingJames RSVP

- Broadcast Marketer of the Year – RSG
- Media Agency of the Year – The Mediashop
- Cape Agency of the Year – Ogilvy Cape
- Durban Agency of the Year – The Hardy Boys
- Personality of the Year – Gary Leih
- Event of the Year – Business Trust Long Run
- The Big Idea – *Joe* Campaign
- Campaign of the Year – Hyundai SA.

Advertising awards

The Loerie Awards are the best-known South African awards that recognise excellence in advertising. The Association of Marketers (ASOM) established these awards in 1978, to coincide with the advent of commercial television in South Africa. The first ceremony took place in 1979.

The Loerie Awards ceremony is a self-liquidating event, with excess monies ploughed directly back into the industry in the form of bursaries for underprivileged advertising and marketing students via the Loerie Education Trust Fund, and as a donation to the Advertising Benevolent Fund.

The main objective of the Loerie Awards is to encourage creative advertising. The Marketing Federation of Southern Africa, which was instituted in 2002 after the merger of ASOM, the Direct Marketing Association and the Institute of Marketing Management, recognises and rewards those creative people who strive for excellence by producing highly creative, mould-breaking advertising.

The organisation has been restructured, starting with the formation of a section 21 company. Through the new committee, the Loerie Awards are now managed by the industry for the industry, and profits will be used to promote the industry and develop its future creative leaders.

The 2005 Loerie Awards presentation was held on 15 and 16 October 2005 in Margate on the KwaZulu-Natal south coast.

Net#work BBDO was judged the most creative advertising agency by winning the most above-the-line awards at the annual Loeries Festival held in 2004. Of the total 115 advertising awards across 12 mediums, Net#work BBDO scooped 32 of them, including one of only two Grand Prix for its successful Virgin Atlantic poster campaign.

The win of one Grand Prix, four golds, 11 silvers and 17 bronzes kept Net#work at the top of the creative ratings for 2004. The agency also did well in below-the-line disciplines.

Other advertising awards

The Vuka! Awards celebrate excellence in public-service announcements where budgets are substantially lighter than they are for product, service or image advertising.

The Pendoring Awards reward excellence in Afrikaans advertising in both verbal and non-verbal form. Categories consist of radio, television, magazines, newspapers, outdoor advertising and campaigns.

Other marketing communication awards

In academic circles, advertising is regarded as one of the core elements of any marketing communication strategy. Marketers are increasingly integrating other core marketing communication elements, such as direct marketing and sponsorship – two of the fastest-growing areas in marketing communication – into their overall campaigns.

The Assegai Awards were introduced in 1998 to honour excellence in direct marketing strategic

In April 2005, the marketing and advertising sectors committed themselves to broader transformation of the industry by adopting the draft Black Economic Empowerment Transformation Charter and Scorecard in Sandton, near Johannesburg.

The commitment represents the culmination of extensive consultation among industry players and government, and over four years of interaction with the Parliamentary Portfolio Committee on Communications.

The development of the charter also follows on the signing of the values statement for the marketing and communication industry, which articulated that transformation of the industry is essential for its long-term growth and the upliftment of people who have been historically disadvantaged.

prowess and innovation, with an emphasis on results. These awards are the only South African marketing communication awards that recognise return on investment – measurable and account- able – talking directly to targeted prospects and existing customers by way of various integrated and actionable media. The awards are recognised as the industry benchmark with a mandate to promote growth and recognise and reward excellence in the direct marketing arena.

Online and offline advertising

In February 2005, the results of the ROAR Online Advertising Awards were announced, with top hon- ours going to Ogilvy One and Saatchi&Saatchi AtPlay.

Sponsored by MPower, Media24 Digital's online advertising sales arm, the ROAR Awards reward creativity and innovation in online advertising.

A judging panel, including industry experts from traditional advertising and online marketing spheres, reviewed a total of 60 submissions in the first year of the competition. Winning entries were awarded in two categories.

Ogilvy One Cape Town picked up the honours for Best Existing Online Advertisers and Saatchi&Saatchi AtPlay Cape Town was awarded Best Online Advertising Newcomers.

The online advertising sector in South Africa posted impressive growth figures of 136,7% for 2004, making it one of the fastest-growing market- ing mediums, according to figures released by OPA and Nielsen Media Research/AIS AdEx in April 2005.

The figures show that the South African online advertising industry was worth R116 million in 2004, meaning that the sector is beginning to grow its share of local advertising spend, which still lags behind other mediums at just under 1% of the total market. These figures represent a more-than-ten- fold increase over growth figures for the previous year.

Advertising Standards Authority (ASA)

The ASA is the protector of the ethical standards of advertising in South Africa and protects consumers against manipulative advertising and unfair claims.

Acknowledgements

Audit Bureau of Circulation

Department of Communications

e-tv

Government Communications (GCIS)

Independent Communications Authority of South Africa

Mr P Diederichs, Department of Journalism, Tshwane University of Technology

M-Net

Print Media SA

Prof Neels van Heerden, University of Pretoria

South African Broadcasting Corporation

South African National Editors' Forum

www.arivia.co.za

www.biz-community.com

www.fxi.org.za

www.gov.za

www.icasa.org.za

www.mtn.co.za

www.mfsa.co.za

www.orbicom.co.za

www.sabc.co.za

www.sapo.co.za

www.sentech.co.za

www.southafrica.info

www.telkom.co.za

www.theworx.biz

www.vodacom.co.za

Suggested reading

A Post Office for the People. Mellville: Chris van Rensburg, 1997.

Ansell, G. *Introduction to Journalism*. Johannesburg: Jacana, 2002.

Chapman, M. ed. *The Drum Decade: Stories from the 1950s*. Pietermaritzburg: University of Natal Press, 2001.

De Beer, A.S. ed. *Mass Media Towards the Millennium: The South African Handbook of Mass Communication*. 2nd ed. Pretoria: Van Schaik, 1998.

Du Plessis, F., Bothma, N., Jordaan, Y. and Van Heerden, N. *Integrated Marketing Communication*. Cape Town. New Africa Books, 2003.

Duncan, J. *Broadcasting and the National Question*. Johannesburg: Freedom of Expression Institute (FXI), 2002.

Duncan, J. and Seleoane, M. eds. *Media and Democracy in South Africa*. Pretoria: Human Sciences Research Council (HSRC) and FXI, 1998.

Evans, N. and Seeber, M. eds. *Politics of Publishing in South Africa*. Scottsville: University of KwaZulu-Natal, 2000.

Fardon, R. and Furness, G. eds. *African Broadcast Cultures: Radio in Transition*. Cape Town: David Philip, 2000.

Gerber, R. and Braun, R. *New Connections: Telecommunications in a Changing South Africa*. Rondebosch: University of Cape Town Press, 1998.

Goldstuck, A. *Hitchhiker's Guide to the Internet: A South African Handbook*. Wynberg, Sandton: Zebra Books, Struik Publications, 1995.

Hadland, A., and Thorne, K. *The People's Voice: The Development and Current State of the South African Small Media Sector*. Cape Town: HSRC, 2004.

Jackson, G.S. *Breaking Story: The South African Press*. Boulder: Westview Press, 1993.

Jacobs, S. *et al. Real Politics: The Wicked Issues.* Cape Town: Institute for a Democratic South Africa, 2001.

Johnson, S. *Strange Days Indeed.* London: Bantam, 1993.

Kaplan, D. *The Crossed Line: The South African Communications Industry in Transition.* Johannesburg: University of the Witwatersrand Press, 1990.

Koekemoer, L (ed). *Marketing Communications.* Cape Town. Juta. 2004.

Kok, P. and Pietersen, J. *Information and Communication Technologies.* Pretoria: HSRC, 2000 (National Research and Technology Project).

Louw, E. *South African Media Policy: Debates of the 1990s.* Durban: Centre for Cultural and Media Studies, University of Natal, 1993.

Manoim, I. *You Have Been Warned: The First Ten Years of the Mail and Guardian.* London: Viking, 1996.

Merrett, C. *A Culture of Censorship: Secrecy and Intellectual Repression in South Africa.* Cape Town: David Philip and University of Natal Press, 1994.

Nel, F. *Writing for the Media in South Africa.* 2nd ed. Oxford: Oxford University Press, 2003.

Oosthuizen, L. *Media Ethics in the South African Context.* Cape Town: Juta, 2002.

Owen, K. *These Times: A Decade of South African Politics.* Johannesburg: Jonathan Ball, 1992.

Retief, J. *Media Ethics: An Introduction to Responsible Journalism.* Cape Town: Oxford University Press South Africa, 2002.

Reynolds, H. and Richard, N. *Women Today: A Celebration: Fifty Years of South African Women.* Cape Town: Kwela Books, 2003.

Ronning, H. and Kasoma, F.P. *Media Ethics.* Cape Town: Juta, 2002

Shaw, G. *The Cape Times: An Informal History.* Cape Town: David Philip, 1999.

Stein, S. *Who Killed Mr Drum?* Cape Town: Mayibuye Books, 1999.

Switzer, L. and Adhikari, M. eds. *South Africa's Resistance Press: Alternative Voices in the Last Generation Under Apartheid.* Ohio: Ohio University Centre for International Studies, 2000.

Tleane, C. and Duncan. J. *Public Broadcasting in the Era of Cost Recovery: A Critique of the South African Broadcasting Corporation's Accountability.* Johannesburg: FXI, 2003.

Tyson, H. *Editors Under Fire.* Sandton: Random House, 1993.

Verwoerd, W. and Mabizela, M. *Chief Truths Drawn in Jest: Commentary on the TRC through Cartoons.* Cape Town: David Philip, 2000.

Wilhelm, P. *The State We're In.* Randburg: Ravan, 1999.

Young, L. *The All Africa Internet Guide.* Johannesburg: M&G Books, 2002.

Economy

South Africa has achieved a level of macro-economic stability not seen in the country for many years. Such advances create opportunities for real increases in expenditure on social services, and reduce the costs and risks for all investors, laying the foundation for increased investment and growth.

By February 2005, the economy was stronger than at any time in the past 20 years.

Economic indicators

Domestic output

Real domestic production responded positively to the growth in real expenditure and registered a growth rate of 3,7% in 2004. This compares favourably with the growth in real gross domestic production of 2,8%, which was recorded in 2003.

The enhanced performance was particularly evident in the middle quarters of 2004 when quarter-to-quarter growth accelerated from an annualised rate of 4% in the first quarter, to 4% and 5% in the second and third quarters, respectively. Growth decelerated somewhat to 4% in the final quarter of 2004, mainly due to the weaker performance of the mining and manufacturing sectors. Up to and including the fourth quarter of 2004, growth in total real gross domestic product (GDP) increased for the 25th successive quarter since the third quarter of 1998.

For 2004 as a whole, the tertiary sector experienced the strongest growth among the major production sectors. Within the tertiary sector, the commerce sector registered the highest rate of increase in real value added, consistent with the brisk pace of expenditure in the economy. In the primary sector, agricultural output recovered somewhat in 2004, following a contraction in 2003. Real value added in mining rose significantly in 2004 in the wake of strong world demand for commodities. Real value added by the secondary sector recorded the slowest rate of increase among the major output sectors in 2004, but still expanded by roughly 3% during the year.

Manufacturing output increased significantly, partly in response to the strong domestic expenditure growth and the strong international demand for certain types of manufactured goods in the global upswing.

The growth in the real value added by the primary sector, which accelerated unabatedly in the first three quarters of 2004, slowed down markedly in the fourth quarter. This slowdown was visible in the real output of both the agricultural and mining sectors. For 2004 as a whole, the level of real output in the primary sector rose by 3% compared with an increase of only 1% in 2003. This was mainly a result of the recovery in the real value added by the agricultural sector following its substantial contraction in 2003.

Following a decline of 6% in 2003, the real value added by the agricultural sector increased by 1% in 2004, mainly on account of higher field crop production, particularly of maize. The output of livestock farmers also increased. Quarter-to-quarter growth in real value added was at its strongest in the middle quarters of 2004. It slowed down, however, from an annualised rate of 11% in the third quarter to 4% in the fourth quarter. Although livestock and horticultural production held up fairly well, the real output in other subsectors of the agricultural sector was weak in the fourth quarter.

The real value added by the mining sector increased for 11 consecutive quarters, but production volumes shrank in the fourth quarter of 2004. The contraction in real output at an annualised rate of 1% in the fourth quarter of 2004, was mainly due to a decline in the real value added by the gold- and platinum-mining sectors, following exceptionally strong output growth in the third quarter.

The strength of the exchange rate left its mark on profitability as export earnings came under pressure. Although coal-mining production increased on account of favourable world demand conditions, this could not offset the decline in the real value added

by the other mining subsectors in the fourth quarter. For 2004 as a whole, growth in the real value added by the mining sector was 4%, which is comparable with the rate of 4% recorded in 2003.

Following an increase of 6% in the third quarter of 2004, growth in the real value added by the secondary sector slowed down to an annualised rate of 3% in the fourth quarter. All three subsectors of the secondary sector recorded slower growth. Nonetheless, their real value added performed sturdily on a year-to-year basis, recording a growth rate of 3% in 2004 against stagnant real output in 2003.

Growth in the real value added by the manufacturing sector slowed down from an annualised rate of 6% in the third quarter of 2004, to 2% in the fourth quarter. This can mainly be attributed to declines in the real output of several subsectors, including food and beverages, petroleum, chemical, rubber and plastic products, and glass and non-metallic mineral products.

However, solid performances were recorded by several other subsectors of the manufacturing sector, which counteracted these declines to some extent. Firm growth in real output was recorded by the subsectors textiles, clothing and leather, wood and wood products, as well as basic iron and steel.

Manufacturing output volumes contracted by 1% in 2003 as a whole, but subsequently rebounded strongly and increased by 2% in 2004. Factors contributing to the improvement included:

- the continued strength of domestic demand
- local manufacturers' proximity to and flexibility in

Real gross domestic product

Percentage change at seasonally adjusted and annualised rates

Sector	2003					2004				
	1st qr	2nd qr	3rd qr	4th qr	Year	1st qr	2nd qr	3rd qr	4th qr	Year
Primary sector	- 0	-2	-2	0	1	5	7	9,5	0,5	3,5
Agriculture	-6,5	-19,5	-21	-5,5	-6	8,5	17,5	11,5	4	1
Mining	3,5	6,5	7	2	4,5	3,5	3	9	-1	4
Secondary sector	-2	-3	-1	0	0	5	6	6,5	3	3
Manufacturing	-3	-4	-2	-1	-1	5	6	6,5	2,5	2,5
Tertiary sector	4	4	4	4,5	4	3,5	4	5	5	4
Non-agricultural sector	2,5	2,5	3	3	3	4	4	5,4	4	4
Total	**2**	**2**	**2,5**	**3**	**3**	**4**	**4,5**	**5,4**	**4**	**3,5**

Source: South African Reserve Bank, *Quarterly Review*

dealing with the domestic market

- well-contained and even declining input costs in certain sectors
- strong international demand for certain types of manufactured goods in the current global upswing.

Under these circumstances, capacity utilisation in manufacturing increased considerably, while business confidence reached its highest level in more than two decades in 2004.

The real value added by the sector supplying electricity, gas and water slowed down from an annualised rate of 3% in the third quarter of 2004 to 3% in the fourth quarter. This modest slowdown was mainly evident in the growth in real value added by the electricity subsector. Higher volumes of electricity exported in 2004 boosted growth in the real value added by the sector supplying electricity, gas and water. The real value added by the construction sector increased further in the fourth quarter of 2004, albeit at a marginally slower pace than in the third quarter. The firm performance was underpinned by robust activity in the residential building sector.

Relatively low interest rates and rising household incomes provided impetus to the demand for new residential buildings. Building conditions in the non-residential sector also showed a substantial improvement, particularly as the demand for retail and entertainment space increased.

By contrast, building activity in the civil engineering sector remained unimpressive. Annual growth in real construction output accelerated from 5% in 2003 to 6% in 2004 – the highest annual growth rate since 1989.

The services sector continued its sterling performance. Growth in the real value added by the tertiary sector was sustained at an annualised rate of 5% in the third and fourth quarters of 2004. This can mainly be ascribed to lively activity in the commerce, transport, storage and communications sectors as well as the finance, insurance, real-estate and business services sectors.

For 2004 as a whole, the real value added by the tertiary sector grew by 4% – the same rate attained in 2003. The growth in the real value added by the commerce sector accelerated from an annualised rate of 5% in the third quarter of 2004, to about 7% in the fourth quarter. The buoyant levels of domestic demand enhanced activity in the wholesale and retail trade subsectors in the fourth quarter of 2004.

Retailers, in particular, benefited from lively consumption demand, especially for durable goods. Prices remained well-contained and even came down in the case of certain items with a high import content, providing a stimulus for consumer demand.

The real value added by the motor trade subsector also rose further in the fourth quarter of 2004. Compared with the other sectors of the economy,

Real gross domestic expenditure

Percentage change at seasonally adjusted annualised rates

Components	2003					2004				
	1st qr	2nd qr	3rd qr	4th qr	Year	1st qr	2nd qr	3rd qr	4th qr	Year
Final consumption expenditure by households	3	3,5	5,5	6	3,5	6	6,5	6,5	7	6
Final consumption expenditure by general government	6	6,5	6,5	14	6,5	6	6	0	13	7
Gross fixed capital formation	8	4 ,5	7	10	9	11,5	10	7,5	9	9 ,5
Change in inventories (R billion) at constant 2000 prices	7,6	10,5	9,2	9,2	9,2	9,6	14,9	13,6	7,6	11,4
Gross domestic expenditure	7	5,5	6	8,5	5,5	5,5	9	2,5	4,5	6,5

Source: South African Reserve Bank, *Quarterly Review*

the commerce sector registered the highest annual growth rate in 2003 and 2004.

The ongoing expansion of the communications subsector, specifically that of cellular telephone and Internet activity, boosted the quarter-to-quarter growth in the real value added by the transport, storage and communications sector to an annualised rate of about 7% in the fourth quarter of 2004. This was slightly higher than the rate of 6% recorded in the third quarter.

In addition, the increased volume of imports and exports boosted the real value added by land transport. Growth in the real value added by the transport, storage and communications sector accelerated from 5,2% in 2003 to 5,5% in 2004.

Following an increase of 5% in the third quarter of 2004, growth in the real value added by the financial intermediation, insurance, real-estate and business services sector accelerated to an annualised rate of 6% during the fourth quarter of 2004. This could be ascribed mainly to higher trading volumes on the JSE Limited (formerly the JSE Securities Exchange) and robust growth recorded in the real-estate subsector. Banks' real output remained high as the demand for financial services continued to increase. The annual growth in the financial intermediation, insurance, real-estate and business services sector in 2004 amounted to about 4%, roughly the same rate as attained in 2003.

Real value added by the general Government increased at an annualised rate of 1% in the fourth quarter of 2004 – similar to the growth in the first three quarters of the year. This stable rate of output growth was largely due to continued moderate increases in general government employment.

The improvement in South Africa's international terms of trade and the lower net primary income payments to the rest of the world, particularly dividend payments, strengthened the level of real gross national income in 2004. As a result, growth in real gross national income accelerated from 3% in 2003 to 5% in 2004. This translated into increases in gross national income per capita of 1% in 2003 and 3% in 2004.

Domestic expenditure

Within an environment characterised by rising income and the lowest inflation and nominal interest rate levels encountered in more than 20 years, all the major components of real domestic final demand rose strongly in 2004. This impacted on the accelerated growth in real gross domestic expenditure for 2004 as a whole.

Growth in aggregate real gross domestic expenditure accelerated from an annualised rate of 2% in the third quarter of 2004 to 4% in the fourth quarter. This acceleration was observed in all three components of domestic final demand – real final consumption expenditure by households and by general government, and real gross fixed capital formation. The slowdown in real inventory investment in the fourth quarter was more than neutralised by the robust increase in the other major spending categories. The level of real gross domestic expenditure was 6% higher in 2004 than in 2003.

Growth in real final consumption expenditure by households accelerated from 6% in the third quarter of 2004 to an annualised rate of 7% in the fourth quarter. The buoyancy in consumer spending was also reflected in a year-on-year growth rate of 6% in 2004 compared with a growth rate of 3% recorded in 2003.

The strong household spending in 2004 was underpinned by several factors, including:
- An increase of 5% in real household disposable income in 2004, partly due to wage settlements that remained above the contemporaneous inflation rate and income tax rates, which were lowered marginally.
- The steady decline in bank lending rates in 2003 and 2004 culminated in the lowest nominal short-term interest rates since 1980. This reduced the debt servicing cost of households as a percentage of disposable income from 8% in 2003 to 6% in 2004.
- The high levels of consumer confidence recorded in 2004, previously observed in 1997.
- The wealth effects arising from the exceptional increase in property and other asset prices.

In the fourth quarter of 2004, most major categories of household spending participated in the spending boom. Annualised growth in real spending on durable goods accelerated from 19% in the third quarter of 2004 to 25% in the fourth quarter. This was mainly a result of households stepping up real outlays on furniture, household appliances and motor cars. Purchases of recreational and entertainment goods also gathered momentum in the fourth quarter.

Growth in real outlays on semi-durable goods accelerated in the fourth quarter of 2004 as spending on household textiles and furnishings and on clothing and footwear picked up substantially. By contrast, real outlays on non-durable goods lost some momentum as households curtailed their purchases of petroleum products in response to the steep rise in petrol and diesel prices during the fourth quarter. Spending on services increased at the same pace as in the third quarter of 2004.

Households financed part of their expenditure by incurring more debt. Household debt as percentage of disposable income accordingly increased from 55% in the third quarter of 2004 to 57% in the fourth quarter. On an annual basis, the ratio increased from 51% in 2003 to 54% in 2004.

After stagnating in the third quarter of 2004, growth in real final consumption expenditure by general government accelerated to 13% in the fourth quarter of 2004.

Real government consumption expenditure on other non-wage goods and services increased at a steady pace from the third to the fourth quarter of 2004. Growth in real compensation of employees was also maintained at the same pace as in the third quarter. The higher level of government expenditure in the fourth quarter lifted the ratio of final consumption expenditure by general government to GDP to 20%, approximating levels previously observed during the period 1992 to 1994.

Growth in real gross fixed capital formation picked up from an annualised rate of 7% in the third quarter of 2004 to 9% in the fourth quarter. The quarter-to-quarter increases throughout 2004 resulted in an annual growth rate of 9,4%, higher than the 9% growth rate recorded in 2003. Firm annual growth in real capital outlays by the private business enterprises in 2004 offset slower growth

in spending by public corporations and general government.

During the fourth quarter of 2004, growth in real capital outlays by the private sector faltered somewhat, while that of public corporations and general government picked up substantially. Growth in real gross fixed capital formation by the private sector slowed down from an annualised rate of 20% in the third quarter of 2004 to 4% in the fourth quarter as enterprises in agriculture and mining reduced their capital outlays.

The agricultural sector's investment expenditure was adversely affected by a decline in the Rand prices of key agricultural products. Platinum mines, whose endeavours have formed the mainstay of mining investment in recent years, postponed several projects given the lustreless Rand prices of their key products. The decline in gross fixed capital formation in the primary sector of the economy was countered by ongoing investment in retail and entertainment space, which benefited from strong consumer spending.

Public corporations stepped up spending considerably in the fourth quarter. The addition of network equipment strengthened investment by the communications sector. In addition, public utilities supplying electricity, gas and water stepped up their capital investment. Real outlays on road infrastructure and urban renewal projects contributed to growth in real gross fixed capital formation by general government.

Business confidence was close to its highest level in July 2005. The South African Chamber of Business' (SACOB) Business Confidence Index (BCI) for July 2005 was 129, just 1,9 points below the record level of 130,9 achieved in September 2004.

According to SACOB, it was not only the highest level of 2005, but a continuation of the renewed rising trend from January 2005 after business confidence slowed during the last few months of 2004.

July's BCI was mainly due to the volume of merchandise exports, share prices and unexpected lower inflation.

An analysis of annual growth rates in capital spending by type of asset confirms that the growth rate of capital outlays on residential buildings not only exceeded that of the other asset types during 2004, but that the growth of investment spending on residential buildings was at its highest since the mid-1960s. The ratio of gross fixed capital formation to GDP improved from 16% in 2003 to 16,5% in 2004. This compares well with an average ratio of 15% from 2000 to 2003.

As may be expected with consistently rising economic activity and sales volumes, real inventory levels rose further throughout 2004. Following a strong build-up in the first three quarters of 2004, inventory accumulation slowed down in the fourth quarter.

Most sectors of the economy reported smaller net additions to inventories – possibly unplanned, as final demand increased strongly in the fourth quarter. In the mining sector, particularly in the gold-mining sector, inventories were actually reduced. Higher sales of gold were probably encouraged by the stronger performance of the gold price while production continued its secular decline. The slowdown in inventory accumulation compressed real expenditure growth by about two percentage points in the fourth quarter of 2004.

As a percentage of non-agricultural GDP, the level of industrial and commercial inventories decreased from 15,7% in the third quarter to 15,5% in the fourth quarter of 2004. On an annual basis, this ratio edged down from almost 16% in 2003 to about 15% in 2004.

The economy grew by 4,8% in the second quarter of 2005.

According to Statistics SA, this was up on a gross domestic product (GDP) figure of 3,5% measured in the first quarter.

The manufacturing industry contributed most to the growth with 1,2 of a percentage point.

GDP for the first six months of the year increased by 4,4% compared with the first six months of 2004.

Price inflation

During recent years, remarkable progress has been made in lowering South Africa's inflation rate to levels more consistent with those of its main trading partners.

Overall consumer price inflation decelerated markedly from a most recent high of 9,2% in 2002 to 5,8% in 2003 and 1,4% in 2004 – the lowest rate of increase since 1962. Also, the year-on-year rate of increase in the consumer price index for metropolitan and other urban areas, less mortgage interest cost (CPIX) decelerated to within the inflation target range of between 3% to 6% in the 21 consecutive months to May 2005.

The waning in price inflation during the recent period resulted mainly from the substantial appreciation in the exchange rate of the Rand since the second half of 2002. Additional factors which contributed to the reduction in inflationary pressures were:

- the consistent application of prudent fiscal and monetary policies
- low increases in food prices over an extended period
- a progressive deceleration in inflation expectations.

A further moderation in price inflation in South Africa was prevented recently. This was consistent with mounting concerns in the international community over the inflationary effects of the increase in commodity prices, particularly crude oil. Year-on-year CPIX inflation rose from a low of 3,1% in February 2005 to 3,9% in May 2005. This acceleration in inflation was almost entirely due to the increase in the domestic price of petrol, which resulted from the higher price of imported crude oil.

The price for mining and quarrying products imported into South Africa, mainly comprising crude oil, increased by as much as 52% in the 17 months to May 2005.

CPIX inflation remained comfortably within the inflation target range and only four categories showed year-on-year rates of price increase in excess of the upper limit of the inflation target range by May 2005. However, some factors were still of concern, necessitating continued vigilance in the application of anti-inflationary policy. These included:

- high and volatile international crude oil prices
- uncertainty concerning exchange-rate developments
- some salary and wage settlements significantly in excess of the inflation target range
- possible second-round effects of the abovementioned factors
- fairly high rates of money supply growth alongside continued buoyancy in domestic demand conditions
- increases in certain administered prices in excess of the inflation target range.

Exchange rates

The weighted average of the Rand, which appreciated by 16,2% between the end of December 2002 and the end of December 2003, improved further by 11,7% between the end of December 2003 and the end of December 2004.

The strengthening in the external value of the Rand coincided with a large surplus on the financial account, which more than made up for the deficit on the current account. The improvement in the external value of the Rand occurred mainly in the fourth quarter of 2004, when, on balance, the nominal effective exchange rate of the Rand strengthened by 6,6%. Factors that probably supported the improvement in the external value of the Rand were:

- the continued weakness of the United States (US) Dollar
- continued prudent economic policies
- improvement in the Reserve Bank's foreign reserve position
- expectations of significant future foreign direct investment (FDI) inflows
- improved international credit ratings
- strong foreign currency prices of South Africa's export commodities
- the positive, although shrinking, interest rate differential between South Africa and its main trading partners.

The external value of the Rand weakened by 3,3% on a trade-weighted basis during January 2005, but strengthened again by 2,2% during February 2005. From the end of December 2004 to the end of March 2005, the nominal effective exchange rate of the Rand appreciated by 4%.

The net average daily turnover in the domestic market for foreign exchange, which decreased to US$10,8 billion in the third quarter of 2004, rose to US$12,4 billion in the fourth quarter of 2004 – its highest level to date.

The value of transactions in which non-residents participated, increased from US$7,4 billion a day to US$9,2 billion a day over the same period. Participation by resident parties decreased from US$3,4 billion a day in the third quarter of 2004, to US$3,2 billion in the fourth quarter.

The average monthly real effective exchange rate of the Rand increased by 4,3% from December 2003 to December 2004.

Foreign trade and payments

The deficit on the current account of the balance of payments widened considerably from R18,9 billion

In August 2005, Fitch Ratings became the third major international agency to upgrade South Africa's sovereign credit ratings in 2005, following upgrades by Moody's and Standard & Poor's.

A better economic growth performance, a stronger external balance sheet, entrenched macro-economic stability, increased public investment and a transparent political system were among the reasons cited by the agencies for their upgrades.

Fitch raised South Africa's long-term foreign currency rating from BBB to BBB+, its short-term rating from F3 to F2, and its country ceiling from BBB+ to A-.

Earlier in August, Standard & Poor's upgraded South Africa's long-term foreign currency rating from BBB to BBB+ and its local currency rating from A to A+.

In January 2005, Moody's lifted South Africa's country ceilings for foreign currency debt and bank deposits from Baa2 to Baa1, with a stable outlook. Ratings on foreign currency-denominated bonds and notes was also raised to Baa1, with a stable outlook.

172

in 2003 to R44,4 billion in 2004. As a ratio of GDP, the deficit rose to 3,2%.

The significant widening of the deficit on the current account in 2004, resulted mainly from the sustained high level of real economic activity and concomitant strong increase in merchandise imports.

Robust domestic demand and the strengthening of the exchange rate of the Rand were reflected in the physical quantity of imported goods, which advanced by no less than 16,5% over the period.

As could be expected against the background of a vigorous upturn in economic activity, South Africa's trade balance with the rest of the world deteriorated considerably from a surplus of R25,6 billion recorded in 2003 to a deficit of R0,2 billion in 2004.

The value of merchandise exports increased throughout 2004. For the year as a whole, export values were 8,8% higher at R278,9 billion from R256,3 billion in 2003. In particular, mining export values increased by no less than 13,5% in 2004, while manufactured goods increased by only 3% over the period.

The Rand prices of goods exported from South Africa in 2004 increased by about 3%, while the Rand prices of commodity exports increased by about 5%.

A stronger world economy and buoyant demand for commodities contributed to the physical quantity of exported goods rising by almost 5,5% in 2004.

The further widening of the current account deficit in 2004 was also brought about by a further decrease of 4% in the value of net gold exports from R34,2 billion in 2003 to R32,8 billion in 2004.

Although the average US$ price of gold on the London gold market increased by 12,6% from US$364 per fine ounce in 2003, to US$409 per fine ounce in 2004, the Rand price of gold decreased by 3,8% over the period from R2 740 per ounce to R2 637 per fine ounce.

The decline in the Rand price of gold was mainly the result of an appreciation of 14,7% of the exchange rate of the Rand against the Dollar over this period.

This had a negative impact on the Rand earnings of gold exporters and their operations in terms of operational cost.

Having remained fairly flat in the first nine months of 2003, the value of merchandise imports rose almost unabatedly for five consecutive quarters up to the end of 2004. The Rand value of imported goods in the fourth quarter of 2004 was no less than 24% higher than in the corresponding quarter of 2003.

All the main categories of imports registered increases of more than 10% from 2003 to 2004.

South Africa's import penetration ratio (i.e. the ratio of real merchandise imports to real gross domestic expenditure) rose from 21,7% in the first quarter of 2004 to 23,9% in the fourth quarter.

For the year as a whole, the volume of merchandise imports rose by 16,5%. The strong rise in the import penetration ratio probably partly reflected the substitution of imported goods for domestically produced goods in response to the decline in the relative prices of imported goods. The average price of imported goods in rands increased by 1,5% in the fourth quarter of 2004 and rose by only half a percent in 2004 as a whole. Increases in the international price of crude oil were offset by the increase in the weighted effective exchange rate of the Rand over the period.

The deficit on the net services, income and current transfer account of the balance of payments widened from R43,4 billion in the third quarter of 2004 to R48,6 billion in the fourth quarter.

This weakening was mainly due to an increase in net income payments, which rose from R26,2 billion in the third quarter of 2004 to R30,6 billion in the fourth quarter as dividend receipts from non-residents decreased.

For 2004 as a whole, the deficit on the net services, income and current transfer account remained virtually unchanged at R44,2 billion compared with 2003.

South Africa recorded substantial inflows of capital on the financial account of the balance of payments during 2004. An inflow amounting to R96,1 billion was recorded during the year; the highest annual inflow ever recorded in a calendar year.

Net financial inflows to the value of R42,2 billion were recorded in the first half of 2004, followed by inflows of R53,9 billion in the second half. These inflows were substantially higher than the inflow of R70,4 billion recorded in 2003.

Inward direct investment decreased during the year to R3,8 billion, compared with an inflow of R5,4 billion in 2003. Outward direct investment recorded an outflow of R10,4 billion in 2004, compared with an outflow of R4,4 billion in 2003. For 2004 as a whole, a net flow of direct investment to the value of R6,6 billion was recorded.

Net portfolio investment increased substantially from an inflow of R6,9 billion in 2003 to an inflow of R38,9 billion in 2004. The inflow in net portfolio investment in 2004 was the highest amount recorded since 1999.

Other foreign investment in South Africa, consisting mainly of loans, trade finance and bank deposits, increased from an inflow of R8,9 billion in 2003 to an inflow of R13,5 billion in 2004. Over the same period, South African entities reduced their other investment assets by R18,1 billion.

The country's net international reserves increased by R52,1 billion during 2004, owing to a strong surplus on the financial account. Total gross gold and foreign exchange reserves increased from R165,5 billion at the end of December 2003 to R184,5 billion at the end of December 2004.

In US dollar terms, South Africa's total gross international reserves rose from US$24,9 billion to US$32,8 billion over the same period.

Import cover, i.e. the value of gross international reserves expressed as a ratio of the imports of goods and services, decreased from 22,5 weeks at the end of 2003 to 21,5 weeks at the end of 2004.

Department of Trade and Industry

The Department of Trade and Industry guides and facilitates access to sustainable economic activity by attracting high levels of investment, increasing access of South African goods and services to international markets, and creating a fair and conducive environment for domestic and international businesses and customers.

The department is working towards a transformed and adaptive economy that generates employment and equity.

To contribute to greater shared growth in the country, the department is pursuing the following goals:
- significantly progressing Broad-Based Black Economic Empowerment (BBBEE)
- increasing the contribution of small enterprises to the economy
- contributing towards providing accessible, transparent and efficient access to redress
- contributing towards building skills, technology and infrastructure platforms from which enterprises can benefit
- increasing market access opportunities for, and export of, South African goods and services
- increasing the overall level of direct investment, as well as in priority sectors
- repositioning the economy in higher value-added segments of value matrices in knowledge-driven manufacturing and services
- contributing towards the economic growth and development of the African continent within the New Partnership for Africa's Development (NEPAD) framework
- building an efficient, effective and accessible organisation to achieve these outcomes.

These strategic objectives will be achieved through the collective effort of the department's divisions and agencies that generate public value for economic citizens and deliver products and services for clients and stakeholders.

These products and services include policy, legislation and regulation, finance and incentives, information and advice, and partnerships. The department also achieves these objectives by pursuing a more targeted investment strategy, improved competitiveness of the economy, broadening the economic participation of historically disadvantaged individuals (HDIs) in the mainstream economy, and policy coherence.

In 2005/06, impetus was added to the achievement of the department's strategic objectives by implementing a number of flagship projects. An average annual budget of R3 billion and about

1 000 employees will be devoted to the implementation of this strategy over the next three years. The department will track its progress through a systematic reporting and measurement system and regular reviews.

Broadening economic participation

Several programmes are aimed at bridging the economic divide and broadening economic participation by HDIs.

These programmes include the Apex Fund that provides micro-finance to micro enterprises; the introduction of the Small Enterprise Development Agency (SEDA) to provide small enterprises around South Africa with a one-stop non-financial support service; the implementation of new policy and legislation to promote the development of co-operative enterprises; the continued implementation of the BBBEE Strategy; and the introduction of a specific strategy to empower women.

The capitalisation of the National Empowerment fund (NEF) commenced with an initial R400 million in the 2005/06 financial year, which allowed the fund to expand the products and services launched in 2004.

The intention is to increase the number of enterprises in the South African economy by creating an enabling environment, reducing regulatory costs for small enterprises and unleashing South Africa's entrepreneurial spirit.

Competitiveness and competition

The competitiveness of many enterprises in the economy continues to be based on the traditional factors of cost and access to raw material rather than on new drivers of competitive advantage. Not enough enterprises have moved into more value-added niche markets.

Furthermore, downstream value-adding beneficiation of raw material is often constrained by high input costs arising from the anti-competitive pricing practices of monopolistic enterprises. An example is the practice of import parity pricing in the steel and chemicals sectors.

The need to strengthen the capabilities of enterprises to compete on factors other than price will be a focus of the Department of Trade and Industry's work in the next three to five years. In this regard, it will undertake reviews of all of its enterprise support measures and incentives for relevance, efficacy and competitiveness compared with those offered by South Africa's competitors.

In addition, an industrial policy framework that extends the work done on the Integrated Manufacturing Strategy (IMS) to include primary sectors and services, will be developed and implemented. A critical element will include the development of policy instruments to address import parity pricing as part of an agreement concluded with government's social partners at the Growth and Development Summit (GDS).

Addressing anti-competitive behaviour and practices will be a focus area over the next three years.

A more targeted investment strategy

Investment levels in the economy remain below the 25% of GDP benchmark required for a sustained acceleration in economic growth rates.

Not only does the level and rate of investment in the economy need to increase, but the type of investment that takes place also needs to be more labour-absorbing if significant numbers of new jobs are to be created.

Over the next three years, the Department of Trade and Industry is expected to develop and implement a more targeted investment strategy. It focuses on identifying and promoting specific investment opportunities in particular sectors, regions, and products, rather than a generic approach of marketing South Africa as an attractive investment destination.

This will require a more co-ordinated approach to investment promotion by national, provincial and local government. Achieving this will be a priority in the first year of the Medium Term Expenditure Framework (MTEF) period. The investment strategy will be informed by the results of the World Bank's Investment Climate Survey of over 500 enterprises, as well as an Organisation for Economic Co-operation and Development review of South Africa's investment policy environment.

The department's work to develop and implement customised sector programmes to unlock the potential of government's priority sectors will be given a higher priority. New growth sectors, including aerospace and paper and pulp, will be added.

Policy coherence and alignment

The Department of Trade and Industry continues to strengthen the Economic and Employment Cluster and promote co-operative governance around economic policy, as well as ensure the strategic alignment and performance of its agencies. The department strengthens the working relationship with social partners through the National Economic Development and Labour Council (Nedlac) and enhances the support provided for organised business, specifically local business chambers.

Market access

International trade and economic development

The International Trade and Economic Development (ITED) Division of the Department of Trade and Industry aims to increase South Africa's access to markets worldwide by negotiating international trade agreements, where possible, on preferential terms.

At the same time, ITED seeks to ensure that the country's commitments are honoured in the multilateral, rules-based trading system underpinned by the World Trade Organisation (WTO).

Internationally, open economies with an export base fare much better in terms of economic growth than closed economies. Production is more and more globally integrated, and South Africa forms a vital part of international supply chains.

Therefore, dismantling barriers to trade, especially those barriers faced by South African exporters, is a critical component of any economic strategy that promotes sustainable growth.

ITED's global economic strategy considers sustainable growth as its departure point. It is not developed in isolation but is part of South Africa's broad industrial strategy. It was formulated in the light of the country's relations with the Southern African Development Community (SADC), the rest of Africa, NEPAD, and economic relations with developed and developing trading partners in the North and the South.

ITED is committed to the pursuit of market access for South Africa, more effective efforts at subregional and continental integration, and the strategic and positive engagement of the region and the continent in the WTO.

Policy and programme developments in international trade development include:

- Continued negotiations with MERCOSUR, a trading bloc consisting of six Latin American countries, namely Argentina, Bolivia, Brazil, Chile, Paraguay and Uruguay.
- Upcoming preferential trade negotiations with India and China, which are expected to gain momentum in 2006.
- Administering various binational commissions (BNCs) with other governments.
- Implementing the new Southern African Customs Union (SACU) Agreement, concluded in September 2001, in which the ITED played a pivotal role.
- Strengthening the trade capacity of the SADC.
- Preparing for and participating in a new trade round under the auspices of the WTO.
- Ongoing analyses of trade threats and opportunities.
- Facilitating the new International Trade Administration Commission's (ITAC) mandate, an independent regulatory agency. The ITAC has taken over the Board of Tariffs and Trade's function of administering the tariff regime and is set to play a central role within the SACU on tariff and related issues.

In the first half of 2004/05, 13 620 permit applications were adjudicated, 7 869 import control permits issued, 1 923 export control permits issued, 12 enforcement investigations launched, 160 unscheduled enforcement inspections undertaken, and 391 container inspections carried out.

In relation to anti-dumping and counter-veiling investigations and reviews, 14 sunset reviews (where something is reviewed after a set period with a view to removing it automatically) and 15 new cases were undertaken. ITAC dispensed 884 duty credit certificates, 1 732 import rebate credit certificates, 466 eligible export certificates, eight rebates of customs tariffs, 14 reductions in customs tariffs and six increases in customs tariffs.

African economic development

Africa forms the focus of South Africa's global economic strategy, within which government pursues a strong developmental agenda. Partnerships with countries on the continent are therefore considered vital and strategic. South Africa's economy is inextricably connected to that of the southern African region, and its success is linked to the economic recovery of the continent through NEPAD.

The developmental challenges must be viewed in light of the mutually beneficial economic and developmental impact on South Africa and Africa's self-enforcing and economic existence.

Africa is an important market for South African exports. In 2003, about 23% of South Africa's exports were destined for the continent. There was a huge increase in imports from the continent. In 2003, only 4% of total imports came from Africa. However, this increased to 40% in 2004.

This trade imbalance has largely been offset by South Africa's investment on the continent, aimed at infrastructural projects designed to enhance the productive capacities of African economies. In addition to forging bilateral trade and economic relations, the Department of Trade and Industry is committed to increasing South Africa's involvement in large capital projects on the continent. The following areas have been prioritised:

- infrastructure and logistics (roads, ports, etc.)
- energy and Information and Communications Technology (ICT)
- water and waste management
- transport
- construction
- oil and gas infrastructure
- agri-business
- mining
- human resource development (HRD).

During meetings of the World Economic Forum (WEF) for southern Africa, the formation of a business forum for southern Africa was announced (a joint initiative between the Department of Trade and Industry and the private sector); established to take advantage of investment opportunities in the region.

The department, through Trade and Investment South Africa (TISA), has established trade and investment promotion offices on the continent to facilitate trade and investment flows. The offices are located in Egypt, Nigeria, Ghana, Kenya, Ethiopia, Tanzania, Zimbabwe, the United Arab Emirates, Saudi Arabia and Angola. New foreign offices were expected to be opened in Zambia, Senegal, Algeria and Angola.

The department is providing supportive services to NEPAD, which is playing a critical role in catalysing trade and economic development on the continent. In southern Africa, South Africa seeks to restructure regional arrangements promoting industrialisation. The department supports a process whereby integrated manufacturing platforms form the basis for an integrated regional industrial strategy. This entails using southern Africa as an integral part of supply chains for globally competitive manufacturing processes.

Through a combination of sectoral co-operation, policy co-ordination and trade integration, South Africa's regional policy aims to achieve a dynamic regional economy capable of competing effectively in the global economy. For instance, South Africa works closely with its neighbours in engaging with multilateral international institutions and agreements – from the WTO to the African-Caribbean-Pacific Declaration.

Southern African Development Community

The SADC is constituted by Angola, Botswana, the Democratic Republic of Congo (DRC), Lesotho, Malawi, Mauritius, Mozambique, Namibia, South Africa, Swaziland, Tanzania, Zambia and Zim-babwe. Madagascar submitted an application for membership during the SADC Heads of State Summit, held in Mauritius during August 2004, and was granted permanent membership in August 2005.

Since attaining democracy in 1994, South Africa has put regional integration by SADC member states on the top of its foreign economic agenda. This approach follows from the belief in the economic benefits that can be brought to all member states by closer economic co-operation in the region. To support this approach, South Africa has reviewed its trade relationship with other SADC members, adopted the SADC Trade Protocol, promoted investment by South African firms in the SADC, and helped to facilitate greater volumes of trade by South Africa and other SADC members.

Implementation of the Southern African Development Community Protocol on Trade

The SADC Protocol on Trade was signed in 1996 in Maseru, Lesotho, and came into force on 25 January 2000.

Since then, negotiations on the operationalisation of the protocol centred on tariff-reduction schedules, rules of origin, dispute-settlement mechanisms, a special trade agreement on sugar, elimination of non-tariff barriers and harmonisation of customs and trade documentation. Agreement was generally achieved on all these issues, hence the launch of the Free Trade Area (FTA) on 1 September 2000.

By mid-2005, all SADC countries, with the exception of Angola, the DRC and Madagascar, were implementing the protocol. Angola has committed itself to the protocol by signing and acceding to it, and is preparing its tariff-reduction offers that are critical in the implementation of the protocol.

By June 2005, the SADC Secretariat was finalising the mid-term review on the implementation of the protocol. The findings of this review will indicate the levels of trade that have taken place under the protocol's preferences, to assess the rules of origin and any other issues that may impact on regional economic integration.

Substantial progress has been made towards customs co-operation with respect to the harmonisation of documentation and procedures, and in preparation for the Memorandum of Understanding (MoU) on Co-operation and Mutual Assistance among Customs Administrations.

Southern African Customs Union

The new SACU Agreement came into force on 15 July 2004. New institutional features include the Council of Ministers, which is the highest decision-making body on all matters pertaining to the SACU Agreement; a SACU tariff board, responsible for making recommendations on tariff and trade remedies to the council; a small SACU secretariat, responsible for rendering administrative and support services to SACU structures; and a dispute-settlement mechanism similar to the one in place in the SADC.

SACU members agreed on the establishment of national bodies responsible for receiving tariff applications from each member state. Consensus was also reached on a new revenue-sharing formula. The new SACU Agreement also provides for member states to develop common policies and strategies with respect to industrial development.

Agreement was reached to co-operate on agricultural issues to ensure the co-ordinated development of the agricultural sector. Member states will also co-operate to ensure fair competition and address unfair trade practices.

Two-way trade between South Africa and the other SADC member states is characterised by the prevailing trade imbalance in terms of exports versus imports from the region. Within the SADC, a smaller group of countries, Botswana, Lesotho, Namibia, Swaziland (the BLNS countries) and South Africa have organised themselves into the SACU. SACU thus shares a common tariff regime without any internal barriers. Customs revenues are shared according to an agreed formula.

A sizeable share of South Africa's exports (estimated at over R38,8 billion at the end of 2004) is destined for SACU and other SADC countries. South African trade with this region increased significantly between 2002 and 2004, from R15 billion to R38,8 billion. Trade with SADC countries also increased from R32 billion to about R38 billion between 2002 and 2004.

This increase was again experienced in the amount of imports from the region, from R4 billion to R6 billion. This gives an overall export:import ratio of 6:1. There is a definite need to reverse this trend and close the trade imbalance between South Africa and its SADC partners.

Zimbabwe is the main destination for South Africa's exports into Africa, absorbing well over R6 billion of South Africa's exports. It is the largest importer within the SADC region, importing over 24,4% of South Africa's exports into Africa.

Mozambique's position is improving. The country is importing more than it did in 2002 (from 16,4% to 19,5%), absorbing over R5 billion of South Africa's exports.

Trade with Europe

Trade relations with Europe, particularly with the European Union (EU), are pivotal to South Africa's economic development. The Trade Development and Co-operation Agreement (TDCA) with the EU forms a substantial element of South Africa's reconstruction and development.

Europe remains South Africa's largest trading region and source of investment. In 2003, Europe accounted for 40% (R92 billion) of South Africa's total exports, and 45,8% (R116,59 billion) of its total imports. During the same year, the EU accounted for the bulk of this trade, with exports to the EU reaching R84,95 billion in 2003 (down from R98,25 billion in 2002), and imports reaching R109 billion in 2003 (down from R115 billion in 2002).

Six European countries are among South Africa's top 10 export destinations, and four European countries are among the top 10 countries from which South Africa's imports originate. Since 2001, Germany has been South Africa's largest source of imports. In 2001, South Africa's imports from Germany totalled R32,35 billion. It reached R43 billion in 2002, and fell to R38,45 billion in 2003.

The United Kingdom (UK) remains South Africa's largest export destination in Europe and the second-largest in the world (after the United States of America [USA]). South Africa's exports to the UK amounted to R24,17 billion in 2003.

European Union

The TDCA, which came under provisional implementation on 1 January 2000, has established an FTA between South Africa and the EU. The TDCA commits South Africa to grant duty-free access to 86% of EU imports over a period of 12 years, while the EU will liberalise 95% of South Africa's imports over a 10-year period.

This agreement is expected to contribute towards the restructuring of the South African economy and its long-term economic growth. The agreement covers trade and related issues, and co-operation in economic, social and political fields. It also provides a legal framework for ongoing EU financial assistance on grants and loans for development co-operation, which amounts to R900 million per year.

Statistics compiled by the South African Revenue Service (SARS) show that increasing use is being made of the tariff preferences in the agreement.

The wines and spirits agreements were signed in January 2002 and are under provisional implementation. The agreements are part of the framework of agreements under the TDCA, and established the basis for trade in wines and spirits between South Africa and the EU. Negotiations on areas related to geographical indications, intellectual property and trademark protection are ongoing.

In 2004, there were two major developments in the relations between South Africa and the EU. The first was the expansion of the EU when 10 more European countries became members of the EU. After 1 May 2004, the enlarged EU became a larger internal market, accounting for 450 million citizens (increasing from 374 million). The second event was the ratification of the TDCA by all EU member countries. The TDCA will now come under full implementation and will elevate South Africa's relations with the EU.

The Americas

North America

The USA is South Africa's number one trading partner in terms of total trade (the sum of exports and imports) recorded in 2004. Exports to the USA increased marginally in nominal terms from R29 billion in 2003 to R30 billion in 2004. Imports from the USA also recorded a paltry increase in nominal terms from R25 billion to R26 billion from 2003 to 2004.

Since 2000, the trade balance has been in South Africa's favour with the trade surplus increasing marginally in nominal terms from R3,5 billion to R4 billion between 2000 and 2004.

South Africa is a beneficiary of the USA's Generalised System of Preferences (GSP), which grants duty-free treatment for more than 4 650 products.

South Africa is also a beneficiary of the Africa Growth and Opportunity Act (AGOA), which was promulgated in May 2000. In terms of the AGOA, an additional 1 783 products were added to the existing GSP products. Although the AGOA was initially due to lapse in 2008, the US Government consented to requests by African countries and extended the measure to 2015 under what is called the AGOA III amendments. The AGOA also allows duty-free entry of clothing and selected textiles into the USA subject to certain criteria and policy reforms. By 2005, about 37 countries had qualified under the AGOA, with Burkina Faso becoming eligible from 10 December 2004. Ivory Coast was removed from the list of AGOA eligible countries with effect from 1 January 2005.

Canada is South Africa's second-largest trading partner in North America. Since the lifting of sanctions in 1994, bilateral trade between South Africa and Canada increased from R904 million in 1993 to R4 billion in 2004.

South Africa is a beneficiary of Canada's General Preferential Tariff (GPT). GPT rates range from duty-free to reductions in the Most Favoured Nation rates. Furthermore, South Africa has an MoU with Canada relating to the export of clothing and textile products to that country.

The MoU allows a certain amount of clothing and textile products from South Africa to enter the Canadian market at a better than Most Favoured Nation tariff rate. The Trade and Investment Co-operation Arrangement, signed in 1998, sought to enhance bilateral and trade investment.

Latin America

South Africa's major trading partners in Latin America are Brazil, Argentina, Colombia, Chile, Mexico and Peru. Most trade is with Brazil and Argentina, which are members of the MERCOSUR

trade bloc. A framework agreement committing South Africa and MERCOSUR to an FTA was signed in 2000. However, as a first step towards achieving this goal, the parties signed a preferential trade agreement (PTA) in December 2004.

Upon ratification by all signatories, the PTA will offer businesses from both sides preferential access on a broad range of product lines.

Trade between South Africa and MERCOSUR grew substantially from R2,7 billion in 1994 to R12,7 billion in 2004. South Africa recorded a trade deficit of about R7,8 billion against the bloc for 2004. About 62,5% of total trade between South Africa and MERCOSUR is with Brazil. Both South Africa and Brazil regard each other as strategic partners, with co-operation taking place in bilateral fora as well as in multilateral fora such as the WTO. Notwithstanding South Africa's strong ties with MERCOSUR, Chile is becoming an increasingly important partner for South Africa. South African mining companies are heavily involved in mining activities in Chile.

After a decline in total trade between South Africa and Mexico from R1,4 billion in 2000 to R1,2 billion in 2003, positive growth was witnessed in 2004. Total trade between the two countries increased to R1,5 billion in 2004. The balance of trade has been in South Africa's favour for a number of years.

Bilateral trade between South Africa and the Andean Community (Peru, Ecuador, Bolivia, Colombia and Venezuela) has been growing at a relatively slow pace since 1994. The Andean Community, more specifically Colombia and Peru, offers great potential for South African companies participating in the mining industry.

Asia

South and south-east Asia and Australasia

India is a key partner for South Africa in South Asia and total trade with that country has been increasing rapidly since 1994. According to the latest figures, total two-way trade between the two countries reached R8,26 billion in 2004.

South Africa and India have enjoyed strong historical ties, which have translated into a firm political commitment. In the light of these shared historical links, closer economic ties are being fostered.

South Africa and India are strengthening and deepening bilateral economic links through mutual strong business and governmental co-operation. The Joint Ministerial Commission (JMC) provides an institutional mechanism for ministerial consultations on political and economic matters, and has facilitated several initiatives, including the conclusion of a general trade agreement, sector co-operation through the India-South Africa Commercial Alliance, and India's pledge of US$200 million for NEPAD.

Developments in building economic relations with India are also expanding to include partners in SACU, as reflected in SACU's decision to pursue FTA negotiations with India.

An FTA between SACU and India will accelerate trade flow between economies, extend the range of traded goods and services and, more importantly, increase the proportion of trade in higher value-added products. This process should stimulate investment, joint ventures and strategic partnerships between South African firms across a range of sectors.

South Africa also co-operates with India in areas of common interest in the WTO and other fora, and works closely in the India-Brazil-South Africa Forum. Furthermore, the two countries co-operate in the G20, a grouping of developing countries that seeks to address developmental challenges in the global economic system.

Bilateral trade with south-east Asia, particularly the Association of South-East Asian Nations (ASEAN) members, increased rapidly off a low base from 1990. The ASEAN presents South Africa with a potential market in excess of 520 million people. Within the ASEAN, partners for South Africa include countries such as Singapore, Thailand, Indonesia, Malaysia, Vietnam and the Philippines. Initiatives are underway to develop and strengthen relations with these economies. South African total trade with the ASEAN region totalled R1,64 billion in 2004, and is set for continued growth.

North-east Asia

The People's Republic of China (PRC) is a key partner for South Africa. The PRC's influence in the global economy has significantly changed in the last few decades as its share of international trade has increased and it is becoming a major pillar of economic growth in the global economy.

Economic and trade relations between South Africa and the PRC have grown rapidly since the formal establishment of diplomatic relations, with total trade growing from R5,3 billion in 1998 to R29,6 billion in 2004.

The two countries engage regularly on economic issues through the Joint Economic and Trade Committee, which is held under the auspices of the BNC. The launching of SACU-China FTA negotiations were recently announced. An FTA with China opens up the possibility, through the subsequent deepening of trade investment relations, for mutually beneficial economic development, greater horizontal and vertical integration, and an environment for strategic partnerships, joint ventures, a greater range of imports and exports, and an increase in the trade of value-added products.

Beyond bilateral and regional initiatives, South Africa and the PRC also co-operate in multilateral fora, including the WTO, based on shared developmental perspectives.

Japan is another important country. It is South Africa's largest trading partner in Asia and is among South Africa's largest overall trading partners. It was South Africa's third-largest export destination during 2004, with total trade between the two countries reaching R47,5 billion.

The Partnership Forum, designed to strengthen bilateral ties between Japan and South Africa, meets regularly and new initiatives are being explored to expand relations.

From March to September 2005, South Africa participated in the World Expo 2005 in Aichi, Japan. The expo not only assisted in showcasing South Africa's goods and services, but also reinforced the vision of pro-poor and ecofriendly sustainable development. South Africa was awarded the Silver Award Trophy for its recognition of poverty and war as a threat to the environment, and for its efforts to create a sustainable economy through ecotourism.

Multilateral economic relations

The WTO, in partnership with the Bretton Woods Institutions, the World Bank and the International Monetary Fund (IMF), have been setting the parameters for and directing the economic development policies of governments around the world.

This has had serious implications for the content, evolution and trajectory of economic development strategies being pursued by developing countries, including South Africa. As the process of globalisation is being questioned, it is imperative for South Africa to influence and shape the configurations of the emerging system of global governance to address the needs and concerns of the developing world. This is best done by participating actively and effectively in all multilateral fora, to ensure that its particular economic interests and developmental goals and objectives, as well as those of the African continent, are taken into account.

United Nations Conference on Trade and Development (UNCTAD)

UNCTAD is an important resource organisation for South Africa and the African continent. The main goals of the organisation are to:
• maximise the trade, investment and development opportunities of developing countries
• help developing countries to face challenges arising from globalisation and integration into the world economy on an equitable basis.

This is pursued through research and policy analyses, intergovernmental deliberations, technical cooperation, and interaction with civil society and the business sector.

UNCTAD focuses much of its energy on assisting developing countries to prepare for mandated and possible future negotiations in the WTO.

UNCTAD holds a conference every four years to set its priorities and guidelines, and to provide an opportunity to debate key economic and development issues.

UNCTAD member states gathered in São Paulo, Brazil, in June 2004 for its 11th Ministerial

Conference. The conference closed with the adoption of a declaration entitled the Spirit of São Paulo, as well as the São Paulo Consensus, which provides more detail on the role of UNCTAD in a globalising world.

The Spirit of São Paulo recognises that most developing countries, especially African and other least-developed countries, have remained on the margins of the globalisation process, and that there is a need to focus on the ability of international trade to contribute to poverty alleviation.

The São Paulo Consensus focuses on:
• development strategies in a globalising world
• building productive capacities and international competitiveness
• assuring development gains from the international trading system and trade negotiations
• partnership for development.

World Trade Organisation

South Africa regards its membership of the WTO as very important because of the enhanced security and certainty in the multilateral trading system provided by WTO rules.

The country is an active participant and contributor towards a strengthened multilateral trading system, whose benefits are equitably distributed across the world community. South Africa wants to participate in the shaping of global governance to ensure beneficial and full integration of its economy, as well as those of other developing nations, into the global trading system.

South Africa's efforts to build an alliance of developing countries within the WTO, based on a common approach and consensus on key issues, bore fruit in late 2001, when an agreement was reached to launch a new round of trade negotiations, this time with a developmental agenda.

The WTO Doha Development Agenda continued to set the work programme of the WTO in 2003/04. However, the work slowed down considerably after the 5th WTO Ministerial Conference held in Cancun, Mexico, during September 2003. At the conference, WTO members failed to reach agreement on key developmental issues due to irreconcilable positions between developed and developing countries.

A positive outcome of the Cancun meeting was the formation of a grouping of developing countries known as the G20. The group succeeded in pushing for significant reforms in agricultural trade, a move that was strongly opposed by the developed world. The failure to reach agreement in Cancun showed that developing countries are now participating more effectively in the WTO to ensure they also benefit from the rule-based trading system and globalisation. The G20 has become an important player in the Doha Development Agenda to ensure that the needs and concerns of the developing world are addressed.

After the failure of Cancun to agree on a work programme for continued Doha development agenda negotiations, the G20 proceeded with its work to highlight agricultural reform as an important development tool. The group was also engaged in trying to narrow the differences between developed and developing countries to put the Doha negotiations back on track.

In July 2004, the WTO General Council adopted a work programme to accelerate progress in the negotiations. This programme, known as the July Package, is focused on a specific set of issues, namely agriculture, non-agricultural market access, services, trade facilitation and rules. The negotiations are scheduled to conclude in 2006.

The G20 consists of Argentina, Bolivia, Brazil, Chile, China, Cuba, Egypt, India, Indonesia, Mexico, Nigeria, Pakistan, Paraguay, Philippines, South Africa, Tanzania, Thailand, Venezuela and Zimbabwe.

Cairns Group

The Cairns Group is an association of countries exporting agricultural products with the objective of free and fair trade in the global agricultural market. It participates as a group in WTO agricultural negotiations. The group consists of Argentina, Australia, Bolivia, Brazil, Canada, Chile, Colombia, Costa Rica, Fiji, Guatemala, Indonesia, Malaysia, New Zealand, Paraguay, Philippines, South Africa, Thailand and Uruguay. The Cairns Group and the G20 worked together in the WTO agriculture negotiations to ensure agricultural reform that would benefit developing countries.

World Economic Forum

The WEF, an annual meeting of world economic leaders, held in Davos, Switzerland, has become the world's global business summit. South Africa is well represented at the forum, and is actively participating in discussions to address economic development and globalisation.

The country hosted the Africa Economic Summit of the WEF in Cape Town in June 2005. The summit focused on the *Commission for Africa Report*, which calls on the G8 to boost African efforts to improve governance and institution-building by doubling aid.

Export and investment promotion

A central task of the Department of Trade and Industry is to promote value-added exports and attract investment. The vision is one of a restructured and adaptive South African economy, characterised by growth, employment and equity (regional, spatial, gender and racial).

Trade and Investment South Africa (TISA)

TISA is a division of the Department of Trade and Industry and has a national mandate to develop the South African economy, focusing on investment facilitation and promotion, export development and promotion, and customised sector policy development.

TISA's mission is to provide strategic vision and direction to key growth sectors in the economy, increase the level of direct investment flow and develop South Africa's capacity to export into various targeted markets.

TISA facilitated investments to the value of R3,6 billion in the first half of the 2003/04 financial year. One-third of these investments were made in the automotive sector. Fifty import and export missions took place during the same period.

Several export training and development seminars were hosted.

Almost 1 000 exporters received financial assistance, while more than 2 500 enterprises received non-financial assistance.

Customised Sector Programme (CSP)

Early in 2002/03, TISA was assigned responsibility for priority-sector development, which is a crucial part of government's Micro-Economic Reform Strategy (MERS) and the Department of Trade and Industry's IMS. Both strategies centre on the accelerated development of priority sectors selected by government for their potential contribution to South Africa's economy, in terms of growth, equity and employment creation.

TISA's aim is to develop strategies for all priority sectors and enhance their growth and competitiveness. The CSP Methodology, which provides a strong and intellectually vigorous platform for optimal sector development, was finalised.

A key characteristic of the CSP Methodology is that it supports a high level of stakeholder interaction. The CSP Methodology also includes interventions to promote and develop investment and exports, and provide input related to policy development.

Export development and promotion

TISA is responsible for the development and promotion of South African goods and services. It contributes directly towards the objectives of the Department of Trade and Industry by:

- identifying, researching and promoting market-access opportunities for South African exporters
- facilitating exports by matching potential exporters with foreign buyers
- developing and helping South African exporters promote their products through the provision of non-financial support.

Investment

Investment promotion and facilitation

TISA is responsible for attracting FDI, and developing and promoting investment by domestic and foreign investors. It offers:

- information on investing in South Africa and the business environment
- detailed sector information
- finance to explore investment opportunities in South Africa

- direct government support in the form of investment incentives
- investment facilitation.

International Investment Council

The council meets twice a year to advise the President on investment promotion and other economic issues.

The 8th International Investment Council meeting was held in March 2005 in Cape Town.

Topics discussed included government's programme of action, the investment climate in South Africa, the investment plans of key public enterprises such as Transnet and Eskom, and international perceptions of South Africa. G7 and EU initiatives regarding Africa and their relation to the strengthening of NEPAD were also discussed.

The meeting also addressed the challenge of integrating the Second Economy into the industrial economy.

The Micro-Economic Reform Strategy (MERS), originally announced by President Thabo Mbeki in 2001 as government's integrated economic action plan, is a coherent framework for action by departments to accelerate growth, equity and employment, and to generate a climate conducive to investment. MERS provides practical actions to exploit strategic domestic and global development opportunities and to remove impediments to growth.

The strategy encompasses the following key elements:

- improving the efficiency of, and expanding access to, services in four input sectors – transport, energy, telecommunications and water
- investing in economic fundamentals that underpin sustainable economic growth
- promoting shared growth through Broad-Based Black Economic Empowerment, women empowerment, small business development, employment and geographic spread
- developing the growth, employment and equity potential of selected priority sectors.

Enterprise and industry development

The Department of Trade and Industry's Enterprise and Industry Development Division (EIDD) is moving trade and industrial policy in South Africa towards an internationally competitive status, capitalising on the country's competitive and comparative advantages.

Old manufacturing support schemes, such as the Tax Holiday Scheme, the Small Medium Manufactur-ing Development Programme, the Regional Industrial Development Programme and the Simplified Regional Industrial Development Programme, have been replaced with a suite of six incentives, namely the:
- Small Medium Enterprise Development Programme (SMEDP)
- Skills Support Programme
- Critical Infrastructure Programme (CIP)
- industrial development zones (IDZs)
- Foreign Investment Grant (FIG)
- Strategic Investment Programme (SIP).

In 2004/05, EIDD developed policy proposals to modernise the South African technical infrastructure. These will culminate in new legislation on the different elements constituting the technical infrastructure, namely:
- strengthening government's recognition of the South African National Accreditation System as the national accreditation authority
- modernising the South African metrology infrastructure and standardising in South Africa
- establishing a new technical regulatory body for the country.

The EIDD established the National Committee on Chemical Safety and Management in 2004/05, which aims to bring all relevant stakeholders together and develop a national position to take to the relevant meetings.

Government's industrial policy strives to achieve a balance between greater openness and improvement in local competitiveness. South Africa has made great strides in opening the domestic economy to international competition.

One of South Africa's key industrial policies remains its commitment to fostering sustainable industrial development in areas where poverty and unemployment are at their highest. This objective is implemented through the spatial development initiatives (SDIs), which focus high-level support on areas where socio-economic conditions require concentrated government assistance, and where inherent economic potential exists.

The SDI programmes focus government attention on the various national, provincial and local government spheres, with the goal of fast-tracking investment and maximising synergies between various types of investments.

The SDI programme consists of 11 local SDIs and four IDZs at varying stages of delivery. They are:
- SDIs: Maputo Development Corridor; Lubombo SDI; Richards Bay SDI, including the Durban and Pietermaritzburg nodes; Wild Coast SDI; Fish River SDI; West Coast Investment Initiative; Platinum SDI; Phalaborwa SDI; and the Coast-2-Coast Corridor
- IDZs: Gauteng, Coega/Ngqura, East London, Saldanha and Richards Bay.

The SDI concept has a variety of focuses, such as:
- industrial – KwaZulu-Natal and Fish River SDIs
- agrotourism – Lubombo and Wild Coast SDIs
- sectoral mix – Maputo Development Corridor
- IDZs – Coega/Ngqura, Saldanha and East London.

IDZs are located near major transport nodes such as ports or airports. The benefits of IDZs are support to investing companies, especially for greenfields development projects; access to transport for exporting purposes; waiver of import duties for products that are produced for export; and subsidies in the provision of skills training for employees.

A precious metals precinct is being established at the Johannesburg International Airport IDZ. The IDZ will allow for duty-free imports and exports of finished goods with great advantage to the industry.

By February 2005, the construction of Ngqura and East London IDZs had proceeded well. The Ngqura development project deep-water sea port was launched. During the first phase of construction, the East London IDZ created 726 jobs, benefiting many people from disadvantaged communities.

The East London IDZ acquired new investors in June 2005 in its bid to become a hub for vehicle and agroprocessing manufacturing. By mid-2005, the Coega/Ngqura IDZ had secured its first investor.

The Enterprise Organisation

The Enterprise Organisation of the Department of Trade and Industry provides incentives to stimulate or catalyse investment in infrastructure, human resource development (HRD), integrated manufacturing and related activities, small business development, specific regions, and technology and innovation.

A number of incentives are being provided to both large and small businesses to improve their competitiveness. This includes incentives under the SMEDP, the Competitiveness Fund, the Sector Partnership Fund and the Black Business Supplier Development Programme.

By mid-2005, more than 12 000 enterprises had benefited from the SMEDP. The Competitiveness Fund had supported more than 1 200 enterprises, the Sector Partnership Fund had assisted over 85 successful partnerships consisting of over 600 individual enterprises, and the Black Business Supplier Development Programme had assisted over 600 small, black-owned enterprises to improve systems, quality, skills and marketability.

The department launched an incentive scheme for the film industry in June 2004, which was to be implemented in 2005/06.

By the end of 2004, the strategic industrial projects incentive scheme had attracted R2,2 billion worth of investments, which will result in 20 107 new direct jobs. More than R100 million will be spent on infrastructure and R122 million on support for small, medium and micro enterprises (SMME).

The draft Enterprise Development Bill was expected to be presented to Cabinet before the end of 2005/06. The Bill is intended to create an enabling regulatory framework for developing and administering economic incentives and other measures for supporting enterprise.

SMEDP investment on approved applications totals R1,4 billion over three years and industrialists will invest R6,8 billion in these projects. These investments represent 1 296 applications and it is estimated that they will generate 27 000 jobs.

Workplace Challenge Programme

This supply-side programme of the Department of Trade and Industry (administered by the National Productivity Institute), assists enterprises and industries to improve their productivity and competitiveness. The programme focuses on improving workplace collaboration, adopting world-class manufacturing practices, and disseminating best practices.

The programme, which was allocated R7 million in 2004/05, focuses on the manufacturing and processing sectors.

The programme assisted eight new clusters, incorporating 57 companies employing 9 487 people. Three new clusters, incorporating 24 companies employing 4 899 people started the orientation phase in May 2004.

National Industrial Participation Programme (NIPP)

Launched in September 1996, the NIPP's principal objective is to raise investment levels and increase exports and market access for South African value-added goods and services by leveraging off government procurement.

This encourages a better geographic spread of investment to create job opportunities and to support value-added manufacturing in strategic sectors of the economy that may not otherwise occur.

Participation in the NIPP becomes obligatory when the imported content of any public-sector purchase exceeds US$10 million.

When the South African Government enters into sizeable contracts with foreign suppliers, they are obliged to participate in economic activities in the country that are designed to increase fixed investment and/or promote international market access for South African value-added goods and services.

The Industrial Participation Secretariat, a business unit within the EIDD of the Department of Trade and Industry, ensures that obligors meet their obligations, in terms of both quantity and time scales,

186

without disrupting the existing local industrial activity, and striving to encourage labour intensity.

Strategic partnership agreements are pro-active arrangements to encourage international companies to identify business opportunities in South Africa.

Obligors can fulfil their obligations either through investment in approved projects or through promoting exports of South African value-added products, by either buying for their own requirements or causing foreign companies to buy from South African companies. In case of investment, Strategic Defence Procurement (SDP) obligors are entitled to sale (exports and local sales) credits arising from those investments in addition to credits for that investment and any technology transfers that may arise.

SDP obligors should fulfil about a third of the obligation from investment and technology transfer credits, and two-thirds from sales. Other obligors, in addition to investment, technology transfer and sales credits, are also entitled to credits arising from job creation, training and skills development, research and development expenses and subcontracting to small and medium enterprises (SMEs). In case of non-SDP obligations, credit multipliers are used to encourage BEE, investment and exports.

These obligations need to be discharged over a period of seven years, with the exception of the BAE/SAAB obligation, which must be discharged over 11 years due to its size.

Manufacturing

South Africa has developed an established and diversified manufacturing base that has demonstrated resilience and the potential to compete in a global economy. The manufacturing sector provides a locus for stimulating the growth of other activities, such as services, and achieving specific outcomes, such as value addition, employment creation and economic empowerment. This platform of manufacturing presents an opportunity to significantly accelerate growth and development.

Key functions of the Department of Trade and Industry include:

- supporting increased investment in the manufacturing sector
- enhancing the establishment of new manufacturing entities
- supporting new sustainable and profitable manufacturing entities.

Some of the key aspects of the Government's IMS involves:

- improving market access for South African products in key markets
- promoting beneficiation and value addition so that value is added to the many natural resources already present in the country
- finding ways to harness the skills and expertise in South Africa so that they can be sold to other countries.

The IMS identifies the need to capture local knowledge, encourages large corporations and companies to make greater use of small businesses, and promotes greater integration between the different sectors of the economy so that they add value to each other.

The IMS also promotes BEE, small-business development, increased use of ICT, job creation, and a more equitable geographic spread of investment and economic activities.

The automotive sector is the leading manufacturing sector and the third-largest economic sector in South Africa. The sector's contribution to GDP in 2003 amounted to 6,4%. Growth in this industry can largely be attributed to the Motor Industry Development Programme (MIDP).

Recommendations on any adjustments to the existing MIDP take account of South Africa's international trade obligations, government's strategic objectives and the simplification of administration procedures. Stakeholders from labour, government and business represented in the MIDP participate actively in this review.

Competition policy

The Competition Act, 1998 (Act 89 of 1998), promotes competition in South Africa to:

- enhance the efficiency, adaptability and development of the economy

- provide consumers with competitive prices and product choices
- promote employment and advance the social and economic welfare of South Africans
- expand opportunities for South African participation in world markets and recognise the role of foreign competition in the country
- ensure that SMEs have an equitable opportunity to participate in the economy
- promote a greater spread of ownership, in particular to increase the ownership stakes of HDIs.

The functions of the Competition Commission include investigating anti-competitive conduct in contravention of the Act, assessing the impact of mergers and acquisitions on competition and taking appropriate action, monitoring competition levels and market transparency in the economy, identifying impediments to competition, and playing an advocacy role in addressing them.

The Competition Commission is independent but its decisions may be appealed to the Competition Tribunal and the Competition Appeal Court.

Small, medium and micro enterprises

Institutional support framework

Small Enterprise Development Agency

In 2004, the National Small Business Act, 1996 (Act 102 of 1996), was amended to provide for the merging of the Ntsika Enterprise Development Agency and the National Manufacturing Advisory Centre and the birth of the integrated, single SEDA on 13 December 2004. The Integrated Enterprise Strategy was also expected to be rolled out during 2005.

SEDA aims to:
- improve geographic outreach
- achieve the desired impact on small enterprises
- provide a single access point for small enterprises
- be inclusive of all relevant stakeholders
- leverage resources in service delivery
- optimise resource utilisation

- align government's strategy of service delivery in a coherent manner.

South African Micro-Finance Apex Fund (SAMAF)

The Department of Trade and Industry launched SAMAF in April 2005. The fund will provide loans of up to R10 000. During the first 18 months, lending is undertaken through various retail channels such as micro-credit organisations, financial services co-ops and the Postbank. The fund aims to introduce a delivery model that is appropriate and applicable to the unique conditions of the South African economy.

Khula Enterprise Finance

Khula is a wholesale agency which provides financial support for small businesses through intermediaries. Its financial products include loans, a national credit-guarantee scheme, grants, institutional capacity-building, equity funds and mentorship schemes. The achievements of Khula can be categorised into providing support to financial intermediaries as retail distribution networks, and direct services to SMMEs.

The Thuso Mentorship Network provides entrepreneurs with pre-loan business plans and post-loan support in the form of technical expertise management.

Furthermore, Khula Enterprise Finance is engaged in a process of repacking its financing activities. It introduced a new strategic direction that is premised on maximising access to finance by increasing its growth in disbursements by 20% a year. Khula will also improve its impact and outreach by introducing new delivery channels such as SEDA access points, as well as by forging new corporate partnerships that have better outreach across the country.

During 2003/04, Khula provided more than 600 loan guarantees to the value of R180 million, disbursed loans worth R100 million, and allocated R20 million through its equity fund. It also set up three new retail finance institutions.

Technology for Women in Business (TWIB)

TWIB aims to enhance the use of technology by

women in business, promote innovation among women, and encourage young girls and women to choose careers in science and technology.

By 2004, TWIB had established itself in a variety of business sectors, including minerals and energy, construction, Information Technology (IT) and ICT, agriculture, arts and culture, and science and technology.

The launch of the Girl Child Initiative is one of TWIB's most important initiatives. This includes the establishment of Techno-Girls, which encourages young girls to pursue a career in the field of science and technology.

South African Women Entrepreneurs Network (SAWEN)

SAWEN assists aspiring and existing business women with their business enterprises. The network advocates policy changes, builds capacity and facilitates the access of women to business resources and information.

SAWEN has been:

- organising networking fora at regional, national and international level
- lobbying and advocating for enabling and supportive policies

The majority of South African women entrepreneurs live in cities since economic resources are located mainly in the urban areas. The average company turnover of a South African woman owning a small to medium enterprise is estimated at R1,5 million a year. Women own enterprises in sectors including services, arts and crafts, manufacturing, agriculture, and clothing and textiles. Their advancement has also led them to enter sectors previously dominated by men.

According to a Southern African Development Community survey on small, medium and micro enterprises conducted by Business Map in 2003, representation and participation of women in different sectors included: agriculture (4%), construction (12%), communications (3%), manufacturing (36%), retail (9%), wholesale (7%), services (42%) and transport (20%). Others accounted for 11%.

- gathering and updating a database of women-owned enterprises and the services rendered by these companies
- facilitating access to pertinent business information
- facilitating capacity-building and training
- providing business mentorship and counselling
- facilitating access to decision-makers.

National Empowerment Fund

The NEF was established by the NEF Act, 1998 (Act 105 of 1998), to promote and facilitate economic equality and transformation.

The fund received R150 million during 2004/05 and a further R400 million for 2005/06.

The NEF leverages its funding by setting up strategic alliances with other private-sector financial institutions to further increase the funding for BEE.

It also operates at several different levels, providing finance and business support to rural women and fledgling entrepreneurs, and large-scale financial support to BEE groups.

The fund also introduced new products and services such as the Group Entrepreneurial Schemes Division (loans and equity finance to BEE SMEs from R250 000 to R10 million), Market Making (larger BEE transactions finance in capital markets, warehousing and strategic projects) and BEE Retail Investment (promoting HDI savings and access to listed equities through new product offerings in design phase).

The NEF partners with key business organisations that are focused on serving women. It deploys its resources to optimise the empowerment dividend to government. The NEF also provides pre- and post-investment management assistance.

The NEF's funding comprises a hybrid of loans and equity, and is designed to lower the cost of capital for BEE participants. This approach to BEE funding is aimed at overcoming the traditional risk aversion of existing funders.

Industrial Development Corporation (IDC)

The IDC plays an increasingly important role in supporting and assisting with venture capital in the formation of new SMEs. The IDC has three operational and client-orientated divisions, namely Services Sectors, Industrial Sectors and Projects.

The Services Sectors Division explores various ways of increasing its development impact on economic growth and job creation. This is increasingly evident in the service sectors. The division fulfils the IDC's mandate of SMME and BEE development, as well as its obligations in line with government's IMS, which identified new sectors of strategic importance that need support.

The Industrial Sectors Division intensifies financing activities in the traditional business areas and concentrates on the development of medium-sized enterprises, focusing on labour-intensive sectors such as agro-industries and entrepreneurial mining.

The Projects Division impacts on the regional economy by using its expertise in evaluating project ideas, participating in and co-funding project pre-feasibility and/or feasibility studies, as well as providing project finance for viable new and/or expanded projects.

In 2004/05, the IDC approved projects worth R6,2 billion, which represented a growth of 26% from the previous financial year. More than 17 000 job opportunities were created by IDC financing.

The IDC established a R50-million fund aimed to assist communities to obtain shareholding in IDC projects, and ultimately, to facilitate socio-economic development related to projects.

IDC collaboration with the EU and the European Investment Bank on the Risk Capital Facility enabled it to reach more black-empowered SMEs. This facility was used in 15% of IDC deals.

Through its financing activities, the IDC made a noteworthy contribution towards addressing the development needs of South Africa.

In the first six months of 2005, the IDC assisted with the creation of 23 211 new job opportunities and generated an estimated R5,7 billion additional export earnings a year.

Business Partners Ltd

Business Partners Ltd is a specialist investment group that provides customised and integrated investment, mentorship and property-management services for SMEs in South Africa.

Business Partners is an unlisted public company whose major shareholders include the Department of Trade and Industry (through Khula Enterprise Finance), Remgro, the Business Partners Employee Share Trust, Sanlam, BHP Billiton SA, Amalgamated Banks of South Africa, Nedcor, FirstRand, Old Mutual Nominees, Standard Bank Investment Corporation of South Africa, Anglo American Corporation of South Africa, De Beers Holdings and Standard Bank Nominees.

The group has been investing in entrepreneurs for over 20 years, providing private equity of up to R15 million for viable start-ups, expansions, outright purchases, management buy-outs and buy-ins, franchises, tenders and contracts. It also provides a range of value-added services, including property broking and management, consulting and mentorship.

In 2004/05, Business Partners boasted an investment portfolio of R1,066 billion, with equity-based investments amounting to 42% of the portfolio. A total of 538 investments valued at R660,5 million were approved in 2004/05. Of these, 213 investments to the value of R265,9 million were approved for historically disadvantaged entrepreneurs, and 159 investments amounting to R154,4 million were approved for women entrepreneurs.

Business Partners also facilitated 7 589 employment opportunities in 2004/05.

The Business Partners Umsobomvu Franchising Fund was established in 2003. With an initial investment allocation of R125 million, the fund aims to make all the opportunities and benefits of franchising available to the country's new generation of entrepreneurs.

During 2004/05, investments amounting to more than R40 million were approved on behalf of the fund.

Business Partners has 22 offices nationwide. It offers free initial consultations to existing or potential entrepreneurs who have viable business plans.

More than 430 mentors are available to assist entrepreneurs with advice, consulting and mentoring.

It also offers a user-friendly business-planning model on its website at *www.businesspartners.co.za*.

State-owned enterprises (SoEs)

In May 2004, President Thabo Mbeki announced during the joint sitting of the third democratic Parliament, that government would unveil five-year investment plans and projects, accompanied by a financing strategy, that will contribute towards economic growth and development.

In this regard, the Department of Public Enterprises has adopted a broader mandate to achieve the overarching objective of faster economic growth and development.

The department's vision is to ensure that SoEs:

- facilitate economic growth through locating them in an optimal industry structure and ensure the efficiency of their operations and the economic effectiveness of their investment programmes
- play a leadership role within the economy in the areas of corporate governance and national policy implementation
- catalyse sector and regional economic development opportunities.

To support this vision, the department has undergone internal restructuring. Four new programmes have been established to fulfil the department's vision, mission and mandate.

These are Analysis and Risk Management, Corporate Strategy and Structure, Secretariat Legal and Governance, and Corporate Finance and Transactions.

The SoEs have embarked on major investment drives that seek to alleviate poverty and unemployment, especially in the Second Economy.

Eskom

Over the next five years, projected investment requirements to meet national energy needs and supply are estimated at R107 billion. This requires R76,9 billion in generation, R10,4 billion in transmission and R13,6 billion in distribution.

Eskom's investment plans are in line with the National Integrated Resource Plan for increased electricity supply. The capital expenditure of the energy utility is estimated at R84 billion if it delivers 70% of the required additional capacity. Due to high

electricity demands, Eskom is rehabilitating three mothballed power stations in Camden, Grootvlei and Komati. (See chapter 16: *Minerals, energy and geology.*)

The programme is expected to create over 63 000 direct and indirect jobs. The other initiative is the construction of two peaking plants, while Eskom will be responsible for the construction of one peaking plant, which will translate into R15 billion in investment.

Transnet

The transportation utility has developed a five-year investment plan for its key business subsidiaries such as rail, ports and pipelines. The plan requires total capital expenditure of R37 billion over the next five years.

Refurbishment of the Phelophepha train, which provides mobile quality healthcare services, is expected to be completed in 2006. The utility is also set to build another health train that will commence operations in 2007.

Eskom and Transnet will embark on a joint venture to locate a modern call-centre operation in a rural area. Dimension Data subsidiary merchants will provide call-centre expertise. This pilot project was expected to start operations by September 2005.

Eskom will dispose of 14 non-core enterprises and assets with a combined asset value of R200 million. Transnet will dispose of 13 non-core entities with an estimated combined asset value of R7,7 billion. It was envisaged that the majority of transactions will be completed in 2005/06. The transactions constitute a major boost to BBBEE.

South African Airways (SAA)

By mid-2005, government was in the process of moving SAA off the Transnet balance sheet to become a stand-alone enterprise that will report to the Ministry of Public Enterprises.

South African Forestry Company (Ltd) (SAFCOL)

By mid-2005, the disposal of forest assets was nearing completion. The remaining key transaction within SAFCOL was the sale of Komatiland Forests, which was expected to go before the Competition Tribunal.

The sale of 9% shareholding interest from SAFCOL to employees was expected to be concluded by the end of 2005.

Consumer and corporate regulation

The Consumer and Corporate Regulation Division of the Department of Trade and Industry is responsible for administering the regulation of the liquor, gambling and lottery industries, as well as commercial competition and consumer-protection policies.

The South African Company Registration Office and the South African Patents and Trademarks Office, have been merged into the Companies and Intellectual Property Registration Office (CIPRO). The overall objective is to ensure that the market is fair, efficient and transparent.

Corporate and consumer regulation has become a creative endeavour that seeks to serve the interests of both business and consumers, and to create a modern and globally competitive national economy. Running a corporate law-reform project and making amendments to the intellectual property-rights regime are ongoing activities.

During 2004/05, three policies were finalised and published for comment. These relate to consumer credit, corporate law reform and consumer protection. The National Credit Bill, which delineates institutional responsibility for consumer-credit education, was drafted. The Liquor Act, 2003 (Act 59 of 2003), and the Gambling Act, 2004 (Act 7 of 2004), were promulgated in 2004. By the end of 2004, the consumer helpline, which became operational in October 2004, had received 472 new cases and resolved 344, while 56 were referred to other institutions. The volume of walk-in complaints continues to increase.

The National Liquor Authority was set up and received about 2 000 applications to convert liquor licences to comply with the Liquor Act, 2003.

CIPRO became a trading entity in July 2002 and has registered over 100 000 close corporations in the past three financial years.

Black Economic Empowerment

Broad-Based Black Economic Empowerment Strategy

In March 2003, government launched its BBBEE Strategy, which aims to address HRD, employment equity, enterprise development, preferential procurement and investment, ownership and control of enterprises, and economic assets. The strategy is the result of an extensive consultation process by government and private-sector role-players, including the BEE Commission, the Department of Trade and Industry, Nedlac and the President's Black Business and Big Business working groups.

The successful implementation of the BBBEE Strategy will be evaluated against the following policy objectives:
- a substantial increase in the number of black people who have ownership and control of existing and new enterprises
- a significant increase in the number of black-empowered and black-engendered enterprises
- a significant increase in the number of black people in executive and senior management positions.

The BBBEE Act, 2003 (Act 53 of 2003), was signed into law in 2004.

Government will use various regulatory means to achieve its BEE objectives, including a balance scorecard to measure progress made by enterprises and sectors in achieving BEE. The use of a common scorecard by different stakeholders provides a basic framework against which to benchmark the BEE process.

The scorecard will measure three core elements of BEE, namely:
- direct empowerment through ownership and control of enterprises and assets
- HRD and employment equity
- indirect empowerment through preferential procurement and enterprise development.

The Minister of Finance, Mr Trevor Manuel, issued the Code of Good Practice for BEE in Public-Private Partnerships (PPPs) in August 2004.

The code sets a clear BEE framework for both public and private parties engaging in PPPs, eliminating uncertainty and ensuring a consistent approach.

The Department of Trade and Industry released the draft codes of good practice in BEE for public comment in December 2004.

The first phase of the codes of practice dealt mainly with the ownership and management control elements of the BBBEE scorecard.

By June 2005, the process of drafting the second phase of the BEE codes of good practice was started. It will deal with employment equity, skills development, enterprise development, preferential procurement and the residual factor. This phase will also give specific attention to the SMME sector. It will deal with the issue of multinationals and the measurement of SoEs for the purpose of BEE. This phase will also go through a public commentary process.

Black Business Supplier Programme (BBSP)

The Department of Trade and Industry launched the BBSP in April 2003.

The BBSP is a 20:80 cost-sharing cash-grant incentive scheme, which offers support to black-owned enterprises in South Africa. The scheme provides such firms with access to business-development services that assist them to improve their core competencies, upgrade managerial capabilities and restructure to become more competitive.

It is aimed at growing black-owned enterprises by fostering links between black SMMEs and corporate and public-sector enterprises.

Any enterprise that is majority black-owned (50 plus one share), has a significant number of black managers, and has a minimum trading history of one year, qualifies for the programme.

Public works programmes

The Department of Public Works plays an important enabling role in service delivery. It acts as the cus-todian of workplace-related immovable assets on behalf of the State, puts in place policies to govern the management of the physical work environment of the Public Service and facilitates the transformation and development of the construction and property industries.

The department is also responsible for putting in place a range of public works programmes to alleviate poverty and unemployment.

The department spent about R3 billion on various capital works projects in 2004/05 regarding its function of providing for the accommodation needs of national government departments.

The department has produced the Government-wide Immovable Asset Management Policy and was drafting a Bill in June 2005 to be tabled in the next session of Parliament. The Bill aims to establish uniformity and ensure the application of minimum norms and standards in the management of immovable assets across all spheres of government.

Between April 1994 and January 2005, the department made great strides in the improvement of public-service delivery, contributing to economic growth and poverty alleviation. In the same period, the department implemented 7 692 construction-related projects worth R10 billion as part of its core function to provide physical accommodation and other essential infrastructure to government.

The department is also implementing the Service-Delivery Improvement Programme as part of its strategic drive to improve customer service and offer value for money to clients.

This programme includes setting service-delivery standards, introducing more business-like management methods and entering into service level agreements with client departments. Problems of capacity are also receiving attention through the recruitment of learners, interns and young professionals onto mentorship programmes in the department.

Expanded Public Works Programme (EPWP)

President Mbeki launched the EPWP at Giyani in Limpopo in May 2004, followed by launches in other provinces.

The aim of the EPWP is to facilitate and create employment opportunities for the poor and vulnerable through integrated and co-ordinated labour-intensive approaches to government infrastructure delivery and service provision.

The Business Trust of South Africa has committed R100 million to provide programme management support to all levels of government to ensure that lack of capacity is not an impediment to implementing the EPWP.

A R20-billion budget has been allocated to take the EPWP into the next five years.

The EPWP is on course to reach its target of one million job opportunities in five years. By September 2005, some 223 400 gross work opportunities had been created from 3 400 EPWP projects nationwide in the first year of the EPWP, yielding at least R823 million in total wages paid. Of those who benefited from these projects in the first year of the programme, 38% were women, 41% youth and 0,5% disabled.

Construction and Property Industry Development Programme (CPIDP)

Both industries have been identified as indispensable to economic growth and social development. Government's socio-economic objectives such as BEE, entrepreneurship and HRD can be further advanced by the transformed industries in line with the reconstruction and development agenda.

The department carried out reviews of some of its existing programmes, including the Repair and Maintenance Programme and the Emerging Contractor Development Programme to assess their contribution to BEE. One of the improvements resulting from these reviews is the department's Contractor Incubator Programme, under which a group of more than 50 medium-sized black contractors have been selected for mentoring and training to develop their management expertise and provide them with the opportunity to become successful large contractors.

The Minister of Public Works, Ms Stella Sigcau, has also launched the Women in Property Project to encourage the participation of women at all levels of the property industry and its associated disciplines. She also launched the Association of Women in Property in August 2005 to champion the cause of women in the sector.

Construction Industry Development Board (CIDB)

The CIDB is a schedule 3A public entity that provides leadership to stakeholders and stimulates sustainable growth, reform and improvement in the construction sector, for effective delivery and the industry's enhanced role in the country's economy. The board, consisting of private and public-sector individuals, is appointed by the Minister of Public Works on the basis of their individual knowledge and expertise.

The board's mandate is to:
- drive an integrated industrial development strategy
- provide strategic leadership to construction industry stakeholders to stimulate growth and reform, and improve the construction sector for effective delivery and the industry's enhanced role in the country's economy.

Council for the Built Environment (CBE)

The CBE promotes the uniform application of policy and improves co-ordination between the building profession and government. It drives the transformation and improved performance of the building profession.

Improving public-service work environment

The departments of public works and of public service and administration are required to develop a framework to improve the physical work environment. Some of the elements of this framework are already being put into place, including the Immovable Asset Management Policy, the Infrastructure Delivery Improvement Programme and the department's Service-Delivery Improvement Programme.

The department will also issue revised space and planning norms for workplace-related accommodation in the Public Service. The revised norms will establish common standards for accommodation, aimed at modernising the workplace. Open-plan offices and building designs that allow for flexible space planning, which make better use of renewable energy, will be promoted.

Together with the Demand-Side Management unit of Eskom, the department will also implement an energy-saving programme at various government facilities such as prisons, magistrate's courts, police stations and office buildings.

Employment and skills development

The Employment and Skills Development Strategy (ESDS) and HRD Branch of the Department of Labour has two areas of legislative responsibility.

It is responsible for the implementation of the Skills Development Act, 1998 (Act 97 of 1998), (amended in 2003), and the Skills Development Levies Act, 1999 (Act 9 of 1999), the latter in co-operation with the SARS.

The branch also manages the Department's responsibilities in relation to the South African Qualifications Authority (SAQA) Act, 1995 (Act 58 of 1995), which is co-managed with the Department of Education.

Legislation

Skills Development Act, 1998, as amended
The following regulations were gazetted during 2004/05:
• Sector education and training authorities' (SETAs) grant regulations were amended in accordance with the Skills Development Amendment Act, 2003 (Act 31 of 2003), and the requirements of the National Skills Development Strategy (NSDS) 2005 – 2010
• new Department of Labour/SETA service level agreement regulations were introduced
• a guideline on the National Skills Fund (NSF) allocations and a procedure manual were developed

• regulations regarding private employment agencies were reviewed
• a learnership sectoral determination issued under the Basic Conditions of Employment Act, 1997 (Act 75 of 1997), is available.

Skills Development Levies Act, 1999
The Skills Development Levies Act, 1999 is used to collect levies from employers to sustain and implement the skills-development initiatives under the NSDS. Eighty percent of the levies collected are transferred to SETAs, based on their scope of coverage. They, in turn, put 10% towards their administration, 60% towards grants to employers, and 10% plus all funds not claimed by a certain date determined by a SETA, towards discretionary projects aimed at benefiting the economic sector in which the SETA is active. Twenty percent is allocated towards the NSF. They, in turn, pay up to 2% of the total levies collected to the SARS, and use 2% of the total NSF allocation towards the administration of the NSF programme.

South African Qualifications Authority Act, 1995
The Minister of Labour jointly administers the Act with the Minister of Education, through whose department funds for the authority are disbursed. Both ministers appointed new members of SAQA during 2004/05 to oversee the development and implementation of an integrated national framework of quality-assured learning achievement, that would:
• facilitate access, mobility and progression within education, training and employment
• enhance the quality of education and training
• accelerate redress of educational and job opportunities
• advance personal, social and economic development.

Both ministers are considering a final policy statement regarding the future of SAQA. This follows the National Qualifications Framework (NQF) review that commenced in 2001, the publication of the NQF review document, and the subsequent report, *An Interdependent National Qualifications Framework Consultative Document,* produced in July 2003.

National Skills Development Strategy

The Minister of Labour launched the country's first NSDS in February 2001, for the period 2001 to March 2005.

The strategy managed to achieve, and in some instances exceed, its targets:

- By March 2005, 3 041 753 workers, which is more than the target of 1 398 033, completed their programmes satisfactorily.
- By March 2005, 53% of firms employing between 50 and 150 workers received skills development grants, against the target of 40%.
- Thirty seven percent of new and existing registered small businesses were supported and benefited from skills-development initiatives against the target of 20%.
- Some 666 new learnerships were registered with the Department of Labour by March 2005. Of these, 619 were learnerships registered on the NQF Level 5 and below, and 47 were learnerships above NQF Level 6. A total of 19 414 learners were engaged in NQF Level 4, followed by 13 826 learners in NQF Level 7 learnerships.
- Eighty one percent of the social development training money allocated under the NSF was already spent by March 2004. A placement rate of 71% was achieved and equity targets met.
- Some 69 000 learners below the age of 35 were registered in learnerships and apprenticeship programmes by the end of March 2004. This number increased to 85 753 by October 2004 against the target of 80 000.

The 2005 – 2010 NSDS was launched at the National Skills Conference in March 2005. Some R21,9 billion was allocated to the strategy over five years.

The new NSDS is expected to play a key role in realising government's goal of halving the country's unemployment by 2014.

The equity targets require that 84% of all beneficiaries of the NSDS be black, 54% female and 4% people with disabilities.

There are two key delivery vehicles for the NSDS, namely the:

- NSF
- 25 SETAs.

Between 2002 and 2005, the NSF disbursed more than R2,3 billion (75%) of its total income of R3,12 billion to fund various projects in provinces and within SETAs. Some R1 billion was allocated towards strategic projects. This represents the single biggest investment in skills development funded under the NSF. By March 2005, the following were achieved under the NSF:

- R883 million (74%) of the total R1 billion for strategic projects had been spent
- 44 838 learners benefited from Adult Basic Education and Training or other programmes at NQF Level 1
- 35 943 people completed structured learning programmes
- 21 107 SMMEs benefited from skills and various other interventions, including mentoring
- 9 332 learners benefited from learnerships funded through strategic projects.

Under the NSF Social Development Funding Window, R700 million was spent between 1999 and 2004 to train about 400 000 unemployed people on skills-development projects.

The 25 SETAs are responsible for about R2,5 billion each year collected through the skills-levy system. The SETAs make grants available, principally to employers who provide skills plans and report on their implementation.

The SETAs are also responsible for the Learnership Programme and the implementation of strategic sector-skills plans. The SETAs have discretionary funds, drawn from their levy income, that can be used for projects designed to assist in the achievement of sector priorities, including the design and implementation of learnerships.

Sector Education and Training Authority Co-ordination Programme

The SETA Co-ordination Programme is responsible for the implementation of the NSDS at sectoral level. It aims to:

- ensure alignment with the SAQA framework and other education and training policies
- oversee and co-ordinate activities of the Department of Labour's Chief Directorate: SETA Co-ordination

- design and implement systems and processes to monitor the use of skills development levy grants, and evaluate the impact and contribution of skills development in enhancing productivity and employment and the number of skilled people in South Africa
- oversee SETA contributions towards the objectives and targets of the NSDS and the HRD Strategy
- facilitate the working relationship between SETAs, Indlela, a subprogramme of the Department of Labour, and provincial offices
- provide relevant analysis to enable the National Skills Authority (NSA), the director-general and the minister to make strategic policy decisions regarding skills development implementation
- facilitate financial skills development levies collection, transfers to SETAs, disbursements to employers and accountability of all stakeholders in the use of funds
- ensure increased access to and relevance of work-based learning and qualifications
- provide support and moderation to learning and assessment initiatives and delivery of training services by the restructured Indlela subprogramme.

Sector Eduction and Training Authority Performance Management

In 2004/05, SETA Performance Management:
- Ensured that all SETAs concluded MoUs with the Department of Labour for the 2004/05 financial year.
- Developed and implemented a formal performance assessment system that produced interim results for each SETA.
- Secured R2 million under the NSF for the capacity development of SETA board members through a formal structured programme on finances and corporate governance matters. A bid was closed on 11 March 2005.
- Adressed historical reporting inaccuracies by SETAs and the capturing of data within the department. This resulted in considerable improvement in SETA performance.

National Skills Authority

The NSA is an advisory body established in terms of the Skills Development Act, 1998 to advise the Minister on the NSDS, its implementation and other relevant matters. Its membership consists of organised business, labour and community organisations, government departments, and representatives from the education and training-provider community.

During 2004/05, the NSA focused and advised the minister on the following:
- the implementation review of the NSDS 2001–2005 during its first three years of implementation through constituency workshops
- the adjusted NSDS 2005 – 2010
- a review of the SETA landscape
- draft regulations relating to the proposed amendments to SETA establishment regulations, proposed amendments to learnership regulations, proposed SETA grants regulations aligned to the Skills Development Amendment Act, 2003, the NSDS 2005 – 2010 and proposed SETA service level agreement regulations
- a draft guide on the NSF funding windows for the NSDS 2005 – 2010, including target beneficiaries, organisations that may apply and access criteria.

The NSA played an important role in the planning, organisation and chairing of the National Skills Conference held in Midrand in March 2005.

National Skills Fund

The NSF, a statutory advisory body to the Minister of Labour on the NSDS, was established in 1999, as legislated by the Skills Development Act, 1998. The Minister of Labour, on advice received from the NSA, allocates subsidies from the NSF. The Director-General of Labour is the accounting officer of the fund.

The NSF is funded by 20% of the skills development levies collected by the South African Revenue Sevice (SARS) (of which 2% is paid to SARS as collection fees and 2% is allocated for administrative costs).

The NSF has funded 66 481 beneficiaries who have completed or are receiving training. Other achievements include:

- From 2002 to the end of December 2004, the NSF awarded 22 955 undergraduate bursaries, to the value of R166,1 million, and 2 286 postgraduate bursaries, to the value of R66,8 million.
- From 2000 to the end of December 2004, 421 710 unemployed people were trained on social development projects – 62% were young black people and 57% were women. The total amount spent on training was R722 million.
- During 2004, 9 513 unemployed people were trained to be accommodated on EPWP projects, of which 6 089 were young black people and at least 5 002 were women.
- Funding of the eight innovation and research projects amounted to R2,1 million. Future plans include funding the NSDS and ensuring the alignment of the newly identified social development funding windows with the objectives and targets of the strategy.

Unemployment Insurance Fund (UIF)

The Unemployment Insurance Amendment Act, 2003 (Act 32 of 2003), is part of the successful turnaround strategy being implemented by the UIF, based on four main pillars. These are legislative reform, IT, human resources and institutional restructuring.

This Act deals with the administration of the fund and the payment of benefits. It also makes provision for the commissioner to maintain a database used to pay benefits to beneficiaries. SARS continues to administer the Unemployment Insurance Contributions Act, 2002 (Act 4 of 2002). SARS collects contributions from all those employers who have workers who pay employees' tax.

The collection of contributions from all other employers is delegated to the Unemployment Insurance Commissioner.

The main tasks of the UIF are to:
- maintain an employer/employee database
- process claims and pay benefits
- invest excess funds
- reduce fraud opportunities
- collect contributions.

Achievements during 2004/05 include:
- By the end of January 2005, the fund had col-

lected R5,1 billion in contributions and paid R2,1 billion to 465 580 beneficiaries.
- The fund's technical reserves at the end of January 2005 totalled R8,455 billion.
- By the end of January 2005, 27 000 domestic workers had received benefits totalling R6 million.
- There were 490 000 domestic workers and 6,1 million commercial workers on the fund's database.
- The regional appeals committees were established.
- The Teba A-Card was successfully piloted in Limpopo and the Free State. A total of 2 913 people received benefits through the A-Card worth R8,7 million.

Occupational Health and Safety (OHS)

The OHS legislative framework consists of the OHS Act, 1993 (Act 85 of 1993), and 20 sets of regulations. Compliance is accomplished by conducting inspections and investigations, providing advocacy and statutory services.

Responsibility for OHS, and workers' compensation in South Africa currently resides in three government departments.

The Department of Labour is responsible for workers' compensation in terms of the Compensation for Occupational Injuries and Diseases Act, 1993 (Act 130 of 1993), and for OHS in terms of the OHS Act, 1993 (Act 85 of 1993).

The Department of Minerals and Energy is responsible for OHS in mines and mining areas in terms of the Mine Health and Safety Act, 1996 (Act 29 of 1996).

The Department of Health is responsible for the compensation of mineworkers in terms of the Occupational Diseases in Mines and Works Act, 1993 (Act 208 of 1993).

These three departments have developed and finalised the Draft National OHS Policy and the National OHS Bill.

Elimination of silicosis

The National Programme for the Elimination of Silicosis was launched in June 2004.

Twenty OHS-focused inspectors were trained at the University of Cape Town on the recognition, identification, evaluation and control of silica dust in the workplace.

Compensation Fund

The Compensation Fund is a public entity of the Department of Labour. The fund's main objective is to compensate workers for occupational injuries sustained and diseases contracted in the course of, and as a result of, their employment, and to compensate dependants in fatal cases. The fund generates revenue for all its operations from the assessments paid by registered employers.

The Compensation Fund administers the Compensation for Occupational Injuries and Diseases Act, 1993, as amended by Act 61 of 1997.

The number of employers registered with the Compensation Fund has increased. On 31 February 2005, 283 732 employers were registered with the fund, compared with 271 237 in 2004.

The fund had more than R14 billion in assets of which R11,5 billion was invested. The accumulated funds consist of more than R6 billion in the Pension Account and R4 billion in the Statutory Reserve Fund.

The fund has developed, published and implemented policies for the compensation of occupational diseases, in consultation with other government departments and medical experts appointed by the Compensation Board. The purpose was to ensure a uniform approach to the handling of occupational diseases in relation to compensation.

The following policies were completed in 2004/05:
• Work Aggravated Asthma
• Upper Airways Disorders.

Between April 2004 and February 2005:
• compensation to beneficiaries amounted to R736 million
• the cost of medical aid totalled R939 million
• pensions amounted to R377 million.

The total claims expenditure amounted to R2 billion.

Labour relations

The Labour Relations Programme's area of work relates to the setting of employment conditions for vulnerable workers, including children, ensuring equity in the workplace, and promoting and monitoring collective bargaining.

The programme continues to administer activities and developments regarding the Labour Relations Act, 1995 (Act 66 of 1995), the Basic Conditions of Employment Act, 1997 and the Employment Equity Act, 1998.

Directorate: Employment Standards

The Directorate: Employment Standards of the Department of Labour focuses mainly on the assessment and completion of applications for variations of minimum wages and conditions of employment received from employers within the agricultural sector. In 2004/05, some 797 applications were assessed, of which 457 were personally verified during provincial visits.

The directorate finalised the Code of Good Practice for the Employment of Children in the Performance of Advertising, Artistic or Cultural Activities.

Employers active within the performing arts are required to apply for permits before they employ children younger than 15 years. The directorate made considerable progress in ensuring that employers and other role-players are aware of this new requirement contained in the Sectoral Determination for the Employment of Children in the Performance of Advertising, Artistic or Cultural

According to the Labour Force Survey, 2005, released by Statistics South Africa in March 2005, the number of employed persons rose from 11,4 million in March 2004 to 11,6 million in September 2004 and 11,9 million in March 2005. The industries that registered the largest increase in employment growth over the period September 2004 to March 2005 were agriculture (up by 107 000 jobs) and trade, up by a similar number. The mining sector posted modest gains – up by 21 000 jobs – from 405 000 in September 2004 to 426 000 in March 2005.

Activities. Between August 2004 and mid-2005, 639 applications for permits were granted.

Sectoral determinations and amendments to sectoral determinations

The Sectoral Determination 1: Contract Cleaning Sector was amended.

Investigations into the following sectoral determinations were completed:

- the Minister of Labour approved the publication of the Sectoral Determination for the Taxi Sector
- the Director-General's report on the forestry sector was submitted to the Employment Conditions Commission for consideration and recommendation.

Investigations into minimum wages and conditions of employment in the welfare sector was announced.

Other highlights on sectoral determinations include:

- minimum wages and conditions of employment for farmworkers are under review
- research has been commissioned to investigate minimum wages and conditions of employment in the hospitality sector
- the investigation into the sheltered employment sector continues.

Child labour

The National Child Labour Action Programme (CLAP) was provisionally adopted in September 2003, with the support of a wide range of government departments and institutions.

Subsequent to the adoption of the CLAP, the department facilitated the formulation in 2004 of the Programme Towards the Elimination of the Worst Forms of Child Labour (TECL) to assist in implementing the key action steps of the CLAP. The TECL is essentially an executing agency for key elements of the CLAP, as partner to relevant government departments. The lead department is the Department of Labour. It is funded through the International Labour Organisation.

Among the flagship projects of the TECL are the running of pilot programmes to devise and test methodologies. Some pilots address the most intolerable forms of child labour, the commercial sexual exploitation of children, child trafficking and children used by adults to commit illegal activities.

Another set of pilots facilitates the prioritisation of water services to households far from the sources of safe water to relieve excessive pressure on children and women (and households generally) carrying water over long distances. The latter project forms part of government's programme to deliver water to all households. Work on all these projects has commenced and the bulk of the initial rapid assessments has been completed.

Bargaining Employment-Equity Registry

During the October 2004 reporting period, the directorate received employment-equity reports detailing workforce profiles and qualitative data from 9 364 employers. This was a significant increase from the 6 990 reports received in October 2002, when both large and small designated employers were required to report.

This improvement may largely be attributed to the co-operation of the social partners at Nedlac, i.e. organised business, organised labour, community and government, who jointly campaigned throughout the country in 2004 to raise the level of awareness of the Employment Equity Act, 1998.

Commission for Employment Equity (CEE)

The CEE meets monthly to assist in the development of policy and to advise the minister on the implementation of the Employment Equity Act, 1998.

The Employment-Equity Registry captures employment-equity reports and maintains a database of these.

This makes it possible to measure the extent of employment equity of designated employers with 50 or more workers.

Employment-Equity Awards System

The CEE has developed the Employment-Equity Awards System. The purpose of this system is to identify employers who excel in implementing the Employment Equity Act, 1998. The system was expected to be implemented in the 2005/06 financial year.

Code on the Integration of Employment Equity into Human Resource Policies and Practices

The CEE completed the draft Code on the Integration of Employment Equity into Human Resource Policies and Practices in March 2005. The draft code aims to provide guidelines on the elimination of unfair discrimination and the implementation of affirmative action measures in the context of key human resource areas, as provided for in the Employment Equity Act, 1998. The guidelines in the draft code will enable employers to ensure that their human resource policies, procedures and practices reflect employment-equity principles.

Directorate: Collective Bargaining

The directorate:
- administers the Labour Relations Act, 1995
- registers trade unions, employers' organisations and bargaining and statutory councils
- publishes bargaining council agreements for the extension thereof to non-parties
- promotes and monitors collective bargaining.

Collective agreements

During 2004/05, 92 collective agreements of bargaining councils were extended to non-parties covering 620 298 workers. These agreements were mainly collective agreements on wage increases and issues such as council levies and medical aid, pension and provident fund benefits.

Of the 52 private-sector councils, 44 (84,6%) reported on the state of applications for exemption from certain provisions of collective agreements extended to non-parties. The majority of applications were from small enterprises. Furthermore, the majority of councils indicated that small enterprises had seats on the council, as well as the independent body to hear appeals.

Dispute resolution

The directorate monitors the Commission for Conciliation, Mediation and Arbitration's (CCMA) activities, ensuring effective and efficient dispute-resolution systems. During 2004/05, the CCMA received R173 million for all its programmes and activities. Between April 2003 and February 2004, the CCMA adjudicated over 115 894 cases; an average of 553 cases a day.

Between April 2004 and February 2005, the CCMA was involved in 169 cases of section 189A (large retrenchments) facilitation. The settlement rate of these cases stood at 60%. The CCMA was also involved in 82 cases of section 188A pre-dismissal arbitration. A total of 43 674 conciliation/arbitration cases and 476 applications for enforcement of arbitration awards as orders of court were handled.

Registration of labour organisations

The registration of labour organisations continues. Efforts are made to identify non-genuine labour organisations and to deregister them if necessary.

In 2004/05, a total of 29 trade unions' registrations were cancelled in terms of Section 106 of the Labour Relations Act, 1995, for reasons ranging from not submitting audited financial statements over a number of years, to not being a genuine union as envisaged by the Act. By mid-2005, there were 341 registered trade unions.

Eight registrations from employers' organisations were cancelled in terms of Section 106 of the Labour Relations Act, 1995. The cancellations were based on similar reasons as for the trade unions. By mid-2005, there were 229 registered employers' organisations.

Acknowledgements

ECONOMY

Business Day
Business Map
Business Partners Ltd
Department of Labour
Department of Public Works
Department of Trade and Industry
Estimates of National Expenditure 2005, published by National Treasury
Office for Public Enterprises
Quarterly Review (March 2005), published by the South African Reserve Bank
South African Reserve Bank
Statistics South Africa
Towards a Ten-Year Review
www.dti.gov.za
www.godisa.net
www.gov.za
www.southafrica.info
www.twib.co.za

Suggested reading

Abratt, R. *Contemporary Cases in South African Marketing*. Cape Town: New Africa Books, 2002.
Ackerman, R. *Hearing Grasshoppers Jump: The Story of Raymond Ackerman as told to Denise Pritchard*. Cape Town: David Philip, 2001.
Adam, H., Van Zyl Slabbert, F. and Moodley, K. *Comrades in Business: Post-Liberation Politics in South Africa*. Cape Town: Tafelberg, 1997.
Adendorff, S.A. and de Wit, P.W.C. eds. *Production and Operations Management: A South African Perspective*. Cape Town: Oxford University Press, 2004.
African National Congress. *The Reconstruction and Development Programme*. Johannesburg: Umanyano Publications, 1994.
Alemayehu, M. *Industrialising Africa: Development Options and Challenges for the 21st Century*. Trenton, N.J.: Africa World Press, 2000.
Allen, V. L. *History of Black Mineworkers in South Africa*. Keighley (UK): Moor Press, 2003. 2v.
Anstey, M. ed. *Employee Participation and Workplace Forums*. Kenwyn: Juta, 1997.
Barker, F. *South African Labour Market*. Pretoria: Van Schaik, 2003.
Barnard, N. and Du Toit, J. *Understanding the South African Macro-Economy*. Pretoria: Van Schaik, 1992.
Baskin, J. ed. *Against the Current: Labour and Economic Policy in South Africa*. Johannesburg: Ravan Press, 1996.
Bendix, S. *Industrial Relations in South Africa*. 3rd edition. Cape Town: Juta, 1996.
Bendix, S. *Basics of Labour Relations*. Cape Town: Juta, 2000.
Best Companies to Work for in South Africa. Cape Town: Zebra Press, 2000.
Beyond the Apartheid Workplace: Studies in Transition. Pietermaritzburg: University of Kwazulu-Natal Press, 2005.
Bhorat, H, *et al*. *Fighting Poverty: Labour Markets and Inequality in South Africa*. Lansdowne: University of Cape Town Press, 2001.
Black, Calitz, Steenkamp and Associates. *Public Economics for South African Students*. Cape Town: Oxford University Press South Africa, 2003.
Bond, P. *South Africa Meets the World Bank, International Monetary Fund and International Finance*. Cape Town: University of Cape Town Press, 2001.
Bond, P. *Talk Left Walk Right: South Africa's Frustrated Global Reforms*. Pietermaritzburg: University of KwaZulu-Natal, 2004.
Botha, H. and Botha, J. *Guide to the New Basic Conditions of Employment Act*. Lynnwood Ridge: Practition IR Publication, 1998.

202

Bothma, C.H. *E-Commerce for South African Managers*. Cape Town: New Africa Books, 2001.
Bruggemans, C. *Change of Pace: South Africa's Economic Revival*. Johannesburg: Witwatersrand University Press, 2004.
Cameron, B. *Financial Freedom for Women*. Cape Town: Zebra Books, 2002.
Cheadle, H. *et al. Current Labour Law 1998: An Annual Review of Key Areas of Labour Law*. Cape Town: Juta, 1998.
Cheru, F. *African Renaissance: Roadmaps to the Challenge of Globalization*. Cape Town: David Philip and Zed Books, 2002.
Clark, I. *et al. More Small Business Opportunities in South Africa*. 2nd ed. Cape Town: Zebra, 1996.
Coetzee J.K. *et al.* eds. *Development: Theory, Policy and Practice*. Cape Town: Oxford University Press, Southern Africa, 2001.
Compiler: Erasmus, J. *Coping Structures of the Unemployed*. Pretoria: Human Sciences Research Council (HSRC), 1999.
Consultative Business Movement. *Building a Winning Nation: Companies and the Reconstruction and Development Programme*. Randburg: Ravan Press, 1994.
Corporate Social Investment and Development Handbook. Rivonia: BML, 1998. Annual.
Creating Action Space: The Challenge of Poverty and Democracy in South Africa. Cape Town: Institute for a Democratic South Africa (IDASA) and David Philip, 1998.
Davids, I, *et al* eds. *Participatory Development in South Africa: A Development Management Perspective*. Pretoria: Van Schaik, 2005
Du Toit, J. and Falkema, H.B. *The Structure of the South African Economy*. Johannesburg: Southern Book Publishers for Absa Bank, 1994.
Hartley, P. ed. *E-Business Handbook: The 2003 Review of Innovation at Work in South African Business*. Cape Town: Trialogue, 2003.
Ehlers, T. and Lazenby, K. *Strategic Management: Southern African Concepts and Cases*, edited by Pretoria: Van Schaik, 2003.
Erasmus, B.J. and van Dyk, P.S. *Training Management in South Africa*. 3rd ed. Cape Town: Oxford University Press, 2004.
Fine, B. and Rustomjee, Z. *The Political Economy of South Africa: From Minerals-Energy Complex to Industrialisation*. Johannesburg: Witwatersrand University Press, 1996.
Ginsberg, A. *South Africa's Future: From Crises to Prosperity*. Basingstoke, Hampshire: Macmillan, 1998.
Grossett, M. and Venter, R. *Labour Relations in South Africa: A Comprehensive Guide for Managers and Practitioners*. Johannesburg: International Thomson Publications, 1998.
Herselman, S. *Dynamics of Diversity in an Organisational Environment*. Pretoria: UNISA Press, 2004.
Hetherington, I. *Heroes of the Struggle*. Kempton Park: National Industrial Chamber, 1998.
Hickey, A. and van Zyl, A. *2002 South African Budget Guide and Dictionary*. Cape Town: IDASA, 2002.
Huber, M. and Sack, P. *Employing a Domestic Worker*. Welgemoed (Cape): Metz Press, 1997.
Hugon, P. *The Economy of Africa*. Pretoria: Protea Book House, 2004.
Huysamen, D. *Rehumanised Productivity Improvement*. Randburg: Knowledge Resources, 1999.
IBC's Guide to Doing Business in South Africa, 1997. Highlands North, Johannesburg: International Business Centres, 1997. Annual.
Ilbury, C. and Sunter, C. *Games Foxes Play*. Cape Town: Human and Rousseau, and Tafelberg Publishers, 2005.
Investment in South Africa. Johannesburg: KPMG, 1997.
Isaacs, S. *South Africa in the Global Economy: Understanding the Challenges: Working Towards Alternatives*. Durban: University of Durban, Trade Union Research Project, 1997.
Jeffrey, A. *Business and Affirmative Action*. Johannesburg: South African Institute of Race Relations, 1996.
Kahn, M. *et al. Flights of the Flamingoes: A Study on the Mobility of R&D Workers*. Cape Town: HSRC, 2004.
Khosa, M. ed. *Empowerment Through Economic Transaction*. Pretoria: HSRC, 2001.
Khoza, R.J. and Mohammed A. *The Power of Governance: Enhancing the Performance of State-owned Enterprises*. Johannesburg: Pan Macmillan, 2005.
Kiloh, M. and Sibeko, A. *A Fighting Union: An Oral History of the SA Railway and Harbour Workers' Union, 1936 – 1998*. Johannesburg: Ravan Press, 2000.
Kok, P. and Pietersen, J. *Manufacturing and Materials*. Pretoria: HSRC, 2000.
Kuzwayo, M. *Marketing Through Mud and Dust*. Cape Town: David Philip, 2000.
Labour Relations in South Africa, edited by R. Venter, rev. ed. Cape Town: Oxford University Press Southern Africa, 2004.
Legum, M. *It Doesn't Have to be Like This! A New Economy for South Africa and the World*. Kenilworth: Ampersand Press, 2002.
Lighthelm, A.A. *The Southern African Development Community: A Socio-Economic Profile*. Pretoria: Bureau of Market Research, University of South Africa, 1997.
Lipton, M. *Capitalism and Apartheid: South Africa, 1910 – 1986*. Cape Town: David Philip, 1986.

Lowry, D. *Twenty Years in the Labour Movement: The Urban Training Project and Change in South Africa, 1971 – 1991.* Johannesburg: Wadmore, 1999.

Macleod, G. *Cultural Considerations: A Guide to Understanding Culture, Courtesy and Etiquette in South African Business.* Cape Town: Spearhead, 2002.

Maganya, E. and Houghton, R. eds. *Transformation in South Africa? Policy Debates in the 1990s.* Braamfontein, Johannesburg: Institute for African Alternatives, 1996.

Mahdi, P. M. *Black Economic Empowerment in the New South Africa. The Rights and the Wrongs.* Randburg: Knowledge Resources, 1997.

Making Affirmative Action Work: A South African Guide. Rondebosch: IDASA, 1995.

Marais, H. *South Africa's Limits to Change: The Political Economy of Transformation.* 2nd reprint. Rondebosch: University of Cape Town Press, 1999.

Marais, H. *South Africa: Limits to Change: The Political Economy of Transition.* 2nd ed. Cape Town: University of Cape Town, 2001.

May, J. ed. *Poverty and Inequality in South Africa: Meeting the Challenge.* Cape Town: David Philip, 2000.

Mbigi, L. *In Search of the African Business Renaissance: An African Cultural Perspective.* Randburg: Knowledge Resources, 2000.

McGrath, S. *et al* eds. *Shifting Understanding of Skills in South Africa: Overcoming the Historical Imprint of Low Skills Regime.* Pretoria: HSRC, 2004.

McGregor's Who Owns Whom in South Africa: Millennium Edition. Grant Park, Johannesburg: Purdey Publishing, 1999.

Mengisteab, K. and Logan, I. eds. *Beyond Economic Liberalisation in Africa: Structural Adjustment and the Alternatives.* London: Zed Books, 1995.

Micro-Finance in Rural Communities in Southern Africa. Pretoria: HSRC, 2002.

Mills, G. *Poverty to Prosperity: Globalisation, Good Government and African Recovery.* Johannesburg: South African Institute of International Affairs and Cape Town: Tafelberg, 2002.

Mostert, J. W. *et al. Micro-Economics.* Cape Town: Juta, 2002.

Naidoo, R. *Corporate Governance: Essential Guide for SA Companies.* Cape Town: Double Storey, 2003.

Nattrass, N. Wakeford, J. and Muradzikwa, S. *Macro-Economics: Theory and Policy in South Africa.* Cape Town: David Phillip, 2000.

Nel, P.S. ed. *South African Industrial Relations: Theory and Practice.* 3rd ed. Pretoria: Van Schaik, 1997.

Nel, P.S. *et al. Successful Labour Relations: Guidelines for Practice.* Pretoria: Van Schaik, 1998.

Nel, P.S. *et al. Training Management: A Multidisciplinary Approach to Human Resources Development in Southern Africa.* 3rd ed. Cape Town: Oxford University Press Southern Africa, 2004.

Nicholson, J. *Measuring Change: South Africa's Economy Since 1994.* Durban: Trade Union Research Project, University of Natal, 2001.

Nicholson, J. *et al.* eds. *User's Guide to the South African Economy.* Durban: Y Press, 1994.

Nieman, G. *et al* eds. *Entrepreneurship: A South African Perspective.* Pretoria: Van Schaik, 2003

Parsons, R. *The Mbeki Inheritance: South Africa's Economy, 1990 – 2004.* Randburg: Ravan Press, 1999.

Preston-Whyte, E. and Rogerson, C. eds. *South Africa's Informal Economy.* Cape Town: Oxford University Press, 1994.

Qunta, C. *Who's Afraid of Affirmative Action: A Survival Guide for Black Professionals.* Cape Town: Kwela Books, 1995.

Ramphele, M. *The Affirmative Action Book: Towards an Equity Environment.* Rondebosch: IDASA, 1995.

Reuvid, J. *Doing Business in South Africa.* 5th ed. London: Kegan Paul, 2001.

Roussouw, D. *Business Ethics in Africa.* Cape Town: Oxford University Press, 2002.

Roux, A. *Everyone's Guide to the South African Economy.* 4th ed. Wynberg, Sandton: Zebra Books, 1996.

Rumney, R. and Wilhelm, J. eds. *Movers and Shakers: An A – Z of South African Business People.* Sandton: Penguin Books, 1999.

Schlemmer, L. and Levitz, C. *Unemployment in South Africa: The Facts, the Prospects and an Exploration of Solutions.* Johannesburg: South African Institute of Race Relations, 1998.

Schrire, R. ed. *Wealth or Poverty: Critical Choices for South Africa.* Cape Town: Oxford University Press, 1992.

Schutz, H, ed. *Organisational Behaviour – A Contemporary South African Perspective.* Pretoria: Van Schaik, 2003.

Sen, A. *Development as Freedom.* Oxford: University Press, 1999.

Shaw, M. *Finding the Rainbow: Organisational Culture: The Key to Corporate Performance.* Johannesburg: Ravan Press, 1997.

Shelley, S. *Doing Business in Africa: A Practical Guide for Investors, Entrepreneurs and Expatriate Managers.* Cape Town: Zebra Press, 2004.

Simpson, J. and Dore, B. *Marketing in South Africa.* Pretoria: Van Schaik, 2002.

Sono, T. *From Poverty to Poverty. Themba Sono's Five Steps to Real Transformation.* Sandton: FMF Books, 1999.

South Africa's Most Promising Companies. Cape Town: Zebra Press, 2000.

Sunter, C. and Ilbur, C. *Mind of a Fox.* Cape Town: Human & Rousseau, 2002.

Tustin, C. and Geldenhuys, D. *Labour Relations: The Psychology of Conflict and Negotiation.* 2nd ed. Cape Town: Oxford University Press Southern Africa, 2000.

Van Zyl, C. *et al. Understanding South African Financial Markets.* Pretoria: Van Schaik, 2003.

Von Holdt, K. *Transition from Below: Forging Trade Union and Workplace Change in South Africa.* Pietermaritzburg: University of Natal Press, 2003.

Visser, W. and Sunter, C. *Beyond Reasonable Greed: Why Sustainable Business is a Much Better Idea.* Cape Town: Human & Rousseau, 2003.

Vosloo, W.B. ed. *Entrepreneurship and Economic Growth.* Pretoria: HSRC, 1994.

Zegeye, A. and Maxted, J. *Our Dream Deferred: The Poor in South Africa.* Pretoria: South Africa History Online and University of South Africa, 2003.

8 Education

The Department of Education aims to develop, maintain and support a South African education and training system for the 21st century.

According to the Bill of Rights contained in the Constitution of the Republic of South Africa, 1996 (Act 108 of 1996), everyone has the right to a basic education, including adult basic education and further education, which the State, through reasonable measures, must progressively make available and accessible.

At almost 5,4% of gross domestic product, South Africa has one of the highest rates of government investment in education in the world.

Formal education in South Africa is categorised according to three levels – General Education and Training (GET), Further Education and Training (FET) and Higher Education (HE).

The GET band consists of the Reception Year (Grade R) and learners up to Grade 9, as well as an equivalent Adult Basic Education and Training (ABET) qualification. The FET band consists of grades 10 to 12 in schools and all education and training from the National Qualifications Framework (NQF) levels 2 to 4 (equivalent to grades 10 to 12 in schools) and the N1 to N6 in FET colleges. The HE band consists of a range of degrees, diplomas and certificates up to and including postdoctoral degrees. These levels are integrated within the NQF provided by the South African Qualifications Authority (SAQA) Act, 1995 (Act 58 of 1995).

In 2004, the South African public education system accommodated more than 11,8 million school learners, more than 450 000 university students, more than 200 000 university of technology students and over 460 000 FET college students. There were almost 26 000 primary, secondary, combined and intermediate schools, with 350 000 educators.

The matric exam pass rate improved from 48,9% in 1999 to 70,7% in 2004. This improvement is due to numerous intervention strategies by the national and provincial education departments, aimed at enhancing the quality of teaching and conditions in the classroom, especially in previously disadvantaged areas.

In 2004, some 85 117 candidates achieved university endorsement compared with 82 010 in 2003 and 537 schools obtained a 100% pass rate. Some 13 480 girl learners passed Mathematics in the Higher Grade (HG) and 17 566 passed Physical Science HG. A total of 40 098 learners passed with merit and 9 213 passed with distinction.

Girl learners' performance in matric Mathematics HG improved, with 74,4% passing the exam in 2004, compared with 50,9% in 1999.

The FET and HE sectors have undergone a major rationalisation process that has reduced the overall number of institutions through mergers.

FET institutions were reduced from 152 to 50. The new institutional landscape for HE consists of eight separate and incorporated universities, three merged universities, five universities of technology and six comprehensive institutions.

Education structures

Ministry of Education
The National Education Policy Act, 1996 (Act 27 of 1996), empowers the Minister of Education to determine national norms and standards for education planning, provision, governance, monitoring and evaluation. The principle of democratic decision-making must be exercised within the context of overall policy goals. In determining policy, the minister must take into account the competence of provincial legislatures and the relevant provisions of any provincial law relating to education.

National and provincial departments of education
The Constitution has vested substantial power in the provincial legislatures and governments to run educational affairs (other than universities and universities of technology), subject to a national policy framework. The national Department of Education is responsible for formulating policy, setting norms and standards, and monitoring and evaluating all levels of education. It also funds HE institutions through subsidies and by providing financial support to stu-

dents through the National Student Financial Aid Scheme (NSFAS).

The national department shares a concurrent role with the provincial departments of education for school education, ABET, Early Childhood Development (ECD) and FET colleges. The South African Schools Act, 1996 (Act 84 of 1996), further devolves responsibility to school level by delegating the governance of public schools to democratically elected school-governing bodies (SGBs), consisting of parents, educators, non-educator staff and (secondary school) learners.

Relations with provincial departments of education are guided by national policy, within which the provincial departments have to set their own priorities and implementation programmes. The National Education Policy Act, 1996 formalised relations between national and provincial authorities, and established the Council of Education Ministers (CEM) and the Heads of Education Departments Committee (HEDCOM) as intergovernmental fora to collaborate in developing the education system.

The role of the national department is to translate the education and training policies of government and the provisions of the Constitution into a national education policy and legislative framework.

The department must ensure that:
- all levels of the system adhere to these policies and laws
- mechanisms are in place to monitor and enhance quality in the system
- the system is on par with international developments.

The core activities of the department are to:
- provide research and policy review
- provide planning and policy development
- provide support to the provinces and HE institutions in their implementation of national policy, norms and standards
- monitor the implementation of policy, norms and standards to assess their impact on the quality of the educational process, and identify policy gaps.

The Department of Education has six branches:
- Administration
- Systems Planning
- Quality Promotion and Development

The Register of Private Higher Education (HE) Institutions provides the public with information on the registration status of private HE institutions.

The HE Act, 1997 (Act 101 of 1997), requires that the registrar of private HE institutions enters the name of the institution in the register. The Act further grants the public the right to view the auditor's report as issued to the registrar in terms of Section 57(2)(b) of the Act.

- GET
- FET
- HE.

Administration

This branch provides administrative support for policy formulation and the overall management of the department, including administrative support to the minister, deputy minister, director-general and internal audit.

It is responsible for personnel; financial, administrative and other office services; as well as Information Technology; security; and asset management.

System Planning

The System Planning Branch has three major functions, namely: costs and financing of education, infrastructure development and human resource planning. The branch provides leadership by:
- developing standards for the provision, utilisation, employment and management of educators
- rendering a professional service to the education and training sector (not HE), as well as financial and physical planning, and information systems
- analysing, developing and planning for policy developments in the education sector
- managing development support and promoting optimal budgeting processes for provinces.

Quality Promotion and Development

The Quality Promotion and Development Branch:
- drives quality improvement by ensuring the availability of credible and up-to-date data on the performance of learners and educational institutions
- promotes and ensures access to both curricular and extra-curricular activities for all learners
- addresses health conditions that constitute barriers to learning and development, and promotes essential health awareness and behaviour
- monitors and evaluates the performance of the education system, individual schools and education institutions; and tracks progress on the achievement of major transformation goals.

General Education and Training

The GET Branch provides leadership through the management and evaluation of programmes for ECD, school education, ABET, learners with special needs, education management and governance programmes, and education human resources.

Key priorities of the branch include expanding ABET programmes; providing Grade R to all children; further developing a truly inclusive system of education, including the consolidation of special schools; ensuring that there are no underqualified educators; and successfully implementing the Revised National Curriculum Statement (RNCS).

The department aims to remove all barriers to learning so that children with special needs, including the most vulnerable, are able to participate fully. The implementation of the *White Paper on Special Needs Education* was expected to begin over the 2005 Medium Term Expenditure Framework (MTEF) period. Progress towards universal Grade R provisioning by 2010 was also to continue in 2005, with access progressively provided to an additional 400 000 children.

Further Education and Training

The FET Branch is responsible for the development of policy for grades 10 to 12 in public and independent schools, as well as public and private FET colleges.

It oversees the integrity of assessment in schools and colleges, and offers an academic curriculum as well as a range of vocational subjects. FET colleges cater for out-of-school youth and adults.

The branch oversees, co-ordinates and monitors the system's response to improved learner participation and performance in Mathematics, Science and Technology. It devises strategies aimed at the use of Information and Communications Technology (ICT) and supports curriculum implementation through the national educational portal called Thutong (*www.thutong.org.za*).

The branch provides leadership by:
- establishing a system to promote open and life-long learning
- promoting the integrity of the assessment of learners
- rendering a professional support service to the FET board.

Private institutions offering FET programmes must register with the department in accordance with the FET Act, 1998 (Act 98 of 1988).

The branch developed a new school-leaving certificate, namely the FET Certificate, to replace the current Senior Certificate in 2008.

Higher Education

HE is central to the social, cultural and economic development of modern societies. The HE Branch provides strategic direction and institutional support for the development of a single co-ordinated system.

The branch provides leadership by:
• developing legislation
• developing policy support to the HE system
• liaising with constituencies in HE
• registering private HE institutions
• overseeing the NSFAS
• implementing the National Plan for HE
• allocating and transferring subsidies to public HE institutions.

There were significant developments in HE in 2004/05. The first set of mergers and incorporations were concluded and over R500 million of restructuring, including recapitalisation funding, was allocated.

Statutory bodies

Council of Education Ministers

The CEM, consisting of the Minister of Education, the Deputy Minister of Education and the nine provincial members of the executive council (MECs) for education, meets regularly to discuss the promotion of national education policy, share information

and views on all aspects of education in South Africa, and co-ordinate action on matters of mutual interest.

Heads of Education Departments Committee

HEDCOM consists of the Director-General of the Department of Education, the deputy directors-general of the department, and the heads of provincial departments of education. The functions of the committee include facilitating the development of a national education system, sharing information and views on national education, co-ordinating administrative action on matters of mutual interest and advising the department on a range of specified matters related to the proper functioning of the national education system.

Council for Quality Assurance in General and Further Education and Training (Umalusi)

The council ensures that providers of education and training have the capacity to deliver, and also assesses qualifications and learning programmes to ensure that they conform to set standards. Umalusi is guided by the General and Further Education Act, 2001 (Act 58 of 2001). The functions of the defunct South African Certifications Council (SAFCERT) were incorporated into those of the council, which was constituted in June 2002. SAFCERT concentrated on quality assurance of the Senior Certificate.

The council has a five-point programme:
• quality assurance of providers
• quality assurance of qualifications and learning programmes
• quality assurance of assessments
• issuing of certificates
• monitoring and reporting on quality in education and training.

South African Qualifications Authority

The SAQA is a statutory body of 29 members appointed by the ministers of labour and of education. The

In September 2005, the Minister of Education, Ms Naledi Pandor, launched the Flag in Every School Project in Cape Town. The project aims to familiarise young people with South Africa's national symbols and build a shared South African identity.

SAQA, through the NQF, ensures that South African qualifications are of excellent quality, and internationally comparable. The authority oversees the:

- development of the NQF by formulating and publishing policies and criteria for the registration of bodies responsible for establishing education and training standards or qualifications
- accreditation of bodies responsible for monitoring and auditing achievements in terms of such standards and qualifications
- implementation of the NQF by ensuring the registration, accreditation and assignment of functions to the referred bodies
- registration of national standards and qualifications on the NQF.

The NQF is a set of principles and guidelines in which records of learner achievement are registered. This enables national recognition of acquired skills and knowledge, thereby ensuring an integrated system that encourages lifelong learning. The NQF also attempts to move the measurement of achievement in education and training away from input towards outcomes.

The SAQA's Centre for the Evaluation of Educational Qualifications determines the equivalence between foreign and South African qualifications in the South African context.

During 2004, the SAQA launched the report: *Trends in Public Higher Education in South Africa, 1992 to 2001.*

The report contains integrated information on education and training trends in all components of the education and training system, and in all sectors of the economy. It provides government and corporate organisations with adequate data necessary for decision-making in terms of the labour market and education and training.

In addition, the report stated that the total number of people in South Africa with qualifications from public HE institutions had almost doubled.

According to the report, South Africa's public HE institutions produced more black and female graduates over a 10-year period spanning 1992 to 2001, with almost 60% of all graduates being black learners, and more than 54% of all qualifications being awarded to women.

By March 2005, there were 8 310 qualifications registered on the NQF.

In June 2005, SAQA launched the *National Qualifications Framework Impact Study Report Cycle 2.* The report was the result of a groundbreaking research project undertaken to measure the impact of the NQF on the transformation of education and training in South Africa. The NQF impact study was a world-first as no other country that has implemented an NQF had, by then, attempted to measure the progress of their NQFs in such a comprehensive manner.

In 2005/06, SAQA received an allocation of R10,421 billion, representing an increase of 48%.

Council on Higher Education

The CHE was established by the HE Act, 1997 as a statutory body responsible for promoting and overseeing quality assurance in HE.

The institutional and programme quality assurance assessment conducted by the HE Quality Committee (HEQC) includes an evaluation of whether:

- an applicant institution has the capacity to provide programmes at HE level
- the programmes an applicant proposes to offer are indeed HE

In August 2005, the Department of Education and the South African Sports Commission hosted the National Girls' Games Festival at the University of the Witwatersrand in Johannesburg.

It aimed at removing barriers which prohibit girl learners from participating in sport, especially in codes that were previously regarded as the preserve of their male counterparts.

The games, among others, sought to:
- address gender issues in sport and education
- promote opportunities to all learners in school sport
- dispose of the gender disparities in school sport.
The National Girls' Games Festival formed part of celebrations of the 50th anniversary of the Freedom Charter by the Department of Education.

More than 2 000 girl learners from all over the country participated in various sporting codes.

- an applicant complies with South African professional practice.

The functions of the CHE include:

- advising the minister either at his/her request or proactively on all matters related to HE
- monitoring and evaluating whether and with what consequences the vision, policy goals and objectives for HE are being realised, including reporting on the state of South African HE
- executive responsibility for quality assurance within HE and training – including programme accreditation, institutional audits, programme evaluation, quality promotion and capacity-building
- contributing to developing HE – providing leadership around key national and systematic issues, producing publications, holding conferences, undertaking research to sensitise government and stakeholders to immediate and long-term challenges of HE, and consulting with stakeholders about HE.

Starting in 2004, the HEQC embarked on its first six-year cycle of audits at public and private HE institutions. The audits focus on the quality of the core functions of learning, research and community engagement in HE institutions.

Each of the insitutions completed their institutional self-evaluations and submitted the audit portfolio. The latter is the core document used by the audit panel of peers to validate the claims made by the institution about its quality management arrangement.

In 2005, the HEQC undertook nine institutional audits, three at public HE institutions and six at private providers.

The report on the *State of the Provision of the MBA in South Africa* was launched on 9 November 2004.

South African Council for Educators (SACE)

The SACE operates under the auspices of the SACE Act, 2000 (Act 31 of 2000). Its main functions are to:

- register and review registration of all educators according to criteria determined by the SACE

- promote and oversee the ongoing professional development of educators
- safeguard ethical standards in the profession
- advise the Minister of Education on pertinent issues pertaining to the profession.

By May 2005, almost 490 000 educators were registered, of which about 18 000 were registered provisionally.

A number of partnership initiatives were undertaken to promote and oversee the ongoing professional development of educators.

These included, among others, the professional development portfolio project (which benefited over 10 000 educators), quality-assurance initiatives with relevant authorities, as well as planning for a coherent framework for teacher education and continuous professional teacher development with the Ministerial Committee on Teacher Education.

In 2004/05, the council received 255 complaints. Of these, 143 were ethics-related, 56 employment-related and 56 were private matters. It also instituted 15 investigations, 10 interviews, five hearings and one mediation. Three educators were struck off the roll and two were given other sanctions.

The council also conducted advocacy workshops, and networked with similar councils and interest groups to forge a collaborative approach to promoting and defending professional ethics.

National Board for Further Education and Training (NBFET)

The NBFET was launched in June 1999 in terms of the National Education Policy Act, 1996. It provides the minister with independent and strategic advice on matters relating to the transformation of FET. The board may, on its own initiative, advise the minister on any aspect of FET, as well as:

- national FET policy, goals and priorities
- norms and standards, including those regarding funding
- norms and the terms, purposes and conditions of earmarked grants
- reports on FET from provincial advisory bodies.

Education Labour Relations Council (ELRC)

The ELRC is a bargaining council for the education sector. The council consists of equal representation of the employer (the national and provincial departments of education) and employees (trade unions representing educators and other employees in the sector).

The ELRC aims to create effective and constructive labour relations in the education sector, and to ensure the promotion and transformation of education at all levels within society.

National Student Financial Aid Scheme

The NSFAS is responsible for:
- allocating loans and bursaries to eligible students in public HE
- developing criteria and conditions for the granting of loans and bursaries to eligible students, in consultation with the minister
- raising funds, recovering loans, maintaining and analysing a database, and undertaking research for the better utilisation of financial resources
- advising the minister on related matters.

By May 2005, the scheme had awarded R4 billion in loans to 360 000 students.

Over the past 10 years, the NSFAS has assisted more than 400 000 students with awards amounting to over R5 billion. A student may receive between R2 000 and R30 000, depending on need that is determined through a national means test.

In 2004/05, R299,6 million was recovered from loans, representing an increase of 34% from 2004/05 to 2005/06.

In 2005/06, the scheme was allocated an additional R776 million, representing a 50% increase in funding over 2004 alone.

Financing education

The total allocation for the Department of Education in 2005/06 was R12,397 billion.

Financial planning in the department occurs within the Government's MTEF, which, through its three-year budgeting horizon, facilitates sustainable and properly planned financing.

In 2005/06, a conditional grant amounting to R912 151 was allocated to the National School Nutrition Programme (NSNP). Responsibility for the NSNP was shifted from the Department of Health to the Department of Education with effect from 1 April 2004.

By November 2005, the Department of Education was providing meals to about 5,3 million learners in 17 000 public schools. The department has set up 2 803 food-production initiatives to sustain the programme.

More than 22 000 adults have been provided with work opportunities through this feeding programme by preparing and serving school meals.

The conditional grant for provincial education departments for HIV and AIDS programmes was increased by R7,714 million in 2005/06. The purpose of the conditional grant was to improve and consolidate HIV and AIDS prevention and mitigation responses at all levels of the education system, and to reach all public schools and FET colleges in nodal areas and informal settlements by the end of the 2005 school year.

Some R40 million was allocated for curriculum writing and implementation of outcomes-based education (OBE) for the FET band in 2004/05.

A further allocation of R7 million in 2005/06 was expected to be used to embark on a comprehensive advocacy campaign to ensure that all stakeholders are sufficiently knowledgeable about the phased implementation of the National Curriculum Statement (NCS) in grades 10 to 12.

Equity in education expenditure

Equity between and within provinces is achieved through the equitable division of national revenue

In 2005/06, R6,9 billion was allocated to the Department of Education to contribute to improving salaries for educators. Some R4,2 billion of the R6,9 billion will be used for expanding pay progression, for performance rewards and for targeted incentives.

between provinces, making use of the Equitable Shares Formula (ESF), the National Norms and Standards for School Funding, and the National Post Provisioning Norms.

The Government's ESF promotes financial equity between provinces, through the distribution of national revenue to provinces on the basis of relative need and backlogs. In the area of education, the size of the school-age population and the number of learners enrolled in public ordinary schools are taken into account, as well as capital-investment needs.

The National Norms and Standards for School Funding, which became national policy in 1999, aim to achieve equality and redress poverty at schools in terms of non-personnel expenditure within a province. The norms are clearly progressive, with 60% of a province's non-personnel expenditure going to the poorest 40% of learners in public schools. The poorest 20% of learners receive 35% of non-personnel resources, while the richest 20% receive 5%.

To enhance the attainment of equity in funding ordinary public schools, the School Funding Norms provide for full, partial and conditional exemption for parents who cannot afford to pay school fees, thus ensuring that learners with financial difficulties cannot be denied access to education.

Considering that about 88% of provincial education expenditure goes towards personnel costs, the distribution of personnel, in particular educators, is a key driver of equity within provinces. Equity in this regard is promoted by the National Post Provisioning Norms. These norms have contributed to the narrowing of inequalities with regard to educator:learner ratios and the availability of more educator posts in historically disadvantaged areas.

Education policy

Legislative framework

Education policy is informed by the following legislation:

- The National Education Policy Act, 1996 identifies the policy, legislative and monitoring responsibilities of the Minister of Education and formalises relations between national and provincial authorities. The Act embodies the principle of co-operative governance.
- The South African Schools Act, 1996 promotes access, quality and democratic governance in the schooling system. It makes schooling compulsory for children aged seven to 15, or learners reaching the ninth grade, whichever occurs first. It also provides for two types of schools – independent schools and public schools. The Act's provision for democratic school governance through SGBs is in place in public schools countrywide.
- The FET Act, 1998 and the *Education White Paper 4 on FET* (1998) provide the basis for developing a nationally co-ordinated system, comprising the senior-secondary component of schooling and technical colleges.
- The HE Act, 1997 provides for a unified and nationally planned system of HE. The HE Act, 1997, *Education White Paper 3 on HE* (1997) and the National Plan for HE form the basis for the transformation of the HE sector.
- The Employment of Educators Act, 1998 (Act 76 of 1998), regulates the professional, moral and ethical responsibilities and competencies of educators.
- The ABET Act, 2000 (Act 52 of 2000), provides for the establishment of public and private adult-learning centres, funding for ABET provisioning, the governance of public centres and quality-assurance mechanisms for the sector.
- The HE Amendment Act, 2002 (Act 63 of 2002), clarifies and brings legal certainty to labour and student matters regarding the mergers of public HE institutions.

A new section was inserted into the Employment of Educators Act, 1998 to enable a provincial department to appoint new recruits or applicants after a break in service, without requiring a recommendation from a governing body. It also enables the fair distribution of qualified educators by allowing provinces to distribute such educators, especially to schools in rural areas.

A new section was inserted into the FET Act, 1998 and the ABET Act, 2000, prohibiting corporal punishment in educational institutions and centres.

215

Tirisano

In January 2000, the Tirisano (meaning 'working together') plan was operationalised. Through it, the department has achieved greater stability in the system, enhanced basic school functionality, improved the ability of provincial education systems to manage human and financial resources and ensured a clear focus on delivery.

The priorities of Tirisano are to:

- deal urgently and purposefully with HIV and AIDS by using the education and training system
- ensure the successful running of provincial systems through successful co-operative governance
- reduce illiteracy among adults and the youth over the next five years
- develop schools as centres of community life
- end conditions of physical degradation in South African schools
- develop the professional abilities of the teaching force
- ensure the success of active learning through OBE
- create a vibrant FET system, which will equip the youth and adults to achieve social goals
- build a rational and seamless HE system that will embrace the intellectual and professional challenges facing South Africans in the 21st century.

These priorities have been organised into the following six core programme areas:

- HIV and AIDS
- school effectiveness and teacher professionalism
- literacy
- FET and HE
- organisational effectiveness of the national and provincial departments of education
- values in education.

The Minister of Education, Ms Naledi Pandor, has prioritised the following eight areas to guide the work of the department:

- Improving access and results through quality of service and opportunity. This includes ongoing reviews to ensure that school education and the curriculum are of a high standard; expanding access to ECD, including accelerating the provision of Grade R to all children by 2010;

improving school infrastructure; and enhancing teacher education and training.

- Equipping pupils and students with appropriate skills, especially with regard to Mathematics, Science and Technology.
- Supporting sectors that are critical to skills development, especially with regard to creating a vibrant, responsive and flexible FET college sector.
- Improving funding for education, especially at provincial level.
- Supporting and enhancing HE, especially in consolidating the merger process at HE institutions and enhancing access to the NSFAS.
- Education for all, especially with regard to adult literacy and education.
- Partnerships in government and beyond, especially those pertaining to the provision of school infrastructure and the alignment of ABET with the Expanded Public Works Programme (EPWP).
- Making the system work, especially with regard to ensuring free access to quality education for those who cannot afford to pay school fees.

Policy developments

Improving access to free and quality basic education

School fees are set at annual public meetings of SGBs where parents vote on the amount to be paid. Parents who cannot afford to pay, or who can only afford a lesser amount, are granted an exemption or reduction in fees.

In his Budget Speech on 23 February 2005, the Minister of Finance, Mr Trevor Manuel, announced that government had developed proposals for improving the targeting of funding for schools and the regulations governing school fee exemptions, especially for poor households.

The plan of action to progressively improve access to free and quality education for all was made public in June 2003 and includes mechanisms to ensure the following:

- Greater interprovincial equity so that learners with similar levels of poverty receive the same minimum level of school funding.
- The abolition of compulsory school fees, where

adequate levels of resourcing are reached for 40% of learners in the poorest schools.

- A national norm based on a minimum basic package of R450 per school term in 2004, to be allocated per learner for non-personnel recurrent items, starting with the poorest 20% of learners. Adequate per-learner funding for the poorest 60% of learners in the poorest schools will be phased in over three years.
- The granting of automatic fee exemptions to learners who qualify for certain social service grants and payments.

e-Education

The collaboration between the departments of education and of communications contributed to the reduction of Internet and telephone tariffs by 50% for schools.

Targets set by the *e-Education White Paper* to be achieved by 2007 are to:

- build an education and training system to support ICT integration in teaching and learning and improved management and administration
- build teachers' and managers' confidence in the use of ICTs
- build a framework for competencies for teacher development in the integration of ICTs into the curriculum
- establish an ICT presence in schools
- ensure that schools use education content of high quality
- ensure that schools are connected, have access to the Internet and communicate electronically
- ensure that communities use and support ICT facilities.

General Education and Training

General school education is structured according to three phases, namely the Foundation Phase, Intermediate Phase and Senior Phase, and constitutes the compulsory component of the education system. The progressive provision of Grade R prior to Grade 1 started in 2002 and will be available to all children by 2010.

Currently, the Foundation Phase lasts three years. Basic learning activities during this phase centre on

three learning programmes, namely Literacy, Numeracy and Life Skills. One additional language is introduced in Grade 3.

During the three-year Intermediate Phase (grades 4 to 6), schools decide on the nature and number of learning programmes based on the resources available to the school. However, these learning programmes should draw on the eight learning areas.

The Senior Phase accounts for grades 7 to 9. During these years, learners have to be offered the following eight learning programmes: Languages, Mathematics, Arts and Culture, Life Orientation, Social Sciences, Natural Sciences, Economic and Management Sciences, and Technology. Grade 9 signals the end of compulsory schooling.

The Ministry of Education's National Environmental Education Project for GET supports educators' implementation of environmental learning in GET schools.

The project has been instrumental in ensuring that environmental learning is included in the principles, learning outcomes and assessment standards of the RNCS.

Curriculum 2005

Curriculum 2005 is the brand name of the National Curriculum Framework introduced in schools in 1998 and based on the concept of OBE. This was revised in 2002.

OBE regards learning as an interactive process between and among educators and learners. The focus is on what learners should know and be able to do (knowledge, skills, attitudes and values). It places strong emphasis on co-operative learning. The goal is to produce active and lifelong learners with a thirst for knowledge and a love of learning.

The RNCS is available in all 11 official languages as well as in Braille. A teacher's guide has been prepared, which assists the educator in developing appropriate learning programmes to achieve the specified outcomes.

A national core training team provided training to officials from every province, including curriculum specialists, subject advisers and other key staff. They, in turn, have been training school principals, who are expected to provide instructional leadership in their schools and to educators.

The Policy on Religion and Education gives directives on how schools should address the issues relating to religious observance, instruction and education, which is a curriculum matter. It recognises diversity among learners and aims to foster tolerance, respect and understanding among learners of different backgrounds.

All the subjects, which make up the NCS, are updated and expanded versions of subjects currently offered in South African schools. In the majority of cases, the names of the subjects have not changed. However, the cognitive demand of all subjects such as Physical Science, History, Geography, Music and Dance has increased. There is also an increased emphasis on Africa – her history, dance, music, etc.

The names of some subjects have changed to reflect international trends and the new content of the subjects. For example, Computer Application Technology replaces Typing and Computyping; Information Technology replaces Computer Studies; Life Sciences replaces Biology; and Consumer Studies replaces Home Economics.

The NCS requires extensive reading and extended writing in all subjects. It requires that learners think carefully about what they learn; that they have strong conceptual knowledge and are able to apply this in a variety of situations; that they are critical and curious learners; and that they are aware of the social, moral, economic and ethical issues which face South Africans and citizens around the world.

School admission policy

The age of admission to Grade 1 is five years if the child turns six on or before 30 June in their Grade 1 year.

However, if a parent has reason to believe that their child is not school-ready at age five turning six, they can choose to send their child to Grade 1 at age six turning seven.

The Education Laws Amendment Bill, 2002 set the age of admission to Grade 1 as the year in which the child turns seven. However, a Constitutional Court challenge to the Bill in 2003 resulted in the school-going age of Grade 1 being changed to age five if children turn six on or before 30 June in their Grade 1 year. This was implemented with effect from the 2004 school year.

When applying for admission, parents must present the school with an official birth certificate and proof that the child has been immunised against communicable diseases.

For non-South African citizens, a study permit, temporary or permanent residence permit, or evidence of application for permission to stay in South Africa, is also required.

Further Education and Training

FET provides learning and training from NQF levels 2 to 4, or the equivalent of grades 10 to 12 in the school system, and FETC General Vocational and FETC Trade Occupational, on NQF levels 2 to 4 in FET colleges.

Learners enter FET after the completion of the compulsory phase of education in Grade 9 or via the ABET route. The long-term vision of this sector includes the development of a co-ordinated FET system; providing high-quality, flexible and responsive programmes; and opportunities for a learning society.

The short-to-medium-term focus is on addressing the weaknesses and deficiencies of the current system, while simultaneously laying the foundations for the next 20 years.

On 5 May 2005, the Minister of Education, Ms Naledi Pandor, officially launched the Learners' Art Exhibition in Pretoria.

The exhibition kick-started the 50th anniversary celebrations of the Freedom Charter at the Sol Plaatje House in Pretoria.

It showcased learners' artwork and creative writing from the World Conference Against Racism and the Department of Education's heritage celebrations.

The minister also launched the National Learners' Competition, which encouraged all learners to interpret the theme *The Doors of Learning and Culture shall be Opened through a Quality Education for All.*

Curriculum development in Further Education and Training

The FET Curriculum is shifting away from the traditional divides between academic and applied learning, theory and practice, to knowledge and skills. The new curriculum moves towards a balanced learning experience that provides flexible access to lifelong learning, HE and training, and productive employment in a range of occupational contexts.

The implementation of the FET Curriculum in 2006 is expected to complete the circle of transformation of the schools' curriculum.

The FET Curriculum provides for a fundamental component comprising four compulsory subjects, namely: two official languages, Mathematical Literacy or Mathematics, and Life Orientation. In addition to the fundamental component, a learner must select three approved subjects.

The NCS grades 10 to 12 (General) as well as the Qualifications and Assessment Policy Framework grades 10 to 12 (General) were developed and declared policy in September 2003.

On 10 March 2005, teachers were honoured during the Aggrey Klaaste Mathematics, Physical Science and Technology Teacher of the Year Awards in Midrand.

The overall winner in the General Education and Training category was Ms Rosie Ruiters from the Free State.

Mr Lazarus Lavengwa from Limpopo took the first prize in the Further Education and Training category.

The provincial winners were:
- Northern Cape – Ms Nina Scheepers and Mr William Botha
- Free State – Ms Elizabeth Maree
- Gauteng – Ms Edith Seabi and Ms Waheeda Mahomed
- Mpumalanga – Mr Richard Twala and Mr Thulani Zulu
- KwaZulu-Natal – Mr Russel Zulu and Ms Rosemary Gumede
- North West – Mr Pieter Cronje and Ms Patricia Majane
- Limpopo – Mr Phillip Mathonsi
- Eastern Cape – Mr Zakhele Sebata and Mr Johnson Ngcape.

Further to the 21 subjects already approved, 13 non-official languages were added to the curriculum.

During November 2004, it was clear from discussions between the Department of Education and the Pan South African Language Board (PanSALB) that the Khoi and San langauge statements were not advanced enough to start with versioning or translating the generic language subject statements of the RNCS grades R to 9 and the NCS grades 1 to 12 (General). PanSALB will determine the level of readiness and inform the Department of Education accordingly.

National Strategy for Mathematics, Science and Technology Education

A profile of 102 schools dedicated to Mathematics and Science was compiled in 2003. Through the 102 Dinaledi schools, the National Mathematics, Science and Technology Strategy assisted in increasing the performance and participation rate in gateway subjects, particularly for African students and girl learners. Performance in Physical Science HG and Mathematics HG has improved considerably in recent years.

In June 2005, the CEM approved a decision by the Minister of Education to increase the Dinaledi schools to 513 in 2006.

Further Education and Training colleges

South African learners need a range of skills and knowledge to keep up with modern technology. Remote rural areas need to be reached, and adult learners need the opportunity to retrain for a second or third career.

Small business entrepreneurs also need courses that cater for their needs, and industry and the community need to be provided with productive people who see learning as a lifelong occupation, and an economy that is being restructured to meet the demands of globalisation.

In this context, the creation of a dynamic, responsive and high-quality FET system to promote wider access and social inclusion; encourage lifelong learning; meet the human resource development

(HRD) needs of the country; contribute towards urban renewal and rural development; and develop an entirely new citizenry in the country, became imperative.

As a result, major transformation of the FET sector took place during 2002/03, in which the existing 152 technical colleges were merged to form 50 multisite-campus FET colleges.

The colleges provide:

- high-level skills training
- a balanced training programme, emphasising both theoretical and practical skills linked to specific industry requirements
- vocational training, which continually exposes students to the demands of the work environment.

Each new college operates under a single governing council appointed to oversee effective and accountable management across and within the various FET college campuses and sites.

The recorded increase in student intake, the development of new programmes and increased participation in learnerships bear testimony to the potential for growth in this sector.

In 2005/06, government invested R1 billion over the next three years for improved facilities, equipment and support for FET colleges.

Some R1 billion will be invested in the recapitalisation of FET public colleges in 2006/07 and 2007/08. In the 2005/06 financial year, R50 million was used to develop a detailed situation analysis and work plans to direct the use of the R1 billion over the 2006/07 to 2007/08 period.

This includes the development of the FET Sector Plan to finalise national, provincial and college recapitalisation plans; collect information on skills shortages and labour market trends; and to ensure that bids and contracts are developed and awarded by the beginning of 2006/07.

Recapitalisation of FET colleges is expected to:

- increase the number of students enrolled in high-quality vocational programmes
- develop high-quality modern and responsive FET programmes
- focus on the development and employment needs and opportunities related to major capital development projects over the next 10 years.

Higher Education

HE and Training is also referred to as tertiary education. The HE band provides the highest level of education. Entry into HE is through a Grade 12 pass or Grade 12 pass with exemption.

Private institutions offering HE must register with the department in accordance with the HE Act, 1997. The role of HE in the South African education system is threefold:

- HRD: Mobilising human talent and potential through lifelong learning to contribute to the social, economic, cultural and intellectual life of a rapidly changing society.
- High-level skills training: Training and providing person power to strengthen the country's enterprises, services and infrastructure. This requires the development of professionals with globally equivalent skills, but who are socially responsible and conscious of their role in contributing to the national development effort and social transformation.
- Producing, acquiring and applying new knowledge: National growth and competitiveness depend on continuous technological improvement and innovation, driven by a well-organised and vibrant research and development system that integrates the research and training capaci-

In March 2005, the ministers of education and of sport and recreation signed a memorandum of understanding on school sport in terms of which it becomes an integral component of a holistic education programme.

Each school is required to allocate time for participation in school sport during or after formal school hours.

Inter-school competition is encouraged in all sport.

The National Co-ordination Committee (NACOC) co-ordinates and manages school sport. NACOC comprises representatives from the departments of education, and of sport and recreation, provincial education departments, the South African Sports Confederation and Olympic Committee, provincial departments that are responsible for sport and recreation, teacher unions, local sports councils and national school-governing bodies.

ty of HE with the needs of industry and of social reconstruction.

Transformation and reconstruction of the Higher Education system

Due to the legacy of apartheid, the HE education sector had to be restructured to meet the social, cultural and economic development imperatives of the new social order, and to establish a single co-ordinated national HE system.

The *Education White Paper 3: A Programme for the Transformation of HE* and the HE Act, 1997 provided the policy and legislative framework for the transformation of the HE system.

National Plan for Higher Education

The National Plan for HE was released in March 2001. The plan establishes indicative targets for the size and shape of the HE system, including overall growth and participation rates, institutional and programme mixes, and equity and efficiency goals.

It provides a framework and outlines the process for the restructuring of the system. It also provides signposts for the development of institutional plans.

The key proposals of the plan are that:
- the participation rate in HE will be increased from 15% to 20% in the long term, i.e. 10 to 15 years
- there will be a shift in the balance of enrolments over the next five to 10 years between the Humanities; Business and Commerce; and Science, Engineering and Technology, from the current ratio of 49:26:25 to 40:30:30 respectively
- institutions will establish student-equity targets with the emphasis on programmes in which black and female students are underrepresented, and develop strategies to ensure equity of outcomes
- institutions will develop employment-equity plans with clear targets for rectifying race and gender inequities
- institutional diversity will be achieved through the approval of a distinct mission and academic-programme profile for each institution
- the academic programme mix at each institution will be determined on the basis of its existing

programme profile, as well as its demonstrated capacity to add new programmes
- redress for historically black institutions will be linked to agreed missions and programme profiles, including developmental strategies to build capacity
- research will be funded through a separate formula based on research output, including, at a minimum, masters' and doctoral graduates and research publications
- earmarked funds will be allocated to build research capacity, including scholarships to promote postgraduate enrolments
- the institutional landscape will be restructured through collaboration at regional level, in programme development, delivery and rationalisation, particularly of small and costly programmes.

Institutional restructuring

The total cost of restructuring the HE system is estimated at R1,9 billion for the period 2001/02 to 2006/07.

The establishment of 24 consolidated HE institutions, including two national institutes for HE, out of the former 36 universities and technikons were finalised in January 2005. The HE system consists of 11 universities, five universities of technology, and six comprehensive institutions.

The new HE landscape consists of the following institutions:
- University of the Witwatersrand.
- University of Cape Town.
- Rhodes University.
- Stellenbosch University.
- University of the Western Cape (incorporating the Dental Faculty of Stellenbosch University on 1 January 2004).
- University of Zululand.
- Venda University.
- University of the Free State (incorporating the QwaQwa Campus of the University of the North on 1 January 2003 and the Bloemfontein Campus of Vista on 2 January 2004).
- North West University (from the merger of the universities of Potchefstroom – which incorpo-

rated Vista Sebokeng Campus on 2 January 2004 – and North West).

- University of Pretoria (which incorporated the Mamelodi Campus of Vista University on 2 January 2004).
- University of KwaZulu-Natal (from the merger of the University of Natal and the University of Durban-Westville).
- University of South Africa (UNISA) (after the merger of UNISA – which incorporated the Vista University Distance Education Campus on 2 January 2004 – with Technikon SA).
- Tshwane University of Technology (from the merger of technikons Pretoria, North West and Northern Gauteng).
- Durban Institute of Technology (from the merger of Natal Technikon and Technikon M.L. Sultan).
- Central University of Technology, Free State (formerly Technikon Free State).
- Mangosuthu Technikon.
- University of Johannesburg (established in January 2005 from the merger of Rand Afrikaans University – which incorporated the Soweto and East Rand campuses of Vista University on 2 January 2004 – with Technikon Witwatersrand).
- University of Limpopo (established in January 2005 from the merger of the Medical University of South Africa and the University of the North).
- Nelson Mandela Metropolitan University (established in January 2005 from the merger of the University of Port Elizabeth – which incorporated the Port Elizabeth Campus of Vista University on 2 January – and Port Elizabeth Technikon).
- Walter Sisulu University for Technology and Science in the Eastern Cape (established in January 2005 from the merger of the University of Transkei, Border Technikon and Eastern Cape Technikon).
- University of Fort Hare (which incorporated the East London Campus of Rhodes University on 1 January 2004).
- Cape Peninsula University of Technology (established in January 2005 from the merger of the Cape and Peninsula technikons).
- Northern Cape Institute of HE, which was launched in June 2003.

- Mpumalanga Institute of HE, which was still to be launched by mid-2005. A detailed planning process was undertaken in 2005.

Adult Basic Education and Training

The 2001 Census showed that at least four million South Africans in the 20 years-and-over age group had no schooling at all, while another four million had limited schooling at primary school level. This translated into at least 18% of the population, excluding school-going children, being in need of basic literacy interventions.

The ABET Act, 2000 provides a legislative framework for the establishment, governance and funding of ABET centres. Through the Adult Education and Training Multi-Year Implementation Plan (MYIP), the quality of ABET provisioning and delivery is improving.

The National ABET Board is an advisory body to the minister, and receives reports from all sectors on the progress of the MYIP.

The department established the South African Literacy Agency (SANLI) to significantly reduce adult illiteracy by:

- mobilising voluntary services in support of a nationwide literacy initiative

The 8th World Conference on Computers in Education took place at the University of Stellenbosch in July 2005 under the theme *40 Years of Computers in Education: What Works*.

The conference focused on the following:
- increasing the Information and Communications Technology (ICT) capabilities of teachers and learners
- providing teachers with the knowledge and skills needed to integrate ICT in teaching and learning
- new and suitable technologies, methodologies and techniques identified through current research and development
- ICT resources available on educational networks and the Internet
- curriculum support and development to access suitable online resources.

- developing training programmes for volunteer educators
- designing, developing and procuring reading and resource material
- setting up local literacy units
- establishing and maintaining a database of learners and providers
- servicing the needs of learners and educators.

Since the establishment of SANLI in 2002, more than 320 000 adults have been reached in various non-formal sites, while more than 635 913 have been reached through the public adult learning centres.

As part of the advocacy campaign to mobilise learners, National Adult Learners' Week was launched as an annual event on 1 September 2000. Award ceremonies are held on International Literacy Day (8 September) to honour and applaud the courage and achievements of adult learners and their educators.

Partnerships to improve literacy levels in the country include the Bridges to the Future Initiative (BFI), a public-private collaboration that includes the Department of Education, Multichoice Africa Foundation, SchoolNet South Africa, UNISA and the International Literacy Initiative.

The BFI aims to provide skills for out-of-school youth and adults in ICT and adult education. Initiatives include the development of community learning and technology centres for lifelong learning and income-generation, the development of tools to improve basic education and literacy through teacher training in selected nodal areas, and the use of ICT for human development in areas such as health, agriculture, and HIV and AIDS prevention.

The Minister of Education launched the national literacy campaign, Readathon 2005, at the Apartheid Museum in Johannesburg on 23 April 2005 (World Book Day). READ Educational Trust, with Nedbank as the major sponsor, co-ordinates the campaign which aims to encourage South Africans to read.

As part of the year-long campaign, material would be distributed to 26 000 schools nationwide to promote reading activities in classrooms, libraries and community centres.

The campaign culminated in International Literacy Week in September 2005 when children read to celebrities, parliamentarians, business leaders and other high-profile patrons and supporters of reading.

Masifunde Sonke is another project set up by the Ministry of Education to address the challenges of illiteracy and to promote a love of reading.

The Department of Education has signed a memorandum of understanding with the United States' Agency for International Development (USAID) to implement a reading and writing project as part of the Unites States' African Education Initiative Textbooks for a Global Society Programme. The project is implemented in partnership with Hampton University and has produced teacher guides and learner workbooks for teaching writing. The ultimate objective of the programme is the production of reading material written by the learners themselves in the different official languages.

The Democracy in the Classroom Project was launched in August 2003. It is the result of a partnership between the United Kingdom's (UK) Department for International Development (DFID), the Independent Electoral Commission of South Africa and the ABET Institute of UNISA, in collaboration with SANLI.

Education of learners with special education needs

The national and provincial departments of education provide a wide range of education services to learners with diverse challenges. These include:

- autism
- behavioural problems
- visual impairment
- tuberculosis
- children in conflict with the law
- physical disability
- neurological and specific learning disabilities
- multi-disability
- intellectual disability
- hearing impairment
- communication disorders
- epilepsy
- over-aged learners.

223

The Department of Education seeks to provide access to all learners, which is a basic right enshrined in the South African Constitution.

The *Education White Paper 6* acknowledges that many children experience barriers to learning. Some of these barriers lie within the learners themselves (intrinsic), while some barriers are systematic, socio-economic and cultural.

In its quest to accommodate learners who experience barriers to learning, the Department of Education is field-testing inclusive education in 30 districts in the nodal areas. Between 2005 and 2006, some 30 selected ordinary primary schools were expected to be made more accessible to learners with physical disabilities.

Assistive devices will also be made available for learners in need. Educators will be trained and empowered to teach children with diverse learning needs. District-based support teams will be developed to provide support mainly to educators in these full-service schools.

This will enable children, the majority of whom could not access education in the past because of the unavailability of specialised services and support in rural and previously disadvantaged areas, to gain access to education.

Once the first phase of implementing inclusive education is completed, the lessons learnt will be applied to the wider education sector incrementally.

Meanwhile, existing special schools will be strengthened so that some of them can serve as resource centres for full-service schools and ordinary schools in their areas.

Early Childhood Development

ECD is a comprehensive approach to programmes and policies for children from birth to nine years of age with the active participation of their parents and caregivers. Its purpose is to protect the rights of children to develop their full cognitive, emotional, social and physical potential.

The Department of Education is responsible for children in grades 1 to 3 as part of compulsory schooling. One of the priorities of the department is to increase access to ECD provisioning through an accredited reception year programme as proposed in *Education White Paper 5*. This policy focuses on expanding ECD provision, correcting the imbalances of the past, ensuring equitable access and improving the quality and delivery of ECD programmes.

It also proposes expanding the provision of services to children from birth to four years through the development and implementation of intersectoral programmes.

The non-profit sector plays a major role in ECD. Most of the 1,03 million places in early learning sites across South Africa have been initiated by the non-profit sector in partnership with communities. Nevertheless, for many poor children, quality ECD is still beyond reach.

The medium-term goal of the department is for all children entering Grade 1 to have participated in an accredited Grade R programme by 2010. With regard to the birth-to-age-four cohort, the Department of Education is leading the ECD Interdepartmental Committee (including the departments of health and of social development), which has developed the Birth-to-Four Integrated Plan.

The plan is closely linked to the Government's EPWP. In ECD, the EPWP will create employment and training opportunities by providing education and care services to young children.

The registration of sites is the responsibility of the Department of Social Development in terms of the Child Care Act, 1983 (Act 74 of 1983). Municipalities/local governments also have constitutional power to provide childcare failities and grants to associations. These regulations are applicable to both public and independent ECD sites.

According to an SACE resolution signed in 2004, all ECD practitioners should be recognised and registered as educators and participate in all professional development programmes.

The *Education White Paper 5* proposes and encourages an integrated cross-sectoral approach to child development. This includes health, nutrition, education and psychosocial factors.

Education management and governance development

The department has developed the education-management policy, which is being used to develop norms and standards for school managers along with a new ladder of education-management qualifications, which will lead to an entry level qualification for principals.

The policy highlights the central role that school and district managers play in improving schools. In school governance, the department is initiating plans to develop structured, accredited courses focused on literacy and community leadership skills while improving the functioning of SGBs.

The focus on improving educational institutional management and governance is supported by improvement in the management of education districts with the development of an operational manual for district managers, as well as the development of two 'model' districts to use as the basis for capacity-building of all district directors.

Teacher development

The following programmes contribute towards teacher development:

- The RNCS project aims to prepare national and provincial teams of trainers who orientate teachers for the delivery of the RNC in the year of implementation. In 2005, 40 000 Grade 7 teachers were targeted.

  About 2 100 provincial officials and 200 000 Foundation Phase and Intermediate Phase teachers across the nine provinces have been orientated to implement the RNC.
- The National Framework for Teacher Education aims to address historical backlogs in levels of teacher performance as well as improve initial professional education of teachers, their continuing professional development and the supporting mechanisms needed.
- The Mathematics, Science and Technology Programme aims to improve the qualifications and skills of teachers in these subjects. Three cohorts have gone through the programme since 2002 with 3 000 teachers graduating with a B.Ed or Advanced Certificate in Education (ACE). In 2005, another 540 teachers were expected to graduate with an ACE as the third cohort, and 630 teachers were to be registered nationally as the fourth cohort.

- The National Professional Diploma for Educators (NPDE) Programme aims to train teachers who do not have teaching qualifications as a result of historical backlogs. Six thousand teachers have received the diploma in two cohorts. In 2005, some 1 300 new NPDE teachers (third cohort) were registered and 500 teachers were expected to graduate (second cohort). An evaluation of the programme was expected to be completed by the end of January 2006.
- The National Teaching Awards acknowledge teachers in eight categories of performance at provincial and national level. The aim for 2005 was to increase the number of schools participating, and improve nominations and adjudication processes at district, provincial and national level.

The School Register of Needs

The School Register of Needs provides an important benchmark for addressing historical inequities.

Considerable progress has been made since 1994 in correcting these inequities. The School Register of Needs 2000 Survey recorded significant improvements in school infrastructure and access to basic services countrywide.

The register indicated that 7 817 schools were without water in 2000. According to provincial departments, 4 774 schools were without water by the end of February 2005. In 2000, there were 12 257 schools without electricity, but by February 2005, 5 233 schools were without electricity.

Unsafe structures declined from 4 389 in 2000 to 1 719 in February 2005. Schools in mud structures declined from 1 751 to 939 in February 2005, and asbestos school structures were reduced from 944 in 2000 to 575 in February 2005.

All zinc school structures, which totalled 311 in 2000, had been replaced by February 2005. The number of platooning schools declined from 1 023 in 2000 to 473 in February 2005. Schools without fencing declined from 5 233 in 2000 to 2 540 in 2004. In 2000, there were 12 192 schools without libraries compared with 7 216 in 2004.

In 2000, 7 520 schools needed laboratories compared with 7 180 in February 2005. In 2000, 453 schools experienced problems with access roads to schools compared with 46 in 2004.

Emphasis on classroom provision has reduced classroom backlogs drastically.

In 2004, the department began developing standards for school infrastructure, including minimum requirements for basic services such as water and sanitation.

Once approved, they will be used to standardise the design and construction of schools. This will result in improved efficiency, quicker turnaround times and the attainment of economies of scale that will translate into improved cost-efficiency.

The department also developed monitoring tools to track progress in reducing the number of learners who are still receiving education under trees, in mud structures or in unsafe conditions.

In April 2005, the departments of education and of public works formed an interdepartmental task team to develop systems to eradicate backlogs in schools' infrastructure. The task team was expected to do an audit of learners who do not have schools and to locate schools that are underused.

Alternative accommodation would be considered for learners without classrooms and more attention would be given to priority provinces such as KwaZulu-Natal, Mpumalanga and Limpopo.

The Department of Education has established systems and databases (including the Education Management Information System) that are used for monitoring output, outcome and impact.

By February 2005, these systems were being refined to ensure that they provided a cross-linked set of information on different aspects of education institutions.

These systems would make it possible to track whether the poor receive a larger share of state resources as a result of poverty-targeting.

Human Resource Development Strategy

In April 2001, the ministries of education and of labour jointly launched the HRD Strategy for South Africa, entitled *A Nation at Work for a Better Life for All*. The strategy is underpinned by a set of institutional arrangements, including sector education and training authorities (SETAs), and the general reshaping of FET and HE to meet the HRD needs of the country.

The strategy ensures that integrated HRD planning and implementation is monitored at national, regional and sectoral level. Progress is measured against approved indicators.

The key mission of the strategy is to maximise the potential of people in South Africa through the acquisition of knowledge and skills. It also seeks to introduce an operational plan and the necessary arrangements to ensure that everyone is productive and works competitively to improve their quality of life.

The goals of the strategy include improving the social infrastructure of the country, reducing disparities in wealth and poverty, developing a more inclusive society, and improving South Africa's position on the International Competitiveness Table over the next 10 years.

The January 2005 Cabinet Lekgotla mandated the urgent revival of the HRD Strategy to ensure integrated HRD planning and implementation that is monitored at national, regional and sectoral level, with progress being measured against approved indicators.

HIV and AIDS

The Ministry of Education works alongside the Ministry of Health to ensure that the national education system plays its part in stemming HIV and AIDS, and ensures that the rights of all those infected with the disease are fully protected.

Between February and September 2005, 87 schools were provided with water and sanitation. Work was underway to extend this to an additional 240 schools.

This priority has been operationalised into three objectives of the Tirisano implementation plan. Each is linked to anticipated outcomes and performance indicators. The three programmes are:

- awareness, information and advocacy
- HIV and AIDS within the curriculum
- planning for HIV and AIDS and the education system.

The ministry's policy on HIV and AIDS for learners and educators has been converted into an accessible booklet aimed at educators, SGBs and district officials.

In 2005, the Department of Education received R150 million from the European Union (EU) to support the HE HIV and AIDS Programme (HEAIDS) to be implemented over four years. HEAIDS is the HE sector's response to HIV and AIDS, designed to enable institutions to prevent, manage and mitigate the impact of HIV and AIDS.

In 2005, the HIV and AIDS conditional grant to provincial education departments was increased by R7,714 billion. The purpose of the grant was to improve and consolidate HIV and AIDS prevention and mitigation responses at all levels of the educa-

In January 2005, the Department of Education launched an educational portal – *www.thutong.org.za* – offering a range of curriculum and learner support material, professional development programmes for educators, and administration and management resources for schools.

Thutong – 'place of learning' in Setswana – features a searchable database of web-based curriculum resources for various education sectors, grades and subjects.

It also carries news and information on the latest developments in education in South Africa, and gives users the chance to interact with experts from the education community, as well as with their peers throughout the country and abroad.

The portal is a free service to registered users, who must go through a once-off, no-cost registration process.

The portal is a partnership venture between the Department of Education and various role-players in the field.

tion system, and to reach all public schools and FET colleges in nodal areas and informal settlements by the end of 2005.

Partnerships, international relations and funding

Central to the education policy framework is the contention that a high-quality education sector cannot be built by government alone. It depends on creative and dynamic partnerships between the public sector, civil society and international partners.

The Department of Education; the three teacher unions; the SACE; the ELRC; and the Education, Training and Development Practices SETA signed a historic declaration at the National Education Convention in November 2002, in which they committed themselves to working together to achieve education transformation goals.

The success of key national initiatives (including SANLI) relies largely on partnerships with the private and non-governmental organisation (NGO) sectors.

Several partnerships have been consolidated, providing working models of educational transformation through public-private partnerships. The Business Trust, a partnership between business and government, works in education through three NGOs, namely the READ Educational Trust, the Joint Education Trust (JET) and the National Business Initiative Colleges Collaboration.

One of JET's largest areas of work has been school development. By September 2004, the organisation was either the lead agent or a senior partner in the management of school development programmes affecting some 3 000 schools spread across all nine provinces, and funded by the South African Business Trust, Britain's DFID, the Swedish International Development Agency (SIDA), and USAID.

Teacher unions

The majority of educators are organised into four teacher unions, namely the National Professional Teachers' Organisation of South Africa, the National

Teachers' Union, the South African Teachers' Union, and the South African Democratic Teachers' Union.

A labour-relations framework has been agreed to jointly by the Ministry of Education and the unions. This encompasses both traditional areas of negotiation and issues of professional concern, including pedagogy and quality-improvement strategies.

Non-governmental organisations

NGOs are emerging as important partners in educational transformation and are often a source of creativity and innovation. The Department of Education is working with NGOs and the private sector to expand relationships, particularly in the areas of educator training, school improvement, ABET, ECD and FET, as well as evaluation, research and monitoring. The private sector in particular is engaging increasingly in the provision of basic education by funding FET initiatives, building schools in needy communities, and supporting the provision of teaching and learning equipment.

The international community

The international community's contribution to the transformation of education is important. The department co-operates with United Nations (UN) agencies and numerous donors to improve access to basic, FET and HE.

Development co-operation partners such as the Australian Agency for International Development, Flanders, France, Germany, Italy, Japan International Co-operation Agency, the Swiss Agency for Development and Co-operation, the Danish Agency for Development Assistance, the USAID, the SIDA, the Canadian International Development Agency, the DFID, the Netherlands, the Irish Agency for International Development, the Finnish Government and the EU have been instrumental in the provision of technical and financial assistance to the national and provincial departments of education.

The governments of the UK and Northern Ireland are making available R226 million to the Limpopo Department of Education. The assistance, which will be spread over six years (2003 to 2009), is known as the Khanyisa Education Support Programme.

The programme aims to improve learning achievement, support, and service delivery across the whole education system.

The ministry also played a leading role in the development of the Southern African Development Community Protocol on Education and Training, which aims to achieve equivalence, harmonisation and standardisation of education in the region.

International partnerships and South-South exchanges are fostered particularly within the African continent.

The department has a strong collaborative relationship with the UN Educational, Scientific and Cultural Organisation. A key initiative of the collaboration is the development of national Education For All (EFA) action plans. As part of regional consultations on the implementation, the department participates in assessing progress in the elaboration of the EFA plans of countries in sub-Saharan Africa, and exchanges information on best practices in the development of these plans.

Libraries

Libraries in the Higher Education sector

The HE libraries hold the bulk of South Africa's scientific and scholarly information resources and fulfil more than half of all the interlibrary loan requests. Pressures on HE libraries include redistribution of educational resources, rising prices and declining

In 2005/06, R10 million was transferred to the Association for the Development of Education in Africa (ADEA).

This was introduced in 2004/05 as an annual contribution to ADEA by African ministries of education, as a way of expressing commitments to ADEA and reinforcing the spirit of partnership between ministries of education and agencies.

student numbers. These libraries have responded by forming consortia, looking at access and exploring digital resources.

Special libraries are libraries that consist of subject-specialised collections, including private organisations' libraries and libraries of government departments. (See also chapter 5: *Arts and culture.*)

Policy Framework for School Libraries

By July 2004, the Department of Education was working on the Policy Framework for School Libraries. This draft document locates itself within the context of the socio-political and educational transformation that is driven by the new legislative framework, and the educational paradigm shift to OBE.

The draft policy argues that educators and learners will only be able to access an OBE curriculum if they have access to learning resources. This has implications for the way school libraries conceptualise, manage and provide resources.

The draft policy recommends different models of school libraries to provide access to resources for learners, and draws attention to the relationship between the school library, the curriculum and learning resources. It also supports the view that the school library is a facility ideally suited to providing learners with a wide range of curriculum-orientated resources in diverse media forms, as required by an OBE system.

Acknowledgements

BuaNews
Department of Arts and Culture
Department of Education
Estimates of National Expenditure 2005, published by National Treasury
Library and Information Association of South Africa
National Library of South Africa
South African Qualifications Authority
www.gov.za
www.umalusi.org.za

Suggested reading

Badat, S. *Black Student Politics, Higher Education and Apartheid: From SASO to SANSCO. 1968 – 1990.* Pretoria: Human Sciences Research Council (HSRC), 1999.
Bisschoff, T. *et al. Project Management in Education and Training.* Pretoria: Van Schaik, 2004.
Bot, M. and Pienaar, L. *TUATA: Transvaal United African Teachers' Association.* Pretoria: HSRC, 1999.
Burger, J.F. and Vermaak, A. *A Directory of HSRC-rated Courses Offered in the Private Education and Training Sector.* Pretoria: HSRC, 1999.
Chinapah, V. *With Africa for Africa: Towards Quality Education for All.* Pretoria: HSRC, 2000.
Chisholm, L. ed. *Changing Class: Education and Social Change in Post-Apartheid South Africa.* Cape Town: HSRC, 2004.
Christie, P. *Right to Learn: The Struggle for Education in South Africa.* 2nd ed. Randburg: Ravan Press, 1991.
Closser, M. *et al. Settling for Less: Student Aspirations and Higher Education Realities.* Cape Town: HSRC, 2004.
Cross, M. *Resistance and Transformation: Education, Culture and Reconstruction in South Africa.* Johannesburg: Skotaville, 1992.
Cross, M. *et al.* eds. *Dealing with Diversity in South African Education: A Debate on the Politics of a National Curriculum.* Kenwyn: Juta, 1998.

Du Toit, C.W. and Kruger, J.S. eds. *Multireligious Education in South Africa.* Pretoria: 1998.

Emerging Voices: Report on Education in South African Rural Communities. Cape Town: HSRC, 2005

Every Step of the Way: The Journey to Freedom in South Africa. Cape Town: HSRC, 2004. Commissioned by the Ministry of Education to commemorate 10 years of freedom in education.

Fleisch, B.D. *Managing Educational Change: The State and School Reform in South Africa.* Sandton: Heinemann, 2002.

Graaf, J. *et al. Teaching in the Gap: Implementing Education Policy in South Africa in the Nineties.* Hatfield: Via Afrika, n.d.

Gravett, S. and Geyser, H. *Teaching and Learning in Higher Education.* Pretoria: Van Schaik, 2003.

Harber, C. *State of Transition.* Oxford: Symposium Books, 2001.

Harley, A. *et al. A Survey of Adult Basic Education in South Africa in the 90s: Commissioned by the Joint Education Trust.* Johannesburg: Sached, 1996.

Hartshorne, K. *Crisis and Challenge: Black Education, 1910 – 1990.* Cape Town: Oxford University Press, 1992.

Heystek, J., Roos, C., and Middlewood, D. *Human Resource Management in Education.* Johannesburg: Heinemann, 2005.

Hutton, B. ed. *Adult Basic Education in South Africa.* Cape Town: Oxford University Press Southern Africa, 2004.

Kallaway, P. *Apartheid and Education: The Education of Black South Africans.* Johannesburg: Ravan Press, 1990.

Kallaway, P. ed. *The History of Education under Apartheid 1948 – 1994.* Cape Town: Pearson Education, 2002.

Kraak, A. and Young, M. eds. *Education in Retrospect.* Pretoria: HSRC and Institute of Education, 2001.

Kraak, A. ed. *Changing Modes: New Knowledge Production and Its Implications for Higher Education in South Africa.* Pretoria: HSRC, 2000.

Maree, K. and Ebersohn, L. *Lifeskills and Career Counselling.* Johannesburg: Heinemann, 2004.

Mboya, M.M. *Beyond Apartheid: The Question of Education for Liberation.* Cape Town: Esquire Press, 1993.

McKinney, C. *Textbooks for Diverse Learners: A Critical Analysis of Learning Materials Used in South African Schools.*

Mncwabe, M.P. *Post-Apartheid Education.* Lanham, Maryland (USA): University Press of America, 1993.

Mokadi, A. *A Portrait of Governance in Higher Education: Taking a Stand for Education.* Johannesburg: Sedibeng Publishing House, 2002.

Morrow, W. and King, K. eds. *Vision and Reality: Changing Education and Training in South Africa.* Cape Town: University of Cape Town, 1998.

Mwamwenda, T.S. *Educational Psychology: An African Perspective.* 3rd rev ed. Johannesburg: Heinemann, 2004.

Nelson, D. ed. *A – Z of Careers: The South African Career Encyclopaedia.* Cape Town, 2004.

Nicolaou, G. and Nicolaou, E. *The School Guide Book.* Johannesburg: G.E.N. Publishing, 1998.

Nkomo, M. ed. *et al. Reflections on School Integration: Colloquium Proceedings.* Pretoria: HSRC, 2004.

Pretorius, F. ed. *Outcomes-Based Education in South Africa.* Randburg: Hodder and Stoughton, 1999.

Roussouw, J.P. *Labour Relations in Education: A South African Perspective.* Pretoria: Van Schaik, 2004.

Saunders, S. *Vice-Chancellor on a Tightrope: A Personal Account of Climactic Years in South Africa.* Cape Town: David Philip, 2000.

Seepe, S. ed. *Towards an African Identity of Higher Education.* Pretoria: Vista University, 2004

Sekete, P. *et al. Deracialisation and Migration of Learners in South African Schools.* Pretoria: HSRC, 2001.

Steyn, J.C. *Education for Democracy.* Durbanville: Wachwa Publishers, 1997.

Taylor, N. *Getting Schools Working: Research and Systemic School Reform in South Africa.* Cape Town: Maskew Miller Longmans, 2003.

Walters, S. ed. *Globalisation, Adult Education and Training: Impact and Issues.* London: Zed Books; Cape Town: CACE Publications, 1997.

Environmental management

In terms of its biological heritage, South Africa is recognised as one of the richest nations in the world.

The vision of the Department of Environmental Affairs and Tourism is a prosperous and equitable society living in harmony with its natural resources. The department manages the development and implementation of policies governing three interrelated components of South Africa's socio-economic development: tourism, the fishing industry and environmental management. Expenditure was expected to increase from R1,1 billion in 2001/02 to R1,7 billion in 2004/05 and R2,1 billion in 2007/08.

The department's mission is to lead the sustainable development of South Africa's environment by:
- promoting the sustainable development and conservation of the country's natural resources
- protecting and improving the quality and safety of the environment
- promoting a global sustainable-development agenda.

In February 2005, the Minister of Environmental Affairs and Tourism, Mr Marthinus van Schalkwyk, announced the establishment of the National Environmental Advisory Forum (NEAF).

The NEAF will play an important role in providing the minister with strategic advice on issues of environmental management from the wide range of stakeholder groupings represented. In addition, the forum will advise the minister on matters concerning environmental management and governance.

At regional level, the provincial conservation agencies are major role-players, and independent statutory organisations such as South African National Parks (SANParks) and the South African National Biodiversity Institute (SANBI) are valuable partners in the country's total conservation effort.

In accordance with the National Environmental Management Act, 1998 (Act 107 of 1998), the Committee for Environmental Co-ordination was established to harmonise the work of government departments on environmental issues and to co-ordinate environmental implementation and national management plans at provincial level. The Act sets principles for effective management of the environment, which all organs of the State have to comply with in their decision-making. The Act also provides for the NEAF.

The National Environmental Management Act, 1998 requires national and provincial departments to compile environmental implementation plans (EIPs) and environmental management plans, thus providing a legal framework for environmental development.

One of the most far-reaching interventions regarding co-operative governance since 1994 has been the introduction of environmental impact assessments (EIAs). Some EIAs are considered at national level, but the vast majority of development applications are processed by the provinces.

The department processes 100 applications a year in terms of the EIA regulations. As part of its law-reform process, the Department of Environmental Affairs and Tourism has identified the need to revise the current approach to the regulation of EIAs.

The aims of the new draft EIA regulations are, among other things, to:

- facilitate a streamlined administrative process
- clearly specify listed activities to remove existing uncertainties
- provide for stricter application in sensitive areas
- provide a mechanism to exclude certain activities in areas which are not sensitive
- provide a mechanism for municipalities to control environmental impact in certain instances through the planning process
- provide for more appropriate public participation and the assessment of issues raised by communities.

The final draft regulations were expected to be promulgated in 2005.

World Wetlands Day: 2 February
National Water Week: 19 to 25 March
Earth Day: 20 March
World Water Day: 22 March
World Meteorological Day: 23 March
World Environment Day: 5 June
World Oceans Day: 8 June
World Desertification Day: 17 June
National Arbour Week: 1 to 7 September
International Day for the Protection of the
 Ozone Layer: 16 September
World Tourism Day: 27 September
World Habitat Day: 4 October
National Marine Day: 20 October

The department has developed a series of information documents on integrated environmental management, which are available in printed and electronic format.

Policy and legislation

The peaceful transition in South Africa presented a unique opportunity for redress and recovery. Starting with the Constitution of the Republic of South Africa, 1996 (Act 108 of 1996), new policies and legislation have been developed across all sectors, with full public consultation and participation.

The National Environmental Management: Biodiversity Act, 2004 (Act 10 of 2004), aims to provide a regulatory framework to protect South Africa's valuable species, ecosystems and its biological wealth. It implements the *White Paper on the Conservation and Sustainable Use of South Africa's Biological Diversity* and multilateral agreements such as the Convention on Biological Diversity (CBD).

South Africa is a signatory to the CBD, which provides the framework, norms and standards for the conservation, sustainable use and equitable benefit-sharing of South Africa's biological resources.

The Act facilitated the transformation of the National Botanical Institute (NBI) into SANBI.

It also enables the development of the National Biodiversity Framework that will provide an integrated, co-ordinated and uniform approach to the conservation and sustainable use of biodiversity in South Africa.

The National Environmental Management: Protected Areas Act, 2003 (Act 57 of 2003), provides for the protection and conservation of ecologically viable areas representative of South Africa's biological diversity and its natural landscapes and seascapes, and the management thereof. The Act envisages a national register of protected areas, with a simplified classification system of special nature reserves, national parks, nature reserves and protected environments.

It introduces the concept of biological diversity protection and ecosystem management for the first time. Biodiversity, conservation and ecosystem management are noted as important aims in policy and legislation that govern marine and coastal resources, freshwater and natural forests.

It also proposes a new system of protected areas, linking various kinds of protected environments to replace the existing fragmented system.

Based on experience with biosphere reserves, and informed by the new bioregional approach to conservation (linking the protected area network along mountains, rivers, wetlands, the coastline and other areas of natural vegetation), the Act will result in an interlocking system of protected areas that explicitly encourages the inclusion of private land.

It recognises that people are the custodians of the land, that they need to be involved in the management of the protected land and that they should benefit from it.

The Act caters for concurrent competence in the management of protected land. For example, an area with national park status can now be managed by another agency, for example, a provincial parks authority. Steps have been taken to ensure that standards are upheld.

South Africa is one of only two countries in the world to have promulgated legislation specifically related to the World Heritage Convention (the other being Australia). The country's World Heritage Convention Act, 1999 (Act 49 of 1999), stipulates that all world heritage sites must have an integrated management plan in place to ensure cultural and environmental protection and sustainable development of the site.

State of the environment

The greatest challenge for South Africa and the rest of the world is to improve the quality of human life for both present and future generations, without depleting its natural resources. This can only be achieved through a healthy natural environment that supplies raw material; absorbs and treats waste products; and maintains water, soil and air quality.

Food security, water provision and climatic stability depend on having properly functioning ecosys-

tems, stable levels of biodiversity, sustainable rates of resource extraction and minimal production of waste and pollution.

To this end, the United Nations (UN) General Assembly Conference on Environment and Development adopted Agenda 21 in 1992 as the global strategy for sustainable development.

South Africa has taken several steps to implement Agenda 21 at national and local level, including reforming environmental policies, ratifying international agreements and participating in many global and regional sustainable-development initiatives.

World Summit on Sustainable Development (WSSD)

Johannesburg hosted the WSSD in September 2002.

The agreements reached in Johannesburg are a guide to action that will take forward the UN Millennium Summit Declaration's goal of halving world poverty by 2015, and incorporate decisions taken by world bodies since the Rio Earth Summit in 1992.

Among the victories of the WSSD was the launch of over 300 partnerships, including 32 energy initiatives, 21 water programmes and 32 programmes for biodiversity and ecosystem management.

The biggest success was getting the world to turn the UN Millennium Declaration into a concrete set of programmes and mobilise funds for these pro-

In March 2005, the Department of Environmental Affairs and Tourism hosted the first-ever Women and the Environment Conference in Muldersdrift near Krugersdorp, Gauteng.

In addition to assessing the contribution and role of women in this sector, the conference aimed to showcase best practice in environmental management as pioneered by women in South Africa.

Some of the key focus areas of the conference involved thematic discussions on women and waste management, women and fishing, and women and conservation.

In August 2005, the Minister of Environmental Affairs and Tourism, Mr Marthinus van Schalkwyk, handed over 18 large hand-crafted wall panels for the Judges Conference Room and entertainment area at the Constitutional Court in Johannesburg. The artwork, commissioned by the Poverty-Relief Programme of the Department of Environmental Affairs and Tourism, was created by 12 embroidery designers from the Northern Cape and six appliqué designers from Limpopo.

The designs for the embroidered panels were inspired by San rock paintings, while the appliqué designs represent life in Johannesburg.

The Poverty-Relief Programme has seen more than R836 million invested in projects since April 1999. It has resulted in the creation of more than 3 000 permanent jobs and more than 4,8 million temporary job-days (equivalent to more than 42 000 job opportunities). Of these job-days, 42% have benefited women and 22% youth.

grammes. The WSSD focused on the most marginalised sectors of society, including women, the youth, indigenous people and people with disabilities.

The Implementation Plan includes programmes to deliver water, energy, healthcare, agricultural development and a better environment for the world's poor. It also incorporates targets for the reduction of poverty and protection of the environment.

Targets set at the summit will have an enormous impact:

- the number of people without basic sanitation and access to safe drinking water will be halved by 2015
- biodiversity loss is to be reversed by 2010, and collapsed fish stocks restored by 2015
- chemicals with a detrimental health impact will be phased out by 2020
- energy services will be extended to 35% of African households over the next 10 years.

South Africa participated in the 12th session of the UN Commission on Sustainable Development (CSD) in 2004, presenting a country report that reflected a positive record of South Africa's progress in meeting the targets agreed to at the WSSD.

The 13th session of the CSD in April 2005, provided South Africa with a further opportunity to highlight the policy options and implementation actions needed at regional, country and international level to meet the Johannesburg Plan of Implementation (JPOI) targets, as well as the internationally agreed development goals outlined in the 2000 UN Millennium Declaration.

The Department of Environmental Affairs and Tourism is leading the co-ordination of South Africa's follow-up to the implementation of the JPOI adopted at the WSSD.

Biodiversity values in South Africa

	Biome	Veld type	Number of species				
			Plant	Mammal	Bird	Amphibian	Reptile
Eastern Cape	6	29	6 383	156	384	51	57
Free State	3	19	3 001	93	334	29	47
Gauteng	2	9	2 826	125	326	25	53
KwaZulu-Natal	3	19	5 515	177	462	68	86
Limpopo	2	14	4 239	239	479	44	89
Mpumalanga	2	20	4 593	160	464	48	82
Northern Cape	4	20	4 916	139	302	29	53
North West	2	10	2 483	138	384	27	59
Western Cape	6	19	9 489	153	305	39	52

Source: Department of Environmental Affairs and Tourism. Plant defined as angiosperm and gymnosperm. Data taken from the National Herbarium Pretoria Computerised Information System Database, May 2003.
Biome counts taken from Rutherford (1997) with thicket from Louw & Rebelo (1998).
Veld types taken from Acocks (1988).

A dedicated directorate for sustainable development co-ordination has been established. It focuses mainly on the promotion of national dialogue, building on partnerships with various major groups, raising awareness and ensuring international follow-up to the WSSD agreements.

National Strategy for Sustainable Development (NSSD)

South Africa is committed to meet the agreements reached at the WSSD, including the development of the NSSD.

The NSSD, a framework for the development of one of the most important targets in the JPOI, was approved by Cabinet early in 2005. The NSSD will bring together programmes like the Integrated Sustainable Rural Development Programme (ISRDP), the Urban Renewal Programme (URP) and the provincial growth and development strategies (PGDS).

Biological diversity

South Africa enjoys the third-highest level of biodiversity in the world. The country's rich natural heritage is vast and staggering in its proportions. For example, over 3 700 marine species occur in South African waters and nowhere else in the world.

The remarkable richness of South Africa's biodiversity is largely the result of the mix of tropical Mediterranean and temperate climates and habitats occurring in the country. Some 18 000 vascular plant species occur within South Africa's boundaries, of which 80% occur nowhere else. More plant species occur within 22 000 hectares (ha) of the Table Mountain National Park (TMNP) (formerly the Cape Peninsula National Park), than in the whole of the British Isles or New Zealand.

In addition to South Africa's extraordinarily varied plant life, an abundance of animal life occurs in the region. The country hosts an estimated 5,8% of the world's total mammal species, 8% of bird species, 4,6% of the global diversity of reptile species, 16% of the total number of marine fish species, and 5,5% of the world's classified insect species. In terms of the number of mammal, bird, reptile and amphibian species that are endemic to this country,

South Africa is the 24th-richest country in the world and the fifth-richest in Africa.

South Africa is home to a diversity of spiders – 66 families comprising more than 6 000 species. The country also boasts 175 species of scorpion.

South Africa's marine life is similarly diverse, partly as a result of the extreme contrast between the water masses on the east and west coasts. Three water masses – the cold Benguela current, the warm Agulhas current, and oceanic water – make the region one of the most oceanographically heterogeneous in the world. According to the *White Paper on the Conservation and Sustainable Use of South Africa's Biological Diversity*, over 10 000 plant and animal species – almost 15% of the coastal species known worldwide – are found in South African waters, with about 12% of these occurring nowhere else.

The easiest way to describe the country's natural heritage is on the basis of a systematic classification of regions, or biomes. A biome is a broad ecological unit representing a major life zone, which extends over a large area, and contains relatively uniform plant and animal life closely connected with environmental conditions, especially climate.

The White Paper states that South Africa is one of six countries in the world with an entire plant kingdom within its national confines. Known as the Cape Floral Kingdom, this area has the highest recorded species diversity for any similar-sized temperate or tropical region in the world.

Other biomes in the country are also of global conservation significance. For example, one-third of the world's succulent plant species is found in South Africa.

There are eight major terrestrial biomes, or habitat types, in South Africa. These biomes can, in turn, be divided into 70 veld types.

The degree to which each of these biomes is threatened varies, depending on the fertility of the soil, the economic value derived from use of the area, human population pressures and the extent to which the biome is conserved in protected areas.

Savanna biome

This biome is an area of mixed grassland and trees, and is generally known as bushveld.

In the Northern Cape and Kalahari sections of this biome, the most distinctive trees are the camel thorn (*Acacia erioloba*) and the camphor bush (*Tarchonanthus camphoratus*). In Limpopo, the portly baobab (*Adansonia digitata*) and the candelabra tree (*Euphorbia ingens*) dominate. The central bushveld is home to species such as the knob thorn (*Acacia nigrescens*), bushwillow (*Combretum spp.*), monkey thorn (*Acacia galpinii*), mopani (*Colophospermum mopane*) and wild fig (*Ficus spp.*) In the valley bushveld of the south, euphorbias and spekboom trees (*Portulacaria afra*) dominate.

Abundant wild fruit trees provide food for many birds and animals in the savanna biome.

Grey loeries, hornbills, shrikes, flycatchers and rollers are birds typical of the northern regions. The subtropical and coastal areas are home to Knysna loeries, purple-crested loeries and green pigeons. Raptors occur throughout the biome.

The larger mammals include lion, leopard, cheetah, elephant, buffalo, zebra, rhinoceros, giraffe, kudu, oryx, waterbuck, hippopotamus and many others.

About 8,5% of the biome is protected. The Kruger National Park, Kgalagadi Transfrontier Park, Hluhluwe-Umfolozi Park, Greater St Lucia Wetlands Park (GSLWP) and other reserves are located in the savanna biome.

Nama-Karoo biome

This biome includes the Namaland area of Namibia, and the Karoo area of South Africa.

Because of low rainfall, rivers are non-perennial. Cold and frost in winter and high temperatures in summer demand special adaptations from plants. The vegetation of this biome is mainly low shrubland and grass, with trees limited to water courses. The

In May 2005, *Afrikan Dream*, South Africa's entry for the 2005 Chelsea Flower Show in London, United Kingdom, won South Africa its 27th gold medal at this annual event. South Africa has exhibited at Chelsea for 30 consecutive years.

bat-eared fox, black-backed jackal, ostrich, suricate and ground squirrel are typical of the area.

Only 1% of the Nama-Karoo biome falls within officially protected areas, of which the Karoo and Augrabies national parks are the largest.

Overgrazing and easily eroded soil surfaces are causing this semi-desert to creep slowly in on the neighbouring savanna and grassland biomes.

Grassland biome

This biome is a summer-rainfall area with heavy thunderstorms and hail in summer, and frost in winter. A number of perennial rivers such as the Orange, Vaal, Pongola, Kei and Umzimvubu originate in, and flow through, the area. Trees are scarce and are found mainly on hills and along riverbeds. Karee (*Rhus lancea*), wild currant (*Rhus pyroides*), white stinkwood (*Celtis africana*) and several acacia species are the most common.

The grassland biome has the third-largest number of indigenous plant species in the country.

Eight mammal species endemic to South Africa occur in a wild state in this biome. Two of these, namely the black wildebeest and the blesbok, occur mainly in the grassland biome.

The area is internationally recognised as an area of high species endemicity as far as birds are concerned. Birds commonly found in the area include the black korhaan, blue crane, guinea-fowl and other grassland birds.

Only 1,1% of the grassland biome is officially protected. The wilderness areas of the KwaZulu-Natal Drakensberg are the most significant.

Succulent Karoo biome

One of the natural wonders of South Africa is the annual blossoming of the Namaqualand wild flowers (mainly of the family *Asteraceae*), which transforms the semi-desert of the Northern Cape into a fairyland. After rain, the drab landscape is suddenly covered from horizon to horizon with a multicoloured carpet (from August to October, depending on the rainfall).

This is a winter-rainfall area with extremely dry and hot summers. Succulents with thick, fleshy leaves are plentiful. Most trees have white trunks to reflect the heat.

The quiver tree (*Aloe dichotoma*) and the human-like elephant's trunk (*Pachypodium namaquanum*) are prominent in the Richtersveld. Grass is scarce.

The animal life is similar to that of neighbouring biomes (fynbos and Nama-Karoo).

The Richtersveld, Tankwa Karoo and Namaqua national parks have improved the conservation status of this biome considerably.

Fynbos biome

The fynbos biome is one of the six accepted floral kingdoms of the world. This region covers only 0,04% of the land surface of the globe.

Fynbos is found mainly in the Western Cape. This is a winter-rainfall area and the fynbos vegetation is similar to that of mediterranean regions.

Fynbos is the name given to a group of evergreen plants with small, hard leaves (such as those in the Erica family). It is made up mainly of three groups of plants, namely the protea, heathers and restio, and incorporates a diversity of plant species (more than 8 500 kinds, over 6 000 of which are endemic).

The fynbos biome's most famous inhabitant is the protea, for which South Africa is renowned. The biome also contains flowering plants, now regarded as garden plants, such as freesia, tritonia, sparaxis and many others.

Protected areas cover 13,6% of the fynbos biome and include the Table Mountain and Agulhas national parks.

This biome is not very rich in bird and mammal life, but does include the grysbok, the geometric tortoise, the Cape sugarbird and the protea seed-eater, which are endemic to the area. The mountains are the habitat of the leopard, baboon, honey-badger, caracal, rhebuck and several types of eagle and dassies.

Forest biome

South Africa has few forests. The only forests of significance are the Knysna and Tsitsikamma forests in the Western and Eastern Cape, respectively.

Other reasonably large forest patches that are officially protected are in the high-rainfall areas of the eastern escarpment, and on the eastern seaboard. Forest giants such as yellowwood

(*Podocarpus spp.*), ironwood (*Olea capensis*) and lemonwood (*Xymalos monospora*) dominate.

The indigenous forests are a magical world of ferns, lichens, and colourful forest birds such as the Knysna loerie, the endangered Cape parrot and the rameron pigeon. Mammals include the endangered samango monkey, bushpig, bushbuck and the delicate blue duiker.

Thicket biome

Subtropical thicket ranges from closed shrubland to low forest, dominated by evergreen succulent trees, shrubs and vines.

It is often impenetrable and has little herbaceous cover. Roughly 20% of the species in the thicket biome are endemic to it.

Desert biome

True desert is found under very harsh environmental conditions, which are even more extreme than those found in the succulent Karoo and the Nama-Karoo biomes. The climate is characterised by summer rainfall, but also by high levels of summer aridity. Rainfall is highly variable from year to year. Desert is found mostly in Namibia, although it does occur in South Africa in the lower Orange River Valley.

The vegetation of the desert biome is characterised by the dominance of annual plants (often annual grasses). This means that after a rare season of abundant rain, the desert plains can be covered with a sea of short annual grass, whereas in drier years, the plains appear bare with the annual plants persisting in the form of seeds.

With over 500 bird species, including black coucals, narina trogons, Pel's fishing owls, crowned eagles, black eagles and the African finfoot, the Kruger National Park is a birding paradise. The park is tapping into its wealth of bird species to boost its income. The park hosts the annual Big Birding Day, which is becoming a very popular event.

The Kruger Park is home to an impressive number of species, namely 336 trees, 49 fish, 34 amphibians, 114 reptiles, 507 birds and 147 mammals.

Perennial plants are usually encountered in specialised habitats associated with local concentrations of water. Common examples of such habitats are broad drainage lines or washes. Nearer to the coast, the role of coastal fog also governs the distribution of certain species commonly associated with the desert.

The desert biome incorporates an abundant insect fauna, which includes many tenebrionid beetles, some of which can utilise fog water. There are also various vertebrates including reptiles, springbok, ostrich, gemsbok, snakes and geckos.

Some areas in the desert biome are formally protected in the Richtersveld National Park.

Preserving biodiversity

Biodiversity plays a crucial role in sustainable development and poverty eradication. Fundamental changes to the legislative, policy and institutional framework for natural resource management have resulted in a shift in focus from an elitist conservation approach, to a management approach based on South Africa's recognition of the contribution of biological resources to food security, science, economy, cultural integrity and well-being.

The country's conservation areas contribute to job creation and socio-economic upliftment, and

Initiatives to bring communities and youth into South Africa's national parks, and to use the parks to drive growth and employment in all provinces, include the R22-million Kids-in-Parks joint venture between South African National Parks, the Department of Education, the Department of Environmental Affairs and Tourism and Pick 'n Pay.

The initiative aims to bring about 7 500 young South Africans and 300 teachers from 150 schools over the next three years into 15 national parks across South Africa. Through other initiatives focused on empowering the youth, about 2 170 job opportunities were created for young South Africans in 2004/05, representing more than 24% of the job opportunities created by the Department of Environmental Affairs and Tourism.

continue to serve as a foundation of the tourism industry.

South Africa is a very popular tourist destination. The main attractions are nature-based tourism facilities such as national parks and private game reserves. There are some 9 000 privately owned game ranches in South Africa, covering about 13% of the country's total land area. The contribution of these areas in maintaining South Africa's unique biodiversity is incalculable.

The Department of Environmental Affairs and Tourism hosted the first National Biodiversity Strategy and Action Plan Workshop in March 2004.

The main strategic objectives of South Africa's National Biodiversity Strategy and Action Plan are to:

- ensure that the protection of biodiversity is a priority for all South Africans and forms an integral part of all economic sectors
- enhance institutional effectiveness and efficiency to ensure good governance in the biodiversity sector
- ensure that benefits derived from biodiversity and the costs of maintaining a sustained flow of environmental goods and services are equally shared
- ensure the direct and indirect consumptive use of biological resources in a sustainable manner
- engage with the international community to promote and develop cross-boundary and international co-operation and partnerships to meet South Africa's international obligations and commitments as far as possible, within the context of national priorities and constraints.

Many successes have been achieved in South Africa by various role-players in terms of the conservation of vulnerable and endangered species, e.g. white rhinoceros, African elephant, the cheetah and the wild dog.

In April 2005, the Minister of Environmental Affairs and Tourism launched the results of the National Spatial Biodiversity Assessment, the first-ever comprehensive spatial evaluation of biodiversity throughout South Africa.

The report shows, among other things, that:

- 34% of territorial ecosytems are threatened and 5% are critically endangered

- 82% of 120 rivers are threatened, and 44% critically endangered
- three of 13 groups of estuarine biodiversity are in critical danger, and 12% of marine bio-zones are under serious threat.

South Africa is the first country to include a comprehensive spatial assessment of biodiversity in its National Biodiversity Strategy and Action Plan.

Conservation areas

South Africa is committed to meeting the World Conservation Union (IUCN) target of 10% of land area under protection.

There are a number of management categories of protected areas in South Africa, which conform to the accepted categories of the IUCN.

The National Environment Management: Protected Areas Act, 2003 seeks to establish a representative system of protected areas as part of a national strategy to protect South Africa's biological diversity, and to ensure that biodiversity is able to bring about sustainable benefits for future generations.

It also enables the Minister of Environmental Affairs and Tourism to acquire private land by purchasing land rights for the creation of protected areas.

The National Environment Protected Areas Amendment Act, 2004 (Act 31 of 2004), further addresses issues of co-operative governance with provincial and local authorities. It empowers the department to conclude fair negotiations with communities and private landowners for the inclusion of some of their land in South Africa's protected areas.

Scientific reserves

Scientific reserves are sensitive and undisturbed areas managed for research, monitoring and maintenance of genetic sources. Access is limited to researchers and staff. Examples of such areas are Marion Island and the Prince Edward Islands near Antarctica.

Wilderness areas

These areas are extensive in size, uninhabited and underdeveloped, and access is strictly controlled since no vehicles are allowed. The highest manage-ment priority is the maintenance of the intrinsic wilderness character. Examples of wilderness areas are the Cedarberg Wilderness Area and Dassen Island in the Western Cape, and the Baviaanskloof Wilderness Area in the Eastern Cape.

Marine protected areas (MPAs)

In June 2004, the Minister of Environmental Affairs and Tourism announced four new MPAs to complement and consolidate the country's existing marine and coastal conservation areas. This brought 19% of South Africa's 3 200-km coastline under protection. MPAs combine conservation with the development of tourism.

South Africa previously had 19 marine protected areas covering approximately 11% of the coastline, which stretches from the country's border with Namibia in the west to Mozambique in the east. The Tsitsikamma National Park was the first to be proclaimed, in 1964.

The new areas are Aliwal Shoal on the south coast of KwaZulu-Natal, the coastal and marine environment of Pondoland in the Eastern Cape, the Bird Island Group at Algoa Bay, and TMNP in the Western Cape.

In August 2005, the Minister of Environmental Affairs and Tourism, Mr Marthinus van Schalkwyk, announced plans for the creation of a new national park in Pondoland in the Eastern Cape.

The new national park will be focused on both conservation and ensuring local economic development and social upliftment.

The park will offer a combination of wildlife viewing, beaches and marine and estuarine escapes in close conjunction with African cultural heritage. This will build on the Pondoland Marine Protected Area, which was proclaimed in 2004. The ultimate aim is to extend the development corridor running along the south coast of KwaZulu-Natal into Pondoland. The longer-term goal is to link it with the Garden Route development corridor.

In October 2005, the minister announced plans for a new national park in the Camdeboo region in the Eastern Cape.

The MPAs do not prohibit tourism activities such as sport-diving operations, but rather aim to regulate them.

Some of the protection measures to be implemented will be restrictions for people who want to fish, as well as restrictions for stowing fishing gear when fishing with a vessel. Spear fishers will not be allowed in these areas. Scuba divers will be required to obtain permits when diving at the restricted zones in the TMNP.

The Pondoland MPA is one of South Africa's largest protected areas. Including 90 km of coastline and extending about 15 km out to sea (to the 1 000 m isobath), it will cover 1 300 km². The extremely narrow continental shelf off Pondoland marks the start of the annual sardine run, which *National Geographic* has rated as the most exciting diving opportunity in the world. The development of tourism in this impoverished region is a priority, and the establishment of the MPA is the first step in realising the potential of this scenic stretch of coastline.

The protection of the Bird Island Group (Bird, Seal and Stag islands) in Algoa Bay is the first step in the seaward extension of the Greater Addo Elephant National Park. Bird Island is home to several species of red-data listed seabirds (such as the Cape gannet, roseate tern and African penguin), while the reefs around the island are important for abalone and linefish, many species of which are threatened.

The TMNP MPA includes all the coastal waters around the Cape Peninsula from Mouille Point in the west to Muizenberg in the east. It is the area that has the longest history of commercial fishing in South Africa.

The MPA is an extension of the TMNP. It includes six areas that are closed to fishing, but the majority of the MPA remains open to fishing. The closed areas have been located for the protection of abalone, rock lobster, linefish and penguin, and for scuba-diving.

The Aliwal Shoal, a subtidal reef situated 5 km off the KwaZulu-Natal south coast near Umkomaas, supports a spectacular coral community, including 15 species of hard corals and four species of soft corals. The diverse fish fauna is a popular attraction for scuba divers, fisherfolk and spear-fisherfolk. Many endangered species of endemic reef fish, as well as ragged-tooth and tiger sharks, are found on the shoal.

National parks and equivalent reserves

SANParks manages various national parks, representative of the country's important ecosystems and unique natural features. Commercial and tourism-conservation development and the involvement of local communities are regarded as performance indicators. These areas include national parks proclaimed in terms of the National Parks Act, 1976 (Act 57 of 1976), provincial parks, nature reserves and indigenous state forests.

Some of these natural and scenic areas are extensive in size and include large representative areas of at least one of the country's biomes. Since 1994, parks under SANParks have expanded by 166 071 ha.

The national parks are: Kruger National Park; Kalahari Gemsbok National Park (part of the

In April 2005, the United Nations Environment Programme (UNEP) gave recognition to President Thabo Mbeki and the people of South Africa for outstanding achievements in the environment field.

The Champion of the Earth Award was presented during the meeting of the UN Commission on Sustainable Development held in New York in the United States of America.

South Africa was recognised both for its own commitment to cultural and environmental diversity, and for its strong leadership role in Africa through the environmental component of the New Partnership for Africa's Development.

The many South African achievements highlighted by UNEP include the fact that South Africa had pioneered the Peace Parks initiative, brought nearly 19% of its coastline under direct protection through the declaration of four new marine protected areas, created specialist environmental courts to back up a wide range of cutting-edge environmental legislation, and was party to more than 43 multilateral environmental agreements.

Kgalagadi Transfrontier Park); Addo Elephant National Park; Bontebok National Park; Mountain Zebra National Park; Golden Gate Highlands National Park; Tsitsikamma National Park; Augrabies Falls National Park; Karoo National Park; Wilderness National Park; West Coast National Park; Tankwa Karoo National Park; Knysna National Lake Area; Marakele National Park; Richtersveld National Park; Vaalbos National Park; Agulhas National Park; Namaqua National Park; TMNP, which incorporates the Cape of Good Hope, Table Mountain and Silvermine nature reserves; and Mapungubwe National Park.

During 2003/04, more land was bought, resulting in the expansion of the Addo Elephant and Mountain Zebra national parks in the Eastern Cape, Marakele in Limpopo, the Namaqua National Park in the Northern Cape, as well as the Cape Agulhas and Table Mountain national parks in the Western Cape.

In July 2004, the Minister of Environmental Affairs and Tourism proclaimed more than 66 480 ha of new land to be incorporated into the country's national park system.

The expansion included the Mapungubwe National Park in Limpopo, which acquired more than 1 725 ha of land; the Western Cape's Agulhas National Park, which acquired 3 636 ha; the Karoo National Park, 17 405 ha; the Namaqua National Park, 34 246 ha; Augrabies Falls National Park, 2 121 ha; the West Coast National Park, 6 772 ha; and the TMNP, 573 ha.

The Free State Government agreed in principle to link the Qwa-Qwa Game Reserve with the Golden Gate Highlands National Park and to bring the two areas under SANParks' management.

Eventually, the consolidated park will span almost 34 000 ha of grassland.

Agreement was also reached with the Eastern Cape Government on the management of Woody Cape Nature Reserve by SANParks, as an integral part of the greater Addo Elephant National Park.

In April 2005, the minister announced the addition of the St Croix and Bird islands to the Addo Elephant National Park, as well as the official opening of the Matyholweni Rest Camp, with local communities set to benefit directly from the revenue generated and the greater influx of tourism to the expanded park.

Visitors to Addo will now be able to experience, for the first time ever in South Africa, the Big Seven in one conservation area, with the extra attraction of whales and great white sharks. The new MPA also cements the park's eastern boundary in Algoa Bay, providing critical protection to the internationally important populations of Cape gannet and African penguin.

Camp Matyholweni, named after the Xhosa expression for 'in the bush', is a 12-unit rest facility in the new southern block of the park. The construction of the camp was made possible by a R6,5-million poverty-relief grant by the Department of Environmental Affairs and Tourism.

Trans-Frontier Conservation Areas (TFCAs)

The South African Government, through the Department of Environmental Affairs and Tourism, is involved in one of southern Africa's boldest and most ambitious programmes of establishing, developing and managing six TFCAs. South Africa is joined in this intitiative by its Southern African Development Community (SADC) neighbours and

Communities bordering the Kruger National Park are expected to benefit from a memorandum of understanding (MoU) signed in February 2005 to help create job opportunities, particularly in the tourism and agriculture sectors.

The park's executive director, Dr Bandile Mkhize, signed the MoU with representatives of the Community Public-Private Partnership Programme and the Tourism Enterprise Programme.

The MoU defines the roles of each of the three organisations in meeting the objective of developing the park's neighbours.

The park already runs a number of empowerment programmes aimed at increasing general economic development in neighbouring communities.

These initiatives include a curio-selling project, a contractor-development programme and ad hoc opportunities for entrepreneurs.

partners, namely Botswana, Lesotho, Namibia, Mozambique, Swaziland and Zimbabwe.

Southern Africa's TFCAs cover almost 100 000 km² and include major biomes and eco-regions. TCFAs contribute significantly to the conservation of biodiversity and to tourism in the region. The diversity of wildlife and presence of large game are Africa's most important competitive advantages in the international tourism industry.

Since the establishment of the first TFCA in 2001, the Kgalagadi Transfrontier Park between South Africa and Botswana, tourism to the area has tripled. A process has been initiated to link the park to Namibia.

The Greater Limpopo Transfrontier Park is located between Mozambique, South Africa and Zimbabwe and includes the Kruger National Park. The Department of Environmental Affairs and Tourism projects that, once the Mozambican side has been completed, 30% of visitors (350 000 people a year) to the Kruger National Park will also travel to Mozambique, thus benefiting one of the world's poorest countries financially.

The Maloti-Drakensberg TFCA situated between South Africa and Lesotho features prehistoric rock paintings, fossils and superb skeletal dinosaur remains that attract international tourists.

On 16 June 2005, the Minister of Environmental Affairs and Tourism, Mr Marthinus van Schalkwyk, launched the first of four hoerikwaggo (sea mountain) hiking trails in the Table Mountain National Park (TMNP).

The new People's Trail forms part of the long-term plan to upgrade and reinvigorate 350 km of trails within the TMNP to help cater for the 4,5 million annual visitors.

This is the first time that TMNP offers overnight accommodation on the mountain.

The minister also launched the new Cape Town Wild Card. Based on the very successful South African National Parks Wildcard, it offers an affordable and innovative new way of accessing the TMNP. The card entitles the owner to 12 entries through any of the TMNP's pay points for a year. Other tourist attractions such as the Two Ocean's Aquarium have also come on board with discounts.

The Ais/Ais-Richtersveld TFCA is situated between South Africa and Namibia.

The proposed Limpopo/Shashe Park between South Africa, Botswana and Zimbabwe will include the important ruins on the Mapungubwe plateau. They were the site of the capital of an African empire built roughly between 1030 and 1290 AD and are thought to precede the Great Zimbabwe Ruins.

The Lubombo Transfrontier Conservation Park borders South Africa, Mozambique and Swaziland and features a level of biodiversity that is greater than that of the Kruger National Park. On the South African side, in the GSLWP, R432 million has been invested, which translates into 900 direct jobs. Further investments of R1,5 billion are intended.

The Department of Environmental Affairs and Tourism intends to create the first Transfrontier Marine Protected Area and the first Transfrontier World Heritage Site in Africa between South Africa and Mozambique, as part of the Lubombo Spatial Development Initiative.

Biosphere reserves

The National Environmental Management: Protected Areas Amendment Act, 2004 protects South Africa's biosphere reserves, which are generally formed around existing core conservation areas.

Biosphere reserves include outstanding natural beauty and biological diversity, exist in partnership with a range of interested landowners and can incorporate development, as long as it is sustainable, while still protecting terrestrial or coastal ecosystems.

South Africa's four biospheres are the:
- Kogelberg Biosphere Reserve, which was registered with the UN Educational, Scientific and Cultural Organisation (UNESCO) in 1998.
- Cape West Coast Biosphere Reserve, which was listed in 2000. It covers 376 900 ha that include a number of threatened vegetation types and important bird breeding sites.
- Waterberg Biosphere Reserve that was listed in 2001 and is located in Limpopo. It covers 1,4 million ha that include the Marakele National Park and the Nylsvlei Ramsar Site.

- Kruger-to-Canyons Biosphere Reserve, which was also listed in 2001, and covers more than 3,3 million ha that span the boundary between Limpopo and Mpumalanga. The core areas comprise 13 declared protected areas, with a major portion of the Kruger National Park as the largest core area.

Natural heritage sites

Initiated in 1984, the Natural Heritage Sites Programme is a co-operative venture between the Department of Environmental Affairs and Tourism, provincial nature conservation agencies, the private sector, private landowners and non-government organisations. Some 325 sites have been registered, representing more than 46 000 ha. Although no legal framework for their protection exists, owners of the sites receive a certificate of appreciation from government.

National and cultural monuments

These are natural or cultural features, or both, and may include botanical gardens, zoological gardens, natural heritage sites and sites of conservation significance.

In May 1997, South Africa ratified the World Heritage Convention. The South Africa World Heritage Convention Committee is responsible for the identification of possible sites in South Africa and the co-ordination of the convention.

The World Heritage Convention Act, 1999 (Act 49 of 1999), allows for cultural and natural sites in South Africa to be granted world heritage status. The convention obliges the South African Government to guarantee its implementation, ensure legal protection, and develop management plans and institutional structures for periodic monitoring.

The Act makes the principles of the convention applicable to South Africa's World Heritage Sites, and further provides for the adequate protection and conservation of these sites to promote tourism in a culturally and environmentally responsible way.

South Africa has seven World Heritage Sites proclaimed by UNESCO, namely Robben Island; the GSWLP; the hominid sites at Swartkrans, Sterkfontein and Kromdraai (known as the Cradle of Humankind); the Ukhahlamba-Drakensberg Park (a mixed natural and cultural site); the Mapungubwe Heritage Site; the Cape Floral Kingdom and the Vredefort Dome.

The Vredefort Dome is an ancient extraterrestrial impact site spanning the Free State and North-West provinces. Formed two billion years ago, it is the world's most ancient meteorite impact site and the third-largest, measuring 140 km wide. The latter was declared a World Heritage Site at the 29th World Heritage Committee meeting held in Durban in July 2005.

Vredefort presents opportunities to engage in geological research and to explore and understand more sensitively the rich culture of the Basotho, Batswana and Khoi-San, as well as the early evidence of human cognitive and artistic endeavour of these cultures. The site is also valued for its rich biodiversity.

Achieving World Heritage Site status has added to Vredefort's economic and tourism potential.

In addition to the R159 million invested in transfrontier conservation area projects during 2004/05, a further R193 million in new projects was invested in 2005/06.

In April 2005, the Minister of Environmental Affairs and Tourism, Mr Marthinus van Schalkwyk, and the Minister of Water Affairs and Forestry, Ms Buyelwa Sonjica, signed a memorandum of understanding (MoU) that marked the single largest transfer of land to South African National Parks (SANParks).

In terms of the MoU, about 97 300 hectares (ha) of state forests, formerly managed by the Department of Water Affairs and Forestry, were earmarked for transfer to SANParks.

This included 35 756 ha of indigenous forests (the Farleigh, Diepwalle and Tsitsikamma estates), about 35 638 ha of mountain catchment area (mostly fynbos in the Outeniqua and Tsitsikamma mountains) and about 25 900 ha of land under pine plantations, which will be clear-felled, rehabilitated and transferred to SANParks over the next 15 years.

The transfer is expected to lay the foundation for the future establishment of a Garden Route mega reserve, encompassing the Tsitsikamma and Wilderness national parks and the Knysna National Lake Area, as well as forests and other public and private conservation land.

Consequently, the Department of Environmental Affairs and Tourism has allocated R18 million from its poverty-relief programme for tourism and infra-structural development at the Vredefort Dome site.

The world heritage status of Sterkfontein's fossil hominid sites was extended in July 2005 to include the Taung skull fossil site in North West and the Mokopane Valley in Limpopo.

By June 2005, there were 788 World Heritage Sites in 134 countries. Africa had 63 sites. A total of 154 were natural sites, 611 cultural sites and 23 were mixed sites.

Habitat- and wildlife-management areas

These areas are subject to human intervention, based on research into the requirements of specific species for survival. They include conservancies; provincial, regional or private reserves created for the conservation of species habitats or biotic communi-ties; marshes; lakes; and nesting and feeding areas.

Protected land and seascapes

These areas are products of the harmonious inter-action of people and nature and include natural environments protected in terms of the Environment Conservation Act, 1989 (Act 73 of 1989), scenic landscapes and historical urban landscapes.

Sustainable-use areas

These areas emphasise the utilisation of products on a sustainable basis in protected areas such as the Kosi Bay Lake System in KwaZulu-Natal. Nature areas in private ownership are proclaimed and man-aged to curtail undesirable development in areas with high aesthetic or conservation potential.

Conservancies are formed to involve the ordinary landowner in conservation. One or more landowners can establish a conservancy where conservation prin-ciples are integrated with normal farming activities.

Wetlands

Wetlands include a wide range of inland and coastal habitats – from mountain bogs and fens to midland marshes, swamp forests and estuaries, linked by green corridors of streambank wetlands.

South Africa became a contracting party to the Ramsar Convention in 1975. The country's Ramsar sites include Nylsvlei Nature Reserve, Blesbokspruit, Barberspan, Seekoeivlei, Ukhahlamba-Drakensberg Park, Ndumo Game Reserve, the Kosi Bay System, Lake Sibaya, the turtle beaches and coral reefs of Tongaland, the St Lucia System, Wilderness lakes, De Hoop Vlei, De Mond State Forest, Langebaan, Verlorenvlei and the Orange River Mouth Wetland.

The Directorate: Biodiversity Management of the Department of Environmental Affairs and Tourism is responsible for the South African Wetlands Conser-vation Programme. The programme ensures that South Africa's obligations in terms of the Ramsar Convention are met.

The programme is aimed at building on past efforts to protect wetlands in South Africa against degradation and destruction, while striving for the ideal of wise and sustainable use of resources, to ensure that the ecological and socio-economic functions of wetlands are sustained for the future.

South Africa is a member of Wetlands Inter-national, an international body dedicated to con-serving the world's wetlands.

South Africa celebrated World Wetlands Day on 2 February 2005 at the GSLWP in KwaZulu-Natal, when the six millionth pine tree from the eastern shores of Lake St Lucia was cut down. Commercial plantations of eucalyptus and pine trees have caused extensive ecological and social damage in that area.

The Working for Wetlands Programme focuses on wetland restoration, while maximising employ-ment creation, support for small, medium and micro enterprises (SMMEs) and transfer of skills to the beneficiaries of the programme's projects.

The programme contributes directly to the objec-tives of the Expanded Public Works Programme (EPWP) and is a partnership between the depart-ments of environmental affairs and tourism, of water affairs and forestry, and of agriculture.

During 2004, R40 million was utilised to employ 1 200 people for the restoration of 45 wetlands around the country.

World Wetlands Day marks the date of the sign-ing of the Convention of Wetlands on 2 February 1971 in the Iranian city of Ramsar.

In 2005, the department intensified its participation in the EPWP. In addition to the R370 million spent in 2004, another R385 million was expected to be spent in 2005/06 on poverty relief and social responsibility projects. The aim is to create more than 1,38 million temporary job days, 12 000 job opportunities, 120 000 training days and more than 300 permanent new jobs.

Botanical gardens

SANBI was established on 1 September 2004 with the renaming of the NBI in terms of the National Environmental Management Biodiversity Act, 2004.

SANBI, with its head office at Kirstenbosch National Botanical Garden in Cape Town, is an autonomous state-aided institute whose vision is to be the leading institution in biodiversity science in Africa, facilitating conservation and the sustainable development of living resources and human well-being. In addition to new biodiversity-related initiatives linked to the Act, traditional activities undertaken by SANBI include the following:

- to collect, display and cultivate plants indigenous to South Africa
- to undertake and promote research into indigenous plants and related matters
- to study, research and cultivate threatened plant species
- to promote the utilisation of the economic potential of indigenous plants
- to run environmental education programmes.

SANBI manages eight national botanical gardens in five of South Africa's nine provinces. The gardens collectively attract over one million visitors a year, are signatories to the International Agenda for Botanic Gardens in Conservation, and founding members of the African Botanic Gardens Network.

The largest garden is Kirstenbosch, situated on the eastern slopes of Table Mountain in Cape Town. It displays 5 300 indigenous plant species, and was voted one of the top seven botanical gardens in the world at the International Botanical Congress in 2000.

Kirstenbosch receives more than 720 000 visitors annually. The Kirstenbosch National Botanical Garden houses the Kirstenbosch Research Centre, the Centre for Biodiversity Conservation, Gold Fields Environmental Education Centre, the Botanical Society Conservatory, two restaurants, a conference venue, gift shops, a coffee bar, concert venues, sculpture exhibits and the Centre for Home Gardening, which includes an indigenous retail nursery.

The other gardens in the national network are the Karoo Desert in Worcester, Harold Porter in Betty's Bay, Free State in Bloemfontein, KwaZulu-Natal in Pietermaritzburg, Lowveld in Nelspruit, Walter Sisulu (formerly Witwatersrand) in Roodepoort/Mogale City and the Pretoria National Botanical Garden.

The Pretoria National Botanical Garden houses the National Herbarium of South Africa, the largest in the southern hemisphere. Research is conducted on the evolution, diversity, distribution and relationships of southern Africa's 24 000 species of plants, based on the SANBI collection of over 1,8 million specimens in its three herbaria. There are also regional herbaria in Durban (KwaZulu-Natal Herbarium) and at the Kirstenbosch Research Centre (Compton Herbarium).

The Harold Porter Botanical Garden boasts Disa uniflora in its national habitat (flowering from mid-December to the end of January), as well as South Africa's national flower, the king protea (*Protea cynaroides*).

The Walter Sisulu National Botanical Garden accommodates more than 600 naturally occuring plant species and more than 230 bird species, as well as a number of reptiles and small mammals. These include jackal and antelope, which occur in the natural areas of the garden.

This garden, which receives some 170 000 visitors annually, is the fastest-growing of the gardens managed by SANBI. It covers over 300 ha and consists of landscaped and natural areas. All the garden's plants are indigenous to southern Africa.

During 2004, SANBI completed new environmental education, restaurant and visitor facilities at the Lowveld, Pretoria, Walter Sisulu and Free State botanical gardens. Many of these capital projects were co-financed by the Department of Environmental Affairs and Tourism's Poverty-Relief Unit.

SANBI is the management agency for the US$20-million Cape Action Plan for People and the

Environment Project, which aims to conserve biological diversity within the Cape Floral Kingdom. Since 1996, SANBI has also served as the implementing agency for the US$5-million Southern African Botanical Diversity Network Project aimed at upgrading facilities and strengthening the level of botanical expertise throughout the subcontinent. The participating countries are Angola, Botswana, Lesotho, Malawi, Mozambique, Namibia, South Africa, Swaziland, Zambia and Zimbabwe.

SANBI has also taken over the management of the Working for Wetlands Programme, with its offices now based at the Pretoria National Botanical Garden.

In addition to the herbarium and taxonomic research, the Kirstenbosch Research Centre in Cape Town is a centre of excellence for biodiversity research. The research programme focuses on the impact of climate change, invasive alien species and land-use on biodiversity, as well as the development of conservation plans for threatened ecosystems and species. The centre has developed a new vegetation map for South Africa and maintains the Protea Atlas Database, one of the most comprehensive plant databases available in South Africa.

The Leslie Hill Molecular Systematics Laboratory is one of the facilities at the Kirstenbosch Research Centre. A DNA-bank has been established at the laboratory, in collaboration with the Royal Botanic Gardens, Kew, in the United Kingdom (UK). The bank is funded by the UK-based Darwin Initiative and the objectives are to archive the DNA of at least one species of all 2 200 genera of South Africa's flowering plants, to train South African researchers and students in high-profile biotechnologies, and to produce a tree of life of South African plants.

SANBI joined the Millennium Seed Bank Project in 2000. This project is a 10-year (2000 – 2010) international programme, conceived and developed by the Seed Conservation Department at the Royal Botanic Gardens, Kew, in the UK, and managed in partnership with 20 countries worldwide. Its central aim is collecting and conserving the seed of 10% of the world's wild plant species.

In South Africa, SANBI co-ordinates this endeavour and ultimately hopes to contribute the seed of about 2 500 of South Africa's indigenous species to this conservation effort, through the collection of verified and well-documented seed collections. This will represent about 10% of South Africa's flowering plants.

Some municipalities have botanical gardens that are not controlled by SANBI. These include the Wilds and Melville Koppies in Johannesburg, the Johannesburg Botanic Garden, the Grahamstown Botanical Garden (now managed by Rhodes University) and the Municipal Durban Botanic Gardens.

Other botanical gardens in South Africa not controlled by SANBI include the Manie van der Schijff Botanical Garden (University of Pretoria), University of Stellenbosch Botanical Garden, North-West University Botanical Garden (Potchefstroom Campus), University of KwaZulu-Natal Botanical Garden (Pietermaritzburg Campus), the Lost City Gardens (near Sun City, North West) and the Garden Route Botanical Garden.

Zoological gardens

The National Zoological Gardens (NZG) of South Africa in Pretoria celebrated its centenary in October 1999. It is the only zoo in South Africa with national status and is a member of the World Association of Zoos and Aquariums; the Pan-African Association of Zoological Gardens, Aquaria and Botanical Gardens; the International Union of Zooculturists; and the International Association of Zoo Educators.

The NZG, considered to be one of the 10 best in the world, extends over an area of about 80 ha. In 2004, the zoo attracted almost 550 000 visitors.

On 1 January 2005, the zoo's collection included 2 586 specimens of 126 mammal species, 1 425 specimens of 158 bird species, 4 189 specimens of 283 fish species, 235 specimens of 21 invertebrate species, 447 specimens of 90 reptile species, and 29 specimens of four amphibian species.

These figures comprise the animals housed at the NZG in Pretoria, as well as the two game breeding centres in Lichtenburg and Mokopane, and the satellite zoo and animal park at the Emerald Animal World in Vanderbijlpark.

In March 2004, the NZG was declared a national research facility, subject to the provisions of the National Research Foundation (NRF). All of the national zoo's assets and liabilities were transferred to the NRF with effect from 1 April 2004.

The NRF is a government agency responsible for supporting and promoting research and the provision of research facilities to facilitate the creation of knowledge, innovation and development in all fields of science and technology. (See chapter 18: *Science and technology*.)

The Johannesburg Zoological Gardens, or Johannesburg Zoo, which houses more than 10 000 animals, celebrated its centenary in 2004.

The Johannesburg Zoo is now registered as a non-profit company. The core business of the zoo is the accommodation, enrichment, husbandry and medical care of wild animals.

The zoo is also renowned for its successful breeding programmes involving several endangered South African bird species such as the wattled crane and ground hornbill.

The zoo's animals are kept in open-air enclosures, separated from the public by dry or water moats. The enclosures include the internationally acclaimed gorilla complex, the pachyderm section and the section for large carnivores.

Of particular interest are the African elephants, golden lion tamarins and sitatunga.

Breeding centres

There are a number of breeding centres in South Africa. The NZG of South Africa is responsible for the management of the Lichtenburg Game-Breeding Centre, which covers an area of some 4 500 ha, and the Game-Breeding Centre near Mokopane, covering an area of 1 334 ha. The two centres supplement the zoo's breeding programme for various endangered animals, and the zoo's own animal collection.

The Lichtenburg Game-Breeding Centre houses, among other animals, Père David's deer, pygmy hippopotamus, white rhino, the endangered addax, and scimitar-horned and Arabian oryx. Large herds of impala, springbok, zebra, blesbok and red hartebeest also roam the area.

About 32 ha of the wetland area at the centre have been developed into a system of dams and pans, which serves as a natural haven for waterbirds such as spoonbills, kingfishers, ibises and herons.

The Mokopane Game-Breeding Centre is home to an abundance of exotic and indigenous fauna such as lemur, rare tsessebe, roan antelope and black rhino.

The renowned De Wildt Cheetah-Breeding and Research Centre, situated near Pretoria, is best known for its highly successful captive-breeding programme that contributed to the cheetah being removed from the endangered list of the *South African Red Data Book – Terrestrial Mammals* in 1986.

De Wildt also breeds a number of rare and endangered African species. The most spectacular of these is the magnificent king cheetah, which is a true cheetah, but with a variation of coat patterns and colouring. De Wildt also plays a major role in the breeding and release of wild dogs. It has donated breeding nucleuses of the highly endangered riverine rabbit and suni antelope to the Kruger National Park.

The Hoedspruit Research and Breeding Centre for Endangered Species in Mpumalanga is another well-known breeding centre. It was initially established as a breeding programme for the then endangered cheetah, but following the success of the cheetah breeding programme, it has evolved into a legitimate breeding programme for other endangered African animal species. The centre caters for, among other things, five species of vulture: Cape

In August 2005, the Department of Environmental Affairs and Tourism held a two-day community workshop on recreational and professional hunting.

Two community representatives – one from Limpopo and the other from the Western Cape – were elected to represent the voice of the communities at a public hearing to the panel of experts on recreational and professional hunting held subsequently.

The panel was appointed to advise on a proper regulatory framework for the hunting industry.

griffins, and whitebacked, hooded, whiteheaded and lappetfaced vultures. Experienced guides show visitors around the centre, where more than 70 cheetahs, including cubs, tame animals and the king cheetah can be viewed. Other attractions include an introduction to the world of the Cape hunting dog and of the vulture.

Aquaria

There are well-known aquaria in Pretoria, Port Elizabeth, Cape Town and Durban.

The Aquarium and Reptile Park of the Pretoria Zoo is the largest inland aquarium in Africa, with the largest collection of freshwater fish. It is also the only aquarium in South Africa that exhibits a large variety of marine fish in artificial sea water.

The Port Elizabeth Oceanarium is one of the city's major attractions. Exhibits include an underwater observation area, a dolphin research centre, various smaller tanks of 40 different species of bony fish, as well as two larger tanks that display sharks and stingrays.

East London has a smaller aquarium, which is also well worth visiting.

At the Two Oceans Aquarium situated at the Victoria and Alfred Waterfront, Cape Town, more than 3 000 specimens represent some 300 species of fish, invertebrates, mammals, birds and plants supported by the waters in and around the Cape coast. More than three million adults and 850 000 children have visited the aquarium since it opened.

uShaka Marine World in Durban incorporates fresh and sea water and is the fifth-largest aquarium in the world by water volume. It comprises Sea World, Dolphin World, Beach World, and Wet and Wild World.

Sea World incorporates a unique shipwreck-themed aquarium, a penguin rookery and a 1 200-seater dolphin stadium (the largest dolphinarium in Africa). It also offers edutainment tours and special interactive activities such as snorkelling and scuba diving. In addition, it features a rocky touch pool, where visitors can touch a starfish or sea cucumber with the help of specially trained guides.

Snake parks

The Transvaal Snake Park at Midrand, between Pretoria and Johannesburg, houses up to 150 species of snakes and other reptiles and amphibians from southern Africa and elsewhere. The emphasis is on the development of breeding programmes for animals in captivity.

The Fitzsimons Snake Park in Durban houses about 250 snakes, including the world's longest (reticulated python), most venomous (boomslang, puff adder and black mamba) and rarest (long-nose tree snake and Madagascar tree boa) snakes. Up to 500 snakes hatch at the park each year. A highlight of the park is the Adventure Walk that enables visitors to view a large variety of snakes that are kept in secure glass viewing enclosures. The park also offers educational, interactive snake demonstrations and junior and advanced herpetology (study of reptiles) classes.

The Port Elizabeth Snake Park at Bayworld has a wide variety of South African and foreign reptiles, including tortoises, boa constrictors, pythons, crocodiles, lizards and deadly venomous snakes such as cobras, mambas and rattlers. Rare and threatened species, including the Madagascar ground boa, are housed safely in realistically landscaped glass enclosures. The park was closed temporarily from the end of June 2005 while the complex was renovated. The completed project was estimated to cost R200 million and was expected to be opened in 2006.

The Aquarium and Reptile Park situated at the national zoo in Pretoria houses 80 reptile species from all over the world.

The Hartbeespoort Dam Snake and Animal Park near Pretoria features one of the finest reptile collections in southern Africa. It offers seal shows and snake-handling demonstrations.

Marine resources

The South African fishing industry, which was once concentrated in the hands of a few, largely white-owned companies, has undergone intensive transformation over the past 10 years.

It is estimated that at least 60% of commercial fishing rights have been allocated to historically disadvantaged individuals (HDIs) or majority HDI-owned companies. Transformation has taken place in a very short space of time, without compromising the principle of sustainable utilisation that is fundamental to the management of fisheries. South Africa's industrial fisheries are widely regarded as being among the best-managed in the world.

The South African coastline covers more than 3 200 km, linking the east and west coasts of Africa. South Africa's shores are particularly rich in biodiversity with some 10 000 species of marine plants and animals having been recorded.

The productive waters of the west coast support a variety of commercially exploited marine life, including hake, anchovy, sardine, horse mackerel, tuna, snoek, rock lobster and abalone. On the east coast, squid, linefish and a wide range of intertidal resources provide an important source of food and livelihood for coastal communities. Marine life that is not harvested, such as whales, dolphins and seabirds, is increasingly recognised as a valuable resource for nature-based tourism.

The responsible utilisation and management of the country's marine and coastal resources is of vital importance to the well-being of South Africa's people and economy. About 29 000 South Africans, many of them from impoverished rural communities, are directly employed by the fishing industry. A further 60 000 people are estimated to be employed in related sectors.

In South Africa, the utilisation of marine resources is regulated by a rights-allocation system.

Through regular scientific research, the Department of Environmental Affairs and Tourism establishes what the optimal utilisation of each fish species should be. This is done annually and ensures that fish stocks are managed sustainably.

The department's functions include the management of commercial, subsistence and recreational fisheries, as well as a wide variety of other activities, including boat-based whale watching and shark-cage diving. Fishing vessels are licensed annually, according to their port of origin and the purpose for which they are used.

The department is also responsible for monitoring the catches of commercial, subsistence and recreational fishers; and the regulation and thorough inspection of fishing boats, fish-processing plants and other places where fish is sold or stored.

Recent developments have led to a dramatic improvement in the field of fisheries compliance:

- An observer programme has been initiated in the offshore fisheries, where on-board observers gather a wide variety of biological data and verify that regulations are adhered to on fishing vessels.
- All commercial fishing vessels are obliged to carry a vessel-monitoring system on board.
- New partnerships between the Department of Environmental Affairs and Tourism, the South African Police Service and the South African National Defence Force have increased investigations, leading to arrests and prosecutions which, in turn, have had a deterrent effect on would-be poachers.
- The first environmental court at Hermanus in the Western Cape has achieved a conviction rate of 75%. In the past, only an estimated 10% of abalone-poaching and related offences were successfully prosecuted and many cases took years to conclude. A second environmental court was opened in Port Elizabeth on 24 February 2004.
- The amending of laws has ensured that loopholes have been closed and that the severity of sanctions has been increased.
- Four purpose-built environmental-protection vessels are boosting the department's capacity to apprehend and inspect non-compliant fishing vessels.

Lilian Ngoyi, the first vessel, was launched in November 2004, followed by Sarah Baartman on 10 January 2005, Ruth First on 18 May 2005 and Victoria Mxenge on 23 September 2005.

In addition to performing fishery-protection duties, the vessels are equipped to conduct oil-spill countermeasure operations. The vessels are further equipped for search-and-rescue work, fire-fighting and limited towing duties. All four ships are certified for operations up to 200 nautical miles from the shore.

They monitor a wide variety of resources, including rock lobster, abalone, line fish and squid, and carry out inspections of the demersal and pelagic fleets. The vessels are capable of operating throughout the SADC region and play a significant role in regional compliance initiatives.

They are 47 m long and 8 m wide and can reach a top speed of about 25 knots (about 40 km per hour), which is roughly twice the speed necessary to catch most poachers.

The much-larger *Sarah Baartman* carries 18 crew members, four cadets and seven fishery inspectors.

Her top speed is in excess of 20 knots. Equipped with a helicopter deck and refuelling facilities, *Sarah Baartman* can accommodate a fully laden Super Puma or Oryx helicopter. It also has hospital facilities and capacity for six 20-foot containers, which can be loaded and discharged by the vessel's own crane.

The patrol vessels are named after women who, through their courage, dedication and commitment, made a significant contribution to South Africa's liberation.

Transformation

With the publishing of the *White Paper on Marine Fisheries Policy* in 1997 and the passing of the Marine Living Resources Act, 1998 (Act 18 of 1998), the fundamental policy and regulatory framework for fisheries management in South Africa was put in place.

A serious challenge facing government after the first democratic election in 1994 was to re-allocate fishing rights (or quotas) in a way that would ensure that the underrepresentation of HDIs and HDI-owned companies in the fishing industry would be corrected.

A revised strategy was introduced in 2000 to build a rational, legally defensible and transparent allocation system to promote government's objective of transforming the fishing industry.

In April 2005, the Minister of Environmental Affairs and Tourism announced plans to reduce application fees for small-scale fisheries by as much as 83%. In the mussel and oyster fisheries, the proposed application fees were reduced from R585 to R100. Traditional line-fishers will no longer be grouped into small-scale commercial (R500) and full commercial (R6 000), but will have only one

component at an application cost of only R400 upfront, and another R204 per crew member for successful applicants.

Under the new proposals, a large company that was allocated 45 000 tons (t) and which paid an application fee of only R6 000 would now pay R2,25 million if allocated that same quantity.

Through the proposed changes, the department plans to recover the full cost of the allocation and verification process from each applicant on a pro rata basis, depending firstly on the value of the respective fishery, and secondly on the value of the right allocated.

On 30 May 2005, the minister launched the final set of 19 fishery-specific policies and one general policy that guides the allocation of long-term commercial fishing rights for periods between eight and 15 years, estimated to be worth about R70 billion.

Approved by Cabinet, these policies set the agenda for a range of post-allocation management issues affecting each commercial fishery. Most importantly, the allocation of these long-term rights is expected to bring real stability to the fishing industry, supporting transformation and smaller businesses by unlocking access to capital financing for successful applicants.

For the first time ever, policy considerations have been codified in significant detail. South Africa is one of only a handful of countries that has codified its fisheries policies, and is perhaps the only country to have done so in such detail.

This provides an unambiguous guarantee for the industry as a whole that, unless decided otherwise by the minister, the department and officials within the department are bound by the words and instructions contained in the policies. The codification therefore provides a level of certainty on critical issues that had not existed before.

The allocation of fishing rights will be managed in terms of the clustered approach to fisheries management. The 19 different fishing sectors remain grouped into four clusters. This was done in response to the call to simplify and streamline the allocation process.

The clusters allow for the design of processes that suit the different fishers involved. Cluster A comprises the most organised and capital-intensive fisheries. Cluster B comprises those fisheries that, although fairly well organised, are significantly less capital intensive. Cluster C comprises large numbers of fishers who are poorly organised, but who have access to valuable fish stocks. Cluster D comprises those fishers who are not only poorly organised, but are also involved in very marginal fisheries. The four clusters are as follows:

Cluster A
- hake deep-sea trawl
- hake inshore trawl
- horse mackerel
- small pelagics
- patagonian tooth fish
- south coast rock lobster
- KwaZulu-Natal prawn trawl.

Cluster B
- west coast rock lobster (off shore)
- hake long line
- squid
- tuna pole
- seaweed
- demersal shark.

Cluster C
- hand-line hake
- west coast rock lobster (near shore).

Cluster D
- oysters
- white mussels
- net fishing (small nets/gillnets and beach seine/trek-nets)
- KwaZulu-Natal beach seine.

The evaluation of every application submitted will take place in terms of rational and judicially sanctioned evaluation criteria.

Deep-sea hake fishery
In 1992, only 21 predominantly white-owned and controlled companies had rights to utilise the deep-sea hake resource. By 2002, this number had more than doubled to 53 right-holders.

The Long-Term Rights Allocation Process, launched in 2005, aims to ensure that transformation achievements are maintained. It also aims to address the viability of small operators through consolidation into fewer, but larger units.

By mid-2004, 74% of right-holders in the deep-sea hake fishery were HDI-owned and managed. In comparison, it is estimated that in 1992, HDI shareholding in the deep-sea hake fishery amounted to less than 0,5%.

Pelagic fishery
Allocation records show that 73% of right-holders in the pelagic fishery are majority HDI-owned companies. These companies hold 75% of the pelagic total allowable catch (TAC). Therefore, access to the pelagic fishery by HDIs increased tenfold, from less than 7% in 1992 to more than 70% in 2002.

South coast rock lobster fishery
The offshore nature of this fishery requires the use of large vessels (30 m – 60 m), which are expensive to purchase and operate. These vessels need to fish a relatively large quota to make their operational costs viable. This makes it difficult for smaller right-holders to participate in the fishery. In spite of these constraints, 65% of south coast rock lobster right-holders are SMMEs in joint ventures with established fishing companies. Remarkably, 77% of the south coast rock lobster resource is controlled by HDIs. This was achieved by allowing new entrants into the fishery, and through substantial changes in the ownership of the larger companies.

West coast rock lobster fishery
As many as 90% of right-holders in the west coast rock lobster fishery were classified as SMMEs in 2002. Sixty-six percent of these companies were majority HDI-owned, compared with 1992 when the majority of the lobster TAC was in the hands of white individuals and white-owned companies. Furthermore, 91,5% of fishing rights that were allocated on a limited scale were allocated to HDIs or HDI-owned SMMEs. This means that about 70% of the global west coast rock lobster TAC is HDI-controlled.

Conservation
Extending the conservation agenda is a key objective. The passing of the Coastal Management Bill

is central to this objective. The promulgation and effective management of four, and eventually five, new MPAs will bring 19% of South Africa's coastline under protection.

Subsistence fishing rights along the coasts of the Eastern Cape and KwaZulu-Natal will also be extended in future. This will allow large numbers of people to legally harvest fish. Plans to open up new commercial fisheries are developing rapidly. The aim is to expand the economy through new fisheries and to create new jobs and associated wealth.

The drive to build a marine science and management capacity of high standing that is able to play a constructive role on the African continent, is well underway. This entails, among other things, formulating an ecosystem approach to fisheries management, exploring the potential of new and underutilised fisheries, developing the legal and scientific framework that is required to boost aquaculture production in South Africa, and assisting other African nations to build equally robust fishery-management regimes.

Sustaining marine resources

Since the 1977 declaration of a 200-nautical mile (370 km) exclusive fishing zone, South Africa has adopted a policy of stock rebuilding in several of its major commercial fisheries. This policy has paid off in the hake, pelagic and rock lobster fisheries, where catches have grown steadily in recent years.

However, while South Africa's offshore fisheries may be among the best-managed in the world, a somewhat different picture has emerged for some of South Africa's inshore stocks. Several species of linefish have collapsed in recent years and the small but valuable abalone fishery is severely threatened by poaching and changing environmental conditions.

Pelagic fishery

Pelagic fish form large shoals in the surface layers of the sea – the pelagic zone where they are targeted by South Africa's purse-seine fleet. Small pelagic fish include sardines, anchovy, round herring and juvenile horse mackerel.

The pelagic fishery is the largest in South Africa in terms of catch volumes, and the second-most valuable after the demersal fisheries. Most of the sardines caught are canned for human consumption. All anchovy, round herring and juvenile horse mackerel are reduced to fish meal, which is an important ingredient in animal feeds.

The by-catch of juvenile horse mackerel is restricted and only makes up a small proportion of the total landed pelagic catch.

The population size of anchovy, sardine and round herring increased markedly over the latter part of the 1990s, from a combined biomass of around 1,5 million tons (mt) to peak at just below 10 mt in 2001. The combined biomass remained at this high level in 2002 and 2003, a large decrease in anchovy biomass being offset by an increase in sardine abundance. Low recruitment of anchovy and sardine in 2003 and 2004, however, has since led to a decrease in overall abundance, although the total biomass is still much higher than was found in the 1980s and early 1990s.

The South African fishing industry, assisted through innovative management of the annual TAC, has made the most of the boom years. Between 2001 and 2004, the purse-seine fleet landed over half a million tons of pelagic fish annually. This feat had been recorded only five times in the past five decades.

Demersal fishery

The demersal fishery has three target species: Cape hakes (*Merluccius paradoxus* and *Merluccius capensis*), horse mackerel (*Trachurus trachurus capensis*) and sole (*Austroglossus pectoralis*). Monkfish (*Lophius vomerinus*) and kingklip (*Genypterus capensis*) are important by-catch species.

In South Africa, the Cape hakes form the basis of the country's demersal fishery, with about 160 000 t being landed each year. Hake is landed by large deep-sea trawlers, smaller inshore trawlers, longlines and by fishers who use small boats to catch hake on hand-lines.

Deep-sea trawling is the most technologically sophisticated and the most capital- and labour-intensive of the four fishing methods. The deep-sea hake fishery catches the largest portion of the annual TAC for hake, with 6% of the TAC being allocated to inshore fishery, and about 10 000 t being landed by line fisheries.

Hake catches have remained steady since the late 1980s. However, scientists and the fishing industry have recorded a downturn in hake total catch rates over the past three years. As a result, the TAC for hake decreased by 5 000 t over the past two years and a further decrease of 3 000 t was expected in 2005.

Lobster fisheries

West coast rock lobsters were first exploited commercially in South Africa late in the 19th century from small row-boats using hand-hauled hoopnets. Catches increased steadily during the early part of the 20th century, peaking at about 10 000 t in the early 1950s. This high level of exploitation was maintained for a while, but by 1965 it had begun to decline, even though the fishing effort was increasing.

Catches stabilised in the 1980s at about 4 000 t a year. However, by 1990, environmental and fishing-related conditions caused the natural growth rate of the west coast rock lobsters to decrease, with fewer young lobsters entering the fishery. By 1996, the TAC was decreased to just below 1 500 t. However, a stock-rebuilding strategy that was instituted in 1996, aimed at achieving a 15% recovery in stocks by 2006, paid off sooner than expected. The global TAC for west coast rock lobster increased from 3 206 t in 2003/04 to 3 527 t in the 2004/05 fishing season.

In total, 745 west coast rock lobster fishing licences were allocated in 2002, compared with only 39 right-holders in 1992. An initial 511 historically disadvantaged fishers were allocated west coast rock lobster rights on a limited scale in 2002, and a further 274 fishers were allocated commercial fishing rights for rock lobster in the newly opened fishing grounds to the east of Cape Hangklip in 2004.

The allocation of rights on a limited scale was part of a strategy by government to encourage the development of SMMEs and to meaningfully address the legitimate demands of disadvantaged fishers who depend on inshore resources such as rock lobster and abalone for their livelihoods. Each licence is valid for four years. Right-holders are only allowed to use hoop nets to catch their quota.

South coast rock lobsters are found in deep-water off the south coast and are caught by traps that are deployed on longlines.

An assessment of the south coast rock lobster resource in 1994 indicated that the population was in decline. A programme of reducing the annual TAC was subsequently introduced. The south coast rock lobster stock has shown signs of recovery and the TAC was increased slightly in 2004. A change in the management strategy in 2000, from TAC to a combined TAC and total allowable effort, led to the cancellation of the licence of a fishing company that was responsible for systematic underreporting and overharvesting. This resulted in a decrease in fishing effort, reducing the overcapacity of vessels and other infrastructure and stabilisation of trap catch rates. Abundance of south coast rock lobster has increased by an average of 7% per year between 2001 and 2005. The TAC increased from a low of 750 t whole mass per year in 2001/02 to 840 t per year in 2004/05.

Abalone fishery

Rampant illegal fishing since 1996, exasperated by adverse ecological shifts, contributed to a severe decline in the abalone resource. This led to the closure of the recreational fishery and the setting of a global TAC of just 237 t in the 2004/05 season.

In 2004, a new system of co-management, based on the Territorial User Rights Fishery (TURF) System was introduced. According to the TURF System, all right-holders are able to catch only their quota in a stipulated zone. The aim of the TURF System is to involve right-holders and members of fishing communities in the management of the abalone fishery.

Line-fishery

Commercial fishing rights for the hake hand-line fishery and the tuna pole fishery were allocated for the first time in 2003.

These fisheries are considered to be stable, with healthy stocks. Many species in the traditional line-fishery, however, are thought to have collapsed.

In December 2000, the Minister of Environmental Affairs and Tourism declared the traditional line-fishery, which targets such species as snoek (*Thysites atun*), yellowtail (*Seriola lalandi*), kob (*Argyrosomus spp.*) and various reef-associated species, to be in a state of environmental crisis.

Many linefish stocks, including kob, rock cod (*Epinephilus spp*), red steenbras (*Petrus rupestris*), white steenbras (*Lithognathus lithognathus*), roman (*Chrysoblephus laticeps*), daggeraad (*C. cristiceps*), poenskop (*Cymatoceps nasutus*) and slinger (*Chryoblephus puniceus*) have collapsed.

A collapsed stock is one that has been fished to levels at which the reproductive capacity of the population has dropped to below 20% of the unfished (pristine) stock. This means that the stock cannot produce sufficient young fish to maintain the population.

The department has taken a three-pronged approach to rehabilitating these stocks.

Firstly, strategically located new MPAs allow for a higher level of stock protection by managing the marine area in terms of sanctuary or no-take zones, as well as by concentrating enforcement strategies and resources in a more defined area.

Secondly, a new line-fish management plan has been devised, which divides the fishery into three subsectors (hake hand-line, tuna and traditional line-fish). Each species has its own set of management measures aimed at reducing catch and/or effort.

Thirdly, the traditional line-fishery is managed in terms of the TAC, restricting effort in this fishery to no more than 450 vessels and 3 450 crew.

New fisheries

The department plans to develop 12 new fisheries over the next five years. Some of the fisheries that have been earmarked for development are the common octopus, ornamental fish, east coast rock lobster, sand soldier and Indian Ocean squid.

The proposed fisheries will initially be managed as exploratory or experimental fisheries to collect data for scientific analysis and ensure that the fisheries do not expand more quickly than the acquisition of information necessary for their management.

Policies and guidelines for an experimental octopus fishery were developed in 2002, and applications for experimental permits were called for in 2003. In 2004, 15 experimental permits were issued to undertake fishing at eight sites around the coast from Saldanha Bay to East London. It is anticipated that the bulk of the octopus catch will be exported to Mediterranean countries and the Far East where there is a high demand for octopus products.

The last foreign fishing boats left South African waters in January 2003, following the termination of South Africa's 25-year-old fisheries agreements with Japan and Taiwan. This paved the way for the development of a South African fishery for large pelagic fish, such as tuna and swordfish.

A policy for the allocation of 10-year fishing rights for catching large pelagic fish by longline method was finalised in 2004. In March 2005, 17 swordfish- and 26 tuna-directed rights were allocated.

Aquaculture

Aquaculture production in South Africa is in the region of 4 000 t a year, of which much is attributable to abalone and mussel production.

Since 2002, abalone farms on the south coast have collectively produced more abalone products for export than the wild abalone fishery.

These farms are creating a substantial demand for fresh kelp fronds, which are fed to cultured abalone. Research into seaweed cultivation is being undertaken by the Department of Environmental Affairs and Tourism to establish whether the nutrient-rich wastewater from abalone farms can be effectively used to cultivate seaweeds for abalone feed. If this method of culture proves to be feasible, it would have the added benefit of purifying the wastewater that is pumped out of abalone farms into the sea.

The success of the abalone farming industry has prompted new interest in the culture of fin fish in South Africa. One of the most exciting local species for the aquaculture industry is the dusky kob. Research carried out in land-based tanks and cages at Rhodes University showed that this species is easily kept in captivity, growing from fingerlings to over one kilogram in less than a year. Subsequently, a number of fishing companies and other interested parties have taken up the challenge of farming dusky kob and are following their own paths to the commercialisation of the species.

The coast

The *White Paper for Sustainable Coastal Development in South Africa* recognises that the co-ordination between the lead department in each province, and other departments and role-players whose work forms part of the overall coastal management effort, is essential. In accordance with the White Paper, a coastal committee was established in each of the four coastal provinces. Progress has been made towards the establishment of a national coastal committee.

It was envisaged that the Coastal Management Bill, which was drafted in 2002, would be promulgated during 2005. The Bill provides for important interventions that will regulate, enhance, preserve or rehabilitate sensitive or overexploited coastal areas. It also ensures equitable access to South Africa's coastline and aligns South African legislation with international laws and conventions.

During 2004/05, a number of initiatives were implemented under the Coastcare banner. These included the formulation of interpretive signage for the coast, the Adopt-a-Beach Programme, and the Coastcare Induction Programme. Adopt-a-Beach aims to increase awareness of coastal-management issues among participant groups, while the induction programme is aimed at building capacity among provincial and local authorities.

In May 2005, South Africa hosted the international Blue Flag Conference in Durban. South Africa was one of the first countries to join the *Blue Flag* Campaign, which is aimed at excellence in beach management and the promotion of tourism. South Africa's beaches are rated amongst the best in the world.

The Blue Flag beaches for 2004/05 were:
- Umhlanga Rocks main beach
- South Beach, Durban
- Hibberdene Beach, KwaZulu-Natal south coast
- Lucien Beach, KwaZulu-Natal south coast
- Margate
- Ramsgate
- Marina/San Lameer Beach, KwaZulu-Natal south coast
- Well's Estate, north of Port Elizabeth
- Humewood, Port Elizabeth
- Dolphin Beach, Jeffrey's Bay
- Grotto Beach, Hermanus
- Kleinmond Beach, near Hermanus
- Mnandi Beach, Strandfontein
- Clifton 4th Beach, Cape Town.

More beaches were added to the list at the end of 2005

Other coastal projects being run by the department include local demonstration projects and sustainable coastal livelihood projects that are being funded by the British Department for International Development.

The proliferation of off-road vehicles in South Africa has created a variety of negative environmental impacts. Bird and turtle nesting areas are particularly susceptible to damage from off-road vehicles, as are certain coastal land forms such as dunes, salt marshes, estuarine sand and mud flats.

The off-road vehicle regulations promulgated by the Minister of Environmental Affairs and Tourism in 2001 were amended during 2004 to increase their effectiveness and ease implementation.

The monitoring of stretches of coast has indicated that the banning of off-road vehicles has enabled several shore-breeding birds – especially the damara tern and the African black oystercatcher – to breed successfully once more. The ban has enabled the damara tern to complete breeding far earlier in the season than in other monitored years.

Against the background of South Africans' concerns about the use of genetically modified organisms, in June 2005, the Department of Environmental Affairs and Tourism established the Directorate: Bio-Safety to co-ordinate and support its work in implementing the Cartagena Protocol on Bio-Safety, and announced that the South African National Biodiversity Institute would work to expand and resource its own bio-safety capacity.

Bird counts have also shown a marked increase in the numbers of sanderlings, common terns, and crowned and blacksmith plovers. The number of birds counted at Bird Island in Lamberts Bay fell after the ban was imposed. Scientists propose that Bird Island acted as a refuge for these birds prior to the ban on off-road vehicles coming into force.

According to conservationists from Ezemvelo KwaZulu-Natal Wildlife, the number of loggerhead and leatherback turtles hatching successfully on the beaches of northern KwaZulu-Natal has increased since the ban was enforced.

Conservation challenges

South Africa faces many of the problems experienced by developing countries, in which rapid industrialisation, population growth and urbanisation pose a threat to the quality of the environment.

The department is reforming environmental law to introduce reform in biodiversity conservation, pollution, waste management and environmental planning.

Climatic and atmospheric change

In South Africa, climate change is evident and will continue, even if greenhouse gas (GHG) concentrations are stabilised. As such, it will continue to undermine sustainable development. Expanded desertification in the semi-arid areas of the country is already a feature of the South African landscape. Climate-change modelling suggests a reduction of the area covered by the current biomes in South Africa by 35% to 55% in the next 50 years.

To address climate-change challenges, government developed the National Climate Change Response Strategy. The strategy, launched on 7 October 2004, provides a comprehensive framework for dealing with climate-change issues in South Africa. The approach used in developing this strategy was to ensure, as far as possible, that climate-change response actions in South Africa facilitate sustainable development.

Government approved accession to the Kyoto Protocol of the UN Framework Convention on Climate Change in March 2002, demonstrating South Africa's commitment to further enhance the effectiveness of environmental legislation.

In August 2005, the Minister of Environmental Affairs and Tourism attended the Greenland Dialogue, a week-long international ministerial meeting to discuss the Kyoto Protocol and climate change. Hosted by the Danish Ministry of the Environment, the Greenland Dialogue followed discussions about climate change at the G8 Heads of State in July 2005. Minister Van Schalkwyk was also invited to the follow-up meeting of the G8 held in London in November 2005 as part of the build-up to the first international meeting of parties under the Kyoto Protocol held in December 2005.

The Kyoto Protocol is a legally binding instrument whereby developed countries undertake to reduce GHG emissions by at least 5% of their 1990 levels. One of the protocol's features is the incorporation of market-based mechanisms designed to allow developed countries to achieve their required emission reductions at the lowest possible cost.

In July 2005, the Department of Environmental Affairs and Tourism announced that Cabinet had approved actions that would help it implement the Climate Change Response Strategy. These included a conference of African scientists and a national conference on climate change held back-to-back with a meeting of all African ministers responsible for the environment.

The second action was a process of scenario-planning to examine the different international models being proposed to reduce GHG emissions. South Africa performed the GHG Inventory in 2005 and is working towards reducing energy demands by 12% by 2015 through the more efficient use of power.

The department is operating three climatic change projects. A sum of US$5 million has been donated to South Africa by the United States of America (USA) in terms of the USA-South Africa Bilateral Agreement on Climate Change Support.

Erosion and desertification

Most South African soil is unstable. The country loses an estimated 500 mt of topsoil annually through erosion caused by water and wind.

About 81% of the total land area of South Africa is farmed. However, only 70% of this area is suitable for grazing.

Overgrazing and erosion diminish the carrying capacity of the veld and lead to land degradation. This process has already claimed more than 250 000 ha of land in South Africa.

The Department of Agriculture administers the Conservation of Agricultural Resources Act, 1983 (Act 43 of 1983), in terms of which various measures are being implemented to prevent or contain soil erosion.

In January 1995, South Africa signed the Convention to Combat Desertification, which was ratified on 30 September 1997. The main objectives of the convention include co-operation between governments, organisations and communities to accomplish sustainable development, especially where water resources are scarce. The convention aims to support member countries in Africa to prevent desertification and its consequences. These countries support one another at technical and scientific level, as they share similar climatic conditions.

South Africa also acts as co-ordinator for the Valdivia Group for Desertification. The group consists of countries in the southern hemisphere, namely Australia, New Zealand, Argentina, Chile, Uruguay, South Africa and Brazil, whose aim it is, among others, to foster scientific and technological co-operation.

In June 2005, South Africa marked the World Day to Combat Desertification, which the United Nations Convention to Combat Desertification (UNCCD) announced and inaugurated, to raise awareness of the effects of land degradation.

In 2002, during the WSSD, the UNCCD was identified as one of the important instruments at the disposal of the international community for food security and for eradicating poverty in arid, semi-arid and subhumid areas, of which South Africa is one.

To address land degradation, government has committed to the Millennium Development Goals, including the overarching goal of halving poverty by 2015. The Department of Environmental Affairs and Tourism has set aside R34 million to address land degradation through community-based natural resource management projects throughout the country from 2005 to 2007.

Waste management

The Department of Environmental Affairs and Tourism takes overall responsibility for integrated pollution and waste management. Within the framework of achieving this, the department, with assistance from the Danish Government, completed the National Waste Management Strategy in 1999.

The department has prioritised four projects within the framework of the National Waste Management Strategy:
- recycling
- waste information system
- healthcare waste
- capacity-building.

Central to these are pilot projects that are being set up countrywide. The department welcomes partnerships with business to ensure that these projects are successful and become a core of better waste management in South Africa.

An agreement containing regulations governing plastic shopping bags was signed in September 2002 by the Minister of Environmental Affairs and Tourism and representatives from various labour and business organisations.

The agreement, which came into effect on 9 May 2003, stipulates that the thickness of plastic bags be 30 microns. However, manufacturers will be allowed to continue using their existing machinery to make bags of 24-micron thickness for the next five years before having to comply with the 30-micron standard.

The agreement states that printing will only be allowed on 25% of the surface area if the ink is not environmentally friendly. In situations where the ink is acceptable, this area can be increased to 50%. The department established a toll-free line to deal with queries about plastic bags.

The plastic bags agreement and supporting regulations have dramatically decreased the environmental impact of this highly visible waste stream, with a 50% reduction in the consumption of plastic bags since the introduction of the regulations.

As part of the implementation of the plastic bag regulations, Buyisa-e-Bag, a non-profit-making company was set up to promote waste minimisation and awareness initiatives in the plastics industry. The company is expected to expand collector networks and create jobs, as well as kick-start rural collection SMMEs and create additional capacity in non-governmental organisations.

Work is in progress to follow this success with targeted and customised agreements in respect of other problem waste streams, including tyres and glass.

The compliance and enforcement of the regulations have been assigned to the South African Bureau of Standards.

Water-quality management

The Directorate: Water-Quality Management of the Department of Water Affairs and Forestry is responsible for the quality management of national water resources in South Africa.

Water-quality management involves the maintenance of the fitness of water resources for use on a sustained basis, by achieving a balance between socio-economic development and environmental protection. From a regulatory point of view, water-

In March 2005, the Department of Environmental Affairs and Tourism, the provincial Department of Health in the Western Cape, the City of Cape Town and a host of coastal local governments, intensified efforts to inform coastal communities, recreational fishers and the public about the effects of the toxic red tide that had occurred along the west coast.

Red tides are natural phenomena that usually occur because of abnormally high production of plankton, following periods of coastal up-welling. Shellfish such as mussels, clams, bait and oysters are particularly vulnerable to red tides because they filter feed.

Collecting and consuming any shellfish brought to shore by a toxic red tide poses a serious health and safety risk to humans.

During the red tide, the department deployed its Coastcare teams along the affected coast to inform communities and the public.

quality management entails the ongoing process of planning, development, implementation and administration of water-quality management policy; the authorisation of water-uses that have, or may potentially have, an impact on water quality; as well as the monitoring and auditing of the aforementioned.

The National Water Act, 1998 (Act 36 of 1998), further enables the Department of Water Affairs and Forestry to manage water quality through source-directed and resource-directed measures. Source-directed measures include the issuing of licences to water users with a potential impact on the resource.

The Act requires that all significant water resources be classified in accordance with the prescribed classification system. (See chapter 23: *Water affairs and forestry.*)

Air pollution

The National Environment Management: Air Quality Act, 2004 (Act 39 of 2004), was promulgated in 2005. The Act, which repealed the Atmospheric Pollution Prevention Act, 1965 (Act 45 of 1965), seeks to give effect to the integrated pollution and waste-management policy to ensure that all South Africans have access to clean air.

The passing of the Act was significant because for the first time in its history, South Africa has in place the basis for scientifically setting minimum air-quality standards and for punishing those who continue to pollute the air.

The next challenge is to create the capacity at provincial and local levels to implement and enforce the new standards, and to create awareness and understanding of the new legislation. In 2005, the Department of Environmental Affairs and Tourism launched a series of community fresh-air izimbizo involving communities across South Africa who are worst-affected by air pollution.

It was envisaged that in 2005, implementation of the new air-quality legislation would be started, draft ambient air-quality standards for comment promulgated, existing air-quality permits reviewed, and the Vaal Triangle declared a priority area for action in terms of the Act. These actions will eventually result in major improvements in South Africa's air quality and will consequently have major public health benefits.

The department was expected to appoint a service-provider by the end of July 2005, to identify the top 50 air-polluting industries or sectors in South Africa. Once identified, the department would, in partnership with provinces and local councils, target these industries to completely review their air-pollution permit conditions.

The review of permit conditions will be an interim measure to address existing air-quality problems in the short term, and under the older laws, while the capacity is being created in provincial and local authorities to implement and enforce the provisions and standards of the Air Quality Act, 2004.

At least 30 air-quality licensing officers were expected to be trained in each province to build the skills needed to apply the new Act.

Marine pollution

More than 80% of marine pollution originates from land-based sources such as pipeline discharges, rivers and stormwater run-off.

There are many places where water or water containing waste is discharged into the sea. Forty sea outfalls have been formalised through exemptions issued by the Department of Water Affairs and Forestry in terms of the Water Act, 1956 (Act 54 of 1956).

The same principles used for the issuing of other water-use licences apply to licences for sea outfalls. Such effluents include raw and treated sewage, industrial effluents, or a mixture of the two. In the past, many of these discharges were made into the surf zone, or even onto the shore, but the current tendency is to extend the pipelines further offshore. Permit conditions generally include the monitoring of adverse effects of such discharges in the marine environment.

An increasing source of concern is non-point-source pollution, especially pollution originating from the burgeoning informal settlements that form part of many coastal cities. Such pollution is generally the result of inadequate sanitation and other infrastructure, and is very difficult to control or monitor.

Shipping also contributes significantly to marine pollution, particularly regarding specific types of pollutants. Of the estimated 6,1 million mt of oil entering the oceans every year, some 45% originates from shipping activities.

The balance comes from industrial discharges, urban run-off, and oil exploration and production – which contributes only 2%. Of the pollution emanating from shipping activities, the majority comes from vessel operations, with only 12% from tanker accidents.

Nevertheless, due to the notorious sea conditions along its coastline, South Africa has experienced a number of major oil spills, and, as a consequence, has a well-developed response capability. This includes contingency plans, salvage tugs, dispersant spraying vessels, a reconnaissance aircraft and a stockpile of oil-spill-response equipment.

Other pollutants linked to the operational activities of ships include sewage and garbage, ballast water discharges, air pollution, and cargoes which enter the sea through accidents. Sewage, garbage and air pollution are regulated by annexes to Marpol, an international convention controlling pollution from ships, to which South Africa is a party. New regulations to control ballast water discharges are being developed.

A major concern is the translocation of alien species, including pathogens, which may have serious ecological, social (public health) and economic consequences. South Africa is involved in an international project aimed at implementing international guidelines on ballast water management in developing countries.

Another potential source of marine pollution is the dumping of waste at sea. This activity is regulated under the Dumping at Sea Control Act, 1980 (Act 73 of 1980), and, since 1995 has excluded industrial waste. The main categories of waste dumped in South Africa are dredged material from the ports; obsolete vessels; and, occasionally, spoiled cargoes.

West Indian Ocean Land-Based Activities Project (WIO-LaB)

WIO-LaB was launched at Robben Island on 5 November 2004. The WIO-LaB Project deals with the protection, prevention and management of marine pollution from land-based activities.

The commitment given to this project by the main donors, the United Nations Environmental Programme (UNEP) and the Global Environmental Facility (GEF), was evident in the appointment of a regional project manager in February 2005. Two task teams were also appointed at regional level, namely the Municipal Waste Water and the Physical Alterations and Destruction of Habitats task teams.

In May 2005, a WIO-LaB steering committee was established at a meeting in Tanzania, and in June 2005, a legal task team was established at a meeting in Madagascar. By August 2005, a process to appoint two legal experts to deal with local issues on the implementation of the WIO-LaB projects was underway.

Task teams were expected to be established in South Africa by September 2005 to develop policies to:
- reduce stress to the ecosystem by improving water and sediment quality
- identify the coastal hot spots for pollution
- recommend the best practices for dealing with pollution from land-based activities
- develop and implement the action plan.

UNEP, UNESCO and GEF reserved R 22 071 725 for the implementation of WIO-LaB for the period 2005 to 2008.

Chemicals

Although relatively small by international standards, the chemical industry is a significant player in the South African economy, contributing about 5% to gross domestic product and providing employment to about 200 000 people. The industry produces 1 301 t of primary and secondary process chemicals annually, making it the largest of its kind in Africa.

Several steps have been taken to align current legislation with the Constitution of the Republic of South Africa and with global chemicals management:
- A special unit has been set up in the Department of Environmental Affairs and Tourism to implement a system aimed at preventing major industrial accidents, as well as systems for emergency preparedness and response.
- The minister has initiated an integrated safety, health and environment approach for the

management of chemicals in South Africa. This government-level initiative, funded by the UN Institute for Training and Research, will involve a multi-stakeholder forum, including labour representatives, aimed at integrating legislation.

The department has embarked on a process to develop the South African National Chemicals Profile. This is intended to contribute to a better understanding of the problems relating to the management and impact of chemicals. It will also help to identify important gaps and weaknesses in the existing system, as a first step in defining whether further efforts may be required.

The development of the profile was motivated by the recommendations of the International Programme on Chemical Safety, as a follow-up to the Rio Declaration on Environment and Development in 1992.

South Africa has signed the Stockholm Convention on Persistent Organic Pollutants and the Rotterdam Convention on Prior Informed Consent Procedure for Certain Hazardous Chemicals and Pesticides in International Trade.

Recycling

Almost every type of paper produced in South Africa has a recycled content. Each ton of waste paper that is recycled saves about 17 pine trees, and a ton of recycled paper saves 3 m^3 of landfill space. South Africa saves 10 million trees annually.

Collect-a-Can celebrated its 12th birthday in April 2005.

Thanks to its efforts, the recycling of colddrink cans increased from 18% in 1993 to 66% in 2003. This is higher than the recycling rate in the USA and the European Union.

Over the past 10 years, more than 530 t of colddrink cans and 400 000 t of scrap metal have been recycled.

According to a survey conducted by Collect-a-Can, more than 37 000 people earn a living by picking up cans for recyling. In excess of R270 million has been paid to can collectors over the past 10 years.

The glass industry in South Africa has taken a proactive stance in driving glass recycling by agreeing on a model of self-regulation. This will involve a section 21 company being established and managed according to guiding principles laid down in the Glass Memorandum of Understanding (MoU), signed on 19 May 2005.

The MoU evolved from extensive research, consultation and negotiation and enjoys the support of the National Glass Recycling Forum, which includes the entire waste-glass value chain, as well as consumer groups. The initiative aims to increase glass-recycling levels from 20% to 50% a year in less than five years.

The official signing of the MoU also marked the launch of a comprehensive national recyling campaign aimed at addressing the challenges posed by waste glass in the environment.

Environmental injustices

The negative effect of asbestos on the environment and other environmental-injustice issues are a priority for the Department of Environmental Affairs and Tourism.

Efforts that are being undertaken by the South African Government to deal with the asbestos problem include:
- eradicating mine-dumps
- developing occupational health and safety regulations on asbestos
- developing safety standards and establishing a single compensation office
- formulating a code of best practice for the maintenance, demolition and disposal of asbestos-containing material
- abolishing the use of asbestos in road construction
- gradually phasing out asbestos-use in housing.

In October 2005, regulations to ban the use of asbestos in South Africa were published for comment. A study on secondary asbestos pollution and its effect on affected communities was also expected to be completed during the course of the year.

There has been a decline of 39% in local asbestos consumption from more than 12 600 t in 200 to just over 7 700 t in 2003. There are fewer than 200 people employed in the domestic asbestos industry.

International co-operation

The department promotes South Africa's interests by participating in a number of international commissions, such as the International Commission for the Conservation of Atlantic Tunas, the Commission for the Conservation of Antarctic Marine Living Resources, and the International Whaling Commission.

South Africa, through the department, has adopted the Benguela Fisheries Interaction and Training (BENEFIT) Programme and the Benguela Current Large Marine Ecosystem (BCLME) Programme as integral parts of the New Partnership for Africa's Development (NEPAD) initiative.

BENEFIT is a joint initiative between South Africa, Namibia and Angola to conduct scientific investigations into commercially important living marine resources and their interaction with the environment in the Benguela region.

The BCLME Programme is another initiative by these three countries to facilitate the sustainable management and protection of the marine ecosystem. It is aimed primarily at improving the structures and capacities of these three countries to deal with problems and issues that occur across national boundaries, so that the ecosystem may be managed as a whole.

The following important instruments have been acceded to, or ratified:
- Agreement for the Implementation of the Provisions of the UN Convention on the Law of the Sea on 10 December 1982 Relating to the Conservation and Management of Straddling Fish Stocks and Highly Migratory Fish Stocks (Straddling Stocks Agreement)
- Agreement on the Conservation of Albatrosses and Petrels (ACAP)
- Convention for the Protection, Management and Development of the Marine and Coastal Environment of the East African Region and Related Protocols (Nairobi Convention)
- Convention for Co-operation in the Protection and Development of the Marine and Coastal Environment of the West and Central African

Region and Related Protocol (Abidjan Convention)
• SADC Protocol on Fisheries.

United Nations Framework Convention on Climate Change (UNFCCC)

South Africa ratified the UNFCCC in 1997. The convention is a global commitment to take collective responsibility for climate change, and is a mandate for action to address the problem.

The convention was signed at the Rio Earth Summit in 1992 by heads of state and other senior representatives from 154 countries (and the European Community), and came into effect on 21 March 1994. Since mid-1998, some 175 states have ratified or acceded to the convention.

The objective of the convention is to stabilise GHG concentrations in the atmosphere at a level that will not have an adverse effect on the climate.

In January 2005, the Minister of Environmental Affairs and Tourism, Mr Marthinus Van Schalkwyk, published norms and standards for the sustainable utilisation of large predators, as well as regulations governing the keeping and hunting of indigenous predators, in the *Government Gazette*.

Since 1997, government has continuously condemned the practice of canned hunting, and the draft norms, standards and regulations support its endeavours to stamp out this practice.

The aims of the draft norms, standards and regulations are to:
• provide a national approach to and minimum standards for all aspects relating to the management of large predators
• regulate the hunting of large predators
• promote the ethical hunting of large predators
• regulate the control of damage-causing animals
• protect the rights of owners of properties adjacent to those on which large predators are introduced
• regulate the import and export of large predators
• protect the genetic integrity of indigenous predator populations
• ensure sustainable use of large predators.

It took effect on 1 July 2005 and is enforced in terms of the provisions of the National Environmental Management: Biodiversity Act, 2004 (Act 10 of 2004).

The convention aims to control this level over a period of time, to:
• allow ecosystems to adapt naturally to climate change
• ensure that food production is not threatened
• enable economic development to proceed in a sustainable manner.

All countries that have ratified the convention are required to:
• develop, update and publish national inventories of anthropogenic emissions by sources, and removals by sinks of GHG (the GHG excludes those listed in the Montreal Protocol)
• formulate, implement and update national and regional programmes containing measures to mitigate climate change
• promote and co-operate in the development and transfer of technology that controls, reduces or prevents anthropogenic emissions of GHG
• promote sustainable management, conservation and enhancement of sinks and reservoirs of GHG
• co-operate in preparing for the adaptation to the impact of climate change
• take climate-change considerations into account where feasible, in relevant social, economic and environmental policies and actions, to minimise the adverse effects on the economy, public health and the quality of the environment
• promote and co-operate in the timeous and transparent exchange of information, including scientific, technological, socio-economic and legal information and research
• promote and co-operate in education, training and public awareness
• report to the Conference of the Parties (COP).

South Africa acceded to the Kyoto Protocol in July 2002. As a signatory party, it is required to submit an initial national communication to the UNFCCC Secretariat reporting, among other things, on national circumstances, the National GHG Inventory, vulnerability and adaptation, mitigation options and preliminary needs assessments. To prepare this document, the Department of Environmental Affairs and Tourism commissioned detailed country studies to be undertaken to evaluate a broad range of likely climate-change impacts in South Africa. The results of these studies were compiled into the initial national communication to the UNFCCC Secretariat, which was submitted during the ninth COP of the UNFCCC that was held in Milan, Italy, in December 2003.

The Kyoto Protocol provides for economic instruments to be used while endeavouring to achieve the objectives of the convention. Three mechanisms have been created and only one, the Clean Development Mechanism (CDM), involves the participation of developing countries like South Africa. The functions of operationalising the CDM have been delegated to the Department of Minerals and Energy. This mechanism allows developed countries to conduct GHG-reducing projects in South Africa, while assisting South Africa with sustainable development.

Convention on International Trade in Endangered Species (CITES)

CITES, also known as the Washington Convention, was negotiated in 1973 when it was realised that international trade in wildlife and wildlife products could lead to the overexploitation of certain species, thereby threatening them with extinction.

CITES came into force in South Africa on 13 October 1975. South Africa, together with the other 149 member countries, acts by regulating and monitoring international trade in species which are, or may be, affected by this trade.

South Africa attended the COP 13 of CITES, which took place in October 2004, in Bangkok, Thailand. The COP's role is to assess the implementation of the convention and to make recommendations to improve its effectiveness, as well as amend the appendices. The parties meet every two and a half years.

Leading up to the COP, parties submit proposals for interpretative resolutions and amendments to the appendices of the convention. Species may be added to the appendices, transferred between appendices, or removed from the appendices. At the COP, procedures for control of the trade in species of fauna and flora listed in the appendices are examined and adapted where necessary.

In 2004, South Africa submitted proposals on the black rhino and leopard.

Montreal Protocol

South Africa, as a signatory to the Montreal Protocol, has a national obligation to safeguard the ozone layer from depletion.

South Africa has phased out chlorofluorocarbons (CFCs), halons, methyl chloroform and carbon tetrachloride – making it the only developing country in the world that has achieved so much in line with the phase-out schedule for developed countries. Although South Africa is classified as a developing country, its consumption of these substances is equal to that of some developed countries.

To demonstrate the country's commitment towards the phasing out of ozone-depleting substances (ODSs), the following control measures constitute the overall position of South Africa on the Montreal Protocol:

- working groups were constituted to assist government to implement the protocol
- regulated ODSs can only be imported or exported after applying for an import/export permit through the Department of Trade and Industry under the Import and Export Control Act, 1963 (Act 45 of 1963)
- ODSs can only be imported after an environmental levy of R5 per kg of CFC has been paid
- information is disseminated to interested and affected parties
- Africa network meetings, as arranged by UNEP, are attended, where views, experiences and problems are shared to improve co-operation within the region and as per NEPAD requirements.

Obligations include:

- ensuring that South Africa, as a party to the protocol, protects human health and the environment against harm from human activities, which modify or are likely to modify the ozone layer
- ensuring the protection of the ozone layer by taking precautionary measures to equitably control total global emissions of substances that deplete the ozone layer, with the ultimate objective of totally eliminating them

- reporting and sending to the Ozone Secretariat data on production, imports, exports and consumption of regulated ODSs as collected from dealers and relevant departments.

The Department of Environmental Affairs and Tourism has embarked on a national project to establish methyl bromide consumption trends and a database of suitable, feasible and economically viable alternatives to methyl bromide. This document will form the basis for an intensive research/ evaluation project to phase out, in the short term, 20% of methyl bromide usage, mainly in the agricultural sector.

As of 1 January 2005, all developing countries were to reduce their respective methyl bromide consumption by 20%, as per the phase-out timetable.

International Agreement on the Conservation of Albatrosses and Petrels

The ACAP, which South Africa ratified in November 2003, came into force on 1 February 2004. South Africa became the fourth country to ratify the agreement, following Australia, Ecuador and New Zealand.

The ACAP aims to reduce the threat of extinction of the 28 species of albatrosses and larger petrels covered by the agreement. All these species are killed as by-catch in longline fishing operations. The birds attempt to snatch baited hooks as they are being deployed, and are then dragged beneath the sea surface and drowned. Simple effective by-catch mitigation measures, such as bird-scaring streamers and line-setting at night, need to be widely adopted if these birds are to be saved from extinction.

The agreement, which includes an action plan, describes a number of conservation measures to be implemented by signatory states to improve the conservation status of the increasingly threatened albatrosses and larger petrels.

Apart from reducing seabird by-catch from longline fishing, these include research and monitoring, the eradication of introduced species such as rats and feral cats at breeding sites, the reduction of disturbance and habitat loss, and the reduction of marine pollution.

South Africa is particularly important in the conservation of albatrosses and petrels, since it is a range state to 15 of the 28 species covered under the ACAP. South Africa's sub-Antarctic Prince Edward islands are important breeding sites for nine of these species, most of which have a formal threatened conservation status.

The Prince Edward islands are particularly important to the wandering albatross, hosting more than 40% of the world's population of this species. The wandering albatross is the largest of all albatrosses, with a wingspan of up to 3,5 m. It is expected that South Africa joining the ACAP will boost conservation-related research on the islands, allowing for the best management of these important populations of threatened species.

Private-sector involvement

Numerous private bodies are involved in conservation activities. There are more than 400 organisations in the country concentrating on conservation, wildlife and the general environment, and more than 30 botanical and horticultural organisations. Among these are:

- BirdLife South Africa
- Botanical Society of South Africa
- Centre for Rehabilitation of Wildlife
- Conservation International
- Delta Environmental Centre
- Dolphin Action Protection Group
- EcoLink
- Endangered Wildlife Trust
- Green Trust
- Keep South Africa Beautiful
- National Conservancy Association of South Africa
- Peace Parks Foundation
- South African National Foundation for the Conservation of Coastal Birds
- Trees and Food for Africa
- Wildlife and Environment Society of South Africa
- Worldwide Fund for Nature South Africa.

Acknowledgements

BuaNews

Beeld

Department of Environmental Affairs and Tourism

Estimates of National Expenditure 2005, published by National Treasury

National Zoological Gardens of South Africa

South African National Biodiversity Institute

South African National Parks

www.southafrica.info

www.collectacan.co.za

www.gov.za

Suggested reading

Beinart, W. *Rise of Conservation in South Africa: Settlers, Livestock and the Environment, 1770 – 1950.* Oxford: Oxford University Press, 2002.

Bethlehem, L. and Goldblatt, M. *The Bottom Line: Industry and the Environment in South Africa.* Rondebosch: University of Cape Town Press, 1997.

Bond, P. *Unsustainable South Africa: Environment, Development and Social Protest.* Pietermaritzburg: University of Natal Press, 2002.

Carruthers, V. and Pearson, M. eds. *Wildlife of Southern Africa: A Field Guide to the Animals and Plants of the Region.* Halfway House, Gauteng: Southern Book Publishers, 1997.

Clarke, J. *Back to Earth. South Africa's Environmental Challenges.* Halfway House: Southern Book Publishers, 1991.

Cock, J. and Koch, E. *Going Green: People, Politics and Other Environment in South Africa.* Cape Town: Oxford University Press, 1991.

Dovers, S. ed. *South Africa's Environmental History: Cases and Comparisons.* Cape Town: David Philip, 2002.

Fuggle, R.F. and Rabie, M.A. Rev. eds. *Environmental Management in South Africa.* Cape Town: Juta, 1996.

Griffiths, T. and Robin, L. eds. *Ecology and Empire: Environmental History of Settler Societies.* Pietermaritzburg: University of Natal Press and Keele University Press, 1997.

Haape, J. ed. *South Africa.* 2nd ed. Basingstoke (UK): GeoCentre International, 1995.

Hattingh, J. *et al.* eds. *Environmental Education: Ethics and Action in Southern Africa.* Pretoria: Human Sciences Research Council (HSRC), 2002.

Hinz, M. *Without Chiefs There Would Be No Game: Customary Law and Nature Conservation.* Windhoek: Out of Africa Publishers, 2003.

Hosking, S. *Exploring the Case for Increasing Glass Recycling Through Regulation.* Pretoria: HSRC, 2000.

Hugo, M.L. *Environmental Management: An Ecological Guide to Sustainable Living in South Africa.* Pretoria: Ecoplan, 2004.

Hulme, D. and Murphee, M. eds. *African Wildlife and Livelihoods: The Promise and Performance of Community Conservation.* Cape Town: David Philip, 2001.

Koch, E. *et al. Water, Waste and Wildlife: The Politics of Ecology in South Africa.* Johannesburg: Penguin, 1990.

Kok, P. and Pietersen, J. *Biodiversity.* Pretoria: HSRC, 2000 (National Research and Technology Foresight Project).

Kok, P. and Pietersen, J. *Environmental Management.* Pretoria: HSRC, 2000.

McDonald, D. ed. *Environmental Justice in South Africa.* Cape Town: University of Cape Town Press, 2002.

Mills, G. and Harvey, M. *African Predator.* Cape Town: Struik, 2001.

Nürnberger, K. *Prosperity, Poverty and Pollution: Managing the Approaching Crisis.* Pietermaritzburg: Cluster Publications, 1999.

Payne, A.I.L. and Crawford, R.J.M. *Oceans of Life off Southern Africa.* 2nd ed. Cape Town: Vlaeberg, 1995.

Phezulu, L. *Leigh Voigt's African Album: A Miscellany of Paintings, Curiosities, Lore and Legend by a Bushveld Naturalist.* Cape Town: David Philip, 1999.

Ramphele, M. ed. *Restoring the Land: Environment and Change in Post-Apartheid South Africa.* London: Panos, 1991.

Ritchie, J. *The Environment Funding Guide: A Comprehensive Guide to Raising Funds for the Environment.* Cape Town: Papillon Books for Nedbank, c.1997.

Spence, C. ed. *Ten Days in Johannesburg: A Negotiation of Hope.* Pretoria: Department of Environmental Affairs and Tourism and the United Nations Development Programme, 2004.

Van der Riet, W. *et al. Environmental Potential Atlas for South Africa.* Pretoria: Van Schaik for the Department of Environmental Affairs and Tourism, 1997.

Van Oudtshoorn, F. *Guide to the Grasses of South Africa.* Photographs by E. van Wyk and F. van Oudtshoorn. Pretoria: Briza, 1999.

Van Wyk, B. and Gericke, N. *People's Plants: A Guide to Useful Plants of Southern Africa.* Pretoria: Briza, 1999.

Weinberg, P. ed. and photographer. *Once We Were Hunters: A Journey with Indigenous People.* Cape Town: David Philip, 2000.

White Paper on the Conservation and Sustainable Use of South Africa's Biological Diversity. Pretoria: Department of Environmental Affairs and Tourism, 1997.

Finance

The Constitution of the Republic of South Africa, 1996 (Act 108 of 1996), lays down a framework for the division of responsibilities between national, provincial and local government. It prescribes an equitable division of revenue between the spheres of government, taking into account their respective functions. It also creates an independent auditor-general and an independent central bank, and sets out the principles governing financial accountability to Parliament, and the annual budget process.

The aim of National Treasury is to promote economic development, good governance, social progress and rising living standards through accountable, economic, efficient, equitable and sustainable public finances.

Fiscal policy framework

The Minister of Finance, Mr Trevor Manuel, presented the Budget for 2005/06 on 23 February 2005.

Highlights included:
- R6,8 billion in tax relief for individuals and households, directed mostly at those earning below R200 000 a year
- no personal income tax for people earning below R35 000 a year (R60 000 for people over the age of 65 years)
- a change in the tax treatment of medical scheme contributions to reduce costs of membership for lower-income families
- scrapping transaction tax on debit entries to credit card and bank accounts, to keep banking services affordable
- increases in the price of beer (11c a bottle and 5c a can) and the price of cigarettes (52c for a packet of 20)
- an increase of 10c a litre in levies on petrol and diesel
- tax relief of R1,4 billion for small business to free up growth resources
- measures to reduce tax compliance costs and red tape for small business
- a drop in the company tax rate from 30% to 29%
- changes to the tax on travel allowances to remove unwarranted benefits for higher-income earners
- a R40 increase in the maximum monthly old-age, disability and care dependency grants to R780, and a R10 increase in the monthly Child Support Grant to R180
- a R6-billion allocation to allow the land restitution programme to complete its work over the next three years

- Regional Services Council (RSC) levies will be eliminated in 2006
- R2 billion for the new comprehensive housing strategy and R3 billion for related community infrastructure
- R1,7 billion for water, sanitation and other municipal infrastructure investment
- R6,9 billion for improving teachers' salaries
- R5 billion to allow for pay progression in police salaries and increased police numbers
- R3 billion for public transport investments and roads

- R3,7 billion for the delivery of municipal services
- R776 million for the National Student Financial Aid Scheme
- R1 billion to revitalise Further Education and Training colleges
- R1,4 billion for South Africa's African development agenda, including peacekeeping operations, the African Union (AU) and the Pan-African Parliament
- R1 billion for the new micro agricultural finance scheme.

Consolidated national, provincial and social security fund expenditure: functional classification[1]

	2003/04		2004/05		2005/06	
	Estimated outcome	% of total	Budget estimate	% of total	Budget estimate	% of total
General government services and unallocatable expenditure[2]	23 158,6	7,7	26 301,1	7,7	28 337,2	7,5
Protection services:	58 982,8	19,5	63 532,0	18,6	71 974,3	18,9
Defence and intelligence	22 291,5	7,4	22 470,7	6,6	25 362,9	6,7
Police	23 688,6	7,8	26 437,5	7,7	30 496,3	8,0
Prisons	7 822,3	2,6	8813,6	2,6	9 715,1	2,6
Justice	5 180,4	1,7	5 810,1	1,7	6 399,9	1,7
Social services:	177 159,7	58,6	202 585,7	59,2	224 306,6	59,0
Education	70 204,7	23,2	76 571,3	22,4	81 995,6	21,6
Health	38 641,6	12,8	42 828,4	12,5	48067,3	12,6
Social security and welfare	51 915,8	17,2	63 532,2	18,6	72 728,4	19,1
Housing	5 636,1	1,9	7 059,1	2,1	7 261,2	1,9
Community development[3]	10 761,4	3,6	12 594,7	3,7	14 254,1	3,7
Economic services:	43 064,3	14,2	49 534,1	14,5	55 571,1	14,6
Water schemes and related services	5 540,7	1,8	5 738,5	1,7	6 336,1	1,7
Fuel and energy	2 285,8	0,8	2 330,3	0,7	2 723,1	0,7
Agriculture, forestry and fishing	6 561,2	2,2	7 541,5	2,2	9 757,3	2,6
Mining, manufacturing and construction	1 497,6	0,5	1 729,1	0,5	2 195,5	0,6
Transport and communications	15 084,7	5,0	18 009,1	5,3	19 533,1	5,1
Other economic services[4]	12 094,2	4,0	14 185,7	4,1	15 026,1	4,0
Subtotal: Votes and statutory amounts	302 365,4	100,00	341 952,9	100,00	380 189,0	100,00
Plus contingency reserves	-	-	-	-	2 000,00	0,5
Total non-interest expenditure	302 365,4	100,00	341 952,9	100,00	382 189,0	100,5
Interest	46 312,9	15,3	48 901,0	14,3	53 125,0	14,0
Total consolidated expenditure	348 678,4	115,3	390 853,9	114,3	435 314,0	114,5

1) These figures were estimated by National Treasury and may differ from data published by Statistics South Africa.
The numbers in these tables are not strictly comparable to those published in previous years, due to the allocation of
some of the unallocatable expenditure for previous years. Data for the history years has been adjusted accordingly.
2) Mainly general administration, cost of raising loans and allocatable capital expenditure.
3) Including cultural, recreational and sport services.
4) Including tourism, labour and multi-purpose projects.

Source: National Treasury

Debt management

South Africa's debt, both domestic rand-denominated bonds and foreign-debt issues, enjoys increasing recognition on international capital markets, and continues to attract a diverse range of investors.

This reflects the country's success in adopting sustainable fiscal and macro-economic policies, the evolution of a sound and transparent approach to debt management, the healthy Balance of Payments position and the maturity of South Africa's financial markets. In recent years, both Standard and Poor's and Moody's Investors' Service upgraded their ratings of South African debt, affirming their confidence in the country's macro-economic and fiscal management. These assessments contribute to broadening South Africa's international investor base and reinforce the favourable outlook for interest rates and the cost of capital.

South African foreign debt continues to trade at tighter spreads than the Emerging Market Bond Index, indicating that investors share the confidence expressed by international rating agencies and regard South Africa positively in comparison with its competitors.

The primary objective of domestic debt management has shifted to the reduction of the cost of debt to within acceptable risk limits, with diversification of funding instruments, and ensuring flexible government access to markets as secondary goals. Recourse to foreign borrowing has been stepped up, allowing the fiscus to contribute to reducing the foreign currency exposure of the South African Reserve Bank in its forward market portfolio.

Domestic-debt-management reforms have addressed several policy and instrument gaps:

- Lower coupon bonds have been introduced, in line with government's approach to reducing inflation in the years ahead.
- The Public-Sector Borrowers' Forum was established in 2001.
- Co-ordination between monetary policy and liability management has been strengthened through more effective liaison between National Treasury and the Reserve Bank.
- Regular meetings with the primary dealers, the

Reserve Bank, and the futures and bond exchanges provide a forum for ensuring a transparent and efficient bond market.

- Debt consolidation has reduced fragmentation on the yield curve and improved liquidity of the benchmark issues. Illiquid bonds were consolidated into five liquid benchmark bonds, thereby smoothing the maturity profile and reducing refinancing risks.
- The integrity and efficiency of the Government securities market has been strengthened by buying back illiquid bonds, including diverse 'ex-homeland' bonds of limited issue size.
- Inflation-linked bonds were introduced to diversify government's investor base and signal confidence in government's macro-economic policy, while also providing an objective measure of inflationary expectations and benchmarks for other issuers.
- The Strips (Separate Trading of Registered Interest and Principal Securities) Programme was introduced to increase demand for the underlying instruments and encourage active portfolio management.

The liquidity in the domestic government-bond market, measured by the increase in nominal trades, has improved substantially during recent years,

In 2004, National Treasury launched the RSA Government Retail Bond, a no-cost, secure, risk-free investment, which offers bond market returns directly to the public.

The main objectives of the RSA Retail Bond are to:
- diversify the financial instruments on offer to the market by government
- target a different source of funding for government
- create awareness among the public of the importance of saving.

By February 2005, sales of the RSA Government Retail Bond had reached R1,248 billion. Some 15 733 people had invested in the bond with a total of 22 523 investments.

National Treasury, through the Asset and Liability Management Division, determines the prevailing interest rates for the two-year, three-year and five-year RSA government retail bonds at the end of each month.

especially since the appointment of primary dealers in government bonds in April 1998.

In actively managing its debt portfolio, National Treasury is responsible for identifying, controlling and managing the risks to which government is exposed. A comprehensive risk-management framework of National Treasury calls for quantitative analyses to model, monitor and manage risk exposure. The framework provides for a set of benchmarks or reference criteria against which the structure and evolution of the debt portfolio can be tested and understood.

Legislation

National Treasury tables a significant amount of legislation in Parliament annually. Legislation passed in 2004/05 included the:
- Appropriation Act, 2004 (Act 15 of 2004)
- Taxation Laws Amendment Act, 2004 (Act 16 of 2004)
- Government Employees Pension Law Amendment Act, 2004 (Act 21 of 2004)
- National Payment System Amendment Act, 2004 (Act 22 of 2004)
- Public Investment Corporation Act, 2004 (Act 23 of 2004)
- Finance Act, 2004 (Act 26 of 2004)
- Adjustments Appropriation Act, 2004 (Act 27 of 2004)
- Securities Services Act, 2004 (Act 36 of 2004)
- Financial Services Ombud Schemes Act, 2004 (Act 37 of 2004)
- Revenue Laws Amendment Act, 2004 (Act 32 of 2004)
- Second Revenue Laws Amendment Act, 2004 (Act 34 of 2004)
- Division of Revenue Act, 2005 (Act 1 of 2005).

Legislation expected to be tabled in 2005/06 included the:
- Appropriation Bill
- Taxation Laws Amendment Bill
- Adjustments Appropriation Bill
- Revenue Laws Amendment Bill
- Second Revenue Laws Amendment Bill.

Draft legislation under consideration and expected to be tabled in 2005/06, pending the outcome of the policy process, internal vetting requirements and the duration of consultation processes, included the:
- Co-operative Banks Bill that proposes a regulatory framework for deposit-taking entities other than banks and mutual banks.
- Dedicated Banks Bill, which will create a new tier of banks. The new tier will introduce financial depth in the banking system by providing basic banking services (savings accounts, transmission services, loans, etc.) to the largely low-income and historically disadvantaged communities. This will improve this market's access to financial services.
- Public Finance Management Amendment Bill, which will amend the Public Finance Management Act (PFMA), 1999 (Act 1 of 1999), to address:
  - practical difficulties encountered in the implementation of the PFMA, 1999
  - the incorporation of recent and intended budget-reform initiatives
  - improved financial regulation of public entities.

Exchange rate of the Rand – percentage changes

	31 Mar 2004 to 30 June 2004	30 June 2004 to 30 Sep 2004	30 Sep 2004 to 31 Dec 2004	31 Dec 2004 to 31 Mar 2005	31 Mar 2004 to 31 May 2005
Weighted average*	2,4	-3,2	6,6	-6,8	-4,4
Euro	2,0	-4,3	3,3	-4,9	-2,7
US dollar	1,0	-2,6	14,3	-9,7	-7,0
British pound	2,6	-2,2	6,6	-7,5	-3,8
Japanese yen	6,1	-0,8	5,7	-5,9	-6,0

*Against a basket of 13 currencies

Source: *Quarterly Bulletin*, June 2005

- Direct Charges Bill, which will authorise certain withdrawals and payments from the National Revenue Fund as direct charges.
- Financial Intelligence Centre (FIC) Amendment Bill, which will provide for various technical and policy amendments to the principal Act.
- The Auditing Professions Bill, which will establish the Independent Regulatory Board for Auditors, to accredit educational institutions and professional bodies, register auditors, and regulate the conduct of registered auditors.

The Public Finance Management Act, 1999

The PFMA, 1999 came into effect on 1 April 2000 for all departments, constitutional institutions and public entities.

The PFMA, 1999 represents a fundamental change in government's approach to the handling of public finances, as it shifts the emphasis away from a highly centralised system of expenditure control by the treasuries. It holds the heads of departments accountable for the use of resources to deliver services to communities. It will also, in time, change the accounting base from cash to accrual.

The Act emphasises:
- regular financial reporting
- independent auditing and supervision of internal control systems
- improved accounting standards
- greater focus on output and performance
- increased accountability at all levels.

Transforming public-sector financial management is one of National Treasury's key objectives. To this end, National Treasury has been implementing the PFMA, 1999 since 2000. It began implementing the Municipal Finance Management Act (MFMA), 2003 (Act 56 of 2003), in 2004.

The Act aims to modernise budget and financial management, and ensure greater transparency and accountability in the finances of municipalities.

Together with the Local Government: Municipal Systems Act, 2000 (Act 32 of 2000), the MFMA, 2003 empowers mayors and councillors to lead municipalities by approving policy and setting performance targets.

Accounting Standards Board

The Accounting Standards Board was appointed in 2002 and is responsible mainly for the implementation of Generally Recognised Accounting Practice in government.

Financial Services Sector Charter

The Financial Services Sector Charter was signed in November 2003, signalling a key milestone in the transformation of the financial sector.

The charter seeks to ensure the broad-based transformation of the sector, based on the following elements: human resource development (HRD), procurement and enterprise development, access to financial services, empowerment financing, ownership, control and corporate social investment.

South Africa's economic growth is expected to improve further in the next three years. Moderation of inflation and the sound and consistent management of monetary policy by the Reserve Bank have brought interest rates down to their lowest levels in 24 years.

Following several years of decline, South African mining production expanded by over 4% a year in 2003 and 2004. Output of gold mines continued to decline, but platinum, coal, diamonds and other minerals benefited from growth in demand and prices on international commodity markets.

Value added in the construction sector grew by over 6% in 2004. There is strong growth in the residential property market. Further impetus will be given to building and construction growth by inner city refurbishment encouraged by the urban renewal tax incentive, accelerated investment in low-income housing and municipal infrastructure, and several large economic infrastructure projects in the next few years.

Official foreign exchange reserves have increased to over US$15 billion, which is more than four times the current short-term debt level. Reserves held by the private banking sector have also increased strongly, contributing to a marked improvement in the nation's overall balance sheet, and reduced vulnerability to the inherent volatility of international financial flows.

National Treasury

Financial expenditure

National Treasury plays a pivotal role in the management of government expenditure.

It determines the financial-management norms and standards, and sets reporting policy that guides the Auditor-General's performance. It also assists Parliament, through the Standing Committee on Public Accounts (SCOPA), with its recommendations and formulation of corrective actions. National Treasury closely monitors the performance of state departments and is obliged to report any deviations to the Auditor-General.

National Treasury, furthermore, maintains transparent and fair bidding processes, as well as accounting, logistic and personnel systems. It sets and maintains standards and norms for treasury and logistics, acts as a banker for national departments, and oversees logistical control of stocks and assets.

Exchange-control reforms

National Treasury continues to follow a policy of gradual relaxation of exchange controls. The following major reforms were announced by the Minister of Finance and implemented in 2004 in relation to resident and non-resident corporates and South African individuals:

- Foreign-owned South African companies were allowed to borrow locally up to 300% of the total shareholder's investment. This debt capital would be used for financing investment in South Africa or as domestic working capital.
- Foreign entities (including foreign governments and multilateral institutions) were allowed to list their securities, both bonds and equities, on South African exchanges (i.e. inward listings). South African institutional investors are allowed to invest an additional 5% of their total retail assets in 'African'-classified inward-listed securities, while South African individuals can invest freely in such African and non-African inward-listed securities.
- Exchange-control limits on outward foreign direct investment (FDI) by South African corporates have been abolished, yet South African corporates are still required to lodge an application with the Reserve Bank.
- In addition, South African companies are no longer compelled to repatriate foreign-earned dividends to South Africa.

Government is working towards the transition from exchange controls to a system of prudential regulation for institutional investors.

Currently, South African long-term insurers, investment managers and pension funds can invest up to 15% of their total retail assets offshore, while collective investment schemes can invest 20% of their total retail assets offshore.

Amnesty Unit

On 26 February 2003, the Minister of Finance announced an amnesty window to enable South Africans to voluntarily declare their foreign assets and to regularise such assets and tax affairs without fear of prosecution. By April 2005, of approximately 43 000 applications received, 35 198 had been adjudicated.

It was estimated that the exchange-control levies could raise about R2,3 billion from the adjudicated applications. The total Rand value of assets disclosed under the processed 35 198 applications was R50,7 billion, of which R26,1 billion was leviable.

Amnesty applicants were subject to a levy of 10% of the leviable amount if assets remained offshore, and 5% of the leviable amount if the assets were repatriated to South Africa. The Amnesty Unit was expected to complete its adjudication process by the end of May 2005.

Deposit insurance

National Treasury intends to introduce legislation that seeks to establish a deposit insurance scheme in South Africa. This legislation was expected to be introduced in the second quarter of 2006.

A deposit insurance scheme is a system in which the Government guarantees a payment to depositors in the event of a bank failure. Under an explicit deposit insurance scheme, the terms and conditions of the scheme are explicitly and publicly stated in statute. The development and implementation of an explicit deposit insurance scheme will bear the following benefits for the South African population:

- provide more certainty about the cost of bank failures to the fiscus
- enhance confidence in the banking system
- improve equitable treatment of depositors through transparency over the nature and extent of reimbursement
- clarify the role and extent of government involvement in the resolution of bank failures.

By assuring timely access to their deposits, a deposit insurance scheme can contain the risk of contagion by reducing the incentive for depositors to make a run on banks. An explicit deposit insurance scheme would also limit the scope for discretionary decisions that may result in arbitrary and possibly inconsistent decisions.

The Securities Services Act, 2004 seeks to facilitate an efficient, fair and secure means of securities trading in the South African capital market by regulating a multiplicity of activities and institutions.

The Act also enhances the power of the Registrar of Securities Services to regulate the interdependence between the various participants in South African markets.

The Financial Services Ombud Schemes Act, 2004 attempts to improve the ability of consumers to enforce their rights and resolve any disputes they may have against the financial services industry. Consumers will have a cost-effective and expeditious way to resolve their complaints, without having their right to take the matter to court impeded.

At the end of 2004, National Treasury issued a retirement fund reform discussion document, inviting stakeholders to provide comment by the end of March 2005. Ultimately, a revised document, which will be the product of wide consultation, will form the basis on which the new Pension Funds Act is drafted.

Treasury norms and standards

In terms of Section 216(1)(c) of the Constitution, National Treasury must prescribe measures to ensure both transparency and expenditure control in each sphere of government, by introducing uniform treasury norms and standards. These treasury norms and standards aim at deregulating financial controls, by granting accounting officers of spending agencies more autonomy in financial decision-making within the ambits of impending financial legislation.

Budget evaluation

National Treasury plays an important role in supporting the economic policy to which government has committed itself. It determines the macro limit on expenditure, which is then matched with requests from departments, in line with the affordability and sustainability of services.

Based on this limit, all national departments are annually requested to submit budget proposals for the following financial year to National Treasury.

Early Warning System

The Early Warning System was first established in 1997. Any likely under- or overexpenditure is brought to the attention of the Cabinet so that the relevant minister can ensure that appropriate action is taken.

The introduction of the system has also assisted in the monthly monitoring of the expenditure trends of provincial departments, by having provincial treasuries report to National Treasury in a prescribed format. The information derived from early warning reports is used for advising the Budget Council and the Cabinet. The Minister of Finance is also informed of the early warning report results.

Financial policies, systems and skills development

National Treasury is responsible for financial management systems and the financial training of government officials.

It delivers services that support the following areas:

- financial systems, which consist of the Personnel and Salary System, Logistical Information System, Financial Management System, Basic Accounting System and Management Information System
- banking services and financial reporting for government
- financial-management capacity-development in national and provincial governments.

Procurement

The preferential procurement regulations, 2000 give substance to the content of the Preferential Procurement Policy Framework Act, 2000 (Act 5 of 2000). This Act and its regulations apply to all three spheres of government.

Bids are evaluated according to a preference point system. A bidder can score a maximum of 80 or 90 points for price, while 20 or 10 points can be scored for contracting or subcontracting historically disadvantaged individuals (HDIs) and promoting/ achieving specified Reconstruction and Development Programme (RDP) goals. A contract is awarded to the bidder who scores the highest total number of points. The way in which the bid is evaluated, including the RDP goals to be promoted or achieved and the allocated points in this regard, forms part of the bid documents.

The implementation of the regulations enhances the involvement of HDIs in the public bidding system and contributes to achieving RDP goals, including the promotion of small and medium enterprises (SMEs).

The Supply-Chain Management Framework replaces outdated procurement and provisioning systems in government with an integrated supply-chain management system, as well as an international best-practice process for appointing consultants.

Financial Intelligence Centre (FIC)

Government has adopted a strong stance on the eradication of money laundering and financing of terrorism in keeping with United Nations (UN) conventions and international standards. In 2001, it passed the FIC Act, 2001 (Act 38 of 2001), and in February 2005, it passed the Protection of Constitutional Democracy Against Terrorist and Related Activities Act, 2004 (Act 33 of 2004). The FIC started functioning in February 2003 as an autonomous government agency reporting to the Minister of Finance.

The Protection of Constitutional Democracy against Terrorism and Related Activities Act, 2004 came into operation on 20 May 2005. The Act makes the Republic of South Africa fully compliant with the UN Counter Terrorism Conventions and Protocols, as well as the AU Convention on the Prevention and Combating of Terrorism. The Act creates a general offence of terrorism and offences relating to terrorist activities, such as recruiting, assistance to commit terrorist activities and facilitating such activities.

The mandate of the FIC is to:
- develop policy that gives effect to government's objectives of combating money laundering and financing terrorism
- identify the proceeds of crime and the financing of terrorism
- exchange relevant information with competent authorities and international equivalent organisations
- prevent and reduce the laundering of the proceeds of crime
- monitor compliance in terms of the Act
- advise the Minister of Finance on all of these matters.

The Act identifies a range of 19 different business sectors, which it defines as being accountable institutions, and which are most vulnerable to abuse by criminals. These include banks, *bureaux de change*, life-insurance companies, stockbrokers, money remitters, as well as casinos, lawyers, accountants, investment advisers, estate agents and motor dealers. These accountable institutions have a range of obligations, including implementing 'know your client' measures and reporting to the FIC when they identify suspicious transactions.

The centre analyses and stores reports from the accountable institutions. It then makes disclosures or information packages available to law-enforcement agencies for investigation. It may also make this information available to similar bodies in other countries. In 2004/05, the FIC received in excess of 22 000 suspicious transaction reports from a range of accountable institutions, mainly banks and money remitters, and referred more than 300 to law-enforcement agencies for investigation.

In 2002, South Africa joined the 14-member-strong Eastern and Southern Africa Anti-Money Laundering Group. South Africa also became a member of the Financial Action Task Force, which is the international standards-setting body. The FIC is a member of the Egmont Group of financial intelligence units, which facilitates the exchange of information, skills and technical assistance between financial intelligence units worldwide.

Financial and Fiscal Commission (FFC)

The commission, which came into operation in April 1994, is a statutory institution and permanent expert commission dealing with intergovernmental fiscal relations.

The FFC is responsible for making recommendations to Parliament and the Cabinet on the equitable division of revenue between national, provincial and local governments yearly, giving advice on fiscal policies and taxes that provinces intend to impose, borrowing by local and provincial governments, and criteria to be considered in determining fiscal allocations. Additional responsibilities can be designated by means of appropriate legislation.

Budget Council

The Budget Council consists of the Minister of Finance and the nine provincial executive committee members responsible for finance. The mission of the council is to ensure that the country uses available resources productively, efficiently and equitably, to the best advantage of its people.

It recommends to the Cabinet the share each province should receive, after taking into account national priorities and FFC proposals.

Public Investment Corporation (PIC)

The PIC, a state-owned institution that manages public servants' pension funds, was corporatised under a new law that came into effect in April 2005.

The PIC Act, 2004 (Act 23 of 2004), which replaces the Public Investment Commissioners Act, 1984 (Act 45 of 1984), protects the PIC as a legal entity and enables it to operate as a modern, professional and world-class investment manager.

The State remains the sole shareholder of the PIC, which reports to Parliament's SCOPA, and whose controlling board is appointed by the Minister of Finance.

The PIC continues to use its current asset managers – RMB Asset Management, Stanlib, Futuregrowth, Sanlam Investment Management and Old Mutual Asset Management.

The biggest contributors to the PIC's assets are public servants through the Government Employees Pension Fund (91,29%). Other contributions come from the Compensation Commission (3,20%), Associated Institution Pension Fund (2,61%), Unemployment Insurance Fund (1,65%), Guardian Fund (0,65%) and Political Office Bearers Pension Funds (0,13%).

The Isibaya Fund – a division of the PIC tasked with the funding of socially responsible investments – funded Black Economic Empowerment (BEE) transactions worth R7,5 billion in 2004/05. These were in the financial, mining, infrastructure, telecommunications and industrial sectors. Combined, these transactions benefited over 221 000 people as owners of the businesses, while a further 10 255 benefited through employment.

PIC funding of BEE has resulted in better vesting for BEE ventures, while also netting good profits for the corporation.

Macro-economic strategy

The positive performance of the South African economy in the wake of a global slowdown is indicative

In July 2005, South Africa took up the presidency of the Financial Action Task Force, which is the international standard-setting body for the prevention of money laundering and terror financing. Cabinet appointed Prof. Kader Asmal to this position.

of a highly resilient economy. The long-term outlook points towards further acceleration of growth over the next few years and reflects a strong improvement in economic fundamentals that include:

- Benefits associated with stricter fiscal discipline, which have resulted in lower budget deficits, and which will eliminate government dissaving and pave the way for higher fixed investment spending.
- Improved domestic competitiveness in foreign markets. This has led to significant improvements in trade and current account balances.

Government's Micro-Economic Reform Strategy (MERS) identifies six key performance areas or objectives:

- economic growth
- employment
- small business development
- BEE
- competitiveness
- geographic spread of growth and development.

The strategy rests on three pillars:

- The first pillar consists of cross-cutting issues: HRD, infrastructure, access to finance, technology, and research and development (R&D).
- The second pillar comprises a set of actions to improve efficiency and lower costs in three input sectors: transport, telecommunications and energy. In addition, access to these sectors needs to be widened to include all South Africans.
- The third pillar consists of growth sectors that demonstrate a high potential for growth and employment, namely tourism, exports, agriculture, Information and Communications Technology and cultural industries.

Government has adopted an integrated way forward that comprises the following:

- fine-tuning the MERS
- continued managed liberalisation and infrastructure investment in key input sectors
- increased attention to the cross-cutting issues that underpin the strategy, including:
  - clarifying the role of individual departments in sectoral HRD strategies
  - adopting a research strategy and allocating the necessary resources to implement it effectively.

- establishing an integrated financing institution that is focused on BEE and small business
- an integrated approach to the planning and implementation of infrastructure investment by government
- developing and implementing an employment-creation framework
- strengthening and co-ordinating government products and services to promote key growth sectors
- an integrated strategy for small business development, emphasising co-ordination and refinement of existing initiatives, addressing access to finance and placing a greater focus on micro enterprises
- implementing three components of the BEE Strategy, namely an enhanced environment for BEE partnership programmes with the private sector, the establishment of the BEE Advisory Council and a review of government procurement
- incorporating a specific geographical dimension into the MERS, to tap the economic and human potential of all nine provinces by co-ordinating current strategies such as the Integrated Sustainable Rural Development Programme, Urban Renewal Programme, spatial development initiatives, industrial development zones and integrated development plans, as well as regional economic integration and the New Partnership for Africa's Development (NEPAD). (See chapter 7: *Economy.*)

South African Revenue Service (SARS)

In accordance with the SARS Act, 1997 (Act 34 of 1997), the service is an administratively autonomous (outside the Public Service, but within the public administration) organ of state.

It aims to provide an enhanced, transparent and client-orientated service to ensure optimum and equitable collection of revenue. Its main functions are to:

- collect and administer all national taxes, duties and levies

- collect revenue that may be imposed under any other legislation, as agreed upon between SARS and an organ of state or institution entitled to the revenue
- provide protection against the illegal importation and exportation of goods
- facilitate trade
- advise the Minister of Trade and Industry on matters concerning control over the import, export, manufacture, movement, and storage or use of certain goods.

Tax system

National Treasury is also responsible for advising the Minister of Finance on tax-policy issues that arise at local, provincial and national government level. In its policy-advice function to government, National Treasury must design tax instruments that can optimally fulfil their revenue-raising function, achieve economic and allocative functions, and strengthen redistributive and social-policy functions. This must be done in a manner that creates a basis for general political acceptability of the selected tax instruments. In designing tax policies, co-operation between National Treasury and SARS is of the utmost importance.

As of 2001, South Africa's source-based income tax system was replaced with a residence-based system. With effect from the years of assessment commencing on or after 1 January 2001, residents are (subject to certain exclusions) taxed on their worldwide income, irrespective of where their income was earned. Foreign taxes are credited against South African tax payable on foreign income. Foreign income and taxes are translated into the South African monetary unit, the Rand.

Capital gains tax was introduced on 1 October 2001. It forms part of the income tax system and includes capital gains made upon the disposal of assets in taxable income.

Value-added tax (VAT) is levied at a standard rate of 14% on all goods and services, subject to certain exemptions, exceptions, deductions and adjustments provided for in the VAT Act, 1991 (Act 89 of 1991), as amended.

Transfer duty, estate duty, stamp duty, marketable securities tax (MST), customs duty and excise duty are also levied by national government.

RSCs levy turnover and payroll taxes. However, these taxes are at fairly low rates and are scheduled for repeal with effect from 1 July 2006. Local governments levy rates on the value of fixed property, to finance the cost of municipal services.

International tax agreements for the avoidance of double taxation

International tax agreements are important for encouraging investment and trade flows between nations. By reaching agreement on the allocation of taxing rights between residence and source countries of international investors, double taxation agreements provide a solid platform for growth in international trade and investment, by providing a certain tax framework.

Agreements for mutual administrative assistance between customs administrations

These agreements cover all aspects of assistance, including the exchange of information, technical assistance, surveillance, investigations and visits by officials.

Sources of revenue

Income tax

Income tax is government's main source of income and is levied in terms of the Income Tax Act, 1962 (Act 58 of 1962).

In South Africa, income tax is levied on South African residents' worldwide income, with appropriate relief to avoid double taxation. Non-residents are taxed on their income from a South African source. Tax is levied on taxable income which, in essence, consists of gross income less allowable deductions as per the Act. The income tax threshold for individuals – the entry level for tax on salaried earnings – was raised by 8,6% to R35 000 in 2005/06.

Companies are taxed at a rate of 29% after a 1% reduction for 2005/06 to stimulate investment and job creation. In addition, secondary tax on companies is levied on companies at a rate of 12,5% on dividend distributions. A formula tax applies to gold-mining companies.

A number of administrative interventions as well as tax-relief measures were announced in the 2005 budget to regularise and stimulate growth for small businesses. Small business corporations (annual turnover limit was increased to R6 million) benefit from a revised graduated tax rate of 0% on the first R35 000 of taxable income and 10% up to R250 000 of taxable income; are eligible for accel-erated depreciation allowances; and can write off investments in manufacturing plant and equipment in the year in which it is incurred.

Additional measures to reduce the administrative and compliance burden on small business were announced in the budget.

Income tax returns are issued annually to regis-tered taxpayers after the end of each year of assessment. The year of assessment for individuals covers a period of 12 months, which generally com-mences on 1 March of a specific year and ends on the last day of February the following year. Companies are permitted to have a tax year ending on a date that coincides with their financial years.

Tax returns must be submitted to SARS within the specified period. A taxpayer may apply for extension for the rendition of a tax return.

People who owe SARS tax are charged interest at a rate as published in the *Government Gazette* that is linked to the rate specified in accordance with the PFMA, 1999. Persons who derive income from sources other than remuneration, e.g. trade, profes-sion or investments and companies, are required to make two provisional tax payments during the course of the tax year and may opt for a third 'top-ping-up' payment six months after the end of the tax year.

Value-added tax

VAT is levied on the supply of all goods and ser-vices rendered by registered vendors throughout the business cycle. It is government's second-biggest source of income.

Effectively, VAT is levied on the value added by an enterprise. As vendors levy and pay over the tax included in their prices, VAT is borne by the final consumer. VAT is also levied on the importation of goods and services into South Africa by any person. It is levied at the standard rate of 14%, but certain supplies are subject to the zero-rate or are exempt from VAT.

The prices of goods and services must be quoted/displayed on an inclusive basis, which means that VAT has to be included in all prices on products, price lists, advertisements and quotations.

Customs duty

South Africa is a signatory to the Southern African Customs Union (SACU) Agreement, together with Botswana, Lesotho, Namibia and Swaziland (BLNS countries). The five member countries of SACU apply the same customs and excise legislation, the same rates of customs and excise duties on imported and locally manufactured goods, and the same import duties on imported goods. The uniform application of tariffs and the harmonisation of procedures simplify trade within the SACU common customs area.

Import duties, including anti-dumping and coun-tervailing duties, are used as mechanisms to protect the local industry.

The renegotiated SACU Treaty is now in force and provides a new dispensation for calculating and affecting transfers based on customs, excise and a development component.

South Africa has entered into agreements on mutual assistance between customs administra-tions. These agreements cover all aspects of as-sistance, including the exchange of information, technical assistance, surveillance, investigations and visits by officials.

Efforts continue to improve the effectiveness of custom controls and trade facilitation.

Excise duty

Excise duty is levied on certain locally manufactured goods as well as their imported equivalents. This duty is levied as a specific duty on tobacco, liquor, and as an *ad valorem* duty on cosmetics, audio-visual equipment and motor cars.

Relief from excise duty is available where excis-able products are exported. In addition, relief is also available in respect of specific farming, forestry and certain manufacturing activities.

Excise duties are imposed both as a means to generate revenue for the fiscus, and to change consumer behaviour.

Transfer duty

Transfer duty is payable on the acquisition of property by individuals at progressive marginal rates between 0% and 8%.

Transfer duty on property acquired by a person other than an individual, e.g. a company or trust, is payable at a rate of 10%.

All transactions relating to a taxable supply of goods that are subject to VAT, are exempt from transfer duty.

Estate duty

For the purposes of estate duty, an estate consists of all property, including deemed property (e.g. life insurance policies, payments from pension funds, etc.) of the deceased, wherever situated. The estates of deceased non-residents consist of only their South African assets.

The duty, at a rate of 20%, is calculated on the dutiable amount of the estate. Certain admissible deductions from the total value of the estate are allowed.

Stamp duty

Stamp duty is levied on certain financial transactions.

Uncertified securities tax (UST)

UST is payable in respect of the issue and change in beneficial ownership of any securities that are transferable without a written instrument and are not evidenced by a certificate. It is levied at a rate of 0,25% and will eventually replace MST.

Skills-development levy

A skills-development levy was introduced on 1 April 2000. This is a compulsory levy scheme for the funding of education and training. SARS administers the collection thereof. The rate has been set at 1% of payroll as from 1 April 2001, and is payable by employers who are registered with SARS for employees' tax purposes, or employers who have an annual payroll in excess of R500 000.

Air passenger departure tax

A tax of R120 per fee-paying passenger departing on international flights, and R60 per passenger departing to the BLNS countries is payable.

Organisational performance

SARS collected R354,9 billion in taxes during the 2004/05 financial year, exceeding its revised target of R333,7 billion by almost R10 billion and its original target of R345,3 billion by R21 billion. The revenue haul will help trim South Africa's budget deficit for 2004/05 from 2,3% to 1,6% of gross domestic product (GDP).

Of the total, personal income tax yielded R1 110,7 billion; company tax yielded R70,6 billion; and VAT yielded R97,8 billion. SARS also collected R7,7 billion in transfer duties; R14 billion in excise duties; R13,1 billion in customs duties; and R18,8 billion in fuel levies.

e-Filing

e-Filing (*www.efiling.gov.za*) is a secure tax return and submission service offered by SARS that removes the risks and inconvenience of manual tax returns. Not only can returns be submitted via the Internet, but users can also make secure tax payments online.

The service offers web-based capture of individual returns as well as facilities for the submission of multiple returns through back-end interfaces.

There is also a facility to apply for tax directives, which can be obtained within 24 hours.

e-Filing in South Africa has been growing significantly since its inception and has been delivering real business benefits to both the taxpayer and SARS.

By 31 March 2005, the number of registrations grew to 290 000, while more than R2,5 billion was paid in electronic transfers between January and March 2005 alone.

The increased use of Information Technology is part of SARS' longer-term objective to move towards a paperless environment where the electronic transmission of information will lead to better service delivery and accuracy.

Filing Season

Filing Season is an extensive marketing and publicity venture to remind taxpayers of their responsibilities to submit their tax returns on time with the correct details, and to ensure that their returns are assessed and processed timeously.

Filing Season also seeks to reduce the number of requests from taxpayers for extensions, and aims to help customers complete their tax returns correctly. Thirty percent of tax returns received by SARS in the past were either incorrectly completed, partially completed, or lacked the necessary substantiating documentation. This caused unnecessary delays for both taxpayers and SARS.

Each year, SARS attempts to simplify complex tax returns for salaried individuals.

The 2005 *Filing Season* was a big success, with SARS receiving about 2,4 million returns before the July deadline, compared with 2,1 million in 2004.

Gambling and lotteries

The National Gambling Board regulates the gambling industry in South Africa by ensuring that the viability, sustainability and integrity of the industry are attained and maintained.

In June 2005, a new court facility, dedicated to resolving tax disputes in Gauteng, was officially opened.

The mandate of the tax court is to strive for the fair and just interpretation and application of tax law as stated in the Income Tax Act, 1962 (Act 58 of 1962).

The court will hear all cases where the tax involved exceeds R200 000 and where the matter could not be resolved in terms of the alternative dispute-resolution process between the South African Revenue Service and taxpayers.

The tax court's pivotal role is strengthened through an appeal procedure that could go to the High Court, the Supreme Court of Appeal and potentially, the Constitutional Court.

The board fulfils its mandate by:
- promoting uniform norms and standards that apply generally throughout South Africa, bringing about uniformity in legislation relating to gambling in the various provinces
- establishing and maintaining a national inspectorate
- monitoring the existence of any dominant or overconcentrated market share in the South African gambling industry
- advising the Minister of Finance and the provinces on gambling matters
- facilitating the resolution of disputes that may arise between the respective provinces regarding the regulation and control of gambling activities
- liaising with similar foreign international bodies.

The South African Advisory Council of Responsible Gambling was created to promote the culture of responsible gambling. It comprises regulators, civil society and the industry.

The National Gambling Act, 1996 (Act 33 of 1996), defines the regulatory framework of the industry. For instance, it limits the number of casinos that can be licensed to 40. There are provincial gambling boards in each of the nine provinces, which are responsible for issuing casino licences.

The National Gambling Act, 2004 (Act 7 of 2004), provides for the co-ordination of concurrent national and provincial legislative competence matters relating to casinos, racing, gambling and wagering, and for the continued regulation of those matters; certain uniform norms and standards applicable to national and provincial regulation; and licensing of certain gambling activities. It also provides for the retention of the National Gambling Board; establishment of the National Gambling Policy Council; and the repeal of the National Gambling Act, 1996.

In September 1999, the Minister of Trade and Industry signed the National Lottery Licence Agreement with Uthingo Management (Pty) Ltd, the official lottery operator. The National Lottery celebrated its fifth anniversary in March 2005.

During this period, the Lotto paid R3 billion to more than 6 100 beneficiary groups. Some 3 920 charities received R1,4 billion. Sport and recreation institutions and arts, culture and national heritage organisations received about R800 million. Disability Sport South Africa received R4 million of that amount. Miscellaneous donations amounted to R27 million.

Auditor-General

The Office of the Auditor-General (OAG) exists as a state institution to support democracy.

The auditor-general is mandated by Section 188 of the Constitution to audit and report on the accounts, financial statements and financial management of:
- all national and provincial state departments and administrations
- all municipalities
- any other institution or accounting entity required by national or provincial legislation to be audited by the auditor-general.

In addition to these duties, and subject to any legislation, the auditor-general may audit and report on the accounts, financial statements and financial management of:
- any institution funded from the national or a provincial revenue fund or by a municipality
- any institution that is authorised in terms of any law to receive money for a public purpose.

The OAG has a budget of R712,3 million and 1 598 employees. These are divided into various centres of excellence that provide auditing services; corporate services; and specialised audit work, namely performance, forensic auditing, computer auditing and technical support. The OAG also boasts an impressive international auditing complement.

The auditor-general must submit audit reports to any legislature that has a direct interest in the audit, and to any other authority prescribed by national legislation. All reports must be made public.

Public-sector auditing involves the investigation and evaluation of government and related institutions regarding financial-management practices, performance and compliance with legal requirements.

Financial sector

South African Reserve Bank

The Reserve Bank and the Ministry of Finance form the monetary authority in South Africa. The Reserve Bank has been given a significant degree of autonomy in terms of the Constitution and must perform its functions independently. However, the Reserve Bank must hold regular consultations with the Minister of Finance. Its management, powers and functions are governed by the South African Reserve Bank Act, 1989 (Act 90 of 1989).

The Reserve Bank formulates and implements monetary policy and regulates the supply of money by influencing its cost. Monetary policy is guided by the objectives of the Reserve Bank, which are formulated to ensure financial stability. Consistent combating of inflation is the cornerstone of the bank's policy. A formal inflation-targeting monetary-policy framework has been adopted since 2000.

Monetary policy is set by the bank's Monetary Policy Committee (MPC). The committee, consisting of the Reserve Bank's governors and other senior officials, usually meets once a quarter, after which the bank issues a statement indicating its assessment of the economy and policy changes, if any.

The Reserve Bank is responsible for:
- assisting government in formulating and implementing macro-economic policy
- formulating and implementing monetary policy to achieve its primary goal in the interest of the community it serves
- ensuring that the South African money and banking system as a whole is sound, meets the

In January 2005, the Minister of Finance, Mr Trevor Manuel, announced that 12 20-foot containers of clothing and footwear would be donated by the South African Government to victims of the tsunami in south-east Asia.

The donated goods were proceeds of smuggling seizures undertaken by the South African Revenue Service.

requirements of the community and keeps abreast of international finance developments
- informing the South African community and all interested parties abroad about monetary policy, and the South African economic situation in general.

The Reserve Bank is managed by a board of 14 directors, seven of whom are elected by the shareholders of the bank and represent commerce, finance, industry and agriculture. The President of South Africa appoints the governor, three deputy governors and three directors.

The Reserve Bank acts as the central bank of South Africa and as a banker to other banking institutions. It provides accommodation to banks and is the custodian of the statutory cash reserves that all registered banks are required to maintain. It also provides facilities for the clearing and settlement of interbank obligations.

The main instrument in managing liquidity in the money market is the repurchase transactions (repo) rate, the price at which the central bank lends cash to the banking system. The repo rate has become the most important indicator for short-term interest rates.

The repurchase agreements entered into between the Reserve Bank and other banks are conducted on the basis of an outright buy-and-sell transaction, with a full transfer of ownership of the underlying assets. The system also provides for a marginal lending facility, which replaces the previous discount window. This facility is available to banks at their initiative to bridge overnight liquidity needs.

The marginal lending facility forms an integrated part of the South African Multiple Option Settlement (SAMOS) System, which came into operation in March 1998.

This enables banks to electronically make payments to, and receive payments from, the Reserve Bank, through their settlement accounts held in the books of the Reserve Bank. Daily settlements of interbank exposures are effected through the SAMOS System.

Payments through the system can only be made if a bank has sufficient funds in its settlement account. Such funds can be obtained through interbank transfers, repurchase transactions, other types of liquidity-creating instruments of the Reserve Bank, or the marginal lending facility. The SAMOS System, however, allows banks to receive funds obtained in the interbank market directly in their settlement accounts in the Reserve Bank's books.

The Reserve Bank uses various instruments to achieve its objectives. These include changes in the repo-rate marginal-lending facility; open-market transactions, including selling its own debentures; changes in requirements with regard to cash reserves of banking institutions; and controlling liquidity in the money market through repurchase transactions.

The bank undertakes national and international transactions on behalf of the State, and acts for government in transactions with the International Monetary Fund (IMF).

The Reserve Bank is the custodian of the greater part of South Africa's gold and other foreign-exchange reserves.

The Reserve Bank issues banknotes (printed by the South African Bank Note Company, a wholly owned subsidiary of the Reserve Bank) and controls the South African Mint Company.

Monetary policy

Growth in broad money supply (M3) exceeded 11% throughout 2004, registering the highest value for the year at 14,9% in October. The accumulation of government deposits late in 2004 and early in 2005, in preparation for sizeable coupon interest

In December 2004, the Communication Division of the South African Revenue Service won the Government Communicator of the Year Award.

It conceptualised and implemented an effective strategy for the *2004 Filing Season*, which focused on improved operational efficiency in reducing the tax gap, and improved service delivery.

The annual awards are co-ordinated by the Government Communication and Information System.

and capital redemption payments on government bonds at the end of February 2005, contributed to the slowdown in M3 growth, as government deposists are not included in M3.

Banks' loans and advances to the domestic private sector accelerated from 9,9% at the beginning of 2004 to 17,6% in February 2005. Throughout 2004 and early in 2005, the growth in total loans and advances was driven mainly by brisk demand for asset-backed credit and a rebound in the corporate sector's use of bank-intermediated funding.

Growth in M3 and banks' total loan and advances were consistent with firm increases in nominal income, expenditure and wealth.

On 12 August 2004, the Reserve Bank's MPC announced a reduction in the repo rate of 50 basis points to 7,50%. However, based on a more neutral assessment of inflationary pressures and risks, the MPC left the repurchase rate unchanged at 7,5% at the October and December 2004, and February 2005, meetings. On 14 April 2005, the repo rate dropped to 7%.

Financial Services Board (FSB)

The FSB is an independent statutory body financed by the financial services industry itself.

The FSB supervises the exercise of control over such institutions and services, in terms of several parliamentary Acts that entrust regulatory functions to registrars of long-term insurance, short-term insurance, friendly societies, pension funds, collective investment schemes, financial services providers, exchanges and financial markets. These

Estimates of revenue before tax proposals, 2004/05

R million	2004/05 Revised estimate	2005/06 Before tax proposals	% change
Taxes on income and profits	189 900	211 350	11,3
Personal income tax	110 950	124 000	11,8
Company tax	65 450	72 100	10,2
Secondary tax on companies	7 600	8 700	14,5
Tax on retirement funds	4 500	4 900	8,9
Other	1 400	1 650	17,9
Taxes on payroll and workforce	4 600	5 000	8,7
Taxes on property	8 928	10 270	15,0
Domestic taxes on goods and services	129 033	141 085	9,3
Value-added tax	95 500	106 250	11,3
Excise duties	14 075	14 400	2.3
Levies on fuel	18 800	19 700	4,8
Other	658	735	11,7
Taxes on international trade and transactions	11 650	13 200	13,3
Stamp duties and fees	1 150	1 250	8,7
Total tax revenue	**345 261**	**382 155**	**10,7**
Department revenue	5 493	8 502	54,8
Transactions in assets and liabilities	533	646	21,1
Less: SACU payments	-13,328	-12 053	-9,6
Main budget revenue	**337 960**	**379 250**	**12,2%**

Source: *Budget Review 2005*

functions converge in the office of the executive officer, acting with the other members of the executive and heads of the various departments of the FSB's administrative infrastructure.

The FSB promotes programmes and initiatives by financial institutions and bodies representing the financial-services industry to inform and educate users of financial products and services. It also acts in an advisory capacity to the Minister of Finance.

Included in such functions is regulatory control over central securities depositories and depository institutions responsible for the safe custody of securities.

The FSB is also responsible for the financial supervision of the Road Accident Fund.

Excluded from the FSB's responsibilities are some areas involving listing requirements or public issues, take-overs and mergers.

The Securities Services Act, 2004 introduces stricter penalties of up to R50 million and/or 10 years' imprisonment for various forms of market abuse.

The executive officer is provided with an armoury of regulatory sanctions, including the cancellation of authorisation to supply financial services.

The executive officer has formal powers of investigation to which criminal sanctions attach in the event of obstruction. The executive officer can, in certain circumstances, also petition for the winding up of, or placing under judicial management or curatorship, certain financial institutions such as insurers and pension funds.

These powers of intervention do not, however, take the risk out of an investment made at a financial institution. All investments carry some degree of risk, whether relating to business or general economic conditions.

In July 2005, Barclays, the third-biggest British bank, concluded a multimillion rand deal for 56,1% control of the Amalgamated Banks of South Africa.
It was the biggest investment yet made in post-apartheid South Africa.

The Inspection of Financial Institutions Act, 1998 (Act 80 of 1998), allows the FSB to obtain warrants for searching and questioning third parties who might have information about unregistered financial institutions, such as those providing insurance or investment services.

The FSB is assisted by an advisory board on financial markets, and advisory committees on financial services providers, long- and short-term insurance, pension funds and collective investment schemes. The Financial Services Consumer Advisory Panel was established to advise the FSB and Registrar of Banks on consumer-protection issues falling within the regulators' jurisdiction.

The FSB maintains a close relationship with all existing industry associations. It liaises with overseas regulatory organisations, and is a member of the International Organisation of Security Commissions, the International Association of Insurance Supervisors, the African Association of Insurance Supervisors and the International Network of Pension Regulators and Supervisors.

On the domestic scene, it liaises with bodies such as the Public Accountants and Auditors, Consumer Affairs Committee and various government departments, as well as with prosecuting authorities such as the South African Police Service, the Directorate of Special Operations, and the National Director of Public Prosecutions.

The banking industry

At the end of December 2004, 35 banks, including 15 branches of foreign banks and two mutual banks, were registered with the Office of the Registrar of Banks. Furthermore, 45 foreign banks had authorised representative offices in South Africa. By the end of December 2004, the banking institutions collectively employed 116 940 workers.

Four major banks dominate the South African banking sector, namely Amalgamated Banks of South Africa (Absa) Bank Limited, the Standard Bank of South Africa Limited, FirstRand Bank Limited and Nedbank Limited. These banks maintain extensive branch networks across all nine provinces and by the end of December 2004 constituted 83,7% of the total assets (R1 498,1 billion) of the banking sector.

The major banks offer a wide range of services to both individual and corporate customers. One-stop relationship banking, instead of isolated services, has gained importance. Nevertheless, several banks specialise in providing services in merchant banking, securities underwriting or other niche areas.

Online banking accounts reached the one-million mark in South Africa for the first time at the end of 2003. According to the World Wide Worx research report, *Online Banking in South Africa 2004,* the number of online bank accounts in South Africa grew by 28% in 2003. The number of online bank accounts reached 1,04 million and was expected to increase by more than 30% in 2004.

Industry-wide net income after tax increased to 1,2% of total assets in 2003. As a percentage of equity, industry-wide net income after tax increased from 11,2% in 2003 to 14,7% in 2004. By the end of 2004, industry-wide net income before taxation had begun to increase to R22,5 billion, compared with R16,4 billion in 2003.

The change in focus of the regulatory authorities, from direct control to deregulation, has been accompanied by an emphasis on proper capitalisation, sound risk-management procedures and greater disclosure. South Africa adheres to the capital-adequacy guidelines for banks issued by the Basel Committee on Banking Supervision, under the auspices of the Bank of International Settlements.

In South Africa, the requirement to maintain capital equal to the full ratio of 10% of risk-weighted assets became effective in October 2001. By the end of 2004, the banking sector as a whole had a ratio of capital-to-risk weighted assets of 13,5%.

Many demands are now being made on South African banking institutions to extend their activities to accommodate the banking needs of the under-privileged, and to provide more funds for housing, export financing, agriculture and small-business development. Several initiatives are underway to develop appropriate structures to provide all sectors of South Africa's populations with access to finance.

The regulations relating to banks, which form part of South Africa's banking legislation, were revised during 2002, ensuring South Africa's continued adherence to best practice. The Bank Supervision Department envisages amending the regulatory framework to allow for the establishment of different classes of banking institutions, such as second-tier and third-tier banks.

A project to consider the establishment of narrow and core banks was initiated during 2002/03. The objective is to increase competition in the banking sector, while also creating greater access to basic banking services, such as savings accounts and housing and educational loans to the under- and unbanked.

The department proposes that such banks be subject to lower-entry criteria, but that their business scope be limited.

To safeguard the stability of the banking system, it is envisaged that narrow and core banks be subject to strict conditions, such as being permitted to take retail deposits, but not to trade or invest in, for example, derivatives. Draft legislation on this was expected in 2005.

The microlending industry

The Micro Finance Regulatory Council (MFRC) was established in 1999. Over the years, the MFRC has made good progress with formalising and regulating the microlending industry. More than 1 400 entities,

The 2005 Protea coin series depicts Chief Albert Luthuli, the first South African to be awarded the Nobel Peace Prize.

The Albert Luthuli coins were launched shortly after the 50th anniversary of the Freedom Charter in June 2005.

On 22 May 2005, the South African Mint minted gold coins on an old fly press on the ancient site of a royal fortress on the Mapungubwe Hill, in the Mapungubwe National Park situated in Limpopo.

The South African Mint's 2005 R2 gold coin series depicted South Africa's world heritage sites.

representing more than 7 000 branches, are registered with the MFRC.

A major problem for the MFRC has been the large number of unregistered lenders and the problems associated therewith. In brief, registered lenders have to comply with the rules of the MFRC, whereas unregistered lenders fall outside the ambit of the MFRC's rules.

The situation, however, improved when the Department of Trade and Industry implemented an amendment to the Usury Act, 1968 (Act 73 of 1968), whereby direct inspection powers were created for the MFRC. The amendment extended the MFRC's mandate to include unregistered microlenders in its regulation process. A number of inspections have been undertaken under this mandate, and there has been a fair level of success in obtaining successful prosecutions, although there appears to be a considerable delay between the completion of investigations and the conclusion of legal prosecutions.

Microlenders are placing an increasing number of credit records onto the National Loan Register (NLR). The MFRC is emphasising measures to combat reckless lending and has formulated a rule compelling all registered lenders to perform affordability assessments. It is believed that these measures will play an important role in curbing overindebtedness, while assisting credit grantors with improving their credit quality and decreasing their credit risk.

As a result of ongoing attention to consumer education and awareness, implementation of measures, such as the NLR, to improve lending practices and consistent disciplinary action against lenders found not to comply with rules and regulations, market conduct and corporate governance in the microlending sector, appear to have improved substantially.

On 30 November 2004, the Microlenders Association was reintroduced as Micro Finance South Africa, the industry's newly branded member association.

Insurance companies

Short-term (non-life) insurance is concerned primarily with risk assessment. The contracts usually run from year to year and can be cancelled by either party. These contracts apply to engineering, guarantee, liability, motor business, accident and health, property, transportation, and miscellaneous insurance. As at 31 March 2004, 97 short-term insurers were registered. The total gross premiums written for 2003 (unaudited figures) amounted to R35,3 billion, while total assets amounted to R39,3 billion (excluding the South African Special Risks Insurance Association Limited).

In essence, long-term insurance consists of life, assistance, sinking fund, health, and disability insurance. Long-term insurance and pension and provident funds are concerned with maximising investment results. Life insurance is dominant. As at 31 March 2004, 78 long-term insurers were registered. The total net premiums received and outstanding for 2003 (unaudited figures) amounted to R156,8 billion, while total assets amounted to R822,1 billion.

The Financial Advisory and Intermediary Services Act, 2002 (Act 37 of 2002), contains many of the provisions incorporated in the policyholder protection rules. In 2004, the FSB was redrafting these rules to ensure that there was no duplication of provisions.

Other financial institutions

Development Bank of Southern Africa (DBSA)

The primary role of the DBSA in terms of the DBSA Act, 1997 (Act 13 of 1997), is to promote economic development and growth, HRD and institutional capacity-building. This is achieved by mobilising financial and other resources from the national and international, private and public sectors for sustainable development projects and programmes. The bank operates in South Africa, in the other Southern African Development Community (SADC) countries, and increasingly as a development agent and knowledge partner in the wider region of Africa south of the Sahara.

Its mandate focuses on infrastructure (economic, social and institutional) both through loans of its own funds and by acting as a catalyst for investments in partnership with the private sector and other development finance institutions.

The bank plays the diversified roles of adviser and partner; acting as a knowledge bank, facilitator and catalyst; and often serving as a development agent to bridge institutional and execution gaps. It is actively involved in project appraisal, evaluation and management, provides development statistics and information, and undertakes policy and sector analysis.

Funding

The DBSA's capital and reserves at 31 March 2004 stood at R11,1 billion. The bank's financial resources are made up of the share capital contribution of National Treasury, borrowings in the financial markets, repayments on loans granted by it, and internally generated funds. In addition to these resources, the bank mobilises loan capital from other international sources. It has established lines of credit with reputable and highly rated international institutions such as the African Development Bank and the European Investment Bank (EIB). It also raises funds from bilateral sources such as the *German Kreditanstalt für Wiederaufbau*, the Japanese Overseas Economic Co-operation Fund and *Agence Française de Développement*.

Strategic direction

The DBSA has adopted a set of stretch targets over a 10-year period to give practical effect to its commitment to the strategic development agenda of South Africa, SADC, NEPAD and the wider international community (the millennium development goals).

The DBSA's institutional vision and strategic plan, Vision 2014, which is also guided by the bank's mandate, focuses on the following key goals:
- reducing poverty by half through economic development, comprehensive social security, land reform and improved household and community assets
- reducing unemployment by half through new jobs, skills development, assistance to small businesses, opportunities for self-employment and sustainable community livelihoods

- massively reducing the incidence of tuberculosis, diabetes, malnutrition and maternal deaths; turning the tide against HIV and AIDS; striving to eliminate malaria throughout the region; improving services to achieve a better national health profile; and reducing preventable causes of death
- positioning South Africa strategically as an effective force in global relations, with vibrant and balanced trade with countries of both the South and the North
- providing the skills required by the economy, building capacity and providing resources across society to encourage self-employment, with an education system that is geared for productive work, good citizenship and a caring society.

The DBSA estimates the impact of its funding operations using economic modelling techniques. According to these, the level of DBSA loan approvals in South Africa and the SADC is projected to grow to R6 billion a year by 2013/14. Between 2004/05 and 2013/14, this in turn should have the effect of creating a total of 127 000 jobs in South Africa, connecting 2,4 million households to one or more basic service, and contributing R22,2 billion to the local economy. To this end, it plans to invest R45,6 billion (loans and equity finance) in infrastructure development and well over R1 billion in technical assistance, capacity-building grants and knowledge development/networking.

Strategic initiatives

In line with its goal of accelerating delivery and growing the economy, especially in historically neglected and poor localities, the DBSA has introduced the Targeted Infrastructure Programme – a multi-year facility of special concessional finance dedicated to poverty-reducing infrastructure services in resource-poor areas. Priority will be given to eradicating backlogs in access to basic water and electricity.

The bank has strengthened and replenished the DBSA Development Fund, a dedicated capacity-building fund recently established as a section 21 company, to enhance and focus the bank's grant and technical support of local capacity-building in several areas, especially feasibility studies, project and programme development, systems design/development and training.

It is also providing concerted financial and institutional support to Project Consolidate, a major local public-sector capacity-building initiative established by government and spearheaded by the Department of Provincial and Local Government. (See chapter 12: *Government system*.)

The bank is in the final stages of launching the Vulindlela Academy, a specialised institutional training facility dedicated to the creation and upgrading of skills required for the economy, in particular infrastructural delivery and improved productivity and sustainability.

The DBSA has also positioned itself to provide strategic and financial support to the South Africa Football Association in its planning and co-ordination of infrastructure development around South Africa's hosting of the 2010 Soccer World Cup.

The bank will continue to serve as a development agent and conduit for a range of national, regional and global partners to bridge institutional and execution gaps. It supports partners such as NEPAD, the World Bank, UN agencies, and the Global Alliance for Improved Nutrition, in addition to government departments.

Land and Agricultural Development Bank (Land Bank)

The Land Bank operates as a development-finance institution within the agricultural and agribusiness sectors, and is regulated by the Land and Agricultural Development Bank Act, 2002 (Act 15 of 2002). The Land Bank provides a range of financing products to a broad spectrum of clients within the agricultural industry. Financing products include wholesale and retail financing to commercial and developing farmers, co-operatives and other agriculture-related businesses.

The Land Bank's objectives are defined within its mandate, which requires that it should achieve:
- growth in the commercial market
- growth in the development market
- business efficiency

- service delivery
- resource management
- sustainability.

(See chapter 4: *Agriculture*.)

Despite operating in a difficult business environment influenced by drought, delayed rains, a strong rand and a lower repo rate, the bank achieved a net profit of R247 million in the 2003/04 financial year, compared with a R1,429-billion loss in the previous reporting year.

The number of loans granted by the bank rose by 14% from 89 967 to 102 527. The development loan book grew by 5,3% to R1 096 billion. Arrears as a percentage of the loan book dropped by 35,4% from 9,6% to 6,2%. For the same period, the total provisions as a percentage of the loan book also declined by 27% from 9,4% to 7,4%. Non-interest income rose 330% from R39 million to R168 million.

Collective investment schemes

The Unit Trusts Control Act, 1981 (Act 54 of 1981), and the Participation Bond Act, 1981 (Act 55 of 1981), which regulated unit trust schemes and participation bond schemes, were replaced on 3 March 2003 by the Collective Investment Schemes Control Act, 2003 (Act 45 of 2003), which regulates all these schemes under the title of collective investment schemes. The structures of these schemes remained basically the same as before, although there is scope for other types of structures.

Collective investment schemes in securities

These open-ended schemes provide for a number of different types of portfolios in the equity, interest-bearing and money markets for those investors who may not have the time, money or expertise to invest successfully in these markets on their own.

The prices of participatory interests (previously known as units) are calculated at net asset value and published daily. Managers create participatory interests for sale to the public as and when the demand arises. Managers may also cancel participatory interests when investors sell their holdings of participatory interests to the manager. The manager is obliged by law to buy back any participatory interests offered to it, at a price determined within 24 hours of receiving a valid notice of a buy-back from an investor.

Various collective investment schemes in South Africa offer similar ranges of investment plans, varying mainly as to the mimimum amounts accepted for investment and certain charges. There are two types of investment plans, namely the open-account or lump-sum plan, and the regular savings plan, which caters for regular monthly investments.

Collective investment schemes in property

Previously known as property unit trusts, these schemes invest mainly in the shares of property-owning companies, direct property and certain other and foreign assets. Their issued participatory interests are listed on the JSE Limited (JSE). As at December 2003, there were seven schemes with an equal number of portfolios, with 2 443 billion participatory interests in issue, of which the market value amounted to R6,756 billion.

Collective investment schemes in participation bonds

Formerly called participation bond schemes, several of these schemes are being wound down. According to the Reserve Bank, the amount invested with these schemes was R3,820 billion as at 31 December 2003. However, by June 2003, only seven of these schemes had invested funds from the general public.

Foreign collective investment schemes

Since 1998, foreign collective investment schemes have been allowed to market their products in South Africa, provided they obtain approval from the FSB.

Individual investors utilising their foreign exposure are the primary investors. At the end of 2003, 78 foreign schemes administering 433 different portfolios had obtained approval to market their products in South Africa. The amount accepted from South African investors amounted to R45,8 billion at the end of 2003.

Stokvels

Stokvels are co-operative rotating saving schemes that mobilise funds among mostly black communities for a variety of purposes. Rotating saving schemes similar to stokvels are also found in countries such as South Korea, Jamaica, Egypt and Japan. An estimated one million stokvels operate in South Africa.

Financial intermediaries and advisers

In accordance with the Financial Advisory and Intermediary Services Act, 2002, the Advisory Committee on Financial Services Providers, established by the Act, has focused its attention on finalising numerous pieces of necessary subordinate legislation (including the codes of conduct for different categories of financial services advisers).

As of 30 September 2004, financial advisory and intermediary entities are no longer able to conduct their business activities without being in possession of a licence issued by the FSB. The FSB was assisted by 12 representative-recognised bodies for the purpose of processing licence applications.

The Office of the Ombudsman for Financial Services Providers was empowered to adjudicate complaints by consumers relating to financial advice and intermediary services from 1 October 2004, when the Act came into full operation.

By the end of February 2005, the FSB had recorded the submission of about 14 500 licence applications in terms of the Financial Advisory and Intermediary Services Act, 2002. Of these, 7 500 applications had been processed fully, considered, and, where successful, licences issued and dispatched to applicants.

Retirement funds and friendly societies

As at 31 December 2003, the FSB supervised 13 752 registered retirement funds and 180 registered friendly societies. These funds exclude the official State funds, Transnet, Telkom and some bargaining-council funds, none of which are registered in terms of the Pension Funds Act, 1956 (Act 24 of 1956).

The total membership of all pension funds at the end of 2002 was 9 779 884, of which 8 567 479 were active members, and 1 212 405 were pensioners, deferred pensioners and dependants. These figures do not reflect the total number of individuals who were members of funds, as some were members of more than one fund.

The total contributions received decreased by 0,9% from R61,097 billion in 2001 to R60,552 billion in 2002. Total contributions to the State, Transnet, Telkom and Post Office funds decreased by 1,4%, while total contributions to self-administered, underwritten and industrial funds in the private sector decreased by 0,7%.

Benefits paid decreased from R111,206 billion in 2001 to R72,492 billion in 2002. Amounts paid in respect of pensions, lump sums on retirement or death and resignations were included.

Total assets of the retirement-fund industry in South Africa increased by 3,7%, from R836 billion in 2001 to R867 billion in 2002.

The net assets of self-administered funds decreased by 4,9% from R370 billion in 2001 to R352 billion in 2002.

Financial markets

Primary capital-market activity

Government bonds
For the 2004/05 fiscal year, total government bond issuance in the primary market amounted to R53,1 billion. Over the same period, a total of R26,3 billion worth of bonds matured, bringing the net financing requirement in the domestic bond market to R26,8 billion.

This is a slight increase from the 2003/04 fiscal year, when total issuance amounted to R51,4 billion, while R26,6 billion was redeemed and net issuance amounted to R24,8 billion. Of the total amount of bonds issued, almost 80% comprised vanilla bonds, with inflation-linked bonds adding about 17% and the remainder being floating rate notes.

The Reserve Bank conducts weekly nominal bond auctions on behalf of National Treasury. For the 2004/05 fiscal year, an average of R850 million was issued weekly, compared with an average weekly issuance of R600 million in 2003/04.

The conditions for issuances in the fixed income market were conducive not only locally, but also globally and the South African Government successfully issued a 10-year US$1,0 billion (R6,5 billion) denominated bond in May 2004 at a spread of 195 basis points over the benchmark United States (US) Treasury Bond.

In addition, R3,2 billion was drawn on the foreign export credit facilities. Foreign bonds redeemed amounted to an equivalent of R5,3 billion, bringing net foreign bond issuance to R4,5 billion. This compares with gross foreign bond issuance of R14 billion in 2003/04, with redemptions totalling about R13 billion. For the 2005/06 fiscal year, no foreign bonds were expected to be issued.

Two new fixed income bonds were launched in 2004/05, namely the R203 and R204 bonds. The R203 bond was launched in May 2004 and carries a coupon of 8,25%, maturing in 2017. By February 2005, R12,3 billion had been issued. The R204 bond was launched in August 2004, carrying a coupon of 8% and maturing in 2018. Over R6 billion was raised via the R204 bond during the 2004/05 fiscal year.

In May 2004, government also launched the RSA government retail bonds, with maturities of two, three and five years. By February 2005, government had raised a total of R1,25 billion through these bonds.

Government's total loan debt increased from R389,3 billion in 2003/04 to R428,1 billion in 2004/05. However, total gross loan debt as a percentage of GDP remained steady at 35,7%.

Non-government bond issuance
In 2004, new bond issuance in the corporate sector amounted to R14,23 billion, compared with R15,34 billion issued in 2003. This figure, however, excludes the total amount of funds raised through other vehicles such as securitisation and private placements. Total issuance related to securitisation amounted to R7,5 billion, bringing total issuance to R29,5 billion by the end of January 2005. Although there was a relatively high volume of issuance in the

securitisation market in 2004, it was 25% less than the R9,9 billion recorded in 2003. Nonetheless, issuance in the non-government sector, whether through corporate bonds, securitisations or private placements, has grown significantly in the past few years. This can be attributed to a diversification of instruments utilised, declining interest rates, narrowing credit spreads indicating investor risk tolerance amid the search for yield, as well as credit upgrades for a number of corporate institutions. The South African corporate market is expected to grow as new asset classes emerge and new issuers continue to enter the market.

Eurorand bonds

Following four years of negative net issuance, the Eurorand bond market expanded in 2004. Improved liquidity conditions in the global financial markets led to improvements in eurorand bond market activities. Gross issuance increased to R6,8 billion in 2004 – a 265% increase compared with the R1,9 billion issued in 2003 and higher than the average of about R4 billion over the past four years. In 2004, R3,6 billion worth of eurorand bonds matured, resulting in a net issuance of R3,1 billion.

The renewed interest in this market can also be attributed to the positive sentiment towards the Rand and an overall positive performance in global fixed income markets in 2004. In the first quarter of 2005, gross issuance amounted to R2,2 billion, while R1,3 billion matured, bringing net issuance to R875 million.

The EIB continued to dominate issuance in the Eurorand bond market, comprising almost 65% of total issuance during 2004. Other issuers were *Rabobank Nederland* (13%) and *Landsman Baden-Wuertemburg* (13%), while *Kredit Wiederauf* and the Republic of Austria issued about 5% and 4%, respectively. The type of credit issued remained predominantly AAA-rated, and the maturity structure changed to longer-dated issues. The 2010 and 2013 bonds account for 56% of total eurorand bond issuance, while the rest is concentrated in bonds maturing in five years or less.

The spreads and yields at which these bonds were issued declined during 2004, with some bonds even issued at spreads below comparable South African benchmark government bonds. The 2013 bond, for example, was tapped by the EIB at a yield of 8,95% in January 2004, and was tapped again in November 2004 at a yield of 8,22%. While coupon rates were as high as 11% in 2003, they declined to between 10% and 8% during 2004.

Secondary capital-market activity

Domestic bonds

South African bond yields declined considerably between May 2004 and February 2005. The yields on government bonds declined to historically low levels, with the yields on two-year R194, five-year R153 and 20-year R186 government bonds declining to 7,22%, 7,40% and 6,98%, respectively, by 28 February 2005.

Factors that contributed to this decline in local yields include the firmer Rand-Dollar exchange rate, reductions in the repo rate, low yields in the developed countries, and a ratings upgrade by Moody's in January 2005. In addition, the inflation outlook has remained promising, with the Consumer Price Index excluding mortgage costs (CPIX) moving to historically low levels, and not expected to breach the upper band of the Reserve Bank's 3% to 6% guideline range over the forecast period.

Improved investor sentiment towards the country's political and economic policies also contributed to the decline in bond yields, as reflected by non-resident interest in the local bond market. After being net sellers of South African bonds to the value of R8,1 billion in 2003, foreigners were net purchasers of bonds to the value of R450 million in 2004.

During March 2005, bond yields increased by an average of 80 basis points, in reaction to external factors, such as increasing US Treasury yields as well as the potential for more rapid US interest rate rises, which affected emerging market debt in general. At the time, investors also did not expect further decreases in the Reserve Bank's repo rate. However, in April 2005, the Reserve Bank cut the repo rate by a further 50 basis points to 7%, and bond yields declined further. For the first quarter of the year, non-residents were net sellers of South African bonds to the value of R1,4 billion. However, during the first half of April 2005, R5,6 billion was bought on a net basis.

Turnover in the domestic bond market declined from about R12 trillion in 2002 to R11 trillion in 2003 and R8 trillion in 2004. This can probably be attributed to declining interest rates, which motivated a buy-and-hold strategy among many investors.

Money-market activity

The South African money market is an over-the-counter market in which a fairly large number of banks and other institutions actively participate. The Reserve Bank implements its monetary policy in terms of a system based on creating a shortage in the money market.

The bank refinances this shortage through weekly repurchase transactions with seven-day maturities at its policy rate, the repo rate. Thus, the bank influences other market interest rates. The daily liquidity requirement in the money market was maintained close to R13 billion throughout the 2004/05 financial year.

The Reserve Bank used mainly four types of open-market operations to drain surplus liquidity from the money market, namely issuing Reserve Bank debentures, conducting longer-term reverse repo transactions, foreign exchange swaps and outright sales/switches of government bonds. Furthermore, with the redemption of the R151 bond and coupon payments made to the Reserve Bank on various bonds during February 2005, the bank was able to permanently drain R10,1 billion worth of liquidity from the market.

The Reserve Bank changed its repo rate once during the 2004 financial year, cutting the repo rate by 50 basis points to a level of 7,5% in August 2004, and money-market rates decreased accordingly. In April 2005, the repo rate was cut again by 50 basis points, justified by a favourable inflation outlook, as the bank expected CPIX to remain within target range over the forecast period.

Equity market

The total value of equity capital raised by companies

listed on the JSE during 2003 was R22,7 billion. It subsequently increased to R41,8 billion in 2004 and R8,3 billion was raised during the first quarter of 2005. The number of new listings doubled in 2004, from eight to 16, while the number of delistings declined from 54 in 2003 to 39 in 2004. Two new listings were recorded in the first quarter of 2005. Some 873 securities were listed on the JSE at the end of 2004 compared with 745 at the end of 2003, increasing to 921 in the first quarter of 2005.

Domestic share prices, as measured by the all-share index (Alsi), increased to new highs during 2004 and the first quarter of 2005. Although the Alsi declined by about 13% from March 2004 to mid-May 2004, the decline was reversed as the Alsi rose by 40,6% to a new high of 13 761 on 17 March 2005. The Alsi rose by almost 32% from the beginning of 2004 until the end of March 2005.

The best performing index during 2004 was the banking index, followed by the financial index and the industrial index, which improved by 62,3%, 45,9% and 42,6%, respectively. The improvement in the domestic equity market occurred despite an appreciation in the exchange rate of the Rand.

Factors that influenced the market during this period were the low interest rate environment, positive economic fundamentals, prudent fiscal and monetary policies, high commodity prices, expectations of continued higher corporate earnings and strong demand from foreign and local investors.

The country's improved ratings outlook and upgrade also added to the positive sentiment within the market, combined with Fitch's upgrading of three local banks. The acquisition of a majority stake in Absa by the United Kingdom's Barclays Bank Plc also added to the improvement in the banking index. Various BEE transactions were also reported during 2004, which were well received by the market.

In contrast with the overall market, the gold index declined by 38,7% and the resources index by 7,2% during 2004. The main reason for the decline in the gold index was the strong Rand, which outweighed the impact of higher commodity prices. Other factors that played a role in the decline of both these indices were the unresolved Harmony/Gold Fields take-over bid, uncertainty about the growth in demand from China, and, to a lesser extent, the downgrading of resource stocks by some equity analysts.

Turnover on the JSE, as measured in terms of the value of shares traded, reached a level of R752 billion in 2003, and increased to a record R1 031 billion in 2004. Liquidity, as measured by turnover as a percentage of market capitalisation, increased from 35% in 2003 to 37% in 2004, with market capitalisation increasing from R1 787,2 billion to R2 566,4 billion over the same period. Market capitalisation in US dollar terms increased almost 70% from US$260,7 billion in 2003 to US$442,5 billion in 2004.

According to the World Federation of Exchanges, South Africa was in 16th position of the world league at the end of February 2005. Foreigners bought a net amount of R31,8 billion worth of equities during 2004 and increased their holdings of domestic equities by a net amount of R9,2 billion during the first quarter of 2005.

The JSE's new interest-rate exchange, Yield-X, commenced trading on 28 February 2005. This interest-rate exchange is the JSE's fourth electronic clearing and settlement platform, alongside equities, financial futures and agricultural products. Yield-X aims to open up the interest-rate market to new players and new products, encouraging liquidity and market diversification.

In addition, Yield-X seeks to ensure proper price discovery for interest-rate products in South Africa. At the heart of the new exchange is an anonymous central order book, allowing for trading via a single platform with automated trade matching and guaranteed settlement. The JSE expects Yield-X to emulate the success of the JSE equities and futures trading systems over time, establishing a sophisticated interest rate derivatives market for the country.

A major benefit of Yield-X will be the elimination of bilateral counter-party risk. The JSE, through clearing-house Safcom, will guarantee all trades and offers a cradle-to-grave audit trail. Yield-X will operate in a fully regulated environment overseen by both the JSE and the FSB. Yield-X is targeting a range of investors, from large institutional investors, banks, corporate treasuries and intermediaries, to

smaller financial institutions and retail investors who may have been previously excluded from the interest rate market.

Domestic currency market

The South African Rand appreciated by almost 20% against the US Dollar during 2004. Although part of this appreciation was due to general US dollar weakness over this period, which caused most emerging-market currencies to appreciate, the Rand was also supported by domestic economic conditions such as the decline in the inflation rate, positive economic growth, improved sentiment and an increase in official foreign exchange reserves.

South Africa's official gross reserves increased from US$8,1 billion at the end of January 2004 to US$15,9 billion at the end of March 2005. Demand for the Rand was also fuelled by foreign portfolio investment, particularly during the last quarter of 2004.

According to Bloomberg's annual ranking report, the Rand was the second-best performing currency against the US Dollar during 2004. The analysis comprises 60 currencies from developed as well as emerging-market countries. The only currency to

The Mzansi bank account for low-income, previously unbanked people saw 557 439 accounts opened by the first week in February 2005.

Launched on 25 October 2004, the Mzansi account was conceived out of the requirements set out in the Financial Services Charter. Mzansi is supported by Absa, First National Bank, Nedbank, Standard Bank and the PostBank.

It was part of an attempt by the banks to draw in about 13 million people who cannot afford the high fees levied by most banks.

Data collected from participating banks showed that more than 6 000 accounts were opened throughout South Africa each day. The target market of the initiative has largely been reached with 56% of new accounts belonging to women and 27,1% to people between the ages of 16 and 25. Most account-holders are from black communities.

Mzansi brought R160 million into the formal banking sector, with an average of R290 held in each Mzansi account.

marginally outperform the Rand was the Polish Zloty. The Rand also appreciated against other major currencies. Against both the Euro and the Pound, the Rand appreciated by almost 10% and compared with the Yen, the Rand appreciated by 13%.

Volatility conditions, as reflected by the implied and historical volatility indicators, rose to as high as 25,6% and 28,4%, respectively, in January 2004, but declined significantly during the rest of the year. At the end of December 2004, the implied and historical volatility indicators were at 14,9% and 13,4% respectively, indicating that volatility in the Rand exchange rate had subsided.

The average turnover in the domestic currency market increased from US$92,9 billion for the 2003 year as a whole, to US$98,0 billion for 2004. The average net daily turnover increased from US$7,7 billion to US$8,2 billion over the same period. These increases occurred mainly in the foreign exchange swap market, and were not out of line with global trends observed in the 2004 Bank for International Settlements survey of global foreign exchange activity. Domestic rand turnover comprises 0,42% of the global foreign exchange market.

During the first quarter of 2005, the Rand depreciated by almost 10% against the US Dollar, mainly as a result of developments in international currency markets. The main reason was the appreciation in the exchange rate of the US Dollar, which began early in January, caused by expectations that the Fed could increase interest rates at a faster pace than previously expected. This affected most emerging market currencies. In addition, commodity prices declined to lower levels during 2005 with a subsequent effect on the Rand, given that it is a commodity currency.

Exchange control

Exchange control is administered by the Reserve Bank on behalf of the Minister of Finance. The Reserve Bank is assisted in this task by a number of banking institutions, which have been appointed by the Minister of Finance as authorised dealers in foreign exchange. These institutions undertake foreign-exchange transactions for their own account with their clients, within limits, and subject to conditions laid down by the Reserve Bank.

The Government is committed to an open capital market and the gradual relaxation of exchange controls. The private individual investment allowance was increased from R400 000 to R500 000 and then to R750 000 in February 2000.

The following dispensations with regard to exchange control are allowed:

Institutional investors

Part of the process of gradual exchange-control liberalisation and financial-sector strengthening is the shift to a system of prudential regulation governing the foreign portfolio investment of institutional investors, such as long-term insurers and pension funds.

Prudential regulations are applied internationally to protect policyholders and pensioners from excessive risk, and typically include restrictions on foreign asset holdings, set at a certain percentage of an institution's total assets or liabilities. As an interim step towards a prudential framework, institutional investors will be:

- Allowed to invest, on approval, up to existing foreign asset limits. These foreign asset limits are 15% of total retail assets for retirement funds, long-term insurers and investment managers registered as institutional investors for exchange-control purposes, and 20% for collective investment scheme management companies.
- Required to submit additional information when making an application for a foreign-investment allowance. The shift to prudential regulation requires improved data reporting on individual institutions' foreign investments and the foreign-diversification levels of the industry as a whole. The new regulation became operational on 1 May 2003, after National Treasury and the Exchange Control Department of the Reserve Bank, in consultation with the FSB, reached agreement with the respective industries on the appropriate revised reporting standards.

South African corporates

The global expansion of South African firms hold

significant benefits for the economy – expanded access to markets, increased exports, and improved competitiveness.

With effect from 26 October 2004, limits on FDI by South African corporates were abolished. Exchange control approval is, however, required. Requests by corporations are considered in light of national interest, such as the benefit to South Africa's international reserves by, for example, generating exports of goods and services. The Exchange Control Department of the Reserve Bank reserves the right to stagger capital outflows relating to very large foreign investments, to manage any potential impact on the foreign exchange market.

Regarding foreign investments authorised before 26 October 2004, corporates will, on application, be permitted to utilise their domestic resources to repay offshore loans raised after 18 February 2004, to finance or partly finance new approved investments. Such transfers will, however, be limited to the greater of R1 million (or R2 million in the case of investments outside Africa) or 20% of the total outstanding loan capital per investment in any given year, provided that, during the first two years of the loan's term, total funds transferred from South Africa do not exceed R2 billion for each new investment, or R1 billion for investments outside Africa.

Interest payments on loans raised abroad to finance or partly finance new approved foreign investments must be repaid from offshore resources.

As a further alternate mechanism of financing offshore investments, applications by corporates to engage in corporate asset/share swap transactions will be considered.

Emigrants' funds

A system of exchange-control allowances for the export of funds when persons emigrate has been in place in South Africa for a number of decades. Emigrants' funds in excess of the emigration allowance were placed in emigrants' blocked accounts to preserve foreign reserves. Reflecting the improved strength and resilience of the South African economy, these blocked assets are now being unwound. The imminent elimination of the net open forward position, and an increasingly diversi-

fied and growing export sector, create an environment conducive to dealing with the foreign reserve problems of the past. As such, the following applies:

- The distinction between the settling-in allowance for emigrants and the private individual foreign-investment allowance for residents has fallen away, and there is now a common foreign allowance for both residents and emigrants of R750 000 per individual (or R1,5 million in respect of family units).
- Emigrant-blocked assets are being unwound. Amounts of up to R750 000 (inclusive of amounts already exited) are eligible for exiting without charge. Holders of blocked assets wishing to exit more than R750 000 (inclusive of amounts already exited) must apply to the Exchange Control Department of the Reserve Bank to do so. Approval is subject to an exiting schedule and an exit charge of 10% of the amount.
- New emigrants wishing to exit more than R750 000 (inclusive of amounts already exited) can similarly apply to the Exchange Control Department to do so, with approval subject to an exiting schedule and an exit charge of 10% of the amount.

Local financial assistance to affected persons and non-residents

To improve access to domestic credit in financing FDI in South Africa or for domestic working capital requirements, foreign companies or foreign-owned South African companies are permitted to make greater use of local finance. With effect from 18 February 2004, foreign companies or foreign wholly owned subsidiaries can borrow locally up to 300% of the total shareholders' investment.

This ratio does not apply to emigrants, the acquisition of residential properties by non-residents or affected persons, and other financial transactions, such as portfolio investments by non-residents, securities lending, hedging, repurchase agreements, etc. In these cases, the 100% ratio still applies.

JSE Limited

Founded on 8 November 1887, the JSE is the sole licensed securities exchange in South Africa. In July 2005, after 188 years as a mutual association, the JSE celebrated its demutualisation and is now known as JSE Limited, a public unlisted company.

The management and control of the JSE vests in the board, which has powers conferred upon it by the Acts, the rules and the Constitution.

On 6 August 2001, the JSE acquired the business and assets of the South African Futures Exchange (SAFEX). SAFEX is now incorporated into the JSE in two divisions, namely the Financial Derivatives Division, which covers the equity and interest-rate futures and options markets; and the Agricultural Products Division, which covers commodities futures and options on maize, sunflowers, soya beans and wheat.

Regulation

As the front-line regulator of its primary and secondary markets, an independent regulatory authority, the FSB, supervises the JSE. The listings division of the JSE together with two independent bodies (the Generally Accepted Accounting Practice [GAAP] Monitoring Panel and the Securities Panel Regulation) enforce compliance with GAAP and the protection of minority shareholders respectively.

The Insider Trading Directorate of the FSB operates a stringent enforcement programme, with the support of the JSE, in respect of the secondary market. The JSE, in turn, regulates its listed companies and broking members by extensive rules and directives in line with the Securities Services Act, 2004.

In November 1995, the JSE permitted ownership by foreign and corporate members for the first time. The move, part of a broader deregulation package designed to entice local and international investors, parallels the London stock market's 'Big Bang' of 1986, although changes were phased in over time. These included closing the open-outcry market floor in favour of automated electronic trading, the introduction of fully negotiable commission, and dual-trading capacity.

International involvement

The JSE is the largest securities exchange in Africa and has a market capitalisation of several times that of all the other African markets combined. It has the third-largest market for single stock market in the world; the ninth-largest market for options and futures in the world; accounts for over 75% of market capital in Africa; and its reserves grew from US$ 31 million in 1999 to US$73 million in 2004.

The JSE is committed to promoting South Africa both regionally and internationally. In this regard, it has led the process of harmonising the listing requirements of the members of the Committee of SADC Stock Exchanges (COSSE). The COSSE envisages an integrated real-time national network of securities markets in the region by 2006. The JSE has offered its trading platform to these members, and the Namibian Stock Exchange has been trading on the JSE's trading platform for the past seven years.

In addition, the JSE has played an instrumental role in the creation of the globally prominent Code of Corporate Practices and Conduct (referred to as King II), a follow-up to the King I Code. The listings requirements of the JSE now require that all companies provide a report in their annual financial statement on their level of compliance with King II, including progress on the novel stakeholder aspects of the code.

Consistent with the objectives of NEPAD and by virtue of the JSE's position in the southern African region, the JSE remains totally committed to the concept of a pan-African board, and is involved in trying to raise money to assist neighbouring countries to participate in this initiative.

Foreign investors

Since 1994, South Africa has restructured its economic policies to attract foreign investment. The transition has led to a significant improvement in the quality and inclusiveness of institutions. Prudent social reform has been coupled with accountable political institutions and sound macro-economic management.

The economic rating agencies' reports confirm the presence of high levels of political stability. The JSE plays a vital role in the South African economy by putting capital providers together with capital seekers. Thus, cash resources are channelled into productive economic activity, building the economy while enhancing job opportunities and wealth creation.

Listing on the JSE enables capital to be raised for expanding the financing of new business and creating new employment opportunities. In addition, it provides a secondary market for dealing in securities by bringing together buyers and sellers in a manner that ensures transparent price discovery. In this way, new investment opportunities in the country are created.

During the February 2004 budget speech, the Minister of Finance continued to further relax exchange controls by approving foreign companies seeking to issue securities on the JSE and Bond Exchange of South Africa (BESA). In line with the approval, international investors have unfettered access to securities listed on the JSE:

- There are no exchange controls of any kind on foreign investors or any non-resident parties.
- There are no limits on the repatriation of capital or income on foreign shareholders.
- There are no withholding taxes or other penalties applied to the repatriation of capital, interest or dividends by foreign investors.
- There are no foreign ownership limits on South African securities.
- There is no separate registration process for foreign investors. Like all other shareholders, such shareholders are reflected in the dematerialised register. Purchases or sales of shares by foreign shareholders are reflected in its electronic share registry by insertion of a flag.
- South Africa has a free-floating exchange rate traded in all global financial centres. The currency is one of the most liquid among upper-middle income countries, with currency equivalent to 24% of South Africa's annual GDP traded every day. The currency is backed by an extremely liquid and deep sovereign bond exchange (not affiliated to the JSE) to which foreign investors similarly have unfettered access.
- JSE member firms and central securities depository participants offer custodian services to foreign investors.

Product developments

The JSE launched the Social Responsibility Index (SRI) in May 2004 to focus on corporate social responsibility and sustainable business practices, and to enable socially responsible investment in South Africa. The SRI is founded on environmental, economic and social sustainability and measures the triple bottom line performance of companies listed in the FTSE/JSE All Share Index.

The SRI criteria are customised to the South African and African context, and could be an aspirational benchmark for all organisations, regarding best practice in the triple bottom line. The background and criteria document are available on the JSE website (*www.jse.co.za*).

Driven by the quest to demystify the market and the desire to broaden the national retail investor base, by encouraging a wider spread of knowledge of the financial market and the growth of investment culture in South Africa, the JSE introduced the University Investment Challenge at the beginning of 2005.

This concept is rooted in the JSE/Liberty Schools Challenge, a simulated trading experience designed to encourage secondary school learners to learn about the market by trading phantom portfolios.

New listings requirements became effective in September 2003. These stipulate that when listed entities wish to de-list, they must make an offer to minorities and obtain a fair and reasonable statement. Listed companies are required to comply with international financial reporting standards for all financial years, starting in 2005.

The Alternative Exchange, better known as ALTX, was launched in October 2003 as a parallel market or alternative exchange for small-to-medium and growing companies. The first listings on ALTX took place in the first quarter of 2004 with a total of 10 listings during the year. ALTX provides an attractive investment area for investors interested in the growth potential of smaller stocks. It is the sum of a partnership between the JSE and government through the Department of Trade and Industry. The ALTX is Africa's first alternative market and a growth exchange for young, innovative companies and investors.

The JSE continually strives to run a low-cost, highly efficient market that offers a wide range of financial products to an ever-broadening investor community. It has served South Africa well for over 100 years and is now moving into the future, determined to take its place among the world's top exchanges.

Bond Exchange of South Africa

BESA is an independent financial exchange operating under a licence granted annually by the country's securities-market regulator, the FSB. BESA is responsible for regulating the debt securities market in South Africa.

Primary debt markets

Although primarily a government-bond market, BESA also lists rand-denominated debt securities issued by local government, public enterprises and major corporates. At 31 December 2004, BESA had 378 fixed-income securities outstanding, issued by 65 borrowers, with a total nominal value of R572 billion. Just over 70% of this debt had been issued by central and municipal government, with a further 11% issued by parastatal and utility organisations. The remaining listed debt had been issued by companies in a wide range of sectors: banking, gold-mining, chemical, food, household goods and textiles, telecommunications and transport. Securitisation issues include vehicle, credit card, loan receivables, equipment receivables and mortgage products.

Vanilla bonds constitute the majority of BESA's listed instruments, but there are variations, including:
- fixed interest-bearing bonds with single and multiple redemption dates
- zero-coupon bonds
- consumer price index-linked bonds
- credit-linked notes
- variable interest-rate bonds/floating rate notes
- strip bonds
- commercial paper.

BESA has appointed the Listings Advisory Technical Committee to provide ongoing advice on its listings disclosure requirements and rules. The aim is to ensure that these contribute to the strengthening of investor protection and market confidence.

Market performance

The South African bond market is one of the most liquid emerging bond markets in the world. Turnover in listed debt declined in 2004, with volumes decreasing from R10,7 trillion nominal in 2003 to R8,4 trillion nominal, which is a drop of 21%. The decrease in nominal turnover was also reflected in the lower number of matched trades for the year, which decreased from 356 000 in 2003 to 328 000 in 2004. Turnover in the spot market increased from 33,6% of total turnover in 2003 to 34,1% in 2004.

Although turnover figures for 2004 dropped significantly, the turnover velocity of listed debt instruments remained healthy at 14 times the market capitalisation for 2004.

While 94% of market turnover in 2004 was in government and utilities stock, there was an ever-increasing amount of listings and turnover in corporate issuances and securitisations which, together in 2004, accounted for 6% of total turnover.

Offshore turnover in listed debt that was settled locally amounted to R2 trillion, or 23,6% of total turnover, indicating that South Africa's local debt has significant attraction for international investors.

Main indices

BESA, in collaboration with the Actuarial Society of South Africa, has introduced a trio of bond indices that provide a simple yet accurate measure of total returns of representative bond portfolios and serve as benchmarks for evaluating performance.

These indices (introduced in August 2000) replaced the previous bond indices used in South Africa. They are published daily by the exchange on its website (*www.besa.za.com*) and are widely disseminated to all members, the asset-management community and the media.

Regulation

BESA is a licensed exchange and, together with its

member firms, must adhere to the Securities Services Act, 2004 and a set of approved rules. As a self-regulatory organisation, BESA undertakes ongoing surveillance over all aspects of bond-market activity in South Africa.

Guarantee Fund

BESA maintains the Guarantee Fund to ensure, as far as possible, the performance of transactions entered on the exchange. The fund provides members and clients with price-risk cover against a member default, to a maximum aggregate of R150 million. Since inception, no settlement defaults or claims on the fund have been recorded.

STRATE Limited

The FSB registered STRATE Limited, the central securities depository for equities, in terms of the Custody and Administration of Securities Act, 1992 (Act 85 of 1992), on 20 September 1999. The depository is responsible for equities and fixed-income securities.

According to a report by GSCS Benchmarks Limited, which is represented by 10 global participating custodians, STRATE is rated sixth in the world in terms of settlement risk, and third in terms of custody risk. These benchmarks measure settlement, safekeeping and operational risk among central securities depositories in a range of major and emerging markets.

Acknowledgements

Bond Exchange of South Africa
Business Day
Development Bank of Southern Africa
Estimates of National Expenditure 2005, published by National Treasury
Financial Services Board
JSE Limited
National Treasury
Office of the Auditor-General
South African Reserve Bank
South African Revenue Service
www.dti.gov.za
www.gov.za
www.jse.co.za
www.landbank.co.za
www.news24.co.za
www.nlb.org.za
www.sagoodnews.co.za
www.samint.co.za
www.sars.gov.za
www.southafrica.info

Suggested reading

Budlender, D. *The Women's Budget.* Rondebosch: Institute for Democracy in South Africa (IDASA), 1996.
Chip, K. and Zenobia, I. *E-Commerce: A Southern African Perspective.* Cape Town: New Africa Books, 2004.
Clark, I., Louw, E. and Myburgh, J. *More Small Business Opportunities in South Africa.* 2nd ed. Cape Town: Zebra Books, 1996.
Dolny, H. *Banking on Change.* Sandton: Penguin, 2001.
Falkena, H.B. *Financial Policy in South Africa.* Halfway House: Southern Book Publishers, 1991.
Falkena, H.B. *Fundamentals of the South African Financial System.* Halfway House: Southern Book Publishers, 1993.
Falkena, H.B. ed. *South African Financial Institutions.* Halfway House: Southern Book Publishers, 1992.
Fölscher, A. *et al. Transparency and Participation in the Budget Process: South Africa: A Country Report.* Cape Town: IDASA, 2001.
Fourie, L.J., Falkena, H.B. and Kok, W.J. eds. *Fundamentals of the South African Financial System.* Students' Edition. Halfway House, Gauteng: International Thompson Publishing, 1996.
Human, P. and Horwitz, F. *On the Edge: How the South African Business Organisation Copes with Change.* Cape Town: Juta, 1992.
Jones, S. *Banking and Business in South Africa.* Basingstoke: MacMillan, 1988.
Kelly, M.V. *Financial Institutions in South Africa – Financial, Investment and Risk Management.* Cape Town: Juta 1993.
Kohn, M. *Financial Institutions and Markets.* 2nd ed. Cape Town: Oxford University Press Southern Africa, 2004.
Kok, P. and Pietersen, J. *Financial Services.* Pretoria: Human Sciences Research Council (HSRC), 2000.
Levin, A. *The Art of African Shopping.* Cape Town: Struik, 2005.
Makinta, V. and Schwabe, C. eds. *Development Funding in South Africa: 1998 – 1999*, Pretoria: HSRC, 2000.
Manuel, Markets and Money: Essays in Appraisal, edited by R. Parsons. Cape Town: Double Storey Books, 2004.
Porteous, D. and Hazelhurst, E. *Banking on Change: Democratising Finance in South Africa 1994 – 2004 and Beyond.* Cape Town: Double Storey, 2004.
Standing, G. and Samson, M. *A Basic Income Grant for South Africa.* Cape Town: University of Cape Town Press, 2003.
Student Guide to the South African Financial System, edited by I.J. Fourie, H.B. Falkena and W.J. Kok. 2nd ed. Cape Town: Oxford University Press Southern Africa, 2004.

Swart, N. *Manage your Money: Basic Financial Skills for South Africans*. Pretoria: Van Schaik, 2004.
Whiteford, A. and Van Deventer, D.E. *Winners and Losers: South Africa's Changing Income Distribution in the 1990s*. Pretoria: HSRC and Warton Econometric Forecasting Services, 2000.

Foreign relations

The role of the Department of Foreign Affairs is to realise South Africa's foreign policy objectives. These are guided by a commitment to promoting:
- human rights and democracy
- justice and international law
- international peace and internationally agreed mechanisms for resolving conflicts
- Africa in world affairs
- economic development through regional and international co-operation.

The department continues to implement its strategic priorities in line with government's foreign policy objectives, outlined in the programme of the International Relations, Peace and Security Cluster. The department's priorities are:
- consolidating the African agenda
- global governance
- South-South co-operation
- strengthening bilateral relations.

South Africa's diplomatic and consular missions help to enhance the country's international profile, and serve as strategic mechanisms for the achievement of South Africa's international interests.

South Africa and Africa

South Africa's development is inextricably linked to the development of Africa and the southern African region. Africa faces the challenge of developing its institutions to combat the marginalisation of the continent, engaging global role-players on socio-economic development, and facilitating a fair and just global order.

African Union (AU)

The AU is the most important institution on the continent. Through the Department of Foreign Affairs, South Africa has played an active role in setting up the AU and making it work. Key AU structures include the:
- AU Commission, which is responsible for the day-to-day running of the AU
- Pan-African Parliament (PAP), which was inaugurated in 2004 and is hosted by South Africa
- Peace and Security Council (PSC), which is operational and tasked with preventing, managing and resolving conflicts.

306

The establishment of the AU was declared on 2 March 2001 at the second Extraordinary Summit in Sirte. The 53-member AU was officially launched in Durban on 9 July 2002, following its inaugural summit. It replaced the Organisation of African Unity, which was established on 25 May 1963 in Addis Ababa, Ethiopia.

The AU's objectives include:
- achieving greater unity and solidarity between African countries and the peoples of Africa
- defending the sovereignty, territorial integrity and independence of its member states
- accelerating the political and socio-economic integration of the continent
- encouraging international co-operation, taking due account of the Charter of the United Nations (UN) and the Universal Declaration of Human Rights
- promoting peace, security and stability on the continent
- promoting democratic principles and institutions, popular participation and good governance
- promoting and protecting people's rights
- establishing the necessary conditions to enable the continent to play its rightful role in the global economy and in international negotiations
- promoting sustainable development at economic, social and cultural level, as well as the integration of African economies
- promoting co-operation in all fields of human activity to raise the living standards of African peoples
- advancing the development of the continent by promoting research in all fields
- working with relevant international partners in eradicating preventable diseases and promoting good health on the continent.

One of the challenges for the AU is the need to involve civil society in continental processes. In this regard, the Constitutive Act makes provision for the establishment of the Economic, Social and Cultural Council (ECOSOCC). The interim ECOSOCC was launched on 29 March 2005 in Addis Ababa.

The South African Chapter was launched with nine civil-society organisations elected as secretariat from the following sectors: women, youth, religious groups, organised labour, non-governmental organisations (NGOs), lawyers, cultural groups and people with disabilities.

The inaugural session of the PAP was held in Addis Ababa from 15 to 20 March 2004. Delegates from 41 member states of the AU witnessed the launch of the continental Parliament on 18 March 2004.

On 16 September 2004, the PAP was inaugurated at Gallagher Estate, near Midrand, in South Africa.

The third session of the PAP took place in Johannesburg from 29 March to 11 April 2005. It adopted, among other things, recommendations on the Africa Land Title System and the World Summit on Information Society.

South Africa has ratified the Protocol on the African Court of Human and People's Rights.

The financial institutions – the African Central Bank, the African Monetary Fund and the African Investment Bank – are expected to take longer to operationalise.

While South Africa hosts the PAP, the Western Region will host the African Central Bank; the

South African representation abroad	Total	Foreign representation in South Africa	Total
Embassies/high commissions	83	Embassies/high commissions	113
Consulates/consulates general	16	Consulates/consulates general	53
Honorary consulates	46	Honorary consulates	73
Other (e.g. liaison offices)	4	Other (e.g. liaison offices)	1
Non-resident accreditations	106	Non-resident accreditations	16
International organisations	7	International organisations	22

Source: Department of Foreign Affairs (www.dfa.gov.za), July 2005

Northern Region will host the African Investment Bank; the Central Region will host the African Monetary Fund; and the Eastern Region will host the Court of Justice.

Promotion of peace, security and stability on the continent

The AU is responsible for the peaceful resolution of conflict among member states, through such appropriate means as may be decided upon by the AU Assembly. The assembly may give directives to the Executive Council on the management of conflict, war, acts of terrorism, emergency situations and the restoration of peace.

The PSC Protocol entered into force in December 2003 and comprises 15 member states, five of which will serve a three-year period, and 10 which will serve for a two-year period each.

The PSC was launched in Addis Ababa in May 2004. Current members are South Africa, Nigeria, Algeria, Ethiopia and Gabon, who will serve three-year terms; and Lesotho, Mozambique, Cameroon, Congo, Kenya, Sudan, Libya, Ghana, Senegal and Togo, who will each serve two-year terms.

As a collective security and early warning arrangement, the PSC will allow for a timely and effective response to conflict and crisis situations in Africa.

In terms of PSC statutes, all African countries should establish their own early warning centres and there should be a continental early warning centre by 2008.

The AU PSC Protocol provides for the creation of the African Standby Force, to be operationalised over a period of 10 years.

The second extraordinary session of the AU Assembly held in Libya in February 2004, adopted the Common African Defence and Security Policy.

Socio-economic development and integration of the continent

The AU is the principal institution responsible for promoting sustainable development at economic, social and cultural level, as well as the integration of African economies. Regional economic communities (RECs) are recognised as the building-blocks of the AU, necessitating the need for their close involvement in the formulation and implementation of all AU programmes.

To this end, the AU must co-ordinate and take decisions on policies in areas of common interest to member states, as well as co-ordinate and harmonise policies between existing and future RECs, for the gradual attainment of the objectives of the AU.

Seven specialised technical committees are responsible for the actual implementation of the continental socio-economic integration process, together with the Permanent Representatives Committee.

New Partnership for Africa's Development (NEPAD)

The adoption of NEPAD is considered to be one of the most important developments of recent times, for its conception of a development programme, placing Africa at the apex of the global agenda, by:
- creating an instrument for advancing people-centered and sustainable development in Africa based on democratic values
- being premised on the recognition that Africa has an abundance of natural resources and people who have the capacity to be agents for change, and so holds the key to its own development
- providing the common African platform from which to engage the rest of the international community in a dynamic partnership that holds real prospects for creating a better life for all.

The expected outcomes are:
- economic growth and development and increased employment
- a reduction in poverty and inequality
- diversification of productive activities
- enhanced international competitiveness and increased exports
- increased African integration.

A major effort of the AU-mandated NEPAD is to continuously factor NEPAD imperatives into the outcomes of international conferences, such as the Conference on Financing for Development, the World Summit on Sustainable Development (WSSD) and the World Trade Organisation (WTO), to ensure the integration of

NEPAD into the multilateral system. In a wider context, countries of the South subscribe to the priorities outlined in NEPAD and have pledged their solidarity and moral support, as well as an appreciation for South Africa's positive role in NEPAD. However, NEPAD does not have a mechanism for South-South co-operation. To this end, improved co-ordination with partners in the South should be pursued.

Structures

Heads of State and Government Implementation Committee (HSIC)

The NEPAD HSIC is required to report annually to the summit of the AU. The chairperson of the AU, as well as the chairperson of the AU Commission, are ex-officio members of the Implementation Committee. The AU Commission is expected to participate in steering committee meetings.

The Implementation Committee comprises 15 states (three per AU geographic region), including the five initiating states: South Africa, Nigeria, Algeria, Senegal and Egypt.

The main function of the Implementation Committee is to set policies, priorities and NEPAD's programme of action.

The 13th NEPAD HSIC meeting held on 19 April 2005 in Sharm-El-Shaik, Egypt, received a NEPAD progress report that reviewed progress since the last HSIC hosted by Algeria in November 2004. The report focused on:
- the NEPAD/AU integration process
- co-operation with international partners, including the G8, the Commission for Africa and the Africa Partnership Forum
- national and subregional integration of NEPAD priorities for the attainment of the millennium development goals (MDGs)
- the enhancement of capacity of RECs.

Steering Committee

The Steering Committee comprises the personal representatives of the five initiating presidents, and is tasked with the development of the Terms of Reference for identified programmes and projects, as well as overseeing the secretariat.

Secretariat

The NEPAD Secretariat co-ordinates implementation of projects and programmes approved by the HSIC. The full-time core staff of the secretariat, located at the Development Bank of Southern Africa in Midrand, provides liaison, co-ordination, administrative and logistical functions for NEPAD.

The AU's mechanisms for peer review and conflict resolution reflect commitment to human rights, democratisation, good governance, and peace and security as being in the interest of Africans.

The African Peer Review Mechanism (APRM) is a process voluntarily acceded to by the member states of the AU as an African self-monitoring mechanism.

The APRM requires that each country develop a programme of action within the framework of specific time-bound objectives.

It enables participating member states to adopt policies and practices that conform to the agreed political, economic and corporate governance values, codes and standards. It also serves as a critical instrument for advancing reforms in governance and socio-economic development, and in building capacity to implement these reforms.

One of the key objectives of the APRM is to identify deficiencies in implementation, with a view to improving its compliance with the Constitutive Act of the AU by member states.

The inaugural meeting of the APRM Forum of participating states was held in Kigali, Rwanda, in February 2004. The second meeting of the forum took place in Algeria in November 2004.

Cabinet has established the focal point (the Minister for Public Service and Administration) and a ministerial committee to lead the APRM in South Africa.

President Thabo Mbeki led a South African delegation to the third summit of the African Peer Review Forum (APRF) held in Abuja, Nigeria, on 19 June 2005.

Ahead of the July 2005 AU Summit, the APRF considered the base country review reports on Ghana and Rwanda.

These two reports constituted the first to emerge from the APRM process and provided useful lessons for country reviews to follow.

South Africa held its first consultative conference on 28 and 29 September 2005. All sectors of society were expected to make submissions in line with the APRM guidelines. The second consultative conference was planned for November 2005. After that conference, a report was expected to be submitted to Cabinet for approval, and the APRM country review team was expected to visit South Africa to review the self-assessment report and programme of action.

Southern Africa

Angola
Following the signing of a ceasefire agreement in April 2002, the Angolan Government started normalising the political situation in that country.

South Africa committed itself to assist with Angola's post-war reconstruction. Consequently, the Joint Commission of Co-operation (JCC) was established in November 2000. The JCC first met at ministerial level on 28 February 2003. Since then, various bilateral agreements have been concluded.

Angolan Prime Minister, Mr Fernando de Piedade Dias Dos Santos, visited South Africa in February 2005 to ratify agreements on bilateral investment protection and promotion, as well as co-operation agreements in the areas of defence, electricity and power supplies, and social reintegration.

Lesotho
The most significant and visible beacon reflecting South Africa's bilateral relations with Lesotho is the Lesotho Highlands Water Project, which, in today's terms, qualifies as a NEPAD project. It was started in 1986 as a joint venture to supply water to South Africa, especially the rapidly growing urban population in Gauteng, and to meet Lesotho's electricity needs. The project delivers about 780 million cubic metres of water to South Africa a year.

South Africa and Lesotho have agreed to engage in a strategic partnership to assist Lesotho in accelerating economic development to raise its status from that of a least developed country.

In June 2005, South Africa and Lesotho signed the Agreement on Scientific Co-operation aimed at sharing South Africa's successes in technologies related to poverty reduction and wealth creation at community level. The agreement provides for the following areas of further engagement:
- public understanding of science, engineering and technology
- biotechnology
- indigenous knowledge
- technology incubation.

Lesotho has requested that South Africa provide training in the areas of food, biotechnology and recycling technology and the development of a database of indigenous knowledge.

Botswana
During President Mbeki's state visit to Botswana in March 2003, the two countries agreed on the establishment of the Joint Permanent Commission for Co-operation (JPCC).

The JPCC covers areas such as agriculture and livestock, water affairs, mining and tourism, environmental co-operation, monetary and financial arrangements, transportation, roads and infrastructure development.

The two countries signed a memorandum of understanding (MoU) on the development and management of the Trans-Kalahari Corridor (TKC) in September 2003. The TKC was formally established in 1998 following the completion of the Trans-Kgalagadi Highway in Botswana, which links Botswana, Namibia and South Africa by road.

Malawi
Malawi is one of South Africa's main trading partners in the southern African region. Like other African trading partners, the trade imbalance with Malawi is in favour of South Africa.

South African-based companies, increasingly interested in linking up with and establishing a presence in Malawi, range from the finance, telecommunications and retail sectors to those involved in the construction industry.

By June 2005, negotiations were underway to establish a commission for co-operation in various fields between the two countries.

Indian Ocean islands

South Africa's political, economic and diplomatic relations with countries in the Indian Ocean islands remain strong.

South Africa, chair of the AU at the time, played a pivotal role in ensuring that peace prevailed in Madagascar, following political instability as a result of election results being disputed in 2000.

South Africa also played a meaningful role in accepting Madagascar's candidature to the Southern African Development Community (SADC) in August 2004.

South Africa, as the co-ordinator of the countries of the region under the aegis of the AU, assisted in diffusing constitutional and political tension that led to the Fomboni Peace Agreement in 2000.

South Africa spearheaded the process of peace-building and reconciliation, as well as the return to constitutionalism, with the result that successful elections were held in 2002. South Africa continues to play an important role in the post-conflict reconstruction and development processes. These include assistance in building institutions of governance, macro-economic planning and development and capacity-building in the area of police training and public-service sectors.

South Africa is also involved in strengthening political and economic bilateral relations with Mauritius and Seychelles. Sectoral relations with these countries include arts and culture, tourism and environmental management, and poverty-alleviation programmes.

On 14 January 2005, South Africa co-chaired the UN High-Level Segment of the International Meeting on the Comprehensive Review of the Barbados Programme of Action for the Sustainable Development of Small Island Developing States (SIDS), held in Port Louis, Mauritius.

As custodian of the WSSD, South Africa closely follows the plight of the SIDS and their sustainable development.

In July 2005, President Mbeki congratulated Mr Navim Ramgoolam on his election as Prime Minister of Mauritius following the National Assembly general elections held in that country on 3 July 2005.

An SADC observer mission to Mauritius declared the elections to be free, fair, professionally managed and transparent, and conducted within the SADC guidelines on elections.

Mozambique

The South African Government supports the democratically elected Government of Mozambique and continues with initiatives to strengthen bilateral relations and the democratic reconstruction and development processes underway in that country.

Both the South African and the Mozambican governments view the expansion of the infrastructural links between the two countries as one of the priority bilateral co-operation areas. The rail and road connections between the two countries serve as the main arteries linking the respective economies.

The Maputo Development Corridor Project has already attracted substantial new investments in Mpumalanga, and is expected to boost the Mozambican economy equally.

The Maputo Corridor Logistics Initiative, launched on 18 February 2004, has resulted in the corridor being a more effective transportation route.

South Africa and Mozambique have made substantial progress in the implementation of so-called borderlands and transfrontier conservation initiatives. (See chapter 9: *Environmental management*.) These are the Lubombo Spatial Development Initiative (SDI), the Great Limpopo Transfrontier Park, as well as the Beira and Nacala corridors, which are in various stages of development.

The fourth JPCC between South Africa and Mozambique was scheduled to take place in South Africa in November 2005. The South Africa-Mozambique Heads of State Economic Bilateral Forum, chaired by the two presidents, met on 15 April 2005, and focused on co-operation in macro-economic projects in Mozambique.

The South African National Defence Force (SANDF) rendered logistical support to Mozambique during the country's third democratic presidential and parliamentary elections in December 2004.

On 2 February 2005, President Mbeki, accompanied by the Minister of Foreign Affairs,

Dr Nkosazana Dlamini-Zuma, attended the inauguration of the new President of Mozambique, Mr Armando Guebuza, in Maputo.

On 15 April 2005, South Africa and Mozambique signed a visa waiver agreement to further South Africa's cordial diplomatic relations with its neighbours and to promote tourism and foreign direct investment (FDI). In terms of the agreement, citizens of the two countries are no longer required to apply for visas if their stay in each other's country does not exceed 30 days.

The signing of the agreement coincided with the visit of President Guebuza to South Africa. Mozambique is South Africa's second-largest export market in Africa, with trade having increased dramatically over the last few years. South Africa is Mozambique's largest investor, with FDI amounting to R8 billion and representing 247 projects.

The South African Government uses the Industrial Development Corporation (IDC) as the primary catalyst for its investment in Mozambique. By mid-2005, the IDC had approved funding for 10 projects geographically spread throughout Mozambique, and was considering six additional projects in the country. Investment ranges from mining and mineral beneficiation, agriculture, tourism, chemicals, forestry and transport infrastructure to energy.

The Mozal Aluminium Smelter remains the IDC's largest investment outside the borders of South Africa.

On 25 June 2005, Deputy President Phumzile Mlambo-Ngcuka represented South Africa at Mozambique's 30th anniversary of independence celebrations.

Namibia

Co-operation in various areas marks the relationship between South Africa and Namibia.

South Africa is the source of between 80% and 90% of Namibia's imports by value, including virtually all commodities. Bilateral trade between the two countries accounts for two-thirds of Namibia's total foreign trade.

The 7 000-km^2 Ai-Ais/Richtersveld Transfrontier Park between South Africa and Namibia features the world's second-largest canyon in the Fish River, a hot-spring game park on the Namibian side, and spectacular arid and desert mountainous scenery on the South African side.

On 21 March 2005, President Mbeki, accompanied by Dr Dlamini-Zuma, attended the inauguration of the President of Namibia, Mr Hifikepunye Pohamba. He was elected following the fourth democratic elections held in November 2004.

Swaziland

Dr Dlamini-Zuma and her Swaziland counterpart, Senator Mabili Dlamini, signed an agreement establishing the Joint Bilateral Commission for Co-operation (JBCC) on 20 December 2004 in Swaziland. This agreement formalised bilateral relations between the two countries.

Swaziland had made considerable progress towards the creation of a new constitution, which was expected to be instituted during 2005.

Tanzania

Trade and investment between South Africa and Tanzania continues to grow at a steady pace. More than 150 South African companies are economically active in Tanzania, which is rated as a premier South African investment destination in Africa.

The proposed Presidential Economic Commission is expected to provide the necessary co-operative framework to manage the development and implementation of bilateral projects as well as the SDI programme, in particular the Mtwara and Central development corridors, which are regional NEPAD priority programmes.

Tanzania's President, Mr Benjamin Mkapa, visited South Africa in September 2005.

Zambia

South Africa enjoys warm relations with Zambia, as evidenced by an increase in trade and investment flow between the two countries.

For many years, South Africa has competed with Britain as the leading source of foreign investment in Zambia. South Africa's investors continue to play an active role in the Zambian economy, which led to the formation of the South African Business Association in Zambia.

By mid-2005, negotiations were underway to establish a formal and structured bilateral forum with Zambia through which a number of issues of mutual interest could be addressed.

A high-level South African delegation paid an official visit to Zambia in June 2005.

Issues discussed included the:

- consolidation of the African Agenda
- implementation of NEPAD
- resolution and prevention of conflict in the region
- reform of global governance, including the reform of the UN and its institutions.

Uganda

Official diplomatic relations between South Africa and Uganda were established on 24 June 1994.

On 17 January 2005, the then Deputy President, Mr Jacob Zuma, met with President Yoweru Museveni and Tanzania's President Benjamin Mkapa in Entebbe, Uganda, for consultations on the Burundi peace process.

Kenya

South Africa and Kenya were expected to sign a JCC agreement in 2005.

Zimbabwe

Zimbabwe celebrated 25 years of independence on 18 April 2005.

South Africa and Zimbabwe, besides their geographic proximity, have a common and long history of regional affiliation and cultural ties. The people of Zimbabwe played an important role in support of the liberation struggle against apartheid in South Africa.

South Africa continues to engage all the stakeholders in Zimbabwe to find ways and means to assist Zimbabweans in their endeavours to find a homegrown solution to their political challenges. South Africa is doing this within the context of the AU and SADC initiatives to the Zimbabwean solution.

South Africa sent the National Observer Mission to observe Zimbabwe's sixth parliamentary elections, held on 31 March 2005. South African observers also participated in the SADC observer elections mission. Both election observer teams declared the Zimbabwean parliamentary elections credible and reflective of the will of the people of Zimbabwe.

On 12 July 2005, Deputy President Mlambo-Ngcuka met with President Robert Mugabe and his Deputy, Ms Joyce Mujuru, as part of ongoing talks between the two countries.

Ethiopia

Bilateral political and economic relations between Ethiopia and South Africa have improved greatly in recent years. The two countries signed the General Co-operation Agreement during Minister Dlamini-Zuma's official visit to Ethiopia in March 2004. This has significantly strengthened bilateral relations between the two countries.

The South Africa-Ethiopia Joint Ministerial Commission (JMC) agreement was also signed in March 2004. This was followed by a series of meetings between senior officials from both sides to expand and strengthen bilateral co-operation in the areas of capacity-building, trade and investment, science and technology, and arts and culture, among others.

Development co-operation

South Africa is not a donor country, but development co-operation with countries in Africa is integral to the country's foreign policy. Assistance is wide-ranging and includes educational visits by agriculturists, the establishment of viable training centres, conservation of the environment, the rendering of medical assistance, and technology-exchange programmes. Technical and financial assistance, with a view to capacity-building, especially to SADC countries, is a major instrument for promoting economic development, peace and stability, democracy, and the African Renaissance, on a regional basis.

South Africa and the Southern African Development Community

South Africa's vision for the southern African region involves the highest possible degree of economic co-operation, mutual assistance, and joint planning consistent with socio-economic, environmental and political realities. Within the region, the SADC is the primary vehicle for South African policy and action to achieve regional economic development.

Originally known as the Southern African Development Co-ordination Conference, the SADC was formed in Lusaka, Zambia, on 1 April 1980, following the adoption of the Lusaka Declaration. The declaration and treaty establishing the SADC was signed at the Summit of Heads of State and Government on 17 August 1992 in Windhoek, Namibia.

The SADC provides for regional peace and security, sectoral co-operation and an integrated regional economy. The SADC member states are Angola, Botswana, the Democratic Republic of Congo (DRC), Lesotho, Malawi, Mauritius, Mozambique, Namibia, the Seychelles, South Africa, Swaziland, Tanzania, Zambia and Zimbabwe.

The SADC is a critical vehicle for the development of the southern African region. South Africa has been engaged in restructuring the SADC to enable it to execute evolving AU mandates and respond to changing development challenges. Considerable work has gone into setting up new institutions, and reviewing existing ones. From August 2004, the focus has been on chairing the SADC Organ on Politics, Defence and Security.

One of the organ's main functions is to ensure that regional peace and security arrangements are linked to continental arrangements. Another challenge is finalising the MoU between the AU Commission and Africa's RECs to ensure a co-ordinated interface for addressing AU themes and activities.

Implementation of the Southern African Development Community Trade Protocol

The SADC Protocol on Trade entered into force on 25 January 2000. The objectives of the trade protocol are to further liberalise intra-regional trade in goods and services, on the basis of fair, mutually equitable and beneficial trade arrangements; ensure efficient production within the SADC, reflecting the current and dynamic comparative advan-

tages of its members; contribute towards the improvement of a climate for domestic, cross-border and foreign investment; enhance the economic development, diversification and industrialisation of the region; and establish a free trade area (FTA) in the SADC region.

At the core of this agreement is the reduction and ultimate elimination of tariff and non-tariff barriers and the setting up of rules of origin by 2008.

By September 2004, South Africa had signed 21 protocols and was in the process of acceding to the Protocol on Immunities and Privileges. South Africa had also ratified the protocols on shared watercourse systems, combating illicit drug trafficking, energy, mining, transport, communications and meteorology, health, and education and training. The Revised Protocol on Shared Water-Course Systems was also ratified.

South Africa is a signatory to the:

• Declaration Towards a Southern Africa Free of Anti-Personnel Landmines
• Declaration on Gender and Development
• Declaration on Productivity
• Declaration Concerning Firearms, Ammunition and Other Related Material.

In June 2005, South Africa and other Southern African Development Community (SADC) countries participated in Exercise Thokgamo at the invitation of the Botswana Defence Force.

More than 300 South African National Defence Force (SANDF) members participated in this peacekeeping exercise near Maun, Botswana.

The objectives were to:

• develop a common understanding of military interoperability and foster mutual trust, respect and co-operation between the SANDF and other participating SADC countries
• give all participating forces practical experience in peace-support operations
• upgrade operational means and methods of multinational peacekeeping
• give SANDF personnel the opportunity to train and function with the necessary confidence in a multinational peacekeeping exercise.

Relations with central Africa

South Africa's diplomatic relations with central Africa have been dominated by attempts to bring peace to the DRC and Burundi, thereby ensuring greater stability in the whole of the central African region.

Gabon

In November 2003, South Africa signed co-operation and tourism agreements with Gabon.

In January 2005, President Mbeki, accompanied by the Minister of Defence, Mr Mosiuoa Lekota, and the Deputy Minister of Foreign Affairs, Mr Aziz Pahad, attended the Summit of the AU PSC in Libreville, Gabon.

Issues on the agenda included the situation in the Great Lakes Region and Sudan.

On 22 March 2005, Minister Dlamini-Zuma held bilateral political and economic discussions with the acting Minister of Foreign Affairs, Co-operation and Francophone of Gabon, Mr Jean-Francois Ndongou.

During the visit, the Protocol for Regular Diplomatic Consultations, a trade agreement and the Convention for the Avoidance of Double Taxation and the Prevention of Fiscal Evasion with respect to Taxes on Income were signed.

President Mbeki and a ministerial delegation paid a state visit to Gabon on 2 and 3 August 2005. The visit focused on bilateral co-operation between the two countries.

The following agreements were signed:
• Merchant Shipping Agreement
• Agreement in the Field of Education, Training and Higher Education
• Agreement in the Field of Arts and Culture.

During 2005/06, the Department of Foreign Affairs commenced the design and construction of two embassies, one in Addis Ababa, Ethiopia, and another in Maseru, Lesotho. The total cost of the embassies is estimated at R60 million. Plans were also underway to build an embassy in Abuja, Nigeria.

Equatorial Guinea

South Africa has enjoyed full diplomatic relations with the Republic of Equatorial Guinea since 5 May 1993.

The two countries signed a general co-operation agreement in December 2003.

Chad

Official relations between South Africa and the Republic of Chad were established on 21 October 1994.

Minister Dlamini-Zuma led a ministerial delegation to Chad in November 2004, and a general co-operation agreement was signed with that country in December 2004. Once implemented, this agreement will open the doors to a number of joint projects in Chad, related to transport, communications and the energy sector.

Rwanda

South Africa and Rwanda maintain good political relations. Co-operation between the two countries focuses on the post-conflict reconstruction of Rwanda and has extended to the co-ordination of NEPAD on the continent.

On 7 April 2005, a high-level South African delegation attended the 11th anniversary of the 1994 Rwanda Genocide, during which an estimated 800 000 people were killed in 100 days, when the ethnic Hutu majority attacked the minority Tutsis.

Relations are growing rapidly between the two countries as evidenced by the signing of the MoU between the City of Tshwane and the City of Kigali, the MoU on Defence Co-operation, and Trilateral Co-operation in the Field of Health, followed by an increase in the frequency of flights between South Africa and Rwanda from three to four a week.

Minister Dlamini-Zuma hosted her counterpart, Dr Charles Murigande, for the third session of the South Africa-Rwanda JCC in July 2004.

To further strengthen this bilateral structure, the Implementation Monitoring Committee (IMC) has been established at director-general level to provide the necessary co-ordinating, planning and monitoring framework to manage effective implementation of approved programmes and to ensure the delivery of cross-cutting training and human resource capacity-building programmes.

More than 200 Rwandan students have been studying at South African tertiary institutions under a bilateral education agreement.

Burundi

South Africa's good relations with Burundi are demonstrated by the leading role the Government played in the Arusha Peace and Reconciliation Agreement signed by representatives of the main Hutu and Tutsi political parties, the Government of Burundi, and the National Assembly on 28 August 2000.

The agreement provided the foundation for the transition to democracy, peace and development in that country. South African diplomacy efforts, under the leadership of former President Nelson Mandela, was central in facilitating the Arusha agreement. The pivotal point of the agreement was the political power-sharing between the Tutsis and the Hutus.

In the constitutional referendum held on 28 February 2005, 91% of voters agreed to a new constitution aimed at reducing the power imbalance between the minority Tutsi and the majority Hutu.

South Africa's contribution towards the establishment of peace and stability in Burundi included the deployment of SANDF troops with an African peace mission in Burundi, now recapped as the UN Operations in Burundi. South Africa has also financially supported the election process by, for example, providing election material for the 2005 referendum and elections.

Burundi held its first democratic elections since 1993 on 4 July 2005. The 21-member South African observer mission concluded in their election report that the elections were executed in a transparent manner.

On 26 August 2005, President Mbeki, accompanied by First Lady Zanele and senior government officials, attended the inauguration of President Pierre Nkurunziza in Bujumbura, Burundi.

Democratic Republic of Congo

The second session of the South Africa-DRC Binational Commission (BNC), co-chaired by President Mbeki and President Joseph Kabila, took place in Pretoria on 29 April 2005. The following agreements were signed:

- The Trilateral MoU between the South Africa-DRC-Sweden Governments on Co-operation in the Area of Public Service and Administration
- The MoU between the South Africa-DRC Governments relating to Co-operation on Capacity-Building for the Congolese National Police Force
- The Agreement on Co-operation between the South Africa-DRC Governments in the field of Agriculture
- The Convention between the South Africa-DRC Governments for the Avoidance of Double Taxation and the Prevention of Fiscal Evasion with respect to Taxes on Income
- The Agreement between the South Africa-DRC Governments regarding Mutual Assistance between the Customs Administrations.

The parties further reviewed progress and challenges in respect of the following areas of co-operation: political and diplomatic consultation; governance and administration; defence and security; and economy, finance and infrastructure. Both presidents agreed that additional structures should be established to increase co-operation between South Africa and the DRC.

The South African Police Service (SAPS) is working closely with the Congolese police forces to ensure security and to assist with the integration of armed forces in the DRC. In addition, South Africa, Britain and the Netherlands formed a partnership to assist the Congolese Government with the integration of their army.

By April 2005, seven countries of the Southern African Development Community (SADC), including South Africa, had ratified the SADC Mutual Defence Pact.

The pact reflects the commitment of the countries in the southern African region to ensuring peace and stability. The SADC Mutual Defence Pact binds South Africa into an SADC community of nations and defines their collective borders.

By mid-2005, the South African Government was also assisting with the DRC's reconstruction and development objectives.

A R25-million contribution from the African Renaissance Fund boosted South Africa's efforts to assist the DRC. The Swedish Government also pledged a further US$3,5 million to the Public-Service programme in the DRC following the Trilateral MoU.

In May 2005, President Mbeki attended the adoption of the DRC's new constitution, which paved the way for democratic elections later in 2005. Following the signing of an MoU between the two countries, South Africa assisted the DRC in its preparation for the elections.

São Tomé and Principe

South Africa, as part of the AU delegation, assisted in the negotiations that restored President Fradique de Menezes to power in July 2003, following the bloodless coup d'état in São Tomé and Principe.

South Africa subsequently donated non-lethal equipment to the armed forces of São Tomé and Principe, and remains committed to the International Committee of Guarantee and Follow-up. This committee ensures that the conditions that led to the coup are addressed to the satisfaction of all parties involved.

Minister Dlamini-Zuma visited São Tomé and Principe in April 2005, where she held bilateral and economic discussions with the Minister of Foreign Affairs, Co-operation and Communities, Mr Ovidio Manuel Barboso Pequeno.

During her visit, the Minister met President de Menezes and held discussions with senior government officials.

The two countries agreed on the need to intensify co-operation in:
- education (especially Higher Education)
- health (particularly medical evacuation, construction of health facilities, and exchange of medical technology)
- air transportation
- tourism
- vocational training
- agriculture, focusing specifically on small- and medium-scale farming

- capacity-building for the São Tomé Diplomatic Service.

The two governments signed a general bilateral co-operation agreement.

Relations with North and West Africa and the Horn of Africa

The countries of North and West Africa and the Horn of Africa are becoming increasingly important trading partners for South Africa, as well as important partners within the context of the AU/African Economic Community.

Algeria

The South African Embassy was established in Algiers in November 1997. Political relations between the South African liberation movement and Algeria dates back to the 1950s.

In October 2004, President Abdelaziz Bouteflika attended the fourth session of the South Africa-Algeria BNC in Pretoria.

The BNC discussed, among other things, bilateral co-operation in fields such as science and technology, health, arts and culture, agriculture, telecommunications, and housing.

Côte d'Ivoire

South Africa established full diplomatic relations with Côte d'Ivoire in May 1992. Given South Africa's firm commitment to the African Renaissance, it continues to promote the restoration of peace and stability in that country.

Following the rebellion of 2002, the Marcoussis Agreement was eventually signed on 25 January 2003 in France by all belligerents. Implementation of the peace process was initially slow, given the political impasse since mid-2004 and early in 2005.

However, in light of South Africa's continued support and the mediation efforts by President Mbeki (as mandated by the AU) towards the resolution of the crisis, the Ivorian Government and opposition parties met for the first time since 2004 during peace talks held in Pretoria in April 2005.

Under the Pretoria Agreement, parties agreed to proceed with the disarmament and demobilisation process and to cease all violence. However, political parties were unable to reach consensus on the adoption of Article 35 of the Ivorian Constitution.

Signatories to the Pretoria Agreement met again in June 2005 to review its implementation.

South Africa's mediation efforts will continue to promote the restoration of peace and stability in Côte d'Ivoire, under the aegis of the AU, the UN and in partnership with the Economic Community of West African States (ECOWAS).

On 10 June 2005, a six-member strong SANDF team left for Côte d'Ivoire to prepare the way for a 40-member South African Military Advisory and Monitoring Team that was to follow. This deployment aimed to assist with the facilitation of the peace process in that country. On 24 June 2005, the UN Security Council extended the UN operation in the Côte d'Ivoire until 24 January 2006, following the unanimous adoption of Resolution 1609 (2005).

Egypt

Bilateral political and economic relations between Egypt and South Africa have improved greatly in recent years. These improvements were underlined in April 1996 with the convening of the first Joint Bilateral Commission (JBC) in Cairo.

Several agreements were signed between South Africa and Egypt during the sixth session of the South Africa-Egypt JBC in Pretoria in July 2003.

In September 2005, President Mbeki congratulated President Hosni Mubarak on his election victory.

Sudan

President Mbeki paid an official visit to Sudan from 30 December 2004 to 2 January 2005.

He held bilateral talks with President Omer Hassan Ahmed Al Beshir on bilateral political and economic relations between South Africa and Sudan, including the work of the AU Committee on the Post-Conflict Reconstruction of Sudan, which is chaired by South Africa; and regional African, and international issues of mutual interest.

South Africa and Sudan signed the MoU on Political Consultations and Co-operation. Issues covered by the MoU included co-operation in inter-national and regional issues of mutual concern, and co-ordination on matters of mutual concern within the framework of the regional and international organisations of which both countries are members. The two countries also agreed to encourage co-operation in the field of oil exploration.

President Al Beshir briefed President Mbeki on progress made with the Naivasha (Kenya) peace process between the Government of Sudan and the Sudanese People's Liberation Movement (SPLM), the situation in Darfur, and the related peace negotiations held in Abuja, Nigeria and N'djamena.

President Mbeki travelled to Naivasha, Kenya, to witness the signing of the Protocol on Implementation Modalities and the Permanent Ceasefire Agreement between Sudan and the SPLM that paved the way for the signing of the comprehensive peace agreement (CPA) in January 2005.

The signing of the CPA ended a 27-year war and marked the start of the six-month pre-interim period (January – July 2005) during which the SPLM had to assemble and constitute a government for South Sudan, and nominate members to form part of central government in Khartoum. This was to be followed by an interim period (July 2005 – July 2011) during which the SPLM will govern South Sudan, with a high degree of autonomy, and participate in central government in Khartoum in a comprehensive and effective manner.

The UN Security Council on 24 March 2004 unanimously adopted Resolution 1590 (2005) on the creation of a peacekeeping operation in South Sudan. The resolution established a UN mission in Sudan (UNMIS) for an initial six-month period to support the implementation of the CPA. The mandate of UNMIS includes monitoring and verifying the ceasefire agreement, assisting with the establishment of disarmament, demobilisation and reintegration programmes, and promoting national reconciliation and human rights.

The Department of Foreign Affairs and the University of South Africa co-hosted a training programme for SPLM cadres in Pretoria in April 2005. This was the second phase of the project, the first of which was launched in New Site, Kapoeta County, in February 2005.

By 6 May 2005, South Africa had deployed 294 South African troops in Sudan as part of the UN Mission and 18 members of the SAPS as part of a co-operation programme.

An additional 46 SAPS members were deployed to Sudan later in May 2005.

Morocco

Diplomatic relations between South Africa and the Kingdom of Morocco were established in 1991 when the South African Interest Office opened in Rabat. The Moroccan Interest Office was opened in Pretoria in April 1992 and both offices were subsequently upgraded to full embassies.

The first JBC Meeting with Morocco took place in Pretoria in 1998.

Sahrawi Arab Democratic Republic (SADR)

On 7 April 2005, Minister Dlamini-Zuma paid an official visit to the SADR, the first such high-level visit by a senior South African minister following recognition of the SADR by South Africa in September 2004.

The minister held bilateral discussions with her counterpart, Mr Ould Salek. She announced that South Africa would provide humanitarian assistance for projects related to nutrition, water and sanitation.

She was also briefed on the status of the UN Baker Plan, a framework through which the current conflict between the SADR and Morocco should be resolved.

South Africa has officially established diplomatic relations at ambassadorial level. South Africa recognises the right of the Sahrawis to self-determination, which is an inalienable right contained in the Charter of the UN.

Mauritania

Full diplomatic relations between South Africa and Mauritania were established in January 1995.

Minister Dlamini-Zuma visited Mauritania in January 2005.

She held bilateral discussions with her counterpart, Mr Mohamed Vail Ould Belial, on different aspects of co-operation, ranging from trade and industry to minerals and energy, fisheries, maritime, transport, infrastructure, and education. The two ministers also signed an agreement on a framework for co-operation, which provides for the establishment of a JCC at ministerial level.

Liberia

Following the signing of the Comprehensive Peace Agreement between the Liberian Government, and the rebel groups Liberians United for Reconciliation and Democracy and the Movement for Democracy in Liberia on 18 August 2003, the socio-political situation in the country has much improved.

In view of the large presence of the UN Mission in Liberia (UNMIL), the security situation has remained stable. With the assistance of the UNMIL, the National Transitional Government of Liberia (NTGL) has greatly advanced the peace process. The NTGL has already deployed a small number of the newly recruited Liberian police force members.

The humanitarian situation has improved although the economy still remains weak. It was anticipated that elections would be held in 2005. South Africa continues to support initiatives towards promoting peace in the country as it has done in the past.

Nigeria

South Africa's bilateral and multilateral relationship with Nigeria remains of strategic importance, particularly in light of the development and promotion of NEPAD.

Nigeria is the current chair of the AU as well as the outgoing chair of the Commonwealth. The sixth session of the BNC was held in Durban in September 2004 while the seventh session was expected to take place in Abuja late in 2005. This co-operation framework is an illustration of the type of South-South co-operation that South Africa seeks to foster. In this regard, Nigeria is a key partner in the promotion of the ideals of the AU, its socio-economic programme NEPAD, as well as the engagement of Africa with the developed states of the G8.

Ghana

During her three-day visit to Ghana in November

2004, Minister Dlamini-Zuma and her counterpart, Mr Nana Akufo Addo, signed agreements on the establishment of a permanent JCC and the avoidance of double taxation.

On 7 January 2005, former Deputy President Zuma attended the inauguration of the President-elect of Ghana, Mr John Agyekum Kufuor, in Accra.

Between 1996 and 2003, there were about 35 South African multinational and small-scale companies registered in Ghana. In April 2004, a South African company, Anglo-Gold, signed a merger deal with Ghanaian Ashanti Goldfields valued at US$1,4 billion. South African investment in the Ghanaian mining sector accounts for more than 60% of total FDI into the sector.

Burkina Faso
South Africa and Burkina Faso established non-resident diplomatic relations in May 1995. The Burkina Faso non-resident ambassador for South Africa is based in Addis Ababa, Ethiopia, while the South African Ambassador to Abidjan, Côte d'Ivoire, is accredited to Burkina Faso on a non-residential basis.

On 13 July 2004, President Mbeki and his counterpart from Burkina Faso, Mr Blaise Compaore, signed a co-operation framework agreement and a MoU in terms of which South Africa will assist Burkina Faso to find and access mineral deposits.

The two leaders also discussed the need to create stability in areas of conflict around West Africa. Though Burkina Faso has limited exploitable resources, opportunities exist for South African mining companies for mining deposits of gold, zinc and manganese. Since agriculture is the dominant industry, opportunities exist for the trade of various agricultural products.

Spoornet is one of the few large South African companies involved in Burkina Faso. Trade between South Africa and that country is limited. In terms of total trade with South Africa, Burkina Faso is South Africa's 11th-largest partner in the West African region.

Republic of Benin
Diplomatic relations between Benin and South Africa were established in May 1994. The South African ambassador to Abidjan, Côte d'Ivoire, is accredited to Benin on a non-residential basis while Benin opened an embassy in Pretoria in 1999.

Former Deputy President Zuma paid a visit to Benin in August 2004 and met with President Mathieu Kerekou. Benin's economy is based largely on subsistence agriculture, cotton production and regional trade. Trade between South Africa and Benin is limited, with main imports into South Africa from Benin being vegetable products, and South Africa's main export products to Benin being base metals and machinery.

Republic of Togo
Diplomatic relations between South Africa and Togo were established in 1997. The South African ambassador to Abidjan, Côte d'Ivoire, is accredited on a non-residential basis to Togo.

Former President Gnassingbe Eyadema visited South Africa in 1997. After his death in February 2005, South Africa strongly opposed the unconstitutional installation of his son as president and welcomed his decision to relinquish the post until further elections.

South Africa also supported the ECOWAS position on restoring Togo to constitutionality following President Eyadema's death.

Economic relations between South Africa and Togo are limited, with phosphates comprising the bulk of South African imports from Togo.

Cape Verde
South Africa and Cape Verde established diplomatic relations on 4 April 1994. South Africa's ambassador to Senegal is also accredited as South Africa's non-resident ambassador to Cape Verde, while the Cape Verdean ambassador to Angola is accredited to South Africa as non-resident ambassador.

The Gambia
In September 2004, the President of The Gambia, Dr Alhaji Yahya AJJ Jammeh, visited South Africa and held bilateral discussions with President Mbeki.

South African exports to The Gambia include motor vehicles, prepared foodstuffs and beverages.

Guinea

Diplomatic relations between South Africa and Guinea were established on 16 February 1995. The first Guinean ambassador to South Africa took up his post in Pretoria in July 1996. The South African ambassador to Senegal is accredited to Guinea on a non-residential basis.

South Africa's trade with and investment in Guinea have increased substantially over the past few years, with the country's rich mineral sector being the main area of focus.

Diplomatic relations between the two countries were expected to be consolidated by an official visit to South Africa by senior officials from Guinea's Ministry of Foreign Affairs in May 2005.

Guinea-Bissau

Diplomatic relations between South Africa and Guinea-Bissau were established in October 1994. The South African ambassador to Senegal is accredited as South Africa's non-resident ambassador to Guinea-Bissau.

In an effort to support post-conflict reconstruction in the country, and in response to the call by the ECOSOCC Ad Hoc Advisory Committee on Guinea-Bissau on the international donor community to give emergency assistance to the people of Guinea-Bissau, the South African Government in February 2004 made a contribution to the UN Development Programme Trust Fund to assist that country.

Mali

Full diplomatic relations between South Africa and

In January 2005, a South African delegation delivered relief aid to Asian communities affected by the tsunami on 26 December 2004.
The South African delegation comprised representatives from government departments and some leading relief organisations.
The donation was mobilised through the non-governmental organisation, the Gift of the Givers Foundation.

Mali were established in May 1994. The latter established an embassy in Pretoria in December 1995. A South African embassy was established in Bamako in November 2002, and the first South African ambassador to Mali was appointed in November 2003.

Mali is a strong supporter of the African Renaissance initiative and NEPAD.

In August 2002, the Agreement of the Preservation of the Ancient Manuscripts in the Ahmed Baba Institute of Higher Learning and Islamic Research in Timbuktu was concluded between the two countries. This followed a pledge made by President Mbeki during his state visit to Mali in November 2001 that South Africa would support a project aimed at improving the preservation of these ancient manuscripts. The manuscripts vary in content from religious treatises and poems, to documentary letters dealing with legal and commercial matters, while others relate to slavery, mathematics, astronomy, medicine, history – all of them subjects of immense interest to scholars and the African population at large. Three major thrusts to the project are to:
- implement a conservation programme to protect and improve environmental storage conditions for the manuscripts
- rebuild the Ahmed Baba Centre to one of international stature while ensuring its architectural harmony with ancient Timbuktu
- promote academic study and public awareness of the magnificent and ancient African and Islamic heritage at Timbuktu.

The two countries share a commitment to the promotion of democracy and good governance, and substantial South African involvement in the Malian gold-mining sector. Anglogold and Randgold run operations in Mali.

The first session of the South Africa-Mali JCC took place in Pretoria in August 2004.

Senegal

Full diplomatic relations between South Africa and Senegal were established in May 1994 and the two countries' representative offices upgraded to embassy level. After closing its embassy in Pretoria in December 1995, the Senegalese authorities re-established it in 2001. The South African ambassador to Senegal is also accredited to Cape Verde, The Gambia, Guinea, Guinea-Bissau and Mauritania on a non-residential basis.

Bilateral relations between South Africa and Senegal are based mainly on the Senegalese Government's strong support for the African Renaissance initiative and NEPAD, as well as strong commitment to the promotion of democracy and good governance.

Senegal is one of the 15 members of the NEPAD HSIC and the AU PSC.

In November 2004, Minister Dlamini-Zuma paid an official visit to Senegal, where she signed an agreement establishing a joint commission for bilateral co-operation (JCBC) between the two countries.

On behalf of President Mbeki, Dr Dlamini-Zuma received the first biannual African Gender Award for 2005 in Senegal in May 2005.

The other recipient was Senegalese President Abdoulaye Wade, in recognition of the leading roles the two leaders played in the 2003 adoption by the AU of the Protocol to the African Charter on Human and People's Rights on the Rights of Women in Africa.

Tunisia
On 9 July 2004, the Minister of Foreign Affairs of the Republic of Tunisia, Mr Habib Ben Yahia, attended the fourth South Africa-Tunisia JBC in South Africa. Several agreement were signed.

In October 2004, President Mbeki and nine Cabinet ministers paid a state visit to Tunisia, where they signed various bilateral agreements.

The fifth session of the South Africa-Tunisia JBC was expected to take place in Tunisia in 2005.

Libya
The long-standing unofficial relations between South Africa and the Great People's Socialist Libyan Arab Jamahiriya (Libya) dates back to the days of the struggle against apartheid.

The first session of the South Africa-Libya JBC was held in Tripoli in June 2002.

Former Deputy President Zuma led a senior government and business delegation on a visit to Libya in March 2005.

Bilateral political and economic discussions aimed to:
- consolidate bilateral political and economic relations between South Africa and Libya
- discuss the operationalisation of the AU and its organs, and the implementation of NEPAD
- consolidate efforts to achieve peace, security and stability in Africa.

This high-level visit to Libya followed that country's denunciation of its nuclear weapons programme and ratification of the Comprehensive Nuclear Test Ban Treaty.

Sierra Leone
Peace and security in Sierra Leone have been sustained with the assistance of the UN Mission in Sierra Leone (UNAMSIL). The Government of Sierra Leone has restored its authority across the entire country and, with the assistance of UNAMSIL, has increased its control over diamond-mining areas.

Although the country remains poor, it has made various accomplishments towards democracy and development. South Africa's Eskom has undertaken to assist the Sierra Leone authorities in improving and managing their electrification system.

Niger
Niger is one of the poorest countries in West Africa and is considered the second-poorest country in the world, according to the UN. It relies solely on foreign aid for its development.

The Minister of Agriculture and Land Affairs, Ms Thoko Didiza, led a South African delegation to the launch of the Implementation of the Comprehensive African Agricultural Development Programme in Accra, Ghana, in May 2005.

As a contribution towards the New Partnership for Africa's Development, the Department of Agriculture initiated the African Agricultural Development Programme. This programme provides a framework for restoring agricultural growth, rural development and food security on the African continent.

Overall, the Niger Government has undertaken several programmes to increase democratisation, improve governance and expand freedom and other civil rights. On 8 December 2004, President Tandja Momadou was re-elected with 65,5% of the vote.

On 6 April 2005, Minister Dlamini-Zuma held bilateral discussions with her Niger counterpart, Mr Achiatou Mindaoudou.

The talks focused on the consolidation of bilateral political and economic relations between the two countries, including the opening of a South African diplomatic mission in Niamey, a bilateral air services agreement and the promotion of South African investment in Niger's mining and agricultural sectors.

South Africa continues to support any initiative aimed at assisting Niger in its development.

Relations with Asia and the Middle East

Asia and Australasia

Since 1994, South Africa's political and economic interaction with Asia and Australasia has increased significantly. By mid-2005, South Africa had 17 residential diplomatic missions in 15 of the 30 countries or territories in Asia, Australasia and central Asia. Eighteen countries from this region maintained 30 diplomatic missions in South Africa.

Over the past two decades, rapid economic growth in the People's Republic of China (PRC), India and south-east Asian countries has made Asia one of the most economically dynamic regions in the world, generating tremendous business opportunities for South Africa.

While Japan, Malaysia and Taiwan already rank among the foremost sources of foreign investment to South Africa, the significance of China and India, as future sources of investment, is expected to grow. South Africa's multinational companies are finding attractive investment opportunities in Australia, China, Indonesia and Thailand in diverse fields such as mining, minerals processing, electronic media and the petrochemical industry.

Greater Asia incorporates five central Asian states, which were formerly part of the Soviet Union.

The five central Asian states (Kazakhstan, Uzbekistan, Turkmenistan, Kyrgyzstan and Tajikistan) offer economic opportunities in, among others, the oil and mining sectors and related technology. Although this region offers a market for South African goods and services, the potential remains largely untapped. South Africa is also expanding and deepening its relations with the Pacific island states. These countries are natural friends of South Africa, sharing its colonial experience and development aims. Therefore, South Africa was expected to conclude diplomatic relations with all the independent and self-governing states of the Pacific, and open a micro-mission in Suva, Fiji, which hosts the Secretariat of the Pacific Islands Forum.

South African diplomatic representation in South Asia will similarly be increased with the establishment of a micro-mission in Colombo, Sri Lanka. During the second half of 2005, the first session of the South African-Pakistan Joint Commission was expected to be held while the sixth session of the JMC with India was also scheduled for 2005.

The assertiveness of this region in both global politics and economics is becoming increasingly visible, as demonstrated by the high-profile role played by key Asian countries in global affairs.

China is the only developing country that is a permanent member of the United Nations Security Council (UNSC); Japan is an influential member of the G8; while India, Japan and Indonesia have publicly declared their intention to lobby for a permanent seat on the reformed UNSC.

South Africa and key Asian countries agree on important multilateral issues, such as the reform of the Bretton Woods Institutions, the WTO and UN, international disarmament and the proliferation of weapons of mass destruction, small arms proliferation, and protection of the environment.

Several important Muslim countries, such as Indonesia, Malaysia, Bangladesh, Pakistan, Brunei, Afghanistan and Indonesia are members of the 52-nation Organisation of Islamic Conference.

Key Asian countries are also committed to contributing to the implementation of NEPAD. NEPAD projects that will make use of the US$200-million credit line offered by India need to be identified.

India has also indicated its willingness to provide funds to electronically connect members of the AU by satellite and fibre-optic network.

Several existing Africa-Asia co-operation fora, such as the Tokyo International Conference on African Development (TICAD) and the Forum on China-Africa Co-operation, are being synchronised with NEPAD to serve as implementing institutions. TICAD is an initiative for African development, launched in 1993 through the joint efforts of the Japanese Government, the UN and the Global Coalition for Africa.

The Vietnam-Africa Forum provides an important venue for greater co-operation between Vietnam and Africa.

As a result of South Africa's participation in the Association of South-East Asia Nations (ASEAN) Summit in November 2002, a decision was taken to launch the Asia-Africa Subregional Organisations Conference (AASROC I) in Bandung in April 2003. South Africa and Indonesia co-host AASROC.

The AASROC II Conference, held in August 2004 in Durban, identified three broad areas of co-operation between Asia and Africa, namely: political, economic, and social and cultural. It further identified the contribution of Asian-African subregional organisations towards the New Asian-African Strategic Partnership (NAASP), which was launched during the Asian-African Summit in Indonesia, in April 2005.

The NAASP will focus on practical, achievable and concrete ways of addressing the development of Asian and African countries in a pragmatic manner. The NAASP will focus on areas such as economic issues, trade, investment, health and human resource development (HRD).

Several key Asian countries are leading role-players of the South. They share common membership with South Africa in international organisations such as the Non-Aligned Movement (NAM), G77 and the Commonwealth. South Africa also plays a leading role in the Indian Ocean Rim Association for Regional Co-operation.

The India-Brazil-South Africa (IBSA) Dialogue Forum remains of strategic importance to all three countries as a powerful global forum to drive South-South co-operation, the agenda of the South, and to champion the needs of the developing world. The second Ministerial Trilateral Commission meeting held in Cape Town in March 2005 provided an opportunity for the further strengthening of co-operation among the three countries.

It is estimated that South Africa's total trade with the Asian region rose from less than R60 billion in 1999 to more than R140 billion by the end of 2003. More than 27% of South African foreign trade is conducted with countries in Asia. Although investment from the region has grown significantly since 1994 and continues to expand, the levels need to be increased.

It remains vital to sharpen South Africa's expertise and capacity throughout the Asian region to raise the trade and investment profile of South African products and services.

The proposed FTA to be negotiated with China, India and Singapore provides an important framework for closer co-operation between the Southern African Customs Union (SACU) and these countries in the quest for mutually beneficial trade links.

East Asia

Japan is by far South Africa's largest trading partner in this region, followed by Greater China and South Korea.

In September 2005, President Mbeki congratulated Prime Minister Junichiro Koizumi on his victory in the September elections.

Bilateral relations with the PRC have expanded substantially since the establishment of diplomatic relations in 1998. There are strong links between the PRC and South Africa at various levels and China is a key global actor with whom South Africa seeks to broaden relations.

South Africa is the PRC's main trade partner in Africa, accounting for 20,8% of the total volume of China-Africa trade. The complementary nature of the two economies provides the impetus for the growth of trade. At the same time, bilateral trade amounts to only a very small percentage of both the PRC and South Africa's international trade profile, suggesting that there is still enormous potential for an increased exchange of goods and services. Total bilateral trade between the PRC and South Africa reached R23,8 billion in 2004, with the balance in favour of the PRC.

Notwithstanding the absence of diplomatic relations, South Africa and Taiwan continue with trade, scientific, cultural and other relations. Taiwanese investors in South Africa continue to enjoy full protection under South African law, as well as all the other benefits extended to foreign investors.

South Africa participated in the fourth session of the TICAD III in Tokyo, Japan, in November 2004.

At the TICAD meeting, Japan committed itself to continued dialogue with Africa as well as to support capacity-building and provide other development assistance.

South Korea remains an important trade partner for South Africa. The second South Africa-South Korea Policy Consultative Meeting took place in Seoul during June 2004.

The strengthening of trade and investment relations was agreed upon. Opportunities for South Africa exist in mining and metal, steel, automotive components, agro-processing, textiles and cosmetics. A science and technology agreement with South Korea was signed during March 2004.

South Asia

South Africa and Afghanistan established diplomatic relations in September 1994. South Africa never recognised the former Taliban regime and has normalised relations with the current Government. The South Africa Liaison Office for Afghanistan was established in 2003, headed non-residentially by the South African high commissioner to Pakistan.

In 2004, South Africa congratulated Mr Hamid Karzai on his election as president of the

By September 2005, the South African pavilion at the World Expo 2005 in Aichi, Japan, had clocked in excess of 2,5 million visitors.

The interest was attributed mainly to the exhibits, texts and audio-visual material on show.

The coelacanth, a fossilised fish dating back more than 400 million years, enjoyed much interest.

Transitional Islamic State of Afghanistan. South Africa intended to monitor developments in Afghanistan through the parliamentary elections scheduled for 2005.

South Africa and Sri Lanka established diplomatic relations in 1994.

An advance team visited Sri Lanka in April 2005, in preparation for the establishment of a South African mission in Colombo. The first session of the Partnership Forum was expected to follow shortly thereafter.

Diplomatic relations between South Africa and Pakistan were established in April 1994. A letter of understanding, establishing a joint commission (JC) between the two countries, was signed in March 1999. The lifting of the Commonwealth suspensions that had been imposed on Pakistan paved the way for the normalisation of South Africa's relations with that country, and created the opportunity to engage on issues of mutual interest.

The first session of the JC was expected to be held in 2005. South Africa supports the ongoing rapprochement between India and Pakistan on the Jammu-Kashmir issue.

India is South Africa's sixth-largest trading partner in Asia. In 2003/04, total trade between the two countries amounted to R6,47 billion.

In September 2004, the President of the Republic of India, Dr Abdul Kalam, paid the first-ever state visit by an Indian head of state to South Africa. Presidents Mbeki and Kalam stressed that the full potential for bilateral trade had not yet been tapped and undertook to maket a concerted effort to at least double the existing volume by 2006. In this regard, a definite role is foreseen for the India-South Africa Commercial Alliance.

The sixth session of the South African-Indian JMC was held in New Delhi in May 2005.

South-east Asia

The ASEAN has emerged as one of the most important groupings within the Asia Pacific region. South Africa maintains embassies and high commissions in six of the 10 member states of ASEAN – Indonesia, Malaysia, Singapore, Thailand, Vietnam and the Philippines. These six ASEAN states, as well as Myanmar (Burma), also maintain embassies and high commissions in South Africa.

Vietnam plays an increasingly important role in south-east Asia and has vast economic potential and opportunities for mining, infrastructure development, and agricultural and manufacturing companies.

In November 2004, during the state visit to South Africa of Vietnamese Prime Minister, Mr Phan Van Khai, South Africa and Vietnam signed an agreement on the establishment of a Vietnam-South Africa partnership forum. He was accompanied by the largest-ever delegation to visit South Africa. South Africa's trade with Vietnam has increased eight-fold in the last 10 years.

Economic relations with Malaysia and Indonesia remain important, due to Malaysian investment in South Africa and the size of the Indonesian market.

The first JC meeting between South Africa and Malaysia was scheduled to take place in Indonesia during the second half of 2005.

Malaysia has indicated its support for NEPAD and has sought to promote the Malaysian-initiated Langkawi International Dialogue aimed at expanding co-operation among countries of the South, including those in southern Africa.

Malaysian Prime Minister Abdullah Ahmad Badawi paid an official visit to South Africa in July 2005.

Total trade with south-east Asia increased significantly from R10 billion in 1999 to R18 billion in 2003.

Central Asia

The economies of Kazakhstan, Uzbekistan, Turkmenistan, Kyrgyzstan and Tajikistan are all at various stages of change and development. Furthermore, all five are developing states and, like South Africa, seek investment. Economic opportunities for South Africa in the Central Asian states include infrastructure development, mining technology, energy exploitation and related mining and engineering technology, agro-processing expertise and exports, water management expertise and infrastructure for adventure and ecotourism.

Australasia and the Pacific islands

South Africa and Australia established diplomatic relations in 1947 and have enjoyed very close political and economic ties. As campaigns for international isolation of South Africa intensified in the 1970s and 1980s, successive Australian governments placed Australia firmly in the anti-apartheid camp, supporting UN resolutions against apartheid and implementing the oil, trade and arms embargo as well as sport boycott against South Africa.

On 7 February 2005, the Deputy Minister of Foreign Affairs, Ms Sue van der Merwe, held bilateral talks with her Australian counterpart, Mr Bruce Billson, in Pretoria. South Africa is Australia's third-largest trading partner in Asia, after Japan and China.

Diplomatic and trade relations between the two countries are valued at R11,4 billion. The merger in the 1990s of Australian BHP Billiton and Gencor created the largest mining company in the world.

New Zealand maintains a high commission in Pretoria, while the high commission in Canberra represents South Africa in New Zealand. The establishment of a resident high commission in Wellington is imminent.

Since 1994, political, economic and social links between the two countries have improved significantly. In 1996, the Cape Town Communique was signed, seeking to strengthen co-operation between South Africa and New Zealand.

The political relationship has been further strengthened through visits by numerous high-level delegations to New Zealand to gain expertise in their different fields and exchange knowledge to enhance capacity-building in central, provincial and local government structures.

South Africa and New Zealand enjoy wide-ranging multilateral relations. Both are members of the Valdivia Group, which aims to promote southern hemisphere views in international environmental meetings and enhance scientific co-operation.

They enjoy a close working relationship within the context of the Antarctic Treaty and Indian Ocean fisheries, and also interact within the context of the WTO and the Cairns Group. South Africa and New Zealand also work closely on Commonwealth issues, particularly those affecting Africa.

The South African Government wants to strengthen relations with the Pacific islands. As a result, a roving ambassador to the Pacific islands was appointed with effect from 1 August 2004.

The ambassador has been accredited to the Independent State of Papua New Guinea, the Fiji Islands and the Solomon Islands.

An advanced team visited Fiji to explore the feasibility of opening a mission there before the end of 2005.

The high commissioner in Canberra, Australia, has been accredited to the Cook Islands, Federated States of Micronesia, the Republic of Marshall Islands, the Republic of Vanuatu and the Independent State of Samoa. By mid-2005, diplomatic relations were being sought with the republics of Kiribati, Palau, Nauru, and Tuvalu.

The Middle East

In the Middle East, the Department of Foreign Affairs distinguishes between two clearly identifiable subregions. On the one hand, there is the Levant, which comprises Israel, Iraq, Jordan, Lebanon, Palestine and Syria, and on the other, the Arabian/Persian Gulf Region, comprising the member states of the Gulf Co-operation Council, namely Bahrain, Kuwait, Oman, Qatar, Saudi Arabia, the United Arab Emirates, Iran and Yemen.

The Middle East is an important economic region as it occupies a unique geopolitical position in the tri-

continental hub of Europe, Asia and Africa. It is the source of 67% of the world's petroleum reserves and commands two of the most strategically important waterways in the world, namely the Arabian/Persian Gulf and the Red Sea, giving access to the Asian hinterland via the Gulf of Aqaba. South Africa places strong emphasis on the expansion of diplomatic representation and activities in this region, where it was formerly underrepresented, particularly in the area of trade, which has grown significantly since 1994.

The South African consulate general in Jeddah, in addition to performing important functions relating to the promotion of trade, also serves members of the South African Muslim community on their annual pilgrimage to Mecca. More than 7 000 South Africans embark on the Hajj pilgrimage each year.

South Africa supports a just, equitable and comprehensive peace process in the Middle East and an end to the illegal occupation of land that has led to conflict and violence between the peoples of the region. Peace and security for the Israelis and the Palestinians cannot be achieved without the fulfilment of the inalienable right of the Palestinian people to self-determination within their own sovereign state.

South Africa has continued to call on all parties to the conflict in Israel and Palestine to avoid actions that could add to an already volatile situation. The country has been consistent in calling for the immediate implementation of the Road Map, without preconditions, to achieve comprehensive and lasting peace between Israel and Palestine.

The Deputy Minister of Foreign Affairs, Mr Aziz Pahad, attended a meeting of the NAM Committee on Palestine convened on 13 May 2004 in Malaysia. This was followed by the NAM Ministerial meeting on Palestine in Durban in August 2004.

A senior delegation of the South African Government, led by President Mbeki and Minister Dlamini-Zuma, met with a senior delegation of the governing Likud Party in Israel, led by Israeli Deputy Minister of Trade, Industry and Labour, Mr Michael Ratzon, in September 2004. The delegations shared experiences and exchanged views on the Israeli-Palestinian conflict as well as the state of bilateral relations.

On 21 April 2005, President Thabo Mbeki paid a state visit to Singapore for bilateral and economic discussions with his counterpart, President Sellapan Ramanathan Nathan.

From 19 to 20 April 2005, President Mbeki paid a state visit to Indonesia for bilateral, political and economic discussions with his Indonesian counterpart, President-General Susilo Bambang Yudhoyono.

President Mbeki attended the Asian-African Summit in Jakarta from 22 to 23 April 2005. On 24 April 2005, he attended the Commemoration Ceremony of the 1955 Bandung Summit in Bandung.

The South African Government sent an election observer delegation to Palestine during the Palestinian Presidential Election, held on 9 January 2005.

In August 2005, South Africa welcomed the withdrawal of Israel from Gaza, effectively ending 38 years of occupation.

During December 2004, Minister Dlamini-Zuma paid an official visit to Kuwait and the Islamic Republic of Iran. She attended the eighth South Africa-Iran JBC, where Iran and South Africa signed an agreement on co-operation in the field of health.

During February 2005, officials from the Iranian Central Bank visited South Africa and met with the deputy governor of the South African Reserve Bank and representatives of South African commercial banks.

Qatar Airways held a gala banquet in Johannesburg on 29 January 2005 to officially launch the new Qatar-Johannesburg-Cape Town air service that commenced on 16 January 2005.

South Africa participated in the Defence Exhibition, held in Dubai in February 2005, at which the South African-manufactured Rooivalk combat helicopter was exhibited.

In mid-2004, a successful first meeting of the South Africa-Saudi Arabia Joint Economic Commission took place in South Africa, during which the South African-Saudi Business Forum was established.

FDI from Turkey into South Africa amounts to US$60 million, mainly in the textile and tourism sectors. Six Turkish companies have set up plants in South Africa. There are also over 50 registered Turkish companies trading or providing services in the tourism and restaurant sectors in South Africa. Several South African companies have also set up business in Turkey.

The official visit of Turkish Prime Minister, Mr Recep Tayyip Erdogan in March 2005, illustrated the growing economic importance of South African-Turkey relations.

South African exports to Turkey (including gold) increased by 20% during 2004 and reached R5,6 billion. South Africa's exports during the same period in 2003 totalled R1,8 billion.

Two successful business summits and exchange visits contributed to bilateral trade during 2004, totaling over one billion US dollars. The conclusion of the trade and economic co-operation and customs agreements during Prime Minister Erdogan's visit is expected to contribute to continued growth in trade, and economic and investment relations between the two countries.

Relations with the Americas

United States of America (USA)

South Africa's bilateral relationship with the USA remains strong. Since 1994, business, civilian and governmental links with the USA have expanded exponentially and a strong, long-term working partnership has been established between the two countries.

The US Administration has identified Africa as a foreign-policy priority and has further identified South Africa as an anchor state in the region in terms of the US National Security Strategy.

The USA remains the largest single foreign investor in the South African economy since 1994, and the largest trading partner, taken as an individual country, as well as the largest donor of official development assistance.

Current economic priorities with regard to the USA are two-fold: the conclusion of the SACU-US FTA negotiations which, once completed, would have the potential of securing Africa Growth and Opportunity Act (AGOA) benefits for the long term; encouraging new investments in South Africa and continuing to market South Africa as a desirable investment destination for US companies, with the emphasis on promoting economic empowerment for previously disadvantaged communities.

The SACU-US FTA negotiations are considered important both in the context of encouraging US support for regional economic development and co-operation, as well as for the effective implementation of NEPAD. The talks have the potential to improve trade flows significantly between the SACU region and the US, and contribute to regional economic growth, stability and prosperity.

Support for NEPAD within the US Administration, US Congress and business sector, with particular focus on the implementation of infrastructure development projects, is a high priority. Building local capacity for research and effective delivery is another area of co-operation with the USA in the continuing battle against communicable diseases such as malaria, tuberculosis, HIV and AIDS.

The USA Presidential Emergency Programme for AIDS committed US$2,8 billion for 2005. US support for South Africa, the region and Africa's social and economic objectives is an important long-term priority.

Consultation between the South African Government, through the Department of Finance and the USA Agency for International Development (USAID), on the alignment of the USAID programmes with the domestic developmental priorities of South Africa, remains ongoing, and is reviewed yearly. USAID programmes in South Africa focus, among others, on strengthening the capacity of educational institutions; improving primary healthcare delivery; providing technical assistance and scholarships to improve economic capacity in the country; and enhancing the quality of, and access to, housing in South Africa.

Under the current co-operation agreement, R234 million will be directly geared towards South African government initiatives. This amount represents 56% of USAID's total annual budget of R546 million to South Africa, which in the past two years has been the top recipient of development assistance from among the 27 African countries supported by USAID.

President Mbeki and Minister Dlamini-Zuma held bilateral discussions with President George W. Bush in Washington in June 2005, ahead of the G8 summit hosted by the United Kingdom (UK) in Scotland in July 2005. Prior to the G8 summit, President Mbeki consulted with various G8 leaders to ensure practical outcomes for Africa and the South during the summit. In addition, presidents Mbeki and Bush discussed conflict resolution and peacekeeping in Africa, the G8 Africa Plan, the AGOA, the Millennium Challenge Account and overseas development aid to Africa.

In 2004, South African exports to the USA totalled US$5 926 million, which was an increase over the total of US$4 888 million in 2003. Imports from the USA came to US$2 977 million in 2004, compared with US$2 698 in 2003.

Canada

The healthy bilateral relations with Canada continue under the Government of Prime Minister Paul Martin. In the multilateral sphere, South Africa and Canada share a like-minded approach to a number of issues such as multilateralism and the need for UN reform. Canada remains a strong supporter of the African Agenda and NEPAD, also in a G8 context.

Canada is actively seeking closer co-operation with South Africa on peacekeeping on the continent.

Intensive interaction takes place between a number of South African government departments and their Canadian counterparts. Closer co-operation has been developing in the fields of health, science and technology, as well as arts and culture, with the emphasis on capacity-building, the transfer of skills, research and funding.

Canada remains the largest foreign investor in the South African mining sector and has indicated its intention of increasing investments in this sector, not only in South Africa, but also on the continent as a whole. Bilateral trade, which has been growing since 1994 and shifted in South Africa's favour in 2004, will receive a further boost with the establishment of the South Africa consulate-general in Toronto.

Canada reconfirmed its commitment to development co-operation with South Africa by making available R100 million a year over the next five years. Its technical assistance programme is aimed at social upliftment, policy development and HRD.

The finalisation of the Country Development Programme Framework between South Africa and Canada, one of the first of its kind, ensures a focused approach to Canadian development assistance to this country.

Annual consultations on a senior official level between South Africa and Canada were instituted in 2004 in terms of the Declaration of Intent signed during President Mbeki's state visit to that country in November 2003. The annual consultations have developed into an effective platform to annually review relations in all spheres and to identify priority areas for co-operation.

The Caribbean

South Africa's relations with the independent member states of the Caribbean community have been strengthened and expanded.

In addition to Jamaica, the high commission also maintains responsibility for Antigua and Barbuda, The Bahamas, Barbados, Belize, Dominica, Grenada, Guyana, Haiti, St Kitts and Nevis, St Lucia, St Vincent and the Grenadines, Suriname, and Trinidad and Tobago. The mission in Havana, Cuba, is responsible for the Dominican Republic.

In formulating South Africa's policy in relation to the emerging markets of the Caribbean, it is important to strengthen relations and develop common positions on global issues such as access to the markets of the industrial North, reform of international institutions, and the promotion of the development agenda. In this regard, special emphasis is placed on how South Africa and the rest of the African continent engage these countries in promoting the ideals of the continent and the Diaspora.

The South African Government will increase its focus on strengthening the relations with the Caribbean region in future. Trinidad and Tobago, the Dominican Republic and Suriname were either in the process or had opened diplomatic missions in South Africa during 2005.

South Africa signed a bilateral co-operation agreement with The Bahamas in May 2005. The first JBC between the two countries was scheduled to take place in 2005, focusing on closer co-operation in the fields of education, tourism and trade.

A JBC with Cuba was also scheduled to be held during 2005, while the fourth Consultative Mechanism meeting, a further instrument in the development of relations with Cuba, was to take place simultaneously. South Africa hoped to strengthen present agreements with Cuba during these meetings.

The South Africa, AU and Caribbean Diaspora Conference held in Kingston, Jamaica, during March 2005, provided specific guidelines on how to take South Africa's relationship with the Caribbean forward.

Latin America

The newly established South American Community of Nations covers 17 million square kilometres, with 361 million inhabitants, a gross domestic product of more than US$973 billion, and exports above US$180 billion.

The developing countries in Central America and the Andean Community are playing an increasingly important role in international political bodies and formations such as the NAM and the UN.

Brazil is a significant player in the multilateral context, particularly regarding the interests of the South. With its like-minded approach to a number of significant issues affecting the developing world, it is a strategic partner for South Africa.

The IBSA Dialogue Forum provides a mechanism for institutionalised engagement. Its second meeting was held in Cape Town in March 2005. In the bilateral sphere, a broad range of contacts and exchanges exist between Brazil and South Africa.

The third meeting of the JC between South Africa and Brazil, which took place in Brasilia in October 2004, gave added impetus to bilateral co-operation and comprised political discussions and technical interaction.

South Africa attaches great importance to its relations with other like-minded countries of the Southern Cone of Latin America such as Chile, Uruguay and Argentina, and efforts are underway to increase co-operation in a number of fields.

A JC agreement has been negotiated with Argentina, and a range of technical and commercial agreements are either in place or in the process of negotiation with several of the countries in the region.

There is furthermore significant potential for co-operation with the MERCOSUR (Southern Common Market) trading bloc, which consists of Argentina, Brazil, Paraguay and Uruguay as full members, and a steadily-increasing number of associate members in the Latin American region.

Since the December 2000 signing by South Africa and MERCOSUR of an FTA, SACU negotiated a partial preferential trade agreement with MERCO-SUR, which was signed in December 2004. Negotiations towards a full FTA continue.

Relations with Europe

The advent of a new democratic political dispensation more than 10 years ago marked the dawn of a new era in South Africa-European Union (EU) relations. The legal framework that governs South Africa's relationship with the EU is the Trade, Development and Co-operation Agreement (TDCA). The agreement is premised on political dialogue, trade and economic co-operation, and development assistance.

The TDCA provides for regular, high-level structured political dialogue at ministerial level. The Political Dialogue Forum enables the Minister of Foreign Affairs and her counterpart, the EU's High Representative for Common Foreign and Security Policy, to discuss bilateral, African and global issues.

These include poverty eradication, NEPAD, peace-building, conflict prevention, respect for human rights, democratic principles, the rule of law, and good governance. The first South Africa-EU Ministerial Troika Meeting in Dublin in April 2004, heralded a new phase in an already good relationship with South Africa.

As a result, President Mbeki visited the European institutions in November 2004. This was followed by the first South Africa-EU Ministerial JCC meeting on 23 November 2004. The JCC is a forum of the TDCA, established to monitor the implementation of the provisions of the agreement. The second Ministerial JCC was expected to take place in South Africa towards the end of 2005.

With regard to trade and economic co-operation, the TDCA provides for an FTA by 2012. The Trade Chapter of the agreement provisionally entered into force in January 2000. The reciprocal elimination of trade tariffs and the resultant access to the EU market improved two-way trade by close to 50% up to a total value of R200 billion.

During this period, South Africa exported to the EU an annual average of R80,6 billion worth of goods and imported R120,2 billion worth of goods from the EU. South Africa and the EU are finalising sectoral agreements on co-operation in investments, mining, information society, agriculture, research, and small, medium and micro enterprises. The TDCA also provides for co-operation in trade-related aspects, which includes co-operation in competition policy, customs, statistics, standards and conformity.

The EU is the largest source of FDI to South Africa. It accounts for 44% of the total FDI flows to South Africa and six out of the top 10 foreign investors in South Africa are member states of the EU.

The TDCA also provides the legal basis for continued EU support for development co-operation activities in South Africa. This support is channelled through the European Programme for Reconstruction and Development (EPRD). The EPRD is funded directly from the EU Commission at 127,5 million euro a year.

The EPRD is the largest single development programme in South Africa financed by foreign donors. Further assistance from the EU comes in the form of soft loans from the European Investment Bank.

A unique feature of the TDCA is that it has a regional development dimension. To this end, up to 15% of the EPRD can be used for regional development. This provision in the agreement created a legal basis for the decision of the first South Africa-EU Ministerial Troika Meeting, that 1,5% of the amount allocated to South Africa under the EPRD would be made available towards the Africa Peace Facility.

Among other things, EPRD funds also serve to strengthen South Africa's democratic institutions. The EU donated R80 million in January 2005 to South Africa's Parliament and the nine provincial legislatures to help strengthen democracy and the rule of law.

South Africa assumed full membership of the Africa, Caribbean and Pacific (ACP) group of countries in 1996. It became a qualified member of the Lome Convention in 1997 and of its successor, the Cotonou Partnership Agreement (CPA), signed in Cotonou, in June 2000. The CPA is a framework for co-operation between the 79 ACP group of countries and the EU. The new EU members which acceded in May 2004 adopted the agreement as part of the EU's legislative infrastructure.

Qualified membership means that South Africa is excluded from the trade regime provided in the agreement as well as from the provisions on development assistance. South Africa can, however, tender for projects in all ACP countries and participate fully in all political instruments of the agreement. South Africa's economic relations with the EU are governed by the TDCA.

The CPA differs significantly from its predecessor in that its duration will be 20 years, with a revision clause every five years and a financial protocol for each five-year period. The agreement underscores the importance of regional economic co-operation.

The most far-reaching changes are to be introduced in the area of trade, through regional economic partnership agreements (EPAs), where non-reciprocal preferences will be gradually abolished and regional integration processes encouraged. The present arrangements are to be maintained until 2008 when the EPAs would have been finalised. South Africa participates in the EPA negotiations as an observer.

One of the key aspects of South Africa's membership of the ACP is its active participation in the three ACP-EU joint political organs, namely the Council of Ministers, the Joint Parliamentary Assembly and the Committee of Ambassadors. South Africa takes part in dialogue on important issues such as peace-building, conflict resolution, respect for human rights, democratic principles and the rule of law.

South Africa regularly participates in ACP summits, council of ministers' meetings, trade ministers' meetings and the ACP Forum on Science and Technology.

The interest and commitment showed by the EU regarding the African continent and its development is encouraging. Within that context, the European Commission (EC) and the NEPAD Secretariat are closely co-operating through established structures and regular dialogue and information sharing.

They have also agreed to increase coherence between EU member states and the EC in support of NEPAD projects, the AU and its institutions, and the RECs.

Alongside political dialogue, there has been phenomenal growth in trade between South Africa and Belgium. The EU is South Africa's top export destination, and Belgian ports remain an important entry point through which South African exports find their way to countries both within and outside of the EU.

The Belgian Government continues to take a keen interest in South and southern Africa and the situation in the Great Lakes Region, particularly the DRC. There is a regular exchange of views between South Africa and Belgium on the issues and the complicated processes necessary to reach a durable solution to the conflicts in the region.

Since 1994, the Dutch Government has consistently supported South Africa in terms of bilateral and multilateral relations. A large number of bilateral agreements have been signed and high-level bilateral ministerial meetings are frequent.

Luxembourg and South Africa enjoy dynamic bilateral relations. High-level visits between the two states take place regularly.

Relations with Germany have expanded considerably since the introduction of the South Africa-Germany BNC in 1996, as the committees of the commission work continuously to enhance economic, scientific, cultural, environmental, defence and development co-operation.

South Africa is Germany's largest trading partner on the African continent. Germany ranks with the UK and USA among the three largest economic role-players in South Africa regarding trade, investment, finance and tourism. More than 370 German companies are investing in South Africa and collectively employ more than 65 000 people.

The Minister of Foreign Affairs of Switzerland visited South Africa in February 2004, during which the Declaration of Intent on the Promotion of Women Rights was signed.

A number of high-level visits, including the South Africa-Swiss Working Group Meeting and the Swiss State Secretary of Science and Technology's visit to South Africa took place during 2004. The Agreement Promoting Trilateral Co-operation in Africa ensures close liaison.

The Irish and South African governments agreed to set up the Ireland-South Africa Partnership Forum to boost co-operation between the two countries. The inaugural meeting of this structured, high-level and multisectoral engagement was expected to be convened late in 2005.

Relations with the UK were strengthened during the sixth meeting of the South Africa-UK Bilateral Forum in Cape Town in August 2004. Thirteen British and South African ministers participated and agreed on a number of new initiatives, including strengthening strategies to address the impact of healthcare personnel migration, as well as a detailed programme of cultural co-operation that is to be finalised through an MoU.

President Mbeki welcomed the report of the Commission for Africa published in March 2005, an initiative by Prime Minister Tony Blair to give impetus to African development.

In September 2004, former Deputy President Zuma visited Poland, where he briefed his Polish interlocutors on the current political situation in South Africa and thanked Poland for its support during the liberation struggle.

He also visited Romania to strengthen political and economic ties between the two countries. As a practical manifestation of this objective, the Agreement on Science and Technology Co-operation as well as the MoU on the Statute of the JC for Economic and Technical Co-operation were signed with that country.

Deputy Minister Pahad paid a successful visit to Croatia where he met, among others, his counterpart and the Croatian business community. To facilitate South Africa's initiatives in Croatia, a South African honorary-consul was appointed in Zagreb.

In December 2004, the Bulgarian Vice President, Mr Angel Marin, paid an official visit to South Africa to strengthen political and economic ties. The two countries signed agreements on police co-operation and co-operation in the fields of culture, healthcare and health science.

Notes were exchanged on the ratification by both parliaments of the Convention on Double Taxation and the Prevention of Fiscal Evasion with respect to Taxes on Income.

The historical links between South Africa and the Russian Federation are strong. The former Union of Soviet Socialist Republics was one of the key supporters of the struggle for liberation in South Africa.

In April 1999, the Intergovernmental Committee on Trade and Economic Co-operation (ITEC) between the Russian Federation and South Africa was established. The fourth session of ITEC was held in Pretoria in November 2004 and resulted in the signing of the bilateral Agreement on Co-operation in the Peaceful Use of Atomic Energy.

During the 5th ITEC session in October 2005 in Moscow, considerable progress was achieved in further strengthening mutually beneficial co-operation.

The Intergovernmental Agreement on Co-operation in the Field of Maritime Transport and an MoU in the sphere of astronomy and nuclear research was signed.

In July 2005, Minister Dlamini-Zuma received the Order of Peter the Great First Class, in recognition of her outstanding achievement in strengthening international peace, security and friendship between Russia and South Africa.

Bilateral relations between South Africa and France are directed by institutionalised mechanisms such as the MoU on Political Dialogue, and joint commissions on trade and industry and education, arts, culture, science and technology, and sport.

Economic relations between France and South Africa continue to strengthen. South African Airways recently procured Airbus aircraft as part of its comprehensive fleet modernisation programme.

Former Deputy President Zuma paid a working visit to Italy in October 2004 and met with his Italian counterpart, Mr Gianfranco Fini, as well as Cardinal Angelo Sodano from the Holy See and representatives from the NGO, St Egidio. He also addressed the World Political Forum in Stresa on *Poverty in the World – A Challenge to Globalisation.*

President Mbeki, accompanied by the Minister of Trade and Industry, Mr Mandisi Mpahlwa, paid a working visit to Italy during May 2005 where discussions were held with President Azeglio Ciampi and Prime Minister Silvio Berlusconi. Issues on the agenda included the consolidation of political and economic bilateral relations, European support for the African Agenda, peacekeeping and conflict management in Africa, the forthcoming G8 Summit and reform of the UN.

During this visit, President Mbeki also met the newly appointed Pope. President Mbeki was one of the first heads of state to be received by His Holiness Pope Benedict XVI. President Mbeki and the Pope discussed issues relating to the role of the Church in contributing to the African Agenda and the global fight against poverty and underdevelopment.

The Executive Programme for Scientific Co-Operation between Italy and South Africa was renewed for another three years. Implementation of the Film Co-Production Agreement saw South Africa participating in numerous film festivals, which culminated in the anniversary of South Africa's 10 years of freedom and democracy being one of the highlights of the Venice Film Festival.

The Forum Barcelona 2004 was the first of a series of international events aiming to bring together civil societies from all over the world to promote the study, reflection and innovative research of the various cultures that constitute the contemporary world.

The South African embassy in Spain participated extensively in this event, which was projected as an important aspect of its programme for the 10 Years of Democracy celebrations in 2004. Various ministers participated in these discussions, as did members of civil society.

The first session of the annual consultations between Deputy Minister Pahad and his former Spanish counterpart took place in February 2004 in Pretoria.

The third-largest Spanish company, El Corte Ingles, selected South Africa as a theme country for countrywide promotion in its 65 outlets in 2005.

In February 2005, President Mbeki paid a state visit to the Hellenic Republic.

Ten Years of Democracy were also celebrated in Greece and commenced with a multidenominational thanksgiving service and performances by three South African music groups. In Cyprus the celebrations were marked by a week-long South African Food Festival presented by South African chefs,

accompanied by performances of the Sibikwa Marimba Band.

Several 10-year celebrations were also held in Portugal.

The South African embassy continues to pursue the hosting of the second Africa-EU Summit with Portugal in 2006.

In January 2005, Minister Dlamini-Zuma attended the fourth session of the Nordic-African Information Consultation in Helsinki, Finland.

Discussions included:

- peace and security architecture in Africa and current challenges
- strengthening human rights, democracy and governance to promote development and prevent conflicts
- the implementation of NEPAD, including the operationalisation of the APRM
- the reform of the global exercise of governance, such as the UN and all its institutions, including the Security Council and the International Monetary Fund.

Multilateral diplomacy

The global challenges for both developing and developed countries, highlighted by the United Nations Secretary-General (UNSG) and many other speakers during the General Debate of the 59th session of the UN General Assembly (UNGA59) in September 2004, renewed the focus on the need to protect and strengthen multilateral mechanisms.

Events and issues that continued to undermine global peace and security and the multilateral system of governance made it clear that, for a collective security system to work, it is essential to address both development and security threats. Recognising the urgency of the matter, a number of member states, including South Africa, called for the speedy finalisation of discussions to restructure the UN.

South Africa remains an active participant in ongoing discussions on the reform of the UN, and believes that the multilateral system should be fully engaged in the endeavour for human development and poverty eradication, starting with the achievement of the MDGs; the common struggle to address

334

environmental degradation; the pursuit of an over-arching human rights agenda; the promotion of democracy and good governance; and all efforts to combat terrorism and the proliferation of weapons, both of mass destruction and small arms.

South Africa maintains that issues such as these pose major threats for world peace and security. Through participation in organisations and groups such as the UN, the AU, the NAM, the Group of 77 and China and the Commonwealth, South Africa seeks to ensure that national interests and objectives, as well as those of the continent and developing countries generally, are taken on board in discussions in multilateral fora and reports.

A major challenge for developing countries such as South Africa, is to be active in the protection and promotion of the agenda of the South in the current global geopolitical power configuration, and to ensure the pre-eminence and centrality of the UN in the eradication of underdevelopment and the maintenance of global peace and security.

International organisations
United Nations
South Africa's current priorities for participation in the UNGA, its main committees and organs, are:
- pursuit of an overarching human rights agenda including the right to development
- promoting global peace and security
- protecting and promoting multilateralism, international law and the centrality of the UN Charter
- addressing human development, poverty eradication and environmental degradation
- advancing the active follow-up and implementation of the MDGs, international development goals and the outcomes of major UN conferences
- advancing South-South co-operation through active participation in the NAM and other South-South co-operation arrangements
- promoting the reform of the UNSC General Assembly, ECOSOCC, and regional organisations, and generally revitalising the UN system
- promoting the Common Africa Position on the reform of the UN, including the equitable representation of Africa on the UNSC

- disarmament, arms control and non-proliferation of both weapons of mass destruction and conventional arms
- implementing the Johannesburg Plan of Action of the WSSD
- humanitarian assistance
- promoting the AU and NEPAD in the UN context
- promoting gender mainstreaming
- supporting the global campaign against terrorism.

President Mbeki used UNGA59 as a platform to expand on these national priorities. In addition, the President also participated in meetings with other world leaders on actions against hunger and poverty, and the social dimensions of globalisation.

In terms of South Africa's priorities, a very important development was the decision of the UNSG to appoint the High-Level Panel on Threats, Challenges and Change and the panel for the UN Millennium Project, to assist it in compiling a comprehensive report for the review of the Millennium Declaration in 2005.

Various other important panels also presented their work to the UNSG, which produced a solid base to offer solutions, in its report, to the global problems and challenges facing mostly the developing world. The announcement of the UNSG thus focused attention on the reform of the UN in many multilateral fora and regional organisations.

Consequently, in pursuance of a common African position, the fourth Ordinary Assembly of the AU held in Abuja, Nigeria, in January 2005, established the Committee of 15 at ministerial level to consider all aspects of the recommendations contained in the Report of the UN High-Level Panel, particularly the reform of the Security Council.

A South African delegation led by Minister Dlamini-Zuma attended the meeting of the Committee of 15 in Swaziland in February 2005 during which an African common position, the Ezulwini Consensus, was adopted and later formally endorsed by the AU Executive Council in Addis Ababa on 7 March 2005.

In March 2005, the UNSG tabled its own comprehensive report, *In Larger Freedom*, which combines elements from the Report of the High-Level Panel and the UN Millennium Project.

In response to the aforementioned reports, South Africa embraced the emphasis that development is an indispensable foundation for a new collective security system and also actively promoted the African Common Position, which calls for the reform of the General Assembly, the ECOSOCC and the Security Council.

South Africa's own candidacy for a permanent seat is pursued in the context of the African Common Position. The aforementioned reports, and consultations on it, provided input for the Millennium Review Summit, which reviewed the implementation of the Millennium Declaration.

The summit was held at the commencement of the 60th Session of the General Assembly (UNGA60) in September 2005.

In pursuit of an overarching human-rights agenda, including the right to development, the greatest challenge faced by the majority in the developing world, including South Africa, is global poverty and under-development notwithstanding advancement in technology and globalisation. Consequently, addressing the issues of poverty and underdevelopment is becoming an increasingly important part of South Africa's foreign policy objectives, also in multilateral fora, and it is a natural extension of government's domestic policy agenda of creating a better life for all.

The latter objective informs South Africa's participation in international organisations and processes that focus on vulnerable groups such as the aged, the youth or physically challenged people.

Recognising the active role South Africa plays in this regard, it was elected to chair the 43rd session of the Commission for Social Development in New York during February 2005.

Through its multilateral diplomacy, South Africa also plays an active role in supporting humanitarian causes internationally. In 2004, the South African Government donated R100 million to the World Food Programme and Food and Agricultural Organisation to address the food security situation in southern Africa in a sustainable manner.

During 2004/05, an additional R8,5 million was transferred to various UN agencies in support of projects alleviating the plight of vulnerable groups such as women, children, internally displaced persons and refugees. South Africa also continues to render in-kind and monetary assistance to countries affected by natural sudden-onset disasters, including the cyclones that affected Madagascar and the devastating tsunami in Asia and East Africa during 2004.

The signing of a number of multilateral environmental agreements (MEAs) and the hosting of the WSSD in 2002 placed South Africa in the forefront of environmental diplomacy. In April 2005, the United Nations Environment Programme (UNEP) listed President Mbeki and South Africa as 'Champions of the Earth'.

As party to the UN conventions on climate change, desertification and biodiversity, South Africa is committed to poverty alleviation and protection against loss of biodiversity by 2010. South Africa is also firmly committed to the protection of the oceans and the sustainable management of its marine resources.

It has put its commitment to the protection of the oceans into practice, by ratifying all the major treaties dealing with marine, maritime, fisheries and Antarctic matters, such as the UN Convention on the Law of the Sea and its related instruments, the International Maritime Convention, the UN Food and Agriculture Organisation Compliance Agreement and the Antarctic Treaty.

South Africa is one of the major participants in intergovernmental discussions relating to all aspects of disarmament, arms control and non-proliferation, as these relate to both weapons of mass destruction

In June 2005, Advocate Albertus Jacobus Hoffmann was elected as a judge to the International Tribunal for the Law of the Sea. This is the first time that South Africa has a judge on the tribunal. The other African candidate to be elected was Ambassador James L. Kateka of Tanzania.

The International Tribunal for the Law of the Sea is an international court established by the United Nations Convention on the Law of the Sea to deal with the peaceful settlement of disputes relating to the use of the seas and oceans and their resources.

and conventional arms, including small arms, light weapons and anti-personnel mines, especially in relation to the continent.

South Africa also continues to promote the importance of ensuring that non-proliferation controls do not become the means whereby developing countries are denied access to advanced technologies required for their development.

On 20 February 2004, South Africa's commitment to combat transnational organised crime was reflected in its ratification of the UN Convention against Transnational Organised Crime and its three supplementary protocols: the Protocol Against the Smuggling of Migrants by Land, Air and Sea; the Protocol to Prevent, Suppress and Punish Trafficking in Persons, Especially Women and Children; and the Protocol against the Illicit Manufacturing of and Trafficking in Firearms, their Parts and Components, and Ammunition. South Africa also ratified the UN Convention against Corruption in 2004.

To ensure that South Africa's interests, as well as those of the African continent and developing countries in general, are adequately catered for in the UN budget, South Africa actively participates in the UN's budgetary and administrative activities. Priority areas for South Africa include the funding of UN structures and programmes that focus on Africa and NEPAD, as well as sufficient funding for peacekeep-

ing operations on the continent. In the context of UN budgetary issues, South Africa plays a prominent role and was elected to the Bureau of the Fifth Committee (Administrative and Budgetary) for UNGA59; and also for a three-year term (2003 – 2005) on the 34-member Committee for Programme and Co-ordination.

For the 2004/05 regular budget of the UN, South Africa's assessed contribution was US$5,196 million. Its contribution to the UN peacekeeping budget was US$1,537 million. It also contributed US$503 648 to the International Criminal Tribunals for Rwanda and former Yugoslavia.

South Africa met its financial obligations to the UN in full, on time and without pre-conditions, resulting in the country being one of a few UN member states meeting its membership obligations on time. As a result, South Africa was honoured again by being included in the Secretary-General's Roll of Honour of countries that paid their dues timeously.

The South African Auditor-General will serve on the UN Board of Auditors until the end of 2006. Three UN member states, nominated by the Fifth Committee and appointed by the General Assembly for a non-consecutive term of six years, constitute the UN Board of Auditors.

South Africa has also been elected to serve on the following UN bodies:

- ECOSOCC (1995 – 1997; 2001 – 2003; 2005 – 2007)
- International Law Commission (2002 – 2006): Professor John Dugard
- International Criminal Tribunal for Yugoslavia (2005 – 2009): Judge J. Moloto
- International Criminal Court (2003 – 2009): Judge M. Pillay
- Committee on Elimination of Racial Discrimination (2005 – 2008): Ambassador P. January-Bardill.

South Africa has been elected by ECOSOCC to serve on the following subsidiary bodies:

- Commission for Social Development (2001 – 2005, 2006 – 2009)
- Statistical Commission (2002 – 2005)
- Commission on Human Rights (2004 – 2006)
- Commission on Status of Women (2002 – 2006)

Various multilateral economic fora, such as the World Trade Organisation, the Organisation of Economic Co-operation and Development, the G8 and the World Economic Forum serve as focal points for South Africa to engage in dialogue with the countries of the North on key global economic issues, ensuring that the Africa and development agendas remain part of the focus of such fora.

The 2005 G8 Summit in Gleneagles, Scotland, provided an important platform for engagement on the New Partnership for Africa's Development.

The G8 announced adopted measures to combat global warming and African poverty, by boosting aid to poor countries in Africa and elsewhere by R170 billion a year by 2010, and cutting farm subsidies.

- Commission on Narcotic Drugs (2002 – 2005) Committee for Programme Co-ordination (2003 – 2005)
- Governing Council on Human Settlements (2004 – 2007)
- Intergovernmental Working Group of Experts on International Standards of Accountancy and Reporting (2003 – 2005)
- Commission on International Trade Law (2005 – 2007)
- Commission on Sustainable Development (2002 – 2005).

United Nations Development Programme (UNDP)

The first agreement South Africa signed with the UN was the Standard Basic Assistance Agreement with the UNDP. The Comprehensive Country Co-operation Framework (CCF) to cover the period 1997 to 2001 followed. The current CCF covers 2002 to 2006.

In terms of the CCF, the UNDP seeks to implement programmes that are relevant to government's transformation and development imperatives. Programmes focus on priority areas such as the eradication of poverty and underdevelopment, strengthening local government, building civil society co-operation and addressing the challenges of globalisation.

South Africa's voluntary contribution to the UNDP for 2004/05 was R950 000, which was utilised by the UNDP towards operational costs of development programmes in South Africa. The UNDP has a country office in Pretoria, which is headed by the Resident Representative, who is also the UN Resident Co-ordinator for all UN operational activities for development in South Africa.

The United Nations Development Assistance Framework (UNDAF) establishes an integrated framework for co-operation for development assistance between the UN System and the Government.

The UNDAF for South Africa currently has three main priorities, namely HIV and AIDS, rural development and regional integration. Regular UNDAF reviews are held, with the participation of all UN agencies with offices in South Africa, as well as all

government departments that interact with these agencies.

The UNDP plays a prominent role in the region. The latest development in this regard is a UNDP Regional Service Centre for eastern and southern Africa. The centre was established in Johannesburg in 2004 in pursuit of the UNDP's objective to use South Africa as a 'hub' to provide technical assistance and expertise for programme implementation in 22 countries in the region.

Commonwealth

The Commonwealth comprises 53 member countries, representing a quarter of the world's population and generating 20% of global trade. Members range from micro-states in Polynesia to members of the G8, from the smallest and poorest to the richest and most populous, with cross-cutting affiliations straddling the North-South divide.

Notwithstanding its geographical, religious and cultural diversity, the Commonwealth is united by its shared ideals and common traditions manifested in similar structures of governance, public administration and law, a common working language, commercial and business practices and understanding.

Its mandate has been determined by consultation, sharing of experience and consensus rather than by vote. The Commonwealth subscribes to the principles of international peace and order, global economic development and the rule of international law, democratic values, individual liberties, human dignity, and racial, gender and other equality.

Its programmes of action are focused on human and government capacity-building, economic and

On 14 September 2005, President Thabo Mbeki joined other world leaders in appending his signature to the United Nations (UN) International Convention for the Suppression of Acts of Nuclear Terrorism in New York.
President Mbeki led a delegation of senior government officials attending the Millennium Summit and the 60th session of the UN General Assembly.

social development, the removal of disparities in living standards across the world and the alleviation of poverty and illiteracy.

In this context, South Africa actively participates in all meetings of the Commonwealth and has played a leading role, also as a voice of the South, in supporting the Commonwealth's commitment to furthering the UN MDGs, relations with NEPAD, poverty relief, debt relief for heavily indebted poor countries, a human rights agenda, assistance to small and island states, Information Technology and human and administrative capacity-building.

Non-Aligned Movement

With the exception of the UN itself, the NAM with its 115 member countries is the largest political grouping of countries in the world. It was founded in 1961 in response to the challenges tabled for the Third World countries of the Cold-War era by the Bandung Summit of 1955. It has since steadfastly adhered to certain guiding principles, seeking consensus through peaceful means, non-interference in domestic affairs of member countries, a multilateral approach to global issues and close South-South

co-operation. It further agitates against marginalisation and impoverishment of the South, and human indignities.

South Africa has played a leading role since joining the NAM in 1994. The XII Summit of Heads of State or Government was hosted in Durban in 1998 when South Africa took over as chair from Colombia until 2003.

In August 2004, South Africa hosted the XIV Ministerial Conference of the NAM. Ministerial conferences, also known as mid-term reviews, are held to review the development and implementation of decisions of the preceding summit and to discuss matters of urgency. In pursuit of the strengthening of multilateralism, South Africa initiated the Durban Declaration on Multilateralism, which was adopted by the conference. The conference also adopted declarations on Palestine and the Gatumba Massacre.

The NAM Co-ordination Bureau meets regularly at ambassadorial level at the UN in New York to review the agenda of the movement and make proposals to further enhance the agenda of the South.

Acknowledgements

BuaNews

Estimates of National Expenditure 2005, published by National Treasury

Department of Foreign Affairs

www.dfa.gov.za

www.gov.za

Suggested reading

Alden, C. and Martin, G. eds. *France and South Africa: Towards a New Engagement with Africa*. Pretoria: Protea Book House, 2003.

Bond, P. *Talk Left, Walk Right: South Africa's Frustrated Global Reform*. Scottsville: University of KwaZulu-Natal Press, 2004.

Chakoodza, A.M. *International Diplomacy in Southern Africa from Reagan to Mandela*. London: Third World, 1990.

Change and South African External Relations. Editors: W. Carlsnaes and M. Muller. Johannesburg: International Thompson Publishing, 1997.

Gill, R. *et al.* eds. *Charting a New Course: Globalisation, African Recovery and the New Africa Initiative*. Johannesburg: South African Institute of International Affairs, 2002.

Hussein, S. ed. *Towards Sustainable Peace: Reflections on Preventive Diplomacy in Africa*. Pretoria: Africa Institute of South Africa, 2003.

Landsberg, C. *The Quiet Diplomacy of Liberation: International Politics and South Africa's transition*. Johannesburg: Jacana, 2004.

Makgoba, M.W. *African Renaissance: The New Struggle*. Sandton: Mafube Publishing; Cape Town: Tafelberg, 1999.

Malan, J.C. *Conflict Resolution Wisdom from Africa*. Durban: ACCORD, 1997.

Mathoma, P., Mills, G. and Stremlau, J. eds. *Putting People First: African Priorities for the UN Millennium Assembly*. Johannesburg: South African Institute of International Affairs, 2000.

Mbeki, T. *Africa: The Time Has Come*. Cape Town: Tafelberg; Houghton: Mafube, 1998.

Mills, G. ed. *From Pariah to Participant: South Africa's Evolving Foreign Relations, 1990 – 1994*. Johannesburg: South African Institute of International Affairs, 1994.

Mills, G. *The Wired Model: South Africa, Foreign Policy and Globalisation*. Cape Town: Tafelberg, 2000.

Mollo, J.K. *Diplomacy Protocol*. Oaklands, Johannesburg: The Author, 1997.

Murray, R. *Human Rights in Africa: From the OAU to the African Union*. Cambridge: University of Cambridge Press, 2004.

Mills, G. and Sideropoulis, E. eds. *New Tools for Reform and Stability: Sanctions, Conditionalities and Conflict Resolution*. Johannesburg: South African Institute of International Affairs, 2003.

Payne, R.J. *The Non-Superpowers and South Africa*. Johannesburg: Witwatersrand University Press, 1990.

Payne, R.J. *Third World and South Africa: Post-Apartheid Challenges*. Westport: Greenwood Press, 1992.

Nel, P. and McGowan, P.J. eds. *Power, Wealth and Global Order*. Cape Town: University of Cape Town Press, 1999.

Sall, A. ed. *Africa 2025: What Possible Futures for Sub-Saharan Africa*. Pretoria: Unisa Press, 2003.

State, Sovereignty and Responsibility: African Resolutions to African Problems. Durban: ACCORD, 1996.

Venancio, M. and Chan, S. *Portuguese Diplomacy in Southern Africa, 1974 – 1994*. Johannesburg: South African Institute of International Affairs, 1996.

Government system

The Constitution

The Constitutional Court (CC) approved the Constitution of the Republic of South Africa, 1996 (Act 108 of 1996), on 4 December 1996. It took effect on 4 February 1997.

The Constitution is the supreme law of the land. No other law or government action can supersede the provisions of the Constitution. South Africa's Constitution is one of the most progressive in the world and enjoys high acclaim internationally.

The Preamble

The Constitution's Preamble states that the Constitution aims to:
- heal the divisions of the past and establish a society based on democratic values, social justice and fundamental human rights
- improve the quality of life of all citizens and free the potential of each person
- lay the foundations for a democratic and open society in which government is based on the will of the people, and every citizen is equally protected by law
- build a united and democratic South Africa able to take its rightful place as a sovereign state in the family of nations.

Founding provisions

According to Chapter One, South Africa is one sovereign, democratic state founded on the following values:
- human dignity, the achievement of equality and the advancement of human rights and freedom
- non-racialism and non-sexism
- supremacy of the Constitution
- universal adult suffrage, a national common voters' roll, regular elections and a multiparty system of democratic government to ensure accountability, responsiveness and openness.

Fundamental rights

The fundamental rights contained in Chapter Two of the Constitution seek to protect the rights and freedom of individuals. The CC guards these rights and determines whether actions by the State are in accordance with constitutional provisions.

Government

Government consists of national, provincial and local spheres, which are distinctive, interdependent and interrelated. The powers of the law-makers (legislative authorities), governments (executive authorities) and courts (judicial authorities) are separate from one another.

Parliament

Parliament is the legislative authority of South Africa and has the power to make laws for the country in accordance with the Constitution. It consists of the National Assembly and the National Council of Provinces (NCOP). Parliamentary sittings are open to the public.

Since the establishment of Parliament in 1994, a number of steps have been taken to make it more accessible. This was done to make the institution more accountable, as well as to motivate and facilitate public participation in the legislative process. One of these steps was the creation of a website (*www.parliament.gov.za*), which encourages comment and feedback from the public.

National Assembly

The National Assembly consists of no fewer than 350 and no more than 400 members elected through a system of proportional representation. The National Assembly, which is elected for a term of five years, is presided over by the Speaker, assisted by the Deputy Speaker.

The National Assembly is elected to represent the people and to ensure democratic governance as required by the Constitution. It does this by electing the President, providing a national forum for public consideration of issues, passing legislation, and scrutinising and overseeing executive action.

National Council of Provinces

The NCOP consists of 54 permanent members and 36 special delegates and aims to represent provincial interests in the national sphere of government. Delegations consist of 10 representatives from each province.

The NCOP must have a mandate from the provinces before it can make certain decisions. It cannot, however, initiate a Bill concerning money, which is the prerogative of the Minister of Finance.

The NCOP has a website, *NCOP Online!* (*www.parliament.gov.za/ncop*), which links Parliament to the provincial legislatures and local government associations. *NCOP Online!* provides information on draft legislation and allows the public to make electronic submissions.

Law-making

Any Bill may be introduced in the National Assembly. A Bill passed by the National Assembly must be referred to the NCOP for consideration. A Bill affecting the provinces may be introduced in the NCOP. After it has been passed by the council, it must be referred to the assembly.

A Bill concerning money must be introduced in the assembly and referred to the NCOP for consideration and approval after being passed. If the council rejects a Bill or passes it subject to amendments, the assembly must reconsider the Bill and pass it again with or without amendments. There are special conditions for the approval of laws dealing with provinces.

The President

The President is the Head of State and leads the Cabinet. He or she is elected by the National Assembly from among its members, and leads the country in the interest of national unity, in accordance with the Constitution and the law.

The Deputy President

The President appoints the Deputy President from among the members of the National Assembly. The Deputy President assists the President in executing government functions.

Cabinet

The Cabinet consists of the President, as head of the Cabinet, the Deputy President and ministers. The President appoints the Deputy President and ministers, assigns their powers and functions and may dismiss them.

The President may select any number of ministers from among the members of the National Assembly, and may select no more than two ministers from outside the assembly.

The President appoints a member of the Cabinet to be the leader of government business in the National Assembly.

Deputy ministers

The President appoints deputy ministers from among the members of the National Assembly.

Traditional leadership

Chapter 12 of the Constitution states that the institution, status and roles of traditional leadership, according to customary law, are recognised, subject to the Constitution.

The Chief Directorate: Traditional Leadership and Institutions in the Department of Provincial and Local Government provides support to traditional leaders and institutions, and is responsible for the development of policy in this regard. It renders an anthropological service, and provides advice and support regarding governance and development matters. It advises and supports the National House of Traditional Leaders and maintains a database of traditional leaders and institutions. It is also responsible for developing and implementing a regulatory framework for the protection of the rights of cultural, religious and linguistic communities.

The Traditional Leadership and Governance Framework Act, 2003 (Act 41 of 2003), seeks to:
- Set out a national framework, norms and standards to define the place and role of traditional leadership within the system of democratic governance.
- Transform the institutions in line with constitutional imperatives.
- Restore the integrity and legitimacy of traditional leadership in line with customary laws and practices.
- Provide guidelines to provincial legislation on traditional leadership and governance. (By mid-2005, provinces were finalising various Bills in this regard).

In October 2004, President Thabo Mbeki appointed the Commission on Traditional Leadership Disputes and Claims in terms of Section 23 of the Traditional Leadership and Governance Framework Act, 2003.

It will investigate and report on all traditional leadership disputes and claims dating from 1 September 1927. The commission will not make any recommendations to the executive. Its decisions will be final and binding.

In terms of Section 25(2) of the Traditional Leadership and Governance Framework Act, 2003, the commission is mandated to hear cases where there is doubt whether a traditional leadership position was established in accordance with customary

President Thabo Mbeki was born on 18 June 1942 in Idutywa, Queenstown, in the Eastern Cape. He joined the African National Congress (ANC) Youth League at the age of 14 and in 1961 was elected secretary of the African Students' Association.

He was involved in underground activities after the banning of the ANC in 1960, until he left South Africa in 1962. He continued his studies in the United Kingdom (UK) and obtained a Master of Arts (Economics) at the University of Sussex. While in the UK, he mobilised the international student community against apartheid and worked at the London office of the ANC for several years. He also underwent military training in what was then the Soviet Union.

From 1973, Mr Mbeki worked in Botswana, Swaziland, Nigeria and Lusaka and became a member of the ANC's National Executive Committee in 1975. Between 1984 and 1989, he was director of the ANC's Department of Information. He led the organisation's delegations, which met groups from inside South Africa in Dakar, Senegal, and elsewhere. In 1989, he headed the delegation that held talks with the Apartheid Government, which led to agreements on the unbanning of political organisations and the release of political prisoners. He also participated in negotiations preceding the adoption of South Africa's Interim Constitution in 1993.

Following the first democratic election in 1994, Mr Mbeki was appointed Executive Deputy President. In 1997, he was elected president of the ANC and in June 1999, after the country's second democratic election, he succeeded Mr Nelson Mandela as President of South Africa.

Mr Mbeki's inauguration as the country's third democratically elected President on 27 April 2004 coincided with the celebration of 10 Years of Freedom.

344

law; cases where the title of an incumbent traditional leader is challenged; claims by communities to be recognised as traditional communities; cases questioning whether any establishment of 'tribes' was legitimate; disputes around traditional authority boundaries and the resultant division or merging of 'tribes'; and any other relevant matters.

Cabinet, as on 1 October 2005	
Mr Thabo Mbeki	President
Ms Phumzile Mlambo-Ngcuka	Deputy President
Ms Nosiviwe Mapisa-Nqakula	Home Affairs
Ms Naledi Pandor	Education
Dr Nkosazana Dlamini-Zuma	Foreign Affairs
Mr Mosiuoa Lekota	Defence
Mr Trevor Manuel	Finance
Mr Sydney Mufamadi	Provincial and Local Government
Mr Jeff Radebe	Transport
Mr Alec Erwin	Public Enterprises
Ms Stella Sigcau	Public Works
Dr Zola Skweyiya	Social Development
Mr Charles Nqakula	Safety and Security
Dr Lindiwe Sisulu	Housing
Mr Mandisi Mpahlwa	Trade and Industry
Ms Brigitte Mabandla	Justice and Constitutional Development
Mr Marthinus van Schalkwyk	Environmental Affairs and Tourism
Ms Geraldine Fraser-Moleketi	Public Service and Administration
Dr Ivy Matsepe-Casaburri	Communications
Mr Membathisi Mdladlana	Labour
Mr Ngconde Balfour	Correctional Services
Ms Thoko Didiza	Agriculture and Land Affairs
Ms Buyelwa Sonjica	Water Affairs and Forestry
Mr Ronnie Kasrils	Intelligence Services
Ms Lindiwe Hendricks	Minerals and Energy
Dr Pallo Jordan	Arts and Culture
Mr Mosibudi Mangena	Science and Technology
Dr Manto Tshabalala-Msimang	Health
Dr Essop Pahad	Minister in The Presidency
Rev Makhenkesi Stofile	Sport and Recreation

The commission will visit all existing royal houses to hold public hearings and meet with royal family members, as well as any other members of communities with an interest in royal affairs.

Houses of traditional leaders

The Constitution mandates the establishment of houses of traditional leaders by means of either provincial or national legislation. The National House of Traditional Leadership was established in April 1997. Provincial houses of traditional leaders were established in all six provinces that have traditional leaders, namely the Eastern Cape, KwaZulu-Natal, the Free State, Mpumalanga, Limpopo and North West.

In terms of the Traditional Leadership and Governance Framework Act, 2003, local houses of traditional leaders will be established in accordance with provincial legislation in district municipalities where traditional leadership exists.

Each provincial house of traditional leaders nominates three members to be represented in the national house, which then elects its own office-bearers.

The national house advises national government on the role of traditional leaders and customary law. It may also conduct its own investigations and advise the President at his request.

Over the 2005 Medium Term Expenditure Framework period, the National House of Traditional Leaders was allocated R24,7 million while the Commission on Traditional Leadership Disputes and Claims received R13 million.

Provincial government

In accordance with the Constitution, each of the nine provinces has its own legislature, consisting of between 30 and 80 members. The number of members is determined in terms of a formula set out in national legislation. The members are elected in terms of proportional representation.

The executive council of a province consists of a premier and a number of members. The premiers are appointed by the President of the country.

Decisions are taken by consensus, as in the national Cabinet. Besides being able to make provincial laws, a provincial legislature may adopt a constitution for its province if two-thirds of its members agree. However, a provincial constitution must correspond with the national Constitution as confirmed by the CC.

According to the Constitution, provinces may have legislative and executive powers concurrent with the national sphere, over:
- agriculture
- casinos, racing, gambling and wagering
- cultural affairs
- education at all levels, excluding university and university of technology education
- environment
- health services
- housing
- language policy
- nature conservation
- police services
- provincial public media
- public transport
- regional planning and development
- road-traffic regulation
- tourism
- trade and industrial promotion
- traditional authorities
- urban and rural development
- vehicle licensing
- welfare services.

These powers can be exercised to the extent that provinces have the administrative capacity to assume effective responsibilities.

Provinces also have exclusive competency over a number of areas, which include:
- abattoirs
- ambulance services
- liquor licences
- museums other than national museums
- provincial planning
- provincial cultural matters
- provincial recreation and activities
- provincial roads and traffic.

The President's Co-ordinating Council (PCC) is a consultative forum where the President discusses issues of national, provincial and local importance with the premiers. The forum meets quarterly and addresses issues such as:

- enhancing the role of provincial executives regarding national policy decisions
- strengthening the capacity of provincial governments to implement government policies and programmes
- integrating provincial growth and development strategies (PGDS) within national development plans
- improving co-operation between national and provincial spheres of government
- improving co-operation on fiscal issues
- ensuring that there are co-ordinated programmes of implementation and the necessary structures in place to address issues such as rural development, urban renewal, and safety and security.

Deputy ministers, as on 1 October 2005	
Ms Cheryl Gillwald	Correctional Services
Ms Susan Shabangu	Safety and Security
Mr Aziz Pahad	Foreign Affairs
Ms Sue van der Merwe	Foreign Affairs
Ms Ntombazana Botha	Arts and Culture
Mr Derek Hanekom	Science and Technology
Ms Lulama Xingwana	Minerals and Energy
Mr Enver Surty	Education
Mr Malusi Gigaba	Home Affairs
Mr Ntopile Kganyago	Public Works
Mr Jabu Moleketi	Finance
Adv Dirk du Toit	Agriculture and Land Affairs
Ms Rejoice Mabudafhasi	Environmental Affairs and Tourism
Mr Rob Davies	Trade and Industry
Ms Elizabeth Thabethe	Trade and Industry
Mr Mluleki George	Defence
Mr Johnny de Lange	Justice and Constitutional Development
Ms Nomatyala Hangana	Provincial and Local Government
Ms Nozizwe Madlala-Routledge	Health
Mr Radhakrishna 'Roy' Padayachie	Communications
Dr Jean Benjamin	Social Development
Mr Gert Oosthuizen	Sport and Recreation

Provincial governments, as on 15 September 2005

Eastern Cape

Ms Nosimo Balindlela	Premier
Mr Gugile Nkwinti	Agriculture
Mr Mkhangeli Matomela	Education
Mr Andre de Wet	Economic Affairs, Environment and Tourism
Mr Billy Nel	Finance
Dr Bevan Goqwana	Health
Mr Sam Kwelita	Housing, Local Government and Traditional Affairs
Mr Thobile Mhlahlo	Safety, Liaison and Transport
Mr Christian Martin	Roads and Public Works
Ms Nomsa Jajula	Sport, Recreation, Arts and Culture
Ms Tkoko Xasa	Social Development

KwaZulu-Natal

Mr Sibusiso Ndebele	Premier
Prof. Lindumusa Nda-bandaba	Agriculture and Environmental Affairs
Ms Ina Cronjé	Education
Mr Narend Singh	Arts, Culture and Tourism
Dr Zweli Mkhize	Finance and Economic Development
Ms Neliswa Nkonyeni	Health
Mr Mike Mabuyakhulu	Local Government, Housing and Traditional Affairs
Inkosi Nyanga Ngubane	Social Welfare and Population Development
Mr Muzikwenkosi Gwala	Public Works
Mr Bheki Cele	Transport, Community Safety and Liaison
Mr Amichand Rajbansi	Sport and Recreation

Free State

Ms Beatrice Marshoff	Premier
Mr Casca Mokitlane	Agriculture
Ms Mantsheng Tsopo	Education
Mr Neo Masithela	Tourism, Environmental and Economic Affairs
Mr France Morule	Public Safety and Liaison
Mr Sakhiwo Belot	Health
Mr Joel Mafereka	Local Government and Housing
Mr Pule Makgoe	Treasury
Mr Seiso Mohai	Transport, Roads and Public Works
Ms Zanele Dlungwana	Social Development
Ms Suzan Mnumzana	Sport, Arts, Culture, Science and Technology

Limpopo

Mr Sello Moloto	Premier
Dr Aaron Motsoaledi	Education
Dr Joyce Mashamba	Provincial Treasury
Mr Thaba Mufamadi	Agriculture
Mr Charley Sekoati	Health and Social Development
Ms Maite Nkoana-Mashabane	Local Government and Housing
Mr Collins Chabane	Development, Environment and Tourism
Ms Dikeledi Magadzi	Agriculture
Mr Joseph Maswanganyi	Sport, Arts and Culture
Mr Stanley Motimele	Roads and Transport
Ms Machwene Semenya	Safety, Security and Liaison

Gauteng

Mr Mbhazima Shilowa	Premier
Mr Khabisi Mosunkutu	Agriculture, Conservation and Environment
Ms Dorothy Mahlangu	Local Government
Ms Angelina Motshekga	Education
Mr Paul Mashatile	Finance and Economic Affairs
Dr Gwen Ramokgopa	Health
Ms Nomvula Mokonyane	Housing
Mr Firoz Cachalia	Community Safety
Ms Barbara Creecy	Sport, Arts, Culture and Recreation
Mr Bob Mabaso	Social Development
Mr Ignatius Jacobs	Public Transport, Roads and Works

Mpumalanga

Mr Thabang Makwetla	Premier
Mr Madala Masuku	Agriculture, Conservation, Environment and Land Administration
Mr William Lubisi	Economic Development and Planning
Mr Siphosezwe Masango	Education
Mr Pogisho Pasha	Health and Social Development
Mr Jabulani Mahlangu	Local Government and Housing
Ms Candith Mashego-Dlamini	Public Works
Ms Mmathulare Coleman	Finance
Mr Nomsa Mtsweni	Culture, Sport and Recreation
Mr Fish Mahlalela	Roads and Transport
Ms Dinah Pule	Safety and Security

Northern Cape

Ms Dipuo Peters	Premier
Ms Tina Joemat-Petterson	Agriculture and Land Reform
Mr Archie Lucas	Education
Mr Pakes Dikgetsi	Finance and Economic Affairs
Ms Shiwe Selao	Health
Mr Boeboe van Wyk	Housing and Local Government
Ms Thembi Madikane	Safety and Liaison
Mr Goolam Akharwary	Social Development
Mr Kagisho David Molusi	Sport, Arts and Culture
Mr Pieter Saaiman	Tourism, Environment and Conservation
Mr Fred Wyngaardt	Transport, Roads and Public Works

North West

Ms Ednah Molewa	Premier
Mr Ndleleni Duma	Arts, Culture and Sport
Mr Mandlenkosi Mayisela	Agriculture, Conservation and Environment
Mr Darkey Africa	Economic Development and Tourism
Mr Frans Vilakazi	Local Government and Housing
Rev Johannes Tselapedi	Education
Ms Nomonde Rasmeni	Health
Ms Maureen Modiselle	Finance
Mr Jerry Thibedi	Safety, Transport and Roads
Mr Howard Yawa	Public Works
Ms Nikiwe Num	Social Development

Western Cape

Mr Ebrahim Rasool	Premier
Mr Kobus Dowry	Agriculture
Mr Leonard Ramatlakane	Community Safety
Mr Cameron Dugmore	Education
Ms Tasneem Essop	Environmental Affairs and Development Planning
Ms Lynne Brown	Finance and Tourism
Mr Pierre Uys	Health
Mr Richard Dyantyi	Local Government and Housing
Mr Marius Fransman	Transport and Public Works
Ms Kholeka Mqulwana	Social Services and Poverty Alleviation
Mr Whitey Jacobs	Cultural Affairs and Sport

Local government

There are 284 municipalities focused on growing local economies and extending the provision of services to previously neglected areas.

In accordance with the Constitution and the Organised Local Government Act, 1997 (Act 52 of 1997), (which formally recognises organised local government and the nine provincial local government associations), organised local government may designate up to 10 part-time representatives to represent municipalities and participate in proceedings of the NCOP.

By July 2005, 67% of the population had access to free basic water, while 64% of South Africa's 284 municipalities were providing free basic electricity to 49% of the population.

South African Local Government Association (SALGA)

SALGA represents the interests of local government in the country's intergovernmental relations system with a united voice.

SALGA aims to:

- continuously improve its ability to deliver high-quality services to its members
- increase the impact and influence of organised local government
- increase the skills base within the local government sector and thus the country as a whole
- increase knowledge-sharing and improve the communication capacity as well as vertical and horizontal connectivity of municipalities
- leverage the collective buying power of municipalities to benefit the local government sector
- ensure that South Africa's local government

Two South African traditional leaders visited Zambia in May 2005 to promote the idea of a continental house of traditional leaders (COHTLA). The ultimate goal is to unite all African indigenous/traditional leaders under the COHTLA banner to enable them to speak with one voice and to contribute towards governance and conflict resolution to the benefit of the entire continent.

plays a critical role in furthering Africa's development at regional and international level.

SALGA is funded through a combination of sources. These include a percentage share of the national revenue allocated to local government, membership fees from municipalities, and donations and grants from a variety of sources that fund specific projects.

Municipalities

The Constitution provides for three categories of municipalities.

As directed by the Constitution, the Local Government: Municipal Structures Act, 1998 (Act 117 of 1998), contains criteria for determining when an area must have a category A municipality (metropolitan municipalities) and when municipalities fall into category B (local municipalities) or C (district areas or municipalities). The Act also determines that category A municipalities can only be established in metropolitan areas.

The Municipal Demarcation Board determined that Johannesburg, Durban, Cape Town, Pretoria, the East Rand and Port Elizabeth be declared metropolitan areas.

Metropolitan councils have a single metropolitan budget, common property rating and service-tariff

The Presidential Municipal Imbizo Programme was initiated in 2005 to align Project Consolidate and government's imbizo programmes. In May 2005, the first Presidential Municipal Imbizo was held in the Bojanala District Municipality in North West. Several others followed.

The National Imbizo Focus Week, held in October 2005, focused on the implementation of Project Consolidate. Attention was paid to practical work in assisting the 136 municipalities identified, as well as others that may be prioritised by provinces, to improve their capacity and to implement projects aimed at reducing poverty and improving sevices to the people.

Members of the executive from all spheres of government interacted directly with the public and communities regarding programmes that require partnership of local, provincial and national government with communities.

systems, and a single employer body. South Africa has six metropolitan municipalities, namely Tshwane, Johannesburg, Ekurhuleni, Ethekwini, Cape Town and Nelson Mandela; 231 local municipalities; and 47 district municipalities.

Metropolitan councils may decentralise powers and functions. However, all original municipal, legislative and executive powers are vested in the metropolitan council.

In metropolitan areas, there is a choice of two types of executive systems: the mayoral executive system where executive authority is vested in the mayor, and the collective executive committee where these powers are vested in the executive committee.

Non-metropolitan areas consist of district councils and local councils. District councils are primarily responsible for capacity-building and district-wide planning.

The Local Government: Municipal Structures Act, 1998 provides for ward committees whose tasks, among others, are to:

- prepare, implement and review integrated development plans (IDPs)
- establish, implement and review a municipality's performance management system
- monitor and review a municipality's performance
- prepare a municipality's budget
- participate in decisions about the provision of municipal services
- communicate and disseminate information on governance matters.

By February 2005, more than 80% of ward committees had been set up.

The two-day National Conference on Public Participation and Strengthening of Ward Committees was held in March 2005. This resulted in draft resolutions and guidelines on the operations and functioning of ward committees and public participation in local government.

Integrated development plans

In terms of the Local Government: Municipal Systems Act, 2000 (Act 32 of 2000), all municipalities are required to prepare IDPs. Integrated development planning is a process by which municipalities prepare five-year strategic plans that are reviewed annually in consultation with communities and stakeholders.

The aim is to achieve service delivery and development goals for municipal areas in an effective and sustainable way. National and provincial-sector departments, development agencies, private-sector bodies, non-governmental organisations and communities all have a key role to play in the preparation and implementation of municipal IDPs.

The Department of Provincial and Local Government provides support to each of these role-players, specifically municipalities, through guidelines, training programmes, hands-on support, funding and capacity-building programmes.

The department also advises role-players on how to co-ordinate and improve development planning, and provide platforms for knowledge sharing. It is also developing a supporting intergovernmental planning framework, which will provide greater clarity as to the type and role of appropriate planning at each government level. The framework will entail policy work, as well as practical initiatives such as the IDP Nerve Centre. The centre will provide an information co-ordination service to strengthen intergovernmental planning.

The IDP review is an annual process required by the Local Government: Municipal Systems Act, 2000. Teams from the Department of Provincial and Local Government will focus on each district and metropolitan municipality which, in turn, will support municipalities with technical engagement to develop credible IDPs that engage key areas of national priority relating to basic service provision, development and work creation.

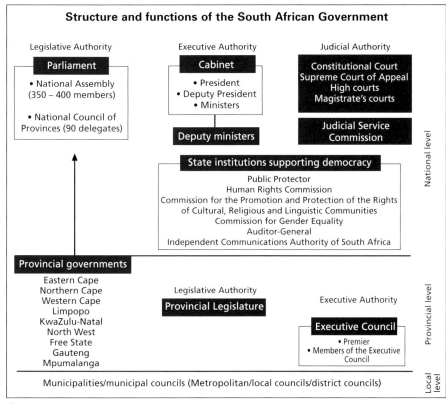

Structure and functions of the South African Government

Source: www.gov.za

By June 2005, the IDP review hearings had been held in nine provinces and the metropolitan councils.

Planning and Implementation Management Support (PIMS) had been established in all 47 district municipalities. The department will continue to support the PIMS centres so that municipalities can be assisted with the development of strategies for integrated development planning and implementation. The PIMS centres provide the ideal conduit for sharing best practice with all municipalities within a district, and are supplementing the efforts of the Knowledge Sharing Facility Project.

Training

The South African Management Development Institute (SAMDI) has been working with the Department of Provincial and Local Government in establishing the Local Government Learning Academy, which will focus on training councillors and senior officials at local level.

Legislation

The Local Government: Municipal Systems Act, 2000 established a framework for planning, performance-management systems, effective use of resources and organisational change in a business context.

The Benoni Declaration was adopted in June 2005 by over 200 municipal mayors, councillors and senior officials. The declaration and its plan of action address gender equality in local government.

The declaration committed local government to:
• continue with skills-development training for women councillors and officials
• voter education and local-governance training for women candidates in local government elections
• monitor gender mainstreaming
• improve and accelerate engendered service delivery and economic development towards eradicating poverty and reducing unemployment, especially among women
• develop and implement strategies to respond to the challenges of communicable diseases, such as HIV, AIDS and tuberculosis.

The Act also established a system for municipalities to report on their performance, and provides residents with an opportunity to compare this performance with others.

It also regulates public-private partnerships. The Act allows municipalities significant powers to corporatise their services, establish utilities for service delivery, or enter into partnerships with other service-providers. The Act provides for the adoption of a credit-control policy for municipalities that will provide for the termination of services in the event of non-payment. Municipalities will have the power to pass bylaws to implement the policy.

The Local Government Municipal Finance Management Act, 2003 (Act 56 of 2003), is aimed at modernising municipal budgeting and financial management. It facilitates the development of a long-term municipal lending/bond market. It also introduces a governance framework for separate entities created by municipalities.

The Act is a critical element in the overall transformation of local government in South Africa. It fosters transparency at local government level through budget and reporting requirements.

The Local Government Municipal Property Rates Act, 2004 (Act 6 of 2004), regulates the power of a municipality to impose rates on property; excludes certain properties from rating in the national interest; makes provision for fair and equitable valuation methods of properties; and provides for municipalities to implement a transparent and fair system of exemptions, reductions and rebates through their rating policies.

Municipal Infrastructure Grant (MIG)

The MIG is a conditional grant aimed at supporting municipal capital budgets to fund municipal infrastructure and to upgrade existing infrastructure, primarily benefiting poor households. It gives effect to earlier Cabinet decisions and policy on the establishment of a single consolidated funding mechanism to support municipal infrastructure.

The MIG started to merge with the following funding programmes in a phased manner in 2004/05:
• the Consolidated Municipal Infrastructure Programme

- the Water Service Capital Fund
- the Community-Based Public Works Programme
- the Local Economic Development Fund
- the Building for Sport and Recreation Programme
- electrification funding in support of addressing the electrification backlogs of permanently occupied residential dwellings that are situated in historically undersupplied areas.

The MIG is geared towards making the system of transfers to municipalities simpler, more certain and direct. Its conditions are more flexible, designed to support the capital budgets of municipalities and to facilitate integrated development planning.

By the end of June 2005, 97,2% of the 2004/05 MIG allocation and 7,4% of the 2005/06 allocation had been spent. Households had benefited from the MIG in respect of water (212 828), sanitation (74 245), roads (122 582), storm water (83 593) and solid waste (55 880). A total of 287 655 person days of employment had been created specifically through the use of labour-intensive methods, in relation to the 2004/05 MIG allocation. Some R135 million was spent on urban nodes and R992 million on rural nodes in the implementation of MIG 2004/05.

Through the MIG programme, the Department of Water Affairs and Forestry has allocated R765 million for eradicating the water supply and sanitation backlogs in the nodes.

Project Consolidate (PC)

The PC is a two-year hands-on programme that allows national and provincial government, with private-sector partners, to find new ways of working with local government.

The Cabinet adopted the PC in February 2004 as the best way to address problems hampering delivery. It provides targeted focus and capacity-building to 136 municipalities identified for assistance.

The specific objectives of the programme are to:
- rally the local government sphere in discharging its service delivery and development mandate
- realise the people's contract and mobilise social partners around this programme
- entrench a people-centred orientation in the entire public sector and a new approach to local government's mode of operation

The Integrated Sustainable Rural Development Programme (ISRDP) and the Urban Renewal Programme (URP), which run projects to improve service delivery and alleviate poverty, continue to focus on their key target groups – the poor, marginalised, underdeveloped and disadvantaged. The programmes aim to maximise the impact of all government resources and know-how in the 21 identified rural and urban nodes. Following a review of progress on the nodes, Cabinet approved the proposed financial interventions to support the nodes, within the framework of government's priority programmes.

A guide for national departments' participation in implementing the ISRDP and URP has been finalised.

- establish a new and practical benchmark for local government performance excellence
- have successful local government elections in 2005/06.

Because backlogs in the 136 municipalities differ, the department partnered with different sectors of society and stakeholders to prepare teams comprising professionals and specialists in different fields.

By September 2005, 38 service-delivery facilitators had been mobilised from the local government and private sectors. Some had been deployed to various municipalities and had undertaken diagnostic assessments. Processes are in place to address the challenges they face. A number of national departments have also identified personnel to support the PC. In addition, representation of national and provincial departments on the steering committees of the PC has improved.

In May 2005, over 4 000 delegates and exhibitors from Africa and beyond gathered in Pretoria for the founding congress of the United Cities and Local Government of Africa. The congress focused on poverty alleviation at the lowest level of government by establishing a strong, unified municipal structure in Africa.

Government and communication

The vision of the Government Communication and Information System is to help meet the communication and information needs of government and the people to ensure a better life for all.

It consists of the following chief directorates:
- The Communication Service Agency is responsible for the production and distribution of government information products (including the *South Africa Yearbook* and *Pocket Guide to South Africa*) and the bulk-buying of advertising space.
- Government and Media Liaison is responsible for strengthening working relations between the media and government, as well as the international promotion of South Africa. It is also responsible for BuaNews, a government news service.
- Policy and Research contributes to the development of policy in the fields of media, communication and the monitoring of government policy in general, from a communication perspective.
- Provincial and Local Liaison provides development communication and information to South Africans to ensure that they have public information that can assist them in becoming active citizens.
- Corporate Services provides financial management, administrative services, and human resource (HR) administration and development.

The chief executive officer of the Government Communication and Information System is the official spokesperson for government.

The Government Communication and Information System is central in developing communication strategies and programmes for government's transversal campaigns. It also assists departments with specific campaigns and events, as well as with developing departmental communication structures.

The Government Communication and Information System is responsible for maintaining the website, Government Online (*www.gov.za*), which includes both an information portal for general information about government, and a services portal, which is a source of information about all the services rendered by national government.

The Government Communication and Information System leads or is involved in various communication partnerships and joint processes, including:
- An intersectoral programme to set up multi-purpose community centres (MPCCs), providing information about how to access government services, as well as some government services at the centres themselves. In September 2005, there were 66 MPCCs in operation. A strategy for setting up one MPCC in each of the country's municipalities by 2014 has been approved.
- Institutional support to the Media Development and Diversity Agency (MDDA), set up under the MDDA Act, 2000 (Act 14 of 2002), for which the Minister in The Presidency is the responsible minister.
- The development of the new coat of arms launched on Freedom Day, 27 April 2000, and the redesign of the national orders.
- The process towards the transformation of the advertising and marketing industry.
- The Academy of Government Communication and Marketing, in collaboration with the Wits School of Public and Development Management, Unilever and the Mandela-Rhodes Foundation.
- The international marketing campaign led by the International Marketing Council (IMC).
- The *Imbizo* Campaign of direct interaction between government and the public.

(See chapters 5 and 6: *Arts and culture* and *Communications.*)

International Marketing Council

The IMC of South Africa was established in 2000 as a public-private partnership aimed at creating a positive, united image for South Africa to give the country a strategic advantage in an increasingly competitive marketplace. The work of the IMC is overseen by a board of trustees, whose members act as advocates for South Africa and provide the council's operational team with strategic guidance.

The IMC's mission is to:

- articulate a brand for South Africa, which positions the country to attract tourism, trade and investment, as well as realise international relations objectives
- establish an integrated approach within government and the private sector towards the international marketing of South Africa
- build national support for Brand South Africa.

The following centres and tools facilitate the work of the council:

- The Communication Resource Centre is a state-of-the-art facility, monitoring media coverage on South Africa anywhere in the world. Government communicators use the rapid-response resource to formulate messaging around various issues covered on South Africa internationally.
- The Information Resource Centre collects, collates and makes accessible a vast spectrum of positive information about South Africa.
- The web portal, *www.southafrica.info,* is the official national gateway to the country for national and international Internet users, realising over 1,5 million page views (nine million hits) per month and containing over 25 000 pages of information updated daily.
- *South African Story Now* is a booklet filled with facts, quotes and anecdotes that illustrate the extraordinary South African story and current challenges. This is the second version of the booklet. It is meant to equip brand ambassadors, but is also a stand-alone marketing tool.
- The Brand Champion Programme tasks skilled professionals with seeping the brand positioning into the bloodstream of South Africa and weaving the values into the fabric of society.
- Country managers in Washington and London lobby the media, maintain supportive relationships with South African and local corporates, and co-ordinate all activities that provide marketing opportunities for South Africa.

The IMC is constantly seizing new and creative opportunities to market South Africa, to:

- encourage patriotism and national pride
- leverage initiatives
- provide leadership
- share research and create strategic frameworks and tools with all institutions wishing to co-ordinate their marketing efforts.

The 10 Years of Freedom celebrations presented the country with a once-in-a-lifetime opportunity to sound its trumpet to the world. For the IMC, this was also an opportunity to garner local support for Brand South Africa and what it stands for. The IMC developed communication, encouraging people to *Join in the Rhythm of this Nation.*

Over 7 000 radio advertisements were flighted, encompassing all of South Africa's 11 official languages

The IMC's first advertising foray into international markets was in the form of a branding exercise using 10 London taxis, each depicting creative, positive headlines about South Africa. This campaign is part of an international strategy to raise awareness of what South Africa has to offer international traders, investors and travellers.

The IMC also started using the international media to conduct surveys, and started using supplements on South Africa more strategically.

Top South African business leaders and IMC representatives visited Europe to search for foreign direct investment (FDI) in trade and tourism. The delegation held investment conferences in Frankfurt, Munich and London.

The visit followed the successful Branding South Africa Mission to the United States of America in June 2004.

Co-operative governance

The importance of co-operative governance and intergovernmental relations in South Africa is reflected in Chapter Three of the Constitution, which determines a number of principles.

A number of intergovernmental structures promote and facilitate co-operative governance and intergovernmental relations between the respective spheres of government.

These include:

- The PCC, comprising the President, the Minister of Provincial and Local Government, and the nine premiers.
- Ministerial clusters, directors-general clusters, and the Forum of South African Directors-General (FOSAD), which promote programme integration at national and provincial level.
- Ministerial fora (or MinMECs) between responsible line-function ministers at national level and their respective counterparts at provincial government level, which normally meet on a quarterly basis. These fora are supported by technical committees.
- A number of intergovernmental fora that facilitate co-operative government and intergovernmental relations.

To improve integration among all spheres of government in both policy development and implementation, the Intergovernmental Relations Framework Act, 2005 (Act 13 of 2005), was promulgated in August 2005. It will be complemented by the alignment of spatial and development strategies and planning cycles among all three spheres of government.

Parties in the National Assembly at midnight, 15 September 2005, after floor crossing				
Party	Seats before	Seats after	Seats won	Seats lost
ANC	279	293	14	-
DA	50	47	2	5
IVP	28	23	-	5
UDM	9	6	-	3
ID	7	5	-	2
NNP	7	-	-	7
ACDP	7	4	-	3
VF Plus	4	4	-	-
Nadeco	-	4	4	-
UCDP	3	3	-	-
PAC	3	3	-	-
MF	2	2	-	-
UIF	-	2	2	-
Azapo	1	1	-	-
UPSA	-	1	1	-
FD	-	1	1	-
PIM	-	1	1	-
Source: *Beeld*				

Elections

The Constitution of South Africa places all elections and referendums in the country in all three spheres of government under the control of the Independent Electoral Commission (IEC), established in terms of the IEC Act, 1996 (Act 51 of 1996).

In the 2004 elections, the African National Congress (ANC) clinched victory in all nine provinces, gaining 279 of the 400 seats in the National Assembly.

The Democratic Alliance (DA) followed with 50 parliamentary seats, the Inkatha Freedom Party was third with 28 seats, the United Democratic Movement won nine seats, while the New National Party and the Independent Democrats secured seven seats each. The African Christian Democratic Party won six seats, the Freedom Front Plus four, and the Pan Africanist Congress and the United Christian Democratic Party three each. The Minority Front and Azanian People's Organisation won two seats each.

The ANC also managed to gain the highest number of votes in the provincial results and won 69,68% of the national votes.

During the floor-crossing window, which closed at midnight on 15 September 2005, the ANC gained 14 members from other parties, including four from the DA, bringing its total in the 400-member house to 293. The DA lost five seats in total. Several new parties emerged (see table). Local government elections are scheduled for March 2006.

Disaster management

The Disaster Management Act, 2002 (Act 57 of 2002), provides for the establishment of the Intergovernmental Committee on Disaster Management and the Disaster Management Advisory Forum.

Since April 2003, the Disaster Management Centre under the departments of provincial and local government and of agriculture have issued a number of early warning systems to notify all those affected about expected weather patterns.

The Government's Early Warning System allows the National Disaster Management Centre to forecast weather patterns.

The centre is developing an electronic database containing extensive information about disasters that occur or may occur in southern Africa, including information on early warning systems.

The Disaster Management Act, 2002 also provides for the establishment of national, provincial and municipal disaster management centres.

In February 2005, Cabinet allocated R15 million towards victims of the tsunami disaster; R75 million for financial needs relating to local disasters; and R130 million for drought relief in various parts of the country, including the Northern Cape. Government also allocated R1 million to the Southern African Development Community (SADC) HIV and AIDS Trust Fund.

The Public Service

The Department of Public Service and Administration leads the modernisation of the Public Service, by assisting government departments to implement their management policies, systems and structural solutions within a generally applicable framework of norms and standards, to improve service delivery.

Size of the Public Service

On 31 December 2004, the Public Service had 1 043 698 people in its employ, of whom 62% were attached to the Social Services Sector (health, social development and education), followed by 19% in the Criminal Justice Sector and 7% in the Defence Sector.

Restructuring of the Public Service

Resolution 7 of 2002 came to an end on 12 September 2003. The resolution aimed to restructure the Public Service in terms of HR to enable the most effective and efficient delivery of services.

Phase One of the programme was completed. Phase Two deals with excess employees not accommodated during the redeployment. Between 2003 and June 2005, the number of excess employees was reduced from 13 383 to 5 298. Restructuring of the Public Service, however, is an ongoing process and a framework will be established to guide its ongoing transformation.

Macro-organisational issues

Government has a range of institutions that render services to citizens. These institutions are generally referred to as the public sector and range from national and provincial government departments, to constitutional institutions, and national and provincial public entities.

National Treasury and the Department of Public Service and Administration have been conducting a review of public entities to develop a coherent and consistent regulatory framework for these entities, broadly aligned with public-service arrangements. It aims to achieve improved governance and oversight, clear and appropriate lines of accountability and performance-orientated human resource management (HRM).

The review focused on schedule 3A and 3B public entities and covered areas of corporate governance, the classification of entities into new corporate forms, HR and performance management, and proposals for legislative amendments to give effect to the governance framework. Reports, with findings and recommendations, were finalised for each of the mentioned areas of review. A consolidated governance framework report was drafted to inform government policy.

Community development workers (CDWs)

CDWs are part of government's drive to ensure that service delivery reaches poor and marginalised communities. CDWs provide a bridge between government and citizens, rendering information on services, benefits and economic opportunities.

Government's Programme of Action 2005/06 is available on Government Online (*www.gov.za*). The information is updated regularly to keep the public informed of the implementation process.

By September 2005, 2 238 full-time CDWs and CDW learners had been recruited and were active in the programme. Of this number, 1 329 had completed their yearlong learnership programme.

By September 2005, provinces were involved in the process of recruiting a further 920 CDW learners, bringing the total of CDWs to 3 158. This will ensure that all municipalities have a substantial number of CDW deployees. Progress made indicated that the initial target of 2 840 CDWs countrywide would be exceeded by March 2006.

Strengthening institutional performance

Integrated Provincial Support Programme (IPSP)

Since its inception, the IPSP has supported five provinces (Eastern Cape, Limpopo, the Free State, KwaZulu-Natal and Mpumalanga) in implementing successful innovative service-delivery initiatives. Some of these initiatives, such as the review of PGDS, have started informing national and provincial policies and approaches aimed at achieving poverty alleviation, effective rendering of basic services and good governance.

The purpose of the programme is to enhance the ability of provincial administrations to achieve service standards as agreed with communities by implementing projects aimed at:

In July 2005, the Electoral Commission (IEC) of South Africa launched the IEC training academy in Kempton Park. The purpose of the academy is to improve the skills levels of election administrators and to produce election officials who will be instrumental in delivering free and fair elections. The academy will initially focus on South Africa, but aims to serve election-management bodies across the continent in future.

To coincide with the launch, the Train-the-Trainer Boot Camp, aimed at equipping people to train electoral staff for the 2006 municipal elections, was also held.

- improving the ability of provincial government to co-ordinate and manage pro-poor policies and development
- improving the utilisation of resources and enhancing the poor's access to basic services
- building capacity to restructure state assets
- ensuring transparency and accountability by the centre of provincial government in the delivery of services to citizens
- maximising shared learning and capacity in the Department of Public Service and Administration and provinces
- achieving effective planning and management of the implementation of projects in IPSP II and the overall implementation of the programme.

Successful projects include:
- functional PGDS with feasible targets in five IPSP provinces
- functional and advanced performance management and development systems in the Free State
- updated HR records in Limpopo, Mpumalanga and the Eastern Cape
- improved integrated planning and budgeting in the Free State
- an established functional platform for intergovernmental co-ordination in KwaZulu-Natal
- an effective project and programme management system at provincial and national level
- effective integrated mobile service-delivery centres in the Eastern Cape and Limpopo
- successful institutional turnaround and restructuring of state asset projects in Limpopo
- institutionalising the MPCC programme within municipalities in Mpumalanga
- eliminating backlogs in child support grants' registration and in the payment of qualifying beneficiaries of social grants in targeted areas
- a functional social development information management system, contract management centre and electronic file-management system in the Eastern Cape.

Service-delivery improvement

A strategy has been formulated to revitalise Batho Pele (People First) in government, identifying new goals and targets in transforming the culture and ethos of the Public Service, thereby improving service delivery.

The *Batho Pele* Campaign encourages a positive attitude in the Public Service.

The campaign focuses on taking services to the people. This involves the development of a comprehensive, integrated 2014 access strategy for the Public Service.

The following will be implemented as part of the campaign:

- public servants dealing directly with the public will be identified by name tags
- the *Know your Services* Campaign will inform the public on how to seek redress for poor service
- management systems will be set up to monitor the rate of service delivery by public servants and to identify the frequency and types of complaints and queries received
- the Department of Public Service and Administration will review its HRM systems in view of Batho Pele
- ministers and public service commissioners will pay unannounced visits to service-delivery centres
- senior managers will be required to spend time in these centres, to assist with service delivery and to learn first-hand of both the challenges and the successes at the grass-roots level of service delivery
- Batho Pele will be infused into the training programme for public servants.

By September 2005, the training of 56 trainers on the Batho Pele Change Engagement was underway in Limpopo. Progress reports on the implementation of name tags, extensions of flexible working hours and signage in departments had been received and a report was being compiled. The Department of Home Affairs had implemented flexible working hours in the spirit of Batho Pele.

Labour relations and conditions of service

By May 2005, recommendations to amend the performance management and development system for the Senior Management Service (SMS) had been drafted. These include the requirement that the implementation of the Batho Pele principles be a factor in assessing managers' performance. The *Batho Pele Change Management* Campaign is being implemented in departments and SAMDI is offering training programmes for SMS and levels 1 to 12. Batho Pele learning sessions are also presented to share best practices on service-delivery improvement.

Medical assistance restructuring

A restricted membership medical scheme for public-service employees called the Government Employees Medical Scheme was registered with effect from 1 January 2005.

During 2005, there was no active enrolment of members in the scheme as it was in the process of developing its operations. Member enrolment was expected to commence on 1 January 2006 according to a member enrolment strategy under negotiation in the Public Service Co-ordinating Bargaining Council (PSCBC). The strategy provides for the phased-in enrolment of public-service employees over a five-year period. The scheme is expected to reach full capacity by 2010.

The scheme is expected to result in the addition of hundreds of thousands of new beneficiaries of medical aid, create new employment opportunities, and reduce patient load on the public health sector while creating new revenue streams for this sector.

The Minister of Public Service and Administration, Ms Geraldine Fraser-Moleketi, announced in May 2005 that South Africa would despatch separate teams of experts to Sudan and the Democratic Republic of Congo (DRC) to help them rebuild their public sectors.

Officials will provide technical and limited financial support to various public-service institutions in the DRC over a three-year period.

She also announced that senior officials from the South African Management Development Institute and her department would visit Sudan to assist in capacitating its public sector, especially skills development.

Pension provisioning restructuring

The PSCBC finalised two collective agreements, namely the PSCBC Resolution 12 of 2002 and PSCBC Resolution 7 of 2003. The agreements provide for the introduction of new benefits (orphans' pension and funeral benefit), the restructuring of identified existing benefits (spouses' pension percentage) as well as a new procedure for changing the employer contribution rate to the Government Employees Pension Fund. The agreements also deal with the recognition of non-contributory service as pensionable service for employees disadvantaged by past discrimination in pensions.

By mid-2005, most aspects of the agreements had been fully implemented while work to address the position of identified groups of employees in respect of the recognition of pensionable service was still underway.

Housing

Resolution 2 of 2004, in terms of which the previous Home-Owner Allowance Scheme, assisting only employees repaying a bond on their property, was repealed and replaced with the Housing Allowance.

The Housing Allowance is a sum of money that the employer pays every month in addition to employees' salaries to assist them to pay for the rent or instalments on their own homes.

Not everybody will immediately receive the maximum value of the Housing Allowance. As part of the agreed phasing-in process, the Housing Allowance will be increased from R100 per month over five years to a maximum of R403 per month. The maximum allowance will also be revised quarterly to provide for changes in the interest rate, whereafter it will be fixed on 1 January 2009.

Leave

With the adoption of Resolution 7 of 2000, the leave benefits of public-service employees was restructured in line with current practices, as well as the requirements of the Basic Conditions of Employment Act, 1997 (Act 75 of 1997). The restructured benefits include annual leave, sick leave, incapacity leave, family responsibility leave, maternity leave, adoption leave, leave for occupa-

tional injuries and diseases, leave for union activities and special leave.

According to the agreement, annual leave became, for the first time, an entitlement. This means that should employees terminate their services in the course of a leave cycle or should they be unable to utilise such leave due to operational reasons, unused credits are payable to the employees. Another added value is the introduction of the benefit of incapacity leave, should employees, after their normal sick leave, require additional leave to recover from a serious illness or injury. The granting of incapacity leave is subject to an investigation by the employer.

Management Policy and Procedure on Incapacity Leave and Ill-Health Retirement (PILIR) for public-service employees

The objectives of PILIR are to set up structures and processes to:
- intervene and manage incapacity leave in the workplace to accommodate temporarily or permanently incapacitated employees
- facilitate the rehabilitation, reskilling, realignment and retirement of temporarily or permanently incapacitated employees, where appropriate.

PILIR adopts a holistic approach to health-risk management; prevents abuse of sick leave by managing incapacity or ill-health as far as possible; adopts a scientific approach to health-risk management based on sound medical, actuarial and legal principles; and implements health-risk management that is consistent, fair, objective, cost-effective and financially sound.

PILIR provides for the appointment of health-risk managers – external companies comprising a multidisciplinary team with the necessary knowledge, skills and capacity in the medical field, specifically occupational medicine. The managers assess cases and make recommendations regarding applications for incapacity leave and ill-health retirements to the heads of departments.

An implementation strategy was developed and approved by Cabinet to inform the implementation of PILIR in the Public Service.

Fighting corruption

The National Anti-Corruption Forum (NACF) is a national structure that brings the public, business and civil-society sectors together to further national consensus against corruption.

The NACF convened the second National Anti-Corruption Summit in March 2005 in Pretoria, Gauteng.

Several resolutions were adopted to form the basis of a national programme to fight corruption. These resolutions pertain to ethics, awareness, prevention, combating, oversight, transparency and accountability. An implementation committee was established to develop the National Anti-Corruption Programme (NAP) that will be implemented within the sectors and as cross-sectoral plans. The summit resolved that the NACF should assume responsibility for driving the NAP and that the NACF should refine representation of sectors in this structure.

By September 2005, an implementation committee had commenced with its first project on the Prevention and Combating of Corrupt Activities Act 2004 (Act 12 of 2004). The project is to develop guidelines on the Act for citizens and public-service and business managers. It will contain a section explaining the Act in plain language, which will be translated into all 11 languages.

Senior Management Service

The overall goal of the SMS initiative is to improve government's ability to recruit, retain and develop quality managers and professionals. To this end, the following have been put in place:
- a modernised employment framework consisting of improved terms and conditions of service
- mechanisms to improve the interdepartmental mobility of senior managers and professionals
- uniform performance management and development systems supported by a competency framework.

The SMS Development Programme is at an advanced stage. The Competency Framework has been converted into the proficiency levels 'competent' and 'advanced'.

An SMS member has to be at either of these levels. If not, development programmes are avail-

able to assist with the development of these competencies. The implementation of the framework will allow the Public Service to plan, recruit, assess and develop its SMS cadre.

The SMS Service-Delivery Challenge (Khaedu) Project entails the deployment of SMS members to service-delivery points as part of a mandatory performance agreement to gain practical experience on the challenges prevalent at these points.

Human resource management

The Human Resource Development (HRD) Strategy for the Public Service was launched in April 2002. The strategy is aimed at improving the State machinery on a sustainable basis through skills development and training programmes. The strategy's vision is to develop a dedicated, responsive and productive cadre of public servants. The development of the strategy is in line with the HRD Strategy for South Africa and the National Skills Development Strategy developed by the departments of labour and of education.

A scarce skills strategy and an internship framework are incorporated in the HRD Strategy for the Public Service. The latter is intended to fast-track the skills development of the youth and unemployed graduates.

The strategy is supported by various laws such as the Skills Development Act, 1998 (Act 97 of 1998), the Skills Development Levies Act, 1999 (Act 9 of 1999), and the 1997 *White Paper on Public Service Training and Education*. The implementation of the strategy is underpinned by the vision of an integrated HRM system.

The Public Service HRM systems propagate the inculcation of a culture of performance, hence the emphasis on strategic and HR planning and the development of human-capital capacity.

The Competency Framework for Senior Managers was introduced to improve the quality of managers and professionals employed in the Public Service. This framework links directly with performance management, training and development, as well as recruitment and selection. Initiatives are underway to develop a similar competency framework for middle managers and lower ranks. It will also involve submitting proposals on how to accelerate the development of middle managers and prepare them for senior management positions.

The State as employer has to comply with the laws of the country on representivity. To this end, the Public Service regulations require that executing authorities prepare strategic plans to inform their annual plans (e.g. service delivery, HR, recruitment, training and development, and change-management strategies) in accordance with their delivery programmes.

In February 2005, the Public Service comprised 2% managers, while 50% of the employees fell within salary levels that were typically labelled as lower-skilled, 40% semi-skilled and a further 8% as highly skilled. Government plans to ensure that the skills profile of personnel and the skills profile required by a developmental state are commensurate with one another.

HR has undertaken a research project to determine ways and methods to strengthen the efficiency of HRM in the Public Service. This will define the roles and responsibilities of HR components. It will also define the competency requirements for HR practitioners and identify necessary interventions to improve service delivery. Work in this regard was completed, and by June 2005 the research findings were being considered for implementation.

Research has been initiated into the Public-Service remuneration framework with specific reference to professionals. Departments are reviewing the grading of certain occupations. Requests for the payment of scarce skills allowances are being considered by the Department of Public Service and Administration. Draft guidelines on the deployment of senior managers within the Public Service have been developed.

Proposals have been made regarding a framework to improve the physical working environment. Draft modernised office norms and a policy on government-wide immovable asset management have been developed. A plan for improving the physical work environment of national departments' headquarters in Pretoria and the Tshwane municipality is being implemented.

Affirmative action

Government's affirmative action policy for the Public Service emphasises the creation of a representative public service within an environment that values diversity and supports the affirmation of those who have been historically disadvantaged.

The overall profile of the Public Service needs to match the population profile in terms of both race and gender.

On 31 March 2005, 73,9% of the Public Service was African; 3,7% Asian; 8,9% coloured; and 13,5% white. Regarding gender, 53,3% was female and 46,7% male. However, at senior management level, 54% were African; 7,5% Asian; 7,7% coloured; and 30% white. The gender breakdown for senior management was 28,5% female and 71,5% male.

HIV and AIDS

The minimum standards for the management of HIV and AIDS in the Public Service were promulgated in 2002. A comprehensive implementation strategy focuses on:

- supporting the implementation of the minimum standards by government departments
- continuously reviewing the minimum standards to ensure relevance and appropriateness
- monitoring the implementation of the minimum standards throughout the Public Service.

The implementation of the minimum standards is proceeding well. The programme has been identified as a good practice model by the International Labour Organisation and is documented as such.

While the current focus on HIV and AIDS will be maintained, a more comprehensive employee health and wellness approach will be adopted over the next few years. The process of developing guidelines for employee health and wellness is already underway. These guidelines will consolidate the following programmes into a comprehensive public-service employee health and wellness programme:

- the current HIV and AIDS Programme
- the Employee Assistance Programme (EAP)
- occupational health and safety
- disaster management

- health promotion and disease prevention
- all other health- and wellness-related programmes.

Over the next three years, other significant projects aimed at supporting government departments in the implementation of the programme include:
- developing a peer educator model for the programme
- developing a model for mainstreaming employee health and wellness
- managing HIV- and AIDS-related stigma and discrimination
- identifying, documenting and distributing good-practice initiatives in the Public Service.

Public-service information

Service delivery, HR and financial information is published on an annual basis by departments to achieve monitoring and evaluation (M&E). The Department of Public Service and Administration, in partnership with National Treasury, is investigating the modernisation and upgrading of HRM information systems.

By June 2005, a proposal on the design of a government-wide M&E system had been developed following Cabinet approval of a framework for such a system. An audit of reporting requirements and departmental M&E systems in the Public Service is underway. An early warning system, which will alert government to imminent service-delivery failures, has been developed.

Government Information Technology Officers' (GITO) Council

The GITO Council was created to serve as an Information Technology (IT) co-ordination and consolidation vehicle to assist in informing government, on a continuous basis, when and how to intervene in the interest of enhanced service delivery. It is premised on the requirement that each GITO is part of the executive team in the respective organ of state, and responsible for the departmental or provincial IT strategy and plan.

The GITO Council has been involved in the investigation, formulation and development of an IT security-policy framework, e-government policy and strategy, and IT procurement guidelines. It also monitors government IT projects to eliminate duplication.

The GITO Council has formed a working group to investigate and make recommendations on the use of open-source software in government. Another working group investigated knowledge management in government.

All Information Communications Technology (ICT) projects will be brought in line with the objectives of the Gateway project.

Batho Pele Gateway Services Portal

The Batho Pele Gateway Services Portal was launched at nine MPCCs countrywide on 3 August 2004.

Responsibility for the content of the Gateway Services Portal (accessed via South Africa Government Online [www.gov.za]) has been transferred to the Government Communication and Information System from the Department of Public Service and Administration. The Government Communication and Information System will be supported by content managers in every department to ensure that services offered to the public are fully and accurately reflected on this website. It is intended that the content of this resource be available in all official languages. By April 2005, the portal was accessible from any computer or from the general service counters at nine MPCCs, over 600 public information terminals in citizen post offices, and from the laptops of 40 CDWs.

The Gateway call centre (1020), is also operational in six of the 11 official languages.

The next phase of the Gateway project involves making service transactions available online.

Centre for Public Service Innovation (CPSI)

The CPSI has driven innovation in the delivery of public services for the past three years. This is achieved through informed, action-orientated research, demonstration of ideas in practice, and addressing the culture and context in which innovation takes place.

In keeping with the emphasis on building the capacity of the Public Service, the CPSI's *2005 Future Watch Research Report* focused on human-capital development in the Public Service. The report identified three forms of human-capital development, namely individual, organisational and stakeholder. The report identified trends in each case to provide government departments with new innovative techniques.

The CPSI strives to create opportunities for enhancing access to government services through innovative means. This was achieved through the piloting of general services counters within MPCCs.

The annual CPSI Public-Sector Innovation Awards recognise projects and programmes that are directed at enhancing public-service delivery, thus improving South Africans' standard of living.

State Information Technology Agency (SITA)

SITA came into operation on 4 April 1999 as a result of the SITA Act, 1998 (Act 88 of 1998).

It consolidates and co-ordinates the State's IT and information-management interests. SITA is managed as a private company, with government as the sole shareholder.

It focuses on the effective provision of ICT products and services across all three spheres of government.

International and African affairs

The Minister of Public Service and Administration, Ms Geraldine Fraser-Moleketi, is the chairperson of the Pan-African Conference of Ministers of Public Service.

The ministry is also active in global organisations involved in public-administration issues and challenges. The minister actively participates in the Commonwealth Association of Public Administration and Management, the International Institute for Administrative Sciences, and in the activities of the United Nations (UN) pertaining to public administration. In addition, the ministry has concluded and continues to conclude various information-sharing and capacity-development bilateral co-operative

agreements with similar ministries and departments across the globe.

South Africa plays an influential role in the international and African governance and public administration community. At the request of the New Partnership for Africa's Development Secretariat, the South African Public Service and Administration Ministry spearheaded the development and adoption of a continental programme on governance and public administration.

The programme focuses on institutional capacity, research and data availability, innovation, and training in public services across all African countries. It has been adopted as a programme of the African Union.

In addition to this comprehensive programme, South Africa has also been called upon to provide direct assistance to other countries. As part of a bilateral agreement, the Democratic Republic of Congo (DRC) requested the South African Government to provide technical assistance in the arena of governance and public administration.

South Africa's participation in the African Peer Review Mechanism process provides an opportunity to achieve various strategic objectives. The Minister of Public Service and Administration was granted overall responsibility for the South African Peer Review Process, which involves consultations with all major role-players to disseminate the questionnaire and to receive input. A self-assessment report must subsequently be drafted, a programme of action implemented and, after consultation with all major role-players, the National Peer Review Governing Council established. (See chapter 11: *Foreign relations.*)

Governance and Administration (G&A) Cluster

A national cluster system comprising six Cabinet committees and five corresponding administrative structures of FOSAD was introduced in 1999.

These structures are the Governance and Administration Cluster; Social Cluster; Economic Cluster; Justice, Crime Prevention and Security Cluster; and International Relations Peace and Security Cluster.

The Governance and Administration Cluster is co-chaired by the directors-general of the Department of Public Service and Administration, the Department of Provincial and Local Government and SAMDI.

The cluster has three broad priorities:
- capability needs of the developmental State
- macro-organisation of the State
- planning, implementation and M&E.

Public Service Commission (PSC)

The PSC derives its mandate from sections 195 and 196 of the Constitution. Section 195 sets out the values and principles governing public administration, which should be promoted by the commission. These values and principles are:
- a high standard of professional ethics
- efficient, economic and effective use of resources
- a development-orientated public administration
- provision of services in an impartial, fair and equitable way, without bias
- responding to people's needs and encouraging the public to participate in policy-making
- accountable public administration
- fostering transparency
- the cultivation of good HRM and career-development practices
- a representative public administration with employment and personnel-management practices based on ability, objectivity, fairness and the need to redress the imbalances of the past.

In terms of Section 196(4) of the Constitution, the functions and powers of the commission are to:
- promote the values and principles, as set out in Section 195, throughout the Public Service
- investigate, monitor and evaluate the organisation, administration and personnel practices of the Public Service, in particular the adherence to the values and principles set out in Section 195 and public-service procedures
- propose measures to ensure effective and efficient performance within the Public Service
- give directives aimed at ensuring that personnel procedures relating to recruitment, transfers, promotions and dismissals comply with the values and principles set out in Section 195

- report on its activities and the performance of its functions, including any findings it may make and directives and advice it may give, and provide an evaluation of the extent to which the values and principles set out in Section 195 are complied with, either of its own accord, or on receipt of any complaint
- investigate and evaluate the application of personnel and public-administration practices and report to the relevant executive authority and legislature
- investigate grievances of employees in the Public Service concerning official acts or omissions, and recommend appropriate remedies
- monitor and investigate adherence to applicable procedures in the Public Service
- advise national and provincial organs of state regarding personnel practices in the Public Service, including those relating to the recruitment, appointment, transfer, discharge and other aspects of the careers of employees in the Public Service.

The PSC is supported by the Office of the Public Service Commission (OPSC), which implements the policy and programmes of the PSC. The commission comprises 14 commissioners and has regional offices in all nine provinces. The work of the OPSC is structured around the following key performance areas:

Labour-relations improvements

Sound labour-relations policies and good HRM have to be advanced to maximise human potential to ensure the effective use of all the resources necessary to promote an acceptable and transparent public administration.

To meet this challenge, the OPSC's Labour-Relations Improvements Unit:
- investigates grievances lodged with the PSC and makes recommendations to executing authorities
- investigates, monitors and evaluates labour-relations policies and trends in the Public Service and makes recommendations in that regard
- monitors and evaluates the capacity and ability

of departments to implement recommendations made
- investigates allegations lodged with the PSC relating to, among others, maladministration, poor conduct and behaviour of staff, and any form of discrimination.

The unit received 435 grievances between 1 April 2004 and 31 March 2005, and finalised 279 grievances.

The PSC also published complaints rules in the *Government Gazette* to provide a mechanism for members of the public (employees and public servants) to lodge complaints with the PSC relating to maladministration, poor conduct and behaviour of staff and any form of discrimination.

The unit is also investigating the performance of SMS members and determining the nature of support to be provided in dealing with poor performance, if any.

Public-administration investigations

This unit is responsible mainly for audits and forensic investigations into public-administration practices. This entails the investigation of complaints lodged and requests emanating from, among others, executing authorities, public servants and whistleblowers. The unit also conducts research on general public-administration trends, and gives advice, makes recommendations and publishes reports on these trends, such as the *Report on Financial Misconduct*.

Most of the investigations relate to anonymous complaints regarding maladministration and irregularities pertaining to HR and procurement practices. Furthermore, the unit undertakes cross-functional investigations in collaboration with other organs of state, such as the Public Protector.

Professional ethics and human resource reviews

The approach of the PSC is to address corruption proactively and in an integrated manner, focusing on the creation of an ethics-management infrastructure.

The implementation of the Anti-Corruption Strategy is co-ordinated by the Anti-Corruption Co-ordinating Committee, which is chaired by the Department of Public Service and Administration. Departments are individually tasked with the implementation of the projects identified in the strategy.

In 2004/05, the commission undertook several activities to implement the strategy and build the capacity of the Public Service to prevent and fight corruption. These included:
- Auditing anti-corruption capabilities in national and provincial departments in conjunction with the Department of Public Service and Administration.
- Anti-corruption training.
- Providing secretariat services to the NACF.
- The successful hosting of the second National Anti-Corruption Summit in March 2005.
- Developing a generic professional-ethics statement to inculcate and maintain a culture of integrity and ethos within the Public Service.
- Ethics awareness and education. An explanatory manual on the Public Service Code of Conduct was developed and published. One million copies were produced and distributed to departments.
- The establishment of the toll-free, 24-hour National Public Service Anti-Corruption Hotline facility (0800 701 701) to which fraud and corruption can be reported. By early 2005, the PSC had referred 419 cases to the provinces and 146 cases to national departments for investigation. Consistent with the resolutions of both the 1999 and 2005 national anti-corruption summits, the hotline is expected to play a crucial role in the fight against corruption.
- The publication of reader-friendly whistleblowing guides to support public-sector managers with the promotion of accountability and transparency.

The PSC is also evaluating the implementation of the policy framework on managing HIV and AIDS in the Public Service and the establishment of EAPs.

Leadership and performance improvement

This unit facilitates the performance management of heads of national and provincial departments and evaluates public-service performance in key government programmes.

The PSC has developed a framework for the evaluation of heads of departments. Their performance agreements are filed with the commission for quality- and compliance-control purposes.

The commission recognises the importance of providing feedback on organisational performance in addition to individual performance. A system to measure organisational performance was being developed and was expected to be implemented in 2005.

Service delivery and quality assurance

The fundamental objective of this unit is to promote improved service delivery through public participation and quality audits that focus either on compliance, performance or management practices. The unit gives advice on the improvement of service processes of departments, including the reconfiguration of organisational structures for more efficient service delivery.

Governance and monitoring

This unit promotes the constitutional values and principles underpinning good governance and, through the implementation of various strategic projects, contributes to improved governance practices in the Public Service.

A key priority of the commission is to ensure the implementation of the Public Service Monitoring and Evaluation System (PSM&ES), which focuses on the performance of individual public-service departments. The PSM&ES is based on the nine values and principles as set out in Section 195 of the Constitution. In applying the system, problem areas are identified, priority areas communicated, good practice noted and departments given an opportunity to reflect on their own performance.

The unit is responsible for managing this system and undertaking departmental assessments on a continuous basis.

The fourth annual edition of the *State of the Public Service Report* afforded the commission the opportunity to once again comment on the state of the Public Service by referring to internal research conducted, as well as limited external research.

In promoting the use of M&E practices and systems within the Public Service, the PSC co-hosted the third African Evaluation Conference with the African Evaluation Association in Cape Town at the end of 2004.

The theme of the conference, which was attended by over 470 participants from 55 countries, 47 of which were African, was *Africa Matters, Evaluation Matters – Joining Forces for Democracy, Governance and Development.*

In April 2005, the PSC partnered with the Joint Africa Institute and African Development Bank to present a development evaluation seminar in Tunis, Tunisia. The eventual aim is to integrate M&E into administrative and governance structures at various levels.

South African Management Development Institute

SAMDI is responsible for:
- creating a public service that understands and encourages the concept of lifelong learning as an investment in human capital
- shaping a public-sector learning framework to address the needs of the two economies through sustained development in a wide range of skills, particularly scarce skills areas such as financial and project management
- supporting the activities of the Governance and Administration Cluster through the provision of an HRD strategy aimed at enhancing the capacity of the State to deliver services to its people
- developing the potential of public-service officials through relevant, practical and targeted skills development and training interventions that are primarily aimed at reducing service-delivery blockages
- determining a structure within which management-development institutes across the continent can contribute to the upliftment and growth of African nations, particularly those experiencing post-conflict processes.

SAMDI has been working closely with the DRC and Sudan in strengthening their post-conflict development processes.

SAMDI has developed a programme for strengthening the capacity of members of the executive to execute their responsibilities. Due to the varying nature of responsibilities at provincial level, SAMDI will develop individual learning strategies, informed by a training development needs analysis, to ensure that the appropriate skills are shared at the right time with the right people. This programme has been piloted in the Northern Cape, and the lessons learnt will be used to further strengthen and shape the programme for other provinces.

The Integrated Management Development Programme (IMDP) was established to ensure a comprehensive approach to the development of public-service managers. It consists of the:

- Presidential Strategic Leadership Development Programme for senior managers on levels 13 to 16
- Advanced Management Development Programme for middle managers on levels 9 to 12
- Emerging Management Development Programme for junior managers on levels 6 to 8.

These programmes are accredited through tertiary institutions. Some 3 632 managers were expected to have been trained through these programmes by 31 March 2005.

SAMDI has developed and plans extensive roll-out of an HR planning course. The SMS and levels 1 to 12 performance-management systems have been revised.

During the past few years, SAMDI has successfully been implementing the IMDP, the development of which was funded by the Republic of Flanders. The IMDP caters for the development of junior, middle and senior managers between levels 6 and 16. SAMDI will also introduce the Foundation Management Programme aimed at the development of officials on levels 3 to 5 to ensure that there is a sustainable pool of potential management candidates on which government can draw to implement its programmes and activities.

During 2004/05, SAMDI delivered 70 079 person training days, of which 6 736 were funded by donors. This resulted in 15 510 persons being trained.

Home Affairs

The Department of Home Affairs provides individual status-determination services.

The department has a network of offices in all provinces. Areas where the establishment of fixed offices is not warranted, are serviced by mobile offices or units on a regular pre-arranged basis.

The department is divided into five functional support and two line-function divisions.

Statutory bodies falling under the department are the:

- Immigration Advisory Board
- Standing Committee for Refugee Affairs
- Refugee Appeal Board.

The Government Printing Works, a division of the Department of Home Affairs, provides printing, stationery and related services to all government departments, provincial governments and municipalities.

It also publishes, markets and distributes government publications. Based in Pretoria, the printing works provides a variety of related services to departments, the printing industry and other African countries, including the manufacture and supply of fingerprint ink to the South African Police Service (SAPS), and the printing of postage stamps for the DRC and Lesotho.

Negotiations on the rationalisation of the Government Printing Works' services with provincial printing facilities are in progress.

Civic services

The Branch: Civic Services is responsible mainly for population registration and civic services. Population registration entails the recording of personal particulars in the Population Register with a view to the issuing of identity documents (IDs); identification by means of fingerprints and photographs; and matters pertaining to the status of persons, such as births, marriages and deaths.

Civic services entail the issuing of passports, registration of foreign births, determining citizenship, and issuing certificates of naturalisation or resumption of South African citizenship.

Between April 2004 and March 2005, about 2 508 480 IDs were issued.

Citizenship matters

South African citizenship is regulated by the South African Citizenship Act, 1995 (Act 88 of 1995), and regulations issued in terms thereof. South African citizenship may be granted by way of:

- birth or descent
- an application for naturalisation as a South African citizen
- an application for resumption of South African citizenship
- the registration of the birth of children born outside South Africa to South African fathers or mothers
- an application for exemption in terms of Section 26(4) of the Act.

Population Register

The current Population Register hosted by the Department of Home Affairs, stores and provides citizenry identification information, including unique identification numbers, addresses, birth dates and marriage status. Information on this system is used for various purposes, including identity validation. In essence, this system forms the core of citizenry information systems within the department.

Evolving technology, modern government structures and the need for more secure systems, led to the department embarking on a programme to re-engineer the Population Register. This will align its function with the current government dispensation and future needs of both the Government and third-party institutions. This redesign project is closely aligned with the implementation of the Home Affairs National Identification System approved by government in January 1996.

The focus and scope of the project is on providing a more scalable, adaptable, efficient, secured and interoperable database. Features will allow integration with the automated biometric fingerprint system, information sourcing from the electronic document management system, an electronic web-based query system, and interrogation from the different deconsole units. As the core component of Home Affairs' electronic systems, it is imperative that the redesigned database also provides for online services, thereby removing current limitations on access to information and thus public services.

Immigration

The Branch: Immigration is responsible for control over the admission of foreigners for residence in and departure from South Africa. This entails:

- processing applications for visas, temporary residence permits and immigration permits
- maintaining a travellers' and foreigners' control system
- tracing and removing foreigners who are considered undesirable or who are in South Africa illegally.

The Refugees Act, 1998 (Act 130 of 1998), gives effect within South Africa to the relevant international legal instruments, principles and standards relating to refugees; provides for the reception into South Africa of asylum seekers; regulates applications for and recognition of refugee status; and provides for the rights and obligations flowing from such status, and related matters. The Act came into effect on 1 April 2000.

In recent years, the department has sought to control illegal immigration through a variety of measures:

- The Immigration Act, 2002 (Act 13 of 2002), provides for a stricter immigration policy. The implementation of administrative fines and other measures came into effect in 2003.
- The department works closely with the South

On 7 April 2005, the Department of Home Affairs launched a national campaign aimed at correcting errors in documents issued by the department. These include identity documents, passports, and birth and marriage certficates.

The *Lokisa Ditokomane/Lungisa Izingcwadi* Campaign was aimed at affording South Africans an opportunity to rectify incorrect details on these documents at no charge. For a period of three months, the department dedicated counters for this purpose, where members of the public received assistance.

African Revenue Service and the SAPS to ensure effective border control.

- A computerised visa system was instituted to curb the forgery of South African visas and is being extended to all South African missions abroad.

The final immigration regulations came into effect on 1 July 2004. The release of these regulations followed the signing of the Immigration Amendment Act, 2004 (Act 19 of 2004), into law on 12 October 2004.

The immigration policy aims to:

- discourage illegal migration into South Africa by encouraging foreign nationals to apply for different permits to legalise their stay in the country
- create an enabling environment for FDI in South Africa
- attract scarce skills required by the economy in accordance with the 2014 vision of eradicating poverty and underdevelopment.

The final immigration regulations furthermore aim to establish a new system of immigration control to ensure that:

- temporary and permanent residence permits are issued as expeditiously as possible and according to simplified procedures
- security considerations are fully satisfied and the State regains control over the immigration of foreigners to South Africa
- economic growth is promoted through the

In May 2005, the Department of Home Affairs launched the first 10 mobile units as a means of achieving the broader strategic objectives intended to bring government services closer to the people. These units will be used to provide the full range of home affairs' civic and immigration services.

Sixty-seven mobile units will be deployed throughout the country and will be fitted with all the necessary equipment and facilities to function like ordinary offices. These vehicles will be located mostly in rural areas, taking into account the population dynamics of the area in accordance with the Urban Renewal Programme's and Integrated Sustainable Rural Development Strategy's nodal points.

employment of needed foreign labour, foreign investment is facilitated, the entry of exceptionally skilled or qualified people is enabled, skilled human resources are increased and academic exchange programmes in the SADC are facilitated

- tourism is promoted
- the contribution of foreigners to the South African labour market does not adversely impact on existing labour standards and the rights and expectations of South African workers
- a policy connection is maintained between foreigners working in South Africa and the training of South African citizens
- a human rights-based culture of enforcement is promoted.

The Directorate: Refugee Affairs manages refugee services in South Africa. It has established two units, namely the Asylum Seekers Unit and Country of Origin Information Unit.

These units advise refugee-reception offices on policy-related matters and on the background information of an applicant's country of origin. After being recognised, refugees are issued with refugee IDs, which give them access to the basic services in South Africa, including basic healthcare, education and employment.

Refugees are also issued with UN travel documents by the South African Government through the Department of Home Affairs. From May 2005, refugees have been issued with a refugee smart ID, which contains security features that are not forgeable.

The Directorate: Information Co-ordination manages information on the National Immigration Branch (NIB) to ensure that the required information is available to the NIB and to facilitate regional and national operations.

The directorate's main objectives are to:

- establish an information repository, which will act on risks and urgent immigration matters
- ensure dynamic real-time support on tactical and legal matters to immigration officers globally
- have a system through which relevant information is readily available to all stakeholders in government.

Future systems include the roll-out of a library system to accommodate paper correspondence, an incident-reporting system to capture and analyse events across the country, and the development of a counter-corruption system, which will be accessible to members of the public for reporting corrupt officials. The establishment of formal mechanisms for exchanging information with stakeholders is also envisaged.

A 24-hour operational centre will be established where immigration-related enquiries and incidents from the department's regional offices, border posts and South African missions abroad will be attended to. The centre will be equipped with all systems available within the department.

Visas

Foreigners who wish to enter South Africa must be in possession of valid and acceptable travel documents. They must also be in possession of valid visas, except in the case of certain countries whose citizens are exempt from visa control. Such exemptions are normally limited to permits, which are issued for 90 days or less at the ports of entry.

The visa system is aimed at facilitating the admission of acceptable foreigners at ports of entry. The visa becomes a permit upon entry, therefore no additional permit will be issued.

Control of travellers

The travel documents of persons entering or departing from South Africa are examined by immigration officers at recognised ports of entry to determine whether such persons comply with the requirements.

Control of sojourn

Foreigners who are in the country illegally and who are therefore guilty of an offence, may be classified into three categories, namely those who:
- entered the country clandestinely
- failed to renew the temporary residence permits issued to them at ports of entry
- breached the conditions of their temporary residence permits without permission, e.g. holiday visitors who took up employment or started their own businesses.

Depending on the circumstances, persons who are in South Africa illegally are either prosecuted, removed or their sojourn is legalised. Officers at the various regional and district offices of the department are in charge of tracing, prosecuting and removing illegal foreigners from the country. Employers of illegal foreigners may also be prosecuted.

Permanent residence

Government allows immigration on a selective basis. The Department of Home Affairs is responsible for:
- Processing applications for immigration permits for consideration.
- Admitting persons suitable for immigration, such as skilled workers in occupations in which there is a shortage in South Africa. The department particularly encourages applications by industrialists and other entrepreneurs who wish to relocate their existing concerns or establish new concerns in South Africa.

The department is not directly involved in an active immigration drive.

In categories where shortages exist, the normal procedure is for employers to recruit abroad independently, and in most cases, initially apply for temporary work permits.

The department considers the applications for immigration permits of prospective immigrants who wish to settle in the relevant provinces. In terms of

South Africa hosted the Regional Hearing for Africa of the United Nations' Global Commission on International Migration in Cape Town from 28 February to 1 March 2005. The theme of the hearing was *To Provide a Framework for the Formulation of a Coherent, Comprehensive and Global Response to International Migration.*

The hearing addressed migration flows from within and to the continent. It covered a wide variety of issues, including the economic aspects of migration; irregular migration; migrants in society and their human rights; as well as the national, regional and global governance of migration.

new regulations, regions will be responsible for issuing permits previously issued by the regional committees in respect of permanent residence. They will also do so in respect of temporary residence.

Enquiries in this regard may be made to the nearest office of the Department of Home Affairs in South Africa, missions abroad, or the Director-General of Home Affairs for attention Directorate: Permitting in Pretoria.

Temporary residence

In terms of the Immigration Act, 2002, temporary residence permits are divided into the following categories:
- visitor's permits
- diplomatic permits
- study permits
- treaty permits
- business permits
- crew permits

New immigration regulations came into effect on 1 July 2005. Amendments to immigration legislation introduced some changes, eliminating the red tape burden imposed on foreigners. Some of these include:
- To curb fraudulent marriages, any foreigner who wishes to marry a South African and thereby obtain permanent residence in the country, should be married in good faith to such a South African citizen for at least five years before the status can be granted to him/her.
- In education, the regulation dealing with study permits provides that a deposit is not required from students of African countries. This is subject to a written undertaking from their governments to pay all deportation expenses in respect of such students, should this become necessary.
- Flexibility that enables mine workers from neighbouring states to be replaced easily upon death by someone from their family without immigration complications regarding the work permit. Workers who are dismissed are also protected; they are no longer forced to leave the country immediately, since they are allowed time to take their case for conciliation or through the courts without relinquishing their right to be in the country.

- medical permits
- relative's permits
- work permits with the following categories:
  - quota work permits
  - general work permits
  - intra-company transfer work permits
  - exceptional skills work permits
  - corporate work permits
  - retired person permits
  - exchange permits
- asylum permits.

In terms of Section 11, a visitor's permit may be issued to a person who intends to enter South Africa for less than 90 days for the purpose of tourism, business, education or medical treatment. Foreigners who are exempt from visa requirements or who are citizens of countries that are exempt from visa requirements for 90 days, may therefore proceed to a port of entry where visitors' permits for the mentioned period will be issued, provided such persons can produce evidence to prove their bona fides.

Foreigners who are citizens of countries that are exempted from visa requirements for less than 90 days may likewise obtain visitors' permits at a port of entry. For the period, such foreigners enjoy an exemption only. Foreigners who require a visa prior to proceeding to South Africa or who intend to enter South Africa for any period longer than the period that they are exempt from the visa requirement, must apply for and obtain a visa prior to proceeding to the country.

Foreigners who intend to accept an offer of employment, start a business, take up studies or enter South Africa for any purpose for which a temporary residence permit is provided for in the Act, must apply for an appropriate temporary residence permit via the South African diplomatic representative in their countries of origin/residence. In countries where there are no representatives, applications must be submitted in the nearest country where there is a foreign representative.

The outcome must be awaited outside South Africa and applicants may only proceed to South Africa once the permit as applied for, has been issued to them.

The overriding consideration when dealing with applications for work permits is whether the employment or task to be undertaken cannot be performed by a South African citizen or an approved permanent immigrant already residing in South Africa.

Applications for the extension of temporary residence permits must be submitted at least 30 days prior to the expiry date of the permit, to the nearest regional/district office of the Department of Home Affairs where the applicant is employed. Any enquiries related to temporary residence permits may be directed to the nearest district/regional office of the Department of Home Affairs in South Africa, South African diplomatic representatives abroad, or the Director-General of Home Affairs, for the attention of the Directorate: Permitting.

Removal of undesirable persons

In terms of legislation, the Minister of Home Affairs may order the deportation of any person (other than a South African citizen) convicted of any of the offences specified, or if such person is deemed by the minister to be an undesirable inhabitant of or visitor to South Africa.

The minister may also order the deportation of any person (other than a South African citizen) if it is deemed to be in the public interest.

Acknowledgements

BuaNews

Bua Briefs

Department of Home Affairs

Department of Provincial and Local Government

Department of Public Service and Administration

Estimates of National Expenditure 2005, published by National Treasury

Government Communication and Information System

International Marketing Council

Office of the Public Service Commission

South African Management and Development Institute

www.cpsi.co.za

www.dplg.gov.za

www.gcis.gov.za

www.gov.za

www.imc.org.za

www.salga.net

Suggested reading

Alexander, N. *An Ordinary Country: Issues in the Transition from Apartheid to Democracy in South Africa*. Pietermaritzburg: University of Natal Press, 2002.

Bond, P. *Elite Transition: From Apartheid to Neoliberalism in South Africa*. 2nd ed. Scottsville: University of KwaZulu-Natal Press, 2005

Bond, P. and Khosa, M. eds. *RDP Policy Audit*. Pretoria: Human Sciences Research Council (HSRC), 1999.

Bratton, M., Mattes, R. and Gyiamh-Boadi, E. *Public Opinion, Democracy and Market Reform in South Africa*. Cambridge: Cambridge University Press, 2005.

Brink, A. *27 April: One Year Later*. Cape Town: Queillerie, 1995.

Calland, R. ed. *The First Five Years: A Review of South Africa's Democratic Parliament*. Cape Town: Institute for Democracy in South Africa (IDASA), 1999.

Calland, R. and Graham, P. eds. *Democracy in the Time of Mbeki*. Cape Town: IDASA, 2005.

Cameron, P. *Democratisation of South African Government: A Tale of Three Cities*. Pretoria: Van Schaik, 1999.

Chidester, D. *What Holds Us Together? Social Cohesion in South Africa*. Pretoria: HSRC, 2003.

Chikane, F. *et al.* eds. *Africa: The Time has Come: Selected Speeches by Thabo Mbeki*. Cape Town: Tafelberg Publishers, 1998.

Constitution of the Republic of South Africa; edited by Juta's Statutes Editors; reflecting the law as at October 2004. Lansdowne: Juta, 2004.

Corrigan, T. *Beyond the Boycotts: Financing Local Government in the Post-Apartheid Era*. Johannesburg: South African Institute for Race Relations (SAIRR), 1998.

Craythorne, D.L. *Municipal Administration: A Handbook*. 4th ed. Kenwyn: Juta, 1997.

Crush, J. and Williams, V. eds. *The New South Africans: Immigration Amnesties and their Aftermath*, Cape Town: Southern African Migration Project, 1999.

D'Engelbronner-Kolff, F.M., Hinz, M.O. and Sindano, J.L. *Traditional Authority and Democracy in South Africa*. Windhoek: Centre for Applied Social Sciences, University of Namibia, 1998.

Daniel, J. *et al*, eds. *State of the Nation: South Africa*. Pretoria: HSRC, 2004.

De Ville, J. and Steytler, N. eds. *Voting in 1999: Choosing an Electoral System*. Durban: Butterworths, 1996.

De Villiers, B. ed. *State of the Nation 1997/98*. Pretoria: HSRC, 1998.

Devenish, G.E. *A Commentary on the South African Constitution*. Durban: Butterworths, 1998.

Direct Access to Key People in South Africa, 2000. Johannesburg: Jonathan Ball, 2000.

Du Toit, D. *et al. Service Excellence Governance*. Johannesburg: Heinemann, 2002.

Ebrahim, H. *The Soul of a Nation: Constitution-Making in South Africa.* Cape Town: Oxford University Press Southern Africa, 1998.

Ergas, Z. *Catharsis and the Healing: South Africa in the 1990s.* London: Janus, 1994.

Erkens, R. and Kane-Berman, J. eds. *Political Correctness in South Africa.* Johannesburg: SAIRR, 2000.

Fakir, E. *et al. Provincial Pocketbook: PIMS 2000 Guide to Politics in the Provinces.* Mackenzie, K. ed. Cape Town: IDASA, 2000.

Faure, M. and Lane, J.E. eds. *South Africa: Designing New Political Institutions.* London: Sage Publications, 1996.

Fick, G. *et al.* eds. *One Woman, One Vote.* Johannesburg: Electoral Institute of South Africa, 2002.

Friedman, S. and Atkinson, D. eds. *Small Miracle: South Africa's Negotiated Settlement.* Randburg: Ravan Press, 1994.

Friedman, S. ed. *South African Review 8.* Johannesburg: Ravan Press, 2000.

Gardner, J. *Politicians and Apartheid: Trailing in the People's Wake.* Pretoria: HSRC, 1997.

Geisler, G. *Women and the Remaking of Politics in Southern Africa: Negotiating Autonomy, Incorporation and Representation.* Uppsala: Nordiska Afrikainstituut, 2004.

Gevisser, M. *Portraits of Power: Profiles in a Changing South Africa.* Cape Town: David Philip, 1996.

Gilliomee, H. and Schlemmer, L. eds. *Bold Experiment: South Africa's New Democracy.* Halfway House: Southern Book Publishers, 1994.

Gilliomee, H. and Simkins, C. eds. *Awkward Embrace: One-Party Domination and Democracy.* Cape Town: Tafelberg Publishers, 1999.

Good, K. *Realising Democracy and Legitimacy in Southern Africa.* Pretoria: Africa Institute of South Africa (AISA), 2004.

Graham, P. and Coetzee, A. eds. *In the Balance. Debating the State of Democracy in South Africa.* Cape Town: IDASA, 2002.

Hadland, A. and Rantao, J. *The Life and Times of Thabo Mbeki.* Rivonia: Zebra Press, 1999.

Hain, P. *Sing the Beloved Country: The Struggle for the New South Africa.* London: Pluto Press, 1996.

Heyns, S. *Down Government Avenue: PIMS Guide to Politics in Practice.* Cape Town: IDASA, 1999.

Heyns, S. *Parliamentary Pocketbook.* Cape Town: IDASA, 1996.

Houston, G. ed. *Public Participation in Democratic Governance in South Africa.* Pretoria: HSRC, 2001.

Human Resource Development in the Reconstruction and Development Programme. Randburg: Ravan Press, 1995.

Hyden, G. and Venter, D. eds. *Constitution-Making and Democratisation in Africa.* Pretoria: AISA, 2001. African Century Publications Series 6.

Ismail, N. *et al. Local Government Management.* Johannesburg: International Thomson Publications, c. 1997.

James, D. *Songs of the African Migrants: Performance and Identity in South Africa.* Johannesburg: Witwatersrand University Press, 1999.

James, W. and Levy, M. *Pulse: Passages in Democracy-Building: Assessing South Africa's Transition.* Cape Town: IDASA, 1998.

Johnson, R.W. and Schlemmer, L. eds. *Launching Democracy in South Africa: The First Open Election, April 1994.* New Haven: Yale University Press, 1996.

Johnson, R. W. and Welsh, D. eds. *Ironic Victory: Liberalism in Post-Liberation South Africa.* Cape Town: Oxford University Press, 1998.

Klug, H. *Constituting Democracy: Law, Globalism and South Africa's Political Reconstruction.* Cambridge: University Press, 2000.

Levy, N. and Tapscott, C. *Intergovernmental Relations in South Africa: The Challenges of Co-operative Government.* Cape Town: IDASA and the University of the Western Cape, 2001.

Lodge, T. *Consolidating Democracy: South Africa's Second Popular Election.* Johannesburg: Witwatersrand University Press for the Electoral Institute of South Africa, 1999.

Lodge, T., Kadima, D. and Poltie, D. eds. *Compendium of Elections in Southern Africa.* Johannesburg: Electoral Institute of Southern Africa, 2002.

Lodge, T. *Politics in South Africa: From Mandela to Mbeki.* 2nd ed. Cape Town: David Philip, 2002.

Lodge, T. *South African Politics Since 1994.* Cape Town: David Philip, 1999.

Maharaj, G. ed. *Between Unity and Diversity: Essays on Nation-Building in Post-Apartheid South Africa.* Cape Town: IDASA and David Philip,1999.

Mail and Guardian A – Z of South African Politics 1999: The Essential Handbook. Compilers: Van Niekerk, P. and Ludman, B. London: Penguin, 1999.

Maltes, R. *Election Book: Judgement and Choice in South Africa's 1994 Election.* Cape Town: IDASA, 1995.

Manganyi, C. ed. *On Becoming a Democracy: Transition and Transformation in South African Society.* Pretoria: Unisa Press, 2004.

374

Mayekiso, M. *Township Politics: Civic Struggles for a New South Africa*. New York: Monthly Review Press, 1996.

Meredith, M. *South Africa's New Era: The 1994 Election*. London: Mandarin, 1994.

Mhone, G. and O. Edigheji, O. eds. *A Look at the Wide-Ranging Effects of Globalisation on South Africa. Governance in the New South Africa: The Challenges of Globalisation*. Cape Town: University of Cape Town Press, 2003.

Milazi, D., *et al*. eds. *Democracy, Human Rights and Regional Co-operation in Southern Africa*. Pretoria: AISA, 2002. African Century Publications Series 9.

Mills, G. *Poverty to Prosperity: Globalisation, Good Governance and African Recovery*. Cape Town: Tafelberg, 2004.

Murray, M.J. *Revolution Deferred: The Painful Birth of Post-Apartheid South Africa*. London: Verso, 1994.

Muthien, Y. ed. *Democracy South Africa: Evaluating the 1999 Election*. Pretoria: HSRC, 1999.

Ndlela, L. ed. *Practical Guide to Local Government in South Africa*. Pretoria: IDASA, 2001.

Nyatsumba, K.M. *All Sides of the Story: A Grandstand View of South Africa's Political Transition*. Johannesburg: Jonathan Ball, 1997.

Policy-Making in a New Democracy: South Africa's Challenges for the 21st Century. Johannesburg: Centre for Development and Enterprise, 1999.

Rautenbach, I.M. and Malherbe, E.F.J. *What Does the Constitution Say?* Pretoria: Van Schaik Academic, 1998.

Reddy, P. S. *et al. Local Government Financing and Development in Southern Africa*. Cape Town: Oxford University Press, 2003.

Reynolds, A. ed. *Elections '94 South Africa: The Campaigns, Results and Future Prospects*. Cape Town: David Philip, 1994.

Rule, S. *Democracy South Africa: Public Opinion on National Priority Issues, March 2000*. Pretoria: HSRC, 2000.

Sanders, M. *Complicities: The Intellectual and Apartheid*. Pietermaritzburg: University of Natal Press, 2002.

Seepe, S. *Speaking Truth to Power: Reflections on Post-1994 South Africa*. Pretoria: Vista University and Skotaville Publishers, 2004.

Sicre, F. and World Economic Forum. *South Africa at 10: Perspectives by Political, Business and Civil Leaders*. Cape Town: Human & Rousseau, 2004.

South Africa Survey, 2000/01. Johannesburg: SAIRR, 2001.

Sparks, A. *Beyond the Miracle: Inside the New South Africa*. Johannesburg: Jonathan Ball, 2003.

Sparks, A. *Tomorrow is Another Country: The Inside Story of South Africa's Negotiated Revolution*. Cape Town: Struik, 1995.

Steytler, N. *et al*, eds. *Free and Fair Elections*. Cape Town: Juta, 1994.

Strand, P. *et al. HIV/AIDS and Democratic Governance in South Africa: Illustrating the Impact on Electoral Processes*. Pretoria: IDASA, 2005.

Sunstein, C.R. *Designing Democracy: What Constitutions Do*. New York: Oxford University Press, 2001.

Sunter, C. *New Century: Quest for the High Road*. Cape Town: Human & Rousseau, 1992.

The Constitution of the Republic of South Africa, 1996. Cape Town: Constitutional Assembly, 1997.

Theron, F. *et al*, eds. *Good Governance for People*. Stellenbosch: School of Public Management, University of Stellenbosch, 2000.

Tutu, D. *Rainbow People of God: South Africa's Victory over Apartheid*. London: Bantam Books, 1995.

Van Niekerk, D., Van der Walt, G. and Jonker, A. *Governance, Politics and Policy in South Africa*. Cape Town: Oxford University Press for Southern Africa, 2001.

Waldmeir, P. *Anatomy of a Miracle: The End of Apartheid and the Birth of a New South Africa*. England: Penguin Books, 1998.

Woods, D. *Rainbow Nation Revisited: South Africa's Decade of Democracy*. London: André Deutsch, 2000.

Wood, E. J. *Forging Democracy From Below: Insurgent Traditions in South Africa and El Salvador*. Cambridge University Press, 2000.

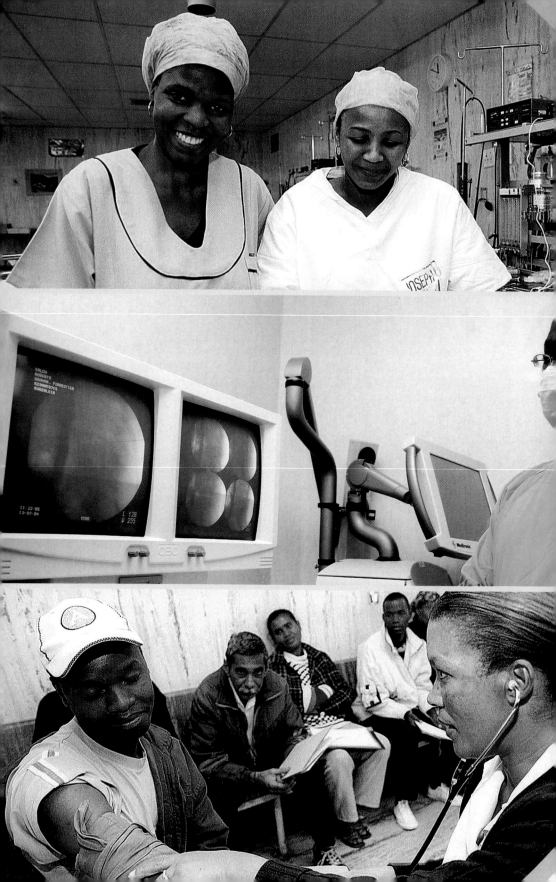

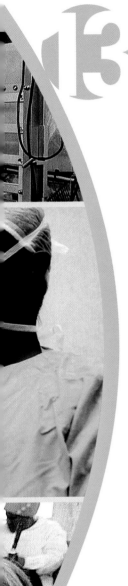

Health

The Department of Health promotes the health of all South Africans through a caring and effective national health system (NHS) based on the primary healthcare (PHC) approach.

Statutory bodies

Statutory bodies for the health-service professions include the Health Professions Council of South Africa (HPCSA), the South African Dental Technicians' Council, the South African Nursing Council (SANC), the South African Pharmacy Council and the Allied Health Professions Council of South Africa (AHPCSA).

Regulations in the private health sector are effected through the Council for Medical Schemes.

The Medicines Control Council is charged with ensuring the safety, quality and effectiveness of medicines.

Health authorities

National
The Department of Health is responsible for:
- formulating health policy, legislation, norms and standards for healthcare
- ensuring appropriate use of health resources
- co-ordinating information systems and monitoring national health goals
- regulating the public and private healthcare sectors
- ensuring access to cost-effective and appropriate health commodities
- liaising with health departments in other international agencies and countries

Provincial
The provincial health departments are responsible for:
- providing and/or rendering health services
- formulating and implementing provincial health policy, standards and legislation
- planning and managing a provincial health-information system
- researching health services to ensure efficiency and quality
- controlling quality of health services and facilities
- screening applications for licensing and inspecting private health facilities

378

- co-ordinating the funding and financial management of district health authorities
- effective consulting on health matters at community level
- ensuring that delegated functions are performed.

Primary healthcare

The policy on universal access to PHC, introduced in 1994, forms the basis of healthcare delivery programmes and has had a major impact on the South African population.

Fifty-three health districts were established in line with the new metropolitan and district municipal boundaries. As a result of the expansion of facilities, the wider range of services on offer, and the free PHC policy, the number of PHC visits per person increased from an estimated 1,8 per year in 1992 to an estimated 2,3 per year in 2001, and in some provinces to 3,5 visits in 2003.

The services provided by PHC workers include immunisation, communicable and endemic disease prevention, maternity care, screening of children, Integrated Management of Childhood Illnesses (IMCI) and child healthcare, health promotion, youth health services, counselling services, taking care of chronic diseases and diseases of older persons, rehabilitation, accident and emergency services, family planning, and oral health services.

Patients visiting PHC clinics are treated mainly by PHC-trained nurses, or, at some clinics, by doctors. Patients with complications that cannot be treated at PHC level are referred to hospitals for higher levels of care.

Beneficiaries of medical aid schemes are excluded from free services.

The complementary medicine industry in South Africa is reportedly growing at a rate of 15% a year. A study published in 1997 showed that due to South Africa's remarkable biodiversity and cultural diversity, about 3 000 species of plants are used as medicines, with some 350 species most commonly used and traded as medicinal plants.

The National Drug Policy is, to a large extent, based on the essential drugs concept, and is aimed at ensuring the availability of essential drugs of good quality, safety and efficacy to all South Africans.

Community health

Government formalised the country's community health worker sector by launching the Community Health Worker (CHW) Programme in February 2004. It is estimated that there are 40 000 such workers in the country.

This category of health workers is an important element of the Presidential initiatives aimed at addressing health and fighting poverty. The massive expansion of the CHW Programme is a vital part of the Socia Cluster's contribution to the Expanded Public Works Programme. The programme will result in the integration of health and social programmes.

By May 2005, the qualifications framework for CHWs had been completed.

An integration programme at National Qualifications Framework (NQF) level 3 aimed at the community care giver was launched in June 2005.

Learning material for a CHW qualification at level 4 is expected to be in place by the end of January 2006. The first group was expected to be trained by June 2006.

Health budget

The budget for 2005/06 was R9,825 billion, representing an increase of 11,4% compared with 2004/05. This allocation is projected to rise to R10,658 billion in 2006/07 and to R11,184 billion in 2007/08.

Health policy

The NHS aims to improve public health through the prevention of diseases and the promotion of a healthy lifestyle. It also strives to consistently improve the healthcare delivery system by focusing on access, equity, efficiency, quality and sustainability.

The strategic priorities for the NHS for 2004 to 2009 are to:

- improve the governance and management of the NHS
- promote a healthy lifestyle
- contribute towards human dignity by improving the quality of care
- improve the management of communicable and non-communicable diseases
- strengthen PHC, emergency medical services and hospital service-delivery systems
- strengthen support services
- plan, develop and manage human resources (HR)
- plan, budget, monitor and evaluate
- draft and implement health legislation
- strengthen international relations.

Telemedicine

The South African Government has identified telemedicine as a strategic tool for facilitating the delivery of equitable healthcare and educational services, irrespective of distance and the availability of specialised expertise, particularly in rural areas.

In 1998, the Department of Health adopted the National Telemedicine Project Strategy.

In September 1999, the national Telemedicine Research Centre was established as a joint project of the Department of Health and the Medical Research Council (MRC).

The objectives of the centre are to:

- evaluate the operations and systems of national telemedicine projects to ensure improved delivery of healthcare services
- use a telemedicine clinical research testbed to test new telemedicine technologies for their clinical abilities and cost-effectiveness
- provide tools for implementing telemedicine, such as training, teaching material and local capacity professional development
- provide research into relevant protocols, standards and medico-legal aspects of telemedicine.

There are a number of telemedicine sites in South Africa.

Legislation

The National Health Act, 2003 (Act 61 of 2003), provides a framework for a single health system for South Africa. It highlights the rights and responsibilities of health-providers and -users and ensures broader community participation in healthcare delivery from a health facility up to national level.

The Act provides for the right to emergency medical treatment, to have full knowledge of one's condition, to exercise one's informed consent, to participate in decisions regarding one's health, to be informed when one is participating in research, to confidentiality and access to health records, to complain about service, and the rights of health workers to be treated with respect.

It establishes provincial health services and outlines the general functions of provincial health departments.

The Traditional Health Practitioner's Act, 2004 (Act 35 of 2004), was promulgated early in 2005. A council for traditional health practitioners was expected to be established during 2005.

The Nursing Bill provides for the introduction of community service for nurses. This should contribute significantly to efforts to ensure equitable distribution of nurses to meet the health needs of communities.

The Bill seeks to ensure that nursing education programmes are registered with the NQF. This means that, unlike in the past, nurses can gain recognisable credit and retain them for future studies. This will do away with the old-fashioned and time-consuming processes of repeating programmes by nurses who wish to further their studies.

In May 2005, in line with the National Health Act, 2003 (Act 61 of 2003), the Department of Health launched the National Health Council, which comprises the Minister of Health, members of executive councils for health and representatives of local government.

The council aims to unite the various elements of the national health system in a common goal to improve universal access to quality health services.

The Mental Healthcare Act, 2002 (Act 17 of 2002), ushered in a process to develop and redesign mental health services in line with the rights of mental healthcare users as guaranteed by the Constitution.

This legislation grants basic rights to people with mental illnesses, and prohibits various forms of exploitation, abuse and unfair discrimination.

The Act provides for:

- empowerment of the users themselves so that they can engage service-providers and society
- allocation of adequate resources
- commitment and leadership for the cause of mental health at all levels of society.

To achieve this, a series of innovative processes and procedures regarding the care, treatment and rehabilitation of mental health users, as well as clear guidelines on good practice in relation to the role of mental healthcare practitioners, will be introduced. This includes the establishment of provincial review boards to conduct systematic reviews of practices for quality assurance.

Although the Act reserves the right to involuntary hospitalisation, it also contains accompanying conditions for strict admission and reviewing processes and procedures before any decision on psychiatric referrals may be made.

National School Health Policy

The national school health policy and guidelines aim to ensure that all children, irrespective of race, colour and location, have equal access to school-health services.

Supplementary healthcare practitioners, May 2005	
Basic ambulance assistants	24 784
Ambulance emergency assistants	4 857
Environmental health officers	2 662
Medical technologists	4 833
Occupational therapists	2 759
Optometrists	2 458
Physiotherapists	4 739
Psychologists	5 875
Radiographers	5 196

Source: Health Professions Council of South Africa

The policy is in line with the United Nations Convention on the Rights of the Child, which affirms the State's obligation to ensure that all segments of society, in particular parents and children, are informed and have access to knowledge of child health and nutrition, hygiene, environmental sanitation and the prevention of accidents.

Department of Health officials will visit all provinces, especially those with a school health programme, to embark on a major training campaign of PHC nurses.

The nurses will be trained to:

- provide children with health education
- impart life skills
- screen children, especially those in Grade R and Grade 1, for specific health problems, and at puberty stage as children undergo physiological changes
- detect disabilities at an early age
- identify missed opportunities for immunisation and other interventions.

The policy was expected to be intensified in 2005.

Social Health Insurance (SHI)

SHI is expected to facilitate access to contributory health cover for families of all employed people. SHI will embrace three major principles:

- risk-related cross subsidies
- income-related cross subsidies
- mandatory cover.

Important groundwork for SHI was done in 2005.

Medicine administration

The Department of Health established the Directorate: Pharmaco-Economic to improve intelligence on medicine pricing. Components dealing with the licensing of pharmacies are being strengthened.

Important progress has been made, in association with the pharmaceutical industry, in making antiretroviral (ARV) medicines more affordable and accessible.

A survey found that the Essential Drug Programme was widely implemented, with 86% of essential drugs found in facilities, 90% of medicines prescribed being from the Essential Drug List, and 97% of facilities having copies of the standard treatment guidelines, compared with 59% in previous surveys

Health team

Health personnel are a crucial component in realising the Department of Health's vision. Major challenges still exist in attracting health personnel to the rural areas.

The department provides rural and scarce skills allowances to attract and retain health professionals in the public health sector in general and rural areas in particular. There are already success stories of young health professionals who settle in rural areas after completing their community service.

The department is interacting with countries like Britain to manage the migration of health workers. An agreement was signed with the Government of Iran to recruit doctors for areas experiencing a shortage of health professionals.

To further advance government's campaign to provide quality healthcare, especially in rural areas, a new cadre of health workers, namely mid-level workers, is being developed. These medical and pharmacist assistants will assist in relieving pressure on doctors and pharmacists and contribute towards improving healthcare delivery.

Draft Framework for Human Resources

The Department of Health presented the draft Framework for the HR for Health Plan in August 2005.

The National Health Act, 2003 requires that the National Health Council develops policy and guidelines for the development, distribution and effective utilisation of HR within the NHS.

The framework, which was approved by Cabinet, is the outcome of prolonged interaction with various role-players in the health sector.

The HR plan for health should provide an overall framework that brings together various interventions to deal with the challenges around HR. These interventions include:

- bilateral and multilateral efforts to manage international migration of health workers

- integrating HR planning in the building and revitalisation of health facilities
- improving overall working conditions for health workers
- providing rural and scarce skills allowances.

The plan should also provide a framework within which all stakeholders can contribute to addressing these challenges either individually or in partnership with government.

Physicians

By August 2005, 32 617 doctors were registered with the HPCSA. These included doctors working for the State, doctors in private practice and specialists. The majority of doctors practise in the private sector. In selected communities, medical students render health services at clinics under the supervision of medical practitioners.

In terms of the Continuing Professional Development (CPD) system, all doctors, irrespective of earlier qualifications, must obtain a specified number of points to retain their registration. The system requires that doctors attend workshops, conferences, refresher courses, seminars, departmental meetings and journal clubs. Non-compliance with the requirements of the system could result in the doctor being deregistered.

Applications of foreign health professionals are subject to assessment by the Examinations Committee of the Medical and Dental Professions Board. Those admitted have to write an examination, after which they can be registered in the particular category for which they applied and were assessed.

Newly qualified interns are required to do remunerated compulsory community service at state hospitals. Only after completion of this service are they allowed to register with the HPCSA, and only then are they entitled to practise privately.

Community service for a range of professional groups, such as physiotherapists, occupational therapists and psychologists, was initiated in 2003. This has helped to provide health services to areas that have been unable to offer such services before. There are about 1 072 doctors, 344 pharmacists, 336 environmental health officers, 292 physiotherapists and 214 radiographers and other categories of health professionals performing community service each year.

To regulate the recruitment of South African health professionals by other countries, the department assisted in the development of a code of ethical recruitment for members of the Commonwealth. A total of 1 658 foreign health professionals sought employment with the department during 2003/04. In addition, the department processed 47 intern and community-service applications from foreign health professionals; 201 work permits; 96 applications for permanent residence; and 594 applications for letters of endorsement for examination, registration and deployment purposes. The department revised its foreign recruitment and employment policy and developed a database on foreign employees.

The first national graduation ceremony of 17 Cuban-trained South African medical doctors took place at the Nelson Mandela School of Medicine in Durban in July 2005. Training in Cuba was part of a government-to-government agreement between South Africa and Cuba, signed in 1995 to address the shortage of health professionals in South Africa.

Medical assistants

In March 2004, the Minister of Health launched a plan to introduce medical assistants. The medical/physician assistant will be part of a team in different units in a district hospital, that is, the emergency unit, maternity and outpatient departments, or medical and surgical units.

In operating theatres, the medical/physician assistant will assist the doctor in basic procedures like incisions and drainage.

The regulation of medical assistants will rest with the HPCSA.

Registered medical interns, practitioners and dentists, 2002 – 2005		
	2002	31 Aug 2005
Dentists	4 560	4 773
Medical interns	2 306	2 535
Medical practitioners	30 271	32 617

Source: Health Professions Council of South Africa

The education and training of medical assistants will take place close to the location where the medical assistant will work. Most learning will take place at district hospitals. A clear link will be maintained with universities through internal training, telemedicine and block learning. The training period will be three years, followed by an internship at the district hospital.

There will be one training site per province with 12 students per site per year in the initial stage. More training sites will be developed within the next five years.

By April 2005, progress had been made in defining the scope of practice and developing the curriculum for medical assistants.

Oral health professionals

By the end of August 2005, 119 dental and oral specialists, 957 oral hygienists and 437 dental therapists were registered with the HPCSA. There were 4 773 dentists at the end of August 2005.

Dentists are subject to the CPD and community-service systems.

Oral health workers render services in the private as well as public sectors.

Pharmacists

Since 20 November 2000, all pharmacists have been obliged to perform one year of remunerated pharmaceutical community service in a public-health facility. Those who have not completed this year of service are not allowed to practise independently as pharmacists.

A section of the Pharmacy Amendment Act, 2000 (Act 1 of 2000), which allows non-pharmacists to own pharmacies, came into effect during May 2003. It aims to improve access to medicine, make them more affordable, improve marketing and dispensing practices, and promote consumer interests.

In May 2005, the South African Pharmacy Council had 11 167 registered pharmacists. About 8 310 and 2 277 of these were rendering their services in the private and public sectors, respectively. Some 494 pharmacists engaged in community service in 2005. Some 501 pharmacist interns registered for 2005 internship.

By May 2005, there were 3 844 pharmacies registered with the council. Of these, 65,56% were community pharmacies, 15,4% public institutional and the remainder wholesale, consultant, manufacturing and private institutional pharmacies.

As of July 2005, every institutional pharmacy is required to have a responsible pharmacist. The public will thus receive exactly the same standard of pharmaceutical service as that experienced in the private sector.

Nurses

The SANC sets minimum standards for the education and training of nurses in South Africa. It accredits schools that meet the required standards and only grants professional registration to nurses who undergo nursing education and training at an accredited nursing school.

The key role of the nursing council is to protect and promote public interest, ensuring delivery of quality healthcare. It does so by prescribing minimum requirements for the education and training of nurses and midwives, approves training schools, and registers or enrols those who qualify in one or more of the basic or postbasic categories.

At the end of 2004, there were 184 459 registered and enrolled nurses and enrolled nursing auxiliaries on the registers and rolls of the council. This represented a growth of 3,8% compared with 2003. The nursing profession represents more than 50% of the total professional HR of health services.

Similarly, 27 157 persons were registered as student and pupil nurses or pupil nursing auxiliaries on the registers and rolls of the council at the end of 2004. This represents a growth of 14% compared with 2003.

Allied health professions

In 2005, the following practitioners were registered with the AHPCSA:

- Ayurveda 122
- Chinese medicine and acupuncture 656
- chiropractors 506
- homoeopaths 726
- naturopaths 158
- osteopaths 62
- phytotherapists 28
- therapeutic aromatherapists 1 123
- therapeutic massage therapists 346
- therapeutic reflexologists 1 935.

National Health Laboratory Service (NHLS)

The NHLS is a single national public entity that consists of the former South African Institute for Medical Research (SAIMR), National Institute for Virology (NIV), National Centre for Occupational Health (NCOH), university pathology departments and public-sector laboratories. It consists of about 250 laboratories.

Their activities comprise diagnostic laboratory services, research, teaching and training, and producing serums for anti-snake venom and reagents.

Registered and enrolled nurses per province, 2004

	Registered nurses	Enrolled nurses	Nursing auxiliaries	Students in training
Eastern Cape	12 025	3 073	5 155	2 908
Free State	7 199	1 302	3 070	966
Gauteng	26 864	8 391	14 749	9 045
KwaZulu-Natal	18 995	10 929	9 039	8 524
Limpopo	7 284	2 913	4 170	1 947
Mpumalanga	4 674	1 768	1 803	568
North West	6 382	2 097	3 884	1 189
Northern Cape	1 919	531	928	210
Western Cape	13 148	4 262	7 905	1 800
Total	98 490	35 266	50 703	27 157

Source: South African Nursing Council (www.sanc.co.za)

All laboratories provide laboratory diagnostic services to the national and provincial departments of health, provincial hospitals, local authorities and medical practitioners.

The NIV and a section of the SAIMR have been combined to form the National Institute for Communicable Diseases (NICD), which is also part of the NHLS. The research expertise and sophisticated laboratories at the NICD make it a testing centre and resource for the African continent, in relation to several of the rarer communicable diseases.

The NCOH has been renamed the National Institute for Occupational Health. It investigates occupational diseases and has laboratories for occupational environment analyses.

Biovac Institute

The Biovac Institute, a public-private partnership for expanding local vaccine productions, was formally launched in 2004. The partnership will ensure the capital injection and expertise needed to revive production and will play a vital support role in local vaccine research.

Provincial health departments

Provincial health departments provide and manage comprehensive health services at all levels of care. The basis for these services is a district-based PHC model. The major emphasis in the development of health services in South Africa at provincial level has been the shift from curative hospital-based healthcare to that provided in an integrated community-based manner.

Clinics

A network of clinics run by government forms the backbone of primary and preventive healthcare in South Africa. Between 1994 and 2004, more than 1 300 clinics were built or upgraded.

Undertaken in collaboration with the Department of Health and various other partners, the Clinic Sanitation Programme was launched in 2005. The programme seeks to improve sanitation services among rural clinics across five provinces, namely KwaZulu-Natal, Mpumalanga, North West, Eastern Cape and Limpopo.

Hospitals

There were 386 provincial public hospitals in 2003, according to the Department of Health.

Ongoing programmes are in place to improve the quality of hospital services. The Charter of Patients' Rights has been developed, as well as procedures to follow when dealing with complaints and suggestions. A service package with norms and standards has been developed for district hospitals and is being extended to regional hospitals.

Steps are being taken to improve the quality of hospital services, with an increasing number of hospitals entering accreditation programmes. New quality-inspection authorities are to be established in terms of the National Health Act, 2003.

All maternal deaths are closely investigated as part of the maternal death surveillance and enquiry process.

Renewal of hospital stock focused initially on renovation and maintenance, but has progressed to major rebuilding under the Hospital Revitalisation Programme. The Hospital Revitalisation Grant increased by 12,7% from R912 million in 2004/05 to R1,027 billion in 2005/06.

In 2004/05, 26 hospitals participated in the Hospital Revitalisation Programme, which is meant to refurbish the infrastructure, strengthen management and improve quality of care.

As part of the programme, the department completed four new hospitals in 2004/05. These were:
- Piet Retief Hospital in Mpumalanga
- Swartruggens Hospital in North West
- Mannie Dipico Hospital in Colesberg in the Northern Cape
- Abraham Esau Hospital in Calvinia in the Northern Cape.

Registered and enrolled nurses, 2003 – 2004		
	2003	2004
Registered nurses	96 715	98 490
Enrolled nurses	33 575	35 266
Nursing auxiliaries	47 431	50 703
Students in training	23 661	27 157
Source: South African Nursing Council		

During 2005/06, government was expected to enrol 16 extra hospitals in the revitalisation programme and to complete the revitalisation of four hospitals, namely:

- Vredenburg and George hospitals in the Western Cape
- Lebowakgomo and Jane Furse hospitals in Limpopo.

The Hospital Association of South Africa represents the interests of more than 70% of private hospitals in South Africa.

Emergency medical services

Provincial departments of health are responsible for emergency medical services, which include ambulance services. Emergency-care practitioners receive nationally standardised training through provincial colleges of emergency care.

Some universities of technology also offer diploma and degree programmes in emergency care. Personnel can receive training to the level of advanced life support.

These services also include aeromedical and medical-rescue services.

Personnel working in this field are required to register with the HPCSA's Professional Board for Emergency Care.

The Department of Health plays a co-ordinating role in the operation, formulation of policy and guidelines, and development of government emergency medical services.

Private ambulance services also provide services to the community, mainly on a private basis. Some also provide aeromedical services to the private sector.

The South African Military and Health Service of the South African National Defence Force plays a vital supporting role in emergencies and disasters. (See chapter 17: *Safety, security and defence*.)

The role of local government

Local government is responsible for rendering the following:

- preventive and promotive healthcare, with some municipalities rendering curative care
- environmental health services, including the supply of safe and adequate drinking water, sewage disposal and refuse removal
- regulation of air pollution, municipal airports, fire-fighting services, licensing and abattoirs.

Many local authorities provide additional PHC services. In some instances, these are funded by provincial health authorities, but in major metropolitan areas the councils carry some of the costs.

The National Health Act, 2003 provides that formal service agreements between provinces and councils will be the basis for the future development of PHC.

Non-profit health sector

Non-governmental organisations (NGOs) at various levels play an increasingly important role in health, many of them co-operating with government to implement priority programmes. They make an essential contribution in relation to HIV, AIDS and tuberculosis (TB), and also participate significantly in the fields of mental health, cancer, disability and the development of PHC systems.

Two particularly high-profile and innovative non-profit organisations are Soul City (*www.soulcity.org.za*) and loveLife (*www.lovelife.org.za*). Both focus on health promotion and the use of the mass media to raise awareness about the prevention of illness, and to enable people to manage their health more effectively.

Soul City pioneered one of the most successful multimedia edutainment initiatives and is known for its sound research-based approach. *Soul Buddyz* is a real-life television drama specifically developed to empower eight to 12-year olds and the adults in their lives. It is the most popular television programme in the country for children. In 2005, running in parallel with the *Soul Buddyz* episodes, was the television programme *Buddyz on the Move (BoM)*. *BoM* was the first actuality programme developed specifically for children and shows *Soul Buddyz* club members' involvement in their communities.

loveLife focuses more on teenage sexuality and relationships and the prevention of HIV-infection and related conditions. It reaches adolescents aged between 12 and 17 and takes a straightforward approach to addressing the underlying factors that fuel the spread of HIV, teenage pregnancy, and sexually transmitted infections (STIs), including society's reluctance to address youth sexuality, the impact of peer pressure and sexual coercion, a sense of pessimism, poverty and the obstacles that keep young people away from South Africa's public health clinics.

Apart from mass-media advertising campaigns backed by a helpline, loveLife focuses on providing services for young people. It has a programme to transform existing reproductive-health and communicable-infection services to make them more 'youth-friendly'. It has also developed drop-in centres where young people can get information and support.

The Health Systems Trust conducts research and helps build appropriate delivery systems for PHC. Funded partly by the Department of Health, it has supported the development of the district health system, monitors the quality of care at public-sector clinics, and facilitates the introduction of services to reduce mother-to-child transmission of HIV.

The South African Cancer Association and the Council Against Smoking share government's approach to the prevention of many chronic non-communicable diseases. They partnered government in the development of tobacco-control measures and their implementation.

Established national health NGOs – such as the St John Ambulance and the South African Red Cross – continue to focus on emergency care and first-aid capacity. They have adapted their services to take account of changing needs, particularly the impact of HIV and AIDS.

Several important organisations in relation to HIV and AIDS are run by people living with HIV or AIDS. The biggest of these is the National Association of People Living with AIDS, which has branches in many areas. There are also many unaffiliated support groups that serve local communities.

Human-rights and health-rights issues in relation to HIV and AIDS have given rise to groups such as the AIDS Law Project and the Treatment Action Campaign, which are pursuing a high-profile campaign in support of expanded treatment.

Faith-based organisations (FBOs) are one of the mainstays of hospice and home-based care for those infected and affected by HIV and AIDS. The Salvation Army was perhaps the first to become meaningfully involved, but in recent years organisations of other faiths and denominations have become increasingly significant sources of care. Many FBOs are also involved in HIV-prevention programmes.

Traditional 'service' organisations like the Lions and Rotary have health projects that boost the public health sector. Fields in which they have made a particular mark are mass immunisation – particularly through the Polio-Free Initiative – and reducing the national backlog of cataract surgery.

The involvement of NGOs extends from the national level, through provincial structures, to small local organisations rooted in individual communities. All are vitally important and bring different qualities to the healthcare network.

Costs and medical schemes

The Council for Medical Schemes regulates the private medical aid scheme industry in terms of the Medical Schemes Act, 1998 (Act 131 of 1998). The council is funded mainly through levies on the industry in terms of the Council for Medical Schemes Levies Act, 2000 (Act 58 of 2000). There are more than 160 medical schemes, with a total annual contribution of about R35 billion, servicing about seven million subscribers.

Medical schemes are the single largest financing intermediary, accounting for nearly 7% of all healthcare expenditure. This is followed by provincial health departments at 33% and households (in terms of out-of-pocket payments directly to healthcare providers) at 14% of all healthcare expenditure.

Tariffs for admission to private and provincial hospitals differ. Cost differences also exist between various provincial hospitals, depending on the facilities offered. Provincial-hospital patients pay for examinations and treatment on a sliding scale in accordance with their income and number of dependants. If a family is unable to bear the cost in terms of the standard means test, the patient is classified as a hospital patient. His/her treatment is then partly or entirely financed by the particular provincial government or the health authorities of the administration concerned.

Provincial hospitals offer treatment to patients with medical aid cover, charging a tariff designed to recover the full cost of treatment. This 'private' rate is generally lower than the rate charged by private hospitals.

The Medical Schemes Amendment Act, 2001 (Act 55 of 2001), improves the regulatory capacity of the Registrar for Medical Schemes and regulates reinsurance. The Act:

- provides improved protection for members by addressing the problem area of medical insurance, revisiting the provision on waiting periods and specifically protecting patients against discrimination on grounds of age
- promotes efficient administration and good governance of medical schemes by insisting on the independence of individuals in certain key positions.
- has introduced mechanisms to address problematic practices in the marketing of medical schemes and brokerage of services.

Minimum benefits are also prescribed. In 2004, several chronic conditions were added to the package of prescribed minimum benefits.

Community health

The most common communicable diseases in South Africa are HIV, AIDS, TB, malaria, measles and STIs.

The appropriate and timeous immunisation of children against infectious diseases is one of the most cost-effective and beneficial preventive measures known.

The mission of the South African Expanded Programme on Immunisation is to reduce death and disability from vaccine-preventable diseases by making immunisation accessible to all children.

In South Africa, it is recommended that children under the age of five be immunised against the most common childhood diseases. Immunisation should be administered at birth, six weeks, 10 weeks, 14 weeks, nine months, 18 months and five years of age. Childhood immunisations are given to prevent polio, TB, diphtheria, pertussis, tetanus, haemophilus influenzae type B, hepatitis B and measles.

Polio and measles

There have been no confirmed measles deaths since 2000, as a direct result of the Measles Elimination Strategy. The last confirmed polio case in South Africa occurred in 1989, but it remains vital to maintain high levels of protection.

The Department of Health observed the National Polio Eradication Week from 4 to 10 April 2005 as part of the *Health Month* Campaign that focused specifically on maternal and child health.

The campaign aimed to complement the World Health Organisation (WHO) 2005 *World Health Day* Campaign slogan *Make Every Mother and Child Count.*

This was in line with the millennium development goals agreed on by the international community in 2000 to reduce maternal deaths by three quarters and child mortality by two-thirds by 2015.

Three committees have been formed, as required by the WHO, to monitor the polio-eradication process. These are the National Certification Committee, the Laboratory Containment Committee and the Polio Expert Committee.

South Africa, Lesotho and Swaziland established the Intercountry Certification Committee to ensure that polio-free certification in the region occurred by December 2005.

Integrated Management of Childhood Illnesses

IMCI promotes child health and improves child survival as part of the National Plan of Action for Children. It is being instituted as part of the Department of Health's policy on the NHS for Universal Primary Care.

South Africa's nurses and doctors are well-trained to treat all diseases using the IMCI strategy. Diseases such as pneumonia, malaria, meningitis, diarrhoea and malnutrition are easily managed. In South Africa, the IMCI strategy has been adapted to include assessment and classification of HIV.

More than 7 000 healthcare providers have been trained in this strategy, which requires that every child brought to a clinic should be examined for difficult breathing, diarrhoea, fever and malnourishment.

Malaria

Malaria is endemic in the low altitude areas of Limpopo, Mpumalanga and north-eastern KwaZulu-Natal. About 10% of the population lives in a malaria risk area.

The prevalence of malaria decreased substantially over the past five years from prevalence levels above 80% in some areas to current levels, which are below 10%. This can be attributed to the success of in-door residual spraying using the insecticide Dichloro-Diphenyl-Dichloromethan (DDT) and the partnership with Mozambique and Swaziland.

Malaria cases reported from January to May 2005 totalled 4 539. This represented a 44,5% decrease from the 8 173 cases reported during the same period in 2004. During the same period, 35 deaths were reported compared with 55 in 2004, which represented a 36,4% decrease in malaria-related deaths.

Through the innovative multinational Lubombo Spatial Development Initiative involving Mozambique, South Africa and Swaziland, malaria prevalence in Mozambique has been reduced by 82%, and in KwaZulu-Natal by 96% compared with 2002. A trans-Limpopo initiative is also being explored between South Africa and Zimbabwe.

South Africa is a signatory to the Abuja Declaration, which undertakes to reduce malaria morbidity and mortality by 50% by 2010.

By September 2005, progress was being made in the development of the Health Charter. The charter aims to strengthen collective efforts within the health system to improve access to affordable and quality healthcare.

There is active co-operation with Zimbabwe on cross-border malaria control. Malaria-control experts are being sent to other Southern African Development Community countries to provide technical assistance and strengthen control programmes in the subregion.

To monitor the disease effectively, the MRC, together with the national and provincial departments of health, developed a malaria-information system to obtain information about the disease and operational aspects pertaining to control programmes. Through these public-private partnerships, malaria is effectively being controlled in southern Africa. However, to ensure that the incidence of malaria remains on a downward trend, increased intercountry collaborations are essential.

Malaria-control teams of the provincial departments of health are responsible for measures such as education, patient treatment, residual spraying of all internal surfaces of dwellings situated in high-risk areas, and detection and treatment of all parasite carriers. It was decided to continue with controlled and restricted use of DDTs because of the growing resistance to pyrethroid insecticides.

The MRC's South African Traditional Medicines Research Group is investigating plants used by traditional healers for the treatment of malaria. Two plants that are effective against malaria parasites in vitro have been identified, and the active compounds in one of the plants have been identified and isolated.

Insecticide-treated nets are another intervention that has had an impact, reducing the number of malaria deaths, particularly among children under the age of five years.

Tuberculosis

Improvements in TB care are confronted by increasing numbers of cases, from 109 328 TB cases reported in 1996 to 255 773 TB cases reported in 2003.

Despite improvements in the TB Control Programme – such as an electronic register, decreased waiting time for test results, and high coverage with Directly Observed Treatment Short Course (DOTS) –

both cure and completion rates are suboptimal, at 53,9% (cured) and 67,8% (successful treatment completion rate). A national surveillance study showed resistant strains in 1,7% of new cases and 6,6% of previous cases returning for treatment.

The Department of Health has implemented DOTS, advocated by the International Union Against TB and the WHO. The focus is on curing infectious patients at the first attempt, by ensuring that:

- they are identified by examining their sputum under a microscope for TB bacilli
- they are supported and monitored to ensure that they take their tablets
- the treatment, laboratory results and outcome are documented
- appropriate drugs are provided for the correct period
- TB control receives special emphasis in terms of political priority, finances and good district health management.

Treatment is free of charge at all public clinics and hospitals in South Africa.

The TB Control Programme is being strengthened by:

- appointing TB co-ordinators in each health district
- strenghtening the laboratory system
- strengthening the implementation of DOTS
- mobilising communities to ensure that patients complete their treatment.

HIV and AIDS

Government's Comprehensive Plan for the Management, Care and Treatment of HIV and AIDS is centred around preventing the spread of HIV-infection and improving the health system to enable the Department of Health to provide a series of interventions aimed at improving the lives of those infected and affected by HIV and AIDS.

While retaining a strong focus on HIV prevention and expanding support for positive living in the early stages of HIV-infection, the plan also provides for ARV treatment in the public health sector as part of government's comprehensive strategy.

The plan envisaged that there would be at least one service point in every health district across the country and, within five years, one service point in every local municipality.

These service points will give citizens access to a continuum of care and treatment, integrated with the prevention and awareness campaign which remains the cornerstone of the strategy.

This involves:

- stepping up the prevention campaign so that the estimated 40 million South Africans not infected stay that way
- a sustained education and community mobilisation programme to strengthen partnerships in the fight against the epidemic
- expanding programmes aimed at boosting the immune system and slowing down the effects of HIV-infection, including the option of traditional health treatments for those who use these services
- improved efforts in treating opportunistic infections for those who are infected but have not reached the stage at which they require ARVs
- intensified support for families affected by HIV and AIDS
- introducing ARV treatment for those who need it, as certified by doctors.

The Department of Health's strategy in dealing with HIV and AIDS operates on two levels. The first level involves a comprehensive strategic response to HIV and AIDS as outlined in the HIV, AIDS and STIs

South Africa was one of the 29 countries and organisations that pledged a total of US$3,7 billion to the Global Fund to Fight AIDS, Tuberculosis and Malaria for the two-year period (2006 and 2007) at the Global Fund Replenishment Conference held in London in September 2005.

The Minister of Health, Dr Manto Tshabalala-Msimang, announced at the conference that the South African Government would continue to support the Global Fund by making a contribution of US$6 million (about R36 million) over the next three years.

The replenishment conference was hosted by the United Kingdom Department for International Development and was the last of three meetings to assess Global Fund performance and resource needs

Strategic Plan for South Africa. Prevention strategies continue to form the backbone of the department's response to HIV and AIDS.

The second level relates to the Comprehensive Plan for Management Care and Treatment. By mid-2005, implementation of the plan was progressing well. Voluntary counselling and testing (VCT) sites continue to see more people than before, while through the Khomanani social mobilisation campaign, the department intensified efforts to spread messages around VCT, as well as prevention.

Regarding care and support for HIV-positive people, messages around positive living and healthy lifestyles are also being intensified.

Budget for the plan increased by 45% from R782 million in 2004/05 to R1,135 billion in 2005/06.

By September 2005, reports from provinces indicated that more than 61 900 patients were receiving ARV treatment. Efforts to improve monitoring systems continue to ensure that these patients and their response to such treatment can be tracked.

By September 2005, there were 178 sites spread across all 53 districts and in about 60% of subdis-

Africa's first dedicated hand-surgery complex is to be established at the Chris Hani Baragwanath Hospital in Soweto.

Once complete, the unit will comprise two hand theatres, therapy areas for physiotherapy and occupational therapy, out-patient rooms, X-ray facilities, an administration section, wards for hand-surgery patients and a dispensary.

The Chris Hani Baragwanath Hospital is the largest referral centre for hand surgery in South Africa, conducting about 120 operations a month.

In 1976, the hospital became the first in the world to successfully conduct a hand replantation operation. It has also pioneered hand reconstruction in cases of congenital deformities in children.

Leading mining and engineering companies, including Impala Platinum, Anglo American, Gold Fields, African Rainbow Minerals and Scaw Metals Group, are expected to inject over R5,3 million into the project, while the Gauteng Health Department will provide trained staff, equipment and donations in kind.

tricts. The department was extending the nutritional interventions by providing nutritional and vitamin supplements.

The South African National AIDS Council serves as a forum for strengthening and integrating programmes within government, as well as between government and civil society.

Improved access to voluntary HIV counselling and testing

Ensuring access to confidential and voluntary HIV counselling and testing is one of the essential elements of the plan, as it provides an important entry into other health interventions, e.g. TB and STI treatment. This goal focuses on expanding access to VCT in both the private and public sectors.

By the end of 2004/05, 3 369 healthcare facilities were providing VCT, mainly at the PHC level, a 100% increase from 1 500 in 2002/03. About 5 000 healthcare facilities were expected to provide VCT by 2005/06.

Preventing mother-to-child transmission (PMTCT) of HIV

The PMTCT programme is expanding. The original research sites continue to provide a full package of care, and help to answer critical operational questions such as the impact of infant-feeding options and the significance of drug resistance.

Most provinces are extending this comprehensive package to more facilities.

By 2003/04, 1 652 facilities had implemented the PMTCT programme, a significant increase from 540 in 2002/03. According to the policy, all PHC facilities should offer VCT and PMTCT programmes by March 2006.

Rape survivors

Cabinet's decision in April 2002 to offer ARVs to victims of sexual assault as part of a comprehensive package of support, is being implemented. The post-exposure prophylaxis programme includes counselling on the effectiveness and risks of using ARVs.

All provinces are working according to national protocols. In some provinces, the focus is on multidisciplinary crisis or victim-empowerment centres, while in others, the service is offered through the emergency rooms of general hospitals.

HIV and AIDS vaccine research and development

The South African AIDS Vaccine Initiative (SAAVI) was established in 1999 to develop and test an affordable, effective, and locally relevant HIV and AIDS vaccine for southern Africa. Since its establishment, SAAVI has made good progress, particularly for a biotechnology project of this nature.

SAAVI is a holistic vaccine development initiative that has three South African developed products undergoing the regulatory process preceding the first phase of human trials. SAAVI activities cover the broad spectrum of vaccine-development components, including laboratory research and development, immunology testing in animals, community education, ethical protocol development, actual modelling, data collection and management, laboratory testing and planning for clinical trials.

SAAVI works closely with many international organisations, including the African AIDS Vaccine Programme and the International AIDS Vaccine Initiative. It receives funding from some of these organisations, including the HIV Vaccine Trials Network of the United States' National Institute of Health, and the European Union.

Training

By February 2005, the Department of Health had ensured the training of 7 658 health personnel nationally, in the management, care and treatment of HIV and AIDS.

Home/community-based care

By May 2005, there were 1 700 projects offering home-based care nationally.

Reproductive health

Government has a number of programmes in place to support women and men in making their reproductive choices. Among these are the Family Planning Programme, which provides for counselling; a range of choices of family-planning meth-

ods such as contraceptives, access to legal termination of pregnancy and sterilisation under specific conditions; as well as education on sexuality and healthy lifestyles. These services are provided free of charge at PHC facilities.

The Department of Health has developed a card for women's reproductive health to improve continued care and to promote a healthy lifestyle. The card is retained by the patient and facilitates communication between health services. Pregnancy Education Week is held annually in February to educate women on their reproductive rights and related issues.

The contraception and the youth and adolescent health policy guidelines promote access to health services for vulnerable groups, by improving the capacity of health and other workers to care for women and children.

The guidelines are aimed at providing quality care, preventing and responding to the needs of young people, and promoting a healthy lifestyle among the youth. The promotion of a healthy lifestyle includes programmes or activities on issues such as:
- life skills
- prevention of substance and alcohol abuse
- provision of a smoke-free environment.

Eight critical areas within the youth and adolescent health policy guidelines have been identified, namely:
- sexual and reproductive health
- mental health

National Condom Week from 13 to 17 February 2005 focused on encouraging people to be more responsible in their sexual behaviour. National Condom Week is aimed at spreading the message that most sexually transmitted infections, with the exception of HIV, are curable. Condom usage has increased by 50% in the last five years from a paltry 15%.

The distribution of male condoms increased from 302 million in 2003 to 346 million in 2004. A total of 1,2 million female condoms were distributed through 203 sites nationwide in 2004.

- substance abuse
- violence
- unintentional injuries
- birth defects and inherited disorders
- nutrition
- oral health.

Guidelines for maternity care deal with the prevention of opportunistic infections in HIV-positive women, and the provision of micronutrient supplements to help ensure the well-being of mothers.

Guidelines for the cervical cancer-screening programme aim to reduce the incidence of cervical cancer by detecting and treating the pre-invasive stages of the disease.

The Cancer-Screening Programme aims to screen at least 70% of women in their early 30s within 10 years of initiating the programme. It allows for three free pap-smear tests with a 10-year interval between each test. Pilot sites for the screening of cervical cancer have been set up in Limpopo, Gauteng and the Western Cape. The project will be rolled out to all provinces.

The Choice on Termination of Pregnancy Act, 1996 (Act 93 of 1996), allows abortion on request for all women in the first 12 weeks of pregnancy, and in the first 20 weeks in certain cases. The Act was amended to improve access and alleviate the pressure on existing termination services. The system of designating services will be changed to ensure that more public health facilities offer termination procedures.

In 1998, the infant mortality rate was measured at 45,4 per 1 000 live births. This decreased in 2003 to 42,5 per 1 000 live births. Mortality of children under five years also decreased from 59,4 per 1 000 live births in 1998 to 57,6 per 1 000 in 2003.

The proportion of births attended to by either a nurse or doctor increased from 84% in 1998 to 92% in 2003. This can be attributed to the increased access to health services both in terms of availability of health facilities in various communities, and free health services for pregnant and lactating women, as well as children under the age of six years

Since the implementation of the Act, about 40 000 women safely terminate pregnancies annually.

The Department of Health continues to support training in abortion care and contraception provision.

The Subdirectorate: Women's Health has developed contraception service-delivery guidelines. The subdirectorate is reviewing the national guidelines on the management of survivors of sexual offences, and developing a policy on the management of survivors of sexual offences.

Environmental health

In terms of the National Health Act, 2003, environmental health services are vested with local government. This shifted the responsibility for rendering environmental health services to metropolitan and district councils from 1 July 2004.

Traditional medicine

In August 2003, South Africa launched the National Reference Centre for African Traditional Medicines to research African herbs and evaluate their medicinal value as part of government's campaign to fight HIV, AIDS, TB and other debilitating and chronic diseases and conditions.

The launch of the centre was the result of a research programme initiated by the Department of Health and the MRC. It aims to test the effectiveness, safety and quality of traditional medicines, as well as to protect people from unscrupulous conduct and unproven medical claims within the traditional healing sector.

To protect the intellectual property rights of traditional peoples, the MRC will conduct biomedical research on medicinal plants. Traditional claims will also be channelled through this centre.

Government supports research by universities and science councils into the efficacy of many traditional medicines used for various conditions.

The WHO estimates that up to 80% of Africa's people use traditional medicine. In sub-Saharan Africa, the ratio of traditional health practitioners to the population is about 1:500, while the ratio of medical doctors is 1:40 000.

Traditional health practitioners have an important role to play in the lives of African people and have the potential to serve as a critical component of a comprehensive healthcare strategy.

In South Africa alone, there are an estimated 200 000 traditional health practitioners. They are the first healthcare providers to be consulted in up to 80% of cases, especially in rural areas, and are deeply interwoven into the fabric of cultural and spiritual life.

Research also indicates that in many developing countries, a large proportion of the population relies heavily on traditional health practitioners and medicinal plants to meet PHC needs. Although modern medicine may be available in these countries, traditional medicines remain popular for historical and cultural reasons.

The MRC will conduct tests to evaluate such medicine, develop substances that could be used for chronic conditions, including immune boosters, and provide information on these medicine to the general public.

Tobacco control

An estimated 25 000 South Africans die each year from tobacco-related diseases.

Regulations of the Tobacco Products Control Amendment Act, 1999 (Act 12 of 1999), include:
- a ban on all advertising for tobacco products from 23 April 2001
- all public places must be smoke-free, but employers and restaurateurs can set aside 25% of their space for smokers, which must be separated by a solid partition
- a fine of R10 000 for those who are caught selling or giving cigarettes to children.

In October 2003, the Minister of Health released details of new provisions designed to protect public health by strengthening South Africa's tobacco control laws. The Tobacco Products Control Act, 1993 (Act 83 of 1993), was amended to provide for, among other things:
- the prohibition of advertising and promotion of tobacco products
- the prohibition of the free distribution of tobacco products and the receipt of gifts or cash prizes in contests, lotteries or games

- the prescription of maximum yields of tar, nicotine and other constituents in tobacco products.

The Act is in line with the provisions of the WHO's International Framework Convention on Tobacco Control (FCTC) and makes it more effective by closing loopholes and increasing fines.

By 2006, the levels of nicotine and tar contents of cigarettes will be reduced even further.

Restrictions on the tar level will be reduced from the current 15 milligrams (mg) to 12 mg, while nicotine will decrease from 1,5 mg to 1,2 mg in all cigarettes sold in South Africa.

South Africa is a co-signatory with 74 other countries of the FCTC that commits governments worldwide to take measures to reduce tobacco use.

In 2005, South Africa became one of the few countries to have satisfied the FCTC.

The Department of Health has set up a tobacco hotline ([012] 312 0180) for the general public to lodge smoking-related complaints.

People who want to stop smoking may contact the National Council Against Smoking's Quit Line on (011) 720 3145.

The results of these interventions are encouraging. Research indicates that smoking prevalence among the adult population decreased from 36% in 1996 to 22% in 2003. Smoking among the youth decreased from 23% in 1999 to 18,5% in 2002.

Alcohol and substance abuse

Foetal Alcohol Syndrome (FAS) is one of South Africa's most common birth defects. It is caused by a mother's consumption of alcohol during pregnancy. Rates in South Africa are the highest recorded anywhere in the world. In the Northern Cape, one in 10 children starting school shows signs of FAS, and in the Western Cape, one in 20.

According to a report by the MRC's Alcohol and Drug Abuse Research Group, released in October 2003, alcohol remains the dominant substance abused in South Africa. Across the five sites in the South African Community Epidemiology Network on Drug Use, between 44% (Cape Town) and 69% (Mpumalanga) of patients in specialist substance-abuse treatment centres list alcohol as their primary substance of abuse.

394

The use of cannabis (dagga) and mandrax (methaqualone) alone or in combination (white pipes) continues to be high. The increase in treatment demand for cocaine addiction reported in Cape Town, Durban and Gauteng, has levelled off.

Over time, there has been a dramatic increase in treatment demand for heroin as the primary drug abused in Cape Town and Gauteng, but this has also levelled off. Demand for long-term treatment appears to be increasing. The abuse of over-the-counter and prescription medicines such as slimming tablets, analgesics and benzodiazepines (e.g. diazepam and flunitrazipam) continues to be a problem, but treatment-demand indicators are stable.

Inhalant/solvent use among young people continues to be an issue of concern. Poly-substance abuse remains high, with 34% of patients in specialist treatment centres in Gauteng and 47% in Cape Town reported to be abusing more than one substance. All sites for which age data are available have shown an increase over the past few years in treatment-demand by persons younger than 20 years of age.

Draft regulations on the labelling of alcoholic beverages were published in the *Government Gazette* in February 2005. The regulations define an alcoholic beverage as any drink for human consumption with an ethyl alcohol content of above 1%.

The regulations propose a number of messages that should be printed in black and white, covering at least 12,5% of the container label or promotional material of an alcohol product.

The health message can be in any of the South African official languages, but must be in the same language as that of the container label or promotional material. The regulations prohibit any claims of health benefits that may be derived from consuming alcoholic beverages.

Contravention of these regulations can lead to a fine or imprisonment of up to five years, or both.

Violence against women and children

The Department of Health has implemented a series of concrete measures to eliminate violence against women and children.

To raise awareness of this grave social problem, the *16 Days of Activism on No Violence Against Women and Children* Campaign is held at the end of every year.

The Domestic Violence Act, 1998 (Act 116 of 1998), was enacted in December 1999, and mass campaigns have been held to create community awareness of the Act. The MRC, through the South African Gender-Based Violence and Health Initiative (SAGBVHI) assisted the Department of Health to compile and adopt the sexual assault policy and clinical management guidelines for the management of sexual-assault cases. These were distributed to provinces for implementation.

Training of health-providers in victim empowerment and trauma management is ongoing. A national pilot project on secondary-level services for victims of violence and other psychological crises is ongoing in Mpumalanga, KwaZulu-Natal and the Eastern Cape.

The training done by SAGBVHI members has raised the awareness of healthcare workers, particularly nurses, about the health impact of violence against women.

Violence prevention

The Department of Health is playing an important role in the prevention of violence. PHC professionals are being trained in victim empowerment and trauma support. Healthcare professionals are also receiving advanced training in the management of complicated cases of violence in the secondary-level victim empowerment centres, established by the department in some provinces. Violence-prevention programmes in schools are also running in some provinces.

The Crime, Violence and Injury Lead Programme, co-directed by the MRC and the University of South Africa's Institute for Social and Health Sciences, aims to improve the population's health status, safety and quality of life. This is achieved through public health-orientated research aimed at preventing death, disability and suffering arising from crime, violence and unintentional incidents of injury. The programme's overall goal is to produce research on the extent, causes, consequences and costs of injuries, and on best practices for primary prevention and injury control.

Birth defects

It is estimated that 150 000 children born annually in South Africa are affected by a significant birth defect or genetic disorder.

The Department of Health's four priority conditions are albinism, Down's syndrome, FAS and neural tube defects. Implementation of policy guidelines for the management and prevention of genetic disorders, birth defects and disabilities will reduce morbidity and mortality resulting from these conditions. This will involve the decentralisation of training, the expansion of the sentinel sites for birth-defect monitoring, and collaboration with NGOs in creating awareness.

South Africa, through the Birth Defects Surveillance System, is a member of the International Clearing House for Birth Defects Monitoring Systems. In the long term, this should result in more accurate diagnoses. Links have been made with those sentinel sites reporting on perinatal mortality, as congenital anomalies have been shown to be among the top three causes of perinatal mortality at some sentinel sites.

The Department of Health participates in regular meetings with NGOs to discuss collaborative issues.

Oral health

In 2005, the National Health Council approved the National Oral Health Strategy.

The strategy aims to improve the oral health of the South African population by appropriately preventing, treating, monitoring and evaluating oral diseases.

The Department of Health is also enganged in a process of amending the regulations on fluoridating water supplies to implement water fluoridation to prevent dental decay.

Chronic diseases, disabilities and geriatrics

The Department of Health has identified the fight against chronic diseases such as cancer, hyperten-

sion, diabetes and osteoporosis as a priority area over the next five years.

The five-year plan is premised on the development of meaningful strategies for preventing diseases such as cancer with special emphasis on healthy lifestyles including physical activity. The department has embarked on an outreach promotion programme – Healthy Lifestyles – that advocates good diet, responsible alcohol consumption, regular exercise and avoiding tobacco use.

Healthcare professionals from each province have been trained in the management of asthma, hypertension, diabetes and eye health. This includes training in a health-compliance model to improve patient compliance.

The department aims to reduce avoidable blindness by increasing the cataract-surgery rate.

Government introduced free health services for people with disabilities in July 2003. Beneficiaries include people with permanent, moderate or severe disabilities, as well as those who have been diagnosed with chronic irreversible psychiatric disabilities.

Frail older people and long-term institutionalised state-subsidised patients also qualify for these free services.

People with temporary disabilities or a chronic illness that does not cause a substantial loss of functional ability, and people with disabilities who are employed and/or covered by relevant health insurance, are not entitled to these free services.

Beneficiaries receive all in- and outpatient hospital services free of charge. Specialist medical interventions for the prevention, cure, correction or rehabilitation of a disability are provided, subject to motivation from the treating specialist and approval by a committee appointed by the Minister of Health.

All assistive devices for the prevention of complications and cure or rehabilitation of a disability are provided. These include orthotics and prosthetics, wheelchairs and walking aids, hearing aids, spectacles and intra-ocular lenses. The Department of Health is also responsible for maintaining and replacing these devices.

The Department of Health made a commitment to eradicate the backlog in terms of the provision of assistive devices for people with disabilities. In this regard, 4 770 wheelchairs and 4 674 hearing aids were provided during 2004/05.

The department continues to develop national policy guidelines on the management and control of priority diseases/conditions of older persons to improve their quality of life and access to healthcare services. These include the development of exercise posters and pamphlets, and guidelines that focus specifically on older persons, e.g. national guidelines on falls in older persons, guidelines on active ageing, national guidelines on stroke and TIA (transient ischemic attacks), and national guidelines on osteoporosis. The National Strategy on Elder Abuse, together with the national guidelines on the management of physical abuse of older persons, have been implemented in all provinces. These raise awareness of abuse in all its subtle forms.

Occupational health

The introduction of legislation such as the Occupational Health and Safety Act, 1993 (Act 181 of 1993), and the Mines Health and Safety Act, 1996 (Act 29 of 1996), has done much to focus the attention of employers and employees on the prevention of work-related accidents and diseases. The Compensation for Occupational Injuries and Diseases Act, 1993 (Act 30 of 1993), places the onus on medical practitioners who diagnose conditions that they suspect might be a result of workplace exposure, to report these to the employer and relevant authority.

The Medical Bureau for Occupational Diseases has a statutory function under the Occupational Diseases in Mines and Works Act, 1973 (Act 78 of 1973), to monitor former mineworkers and evaluate present miners for possible compensational occupational lung diseases until they either die or are compensated maximally.

The Compensation Commissioner for Occupational Diseases is responsible for the payment of benefits to miners and ex-miners who have been certified to be suffering from lung-related diseases contracted as a result of working conditions.

Mental health

The promotion of mental health is one of the corner-stones of South Africa's health policy. The Mental Healthcare Act, 2002 provides for the care, treatment, rehabilitation and administration of mentally ill persons. It also sets out the different procedures to be followed in the admission of such persons.

There are 18 state institutions with some 10 000 beds.

Private psychiatric hospitals and clinics cater for patients requiring hospitalisation for less severe psychiatric illnesses. General hospitals have some psychiatric beds. A further 7 000 beds are hired from the private sector for treatment of long-term chronic psychiatric and severely intellectually challenged patients.

In keeping with government policy of promoting care of the severely intellectually challenged within the community, these persons receive care-dependency grants to reimburse their families for personal expenses. This allows persons to remain with their families in the community. These grants are administered by the Department of Social Development. In recent years, the focus of treatment has shifted from medication only, except where necessary, to patient rehabilitation.

A comprehensive psychiatric community service is managed by health authorities countrywide. Where possible, consultations are undertaken by multidisciplinary teams comprising psychiatrists, psychiatric nurse practitioners, psychologists, pharmacists, social workers and occupational therapists.

According to the Mental Healthcare Act, 2002, mental health is a health issue like any other. The purpose is to bring community services closer to mentally ill patients instead of simply placing them in institutions.

The Act focuses on a strong human-rights approach to mental health. It also makes the process of certifying a person more complex, and introduces a 72-hour assessment period before a person can be certified. Previous legislation relied on psychiatrists and doctors to make the decision, but the new Act recognises that there are not enough psychiatrists, especially in rural areas.

According to the Act, a mental-healthcare practitioner may make such a decision. It also introduces a review board, comprising a mental-healthcare practitioner, a legal expert and a community representative to examine the certified patient's case. The patient and the family will be able to appeal to the board, and all certified cases will be reviewed at least once a year.

The Mental Health Information Centre (MHIC) is situated at the Health Sciences Faculty of the University of Stellenbosch and has been in operation since 1995. It forms part of the MRC's Unit on Anxiety and Stress Disorders and aims to promote mental health in South Africa.

The MHIC is also actively involved in research, and conducts academic and clinical research trials for conditions such as obsessive-compulsive, panic, post-traumatic stress and generalised anxiety disorders. Research is also undertaken on mood, psychotic and dementia disorders, as well as other major psychiatric disorders. A key focus area is mental health literacy. The MHIC regularly conducts mental health attitude and stigma surveys among various population and professional groups.

As part of a national campaign to educate and inform the public on mental illness, Mental Health Awareness Month was held in July 2005. Special attention was paid to encouraging healthy practices through education and training programmes, as well as to the development and maintenance of working conditions that support and contribute to the well-being of employees with mental problems.

Quarantinable diseases

The Port Health Service is responsible for the prevention of quarantinable diseases in the country as determined by the International Health Regulations Act, 1974 (Act 28 of 1974). These services are rendered at sanitary airports (Johannesburg, Cape Town and Durban international airports) and approved ports.

An aircraft entering South Africa from an epidemic yellow-fever area must make its first landing at a sanitary airport. Passengers travelling from such areas must be in possession of valid yellow-fever vaccination certificates. Every aircraft or ship on an international voyage must also obtain a pratique from a port health officer upon entering South Africa

Consumer goods

Another function of the Department of Health, in conjunction with municipalities and other authorities, is to prevent, control and reduce possible risks to public health from hazardous substances or harmful products present in foodstuffs, cosmetics, disinfectants and medicines; from the abuse of hazardous substances; or from various forms of pollution.

Food is controlled to safeguard the consumer against any harmful, injurious or adulterated products, or misrepresentation as to their nature, as well as against unhygienic manufacturing practices, premises and equipment.

Integrated Nutrition Programme (INP) and food security

The INP aims to ensure optimum nutrition for all South Africans by preventing and managing malnutrition. A co-ordinated and intersectoral approach, focusing on the following areas, is thus fundamental to the success of the INP and include:

The Department of Health, in partnership with the Nutrition Society of South Africa, the Medical Research Council, the Association for Dietetics in South Africa and the South African Society of Parenteral and Enetral Nutrition, hosted the 18th International Congress of Nutrition (ICN) for the first time on African soil in Durban in September 2005.

The ICN is held every four years under the auspices of the International Union of Nutritional Sciences. The congress, under the theme *Nutrition Safari for Innovative Solutions*, aimed to positively position the role of nutrition in health, human development and well-being, equity, and quality of life in Africa and other developing countries.

It also provided a platform for experts and role-players from all over the world to explore and exchange knowledge about nutrition, generate new insights and define innovative solutions for global nutrition problems.

- disease-specific nutrition support, treatment and counselling
- growth monitoring and promotion
- nutrition promotion
- micronutrient malnutrition control
- food-service management
- promotion, protection and support of breast-feeding
- contributions to household-food security.

The INP targets nutritionally vulnerable/at-risk communities, groups and individuals for nutrition interventions, and provides appropriate nutrition education to all.

The Food Fortification Programme was launched in April 2003. With effect from 7 October 2003, millers are compelled by law to fortify their white and brown-bread flour and maize meal with specific micronutrients.

The regulations on food fortification stipulate mandatory fortification of all maize meal and wheat flour with six vitamins and two minerals, including Vitamin A, thiamine, riboflavin, niacin, folic acid, iron and zinc.

Environmental health practitioners at local government level are responsible for compliance monitoring and law enforcement. Fines of up to R125 000 can be imposed upon millers who fail to comply.

The National School Nutrition Programme is based on community participation and mobilises communities to develop food gardens. The primary goal of the programme is school feeding, while also utilising resources invested by government to create sustainable livelihoods for local communities.

The programme has been transferred from the Department of Health to the Department of Education. (See chapter 8: *Education*.)

It also focuses on creating employment opportunities for women. The focus is on the 21 Presidential nodes where women are encouraged to form small businesses to administer the school-feeding programme for schools in the area.

Acknowledgements

BuaNews

Department of Health

Estimates of National Expenditure 2005, published by National Treasury

Health Professions Council of South Africa

Medical Research Council

National Health Laboratory Service

South African Nursing Council

South African Pharmacy Council

www.gov.za

www.hasa.co.za

www.lovelife.org.za

www.nhls.ac.za

www.soulcity.org.za

Suggested reading

AIDS and Governance in Southern Africa: Emerging Theories and Perspectives, compiled by K. Chirambo and M. Caesar. Pretoria: Institute for Democracy in South Africa (IDASA), 2003. Report on the IDASA/United Nations Development Programme Regional Governance and AIDS Forum, 2 – 4 April 2004.

Arden, N. *African Spirits Speak: A White Woman's Journey into the Healing Tradition of the Sangoma*. Rochester, Vermont: Destiny Books, 1999.

Baldwin-Ragaven, L., De Gruchy, J. and London, L. *An Ambulance of the Wrong Colour: Health Professionals, Human Rights and Ethics in South Africa*. Cape Town: University of Cape Town Press, 1999.

Barnett, T. and Whiteside, A. *AIDS in the 21st Century. Disease and Globalisation*. Hampshire: Palgrave Macmillan, 2002.

Bayer, R. and Oppenheimer, G.M. *AIDS Doctors: Voices from the Epidemic*. Cape Town: Oxford University Press, 2002.

Booysens, S.W. ed. *Introduction to Health Services Management*. Kenwyn: Juta, 1996.

Bradshaw, D., Groenewald, P., Laubscher, R., Nannan, N., Nojilana, B., Norman, R., Pieterse, D. and Schneider, M. *Initial Burden of Disease Estimates for South Africa, 2000*. Medical Research Council Technical Report. Cape Town, 2003.

Campbell, C. *Letting Them Die – Why HIV/AIDS Intervention Programmes Fail*. London: International African Institute and Cape Town: Double Storey Books, 2003.

Campbell, S. *Called to Heal: Traditional Healing Meets Modern Medicine in Southern Africa*. Halfway House: Zebra Press, 1998.

Couvadia, H.M. and Benatar, S. eds. *Tuberculosis With Special Reference to Southern Africa*. Cape Town: Oxford University Press, 1992.

Crewe, M. *AIDS in South Africa: The Myth and the Reality*. London: Penguin, 1992.

De Haan, M. *Health of Southern Africa*. 6th ed. Cape Town: Juta, 1988.

De Miranda, J. *The South African Guide to Drugs and Drug Abuse*. Cresta, Randburg: Michael Collins Publications, 1998.

Dennill, K., King, L. and Swanepoel, T. *Aspects of Primary Healthcare*, 2nd ed. Cape Town: Oxford University Press Southern Africa, 2004.

Dreyer, M. *et al. Fundamental Aspects of Community Nursing*. 2nd ed. Halfway House: International Thomson Publishing, 1997.

Engel, J. *The Complete South African Health Guide*. Halfway House, Gauteng: Southern Book Publishers, 1996.

Evian, C. *Primary AIDS Care: A Practical Guide for Primary Healthcare Personnel*. 3rd ed. Johannesburg: Jacana, 2003.

Felhaber, T. ed. *South African Traditional Healers' Primary Healthcare Handbook*. Traditional aspects compiled by I. Mayeng. Cape Town: Kagiso, 1997.

Ferreira, M., Keikelame, M. and Mosaval, Y. *Older Women as Carers to Children and Grandchildren Affected by AIDS: A Study Towards Supporting the Carers*. Cape Town: Institute of Ageing in Africa, University of Cape Town, 2001.

Fertility: Current South African Issues of Poverty, HIV/AIDS and Youth: Seminar Proceedings. Cape Town: Human Sciences Research Council (HSRC), 2003.

Gow, J. and Desmond, C. eds. *Impacts and Interventions: The HIV/AIDS Epidemic and the Children of South Africa*
    Pietermaritzburg: University of Natal Press, 2002.
Green, A. *Introduction to Health Planning in Developing Countries*. London: Oxford University Press, 2004
Gumede, M.V. *Traditional Healers: A Medical Doctor's Perspective*. Johannesburg: Skotaville, 1990.
Hammond-Tooke, W.D. *Rituals and Medicines: Traditional Healing in South Africa*. Johannesburg: Donker, 1989.
Hattingh, S. *et al. Gerontology: A Community Health Perspective*. Johannesburg: International Thomson Publishing, 1996.
Holland, H. *African Magic: Traditional Ideas that Heal a Continent*. Sandton: Penguin, 2001.
*Impact of HIV/AIDS on the Health Sector: National Survey of Health Personnel, Ambulatory and Hospitalised Patients and
    Health Facilities 2002*. Pretoria: Department of Health, 2003.
Katzenellenbogen, J.M. *et al. Epidemiology: A Manual for Southern Africa*. Cape Town: Oxford University Press Southern
    Africa, 2004.
Kauffman, K. and Lindauer, D. eds. *AIDS and South Africa: The Social Expression of a Pandemic*. Basingstoke: Palgrave
    Macmillan, 2004.
Kibel, M. and Wagstaff, L. eds. *Child Health for All: A Manual for Southern Africa*. Cape Town: Oxford University Press.
    1992.
Kok, P. and Pietersen, J. *Health*. Pretoria: HSRC, 2000.
Labonde, R., *et al. Fatal Indifference: The G8, Africa and Global Health*. Cape Town: University of Cape Town Press, 2004
Martin, H.G. *A Comparative Analysis of the Financing of HIV/AIDS Programmes in Botswana, Lesotho, Mozambique, South
    Africa, Swaziland and Zimbabwe*. Cape Town: HSRC, 2003.
Mashaba, T.G. *Rising to the Challenge of Change: A History of Black Nursing in South Africa*. Kenwyn: Juta, 1995
Mbuya, J. *The AIDS Epidemic in South Africa*. Johannesburg: The Author, 2000.
Mendel, G. *A Broken Landscape: HIV and AIDS in Africa*. Johannesburg: M & G Books, 2002.
Nadasen, S. *Public Health Law in South Africa: An Introduction*. Durban: Butterworths, 2000.
Parry, C. and Bennetts, A. *Alcohol Policy and Public Health in South Africa*. Cape Town: Oxford University Press Southern
    Africa, 2004.
Reddy, S.P. and Meyer-Weitz, A. *Sense and Sensibilities: The Psychosocial and Contextual Determinants of
    STD-Related Behaviour*. Pretoria: MRCI and HSRC, 1999.
*South African First-Aid Manual: The Authorised Manual of the St John's Ambulance and the South African Red Cross
    Society*. 3rd ed. Cape Town: Struik, 1997.
Swartz, L. *Culture and Mental Health: A Southern African View*. Cape Town: Oxford University Press Southern Africa. 2004
Uys, L. *Home-Based HIV/AIDS Care*. Cape Town: Oxford University Press Southern Africa, 2004.
Van Rensburg, H.C.J. *Healthcare in South Africa: Structure and Dynamics*. Pretoria: Academica, 1992
Van Wyk, B.E. and Gericke, N. *Medicinal Plants of South Africa*. Pretoria: Briza Publications, 1999.
Walker, L., Reid, G., and Cornell, M. *Waiting to Happen: HIV/AIDS in South Africa*. Cape Town: Double Storey, 2004
Webb, D. *HIV and AIDS in Africa*. London: Pluto; Cape Town: David Philip, 1997.
Whiteside, A. and Sunter, C. *AIDS: The Challenge for South Africa*. Cape Town: Human & Rousseau, 2000.
Wilson, D. *et al.* eds. *Handbook of HIV Medicine*, Cape Town: Oxford University Press Southern Africa. 2004
Wood. M. *No Turning Back*. London: Michael Wood Memorial Fund, 2001

Housing

Access to housing and secure accommodation is an integral part of government's commitment to reduce poverty and improve the quality of people's lives.

The Department of Housing determines, finances, promotes, co-ordinates, communicates and monitors the implementation of policy for housing and human settlement.

Since the launch of the *White Paper on Housing* in December 1994, housing in South Africa has undergone fundamental changes. Between 1994 and June 2005, the housing programme provided more than 1,7 million housing units to more than seven million people. During the same period, a total of 2,4 million subsidies were approved.

In 2004/05, 178 612 housing units were made available.

Legislation and policy

Comprehensive housing plan

The Minister of Housing, Dr Lindiwe Sisulu, announced the Comprehensive Housing Plan for the Development of Integrated Sustainable Human Settlements in September 2004.

Cabinet approved the plan as a framework for housing programmes in the next five years. It provides for comprehensive oversight by government in promoting the residential property market. This includes the development of low-cost housing, medium-density accommodation and rental housing; stronger partnerships with the private sector; social infrastructure; and amenities. The plan also aims to change spatial settlement patterns, informed by the need to build multicultural communities in a non-racial society.

It is estimated that more than 108 000 additional households will benefit from this venture.

The following benefits will be achieved:
• Housing delivery will be demand-driven and will involve a great deal of flexibility.
• The role of the private sector will be enhanced through the collapsing of subsidy bands, as well as the removal of blockages relating to down-payments for indigents and pensioners. Beneficiaries' spousal income will also be assessed. A fixed rate and other new loan products will be developed, including an option to convert the capital grant, where linked to home ownership or rental, into an annuity-based grant or benefit.

Housing subsidiy bands, 2005/06				
Income category	Previous subsidy	New subsidy	Contribution	Product price
Individual, project-linked and relocation assistance subsidies				
R0 – R1 500	R25 800 + contribution	R31 929	None	R31 929
R1 501 – R3 500	R15 700	R29 450	R2 479 + shortfall	R31 929
Indigent: Aged, disabled and health stricken	R28 279	R31 929	None	R31 929
Institutional Subsidy				
R0 – R3 500	R25 800	R29 450	Indirect institution must add capital	At least R31 929
Consolidation subsidies				
R0 – R1 500	R14 102	R18 792	None	R18 792
R1 501 – R3 500	New category	R16 313	R2 479	R18 792
Consolidation subsidy for aged, disabled or health-stricken groups R1 501 – R3 500	R16 581	R18 792	None	R18 792
Rural housing subsidies				
R0 – R3 500	R25 800	R29 450	None	R29 450
People's housing subsidies				
R0 – R3 500	R25 800	R31 929	None	R31 929
Emergency Housing Programme				
Temporary assistance	R23 892	R26 874	Shortfall	R26 874
Services	R11 698	R13 137	None	R13 137
Houses	R16 581	R18 792	None	R18 792
Public-Sector Hostels Redevelopment Programme		Previous grant		New grant
Family units		R25 800		R29 450
Individual units (per bed)		R6 400		R7 234

Source: Department of Housing

- Employers will be encouraged to make their contribution through employer-assisted housing.
- Barriers to housing trade will be removed through amendments to the Housing Act, 1997 (Act 107 of 1997), to reduce the period during which resale on the private market is prohibited from eight to five years.
- Access to title deeds will be enhanced through the implementation of measures to stimulate a renewed uptake in the Discount Benefit Scheme, and the establishment of a high-priority focus on completing the registration of transfer in respect of houses constructed under the existing housing programme.
- All programmes will be focused on ring-fencing informal settlements and replacing these with more adequate forms of housing.

Additional funding amounting to R500 million in 2006/07 and R1,5 billion in 2007/08 has been allocated to step up the housing programme so that all informal settlements can be upgraded by 2014.

A number of pilot projects will inform the further development of the informal settlement upgrading programme.

Key focus areas identified by the comprehensive housing plan include:

- accelerating housing delivery as a key strategy for poverty alleviation
- utilising housing provision as a major job-creation strategy
- ensuring that property can be accessed by all as an asset for wealth creation and empowerment
- leveraging growth in the economy, combating crime and promoting social cohesion

- using housing development to break barriers between the First Economy residential property boom and the Second Economy slump
- utilising housing as an instrument for the development of sustainable human settlements in support of spatial restructuring
- diversifying housing products by placing emphasis on rental stock.

Rental Housing Act, 1999

The Rental Housing Act, 1999 (Act 50 of 1999), which came into operation on 1 August 2001, defines the responsibility of government in respect of the rental housing market.

It sets out the duties and responsibilities of both landlords and tenants, and provides for the establishment of rental housing tribunals in the provinces, thus allowing for a speedy and cost-effective resolution of disputes between landlords and tenants.

Among other things, the Act prescribes that:
- Leases may be oral or in writing. Tenants can demand a written lease.
- The landlord must give the tenant a written receipt.
- The landlord may require the tenant to pay a deposit before moving in.
- The balance of deposit and interest must be refunded to the tenant by the landlord not later than 21 days after the expiration of the lease.

Three rental housing tribunals were set up in Gauteng, the Western Cape and North West. Other provinces are in the process of establishing similar tribunals. The Act gives these tribunals the power to make rulings in line with those of a magistrate's court.

Home Loan and Mortgage Disclosure Act, 2000

The Home Loan and Mortgage Disclosure Act, 2000 (Act 63 of 2000), provides for the establishment of the Office of Disclosure and the monitoring of financial institutions serving the housing-credit needs of communities. It requires financial institutions to disclose information, and identifies discriminatory lending patterns. The Act aims to promote equity and fairness in lending and disclosure by financial

institutions, and will be implemented as soon as the regulations of the Act have been promulgated.

The Act also aims to eradicate discrimination and unfair practices, by encouraging banks and financial institutions to grant home loans to all its clients. It compels banks and financial institutions to disclose annual financial statements so that their lending practices in respect of home loans can be monitored.

In March 2005, the Department of Housing revived the Financial Services Charter by signing a memorandum of understanding (MoU) with four major banks – the Amalgamated Banks of South Africa (Absa), First National Bank, Standard Bank and Nedcor.

The banks pledged R42 billion to be released into the affordable housing market by 2008.

As part of the MoU, the department was negotiating the National Home Loan Code of Practice with appropriate role-players.

Housing Consumer Protection Measures Act, 1998

In terms of the Housing Consumer Protection Measures Act, 1998 (Act 95 of 1998), residential builders have to register with the National Home-Builders Registration Council (NHBRC) and are obliged to enrol all new houses under the NHBRC's Defect Warranty Scheme.

The Act aims to protect home owners from inferior workmanship. Builders are responsible for design and material defects for three months, roof leaks for a year, and any structural failures of houses for five years. NHBRC inspectors may assess workmanship during and after the building process.

Banks are compelled by law to insist on home-builder registration and enrolment prior to granting a mortgage loan or finance.

All new government-subsidised housing units constructed as part of approved projects enjoy protection against shoddy workmanship by housing contractors.

Through the Act, properties that were built with funding from the Government's housing subsidy grant only, enjoy protection against structural defects and must comply with minimum technical norms and standards.

Previously, the properties of the poor did not qualify for such protection. The NHBRC ensures that registered builders deliver within the minimum housing standards.

Prevention of Illegal Eviction and Unlawful Occupation of Land Act, 1998

The Prevention of Illegal Eviction and Unlawful Occupation of Land Act, 1998 (Act 19 of 1998), prohibits unlawful eviction and sets out detailed procedures for the eviction of unlawful occupiers.

It also prohibits the receipt of payment as a fee for arranging the occupation of land without the consent of the owner, and repeals obsolete laws relating to illegal squatting.

The Act provides a process for fair eviction of unlawful occupiers, and distinguishes between occupiers who have been residing on land for less than six months and those who have been residing on land for more than six months.

Social housing

On 15 August 2004, Minister Sisulu and the European Union Ambassador, Mr Michael Lake, launched the R160-million Social Housing Programme in Pretoria.

The Social Housing Bill was expected to assign the responsibilities of national, provincial and local government on matters pertaining to social housing.

In May 2005, the Minister of Housing, Dr Lindiwe Sisulu, was nominated to serve on the United Nation's High Level Commission on the Legal Empowerment of the Poor.

Minister Sisulu is one of the only two serving ministers from sub-Saharan Africa nominated to serve on this commission, comprising primarily heads of government.

The commission is based on the conviction that the fight against poverty can only be achieved if governments succeed in democratising the rule of law.

The commission was expected to start operating in September 2005.

It will also ensure that relevant institutional arrangements and capacities required by the Social Housing Programme are in place, including the establishment of the Social Housing Regulatory Authority.

Public-Sector Hostel Redevelopment Programme

The Department of Housing is replacing the hostels policy with a policy that will create humane living conditions, and provide affordable and sustainable housing on either a rental or home-ownership basis.

Several pilot redevelopment projects have been launched.

The department has also prepared a set of technical specifications for the upgrading or provision of new services, and the upgrading (redevelopment) of hostel buildings. The new technical norms and standards for redeveloping hostels will give rise to new guidelines for turning sector hostels into family units.

Housing Development Bill

The Housing Development Bill is expected to put in place a broad framework for residential development, facilitate spatial restructuring and set aside a certain proportion of all housing developments for affordable housing.

Funding

The Department of Housing received R5,1 billion in 2005/06 to finance national and provincial housing programmes.

The allocation is made annually on the basis of a formula that takes into account the backlog in each province, the number of households in the various income categories of the subsidy scheme, the ratio between urban and rural housing, and the performance of the relevant provincial Government.

Total departmental expenditure was expected to increase from R3,7 billion in 2001/02 to R7,4 billion in 2007/08, an average annual growth rate of 12,1%.

The People's Housing Process (PHP) recognises the efforts and initiatives of those who prefer to build their own houses and are prepared to commit their resources, skills and energies to this task. It provides technical, financial and other support to these people. Funding is administered through the provincial housing departments, while the People's Housing Partnership Trust (PHPT) helps build the capacity to speed up delivery.

Capacity-building

One of the major constraints in housing delivery is the lack of capacity. This includes an efficient workforce and the installation of appropriate technology, equipment and systems for monitoring, evaluation and reporting purposes.

The Department of Housing continues to assist provinces to ensure effective and efficient implementation of the National Housing Programme. The strategy and guidelines for housing capacity-building, as well as guidelines for provincial housing-capacity business plans, have been developed.

In 2005/06, the Department of Housing set aside R10 million to train emerging contractors country-wide to meet the challenge of sustainable provision of human settlements.

Emergency housing

In April 2004, the department announced the amended version of the National Housing Programme dealing with housing assistance in emergency circumstances.

The National Housing Programme for Housing Assistance in Emergency Housing Circumstances was instituted in terms of the Housing Act, 1997.

The amendment relates to the provision of the Constitution that everyone has the right to have access to adequate housing, and that the State must take reasonable legislative and other measures within its available resources to achieve the progressive realisation of this right.

The main objective of this programme is to provide temporary housing relief to people in urban and rural areas who find themselves in emergency situations, such as when:

- their existing shelters have been destroyed or damaged

- their prevailing situation poses an immediate threat to their lives, health and safety
- they have been evicted or face the threat of eviction.

The assistance involves prioritising funds from the provincial housing allocations to municipalities to accelerate land development, and the provision of basic municipal engineering services and temporary shelter.

Housing Consumer Education (HCE) Programme

The HCE programme educates and trains housing consumers (owners and rental users) on their rights and responsibilities, thereby:

- protecting and strengthening low-cost housing as a national asset
- enhancing the market value of low-cost housing
- using low-cost housing as collateral for leveraging credit by the poor
- building strong and vibrant communities, in collaboration with other programmes such as community development workers, the Expanded Public Works Programme, and HIV and AIDS awareness
- enhancing the maintenance culture of housing consumers
- improving the sustainability of the housing unit as an inclusive element of living environments.

Furthermore, the HCE programme empowers housing consumers to understand their housing rights and responsibilities, as well as the different types of subsidies offered by government.

The N2 Gateway Lead Project in Cape Town forms part of the Comprehensive Housing Plan for South Africa, adopted by Cabinet on 2 September 2004.
The plan aims to eradicate informal setlements in South Africa in as short a period as is physically possible.
The project will build sustainable human settlements designed to uplift the standard of living of more than 100 000 residents of the City of Cape Town.

It also ensures that housing consumers are educated on existing and new housing legislation, strategies and approaches.

Housing subsidies

New housing-subsidy programmes are being developed and certain existing programmes have been enhanced, including rental and social-housing subsidies. The housing-subsidy programmes, including project-linked subsidies, are being revised to introduce a procurement-compliant regime, consolidation subsidies, PHP, rural subsidies and institutional subsidies.

The Department of Housing increased housing subsidies by up to 11,68% with effect from April 2005.

The department designed a housing scheme to effectively cater for people with disabilities. People with visual impairment and other disabilities will receive an additional amount to the normal subsidy to make their homes more accessible and comfortable, in accordance with their physical needs.

Disabled beneficiaries may receive special additions to their houses to enable them independent living in normal residential areas. These additions have been tailor-made to accommodate the variety of special housing needs.

Such special additions to houses entail concrete aprons and ramps to facilitate access, special grab rails in bathrooms, kick plates on doors, visible doorbells and special access arrangements to toilets.

Project-linked subsidies

This housing subsidy mechanism enables a qualifying household to access a complete residential unit, which is developed within an approved project-linked housing subsidy project for ownership by the beneficiary.

Individual subsidies

An individual subsidy provides qualifying beneficiaries with access to housing subsidies to acquire ownership of serviced stands. It also allows the beneficiary to enter into house-building contracts, or to purchase existing, improved residential property which is not part of approved housing-subsidy projects.

This subsidy furthermore helps qualifying beneficiaries who wish to increase their subsidies by accessing credit, as well as beneficiaries who do not qualify for credit.

Consolidation subsidies

This subsidy mechanism affords former beneficiaries of serviced stands, financed by the previous housing dispensation (including the Independent Development Trust's site and service schemes), the opportunity to acquire houses.

Institutional subsidies

The institutional subsidy is available to qualifying institutions to enable them to create affordable housing stock for persons who qualify for housing subsidies.

The subsidy is paid to approved institutions to provide subsidised housing on deed of sale, rental or rent-to-buy options, on condition that the beneficiaries may not be compelled to pay the full purchase price and take transfer within the first four years of receiving the subsidy.

Institutions must also invest capital from their own resources in the project.

Relocation assistance

Relocation assistance provides an alternative option to defaulting borrowers who were three months in arrears on 31 August 1997, and where the option of rehabilitating these mortgage loans is not affordable.

This alternative provides an opportunity to obtain affordable housing with the assistance of the housing subsidy.

A person who is eligible for relocation assistance must enter into a relocation agreement to relocate to affordable housing.

Discount Benefit Scheme

The Discount Benefit Scheme promotes home ownership among tenants of state-financed rental stock, including formal housing and serviced sites. In terms of this scheme, tenants receive a maximum discount of up to R7 500 on the selling price of the property.

Where the discount amount equals or exceeds the purchase price or loan balance, the property is transferred free of any further capital charges.

Rural subsidies
This housing subsidy is available to beneficiaries who enjoy only functional tenure rights to the land they occupy. This land belongs to the State and is governed by traditional authorities.

The subsidies are only available on a project basis and beneficiaries are supported by implementing agents. Beneficiaries also have the right to decide on how to use their subsidies, either for service provision, the building of houses or a combination thereof.

Housing institutions

The Department of Housing's support institutions play an important role in enhancing the norms and standards of housing, as well as making housing more accessible to all South Africans.

The institutions are the NHBRC, the National Housing Finance Corporation (NHFC), the National Urban Reconstruction and Housing Agency (NURCHA), Servcon Housing Solutions, Thubelisha Homes, the Social Housing Foundation (SHF), the South African Housing Fund, the PHP and the Rural Housing Loan Fund (RHLF).

National Home-Builders Registration Council
The NHBRC was established in terms of the Housing Consumer Protection Measures Act, 1998 (Act 95 of 1998). The council protects the interests of consumers and regulates the home-building industry.

The NHBRC is a section 21 company established to provide for the protection of housing consumers through a home warranty scheme, to regulate the home-building industry through the registration of builders and setting of ethical and technical standards for the residential building industry.

The Housing Consumer Protection Measures Act, 1998 extends the NHBRC home warranty scheme to government housing subsidy schemes.

The NHBRC raises revenue from fees charged for the registration of home-builders and the enrolment of new houses under its warranty scheme. Revenue increased significantly from R164,9 million in 2001/02 to R355 million in 2004/05, representing an average annual increase of 29,1%.

Expenditure has remained relatively stable, fluctuating between R77,7 million in 2001/02 and R88,3 million in 2003/04.

Expenditure is driven largely by the claims on the warranty scheme resulting from poor construction, and is therefore difficult to predict. As a result of the limited claims against the warranty scheme, the NHBRC accumulated significant reserves – R945,4 million in 2004/05.

The NHBRC improved its effectiveness following an aggressive publicity campaign, registering 3 739 home-builders by March 2004 (an increase of 23,7% from 2003) and enrolling 48 305 housing units (an 11,5% increase from 2003).

From 2003 to 2004, complaints handled recorded a decrease of 6,9%, inspections increased by 51,8% and renewals increased by 6,9%. Conciliation cases decreased by 21,9% and suspensions increased by 67,1%, resulting in more home-builders being suspended for the year ending 2004 compared with 2003.

National Housing Finance Corporation
The Department of Housing established the NHFC as a development finance institution in 1996, to ensure that every low- and moderate-income household gains access to housing finance.

As a wholesale funder and risk manager, the NHFC is mandated to:
- undertake funding as a wholesale intermediary to promote broader access to housing
- underwrite the flow of wholesale funds to retail intermediaries (provide cover, security or guarantee)
- undertake proactive programmes aimed at building institutional and financial capacity at retail level
- specialise in identifying, assessing, pricing, monitoring and managing risks associated with the placement of wholesale funds with retail intermediaries.

The NHFC defines the low- and moderate-income market as any South African household with a regular monthly income of between R1 500 and R7 500. This market sector is able to contribute towards its housing costs, but finds it hard to access bank-funded housing finance.

The corporation is a registered public company and has been granted the necessary exemption in terms of the Banks Act, 1990 (Act 94 of 1990). As a national public entity, the NHFC adheres to the regulatory framework of the Public Finance Management Act, 1999 (Act 1 of 1999).

The NHFC has made significant strides towards making affordable housing finance accessible to low- and moderate-income communities. Through its various intermediaries and partners, the corporation has, in its eight years of existence, disbursed more than R1,7 billion.

Through its funding, the lives of almost two million people have improved.

The NHFC's commitment to supporting emerging lenders has resulted in the funding of niche lenders and housing institutions.

National Urban Reconstruction and Housing Agency

NURCHA was formed in May 1995 as a partnership between the South African Government and the Open Society Institute of New York, United States of America (USA), to arrange finance for housing.

Over the years, NURCHA has raised additional financing through Swedish, Norwegian and US agencies, and through the Futuregrowth Fund, Overseas Private Investors' Corporation and Rand Merchant Bank. It is a tax-exempt, non-profit-making company. By the end of 2004/05, NURCHA had supported the building of 146 984 houses.

Programmes

NURCHA uses a variety of interventions to arrange and package finance for those delivering housing to low-income households, infrastructure and community facilities:

- Bridging-finance loans for small contractors: NURCHA lends money to small/emerging contractors building subsidy housing. To assist con-

tractors and developers who are unable to access bridging finance from a bank, NURCHA has developed innovative finance programmes and entered into agreements with financial intermediaries who ensure the appropriate flow of finance to projects. Applicants requiring this form of funding are normally contractors who also require financial-management support.

- Bridging finance loans for established contractors: NURCHA lends directly to established developers and contractors developing subsidy housing, credit-linked housing in the R50 000 to R180 000 selling price range, infrastructure and community facilities. Established contractors are required to provide a minimum of 30% of the project-bridging finance required upfront.
- Financing for rental housing: NURCHA provides finance and guarantees for the construction and upgrading of rental stock for the affordable housing market sector. These facilities are provided subject to the specific requirements of the negotiated package.

Servcon Housing Solutions

Servcon was established in 1994 as a 50-50 joint venture between the Department of Housing (representing government) and the Council of South African Banks, now the Banking Association of South Africa.

When the agreement was renewed in 1998, Servcon was mandated to provide exclusive management services in respect of the designated portfolio, comprising 33 306 properties in possession (PIPs), and non-performing loans (NPLs) with a value of R1,277 billion, for a period of eight years from 1 April 1998 to 31 March 2006.

In terms of the normalisation programme, Servcon's mission is to normalise the lending process by managing PIPs and NPLs in areas where the normal legal process has broken down.

By 31 March 2005, Servcon had normalised 21 953 properties, and anticipated achieving the full target of 33 306 by 31 March 2006. It receives funding from the department on a quarterly basis to cover 50% of its operating costs while 50% of interest on the value of the undischarged guarantee is paid to banks.

Thubelisha Homes

Thubelisha Homes is a housing-support institution reporting to the Minister of Housing. Its primary function is to build affordable houses for South Africans using government's capital subsidy. Thubelisha does this in three stages: securing land for development, servicing stands with water and sewerage infrastructure, and building top structures.

In 2004/05, Thubelisha serviced 3 000 stands and built 3 674 houses, using skills such as project and construction management; subsidy administration; beneficiary relocations; acting as a support organisation for 'managed' PHP projects; community liaison and contractor development; and skills transfer.

Thubelisha is undergoing major structural changes to accommodate government's Comprehensive Plan for the Development of Sustainable Human Settlements. The repositioning will enable Thubelisha to assist provincial housing departments and local authorities to provide more houses through delivery-enhancing interventions such as unblocking slow-moving projects.

Thubelisha will assist government's housing plan in the following areas:
- informal settlements
- social and community facilities
- social (medium-density) housing
- job creation
- appropriate technology
- delivery-enhancing interventions.

To help government in the implementation of these six key areas, Thubelisha has established a head office in Johannesburg and opened provincial offices in Gauteng, Mpumalanga, Eastern Cape and Western Cape. More offices were expected to be opened in North West and KwaZulu-Natal in 2005.

Social Housing Foundation

The SHF was established as a section 21 company by the Department of Housing in 1997. It is mandated by the department to develop and build capacity for social housing institutions (SHIs) and to develop a policy framework for the sector.

The strategic objectives of the organisation, based on its mandate, mission and vision, are to:

- provide social-housing-sector strategic information
- mobilise resources for the social housing sector
- facilitate the capacitation of sectoral participants
- promote the social housing sector
- facilitate sectoral stakeholder alignment
- achieve SHF business-service excellence.

The SHF and the social housing sector have shown significant growth and development in recent years. By March 2004, there were 83 SHIs in South Africa.

The most significant agreement relating to social housing is that between the European Commission (EC) and the South African Government.

The EC has pledged 20 million euros (about R200 million) for social housing over the next five years.

The EC programme has been strengthened, with a considerable amount of work conducted around building the internal staff capacity, systems, procedures and manuals of the SHF. Three SHIs were successful in applying for grant funding for capacity-building and development, and plans for a number of additional institutions are in the pipeline.

In 2005/06, government awarded a grant of R18 118 000 to the SHF.

South African Housing Fund

The South African Housing Fund aims to provide adequate funds to enable provincial governments to establish and maintain habitable, stable and sustainable residential environments.

This includes the provision of:
- permanent residential structures with secure tenure and privacy, and which provide adequate protection against the elements
- potable water, adequate sanitation facilities and domestic electricity supply.

People's Housing Process

The National Housing Policy: Supporting the PHP was adopted by the Minister of Housing in 1998. The policy focuses on poor families in both urban and rural areas, using capital subsidies to allow people to build their own homes.

It also assists people in obtaining access to technical, financial, logistical and administrative support to build their own homes, on either an individual or a collective basis.

Peoples' Housing Partnership Trust

The broad mandate of the PHPT is aligned with the National Housing Policy: Supporting the PHP, which stipulates and defines the PHPT mandate as capacitating and engaging with national, provincial and local governments and civil society to meaningfully participate and support the PHP. To create adequate capacity for the PHP, the department established the PHPT in June 1997 to implement the Capacitation Programme to Support the PHP.

The main objective of the programme is to develop capacity at all levels of government, and in non-governmental organisations, community-based organisations and communities to support the PHP.

The PHPT has five programmes:

- Communication
- Training
- Research and Development
- Technical Advisory Services
- Corporate Services.

The PHPT is funded by the United Nations (UN) Development Programme, the UN Centre for Human Settlement and the US Agency for International Development. Government assists the PHP by way of subsidies, facilitation grants and housing-support funding.

Rural Housing Loan Fund

The RHLF's core business is providing loans, through intermediaries, to low-income households for incremental housing purposes. Incremental housing is a people-driven process and the RHLF aims to empower low-income families in rural areas to access credit that enables them to unleash the potential of their self-help skills, savings and local ingenuity to build and improve their shelters over time.

Until 31 March 2002, the RHLF was a subsidiary of the NHFC. From 1 April 2002, it became a separate entity. The RHLF has channelled funds to homeowners in several rural areas in all nine provinces in South Africa through 20 medium and small retail lenders.

The RHLF has set up a peer-support network to support capacity-building and loyalty to the RHLF mission among intermediaries. This unique approach to development finance seeks to institutionalise peer interaction among non-competitive start-ups.

Urban renewal

The Special Integrated Presidential Project for Urban Renewal was identified as one of the first Presidential lead projects.

The project aimed to kick-start development in major urban areas, focusing on violence-torn communities and those in crisis.

It was developed to ensure an integrated approach to the provision of infrastructure, housing, community and recreation facilities, and job opportunities. It aimed to transform previously disadvantaged communities and create sustainable and habitable living environments.

In addition, the project has been viewed as an ideal opportunity to promote the business-planning concept and to provide provincial governments with the opportunity to improve co-ordination.

Several such projects within 31 communities have been identified as beneficiaries. The projects are:

- Eastern Cape: Duncan Village and Ibhayi
- Free State: Thabong
- Gauteng: Katorus
- KwaZulu-Natal: Cato Manor
- Limpopo: Mahwelereng
- Mpumalanga: Masoyi and Siyabuswa
- Northern Cape: Galeshewe
- North West: Molopo River Basin
- Western Cape: Integrated Service Land Project in the Cape Metropolitan Area.

These projects include the provision of housing, and the upgrading of hostels and infrastructure (such as roads and the provision of electricity and street-lighting). Projects include child-care facilities, schools, clinics, sports fields, libraries, police stations, centres for the aged, post offices and playgrounds.

Providing areas for markets, community gardens and skills training creates opportunities for business development. These activities are planned and implemented in an integrated manner to ensure sustainable and habitable living environments.

The Department of Housing plans to construct homes with two or three storey 'walk ups' as part of dealing with the housing backlog. Existing buildings will also be acquired and converted for housing purposes.

Urban Upgrading and Development Programme (UUDP)

The UUDP is a joint bilateral undertaking between South Africa and Germany, which was established in 1994 between the national Department of Housing and German Technical Co-operation.

The department is playing a key facilitation and co-ordination role in implementing the programme in the Free State and Eastern Cape. Assistance to the two provinces and housing institutions involved:

- support to the Masilonyana Municipality in the Free State in bridging the bufferzone, by promoting the integration of the Masilo township with the former town through territorial marketing
- support for the implementation of the PHP projects in Mount Fletcher, Elliotdale and Tarkastad in the Eastern Cape
- support for the national review of the PHP by the PHPT
- the piloting of a municipal housing-sector plan as part of the Integrated Development Plan of the local municipality of Mohokare in the Free State.

By March 2004, the UUDP had:

- assisted roughly 2 500 beneficiaries of housing subsidies, through integrated planning, self-help and management of construction processes to gain a foothold in the urban economy by owning a transferable asset
- fast-tracked the delivery of roughly 18 000 housing units within the framework of the Housing Support Programme without losing sight of quality
- conceptualised and scaled-up a national programme for educating thousands of prospective or existing house owners about citizens' rights and responsibilities as housing beneficiaries

- empowered 550 household beneficiaries of housing subsidies to grow the value of their national assets by investing more than R3 million in the upgrading and improvement of their houses
- empowered community members to gain a better understanding of housing policy so as to better articulate demand, make an informed choice and be part of decision-making on appropriate delivery
- trained many of its staff and community members to improve their understanding of urban service-delivery markets and fill some of the delivery gaps with rare skills.

Settlement policy and urban development

In June 1996, South Africa made a commitment at the Habitat II Conference in Istanbul, Turkey, to implement the Habitat Agenda. The agenda is the guiding international policy for human settlements.

The Department of Housing is charged with the responsibility of co-ordinating the implementation of the agenda. To do this, national policies that support the principles and the vision of the agenda should be in place.

The Urban Development Framework is essentially the key policy document that will guide the implementation of the Habitat Agenda in South Africa. Besides the framework, the department has taken the opportunity offered by the Global Urban Observatory, and initiated the Urban Indicators Programme and Local Best Practice Strategy.

African Solutions Network, a website hosted by the department, features:

- information about the African Solutions Conference and others in the region, which deal with issues relating to sustainable development
- contact details of individuals and organisations active in the field of sustainable human-settlement development
- a database of relevant good practices
- information on technologies, building material and practices that support sustainable human-settlement development
- links to relevant research databases to source

the latest research relating to sustainable human settlement.

African Solutions Network also provides links to other websites and Internet resources.

Another initiative driven by the department, which relates to Habitat II, is the Environmentally Sound Low-Cost Housing Task Team. The team has been tasked with promoting environmental efficiency in the housing sector, and is working on the development of standards and guidelines, incentive programmes, a financing mechanism and general awareness-raising initiatives.

Acknowledgements

A Review of the UUDP's Support to the South African Housing Sector, published by the German Technical Co-operation

BuaNews

Department of Housing

Estimates of National Expenditure 2005, published by National Treasury

Social Housing Foundation

Thubelisha Homes

National Urban Reconstruction and Housing Agency

www.gov.za

Suggested reading

Bond, P. *Cities of Gold: Townships of Coal: Essays on South Africa's New Urban Crisis*. Trematon, New Jersey: African World Press, 2000.

Boraine, A. ed. *State of the Cities Report 2004*, Johannesburg: South African Cities Network, 2004.

Bundy, C. *Rise and Fall of the South African Peasantry*. 2nd ed. Cape Town: David Philip, 1988.

Harrison, P. *et al.* eds. *Confronting Management: Housing and Urban Development in a Democratising Society*. Cape Town: University of Cape Town Press, 2003.

Housing and the World of Work. Produced by the National Housing Initiative in association with AECI and Matthew Nell and Associates. Auckland Park, Johannesburg: National Business Institute, 1998.

James, W. ed. *Houses for Africa: An Inspirational Source Book for Building and Finishing Your Home*. Johannesburg: Emden Publishing, n.d.

Keegan, T.J. *Facing the Storm: Portraits of Black Lives in Rural South Africa*. Cape Town: David Philip, 1988.

Khan, F. and Thring, P. *Housing Policy and Practice in Post-Apartheid South Africa*. Johannesburg: Heinemann, 2003.

Rust, K. and Rubenstein, S. eds. *A Mandate to Build: Developing Consensus Around a National Housing Policy in South Africa*. Johannesburg: Ravan Press, 1996.

South African Home-Owners Buyers' Guide: Design, Building, Renovating, Decorating, Garden and Outdoor, 1998/99. Johannesburg: Avonwold, 1998. Annual.

Justice and correctional services

The Department of Justice and Constitutional Development aims to uphold and protect the Constitution of the Republic of South Africa, 1996 (Act 108 of 1996), and the rule of law. It also aims to render accessible, fair, speedy and cost-effective administration of justice in the interest of a safer and more secure South Africa.

The department has four core branches at national level, namely Court Services, Master of the High Court, Legal Advisory Services and Legislation and Constitutional Development. There are four support branches, namely Human Resources, Public Education and Communication, Information Systems Management and Financial Management. The National Prosecuting Authority (NPA) forms a separate programme on the department's vote.

To ensure the efficiency of its service and enhance accessibility, the NPA, Court Services and the Master of the High Court have established provincial and local structures linked to courts to co-ordinate the implementation of national policy. Legal Advisory Services has also established state attorney offices in Pretoria, Johannesburg, Cape Town, Bloemfontein and Durban to provide services at a decentralised level.

The following constitutional institutions form part of the department:
- the South African Human Rights Commission (SAHRC) promotes and monitors the observance of human rights in South Africa
- the Commission on Gender Equality (CGE) aims to create a society free from gender discrimination and any other forms of oppression
- the Public Protector investigates any conduct in state affairs, or in public administration in any sphere of government, that is alleged to be improper, or which results in any impropriety or prejudice.

The department administers the following public entities:
- the Special Investigating Unit (SIU) provides professional forensic investigating and litigation services to all state institutions at national, provincial and local level to combat maladministration, corruption and fraud, and to protect state assets and public money
- the Legal Aid Board provides legal aid and representation to as many indigent people as possible at the State's expense.

The department's Medium Term Expediture Framework (MTEF) baseline allocation will grow from R5,072 billion in 2005/06, to R5,598 billion in 2006/07 and to R6,046 billion in 2007/08. This equates to an average increase of 9,2% over the MTEF period.

Judicial system

The Constitution is the supreme law of the country and binds all legislative, executive and judicial organs of the State at all levels of government.

In terms of Section 165 of the Constitution, the judicial authority in South Africa is vested in the courts, which are independent and subject only to the Constitution and the law.

No person or organ of state may interfere with the functioning of the courts, and an order or decision of a court binds all organs of state and persons to whom it applies.

Chapter 8 of the Constitution makes provision for the following courts:

- Constitutional Court
- Supreme Court of Appeal
- high courts, including any high court of appeal that may be established by an Act of Parliament to hear appeals from high courts
- magistrate's courts
- any other court established or recognised in terms of an Act of Parliament, including any court of a status similar to either high courts or magistrate's courts.

In line with this, Parliament also established special income tax courts, the Labour Court and the Labour Appeal Court, the Land Claims Court, the Competition Appeal Court, the Electoral Court, divorce courts, consumer courts, 'military courts' and equality courts.

By June 2005, the Minister of Justice and Constitutional Development, Ms Brigitte Mabandla, was leading a process to rationalise high courts. The Superior Courts Bill, which was introduced in Parliament in 2005, will abolish the last remnants of the homeland-based supreme courts and usher in new provincial divisions of the High Court in each province. Their jurisdiction and capacity will be determined in accordance with people's needs. This will result in the opening of high courts in Mpumalanga and Limpopo, which are currently serviced by the Pretoria High Court.

Constitutional Court

The Constitutional Court, situated in Johannesburg, is the highest court in all constitutional matters. It is the only court that may adjudicate disputes between organs of state in the national or provincial sphere concerning the constitutional status, powers or functions of any of those organs of state or decide on the constitutionality of any amendment to the Constitution or any parliamentary or provincial Bill. The Constitutional Court makes the final decision whether an Act of Parliament, a provincial Act or conduct of the President is constitutional. It consists of the Chief Justice of South Africa, the Deputy Chief Justice and nine Constitutional Court judges.

Justice Pius Langa was appointed the Chief Justice of South Africa with effect from 1 June 2005, following the retirement of Chief Justice Arthur Chaskalson. Justice Dikgang Moseneke became Deputy Chief Justice.

Supreme Court of Appeal

The Supreme Court of Appeal, situated in Bloemfontein, in the Free State, is the highest court in respect of all other matters. It consists of the President and Deputy President of the Supreme Court of Appeal and a number of judges of appeal determined by an Act of Parliament. The Supreme Court of Appeal has jurisdiction to hear and determine an appeal against any decision of a high court.

Decisions of the Supreme Court of Appeal are binding on all courts of a lower order, and the decisions of high courts are binding on magistrate's courts within the respective areas of jurisdiction of the divisions.

High courts

There are 10 high court divisions: Cape of Good Hope (with its seat in Cape Town), Eastern Cape (Grahamstown), Northern Cape (Kimberley), Orange Free State (Bloemfontein), Natal (Pietermaritzburg), Transvaal (Pretoria), Transkei (Umtata), Ciskei (Bisho), Venda (Sibasa), and Bophuthatswana (Mmabatho). Each of these divisions, with the exception of Venda, is composed of a judge president and, if the President so determines, one or more deputy judges president, and as many judges as the President may determine from time to time.

There are also three local divisions: the Witwatersrand Local Division (Johannesburg),

Durban and Coast Local Division (Durban) and South-Eastern Cape Division (Port Elizabeth). These courts are presided over by judges in the provincial courts concerned.

A provincial or local division has jurisdiction in its own area over all persons residing or present in that area. These divisions hear matters that are of such a serious nature that the lower courts would not be competent to make an appropriate judgment or impose a penalty. Except where minimum or maximum sentences are prescribed by law, their penal jurisdiction is unlimited and includes life imprisonment in certain specified cases.

Circuit local divisions

These are itinerant courts, each presided over by a judge of the provincial division. These courts periodically visit areas designated by the Judge President of the provincial division concerned.

Other high courts

The Land Claims Court and the Labour Court have the same status as the High Court. The Land Claims Court hears matters on the restitution of land rights that people lost after 1913 as a result of racially discriminatory land laws. The Labour Court adjudicates matters relating to labour disputes, and appeals are made to the Labour Appeal Court.

Decisions of the Constitutional Court, the Supreme Court of Appeal and the high courts are an important source of law. These courts are required to uphold and enforce the Constitution, which has an extensive Bill of Rights binding all state organs and all persons. The courts are also required to declare any law or conduct that is inconsistent with the Constitution to be invalid to the extent of that inconsistency, and to develop the common law in a manner consistent with the values of the Constitution and the spirit and purpose of the Bill of Rights.

Regional courts

The Minister of Justice and Constitutional Development may divide the country into magisterial districts and create regional divisions consisting of districts. Regional courts are then established per province at one or more places in each regional division to hear matters within their jurisdiction. Unlike the High Court, the penal jurisdiction of regional courts is limited by legislation.

Magistrate's courts

Magisterial districts have been grouped into 13 clusters headed by chief magistrates. This system has streamlined, simplified and provided uniform court-management systems applicable throughout South Africa, in terms of judicial provincial boundaries.

It facilitated the separation of functions pertaining to the judiciary, prosecution and administration; enhanced and developed the skills and training of judicial officers; optimised the use of the limited available resources in an equitable manner; and addressed the imbalances in the former homeland regions. The department communicates through cluster heads.

In terms of the Magistrates Act, 1993 (Act 90 of 1993), all magistrates in South Africa fall outside the ambit of the Public Service. The aim is to strengthen the independence of the judiciary. Although regional courts have a higher penal jurisdiction than magistrate's courts (district courts), an accused person cannot appeal to the Regional Court against the decision of a district court, only to the High Court.

By March 2005, there were 366 magistrate's offices, 50 detached offices, 103 branch courts and 227 periodical courts in South Africa, with 1 767 magistrates.

The department expected to appoint 40 new magistrates in 2005/06 and fill 1 000 vacancies at courts in support of the judiciary and the prosecution.

Criminal jurisdiction

Apart from specific provisions of the Magistrate's Courts Act, 1944 (Act 32 of 1944), or any other Act, jurisdiction regarding sentences imposed by district courts is limited to a period of not more than three years' imprisonment or a fine not exceeding R60 000. A regional court can impose a sentence of not more than 15 years' imprisonment or a fine not exceeding R300 000.

Any person charged with any offence committed within any district or regional division may be tried either by the court of that district or the court of that regional division. Where it is uncertain in which of several jurisdictions an offence has been committed, it may be tried in any of such jurisdictions. Where, by any special provision of law, a magistrate's court has jurisdiction over an offence committed beyond the limits of the district or regional division, the court will not be deprived of such jurisdiction.

A magistrate's court has jurisdiction over all offences except treason, murder and rape. A regional court has jurisdiction over all offences except treason. However, the High Court may try all offences. Depending on the gravity of the offence and circumstances pertaining to the offender, the Director of Public Prosecutions (DPP) decides in which court a matter will be heard and may even decide on a summary trial in the High Court.

Prosecutions are usually summarily disposed of in magistrate's courts, and judgment and sentence passed. The following sentences may, where provided for by law, be passed upon a convicted person:

- imprisonment
- periodical imprisonment
- declaration as a habitual criminal (regional courts and high courts)
- committal to an institution established by law
- a fine with or without imprisonment as an alternative, correctional supervision or a suspended sentence
- declaration as a dangerous criminal (regional courts and high courts)
- a warning or caution
- discharge.

The sentencing of 'petty' offenders to do community service as a condition of suspension, correctional supervision or postponement in appropriate circumstances, has become part of an alternative sentence to imprisonment. Where a court convicts a person of any offence other than one for which any law prescribes a minimum punishment, the court may, at its discretion, postpone the passing of sentence for a period not exceeding five years and release the person convicted on one or more conditions, or pass sentence, but suspend it on certain conditions.

If the conditions of suspension or postponement are not fulfilled, the offender may be arrested and made to serve the sentence. This is done provided that the court may grant an order further suspending the operation of the sentence if offenders prove that circumstances beyond their control, or any other good and sufficient reason, prevented them from complying with the conditions of suspension.

Other criminal courts

In terms of statutory law, jurisdiction may be conferred upon a chief or headman or his deputy to punish an African person who has committed an offence under common law or indigenous law and custom, with the exception of certain serious offences specified in the relevant legislation. The procedure at such trials is in accordance with indigenous law and custom. The jurisdiction conferred upon a chief and a magistrate does not affect the jurisdiction of other courts competent to try criminal cases.

Community courts

In line with President Thabo Mbeki's directive during the State of the Nation Address in February 2005, the establishment of community courts will be accelerated beyond the pilot projects. Unlike normal courts, these operate with flexible hours, like the Hatfield Community Court in Pretoria.

The business community and other formations of civil society continue to contribute significantly to the establishment and sustainability of these courts.

By May 2005, 13 community courts had been established. Four were fully operational and had been formally launched. They were Hatfield, Fezeka (Gugulethu), Mitchell's Plain and Cape Town. Another nine pilot sites commenced in Durban (Point), KwaMashu, Umtata, Bloemfontein, Thohoyandou, Kimberley, Phutaditjaba, Hillbrow and Protea (Lenasia).

By June 2005, 9 685 cases had been finalised since the start of the first Community Court in April 2004, with a 96% conviction rate.

Courts for income tax offenders

In October 1999, the South African Revenue Service

(SARS) opened a criminal courtroom at the Johannesburg Magistrate's Office dedicated to the prosecution of tax offenders. The court deals only with cases concerning failure to submit tax returns or to provide information requested by SARS officials. It does not deal with bigger cases such as tax fraud.

Another SARS court is operating twice a week at the Magistrate's Office in Roodepoort. Discussions to decentralise and expand such courts to the bigger centres in the country have taken place between SARS and the Department of Justice and Constitutional Development. These courts will be established on request of SARS.

Family court pilot project

A specialised family court structure and extended family advocate services are priority areas for the department. The establishment of family courts in South Africa is motivated by three broad aims, namely to:

- provide wide and specialised protection and assistance to the family as the fundamental unit in society
- facilitate access to justice for all in family disputes
- improve the quality and effectiveness of service delivery to citizens who have family law disputes.

The Family Court Blueprint recommended that 17 interim projects be established to strengthen existing pilot projects. The department is implementing these recommendations as part of the overall restructuring of courts.

Municipal courts

Municipal courts are being set up in the larger centres of South Africa in conjunction with municipalities. They are magistrate's courts, but deal only with traffic offences and contraventions of municipal by-laws. They are set up in a partnership agreement in that administrative and infrastructural support is supplied by the municipality, while magistrates are provided by the Magistrate's Commission, with the support of the department.

One court is envisaged per major centre per province.

Equality courts

The role of equality courts, which are to be rolled out countrywide, is to enforce the provisions of the Promotion of Equality and Prevention of Unfair Discrimination Act, 2000 (Act 4 of 2000). The Act outlaws unfair discrimination and allows for the creation of equality courts within magistrate's and high courts, each to be presided over by an equality court presiding officer. The Act further authorises the Minister of Justice and Constitutional Development to appoint the Equality Review Committee to monitor the implementation of the Act's provisions.

By May 2005, 220 equality courts were in operation.

More than 800 magistrates have been trained in equality matters. The training will be extended to include more magistrates to ensure that all equality courts have a sufficient number of trained presiding officers.

Civil jurisdiction

Except when otherwise provided by law, the area of civil jurisdiction of a magistrate's court is the district, subdistrict or area for which the court has been established. South African law, as applied in the Western Cape, is in force on Prince Edward and Marion islands which, for the purpose of the administration of justice, are deemed to be part of the Cape Town magisterial district.

On 1 May 1995, the civil jurisdictional limits of magistrate's courts were increased for both liquid and illiquid claims, from R50 000 and R20 000 respectively, to R100 000. In addition to the considerable increase, the previous distinction between

In 2004/05, district courts managed a conviction rate of 87%.

Regional courts attained their conviction rate target of 70% for the first time since 2000, while the high courts also attained their conviction rate target of 85% for the first time.

jurisdictional limits regarding the different causes of action was abolished. Unless all the parties in a case consent to higher jurisdiction, the jurisdiction of a magistrate's court is limited to cases in which the claim value does not exceed R100 000 where the action arises out of a liquid document or credit agreement, or R50 000 in all other cases.

Small claims courts

The limit of cases involving civil claims is R7 000. By June 2004, there were 152 small claims courts throughout the country. The Commissioner of Small Claims is usually a practising advocate or attorney, a legal academic or other competent person, who offers his/her services free of charge.

Neither the plaintiff nor the defendant may be represented or assisted by counsel at the hearing. The commissioner's decision is final and there is no appeal to a higher court.

By May 2005, a national plan of action to transform and re-engineer small claims courts throughout South Africa had been established to ensure greater access to civil justice. A dynamic partnership with the Swiss Agency for Development and Co-operation, the South African Law Society and tertiary institutions had also been formed to pursue the blueprint for small claims courts.

Other civil courts

An authorised African headman or his deputy may hear and determine civil claims arising from indigenous law and custom, brought before him by an African against another African within his area of jurisdiction.

Courts constituted in this way are commonly known as chief's courts. Litigants have the right to choose whether to institute an action in the chief's court or in a magistrate's court. Proceedings in a chief's court are informal. An appeal against a judgment of a chief's court is heard in a magistrate's court.

Towards transforming partnerships

A key aspect of the transformation of the justice system concerns the department's key strategic partners and stakeholders. The considerable effort put behind transforming prosecution and allied services into a prestigious professional force, in accordance with the Constitution, is paying off.

At the end of February 2005, of the 199 judges, 54% (108) were white, 29% (58) were African, 8% (15) were coloured and 9% (18) were Indian. Overall, 14% were female and 86% male. In terms of the lower court judiciary, as at the end of February 2005, of the 1 767 magistrates, 49% (861) were white, 38% (672) were African, 6% (103) were coloured and 7% (131) were Indian. Overall, 30% were female and 70% male.

A comprehensive human resource development strategy to widen the pool of women and black legal practitioners is expected to be finalised during 2006/07.

The transformation of the judiciary is intimately linked with the transformation of the legal profession and of legal scholarship. The department has already worked in partnership with law schools in transforming the curriculum of the basic law degree to bring it in line with modern best practices. In addition to encouraging law schools to widen access to students from previously disadvantaged communities, these institutions will further be encouraged to forge linkages with leading law firms, with prominent practitioners and with relevant international organisations. This will:

- ensure the relevance of the training they offer to the practical demands of the cutting edge of the profession
- expose students, especially those from previously disadvantaged communities, to the profession and vice versa to facilitate professional training prospects
- engage the legal profession in the evolution of a new legal system that fully expresses the constitutional and cultural aspirations of the new dispensation.

The department will play its part in assisting law graduates through its internship programme. The internship programme will also provide research training to give much-needed assistance to state legal officers, prosecutors, public defenders, the judiciary and the magistracy.

Transformation of the legal profession includes ensuring that judicial services are accessible to the poor, the uneducated and the vulnerable. This entails physical presence in rural areas and in townships, as well as affordable fees and speedy and empathetic services. It also entails active assistance in opening up accessibility of all aspects and levels of the profession to aspirant lawyers, especially to those from previously marginalised backgrounds.

The provision of alternative dispute-resolution mechanisms is another key aspect of transforming justice services. This helps make justice more accessible and more affordable.

The department gives prominence to integrating and modernising justice services through technology. It seeks to evolve simplified, cheaper and faster processes geared for the poor and vulnerable in townships and rural areas. It wants to achieve this in partnership with its customers, with other government departments and with stakeholders.

Capacitating courts and restructuring the court system

The department is implementing its five-year courts turnaround strategy, through the *Re Aga Boswa* ('We are rebuilding') Project to enhance court efficiency. It will complete the restructuring programme for courts. The project also institutionalises a new customer-focused court-management model that ensures that court managers are entrusted with managing courts and that judges and magistrates invest more time in their judicial work. This will result in increased court hours and better-quality judgments.

The rationalisation of high courts and the redemarcation of magisterial districts are also part of the restructuring programme. This entails the rationalisation of service areas of the supreme courts in the former homelands and self-governing states to bring them in line with the new constitutional order. In 2004, the Minister of Justice and Constitutional Development proclaimed new magisterial districts aligned to the new municipal boundaries.

Saturday courts and other additional courts were established to assist with decreasing the backlog of cases. This came to an end in September 2004.

Between 2001 and 2004, Saturday courts finalised 76 836 cases. Twenty additional courts that dealt mainly with sexual offences continued until the end of 2004/05. At least 47 new regional court posts were created and filled, impacting positively on decreasing case backlogs.

The department operates 46 integrated justice court centres throughout the country to improve co-operation between criminal justice role-players in case management. This initiative led to a reduction in the case cycle from 105 to 78 days between 2001 and 2003.

National Prosecuting Authority of South Africa

Section 179(1) of the Constitution established a single NPA, which consists of the National Director of Public Prosecutions (NDPP), who is the head of the NPA, DPPs and prosecutors as determined by an Act of Parliament.

The NPA structure includes the National Prosecuting Services (NPS), the Directorate: Special Operations (DSO), the Witness-Protection Programme, the Asset Forfeiture Unit (AFU) and specialised units such as the Sexual Offences and Community Affairs (SOCA) Unit, the Specialised Commercial Crime Unit, the Priority Crimes Litigation Unit and the Integrity Management Unit.

In terms of the NPA Act, 1998 (Act 32 of 1998), the DSO is a distinct and autonomous directorate.

In May 2005, President Mbeki appointed the Commission of Inquiry into the Mandate and Location of the DSO.

Office of the National Director of Public Prosecutions

The Office of the NDPP is the head office of the NPA. The prosecuting authority vests in the NDPP and the DPP. This authority has been delegated to other members of the NPA. They have the power to:

- institute and conduct criminal proceedings on behalf of the State
- carry out any necessary functions incidental to instituting and conducting such criminal proceedings
- discontinue criminal proceedings.

Directorate: Special Operations

The DSO pursues its objectives and complies with its legislative mandate through the application of numerous legislative tools. In addition to the NPA Act, 1998, other statutes include the Prevention of Organised Crime Act, 1998 (Act 121 of 1998), International Co-operation in Criminal Matters Amendment Act, 1996 (Act 75 of 1996), and the Extradition Amendment Act, 1996 (Act 77 of 1996).

The objective of the DSO is to prioritise, investigate and prosecute particular manifestations of serious and organised crime that threatens the South African democracy and economy.

Consequently, focus areas have been defined to include complex financial crime, syndicated organised crime and high-level corruption affecting business integrity and state administration. The core business of the DSO has been layered by a selection of investigations, where racketeering, money laundering and the forfeiture of the proceeds of crime form the main activities.

The primary client of the DSO is government, which has a fundamental interest in combating and suppressing insidious (and apparently victimless) organised crime. Equally, complainants from the private sector and regulatory bodies (for example the SARS, the Financial Services Board and the South African Reserve Bank) base their expectations on how the DSO deals with financial crimes.

Individual complainants, who are rare, form part of the DSO's client and customer base, when they are affected by large-scale money rackets or organised violence.

The DSO renders services that include the determination, investigation and prosecution of crime to restore justice, enhance public confidence in governance and reduce crime through deterrence.

Products are realised through accurate assessments of crime threats, impact-driven and opportune investigations, successful prosecutions, confiscation of contraband, forfeiture of ill-gotten gains and compensations, where warranted.

In 2004/05, the DSO achieved a conviction rate of 93%, well over the 80% target for the year. Proceeds of crime value for the year ending February 2005 was R255,7 million.

Asset Forfeiture Unit

The AFU was created in 1999 in terms of the Prevention of Organised Crime Act, 1998. The AFU can seize and forfeit property that was bought from the proceeds of crime, or property that has been used to commit a crime.

The AFU has two major strategic objectives, namely to:
- develop the law by taking test cases to court and creating the legal precedents necessary to allow for the effective use of the law
- build capacity to ensure that asset forfeiture is used as widely as possible to make a real impact in the fight against crime.

The use of asset forfeiture to fight crime has been one of government's most important innovations.

Between January and August 2005, the AFU completed more than 132 cases and seized assets worth R184 million. The money is held in a special 'criminal assets recovery account', established under the Prevention of Organised Crime Act, 1998, which empowers the Cabinet to make special disbursements only for law enforcement or victim empowerment.

More than R66 million was paid to victims of financial crime in 2005 – most of it in the form of compensation to 35 defrauded workers.

Special Investigating Unit

The broad legislative mandate of the DSO has been reduced to four crime focus areas to enable the DSO to carry out its mandate successfully:
- organised crime
- organised corruption
- serious and complex financial crime
- racketeering and money laundering.

Sexual Offences and Community Affairs Unit

The SOCA Unit was established in September 1999 through a Presidential proclamation and with a specific mandate that includes:
- formulating policy regarding capacity-building, sensitising and scientific functional training in respect of the prosecution of sexual offences and gender-based violence

- co-ordinating the establishment of special courts for the adjudication of sexual offences and gender-based violence
- facilitating and/or formulating research techniques for the prosecution of sexual offences, gender-based violence, maintenance and child justice
- developing and implementing community awareness programmes and plans for the participation of non-governmental organisations (NGOs) in the processes and procedures aimed at the prevention or containment of sexual offences
- developing training, plans and mechanisms regarding the prosecution of sexual offences, gender-based violence, maintenance and child justice from the President, the Minister of Justice and Constitutional Development and the NDPP.

The unit received two prestigious achievement awards in acknowledgement of the interventions regarding sexual offences management, namely the Impumelelo Innovations Trust Award and the Standard Bank Innovations Award. It was also nominated for a United Nations (UN) award and the head of the unit was appointed as an innovations ambassador.

The Department of Justice and Constitutional Development, in conjunction with the South African Police Service (SAPS) and the departments of social development and of health, have established several Thuthuzela care centres for victims of sexual offences.

The Thuthuzela care centres are 24-hour one-stop service centres where victims have access to all services that include police, counselling, doctors, court preparation and prosecutors. The main objectives of these centres are to eliminate secondary victimisation, reduce case cycle time and increase convictions.

Specially trained police investigators, medical personnel, community volunteers, social workers and prosecutors work together. They ensure that the victim is not further traumatised in the process of reporting the incident, and that the information needed to secure a prosecution and conviction is passed seamlessly from one person to another.

These multi-purpose centres render the services of these departments to communities where these services either do not exist, or do exist but are not easily accessible (especially in rural areas).

The centres are situated at Thembalethu (George, Western Cape), Nsimbi (Umbumbulu, KwaZulu-Natal), Leboeng (Praktiseer, Limpopo), Khutsong (Oberholzer/Carletonville, Gauteng), Tshidilamolomo (Molopo, North West) and Centane (Eastern Cape).

Sexual offences courts

The fight against sexual offences is a national priority. The department is providing facilities at courts where child witnesses, especially in child-abuse cases, can testify in a friendly and secure environment without the risk of being intimidated.

New child-witness rooms are fitted with one-way glass partitions adjacent to the courtrooms. Where it is impossible to provide such rooms in existing buildings, other rooms away from the courts are utilised by providing a closed-circuit television link.

Intermediaries act as buffers against hostile and potentially protracted cross-examinations of child witnesses in an open court, particularly necessary in cases of sexual victimisation. Most intermediaries are social workers by profession, and fulfil their intermediary functions on a part-time basis or as volunteers. Given the specialised nature of the work and the scarcity of the resource, the department has decided to appoint about 53 full-time intermediaries. The Draft Criminal Law (Sexual Offences) Amendment Bill, 2003, aims to provide intermediaries to all vulnerable witnesses in sexual-offence cases, where appropriate. While awaiting the finalisation of the legislation and the workstudy-investigation into the post-class of 'intermediary', the department appointed 53 intermediaries on contract in especially dedicated and additional sexual offences courts.

By May 2005, 54 sexual offences courts, with a conviction rate of 62%, had been established. Twenty-six of the 54 courts are blueprint-compliant and attention is given to provide the infrastructure to make the remainder blueprint-compliant. Permanent positions will be created in conjunction with the Magistrate's Commission to capacitate the approved sexual offences courts.

National Prosecuting Services

The mission of the NPS is to raise the levels of productivity in the NPA and make it efficient and credible.

It has to ensure proper planning of court rolls, prioritisation, proper preparation and arrangement for all cases to be heard, as well as the avoidance of unreasonable delays.

Specialised Commercial Crime Unit

The Pretoria-based Specialised Commercial Crime Unit was established in 1999 as a pilot project to bring specialisation to the investigation and prosecution of commercial crimes emanating from the commercial branches of the SAPS in Pretoria and Johannesburg, respectively.

Three new courts and offices were established in the Johannesburg and Pretoria central business districts for specialised commercial crime cases. Similar courts were created during 2004 in Durban and Cape Town.

The Specialised Commercial Crimes Unit continues to achieve an above-average conviction rate.

Witness-Protection Programme

The Office for Witness Protection falls under the auspices of the NPA. The office is responsible for the protection of witnesses in terms of the Witness Protection Act, 1998 (Act 112 of 1998), and its regulations.

The office aims to:
- combat and reduce crime
- create a culture of civil morality
- enhance public confidence in the office and the criminal justice system (CJS)
- enhance prosecutions through the evidence of vulnerable and intimidated witnesses.

It also provides for placing a person related to the witness under protection at the request of the witness, prospective witness or a person who has given evidence or is required to give evidence in criminal proceedings or before a commission of inquiry.

The programme does not offer incentives such as those offered by the SAPS to witnesses of serious crimes.

Instead, the programme offers sustenance in the form of a food allowance; replacement of salary if employment has been lost; free accommodation, including all municipal services; a clothing allowance; transport; a housing allowance for school-going children; medical expenses, etc.

Legal practitioners

The legal profession is divided into two branches – advocates and attorneys – who are subject to strict ethical codes.

Advocates are organised into Bar associations or societies, one each at the seat of the various divisions of the High Court. The General Council of the Bar of South Africa is the co-ordinating body of the various Bar associations. There is a law society for attorneys in each of the provinces. A practising attorney is *ipso jure* a member of at least one of these societies, which seek to promote the interests of the profession.

The Law Society of South Africa is the co-ordinating body of the various independent law societies.

In terms of the Right of Appearance in Courts Act, 1995 (Act 62 of 1995), advocates can appear in any court, while attorneys may be heard in all of the country's lower courts and can also acquire the right of appearance in the superior courts. Attorneys who wish to represent their clients in the High Court are required to apply to the registrar of a provincial division of the High Court. Such an attorney may also appear in the Constitutional Court. All attorneys who hold an LLB or equivalent degree, or who have at least three years' experience, may acquire the right of audience in the High Court.

The Attorneys Amendment Act, 1993 (Act 115 of 1993), provides for alternative routes for admission as an attorney. One of these routes is that persons who intend to be admitted as attorneys and who have satisfied certain degree requirements prescribed in the Act are exempted from service under articles or clerkship. However, such persons must satisfy the society concerned that they have at least five years' appropriate legal experience.

State law advisers give legal advice to ministers, government departments and provincial administrations, as well as to a number of statutory bodies. In addition, they draft Bills and assist the minister concerned with the passage of Bills through Parliament. They also assist in criminal and constitutional matters.

Other legal practitioners

In terms of the NPA Act, 1998, state advocates and prosecutors are separated from the Public Service in certain respects, notably the determination of salaries.

State attorneys derive their power from the State Attorney Act, 1957 (Act 56 of 1957), and protect the interests of the State in the most cost-effective manner possible. They do this by acting on behalf of the State in legal matters covering a wide spectrum of the law.

State attorneys are involved in the drafting of contracts where the State is a party, and also act on behalf of elected and appointed officials acting in the performance of their duties, e.g. civil and criminal actions instituted against ministers and government officials in their official capacities.

Human rights

Human rights, in terms of Chapter Two (Bill of Rights) of the Constitution, bind all legislative and executive bodies of state at all levels of government.

They apply to all laws, administrative decisions taken, and acts performed during the period in which the Constitution is in force. In terms of the Constitution, every person has basic human rights such as:

- freedom from unfair discrimination
- a right to life.

Since 1994 and in keeping with the cultivation of a human-rights culture, the focus is gradually shifting from an adversarial and retributive CJS to that of a restorative justice system. The Service Charter for Victims of Crime seeks to consolidate the present legal framework in South Africa relating to the rights of and services provided to victims of crime, and to eliminate secondary victimisation in the criminal justice process.

The ultimate goal is victim empowerment through meeting victims' needs, whether material or emotional.

Crime prevention

The Department of Justice and Constitutional Development is one of the five core departments in the Justice, Crime Prevention and Security (JCPS) Cluster that has been tasked with the implementation of the National Crime Prevention Strategy (NCPS). This is government's official strategy to combat, control and prevent crime. (See chapter 17: *Safety, security and defence*.)

The main responsibilities of the department in the implementation of the NCPS are to:

- promote legislation to create an effective CJS
- create an effective prosecution system
- create an effective court system for the adjudication of cases
- co-ordinate and integrate the departmental activities of all role-players involved in crime prevention.

Integrated justice system (IJS)

In recent years, departments within the JCPS Cluster have taken significant steps towards modernising and integrating the CJS. Following government's approval of the NCPS in 1996, the IJS Board was formed in 1997 to integrate the activities of departments in the cluster in a co-ordinated manner.

The IJS, approved in 2002, aims to increase the efficiency and effectiveness of the entire criminal justice process by increasing the probability of successful investigation, prosecution, punishment for priority crimes and ultimately rehabilitation of offenders.

A second version of the IJS was published in May 2003.

Issues that are receiving specific attention include overcrowding of prisons and awaiting-trial prisoner problems (currently dealt with by the Department of Correctional Services), as well as bail, sentencing and plea-bargaining (currently dealt with by the Department of Justice and Constitutional Development).

Government at all levels wants to eliminate duplication of services and programmes. The need for strategic alignment of cluster activities was also raised at a series of other governmental meetings and fora.

Benefits of proper alignment include:
- less duplication of services
- effective use of scarce and limited resources and skills
- joint strategic planning and programmatic approach instead of reacting to problems.

During the latter half of 2002, the IJS Board responded to the challenge and initiated a process to co-ordinate and align activities beyond the IJS. In response to this, a development committee was established in 2003 and mandated to align the shared objectives of cluster departments.

The JCPS has structured itself to focus on two main areas of responsibility, namely operational and developmental issues relating to the justice system, and improved safety and security of citizens.

Modernisation of the justice system

This includes the establishment of proper governance structures, effective monitoring mechanisms based on proper review findings, as well as the integration and automation of the justice system.

Key projects already receiving attention are:

Criminal Justice Review Commission

The 2004 Cabinet Lekgotla identified, as one of government's priorities, the need for a comprehensive audit and review of the CJS. The review is intended to look at how the CJS works and to establish whether processes underway and steps undertaken are feasible and in line with international best practice. By September 2005, the Cabinet had endorsed proposals by the JCPS Cluster to review the CJS.

The review of the CJS will also design a programme for the empowerment of the NPA as a key pillar with respect to the dispensation of social justice in South Africa. A development committee was formed to facilitate cluster co-operation and co-ordination with respect to the IJS.

Integration and automation of the Criminal Justice System

While each department within the JCPS Cluster must have its own Information Technology (IT) Plan to achieve the vision, mission and departmental specific objectives, the IJS Board co-ordinates the broader and shared duty to integrate the information flow throughout the CJS.

Effective and efficient management of cases and persons through the justice chain

This goal focuses specifically on women, children and vulnerable groups, as well as improved court and case administration.

Child justice

Key activities include:
- Implementing the Child Justice Bill, once enacted.
- Trend analyses of children at risk and in custody – improving the situation of children awaiting trial in practice by monitoring their numbers monthly, which has resulted in about 2 500 children monthly awaiting trial in jail in 1998, being reduced to 1 381 in May 2005.
- A plan of action to fast-track the processing of children in the justice system.
- Standardising diversion programmes for children.
- Reviewing 60 places of safety and secure-care facilities.
- Establishing one-stop child justice centres – at least one in each province by 2009. A draft policy has been finalised and draft guidelines are receiving urgent attention.
- Training in restorative justice and family-group conferencing.

Victim-Empowerment Programme (VEP)

This programme aims to improve services rendered to victims of crime.

The NPA has 66 court-preparation officials on contract who provide support to crime victims, especially abused children, in preparing them for court proceedings. By June 2005, 41 077 victims had been prepared for court by the court-preparation officials.

Establishing dedicated courts

Immediate priorities are the establishment of special commercial crimes courts and sexual offences courts. Environmental courts also received attention with two being established at Hermanus and Port Elizabeth respectively to deal with syndicated crimes pertaining to the environment in particular.

On 29 November 2004, the Minister of Justice and Constitutional Development launched the Specialised Commercial Crimes Court in Durban.

Integrated justice case-flow management centres

Case-flow management centres provide an integrated solution to managing cases through the court system, facilitated by IT that allows the monitoring of aspects such as case cycle time and court rolls. The aim is to facilitate co-ordination between the IJS partners around case-flow management, and ensure the development of case-management capacity at court level.

Some 46 case-flow management centres have been established, which led to reductions in case cycle times, increased court hours, increased number of cases finalised, reductions in awaiting-trial prisoners and reductions in outstanding court rolls.

Contributing to interdepartmental and cluster co-ordination and co-operation

The Development Committee is mandated to align and co-ordinate cluster activities across the various departments, with the ultimate aim of improving service delivery, policy co-ordination and planning.

It consists of senior representatives from each of the partner departments participating in the IJS and is chaired by the Department of Justice and Constitutional Development. National Treasury, the judiciary and the Department of Home Affairs are also represented on the Development Committee.

Children awaiting trial

National and provincial action plans to fast-track all children awaiting trial in prisons and police cells, have led to a reduction in children awaiting trial from 2 200 a month, to 1 500 a month since October 2004.

Specific interventions to address the backlog of cases pending trial, include the shifting away from placing children who are in trouble with the law in correctional detention centres. Children awaiting trial will be placed under home-based supervision, in places of safety or in the care of parents or caregivers. Three child justice centres have been established in Port Elizabeth, Bloemfontein and Port Nolloth respectively.

e-Justice Programme

The e-Justice Programme supports the fundamental reforms necessary to establish a more fair, accessible and efficient justice system in South Africa.

The purpose of this programme is to reform and modernise the administration and delivery of justice through re-engineering work processes by using technologies, strengthening strategic planning and management capacity, organisational development and human resource interventions.

The e-Justice Programme has evolved into the Information and Systems Management Programme which has 25 projects in addition to the three main projects, i.e. Court Process Project (CPP), Digital Nervous System (DNS) Project and Financial Administration System (FAS) Project. The e-Justice Programme is funded mainly by the Justice Vote Account, but is supplemented with donor funding from the European Union Commission, the Royal Netherlands Embassy and the Irish Embassy.

By June 2005, the e-Justice Programme had achieved the following:
- successful completion of the DNS I project which provided Information and Communications Technology (ICT) infrastructure, connectivity, ICT equipment (desktops, printers, etc.), e-mail and training to 221 sites
- computer literacy training to an estimated 10 000 users
- the department's Intranet
- successful roll-out of the Guardian's Fund system to all master's offices

- development and implementation of the State Attorneys System.
- development of a monitoring and evaluation framework for the department.

Court Process Project

The CPP, which was initiated in 2000, seeks to re-engineer the way in which court services are delivered. It is aimed at providing courts with the necessary tools to deal with caseloads and general management in a more effective manner. This project also links, for the first time, the police, prosecutors, courts, prisons and social-welfare facilities at selected pilot sites. It incorporates the flow of processes that affect departments in the IJS, namely the departments of safety and security, of correctional services, of social development and of justice and constitutional development and the NPA.

Its benefits include:
- improved administration and tracking of dockets and case files
- reduced delays leading up to trials
- reduced duplication of data entry
- improved access to information
- timeous notification of events
- verification of identities
- reduced number of lost case dockets
- reduced postponement of cases due to misplaced files/exhibits
- improved administration of prisoner admissions and releases
- improved docket/exhibit administration.

Financial Administration System

The FAS is tasked with automating and administering trust accounts in the magistrate's courts, the State Attorneys' offices and the Guardian's Fund in the master's offices. The FAS comprises the following projects:
- The Guardian's Fund administers monies kept in trust for persons including minors, state patients, unborn heirs, and persons having usufructuary, fiduciary or fideicommissary interests.
- The Justice Deposit Account System administers monies received at court in lieu of maintenance,

bail, admission of guilt, civil cases, contributions, court cases and estates.
- The State Attorneys' System assists state attorneys with registering and administering case files, collecting money and administering payments to applicable parties, and the handling of litigation processes.
- The Masters' Administration System for Estates and Insolvencies enables officials to manage cases and track records. It has also resulted in better service delivery through quick and efficient response times to queries.

Legislative and constitutional development

The Legislative and Constitutional Development Branch of the Department of Justice and Constitutional Development is responsible for promoting, maintaining and developing the Constitution and its values by researching, developing and advancing appropriate legislation.

It includes research activities of the South African Law Reform Commission (SALRC), which involve extensive reviews of wide areas of law and legal practice.

The legislative development component of the branch is, among other things, responsible for researching, developing and promoting appropriate legislation that has a bearing on the line functions of the department.

The constitutional development component of the unit is also responsible for promoting the independence and effectiveness of chapter 9 institutions and administering the Constitution, which includes monitoring the implementation of the Constitution and the Bill of Rights.

Between 1994 and 2004, the department promoted more than 108 Bills. The department's legislative programme was dominated by three main themes, namely, legislation to give effect to the spirit of the constitutional dispensation, legislation to address the crime problem prevailing in South Africa, and legal reform.

By May 2005, legislation to repeal the Black Administration Act, 1927 (Act 8 of 1927), and to bring the Customary Law of Succession in line with the Constitution was being finalised.

During 2005, a draft Bill intended to address the concerns raised by the Constitutional Court in the case involving the attachment of low-cost housing, was also being finalised.

Legislation

Some important legislation that is being promoted by the department includes:

Child Justice Bill

The proposed Child Justice Bill will create a new system for dealing with children in trouble with the law.

By May 2005, the Bill had been redrafted and submitted to Parliament.

Superior Courts Bill

The Bill is intended to rationalise the structure and functioning of South Africa's superior courts.

Compulsory HIV-Testing of Alleged Sexual Offenders Bill

The purpose of the Bill is to provide a speedy and uncomplicated mechanism whereby a victim of a sexual offence can apply to have the alleged offender tested for HIV and have the test results disclosed to the victim.

Criminal Law (Sexual Offences) Amendment Bill

The Criminal Law (Sexual Offences) Bill emanates from an investigation by the SALRC and proposes a comprehensive review of existing legislation dealing with sexual offences. It aims to bring this area of law into line with the new constitutional dispensation and to provide greater protection to victims of sexual offences.

Maintenance Act, 1998 and the Domestic Violence Act, 1998

The department implemented the Maintenance Act, 1998 (Act 99 of 1998), and the Domestic Violence Act, 1998 (Act 116 of 1998), in November 1999 to improve the lives of vulnerable women and children.

By mid-2005, maintenance investigators had been appointed to 140 maintenance courts. Maintenance clerks were also appointed in hot-spot courts. Constant monitoring of the situation on ground level ensures that service delivery and access to justice improves for all vulnerable groups, especially children, women, people with disabilities, the elderly and victims of crime.

Promotion of Access to Information Act, 2000

The Promotion of Access to Information Act, 2000 (Act 2 of 2000), grants the right of access to information referred to in Section 32 of the Constitution.

The Act generally promotes the transparency, accountability and effective governance of all public and private bodies.

Promotion of Administrative Justice Act, 2000

The Promotion of Administrative Justice Act, 2000 (Act 3 of 2000), is aimed at the provision of lawful, reasonable and procedurally fair administrative action as contemplated in Section 33 of the Constitution.

Promotion of Equality and Prevention of Unfair Discrimination Act, 2000

The objectives of the Promotion of Equality and Prevention of Unfair Discrimination Act, 2000 include prevention, prohibition and progressive eradication of unfair discrimination as well as redress for unfair discrimination and the promotion of equality.

Prevention and Combating of Corrupt Activities Act, 2004

The Prevention and Combating of Corrupt Activities Act, 2004 (Act 12 of 2004), provides for the strengthening of measures to prevent and combat corruption and corrupt activites.

State Legal Services

State Legal Services provides government with legal services and facilitates constitutional amendments through three subprogrammes.

State Legal Services provides for the work of the State Attorney and state law advisers. The former acts as attorney, notary and conveyancer for government.

State law advisers provide legal opinions, scrutinise and amend international agreements, draft legislation and attend relevant parliamentary portfolio committees as legal advisers for all national departments. The component hosts the National Forum Against Racism and facilitates South Africa's participation in the International Court for Criminal Justice.

Plans to establish a constitutional litigation unit in the department are at an advanced stage.

International affairs

The functions of the Directorate: International Affairs in the Department of Justice and Constitutional Development are mainly to identify and research legal questions that relate to matters pertaining to the administration of justice between South Africa and other states.

The directorate is involved in direct liaison and negotiations at administrative and technical levels with foreign states to promote international legal co-operation, and for the possible conclusion of extradition and mutual legal-assistance agreements.

The directorate also aims to establish greater uniformity between the legal systems of southern African states, especially the Southern African Development Community (SADC). It thus promotes and establishes an efficient administration of justice in the southern African region.

The directorate co-ordinates human-rights issues at international level under the auspices of the UN and the African Union (AU).

The functions of the directorate are divided into six broad categories:
- regular liaison with SADC states
- co-ordinating all Commonwealth matters pertaining to the administration of justice
- interacting with other international bodies, such as the UN, the Hague Conference and the International Institute for the Unification of Private Law
- interacting with foreign states outside the SADC region

- negotiating extradition and mutual legal-assistance agreements with other countries
- preparing Cabinet and Parliament documentation for the ratification of human-rights treaties, including report-writing.

International Criminal Court (ICC)

As required by the Rome Statute of the ICC, South Africa has promulgated the Implementation of the Rome Statute of the ICC Act, 2002 (Act 27 of 2002).

This Act provides for a framework to:
- ensure the effective implementation of the Rome Statute of the ICC in South Africa
- ensure that South Africa conforms with the obligations set out in the statute
- address the crime of genocide, crimes against humanity, and war crimes
- address the prosecution in South African courts of persons accused of having committed the said crimes in South Africa and beyond the borders of the country in certain circumstances
- deal with the arrest of certain persons accused of having committed the said crimes and their surrender to the ICC in certain circumstances
- enhance co-operation by South Africa with the ICC.

Legal structures

Masters of the High Court

The Masters of the High Court are involved with the administration of justice in estates of deceased persons and those declared insolvent, the liquidation of companies and close corporations, and the registration of trusts.

Each year, the value of estates under the supervision of the masters' offices amounts to about R18 billion. This includes about R2,5 billion in the Guardians' Fund.

The key statutory functions of the masters' offices are to:
- control the administration of deceased and curatorship estates
- control the administration of insolvent estates and the liquidation of companies and close corporations

- control the registration and administration of both testamentary and *inter vivos* trusts
- manage the Guardian's Fund, which is entrusted with the funds of minors, mentally challenged persons, unknown and/or absent heirs, and creditors for administration on their behalf
- assess estate duty and certain functions with regard thereto
- accept and take custodianship of wills in deceased estates
- act as an office of record.

Deceased estates

On 15 October 2004, the Constitutional Court declared Section 23 and regulations of the Black Administration Act, 1927 unconstitutional.

By mid-2005, legislation to repeal the Black Administration Act, 1927 was being finalised.

This decision implied that the Master of the High Court takes over the powers of supervision in all deceased estates, and that all estates have to be administered in terms of the Administration of Estates Act, 1965 (Act 66 of 1965), as amended. All intestate estates must be administered in terms of the Intestate Succession Act, 1987 (Act 81 of 1987), as amended.

This will ensure that all South Africans are treated equally, and that the dignity of each person is respected.

The institutional structures are:
- The Chief Master heads the national office and is responsible for co-ordinating all the activities of the masters' offices.
- There are 14 masters' offices: Bisho, Bloemfontein, Cape Town, Durban, Grahamstown, Johannesburg, Kimberley, Mafikeng, Polokwane, Port Elizabeth, Pietermaritzburg, Pretoria, Thohoyandou and Umtata.
- Suboffices are located in places where the High Court does not have a seat, but workloads require the presence of at least one assistant master.
- At service points, officials attached to the Branch: Court Services deliver services on behalf of, and under the direction of, the master. Each magistrate's court is a service point. Each ser-

vice point has at least one designated official, who is the office manager or a person of equal rank. They only appoint masters' representatives in intestate estates of R50 000 or less, in terms of Section 18(3) of the Administration of Estates Amended Act, 2002 (Act 49 of 2002).

Curatorships

On 26 December 2004, the Mental Healthcare Act, 2002 (Act 17 of 2002), came into operation recalling the Mental Health Act, 1973 (Act 18 of 1973).

The new Act provides that where a person falls within the ambit of this Act, the master can appoint an administrator to handle the affairs of the person. The administrator, in this instance, replaces the appointment of a curator, as done in the past.

In terms of the Prevention of Organised Crime Act, 1998, the master also appoints curators in these estates to administer the assets of persons and legal entities attached by the AFU, in terms of a court order.

Guardian's Fund

The fund holds and administers funds which are paid to the master on behalf of various persons known or unknown. These include minors, persons incapable of managing their own affairs, unborn heirs and missing or absent persons or persons having an interest in the money of an usufructuary, fiduciary or fideicommissary nature.

The money in the Guardian's Fund is invested with the Public Investment Commission and audited annually. Interest is calculated on a monthly basis at a rate per year determined from time to time by the Minister of Finance. The interest is compounded annually at 31 March. Interest is paid for a period from a month after receipt up to five years after it has become claimable, unless it is legally claimed before such expiration.

After a lapse of five years after the money has become claimable, the master pays the unclaimed money to the Receiver of Revenue Payment Register. This does not mean that the owner of the money cannot claim the money from the Guardian's Fund. However, after a lapse of 30 years after the money has become claimable, the money is forfeit-

434

ed to the State. Every year in September, the master advertises unclaimed amounts in the *Government Gazette*.

Rules Board for Courts of Law

The rules board is a statutory body empowered to make or amend rules for high courts, the Supreme Court of Appeal and the lower courts.

It also develops rules and court procedures to ensure a speedy, inexpensive civil justice system, which is in harmony with the Constitution and technological developments, and accessible to all South Africans.

Justice College

The Justice College provides vocational training to all officials of the Department of Justice and Constitutional Development. It also presents training to autonomous professions such as magistrates and prosecutors.

Office of the Family Advocate

The Office of the Family Advocate functions in terms of the Mediation in Certain Divorce Matters Act, 1987 (Act 24 of 1987).

The family advocate, assisted by family counsellors, reports to the court and makes recommendations. These serve the best interest of children in cases where there is litigation relating to children in divorce actions or applications for the variation of existing divorce orders.

Inquiries take place at the request of the court, one or both parties to the litigation, or on the initiative of the family advocate, in which case authorisation of the court must be obtained.

Family advocates operate in the provincial and local divisions of the High Court.

The Hague Convention on the Civil Aspects of International Child Abduction Act, 1996 (Act 72 of 1996), came into effect in October 1997 and the Natural Fathers of Children Born out of Wedlock Act, 1997 (Act 86 of 1997), in September 1998. The promulgation of these Acts extended the service delivery of the Office of the Family Advocate countrywide.

The Office of the Family Advocate provides support services for the family court pilot project. Most offices are involved in mediation training for a large contingent of social workers and other mental-health professionals.

The Office of the Family Advocate co-ordinates community-outreach programmes to assist children involved in family disputes.

The Children's Bill provides for the extension of the role of the family advocate to areas such as mediation and the facilitation of family-group conferences.

Legal Aid Board

The Legal Aid Board has completed the roll-out of a national infrastructure of four regional offices, 57 justice centres and 35 satellite offices. They employ more than 1 500 staff of whom more than 1 000 are legal professionals.

The board continues to provide legal assistance to the indigent, in accordance with the Constitution and other legislative requirements. This is carried out through a system of in-house outsourcing to private lawyers (a system of judicare) and co-operation partners.

With its national infrastructure in place, the board focuses on improving access to clients and communities, and on improving the quality of delivery of legal services.

Public Protector

The Public Protector receives and investigates complaints from the public against government or its officials, and has the power to recommend corrective action and to issue reports.

The Public Protector's services are free and available to everyone.

Complainants' names are kept confidential as far as possible.

The President appoints the Public Protector on recommendation of the National Assembly and in terms of the Constitution, for a non-renewable period of seven years.

The Public Protector is subject only to the Constitution and the law, and functions independently from government and any political party.

No person or organ of state may interfere with the functioning of the Public Protector.

The Public Protector has the power to report a matter to Parliament, who will debate on it and ensure that the Public Protector's recommendations are followed.

Magistrate's Commission

The Magistrate's Commission ensures that the appointment, promotion, transfer or discharge of, or disciplinary steps against, judicial officers in the lower courts take place without favour or prejudice, and that the applicable laws and administrative directions in connection with such actions are applied uniformly and correctly.

The commission also attends to grievances, complaints and misconduct investigations against magistrates. It advises the minister on matters such as the appointment of magistrates, promotions, salaries and legislation.

The commission has established committees to deal with appointments and promotions; misconduct, disciplinary inquiries and incapacity; grievances; salary and service conditions; and the training of magistrates.

South African Law Reform Commission

The SALRC is an independent statutory body, established by the SALRC Act, 1973 (Act 19 of 1973). The SALRC and its secretariat are responsible for research in respect of the law of South Africa with a view to advising government on the development, improvement, modernisation and reform of the law of South Africa in all its facets by performing, among others, the following functions:

- executing the law-reform programme of the SALRC by conducting legal research, including legal comparative research, by developing proposals for law reform and, where appropriate, by promoting uniformity in the law
- preparing legislative proposals
- establishing a permanent, simplified, coherent and generally accessible statute book, complying with the principles of the Constitution
- consolidating or codifying any branch of the law
- assisting parliamentary committees during the

deliberation of draft legislation emanating from the SALRC
- advising ministers and state departments on proposed legislation and recommendations of the SALRC.

Judicial Service Commission (JSC)

In terms of the Constitution, the Chief Justice and the Deputy Chief Justice, and the President and Deputy President of the Supreme Court of Appeal are appointed by the President after consulting with the JSC. Other judges are appointed by the President on the advice of the JSC.

In the case of the Chief Justice and the Deputy Chief Justice, the leaders of parties represented in the National Assembly are also consulted.

The JSC was established in terms of Section 178 of the Constitution to perform this function.

It also advises government on any matters relating to the judiciary or the administration of justice.

When appointments have to be made, the commission gives public notice of the vacancies that exist and calls for nominations.

Suitable candidates are short-listed by the JSC and invited for interviews. Professional bodies and members of the public are afforded the opportunity to comment before the interviews or make representations concerning the candidates to the commission.

The JSC has determined criteria and guidelines for appointments, which have been made public.

The interviews are conducted as public hearings and may be attended by anyone who wishes to do so. Following the interviews, the JSC deliberates and makes its decisions in private. Its recommendations are communicated to the President, who then makes the appointments.

South African Human Rights Commission

In terms of Section 184(1) of South Africa's Constitution, the SAHRC must:
- promote respect for human rights and a culture of human rights
- promote the protection, development and attainment of human rights

- monitor and assess the observance of human rights in South Africa.

The work of the commission is divided into the following programmes:

- Strategic Management and Support Services
- Commissioners
- Legal Services
- Research and Documentation
- Education and Training
- Provincial Offices.

Strategic Management and Support Services ensures that the operations of the commission comply with constitutional and legislative imperatives, guides the functioning of the commission to align with its strategic objectives and national priorities, and positions the commission favourably within the human-rights field regionally, nationally and internationally.

Commissioners raise the profile of the SAHRC, make strategic interventions, provide leadership in relation to human-rights issues and contribute to the development of human-rights-related and organisational policy.

The commission plays a special role in the development of human rights in Africa through work with the relevant organs of the SADC, AU and the African Commission on Human and People's Rights. It is a member of the International Co-ordinating Committee of African National Human Rights Institutions, hosts the Secretariat of the committee and has been instrumental in setting up other national human-rights institutions in Africa.

Legal Services investigates individual and systemic human-rights violations and provides appropriate redress. Some 12 124 individual complaints of human-rights violations were received in 2004/05. Mediations, decisions, findings and opinions of the commission and litigation are used to secure redress for individuals and communities.

An important mechanism through which the commission addresses systemic violations of human rights is through the convening of public inquiries and hearings.

Research and Documentation monitors and assesses the observance of human rights, in particular economic and social rights, the right to equality and the right of access to information. In addition, the programme monitors and intervenes in the legislative process and liaises with Parliament. It maintains a leading human-rights library and documentation centre.

The commission is mandated by the South African Constitution to request annual reports from government on progress made in the realisation of economic and social rights. This function is carried out by the Economic and Social Rights Unit.

The Promotion of Equality and Prevention of Unfair Discrimination Act, 2000 gives the commission specific responsibilities in addition to its overall mandate to secure the right to equality. The Equality Unit functions as the focal point for the commission's activities in this area. The unit monitors equality courts and contributes to legislative developments and reform. Once the promotional aspect of the Act comes into place, the programme will receive and analyse equality plans, request regular reports relating to the number of cases adjudicated by the equality courts, and submit an annual report to Parliament.

The Promotion of Access to Information Act, 2000 places specific obligations on the commission. It co-ordinates implementation in this arena, including monitoring and research, making recommendations for the improvement and development of the Act, and providing an annual report to Parliament.

Education and Training conducts educational interventions on human rights and the commission's focus areas, conducts community outreach and awareness programmes, develops human-rights education and training material, and ensures the institutionalisation of human-rights education.

Public outreach activities within the commission focus on poverty-stricken communities in rural and peri-urban areas. The commission has developed the Omnibus Outreach Programme. The omnibus is a multifaceted tool for engaging with communities, encompassing a large range of educational interventions ranging from workshops, seminars, presentations, site visits and walkabouts to widespread campaigns, events and advocacy initiatives.

SAHRA's head office is based in Gauteng. It also has provincial offices in all provinces except North West, which is served by the adjacent offices.

Provincial offices implement the programmes of the commission at provincial and local level.

National Centre for Human-Rights Education and Training (NACHRET)

The NACHRET was established in April 2000. The centre provides a platform for debate on human-rights issues aimed at enhancing an understanding of these issues and practices. The centre also provides training and builds capacity both in South Africa and on the African continent regarding human-rights themes, challenges and issues.

Commission on Gender Equality

Chapter 9 of the Constitution provides for the establishment of the CGE. Section 187 of the Constitution specifically grants the CGE powers to promote respect for, and to protect, develop and attain gender equality. The composition, functions and objectives of the CGE are outlined in the CGE Act, 1996 (Act 39 of 1996).

The CGE is responsible for:
- gathering information and conducting education on gender equality and the human rights of women
- monitoring and evaluating the policies and practices of state organs, statutory and public bodies, as well as the private sector, to promote gender equality
- evaluating Acts in force, or Acts proposed by Parliament, affecting or likely to affect gender-related rights and women's human rights
- investigating any gender-related complaints received or on its own initiative
- liaising with institutions, bodies or authorities with similar objectives
- conducting research to further the objectives of the CGE.

The CGE works in partnership with various civil-society structures and other organisations with similar objectives.

Most complaints are handled telephonically or are referred. Others are conveyed personally for face-to-face intervention and are later referred to relevant institutions. By the end of March 2005, the CGE had handled 429 cases. Of these, 189 were maintenance cases; 121 gender-based violence; 25 labour; eight culture, tradition and religion; 16 social security; 15 inheritance; 26 court processes; and 29 sexual harassment.

The CGE supports strategic interventions in litigation, with the aim of encouraging law reform.

It also monitors most Bills that are introduced in Parliament to ensure that gender sensitivity is considered and that the rights of women are integrated.

Truth and Reconciliation Commission (TRC)

The TRC was established in terms of the Promotion of National Unity and Reconciliation Act, 1995 (Act 34 of 1995), to help deal with human-rights abuses that were perpetrated under South Africa's apartheid government.

Some 22 000 individuals or their surviving family members appeared before the commission. Of these, 19 000 required urgent reparations, and virtually all of them, where the necessary information was available, were attended to as proposed by the TRC with regard to interim reparations.

President's Fund

In 2003, government announced the creation of the President's Fund, from which victims of apartheid, as declared by the TRC, would be granted a once-off R30 000 as part of the reparations.

Correctional services

The Department of Correctional Services contributes towards maintaining and protecting a just, peaceful and safe society by enforcing court-imposed sentences and detaining inmates in safe custody while maintaining their human dignity.

It is also responsible for facilitating the correction of offending behaviour and the general development of all offenders as part of their rehabilitation, including those subject to community corrections.

In pursuing these objectives, the department has developed the *White Paper on Corrections* that embodies its long-term strategic policy and operational framework. These recognise corrections as a societal responsibility and puts rehabilitation at the centre of all the department's activities.

The White Paper on Corrections, which was approved by Cabinet in February 2005, is the culmination of a protracted process that included extensive consultations, both within the organisation and in the external environment.

The department has identified 36 correctional centres countrywide for inclusion in a White Paper implementation project. These centres will be known as centres of excellence. The project aims to develop best practice in the implementation of the White Paper under ideal, well-managed, and well-resourced circumstances and roll it out to other correctional centres. The intervention programmes which are designed to address the offending behaviour of individual inmates will also be rolled out at the centres of excellence.

The White Paper roll-out is a deliberate effort aimed to promote partnership, ownership and participation from correctional staff, NGOs, government departments, individuals and collectives.

The key to the realisation of the objectives of the White Paper is the department's ability to ensure a secure, safe and enabling environment within correctional centres and the transformation of its staff members from prison warders to correctional officials.

To this end, the department has initiated intensive training of junior and middle managers to empower them to successfully carry out their responsibilities.

The *White Paper on Corrections* recognises the role of the family and community institutions in correcting offending behaviour among its own members before it turns into criminal activities that lead to imprisonment.

The ultimate solution to crime and to the severe overcrowding of correctional centres lies in the prevention of criminal activity. The responsibility for this lies primarily within the family unit and community institutions.

Budget and scope of work

During 2004/05, the budget allocation for the Department of Correctional Services was spent as follows:

- R2,707 billion on security
- R503 million on corrections
- R765 million on care
- R1,622 billion on facilities
- R318 million on after-care
- R407 million on development
- R2,707 billion on administration.

By 31 January 2005, the department had a staff complement of 33 076, with 187 446 offenders incarcerated in 238 correctional centres countrywide. By 31 October 2004, there were 50 220 parolees and 26 918 probationers within the system of community corrections.

Strategies have been adopted to balance the need for security with the need for conditions that are conducive to rehabilitation. The Gearing Department of Correctional Services for Rehabilitation Project was introduced in 2002/03. It involved a substantial review of rehabilitation, and identified key service-delivery areas: corrections, development, security, care, facilities and after-care.

This comprehensive approach entails all aspects of the department's core business. It requires developing new policy regarding the types of correction programmes offered and the recruitment and training of prison personnel.

In line with the Vienna Declaration on Crime and Justice, the department has embraced the restorative-justice approach aimed at reducing crime and promoting healing between offenders, victims and the community.

The process to conduct public education campaigns has begun to raise awareness of the implementation of restorative-justice programmes and policies. This project aims to facilitate the mediation process between crime victims and offenders in an attempt to bring about restitution and reparation. This will be achieved through restorative-justice and victim-empowerment programmes.

The department has implemented a seven-day-week regime to save money for the recruitment of more correctional officials. Weekend work was previously regarded as overtime, costing the department R916 million in 2004/05 alone.

The department plans to recruit 8 311 officials over a three-year period. About R270 million was set aside for the recruitment of 3 000 new members in 2005/06.

Offender accommodation

The department strives to provide adequate prison accommodation that complies with accepted standards. Offenders are housed in 238 prisons countrywide, including:

- eight correctional centres for female offenders only
- 13 youth correctional facilities
- 141 correctional centres for male offenders only
- 72 correctional centres for both male and female offenders
- four temporarily inactive correctional centres (closed down for renovations).

In prisons where male, female and juvenile offenders are accommodated, female and juvenile offenders are housed in separate designated sections.

Overcrowding in prisons

The problem of prison overcrowding remains the most important influence on the department's budget and performance, especially in relation to rehabilitation.

By 31 January 2005, South Africa's correctional centres collectively housed 187 446 inmates, while accommodation was available for only 113 825. This means that the general overcrowding was in the region of 164%. Of the total population, 52 326 inmates were unsentenced.

The daily average prisoner population is projected to increase to 195 300 in 2005/06 and 202 400 in 2006/07.

To address these challenges, the department is implementing a number of strategies:

- The building and staffing of new correctional centres, designed cost-effectively.
- The finalisation of prison procurement models.
- The Department of Correctional Services is co-operating with other departments in the IJS, notably the Department of Justice and Constitutional Development, on a range of projects to reduce the number of prisoners.
- The department is also promoting awareness in the IJS of alternative sentencing options and diversion programmes.

- The JCPS Cluster Task Team on Overcrowding, established at the end of 2002, monitors the CJS to identify and eliminate blockages that result in increased prisoner numbers.
- Since 1994, 10 new prisons have been constructed and two rebuilt to address the problem of overcrowding. Two of the 10 prisons are public-private partnership prisons. They have a combined capacity of 5 952.

Four new-generation prisons in Kimberley, Klerksdorp, Leeuwkop and Nigel are expected to be completed by April 2007. Similar facilities are expected to be built in the Eastern Cape, Western Cape, KwaZulu-Natal and Limpopo. All eight prisons will have 3 000 beds each.

Over the next three years, accommodation capacity in correctional services is expected to increase by 12 000 beds.

Safety and security

One of the core objectives of the department is to ensure that every correctional centre has a secure environment with a correcting influence. This does not only refer to the prevention of escapes from custody but also to the creation and maintenance of an environment in which there is a significantly low prevalence or absence of inmate abuse, violence, corruption and negligence.

The department has put in place various measures aimed at combating escapes. These include the optimal utilisation of existing security aids and equipment, continued evaluation of security directives, upgrading of personnel training, disciplinary action against negligent personnel, rewarding

A permanent exhibition in the women's jail and the new head offices of the Commission on Gender Equality at Constitution Hill was launched on 2 August 2005.

The exhibition in the women's jail, once a place of incarceration and oppression of women, consists of permanent and temporary displays informed by generations of women who fought for their basic human and gender rights.

offenders who report or warn of planned escapes, and the installation of electronic fences and X-ray scanners in high-risk prisons.

Through the implementation of national and regional escape prevention strategies, the department succeeded in reducing the number of escapes from 195 in 2003/04 to 171 in 2004/05.

To protect society by preventing escapes and supervising offenders, expenditure increased to R2,7 billion in 2004/05, and is expected to reach R4,2 billion by 2007/08.

The bulk of the increase is linked to the initial increase in operating costs associated with appointing additional personnel to implement the seven-day working week.

The department is upgrading and intensifying the use of equipment to increase the level of security in prisons. This will ensure the protection of offenders, officials and the public. The department has created a culture of security awareness among its staff. All managers are involved in monitoring and ensuring adherence to security policies and procedures, through strict supervision, control mechanisms and disciplinary action against negligent officials.

From 2005/06, special emphasis will be placed on measures to prevent dangerous weapons and firearms from entering correctional facilities.

To achieve this, R80 million was expected to be spent in 2005 on the installation of advanced technological equipment at the 36 centres of excellence and 30 other identified high-risk centres.

Equipment to be installed includes items such as closed-circuit television cameras, biometric readers and scanning devices. In addition, the National Security Plan and minimum security standards for correctional centres were expected to be implemented during 2005.

In November 2004, the Minister of Correctional Services, Mr Ngconde Balfour, launched South Africa's inmate tracking system at the Durban Westville Correctional Centre.

The pilot project has since been extended to the Johannesburg Medium A Correctional Centre. The main functions of the project are to accurately identify awaiting-trial detainees (ATDs), to decrease the time spent in processing ATDs for court appearances and visits, and to monitor the movements of ATDs through a personal tracking device.

The system has the added advantage of being able to pinpoint the whereabouts of inmates at the time of a transgression being committed inside the monitored area, which should ease investigative work.

The pilot project has assisted in identifying weaknesses in the system, especially regarding the tracking device that is attached to the wrists of ATDs. However, the tracking system has greatly benefited identifying ATDs on a daily basis through the use of the biometric fingerprint reader and the electronic facial photograph facility. The pilot project at Johannesburg has yielded positive results, but consideration will only be given to extending its use after the completion of an intensive evaluation of the current pilot projects.

Classification

Offenders undergo safe-custody classification upon admission to determine the level of security required to detain them.

Offenders are classified into minimum, medium or maximum custodial categories. Variables taken into account include the type of crime committed, the length of the sentence and previous convictions. The safe-custody classification of all offenders is reviewed regularly, and if their behaviour, or any other aspect affecting their security risk, justifies it, reclassification takes place.

Categories

There are five categories of offenders in South African prisons, namely:

- unsentenced offenders (mainly offenders standing trial on a charge and detained in prison pending the conclusion of the judicial process)
- short-term offenders (offenders serving a sentence of less than two years)
- long-term offenders (offenders serving sentences of two years and longer)
- unsentenced children/juveniles and youths between the ages of 14 and 25

- sentenced children/juveniles and youths between the ages of 14 and 25.

Young offenders

In terms of the Constitution, a child is a person under the age of 18 years. The Department of Correctional Services regards a person between the ages of 14 and 25 years as a youth. The department is responsible for the detention, treatment and development of sentenced juveniles.

Section 7(2)(c) of the Correctional Services Act, 1998 (Act 111 of 1998), stipulates that children must be kept separate from adult offenders and in accommodation appropriate to their age, as young offenders are predisposed to negative influence.

The aim of this separation is the provision of distinctive custodial, development and treatment programmes, as well as spiritual care, in an environment conducive to the care, development and motivation of youths to participate and to develop their potential.

The nature of serious offences committed or allegedly committed by children under the age of 18 who were awaiting trial or sentenced is alarming. A breakdown of the nature of the crimes of those in custody on 31 January 2005 revealed that there were 604 economic-related offences, 804 aggressive offences and 230 sexual offences. A further 93 were detained for drug-related and other offences.

Of the crimes committed by 57 760 sentenced youths between the ages of 18 and 25, 29 103 were aggressive, 17 239 economical, 7 466 sexual, and 3 952 drug-related and other types of offences.

There are 13 youth correctional facilities in the country, namely Hawequa, Brandvlei, Drakenstein Medium B and Pollsmoor Medium A (Western Cape); Leeuwkop, Emthonjeni and Boksburg (Gauteng); Rustenburg (North West); Durban and Ekuseni (KwaZulu-Natal); Groenpunt and Kroonstad (Free State); and Barberton Prison (Mpumalanga).

The development and support of youth offenders form an essential part of their incarceration. The aim of rendering professional services (education, reskilling, learning a trade, moral and spiritual enlightenment, and personal development) is to rehabilitate youth offenders, contribute towards their behavioural change, and prepare them for their reintegration into the community.

The focus is on the promotion and development of leadership qualities. A holistic approach is followed in which:

- young offenders are motivated to actively participate in their own development and the realisation of their potential
- a culture and atmosphere of development prevails
- sound discipline and co-operation between personnel and offenders, and among offenders, are fostered and maintained.

Mother-and-child units

Mother-and-child units have been established in eight female correctional centres nationally. By 31 March 2005, there were 173 infants under the age of five in correctional centres with their mothers. Policy on such infants clearly stipulates that mothers and children are kept in a separate unit within the correctional centre, where the surroundings and facilities are complementary to the sound physical, social and mental care and development of children.

The policy also stipulates that the admission of an infant with a mother is permitted only if no other suitable accommodation and care are available at that stage, and that it should be regarded as a temporary measure.

The right of the mother to have her child with her during admission promotes a positive relationship between mother and child. The policy emphasises that the mother should be taught good child-care practices for her own self-esteem and self-confidence, and for the benefit of the child.

The privilege system

The main objectives of the privilege system are to encourage offenders to display good behaviour, engender a sense of responsibility in them, and ensure their interest and co-operation in treatment programmes.

The system consists of primary and secondary privileges. Primary privileges are aimed at the retention, maintenance or furthering of family ties to, among other things, facilitate reintegration into the community. These privileges are divided into A, B and C groups. The entry level for all new admissions is the B group and, depending on behaviour, an offender may be promoted or demoted to either the A or the C privilege group.

Secondary privileges are aimed at leisure-time activities such as participation in sport and watching television. No sentenced offenders are allowed to receive food from outside prison or to use private electrical appliances.

Healthcare services

The healthcare of offenders is regarded as an important responsibility of the department. It includes nutrition, personal care, environmental hygiene and pharmaceutical services. The department endorses the fundamental rights and privileges of all offenders.

In accordance with the Correctional Services Act, 1998, an independent judicial inspectorate regularly inspects all prisons and reports on their conditions and the treatment of offenders.

The policy and administrative framework for the maintenance of an adequate, affordable and comprehensive healthcare service is based on the principles of primary healthcare (PHC). The service includes mental, dental and reproductive health, supplementary healthcare, health-promotion management of communicable diseases (including HIV, AIDS and sexually transmitted infections [STIs]) and referrals where necessary, through the acknowledgement of national and international norms and standards, within the limited available resources.

The approach to healthcare in South Africa's correctional facilities focuses on:
- the strict pursuance of ethical codes by health professionals
- regular health-quality inspections
- strict compliance with rules of confidentiality and privacy regarding the medical records of patients
- the continuous evaluation and upgrading of medical emergency services.

The Department of Correctional Services provides a system in which offenders are treated in the same way as other patients in the State sector through PHC principles.

Offenders in need of further healthcare are, as far as possible, treated in state hospitals. The use of private hospitals for offenders is permitted in cases where public hospitals are unable to provide access to healthcare and only after approval by the Provincial Commissioner of Correctional Services.

The department's objective is to maintain a high standard of personal hygiene by ensuring that the following are provided to offenders:
- toilet and bathing amenities with warm water
- suitable clothing and comfortable shoes
- adequate bedding
- a clean and healthy environment
- safe water-supply
- the promotion of a smoke-free prison environment.

The Minister of Correctional Services approved the department's HIV and AIDS Policy in October 2002. The department will be involved in the roll-out of government's antiretroviral implementation plan to HIV-positive prisoners during the medium term.

The department's HIV and AIDS Policy caters for:
- prevention, which involves the promotion of safe sexual practices, management and control of STIs, provision of condoms and access to voluntary counselling and testing
- treatment, care and support
- respect for human rights
- awareness campaigns and the commemoration of HIV and AIDS calendar events
- partnerships with other government departments, the private sector, NGOs and educational institutions
- peer-led education programmes to introduce behavioural changes among peers
- the appointment of employee-assistance practitioners to implement employee-wellness programmes
- principles of universal precautions, which provide personnel and offenders with guidelines and procedures regarding the handling of all body fluids.

Expenditure under the Healthcare Programme was expected to increase from R777 million in 2004/05 to R1,2 billion in 2007/08. This will fund the department's commitment to managing HIV- and AIDS-related diseases and making available health services previously provided as free by provincial health departments. The department plans to improve these services by upgrading healthcare facilities in correctional centres and appointing medical practitioners, pharmacists and nursing personnel.

Nutrition

The department is committed to maintaining the health and strength of those entrusted to its care by satisfying their nutritional needs according to the Recommended Daily Allowance for food intake.

The objective is to provide all offenders with three nutritious meals per day and to provide for therapeutic and special diets when prescribed by a medical doctor. The system also allows for religious and cultural diets.

In its efforts to ensure compliance in this regard, a contract was negotiated with an external service-provider to render catering services to the offenders and to train staff and offenders who work in the kitchens.

Because of budgetary constraints, the department decided on phased implementation. The first phase has seen implementation at seven large management areas, which benefit about one third of the inmate population. An added advantage is that trained offenders will on release be able to participate effectively in the catering arena.

Rehabilitation

Rehabilitation aims to provide treatment and development programmes to offenders in partnership with the community. This will enhance personal and social functioning, and prepare them for reintegration into the community as productive, well-adapted and law-abiding citizens.

A multidisciplinary team, consisting of social workers, psychologists, chaplains, educators, correctional officers and others (the external community), addresses the basic needs of offenders by means of comprehensive assessments and various needs-based programmes.

The development and rehabilitation processes, which enable offenders to improve their mental health, social functioning, competencies, knowledge, skills and spiritual well-being, are focused on the following key strategies, namely to:

- positively combat illiteracy within the prison environment
- actively engage the community to assist with development programmes for the people entrusted to the department's care
- develop and implement a needs-based development programme
- establish training centres at large prisons as well as capacity-building in small prisons
- market rehabilitation programmes to offenders and the community
- promote and implement restorative justice principles to ensure the involvement of offenders, victims and the community in the rehabilitation process.

The further establishment of training centres in the various provinces is aimed at equipping offenders with basic technical skills in a variety of fields such as brick-making, brick-laying, woodwork, welding, garment-making, etc. Training is also provided in business skills to equip individuals to operate their own small businesses following their release.

The department is in the process of researching, designing and developing needs-based correctional programmes to target and address the offending behaviour of individual offenders.

In March 2005, the Department of Correctional Services, in conjunction with the Department of Arts and Culture, launched the Arts Against Crime Project. The project involves artists visiting correctional centres and engaging with offenders to impart their love of the various art forms. It also aims to assist offenders in discovering and honing their own artistic skills. The Department of Correctional Services believes that exposure to, and participation in, the various art forms by offenders is of therapeutic value to them.

Institutional committees

Institutional committees at each prison are responsible for ensuring a professional and co-ordinated approach towards the incarceration, treatment, training and development of all offenders.

This is implemented by means of a multidisciplinary approach in which all role-players are involved, i.e. those concerned with custodial, training, educational, psychological, religious-care and social-work functions, recreational sport and library projects, as well as self-sufficiency and life skills programmes.

Institutional committees have statutory decision-making competency regarding the safe custody of offenders, individual participation, subgroup and group programmes, as well as the prompt rewarding of positive behaviour.

Education and training of offenders

All offenders have a right to basic education and training. The aim is to enhance the education level and improve the skills of offenders to facilitate their reintegration into the community.

Services are provided to sentenced and unsentenced offenders in collaboration with external partners (government institutions, training boards, NGOs, etc.) and are in line with the provisions of the South African Qualifications Authority and the National Qualifications Framework.

Education and training programmes include:
• Adult Basic Education and Training (ABET)
• mainstream education (grades 10 – 12)
• business and engineering
• correspondence studies
• technical studies
• vocational training
• occupational skills training
• instruction in recreation and sport
• arts and culture programmes
• life-skills training and development
• entrepreneurial skills training
• computer-based training.

The main emphasis is on the provision of literacy and numeracy programmes, which include training in occupational, life and entrepreneurial skills. This should enhance the chances of the successful reintegration of the offender into the community and labour market.

Inmates are encouraged to take part in sport, recreation, and arts and culture activities as far as possible.

During 2004/05, 8 876 offenders benefited from the ABET Programme, while 5 205 and 5 723 respectively participated in Further Education and Training (FET) studies (grades 10 – 12 and N 1 – 3 business and engineering) and 1 710 in the Higher Education and Training field (certificate, diploma and degree studies).

Offenders who are of school-going age are provided with formal school education opportunities to complete their General Education and Training Certificate (Grade 9) to further their studies within the FET band.

Partnership agreements and formal working relationships were established with external service-providers of voluntary services in relation to formal education and skills development.

Within the Department of Correctional Services, the READY (Reintegration and Diversion for Youth) Programme is presented to young offenders by correctional officials. During 2004/05, 1 797 young offenders between the ages of 18 and 25 years competed in at least one of the three programme levels, i.e. bronze, silver and gold. From these, 97 young offenders were awarded gold certificates, representing the Western Cape, Free State, Northern Cape and Gauteng regions.

Some 300 offenders were trained during the 2004 academic year by 238 Readucate instructors, in a project facilitated by the Readucate Trust. The core of the Readucate approach is to teach literate prisoners how to become Readucate instructors, who in turn will teach functionally and/or totally illiterate prisoners how to read. This programme contributes towards the literacy tuition programme and serves as a conduit to the ABET programmes of the Department of Correctional Services.

Inmates are trained in 14 of the department's training centres throughout the country in various fields such as IT, brick-laying, woodwork, welding, etc. In 2004, about 11 government departments purchased a range of items produced in the department's workshops, generating revenue of about R3 million.

These training facilities are also available to members of the neighbouring communities to empower themselves. The Vukukhanye Youth

Development Project in the Western Cape is a prime example where trainees from Paarl and Franschoek graduated with technical skills in garment-making, cabinet-making, upholstery and other fields in early 2005.

Psychological services

Psychological services are provided for sentenced offenders and persons subject to community corrections, to maintain or enhance their mental health and emotional well-being.

By May 2005, there were 25 permanent psychologists within the department. The department has registered with the Department of Health as an institution for psychologists who have to do one year of compulsory community service. Thirty-three psychologists completing a compulsory one-year community service joined the department in 2005. This positively impacted on the rendering of services in 2005. This venture is also supporting the Department of Correctional Services' rehabilitation drive and serves as a solution for continual recruitment.

In areas where there are no departmental psychologists, the department uses the following procedures to address the emotional needs of offenders:

- external registered psychologists can be contracted in if a medical practitioner has referred the offender for psychological treatment
- offenders can see a private psychologist at their own expense
- final-year students who are completing their MA degrees in Clinical or Counselling Psychology provide services without remuneration under the supervision of their respective universities.

Social Work Services

Social Work Services aims to provide professional services to help offenders cope more effectively with problems relating to social functioning, and to prepare them for reintegration into the community.

Social Work Services provides structured treatment programmes on issues such as life skills, family care and marriage, alcohol and drug abuse, orientation, sexual offences, trauma, pre-release, and HIV and AIDS.

On 30 April 2005, the department employed 462 social workers. The increasing number of people living with HIV and AIDS is a major challenge, as not all social workers are trained HIV and AIDS counsellors.

Research on the rehabilitation of offenders shows that rehabilitation interventions should be systematic and needs-based. A framework/model of intervention to assist in the consistent and intensive assessment and evaluation of offenders' needs and rehabilitation programmes, was subsequently developed.

All social workers in the department received training on the intervention model to assist in the consistent assessment of offenders and the provision of needs-based rehabilitation programmes.

However, other structured programmes are still being offered as a preventative measure, e.g. the programme on HIV and AIDS offered to young offenders.

Spiritual care of offenders

Spiritual-care services are rendered through needs-based programmes within a multidisciplinary context to persons who are in the care of the department. This is done in partnership with churches or faith-based organisations (FBOs) and other role-players to rehabilitate offenders and reintegrate them into the community.

It also aims to contribute to changing the offenders' behaviour, based on a lifestyle which is in accordance with the acceptable values and norms of their faith.

Spiritual-care services are rendered to sentenced and unsentenced offenders, probationers, parolees and personnel on an ad hoc basis.

The department employs full-time chaplains and part-time spiritual workers from various religious backgrounds.

The extent of religious/spiritual counselling is reflected by the 43 437 spiritual services, 71 595 group sessions and 71 841 individual sessions held for offenders in 2004/05.

Quarterly meetings are held with the chaplains of the South African National Defence Force and the SAPS to discuss issues of common concern.

The department is a member of the International Prison Chaplaincy Association (IPCA). A working relationship also exists with FBOs like Prison Fellowship International, Alpha, New Life Behaviour Ministries and Kairos.

Provision is made for offenders to observe the main religious festivals and holy days such as Ramadan, Passover, Good Friday and Christmas. Religious and spiritual literature, such as the *Bible* and the *Qur'an*, is supplied to offenders.

Release of offenders

The Correctional Services Act, 1998 provides for the creation of independent regional correctional supervision and parole boards throughout the country, with greater powers to consider and approve which offenders, serving sentences exceeding 12 months, should be granted parole. In the interest of protecting the community, the department has abolished the concept of remission of sentence.

The Minister of Correctional Services inaugurated the correctional supervision and parole boards (CSPBs) in July 2005.

The new boards mark a historic departure from the past as key decision-making powers will be vested with community representatives appointed to chair the boards. All applications from offenders for parole will be considered and approved by CSPBs, with the exception of decisions on some categories of crimes committed by offenders as outlined in the Criminal Procedure Act, 1977 (Act 51 of 1977).

By July 2005, 42 chairpersons of the CSPBs had assumed duties. Fifty-two CSPBs will be established countrywide.

The victim of a criminal act may now also participate or be represented at the parole hearing. This allows, for the first time, the direct participation of victims in the justice system instead of them being called upon only as prosecution witnesses.

The parole and correctional-supervision policy deals with and also provides for a non-parole period. In terms of the Correctional Services Act, 1998, offenders are not considered for parole until they have served at least half of their original sentences or the non-parole period, whichever is the longer.

Courts are empowered to build a non-parole period into the sentence of any convicted criminal. This period may be as much as two-thirds of the total sentence. A person declared a habitual criminal may not be considered for parole before having served at least seven years in prison. Offenders serving a life sentence may not be considered for parole until they have served at least 25 years of their sentence.

Reintegration into the community

The department aims to equip offenders with the skills required for effective reintegration into society after release. Offenders sentenced to longer than six months' imprisonment undergo a basic pre-release programme before release. Aspects receiving attention include how to secure employment, personal finance management and street law.

Specialists from the community are also involved in the presentation of the programme. Care and support for an offender are prerequisites for placement in the community. Before offenders are placed, they are assisted with obtaining employment and accommodation, or at least care and support. Community involvement in supporting offenders after release is encouraged.

Offenders are provided with financial and material assistance before they are released from prison.

Community corrections

Plans are being implemented to make community correction offices more accessible to the majority of offenders and the community, especially in rural areas. The final location and decentralisation of the offices is envisaged by the end of 2006/07. On 31 March 2005, there were 172 fully functional offices and 21 suboffices.

By mid-2005, a revised classification system for offenders subject to community corrections was being developed. The intention is to align offenders' classification with the principles of rehabilitation, requiring more interaction between offenders and their supervision officials.

Supervision of parolees

Parolees are subject to certain conditions as well as

supervisory measures aimed at gradually re-integrating them into the community.

To achieve these goals, parolees are allocated to a supervision official of the department, who ensures that they are regularly monitored. Contravention of parole conditions leads to stricter conditions and increased supervision or reimprisonment for a part of or the entire remainder of the parole period.

Volunteers from the community are encouraged to assist the department in the monitoring of parolees.

Based on their risk profile, parolees are placed in minimum, medium or maximum supervision categories. The conditions for parole may include periods of house-arrest, restriction to a specific magisterial district, compulsory attendance of treatment programmes and the rendering of compulsory community service.

Persons awaiting trial may also be placed under correctional supervision. Because little is known about their criminal record prior to conviction, they are classified under the maximum supervision category.

Monitoring includes visits to the parolee's home and workplace, telephonic liaison and reports to the Community Corrections Office.

The department aims to increase the number of personnel responsible for managing and controlling persons sentenced to community corrections.

Correctional supervision

Correctional supervision, an alternative sentencing option available to law courts, entails that upon conviction, offenders are sentenced to a period of correctional supervision. Correctional supervision provides the opportunity to deal with some offenders outside the walls of correctional centres. Offenders who pose a real threat to the community and who have chosen crime as a career, however, do not qualify for correctional supervision.

A person sentenced to correctional supervision is placed under the control of a correctional supervision official. This official ensures that the probationer complies with whichever of the following conditions he or she may be subject to:

- house arrest
- community service, rendered free of charge
- victim's compensation

- restriction to a magisterial district
- prohibition on alcohol usage or abuse
- participation in certain correctional programmes.

If the set conditions are violated, probationers can be referred to the court of first hearing for consideration of an alternative sentence or, in certain cases, be admitted directly to correctional centres to serve the remainder of their sentences.

According to Section 117(e) of the Correctional Services Act, 1998, it is an offence for a probationer or parolee to abscond from the system of community corrections. If found guilty, they may receive an additional sentence of up to 10 years' imprisonment.

On 31 October 2004, the community corrections population, comprising parolees and probationers, totalled 77 138 compared with the 184 871 sentenced offenders who were serving their sentences inside correctional centres at the same time.

Day parole

A small number of offenders are placed on day parole either because they are institutionalised or they have a doubtful prognosis and pose a high security risk to the community. These offenders are gradually resettled into the community as a bridging measure, instead of being released upon termination of sentence. Day parolees have to comply with certain conditions. Contravention leads to withdrawal of privileges, stricter conditions or suspension of day parole.

Offenders whose parole has already been approved may under certain circumstances be allowed to spend weekends at home for the consolidation of family ties, preparation for release, or for reasons that involve the reintegration of the offender into society. Offenders may also be granted compassionate leave under certain circumstances, such as attending burials of close family members.

The offender has to observe strict conditions, which include abstaining from drugs and alcohol, being in the care of a specific person and at a specific address, personally accepting liability for any event that might result in expenses for the State, and not being found guilty of any misconduct.

Administration

The Administration Programme funds the overall management of the department. It includes policy formulation by the minister, the national commissioner, and other members of senior management, and facilitates prison inspections by the inspecting judge.

The programme accounted for about 28% of the budget of the department in 2005/06, and increases by about 5% each year.

Employee organisations

Employees of the Department of Correctional Services subscribe to the Labour Relations Act, 1995 (Act 66 of 1995). Two labour unions are active in the department, namely the Police and Prisons' Civil Rights Union and the Public Servants' Association.

Because the department renders an essential service, its members are not allowed to embark on strike action. Participation in illegal strikes led to the dismissal of 462 staff members during 2004/05.

Social responsibility

The department actively participates in the initiative of the NCPS to establish community safety centres. These centres aim to provide integrated services in South Africa's disadvantaged communities. The departments of correctional services, health, social development, justice and constitutional development and the SAPS provide these integrated services to the community under one roof.

The department has embarked on a poverty-alleviation programme that entails the deployment of offender-generated goods and services for poverty alleviation, disaster relief and rural development. The majority of prisons had engaged in projects by May 2005. In 17 areas they have managed to realise surplus produce in agriculture, which is donated to needy entities in the community, such as old-age homes, children's homes and orphanages.

Anti-corruption

A three-pronged anti-corruption strategy was approved by Cabinet in 2002. The strategy focuses on:

- corruption prevention
- investigation of corruption, fraud and serious maladministration
- disciplinary sanction of members found to be involved in corruption, fraud or serious mismanagement.

In implementing the strategy, it was necessary to forge a partnership with the Special Investigating Unit (SIU) that was called into being earlier by President Mbeki. The aim was to bolster the department's own investigative capacity and to deploy an independent specialist investigating agency.

While serious gains have been made in cleansing the department of corruption over the past three years, it requires a sustainable and prioritised anti-corruption programme to seriously impact on corruption. In the process, the mandate of the SIU was extended to allow it to investigate all incidents up to and including November 2004.

The department in the interim established its own Departmental Investigation Unit (DIU). It is a fully fledged agency with three main divisions whose scope of work follows the three-pronged anti-corruption strategy, namely prevention, investigation and sanctioning.

During 2004, 161 cases were investigated. Of these, 96 were for corruption, 28 for theft and 37 for fraud. Ninety-nine were finalised with 62 still under investigation. Sanctioning resulted in 30 dismissals and six final written warnings, while two staff members resigned prior to the conclusion of disciplinary proceedings.

Other DIU successes include:
- an understanding of the most common manifestations of corruption within the department
- an internal capacity to effectively deal with corruption
- a whistle-blowing policy
- training of managers on anti-corruption awareness
- training aimed at ensuring consistent application of the department's Disciplinary Code and Procedure
- a database of corruption and maladministration-related information.

International co-operation

The department of Correctional Services has established relations with organisations such as the American Correctional Association, the IPCA and the International Corrections and Prisons Association (ICPA).

The department endorsed the Charter of Fundamental Rights for Prisoners at the 11th UN Congress on Crime Prevention and Criminal Justice in April 2005. It will continue to participate in multilateral fora such as the ICPA, the Conference of Commissioners for East and Southern Africa and the UN.

In conjunction with other African states, the department is developing a programme that will result in full compliance with the UN minimum standards on the treatment of offenders. Participation in binational commissions and joint commissions of co-operation has resulted in the department hosting several delegations from various countries, as well as the Commission on Human and Peoples' Rights under the AU.

Ministers responsible for prison management and correctional services in SADC countries are continuing efforts to implement the July 2003 Johannesburg Declaration on Corrections. The declaration seeks to include the field of corrections in the work of regional and continental multilateral structures.

The department is considering the development of policy guidelines to enable government to enter into prisoner transfer agreements with other countries. This policy advocates for the return of prisoners sentenced in foreign countries to enable them to complete their sentences closer to their families and the communities they will be released into. This affects South Africans in foreign prisons, as well as foreigners in South African prisons.

The policy has yet to go through government processes for final approval by Cabinet.

Acknowledgements

Beeld

BuaNews

Commission on Gender Equality

Department of Correctional Services

Department of Justice and Constitutional Development

Estimates of National Expenditure 2005, published by National Treasury

South African Law Reform Commission

www.financialmail.co.za

www.gov.za

www.southafrica.info

Suggested reading

Abel, R.L. *Politics by Other Means: Law in the Struggle Against Apartheid, 1980 – 1994*. London: Routledge, 1995.

Ajibola, B. and Van Zyl, D. *The Judiciary in South Africa*. Cape Town: Juta, 1998.

Albertyn, C. *et al*, eds. *Introduction to the Promotion of Equality and Prevention of Unfair Discrimination Act (Act 4 of 2000)*. Johannesburg: Witwatersrand University Press, 2001.

Andrews, P. and Ellman, S. eds. *The Post-Apartheid Constitution: Perspectives on South Africa's Basic Law*. Johannesburg: Witwatersrand University Press, 2001.

Asmal, K., Asmal, L. and Roberts, R.S. *Reconciliation Through Truth: A Reckoning of Apartheid's Criminal Governance*. 2nd ed. Cape Town: David Philip, 1997.

Asmal, K., Chidester, D. and Lubisi C. eds. *Legacy of Freedom: The ANC's Human Rights Tradition: Africans' Claims in South Africa, the Freedom Charter, the Women's Charter and Other Human Rights Landmarks of the African National Congress*. Johannesburg: Jonathan Ball, 2005.

Bell, T. *Unfinished Business: South Africa, Apartheid and Truth*. Observatory: Redworks, 2001.

Bennett, T.W. *Customary Law in South Africa*. Cape Town: Juta, 2004.

Bezuidenhout, C., and Joubert, S. eds. *Child and Youth Misbehaviour in South Africa: A Holistic View*. Pretoria: Van Schaik, 2003.

Burchell, J., and Erasmus., A. *Criminal Justice in a New Society: Essays in Honour of Solly Leeman*. Cape Town: Juta, 2004.

Chanock, M. *The Making of South African Legal Culture, 1902 – 1936: Fear, Favour and Prejudice*. Cambridge: University Press, 2001.

Chubb, K. and Van Dijk, L. *Between Anger and Hope: South Africa's Youth and the Truth and Reconciliation Commission*. Johannesburg: Witwatersrand University Press, 2001.

Coleman, M. ed. *Crime Against Humanity: Analysing the Repression of the Apartheid State*. Johannesburg: South African Human Rights Commission; Cape Town: David Philip, 1998.

Corder, H. ed. *Democracy and the Judiciary*. Cape Town: Institute for Democracy in South Africa, 1989.

Cries Without Tears: An Anthology of Writings from Rehabilitating Offenders. Johannesburg: Corrective Action Holdings and Sandton: Sizwe, 1999.

Doxater, E. and C. Villa-Vicenco, C. eds. *Repairing the Unforgivable: Reparations, Restoration and Renewal*. Cape Town: David Philip, 2003.

Doxater, E. and Villa-Vicenco, C. eds. *Provocation of Amnesty: Memory, Justice and Impunity*. Cape Town: David Philip, 2003.

Edelstein, J. *Truth and Lies: Stories from the Truth and Reconciliation Commission in South Africa*. Johannesburg: M & G Books, 2001.

Gibson, J.L. *Overcoming Apartheid: Can Truth Reconcile a Divided Nation*. Cape Town: Human Sciences Research Council (HSRC) Press, 2004.

Glauber, I. *The Death Penalty as a Deterrent*. Johannesburg: The Author, 2004.

Goldstone, R. *For Humanity: Reflections of a War Crimes Investigator*. Johannesburg: Witwatersrand University Press, 2000.

Gutto, S. *Equality and Non-Discrimination in South Africa: The Political Economy of Law and Law-Making.* Cape Town: New Africa Books, 2001.

Hund, J. ed. *Law and Justice in South Africa.* Cape Town: Centre for Intergroup Studies, 1986.

Hund, J. *Witchcraft, Violence and the Law in South Africa.* Pretoria: Protea, 2003.

James, W.G. and Van de Vijver, L. eds. *After the TRC: Reflections on Truth and Reconciliation.* Cape Town: David Philip, 2000.

Jeffrey, A. *The Truth About the Truth Commission.* Johannesburg: South African Institute of Race Relations, 1999.

Krog, A. *Country of My Skull.* Johannesburg: Random House, 1998.

Lange, C. and Wessels, J. *The Right to Know: South Africa's Promotion of Administrative Justice and Access to Information Acts.* Cape Town: Siberink, 2004.

Law of South Africa (LAWSA), Encyclopaedia of South African Law. Durban: Butterworth, 1976.

Leggett, T. *The Market for Drugs and Sex in South Africa.* Cape Town: New David Philip Publishers, 2001.

Lewis, D. *Parliamentary Support Programme: A Review, 1996 – 2001.* Cape Town: Parliamentary Support Programme, 2002.

Lewis, S. *Dealing with Rape.* Johannesburg: Sached, 1997.

Lobban, M. *White Man's Justice: South African Political Trials in the Black Consciousness Era.* Oxford: Clarendon Press, 1996.

Mamdani, M. ed. *Beyond Rights Talk and Culture Talk: Comparative Essays on the Politics of Rights and Culture.* Cape Town: David Philip, 2000.

McQuoid-Mason, D. ed. *Street Law South Africa: Practical Law for South Africans.* Cape Town: Juta, 2004.

Murray, C. and Nijzinky, L. *Building Representative Democracy: South Africa's Legislatures and the Constitution.* Cape Town: Parliamentary Support Programme, 2002.

Murray, J. *The Law in South Africa: A Practical Guide.* 5th ed. Gardenview: Legal and General Publishers, 2002.

Ncube, W., ed. *Law, Culture and Tradition: Children's Rights in Eastern and Southern Africa.* London: Ashgate, 1998.

Ndima, D. *The Law of Commoners and Kings: Narratives of a Rural Transkei Magistrate.* Pretoria: UNISA Press, 2004.

Ndung'u, S. *The Right to Dissent: Freedom of Expression, Assembly and Demonstration in South Africa.* Johannesburg: Freedom of Expression Institute, 2003.

Orr, W. *From Biko to Basson: Wendy Orr's Search for the Soul of South Africa as a Commissioner of the Truth and Reconciliation Commission.* Johannesburg: Contra, 2000.

Pistorius, M. *Catch Me a Killer: Serial Murders: A Profiler's True Story.* Sandton: Penguin, 2000.

Pistorius, M. *Strangers on the Street: Serial Homicide in South Africa.* Sandton: Penguin, 2002.

Rautenbach, F. *Liberating South African Labour from the Law.* Cape Town: Tafelberg, 1999.

Richter, L., *et al.* eds. *Sexual Abuse of Young Children in Southern Africa.* Pretoria: HSRC, 2004.

Shaw, M. *Crime and Policing in Post-Apartheid South Africa: Transforming Under Fire.* Cape Town: David Philip, 2002.

Sibanyoni, C, comp. *Directory of Human Rights Organisations.* Pretoria: HSRC, 1999.

Steinberg, J. *Farm Murders, Crime.* Johannesburg: Jonathan Ball, 2002.

Truth and Reconciliation Commission. Report. Cape Town: Juta, 1998. 3 vols.

Truth and Reconciliation Commission of South Africa Report, vols 6 and 7. Cape Town: Juta, 2003. 2 vols.

Tshiwula, L. *Crime and Delinquency.* Pretoria: Kagiso Publishers, 1998.

Turrell, R. *White Mercy: A Study of the Death Penalty in South Africa.* Westport. Cape Town: Praeger, 2004.

Vale, P. *Security and Politics in South Africa: The Regional Dimension.* Cape Town: University of Cape Town Press, 2003.

Villa-Vicencio, C. and Verwoerd, W. *Looking Back, Reaching Forward: Reflections on the Truth and Reconciliation Commission of South Africa.* Cape Town: University of Cape Town Press, 2000.

Minerals, energy and geology

The Department of Minerals and Energy is responsible for ensuring exploration, development, processing, utilisation and management of South Africa's mineral and energy resources.

The department's Electricity and Nuclear Branch is responsible for electricity and nuclear-energy affairs. The Hydro Carbons and Energy Planning Branch is responsible for coal, gas, liquid fuels, energy efficiency, renewable energy and energy planning, including the energy database.

The objective of the Mineral Development Branch is to transform the minerals and mining industry and to promote the sustainable development of the industry for the benefit of all South Africans.

The Mine Health and Safety Inspectorate (MHSI) is responsible for implementing mine health and safety legislation.

Policy

The Minerals and Petroleum Resources Development Act (MPRDA), 2002 (Act 28 of 2002), was promulgated in May 2004 and became law in May 2005. The Act recognises the State's sovereignty and custodianship over the country's mineral resources, provides for equitable access to mineral resources, opportunities for historically disadvantaged individuals (HDIs), economic growth, employment and socio-economic welfare, and security of tenure. Meaningful and substantial participation of HDIs in the mining sector is guided by principles contained in the Broad-Based Socio-Economic Empowerment Charter. A scorecard for the charter has been introduced to facilitate its application in terms of the requirements of the MPRDA, 2002, for the conversion of all the old-order rights into new rights.

The provisions of the MPRDA, 2002 have necessitated the establishment of the National Mining Promotion System (NMPS). This online system allows the department to improve mineral licensing administration, investment promotion and the registration of rights. The NMPS enables the department to improve on turnaround time when processing applications and to maintain the proper management and administration of mineral-related rights and permits.

By May 2005, the department had processed 57 conversions for both exploration and mining, of which 22 had been granted and 35 returned to applicants for further information.

The Mining Titles Registration Amendment Act, 2003 (Act 24 of 2003), was promulgated on 26 November 2003. The purpose of the Act is to re-regulate the registration of mineral and petroleum titles and related rights, to effect certain amendments that are necessary to ensure consistency with the MPRDA, 2002 and to amend the Deeds Registries Act, 1937 (Act 47 of 1937). This transfers the functions relating to the registration of minerals rights from the ambit of the Act into the duties and functions of the Director-General of the Department of Minerals and Energy.

The Precious Metals Bill and Diamond Amendment Bill were expected to be promulgated in 2005. In addition, incentives for the beneficiation of minerals and metals were being developed.

The Bills will assist in providing access to precious metals and diamonds to promote the culture of local value addition/beneficiation. This will also go a long way towards creating jobs, promoting skills development and increasing foreign direct investment and export earnings.

Mine environmental management

Mine environmental management forms an integral part of the management of mineral and petroleum resources. It focuses on the following national priority programmes:

- Strengthening enforcement to prevent mining legacies from occurring. This relates to the effective implementation of the MPRDA, 2002 and other short- and long-term strategies to strengthen environmental enforcement.

On 3 March 2005, Cabinet approved cleaner fuels for South Africa with effect from January 2006. This will see an end to lead being added to petrol and lower sulphur standards for diesel. This decision is part of a process that will see newly formulated fuels being introduced, which will contribute to the improvement of urban air quality.

- Identifying mine-pollution 'hot spots' and implementing regional closure strategies to direct operational mines in addressing and managing pollution and mining waste within these areas.
- Rehabilitating abandoned and ownerless mines in accordance with a priority ranking system and a dedicated database.

To address the water ingress and decanting problems within the Witwatersrand gold-mining area, which includes the central, eastern, western and far western basins, the Department of Minerals and Energy, in conjunction with the Council for Geoscience (CGS) and several other government departments, is developing a comprehensive strategy to prevent water ingress and to manage decant water in a sustainable way.

Such preventative measures will reduce safety hazards within operational mines underground and the impact on the receiving environment and will substantially decrease mining costs within the area.

For the prevention of water ingress, a programme aimed at implementing engineering interventions in the central and eastern mining basins was implemented in 2003/04. Engineering solutions such as limiting water losses through leaking water pipes to prevent ingress, and other water-management options such as building canals and tunnels to manage decanting water, are under consideration.

A phased work plan is also underway in terms of the rehabilitation of 75 abandoned and ownerless mine shafts, ventilation shafts and other mine-related openings.

Mining outcomes of the World Summit on Sustainable Development (WSSD)

Representatives from nearly 200 countries assembled at the WSSD in Johannesburg in September 2002 to reaffirm their commitment to sustainable development.

As a follow-up to the WSSD outcomes for mining, the Department of Minerals and Energy finalised a strategy with specific programmes, plans and time frames to achieve the objectives and priorities regarding the implementation of the Johannesburg Plan of Implementation (JPI).

The WSSD outcomes for mining include:
- poverty eradication
- changing unsustainable patterns of consumption and production
- protecting and managing the natural resource base for economic and social development
- globalisation
- initiatives for sustainable development in Africa.

Apart from the national processes being established to take the WSSD outcomes forward, international processes and structures such as the African Mining Partnership will be established to champion, among others, the New Partnership for Africa's Development's (NEPAD) mining and mineral-related initiatives. The Global Mining Dialogue was also established to promote WSSD mining outcomes in the international arena.

The dialogue has achieved its objective of bringing together interested governments to prepare for the launch of the Intergovernmental Forum on Mining, Minerals, Metals and Sustainable Development.

The second preparatory meeting of the Global Dialogue on Mining/Metals and Sustainable Development took place in Geneva, Switzerland, in June 2004.

The JPI has implications for a number of national departments, because of its integrated nature to address poverty eradication, sustainable production and consumption, management of the natural resource base and socio-economic aspects. Many of the relevant national departments have been requested to submit follow-up action plans to the Department of Environmental Affairs and Tourism. The departments' input ranges from national to international actions as well as policy reform and priorities.

Mineral and Mining for Sustainable Development

An international initiative as well as a southern African initiative for sustainable development have been embarked on. The purpose of these initiatives is to undertake research into sustainable development through mining, to identify critical issues and priorities, and to make recommendations regarding the implementation of such initiatives.

The key challenges include:
- poverty alleviation through employment, job creation, skills development and training, and ensuring that communities benefit from the exploitation of natural resources
- addressing the social and environmental legacies of the past
- HIV and AIDS
- ensuring the viability of the mining industry on global, national and regional bases where markets for minerals must develop in a way that enables rather than limits the transition to sustainable development, notably in terms of internalising costs over time, while maintaining viable enterprises and rewarding good practice
- good governance and strengthening enforcement
- issues relating to market access and, in particular, the beneficiation of minerals.

A task team has been established, consisting of government departments, the mining industry, labour and non-governmental organisations. Its role is to determine how the recommendations emanating from the initiatives can be taken forward.

Sustainable development on the African continent

In support of the implementation of mining-related NEPAD issues, the department played an important role in conceptualising the African Mining Partnership, a mining ministers' partnership that drives the minerals and mining agenda of NEPAD.

During 2005/06, the department continued to participate in projects addressing beneficiation, small-scale mining, environment/sustainable development, human resource development, foreign investment and indigenous/local participation.

A collaborative programme among coastal states has been put in place under the auspices of the African Mining Partnership. The programme provides a platform for African coastal states to share expertise in compiling their respective submissions supporting their claims to extend their exclusive economic zones. The submission to the United Nations should be made by May 2009. The project is led by South Africa's CGS and Senegal.

The Intergovernmental Memorandum of Understanding (MoU) on the Western Power Corridor Project (WESTCO) was signed in October 2004. WESTCO is a NEPAD flagship programme intended to pilot hydroelectric energy of the Inga rapids site in the Democratic Republic of Congo (DRC). It will ensure security of supply in the Southern African Development Community (SADC). The participating utilities are those of Namibia, South Africa, the DRC, Botswana and Angola. A joint venture company has been formed to initiate studies determining the viability of the project and to build, own, and operate the infrastructure.

Rehabilitation of mines

About R120 million has been allocated over the 2005/06 to 2007/08 financial years towards the rehabilitation of ownerless and derelict mines. The cleaning up of abandoned and ownerless asbestos dump sites was the Department of Minerals and Energy's first rehabilitation priority. By mid-2005, 65% of the identified 578 sites, mainly in the Northern Cape and Limpopo, had been cleaned up.

The rehabilitation programme for 2005/06 included the following:
- Some R48 million was allocated to asbestos rehabilitation, which continues to be a priority as asbestos is a serious health hazard.
- In North West, Northern Cape and Mpumalanga, the CGS has identified about 490 abandoned shafts, which pose a severe safety risk to nearby communities.
- Some R18 million was allocated towards the rehabilitation of abandoned uranium mines in the Karoo and the Free State.

Gold panners from around the world gathered at Pilgrim's Rest in Mpumalanga for the eight-day World Gold Panning Championships in September 2005.
South Africa was the first country in Africa to host the championships.
The championships are held annually in one of 22 countries that are members of the World Gold Panning Association.

- Bids worth R104 million were expected to be published as part of the rehabilitation programme in 2005/06. Each of the rehabilitation projects will incorporate dedicated enterprise development and intensive job creation.

Excellence in Mining Environmental Management (EMEM) Award System

The EMEM Award System was implemented in March 2000 to motivate the mining industry to excel in environmental management and to recognise mining companies that have excelled in their field. The awards are presented to both regional and national companies.

Black Economic Empowerment (BEE)

The New Africa Mining Fund (NAMF), a private equity fund, was established in 2002 to exclusively finance exploration activities, while facilitating the entry of HDIs into the mining industry.

By June 2004, the NAMF had received 130 applications for funding. During 2004, eight BEE transactions to the value of R10 billion were finalised.

The Department of Minerals and Energy continues to support BEE suppliers in pursuance of the Liquid and Petroleum Charter. On 30 November 2004, the department and individual members of the Southern African Petroleum Industry Association signed an MoU aimed at the creation of the Supplier Development Agency. The agency opened its doors for trading on 1 April 2005.

The primary objectives of the agency are to source potential BEE suppliers, accredit the suppliers to combat fronting, develop suppliers to meet the performance levels of the industry, and source opportunities for BEE suppliers from industry.

Mining industry

Preliminary figures for 2004 indicate that South Africa's mining contributed R87,1 billion or 7,1% gross value added, an increase of R8,6 billion from the previous year. The trend where foreign revenue earnings are dominated by platinum-group metals (PGMs) at US\$4,6 billion, followed by gold at US\$4,5 billion, also continued in 2004.

However, the gold sector has been declining due to the challenges of aging infrastructure in deep mines. The industry faces challenges of commodity price cycles and is also affected by the currency fluctuations and business models that are not aligned with current rand value.

The Department of Minerals and Energy, in collaboration with its partners, labour and business, is evolving a strategy to manage the decline of the sector and the impact on workers.

South Africa produces 14% of the world's gold, and has 41% of the world's known reserves. Solutions and new ways to mine the remaining gold will be investigated.

Over the last few years, South African mining houses have transformed into large focused mining companies that include Anglo Platinum, Anglogold, De Beers, Implats and Iscor.

The Government is the only shareholder of Alexkor, a diamond mine situated on the west coast of Namaqualand. Mining takes place on land and in certain sea concession areas.

The Alexkor Limited Amendment Act, 2001 (Act 29 of 2001), provides for the sale or disposal of shares held by the State.

Government is involved in the Alexkor Diamond Mine Board and Audit Committee.

In October 2003, the Constitutional Court returned the land and mineral rights owned by Alexkor to the Richtersveld community, which was forcibly removed from the land in the 1920s.

Negotiations regarding the future of the mine continue.

Mineworkers

Gold mining, with 45,7% of the mining industry's labour force, was the largest employer in 2003, followed by PGM mining with 28,8%. The coal industry employed 11% of the labour force in 2003.

Taking into account the multiplier effect of the supply and consumer industries, including dependants, many millions rely on the mining industry for their livelihood.

Employers and trade unions in the mining industry have agreed to establish measures that will help create jobs and alleviate poverty. The parties committed themselves to ensuring that skills development becomes a priority in the industry.

Mine health and safety

The MHSI, established in terms of the Mine Health and Safety Act (MHSA), 1996 (Act 29 of 1996), is responsible for protecting the health and safety of persons working at mines or affected by mining activities.

The activities of the MHSI are unequivocally focused towards achieving a safer and healthier mining industry for all.

The mining industry's safety performance improved in 2004. A fatality rate of 0,56 deaths per 1 000 employees was recorded compared with a fatality rate of 0,65 deaths per 1 000 employees in 2003. Regrettably, these rates correspond to 246 deaths in 2004 and 270 deaths in 2003. The reportable injury rates also improved from 10,32 per 1 000 employees in 2003 to 9,63 in 2004. These rates correspond to 4 254 injuries in 2004 and 4 301 injuries in 2003. Considering that the number of persons employed at mines increased by 24 952, from 416 660 in 2003 to 441 612 in 2004, a dedicated effort was required from all stakeholders to realise the improvement.

At the Mine Health and Safety Summit held in 2003, employers, labour and government agreed to work towards achieving national health and safety milestones. The following milestones necessitate steady improvement in occupational health and safety over the next decade (ending December 2013), including:

- Reducing the fatality and disabling injury rate by 20% in the industry as a whole (by 2% per year). Safety performance during 2004 was well within target and reflected an annual decrease of 14% in fatalities and 7% in disabling injuries.
- Reducing the fatality and disabling injury rate by 50% in the gold sector to achieve performance comparable with other internationally recognised levels in metalliferous underground mines (a reduction of 5% per year.) This target was

achieved during 2004 with a 24% annual decrease in fatalities, with disabling injuries realising a 4,5% decrease.

- Eliminating silicosis and noise-induced hearing loss by 2013. By mid-2005, work towards improving the quality of reporting, collecting and analysing occupational health and disease data was in progress and was expected to start yielding meaningful results in 2005/06.

The expansion in the platinum sector resulted in total labour at work increasing from 111 745 in 2003 to 140 287 in 2004. However, this resulted in an increase in fatalities from 58 to 64 respectively. This is a 12% improvement of fatality rates per 1 000 employees, from 0,52 in 2003 to 0,46 in 2004.

The Mine Health and Safety Council (MHSC) provides extensive advice to the minister on the continued development of a revised regulatory framework for the industry. These recommendations led to the promulgation of new regulations and guidelines for mandatory codes of practice at mines. The following MHSA, 1996 regulations were promulgated in 2004/05:

- Underground Railbound Transport
- Survey, Mapping and Mine Plans
- Protection of the Surface and Workings.

The Chief Inspector of Mines issued guidelines for mandatory codes of practice dealing with slope stability-related accidents on surface mines.

The MHSI also prepared and published an internal guideline document on the enforcement of the MHSA, 1996, for use by inspectors.

There are five projects aimed at raising awareness on the prevention, treatment and care of HIV and AIDS in the mining industry. These include the:

- Powerbelt Project, which focuses on coal-mining areas
- Lesedi Project in Virginia, Free State
- Lechabile Project in Welkom
- Bambisanani Project in Lusikisiki, Eastern Cape
- Carletonville Home-Based Care Project, Gauteng.

The Chief Inspector of Mines also proposed a strategy on dealing with deaths associated with HIV and AIDS following a non-life threatening mine accident.

The Safety in Mines Research Advisory Committee has a programme to overcome barriers to improved occupational health and safety performance. The programme comprises the following nine major thrust areas:

- cultural change
- rockfalls
- rockbursts
- explosions and fires
- machinery and transport systems
- airborne pollutants
- physical hazards (noise, temperature, radiation, etc.)
- occupational diseases (effect of HIV and AIDS on tuberculosis and silicosis)
- special projects (surveys for quantifying risk prevalence).

South Africa's mineral reserves, 2004

Commodity	Unit	Reserves	%	World ranking
Alumino-silicates	Kt	50	37	1
Antimony	t	250	6,4	3
Chrome ore	Mt	5 500	72,4	1
Coal	Mt	33,8	3,6	7
Copper	Kt	13	1,4	14
Fluorspar	Mt	80	17	2
Gold	t	36 000	40,7	1
Iron ore	Mt	1 500	0,9	9
Lead	Mt	3	2,1	7
Manganese ore	Kt	4 000	80,0	1
Phosphate rock	Kt	2 500	5	n/a
Platinum-group metals	Kg	70 000	87,7	1
Silver	t	10	1,8	9
Titanium minerals	Kt	244	29	2
Uranium	t	298	1,0	4
Vanadium	Kt	12 000	44,4	1
Vermiculite	Kt	14	40	1
Zinc metal	Kt	15	3,3	6
Zirconium minerals	Kt	14	19,4	2

Mt=megaton, Kt=kiloton, t=ton, n/a=not available, Kg=Kilogram

Source: Minerals Bureau

Mine Qualifications Authority (MQA)

The overall aim of the MQA is to facilitate the development of appropriate knowledge and skills in the mining, minerals and jewellery sectors, to:

- enable the development and transformation of the sector
- contribute to the health, safety and competitiveness of the sector
- improve access to quality education and training for all
- redress past inequalities in education and training.

The MQA was established as a sector education and training authority under the leadership of the Department of Labour. The responsibilities of the MQA are to:

- develop and monitor the implementation of a sector skills plan
- register skills-development facilitators at workplaces within the sector
- approve work skills plans and annual training reports of companies in the sector
- develop unit standards and qualifications
- maintain the quality of standards, qualifications and learning provision in the sector
- establish, register, administer and promote learnerships
- administer existing apprenticeship systems
- administer and disburse skills-development levies.

Employment equity in the mining sector is supported through the following initiatives:

- The Mining Executive Preparation Programme specifically aims to address the needs of HDIs. Thirty-seven participants completed the course in 2004 and a further 41 started the course in February 2005.
- The MQA awarded bursaries to 196 students for scarce skills and tertiary-education assistance.
- In March 2004, 273 adult basic education and training practitioners started their learnerships. The second intake was planned for March 2005. The aim was to train 70% of these workers in basic literacy and numeracy skills by March 2005.
- By January 2005, 1 795 learners were registered in different skills programmes.

Chamber of Mines

Established in 1889, the Chamber of Mines consists of independent mining finance corporations, individual mines and mining companies. The members account for more than 85% of South Africa's mineral output.

The Chamber of Mines provides an advisory and service function to its members and to the industry on a co-operative basis. It covers areas such as industrial relations; education and training; security and healthcare; technical, legal and communication services; and the provision of statistical data.

The following services are provided by subsidiary companies to the South African mining industry and, in some instances, also to customers outside the mining industry: training, examination administration, visits to operational gold and diamond mines, the monthly newspaper *Mining News*, mine-rescue, environmental management, and centres for human development.

Other areas of industry networking include:

- The Employment Bureau of Africa (TEBA)
- TEBA-Bank, providing efficient and cost-effective banking services for mineworkers
- Rand Mutual Assurance, providing workers' compensation benefits for accidental injury or death arising out of and in the course of employment
- Rand Refinery Ltd, the world's largest gold refinery
- the Nuclear Fuels Corporation (NUFCOR)
- Colliery Technical Services, which includes the Colliery Training College
- Rescue Drilling Unit
- Collieries Environmental Control Services
- the Council for Scientific and Industrial Research's Mining Technology Division (Miningtek).

Junior and small-scale mining

The National Small-Scale Mining Development Framework assists small-scale miners with the challenges they face. The small-scale mining sector makes a significant contribution to job creation in the mining industry.

It is estimated that about 1 000 jobs can be created for every seven to 10 sustainable small-scale mining projects assisted. Experience has shown that it is not enough just to provide institutional support. There is also a need to involve technical partners or business professionals to mentor the project to its completion.

The target market for assistance by the framework are:
- illegal or unacceptable operations to legalise and convert them into sustainable operations
- undercapitalised operations which require expansion or optimisation

- first-time entrepreneurs interested in greenfield projects.

The South African Small-Scale Mining Chamber (SASSMC) was launched in July 2005 in Kimberley in the Northern Cape.

The SASSMC represents the interests of small-scale miners nationally. Its objectives include positioning small-scale mining member companies to utilise available mining opportunities in and beyond South Africa's borders. It also aims to provide a model for small-scale mining that can be used as a basis to link up with the SADC and the African Mining Partnership.

The launch of the chamber supports government's objective to encourage and facilitate the sustainable development of small-scale mining, to ensure the optimal exploitation of small mineral deposits and to enable this sector to make a positive contribution to the economy.

Mineral wealth

South Africa's mineral wealth is found in diverse geological formations, some of which are unique and extensive by world standards. Some of the country's minerals include:
- Gold – the unique and widespread Witwatersrand Basin yields some 96% of South Africa's gold output.
- Diamonds (in kimberlites, alluvial and marine) – the country is among the world's top producers.
- Titanium – heavy mineral-sand occurrences containing titanium minerals are found along the coasts.
- Manganese – enormous reserves of manganese are found in the sedimentary rocks of the Transvaal Supergroup.
- PGMs and chrome – these minerals occur in the Bushveld Complex in Mpumalanga, Limpopo and North West. More than half of the global reserves of chrome and platinum are found in this deposit.
- Coal and anthracite beds occur in the Karoo Basin in Mpumalanga, KwaZulu-Natal and Limpopo.
- Copper phosphate, titanium, iron, vermiculite and zirconium are found in the Phalaborwa Igneous Complex in Limpopo.

South Africa's mineral production, 2004

Commodity	Unit	Production	%	World rank
Aluminium	Kt	866	2,6	10
Alumino-silicates	Kt	234,4	54,4	1
Antimony	t	4 967	3,1	3
Chrome ore	Mt	7,4		
Coal	Mt	243	4,7	5
Copper	Kt	102,6	0,7	18
Diamonds	Kcar	14 400	9	4
Ferrochromium	Mt	2,8		
Ferromanganese	Kt	907,8		
Ferrosilicon	Kt	131 555		
Fluorspar	Kt	–	–	–
Gold	t	340,2	13,8	1
Iron ore	Mt			
Lead	Kt	37,5	1,2	13
Manganese ore	Kt	4 206,7		
Nickel	Kt	40		
Phosphate rock	Kt	–	–	–
Platinum-group metals	Kg	286 733	57,8	1
Silicon metal	Kt	50 470		
Silver	t	72		
Titanium minerals	Kt	–	–	–
Uranium	t	887	2	4
Vanadium	Kt	27	41	1
Vermiculite	Kt	194,5	52,6	1
Zinc metal	Kt	105	1,2	22
Zirconium minerals	Kt	–	–	–

Mt=megaton, Kt=kiloton, t=ton, Kg=kilogram, K car=kilocarats

Source: Minerals Bureau

South Africa's reserves of five commodities rank highest in the world. These are:

- manganese
- chromium
- PGMs
- gold
- alumino-silicates.

Due to the small domestic market for most commodities, South Africa's mineral industry is export-orientated. Vanadium contributes 79% of world exports, antimony 26%, alumino-silicates 38%, ferrochromium 57%, chrome ore 57%, and manganese ore and ferromanganese 22% and 24% respectively.

South Africa is the world's largest exporter of these commodities, as well as of gold, zirconium and vermiculite. Other important export commodities include coal and titanium minerals.

Because of its vast mineral resource base, South Africa is, to a large degree, self-sufficient with respect to the supply of minerals.

However, some minerals and mineral products need to be imported.

South Africa's total primary minerals decreased by 12,6% to R117,7 billion in 2003. Total processed mineral sales increased by 10% from R30,9 billion in 2002 to R27,8 billion in 2003.

The combined total for primary and processed mineral sales is estimated to have decreased by 12,2% from R165,7 billion in 2002 to R145,5 billion in 2003.

Domestic primary mineral sales revenue increased in 2003 by 12,8% to R30,9 billion, from 27,4 billion in 2002.

The value of exports of primary minerals in 2003 decreased by 19,1% to R86,8 billion.

The Directorate: Mineral Economics (Minerals Bureau) of the Department of Minerals and Energy monitors and analyses all mineral commodities regarding South African and world supply and demand, marketing and market trends.

Gold

World demand for gold decreased by 7,2% to 3 851 tons (t) in 2004. The average gold price traded at a 15-year high of US$409/oz.

World mine supply decreased by 128 t to 2 462 t, but South African gold production fell by 8,7% to 340,2 t in 2004. Provisional data for 2004 indicates that total gold sales increased by 4,1% to US$4,55 billion.

Coal

In 2004, South African mines produced 242,82 megaton (Mt) of coal. Of this figure, 178,37 Mt was used locally, at a value of R13,6 billion, with export sales totalling 67,94 Mt, at a value of R14,47 billion.

South Africa has around 28,6 billion t of recoverable coal reserves, making it the seventh-largest holder of coal reserves in the world.

Platinum-group metals

South African PGM production increased by 7,7% to 286,7 t in 2004, while PGM revenue increased by 35,7% to US$5,17 billion. The average platinum price for 2004 was 22,2% higher at US$846/oz, while the average palladium price was 14,7% higher at US$230/oz.

Non-ferrous minerals

Refined copper, nickel, cobalt, titanium and zirconium concentrates dominate this sector, with support from zinc, lead and arsenic concentrates. The sector contributes some 12% and 4% respectively to total primary local sales and total primary export sales. About 44% of total revenue is from local sales for further added-value operations.

Ferrous minerals

This sector consists of manganese and chrome, and is dominated by iron ore. It has been a leading performer in the primary minerals industry in recent years, with revenue in dollar terms growing at about 10,3% annually. Demand depends on the fortune of the world's steel and stainless steel industries.

Export earnings from ferrous minerals increased by 16,3% from R4,16 billion in 2003 to R4,84 billion in 2004, despite the fact that higher dollar earnings were severely discounted by a much higher average rand-dollar exchange rate ratio for 2004. Higher prices also affected total ferrous sales, which rose by 18,9% to R6,81 billion.

Industrial minerals

This sector comprises a wide variety of mineral products, from which over 80% of revenue is local sales. In dollar terms, domestic total sales increased by 25% in 2004 to US$942 million. In rand terms, local sales increased by 15% to the value of R5 billion, and export sales decreased by 21% to R1 billion.

During 2004, 83% of local sales comprised aggregate and sand (38%), limestone and lime (24%), phosphate rock concentrate (data withheld) and sulphur (4%).

Exports were dominated by dimension stone (33%), vermiculite (14%), andalusite (20%), fluorspar (17%) and phosphate rock concentrate (data withheld).

Processed minerals

Ferro-alloys and aluminium dominate this sector, with solid support from titanium slag, phosphoric acid, vanadium, zinc metal and low-manganese pig-iron. Through investment in beneficiation, it has been the outstanding performer in the mineral industry over the last 20 years, with revenue in dollar terms growing by 6,3% annually.

International prices of processed minerals surged strongly during 2004 on the back of vigorous growth in demand in China and the East. As a result, export sales earnings were at an all-time high of US$4,096 billion in 2004, up 42% from US$2,889 billion in 2003.

Other minerals

This sector is dominated by diamonds, with support from hydrocarbon fuel, uranium oxide and silver.

Due to the strong Rand, revenue from these minerals slumped by 12,6% to R117,8 million in 2003.

New investment potential remains strong in this sector, which has recovered enormously through new investments in operations since 1994. This compensates for the rapid demise in the demand for uranium oxide in nuclear applications since the late 1980s.

Energy

The Department of Minerals and Energy's Energy Policy is based on the following key objectives:

- attaining universal access to energy by 2014
- accessible, affordable and reliable energy, especially for the poor
- diversifying primary energy sources and reducing dependency on coal
- good governance, which must also facilitate and encourage private-sector investments in the energy sector
- environmentally responsible energy provision.

Estimates suggest that R107 billion will be needed between 2005 and 2009 to meet the country's growing energy needs. Eskom will invest R84 billion over the next five years. The balance of R23 billion is reserved for independent power producer (IPP) entrants.

By May 2005, the department was in the process of procuring 1 000 megawatt (MW) through IPPs, which are expected to be commissioned in 2008.

The refurbishment of three power stations – Camden in Ermelo, Grootvlei in Balfour, and Komati in Middelburg – will result in an additional 3 800 MW to the system.

Eskom will spend about R12 billion (nominal rand) on the recommissioning of these stations. This is about 40% of the cost of a new station. About 10% of the costs will go towards improving environmental performance such as particulate emissions and water controls.

At least 36 000 jobs are expected to be created, directly and indirectly, until 2007, during both construction and operational phase activities.

Energy in the economy

Energy comprises about 15% of South Africa's gross domestic product (GDP), creating employment for about 250 000 people. The total electricity sales by Eskom in 2003 grew to 196 980 gigawatt-hour (GWh). The peak demand on the integrated system totalled 31 928 MW. Total liquid-fuels sales in 2001 grew by 0,3% to 20 934 million litres (ML). These figures demonstrate the growth of the South African economy and the importance of energy as a key driver of the country's economy.

This energy intensity is above average, with only 10 other countries having higher commercial primary energy intensities. It is largely a result of the economy's structure, with dominating large-scale, energy-intensive primary mineral beneficiation and mining industries.

In addition, coal is relied on for the generation of most of the country's electricity and a significant proportion of its liquid fuels. Furthermore, South Africa's industry has not generally used the latest in energy-efficient technologies, mainly as a result of relatively low energy costs.

Government has been persistently engaging members of the Organisation of Petroleum Exporting Countries through diplomatic channels to increase production.

Energy efficiency

The Energy Efficiency Strategy, which was approved in March 2005, sets a national target for energy efficiency improvement of 12% by 2015.

South Africa has a history of overcapacity in electricity, which has made its power cheap and reliable. Electricity has been a contributor to the country's economic growth and service delivery to the poor.

The strategy includes Eskom's demand-side management. Municipalities are also implementing their own energy efficiency strategies. In addition, 32 large companies have joined forces with the Department of Minerals and Energy and Eskom by signing an energy-efficiency accord, committing themselves to targets contained in the department's strategy.

To assist households to be more energy efficient, the Department of Minerals and Energy initiated an appliance-labelling campaign. Labels on household appliances inform consumers how energy efficient their appliances are.

The department, in collaboration with the Department of Public Works and Eskom, is retrofitting government buildings to make them more energy efficient. This contributes a saving of about R600 000 in electricity bills per year.

Energy demand by the economic subsector

Households

Energy consumed by households represents some 17% of the country's net use. Most household energy is obtained from fuel wood (50% of net household energy), primarily in rural areas, with the remainder obtained from coal (18%), illuminating paraffin (7%) and a small amount from liquid petroleum gas.

Rural households comprise the majority of poor homes and are characterised by severe poverty. In terms of basic energy services, their energy 'poverty' is exacerbated by the increasingly widespread scarcity of fuel-wood resources. Wood and paraffin are their main energy sources, with few having access to electricity.

Coal

South Africa's indigenous energy resource base is dominated by coal. Internationally, coal is the most widely used primary fuel, accounting for about 36% of the total fuel consumption of the world's electricity production.

About 77% of South Africa's primary energy needs are provided by coal. This is unlikely to change significantly in the next two decades, owing to the relative lack of suitable alternatives to coal as an energy source.

Many of the deposits can be exploited at extremely favourable costs and, as a result, a large coal-mining industry has developed.

In addition to the extensive use of coal in the domestic economy, some 28% of South Africa's production is exported internationally, mainly through the Richards Bay Coal Terminal, making South Africa the fourth-largest coal exporting country in the world.

South Africa's coal is obtained from collieries ranging from among the largest in the world to small-scale producers. As a result of new entrants in the industry, operating collieries were increased to 64 during 2004. Of these, a relatively small number of large-scale producers supply coal primarily to electricity and synthetic fuel producers. About 51% of South African coal mining is done underground and about 49% is produced by opencast methods.

The coal-mining industry is highly concentrated, with five companies, namely Ingwe (BHP Billiton), Anglo Coal, Sasol, Eyesizwe and Kumba, accounting for 85% of the saleable coal production. Production is concentrated in large mines, with 11 mines accounting for 70% of the output.

South African coal for local electricity production is among the cheapest in the world. The beneficiation of coal, particularly for export, results in more than 65 Mt of coal discards being produced annually.

Twenty-one percent of the run-of-mine coal produced is exported, and 21% is used locally (excluding power-station coal). The rest is not saleable and is discarded.

The remainder of South Africa's coal production feeds the various local industries: some 62% is used for electricity generation, 23% for petrochemical industries (Sasol), 8% for the general industry, 4% for the metallurgical industry (Mittal), and 4% is purchased by merchants and sold locally or exported.

The key role played by South Africa's coal reserves in the economy is illustrated by the fact that Eskom ranks first as steam coal user and seventh as electricity generator in the world. Sasol is the largest coal-to-chemicals producer.

South Africa's coal reserves are estimated at 28,6 billion t. With the present production rate, there should be more than 50 years of coal supply left.

By international standards, South Africa's coal deposits are relatively shallow with thick seams, which make them easier and, usually, cheaper to mine.

Coal is expected to maintain its share of the overall electricity generation market until 2020. Total discards on the surface could reach more than two billion tons by 2020, should none of this material be utilised. As a result, the Department of Minerals and Energy is investigating ways to promote and encourage the economic use of the discards.

Environmental concerns pose the main challenge to coal as energy source. Not only does the burning of coal cause air pollution, but the mining activities to extract coal also impact negatively on the environment. The department and the coal-mining industry are therefore fostering the introduction of clean coal technologies into the South African arena.

Nuclear

The nuclear sector in South Africa is mainly governed by the Nuclear Energy Act, 1999 (Act 46 of 1999), and the National Nuclear Regulator (NNR) Act, 1999 (Act 47 of 1999). These Acts are administered by the Department of Minerals and Energy; while part of the Hazardous Substances Act, 1973 (Act 15 of 1973), related to groups III and IV of hazardous substances, is administered by the Department of Health.

The main organisations directly involved in the nuclear sector are the following:

- The Department of Minerals and Energy plays a leading governance role regarding nuclear technology, non-proliferation and safety. The Minister of Minerals and Energy is the executive authority responsible for overseeing the Nuclear Energy Corporation of South Africa (Necsa) and the NNR.

- Necsa undertakes and promotes research and development in the fields of nuclear energy, radiation sciences and technology, medical-isotope manufacturing, nuclear liabilities management, waste management and decommissioning. Necsa's reactor-produced radioisotopes are exported to more than 50 countries.

- The NNR oversees safety regulation of nuclear installations at Necsa's Pelindaba site, Vaalputs Radioactive Waste Disposal Facility, the Koeberg Nuclear Power Station, certain mines and other small users. It is a public entity reporting to the Minister of Minerals and Energy.

- The Department of Health (Directorate: Radiation Control) issues licences for group III hazardous substances (electronic product generating X-rays, other ionising beams, electrons, neutrons or other particle radiation or non-ionising radiation) and group IV hazardous substances (radioactive material outside a nuclear installation, which does not form part of or is used or intended to be used in the nuclear fuel cycle, and which is used or intended to be used for medical, scientific, agricultural, commercial or industrial purposes).

- The Koeberg Nuclear Power Station is responsible for electricity generation. It is government-owned through the public entity, Eskom, which reports to the Minister of Public Enterprises.

- iThemba Laboratories is responsible for medical isotopes and medical applications. This public entity falls under the Department of Science and Technology.
- NUFCOR is responsible for uranium-ore refinement and export. It is privately owned by AngloGold.

The South African nuclear sector employs about 2 700 people. The Koeberg Nuclear Power Station contributes about 6% of total electricity, and contributions to GDP are in excess of R1,5 billion from uranium exports (last five years) and Necsa's direct commercial sales of about R300 million per year.

Liquid fuels

The liquid fuels industry was, for the first time, licensed in 2005. The objectives of the licensing framework as detailed in the Petroleum Products Amendment Act, 2003 (Act 58 of 2003), include:

- promoting an efficient manufacturing, wholesaling and retailing petroleum industry
- facilitating an environment conducive to efficient and commercially justifiable investment
- promoting the advancement of HDIs
- creating employment opportunities and small businesses in the petroleum sector.

South Africa consumed 21 267 ML of liquid-fuel products in 2002 and 25 338 ML in 2003. Thirty-six percent of the demand is met by synthetic fuels (synfuels) produced locally, largely from coal and a small amount from natural gas. The rest is met by products refined locally from imported crude oil.

The petrol price in South Africa is linked to the price of petrol in United States (US) dollars in certain international petrol markets. This means that the domestic price is influenced by supply and demand for petroleum products in the international markets, combined with the Rand/Dollar exchange rate.

The National Petroleum, Gas and Oil Corporation of South Africa (PetroSA) was officially launched in Cape Town in October 2002.

PetroSA is responsible for exploring and exploiting oil and natural gas, as well as producing and marketing synthetic fuels produced from offshore gas at the world's largest commercial gas-to-liquids plant in Mossel Bay, in the Western Cape.

Sasol

Sasol operates the world's only coal-based synthetic fuels facility, producing liquid petroleum gas (LPG) from low-grade coal. Sasol mines coal and converts it into synthetic fuels and chemicals through proprietary Fischer-Tropsch technologies. The company also has chemical manufacturing and marketing operations in Europe, Asia and the Americas. Its larger chemical portfolios include polymers, solvents, olefins and surfactants and their intermediates, waxes, phenolics and nitrogenous products.

Sasol produces crude oil in offshore Gabon, refines crude oil into liquid fuels in South Africa, and retails liquid fuels and lubricants through a growing network of retail centres and service stations. In the first quarter of 2004, Sasol started supplying Mozambican natural gas to customers and to its petrochemical plants in South Africa. The company is also developing two gas-to-liquids fuel joint ventures that will incorporate the proprietary Sasol Slurry Phase Distillate Process.

Sasol's focus is on the manufacturing, refining and marketing of automotive and industrial fuels

The 18th World Petroleum Congress (WPC) was held in Johannesburg from 25 to 29 September 2005.

For the first time in its 72-year history, the WPC was held on the African continent. Many African countries such as South Africa, Algeria, Angola, Libya and Nigeria are already major energy suppliers in world terms, while new energy powers such as Egypt and Equatorial Guinea are experiencing rapid growth. Hotspots such as Mauritania are emerging as exploration pushes new frontiers.

The WPC focused on the theme *Shaping the Energy Future: Partners in Sustainable Solutions*.

Delegates explored international business opportunities and threats; exchanged ideas on global issues; networked; and shared the latest information on technological, economical, environmental and social developments.

and oils, with a growing interest in gas. Its entry into hydrogen- and methane-rich gas production and exploration has extended into southern and West Africa.

In industry, Sasol provides premium fuels and lubricants that meet or exceed stringent specifications. It also produces jet fuel, fuel alcohol and illuminating kerosene.

Sasol is a signatory of Responsible Care, a worldwide initiative that strives to improve performance in safety, health and the environment.

Central Energy Fund (CEF)

The CEF is involved in the search for appropriate energy solutions to meet the future energy needs of South Africa, SADC and the sub-Saharan African region. This includes oil, gas, electrical power, solar energy, low-smoke fuels, biomass, wind and renewable energy sources. The CEF also manages the operation and development of the oil and gas assets and operations of the South African Government.

The CEF, through its integrated oil company subsidiary, PetroSA, is involved in the exploration for oil and gas onshore and offshore in South Africa and the rest of Africa. It is also involved in the production of environmentally friendly petroleum fuels and petrochemical products from gas and condensate at its synfuels refinery outside Mossel Bay and the management of oil-storage facilities. The Strategic Fuel Fund manages South Africa's strategic crude oil reserves.

Implementation of the Kyoto Protocol came into effect on 16 February 2005. Government established the Designated National Authority (DNA) in the Department of Minerals and Energy to handle clean development mechanism transactions. It opened its doors on 1 December 2004. The DNA is receiving a number of project proposals for review from the private sector. These projects will, by the year 2012, reduce South Africa's carbon dioxide emissions by 21 million tons and generate revenue of R618 million from sales of certified emission reductions.

CEF subsidiary company, Oil Pollution Control SA, provides oil prevention, control and clean-up services, mainly in South African ports and coastal areas, in terms of South Africa's National Environmental Management Act, 1998 (Act 107 of 1998).

Through its subsidiary, the Petroleum Agency of South Africa (PASA), the CEF manages the promotion and licensing of oil and gas exploration, development and production in South Africa and the coastal areas offshore, as part of creating a viable upstream oil industry in the country.

CEF subsidiary iGas acts as the official agent of the South African Government for the development of the hydrocarbon gas industry, comprising liquified natural gas and LPG in South Africa.

Indigenous oil and gas resources and production

The Department of Minerals and Energy is committed to the promotion of LPG, which is cleaner and safer and can serve as an efficient burning energy source. It is better-burning fuel for cooking and heating and does not generate smoke, dust and choking fumes like most other hydrocarbon fuels.

Government is committed to making it more affordable for cooking and heating to reduce the need for large investments in power generation. The LPG Association undertook to connect 250 000 low-income households by March 2005 and a further three million by 2008. However, only 23 000 households were connected by March 2005. Among the obstacles encountered was the price of LPG and the cost of cylinders. Once these become affordable, a large market will open up. The department is addressing these problems.

Eskom is supporting the initiative. By May 2005, the industry had donated 120 LPG cylinders to members of Parliament for use in their constituencies and homes to educate themselves and the public.

PASA has been successful in further encouraging international exploration companies to evaluate the country's oil and gas opportunities.

The EM gas-field complex off Mossel Bay started production in the third quarter of 2000. It will ensure sufficient feedstock to PetroSA to maintain current liquid-fuel production levels at 36 000 barrels (bbls) of petroleum products a day until 2009.

Parallel exploration is being carried out in various other sections of the Bredasdorp Basin off the coast of Mossel Bay to locate reserves for PetroSA beyond 2009.

PetroSA's gas-to-liquid plant supplies about 7% of South Africa's liquid-fuel needs. The products are supplied to oil companies that market them under their own brand names.

PetroSA also produces anhydrous alcohols and speciality fuels that are exported and earn the company more than R500 million per year.

PetroSA's oilfield, Sable, situated about 150 km south off the coast of Mossel Bay, is expected to produce 17% of South Africa's oil needs.

The field, which came into operation in August 2003, was initially projected to produce 30 000 to 40 000 bbls of crude oil a day and 20 million to 25 million bbls in the next three years.

The net savings in foreign exchange to the country would be equivalent to PetroSA's bottom-line profit of between US$10 million and US$15 million a year.

PetroSA holds 60% working interest in Sable, while Dallas-based partner company Pioneer Natural Resources holds the remaining 40%.

Import and export of fuel products

The import of refined products is restricted to special cases where local producers cannot meet demand. It is subject to state control to promote local refinery utilisation.

When overproduction occurs, export permits are required and generally granted, provided that both South Africa's and other Southern African Customs Union members' requirements are met.

More diesel than petrol is exported, owing to the balance of supply and demand of petrol and diesel relative to refinery configurations. Although petrol and diesel make up 55% of total liquid-fuel exports, South Africa is also the main supplier of all other liquid fuels to Botswana, Namibia, Lesotho and Swaziland.

Gas

In addition to coal gas and LPG, South Africa produced some 930 000 t of natural gas and 104 860 t of associated condensate in 2003.

The entire gas and condensate output is dedicated to PetroSA's liquid-fuel synthesis plant, and accounts for about 1,5% of total primary energy supply. Gas manufactured from coal accounted for 5% of net energy consumption, while LPG accounted for about 6%.

Natural and coal gas play separate roles in the energy system, with natural gas being used solely as a feedstock for the production of synthetic fuels, and coal gas as an industrial and domestic fuel.

However, current development of regional gasfields will lead to natural gas becoming a more important fuel in South Africa.

Infrastructure

South Africa's gas infrastructure stretches from Sasolburg in the northern Free State, through the

In July 2005, the Minister of Minerals and Energy, Ms Lindiwe Hendricks, announced that the SAFARI-1 nuclear research reactor of the South African Nuclear Energy Corporation, located at Pelindaba, will be converted from using high enriched uranium (HEU) to low enriched uranium.

SAFARI-1 was commissioned in the 1960s as a material test reactor and is now mainly used for the production of radioisotopes for nuclear-medicine applications. The remaining HEU will generally be applied to the manufacturing of medical isotopes, mainly Molybdenum-99, which are used in nuclear-medicine diagnostics.

The conversion of SAFARI-1 ensures that the future of South African medical-isotope production can be guaranteed for a longer period.

The conversion will be undertaken over a period of about three years and will provide opportunities for young scientists to be engaged in new development projects.

The process will be regulated by the National Nuclear Regulator and monitored by the International Atomic Energy Agency.

industrial areas of Vereeniging, Johannesburg and the East Rand, and from Secunda to Witbank, Middelburg, Newcastle, Richards Bay and Durban.

Through the Sasol Gas Division, Sasol Oil markets industrial pipeline gas produced by Sasol Synthetic Fuels and Sasol Chemical Industries to about 700 industrial customers. These customers are mostly situated in the greater Johannesburg-Pretoria region and the industrial areas of Witbank-Middelburg and Durban. Its pipeline network consists of about 1 500 km of underground pipelines.

Most of the remaining 10% of gas sales in South Africa is on selling of Sasol gas by Metro Gas in Johannesburg, which owns 1 300 km of distribution pipe, and supplies 12 000 domestic and 3 000 industrial customers.

The privatisation of Metro Gas was completed in 2000. It is now owned by Egoli Gas (Pty) Ltd, a joint venture company owned by Cinergy Global Power Inc. Egoli Gas intends to invest R276 million in Metro Gas.

Petronet owns and operates a gas pipeline, known as the Lily Line. It is about 600 km long and transports methane-rich gas from Sasol's Secunda plant as far as the Durban area. Easigas (Shell) has a small LPG/air pipe network in Port Elizabeth. A privately owned company in Port Elizabeth distributes a small amount of LPG/air blend by pipe.

Industrial customers use 87% of the gas, and domestic consumers the rest. The supply of cost-competitive pipeline gas is complemented by the fuel oils range of low-sulphur residual and distillate fuel oils derived from coal and other synthesised forms, as well as crude oil.

PASA markets offshore gas exploration and exploitation.

The Gas Act, 2001 (Act 48 of 2001), aims to:
• promote the orderly development of the piped gas industry
• establish a national regulatory framework
• establish the National Gas Regulator as the custodian and enforcer of the national regulatory framework.

To facilitate the movement of gas across international borders, a cross-border gas trade agreement was signed with Mozambique.

Electricity

South Africa supplies two-thirds of Africa's electricity and is one of the four cheapest electricity producers in the world. Almost 90% of South Africa's electricity is generated in coal-fired power stations. Koeberg, a large nuclear station near Cape Town, provides about 5% of capacity. A further 5% is provided by hydroelectric and pumped storage schemes. In South Africa there are few, if any, new economic hydro sites that could be developed to deliver significant amounts of power. Generation is currently dominated by Eskom, the national wholly State-owned utility, which also owns and operates the national electricity grid. Eskom currently supplies about 95% of South Africa's electricity.

In global terms, the utility is among the top seven in generating capacity, among the top nine in terms of sales, and has one of the world's biggest dry-cooled power stations, Matimba Power Station.

Eskom was converted into a public company on 1 July 2002. It is financed by net financial market liabilities and assets as well as reserves.

While Eskom does not have exclusive generation rights, it has a practical monopoly on bulk electricity. It also operates the Integrated National High-Voltage Transmission System and supplies electricity directly to large consumers such as mines, mineral beneficiators and other large industries. In addition, it supplies directly to commercial farmers and, through the Integrated National Electrification Programme (INEP), to a large number of residential consumers. It sells in bulk to municipalities, which distribute to consumers within their boundaries.

INEP is one of South Africa's major achievements and unprecedented internationally. Some 3,5 million homes had been electrified by mid-2005, translating into over 435 000 homes per year.

Between January 2003 and January 2004, South Africa increased its electricity output by 7,1% with a peak demand of 34 195 MW on 13 July 2004, as opposed to the 31 928 MW peak in 2003. Of the new capacity to be built, Eskom will target about 70% (in MW), with the balance from IPPs.

In 2004, Eskom announced major plans to expand its generation and transmission capacity to ensure supply for the future. The first step is the reintroduction of three of its previously mothballed power stations.

These are Camden in Ermelo, Grootvlei in Balfour, and Komati, between Middelburg and Bethal, with a combined nominal capacity of 3 800 MW. The first unit of Camden was expected to be returned to service in 2005, followed by Grootvlei in 2007 and Komati in 2008.

Restructuring of the electricity supply industry (ESI)

In December 1998, government released the *Energy White Paper*, which sets out its policy objectives for the entire energy sector. These objectives are to increase access to affordable energy services, improve energy governance, stimulate economic development, manage energy-related environmental impacts and secure energy supplies through diversity.

Restructuring aims to improve the quality of life of all South Africans and to increase economic growth and redeploy assets.

To ensure non-discriminatory and open access to transmission lines, and taking into consideration the financial stability of Eskom, government, in the medium term, is to establish a separate state-owned transmission company. It will be independent of generation and retail businesses, with a ring-fenced transmission-system and market-operation functions. Initially, this transmission company will be a subsidiary of Eskom Holdings and will be established as a separate state-owned company before any investments are made in current or new generation capacity.

Over time, a multimarket electricity-market framework will ensure that transactions between electricity generators, traders and power purchasers take place on a variety of platforms, including bilateral deals, and future and day-ahead markets.

A regulatory framework is in place that will ensure the participation of IPPs and that diversified primary energy sources be developed within the electricity sector without hindrance.

The planning and development of transmission systems will be undertaken by the trans-

mission company, subject to government's policy guidelines.

During 2003, Eskom implemented a revised business model to prepare for capacity requirements and the impending restructuring by splitting its business into regulated and non-regulated divisions.

Eskom's core business, its strategic support businesses, and target markets were reviewed and agreed upon.

The Generation Division will continue to be part of Eskom. In 2003, the power stations in the division were paired together to form clusters to prepare the generation sector for flexibility to accommodate different options in a changing ESI.

The Transmission Division takes responsibility for the electricity grid. Worldwide transmission is a natural monopoly. In South Africa, an efficient regulatory body must be established that will grant all players access to the grid. For example, customers could buy from sources other than Eskom, such as the SADC electricity pool or IPPs, but still use the same transmission infrastructure to have power delivered to them.

The Distribution Division will undergo the most radical change. Government's policy on the electri-

In 2005, the Department of Public Enterprises gave decisive impetus to the Pebble-Bed Modular Reactor (PBMR) Project. The project is now factored into the department's future energy planning and a major intention-to-purchase agreement between Eskom and the PBMR was negotiated. It was probably a world-first and forms the foundation for the further development and industrialisation of this technology.

Due to the urgency with which climate change has to be addressed and the hopes for future hydrogen energy sources, the PBMR assumes a key place in the department's long-term planning.

Cabinet approved the Human Capital Research and Innovation Frontier Programme to build the science base needed to ensure the long-term sustainability of the PBMR project, which is a uniquely South African nuclear technology innovation.

city distribution industry (EDI) requires the division to be separated from Eskom and merged with the electricity departments of municipalities to form a number of financially viable regional electricity distributors (REDs). An interim body, called EDI Holdings Company, is overseeing the transition period. The REDs will be subsidiaries of the company until they can become independent. They will be responsible for distributing electricity and collecting revenue.

Electricity distribution industry

The EDI is valued at R50 billion. The Minister of Minerals and Energy, Ms Lindiwe Hendricks, launched South Africa's first RED in July 2005 in Cape Town. RED 1 leads the way for the other five distributors.

REDs will provide competitive electricity tariffs and offer an efficient electricity service, thus ensuring that consumers get a reliable electricity supply. These entities will in the long term enable access to electricity for all.

REDs will consist of Eskom Distribution and the local authorities. They will buy electricity from power generators such as Eskom on wholesale prices determined by the National Electricity Regulator (NER).

The launch was highlighted by the signing of the Service Delivery Agreement and the Agreement on Operating and Transition Plan for Transfer between RED 1 and the City of Cape Town; and RED 1, City of Cape Town and Eskom respectively.

National Electricity Regulator

The NER was the regulatory authority which presided over the ESI in South Africa. In November 2005, the National Energy Regulator (NERSA) replaced the NER. NERSA also undertook the functions of the Gas Regulator and the Petroleum Pipelines Regulatory Authority.

The NER was funded through a levy imposed on electricity generators, which was passed on to all electricity customers. The role of the NER was to license generators, transmitters and REDs, to approve the prices at which electricity is sold and to set minimum standards for quality of supply and service.

National and regional co-operation

The NER was elected the first chairperson of the formalised African Forum for Utility Regulators. The NER was also the founding member of the Regional Electricity Regulators' Association (RERA) and the South African Utility Regulators' Association (SAURA), which were launched in September and October 2002 respectively. The NER is the chairperson of SAURA and a chairperson of one of RERA's portfolio commitees.

The main purpose of RERA is to provide a platform for co-operation between independent electricity regulators within the SADC region.

Integrated National Electrification Programme

The INEP remains the flagship of the Department of Minerals and Energy. By May 2005, the INEP had delivered connections to 232 287 households at a cost of R582 million, 2 233 school connections at R100 million, and 50 clinic connections at R118 million.

Government announced in February 2004 that it would allocate R200 million towards providing free, basic electricity to poor people in an effort to improve their living conditions. The National Electricity Basic Services Support Tariff Policy was gazetted in July 2003. The policy aims to bring relief, through government intervention, to low-income households and to ensure optimal socio-economic benefits from the INEP. Qualifying customers are eligible for 50 kilowatt-hours (kWh) of free electricity per month. Eskom is a service-provider for free basic electricity in its areas of supply. By December 2003, 35% of the municipalities, which have about 425 000 customers, entered into agreements with Eskom. Formal procedures to roll out the implementation of free basic electricity to these customers have started.

By providing this basic service, government hopes to offer social relief to those who earn less than the national minimum wage levels.

Although users have access to a basic quantity of 50 KWh per household per month in terms of the policy, users will pay the normal tariff for any consumption exceeding 50 KWh per month.

By May 2005, the Department of Minerals and Energy was ready to hand over free basic electricity policy implementation to the Department of Provincial and Local Government. The department's intervention added 3,5 million qualifying recipients.

New jobs and small, medium and micro-enterprise opportunities in KwaZulu-Natal, the Eastern Cape and Limpopo have been created as a result of the Non-Grid Electrification of Schools Programme.

By May 2005, about 1 100 schools had been electrified through the programme. Achieved in one year, this represents more than 50% of the total number of schools electrified in the previous five years. School electrification is done parallel to the installation of e-learning facilities to ensure that learners become computer literate.

Rural households using solar energy will benefit from a limited operation and maintenance subsidy up to a maximum of R40 per household.

Rural solar-energy users will then be liable for paying any amount above the R40 monthly subsidy.

To make paraffin more affordable, the Department of Minerals and Energy removed the levying of value-added tax on it.

Southern African Power Pool (SAPP)

The SAPP is the first formal international power pool in Africa.

The objectives of the SAPP are, among others, to:

- co-ordinate and co-operate in the planning and operation of electricity power systems to min-imise costs, while maintaining reliability, auto-nomy and self-sufficiency
- increase interconnectivity between SADC countries to increase the reliability of power supplies
- facilitate cross-border electricity trading
- fully recover costs of operations and equitably share benefits, including reductions in generat-ing capacity and fuel costs, and improved use of hydroelectric energy.

Member countries are Angola, Botswana, Lesotho, Malawi, Mozambique, Namibia, Swaziland, Tanzania, Zambia, Zimbabwe and the DRC.

The SAPP faces the following challenges:

- lack of infrastructure to deliver electricity
- lack of maintenance of infrastructure
- funds to finance new investments
- insufficient generation – running out of excess capacity by 2007
- high losses.

To lay down the rules governing electricity exchange between utilities, the SAPP Agreement between operating members has been drafted. By mid-2005, it had been signed by the following nine national utilities: BPC (Botswana), EDM (Mozambique), Eskom (South Africa), SNEL (Zaire), ZESA (Zimbabwe), NAMPOWER (Namibia), ZESCO (Zambia), SEB (Swaziland) and LEC (Lesotho).

The success of the SAPP can be measured by the following changing volumes of energy traded by Eskom since its inception:

- 1996: 4 648 GWh
- 1997: 5 513 GWh
- 1998: 3 197 GWh
- 1999: 3 128 GWh
- 2000: 3 872 GWh
- 2001: 6 710 GWh
- 2002: 6 956 GWh
- 2003: 9 977 GWh.

It is now possible for SAPP members to delay capital expenditure on new plants due to the existence of interconnections and a power pool in the region. This is an important aspect in developing the economies of southern Africa.

Biomass

Fuel wood obtained mainly from natural woodlands is the primary source of energy used by households in most rural areas for cooking and heating. In some areas, this resource is almost completely depleted and in others it is under heavy pressure.

The total annual sustainable supply of wood from natural woodlands in communal rural areas is esti-mated at about 12 Mt. However, probably no more than half of it is usable as fuel wood. In addition to these sources, residues from commercial forestry total about 4,2 Mt per year. Much of this, as well as wood from bush clearing on commercial farmland is increasingly being used as fuel.

To be effective, planning for a sustainable fuel-wood supply requires decentralisation, understanding of local conditions and flexibility.

Supply-side interventions focus on satisfying a range of local needs and the realisation that community forestry involves not only the planting of trees, but also community participation, which is central to all activities.

Planning must ensure their integration into broader rural development, land use, natural resource management, and agricultural and energy planning. Interventions should build on the best indigenous practices identified. (See chapter 23: *Water affairs and forestry*.)

By mid-2005, Eskom was looking at harnessing biomass as a grid-supply option, while also planning to pilot new technology aimed at providing rural power in a remote area in the Eastern Cape. This technology, called a gasifier system, will use waste from a rural sawmill to provide electricity to power the creation of business ventures in the area. The system was expected to be installed towards the end of 2005.

Renewables

Renewable energy sources, other than biomass, have not yet been exploited optimally in South Africa.

The department strengthened international relationships in this area through the support offered to partnerships established during the WSSD in 2002. Such partnerships will overcome market barriers, promoting widespread use of sustainable energy solutions. These include the Global Village Energy Partnership and the Renewable Energy and Energy Efficiency Partnership.

The department's capacity-building programme for renewable energy and energy efficiency (CaBEERE) is funded by the Danish International Development Agency. It is yielding significant value in capacity-building in the department, as well as various strategies and studies to support the enabling environment created by government.

The White Paper addresses four key strategic areas, namely:
- financial instruments to promote the implementation of sustainable renewable energy through

the establishment of appropriate financial instruments
- legal instruments to develop, implement, maintain and continuously improve an effective legislative system to promote the implementation of renewable energy
- technology development to promote, enhance and develop technologies for the implementation of sustainable renewable energy
- building capacity and education to develop mechanisms to raise awareness of the benefits and opportunities that renewable energy offers.

Technological feasibility studies will be conducted for possible implementation in the medium to longer term. These include:
- Grid-connected wind farms.
- Wind farm/pumped storage as a means of addressing peak loads on the national electricity grid.
- The local production and commercial dissemination of solar cookers, which is a collaborative project between the German Development Agency and the Department of Minerals and Energy.
- Solar thermal-power generation, which is a collaborative programme with Eskom. It also involves the SolarPACES Programme of the International Energy Agency.
- Small-scale hydropower.
- Landfill gas exploitation.
- Rural water supply and sanitation.

Following Cabinet approval of the *White Paper on Renewable Energy*, the department proceeded with the development of its Renewable Energy Strategy. This is essentially the implementation plan for widespread roll-out of the various technologies identified in a macro-economic study undertaken in the latter half of 2003.

The White Paper's target of 10 000-GWh renewable energy contribution to final energy consumption by 2013 was confirmed to be economically viable with subsidies and carbon financing. Achieving the target will add about 1 667 MW new renewable energy capacity, with a net impact on GDP as high as R1,071 billion per year; additional government revenue of R299 million; additional income that would flow to low-income households of as much as R128 million, creating just over 20 000 new jobs; and water savings of 16,5 million kilolitres, which translates into a R26,6-million saving.

The study also highlighted the technologies to be implemented first, based on the level of commercialisation of the technology and natural resource availability. These technologies include:

- sugar-cane bagasse for cogeneration
- landfill gas extraction
- mini-hydroelectric schemes
- commercial and domestic solar water heaters.

These technologies are to be deployed in the first phase of the target period, from 2005 to 2007. The department will introduce nominal, once-off capital subsidies to assist project developers in producing economically sound projects that are readily financed by financial institutions.

Solar

Most areas in South Africa average more than 2 500 hours of sunshine per year, and average daily solar-radiation levels range between 4,5 and 6,5 kWh/m^2 in one day.

The southern African region, and in fact the whole of Africa, is well endowed with sunshine all year round. The annual 24-hour global solar radiation average is about 220 W/m^2 for South Africa, compared with about 150 W/m^2 for parts of the USA, and about 100 W/m^2 for Europe and the United Kingdom. This makes the local resource one of the highest in the world.

The solar resource is the most readily accessible in South Africa. It lends itself to a number of potential uses.

The country's solar-equipment industry is developing. Annual photovoltaic (PV) panel-assembly capacity totals 5 MW, and a number of companies in South Africa manufacture solar water-heaters.

The *White Paper on Energy Policy* identifies universal access to electricity as one of the primary goals of South Africa's energy policy.

To achieve this goal, it was decided to integrate non-grid technologies into the INEP as complementary supply-technologies to grid extension. A pilot programme has been launched to establish a limited number of public-private sector institutions in conjunction with the relevant municipalities to pro-

vide electricity services on an integrated basis. The service-provider will own and maintain the systems, allowing longer-term financing to ameliorate monthly payments. It will provide the service against a monthly fee.

Once the underlying managerial and funding issues have been resolved, the process will be expanded to cover all rural areas.

Solar power is increasingly being used for water-pumping through the rural water-provision and sanitation programme of the Department of Water Affairs and Forestry.

Solar water-heating is used to a certain extent. Current capacity installed includes domestic 330 000 m^2 and swimming pools 327 000 m^2 (middle to high income), commerce and industry 45 000 m^2 and agriculture 4 000 m^2.

Three co-operatives with over 10 permanent employees each have been started in the Eastern Cape to maintain 8 000 solar home systems installed under the previous electrification programme.

Solar-passive building design

Houses and buildings in South Africa are seldom designed from an energy consumption or energy-efficiency perspective. The energy characteristics of low-cost housing are particularly bad, resulting in high levels of energy consumption for space heating in winter. The net result is dangerously high levels of indoor and outdoor air pollution in townships, due mainly to coal burning.

Research has shown that low-cost housing could be rendered 'energy smart' through the utilisation of elementary 'solar-passive building design' practice. This can result in fuel savings of as much as 65%. Such savings on energy expenditure will have a major beneficial impact on the household cash-flow situation. Energy-efficient homes may be constructed at the same direct cost (and lower life-cycle cost) as energy-wasteful houses. The challenge is to develop awareness and to ensure implementation of basic energy-efficiency principles.

National solar water-heating programme

Water-heating accounts for a third to half of the

energy consumption in the average household. In South Africa, this derives mainly from electricity, being the most common energy-carrier employed. Removing this expenditure could lead to significant improvements in the disposable incomes of the lower-income sector.

Furthermore, the equivalent of a large coal-fired power station (2 000 MW+) is employed to provide hot water on tap to the domestic sector alone. Since the inception of the accelerated domestic electrification programme through grid extension, a major distortion of the national load curve has emerged, with the early evening load peak growing significantly.

Modelling indicates that the introduction of solar water-heating can ameliorate the situation substantially.

Switching from electrical to solar water-heating can, therefore, have significant economic and environmental benefits.

There are economic benefits for home owners in reducing their energy bills. Expensive generation capacity to address load peaks will be obviated, and the introduction of new base-load capacity will be postponed. Benefits for the country include reducing greenhouse gas (GHG) emissions, and the release of scarce capital for other pressing needs.

A roll-out programme of solar heaters has commenced, with the focus on middle- to high-income households in Gauteng, the Western Cape and KwaZulu-Natal. The initiative is spearheaded by the CEF.

Solar-thermal power generation

The minimum direct normal radiation (DNR) to justify a combined solar thermal power plant is 1 800 kWh/m^2 per year. According to the Renewable Energy Resource Database, the area exceeding the minimum required DNR in South Africa covers about 194 000 km^2. A 100-MW solar thermal plant requires roughly 3 km^2 (1800 kWh/m^2 per year). If 1% (1 940 km^2) of the identified area is available for solar thermal power generation, South Africa has an installed potential of 64,6 GW, which is about 36 217 GWh/year.

Back-up and energy-storage constraints are limiting the wider economical utilisation of solar electricity generation (solar thermal and PV).

Stirling Dish Demonstration Project

The system consists of a mirror collector that follows the sun during the day and a Stirling engine mounted at the focal point of the mirror collector. As the collector follows the sun, the working gas inside the engine is heated, which is converted to mechanical energy and drives a generator to generate electricity. Eskom's Research, Development and Demonstration Division Project is aimed at assessing the technical and economic feasibility of this new technology. To achieve these objectives, a 25-kW unit was installed at the Development Bank of Southern Africa in Midrand, Johannesburg, in 2002.

Wind

Eskom's demonstration wind farm at Klipheuwel is exploring the use of wind energy for bulk electricity-generation. Of the turbines, the most basic unit is actually performing the best under high wind (summer) conditions, while the largest turbine is performing the best under weak wind (winter) conditions. Overall, the total production annually has been just more than 4 GWh. The Klipheuwel wind farm has a total capacity of 3,2 MW, and is expected to generate at a load factor of between 20% and 30%.

The wind farm consists of three units, i.e. two Vestas (Danish) turbines of 660 kW and 1 750 kW respectively, and a Jeumont (French) turbine of 750 kW. The blade spans are 47, 66, and 48 metres respectively. The first unit started generating on 16 August 2002 and the last on 20 February 2003. Each wind generator has its own small meteorological station on top of the turbine, as well as an aircraft warning light. The wind turbines at Klipheuwel generate at wind speeds between 11 and 50 km/hour. Full power is reached at 50 km/hour.

The proposed wind farm in the Darling district of the Western Cape was approved in March 2005.

This facility will consist of four Danish-designed wind turbines that will produce 1,3 MW of electricity each, bringing the total output of the wind farm to 5,2 MW.

This is the first renewable energy power-generating facility to be developed by a private company, which will feed into the national power network. It will also be the first commercial wind farm in South Africa.

The project will be developed with financial assistance from the Danish Government through its funding agency, Danida. Referred to as the National Demonstration Project, it will be used as an example for future public-private partnerships in the establishment of electricity generation. Historically, this was largely the sole domain of Eskom.

The installation is to be erected below Moedmaag Hill about 12 km from Darling along the way to Yzerfontein on the West Coast. The structures will be 50 m high and the blades will have a span of 31 m.

Approval was granted after the Environmental Impact Assessment as prescribed by legislation. The Department of Environmental Affairs and Tourism established that the positive impacts will far outweigh any possible negative environmental impacts.

One of the activities of the Global Environment Facility-funded South African Wind Energy Programme, which is supported through CaBEERE, is to quantify South Africa's commercial exploitable wind resources.

Moderate wind regimes, for example the large sparsely populated areas of the Karoo and Northern Cape, can be economically exploited in stand-alone or hybrid electricity-generation configurations with PV and/or diesel-generator sets. A small local supply industry focusing on small stand-alone battery-charging systems already exists.

Hydro

An assessment conducted by the Department of Minerals and Energy, the *Baseline Study on Hydropower in South Africa*, indicated that specific areas in the country show significant potential for the development of all categories of hydropower in the short and medium term.

The Eastern Cape and KwaZulu-Natal are endowed with the best potential for the development of small, i.e. less than 10-MW hydropower plants. The advantages and attractiveness of these plants are that they can either be stand-alone or in a hybrid combination with other renewable energy sources. Advantage can be derived from the association with other uses of water (e.g. water supply, irrigation, flood control, etc.), which are critical to the future economic and socio-economic development of South Africa.

The SAPP allows the free trading of electricity between SADC member countries, providing South Africa with access to the vast hydropower potential in the countries to the north, notably the significant potential in the Congo River (Inga Falls).

The main project outside South Africa's borders is Westcor. It entails a five-way intergovernmental MoU signed between the utilities of the DRC, Angola, Namibia, Botswana and South Africa. A Westcor office has been set up in Gaborone, Botswana, and will comprise staff from the five national utilities. Westcor will tap into some of the potential in the DRC. The first project is Inga III, a 3 500-MW hydro plant on the Congo River.

At the same time, the countries to the north could benefit through access to the coal-fired power resources in the south. Such an arrangement should stabilise the energy requirements of the region well into this century.

Exploitation of the vast hydropower resources will constitute a significant infusion of renewable energy resources into the energy economy of the region over the medium to long term. The Lesotho Highland Water Project can contribute some 72 MW of hydro-electric power to the system in the short term. Global pressures regarding the environmental impact and displacement of settlements by huge storage dams will likely limit the exploitation of hydropower on a large scale.

Irrespective of the size of installation, any hydropower development will require authorisation in terms of the National Water Act, 1998 (Act 36 of 1998).

Ocean energy

Ocean energy could potentially be derived from the various characteristics of the sea. For example, the rise and fall of the waves can be converted into hydraulic pressure by mechanical compression devices. The pressure can drive a turbine generator to produce electricity, while the tidal variation, sea current and different thermal layers in the ocean can also be used.

The main reason why this energy resource is not currently harnessed is that no reliable technology exists that can generate electricity from this resource. Various companies are testing systems internationally to develop technically viable solutions. Once technical reliability has been proven, cost-effectiveness in relation to other solutions will have to be proven.

Eskom is monitoring the development of these technologies and will take a decision whether to investigate them further upon completion of their initial tests.

Energy and the environment

Energy and the global environment
On a global scale, South Africa's contribution to GHG emissions is small. On a per-capita basis, however, it is well above global averages and that of other middle-income developing countries.

Furthermore, the economy is carbon-intensive, producing only US$259 per ton of carbon dioxide emitted, as compared with US$1 131 for South Korea, US$484 for Mexico and US$418 for Brazil.

Sources of greenhouse gas emissions
The energy sector is a major source of GHG because of the heavy reliance on coal for electricity generation, the Sasol oil-from-coal process and a variety of other indigenous energy uses such as household coal burning.

In addition, 57% of the coal-mining methane emissions can be attributed to these two uses of coal.

Energy and the national environment
There is some contention regarding the polluting effects of the energy sector, particularly in the Mpumalanga highveld – the location of most of Eskom's coal-powered stations and the largest Sasol plants.

As is the case internationally, there is ongoing debate about the desirability of nuclear energy.

Energy and the household environment
Coal is used by about 950 000 households countrywide. This causes indoor air-pollution problems, which have a serious health impact.

It has been found that in some cases, especially regarding particulate matter, exposure can exceed World Health Organisation (WHO) standards (180 mg.m^{-3}) by factors of six to seven during winter, and two to three in summer. A national programme has been established to introduce low-smoke alternatives into the townships.

Fuel wood is used by three million rural households as their primary energy source. Studies have shown that fuel-wood users are exposed to even higher levels of particulate emissions than coal users. In one study, exposure levels were found to exceed the WHO lowest-observed-effect level by 26 times.

The Department of Minerals and Energy participates in the National Housing Interdepartmental Task Team and has contributed towards the development of norms and standards for solar-passive and thermally efficient housing design.

The department is investigating the introduction of improved woodstoves and other alternatives, such as solar cookers and biogas, in an attempt to address these pollution problems.

More widespread is the use of paraffin by low-income households, rural as well as urban. Paraffin has, however, associated health and safety problems. The distribution of child-proof caps and the dissemination of information on the safe storage and use of paraffin are some of the measures being taken by the department and other role-players to address the problem.

Integrated Energy Planning (IEP)
The Department of Minerals and Energy published the first IEP for South Africa in March 2003. A full copy of the IEP is available on the department's website.

The department is embarking on a second phase of integrated energy planning, as required by the *1998 White Paper on Energy Policy*.

IEP2 will focus on addressing the gaps identified in the first IEP and through a proper consultative process will identify the scenarios and sensitivity studies that will be considered in the second IEP.

Integrated energy centres (IeCs)

The Department of Minerals and Energy initiated the IeC Programme in 2002/01 as part of its contribution to the Integrated Sustainable Rural Development Programme (ISRDP) in support of government's strategy on service delivery and poverty eradication. The programme targets the Presidential nodal areas

The department's main strategies for increasing the ability of rural communities to get improved energy supplies to assist ISRDP are:

- raising community awareness and empowering a cadre of rural energy activists, so that they can express their needs and provide an informed constituency to understand and respond to government policies
- establishing IeCs in rural areas
- assisting local authorities to incorporate energy planning into their integrated development plan processes (especially in the context of electrification planning and non-grid electrification).

By mid-2005, there were three operational IeCs, namely Kgalagadi IeC in Kuruman (Northern Cape), Eshane IeC in Greytown (KwaZulu-Natal) and Caba Mdeni IeC in Matatiele (Eastern Cape). The department was preparing a strategy to roll out more centres. The centres are to be established as co-operatives of the local community and will provide sales outlets for energy products, such as petrol, diesel, paraffin, gas, and energy-efficient appliances. The communities around IeCs are benefiting from the programme in that:

- energy sources such as paraffin, LPG, petrol, diesel, lubricants and other petroleum products are now more accessible
- energy products and gadgets, such as efficient bulbs, Eskom pre-paid cards, solar cookers, etc. are also available at these centres

- information on energy in general (including free basic electricity) is provided
- training on paraffin and LPG safety is provided by the Paraffin Safety Association of South Africa and the LPG Association, respectively.

The IeC progamme is supported by Total SA and Sasol. Other stakeholders include the National Development Agency and Eskom Rural Development.

Energy data

The Department of Minerals and Energy is responsible for collecting and publishing energy data. The department and Statistics South Africa are in the process of signing an MoU that will, among other things, enable energy data to be regarded as official statistics.

Detailed, complete, timely and reliable statistics are essential to monitor the energy situation at national and international level. As part of a process to ensure that energy data meets national and international standards, the department intends to make the provision of energy data mandatory.

The department produces annual energy balances of the energy economy in South Africa, which conforms to internationally accepted standards. It also regularly produces a price report of energy commodities in the country.

Geology

South Africa has a geological wonderland, which comprises 10 different and unique areas across the country.

Barberton mountain land

This beautiful and rugged tract of country with some of the oldest rocks on Earth is situated in Mpumalanga. The renowned Barberton Greenstone Belt, the largest of its kind in South Africa, represents remnants of original crust, dated around 3,5 billion years. The greenstone formations represent the earliest clearly decipherable geological events on the Earth's surface. Silica-rich layers within the greenstone have revealed traces of a very early life form – minute blue-green algae.

The formations are surrounded by granites and gneisses more than 3 000 million years old.

Gold, iron ore, magnesite, talc, barite, chrysotile asbestos and verdite are mined in the area.

Bushveld Complex and escarpment
The Bushveld Complex extends over an area of 65 000 km² and reaches up to 8 km in thickness. It is by far the largest layered igneous intrusion in the world and contains most of the world's resources of chromium, PGMs and vanadium. This mega-complex was emplaced in a molten state about 2,060 billion years ago into pre-existing sedimentary rocks, through several deep feeder zones.

The impressive igneous geology of the Bushveld Complex is best viewed in Mpumalanga, in the mountainous terrain around the Steelpoort Valley. In abundance here are the imposing Dwars River chromitite layers, the original platinum-bearing dunite pipes, the discovery site of the platinum-rich Merensky Reef, and extensive magnetite-ilmenite layers and pipes near Magnet Heights and Kennedy's Vale.

The great escarpment is one of South Africa's most scenic landscapes. This area features potholes (at Bourke's Luck), the Blyde River Canyon and the dolomite formation in which giant stromatolites bear witness to the 2,5 billion-year-old fossiled remains of vast oxygen-producing algae growth.

Drakensberg escarpment and Golden Gate Highlands National Park
The main ramparts of the Drakensberg range, reaching heights of more than 3 000 m, lie in KwaZulu-Natal and on the Lesotho border. These precipitous mountains are the highest in southern Africa and provide the most dramatic scenery.

They are formed from outpourings of basaltic lava more than 1 500 m thick, covering the Clarens sandstones. Only a small remnant of the once-vast continental basalt field that covered much of the continent now remains, mostly in the Lesotho highlands.

The northern area of the Drakensberg has been declared a World Heritage Site. More than 40% of all known San cave paintings in southern Africa are found here.

The Golden Gate Highlands National Park features spectacular sandstone bluffs and cliffs. The sandstone reflects a sandy desert environment that existed around 200 million years ago. Dinosaur fossils can still be found in the area.

Karoo
The Karoo Supergroup covers most of South Africa and reaches a thickness of several thousand metres. The sedimentary rock sequence reveals an almost continuous record of deposition and life, from the end of the Carboniferous into the mid-Jurassic periods, between 300 million and 180 million years ago.

Karoo rocks are internationally renowned for their wealth of continental fossils, and particularly for the fossils of mammal-like reptiles that show the transition from reptiles to early mammals, and for early dinosaur evolution.

During this long period of the history of the Earth, southern Africa was a lowland area in the centre of the Gondwana supercontinent.

Initially, the prehistoric Karoo was a place of vast glaciation, then a shallow inland sea, followed by huge rivers, lush flood plains and swampy deltas, ending in sandy desert and finally, vast outpourings of continental basaltic lava heralding the Gondwana break-up.

Diamond fields
Kimberlite is the primary host-rock of diamonds and was first mined as weathered 'yellow ground' from the Kimberley mines, starting in 1871 at Colesberg koppie, now the site of the Big Hole of Kimberley.

At increasing depths, less-weathered 'blue ground' continued to yield diamonds.

The discovery of kimberlite-hosted diamonds was a key event in South Africa's economic and social development, and paved the way for the later development of the Witwatersrand goldfields.

Kimberlite originates as magma from very deep below the surface, and typically occurs as small vulcanic pipes and craters at the surface. Included within solidified kimberlites are fragments of deep-seated rocks and minerals, including rare diamonds of various sizes.

The Orange and Vaal rivers' alluvial diamond fields and the rich West Coast marine diamond deposits all originated by erosion from primary kimberlite pipes.

Meteorite impact sites

Impacts by large meteoritic projectiles played a major role in shaping the surface of the Earth.

One such site is the Vredefort Dome, the oldest and largest impact structure known on Earth.

Recently declared a World Heritage Site, it is located some 110 km south-west of Johannesburg, in the vicinity of Parys and Vredefort in the Free State and North West.

This spectacular and complex geological feature, measuring 70 km across, has been proved to be the remnant of the original catastrophic impact by a large meteorite or asteroid, some two billion years ago. The original impact crater has long since eroded.

The Vredefort structure consists of a 50-km wide core zone made up of granitic rocks, surrounded by the ring-like collar zone of younger bedded formations. Younger Karoo sediments cover the structure in the south-east.

Pilanesberg

The Pilanesberg complex and National Park, located some 120 km north-west of Johannesburg in North West, is a major scientific attraction which includes a number of unique geological sites.

The complex consists of an almost perfectly circular, dissected mountain massif some 25 km in diameter, making it the third-largest alkaline ring complex in the world.

The geology reflects the roots of an ancient volcano that erupted around 1,5 billion years ago.

The remains of ancient lava flows and vulcanic breccias can be seen.

The dominant feature of the complex is the concentric cone sheets formed by resurgent magma that intruded ring fractures, created during the collapse of the vulcano. There are old mining sites for fluorite and dimension stone, and a non-diamond-bearing kimberlite pipe in the region

Cradle of Humankind

Located mainly in Gauteng, this World Heritage Site extends from the Witwatersrand in the south to the Magaliesberg in the north, and is considered to be of universal value because of the outstanding richness of the fossil hominid (family of man) cave sites.

The Sterkfontein area near Krugersdorp stands supreme as the most prolific and accessible fossil hominid site on Earth. It comprises several scientifically important cave locations, including Sterkfontein, Swartkrans, Drimolen, Kromdraai, Gladysvale and Plover's Lake, all of which have produced a wealth of material crucial to palaeoanthropological research.

Table Mountain and the Cape Peninsula

Table Mountain is arguably South Africa's best known and most spectacular geological site, being made up of five major rock formations.

The earliest of these are the deformed slates of the Malmesbury group which formed between 560 million and 700 million years ago.

Coarse-grained Cape granite intruded around 540 million years ago.

The Table Mountain Group, deposited from 450 million years ago, consists of basal, reddish mudstone and sandstone, very well exposed along Chapman's Peak. Overlying this is the light-coloured sandstone that makes up the higher mountains and major cliff faces of the Cape Peninsula, as far south as Cape Point.

Much younger sandy formations make up the Cape Flats and other low-lying areas.

The Table Mountain group continues further inland across False Bay in the strongly deformed Cape Fold Belt.

Witwatersrand

The geology and gold mines of the 'Ridge of White Waters' are world-famous. Nearly half of all the gold ever mined has come from the extensive Witwatersrand conglomerate reefs that were discovered in 1886, not far from the Johannesburg city centre

The Witwatersrand is the greatest goldfield of all time. More than 48 000 t of gold have been produced from seven major goldfields distributed in a crescent-like shape across the 350-km long basin, from Welkom in the Free State in the southwest, to Evander in the east.

The geology of the region can be seen at many excellent outcrops in the suburbs of Johannesburg.

The sequence is divided into a lower shale-rich group and an upper sandstone-rich group. The latter contains the important gold-bearing quartz-pebble conglomerates. These 'gold reefs' were formed from gravels transported into the basin and reworked 2,75 billion years ago. The gold and uranium originated from a rich source in the hinterland.

Acknowledgements

Business Day

Central Energy Fund

Chamber of Mines of South Africa

Council for Geoscience

Department of Minerals and Energy

Eskom

Estimates of National Expenditure 2005, published by National Treasury

Gavin Whitfield

National Electricity Regulator

Nuclear Energy Corporation of South Africa

PetroSA

www.southafrica.info

www.globaldialogue.info

www.gov.za

www.sasol.co.za

Suggested reading

Allen, V.L. *History of Black Mineworkers in South Africa.* Keighley: Moor Press, 1992.

Anhaeusser, C.R. ed. *Century of Geological Endeavour in Southern Africa.* Johannesburg: Geological Society of South Africa, 1997.

Brooke-Simons, P. *Cullinan Diamonds: Dreams and Discoveries.* Cape Town: Fernwood Press, 2004.

Cruse, J. and James, W. eds. *Crossing Boundaries: Mine Migrancy in a Democratic South Africa.* Claremont, Cape Town: Institute for Democracy in South Africa. 1995.

Fig, D. *Uranium Record: Questioning South Africa's Nuclear Direction.* Johannesburg: Jacana, 2005.

Flynn, L. *Studded with Diamonds and Paved with Gold Mines. Mining Companies and Human Rights in South Africa.* London: Bloomsbury, 1992.

Gustafsson, H. *et al. South African Minerals: An Analysis of Western Dependence.* Uppsala: Scandinavian Institute of African Studies, 1990.

Kamfer, S. *Last Empire: De Beers, Diamonds and the World.* London: Hodder & Stoughton, 1994.

Katz, E. *The White Death: Silicosis on the Witwatersrand Gold Mines, 1880 – 1910.* Johannesburg: Witwatersrand University Press, 1994.

Lang, J. *Bullion Johannesburg: Men, Mines and the Challenge of Conflict.* Johannesburg: Jonathan Ball, 1986.

Lang, J. *Power Base: Coal Mining in the Life of South Africa.* Johannesburg: Jonathan Ball, 1995.

Roberts, J.L. *A Photographic Guide to Minerals, Rocks and Fossils.* London, Cape Town: New Holland, 1998.

South Africa Minerals Yearbook, 1997. University of the Witwatersrand: Minerals and Energy Policy Centre, 1997.

Strategic Overview of the South African Mining Industry: Gold, Coal, Platinum Group Metals, Diamonds, Vanadium. Johannesburg: Industrial Development Corporation, 2000.

Wilson, M.G.C. and Anhaeusser, C.R. eds. *The Mineral Resources of South Africa: Handbook.* Pretoria: Council for Geoscience, 1998.

Walton, J. and Pretorius, A. *Windpumps in South Africa: Wherever You Go, You See Them; Whenever You See Them, They Go.* Cape Town: Human & Rousseau, 1998.

Ward, S. *The Energy Book for Urban Development in South Africa.* Noordhoek: Sustainable Energy Africa, 2002.

Safety, security and defence

The South African Police Service (SAPS) is responsible for internal security and crime prevention, while the South African National Defence Force (SANDF) is responsible for defending South Africa against external military threats.

Safety and security

In accordance with the Constitution of the Republic of South Africa, 1996 (Act 108 of 1996), the Minister of Safety and Security is responsible for policing in general and is accountable to the Cabinet and Parliament. Important features of the minister's responsibility are the determination of national policing policy and the provision of civilian oversight. The following three structures fall under the Minister of Safety and Security:
- Secretariat for Safety and Security
- Independent Complaints Directorate (ICD)
- SAPS.

Based on its legislative mandate, the Department of Safety and Security has identified the following key objectives for the medium term, namely to:
- enhance the safety and security of South Africans
- ensure proper investigation of criminal cases and the provision of sound crime intelligence
- protect prominent people
- efficiently manage the SAPS, including its resources, development and operations.

These objectives have been aligned with the goals of the integrated justice system and the Justice, Crime Prevention and Security (JCPS) Cabinet Cluster, which coordinates joint crime-prevention initiatives.

The SAPS Strategic Plan (2004 – 2007) includes four key strategic priorities for the medium term. These are to:
- combat organised crime by focusing on drug and firearm trafficking, vehicle theft and hijacking, as well as commercial crime and corruption among public officials
- address serious and violent crime to counter the proliferation of firearms; improve safety and security in high-crime areas; combat crimes such as taxi and gang violence and faction fighting; and maintain security at major public events
- reduce the incidence of crimes committed against women and children and improving the investigation and prosecution of these crimes
- improve service delivery at police stations.

The National Crime Combating Strategy (NCCS) involves the establishment of crime-combating task groups targeting serious and violent crime in designated high-crime zones.

The NCCS informs and directs operations and resources at police-station level. Furthermore, police resources are focused on identified high-crime areas and priority stations in terms of a multi-disciplinary geographical approach. A service-integrity framework has been developed to encourage members to resist and expose corruption, and to improve management and supervision.

Secretariat for Safety and Security

In terms of the SAPS Act, 1995 (Act 68 of 1995), the functions of the Secretariat for Safety and Security are to:
- advise the minister
- promote democratic accountability and transparency in the SAPS
- provide the minister with legal services and advice on constitutional matters
- monitor the implementation of policy
- conduct research on any policing matter in accordance with the instructions of the minister, and evaluate the performance of the SAPS.

The secretariat emphasises the importance of moral regeneration in efforts to combat crime, in the belief that a major problem affecting criminality is moral degeneration. The Moral Regeneration Movement calls on all cardinal role-players – the family, church, school system, government departments, various constitutional commissions such as the National Youth Commission and the Commission on Gender Equality, and business – to come on board.

Independent Complaints Directorate

The ICD investigates complaints of alleged criminality and misconduct against members of the SAPS.

Criminality includes offences such as theft, corruption, robbery, assault and rape.

The primary role of the ICD is to ensure that complaints about offences and misconduct committed by SAPS members are investigated in an effective manner. Police conduct or behaviour which is prohibited in terms of the SAPS standing orders and police regulations, includes neglect of duties and failure to comply with the SAPS Code of Conduct. It is governed by Chapter 10 of the SAPS Act, 1995.

The ICD has additional mandates in respect of monitoring the implementation of the Domestic Violence Act, 1998 (Act 116 of 1998), by the SAPS, and in respect of civilian oversight over municipal policing services.

The ICD investigates all deaths in police custody or as a result of police action. An investigation is conducted to determine any indications of criminal conduct by the SAPS. Where there are no indications of criminal conduct, the matter is left to the police themselves to investigate, while the ICD monitors/supervises the investigation. If information is subsequently received indicating criminal conduct on the part of the police, the ICD conducts a full investigation.

Upon completion of an investigation, the ICD may make recommendations to the Director of Public Prosecutions about the prosecution of any SAPS member(s) implicated. It may also make recommendations to the SAPS management regarding the departmental prosecution of a police member.

The ICD is compelled by law to investigate complaints or reports of deaths in police custody, or as a result of police action.

The ICD reports to Parliament through the Minister of Safety and Security. However, it is operationally independent from the SAPS.

The number of complaints handled by the ICD in 2004/05 amounted to 5 790, representing a decrease of 2% compared with 2003/04, when 5 903 complaints were received.

There has been a decrease of 9% in deaths in police custody or as a result of police action, compared with the same period in 2003/04.

There were 652 deaths in 2004/05 compared with 714 in 2003/04. The majority of deaths, most of which were shootings, occurred in KwaZulu-Natal (26,8%).

Gauteng accounted for 22,7%, comprising mainly shootings, suicides and natural deaths. The Eastern Cape had 10,7% deaths; Western Cape

10%; Mpumalanga 8,4%; Limpopo 8%; North West and the Free State 5,8%; and the Northern Cape 1,7%.

Incidents of misconduct reported to the ICD decreased by 8,3% compared with 2003/04.

The reduction of deaths is partly attributed to the joint ICD-SAPS committee, which meets monthly to monitor death incidents. The decrease also confirms a growing human-rights ethic within the SAPS.

South African Police Service

Ten years of policing in a democracy

The SAPS was established in 1995 after the amalgamation of the 11 independent policing agencies that existed before the nation's transition to democracy. On 27 January 2005, the SAPS celebrated 10 years of policing in a democracy.

To mark the occasion, a prestigious commemorative publication, *South African Police Service, 10 Years of Policing in a Democracy 1995 – 2005*, was published.

A series of 10 postage stamps was also launched, in co-operation with the South African Post Office and the Department of Communications.

National Police Day, 27 January

Cabinet declared 27 January as National Police Day to coincide with the 10th anniversary of the SAPS on 27 January 2005.

The purpose of National Police Day is to:
- signify the date and anniversary of the establishment of the SAPS
- recognise the service rendered by members of the SAPS
- honour those members who have paid with their lives to protect and serve all South Africans
- indicate to both local and international communities that the SAPS is honoured and respected for the law, order, safety and security it provides for South Africa and its people, and that the SAPS has the full backing of its government

- make it possible for all sectors of communities to be informed and to feel actively engaged in safety and security matters.

Strategic overview and key objectives

The key aims and programmes of the SAPS are based on the objectives provided for in Section 205 of the Constitution. The SAPS is responsible for:
- preventing, combating and investigating crime
- maintaining public order
- protecting and securing South Africans and their property
- upholding and enforcing the law.

The vision of the SAPS is to create a safe and secure environment for all South Africans.

The values held by the SAPS are to:
- protect everyone's rights and be impartial, respectful, open and accountable to the community
- use its powers in a responsible way
- provide a responsible, effective and high-quality service with honesty and integrity
- evaluate its service continuously and make every effort to improve it
- use its resources in the best way possible
- develop the skills of all its members through equal opportunities
- co-operate with the community, all levels of government and other role-players.

The budget of the SAPS has been increasing by an annual average of 10,7% since the 2000/01 financial year, when it stood at R15,6 billion. It is expected to increase to R28,7 billion by 2006/07.

In 2005/06, the SAPS was allocated R4,4 billion to improve police salaries and R600 million to employ an additional 1 200 police officers in 2005.

Enhancing policing presence

Crime prevention in South Africa is based on the principles of community policing, that is, partnerships between the community and the SAPS. Partnerships between police officers (who are appointed as sector managers) and communities strengthen existing community police fora.

Sector policing was introduced in 2002/03 to increase the visibility and accessibility of police officers, particularly in areas that have limited infrastructure and high levels of crime. In 2003/04, sector policing was implemented at the 50 priority stations and the 14 Presidential stations.

The implementation of sector policing continues and funds will be provided to increase the number of personnel to 156 760 by the end of March 2007, which is a 31,1% increase. This labour input will be complemented by a concomitant expansion of the vehicle fleet, equipment supplies and Information Technology (IT) infrastructure.

Restructuring

The National Intervention Unit (NIU) was established in 2002/03 to deal with medium- and high-risk operations to stabilise volatile situations.

It provides specialised operational support to police stations, sections and units. Area crime-combating units are responsible for combating serious and violent crimes, policing public gatherings and providing specialised operational support in the areas where they are situated.

At national level, the specialised investigation units comprise the Serious Economic Offences Unit and organised crime and serious and violent crime task teams. Provincial and area specialised units include commercial branches; organised crime units; serious and violent crime units; precious metals units; diamond units; vehicle identification and safeguarding units; stock theft units; and family violence, child protection and sexual offences units.

Owing to the unique functions performed by the Forensic Science Laboratory and the Criminal Record Centre, a new division, the Criminal Record and Forensic Science Services, responsible for functions related to these two centres, was established in 2004.

By May 2005, the Forensic Science Laboratory was being upgraded and the Laboratory Information Management System implemented. The Automated Fingerprint Identification System (AFIS) has been fully implemented and rolled out.

SAPS divisions

Career Management

This division recognises the substantial corporate investment in human capital and delivers effective career-management systems, practices and methodologies required by the SAPS.

The division renders a people-centred human-resource (HR) service to all personnel and ensures their optimal utilisation.

A strong knowledge of critical skills resident in the workforce, paired with essential emerging technologies, can solve HR problems and effectively service the people in times when surge capacity is required.

Career Management provides HR support and capacity-building to the SAPS, including management interventions, career coaching, career alignment and strategic workforce planning.

Crime Intelligence

The Crime Intelligence Division of the SAPS is responsible for managing information gathering and centralised intelligence management, co-ordination and analysis. It also provides technical intelligence support to the operational components of crime intelligence and, where necessary, to other operational divisions of the SAPS.

Crime Prevention

Crime Prevention aims to reduce opportunities to commit crime by optimising visible policing. The division is also responsible for developing, maintaining and monitoring policy standards and directives regarding crime prevention and uniformed services in general.

The division's three main components are Social Crime Prevention, Visible Policing and Police Emergency Services.

Social Crime Prevention deals with crimes affecting the social fabric of society, including crimes against women and children, as well as community-based crime prevention.

Visible Policing is responsible for combating crime through crime operations, police station activities and high visibility, and the availability of police officials at grassroots level.

Police Emergency Services renders a rapid-response service in respect of crimes in progress, and provides dog and mounted services.

Criminal Record Centre and Forensic Science Laboratory

The Pretoria laboratory does advanced work such as voice comparison and the detection of fraudulent documents, including cheques. By mid-2004, the decentralisation of the DNA analysis capacity to KwaZulu-Natal had been commissioned and a new multimillion rand project for expansion work at the Forensic Science Laboratory in the Western Cape was underway.

Automated Fingerprint Information System

The AFIS is fully operational at national level as well as at 35 sites throughout the country. The AFIS Palm was expected to be implemented in 2005. This technology will enable the SAPS to read latent palmprints along with the current ability to read latent fingerprints. The AFIS is contributing towards an increase in accuracy, productivity and service delivery. Faster response times lead to an increase in the production of previous conviction reports.

Integrated Ballistics Information System (IBIS)

The IBIS, which enables the SAPS to link bullets and cartridge cases to firearms and crime scenes, was upgraded in 2003/04. More than 24 566 exhibits have been placed on the system since its upgrading.

Detective Service

The Detective Service is responsible for maintaining an effective crime-investigation service. Its main functions involve conducting investigations into organised crime, serious and violent crime, general crime and commercial crime. The Detective Service is also responsible for curbing corruption, drawing up strategic crime reports and establishing crime-pattern analysis capabilities at all levels in the SAPS

The Detective Service consists of the following components:
- General Investigations

- Organised Crime
- Commercial Crime
- Serious and Violent Crime.

Financial and Administration Services

This division ensures that the SAPS' budget is managed in a cost-effective manner and that an effective auxiliary service is rendered. The division consequently manages financial and auxiliary services, and also oversees the management and utilisation of all resources in accordance with relevant directives and legislation. The division has a capacity for support and interventions at national level pertaining to, among other things, the management of the national budget.

Legal Services

This division mainly renders a legal advisory service to the SAPS in respect of, among other things, the development, interpretation, application and implementation of policy; the drafting of legislation; the management of litigious matters; the administration and management of contracts and agreements arbitration; the management of national and inter

In September 2005, the South African Police Service released crime statistics for 2004/05:
- attempted murder decreased by 18,8%
- assault decreased by 4,5%
- common assault decreased by 5,1%
- robbery with aggravating circumstances decreased by 5,5%
- common robbery decreased by 5,3%
- burglary at residential premises decreased by 8,1%
- theft of motor vehicles and motorcycles decreased by 5,3%
- theft out of or from motor vehicles decreased by 14%
- stock-theft decreased by 21,2%
- illegal possession of firearms and ammunition decreased by 8,3%
- drug-related crimes increased by 33.5%
- car hijackings decreased by 9,9%
- shoplifting decreased by 7,9%
- commercial crime decreased by 3,8%
- murder decreased by 5,6%
- rape increased by 4%.

national crime operations; special projects; the promotion of corporate identity and good governance; and the general administration and management of legal services.

The division is also responsible for formulating national standards and policy relating to these aspects. The division has seven components, namely:

- Contracts and Agreements
- Crime Operations
- Crime Prevention
- Litigation
- Legislation
- Policy Standards
- Property and Asset Management.

The division has, over the past 10 years, made a considerable contribution towards establishing the legal framework pertaining to policing nationally and internationally. All principal legislation administered in the department has been reviewed and as a result, substituting legislation has been enacted.

The division was instrumental in the drafting of international police co-operation agreements. It also participated in the drafting processes of international instruments pertaining to the combating of transnational organised crime, the proliferation of firearms and terrorism.

Management Services

This division provides a support function to the SAPS. It supports management in respect of communication and liaison services; strategic planning; information and systems management; and organisational development such as the maintenance of organisational structures, procedures, methods, forms and registers.

Although there are management service components at area and provincial levels reporting operationally to the area commissioner and provincial commissioner respectively, such components function in accordance with national policies and guidelines issued by this division.

The division, which has a national capacity for service delivery and interventions at national level, comprises the following components:

- Efficiency Services

- Strategic Management
- Information and Systems Management
- Communication and Liaison Services.

National Evaluation Service

This division supports management in the assessment of service-delivery standards and performance. It strives not only to determine the level of service delivery, but also to assist provinces, areas, stations and units to improve their level of service delivery.

Operational Response Services

This division deals with abnormal policing situations through the utilisation of highly skilled and specialised police officers. These include patrolling South Africa's land, sea and air borderline.

The division is nationally responsible for the maintenance of public order, the execution of medium- and high-risk operations, including the prevention of rural and urban terror, the execution of search-and-rescue operations, the stabilisation of volatile crime situations and the prevention of cross-border crime. The division, which has a national capacity for dealing with matters requiring such responses, consists of the following components:

- area crime-combating units that maintain public order
- NIUs that deal with medium- to high-risk situations such as cash-in-transit heists
- Border Police that prevents the illegal entry and exit of people and goods to and from South Africa at the air, sea and land borders
- the Air Wing that renders an efficient and cost-effective airborne law-enforcement service to police line functions
- the Special Task Force that deals with high-risk situations such as hostage-release operations on land, at sea and in the air.

Most of the personnel in this division are formally trained in basic policing, as well as in a variety of specialised and operational fields, such as crowd management and medium- to high-risk operations.

The division underwent significant changes in 2004, specifically pertaining to recruiting and training female members at previously male-dominated units such as the Special Task Force, NIU and the Air

Wing. The empowerment of women is a main priority within the division.

The Special Task Force became one of the first units of its kind to accept 35 female members on its selection course. Five female members completed the course.

In 2004, the NIU, which already boasted six female operational members, recruited another 23 female members. They completed the selection course successfully to become fully operational members of the NIU.

The Air Wing, which already had three female pilots, embarked on the Designated Pilot Training Programme in 2002, during which various designated members, including women, were identified through a screening process to be trained as pilots. By mid-2005, these members were undergoing training to become fully fledged pilots.

The SAPS, by virtue of its world-class training, is in demand in respect of technical and operational assistance to neighbouring countries, as well as internationally.

The Air Wing participated in various cross-border initiatives in 2004, such as Operation Rachel in Mozambique, during which arms caches were located and destroyed. Operation Rachel has been conducted since 1999 with the active support and assistance of the Mozambican authorities.

The division also assisted with training members of the Democratic Republic of Congo (DRC) Police, as well as with anti-terrorism training and other training needs of the Southern African Regional Police Chiefs Co-operation Organisation.

Personnel Services

Personnel Services manages personnel-related matters in support of the operational priorities of the SAPS. The division consists of three components, namely:
- Employee Assistance Services
- Personnel Provisioning and Maintenance
- Service Terminations and Behaviour Management.

Protection and Security Services

Protection and Security Services minimises security violations by protecting prominent foreign and local people, and securing strategic areas to ensure a safer South Africa.

The division started a programme designed to introduce focused capacity within the environments of railway policing and ports of entry.

After completing their field training in June 2005, 600 members were deployed at Johannesburg International Airport (JIA) and 400 at the Metro rail system in Cape Town.

Phase one of the pilot project for the protection and security of Durban Harbour will commence with the recruitment of 800 members.

All high courts in South Africa have been assessed regarding their physical security. Proposals have been forwarded to the Department of Justice and Constitutional Development to take the matter forward.

The process to transfer excess SANDF personnel to the SAPS started in 2004.

More than 3 600 excess personnel were identified within the SANDF. The integration is expected to be completed within two years.

Supply Chain Management

Supply Chain Management is responsible for meeting the total logistical needs of the SAPS.

On 19 August 2005, the South African Post Office (SAPO) and Business Against Crime SA signed the Statement of Purpose of the Forum for the Alignment of Industry Body Crime-Combating Initiatives. The SAPO was the 10th industry body to sign the statement of purpose, which is part of the initiative by public and private institutions in South Africa to form partnerships aimed at fighting crime, fraud and corruption across a broader spectrum.

Objectives include developing collaborative crime-prevention and combating strategies, sharing crime intelligence and influencing government crime-prevention strategies, including legislative processes that impact on crime-related matters and the economy in general.

The SAPO has embarked on various initiatives internally. This has resulted in losses arising from criminal incidents decreasing by 33%, while reported incidences of crime decreased by 12% in 2004/05.

The SAPS has made great strides in upgrading and providing facilities. Some 110 police stations and cells received attention in 2004/05. Special attention is being paid to facilities in historically disadvantaged communities.

The digital radio communication trunking system in Gauteng is expected to be completed and fully functional by December 2006.

Other major projects include procuring more vehicles; building new police stations; refurbishing existing ones; as well as providing victim-empowerment sections and identity-parade rooms and entrances for people with disabilities.

Seven new police stations were completed during 2004/05, while 41 existing ones were renovated and upgraded. By mid-2005, construction work was underway to build 23 more stations. Twelve of these were expected to be completed during 2005/06.

Training

The functions of the division are to:

- provide effective learning programmes for policing-related education, training and development
- generate, implement and maintain Education, Training and Development (ETD) system standards and the quality assurance of ETD
- facilitate skills development within the SAPS
- manage basic training within the SAPS
- manage in-service training within the SAPS
- manage generic skills provision and international training support within the SAPS
- manage and use all resources in accordance with relevant directives and legislation.

Community involvement

The Crime-Prevention Development Programme facilitates the development and implementation of community-based crime-prevention strategies.

The programme has made a significant contribution towards intersectoral co-operation. It serves as a tool for local service-providers such as local government to integrate community-based crime-prevention strategies in their core business. Communities have participated through applying indigenous knowledge during the conceptual phase of projects.

The programme was successfully completed in the urban-renewal nodes of KwaMashu and Inanda in KwaZulu-Natal. It has been extended to the following areas:

- Limpopo (Thohoyandou and Bolobedu)
- KwaZulu-Natal (KwaDukuza, Mtubatuba and Umhlathuze)
- Eastern Cape (Motherwell and Mdantsane)
- Mpumalanga (Driefontein).

Sector policing

Over and above efforts to concentrate on the generators of contact crimes, such as firearms and drug and substance abuse, the SAPS intensified its efforts in 2004 to implement sector policing. The increase in police visibility not only serves as a crime deterrent, but it also contributes to an increased feeling of safety and security among communities.

To strengthen community policing, the SAPS introduced sector policing in 2002 through which station precincts are divided into smaller manageable parts. By May 2005, sector policing had been implemented in 97 of the 126 sectors at Presidential police stations and in 217 of the 394 sectors in high-crime stations.

Community policing fora (CPFs), which have been in place since 1993, are functioning well at most police stations. This is the cornerstone of the partnership between police and communities. CPFs are actively involved in crime prevention and awareness programmes, and allow police to mobilise and involve communities in the fight against crime. CPFs also assist police by mobilising partnerships with business and other stakeholders in communities to address crime concerns.

Community safety centres

The SAPS is dedicated to the upliftment of historically disadvantaged communities. This includes the building of community safety centres. These centres focus on delivering basic and easily accessible services to communities, especially in deep rural and informal settlement areas.

Community safety centres bring all relevant departments under one roof. It involves the SAPS, the departments of justice and constitutional development, correctional services, health, and social development. Community safety centres are fully operational in Thembalethu in the Western Cape, Ntsimbini in KwaZulu-Natal, Leboeng in Limpopo and Khutsong in Gauteng.

Victim-Empowerment Programme

Some 227 victim-friendly facilities have been established at police stations. The SAPS aimed to establish an additional 150 such facilities in 2005/06. In new or upgraded police stations, provision is made for private facilities where victims can provide statements and access information.

The SAPS Victim Support Programme has been reviewed to ensure that SAPS training and guidelines support the Victims' Charter of Rights. By mid-2005, a youth crime-prevention and development programme that defines the roles and responsibilities of the SAPS was being developed. This is linked to the training of SAPS members to deal with child offenders and youth crime prevention.

The Safer Schools Programme, which resulted from a partnership between the SAPS and the Department of Education, continues to ensure a safe learning environment. This programme is implemented jointly at provincial level and addresses issues such as drugs and firearms in schools, sexual offences and bullying.

By September 2005, 1 253 schools were visited as part of the programme.

During 2004, the SAPS endeavoured to address the plight of homeless children and to mobilise relevant stakeholders to assist children in need. Programmes for homeless children were established in Hillbrow, Johannesburg, and Sunnyside, Pretoria. These provide safe and educational alternatives for children who would normally spend their time on the streets.

By September 2005, the ministries of education and of safety and security were finalising the details of a project to declare all schools in South Africa firearm-free zones.

Firearms control

The Firearms Control Act, 2000 (Act 60 of 2000).

and the Firearms Control Amendment Act, 2003 (Act 43 of 2003), intend to assist the SAPS in preventing the proliferation of illegal firearms and removing them from society, as well as to control legally owned firearms. The Firearms Control Act, 2000 came into effect on 1 July 2004. People seeking firearm licences are compelled to undergo a competency test before being granted a licence.

In November 2004, the Minister of Safety and Security, Mr Charles Nqakula, declared amnesty for people in possession of illegal firearms and ammunition. In terms of the amnesty, as defined in Section 138 of the Firearms Control Act, 2000, illegal firearms and ammunition had to be surrendered at police stations nationwide from 1 January to 31 March 2005. This period was subsequently extended to 30 June 2005.

By June 2005, the SAPS had intensified the accreditation of non-official and official institutions to ensure that potential firearm owners received the necessary mandatory training.

During the same period, the SAPS accredited 510 non-official firearm institutions, 144 shooting ranges and 158 training-providers. Some 3 788 applications for renewal of firearm licences, permits and authorisations were received.

International obligations and involvement in Africa

The SAPS formed part of the South African contingent that assisted the people of the DRC to prepare for their general election in 2005. It was also a key component of the civilian police structure built into the programme of the African Union (AU) Mission in Sudan (AMIS), working towards permanent peace in that country.

On 15 August 2005, the total staff establishment of the South African Police Service was 148 113. Some 11 000 trainees were allocated for 2005/06. In July 2005, 4 410 reported for basic training. The remaining recruits were scheduled to start their training on 6 January 2006.

The AMIS civilian police comprised members of police services from 16 African countries. The SAPS, among others, assisted the Sudanese Police by:

• facilitating communication between them and local communities

• providing technical assistance requested by the Sudanese Government and police authorities.

The SAPS has co-operation agreements with France, Argentina, Chile, Brazil, the Russian Federation, Hungary, Egypt, China, Nigeria, Mozambique, Portugal, Swaziland and the People's Republic of China. Negotiations are ongoing to include more countries on its list of international partners against organised crime.

South Africa is among 182 countries whose police structures are affiliated with Interpol. It has 12 liaison officers based at South African missions abroad to interact on a continuous basis with its counterparts in the detection of international crime.

In 2004, the French Government pledged to support a second three-year programme (2005 – 2007), focusing on the fight against transnational organised crime and terrorism.

Since 2000, the French Government has spent more than R3,7 million to purchase state-of-the-art equipment used to collect and process fingerprints more quickly.

Other projects included equipping the detective and intelligence academy in Hammanskraal with closed-circuit television equipment and a fully fledged computer room to assist in the training of investigators.

Commandos and reservists

The SAPS' drive to increase its capacity will be enhanced by the recruitment of commandos, whose units are being phased out. Many of these will have the opportunity to be recruited into the revised SAPS reservist system.

The reservists will be deployed as part of the programme to reduce crime in the 169 priority areas, as well as implement specific operational concepts such as rural protection.

Career centres

To market career prospects in the SAPS, career centres were launched in:

• Sharpeville, Gauteng

• Bellville, Western Cape

• Pinetown, KwaZulu-Natal.

Two more were scheduled for Thabong and Galeshewe in 2005.

Women's Network

The SAPS Women's Network was launched in July 2004 to assist and support women in the service. The network aims to enhance the rendering of service by the SAPS through facilitating greater co-operation, equality and empowerment among all employees of the SAPS. Activities are aligned to government initiatives to improve the overall quality of life of women.

The network will run at station, provincial and national levels.

Defence

The Constitution, the Defence Act, 2002 (Act 42 of 2002), the *White Paper on Defence* and the *Defence Review*, mandate the Department of Defence. These laws and policies direct and guide the functions of the Department of Defence and the SANDF.

The mission of the Department of Defence is to provide, manage, prepare and employ defence capabilities commensurate with the needs of South Africa, as regulated by the Constitution, national legislation, and parliamentary and executive direction.

The mission success factors of the department involve the following:

• national consensus on defence

• excellent strategic direction

In April 2005, the South African Police Service and the three cellphone operators – Cell C, Vodacom and MTN – signed an agreement to blacklist all stolen handsets.

In terms of the agreement, operators can blacklist a reported stolen cellphone and render it useless.

- excellent resource management
- effective combat and support forces
- professionalism in the conduct of operations
- successful implementation of the transformation process.

Ongoing transformation has drastically changed the functions of the department from offensive to defensive. It is gradually withdrawing from its involvement in support of the police and other protection agencies.

As a key player in regional peace efforts, and as a committed member of the Southern African Development Community (SADC) and the AU, the department is participating in various initiatives aimed at securing peace and stability on the continent.

The defence budget was expected to remain constant over the next three years, with R22,4 billion set aside for 2005/06, R22,5 billion for 2006/07 and R22,1 billion for 2007/08.

An additional R361 billion has been allocated for the ongoing integration of defence systems and military health services, as well as the upgrading and maintaining of facilities.

Legislation

Defence Act, 2002
The Defence Act, 2002 regulates the defence function.

National Conventional Arms Control Committee (NCACC) Act, 2002
The NCACC Act, 2002 (Act 41 of 2002), establishes, among other things, the NCACC (a committee of ministers of which the Minister of Defence is a member) as a statutory body to ensure compliance with government policies in respect of arms control, and provide guidelines and criteria to be used when assessing applications for permits.

National conventional arms-control regulations dealing with applications for permits and the list of dual-use goods, technologies and munitions that are subject to control were published in May 2004. The NCACC's Policy for the Control of Trade in Conventional Arms was promulgated in January 2004.

Protection of Constitutional Democracy and Related Activities Act, 2004
The Protection of Constitutional Democracy and Related Activities Act, 2004 (Act 33 of 2004), came into force on 20 April 2005. Given the scale and nature of contemporary terrorist threats and activities, it is conceivable that military action, including action in the fulfilment of international obligations and action surpassing the usual service in co-operation with the SAPS, could be required in future.

Any military action surpassing service in co-operation with the SAPS and aimed at preventing or combating terrorism within South Africa must be in defence of the country, its sovereign territory, its citizens or its political independence.

Only the President may authorise the deployment of the SANDF in defence of South Africa or in co-operation with the SAPS.

Functions
The SANDF is responsible for:
- the defence of South Africa, and for the protection of its sovereignty and territorial integrity
- compliance with South Africa's international obligations regarding international bodies and other states
- the preservation of life, health and property
- the provision and maintenance of essential services
- upholding law and order in South Africa in co-operation with the SAPS, under circumstances set out in legislation, where the SAPS is unable to maintain law and order on its own
- the support of any state department for the purpose of socio-economic upliftment.

Objectives
The SANDF's military strategic objectives and tasks are to:
- enhance and maintain comprehensive defence capabilities by:
  - providing military defence capabilities for defending South Africa against external military threats, and executing military operations in defence of South Africa, its interests and its citizens when so

494

ordered by the President in his/her capacity as commander-in-chief of the SANDF
- promote peace, security and stability in the region and the continent by:
  - promoting regional security through defence co-operation within the SADC/AU/United Nations (UN)
  - promoting international security through military co-operation in support of South Africa's foreign policy
  - providing a military capability for participation in regional and international peace-support operations
- support the people of South Africa by providing:
  - defence capabilities against internal threats to the constitutional order, and the execution of such operations in a state of emergency when so ordered by the President
  - forces for land, air and maritime border protection against non-military threats
  - capacity to maintain law and order in co-operation with the SAPS on an ongoing basis, which will remain necessary until the SAPS is able to fulfil the task without assistance from the military other than in exceptional circumstances
  - surveillance and enforcement support to the relevant authorities for the protection of marine resources, control of marine pollution, and maritime law and enforcement
  - air-traffic control services in support of civil-aviation authorities
  - military support for the preservation of life, health and property in emergencies where the scale of the emergency temporarily exceeds the capacity of the relevant civil authority
  - emergency capabilities for the maintenance of essential services which have been disrupted temporarily and where the capacity of the relevant civil authority is exceeded
  - medical and health services in support of relevant authorities
  - search-and-rescue support for relevant authorities in accordance with domestic agreements and South Africa's international obligations
  - an air transport service for diplomatic commitments in accordance with approved policy
  - support for other state departments for missions to the Antarctic and southern oceans
  - hydrographic services to South African mariners in compliance with the country's international obligations
  - an infrastructure for the management of the Service Corps
  - a communications-security service for other state departments.

Defence Strategy
The Department of Defence's Defence Strategy is based on the Constitution, the *White Paper on Defence,* the *Defence Review* and the National Security Strategy.

The Defence Strategy endeavours to perform the functions as set out in legislation and policy, which includes defence of the sovereignty, territorial integrity and the people of South Africa. It also includes promoting the regional and continental security initiatives of the South African Government.

The Defence Strategy promotes good departmental governance and the continuous improvement of defence capabilities, and also ensures that resources are provided to all required elements of the Department of Defence.

Military Strategy
The Military Strategy of South Africa is derived from the Constitution, the *Defence Review*, the *White Paper on Defence* and the National Security Strategy.

The National Security Strategy is derived from implied national interests, the Department of Foreign Affairs and the International Relations, Peace and Security and JCPS cluster objectives.

Missions
The SANDF uses a mission-based approach to achieve the military strategic objectives of the Department of Defence. This approach uses wartime and peacetime missions to direct the peacetime strategy for force preparation, and to guide joint and combined force preparation and force employment during times of conflict. The missions envisaged for the next 10 years include:
- borderline control

- co-operation with the SAPS
- defence against a biological and/or chemical onslaught
- defence against an information onslaught
- disaster relief and humanitarian assistance
- international or regional humanitarian intervention
- international or regional observers
- international, regional or subregional peace-building and peacemaking
- international or regional peace enforcement
- international or regional search-and-rescue
- maintenance of the health status of members of the SANDF
- maritime support
- pre-emptive operations
- Presidential healthcare
- Presidential tasks
- protection of foreign assets
- repelling of conventional and non-conventional onslaught
- show-of-force
- special operations
- subregional disaster-relief and humanitarian assistance
- support to military diplomacy
- support to government departments
- air transport for diplomatic commitments

Military strategic concepts

The military strategic concepts describe the procedures to be followed to meet the military strategic objectives:

- Provision of mission-essential training: The SANDF educates, trains and develops its soldiers in the essential skills required to execute the tasks necessary to accomplish its missions. It focuses on force training/preparation and is aligned with the allocated budget. In April 2005, the Minister of Defence, Mr Mosiuoa Lekota, announced that SANDF officers were to receive multidisciplinary training, including training on conflict resolution, negotiation and humanitarian actions.
- Establishing a mission-trained force: The SANDF is to have the capability to establish a mission-trained force that can engage in specific missions. The force will be relatively small, but must ultimately be prepared according to the missions and capabilities required.
- Selective engagement where possible: The SANDF will execute all the missions as ordered, but will be selective in the courses of action it will follow, the force levels it will field, as well as the capabilities and resources it will provide and maintain. It focuses on the conscious taking of calculated strategic and operational risks.
- Strategic positioning: This entails the establishment of early-warning mechanisms, such as the placement of military attachés and involvement in subregional institutions to enhance peace and security in the region. This supports development initiatives such as the SADC and AU.

Military strategic capabilities

The capabilities of the SANDF constitute the means of the strategy and consist of:

- command and control, communications, computers, information, intelligence, infrastructure, reconnaissance and surveillance capabilities
- light mobile capability
- conventional warfare capability
- support capability.

Organisational structure

Defence administration

The Department of Defence adheres to the principles of civil control and oversight through the Minister of Defence, through various Parliamentary committees such as the Joint Standing Committee on Defence (JSCD) and the Defence Secretariat.

While the minister is responsible for providing political direction to the department, the JSCD ensures that the Executive Authority (Minister of Defence) remains accountable to Parliament. However, for day-to-day administration and the co-ordination of strategic processes, the Minister of Defence relies on the Defence Secretariat, which is the civilian leg of the department

Defence Secretariat

The Defence Secretariat is headed by the Secretary for Defence.

In terms of the Defence Act, 2002, the Defence Secretariat is responsible for:

- supporting the Secretary for Defence in his/her capacity as the head of the department, the accounting officer for the department and the principal departmental adviser to the Minister of Defence
- performing any functions entrusted by the minister to the Secretary for Defence, in particular those necessary or expedient to enhance civil control by Parliament over the Department of Defence, parliamentary committees overseeing the Department of Defence and the Minister of Defence over the Department of Defence
- providing the SANDF with comprehensive instructions regarding the exercise of powers
- monitoring compliance with policies and directions issued by the Minister of Defence to the SANDF, and reporting thereon to the minister
- ensuring discipline of, administrative control over, and the management of employees, including effective utilisation and training
- instituting departmental investigations as may be provided for by the law.

Chief of the South African National Defence Force

The functions of the Chief of the SANDF include:

- advising the Minister of Defence on any military, operational and administrative matters
- complying with directions issued by the Minister of Defence under the authority of the President, as contemplated in the Constitution
- formulating and issuing policies and doctrines
- exercising command by issuing orders, directives and instructions
- directing management and administration
- executing approved programmes of the defence budget
- employing the armed forces in accordance with legislation
- training the armed forces
- maintaining defence capabilities

- planning contingencies
- managing the defence force as a disciplined military force.

Inspector-General

The Inspector-General provides management information to the Secretary for Defence. This is derived from performance and regulatory internal audits based on the risks derived from the Department of Defence Risk Register and results depicted from survey analyses.

Policy and planning

The Division: Policy and Planning is one of the subprogrammes of the Defence Administration Programme. It comprises Defence Policy, HR Policy and Strategic Management. The functions of this subprogramme include, but are not limited to, the following:

- providing expert input relating to general defence policy to the Minister of Defence, Deputy Minister of Defence, Secretary for Defence and the Chief of the SANDF
- the strategic management, planning and strategic control processes of the department
- managing the policy-formulation process of the department
- drawing up, promulgating and presenting the departmental plan to Parliament
- the integration and performance analysis of management systems in the department
- interpreting input and influences that could affect the overall national defence strategy
- regulating conventional arms transfers in accordance with government policy
- co-ordinating the drawing up of national contingency plans for a state of national defence (war).

Management of transformation

Since 1996, the Department of Defence has been undergoing a formal transformation process through which the Transformation Project was registered. The project's goals are to:

- maximise defence capabilities through an affordable and sustainable force design and structure
- minimise defence costs using business

processes, i.e. engineering and restructuring of especially the support structures

- institutionalise appropriate leadership, command and management practices, philosophy and principles
- align defence policies, plans and management with the overall government transformation and administrative-reform initiatives
- ensure compliance with the Public Finance Management Act, 1999 (Act 1 of 1999), as amended by Act 29 of 1999 and National Treasury regulations.

After comprehensive research, a set of seven shared values for the department was approved:

- military professionalism
- human dignity
- integrity
- leadership
- accountability
- loyalty
- patriotism.

Operations

Conventional

In the event of a conventional military threat against South Africa, the broad joint concept of operations will be as follows:

- land operations: the SANDF will conduct offensive, proactive and reactive land operations directed at stopping and destroying the enemy before it can penetrate South African territory
- air operations: enemy air power will be neutralised mainly through defensive counter-air operations assisted by air-mobile land operations aimed at destroying the enemy air force on the ground
- maritime operations: enemy maritime forces will be attacked at range, while the defence of own and friendly shipping will be enhanced by defensive patrols and escort
- South African Military Health Service (SAMHS) operations: during conventional operations, the SAMHS deploys its mobile formation in direct support of land, air and maritime operations.

Non-conventional

The broad non-conventional concepts of operations are as follows:

- support to the SAPS in the maintenance of law and order will be provided by general support tasks and focused rapid-reaction operations directed at priority crime and the conduct of special operations
- border control will be exercised on land, sea and air by high-technology surveillance supported by rapid-reaction forces
- general area protection will be provided by a combination of high-density and rapid-reaction operations.

Operational commitments

Operational commitments include:

- The achievement of international and regional defence co-operation aims.
- The execution of limited peace operations.
- Effective land, sea and air-border control.
- The maintenance of law and order in support of the SAPS, with special attention to the combating of taxi violence, robberies and heists.
- Control of the South African maritime areas of responsibility, including the Exclusive Economic Zone (EEZ).
- When requested, providing support to civil authorities within the scope of regulations regarding:
  - the preservation of life, health and property
  - the maintenance of essential services
  - the provision of medical and health services
  - search-and-rescue operations
  - missions to the Antarctic and the southern oceans
  - diplomatic initiatives.
- Air-transport missions, including for diplomatic commitments and departmental scheduled flights.
- Area-defence operation missions.
- Multinational and joint-force preparation missions.
- Special forces missions.
- Borderline control – the SANDF deploys forces in support of the SAPS along South Africa's

international borders. The SANDF will gradually phase out its role in this regard. SANDF deployment consists of an average of nine infantry companies patrolling selected stretches of the borderline as the situation demands, supported by elements of the SAMHS and the South African Air Force (SAAF). The SAAF contributes aircraft to deploy land forces along the land borders where necessary. It also carries out reconnaissance flights along the land and sea borders where they assist the South African Navy patrolling the EEZ. The navy patrols the coastline, assisting the Department of Environmental Affairs and Tourism with the prosecution of illegal fisherfolk, while also maintaining a presence at sea and thereby deterring other criminal activities such as drug smuggling.

The SAAF further assists the Civil Aviation Authority and the SAPS border component in reducing the incidence of illegal aircraft flights into the country which, in most cases, are involved with smuggling.

Other defence commitments

Other defence commitments of the Department of Defence are to:

- achieve a reasonable level of military diplomacy through:
  - the placement and control of defence attachés
  - the establishment and maintenance of bi- and multilateral agreements
  - participating in the activities of the defence structures of multinational organisations such as the UN, AU and SADC (especially in the Interstate Defence and Security Committee)
- meet the international obligations of the Department of Defence in line with international agreements, which may include search-and-rescue, and hydrography
- provide communications-security services to other state departments
- administer the National Key Points Act, 1980 (Act 102 of 1980)
- provide healthcare for the President and Deputy President.

Force employment

In accordance with the Force Employment Strategy

approved in 2002, force employment structures provide for operational level structures to enhance command and control, cost-efficiency and functional differentiation at military-strategic, operational and tactical levels of the Joint Operations Division. This will ensure that the core strategic objectives of the department are effectively addressed.

For internal operations, nine tactical level headquarters were established, one in each province. If required, temporary joint task force headquarters may be created for specific operations. Combat-ready units are prepared, provided and supported, as required.

Bases

Bases are lower-level structures provided by all the services. Units are generally clustered in or around bases and share common facilities and services.

Bases exercise administrative control, but not command over attached units.

One Force

The 'One Force' concept comprises the regular and reserve force components of the SANDF.

The Regular Force consists of highly trained soldiers to operate and maintain a core capability, sophisticated equipment and defence systems.

The Reserve Force is the former part-time component of the SANDF. Members are trained to bolster the core defence commitment. Other components are the Army Conventional Reserve (ACR), the Army Territorial Reserve (ATR), which includes the commandos, the SAAF, the Naval Reserve and the SAMHS Reserve.

The ATR operates mainly in co-operation with other government departments, especially the SAPS. Approval has been granted for the expansion of the Defence Reserve Force divisions to include offices in 10 regions. These offices will carry out the mandate of the Chief of Defence Reserve at regional level.

This is aimed at involving reserve force members in the command, management and decision-making processes, and providing them with enhanced career-development opportunities.

Force preparation

The chiefs of the services (army, SAAF, navy and SAMHS) are responsible for the 'provide forces' processes of their respective services. Formations are basic building-blocks in this process.

Each formation has its own commander. A formation includes, where practical, all units and support elements related to a specific user-system type. It is capable of providing a fully supported user system to a commander responsible for the exercising and combat-readiness of land, air, maritime and military-health capabilities, such as a brigade or division commander.

A formation can provide the same service to a task-force commander appointed by the Chief of Joint Operations.

This is a considerable improvement in cost-effectiveness, while it also provides the best way of retaining core defence capabilities, especially expertise in critical mass function. Some examples of formations established by the different services are:

- army – infantry, artillery or armour formations
- SAAF – direct combat system
- navy – the fleet
- SAMHS – military-health formations.

A formation's specific geographical location depends on where its combat and support units are concentrated.

Force support

Support formations are intermediate structures with their own formation commanders. Their task is to provide combat support to type formations and other system structures.

Reserve Force

The majority of reserve force units reside in the South African Army. Currently, the army comprises the ACR and the ATR, or the commandos, as they are commonly known.

As an integral and essential part of the army, the reserve force element will, during times of war, provide the expansion capability of the army. The South African Army Reserve is being aligned with force-employment capability requirements.

The Chief Directorate: Army Reserve is the advisory body to the Chief of the Army on all issues pertaining to the Reserve Force. Furthermore, it provides policy and strategy input to the army's planning fora. Senior reserve officers from both the ex-statutory and non-statutory forces were appointed to provide a balanced input and to be part of the planning processes in the army.

With the implementation of the Military Strategy and the Force Employment Strategy, the SANDF (regular and reserve) will gradually withdraw from providing support to the SAPS, which will rightfully assume full responsibility. The ATR as a system is being phased in and is expected to be completed by 2009.

The process to transfer functions and personnel from the SANDF to the SAPS' Protection and Security Services Division was underway by 2005.

It forms part of the phasing out of the commando system by closing down 183 commando units by 2009. At least 17 units were expected to be closed down by the end of March 2005 and 55 units by 2006.

This process is intended to release SANDF forces to pursue government's regional and continental obligations to peace-support, conflict resolution and post-conflict reconstruction.

Military veterans

The Military Veterans Affairs Act, 1999 (Act 17 of 1999), came into effect on 1 February 2001. The regulations in terms of the Act were approved by the Minister of Defence for promulgation.

The minister appointed the chairperson and members of the Advisory Board on Military Veterans' Affairs from nominations received from the recognised military veterans' organisations. The President is designated as the Patron-in-Chief of all military veterans in terms of the Act.

Staff complement

The Department of Defence strives towards representivity at all levels in terms of gender and race. The department's baseline target for race is 65% black, 10% coloured, 0,75% Indian and 24% white.

By September 2003, the Department of Defence was employing 446 persons with disabilities. To achieve its target, the department will have to employ 1 400 persons with disabilities.

Resettlement

The Directorate: Personnel Separation has executed programmes at various levels in terms of the department's HR Strategy 2010. The directorate is serving as a nodal point for redeployment and resettlement.

The Department of Defence established the Personnel Rationalisation Advisory and Co-ordinating Committee for the management of this process to ensure efficient and cost-effective support programmes for both the resettlement and redeployment of the department's members and employees affected by separation.

The directorate has established and implemented the Social Plan, which addresses the reskilling and psychosocial needs of the department's employees.

Professional multidisciplinary teams execute this support programme.

The Department of Defence has put in place the HR Planning Instruction that guides the process of interdepartmental transfers of redeployable members and employees.

Peace support

Based on the *White Paper on South African Participation in International Peace Missions*, the SANDF continues to prepare for support in peace missions. Various members of the Department of Defence have been trained for participation in these missions.

Cabinet authorised the SANDF to deploy up to 1 600 South African soldiers as part of the 3 200-strong AU Mission in Burundi, consisting of soldiers from South Africa, Mozambique and Ethiopia.

On 21 May 2004, the UN Security Council adopted Resolution 1545 of 2004, authorising and mandating the UN Operation in Burundi (ONUB), which came into effect on 1 June 2004. The UN Department of Peacekeeping Operations requested South Africa to contribute to the ONUB.

Three South African staff officers were deployed to the UN Mission in Liberia. The first two members were deployed in November 2003 and the third in January 2004.

On 19 February 2005, 27 SANDF members were deployed to the DRC to assist with integration and training of the DRC armed forces. By April 2005, 1 400 members were deployed as part of the UN Mission in the DRC.

Some 1 200 members were deployed to Burundi, while three members were deployed as staff officers to the UN Military Headquarters in Liberia.

Some 257 members (military observers, staff officers and contingent members) were deployed in support of the AU Observer Mission in Sudan. Seven military observers and staff officers were deployed to Ethiopia and Eritrea as part of the UN and AU missions.

Acquiring of main equipment

The Department of Defence has completely revised and consolidated its policies for the acquisition of weapon systems. Whereas the old approach placed emphasis mainly on meeting local systems and technological needs, the new direction takes into account that South Africa is part of the global environment within which opportunities should be exploited to the benefit of the Department of Defence.

Directorate: Army Aquisition

The Artillery Target Engagement System was integrated into the first of four regiments. The system also paves the way for digitalisation of the landward battlefield. The second regiment was contracted during February 2005 and delivery is scheduled for 2007/08.

The 40-mm Automatic Grenade Launcher System was delivered to the army for its operating phase.

Directorate: Air Force Acquisition

Operational test and evaluation of the Hawk fighter aircraft was expected to start in September 2005. The aircraft will be operated from Air Force Base Makhado (85 Combat Flying School). Training of students is expected to start in April 2006.

The Gripen is still under development and the first dual-seater aircraft is scheduled for delivery in 2008. Delivery of the single seater aircraft is scheduled to start in 2009 with the last aircraft to be delivered in 2011.

The light utility helicopter from Agusta has been commissioned at the various helicopter squadrons. The final handover of these aircraft to the SAAF is scheduled for 2006. The delivery of the maritime helicopter currently under development is scheduled for 2007 and handover to the SAAF in 2008.

As part of a government initiative, an international partnership with Airbus Military has been formed to rejuvenate the local aviation industry. The acquisition of eight A400M aircraft has been contracted, with the delivery of the first aircraft expected in 2010.

Directorate: Naval Acquisition

The *SAS Isandlwana* was launched and named by Ms Nozizwe Madlala-Routledge, the then Deputy-Minister of Defence, on 5 December 2002. The vessel arrived in Table Bay, Cape Town, on 25 February 2004.

The *SAS Spioenkop* was launched and named by Ms Thandi Modise, the then chairperson of the Parliamentary Standing Committee on Defence, on 4 June 2003. The vessel arrived in Simon's Town on 31 May 2004. The *SAS Mendi* was launched and named in Kiel on 15 June 2004 and arrived in South Africa in early November 2004.

These ships, each with a range of 6 200 nautical miles, are the first new warships for South Africa in 16 years and are specifically designed for South African maritime conditions.

By mid-2005, South Africa was also in the process of acquiring three type 209 Mod 1400 submarines from Germany. The first was launched by Ms Ruth Mompati, a veteran of the apartheid struggle, in Kiel on 15 June 2004. After completing sea trials, the submarine was expected to arrive in South Africa towards the end of 2005.

The submarines will be delivered at approximately 12-month intervals, with final delivery expected by December 2008.

Facilities, land and environment

Facilities, Land and Environmental Management in the Department of Defence strives for the efficient management of these entities. The department has adopted the process of base conversion. The focus is on the role and responsibilities of the military process of conversion aimed at assisting role-players in closing down and re-using military bases in a sustainable manner.

The Military Integrated Training Range Guide provides military environmental managers with information that will ensure the long-term continuation of environmentally sound management practices. It will also enhance the ability of the defence sector to sustain long-term and cost-effective range operations.

The department continues to demonstrate its responsibility as the custodian of land entrusted to it through active co-operation in government's land redistribution and restitution policies.

It co-operated in a pilot study regarding the closing down and re-use of redundant military bases for the purposes of alternative economic land-use initiatives. These are aimed at achieving co-operative environmental governance as advocated in national environmental policies.

Over the past decade, the department has been rationalising its land portfolio and has made one third (close to a quarter million hectares) of its original estate available for non-military use.

The Military Skills Development System (MSDS), launched in 2003, aims to ensure a continuous intake of young, healthy South Africans into the South African National Defence Force (SANDF). This is to rejuvenate the Regular Force and supply the Reserve Force.

The MSDS not only provides young South Africans with military skills, but also contributes to their social upliftment by providing them with skills that they will use in their civilian lives after completing their military service. It also provides the youth with employment opportunities. By September 2005, the SANDF was providing opportunities for 6 000 young South Africans. This figure is expected to grow to 10 000 within the next two years.

Armaments

Armaments Corporation of South Africa (ARMSCOR)

ARMSCOR is a statutory body established in accordance with the ARMSCOR Limited Act, 2003 (Act 51 of 2003). The Minister of Defence is the executive authority responsible for ARMSCOR. The management and control of ARMSCOR reside with a board of directors, while its day-to-day management vests in the hands of the management board.

In the execution of its functions, ARMSCOR maintains capabilities and technologies that are required to fulfil its mandate. These include appropriate programme management systems, the Defence Industrial Participation Programme, the management of technology projects and strategic facilities.

ARMSCOR acquires defence material for the Department of Defence and for any organ of state that may require such services, such as the SAPS.

Quality assurance

ARMSCOR provides for a quality assurance capability in support of acquisition and technology projects as well as for any other service required by the Department of Defence. To enhance this capability, ARMSCOR is a certified ISO 9001:2000 organisation.

ARMSCOR Business (Pty) Ltd

This subsidiary of ARMSCOR offers defence support services of exceptional standard to the Department of Defence. The core of these services includes defence research and development, test and evaluation, defence material disposal and logistic support services. To fulfil this mandate, ARMSCOR Business is structured into three groups:

Defence, Science and Technology Institute

- The Institute for Maritime Technology aims to satisfy strategic needs for technomilitary maritime support, products and services; and to establish applicable technology and systems to further the interests of the SANDF.

- Protechnik Laboratories conducts research, and develops and implements projects in the fields of chemical and biological defence, and non-proliferation of chemical weapons.
- The Defence Institute assists the defence community in developing informed solutions to decision-making problems over the full life cycle of defence capabilities.
- Hazmat Protective Systems manufactures and distributes protective equipment such as filter canisters, cartridges and masks, and also impregnates activated carbon.
- Ergonomics Technologies provides services on ergonomics to enhance and optimise human machine interaction within the working environment.
- Flamengro provides computer-based simulation and failure-analysis support, and consultative services to the department and the defence industry during product and system development.
- Armour Development provides a research and development capability for armour protection and anti-armour attacks.

Test and Evaluation Group

- Gerotek Test Facilities provides specialised services such as testing and evaluating vehicles and vehicle components, research and developing of vehicle-testing technologies and methods. VHF/UHF and microwave antenna-testing and evaluation, environmental testing, and verifying military products against specification.
- Alkantpan offers an all-purpose weapon and ammunition test range, compiles specifications and analyses test data.
- Sidibane/Gerotrain offers restaurant and conference facilities, independent driver-assessment and development facilities.

Defence Support Group

- ARMSCOR Defence Asset Management Centre provides decision-making support in the acquisition, operational and phasing-out phases of systems by providing data and asset-management services.

- Defence Material Disposal is the appointed agent of the Department of Defence to dispose of excessive military defence equipment.

The activities of ARMSCOR are financed mainly by an annual transfer payment from the Department of Defence, interest received on investments, the hiring of some of their buildings, commission from stock sales and income from subsidiaries.

The acquisition of arms is transparent. ARMSCOR publishes the monthly *Contracts Bulletin*, which contains all requests for proposals and bids awarded. A daily electronic bulletin is also available to the industry through a secure computer network.

Denel Group of South Africa

Specialising in aerospace and defence, Denel is recognised globally for leading defence capabilities, notably integrated artillery systems. Unmanned aerial vehicles (UAVs), precision-guided weapons and the Rooivalk attack helicopter, now operational in the SAAF, are testimony to Denel's sophisticated aerospace capabilities.

Following Denel's proven capabilities in defence-technology development and manufacturing, it has also emerged as a leader in commercial fields such as property development, innovative food technology, industrial manufacturing and IT.

Denel is a state-owned profit-driven corporation registered under the South African Companies Act, 1973 (Act 61 of 1973). Its defence capability dates back more than 50 years, when its oldest manufacturing plants were established.

The company has international technology alliances and joint ventures with some of the world's major aerospace and defence companies. Denel provides invaluable humanitarian services around the world through cost-effective mine-action contracts.

Reflecting South Africa's priorities of empowering, uplifting and educating people, Denel has established learning and development centres, focusing on education, training and job creation.

Denel's defence manufacturing is grouped as follows:
- Aerospace Group
- Land Systems Group.

Aerospace Group

Airframe Manufacturing

As part of Denel Aviation in Kempton Park, adjacent to the Johannesburg International Airport (JIA), this facility specialises in a range of manufacturing disciplines.

It includes comprehensive machine shops, a fabrication plant, an assembly line and a composites department. It is well positioned for the manufacture of aircraft detail components and aerostructure sub-assemblies, as well as the assembly and integration of airframes, mainly for:
- Saab
- BAE Systems
- detail machine parts for commercial airplanes, including B747, B737 and B777.

Denel Aerospace Systems

Located in Irene, Centurion, this unit is responsible for systems development, comprising ground-based air defence systems (GBADs) for the SANDF.

Denel is prime contractor on the first phase of the South African Army's requirement for GBADs. This phase, for the local warning segment, will provide the army with an integrated short-range defence system capability consisting of a man-portable air defence system, radar sensor and relevant air-defence command and control.

Rooivalk attack helicopter

The Rooivalk attack helicopter was designed from the outset to operate in all-weather conditions, suitable for high-mobility warfare, with low detectability and high manoeuverability, low pilot workload, extreme agility and cost-efficiency. It can be rapidly deployed and has very low maintenance costs.

Missiles and guided weapon systems

As a leader in systems technology, Denel's range of missiles and guided weapons include the following:
- anti-armour missiles, like Ingwe and Mokopa
- surface-to-air missiles
- air-to-air missiles
- the Raptor family of long-range precision-guided weapons.

Unmanned aerial vehicles

Denel is a world pioneer of UAV systems and is the leading technology house in Africa regarding design, production and operation of UAV systems. It not only produces short-to-medium range tactical UAV systems like the Seeker II, but is also a leading force in the design, production and operation of multipurpose high-speed aerial targeting systems such as Skua.

Aerospace Engineering

Aerospace Engineering is undertaken at Denel's Kempton Park facilities adjacent to the JIA and at Irene in Centurion. Its activities include:

- airframe structural and system design, structural testing, subsystem design and integration
- aerodynamic design and analysis
- weapons and stores integration and clearance
- avionics system engineering and software development
- electrical system design and analysis
- mission planning and debriefing systems
- test and integration, including ground-testing and full-flight testing capability.

Aircraft Logistics

Aircraft Logistics, based at Denel's Kempton Park facilities near the JIA, undertakes the following:

- Integrated system and product support for transport aircraft (including C-130) and tactical aircraft, like the Rooivalk combat helicopter, the Oryx medium transport helicopter, and the SAAF Cheetah fighter fleet. It is geared to undertake similar work on the future SAAF fleet of the Hawk LIFT and Gripen swing-role jet aircraft.
- Component repair, and laboratory/calibration services.
- Aircraft refurbishment/modernisation, including full-service painting.

OTB Multi-Purpose Test Range

Located near Bredasdorp in the Western Cape, OTB is renowned for specialised in-flight system-performance measurements on sophisticated weapons and aviation systems for local and international aerospace industries.

Denel Optronics

Comprising a wide range of capabilities, Denel Optronics undertakes:

- design and manufacture of optical and laser products
- electro-optical stabilised observation and surveillance systems
- helmet-mounted sighting and tracking systems.

Land Systems Group

Denel Land Systems

The Systems Unit within Denel Land Systems is located in Lyttelton, Centurion. Its activities include the design, development, manufacture, integration and product support of:

- 155-mm and 105-mm artillery ballistic systems, renowned for accurate extended range fire
- advanced combat turrets in various calibres
- infantry weapons
- rapid fire cannons
- naval air-defence gun systems.

Large Calibre Ammunition

The Large Calibre Ammunition plant in Potchefstroom in North West, in conjunction with the forging facility in Boksburg designs, develops and manufactures:

- heavy calibre ordnance consumables
- a comprehensive range of 60-mm and 81-mm mortar bombs
- naval ammunition
- turnkey ammunition filling plants.

Explosives and Pyrotechnic Ammunition

Located in the Western Cape, Denel's Explosives and Pyrotechnic Ammunition plants offer research, design, development, and the manufacture of:

- propellants in small and medium calibre
- gun propulsion
- rocket propulsion for all tactical rockets and missile applications, UAVs and propellant grains for rocket motors and ejection seats
- warhead systems, high explosives and energetic raw material for defence and civilian applications

- minefield breaching systems
- pyrotechnics and explosive devices for riot control
- high explosive and phosphorus devices, as well as pyrotechnics for signalling, screening, illumination, training simulation and battlefield application
- low velocity and high velocity 40-mm grenades
- commercial products, including distress flares, industrial cartridges and rock-breaking devices.

Small and Medium Calibre Ammunition
In its Small and Medium Calibre Ammunition plant, Denel produces:
- small arms ammunition for military and commercial applications
- medium-calibre ammunition
- brass products
- detonics
- industrial products for mining, aircraft escape systems and cutting charges.

Mechem
Mechem delivers humanitarian mine clearance and other forms of mine-action services. Its product line comprises:
- landmine-clearing equipment and landmine-protected vehicle platforms
- cost-effective and professional execution of mine-clearing contracts.

National Conventional Arms Control Committee
The NCACC, consisting of ministers and deputy ministers, oversees policy and sets control mechanisms for the South African arms trade. It also ensures that arms-trade policies conform to internationally accepted practices.

Companies interested in exporting arms have to apply for export permits, after which the Ministry of Defence processes the application.

Each application is also sent for scrutiny to the relevant government departments, such as foreign affairs or trade and industry. The application is then referred to the various directors-general to make their recommendations, whereafter the NCACC makes the final decision.

An independent inspectorate ensures that all levels of the process are subject to independent scrutiny and supervision, and conducted in accordance with the policies and guidelines of the NCACC. The inspectorate submits periodic reports to the Standing Parliamentary Committee on Defence.

Intelligence services

There are two civilian intelligence structures, namely the National Intelligence Agency (NIA) and the South African Secret Service (SASS).

The intelligence community provides evaluated information to:
- safeguard the Constitution
- promote the interrelated elements of security, stability, co-operation and development, both within South Africa and in relation to southern Africa
- uphold the individual rights enshrined in the Bill of Rights contained in the Constitution
- promote South Africa's ability to face foreign threats and enhance its competitiveness in a dynamic world.

National Intelligence Agency
The NIA's mandate is divided into seven areas of interest: counter-intelligence, political intelligence, economic intelligence, border intelligence, terrorism, organised crime and corruption.

South African Secret Service
The SASS provides the country's foreign intelligence capacity. It aims to provide government with accurate, topical, policy-relevant and timeous foreign intelligence to promote, enhance and protect the national security and interests of South Africa and its citizens.

The objective of the SASS is to forewarn, inform and advise government on real and potential threats to South Africa's security, and on opportunities for South Africa. It is subject to comprehensive accounting and oversight regulations, making the organisation accountable to the public. Executive control is exercised by a civilian ministry and a cabinet committee. The civilian intelligence services are accountable to the Minister of Intelligence Services, who reports to Cabinet through the Cabinet Committee on Security and Intelligence Affairs.

Parliament has appointed the Joint Standing Committee on Intelligence (JSCI), which may order investigations into the intelligence community's activities. In addition, the Constitution provides for protection against state abuse through the Public Protector and South African Human Rights Commission.

The National Strategic Intelligence Amendment Act, 1998 (Act 37 of 1998), allows South Africa to conduct a counter-intelligence service overseas, under the SASS. The Act gives the Minister of Intelligence Services a seat on the National Intelligence Co-ordinating Committee, and clearly defines his/her powers and functions. The minister is also accountable to Cabinet for co-ordinating intelligence through the national intelligence structures.

Intelligence oversight

Joint Standing Committee on Intelligence

Integral to the *White Paper on Intelligence,* drafted in 1994, was the establishment of legislative oversight mechanisms.

The JSCI is an oversight parliamentary body comprising members of the six largest political parties. Selection to the committee is based on proportional representation decided on by the percentage of votes received in the last national election.

The JSCI hears complaints from the public, scrutinises the finances and operations of the services and reports to Parliament on these matters.

Parliamentary members serving on the JSCI take an oath of secrecy and undergo security screening to ensure that they do not compromise the work of the services in the course of performing their duties.

Inspector-General

The Inspector-General monitors compliance with the Constitution, laws and policies of the country. The Office of the Inspector General reports to the Minister of Intelligence Services.

The office reviews the activities of the services, receives and investigates complaints from the general public and the JSCI, or is tasked by the Minister of Intelligence Services.

The Inspector-General is appointed by the President following approval by two-thirds of the members of the National Assembly.

Other civilian intelligence structures

South African National Academy of Intelligence (SANAI)

SANAI plays a central role in providing quality training to members of the intelligence services.

Training at SANAI, which was established in February 2003, is geared towards producing officers who understand the political and security realms of South Africa and Africa.

The academy comprises the Academic Faculty, the Intelligence Research Institute and the Education, Training and Development Support Component.

Located in Mafikeng, North West, the SANAI campus is named after the late Mzwandile Piliso, a veteran intelligence officer who played an important role in the establishment of a non-statutory intelligence body that served the liberation movement.

Intelligence Services Council (ISC)

The ISC conducts continuous research towards developing effective and competitive working conditions for members as they are recruited and receive multiskill training and development, commensurate benefits, career options and eventually retirement benefits.

The council oversaw the establishment of a new staff association and is in the process of establishing a united veterans' association for former members.

Electronic Communications Security (Pty) Ltd (COMSEC)

COMSEC was established as a private company in

February 2003 to ensure that critical electronic communications of government and related organs are protected and secured.

COMSEC's functions include securing government communications against unauthorised access and from technical, electronic or any other related threats. The company will, in concurrence with the NIA, provide verification services for electronic communications security systems, products and services used by the State.

COMSEC strives for greater co-ordination, integration, alignment and the maintenance of communications security.

National Communications Centre (NCC)

The NCC serves as an advisory structure to the Minister of Intelligence Services on matters related to signals-intelligence procurement, management and direction. This includes areas such as the Signals Intelligence Evaluation Centre and the soon to be established Office of Interception Centres.

The centre will regulate the applications and authorisation for interceptions and monitor all interception of communications. It will eliminate duplication and possible mismanagement of resources.

Acknowledgements

Armscor
BuaNews
Denel
Estimates of National Expenditure 2005, published by National Treasury
National Intelligence Agency
National Treasury
Independent Complaints Directorate
Secretariat for Safety and Security
South African National Defence Force
South African Police Service
South African Secret Service
www.gov.za

Suggested reading

A Navy for Three Oceans: Celebrating 75 Years of the South African Navy. Roggebaai: BP Southern Africa, 1997.
Batchelor, P. and Willet, S. *Disarmament and Defence: Industrial Adjustment in South Africa*. Oxford: Stockholm
 International Peace Research Institute. Oxford University Press, 1998.
Bornman, E. *et al. Violence in South Africa: A Variety of Perspectives*. Pretoria: Human Sciences Research Council (HSRC),
 1998.
Bremer, J.D. *Black and Blue: Policing in South Africa*. Oxford: Clarendon Press, 1994.
Brogden, M. and Shearing, C. *Policing for a New South Africa*. London: Routledge, 1993.
Cawthra, G. *Policing South Africa: The South African Police and the Transition from Apartheid*. Cape Town: David Philip,
 1993.
Cock, J. and Mackenzie, P. eds. *From Defence to Development: Redirecting Military Resources in South Africa*. Cape Town:
 David Philip for the Group for Environmental Monitoring, 1998.
Cohen, D. *People Who Have Stolen From Me*. Johannesburg: Picador, 2004.
Davis, D. and Slabbert, M. eds. *Crime and Violence in South Africa: Critical Studies in Criminology*. Cape Town: David
 Philip, 1985.
Dixon, B. and van der Spuy, E. *Justice Gained? Crime and Crime Control in South Africa's Transition*. Cape Town: University
 of Cape Town Press, 2004.
Du Plessis, L. and Hough, M. eds. *Managing African Conflicts: The Challenge of Military Intervention*. Pretoria: HSRC, 2000.
Du Plessis, L. and Hough, M. eds. *Protecting Sub-Saharan Africa: The Military Challenge*. Pretoria: HSRC, 1999.
Emmett, T. and Buthcart, A. eds. *Behind the Mask: Getting to Grips with Crime and Violence in South Africa*. Pretoria:
 HSRC, 2000.
Gamba, V. ed. *Governing Arms: The Southern African Experience*. Pretoria: Institute for Security Studies, 2000.
Gamba, V., Meek, S. and Potgieter, J. eds. *Society Under Siege: Crime, Violence and Illegal Weapons*. Halfway House:
 Institute for Security Studies, 1997.
Gutteridge, W. and Spence, J.E. *Violence in Southern Africa*. London: Frank Cass, 1997.
Hansson, D. and Van Zyl-Smit, D. eds. *Towards Justice? Crime and State Control in South Africa*. Cape Town: Oxford
 University Press, 1990.
Kok, P. and Pietersen, J. *Safety and Security of Citizen and Society*. Pretoria: HSRC, 2000.
Louw, M.N. and Bouwer, J.S. *The South African Air Force at War: A Pictorial Appraisal*. 2nd ed. Johannesburg: Chris van
 Rensburg Publications, 1995.
Machel, G. *Impact of War on Children*. London: Hurst, 2001.
Manganyi, N. and Du Toit, A. eds. *Political Violence and the Struggle in South Africa*. Halfway House: Southern Book
 Publishers, 1990.
Marks, M. *Young Warriors: Youth Politics, Identity and Violence in South Africa*. Johannesburg: Witwatersrand University
 Press, 2004.
Marsh, R. *With Criminal Intent: The Changing Face of Crime in South Africa*. Kenilworth: Ampersand Press, 1999.

Matthews, M.L. *et al.* eds. *Policing the Conflict in South Africa*. Gainesville: University Press of Florida, 1995.

McKendrick, B. and Hoffman, W. eds. *People and Violence in South Africa*. Cape Town: Oxford University Press, 1990.

Melville, N. *The Taming of the Blue: Regulating Police Misconduct in South Africa*. Pretoria: HSRC, 1999.

Minaar, A. and Hough, M. eds. *Conflict, Violence and Conflict Resolution: Where is South Africa Heading?* Pretoria: HSRC 1997.

Myerson, L. *Hijackings, Burglaries and Serious Crime: How to Protect Your Family, Your Home and Your Valuables*. Sandton: LAD, 1995.

Nöthling, C.J. and Becker, D. compilers. *The Pride of the Nation: A Short History of the South African Air Force, 1920 – 1995*. Pretoria: The Air Force, 1995.

Pelser. E. ed. *Crime Prevention Partnerships: Lessons from Practice*, Pretoria: Institute of Strategic Studies, 2003.

Pistorius, M. *Catch Me a Killer: Serial Murders*. Johannesburg: Penguin Books, 2000.

Pistorius, M. *Strangers on the Street: Serial Homicide in South Africa*. Johannesburg: Penguin Books, 2002.

Reyneke, E. compiler. *Small Arms and Light Weapons in Africa*. Pretoria: Institute for Security Studies, 2000.

Safe, Secure and Streetwise: The Essential Guide to Protecting Yourself, Your Family and Your Home from Crime. Cape Town: Reader's Digest Association, 1997.

Schonteich, M. *Unshackling the Crime Fighters: Increasing Private-Sector Involvement in South Africa's Criminal Justice System*. Johannesburg: South African Institute of Race Relations, 1999.

Seegers, A. *The Military in the Making of Modern South Africa*. London: Taurus Academic Studies, 1996.

Shaw, M. *Crime and Policing in Post-Apartheid South Africa*. Cape Town: David Philip, 2002.

Smith, L. *A Guide to a Safer Lifestyle: A Practical Guide to Surviving the Urban Jungle*. Johannesburg: Chris van Rensburg Publications, 2000.

Solomon, H. ed. *Towards a Common Defence and Security Policy in the Southern African Development Community*. Pretoria: Africa Institute of South Africa, 2004.

Steinberg, J. ed. *Crime Wave: The South African Underworld and its Foes*, Johannesburg: Witwatersrand University Press, 2001.

Van der Merwe, H.W. *Peace-Making in South Africa: A Life in Conflict Resolution*. Cape Town: Tafelberg, 2000.

Science and technology

Policy and funding

The vision of the Department of Science and Technology is to realise the full potential of science and technology (S&T) in social and economic development, through the development of human resources (HR), research and innovation.

National S&T policy is the responsibility of the Minister of Science and Technology.

The intellectual framework for policy is the National System of Innovation (NSI), in which a set of functioning institutions, organisations, individuals and policies interact in the pursuit of a common set of social and economic goals.

National System of Innovation

The NSI focuses on the role of technology in economic growth and supports innovation and technology diffusion. Since 1994, institutions such as the National Advisory Council on Innovation (NACI) have been established to advise the minister on policy and the allocation of funding.

Some funds allocated to science councils were earmarked to address specific South African problems. The funding of science councils has been substantially reformed: core funding through parliamentary grants is complemented with allocations through a competitive bidding process from the Innovation Fund (IF). The IF applies three major criteria when making its selections: competitiveness, quality of life and environmental sustainability. Projects funded by the IF have led to new businesses, products and services in the marketplace.

Innovation Fund

The IF, a policy instrument of the Department of Science and Technology, was created to promote technological innovation; increased networking and cross-sectoral collaboration; and competitiveness, quality of life, environmental sustainability and the harnessing of Information Technology (IT).

The National Research Foundation (NRF) claims a management and administration fee from the allocated budget for support services rendered.

The IF's strategic objectives include creating a knowledge base in key technology and economic sectors; facilitating the exploitation and commercialisation of research and development (R&D) results from the existing knowledge base; investing in technological innovations that will benefit South Africa; and supporting historically disadvantaged individuals (HDIs) in terms of infrastructure, knowledge and technology transfer. The IF enables the expansion and migration of existing industries to new value-added areas and the establishment of R&D-intensive industries. It fosters the establishment and growth of technology-based small enterprises.

The strategic direction of the fund identified a series of new funding initiatives that seek to enhance innovation in South Africa. They are:

- technology missions to support the development of long-term, high-risk, market-driven, enabling technology that will benefit an existing economic sector

South Africa's spending on research and development (R&D) increased to R10,1 billion in 2003/04 from R7,5 billion in 2001/02. According to a survey by the Centre for Science, Technology and Innovation Indicators, this contributed to the country's economy becoming more competitive in 2003/04.

South Africa spends more in this field than Argentina, which spends 0,41% of its gross domestic product (GDP) on R&D. Lagging behind countries such as China, which spent 1,22%, and the Russian Federation's 1,28% of GDP, South Africa spent 0,81% of GDP on R&D in 2003/04.

The Organisation for Economic Co-operation and Development country with the highest R&D intensity was Sweden, which spent 4,27% of GDP, followed by Finland with 3,46%.

South Africa's R&D expenditure is fairly high compared with that of other developing countries. However, the total number of researchers is low at 2,2 researchers per 1 000 employees.

Women researchers make up 38% of the total researchers, compared with 11,2% in Japan and 28,4% in Norway. In developing countries, Argentina leads the way with 50,5% women researchers.

The largest percentage, 28% of R&D, is performed in the field of engineering sciences. This is followed at 21,9% in natural sciences and 13,5% in the medical and health sciences.

The major performer and financier of R&D is the business sector, which performs 55,5% of all R&D undertaken and finances 52% of the total spent in this field.

Government financed 28%, while 10% of R&D is financed from abroad.

Higher Education performs 20,5% of national R&D and government 21,9%.

- technology-advancement programmes to promote innovation in new technology frontiers
- various competitive initiatives to promote entrepreneurship through the commercialisation of the innovative ideas of young entrepreneurs and to promote R&D collaboration and entrepreneurship within the business and research community, emphasising networking among racial groups and across cultures
- the IF Commercialisation Office, which offers a comprehensive service regarding patent applications and technology transfer for publicly funded research
- seed and start-up financing for the development of a product or prototype, proof of concept and initial marketing.

The IF's budget increased to R182 million in 2005/06.

National Research and Development Strategy

The National R&D Strategy focuses on three broad areas:

- Innovation enhancement, primarily through technology missions: The emphasis is on technological innovation, demonstrating technology, incubating new technology-based businesses, and enhancing networks of knowledge workers and organisations in specific areas of technology.
- Strengthening science, engineering and technology (SET), human resources (HR) and transformation: The emphasis is on establishing centres of excellence (CoEs); establishing and funding networks for the New Partnership for Africa's Development (NEPAD) and Southern African Development Community (SADC); strengthening global science networks; formulating strategies aimed at sourcing new financing for R&D equipment; strengthening institutional and individual research capacity in science focus areas through the NRF; and increasing public understanding and engagement.
- Creating an effective government S&T system: A clear distinction needs to be drawn between the roles of line-function departments and the

integrative role of the Department of Science and Technology. This focus area is involved in generating three-year R&D plans for science councils in line with the Medium Term Expenditure Framework (MTEF) process, developing standard-reporting frameworks and a performance management system for all institutions, and giving the department central responsibility for producing an integrative budget for all S&T initiatives.

The department has committed itself to the 2002 R&D Strategy target of 1% of gross domestic product to be invested in R&D by both the public and private sectors by 2008. This implies an annual increase of about R1 billion in government expenditure on R&D. The R25-million grant to six CoEs over the next 10 years in engineering, biotechnology, biodiversity and disease research continues to support R&D.

Advanced Manufacturing Technology Strategy

The Advanced Manufacturing Technology Strategy was launched in October 2003 and resources are being allocated towards its implementation. Planning is underway for developing innovation programmes in the energy, mining and mineral-beneficiation domains of resource-based industries.

National Technology Transfer Strategy

The National Technology Transfer Strategy is based on the inevitable role that technology plays in wealth creation and in addressing the challenges of social development.

National Energy Research Institute (NERI)

Cabinet approved the establishment of the NERI in 2004.

The institute, jointly run by the departments of minerals and energy and of science and technology, will conduct research on the energy sector.

The NERI, through R&D, provides for:

- cost-effective and efficient energy generation, transformation, transport, end-use and decision-support technologies

- energy-technology innovation
- sustainable development and utilisation of energy resources
- improving the quality of life of all South Africans
- promoting and conducting training of energy researchers
- establishing and expanding industries in the field of energy
- commercialising energy technologies resulting from its research development and innovation programmes.

Pebble Bed Modular Reactor (PBMR) Human Capital Research and Innovation Frontier Programme

In support of the Government's vision for the PBMR, the Department of Science and Technology has undertaken to establish a co-ordinated programme to advance skills and innovation frontiers along the entire technology value chain of the PBMR programme. This ranges from basic and applied research of all applicable science and engineering disciplines, to manufacturing and the distinctive aspects of waste management.

The PBMR Human Capital Research and Innovation Frontier Programme is a consensus of

The Department of Science and Technology recognises the wealth of indigenous knowledge through various projects. These include:
- drafting the Indigenous Knowledge Systems (IKS) Bill
- financial support for the IKS of the South Africa Trust
- establishing interdepartmental committees on IKS
- dedicated ring-fenced funding from the National Research Foundation for IKS research
- developing a framework for the establishment of the South African Indigenous Knowledge Digital Library based on the Traditional Knowledge Digital Library in India.

The IKS Policy and Bill were adopted by Cabinet in November 2004. The policy builds on initiatives already in place, such as the National Language Policy, the promotion and copy-writing of indigenous music and art forms, and the Traditional Health Practitioners Act, 2004 (Act 35 of 2004).

key stakeholders, including the departments of minerals and energy and of trade and industry; Eskom; the Nuclear Energy Corporation of South Africa; universities; and science councils.

The PBMR programme represents a significant development for South Africa in the field of nuclear S&T. This programme is about four years ahead of any other high-temperature gas-cooled reactor programme in the world. To maintain this competitive edge, rapid development of the research and skills base in South Africa is essential.

This fast-track five- to 10-year programme is aimed at:
• utilising and co-ordinating existing capacity and instruments to grow a critical research and skills base to support the PBMR programme for a sustainable nuclear industry in South Africa
• promoting new programmes at universities to stimulate innovation and high-calibre intellectual capacity in PBMR-specific science and engineering disciplines, with a special focus on HDIs
• stabilising attitudes towards nuclear technology in society, through the creation of awareness programmes.

National Advisory Council on Innovation
The NACI is appointed by the Minister of Science and Technology to advise on the role and contribution of innovation, including S&T in promoting and achieving national objectives. These include:
• improving and sustaining the quality of life of all South Africans
• developing human resources for S&T
• building the economy
• strengthening the country's competitiveness in the international sphere.
NACI membership is broadly representative of all sectors and is constituted to ensure a spread of expertise and experience regarding national and provincial interests, scientific and technological disciplines, innovation regarding the needs and opportunities in different socio-economic fields and R&D in all sectors.

Public understanding of science, engineering and technology (PUSET)
The department's efforts in this regard include:
• The South African Reference Group on Women in S&T, established in March 2003. This ministerial body advises on ways to increase the visibility and development of women, and on making science more relevant to the needs of society by incorporating women's needs and expectations.
• The Women in Science Awards, first awarded in 2003, to honour female scientists and their achievements.
• The SET Week project, implemented for the first time in 2000. The 2005 National Science Week (NSW) was launched in May 2005 by the Minister of Science and Technology, Mr Mosibudi Mangena, under the theme *Tomorrow's Science and Technology is in our Youth's Hands.* The NSW is an annual week-long event aimed at highlighting the important role that science plays in everyday life and encouraging more youth to participate in Science, Mathematics, Engineering and Technology-related studies and careers. Over 40 sites throughout the country offered SET awareness events during the NSW.

National Biotechnology Strategy (NBS)
The 1996 *White Paper on Science and Technology* set the course for the transformation of South Africa's S&T system into a better co-ordinated and inclusive system aimed at benefiting all South Africans.

The biotechnology industry in South Africa is growing rapidly off a small base. Funding for genetic engineering grew by 360% between 2002 and 2004. The growth in all related fields, namely biochemistry, genetics and molecular biology, microbiology, genetic engineering and biotechnology, exceeded 46%.

The NBS, which was launched in 2001, sets the agenda for the development of South Africa's biotechnology industry.

Other initiatives include the establishment of biotechnology regional innovation centres (BRICs), namely: BioPAD, Cape Biotech, LIFElab and the Plant Biotechnology Innovation Centre (PlantBio). BRICs were created to act as instruments for the implementation of the NBS.

BRICs' focus areas cover a wide spectrum of the subdisciplines in biotechnology. These include human and animal health, biopharmaceuticals, industrial bioprocessing, mining biotechnology, bioinformatics and plant biotechnology. One of the challenges facing the South African biotechnology sector is the public's lack of understanding and knowledge of biotechnology applications and benefits.

Another programme initiated as a result of the NBS is the Public Understanding of Biotechnology (PUB) Programme. The PUB Programme provides the South African public with information, enabling them to participate meaningfully in debates about biotechnology and to make informed decisions.

Godisa Programme

The Godisa Trust is bringing about fundamental development in South Africa through the application of technological innovation.

Enhancing the competitiveness, productivity and sustainability of small, medium and micro enterprises (SMMEs), Godisa aims to induce long-term employment, economic growth and sustainable development as an imperative factor in the overall development of South Africa.

Since its establishment in 2001, Godisa has assisted 1 280 small business enterprises through its centres across South Africa.

The Godisa Trust is partnered by the departments of science and technology and of trade and industry, with additional support provided by the European Union (EU).

Godisa derives its name from the Setswana word meaning 'nurturing' or 'helping to grow'. As such, it incubates and nurtures SMMEs to play an increasingly vital role in developing sustainable employment and advancing essential skills and technologies.

The Godisa Trust is helping South Africans to cultivate their innovations and business ideas, and in the process, uplifting and empowering individuals and their communities.

Tshumisano

The Tshumisano partnership programme aims to encourage a closer partnership between stations based at participating universities of technology and SMMEs. The Tshumisano Trust, a joint venture between government, the German Agency for Technical Co-operation and the Committee of University of Technology Principals, is generating stronger working relationships between the departments of science and technology and of labour.

The Tshumisano technology stations offer support to South African enterprises for technology transfer and innovation. In 2003/04, 67 students involved in work programmes at the Tshumisano stations, gained practical exposure to real industry challenges as part of their training, which generally requires certain periods of work-integrated learning.

By June 2004, there were nine Tshumisano stations operating from the universities of technology environment in specific sectors to enrich their R&D, teaching and learning activities with better equipment and more realistic understanding of the industry and its needs. The sectors include chemicals, textiles, electronics, metals processing, mechanical engineering and food technology.

A key objective of these programmes is Black Economic Empowerment (BEE) through new small and medium enterprise (SME) development, and

On 7 June 2005, the Deputy Minister of the Department of Science and Technology, Mr Derek Hanekom, launched the South African Biodiversity Facility (SABIF) and its portal at the Innovation Hub in Pretoria.

SABIF aims to contribute to South Africa's sustainable development by facilitating access to biodiversity and related information on the Internet. The SABIF portal serves as South Africa's national gateway to open and free scientific biodiversity information. In doing this, SABIF will contribute towards a co-ordinated international scientific effort to enable users throughout the world to discover and put to use vast quantities of biodiversity data.

South Africa, as a voting member of the Global Biodiversity Information Facility (GBIF), has established the SABIF as a national node to the GBIF.

productivity improvement, technical mentoring and innovation services for existing SMEs.

Poverty-reduction programme

The Department of Science and Technology believes in a multipronged approach to fighting poverty.

Its poverty-alleviation projects have had positive outcomes in businesses and co-operatives focused on, among other projects, bee-keeping, paper-making, African design incorporation in clothing and textiles based on natural fibres, and indigenous cattle production. These projects are concentrated in the poverty nodes as identified by the Government's Integrated Sustainable Rural Development Strategy.

International science and technology co-operation

Science is an increasingly global activity and international funding for South African science rose from essentially nil in 1994 to 6% in 2002.

The strategy to use southern Africa's local (geographical) advantages and efforts to attract large international science-based investments are paying off. Key examples include the construction of the High-Energy Stereoscopic System (HESS) observatory in neighbouring Namibia and the Southern African Large Telescope (SALT) in Sutherland in the Northern Cape, as well as winning the bid to host the European Developing Countries Clinical Trials Partnership. Added to this are bold efforts to bolster South Africa's bid to site the Square Kilometre Array (SKA) radio telescope in South Africa. A 1% SKA demonstrator called Pathfinder is being built, which will enable the South African industry and academia to participate in the technology development process.

SALT is a multimillion-rand project involving Germany, Poland, the United States of America (USA), New Zealand and the United Kingdom (UK). SALT is the largest single optical telescope in the southern hemisphere. It was officially inaugurated on 10 November 2005.

The Department of Science and Technology is committed to building strong international relations.

It manages over 30 S&T bilateral agreements with various countries and is a key player in many multilateral fora, including the Commonwealth; the African, Caribbean and Pacific Group of States; the EU; and the Organisation for Economic Co-operation and Development.

The main areas of S&T co-operation between South Africa and its international partners are material science, manufacturing technology, biotechnology, environmental management, sustainable exploitation of natural resources and minerals, medical research and public health, engineering science and the advancement of technologies, water-supply projects, and Agriculture, Mathematics and Science education.

The NRF manages the implementation of the agreements.

South Africa's role at the forefront of NEPAD is, to a significant extent, based on its ability to deploy scientific knowledge and technological solutions on the continent.

In 2002, the International Council for Science (ICSU) took a decision to establish four regional ICSU offices in the developing world. In September 2005, the council's Regional Office for Africa was launched in Pretoria. The office is located at the premises of the NRF and is hosted by South Africa.

The department has successfully promoted South Africa's participation in strategic multilateral organisations, of which the International Centre for Genetic Engineering and Biotechnology (ICGEB) is a good example. A number of South Africans have been nominated for key positions on ICGEB, including the role of external auditor.

The Department of Science and Technology has taken a leadership role in the international process to establish the Global Earth Observation System of Systems (GEOSS). Acting through the department, South Africa participated in the development of the 10-year implementation plan and was elected co-chair of the Group on Earth Observations. GEOSS aims to enable globally co-ordinated earth observations, across a number of domains, to provide better and more reliable data in areas of benefit to society, including agriculture, weather, climate, water, disasters, health, energy, biodiversity and ecosystems.

Science councils

The statutory science councils are a key part of South Africa's NSI. Through them, government is able to directly commission research in the interest of the nation and support technology development in its pre-competitive phase.

National Research Foundation

The NRF is the key public entity responsible for supporting the development of HR capacity for research, technology and innovation in all fields of S&T. Within the context of the National R&D Strategy and NEPAD objectives, the NRF is one of the major players in educating and training a new generation of scientists able to deal with South African and African needs.

The NRF is guided by corporate core missions and strategic priorities based on the needs of the NSI and the imperatives outlined in the National R&D Strategy.

The four corporate core missions of the NRF are to:

- develop and support high-quality HR in substantially increased numbers
- generate high-quality knowledge in prioritised areas that address national and continental development needs
- use knowledge, technology transfer and innovation to ensure tangible benefits to society from the knowledge created
- provide state-of-the-art research infrastructure that is essential to develop high-quality HR and knowledge.

The six cross-cutting corporate strategic priorities are:

- redressing inequalities in race and gender
- adhering to quality
- internationalising research
- focusing on Africa
- positioning the NRF within the NSI
- transforming the NRF organisationally.

With a growth of 25% in its budget from R766 million in 2003/04 to R956 million in 2004/05, the NRF is becoming a major player in the NSI. This budget includes ring-fenced funds, and the budget for national research facilities and CoEs. It excludes funds for the IF and Technology and Human Resources for Industry Programme (THRIP).

As one of the key players in the NSI, the NRF focuses on positioning itself squarely in government's strategy to deliver on the creation of wealth and the improvement of the quality of life. Achievement of these goals in the long run depends critically on highly-skilled people who can generate new knowledge, develop and use new technologies, innovate, and drive the competitiveness of the country in international world markets.

Recommitment to support for 'Big Science'

The NRF will continue to promote the competitive advantage of South and southern Africa for capital-intensive 'Big Science' initiatives among the international community of scientists. The decision on the siting of the SKA radio telescope is expected in 2008. It is anticipated that the success of the SALT will positively influence the deliberations.

Both the African Coelacanth Ecosystems Programme (ACEP) and Inkaba ye Africa (a multi-institutional German/South African collaborative research programme in the Earth and space

The Minister of Science and Technology, Mr Mosibudi Mangena, officially opened the Women in Science Awards in August 2005, in Johannesburg. Hosted by the Department of Science and Technology, the awards are aimed at celebrating the significant contribution of outstanding women in scientific research that has led to economic growth and an improvement in the quality of life of all South Africans.

The 2005 awards were supported by L'Oreal South Africa as part of the company's partnership with the United Nations Educational, Scientific and Cultural Organisation. Ten winners were identified in eight award categories.

The Women in Science Awards underscore the Department of Science and Technology's efforts to radically increase the number of women entering the sciences and remaining there, as part of the national pursuit of sustainable economic growth.

sciences) are evolving into two major internationally co-sponsored flagship programmes.

The conceptualisation of the Major Radiation Medicine Centre, using the unique infrastructure and expertise at iThemba LABS that includes a separated sector cyclotron, is at an advanced stage. It was anticipated that financing for this project would be secured in 2005/06.

The first of several South African Environmental Observation Network nodes was launched in September 2004. The NRF was requested by the Department of Arts and Culture to assist with the establishment and management of the Human Language Technologies Facility. In line with policy to support 'Big Science', the NRF is committed to ensure that South African scientists gain access to major international research facilities.

Research and Innovation Support Agency (RISA)

The purpose of RISA is to advance the promotion and support of research and research-capacity development in all fields of knowledge and technology. This is done by investing in knowledge, people and infrastructure; promoting basic and applied research and innovation; as well as developing research capacity and advancing equity and redress to unlock the full creative potential of the research community. RISA facilitates strategic partnerships and knowledge networks, while upholding research excellence.

The South African Government aims to transform South Africa into a knowledge society that competes effectively in a global system. Because this requires educated and appropriately skilled people, much effort has been directed towards ensuring that RISA-supported research is focused on areas that are relevant to the development challenges of South Africa in a rapidly changing, highly competitive and knowledge-driven environment.

RISA has restructured to build its activities around the NRF key driver to produce large numbers of high-quality doctorates. The Knowledge Field Development function promotes new knowledge and research capacity. Institutional Capacity Development promotes the capacity of Higher

Education (HE) and other research institutions in South Africa to deliver skills of the quality and quantity required by the national R&D challenges. Knowledge Management and Strategy provides policy advice and ensures rational decisions in grants management and administration.

RISA's granting functions centre on nine focus areas, which provide a framework for generating new knowledge and training HR through research. The focus areas are:

- unlocking the future: advancing and strengthening strategic knowledge
- identifying distinct South African research opportunities
- conservation and management of ecosystems and biodiversity
- economic growth and international competitiveness
- education and the challenges for change
- indigenous knowledge systems (IKS)
- Information and Communications Technology (ICT) and the information society in South Africa
- socio-political impact of globalisation: the challenge for South Africa
- sustainable livelihoods: the eradication of poverty.

Research Capacity Development (RCD)

RCD programmes focus on boosting historically black universities and universities of technology committed to the research process. In addition, the Thuthuka Programme supports individual researchers. It comprises researchers in training, women in research, and research development for black academics. All the NRF's RCD initiatives aim to boost the output of high-level black HR (both academics and research students at all HE institutions); develop a postdoctoral research culture; strengthen weak, yet critically important disciplines; improve gender equity; and renew outdated research equipment.

Student support

The NRF provides two complementary types of postgraduate student support.

Free-standing bursaries, scholarships and fellowships are awarded directly to postgraduate students on a competitive basis, while grantholder-linked bursaries are granted to researchers within their NRF support package and may be awarded to students selected by the NRF grantholder. The NRF offers a limited number of travel grants for research abroad.

Knowledge management

The NRF's Knowledge Management Directorate includes Information and Strategy Advice, the Evaluation Centre and the IT Department. Knowledge management, including records management, and expanding communities of practice are high on RISA's agenda.

Internationalisation

Internationalisation has been identified as a strategic priority for the NRF. The goal of becoming globally competitive requires local professionals and researchers to collaborate with the best in the world. This collaboration enhances knowledge transfer and the sharing of expertise, improves knowledge production and offers opportunities to train research students.

A new vision will be formulated for leveraging international capacity to build South Africa's R&D capacity. In the short term, the strategy will be designed and tested within the research community, for implementation in the longer term. It will be expected of all RISA funding programmes to indicate their contribution to internationalisation in all knowledge domains.

Several other initiatives in internationalising South African science are vested within granting programmes and other sections of the RISA:
- Inkaba ye Africa
- the Royal Society/NRF programme, which has received approval for continued funding for a second cycle
- continued support to the steering committee of the International Group of Funding Agencies for Global Change Research
- support to the ICSU African Regional Office at the NRF in Pretoria
- implementation of newly identified ICSU priority areas
- National Science Foundation/NRF collaboration

in science education research, involving partners in the UK and Australia.

An amount of R10,9 million was allocated for the internationalisation of science during 2005/06.

Technology for Human Resources for Industry Programme

Managed by the NRF, advised by the THRIP Board and sponsored by the Department of Trade and Industry, this programme supports projects that address the technology and HR needs of industry on a cost-sharing basis with industrial partners.

During 2005/06, THRIP was expected to implement recommendations made in the new five-year strategic plan approved by the Department of Trade and Industry. The programme would thus be better aligned to key strategies that government uses to guide increased R&D competitiveness, grow the economy, create jobs, eradicate poverty and provide equity within South Africa. There is also a strong focus on monitoring and mentoring to broaden participation.

The programme is focusing on increasing participation by SMMEs, BEE entities and black and women researchers and students. It also aims to increase the share of the THRIP budget allocated to HDIs and universities of technology.

In 2005/06, the MTEF budget allocation for THRIP was R143 million.

Science and Technology Agreements Committee (STAC)

The NRF is responsible for managing and administering STAC-related activities and grants and overseeing projects. The Department of Science and Technology retains the responsibility for negotiating bilateral or multilateral agreements with international partners and drafting framework programmes. These agreements develop scientific relations between the research communities of the intergovernmental signatories and establish long-term, scientific co-operation. Emphasis is placed on training, the inclusion of doctoral students and the exchange of postdoctoral fellows.

During 2005, the Swiss National Science Foundation's bilateral agreement activities and funds were expected to be transferred to STAC. The support for activities within the IBSA (India, Brazil and South Africa) agreement was also expected to be launched. The co-operation within the EU Framework will continue through marketing and workshops around the EU research platforms.

In 2005/06, the STAC budget increased to R26,5 million.

Scarce Skills Development Fund

The Department of Labour, in conjunction with the departments of education and of science and technology, is responsible for ensuring training in scarce skills, both in HE and other training institutions, especially in S&T. To deliver on this objective, the Department of Labour recommends the allocation of resources from the National Skills Fund (NSF) for bursaries and scholarships. The NRF has become the implementing agency for the Department of Labour to provide and support scarce skills at postgraduate levels in S&T.

Biodiversity programmes

The Department of Science and Technology requested the NRF to manage some initiatives linked to the biodiversity science thrust of the National R&D Strategy. These include the South African Biodiversity Initiative and the South African Biodiversity Information Facility.

The NRF manages the Sea and Coast Programme with the Department of Environmental Affairs and Tourism as a co-investor. This research programme provides information, advice and training in support of optimal and sustainable use and the development of sea, coasts and estuaries. The Sea and Coast Programme ends in 2006 and the South African Network for Coastal and Oceanic Research (SANCOR), administered by the NRF, was expected to undertake an independent evaluation of this programme in 2005.

The NRF will continue to manage the provincial research projects of the Branch: Marine and Coastal Management of the Department of Environmental Affairs and Tourism. These projects have a strong applied research focus which feeds into the management of marine and coastal

resources, including resource allocations for the fishing industry.

South African National Antarctic Programme (SANAP)

In 2004, the Department of Science and Technology appointed the NRF as implementing agency to administer the grant award process for SANAP in conjunction with the Department of Environmental Affairs and Tourism, which will continue to administer the logistics of the programme. The programme aims to create a demographically balanced Antarctic research programme that strives for high-quality international research, and links to other African countries and interdisciplinary research. The estimated budget is R5 million.

Indigenous Knowledge Systems

Similar to STAC, the NRF receives a ring-fenced grant for IKS from the Department of Science and Technology to support research and HR development in the field of indigenous knowledge. RISA reports separately to the Department of Science and Technology on the outcomes of this programme. The IKS grant from the Department of Science and Technology amounts to R10 million annually.

Additional initiatives

- The NRF has taken on management responsibility for CoEs. The Department of Science and Technology has entrusted the NRF with managing these centres to stimulate research, generate high-quality HR development and to impact meaningfully on key national and international R&D issues.
- The Department of Trade and Industry has recognised the need for greater innovation and skills development and will fund centres that focus on national priorities and sectors for which the Department of Trade and Industry is the primary custodian. Managed by the NRF, the CoEs in industrial R&D will maximise co-operation and synergies with other relevant NRF programmes.
- Following international trends of funding-endowed chairs at HE institutions to provide

leadership and guidance in a specialist field, the Department of Trade and Industry has decided to support endowed chairs of entrepreneurship and enterprise development.
- Postgraduate bursaries for the disabled are made possible through a grant of R5 million per year by the Department of Labour's NSF.
- The Department of Trade and Industry has asked the NRF to manage the Mathematics and Science Teachers' Training Programme to enhance Science and Mathematics educators' teaching skills. A budget of R20 million was allocated for this initiative in 2004/05.
- The NRF manages the Innovation Postdoctoral Fellowship Programme on behalf of the Department of Science and Technology. It is a five-year programme that aims to support up to 100 new postdoctoral fellowships with R15 million per year from the department.

South African Agency for Science and Technology (SAASTA)
Facilitating the interface between science and society, SAASTA's mandate is to promote public awareness, appreciation and engagement of SET in South Africa. SET education, through pre-tertiary, tertiary and lifelong learning initiatives, provides the base for creating the required human capital for South Africa's SET endeavours. SAASTA aims to increase the number of previously disadvantaged learners who enrol for and perform in Mathematics and Science.

SAASTA makes a major contribution towards raising the quality of and expanding the feeder system that inputs into other NRF HR development strategies. The agency enhances the NRF's seamless approach to HR development. This approach entails the promotion of appropriate human capital from schools level to building student capacity, research expertise, entrepreneurship, technological capacity and eventually innovation. This, in turn, creates economic growth and improved quality of life.

SAASTA's three strategic pillars for the science promotion and awareness programmes of the NRF are:
- education-related programmes (preparing tomorrow's scientists and innovators)

- a SET awareness platform, incorporating a reconstituted museum, the National Zoological Gardens (NZG), the Johannesburg Observatory, and infrastructure available through the national research facilities (engaging with the phenomena of science)
- science communication (communicating the research advances of science to the public).

National research facilities
The NRF manages the following:
- South African Astronomical Observatory (SAAO)
- Hartebeesthoek Radio Astronomy Observatory (HartRAO)
- Hermanus Magnetic Observatory (HMO)
- South African Institute for Aquatic Biodiversity (SAIAB)
- South African Environmental Observation Network (SAEON)
- NZG
- iThemba Laboratory for Accelerator-Based Sciences (iThemba LABS).

South African Astronomical Observatory and Southern African Large Telescope
The SAAO is the national research facility for optical/infrared astronomy in South Africa. Its prime function is to further fundamental research in astronomy and astrophysics at national and international level.

As the premier optical/infrared astronomy facility in Africa, SAAO also plays a leading role in the promotion of astronomy on the continent. In terms of research, it is one of the most productive scientific

Two 190-million-year-old dinosaur embryos from a group of seven eggs have been identified as the oldest dinosaur embryos yet found. Discovered in South Africa, they are also the oldest known embryos for any terrestrial vertebrate.

522

institutions. There are strong international links worldwide through scientific collaboration and technological exchange. SAAO's research excellence is underpinned by strong technical competencies in niche areas.

In 2005, SAAO made the transition from the SALT construction phase to the SALT operation phase. Through devising a vastly superior spherical aberration corrector, and a variety of other innovations, SAAO has contributed to making SALT more capable than its prototype, the Hobby-Eberly Telescope in Texas.

SALT represents a paradigm shift for the SAAO in terms of the level and complexity of technology. It will open up new areas of research, which are currently not possible to pursue at SAAO. SAAO scientists will be responsible for spearheading the South African scientific use of SALT and training the southern African user community. Therefore, a major challenge to SAAO in 2005/06 will be the reorientation of scientific effort towards SALT science.

From the outset, SALT was conceived as an African facility. With the advent of large-scale facilities such as SALT and the HESS, and other initiatives such as SKA, Inkaba ye Afrika and ZASat, southern Africa is emerging as a regional space S&T hub.

Hartebeesthoek Radio Astronomy Observatory

HartRAO is the national research facility responsible for research and training in radio astronomy and space geodesy in South Africa. The radio telescope is available for research either as a single, independent instrument or in global networks of radio telescopes, using the technique of very long baseline interferometry (VLBI).

HartRAO is one of only five permanent fundamental space geodesy stations worldwide and participates in geodetic VLBI through the International VLBI Service, in satellite laser ranging (through the International Laser Ranging Service) and in the Global Positioning System (GPS) (through the International GPS Service). The data is available to the international community.

The radio astronomy group is repositioning itself to meet the expectations and demands of the National Astrophysics and Space Science Programme, SKA and increased university involvement. The space geodesy group is aligning itself with a multidisciplinary approach and capacity-building initiatives through expansion, collaboration and new projects.

Hermanus Magnetic Observatory

The HMO functions as part of the worldwide network of magnetic observatories. Its core function is to monitor and model variations of the Earth's magnetic field. It is primarily the HMO's scientific achievements, critical location, and unique facilities that make it indispensable in the global network of magnetic observatories.

The density of geomagnetic recording stations in Africa is significantly less than in other continental landmasses. The continuous recording stations operated by the HMO are the only operational sources of ground-based geomagnetic field data south of the equator in Africa. The HMO is one of only four geomagnetic observatories whose data is used by the World Data Centre for Geomagnetism in Kyoto, Japan, for measuring geomagnetic storm intensity.

South African Institute for Aquatic Biodiversity

The SAIAB is an interactive hub focused on serving the nation by generating, disseminating and applying knowledge to understanding and solving problems on the conservation and wise use of African fish and aquatic biodiversity.

The SAIAB cares for and develops the National Fish Collection; generates knowledge through research on aquatic biodiversity and the fundamental processes and conservation of aquatic biodiversity in Africa; and trains and educates knowledge workers in aquatic biodiversity. It addresses national and international issues in aquatic biodiversity through the priorities set by national and international funding agencies.

The most direct challenges facing SAIAB are to ensure continued funding for the ACEP; develop research capacity; develop biosystematic skills capacity; and inspire, educate and train a new generation of South African aquatic biosystematic and conservation scientists. The SAIAB is working on a knowledge management system required to develop and manage aquatic biodiversity databases. The facility is also working on consolidating its position within the NSI, especially in relation to the South African National Biodiversity Institute (SANBI).

iThemba Laboratory for Accelerator-Based Sciences

Providing modern research facilities to users in science, medicine and industry, iThemba LABS has established itself as a major commercial centre for radiation medicine. It is also forging strategic partnerships with the private and public sectors to leverage capital, skills and the expertise required for an initiative of this magnitude. iThemba LABS focuses on providing scientifically and medically useful radiation through the acceleration of charged particles. It is the primary centre of expertise in radiation medicine and nuclear S&T in South Africa.

iThemba LABS is expanding its research facilities and infrastructure to enhance training, HR development and transformation, as well as building international collaborations (especially in Africa) to improve the S&T profile. There is a strong focus on facilitating a quantum increase in postgraduates in S&T. This is essential for transforming the South African S&T workforce and for building a successful economy to minimise the impact of poverty.

National Zoological Gardens

The NZG was declared a national research facility in April 2004. It has since been engaged in a strategic reorientation process to align with, and make a contribution to, the core missions and strategic priorities of the NRF.

The NZG is undergoing radical transformation from being a traditional zoological garden, to being a national facility for and an active participant in terrestrial biodiversity research. It has the potential to offer South Africa, Africa and the international community at large the infrastructure required to conduct world-class, and knowledge-generating research.

The NZG houses one of the largest animal collections in the world. It operates three breeding centres and covers an area of over 6 000 hectares. The NZG is well placed as an education platform, receiving close to 600 000 visitors a year, comprising learners, educators and the general public.

South African Environmental Observation Network

The purpose of the SAEON is to generate long-term information relevant to the sustainable management of natural resources and habitat over a range of ecoregions and land uses. These include pristine (wild) landscape, partially pristine (managed) landscape, agriculturally (rural) transformed landscape and urban transformed landscape.

SAEON will establish innovative research platforms and information-management systems for long-term multidisciplinary, multi-institutional and participatory ecosystem studies with strong regional and global linkages. These research platforms are co-ordinated as nodes, with the first one – the Ndlovu Node – established during 2004 in Phalaborwa. The SAEON Fynbos Node and the Marine and Coastal Node were expected to be launched during 2005/06.

Agricultural Research Council (ARC)

The ARC is a statutory parastatal body established in terms of the Agricultural Research Act, 1990 (Act 86 of 1990). It is committed to the promotion of agriculture and related sectors through research, and technology development and transfer.

Through its wide network of research institutes and experimental farms, the ARC provides a strong scientific base and a broadly distributed technology-transfer capacity for the entire agricultural industry in South Africa. In support of national and household food security, ARC research empowers both commercial and resource-poor farmers.

Farmers are provided with appropriate technologies to improve production. Training of farmers and agricultural extension staff in new technologies is an integral part of the ARC's activities.

The ARC is also active in international collaboration, especially with universities in the USA, UK, Europe, Australia, New Zealand and Africa. It has memoranda of understanding with numerous scientific role-players in other countries.

The ARC's institutes have localised research and demonstration trials at about 40 sites. These include strategic research farms and satellite stations located within some provincial departments of agriculture.

ARC Institute for Soil, Climate and Water

This institute in Pretoria, Gauteng, promotes the characterisation, sustainable utilisation and protection of natural resources.

Research activities cover soil science, agrometeorology, water utilisation and analytical services.

ARC Institute for Agricultural Engineering

Situated in Pretoria, the institute is active in agricultural mechanisation, resource conservation, farm structures, irrigation, alternative energy, aquaculture and product-processing.

Research is directed at a wide range of clients, from subsistence farmers using animal traction to commercial farmers and manufacturers requiring scientific performance evaluations of advanced equipment. Innovative energy sources and applications are developed for rural areas.

ARC Plant-Protection Research Institute

The ARC Plant-Protection Research Institute in Pretoria concentrates on national agricultural and environmental problems. It is committed to the promotion of economic and environmentally acceptable pest control. Research focuses on biosystematics, ecology and epidemiology of vertebrates, as well as fungi, and pathogenic and useful bacteria and viruses.

The institute researches the control of pests and invasive plants through effective pesticide management, as well as biological and integrated control strategies. A variety of services are provided.

The institute also houses the Plant Genetic Resource Unit.

ARC Grain Crops Institute

This institute, situated in Potchefstroom, North West, is responsible for research into the improvement and cultivation of grain crops such as maize, sorghum and millet, as well as oil-and-protein seeds such as sunflower, ground-nuts, soya beans, dry beans, cowpeas, sweet white lupin and bambara. Research activities involve plant-breeding, evaluation of cultivars and grain quality, plant physiology and other production factors.

ARC Small Grain Institute

The ARC Small Grain Institute in Bethlehem, Free State, concentrates on the improvement and cultivation of small grain crops such as barley, wheat, oats, triticale and rye. Research activities include plant-breeding, evaluation of cultivars and grain quality, plant physiology, tillage, weed science, plant pathology, entomology and yield potential.

ARC Institute for Industrial Crops

This institute in Rustenburg, North West, is involved in all fundamental and applied research in the interest of the tobacco and cotton industries. Research is also conducted on other fibre crops such as hemp, sisal and flax, which have potential as new crops in rural areas.

ARC Institute for Tropical and Subtropical Crops

The ARC Institute for Tropical and Subtropical Crops in Nelspruit, Mpumalanga, is responsible for research into all aspects of the cultivation of tropical and subtropical fruits.

Other crops on which production research is conducted include tea and coffee, spices such as ginger, as well as pecan, macadamia and cashew nuts. Lesser-known exotic crops being evaluated are pitanga, feijoa, annona types, carambola and jaboticaba.

ARC Roodeplaat Vegetable and Ornamental Plant Institute

Situated outside Pretoria, this institute concentrates on a wide range of horticultural crops. Research is conducted on commercial vegetables such as onions, potatoes, tomatoes and sweet potatoes. Traditional and indigenous vegetables receiving attention include amaranthus, cassava, plectranthus, Zulu round potato, pigeonpeas, cowpeas and bambara.

Research on the production and development of ornamentals and indigenous flora such as fynbos, woody ornamentals and bulbs, has led to a new growth industry.

ARC Infruitec/Nietvoorbij
ARC Infruitec/Nietvoorbij in Stellenbosch, Western Cape, is responsible for research on the cultivation and post-harvest technology of deciduous fruit.

Other assigned crops are berry fruits, tree-nut crops, rooibos tea, honeybush tea, dates, olives, kiwi fruit and hops. It is also responsible for research on the cultivation of table, raisin and wine grapes, as well as on the production of wine and brandy.

ARC Animal-Improvement Institute
The ARC Animal-Improvement Institute at Irene, near Pretoria, provides the livestock industry with technologies for the improved quality of animals.

It has established genetic and physiological methods to identify and study superior breeding material to improve the efficiency of the national herd.

ARC Animal Nutrition and Animal Products Institute
Situated at Irene, near Pretoria, this institute develops environment-friendly technologies to promote animal production through improved nutrition.

Research is conducted on beef and dairy cattle, sheep, pigs, goats and poultry. The institute also evaluates technologies to enhance the quality of meat and dairy products.

ARC Onderstepoort Veterinary Institute
The ARC Onderstepoort Veterinary Institute, north of Pretoria, is responsible for preventing and controlling animal diseases. It also provides a public health service regarding animal products such as milk, meat and eggs.

The institute conducts research on specialised diagnostics, parasitology, toxicology and related disciplines. Various vaccines and other biological products are developed and produced. The institute also houses a high-security facility for research into infectious diseases such as foot-and-mouth disease and African swine fever. It serves as a regional centre for diagnostic services, advice and training.

ARC Range and Forage Institute
The institute, situated in Pretoria, focuses on the development of holistic and integrated land-use strategies. It provides guidelines for sustainable livestock and rangeland management systems.

Council for Scientific and Industrial Research (CSIR)
Constituted by an Act of Parliament in 1945, the CSIR is one of the largest scientific and technology research, development and implementation organisations in Africa. It is situated in Pretoria and is represented in each of South Africa's nine provinces.

The council undertakes and applies directed research and innovation in S&T to improve the quality of life of the country's people. Building measurable value into its work through local and international partnerships remains a key component of its endeavours to provide world-class technology.

Supporting national imperatives
South Africa's national imperatives and global challenges provide the macro-strategic framework within which the CSIR conducts its research. In an effort to contribute to placing Africa on a path of sustainable growth and development, the organisation supports and actively participates in NEPAD. The CSIR's current five-year strategy, which largely shapes its agenda until 2008, highlights the following five strategic initiatives:
- aligning with and contributing to key government initiatives
- consolidating excellence in SET
- contributing to excellence in business and innovation

- contributing to sustainable development
- accessing and developing the best minds.

The CSIR's portfolio includes:

- research, development and implementation
- technology transfer and assessment
- scientific and technical education and training
- policy and strategic decision support
- global S&T links as well as perspectives
- specialised technical and information consulting
- prototyping and pilot-scale manufacturing
- commercialising intellectual property, including venture establishment.

The organisation's staff complement is about 2 500 with a core of technical and scientific specialists. HR development and transformation in the CSIR are clearly influenced by the CSIR's emerging challenges. Processes have been developed in accordance with the dictates of a knowledge economy in a global world and the challenges facing South Africa.

The CSIR's parliamentary grant is intended to keep its knowledge base and facilities at the leading edge of technological development. The grant is invested in developing new areas of expertise in emerging research fields, undertaking 'pre-competitive' research too risky for the private sector to fund, and for training young researchers.

Mintek

Mintek, South Africa's national mineral research organisation, is one of the world's leading technology organisations specialising in mineral processing, extractive metallurgy and related areas. Working closely with industry and other R&D institutions, Mintek provides service testwork, process development, consulting and innovative products to clients worldwide.

Mintek is an autonomous statutory organisation and reports to the Minister of Minerals and Energy. About 35% of the annual budget of R278 million is funded by the State's science vote, with the balance provided by contract R&D, sales of services and products, technology licensing agreements and joint-venture operating companies. Mintek has some 480 permanent staff members, over half of whom are scientists, engineers and other technical R&D personnel.

Mintek's objectives are to research, develop and transfer to industry novel and improved techniques for processing, extracting, refining and utilising minerals and mineral products, to:

- enhance the competitiveness of South Africa's minerals industry in the global market
- assist local mining and engineering companies to expand internationally
- promote job creation, economic growth and regional development.

Specific goals are:

- promoting increased beneficiation of South Africa's minerals and mineral commodities by developing competitive and innovative processing technology and equipment
- strengthening South Africa's international position as a supplier of mineral technologies, capital goods and services
- developing regional strategies for the mineral-processing sector, concentrating on value-addition, capacity-building and broad-based development.

Mintek's activities include:

- providing essential services (information, consulting and experimental)
- increasing the competitiveness of industry by developing appropriate technology to cut costs and improve recoveries
- developing 'breakthrough' process technologies and novel uses for metals and their products
- marketing its commercial products and technologies to industry
- establishing strategic partnerships and joint ventures
- participating in regional development initiatives and SADC activities and projects
- maintaining and expanding international scientific links
- developing the HR potential of the region through educational and training activities.

To ensure focus and market orientation, Mintek's R&D activities are grouped into programmes that are based largely on industry structure:

- The Gold Industry Programme focuses on developing and introducing improved technologies such as biotechnology and ion-exchange processes, to simplify processing and increase recoveries, particularly from ores that are difficult to treat. A major joint venture with industry and other research groups is exploring new industrial uses of gold.

- The Platinum-Group Metals (PGMs) Industry Programme aims to increase the cost-effectiveness of PGM production and stimulate industrial demand for PGMs.
- The Ferrous Metals Industry Programme develops products and technical services to increase the cost-effectiveness of ferro-alloy production, as well as stainless steels and other alloys with improved properties.
- The Non-Ferrous Metals Industry Programme includes the processing of aluminium, cobalt, copper, lead, magnesium, nickel and zinc. Major emphasis is placed on the introduction of cleaner technologies.
- The Industrial Minerals Industry Programme includes the beneficiation and processing of commodities such as heavy minerals, chromite, iron and manganese ores, andalusite, phosphates, fluorite and diamonds. Mintek's research into waste management and environmental problems also fall under this programme.

Promoting industrial growth

Mintek is promoting a number of major new industrial projects based on mineral beneficiation, and utilising both existing and newly developed technologies. These include recovering PGMs from chromite tailings, producing ferronickel and electrolytic manganese dioxide, and establishing a local magnesium industry using a novel thermal production route.

Regional development

Mintek carries out surveys, evaluations and commodity and market studies to support initiatives by international, governmental, regional or industry associations. It also identifies and evaluates potential development projects, assesses and provides technology, and conducts feasibility studies. Mintek supports the activities of the SADC Mining Coordination Unit and was closely involved in develop-

ing the economic growth strategy for NEPAD and the African Mining Partnership.

Mintek's Small-Scale Mining (SSM) Division supports the SSM sector by developing appropriate technologies, providing consulting services and training, and promoting sustainable mining, downstream processing and value-addition through integrated development programmes.

Environment

Mintek focuses on the development of environmentally responsible technologies for the recovery and recycling of metals from metallurgical residues. A major programme is in place to monitor cyanide species after discharge in various locations around gold plants, from both an environmental and a processing point of view.

Mintek's environmental management system has been certified as meeting the requirements of the International Organisation for Standardisation (ISO) 14001 standard.

Education

The development of appropriate HR is crucial for the long-term sustainability of the minerals industry. Mintek's educational and training initiatives are provided through a section 21 company that was set up to develop technicians, technologists, engineers and others with appropriate skills from previously disadvantaged communities. The specific programmes include:

- artisanal and SSM training
- jewellery manufacturing
- upgrading of Mathematics and Science skills
- undergraduate and postgraduate bursary schemes
- in-training programmes for recently qualified engineers and technicians.

Human Sciences Research Council (HSRC)

The HSRC is South Africa's statutory research agency dedicated to the applied social sciences. It has about 130 researchers, mainly specialists, 30 interns and 110 support staff. Its revenue is derived roughly equally from its parliamentary grant and from earnings through tenders, commissions and local and international foundation grants.

The HSRC conducts social-science research concerned with all aspects of development and poverty alleviation in South Africa, the region and in Africa.

Research programmes

The HSRC's research is organised into 10 interdisciplinary programmes:

Assessment Technology and Education Evaluation (ATEE)

ATEE focuses on the monitoring and evaluation of education change at national, provincial, district, school and classroom level. It also develops instruments and techniques for assessing individuals in the workplace.

The research programme provides valuable information to address quality, equity, access and redress issues for transforming the education and training sector. It focuses on the following areas:
- language and literacy studies, including language policy development and implementation
- Science, Mathematics and Technology education, including research to provide information to policy-makers to plan for Science, Mathematics and Technology education at school level
- school reform and policy analysis, including understanding the school system, and how to transform and measure change
- methodology, modelling and analysis.

Child, Youth and Family Development (CYFD)

CYFD is dedicated to national social development through innovative research that has significant intervention and policy implications.

It works in seven priority areas:
- early childhood development and intervention, including nutrition, psycho-social development, health, illness and pre-school education
- rights and protection, including violence and abuse, child labour, children and youth in care, and law and justice as it affects children, youth and families
- socialising and learning, including language and literacy, schools, neighbourhoods and social identity
- youth development, including civic engagement,

work, livelihoods and life skills, subcultures and networks
- risk and resilience, including context and determinants, risk behaviours, prevention and intervention to reduce high-risk conditions and behaviour
- sexuality and reproductive health, including HIV and AIDS, teenage pregnancy and parenthood, sexual violence, gender and relationships
- families and households, including family formation and security, dissolution and coping, roles and responsibilities, culture and values, and the impact of HIV and AIDS.

Democracy and Governance (D&G)

D&G explores contributions to and constraints upon democratisation in South Africa and the African continent. Researchers evaluate the policies, institutions and impact of government, business and civil society regarding their capacity to reduce inequality and poverty, while empowering communities to promote local, regional and national sustainable development. D&G has three major thrusts, namely democratisation, local government and delivery, and public service and development.

The programme focuses on:
- evaluating legislation, policies and administration of government in terms of its ability to reduce inequality and poverty
- exploring the linkages between state institutions and the characteristics of African political economies which contribute to, or threaten, democratic consolidation.

Employment and Economic Policy Research (EEPR)

EEPR seeks to improve and disseminate an understanding of the nature and causes of persistent unemployment and underemployment. This work feeds directly into strategy and action by enabling public and private interventions. To ensure relevance and uptake, each new step involves critical stakeholder groups and government departments.

EEPR's priority areas include:
- labour-market analysis, including skills development, regional labour-market studies, the eco-

nomic impact of HIV and AIDS and the design of active labour-market policies
- sector strategies, with an emphasis on employment creation, including industrial competitiveness studies and basic needs industries
- integrated employment studies, including evidence-based employment scenarios, such as in-depth analysis of employment statistics.

Human Resource Development (HRD)

This research programme undertakes research on the development of HR, orientated largely towards the creation of an improved information and analysis infrastructure to support government decision-making in this area.

Its primary focus is the study of the pathways of learners from school into Further Education and HE, and into the world of work. HRD is a cross-sectoral research issue, shaped by and affecting a number of related government policy domains. It aims to yield the appropriate human and technological capabilities necessary for human development, equity, and future national economic success.

Integrated Rural and Regional Development (IRRD)

IRRD promotes rural development in South and southern Africa through user-driven policy, monitoring and evaluation, and problem-orientated research. With poverty reduction as the unifying, overarching theme, the programme's objectives, orientation and activities are designed specifically to address key regional, national and Africa-wide policy priorities.

There are four distinct, but interlocking, subprogrammes:
- land and agrarian reform, which investigates land tenure, land use, land redistribution and restitution, farm labour and employment and environmental and related issues
- rural non-farm development, which investigates rural livelihoods, rural infrastructure and service delivery, rural micro-enterprise support, and eco-tourism
- regional resource flows, which investigates HR, trade and capital flows into, out of, and within southern Africa

- poverty reduction, which investigates a wide range of issues related to policy, strategy and practice to reduce poverty in South and southern Africa.

Knowledge Management (KM)

KM focuses on knowledge production, measurement and sharing, and interacting with peers nationally and internationally. It covers three overlapping domains:
- The information society, which has developed a strong working relationship with the Presidential National Commission for the Information Society and Development.
- The NSI studies, which consist of the *Research and Experimental Development Surveys* of 2001/02 and 2003/04. These important studies go to the core of information decision-making in respect of funding for the NSI.
- Knowledge-intensive research organisations, which measure KM practices that could be deployed across government.

Social Aspects of HIV/AIDS and Health (SAHA)

There is a high demand for quality research into the social aspects of HIV and AIDS. SAHA conducts research that is relevant to policy-making and has become both a national and SADC resource.

This research programme focuses on the following areas:
- the key socio-cultural, political, economic and demographic determinants that increase or reduce vulnerability to HIV-infection
- aspects that facilitate or hinder change in risky behaviour, enable or delay progress towards care, and prevent or mitigate the impact of HIV and AIDS
- the social epidemiology of HIV and AIDS and major public health conditions in South Africa and the SADC
- health-system issues necessary for disease control within a social development context.

SAHA has established the Social Aspects of AIDS Research Alliance (SAHARA), a vehicle for facilitating the sharing of research expertise across sub-Saharan Africa to prevent the further spread of the epidemic and to mitigate the impact of the disease.

SAHARA conducts multisite and multicountry research projects that are exploratory, cross-sectional, comparative or intervention-based.

Surveys, Analyses, Modelling and Mapping (SAMM)

SAMM is a cross-cutting entity that brings together the HSRC's capacity in surveys, quantitative and qualitative analyses, geographical information systems (GIS), statistical and econometric modelling, and data management.

SAMM consists of the following units:

- Surveys, which designs appropriate survey methods and instruments to gather relevant and up-to-date information on public attitudes, and assists other research programmes with their survey-based project needs
- Analyses, Modelling and Statistics, which provides technical research support and expertise internally and externally in data analysis, modelling and statistics
- Data Management, which is responsible for a range of data-management archiving, quality control and related data-support services
- the GIS Centre, which provides analytical and technical GIS support and services in project design, implementation and management
- Urban Renewal and Development, which is a dedicated urban research facility.

Social Cohesion and Identity (SCI)

SCI explores what constitutes South African identity, and the historical traditions and social processes that have shaped leadership in South Africa.

The programme also explores how South Africans view themselves within the emerging discourses of the African Renaissance, and how African leadership responds to the broader challenges facing the African continent within a rapidly changing and fluid global political order.

Medical Research Council (MRC)

The MRC's mission is to improve the nation's health status and quality of life, through relevant research aimed at promoting equity and development.

The MRC is an autonomous body, but reports to the national Department of Health. It receives 60% of its budget from the Department of Science and Technology. Its head office is situated in Cape Town, with provincial offices in Pretoria and Durban.

The MRC's research activities are aligned with the health priorities of the nation, and in accordance with the national S&T imperatives and the health priorities defined by the Department of Health under the philosophy of essential national health research. Activities are grouped into the following national programmes:

National Programme for Research in Molecules to Disease

This programme undertakes research on human and microbial genetics, genomics, bio-informatics, cell and molecular biology, tissue engineering, oesophageal cancer, molecular hepatology, microbacteriology, and liver and bone disease.

National Programme for Health Systems and Policy Research

The scientists in this programme conduct research on health systems, clinical epidemiology, biostatistics, health policy, burden of disease and telemedicine.

National Programme for Infection and Immunity Research

The research units in this programme are involved in research on tuberculosis, malaria, immunology of infectious diseases, diarrhoeal diseases, inflammation and amoebiasis, genital ulcer diseases, respiration and meningeal pathogens, and South African traditional medicines.

It also incorporates the MRC National HIV and AIDS Lead Programme, whose divisions co-ordinate the South African AIDS Vaccine Initiative; various aspects of biomedical research, including mother-to-child transmission and microbicides; and prevention of transmission through behavioural change. (See chapter 13: *Health*.)

National Programme for Non-Communicable Disease Research

This programme undertakes research on heart disease (both laboratory, clinical and public health research), nutritional intervention, diabetes, crime, violence and injury, anxiety and stress disorders, dental issues, medical imaging, chronic diseases of lifestyle and cancer epidemiology.

National Programme for Environment and Development Research

In this entity, research is undertaken on health promotion, health and development, exercise and sports science, occupational and environmental health, alcohol and drug abuse, and technology transfer.

National Programme for Women and Child Health Research

This programme undertakes research on many aspects of women's health, including high blood pressure during pregnancy, healthcare strategies in maternal and infant health, perinatal mortality, gender and health, mineral metabolism and nutritional intervention.

South African National Health Knowledge Network

The South African National Health Knowledge Network was established in 1999 at the MRC with funding from the Government's IF.

The network operates under the tradename *SA HealthInfo* and is available on the Internet at *www.sahealth-info.org*. It provides a one-stop interactive forum or resource for quality-controlled and evidence-based health-research information.

Council for Geoscience (CGS)

The main functions of the CGS are:
- the systematic documentation of the surface of the Earth within the borders of South Africa; the compilation of geological, geophysical, geochemical and other geoscientific information; and the publication of this information in the form of maps and documents
- geoscientific research on rocks, minerals, ores, fossils, etc. in South Africa, and the publication of research results in national and international journals

- the collection and conservation of all geoscientific information and data on South Africa in national collections and electronic databases
- the supply of geoscientific services and advice to the national and provincial governments, to ensure informed decisions regarding the optimal and efficient use of the Earth's surface.

The objectives of the CGS are to:
- minimise the geological and geoscientific investment risk for national and international entrepreneurs in the South African mining sector (the quality of available geological information, which is known as the 'geological risk grading', contributes to about 61% of the investment risk in any country)
- supply the country with basic geoscience data to establish a safe, cost-effective physical infrastructure
- supply basic knowledge to ensure safe, cost-effective and environmentally acceptable urbanisation and housing development
- carry out research on raw material needed to clothe, transport, feed and provide shelter for the nation.

To accomplish these functions and objectives, the CGS maintains a specialised workforce, consisting of Earth scientists supplemented by technical, support and administrative staff at its headquarters in Pretoria, as well as branch offices in the Western Cape, Northern Cape, Limpopo, North West and the Eastern Cape.

The following national institutions are maintained by the CGS:
- The National Geoscience Library in Pretoria is probably the most comprehensive geoscience library in Africa. It includes the National Geoscience Map Library, which contains a collection of South African and African geoscience maps.
- The National Core Library contains a representative stratigraphic-borehole core collection, representing most of the lithological units located within the borders of South Africa. This collection is housed at Donkerhoek, east of Pretoria.
- The Geoscience Museum in the Transvaal Museum in Pretoria contains a unique collection of minerals and fossils, catering for the Earth-

science education of the public, especially schoolchildren.

- An extensive laboratory analyses of rock and soil samples, using various specialised techniques.

The geoscience information and services provided by the CGS are particularly important for sustainable development of the country. In South Africa's arid regions, the management of groundwater resources (both the quantity and quality thereof) is aimed at providing enough clean water to communities.

Although South Africa is situated on a relatively stable part of the Earth's crust, the CGS maintains a seismic network for the recording of seismic events within the national borders and coastal waters off South Africa's coastline. This information is available to interested parties and helps mitigate the problems associated with mining-related seismic events.

The council is a world leader in the domain of geophysical surveys, using a detection system deployed on light aircraft. This significantly reduces the cost of very high-resolution geophysical data for mineral exploration.

Through its membership of the National Steering Committee of Service-Providers to the SSM Sector, the CGS helps mining entrepreneurs, particularly those from historically disadvantaged groups, to exploit South Africa's mineral resources in a cost-effective and environmentally friendly way.

The CGS plays a leading role in the SADC and as a result, several geoscience publications covering the region have been produced, describing heavy mineral sand, diamond, gold, bauxite and dimension-stone deposits in the region. A seismic hazard map of the region, a litho-stratigraphic table comparing the geological formations in the region, and maps of the Kalahari Basin have also been produced. A geological map of the region is in preparation.

In addition to its national responsibilities, the CGS is also active internationally, mainly in Africa. Geological and metallogenic maps of, among other countries, Angola, the Democratic Republic of Congo, Mozambique, Gabon and Morocco have been produced. The supervision of projects in Mauritania and Mozambique is also underway.

South African Bureau of Standards (SABS)

The SABS was established in 1948 with the purpose of developing, maintaining and disseminating standards in South Africa. Although this core objective has remained unchanged over the years, the mission of the SABS has changed to provide different focus relevant to the times. The SABS currently sees its mission as 'improving the quality of life of all South Africans, through the process of standardisation'.

Standards South Africa (StanSA)

StanSA is the SABS' core function and is responsible for the development, maintenance and dissemination of the country's national standards.

Through its main Standards Sales Division in Pretoria, as well as its offices in Durban, Cape Town and Port Elizabeth, all national standards as well as those of the International Electrotechnical Commission, the ISO and a host of other foreign standards are made available to the public.

Regulatory Affairs and Consumer Protection

This division of the SABS is responsible for the administration of certain national regulations, mainly on behalf of the Department of Trade and Industry. Legal Metrology forms a part of the division and ensures the protection of consumers against incorrect metrological practices such as the sale of underweight or undersized products. A specific function directed towards the provision of conformity-assessment services to the SME sector, and other Presidential imperatives and social responsibility activities, are also located in this division.

South African Bureau of Standards Holdings (Pty) Ltd.

All the conformity assessment services of the SABS are located in this company. These include the testing of products, providing system and product certification schemes, inspecting consignments and the training of people in these matters. SABS Holdings is a separate company, which competes in the private sector and charges for the services that it renders.

This is unlike SABS Regulatory Affairs and StanSA, which recover their costs from monies allocated for those purposes under the science budget vote of the Department of Science and Technology.

A corporate function provides overhead services such as finance, HR, legal, marketing and communication, risk management and IT.

Other scientific and research organisations and structures

Biotechnology Partnership for Africa's Development (Biopad)

Biopad was initiated early in 2003 by a community of biotechnologists and professionals as a means to put South Africa among the world leaders in the application of biotechnology.

Sasol

Sasol is an integrated oil and gas company with substantial chemical interests. In South Africa, these operations are supported by mining coal and converting it into synthetic fuels and chemicals through proprietary Fischer-Tropsch technology.

Sasol also has chemical manufacturing and marketing operations in Europe, Asia and the Americas. Its larger chemical portfolios include polymers, solvents, surfactants and their intermediates, waxes, phenolics and nitrogenous products.

The group explores and produces crude oil in offshore Gabon, refines crude oil into liquid fuels in South Africa, and retails liquid fuels and lubricants through a growing network of retail service centres. During the first quarter of 2004, Sasol started extracting Mozambican natural gas, some of which has been used as feedstock for fuels and chemical production in South Africa since mid-2004.

Sasol is also developing two joint-venture gas-to-liquid plants in Qatar and Nigeria based on its Sasol slurry phase distillate process.

Eskom

Eskom's Technology Services International group is a multidisciplinary industrial laboratory and consulting organisation. It undertakes testing, investigation studies, project management, engineering services and applied research for Eskom and other customers.

Mittal Steel SA

Mittal Steel SA is the dominant steel producer on the African continent, producing 7,1 million tonnes of liquid steel per year. Mittal Steel SA's global standing is further underpinned through becoming part of the world's largest steel producer, Mittal Steel Company N.V.

Through this agreement, Mittal Steel SA has access to world-class R&D, best practice processes, aggressive procurement contracts and international market leverage to ensure the company remains at the cutting edge of the international steel industry.

National Health Laboratory Service (NHLS)

The NHLS conducts research into the prevention and treatment of human diseases.

The NHLS comprises about 240 laboratories countrywide, including the former South African Institute for Medical Research, the National Institute for Virology, the National Centre for Occupational Health, all provincial diagnostic pathology laboratories (excluding those in KwaZulu-Natal), and tertiary laboratories used by universities' medical schools. It has approximately 4 000 employees and consists of four divisions: Research, Diagnostic Laboratory Services, Production (serum and laboratory reagents), and Teaching and Training. The NHLS conducts medical research as well as pathology laboratory tests for all provincial hospitals, excluding those in KwaZulu-Natal. Research is conducted on diseases and health dangers that are of specific importance to South Africa.

Bureau for Economic Research

The Bureau for Economic Research at the University of Stellenbosch, Western Cape, is an independent and objective economic research organisation. It renders a service to organisations ranging from

SOUTH AFRICA YEARBOOK 2005/06

small one-person businesses to policy-makers at the highest level of government.

National Institute for Tropical Diseases

The National Institute for Tropical Diseases in Tzaneen, Limpopo, is responsible for the ongoing assessment of malaria-control programmes carried out by various authorities in South Africa.

Control methods are assessed, and recommendations made to the appropriate authorities regarding equipment, insecticide usage and application. A malaria-reference service is also provided. Tests for malaria are carried out by the institute, and statistical analysis of data pertaining to the programme is undertaken.

General research areas

Mine-safety research

The activities of the Safety in Mines Research Advisory Committee are aimed at the advancement of the safety of workers employed in South African mines. The committee is a statutory tripartite sub-committee of the Mine Health and Safety Council. It has a permanent research-management office managing the fields of research, namely rock engineering, engineering and mine occupational health.

Energy research

The Chief Directorate: Energy of the Department of Minerals and Energy manages a policy-directed research programme. This includes transport energy, renewable energy and energy for developing areas, coal, electricity, energy efficiency, energy economy, and integrated energy-policy formulation.

Agricultural research

Agricultural research is conducted by the ARC, several universities and various organisations in the private sector. Provinces are responsible for farm management and technological development. These activities are aimed at improving managerial efficiency on farms.

The Directorate: Scientific Research and Development in the Department of Agriculture co-ordinates all agricultural R&D activities.

Biannual meetings are held to debate and agree on research needs, programmes and budgeting. Efforts are made to ensure that the bulk of research serves the needs of small-scale producers.

Research initiatives have been integrated into the various industries in line with the overall objectives of each agricultural sector.

Water research

Water research in South Africa is co-ordinated and funded by the Water Research Commission (WRC) in Pretoria. The WRC was established in 1971 through the Water Research Act, 1971 (Act 34 of 1971), following a period of water shortage. It was deemed to be of national importance to generate new knowledge and to promote the country's water research purposefully.

The WRC is a dynamic hub for water-centred knowledge, innovation and intellectual capital. It provides leadership for R&D through the support of knowledge creation, transfer and application. The WRC engages stakeholders and partners in solving water-related problems which are critical to South Africa's sustainable development and economic growth, and are committed to promoting a better quality of life for all.

As reflected in the WRC's mission and its various undertakings, the WRC functions as a 'hub' for water-centred knowledge. It is a networking organisation, linking the nation and working through partnerships.

The WRC continues to play a leading role in building a sustainable water-related knowledge base in South Africa by:
- investing in water R&D
- building sustainable and appropriate capacity
- developing skills for the water sector
- being adept in forming strategic partnerships to achieve objectives more effectively while making optimal use of the latest global information/knowledge and other technologies available.

The Water Research Act, 1971 provides for the establishment of the Water Research Fund, which derives income primarily from levies on water consumption.

In supporting the creation, dissemination and application of knowledge, the WRC focuses on five key strategic areas:
- water-resource management
- water-linked ecosystems
- water use and waste management
- water utilisation in agriculture
- water-centred knowledge.

The WRC also calls for specific mechanisms to address key strategic issues of national importance. These issues are dealt with in four cross-cutting domains:
- water and society
- water and the economy
- water and the environment
- water and health.

The organisations most active in water research are:
- universities and universities of technology (56,25% of the total number of contracts)
- professional consultants (16,6%)
- science councils (22,9%)
- water/waste utilities (2%)
- non-governmental organisations (NGOs) (2%).

The main areas of research are surface hydrology, groundwater, hydrometeorology, agricultural water utilisation, water pollution, municipal effluents, industrial water and effluents, drinking water, membrane technology, water ecosystems, hydraulics, mine-water management, water policy, developing communities, and the transfer of technology.

The Division: Water, Environment and Forestry Technology (Environmentek) of the CSIR specialises in research into water quality, including technology to meet effluent and water-quality standards, and to establish reclaimed water as an additional water source. Environmentek is a world leader in research into activated sludge processes and the biological monitoring of water to detect potentially toxic substances. It is also involved in research on the effects of afforestation and veld management on the quantity and quality of catchment water-yield.

Environmental research

The Chief Directorate: Environmental Management of the Department of Environmental Affairs and Tourism annually finances several research and monitoring programmes.

The programmes comprise subjects such as waste management and pollution, nature conservation, river management, the coastline and marine environment, and the atmosphere.

Some programmes are conducted in collaboration with the NRF, while others are undertaken on behalf of the department by the CSIR and universities.

Research on human-environment interaction sponsored by the department is co-ordinated by the HSRC.

In addition, institutes of the ARC are concerned with environmental research insofar as environmental problems impact on agriculture or are caused by agricultural practices.

The Department's National Environmental Potential Atlas (ENPAT) provides a visual overview of South Africa's environmental resources. The most important advantage of ENPAT is that environmental implications of land-use decisions are available before any actions are initiated. ENPAT-National contains two main data types, namely environmental and population data. The atlas also identifies possible conflict areas in the utilisation of natural resources.

The South African Weather Service (SAWS) is a statutory body functioning under the Department of Environmental Affairs and Tourism.

The SAWS delivers public-good services, mainly for the protection of life and property, as well as commercial services to the private sector, as stipulated in the Weather Service Act, 2001 (Act 8 of 2001).

Public-good services are funded by government while commercial services are paid for by the user. Public-good services include weather and climate forecasting, a weather-disaster warning system, services to subsistence farmers and fishers, the provision of information and advice to government, meeting regional and international treaty and agreement obligations, maintaining a national meteorological library, technical and scientific training in meteorology, and undertaking research to improve services.

In 2004/05, SAWS has taken a number of steps to further improve its services and capacity to deliver a world-class service.

Among other activities, SAWS has been running the Global Atmospheric Watch Programme, which measures and monitors greenhouse gas datasets. The SAWS has also rolled out a number of ozone-monitoring stations in the SADC region.

In keeping with its public-good obligations, SAWS plays a key role in offering early warning in the case of impending disasters. To this end, SAWS has increased its weather observation network in South Africa. The Mtata Radar launch in October 2004 improved the organisation's understanding of weather patterns in the Eastern Cape and the hard-to-predict East Coast. The project also involved the installation of five automatic weather stations in data-sparse areas of the province. The project provided temporary employment and training to a number of people from the involved and surrounding rural areas. In addition, SAWS has taken the first steps to acquire a lightning detection network for the country.

The NRF directs the multidisciplinary Conservation and Management of Ecosystems and Biodiversity Focus Area, primarily in collaboration with universities and museums, to promote and support research on living resources and terrestrial, freshwater, marine, coastal and atmospheric ecosystems.

Some 170 projects are approved annually, and global issues such as climate change and biological diversity are also included. The sustainable use of natural resources is a priority area, resulting in an increase in projects relying on sociology and the humanities. The NRF also supports a range of environmental research network organisations such as the Arid Zone Ecology Forum, the Fynbos Forum, the Indigenous Plant-Use Forum and the Savanna Ecology Forum.

Fisheries research

Research into South Africa's fish resources, and their conservation and judicious exploitation is carried out by research personnel of the Chief Directorate: Marine and Coastal Management, a division of the Department of Environmental Affairs and Tourism, and by several universities and NGOs. Research is designed to provide parameters for estimates of stock sizes and sustainable yields for the different fisheries.

Coastal and marine research

The Chief Directorate: Marine and Coastal Management advises on the utilisation of marine living resources and the conservation of marine ecosystems, by conducting and supporting relevant multidisciplinary scientific research and monitoring the marine environment. Sustainable use and the need to preserve future options in the utilisation of marine ecosystems and their resources are guiding objectives in the research and advice provided by the chief directorate.

The NRF supports marine and coastal research in partnership with the Department of Environmental Affairs and Tourism and SANCOR.

Private-sector involvement

South Africa's gold-mining industry works at deeper levels and under more difficult conditions than any other mining industry in the world. The research on gold mining conducted by the CSIR's Mining Technology is concerned primarily with ensuring the health and safety of the workforce. It includes those working in the areas of rock engineering and the underground environment.

Mining Technology's coal-mining research takes place on a smaller scale than that of gold mining, because the coal-mining industry can make use of various overseas developments. Areas in which research is undertaken include strata control, mining, maximising extraction of coal, and the underground environment.

Research is also carried out by a large number of industrial companies with facilities to meet their specific needs.

The more important ones are the Anglo American Corporation of South Africa (applied metallurgy, processing of precious metals, base metals and coal),

Agricura (synthesis and testing of veterinary remedies, insecticides, herbicides and entomology), Cullinan Holdings (refractories and electrical porcelain), De Beers Industrial Diamond Division (manufacture and application of synthetic diamonds and other super-hard material), Johannesburg Consolidated Investment Company (metallurgy, mineralogy, chemistry and chemical engineering), National Chemical Products (chemistry, microbiology and animal nutrition), Metal Box Company of South Africa (corrosion mechanism and microbiology), Tellumat (development of electronic instruments), the Rembrandt Group (development and improvement of tobacco and liquor products), South African Pulp and Paper Industries (wood technology, paper manufacture and water treatment) and Standard Telephones and Cables SA (long-distance transmission of information and lightning protection).

Acknowledgements

BuaNews
Council for Geoscience
Department of Science and Technology
Estimates of National Expenditure 2005, published by National Treasury
Human Sciences Research Council
Medical Research Council
Mintek
National Department of Agriculture
National Health Laboratory Service
National Research Foundation
South African Bureau of Standards
Water Research Commission
www.csir.co.za
www.gov.za
www.iscor.co.za
www.sabs.co.za
www.southafrica.info

Suggested reading
Austin, B. *Schonland.* Johannesburg: Witwatersrand University Press, 2001.
Basson, N. *Passage to Progress: The Council for Scientific and Industrial Research's (CSIR) Journey of Change, 1945 – 1995.* Johannesburg: Jonathan Ball, 1995.
Brooke-Simons, P. *Cullinan Diamonds: Dreams and Discoveries.* Cape Town: Fernwood Press, 2004.
Crouch, M. ed. *Sparkling Achievements.* Johannesburg: Chris van Rensburg Publications, 2001.
Fig, D. *Uranium Record: Questioning South Africa's Nuclear Direction.* Johannesburg: Jacana, 2005.
Harrison, P. *South Africa's Top Sites: Science.* Cape Town: Spearhead, 2004.
Kok, P. *et al. Development Research in South Africa.* Pretoria: Human Sciences Research Council, 1994.
Liebenberg, L. *Tracking: The Origin of Science.* Cape Town: David Philip, 1990.
Macrae, C. *Life Etched in Stone: Fossils of Southern Africa.* Johannesburg: Geological Society of South Africa, 1999.
Prout-Jones, D. *Cracking the Sky.* Pretoria: University of South Africa, 2002.

Social development

The Department of Social Development seeks to build a caring and integrated system of social development services that facilitates human development and improves the quality of life of all South Africans.

It works in partnership with non-governmental organisations (NGOs), faith-based organisations (FBOs), the business sector, organised labour and other role-players in the spirit of Batho Pele (People First).

The department provides implementation support to the provincial departments of social development, and monitors and evaluates the range of social development programmes. Provincial departments are responsible for most of the service delivery.

Some of the direct services provided by the Department of Social Development include:

- relief payment to victims of declared disasters
- registration of non-profit organisations (NPOs)
- payment of subsidies to national councils
- poverty-relief projects
- home- and community-based HIV and AIDS projects
- a national call centre for social-grant enquiries.

The department's strategic plan is informed by the Ten Point Plan, which sets out the priorities to be addressed by the social development sector:

- rebuilding family, community and social relations
- an integrated poverty-eradication strategy
- a comprehensive social security system
- preventing violence against women and children, older persons and other vulnerable groups
- HIV and AIDS
- youth development
- accessibility of social welfare services
- services to people with disabilities
- commitment to co-operative governance
- training, educating, redeploying and employing a new category of workers in social development.

The department is responsible for policy and oversight in the critical areas of social assistance (means-tested cash benefits to vulnerable categories of South Africans) and social welfare services (including probation and adoption services, child and family counselling and support services, and secure centres).

Over the last three years, the department has overseen a large expansion of the social assistance system, with beneficiary numbers increasing from 3,8 million in April 2001 to more than 10 million in September 2005.

The departmental mandate has also widened in recent years, with growing responsibility for a broad set of initiatives to improve the livelihoods of South Africans through the co-ordination of home-based care for people with HIV and AIDS, food-relief programmes, a focus on programmes for particularly vulnerable groups, and overseeing the National Development Agency (NDA).

Legislation

Older Persons Bill

The Older Persons Bill was expected to be finalised in 2005. By April 2005, the department had drafted the accompanying guidelines on frail-care services and service standards for community-based care for older persons.

The Bill proposes a law that will deal effectively with the plight of older persons, promoting their empowerment and protection, as well as maintaining their status, rights, well-being, safety and security.

Child-care legislation

The South African Law Reform Commission (SALRC) finalised its research on the review of the Child Care

On 7 April 2005, the South African Council for Social Service Professions, together with the Department of Social Development, inaugurated the boards that will oversee the improvement of social work and child- and youth-care services.

The boards aim to further enhance the transformation of social service professions by making them more inclusive and ensuring uniform standard services for everyone.

The boards are responsible for the education, training and development of social service professionals, as well as the development of regulations pertaining to their registration.

Act, 1983 (Act 74 of 1983). The SALRC proposed the Draft Children's Bill in January 2003. Close liaison with the various role-players followed.

On 23 July 2003, Cabinet approved that the Children's Bill be submitted to Parliament for consideration.

The Children's Bill defines both the rights and responsibilities of children, as well as parental responsibilities and rights. It also specifies principles and guidelines for the protection of children and the promotion of their well-being. In addition to consolidating the laws relating to the welfare and protection of children, the Bill provides for assistance to orphaned children and child-led households.

By April 2005, the Policy Framework and Strategic Plan for the Prevention and Management of Child Abuse was in the process of being approved and was expected to be implemented in 2005/06. This will ensure the swift implementation of the Child Protection Register, which will link provincial and national databases of children under 18 years who have allegedly been abused.

Early childhood guidelines were expected to be implemented in 2005/06. The department participated in the development of the draft Integrated Early Childhood Development Strategy, in collaboration with the departments of education and of health.

To prevent child trafficking and to manage intercountry adoptions more effectively, a permanent central authority for intercountry adoptions will soon be in place.

Social assistance

Social assistance and security

In 2004, the Social Security Agency Act, 2004 (Act 9 of 2004), and the Social Assistance Act, 2004 (Act 13 of 2004), were signed into law.

These Acts provide for the establishment of the South African Social Security Agency (SASSA). SASSA, which started operating in April 2005, is expected to be fully functional by 2007. Some R60 million was set aside in 2005/06 and over R133 million over the Medium Term Expenditure Framework (MTEF) period to ensure that this goal is met.

By September 2005, staff were being employed in the national office with over 5 000 existing social security staff in provinces awaiting transfer to the agency.

The agency is tasked with the management, administration and payment of social grants.

The Social Security Agency Act, 2004 creates a unitary but flexible service-delivery mechanism to ensure that government pays the right grant amount to the right person, at the right time and in a dignified manner.

The establishment of SASSA is part of government's efforts to provide services to the poorest of the poor and to restore the dignity of the most vulnerable, especially older people, people with disabilities, women and children.

The Social Assistance Act, 2004 creates uniform norms and standards that apply countrywide. It provides for the publishing of regulations on performance management and on adherence to the Batho Pele principles of customer service.

The Act provides for the rendering of social assistance to persons, mechanisms for the rendering of such assistance, the establishment of an inspectorate for social assistance, and related matters.

With a view to operationalising SASSA, government has committed itself to ensuring that ordinary citizens of South Africa see visible changes to the social security administration system, particularly as improved service delivery will affect them directly.

Operation Isidima is an endeavour by the Department of Social Development to ensure that Section 2 of the Constitution of the Republic of South Africa, 1996 (Act 108 of 1996), is given effect, with its primary objective to restore dignity to citizens who are recipients of social grants.

The main focus areas of Operation Isidima include:

- reducing the application and processing time for grants to 21 days
- enhancing human resource capacity to a ratio of 1:1000
- upgrading pay and service points in nodal areas
- paying contractors to deliver an improvement package

- enhancing communication by uniform messaging
- standardising the disability application process
- deploying dedicated fraud prevention/detection teams.

The department's national facilities to combat fraud and corruption in the social security system consist of:

- a toll-free national security fraud hotline (0800 60 10 11) that operates 24 hours a day, seven days a week
- an e-mail address (*fraud@socdev.gov.za*) and a free-call fax service number (0800 61 10 11).

As part of the Anti-Corruption and Fraud Prevention Strategy, launched in 2001, internal control systems have been improved, and forensic and investigating teams deployed in all provinces.

In December 2004, the department launched a nationwide anti-fraud and anti-corruption campaign.

It granted indemnity to all people illegally accessing social grants and requested them to come forward before 31 March 2005.

Over 30 000 people responded and their fraudulent payments were stopped. This translated into an estimated saving of R12 million per month and over R446 million over the MTEF period. These savings are expected to result in an additional 66 000 children receiving the Child Support Grant (CSG).

To root out fraud and corruption, the department has set aside R57,9 million and entered into a co-operation agreement with the Special Investigating Unit (SIU).

Some 200 staff members were trained and used in the fight against fraud and corruption, and probed the details of all grant beneficiaries.

Amounts of grants per month as at 1 April 2005	
Grant type	Amount
Old-Age Grant	R780
Disability Grant	R780
War Veterans' Grant	R758
Foster Care Grant	R560
Care Dependency Grant	R780
Child Support Grant	R180
Grant-in-Aid	R170

The department, in collaboration with all national and provincial law-enforcement agencies, including the South African Police Service (SAPS) and the SIU, was expected to establish the Inspectorate for Social Security by March 2006.

In June 2005, the Minister of Social Development, Dr Zola Skweyiya, met with members of the Banking Association of South Africa to agree on areas of co-operation in fighting poverty, developing rural communities and improving access to banking for the poor and vulnerable.

Representatives of Nedbank, Absa, First National Bank, Nedcor, Standard Bank and the co-operatives sector agreed to collaborate with the department, to, among other things:

- create access and affordable banking for social-grant recipients
- have a common approach to assist the delivery of quality services to social-grant recipients
- provide financial and technical know-how in establishing SASSA.

Payment of social grants

By September 2005, more than 10 million South Africans were accessing social grants, with 6,2 million children making up the majority of recipients. These figures were reached despite significant decreases in some grants after a number of people exited the system during the Department of Social Development's anti-fraud and corruption campaign.

Total government expenditure on social grants increased from R10 billion in 1994 to R48 billion in 2005. An additional R105 billion has been budgeted for the 2006/08 period. Social grants have been equalised between racial groups and extended to all in need who qualify.

Some R6,9 billion was set aside for 2005/06 and an additional R19 billion has been set aside over the MTEF period for the further extension of the CSG to children under the age of 14 years.

Growth in the total number of beneficiaries doubled between 1999 and September 2005, reaching staggering heights as the CSG was extended to children between the ages of seven and 14 years.

The department has reached almost all the elderly people with old-age and disability grants. The real growth for disability has only been around 1% since April 2004. By September 2005, the coverage for the Old-Age Grant was about 2,1 million and for disability grants about 1,3 million.

The Old-Age Pension Grant is the second-largest social grant. Women qualify at the age of 60 years and men at the age of 65.

The Disability Grant is paid to people who have been assessed as permanently or temporarily disabled.

By April 2005, the department had reviewed 260 000 recipients of temporary disability grants. As a result of the reviews, by September 2005, 100 000 cases of temporary disabilities had been terminated, saving the State more than R200 million.

In partnership with the Department of Health, the Department of Social Development has embarked on a project to retrain health practitioners in disability assessment and the rehabilitation of people with disabilities. Such rehabilitation is expected to enable people with disabilities to access training and job opportunities.

Foster care grants are paid to caregivers of children who have been placed with them by the courts. Caregivers of children with disabilities up to the age of 18 years are eligible for the Care Dependency Grant. Once these children turn 18 years, they are eligible for the Disability Grant. By September 2005, foster care grants were being paid to 286 131 people, while 87 093 received care dependency grants.

Other grants provided by the Department of Social Development include the War Veterans' Grant and the Grant-in-Aid. By September 2005, 3 076 people were receiving the War Veterans' Grant and 24 460 Grant-in-Aid.

Poverty-relief pogramme

The eradication of poverty is the highest priority in government's efforts to build a better life for all.

In addition to the provision of social assistance, the Department of Social Development also manages the Poverty-Relief Programme. This programme aims to assist communities in a range of developmental projects.

The programme entrusts state resources to communities to undertake and dictate development for themselves by themselves.

The programme emphasises access to economic opportunities for specific targeted groups and the establishment of local structures that are able to identify, own and manage the ongoing implementation of development initiatives in the community.

The programme has established 408 projects throughout the country, 80% of which are in the hands of women. A study done by the Independent Development Trust (IDT) has indicated that these projects are at different stages of development. According to the study, 20% are ready for graduation into small, medium and micro enterprises (SMMEs). The IDT and the department are negotiating with relevant stakeholders, such as the Department of Trade and Industry, the Umsobomvu Youth Fund and the National Empowerment Fund, to provide the necessary support to this process.

The department embarked on a series of provincial visits to undertake an audit of a sample of projects and establish relationships with provinces and municipalities. These relationships will facilitate a smooth handover of projects and promote ownership of all national projects by provinces and municipalities.

An assessment of the status and needs of poverty-relief projects in the 21 Integrated Sustainable Rural Development Programme and Urban Renewal Programme nodes is expected to be done in 2006/07.

Food security

The department's National Food Emergency Scheme, introduced by Cabinet in 2002, is aimed at distributing food parcels to the most vulnerable sections of the population. These include children and child-headed households, people with disabilities, female-headed households with insufficient or no income, and households affected by HIV, AIDS and tuberculosis.

In 2005/06, the department set aside R388 million to ensure improved access to food in vulnerable and impoverished families.

The distribution of food parcels is a temporary measure to assist poor people spending less than R300 per month on food. Most of the people who receive food parcels are identified by NGOs and FBOs. In 2004/05, the scheme distributed over 490 000 food parcels for each of the three months of distribution. By mid-2004, the scheme had benefited over 1,5 million people at a cost of R360 million. Each beneficiary household received food parcels worth R300.

The scheme forms part of government's Integrated Food Security and Nutrition Programme (IFSNP).

The five elements of the IFSNP are:

- Developing comprehensive food-production and trade schemes to enhance the capacity of communities to produce food for themselves through the setting up of household and communal food gardens.
- Initiating a community-development scheme aimed at providing employment to local communities through community-based and community-owned public works programmes. This involves setting up community-based income-generating projects and activities to ensure sustainable food security.
- Developing a nutrition and food programme that focuses primarily on the improvement of nutrition levels in communities, to ensure that every child has at least one nutritious meal a day.
- Developing a fully funded communication strategy to ensure the maintenance of government's communication lines with all its people.
- Building a safety net and establishing a food emergency scheme to ensure that the poorest families, especially children and child-headed households, have food on the table.

By September 2005, more than 22 000 people nationwide, ranging from young people to unemployed women, had been provided with work opportunities to prepare and serve school meals, thus enabling them to gain income through stipends. The scheme also supported the emergence of a number of SMMEs and co-operatives, which render various services in support thereof. In addition, a number of schools in the National School Nutrition Programme had established vegetable gardens to enrich the nutritional value of the meals served in schools.

Responding to the impact of HIV and AIDS

The Department of Social Development has developed a social-development framework for an integrated and co-ordinated response to HIV and AIDS.

The framework includes sourcing reliable research and information; providing social protection to those infected and affected, especially children; protecting children's rights; providing services; special programmes such as the Home-Based/Community-Based Care Programme; empowering women; and capacitating officials to deal with HIV and AIDS.

The department's response to HIV and AIDS is underpinned by working in partnership with other government departments, NGOs, community-based organisations (CBOs), FBOs, the business sector, volunteers and international agencies.

HIV and AIDS Youth Programme

The expansion of the loveLife Groundbreaker Partnership Programme has been approved. This aims to strengthen the loveLife Mphintshi Initiative by linking it to the Expanded Public Works Programme (EPWP) and the prevention programme in relation to home- and community-based care and support. The programme will also expand its services to enable it to reach marginalised and vulnerable youth in rural areas.

HIV and AIDS Workplace Policy and Strategy

The existing HIV and AIDS Workplace Policy and Strategy was reviewed in March 2004, when strategic focus areas for the next three years were outlined. The department's initiatives will be managed according to these focus areas. In addition, a set of

indicators has been developed to monitor the implementation of the workplace strategy. Research will be commissioned to assess the impact of the department's initiatives.

Home-Based/Community-Based Care Programme

The social impact of HIV and AIDS is evidenced by an increase in the number of orphans and child-headed households, manifesting itself in the disintegration of families and communities. Close to a million children in South Africa have lost one or both parents to HIV and AIDS. This number is expected to increase in future. The extended family's capacity to cope with the demand to care for children who are affected and/or infected by HIV and AIDS is over-stretched.

The social impact of the epidemic on families and communities calls for an integrated approach to mitigate such impact.

The National Action Committee for Children Affected by HIV and AIDS has been established at national and provincial level. In some provinces, the structure has been cascaded to district level. The primary purpose of the co-ordinated action structure is to improve on programmes and service delivery.

By mid-2005, a draft policy framework for orphans and other children made vulnerable by HIV and AIDS had been developed and was communicated to stakeholders for consultation purposes.

The policy framework is a culmination of processes undertaken to ensure that government meets its constitutional obligations in providing appropriate and protective services to orphans and other children made vulnerable by HIV and AIDS. It intends to create and promote an enabling environment for more effective co-ordination in service delivery in relation to the existing commitments made towards the promotion and protection of children's rights.

During the first three quarters of 2004/05:
- Some 116 811 orphans and other children made vulnerable by HIV and AIDS were identified and were receiving appropriate care and support. The services included food parcels; the provision of clothing, counselling and support; the provision

of day-care and after-school care at drop-in centres; and referrals for foster care.

- Some 169 663 families received support such as food parcels, cooked meals, counselling and the linking of families with income-generating projects. Some 78 260 food parcels were distributed.
- Some 627 child-care fora were established as a community-based mechanism to address the needs of orphans and vulnerable children.

A bid has been advertised to do an audit on caregivers rendering a service within the Home-Based/Community-Based Care Programme. On its completion, caregivers will be provided with accredited National Qualifications Framework level training, as part of the EPWP.

The EPWP is a nationwide programme to draw significant numbers of unemployed people into productive work, accompanied by appropriate training and skills development. The aim is to build the capacity of unemployed persons to earn an income.

The Home-Based/Community-Based Care and Support Programme was identified as one area for such expansion. The number of sites for community- and home-based care support increased from six projects in 2001 to 400 in 2003.

The integrated programme teaches life skills to children and the youth, and provides voluntary testing and counselling services, and a range of care and support services focusing on families and on children orphaned through the AIDS-related death of their parents. There has been significant progress regarding the initial implementation of home- and community-based care and support.

It is estimated that the home- and community-based care sector has about 2 500 full-time caregivers and 20 000 volunteers. Only a quarter of these volunteers receive stipends of any kind.

In 2005, the department set aside R74 million to accelerate the delivery of care facilities.

Services for children

The HIV and AIDS drop-in centres established by the Department of Social Development received a budget of R16,4 million in 2003/04. Each food parcel these centres provide costs about R300. The drop-in centres were identified through the HIV and AIDS database of home- and community-based care centres. Each province has identified drop-in centres to be contracted to provide cooked meals to identified beneficiaries. These beneficiaries are classified as people who are not able to cook for themselves, e.g. as in the case of child-headed households.

The department has developed the integrated and consolidated Five-Year National Social Development Strategic Plan, which is being implemented in partnership with other stakeholders such as the United Nations Children's Fund (UNICEF).

Partnerships

Since 2000, the department has strengthened its partnership with national and international organisations involved in the fight against HIV and AIDS. The department chairs the National AIDS Children's Task Team (NACTT), a multisectoral task team focusing on the care and support of children infected with and/or affected by HIV and AIDS.

United Nations Children's Fund

UNICEF conducted studies on caring for vulnerable children and children orphaned through AIDS-related illnesses, as well as on the cost-effectiveness of several models of care for vulnerable children.

The department has implemented the results of UNICEF studies in its design of programmes for children. UNICEF has indicated interest in providing further support to the department in fast-tracking the Home-Based/Community-Based Care Programme.

In May 2005, the Minister of Social Development, Dr Zola Skweyiya, launched the green ribbon as the new national symbol for child protection. It marked the beginning of Child Protection Week from 30 May to 5 June 2005.

Some 197 activities were planned throughout the country to commemorate Child Protection Week.

Save the Children Fund

This organisation provides secretariat and other assistance to the NACTT and has undertaken research on abused children and children affected by HIV and AIDS. It has compiled a directory of services and children's organisations.

Faith-based organisations and the business sector

The department has strengthened its partnership with churches and other FBOs, the business sector, volunteer organisations, and individuals, to assist with poverty-relief, HIV and AIDS, and social-grant registration programmes.

Promoting and protecting the rights of vulnerable groups

Children and the youth

In addition to providing social assistance to children through the CSG and the Foster Care Grant, the Department of Social Development facilitates the provision of services to children and the youth through the provincial departments of social development and NGOs.

Through the National Youth Service Programme, the department was expected to train 940 young people in assistant probation services in 2005.

Social crime prevention

The department is tasked with the implementation of the Probation Services Act, 1991 (Act 116 of 1991), as amended. As such, it has to fulfil various obligations at national and provincial level, such as early intervention services (reception, assessment and referral services, restorative justice programmes and diversion programmes), prevention programmes, services to crime victims and statutory services.

The proposed Child Justice Bill will augment the responsibilities of probation services to ensure that sufficient diversion programmes in all areas (rural and urban) are in place. It will also ensure that every arrested child is assessed within 48 hours; addition-

al home-based supervision programmes are provided; the numbers of probation and assistant probation officers are increased; and that sufficient and secure care facilities to accommodate children awaiting trial are put in place.

The department's contribution towards the implementation of the Child Justice Bill was strengthened through donor-funding from the Royal Netherlands Embassy. Service-providers have been contracted to deliver a range of projects, namely minimum standards for diversion; the establishment of a professional board and standard-generating body for probation services; the roll-out of the home-based supervision programme; the appointment of additional assistant probation officers; the training and retraining of probation practitioners; restorative justice training to probation practitioners in all provinces; and the evaluation of the assistant probation and crime-buster programmes.

Some 1 000 children benefited from the home-based supervision programmes, 750 probation practitioners received training in restorative justice and probation-practice principles; and 72 assistant probation officers received in-service training. New secure care facilities in Gauteng, the Western Cape and KwaZulu-Natal have been completed.

In 2004, about 30 000 children were diverted from the criminal justice system (CJS). The National Youth Service Programme will ensure the appointment of additional assistant probation officers in all provinces.

The department, as one of the Justice, Crime Prevention and Security (JCPS) cluster core integrated justice system (IJS) partners, has been included in a capacity-strengthening programme to ensure departmental delivery on the IJS and JCPS strategic focus areas.

A special intersectoral programme, under the leadership of the Deputy Minister of Social Development, Dr Jean Benjamin, to reduce the number of children awaiting trial, was initiated in October 2004. By early 2005, some 300 children had been moved from Department of Correctional Services, SAPS and Department of Social Development facilities into alternative care programmes.

Child abuse and neglect

The department's priority is fighting child abuse and neglect, as illustrated by the following initiatives:

- Child Protection Register: This programme, tested and revised in 2004, has been implemented in seven provinces. It aims to develop an electronic database in all provinces linked to a central database at the Department of Social Development on children younger than 18 years who have been abused or neglected.
- Draft Policy Framework and Strategic Plan on the Prevention and Management of Child Abuse, Neglect and Exploitation: The framework has been completed. Effective implementation is expected to reduce the incidence of abuse and neglect, and clarify the roles and responsibilities of stakeholders.
- *Isolabantwana* (Eye of the Child): The South African National Council for Child Welfare received donor funding from the department for the replication of a prevention programme in communities to eliminate child abuse and to promote child protection. The programme aims to provide a safety net for children within a community where services and support could be provided to children at risk on a 24-hour basis, and in areas were resources are limited. Community members contribute to the success of the child-protection services, as they reside in the communities and are familiar with the people, structures and traditions. The programme has been implemented (with a minimum of three sites per province) in all nine provinces according to community needs.

Childline South Africa

Childline offers a toll-free crisis line (0800 55 555) to children and families across South Africa on a 24-hour basis. The line provides immediate assistance to children and families in crisis who need brief counselling and information.

Apart from the 24-hour toll-free helpline, services also include treatment centres for individual, family and play therapy; prevention programmes; community safehouses; and training and awareness programmes.

Integrated justice system

The IJS Project ensures the integration of case management and offenders through four departments, namely the SAPS, and the departments of justice and constitutional development, of correctional services and of social development, supported by enabling technologies. A number of projects have been initiated to this end, including the Awaiting-Trial Prisoner Project.

Children awaiting trial in any residential-care facility are a priority of the Department of Social Development. Active participation from the provincial social-service representatives and management teams has yielded positive results. An interdepartmental committee of senior officials monitors the cases of children awaiting trial.

The computerised Child Protection Register has been developed. Technological improvements in the SAPS Crime Administration System have enabled the departments to track children through the system and assist in monitoring their cases.

The Court Process Project provides for the electronic management of court processes from arrest to final court appearances. The project is running in six pilot sites and is increasing efficiency and reducing court delays.

Women

Social-development services for women are another priority. This derives from the premise and concern that the inequality that exists between men and women in South Africa is deeply entrenched and has characterised South African society for many decades. Women are subject to discrimination, exploitation and violence despite the Constitution, which affirms the democratic values of human dignity, equality and freedom. An unprecedented effort is therefore required to ensure that the status of women is elevated to protect their rights and speed up gender equality.

Economic empowerment

The department has established the Flagship Programme: Developmental Programmes for Unemployed Women with Children under Five Years. The programme provides economic and development opportunities and services to unemployed women with children under the age of five years, living in deep rural areas and previously disadvantaged informal settlements. Sixteen projects create income that is distributed among the participating women.

The various projects include activities such as eating-houses, overnight facilities, car washes, beauty salons, vegetable gardens, garment-making, poultry and egg production, bread-baking, leather works, offal-cleaning, child-minding and paper-and-fabric printing.

A considerable number of women and children are benefiting from the programme. The flagship programme has developed a creative form of early childhood intervention, which provides developmentally appropriate education to children younger than five to increase their chances of healthy growth and development.

People with disabilities
There are more than three million people with disabilities in South Africa. The majority of these are women.

The Office on the Status of Disabled Persons is part of The Presidency and is duplicated in the offices of the premiers. Together they have co-ordinated work to mainstream disability issues in all government policies and programmes.

The *White Paper on an Integrated National Strategy* provides a policy framework for implementation across the whole of society and through all spheres of government.

By mid-2004, 0,25% of the Public Service was made up of people with disabilities, while the target was to reach 2% by 2005.

The National Skills Development Strategy calls for 4% of all people trained to be people with disabilities.

The national councils supported by the Department of Social Development are the:
• National Council for Persons with Physical Disabilities
• Deaf Federation of South Africa
• South African National Epilepsy League
• South African Federation for Mental Health

• Cancer Association of South Africa.
During 2000/01, the department reviewed the procedures for assessing applicants for the Disability Grant and proposed amendments to the regulations of the Social Assistance Act, 1992 (Act 20 of 1992). The amendments provide for the use of community-based assessment panels as an alternative to district surgeons, who are not easily accessible to people in rural areas. The Committee of Inquiry into a Comprehensive Social Security System made recommendations to improve social protection for people with disabilities.

Victim-Empowerment Programme (VEP)

The VEP facilitates the establishment and integration of interdepartmental/intersectoral programmes and policies for the support, protection and empowerment of victims of crime and violence, with a special focus on women and children.

It also ensures that the implementation of such programmes and policies is monitored and evaluated.

Some 120 projects have been established since the inception of the VEP in 1999. The projects provide trauma support and counselling services to the victims of violence and crime. Some of these projects focus on empowering community workers and professionals with skills and knowledge for the effective delivery of services to such victims.

One such project, which has been provided with technical and financial support through the VEP, is the Stop Abuse Helpline of the Johannesburg Life Line.

Other organisations that are financially supported by the VEP include the National Network on Violence Against Women, the Ilitha Psychological Services NGO in Fort Hare, the Soshanguve Trauma Centre, the University of South Africa's Department of Industrial Psychology, the Themba Lesizwe NGO, and the Walk the Talk Challenge from Durban to Cape Town.

Achievements and progress in the area of victim empowerment include the updating of the 2003 National Resource Directory of Services to promote the accessibility of services to victims of crime and violence.

One-stop centres for abused women and children

The VEP is a major component of the joint agreement between the Department of Social Development and the United Nations Office for Drug Control and Crime Prevention for the establishment of one-stop centres for women and children who are victims of abuse, especially domestic violence.

Anti-Rape Strategy

The Interdepartmental Management Team (IDMT) comprises representatives from the departments of health, of safety and security, and of social development, as well as the Sexual Offences and Community Affairs Unit of the National Directorate of Public Prosecutions. The IDMT was tasked to develop the Anti-Rape Strategy for the prevention of sexual violence against women and children.

The strategy encompasses an approach that enables both prevention of and response to violence, improves effectiveness of the CJS, increases the reporting rate of sexual assault, and improves the effectiveness of survivor-support programmes.

The SAPS has also established partnerships with several community-based role-players, including businesses. These links have improved the implementation of crime-prevention initiatives.

Non-profit organisations

The Non-Profit Directorate of the Department of Social Development registers organisations under the NPO Act, 1997 (Act 71 of 1997).

The NPO Directorate is reviewing the NPO Act, 1997.

The primary purpose of the Act is to encourage and support organisations by creating an enabling environment for NPOs to flourish in, and setting and maintaining adequate standards of governance, accountability and transparency.

An NPO is defined as a trust, company or association of persons that has been established for public purpose, and of which the income and property

are not distributable to its members or office bearers except as reasonable compensation for services rendered.

This includes NGOs, CBOs, FBOs, public-benefit organisations, section 21 companies, trusts and other voluntary organisations.

The registration process to attain NPO status takes two months on average and is free of charge. The benefits of registration include improving the credibility of the sector, as NPOs can account to a public office and receive help in accessing benefits such as tax incentives and funding opportunities.

By March 2005, 29 000 organisations had registered for NPO status, while just over 2 000 had deregistered and 22 dissolved.

Statutory bodies

National Development Agency

The NDA is a government agency mandated by the NDA Act, 1998 (Act 108 of 1998), to contribute towards poverty eradication through funding, capacity-building, research and development.

The NDA's primary sources of income are an allocation from the National Revenue Fund and donor funding.

Transfers to the NDA will increase from R103,3 million in 2003/04 to R123 million in 2006/07.

The key strategic objectives of the NDA are to:
- grant funds to civil-society organisations to meet the development needs of poor communities

In August 2005, the South African Human Rights Commission hosted a two-day convention to establish a national forum for older persons.

The convention was a follow-up to the International Conference on Ageing held in Spain in 2002, as well as the Ministerial Committee of Inquiry into the Neglect and Abuse of Older Persons.

The forum will, among other things, assist in monitoring the levels of service provided to older persons, especially at pension pay points.

- strengthen organisations' institutional capacity for long-term sustainability
- proactively source funds for the NDA
- promote consultation, dialogue and the sharing of development experiences, and debate and influence developmental policy
- develop strategies to collaborate with local-community development trusts, foundations, government clusters and civil-society organisations.

Relief boards
The Fund-Raising Act, 1978 (Act 107 of 1978), provides for relief boards to offer social relief to people in distress as a result of disasters or displacement from another country.

In October 2005, the Minister of Finance, Mr Trevor Manuel, announced in the Medium Term Budget Statement that R32 million would be allocated to the Disaster Relief Fund.

In October 2005, the Minister of Social Development, Dr Zola Skweyiya, was elected president of the United Nations (UN) Educational, Scientific and Cultural Organisation's Management of Social Transformation Programme's (MOST) Intergovernmental Committee (IGC) in Paris, France.

The MOST IGC president is elected in his/her personal capacity as a renowned social scientist or social policy-maker whose commitment to the MOST programmes has already been established through prior co-operation.

Dr Skweyiya has demonstrated his commitment to the MOST through a number of actions, including:
- convening the Cape Town Ministerial Forum of Southern African Development Community Ministers of Social Development in November 2004
- chairing, on behalf of MOST, an informal gathering of ministers of social development within the framework of the Copenhagen +10 review process, during the annual session of the UN Commission on Social Development in New York, United States of America, in February 2005
- active participation in meetings of the International Steering Committee of the MOST International Forum on the Social Science-Policy Nexus, to be held in Buenos Aires and Montevideo in February 2006.

Central Drug Authority (CDA)
The CDA has started an extensive process of reviewing the National Drug Master Plan, which involves drug fora established in all provinces. All provinces have, with support from the Department of Social Development, developed mini-drug master plans to ensure that there is a co-ordinated approach to service delivery.

The review process in terms of the Drug Master Plan was expected to be finalised in 2005/06. The Ke Moja Project, launched in the Western Cape, is a prevention programme which has successfully targeted the youth. The department successfully trained service-providers in two provinces on the management of substance abuse. This project will be extended to other provinces in the ensuing year. The Youth Best Practice Treatment Model was developed.

A significant achievement has been the development of minimum standards for in-patient treatment centres.

The standards are being used to transform service delivery in government facilities as a first priority and to ensure that appropriate services are provided at these centres. These standards will also set the framework for the registration of treatment centres run by civil-society structures in the country.

The proliferation of unregistered treatment centres is being addressed. Notices have been sent out to sensitise the sector about the legal requirement for registration and to ensure that these facilities are registered in terms of the Prevention and Treatment of Drug Dependancy Act, 1992 (Act 20 of 1992).

The Act, which is outdated and does not meet current demands for effective service delivery, is being reviewed.

The department wants to ensure that human rights and minimum standards for treatment are upheld. The Policy on Substance Abuse has been drafted and was expected to be finalised in 2005/06.

The process of reviewing the Prevention and Treatment of Drug Dependency Abuse Act, 1992 (Act 20 of 1992), an outdated Act which does not meet current demands for effective services delivery, has begun.

United Nations Population Fund (UNFPA) Second Country Support Programme for South Africa

The implementation of the Second UNFPA Country Support Programme for South Africa has been initiated in three priority provinces: KwaZulu-Natal, the Eastern Cape and Limpopo. Details of programme implementation have been outlined in collaboration with provincial representatives and key stakeholders in the three provinces.

In 2004, preparations began for a mid-term review (MTR) of the progress made with the implementation of the country programme, in partnership with the UNFPA country office in South Africa.

Preparations included establishing the required structures at provincial level and conducting a series of capacity-building workshops in the three provinces to facilitate the MTR process. In November 2004, the UNFPA country representative and the Chief Directorate: Population and Development in the Department of Social Development reached an agreement on the procedure to be followed.

The MTR process was scheduled to be concluded in 2005. This was expected to be followed by a final evaluation report with recommendations for the next country programme to be submitted to the UNFPA.

Acknowledgements

BuaNews
Department of Social Development
Estimates of National Expenditure 2005, published by National Treasury
National Development Agency
www.childline.org.za
www.gov.za
www.socdev.gov.za

Suggested reading

Barnard, D. and Terreblanche, Y. eds. *PRODDER: The Southern African Development Directory 1999/00.* Pretoria: Human Sciences Research Council (HSRC), 1999.
Bartley, T. *Holding Up the Sky: Love, Power and Learning in the Development of a Community.* London: Community Links, 2003.
Cassiem, S. *et al. Are Poor Children Being Put First? Child Poverty and the Budget.* Cape Town: Institute for Democracy in South Africa, 2000.
Donald, D., Dawes, A. and Louw, J. eds. *Addressing Childhood Adversity.* Cape Town: David Philip, 2000.
Eckley, S.A.C. *Transformation of Care for the Aged in South Africa.* In: *Social Work Practice, 2,* 1996, pp 47 – 51.
Gray, M. ed. *Developmental Social Work: Theory and Practice in South Africa.* Cape Town: David Philip, 1999.
Hart, G. *Disabling Globalisation: Places of Power in Post-Apartheid South Africa.* Pietermaritzburg: University of Natal Press, 2002.
Isbister, J. *Promises Not Kept: The Betrayal of Social Change in the Third World.* 4th ed. West Hartford. Connecticut, Kumarian Press: 1998.
Kok, P. and Pietersen, J. *Youth.* Pretoria: HSRC, 2000.
Laubscher, J. ed. *Interfering Women. No Place: National Council of Women of South Africa,* n.d.
Leggett, T., Miller, V. and Richards, R. eds. *My Life in the New South Africa: A Youth Perspective.* Pretoria: HSRC, 1997.
Luirink, B. *Moffies: Gay and Lesbian Life in Southern Africa.* Cape Town: David Philip, 2000.
Magubane, B.M. *African Sociology: Towards a Critical Perspective.* Trenton, N.J: Africa World Press, 2000.
Marais, H.C. *et al.* eds. *Sustainable Social Development: Critical Issues.* Pretoria: Network Publishers, 2001.
May, J. ed. *Poverty and Inequality in South Africa: Meeting the Challenge.* Cape Town: David Philip, 1999.
Midgley, J. *Promoting a Developmental Perspective in Social Welfare.* In: *Social Work Practice, 32,* 1996, p 1 – 7.
Morrell, R., ed. *Changing Men in South Africa.* Pietermaritzburg: University of Natal Press, 2001.
Morris, A. *Bleakness and Light: Inner-City Transition in Hillbrow.* Johannesburg: Witwatersrand, 1999.
Pistorius, P. ed. *Texture and Memory: The Urbanism of District Six.* Cape Town: Cape Technikon, 2002. 2nd ed.
Ratele, K.R., *et al.* eds. *Self, Community and Psychology.* Cape Town: University of Cape Town Press, 2004.
Report of the Land Committee on Child and Family Support. August 1996.
Sarandon, S. *Children of AIDS: Africa's Orphan Disaster.* Pietermaritzburg: University of Natal Press, 2001.
Seleoane, M. *Socio-Economic Rights in the South African Constitution.* Pretoria: HSRC, 2001.
Sono, T. *Race Relations in Post-Apartheid South Africa.* Johannesburg: South African Institute of Race Relations,1999.
The Apartheid City and Beyond: Urbanisation and Social Change in South Africa. London: Routledge; Johannesburg: University of the Witwatersrand, 1992.
The Road to Social Development: Department of Social Development, April 2001.
The State of South Africa's Population: 2000: National Population Unit, Department of Social Development, September 2000.
Vergnani, L. *Getting Rid of the Welfare Dinosaurs.* In: *Landing Edge, 6,* 1996, pp 29 – 33.
Visvananathan, N. *et al.* eds. *The Women, Gender and Development Reader.* Cape Town: David Philip, 1997.
Women Marching into the 21st Century: Wathint' Abafazi, Wathint' Imbokodo. Pretoria: HSRC, 2000.
Wylie, D. *Starving on a Full Stomach.* Charlottesville: University Press of Virginia, 2001.
Zegeye, A. ed. *Social Identities in the New South Africa.* (*After Apartheid, Vol. 1*). Cape Town: Kwela Books, 2001.

Sport and recreation

Sport and Recreation South Africa (SRSA) aims to improve the quality of life of all South Africans by promoting participation in sport and recreation in the country, and through the participation of sportspeople and teams in international sporting events.

The key objectives of the SRSA are to:
- increase the level of participation in sport and recreational activities
- raise the profile of sport
- maximise the probability of success in major sporting events
- place sport at the forefront of efforts to address issues of national importance.

The SRSA is responsible for:
- Co-ordinating and contributing to the drafting of legislation on sport and recreation.
- Interpreting broad government policy, translating government policy into policies for sport and recreation, revising such policy if and when necessary, and monitoring the implementation thereof.
- Aligning sport and recreation policy with the policies of other government departments in the spirit of integrated planning and delivery.
- Providing legal advice to all stakeholders in sport and recreation from a government perspective.
- Subsidising clients of the SRSA in accordance with the Public Finance Management Act, 1999 (Act 1 of 1999), its concomitant regulations, as well as the SRSA funding policy; monitoring the application of such funds; and advising clients on the management of their finances.
- Managing inter- and intragovernmental relations.
- Acknowledging the outstanding contributions of sportspeople to South African society.
- Procuring resources from abroad for sport and recreation, through the appropriate structures in National Treasury.
- Communicating sport- and recreation-related matters from a government perspective.
- Co-ordinating and monitoring the creation and upgrading of sport and recreation infrastructure through the Building for Sport and Recreation Project (BSRP). Projects have been identified in line with the Integrated Sustainable Rural Development Programme and the Urban Renewal Strategy.

The main focus of the BSRP is the construction of outdoor and indoor facilities and the rehabilitation and upgrading of existing ones. Key elements of this project are the provision of training in facility management, and the implementation of sustainable maintenance projects.

The majority of the projects are located in rural poverty nodes.

By the end of 2004/05, government had invested R550 million in basic outdoor and indoor sports facilities in disadvantaged communities throughout the country. A further R140 million was allocated to such facilities in 2004/05. Since 2001, government had built more than 360 basic, multi-purpose facilities and established some 360 community sports councils. More than 15 500 temporary jobs were created over a four-year period.

The allocation for 2004/05 also allowed the SRSA to undertake projects in the areas where the 2010 Soccer World Cup matches are planned, to benefit the poor in those urban areas. The projects are, however, not restricted to soccer or to these areas alone.

In May 2005, South Africa sent five athletes to the inaugural Paralympic World Cup in Manchester, England.

They brought home seven gold medals between them – boasting two world records in the pool and a sprint double on the track by two people who are bridging the gap between able-bodied and disabled athletes.

Natalie du Toit established new world records in the 50-m and 100-m freestyle, breaking both world records in the heats and then smashing them in the finals. She completed the 50 m in 29,35 seconds and the 100 m in 1:01.68.

Double leg-amputee Oscar Pistorius claimed the 100 m in 11,23 seconds and the 200 m in 22.01.

Ernst van Dyk, the wheelchair marathon world record holder and winner of the Boston Marathon wheelchair division for a record fifth consecutive time, added two more golds to the South African haul. He claimed the pursuit title in 4:20.80, and also won the 1 500 m in 3:21.85.

High jumper David Roos came close to a medal in Manchester, finishing fourth, while Dewald Reynders settled for seventh place in the discus.

From 2005/06, the allocation became part of the Municipal Infrastructure Grant, which is located in the Department of Provincial and Local Government. The SRSA will continue with its policy, advocating and monitoring roles. In accordance with a contract concluded with the SRSA, local authorities own the facilities once they have been completed and are responsible for their maintenance.

The SRSA assists with the creation of sports councils in the communities where facilities are built, and empowers individuals to manage and run activities at these venues.

Sport and recreation benefits from the proceeds of the National Lottery, subject to the Lotteries Act, 2000 (Act 10 of 2000). The Distribution Agency for Sport and Recreation was established to create and consolidate thriving, sustainable, mass-based sport and recreational structures and programmes, especially in disadvantaged rural communities.

Programmes

Sports Tourism Project

The primary motivation of the Sports Tourism Project is to exploit the substantial benefits that the tourism industry presents for job creation in South Africa.

Tourism is widely recognised as a major growth sector internationally and it is estimated that 30% of all tourism comprises sports tourism.

A survey conducted by Standard Bank indicated that tourism outstripped gold earnings as a revenue generator for South Africa.

SRSA aims to enhance the sustainability of the project by:

- promoting 'home-grown' events such as the Comrades Marathon, Dusi Canoe Marathon, Argus Cycle Tour, Midmar Mile (swimming), Berg and Breede river canoe marathons and the Two Oceans Marathon, which attract large numbers of international participants and spectators
- working closely with South African Tourism and the Department of Environmental Affairs and Tourism to promote more attractive tourist packages for spectators who want to accompany touring sports teams to South Africa

- assisting agencies, in line with a major events strategy and the hosting and bidding regulations, to attract major international sports events to South Africa
- marketing South Africa's sport and recreation facilities, such as golf courses and beaches, abroad
- producing an interactive CD-ROM to provide information on sport and recreation events and associated information on South Africa.

Mass participation

The Mass Participation Programme was launched in 2005 to facilitate access to sport and recreation by as many South Africans as possible, especially those from historically disadvantaged communities. Previously, this programme's activities comprised the development programmes of federations and the recreation programme of the department.

It has proven to be highly successful and should meet some of government's priorities such as moral regeneration and social cohesion. The programme exceeded its target of 36 hubs (four in each province) in 2004/05, by launching 60 hubs. A further 36 were expected to be launched in 2005/06.

The programme provides opportunities for identifying talent. Athletes will be channelled into the support systems, including the National Sports Academy, and nurtured throughout the development continuum to reach their maximum potential. This system should contribute to greater representation at all levels, particularly of athletes from historically disadvantaged backgrounds. Unemployed youth from the communities where the programme has been launched, have been trained as co-ordinators and are running the hubs' activities.

Young Champions Project

The project is a joint effort of the SRSA, the South African Police Service, provincial and local departments responsible for sport and recreation, the Office of the Public Prosecutor, the Department of Justice and Constitutional Development, and national and provincial sports federations.

It forms part of the SRSA's commitment to encourage the youth, especially those in crime nodes, to take part in sport.

Transformation in sport

Sports Transformation Charter

The Sports Transformation Charter guides all macro-bodies, national and provincial federations, and clubs on the need to transform sport.

The charter is complemented by performance agreements that national federations enter into with the Minister of Sport and Recreation. The main focus of the charter and the performance agreement is to:

- increase participation levels in sport and recreation
- make sport and recreation accessible to all South Africans
- ensure that provincial and national teams reflect South African society
- ensure that all sport and recreation bodies meet their affirmative-action objectives
- promote greater involvement of marginalised groups – such as women, people with disabili-

South Africa will host the 2010 Soccer World Cup. This will create significant direct and indirect economic benefits for the country.

South Africa expects some 400 000 visitors for the 2010 World Cup, which is the first to be held in Africa.

Television coverage of the World Cup will bring South Africa into the homes of new tourism markets such as Brazil, Argentina, eastern Europe, Russia, Japan and South Korea.

An economic-impact study predicts that 2,72 million tickets will be sold, generating revenue of R4,6 billion.

Capital expenditure on the upgrades of stadia and other infrastructure is expected to amount to R2,3 billion. The event will lead to an estimated direct expenditure of R12,7 billion, while contributing R21,3 billion to the country's gross domestic product. Some 159 000 new employment opportunities are expected to be created and an estimated R7,2 billion will be paid to government in taxes.

558

ties, people living in rural communities and the youth – in sport and recreation.

Ministerial task team into high-performance sport

In December 2004, the first steps were taken towards the implementation of the ministerial task team's recommendations into high-performance sport that were approved by Cabinet. The South African Sports Confederation and Olympic Committee (SASCOC) opened its doors and SRSA took over the functions of the South African Sports Commission (SASC) and its personnel.

The expanded SRSA has the capacity to provide mass-based sport and recreation at community level in the most remote parts of the country. Government resources for sport and recreation will be channelled into the Mass Participation Programme.

SASCOC has taken over all the high-performance sport activities and works in close co-operation with national federations that constitute their primary stakeholders.

National Sports Academy

The National Sports Academy was launched in 2004 to improve sports performance and to bring South Africa on par with other sporting nations. The academy seeks to create opportunities for talented athletes to exploit their potential to the full.

Its short-term focus is to provide a one-stop, world-class training and support environment for identified sport, offering elite athletes the opportunity to prepare for the Olympic and Paralympic games.

The academy's work is complemented by the Mass Participation Programme.

The sports academy system comprises a significant aspect of the delivery system in sport and recreation at the high-performance level that will eventually provide the necessary support for talented athletes. It will ensure that talented athletes from disadvantaged backgrounds receive the support they need.

Government allocated R15 million to sports academies in 2005/06.

During 2004/05, 300 athletes received high-performance training for the first time through the National Sports Academy Programme. This contributed to the South African team winning a total of six medals (one gold, three silver and seven bronze) at the Olympic Games in Athens, 35 at the Paralympics (15 gold, 13 silver and seven bronze), 66 in the Zone VI Games, and 56 at the Junior Commonwealth Games.

Sporting accolades

South African Sports Awards

The South African Sports Awards are the highest honour a South African athlete can receive, short of Presidential honours.

South Africa's sports heroes who excelled during the past year were honoured in Johannesburg on 25 November 2005.

In 2004, Roland Schoeman, Olympic swimming sensation, was voted Sports Star of the Year.

The Order of Ikhamanga

In September 2005, President Thabo Mbeki bestowed the Order of Ikhamanga (silver class) to Fanie Lombaard (Paralympic gold medallist) and Lucas Radebe (soccer) respectively, for their exceptional contribution to sport.

Sports organisations

South African Sports Confederation and Olympic Committee

The SASC Act, 1998 (Act 109 of 1998), provided for a commission to administer sport and recreation under the guidance of the Minister of Sport and Recreation. In 2005, the SASC Repeal Act, 2005 (Act 8 of 2005), de-established the SASC. The functions of the SASC are now shared between SRSA and the newly established SASCOC.

SASCOC is the controlling body for all high-performance sport in South Africa. It also controls the preparation and delivery of Team South Africa at all multisport international games, including the Olympics, Paralympics, Commonwealth Games, World Games and All Africa Games.

It has assumed functions relating to high-performance sport that were carried out by the following controlling bodies: Disability Sport South Africa, the National Olympic Committee of South Africa, South African Commonwealth Games Association, SASC, South African Student Sports Union, and the United School Sports Association of South Africa.

SASCOC will also:

- affiliate to and/or be recognised by the appropriate international, continental and regional sport organisations for high-performance sport
- initiate, negotiate, arrange, finance and control multisport tours to and from South Africa
- ensure, and if necessary, approve that the bidding process relating to the hosting of international or any other sporting events in South Africa complies with the necessary rules and regulations
- facilitate the acquisition and development of playing facilities, including the construction of stadia and other sports facilities
- ensure close co-operation between government and the private sector relating to all aspects of Team South Africa
- ensure the overall protection of symbols, trademarks, emblems or insignia of the bodies under its jurisdiction.

In October 2005, SASCOC announced that it would be sending 252 athletes to the 2006 Commonwealth Games in Australia. South Africa will be participating in all 12 individual sport codes.

Boxing South Africa

Boxing South Africa was established in terms of the South African Boxing Act, 2001 (Act 11 of 2001), and is partly funded with public money.

Its function is to promote boxing and protect the interests of boxers and officials. Its main responsibilities are to:

- consider applications for licences from all stakeholders in professional boxing

- sanction fights
- implement the regulations pertaining to boxing
- promote the interests of all stakeholders in boxing.

Boxing South Africa's new academy was launched in August 2003.

The boxing academy was established using part of the R27 million invested in boxing by cellular service-provider Vodacom. The academy is spearheaded by the Sports Information and Science Agency in conjunction with the University of Pretoria's High-Performance Centre.

The academy offers boxers high-performance, physical fitness, athletics and life skills. In 2004, Boxing South Africa trained 67 boxers, promoters, ring officials, trainers/managers and administrators against the expected target of 62.

South Africa's professional boxing categories comprise 17 weight divisions.

South African Institute for Drug-Free Sport (SAIDS)

The SAIDS is a public entity established by the SAIDS Act, 1997 (Act 14 of 1997). It is funded by the SRSA with a mandate to promote participation in sport free from the use of prohibited substances or methods intended to artificially enhance performance, in the interest of the health and well-being of sportspeople. The SAIDS is the only recognised body in the country permitted to authorise and enforce national anti-doping policy.

It has 54 certified doping control officers who conduct testing throughout South Africa, assisted by 70 trained and certified chaperones. SAIDS is one of

In November 2005, South Africa's rugby wing sensation Bryan Habana and Protea cricket team star Jacques Kallis were named as the joint winners of the SA Sportsman of the Year award, while swimmer Natalie du Toit scooped the SA Sportswoman of the Year title, at the SA Sports Awards held in Midrand, near Johannesburg.

the few national anti-doping agencies worldwide to achieve ISO 9001:2000 certification in compliance with the International Standard for Doping Control. This is the internationally recognised benchmark for quality assurance and excellence, and represents world best practice in doping control in sport.

SAIDS' key focus areas are:

- Drug testing: The institute conducts a comprehensive, independent and effective national drug-testing programme on South African athletes from 54 sporting disciplines competing at regional, national and international level. Over 2 300 tests were conducted in 2004. SAIDS also provides testing services for international sports federations and anti-doping organisations.
- Education: The SAIDS provides accessible education and information resources and services to its target groups. These include a telephone information service manned by qualified pharmacists (Tel 021 448 3888); a website with up-to-date information on anti-doping issues (*www.drugfreesport.org.za)*; and monthly workshops and seminars for athletes, sports federations, sports coaches, school learners, educators, and members of the medical, pharmaceutical and sports science professions. The SAIDS collaborates with the South African National Council on Alcoholism and Drug Dependence and other organisations and facilitators providing

drug education and awareness programmes at schools and in communities throughout South Africa, to incorporate information about sports drugs into their education programmes. Sports drugs are included in the Department of Education's National Policy on the Management of Drug Abuse by Learners in Public and Independent Schools and Further Education and Training Institutions.

- Research: The SAIDS conducts sociological research into the knowledge, attitude and use of performance-enhancing drugs among South African sportspeople, for the purpose of planning and implementing effective drug-testing and education programmes.
- International collaboration: South Africa and the SAIDS are active participants in the global effort to combat drugs in sport. The SAIDS collaborates closely with its counterparts throughout the world to achieve international harmonisation and improvement of standards and practice in anti-doping. South Africa is a member of the 13-country International Anti-Doping Arrangement.

World Anti-Doping Agency (WADA)
The Africa regional office of WADA was established in Cape Town in 2004. Its role is to coordinate the anti-doping activities of WADA throughout Africa. This includes promoting and maintaining effective lines of communication between WADA and all the relevant stakeholders, governments and public authorities, the broad sports movement, national anti-doping agencies and laboratories.

2005 sports highlights

Athletics
In January 2005, Oscar Pistorius, the 18-year-old 200-m paralympic champion and world record holder for double leg amputees, set a new global 400-m record in the same category with a time of 47,43 sec at Pilditch Stadium in Pretoria.

Boxing
In October 2005, almost all South African fighters holding World Boxing Council (WBC) international

The South Africa Games 2005 took place in Durban in September 2005. At least 5 500 athletes from all over South Africa participated.

The games, under the theme *Today's Youth, Tomorrow's Stars,* were aimed at unearthing sporting talent among South African youth. Thirteen different sporting codes were included, namely athletics, gymnastics, table tennis, golf, rugby, boxing, tennis, netball, goal ball, soccer, swimming, hockey and cricket.

To ensure that different communities received a slice of the action, the games were played in Pinetown, Umlazi, KwaMashu, Cleremont, Cato Manor and at Kingspark Stadium in Durban.

titles had their ratings boosted, following the WBC Convention in Spain.

The big movers were Border fighters Hawk Makepula (WBC international junior bantamweight champion), Mhikiza Myekeni (WBC international fly-weight) and Gabula Vabaza (World Boxing Association international junior featherweight).

Vabaza moved from sixth to fourth spot, Makepula moved from ninth to seventh position and Myekeni moved from ninth to sixth spot.

Another big mover was South African and WBC International welterweight champion Joseph Makaringe, who gate-crashed to sixth spot from ninth in the most competitive division in the world.

This, despite the fact that Makaringe was yet to defend his WBC B-grade belt which he won when stopping Philip Kotey in 11 rounds in September 2005.

Cricket

In February 2005, Ashwell Prince scored his maiden half-century at Supersport Park in Centurion to steer South Africa to a three-wicket win over England. This also wrapped up a 4-1 series victory in the seventh and final one-day international.

In March 2005, South Africa won the one-day series against Zimbabwe by 3-0. They also clinched the test series.

Also in March, more than 120 women from eight countries gathered in South Africa for the eighth Women's Cricket World Cup. It was won by Australia.

In April 2005, Protea fast bowler Makhaya Ntini claimed the best bowling figures in South African test history, helping his team dismiss the West Indies on the final day of the second test at Queen's Park Oval in Trinidad.

Ntini took seven wickets for 37 as the home team slumped from 170 for five at the start of the day to 194 all out. South Africa then reached 45 without loss at lunch, 99 short of victory. Ntini already had six for 95 in the first innings – a record for a South African team against the West Indies. That completed overall match figures of 13 for 132, beating off-spinner Hugh Tayfield's record 13 for 165 against Australia in 1952. South Africa won the test series 2-0.

Cycling

In February 2005, South African cyclist Ryan Cox won the Tour de Langkawi in Malaysia. Cox, from the Barloworld team, won the 10-day tour in 30 hours, 18 minutes and 18 seconds. South Africa also retained the team title.

Golf

Women's World Cup of Golf

Early in 2005, South Africa hosted the first Women's World Cup of Golf. Twenty countries participated.

The competition was endorsed by the Ladies European Tour, the Ladies Professional Golf Association Tour, and South Africa's Women's Professional Golf Association and drew a host of top names from around the world.

The event featured a different format on each day. Day one was 18 holes of foursomes, followed by 18 holes of four-ball on day two. The third day was stroke-play. The purse was US$1 million.

South Africa's Ashleigh Simon, one of two amateurs in the field, was the youngest player in the competition.

The event was won by Japan with Ai Miyazato leading her country to a two-shot victory. The 19-year-old fired a six-under-par 67 in the last-day singles, while her playing partner Rui Kitada managed 82 as the Japanese duo finished on three-under 289.

The South African Sports Commission hosted the Indigenous Games Best of the Best event in March 2005 at the Mmabatho Stadium in North West. North West was the overall winner at the first Indigenous Games Festival held in Limpopo in 2003 and was the province that had the most delegates represented in the team to Canada for the World Indigenous Games in 2004.

The provinces that took part in the 2005 games were Gauteng, Mpumalanga, North West, Western Cape, Eastern Cape and Limpopo. More than 90 athletes participated in five indigenous games, namely kho-kho, dibeke, intonga, ncuva and jukskei.

The Philippines came second and South Korea third. South Africa finished in 12th position.

Dubai Desert Classic

In March 2005, Ernie Els won an unprecedented third Dubai Desert Classic in dramatic style, holing an eagle putt from 18 feet at the last hole for a one-shot victory.

He went into the final round a stroke behind leader Miguel Angel Jimenez and fired a four-under-par 68 to finish at 19-under 269.

Qatar Masters

In March 2005, Els fired a seven-under 65 to storm to a one-shot win over Sweden's Henrik Stenson at the Qatar Masters.

It gave the South African, who carded eight birdies and one bogey, a 12-under aggregate 276, and a second victory in seven days after his Dubai Desert Classic success the previous weekend.

In May 2005, *Golf Digest USA* ranked the top 100 golf courses outside the United States of America (USA). South Africa achieved five listings, with Leopard Creek Golf Estate and Country Club in Mpumalanga, coming in at number 25.

The survey covered 1 005 golf courses around the world and was overseen by a panel of over 800 course-rating specialists, 22 editors of *Golf Digest* and its affiliates, and an undisclosed number of other expert panelists.

The magazine ranked the Old Course at St Andrews first among courses outside the USA, followed by Australia's Royal Melbourne Golf Club and Ireland's Royal Portrush.

Five South African courses, all regular stops on the Sunshine Tour annual calendar, ranked in *Golf Digest's* top 100.

Leopard Creek ranked 25th, followed by the Gary Player Country Club at Sun City, home to the multimillion-dollar Nedbank Golf Challenge and the Dimension Data Pro-Am, at 29th.

The Links at Fancourt, venue for the 2003 President's Cup, joined the list at number 59, followed at number 62 by the Durban Country Club. Arabella Estate and Country Club, which plays host to the annual Nelson Mandela Invitational, completed the list at number 100.

Asian Tour

At the beginning of May 2005, Els recorded his third win of the season in record-breaking style at the Tomson Shanghai Pudong Golf Club in Shanghai. He carded a tournament best 26-under par 262 to win by 13 shots.

Scottish Open

In July 2005, South African Tim Clark holed a 20-foot birdie putt at the last to shoot a four-under 67 and clinch his third European tour title by two shots at the Scottish Open in Loch Lomond.

International

In August 2005, Retief Goosen beat Brandt Jobe to win the International at Castle Rock, Colorado. Goosen averaged only 1,596 putts per green he hit in regulation, which was the best showing of the tournament. His total of 27 putts per round was also the sixth-best putting performance of the event.

China Masters

In September 2005, Goosen won the China Masters by six shots over Michael Campbell.

German Masters

In September 2005, Goosen shot a five-under 67 to win the German Masters by a stroke.

The two-time United States (US) Open champion's total score was 20-under 268.

Hockey

In October 2005, South Africa's women hockey team thrashed Ghana 6-1 in the final to win the Africa Cup of Nations.

Marathons

In April 2005, South African wheelchair athlete Ernst van Dyk won the Boston Marathon for a record fifth consecutive time, coming home almost six minutes clear of his nearest challenger.

Van Dyk's winning time of one hour, 24 minutes and 11 sec was some way off the world record 1:18:27 he posted in 2004.

Another South African, Krige Schabort, claimed second place in 1:30:03.

A week prior to the Boston Marathon, Van Dyk won the Paris Marathon.

On 16 June 2005, Sipho Ngomane from Mpumalanga won South Africa's annual premier athletic event, the Comrades Marathon.

Paddling

In May 2005, South African ski paddler Oscar Chalupsky won a record 11th Molokai Challenge, widely regarded as the unofficial world surf ski championship.

Swimming

In February 2005, South African swimmer Ryk Neethling won the 50- and 200-meter freestyle short-course races, capturing the overall Fina World Cup title.

Neethling won a total of five races in the World Cups' last leg in Belo Horizonte, Brazil. The 27-year-old won the 50-m butterfly, the 100-m freestyle and the 100-m individual medley.

Neethling, who won 21 gold medals in the World Cups' eight events, finished ahead of countryman Roland Schoeman in the overall standings and took home US$50 000 for the title.

In July 2005, Schoeman set a world record in the semi-finals of the men's 50-m butterfly at the World Championships in Montreal. He went on to win South Africa's first world swimming title by setting another world record in the final of the men's 50-m butterfly.

He also won the men's 50-m freestyle final in 21,69 sec, the second-fastest time in history and only 0,05 outside Alexander Popov's world record of 21,64.

The South African team brought home a total of five medals.

In November 2005, Neethling won six gold medals at the first leg of the Fina World Cup Series in Durban.

Rugby

In April 2005, the Baby Boks retained the 2005 International Rugby Board Under-19 Rugby World Championship title when they defeated New Zealand 20-15 at the Absa Stadium in Durban.

In June 2005, South Africa defeated Australia 24-20 to win the U-21 Rugby World Championship.

Also in June, South Africa defeated the French 27-13 in Port Elizabeth to clinch the series. The first test was drawn 40-all.

In July 2005, the Springboks ensured that the Nelson Mandela Challenge Plate stayed in South Africa by beating Australia 33-20 at Ellis Park in Johannesburg. Two weeks earlier they went down 12-30.

At the end of July 2005, South Africa beat Australia 22-16 in the first match of the Tri-Nations. A week later they also beat the All Blacks 22-16 at Newlands.

In August 2005, Bryan Habana scored two amazing long-range tries to give South Africa a 22-19 victory over Australia in their Tri-Nations match in Perth. However, later in August, they went down 27-31 against the All Blacks in Dunedin. New Zealand beat Australia in the final to win the Tri-Nations Cup.

Soccer

In February 2005, South Africa's national soccer squad, Bafana Bafana, were held to a 1-1 draw by Australia in a hard-fought friendly international played at Durban's Absa Stadium. Bafana led 1-0 at halftime.

At the end of February 2005, Bafana Bafana went through to the final stage of the Confederation

Protea fast bowler Makhaya Ntini was named the 2005 Mutual and Federal South African Cricketer of the Year.

Ntini bagged 58 wickets in 14 tests, including a South African record 13 for 132 against the West Indies in the second test. He knocked over six for 95 and then devastated the islanders' second innings with a haul of seven for 37 during this test.

The Border paceman's fine performances lifted him to a career-high fourth in the LG International Cricket Council test bowling rankings.

In October 2005, Jacques Kallis and England's Andrew Flintoff shared the International Cricket Council's 2005 Player of the Year Award.

of Southern African Football Association Cup when they defeated Mauritius 1-0 in the A Group final.

In June 2005, Bafana Bafana came through with a vital 2-1 World Cup qualifying win over the Cape Verde Islands to move three points clear at the top of Africa Group Two. However, they later lost crucial matches and failed to qualify for the 2006 World Cup.

In July, Jamaica and South Africa drew 3-3, joining the USA and Costa Rica in the quarterfinals of the Concacaf Gold Cup, while Mexico beat Guatemala 4-0 to recover from their upset loss to Bafana Bafana two days earlier. However, South Africa lost narrowly to Panama in the quarter-final in Houston, in the USA.

In October 2005, South Africa and the Democratic Republic of Congo drew 2-all in their final 2006 World Cup qualifier at Absa Stadium to finish joint second in their group on 16 points. Bafana Bafana's draw in Durban was enough, however, to secure South Africa a spot in the 16-nation 2006 Africa Cup of Nations in Egypt.

Surfing

In March 2005, Nikita Robb outclassed a field of top junior surfers to win the inaugural Rip Curl GromSearch International Final at Bells Beach in Australia.

Tennis

Second seeds Cara Black of Zimbabwe and Liezel Huber of South Africa won the Wimbledon women's doubles title for their first Grand Slam title since joining forces at the beginning of the year.

They defeated the duo of Amelie Mauresmo of France and Svetlana Kuznetsova of Russia 6-2, 6-1 in the final.

South Africa's Wesley Moodie teamed up with Australia's Stephen Huss to beat Bob and Mike Bryan, the American second seeds, 7-6 (7/4), 6-3, 6-7 (2/7), 6-3, to become the first qualifiers to clinch the title.

In October 2005, Moodie earned his first single career victory at the Japan Open tennis tournament in Tokyo. The win improved his ranking by 41 places, to a career high of 57.

Mountaineering

In June 2005, South African game ranger Sibusiso Vilane summited Mount Everest with fellow mountaineer Alex Harris. Vilane became the first black African to reach the top of Everest in 2003.

Yachting

In April 2005, Team Shosholoza, South Africa's America's Cup challenger, unveiled the hull of the world's first fully constructed new generation V5.0 America's Cup class yacht.

The Shosholoza RSA 83, sponsored by German firm T-Systems, is the first America's Cup class yacht to be designed and built in South Africa, and the first in the world to meet the new Version 5.0 rule of the 2007 America's Cup.

The crew left for Europe in May to take part in six 2005 Louis Vuitton Acts, or pre-America's Cup regattas in Spain, Sweden and Sicily.

Acknowledgements

Beeld

Disability Sport South Africa

Estimates of National Expenditure 2005, published by National Treasury

National Olympic Committee of South Africa

news24.com

Standard Bank

South African Institute for Drug-Free Sport

South African Sports Commission

Sowetan

Sport and Recreation South Africa

The Star

www.gov.za

www.sapa.org.za

www.southafrica.info

www.supersport.co.za

www.superswimmer.co.za

www.news24.com

Suggested reading

Alegi, P. *Laduma! Soccer, Politics and Society in South Africa*. Scottsville: University of KwaZulu-Natal Press, 2004.

Alfred, L. *Lifting the Covers: The Inside Story of South African Cricket*. Cape Town: Spearhead, 2001.

Alfred, L. *Testing Times: The Story of the Man Who Made South African Cricket*. Cape Town: Spearhead Press, 2003.

Alswang, J. *South African Dictionary of Sport*. Cape Town: David Philip, 2003.

Beaumont, F. *In the Presence of Gary Player: A Perspective on the Life and Philosophy of One of the World's Greatest Golfers*. Hatfield, Pretoria: Undaus Press, 2004.

Berkowitz, A. and Samson, A. *Supersport Factfinder*. 5th ed. Cape Town: Don Nelson, 1997.

Bryden, C. *Story of SA Cricket, 1990 – 1996*. Cape Town: Inter-African Publications, 1997.

Burke, L. *et al. The Complete South African Guide to Sports Nutrition*. Cape Town: Oxford University Press, 1998.

Capostagno, A. and Neild, D. *Fancourt: The Road to the President's Cup*. Johannesburg: Viking, 2003.

Chesterfield, T. and McGlew, J. *South Africa's Cricket Captains*. Cape Town: Zebra Press, 2002.

Colquhoun, A. ed. *South African Rugby Annual 2004*. Johannesburg: SA Rugby and MWP Media, 2004.

Cottrell, T. *Old Mutual's Runner's Guide to Road Races in South Africa*. Parklands: Guide Book Publications, 2003.

Cottrell, T. *et al. Comrades Marathon Yearbook*. Halfway House: Southern Books, 1998.

Cottrell, T., Laxton, I. and Williams, D. *Comrades Marathon: Highlights and Heroes, 1921 – 1999*. Johannesburg: Jonathan Ball, 2000.

Cottrell, T. ed. *Nedbank Runners' Guide to the Road Races in South Africa*. Parklands: Guide Book Publications, 2005.

Desai, A. *et al. Blacks in Whites: A Century of Cricket Struggles in KwaZulu-Natal*. Pietermaritzburg: University of Natal Press, 2002.

Evans, G. *Dancing Shoes is Dead*. London: Doubleday, 2002.

Griffiths, E. *Bidding for Glory: Why South Africa Lost the Olympic and World Cup Bids, and How to Win Next Time*. Johannesburg: Jonathan Ball, 2000.

Griffiths, E. *Glory Days: Forty Years of One-Day Cricket*. Johannesburg: Viking, 2003.

Griffiths, E. *The Captains*. Johannesburg: Jonathan Ball, 2001.

Grundelingh, A. *et al. Beyond the Tryline: Rugby and SA Society*. Randburg: Ravan Press, 1995.

Heyns, P. and Lemke, G. *Penny Heyns*. PHBH Publications, 2004.

Jaffee, J and Wolfaardt, F. *And Away They Go*. Johannesburg: Sharp Sharp Media, 2004.

Keohane, M. *Springbok Rugby Uncovered: The Inside Story of South African Rugby Controversies*. Cape Town: Zebra Press, 2004.

Kirsten, G. and Manthrop, N. *Gazza: The Gary Kirsten Autobiography*. Cape Town: Don Nelson, 2004

Knowles, R. *SA Versus England: A Test History*. Cape Town: Sable Media, 1995.

Lambson, B. *The South African Guide to Cricket with Barry Lambson and Brian Basson*. Editor: M. Collins. Cresta: Michael Collins Publications, 1998.

Lediga, S. *Ndizani 1992 – 2003 Bafana Bafana*. Polokwane: Sello Lediga, 2003.

Leppan, L. *South African Book of Records*. Cape Town: Don Nelson, 1999. Greenhouse, 2004.

Mazwai, T. ed. *Thirty Years of South African Soccer*. Cape Town and Randburg: Sunbird Publishing and Mafube Publishing, 2003.

Murray, B. and Merrett, C. *Caught Behind: Race and Politics in Springbok Cricket*. Johannesburg: Wits University Press and Scottsville: University of Kwazulu-Natal Press, 2004.

Nauright, J. *Sport, Cultures and Identities in South Africa*. Cape Town: David Philip, 1998.

Oborne, P. *Basil d'Oliveira – Cricket and Conspiracy: The Untold Story*. London: Little Brown, 2004.

Odendaal, A. *The Story of an African Game*. Cape Town: David Philip, 2003.

Raath, P. *Soccer Through the Years 1862 – 2002: The First Official History of South African Soccer*. Cape Town: The Author, 2002.

Ramsamy, S. *Reflections on a Life in Sport*. Cape Town: Publishing Partnership for Greenhouse, 2004.

Winch, J. *Cricket in Southern Africa: Two Hundred Years of Achievements and Records*. Rosettenville, Johannesburg: Windsor, 1997.

Tourism

South Africa is a tourist paradise – offering scenic beauty, diverse wildlife, a kaleidoscope of cultures and traditions, and endless opportunities to explore the outdoors through sport and adventure activities.

Tourism is South Africa's fastest-growing industry and contributes about 7,1% of the Gross Domestic Product (GDP).

In 2004, total international arrivals increased by 2,7%. Although European arrivals decreased by 2,4%, arrivals from North America increased by 10,4%, Central and South America by more than 12%, Australasia by 4,4%, Asia by 3,1% and other African countries by 4,2%.

In the first quarter of 2005, there were 1,7 million foreign tourist arrivals – the highest in South African history, representing exceptional growth of more than 10%. At the same time, foreign tourism spending increased by more than 25% to R12,9 billion.

The tourism industry employs an estimated 3% of South Africa's workforce, and is regarded as potentially the largest provider of jobs and earner of foreign exchange. Some 27 000 new direct tourism jobs were created in 2004.

The fastest-growing segment of tourism in South Africa is ecological tourism (ecotourism), which includes nature photography, birdwatching, botanical studies, snorkelling, hiking and mountaineering.

Community tourism is becoming increasingly popular, with tourists wanting to experience South Africa's rural villages and townships. (See chapter 5: *Arts and culture*.)

Another key aspect of South Africa's tourism vision for the next three years, is the vast business tourism potential. Injecting about R20 billion annually into the economy, business tourism is estimated to sustain almost 260 000 jobs, paying an estimated R6 billion in salaries and accounting for R4 billion in taxes every year.

South Africa ranks as the 28th most popular global business tourism destination. To improve this ranking, the *Business Tourism* Campaign was launched in November 2005 to industry and business leaders in Amsterdam. The campaign was also launched in London in 2005, and an Asian and American roll-out is planned for 2006.

Tourism policy and initiatives

At national level, the Tourism Branch in the Department of Environmental Affairs and Tourism leads and directs tourism-policy formulation and implementation. It works in partnership with South African Tourism, provincial tourism authorities, the tourism industry and other relevant stakeholders. It aims to ensure and accelerate the practical delivery of tourism benefits to the broad spectrum of South Africans, while maintaining sustainability and quality of life.

The *White Paper on Tourism* provides a policy framework for tourism development, and entails, among other things:

- empowerment/capacity-building
- a focus on tourism-infrastructure investment
- aggressively marketing South Africa as a tourism destination to international markets
- a domestic tourism and travel campaign.

Raising general awareness about the opportunities for domestic travel continues to be a priority. The aim is to encourage South Africans to travel within their country, to make tourism products accessible to all, to facilitate the development of a culture of tourism, and to create a safe and welcoming environment for visitors.

Poverty-relief funding

The Department of Environmental Affairs and Tourism's poverty-relief projects promote the development of community-owned tourism products and the establishment of tourism infrastructure, including roads, information centres and tourism signage.

These poverty-relief projects are categorised into product development, infrastructure development, capacity-building and training, the establishment of

Government will spend R12 million over the next three years to implement the Tourism Satellite Account in partnership with StatsSA, the Reserve Bank and others. Among the most important information that this will generate for South Africa's tourism industry is the specific contribution of tourism to gross domestic product, the actual number of direct and indirect jobs in tourism, the quantity of tourism investment and revenue generated by tourism throughout South Africa.

small, medium and micro enterprises (SMMEs), and business-development projects.

Welcome Campaign

The *Welcome* Campaign encourages all South Africans to embrace tourism and share South Africa's rich natural and cultural heritage. It is run as a national general-awareness campaign, through roadshows and community-outreach programmes.

Another facet of the campaign is the celebration of Tourism Month. This annual promotion, held in September, aims to promote a culture of tourism among all South Africans.

SA Host

SA Host, a national customer-service training programme, was introduced in December 2001. The programme aims to develop and promote a culture of customer service in South Africa by creating awareness of the importance of the individual's role in delivering superior customer service in their place of work and their community.

The programme was originally developed in Canada and has been successfully run in 14 countries.

Successful workshop participants become South African hosts and are awarded a certificate and a lapel pin identifying them as people who are committed to excellent service and who are ambassadors for their community and South Africa.

The objectives of SA Host programmes are to:

- improve service-delivery standards through training
- change attitudes towards visitors by creating an awareness of the value of the visitor industry to the country and the role played by every resident
- elevate national pride.

The Department of Environmental Affairs and Tourism provided funding to develop seven regional trainers.

Sho't Left Campaign

The second *Sho't Left* Campaign was launched in February 2005. This R20-million domestic marketing campaign aims to increase the number of domestic tourists nationally. The campaign showcases accessible holiday opportunities in all nine provinces.

Sho't Left focuses on converting interest into the actual booking of accommodation and inspiring people to discover the country. The campaign facilitated closer co-operation with the private sector, and particularly the Association of Southern African Travel Agents (ASATA). As a result, the public can book affordable *Sho't Left* holidays through the retail network of more than 5 000 agents, all of whom are equipped with brochures and educational leaflets. ASATA was also working with South African Tourism to develop the *Sho't Left* Enterprise Programme where travel agencies employ domestic agents to stimulate the domestic travel market.

In alignment with the Tourism Black Economic Empowerment (BEE) Charter, this project also addresses unemployment and skills transfer.

International tourism

Cabinet approved the International Tourism Growth Strategy in June 2003. The strategy includes an analysis of core markets and their segments.

Priority markets have been identified in Europe, Asia and Africa.

The strategy not only aims to increase arrivals, but also to:
- increase the duration tourists spend in South Africa
- increase the spending of tourists
- ensure that tourists travel throughout the country, and not just in a few provinces
- facilitate transformation and BEE in the local tourism industry.

South Africa has made its mark as a world meetings, incentives, conferences and exhibitions destination.

In February 2004, South African Tourism launched its *Woza 2004* Campaign. This deal-driven consumer campaign is aimed at encouraging German travellers to visit South Africa in large groups, particularly during the low tourist season. It is also intended to increase awareness about South Africa and entrenches the country as an affordable, year-round, preferred tourist destination.

The *Woza* Campaign offers two value-for-money packages that include return flights into South Africa, airport taxes, world-class accommodation at some of the country's leading quality-graded establishments, and hotel and airport transfers.

The New Partnership for Africa's Development (NEPAD) identified tourism as an important sector to address the development challenges facing Africa. The NEPAD Tourism Action Plan has been developed, providing a more detailed framework for action at national and subregional levels. The action plan proposes concrete interventions in the following focus areas:
- the creation of an enabling policy and regulatory environment
- institution-building aimed at promoting tourism
- tourism marketing
- research and development
- investment in tourism infrastructure and products
- human resource development (HRD) and quality assurance

Some of the tourism initiatives South Africa is actively participating in, include the:
- Okavango Upper Zambezi International Tourism Spatial Development Initiative (SDI)
- Coast-2-Coast SDI.

Domestic tourism growth

The Department of Environmental Affairs and Tourism, in conjunction with South African Tourism,

In April 2005, the Minister of Environmental Affairs and Tourism, Mr Marthinus van Schalkwyk, announced that the South African Government would, over the next three years, invest another R193 million in transfrontier conservation areas, creating visitor centres, upgrading access routes, building camps and improving tourism infrastructure.

Originating in Africa, the transfrontier conservation initiative has been spearheaded by the Southern African Development Community. By April 2005, there were 169 such areas worldwide, involving 113 countries and 667 protected areas.

launched the Domestic Tourism Growth Strategy at the Tourism Indaba in Durban in May 2004.

Domestic tourism is particularly valuable to the country because unlike foreign tourism, it is not seasonally based. It contributes R47 billion to South Africa's economy and there is huge potential for growth.

Some 49,3 million trips are made annually by South Africans within their own country. This comprises 46% of the country's total income from travel expenditure.

A study conducted by the department and South African Tourism, as part of developing the strategy, found that nearly two-thirds of trips were conducted to visit friends and relatives. Although holiday travel accounts for only 16% of trips, it accounts for 44% of all expenditure. Therefore, by focusing on holiday travel, the overall value of the domestic tourism market will be increased.

Some 64% of local people who travel reside in KwaZulu-Natal, Gauteng and the Eastern Cape. These three provinces, in turn, receive 60% of the domestic tourist trade.

Some 60% of domestic travel is undertaken in the province in which people live (intraprovincial travel), while only 40% of trips taken are to another province (interprovincial travel).

To continuously support the growth of the domestic industry, the following have been implemented:

- greater promotion of the domestic tourism brand
- promoting a set of experiences that relate to South African consumers
- distributing appropriate information in specific places
- facilitating the development of co-operative product packages
- developing marketing and distribution channels
- promoting repeat visitation.

Tourism Enterprise Programme (TEP)

TEP was initially launched as a four-year job-creation initiative in July 2000, with R60,4 million in funding from the private sector through the Business Trust. The primary thrust of the pro-gramme is to facilitate the growth and expansion of SMMEs in the tourism economy, resulting in job creation and income-generating opportunities.

TEP exceeded all its targets during Phase I. As a result, the programme was renewed for a further three years with R80 million provided jointly by the Business Trust and the Department of Environmental Affairs and Tourism.

In TEP Phase II, the core transaction facilitation model that was developed in Phase I was retained. In addition, systemic issues designed to maximise the growth and development of tourism SMMEs are addressed. These include implementing tourism-specific training programmes for SMMEs; assistance in strengthening and establishing local tourism associations; developing HIV and AIDS workplace programmes for SMMEs; and strategies to help SMMEs gain maximum benefit from the Tourism Industry BEE Scorecard.

In June 2004, TEP was instrumental in establishing South Africa's premier contemporary arts trade show, *One of a Kind*. The show was hosted in conjunction with Decorex SA in August 2005 at Gallagher Estate in Midrand, Gauteng.

Some 177 crafters, representing 40 individual exhibitors, financially assisted by the TEP, and 137 provincial exhibitors, assisted by the Department of Trade and Industry, as well as various provincial departments, showcased their crafts. These were highly acclaimed by international buyers from as far afield as Canada, the United States of America (USA), Japan, France and Germany. Total funds leveraged were in excess of R3,5 million.

Human resource development

Tourism HRD is considered one of the pillars of the development of a new responsible tourism culture in South Africa.

The department supports the full introduction of Travel, Tourism and Hospitality studies as a subject in schools. Travel and Tourism was introduced in 2000 in all schools wishing to offer the subject from grades 10 to 12.

Tourism and Hospitality Education and Training Authority (THETA)

The THETA comprises the following chambers:

- Hospitality
- Conservation and Tourist Guiding
- Sport, Recreation and Fitness
- Tourism and Travel Services
- Gaming and Lotteries.

Every chamber has its own committee that helps the THETA to identify industry needs. The Tourism Learnership Project (TLP) is a multimillion rand partnership between the Business Trust, THETA and the Department of Labour.

The TLP aims to raise the standards of South Africa's tourism industry by ensuring the development of useful, transferable and accredited skills. The TLP's three core objectives are to:

- accelerate the development of national qualifications for all primary subsectors of the tourism sector
- ensure the availability of national qualifications, which will trigger increased investment in training by employers
- develop systems and support the training of unemployed people through learnerships that provide them with the necessary skills to find jobs.

South African Tourism Institute (SATI)

The SATI was established with the assistance of the Spanish Government, which provided some R13 million for the project.

The SATI has initiated a number of projects that create a supportive learning environment for teachers, high-school learners and employees in the tourism industry.

The SATI focuses on teacher-development programmes aimed at enhancing the quality of the Travel, Tourism and Hospitality subjects.

The project started with 14 schools and 800 learners in 1996. By 2004, more than 700 schools and 150 000 learners had participated in the project.

There is also emphasis on capacity-building of Department of Education officials and educators.

In 2004, the SATI launched an information pack on tourism and hospitality careers, which contains videos, presentations, leaflets and notes on these careers.

A SATI resource centre has also been established, containing electronic and physical resources on many aspects of tourism and its related industries. The centre is open to the public. Other developmental projects are also underway that include working with tourism role-players to develop levels of customer service and staff training.

Black Economic Empowerment

The department has embarked on a legislative reform process to reflect the guidelines set out in the *White Paper on Tourism*.

The Tourism Transformation Strategy was approved by Cabinet in November 2001. More emphasis has since been placed on developing BEE businesses within the tourism industry, by having raised the proportion of government expenditure going to these businesses from 30% in 2001/02 to 50% in 2004/05.

A database of BEE tourism enterprises was compiled to assist government departments to meet affirmative-procurement targets.

All these initiatives have culminated in the Tourism BEE Charter and the Tourism Scorecard launched by

The School for Tourism and Hospitality in Johannesburg, the first combined hospitality and tourism training school in the country, was officially opened by Deputy President Phumzile Mlambo-Ngcuka in August 2005.

The school is situated on the Auckland Park campus of the University of Johannesburg. Some 750 students enrolled, but the intake was expected to increase to 1 000 a year.

The school has various modern facilities, including, among others, two restaurants catering for fine dining, à la carte, buffet and fast food; a bar; a wine cellar; six en-suite bedrooms; computer rooms; and museums featuring the hotel school and the history of catering and cuisine in South Africa.

Students can obtain national diplomas or master's degrees in Technology (MTech) in Hospitality Management, Tourism, and Food and Beverage Management, preparing them for employment in all sectors of the tourism and hospitality industry.

the Minister of Environmental Affairs and Tourism, Mr Marthinus van Schalkwyk, in May 2005. The charter is the result of intensive negotiations with the tourism industry, and represents the commitment of this industry to transformation.

The scorecard comprises seven indicators, namely ownership, strategic representation, employment equity, skills development, preferential procurement, enterprise development and social development. Weightings and targets for each of these indicators have been set for two milestone dates in 2009 and 2014. It applies to large and small businesses alike.

Hints for the tourist

Every traveller to South Africa must be in possession of a valid passport and, where necessary, a visa.

The Immigration Act, 2002 (Act 13 of 2002), stipulates that all visitors to South Africa are required to have a minimum of one blank page (both back and front) in their passport to enable the entry visa to be issued. If there is insufficient space in the passport, entry will be denied.

Enquiries may be directed to South African diplomatic representatives abroad or to the Department of Home Affairs in Pretoria. Visas are issued free of charge. Visitors who intend travelling to South Africa's neighbouring countries and back into South Africa are advised to apply for multiple-entry visas.

The top 10 tourist attractions in South Africa are:
1. Kruger National Park
2. Table Mountain
3. Garden Route
4. Cape Town's Victoria and Alfred Waterfront
5. Robben Island
6. Beaches
7. Sun City
8. Cultural villages
9. Soweto
10. The Cradle of Humankind
Source: SA Venues

Passport-holders of certain countries are exempt from visa requirements. Tourists must satisfy immigration officers that they have the means to support themselves during their stay and that they are in possession of return or onward tickets. They must also have valid international health certificates.

Visitors from the yellow-fever belt in Africa and the USA, as well as those who travel through or disembark in these areas, have to be inoculated against the disease.

Malaria is endemic to parts of KwaZulu-Natal, Mpumalanga and Limpopo. It is essential to take precautions when visiting these areas.

Foreign tourists visiting South Africa can have their value-added tax (VAT) refunded, provided the value of the items purchased exceeds R20.

VAT is refunded on departure at the point of exit.

South Africa's transport infrastructure – airlines, railroads, roads, luxury touring buses (coaches) and motor cars – is such that tourists can travel comfortably and quickly from their port of entry to any part of the country. A number of international airlines, including South African Airways, operate regular scheduled flights to and from South Africa. Several domestic airlines operate in the country. There are also mainline trains to all parts of the country. (See chapter 22: *Transport.*)

A brochure entitled *Helpful Hints to Make Your Stay Enjoyable and Safe* is distributed to tourists at international airports.

South African Tourism's state-of-the-art global call centre in Johannesburg offers information on travelling to South Africa.

Operated 24 hours a day and equipped with 19 international operators, the centre provides information telephonically and via e-mail to English, French, German, Italian, Dutch, Portuguese and Mandarin-speaking customers. The centre, which became operational in October 2004, handled over 7 000 contacts in the first month. Calls and e-mails are handled from 16 countries.

Accommodation

The tourist accommodation industry in South Africa provides a wide spectrum of accommodation, from formal hotels to informal holiday flats and cottages, game lodges and reserves, guest-houses, youth hostels and bed-and-breakfast establishments.

A variety of promotional material on South Africa is available. Comprehensive guides and maps cover all the regions and aspects of interest to tourists, including accommodation. Various useful tourism websites can be found on the Internet.

Quality assurance

The Tourism Grading Council of South Africa (TGCSA) inspects the standards in the hospitality and accommodation industry.

This voluntary grading system, which was launched in 2001, uses internationally recognised star insignia to rate accommodation establishments and will be extended to include relevant businesses in classified sectors of the tourism industry. Once graded, establishments will be encouraged to utilise the star system for marketing and advertising purposes.

Establishments will be assessed according to the type of accommodation they provide. There are currently nine types of establishments:

- bed-and-breakfast
- guest-house
- hotel
- self-catering
- backpacker and hostelling
- caravan and camping
- country house
- meeting, exhibitions, special events
- restaurants.

Grading assessors undergo training to receive the National Certificate in Tourism Grading. The awarding of such a qualification is a world-first. Assessors are accredited with the THETA and registered with the TGCSA before being recommended to the industry. Larger hotel groups with their own internal assessors will also be accredited with the THETA. Independent auditors conduct random audits. These auditors also assist in ensuring that the assessors adhere to a code of conduct.

Star grading is the only system recognised by government and the TBCSA.

By March 2005, 54% of all accommodation rooms in South Africa had been star graded. Some 30 000 accommodation establishments and more than 40 conference venues had been graded. The grading scheme for the food and beverage sector was also operational and restaurants were invited to apply for grading.

Tourist safety

South African Tourism has launched several initiatives aimed at ensuring the safety of travellers to the country.

These include a partnership initiative with the oil company Engen and the Tourism Information and Safety Call Line, 083 123 2345, which provides tourists with information on what to do in an emergency and where to locate services.

The Department of Environmental Affairs and Tourism established the National Tourism Safety Network, a multistakeholder forum comprising provincial representatives, the South African Police Service, Business Against Crime, the departments of foreign affairs and of justice, the Metro Police, organised local government, community policing structures, South African Tourism and other key stakeholders.

The forum has developed the Tourism Safety Communications Strategy and redrafted the National Tourism Safety Tips.

The Department of Environmental Affairs and Tourism also hosted a tourism safety workshop in early February 2005 to address the needs and challenges facing the tourism industry.

The National Tourist Guide of the Year and Emerging National Tourist Guide of the Year Awards recognised and encouraged tour-guiding excellence.

In 2005, the National Tourist Guide of the Year was Mr Alan Weyer and the Emerging Tourist Guide of the Year was Mr Tebogo Ramathunya. These awards will be incorporated with the new Welcome Awards in 2006.

Tourism in the provinces

Western Cape

The Western Cape lies at the southern tip of the African continent. Considered one of the most beautiful regions in Africa, it is also the place where two oceans meet and the home of the famous fynbos vegetation.

The paternal presence of Table Mountain, the pristine coastline with its white sandy beaches, the magnificent countryside with its bountiful rivers, vleis and dams, fauna and flora, together with the warm summer climate and friendly community, makes the Western Cape the perfect holiday destination.

Cape Metropole

Tourism in the city of **Cape Town** centres around the Victoria & Alfred (V&A) Waterfront, a working harbour offering everything from upmarket shopping malls, arts and craft markets, theatres and live music, to museums.

Other major attractions in the city include the Bo-Kaap Museum, the Castle of Good Hope, the Company's Garden, the District Six Museum, flea markets, the Grand Parade, the houses of Parliament, the South African Cultural History Museum and the South African National Gallery. Also worth a visit are historical buildings in the Bo-Kaap and District Six.

In June 2005, South Africa was one of the most affordable holiday destinations in the world.

The findings were from the annual American Express Foreign Exchange Holiday Cost of Living Index, which compares prices in 12 popular holiday resort areas for 13 'shopping basket' items.

Even with the strength of the Rand, South Africa offered significant value for overseas tourists, finishing second only to Thailand.

South Africa was ranked the cheapest on five of the 14 shopping items surveyed, making it the country with the highest number of cheapest items. South Africa also didn't have a product ranked most expensive of all the 14 items listed.

The Gold of Africa Museum established by Anglo Gold is home to a celebrated collection of more than 350 gold artefacts.

Air flips and trips are available, as well as many boat and yacht trips from Table Bay Harbour, including trips to Robben Island (proclaimed a World Heritage Site and also the place where former President Nelson Mandela was imprisoned for several years).

The Nelson Mandela Gateway to Robben Island is situated in the Clock Tower Precinct at the V&A Waterfront. The gateway houses interactive multimedia exhibitions, an auditorium, boardrooms, the Robben Island Museum and a restaurant.

Jazz is big in Cape Town. From traditional blues through progressive jazz to African-influenced jazz, every taste is catered for at a number of restaurants, jazz cafés, cigar bars, pubs and at some of the wine farms. The top jazz event in the Western Cape is the annual Cape Town International Jazz Festival.

Table Mountain, which forms part of the Table Mountain National Park (TMNP) is a popular attraction for visitors and provides a majestic backdrop to the vibrant and friendly Mother City. An ultra-modern cableway takes visitors to the top of the mountain, providing spectacular views.

Newlands is home to the renowned Kirstenbosch National Botanical Garden. In summer, various open-air concerts are held here.

The South African Rugby Museum in Newlands reflects the history of the sport as far back as 1891.

The Rhodes Memorial is situated at **Rondebosch** on the slopes of Table Mountain. It was built of granite from the mountain as a tribute to the memory of Cecil John Rhodes, prime minister of the Cape from 1890 to 1896.

The University of Cape Town is worth a visit for its historic Middle Campus and many buildings designed by Sir Herbert Baker.

Cape Point, part of the TMNP, offers many drives, walks, picnic spots and a licensed restaurant. Care has been taken to protect the environmental integrity of this 22 100-hectare (ha) reserve of indigenous flora and fauna.

Simon's Town's naval atmosphere and Historic Mile are major attractions in the area. A statue of the famous dog and sailor's friend, Able Seaman Just Nuisance, stands at Jubilee Square.

Other attractions include the South African Naval Museum and the Warrior Toy Museum. One of only two of the mainland African penguin-breeding colonies in the world can be found at Boulders Beach, also part of the TMNP.

Hout Bay is well-known for its colourful working harbour. Seafood outlets, round-the-bay trips to the nearby seal colony, shell and gift shops, and a famous harbourfront emporium attract many visitors. Duiker Island is a seal and sea-bird sanctuary. The World of Birds Wildlife Sanctuary is one of the largest bird parks in the world and is home to some 3 000 birds.

In **Oostenberg**, visitors can enjoy some fine wine and flower farms, such as Zevenwacht Wine Estate with its graceful Cape Dutch homestead. Tygerberg Zoo boasts a collection of exotic animals. Endless stretches of quiet beaches provide popular surfing and windsurfing spots. Big Bay in **Bloubergstrand** is a surfer's paradise and host to an international windsurfing event. Rietvlei Nature Reserve is a unique wetland area, boasting over 110 bird species, including pelicans and flamingos.

Canal Walk Century City is the largest shopping centre in Africa, with close to 400 shops and home to the largest cinema complex in South Africa.

Tygerberg is a vibrant and fast-growing area with a well-developed business centre, numerous sports fields, an international indoor cycle track, well-kept golf courses and a racecourse.

New Year in Cape Town is a festive affair, when the Cape minstrels take to the streets with their upbeat music and fancy costumes.

Garden Route

This area features the pont at **Malgas**, which is the only remaining pont in the country, ferrying vehicles and livestock across the Breede River. Whale-watching attracts tourists at **Witsand** and **Port Beaufort** from June to November.

The Grootvadersbosch Nature Reserve outside **Heidelberg** comprises the popular Bushbuck Trail, a wilderness trail and two mountain-bike trails.

Riversdale is one of South Africa's most important fynbos export areas. Other attractions include the Julius Gordon Africana Museum.

At the historical Strandveld Architectural Heritage Site at **Still Bay**, visitors can watch tame eels being fed. Ancient fish-traps can be seen at Morris Point and the harbour.

At the aloe factories at **Albertinia**, aloe juice is extracted for medicine and high-quality skin-care products.

Nearby, bungee-jumping on the Gourits River Gorge, hiking, mountain-biking and angling are popular pastimes.

The Point in **Mossel Bay** is not only popular among surfers, but its natural pool formed by rock, is also a favourite swimming spot at low tide. The St Blaize trail starts here and it is the ideal place to watch the whales and dolphins at play in season.

The harbour at Mossel Bay is one of the most modern commercial and recreational harbours on the southern Cape coastline. PetroSA's Information Centre informs visitors about the production of synthetic fuels from Mossel Bay's offshore gas fields. Other attractions include the Attequas Kloof Pass, Anglo-Boer/South African War blockhouses and the Bartolomeu Dias complex.

Great Brak River offers a historic village with many opportunities for whale and dolphin watching along the extensive coast.

George is at the heart of the Garden Route. It is the mecca of golf in the southern Cape, as it is home to the renowned Fancourt Country Club and Golf Estate, as well as various other acclaimed golf courses. Board the Outeniqua Choo-Tjoe on its daily trip along the coastline between George and Knysna (except Sundays) at the Outeniqua Transport Museum.

Visitors can also board the Power Van here, and enjoy a glimpse of the Garden Route Botanical Garden from this rail bus.

The George Museum, with its theme of timber history, offers ongoing exhibitions. The Montagu and Voortrekker passes are national monuments, providing spectacular views of the Outeniqua Nature Reserve, which offers several hiking trails.

The George Airport, the Outeniqua Pass, the railway line and the N2 offer convenient access to this region, making George the ideal hub from which to explore the Garden Route and Little Karoo.

Victoria Bay and **Wilderness** are popular for their unspoilt beaches. Wilderness is the western gateway to the southern Cape lakes area. It is a nature lover's paradise, best known for its beaches, lakes, placid lagoon and lush indigenous forests. Birdwatchers flock to the Langvlei and Rondevlei bird sanctuaries in the Wilderness National Park, which hosts over 230 different bird species.

Sedgefield borders Swartvlei Lagoon, the largest natural inland saltwater lake in South Africa. Activities include beach horse-riding, hiking, angling and birdwatching.

Knysna nestles on the banks of an estuary, guarded by The Heads (two huge sandstone cliffs) and surrounded by indigenous forests, tranquil lakes and golden beaches.

This natural wonderland is home to the largest and smallest of creatures, from the Knysna seahorse to the Knysna elephants, rare delicate butterflies and the endemic Knysna loerie, a colourful forest bird. Over 200 species can be found in the abundant fynbos and forest settings.

Knysna is also famous for its delectable home-grown oysters, enjoyed with locally brewed beer in quaint pubs and restaurants. An eclectic mix of art galleries showcases the diversity of talent in the area. The area also offers lagoon cruises, forest hikes, golf and adventure sports.

Plettenberg Bay is adventure country, offering boat-based whale watching, black-water tubing, hiking, and forest and cycling trails.

The Keurbooms River Nature Reserve at Plettenberg Bay offers a canoeing trail, while the Robberg Nature Reserve is a treasure trove of land, marine, geological and archaeological wealth.

At 21,6 m high, the bungee jump from the Bloukrans River Bridge is the highest commercial bungee jump in the world.

Little Karoo

The Little Karoo's spectacular landscape is fashioned almost entirely by water. Its vegetation ranges from lush greenery in the fertile river valleys to short, rugged Karoo plants in the veld. Gorges follow rivers that cut through towering mountains, while breathtakingly steep passes cross imposing terrain. The region is also home to the largest bird in the world – the ostrich. The Little Karoo is rich in culture and history.

Excellent wines and port are produced in the **Calitzdorp** and **De Rust** areas.

Oudtshoorn, the world's ostrich-feather capital, is the region's main town. The Swartberg Nature Reserve and Pass with its gravel roads, are also worth a visit. The *Klein Karoo Nasionale Kunstefees* is held in the town annually. Some 29 km from Oudtshoorn lie the remarkable Cango caves, a series of spectacular subterranean limestone caverns. Bearing evidence of early San habitation, the 30-cave wonderland boasts magnificent dripstone formations.

Amalienstein and **Zoar** are historic mission stations midway between Ladismith and Calitzdorp. Visitors can go on donkey-cart and hiking trails through orchards and vineyards, while the Seweweekspoort is ideal for mountain-biking, hiking, and protea and fynbos admirers.

Calitzdorp boasts four wine estates, three of which are open to the public. The spring water of the Calitzdorp Spa is rich in minerals and is reputed to have medicinal properties. The Gamka Mountain Reserve is home to the rare and endangered Cape mountain zebra.

De Rust lies at the southern entrance to Meiringspoort. The Meiringspoort Gorge extends 20 km through the Swartberg Mountain Range. Halfway through, a beautiful 69 m-high waterfall can be seen. Wine farms in the area are open to the public.

Ladismith is home to the Towerkop Cheese Factory. There are various hiking, mountain-biking and 4x4 trails in the area. The Anysberg, Klein Karoo and Towerkop nature reserves are also worth a visit.

Uniondale, on the main route between George and Graaff-Reinet, features the largest water-wheel in the country, the Old Watermill. Uniondale Poort is a scenic drive linking Uniondale with Avontuur in the Langkloof Valley.

At **Vanwyksdorp**, visitors can see how fynbos is dried and packed for the export market. Donkey-cart rides take visitors to Anglo-Boer/South African War grave sites.

Central Karoo

The Central Karoo, a fascinating semi-desert area, lies in the heart of one of the world's most unique and interesting arid zones.

This ancient, fossil-rich land, which is five times the size of Great Britain, is also home to the richest desert flora in the world.

In the Central Karoo, visitors will find the largest variety of succulents found anywhere on Earth.

Beaufort West, the oldest town in the Central Karoo, is often referred to as the Oasis of the Karoo. Awards presented to heart-transplant pioneer, the late Prof. Chris Barnard, a son of this town, are on display in the local museum.

A township route introduces visitors to the Xhosa culture in the area. At the Karoo National Park on the town's doorstep, visitors can experience the flora and game of the Karoo. A challenging 4x4 route takes visitors to the escarpment and new areas of ecological discovery. The park is also home to a variety of game, as well as the highly endangered riverine rabbit.

Matjiesfontein, a national monument, offers tourists a peek into yesteryear and the opportunity to overnight in Victorian splendour. The village houses a small railway museum, a private motor museum and the largest privately owned museum in South Africa.

Experience the vastness of the Great Karoo in **Murraysburg**, an ecotourist and hunter's paradise.

Laingsburg, a tiny village almost totally wiped out by floods a century after it was established, is the best place to study the geology of the region.

Prince Albert is a well-preserved town which nestles at the foot of the Swartberg mountains. It is the ideal place to sample the great variety of Karoo cuisine, see examples of local architecture dating back to the early 1800s and enjoy several scenic drives. The Fransie Pienaar Museum introduces visitors to the cultural history of the area. It has a fossil room and an exhibit covering the gold rush to this area in the 19th century. The museum has a licence to distil and sell witblits (white lightning).

Prince Albert is the closest town by road to Gamkaskloof.

The Hell, a little valley in the heart of the Swartberg mountains, was the home of one of the world's most isolated communities for almost 150 years. Today, Gamkaskloof is a nature reserve and national monument managed by Cape Nature Conservation. It has overnight facilities and can be accessed by a 57-km long (but two-hour drive) winding road which starts at the peak of the Swartberg Pass.

Cape winelands

The Cape winelands, including the former Breede River Valley, are situated in close proximity to Cape Town.

The Cape winelands are a rural enchantment of dramatic mountains, rolling farmlands and peaceful vineyards.

They are home to Route 62, the world's longest wine route.

Stellenbosch, the oldest town in South Africa, is also known as the *Eikestad* (City of Oaks). Various historical walks delight visitors. The town is a gracious blend of old Cape Dutch, Georgian and Victorian architecture. Dorp Street consists of one of the longest rows of old buildings in the country. The Stellenbosch Village Museum consists of four homesteads and gardens ranging from the late 17th to the middle 19th centuries.

The Spier Summer Arts Festival livens up sultry summer nights from November to March at the Spier Wine Estate near Stellenbosch. The Stellenbosch Wine Route comprises over 100 wine estates, most of which offer cellar tours.

South Africa's Blue Train is one of the world's most luxurious railway services. The train runs between Cape Town and Pretoria, to Hoedspruit in Mpumalanga, and along a section of the Garden Route between Cape Town and Port Elizabeth. It also travels to the Victoria Falls in Zimbabwe.

The Freedom Monument at Pniel, which was built in 1992, commemorates the freed slaves who were the first settlers at the mission station, which was established in 1843.

Franschhoek has become known as the gourmet capital of the Cape. Originally known as *Oliphantshoek*, it was named after the arrival of Huguenots who were predominantly French. The Huguenot Monument was built in 1944 to commemorate their arrival in 1688.

Visitors can also enjoy various hiking trails and historical walks, as well as the *Vignerons de Franschhoek* wine route.

Paarl lies between the second-largest granite rock in the world and the Du Toit's Kloof mountains. It is famous for its architectural treasures found along a 1-km stretch of the main street featuring Cape Dutch and Victorian architecture.

The area's fynbos vegetation supports a number of south western Cape endemics, such as the Cape sugarbird and the orange-breasted sunbird.

The *Afrikaanse Taalmonument* is situated on the slopes of the Paarl Mountain, while the *Afrikaanse Taalmuseum* is in the centre of the town.

The town of **Wellington** lies in a picturesque valley, with the majestic Hawequa mountains on its eastern boarder. Apart from three renowned co-operative wineries, one can visit a number of prestigious wine cellars situated on historic Huguenot farms with Cape Dutch homesteads.

Flower lovers will enjoy the chrysanthemum show in May, the longest-running show of its kind in South Africa. More than 90% of South Africa's vine-cutting nurseries are found in Wellington. The town is also the home of South Africa's dried-fruit industry.

Experience life as the pioneers lived in years gone by at the Kleinplasie Living Open Air Museum. The KWV Brandy Cellar, the largest of its kind in the world, offers cellar tours and brandy tasting.

Tulbagh is famous for its heritage, historical homesteads and magnificent country living. Church Street, home to 32 national monuments, constitutes the largest concentration of national monuments in one street in South Africa.

Ceres, named after the Roman goddess of fruitfulness, is the largest deciduous fruit-producing region in South Africa. Tours are offered at various fruit farms. The area also boasts several 4x4 trails, horse-riding, mountain-biking and abseiling.

The **Hex River Valley** is the largest producer of table grapes in southern Africa. Visitors can pick their own grapes at harvest time and sample the variety of export-quality produce. The well-known Hex River 4x4 trail and the Ochre San rock art trails are a must for nature lovers.

De Doorns is situated in the heart of the Hex River Valley.

Situated on the Breede River, **Bonnievale** features several cheese factories. For the adventurous outdoor enthusiast there are canoe trips, birdwatching and riverboating.

Known as The Valley of Wine and Roses, **Robertson** is one of the most beautiful areas in South Africa. Surrounded by vineyards, orchards, delectable fruit and radiant roses, Robertson produces connoisseur-quality wines and is also known for its thoroughbred horses.

Renowned for its muscadel wines, **Montagu** is the gateway to the Klein Karoo and is set in a fertile valley. Relax in the healing waters of the Avalon Springs or visit the waterfowl breeding camp, the largest of its kind in the Western Cape.

The area also offers several hiking trails, game-viewing drives, guided cultural tours and excellent rock climbs.

The picturesque village of **Gouda** is renowned for the Parrotts Den Pub, a living museum in the Gouda Hotel.

McGregor has a wealth of fascinating whitewashed, thatched cottages and well-preserved Victorian houses, making it one of the best-preserved examples of mid-19th century architecture in the Western Cape.

Prince Alfred Hamlet is the gateway to the Gydo Pass, known for its scenic views. This quaint village lies in an important deciduous-fruit farming area.

Hidden amidst vineyards and wine estates lies the picturesque town of **Rawsonville**, renowned for its array of award-winning wines. Tourists can enjoy an afternoon drive along the awe-inspiring Slanghoek Valley, with its lush vineyards and breathtaking views, or relax in the warm-water mineral springs at Goudini Spa.

West Coast

The West Coast is a region of extreme beauty and contrast. The solitary coast's scenic beauty is challenged only by rich culinary experiences of mussels, oysters, calamari, crayfish and abalone in season, or linefish pulled from the Benguela current's cold waters. The area is a birdwatcher's paradise. In addition, every year migrating whales visit the coastal waters from July.

Within the first two months of the first good winter rains, wild flowers on the West Coast explode in a brilliant array of colour.

The Swartland region is known for its undulating wheat fields, vineyards, wineries and outdoor activities. Further north, visitors encounter the fertile Olifants River Valley and the vast plains of the Knersvlakte with its wealth of indigenous succulent plants.

The town of **Darling** draws visitors to its country museum and art gallery, annual wild flower and orchid shows, basket factory and wine cellars. The entertainment venue Evita se Perron is situated at the old Darling Railway Station and offers top entertainment from South African entertainers.

Malmesbury is the biggest town in the Swartland. Major attractions include Bokomo Mills, the Malmesbury Museum, the Sugarbird glazed fruit factory and the historical walk-about.

The Riebeek Valley is known for its scenic beauty. The area has become a popular haven for well-known artists of various disciplines. Wines and olives can be tasted at various cellars.

Elands Bay is a popular holiday resort and surfer's paradise. Khoi and San rock art can be viewed at the Elands Bay caves.

Moorreesburg and **Koringberg** are major wheat-distributing towns. Tourists can visit the Wheat Industry Museum, one of only three in the world. Birdwatching, hiking, 4x4 routes, clay-pigeon shooting, mountain-bike trails, canoeing and water-skiing at Misverstand are popular activities.

Yzerfontein is famous for its unspoilt beaches, fynbos, beautiful views and whale watching. Another major attraction is the historical lime furnaces.

Langebaan is a popular holiday destination. The West Coast National Park, an internationally renowned wetland which houses about 60 000 waterbirds and waders, attracts thousands of visitors each year. The park is also the site where the oldest anatomically modern fossilised human footprints were discovered.

The Langebaan Lagoon forms part of the park and is zoned for specific activities. The Postberg section of the park, across the lagoon, is famous for its wild flowers blooming mainly during August and September.

Cape Columbine at **Paternoster** is the last manned lighthouse built on the South African coast. The Columbine Nature Reserve is home to many seabird species.

Saldanha is a watersport enthusiast's paradise. Other attractions include Doc's Cave, a landmark on the scenic breakwater drive, and the Hoedjieskoppie

Southern Africa has become one of the most popular big-game hunting regions in the world. It offers a great variety to trophy hunters, including the Big Five, namely elephant, white rhino, lion, leopard and buffalo, as well as 26 species of antelope.

The hunting proclamations of the various provinces differ and are promulgated annually. The hunting season is normally during the winter months, from May to the end of July.

Most species may be hunted legally by non-landowners during the hunting season, provided they have the written consent of the landowner and a valid hunting permit issued by the appropriate conservation authority.

Trophy hunting by overseas clients is subject to uniform legislation throughout South Africa, and all hunters are required to be accompanied by registered professional hunters and have their hunts arranged by approved hunting outfitters.

All nine provinces provide schedules of ordinary, protected and specially protected game. Ordinary game may be hunted under licence during an open season. Protected game may be hunted only under permit and licence, the fee depending on the species. Specially protected game, which includes grysbok, klipspringer, red hartebeest, giraffe, black rhinoceros, pangolin and antbear, may not be hunted at all.

Nature Reserve. There are various hiking trails in the SAS Saldanha Nature Reserve.

St Helena Bay is best known for the Vasco Da Gama Monument and Museum. Fishing (snoek in season), hiking, bird and whale-watching opportunities also draw many visitors.

Vredenburg, the business centre of the area, offers shopping opportunities, cinemas and a golf course with a bird hide where various species can be viewed.

Lambert's Bay is a traditional fishing village with Bird Island as a tourist attraction. It is a breeding ground for African penguins, Cape cormorants and other sea birds. Visitors can also watch southern right whales from July to November.

Piketberg offers arts and crafts, fauna and flora, wine culture and recreation. The Goedverwacht and Wittewater Moravian mission stations are situated close to the town.

Porterville is famous for its Disa Route (best in January and February). The Groot Winterhoek Mountain Peak in the Groot Winterhoek Wilderness Area is the second-highest in the Western Cape. The Dasklip Pass is popular with hang gliders.

At **Velddrif/Laaiplek**, visitors can indulge in some bokkem (a West Coast salted-fish delicacy) at factories along the Berg River. Tourists can also visit the salt-processing factory or the West Coast Art Gallery in town.

The citrus area in the Olifants River Valley is the third-largest in South Africa. The wine route from Citrusdal to Lutzville boasts a selection of internationally acclaimed wines. The world-renowned rooibos tea is also produced here.

Citrusdal is famous for its citrus products and wines. The Citrusdal Museum depicts the pioneering days of the early colonists. The Goede Hoop Citrus Co-op is the largest single packing facility in South Africa. The annual Citrusdal Outdoor Calabash features, among others, 4x4 outings, lectures and visits to rock-art sites, and an arts and crafts market.

The Sandveldhuisie is a recently built example of a typical Sandveld dwelling. There are several recognised mountain-biking, walking, hiking and canoeing trails and a sky-diving club. The Cederberg Wilderness Area features the elephant's foot plant, the rare snow protea, and some of the best examples of San rock art in the Western Cape.

Visitors to **Clanwilliam** can visit the rooibos and velskoen factories and the grave of the well-known South African poet Louis Leipoldt. Various historical buildings can also be viewed. The Clanwilliam and Bulshoek dams are popular among watersport enthusiasts.

Wupperthal, at the foot of the Cederberg mountains, features the oldest Rhenish Mission Station. Proceeds from 4x4 trails in the area go to community coffers for establishing new hiking trails and building more overnight huts and guest-houses.

Vredendal is the centre of the Lower Olifants River Valley. Major attractions include marble-processing and manufacturing, industrial mines (dolomite and limestone), the KWV Grape Juice Concentrate Plant and Distillery, and the South African Dried Fruit Co-op. The town is also home to the Vredendal Wine Cellar, the largest co-operative wine cellar under one roof in the southern hemisphere.

The picturesque town of **Doringbaai** with its attractive lighthouse is well known for its seafood.

Strandfontein, situated about 8 km north of Doring Bay, is essentially a holiday and retirement resort. It offers a breathtaking view of the ocean.

Klawer was named after the wild clover growing in the area. During the flower season, the area is a kaleidoscope of colour. There are hiking trails and river-rafting along the Doring River.

Lutzville and **Koekenaap** are synonymous with wine and flowers in season.

Visitors can also view the Sishen-Saldanha Railway Bridge. Where the railway line spans the Olifants River, it is divided into 23 sections, each 45 m long. The 14 100-ton deck was pushed into position over teflon sheets with hydraulic jacks from the bridgehead. It is the longest bridge in the world built using this method.

Vanrhynsdorp houses the largest succulent nursery in South Africa. The Latsky Radio Museum houses a collection of old valve radios, some dating back to 1924. Birdwatching, mountain-biking, day walks, and hiking and 4x4 trails abound. The Troe-

Troe and Rietpoort mission stations are a must-see for historians.

Overberg

In the most southerly region of Africa, only one hour east of Cape Town, lies a fertile area surrounded by mountains and sea, called the Overberg.

The **Hangklip-Kleinmond** area comprises **Kleinmond**, **Betty's Bay**, **Pringle Bay** and **Rooiels**. It is a popular holiday region, ideal for whale watching, and includes the Kleinmond Coastal Nature Reserve and the Harold Porter Botanical Garden.

The Penguin Reserve at Stoney Point, **Betty's Bay**, is one of two breeding colonies of the jackass penguin on the African continent.

South Africa's first international biosphere reserve, the Kogelberg Biosphere Reserve, was proclaimed by the United Nations Educational, Scientific and Cultural Organisation in 1999. It runs along the coast from Gordon's Bay to the Bot River Vlei, stretching 2 km out to sea, and inland to the Groenlandberg, the mountains near Grabouw.

Hermanus is a popular holiday resort, famous for the best land-based whale watching in the world.

Stanford is one of the few villages in South Africa where the market square has been retained. The central core of the village has been proclaimed a national conservation area.

Gansbaai is known for its excellent rock and boat angling, diving, shark-cage diving and whale watching. The Danger Point Lighthouse, named as such because of the ships that have been wrecked and lives that have been lost on this dangerous coast, is open to the public.

De Kelders is the only freshwater cave on the African coast. Spectacular views of southern right whales can be enjoyed from the cliffs at De Kelders and along the coast to Pearly Beach. Also popular are white-shark tours, diving safaris and fishing trips.

Elim was founded by German missionaries in 1824, with its only inhabitants being members of the Moravian Church. Visitors are welcome to attend services. The Old Watermill (1833) has been restored and declared a national monument.

Popular sites in **Napier** include the Militaria Museum and Rose Boats and Toy Museum. The Shipwreck Museum in **Bredasdorp**, founded in 1975, specialises in shipwrecks found along the South African coastline.

De Mond Nature Reserve boasts rare bird species including the damara tern and giant tern.

The Geelkop Nature Reserve derives its name from the mass of yellow flowering plants, particularly leucadendrons, which cover the hill during spring.

The lighthouse at **L'Agulhas**, which forms part of the Agulhas National Park, is the country's second-oldest working lighthouse. It celebrated its 150th anniversary in 1999.

The Agulhas National Park, home to a rich and diverse plant population, includes more than 110 *Red Data Book* species. Among these are the endangered Cape platanna and microfrog, and rare coastal birds such as the African oystercatcher. The damara tern finds the area ideal for breeding.

At **Cape Agulhas**, the southernmost tip of the continent, the waters are cleaved into the Indian and Atlantic oceans.

Struisbaai has the longest white coastline in the southern hemisphere.

Arniston was named Waenhuiskrans (coach-house cliff) by the local fishers in honour of the huge sea cave capable of housing several ox-wagons. For outsiders it was named after the *Arniston*, a ship wrecked here in 1815. The Waenhuiskrans Cave can be explored at low tide.

The De Hoop Nature Reserve on the way to Swellendam includes an internationally renowned wetland and bird sanctuary. It is a winter retreat for the southern right whale and the Western Cape's only Cape griffen vulture colony.

The red Bredasdorp lily and many species of protea and erica are found in the Heuningberg Nature Reserve.

Swellendam is well-known for its youngberries and eclectic architecture. The Drostdy Museum consists of a group of buildings containing a huge selection of period furniture. The Bontebok National Park, about 7 km from Swellendam, provides sanctuary to the threatened bontebok.

Known for its world-class wine, **Barrydale** offers the visitor fruit and fresh air in abundance.

Situated on the N2, about 160 km from Cape Town, **Riviersonderend** offers beautiful mountain and river scenery, a nine-hole golf course and sightings of the blue crane.

Caledon is famous for its natural mineral waters, hot springs and wild-flower shows. Southern Associated Maltsters is the only malt producer for the South African lager beer industry and the largest in the southern hemisphere.

Genadendal is the oldest Moravian village in Africa, with church buildings and a school dating back to 1738. The Genadendal Mission and Museum Complex documents the first mission station in South Africa.

The Theewaterskloof Dam outside **Villiersdorp** is the seventh-largest dam in the country. The Villiersdorp Wild Flower Garden and Nature Reserve boasts an indigenous herb garden and a reference library.

The **Grabouw/Elgin** district produces about 60% of South Africa's total apple exports. The valley is also renowned for cultivating fresh chrysanthemums, roses and proteas. The Elgin Apple Museum is one of only two in the world. Sir Lowry's Pass offers spectacular views of False Bay from Gordon's Bay to Cape Point.

Northern Cape

Characterised by its vast expanses of space and silence, blazing summer sunshine and interesting and friendly people, the Northern Cape is a province rich with culture.

Diamond fields

The Big Hole in **Kimberley** is the largest hand-dug excavation in the world. In 1871, diamonds were discovered at the site and mined manually by prospectors. The Kimberley Tram Service dates from the beginning of the century and still transports passengers from the City Hall to the Mine Museum.

Underground mine tours are a big attraction, as are the famous ghost tours, during which many historical buildings are seen from a different perspective. Hand and mechanical diamond-digging by private diggers can be viewed by appointment.

The McGregor Museum houses invaluable collections of the archaeological finds in the area, as well as San art works. The house where Sol Plaatje (African National Congress founding member and human-rights activist) lived in Kimberley, boasts a library of Plaatje's and other black South African writers' works, and several displays, including a portrayal of black involvement in the Anglo-Boer/South African War.

A township tour of **Galeshewe** provides a fresh perspective on South Africa's socio-historical realities. Pan African Congress founder Robert Sobukwe's house is worth a visit.

The Magersfontein Battlefield outside Kimberley with its original trenches and other defences intact, is the site of the Boers' crushing defeat of the British during the siege of Kimberley.

A cultural centre at Wildebeestkuil outside Kimberley features !Xun and Khwe artwork for sale and a tour of rock engravings by these indigenous people.

A short distance from Kimberley is the mining town **Barkley West**, which, due to its proximity to the Vaal River, is a favourite spot for many water-sport enthusiasts and anglers.

Tucked along the Vaal River near Barkley West lies the Vaalbos National Park. The park is not only home to large raptors, but is also a breeding centre for endangered African herbivores such as rhino, roan, sable and disease-free buffalo.

Kalahari

At **Black Rock**, visitors are afforded the opportunity to view a worked-out manganese mine.

Danielskuil lies at the foot of the Kuruman hills. The Tswana people occupied it before it became home to the Griquas. Boesmansgat, on the farm Mount Carmel outside Danielskuil, is a unique natural sinkhole – the second-deepest and largest of its kind in the world.

Known as the Oasis of the Kalahari, **Kuruman** is blessed with a permanent and abundant source of water. Its water flows from Gasegonyana (Tswana for 'the little water calabash') – commonly called the Eye of Kuruman.

Moffat's Mission in Kuruman is a tranquil place featuring the house of missionary Robert Moffat, the church he built, and several other buildings. Moffat translated the Bible into Setswana – the first African language in which the Bible was made accessible.

The printing press on which he printed the first 2 000 copies can still be viewed. The church seats 800 people and is still in use. David Livingstone married Moffat's daughter and started many famous travels from this mission station.

The Wonderwerk Cave at Kuruman features extensive San paintings that may be viewed by appointment.

The Kalahari Raptor Centre cares for injured birds and many of these majestic birds can be seen at close quarters. Another marvel is the Witsand Nature Reserve situated about 80 km south-west of **Postmasburg**, which features a 100-m high dune of brilliant white sand. It stretches for about 9 km and is about 2 km wide.

Green Kalahari

The roaring sands on the farm Doornaar near Groblershoop is an interesting site. The white dunes, surrounded by typically red Kalahari dunes, are said to 'roar' when the wind blows.

Eleven water wheels are still used today along the hand-built irrigation canals at **Kakamas**. The Orange River Wine Cellar Co-op Rockery Route runs between Keimoes and Kakamas.

Kanoneiland is a settlement on the biggest island in the Orange River.

At **Keimoes**, the Orange River flows at its widest. The Tierberg Nature Reserve offers spectacular views of the Keimoes Valley and the many islands in the Orange River. The original irrigation canal system is still in use. The Orange River Wine Cellar Co-op's largest cellar is situated here.

Kenhardt is the oldest town in the Lower Orange River area. The Quiver Tree Forest and Kokerboom Hiking Trail, consisting of between 4 000 and 5 000 quiver trees, are within easy driving distance of the town.

Upington is the commercial, educational and social centre of the Green Kalahari, owing its prosperity to agriculture and its irrigated lands along the Orange River. A camel-and-rider statue in front of the town's police station pays tribute to the 'moun-

ties', who patrolled the harsh desert territory on camels.

The South African Dried Fruit Co-operative is the second-largest and one of the most modern of its kind in the world. Tours of the plant are offered and freshly packed dried fruit is sold.

The Orange River displays its impressive power at the Augrabies Falls, also known as the Place of Great Noise, in the Augrabies Falls National Park. Visitors can hire canoes to ensure closer contact with the natural heritage surrounding the world's sixth-largest waterfall.

The Kgalagadi Transfrontier Park comprises half-a-million hectares of sparsely vegetated, red sand dunes and dry riverbeds within South Africa's borders. Straddling the Green Kalahari and Botswana, the park is a two-million ha sanctuary for antelope, gemsbok, springbok, blue wildebeest, red hartebeest, eland, the Kalahari lion, leopard, cheetah and smaller game, including mongoose, porcupine and honey badger.

Fifty-eight mammal, 55 reptile, countless insect and a host of plant species share the desert and dry savannah, while 260 species of bird, including at least 20 species of raptor, share the endless skies.

Namaqualand

The indigenous people of the Namaqualand region are the Namas. They speak their own language and can still be found in Namaqualand. Their traditional Nama reed huts still abound in **Leliefontein**, **Nourivier** and **Steinkopf**.

Namaqualand annually puts on a spectacular show in spring when an abundance of wild flowers cover vast tracts of desert. The flowers sprout and survive for a brief period before they wilt and disappear just as suddenly in the blistering heat and dry conditions.

The small town of **Garies** is the centre for those setting out to enjoy spring's show of exuberance in the Kamiesberg.

After diamonds were discovered along the West Coast in 1925, **Alexander Bay** was known for its mining activities. The town is no longer a high-security area and no permits are needed to enter. The Alluvial Diamond Mine paints a picture of the history of the area. The town also features the world's largest desert lichenfield with some 26 species.

At **Hondeklip Bay**, visitors can dive for crayfish and watch the local fishermen conduct their trade.

Established as a small-vessel harbour and railway junction in 1954 for the copper-mining industry, **Port Nolloth** is a centre for the small-scale diamond recovery and crayfish industries. It is the only holiday resort on the Diamond Coast. Fish and crayfish can be bought from the local factory when in season.

Set in a narrow valley bisecting the granite domes of the Klein Koperberge lies **Springbok**.

South of Springbok, near Kamieskroon, lies the Skilpad Wild Flower Reserve, part of the Namaqua National Park, which captures the full grandeur of the flower season. The 1 000-ha reserve operates only during the flower season.

The Goegap Nature Reserve comprises 15 004 ha of typically granite, rocky hills and sandy flats. The reserve also offers a 4x4, and several hiking and mountain-biking trails.

Namaqualand is also home to the Richtersveld National Park, the only contractual national park.

Upper (Bo-Karoo)

One of the Northern Cape's most beautiful towns, Colesberg, is flanked by the Towerberg.

The town features one of the country's last working horsemills. An Anglo-Boer/South African War tour is also on offer. A weekend tour includes a visit to the Norvalspont prisoner-of-war camp and cemetery. Colesberg has bred many of the country's top merino sheep. It is also renowned for producing high-quality racehorses.

De Aar is the most important railway junction in South Africa. The author Olive Schreiner lived in the town for many years. Visitors can dine in her house, which has since been converted into a restaurant.

Hanover is known for its handmade shoes and articles, made mostly from sheepskin and leather.

The Star of South Africa diamond was discovered at **Hopetown**. The town, which is steeped in history, also features an old toll house and a block house dating from the Anglo-Boer/South African War.

At **Wonderdraai** near **Prieska**, visitors can visit the horseshoe-shaped island formed by the flow of the Orange River. It seems as if the river turns to flow uphill.

Vanderkloof was built to house people building the Vanderkloof Dam. Today, it is a flourishing holiday resort. Visitors can enjoy waterskiing, boardsailing, boating and swimming, or visit the Eskom Hydroelectric Power Station situated within the dam's wall.

Victoria West is home to the Apollo Theatre, South Africa's last operational art deco movie theatre from the 1950s. The theatre comes alive each September with the Apollo Film Festival.

The Victoria West Nature Reserve is the habitat of the rare riverine rabbit.

Hantam Karoo

Near the small town of **Brandvlei** lies Verneukpan, where Sir Malcolm Campbell unsuccessfully attempted to break the world land-speed record in 1929.

Carnarvon is well-known for its corbelled domed-roofed houses built of flat stones because of a lack of wood. The floors of these interesting houses were smeared and coloured with a rich red mixture of fat and oxblood, polished with smooth stone.

The mountain tortoises at the Carnarvon Nature Reserve each respond to their name and fetch a titbit from visitors when called.

A few kilometres outside **Fraserburg** lies the Gansfontein Palaeosurface. Discovered in 1968, it comprises several trackways of large, four-footed, five-toed mammalian reptiles. The prints are estimated to be some 190 million years old.

Sutherland, birthplace of well-known Afrikaans author and poet N.P. van Wyk Louw is known for its brilliant night skies and cold, biting winters.

The *sterboom* (star tree), which blossoms in September, is found only in Sutherland.

The Southern African Large Telescope at Sutherland will boast a science-education centre based in Sutherland and a visitor's centre adjacent to the telescope sites on the mountainside. Observation telescopes will be available to the public on open nights.

Free State

The Free State lies in the heart of South Africa with the Kingdom of **Lesotho** nestling in the hollow of its bean-like shape. Between the Vaal River in the north and the Orange River in the south, this immense rolling prairie stretches as far as the eye can see. This central region is characterised by endless rolling prairies of wheat, sunflower and maize fields, and forms the principle bread basket of South Africa.

Motheo

With its King's Park Rose Garden containing more than 4 000 rose bushes, the Free State's major city, **Bloemfontein**, has rightfully earned the nickname City of Roses. The city also hosts an annual rose festival.

The *Eerste Raadsaal* (First Parliament Building), built in 1849 as a school, is Bloemfontein's oldest surviving building. Still in its original condition, this historical building is used as the seat of the Provincial Legislature.

The National Afrikaans Literary Museum and Research Centre has a repository of works by prominent Afrikaans authors. Exhibits in the Afrikaans Music Museum and the Theatre Museum (part of the centre) include old musical instruments, sheet music, costumes, photographs and furniture.

The national museum is notable for its wide collection of fossils, cultural-historical exhibits and archaeological displays, including the Florisbad skull, which was discovered in the 1930s at the Florisbad spring, about 50 km north of Bloemfontein.

The National Women's Memorial is a sandstone obelisk, 36,5 m high, which commemorates the women and children who died in concentration camps during the Anglo-Boer/South African War from 1899 to 1902. Visitors are afforded a glimpse into life in the concentration and prisoner-of-war camps. The research library contains an extensive collection of Africana.

The Old Presidency dates back to 1885 and was the official residence of three presidents of the former Republic of the Orange Free State. It houses a museum depicting their respective terms of office, and a cultural centre for art exhibitions, theatrical productions and musical events.

The Observatory Theatre in Bloemfontein's game reserve is a unique attraction.

Bloemfontein has a busy cultural and social events calendar. One of the annual events not to be missed is the Manguang African Cultural Festival, popularly known as the Macufe Arts Festival, in September.

The Sand du Plessis Theatre and Art Gallery at Oliewenhuis are also worth visiting.

Botshabelo (Place of Refuge) is 45 km from Bloemfontein on the N8 road to Lesotho, and is believed to be the largest township settlement in the Free State – and the second-largest in South Africa after Soweto.

Nearby, the town of **Thaba Nchu** features luxury hotels and a casino, with the Maria Moroka Nature Reserve surrounding Thaba Nchu Sun and the Setlogelo Dam.

Xhariep

Bethulie used to be a London Missionary Society station. The original mission buildings still stand.

The Pellissier House Museum depicts the history of events in the area.

The Gariep Dam, more than 100 km long and 15 km wide, is part of the Orange River Water Scheme, the largest inland expanse of water in South Africa.

Situated between the dam and Bethulie lies the Gariep Dam Nature Reserve. On the southern side of the dam lies the Oviston Nature Reserve.

Philippolis, the oldest town in the Free State, was founded as a London Missionary Society station in 1824. It was the first mission station in the province.

Trompsburg is the hub of the Free State Merino sheep-farming industry.

The Tussen-die-Riviere Nature Reserve reputedly supports more game than any other sanctuary in the Free State. It is reserved for hunters in autumn and winter.

A fountain near **Koffiefontein** was a favourite outspan for transport riders in the 19th century. In June 1870, one of these transport riders picked up a diamond near the fountain. This prompted the usual diamond rush and by 1882, Koffiefontein was a booming town with four mining companies.

Thabo Mofutsanyana

With its beautiful snow-capped mountains providing a backdrop to numerous romantic hide-aways, this untouched, pristine area with its breathtaking scenery possesses a grandeur of majestic proportion.

The Basotho Cultural Village in the QwaQwa Nature Reserve is a living museum where visitors can witness the Sotho traditions and lifestyle in the chief's kraal.

Clocolan is known for its cherry trees, which provide a spectacular sight when they blossom in spring. San rock paintings and engravings are also found in the area.

Clarens is often described as the Jewel of the Free State, owing to the spectacular scenery. San paintings are found on farms in the area. Close by, the Highlands Route meanders along the foothills of the Maluti mountains. One can also explore the magnificent mountain scenery by bike.

Ficksburg is known for its cherry and asparagus farms. A cherry festival is held annually in November. The town is a gateway to the Mountain Kingdom of Lesotho.

The Golden Gate Highlands National Park, known for its beautiful scenery, is a very popular holiday destination. A vulture restaurant enables visitors to observe these scavengers closely. San paintings can also be viewed.

The Highlands Route follows the Lesotho border via **Ladybrand** and ends at **Zastron** in the south. San caves and rock art are some of the main features of the route.

The birdwatching mecca of Seekoeivlei Nature Reserve near **Memel** constitutes a wetland with Ramsar status, and is surrounded by private game and holiday farms.

Lejweleputswa region

Bethlehem lies on the banks of the Jordaan River and was founded by the Voortrekkers during the 1840s. The museum in Miller Street depicts the history of the area. The banks of the Jordaan River form part of the Pretoriuskloof Nature Reserve – a sanctuary for birds and small game.

Van Reenen's Pass winds through the Drakensberg, and was originally used by migrating herds of zebra, hartebeest, blesbok and wildebeest. The Llandaff Oratory in the nearby village of **Van Reenen** is believed to be the smallest Roman Catholic church in the world.

At **Harrismith**, there are various memorials in honour of those who fought in the Anglo-Boer/South African War and World War I. Of particular interest is a memorial for the Scots Guards and Grenadier Guards. Platberg, the 2 394 m 'flat mountain', is the town's landmark. A well-known race, claimed by some to be the toughest in the country, is run annually up, along and back down the mountain. Sterkfontein Dam is ideal for water sports and fishing.

The Riemland Museum in **Heilbron** depicts the heritage and agricultural activities of the region.

The QwaQwa district is a traditional home to the Basotho people. Karakul carpets, mohair, wall hangings, copper, glassware and brass are made and sold at **Phuthaditjhaba**. The Metsi Matsho and Fika Patso dams are renowned for trout fishing.

Welkom is known for its gold mines. It is also the only city in the country where traffic circles are used instead of traffic lights.

The world's deepest wine cellar is at the St Helena Mine which is 857 m below the Earth's surface.

Bothaville is regarded as the centre of the Free State Maize Route. The NAMPO Harvest Farm and Festival attracts more than 20 000 visitors each year and is the second-largest private agricultural show in the world. Bothaville also hosts the annual Food and Witblits Festival, drawing visitors from all over South Africa.

Winburg is the oldest town and first capital of the former Republic of the Orange Free State. The Voortrekker Museum, using life-size models, depicts the daily routine of the trekkers. A concentration camp cemetery is situated close by.

Sasolburg originated in 1954 with the establishment of Sasol, the synthetic fuel producer.

Parys, which is situated on the banks of the Vaal River, is a popular holiday destination.

The Vredefort Dome is a crater, caused by the collision of a meteorite with the Earth many years ago. In July 2005, it was declared a World Heritage Site.

It features unique fauna and flora, including 100 different plant species, more than 300 types of birds and a variety of small mammals. Various hiking and mountain-bike trails are also on offer.

Eastern Cape

The main feature of the Eastern Cape is its magnificent coastline. With its wide open sandy beaches, secluded lagoons and towering cliffs, the Indian Ocean coastline provides the province with a rich natural tourist attraction, which is also a paradise for watersports enthusiasts.

Added to the diverse coastal experiences are more than 60 state-owned game reserves and more than 30 private game farms, which collectively cover an area greater than the Kruger National Park.

Amatola Mountain region

The Amatola mountains are famous for their scenery and history, and stretch from **Adelaide** in the east to **Stutterheim** in the west. With its lush forests and ancient battlefields, it is an area steeped in Xhosa culture and early settler history.

The dense forests of the Amatolas are a haven for the endangered Cape parrot. It was also home to the first dinosaur to be identified in South Africa, 'The Blinkwater Monster', a large fossilised reptile discovered near **Fort Beaufort**.

Outdoor enthusiasts enjoy **Cathcart**, where trout-fishing, hiking, riding and birdwatching are among the attractions.

The Amatole Hiking Trail is a well-known scenic but strenuous trail.

The coastal city of **Port Elizabeth**, which has earned the name of Friendly City, is a superb holiday destination, offering a diverse mix of eco-attractions. The Isuzu National Sailing Week is held annually in April in the waters of Algoa Bay.

The city boasts various scuba-diving sites. Visitors can also visit Bay World with its oceanarium and snake park, and many splendid museums. Other attractions include the Greater Addo Elephant National Park and game reserves; the traditional healing village, Kaya Lendaba; birdwatching; air tours; canoeing; various mountain-bike and horse-riding trails; and organised outdoor excursions.

The Greater Addo Elephant National Park nurtures some 400 elephants; one of the largest concentrations of elephant to be found in the world. Plans are underway to expand the park to incorporate a marine reserve from the Sundays River Mouth to Cape Pardone, including off-shore islands. It will feature the Big Five as well as southern right whales and great white sharks.

Tourists can also explore the Donkin Heritage Trail, take a ride on the famous Apple Express and go hiking along the site of ancient shipwrecks on the Sacramento Trail.

Wild Coast

Since Portuguese mariners first pioneered the sea route around the Cape to India, this notorious coast has claimed countless ships.

Southern right and humpback whales and their calves are regularly spotted from the high dunes, usually between May and November, while common and bottlenose dolphins are often seen close to shore.

The entire region, once known as the Transkei homeland, is the home of a major section of the Xhosa-speaking southern Nguni (or Pondo) tribes. Brightly coloured examples of their beadwork, together with traditional pottery and basketry can be bought from roadside vendors and at some trading posts.

Visitors to the rural village of Qunu can view the childhood home of former President Mandela. In the city of Umtata, the Nelson Mandela Museum tells the story of this great figure.

The alignment of the N2 national route along the Wild Coast will help open up investment opportunities in this area.

Coffee Bay is popular among surfers, anglers and shell collectors.

Near **Coffee Bay** to the south, is the prominent rock formation called the Hole-in-the-Wall. The local Xhosa call this place *Izi Khaleni*, which means Place of the Thunder. During high tide, the waves move through the hole in such a way that the concussion can be heard throughout the valley.

Karoo

The vast plains of the Karoo have an air of grandeur and its many picturesque towns are steeped in history.

The Owl House in **Nieu Bethesda** displays the creative talent of the late Helen Martins. Statues of mermaids, wise men, camels, owls and churches create a wonderland in the garden. All the artworks were created with broken bottles, bits of mirror and cement.

More than 200 houses in **Graaff-Reinet** have been restored to their original Victorian appearance, and proclaimed national monuments. The Old Library Museum houses the Lex Bremner Fossil Collection of Karoo reptile fossils and a collection of Khoi and San art reproductions. Urquhart House has a popular genealogical research centre.

Almost 50 km south-west of Graaff-Reinet is the Kalkkop Crater, a gigantic circular impact. Kalkkop is of major scientific importance.

To the north-west of Graaff-Reinet lies the Valley of Desolation. A steep and narrow road leads into the mountains that surround the valley.

The Valley of Desolation is a national monument within the Karoo Nature Reserve, and was formed millions of years ago by weathering erosion.

The first evidence of the presence of dinosaurs in South Africa can be viewed at **Maclear**.

The Mountain Zebra National Park is a haven for the Cape mountain zebra species, which at one time inhabited most of the Cape.

The park saved these animals from extinction and today their population stands at about 350.

Other species found in the park include antelope, eland, African wildcat, bat-eared fox, and more than 200 bird species, including the pale-winged starling, booted eagle and the blue crane.

N6 Route

The route runs from Bloemfontein to East London. Popular attractions include the slopes of the Tiffindell Ski Resort and the streams filled with trout, as well as the many caves adorned with ancient rock art.

Several historic towns can be found in the region, including Barkly East, Rhodes, Lady Grey, Elliot, Aliwal North, Burgersdorp and Queenstown.

Sunshine Coast

The Sunshine Coast comprises miles of unspoilt sun-drenched beaches.

Port Alfred lies at the mouth of the Kowie River. Coastal hills are home to the oribi – a small territorial buck that was recently near extinction.

Inland, **Grahamstown** is sometimes referred to as the City of Saints, because of the more than 40 churches found in the town. The town is also known for the National Arts Festival, which is held here annually. During this time, Grahamstown is transformed into a dedicated arts venue where performers, visual artists, audiences, writers and craftspeople fuse in a celebration of creative energy.

Other attractions include various museums and historical buildings, the oldest post-box in South Africa, botanical gardens, the cathedrals of St Michael and St George, nature reserves and hiking trails.

Situated north-east of Grahamstown, the Great Fish River Reserve consists primarily of valley bushveld habitat and is surrounded by both tribal land and commercial game reserves and farms.

The reserve boasts abundant wildlife such as white rhino, giraffe, waterbuck, Cape buffalo, hippo, kudu, springbok and eland.

There are several historic forts and remains from the legendary frontier wars located in the area.

East London, South Africa's only river port city, was originally established as a supply port to serve the military headquarters at King William's Town. The city's own waterfront development, Latimer's Landing, is situated on the banks of the Buffalo River. The East London Aquarium houses approximately 400 different species of marine and freshwater animals.

The East London Museum depicts the natural environment and rich heritage of the region. Best known for the prehistoric coelacanth, the museum also displays reconstructions of the extinct dodo of Mauritius, along with the only extant dodo egg in the world.

The Baviaanskloof Wilderness Area is the largest of the inland protected areas and provides opportunities to visit spectacular fynbos-covered mountains on foot or in off-road vehicles.

Tsitsikamma

This region, stretching from **Plettenberg Bay** to **Jeffreys Bay**, is renowned for its dense forests, majestic mountains and deep river gorges. It forms the eastern end of the Garden Route.

The word tsitsikamma is derived from the Khoekhoen words *tse-tsesa* meaning clear and *gami* meaning water.

South Africa's first marine park, the Tsitsikamma National Park, extends along a rocky coastline of 50 km, and 3 km out to sea.

Inland, adventure seekers will find deep gorges and temperate evergreen forests criss-crossed by six hiking trails, including the five-day Otter Trail. The varied wildlife includes dolphins and whales, caracal, genet, chacma baboon, dassie and mongoose.

Another popular adventure is a black-water tubing experience on the Storms River.

Prominent bird species in the area are the African black oystercatcher, the orange-breasted sunbird, the Nerina trogan and the colourful Knysna loerie. A lucky few may catch a glimpse of the rare Cape clawless otter, after which the Otter Trail is named.

Limpopo

Limpopo is a land of dramatic contrasts characterised by hot savanna plains and mist-clad mountains, age-old indigenous forests and cycads alongside latter-day plantations, ancient mountain fortresses and the luxury of contemporary infrastructure and modern-day facilities.

Steeped in history, Limpopo celebrates a rich cultural heritage and at many archaeological sites the mysteries of the past and ancient peoples are still being unearthed. The present tranquillity of the province belies a turbulent past, to which many monuments and museums attest.

Much of the land, particularly in the Kruger National Park and other game and nature reserves is unspoilt, providing sanctuary to large numbers of game.

Waterberg

The Nylsvley Nature Reserve boasts one of the greatest concentrations of waterfowl and bushveld birds in South Africa. More than 400 species frequent the area.

The **Mokopane** vicinity has several nature reserves. The Arend Dieperink Museum features a fine cultural-historical collection and the Makapan caves are notable for their fossils. The caves are being developed into an archaeological site.

In July 2005, Makapan Valley was inscribed as an extension of The Cradle of Human Kind World Heritage Site. The Makapansgat caves and limeworks near Mokopane represent an archaeological site of global importance.

The **Thabazimbi** district has a large concentration of private game reserves and is one of the fastest-growing ecotourism areas in the country. The Marakele National Park is home to some rare yellowwood and cedar trees and is the world's largest colony of Cape vultures. It is a leader in the conservation of the black rhino outside of the Kruger National Park and the KwaZulu-Natal parks.

Bela-Bela is known for its hot springs. There are also a number of game reserves and leisure resorts in the area.

The Waterberg range is rich in indigenous trees, streams, springs, wetlands and bird life. Cliffs known as the Palace of the Vultures harbour a large breeding colony of Cape vultures. **Modimolle** is the region's main town.

Capricorn district

The Bakone Malapa Open-Air Museum outside **Polokwane** is a traditional Northern Sotho kraal. Men and women practise traditional skills such as making baskets, clay pots, furniture and utensils, and preparing hides.

Zion City at Moria near Polokwane is the headquarters of the Zion Christian Church, which attracts more than a million pilgrims every Easter.

Polokwane hosts a great variety of museums and art galleries.

Vhembe district

The Mapungubwe Archaeological Site, situated 80 km west of **Musina**, lies within the boundaries of the Mapungubwe National Park, (formerly known as Vhembe/Dongola National Park). It is one of the richest of its kind in Africa and is a World Heritage Site. Excavations in the 1930s uncovered a royal grave-yard, which included a number of golden artefacts, including the famous gold foil rhinoceros.

The Schoemansdal Voortrekker Town and Museum, west of **Makhado** (formerly known as Louis Trichardt), is built on the site of an original Voortrekker village and depicts their lifestyle between 1848 and 1852.

Also worth visiting is the Big Tree in the Mutale Municipality, which is the largest known baobab in southern Africa; the Tshatshingo potholes; the mystical lake of Dzivhafundudzi; and the holy forest and waterfalls at Phiphidi.

Mopani district

The Modjadji Nature Reserve, north of **Tzaneen**, is named after the legendary Rain Queen, Modjadji, who is believed to have settled in the area early in the 16th century. The reserve encompasses the world's largest concentration of the cycad species *Encephalartos transvenosus*, also known as the Modjadji cycad.

The Hans Merensky Nature Reserve and Mineral Spa on the southern banks of the Great Letaba River supports a large variety of game.

At the Tsonga Kraal Open-Air Museum, arts, crafts and traditional huts reflect the Tsonga lifestyle of 100 years ago.

The Kruger National Park (northern section) is one of South Africa's major tourist attractions. The park is home to a large number and wide variety of amphibians, reptiles and birds, as well as 147 mammal species, including the Big Five.

Thulamela, in the northern part of the Kruger National Park, was opened to guided groups in June 1997. This followed seven years of archaeological excavations, which brought to light the skeletons of two ancient royals and a multitude of artefacts, including gold bangles, beads and a double gong.

Bohlabela district

On the way to the Kruger National Park, visitors can enjoy the wildlife experiences at **Manyeleti**, the home of the Big Five. Adventurers can attempt mountain-climbing at the Mangwazi Nature Reserve and enjoy the Mapulaneng Trail at Zoeknog.

The Inyaka Dam at **Bushbuckridge** is also worth a visit.

North West

The North West is blessed with several cultural villages that entertain and enrich.

A number of excellent game reserves have been established, including the Pilanesberg National Park, known as the Jewel of the North West. It is set in a crater on an extinct volcano and is home to the Big Five as well as a wide variety of smaller game and birds.

Central district

The historic route of **Mafikeng** includes an Anglo-Boer/South African War siege site, the Molema House where Sol Plaatje lived while writing his *Mafikeng Diary*, and the Mafikeng Museum.

The Lichtenburg Game-Breeding Centre and the Botsalano Game Reserve are well worth a visit.

The Groot Marico region is known as mampoer country and visitors can embark on a mampoer and tobacco route. The Kortkloof Cultural Village is dedicated to the Tswana people.

Other attractions include the Wondergat; the Bosbult Monument, which commemorates a battle during the Anglo-Boer/South African War; the Kaditshwene Iron Age Village Ruins; and various hiking trails.

Eastern district

The Hartbeespoort Dam is a popular spot for week-end outings, breakfast runs and yachting. The Hartbeespoort Reptile and Animal Park is situated on the banks of the dam.

Cultural experiences in the area include the popular Mapoch and Gaabo Motho cultural villages as well as the Ring Wagon Inn.

The De Wildt Cheetah-Breeding and Research Centre specialises in the breeding of cheetah and other endangered wildlife species. Other places of interest include the Borakalalo Game Reserve, the Margaret Roberts Herb Farm and the Phaladingwe Nature Trail.

Bophirima district

The Taung skull fossil site and the blue pools are renowned for the Taung skull found in the Buxton quarries. In July 2005, the World Heritage Committee declared the Taung skull fossil site an extension of the Sterkfontein fossil hominid site. This region is popular with adventure-seekers – especially the 4x4 routes and hunting farms.

Rustenburg district

The Pilanesberg National Park supports more than 7 000 head of game and 350 bird species.

The Madikwe Game Reserve is home to a major game-relocation programme. Over 10 000 animals of 27 major species have been reintroduced under Operation Phoenix. A hot-air balloon ride, day and night game drives, and bushwalks are available. Sun City and the Palace of the Lost City are very popular tourist attractions offering gambling, golf, extravaganza shows, watersport and an artificial sea.

There are various hiking trails in the region. The Heritage Route starts at the Sterkfontein caves World Heritage Site and ends at Pilanesberg.

Southern district

The O.P.M. Prozesky Bird Sanctuary in **Potchefstroom** has over 200 bird species and is situated adjacent to the Mooi River. The Oudorp Hiking Trail takes visitors through the old part of **Klerksdorp** where 12 Voortrekker families settled.

Other attractions in the region include the Potchefstroom Lakeside Resort, the Faan Meintjies Nature Reserve in Klerksdorp, mine tours at **Orkney**, the Diggers Route at **Wolmaransstad** and the Bloemhof Dam Nature Reserve.

Mpumalanga

Mpumalanga – The Place Where The Sun Rises – epitomises every traveller's dream of the true African experience. Located in the north-eastern part of South Africa, the province is bordered by Mozambique to the east and the Kingdom of Swaziland to the south and east.

The climate and topography vary from cool highland grasslands at 1 600 m above sea level, through the middleveld and escarpment, to the subtropical Lowveld towards the Kruger National Park and many private game reserves. Scenic beauty, climate and wildlife, voted the most attractive features of South Africa, are found in abundance in this province.

Attractions range from game viewing and bird-watching to scenic drives across the valleys and peaks of the vast Drakensberg escarpment, and include agritourism, industrial and adventure tourism and cultural experiences. Historical sites and villages, old wagon routes and monuments mark events and characters who passed this way in search of adventure and wealth.

The cultural heritage of the province is varied and fascinating. The Ndebele beadwork and wall-painting in the north-west, the arts and crafts of the Lowveld and the different traditional villages throughout the province offer a unique insight into the people's history.

Nelspruit

Nelspruit is the capital of Mpumalanga and the commercial and administrative hub of the Lowveld. The Nelspruit Historical Trail is an hour-long route stretching from the Promenade Centre to the Civic Centre.

The Blue Train runs between Pretoria and Nelspruit from May to September on a trip called the 'Lowveld Experience'. Rovos Rail's trains also travel to Nelspruit.

The Green Heritage Hiking Trail in the Nelspruit Nature Reserve is one of several walks in the reserve and one of many in the region.

Not to be missed is the Lowveld Botanical Garden, as well as the Reptile Park, the Sudwala caves, P.R. Owen Dinosaur Park, and the tranquil town of **White River**. Well-known as an artists' haven and a gateway to the Kruger National Park, White River also boasts an orange winery.

Panorama

Barberton features many reminders of the early gold-rush era. Museums include Belhaven, Fernlea House and Stopforth House. The only known verdite deposits in the world are found in the rocks of the Barberton district. An annual Diggers Festival is held in September.

The Blyderivierspoort Nature Reserve near **Graskop** is characterised by striking rock formations and a rich diversity of plants. Within the reserve, the Bourke's Luck potholes were formed by river erosion and the action of flood water.

The spectacular Blyde River Canyon is a 26 km-long gorge carved out of the face of the escarpment, and is one of the natural wonders of Africa. The canyon is the third-largest in the world but the only green canyon, and hosts three rivers which feed the Blydepoort Dam at **Swadini**. God's Window provides a magnificent panoramic view across miles of densely forested mountains, the green Lowveld and the canyon. The Blyderivierspoort Hiking Trail is one of the most popular in the country. A number of other hiking trails are also available.

The southern section of the Kruger National Park, which is a major tourist attraction, falls within this region.

Kaapsehoop is a quaint historical village known for the wild horses that frequent the district. Blue swallows are regular visitors from September to April.

The **Lydenburg** Museum is situated in the Gustav Klingbiel Reserve, which is the site of archaeological ruins from the Later Iron Age. The Lydenburg heads, human-like masks dated to 500 AD, were discovered in this area.

Sabie is the centre of the largest man-made forest in South Africa. The Cultural Historical Forestry Museum depicts various aspects of the country's forestry industry. The Bridal Veil, Horseshoe and Lone Creek waterfalls, and Mac Mac pools and falls just outside **Sabie** are well worth a visit.

The 69-km Prospector's Trail starts at the Mac Mac Forest Station and leads to Bourke's Luck potholes.

At the Montrose Falls in **Schoemanskloof**, the Crocodile River cascades 12 m into a series of rock pools. It is also the starting point of the annual Lowveld Crocodile Canoe Marathon, held in February.

Pilgrim's Rest is a living museum and a replica of the early gold-mining town. The Alanglade House Museum offers guided tours of the former mine-manager's house, while the Diggings Museum just outside the town arranges guided tours of gold-panning activities. This area was the setting for *Jock of the Bushveld*, the novel by Sir Percy Fitzpatrick about the experiences of a man and his dog as they shared adventures in the world of African gold-mining. The Dredzen Shop Museum consists of a store stocked with a range of items in use nearly a century ago. The Pilgrim's Rest Festival is held annually in December.

Mount Sheba Nature Reserve, south of Pilgrim's Rest, is best known for its indigenous forest — one of few left in the region.

Highlands Meander

The Highlands Meander is a mecca for fly-fishers. It is in the placid and pristine waters of this region that one finds various stocks of fish, with trout as the major drawcard. The meander also offers numerous other activities.

At the Verloren Vlei and Steenkampsberg nature reserves (**Dullstroom**), one can get a rare glimpse of the three endangered crane species (the blue, wattled and crowned cranes).

The Loskop Dam Nature Reserve offers game watching, boating and fishing.

A large number of hiking trails are available, such as the Elandskrans Trail, which includes a 30-minute train ride between **Waterval-Boven** and **Waterval-Onder**.

Cultural Heartland

Visitors to the Cultural Heartland can immerse themselves in the true cultural heritage of Mpumalanga. Here, one can learn about the proud and welcoming Ndebele people, revered for the striking and colourful geometric patterns on their houses, clothing and beadwork.

This region also has illuminating historical sites such as the Botshabelo Historical Village, near Middelburg.

Cosmos Country

Cosmos Country covers parts of what is known as the energy belt of Mpumalanga, which is home to a number of power stations. This region also boasts the world's largest underground coal-mining complex and the Sasol plant renowned for its technology of extracting oil from coal.

The carpet of cosmos flowers that blossoms in late summer lures visitors to this region.

Wild Frontier

Various archaeological discoveries dating back almost three billion years were made in the imposing mountains of this region.

Visitors to this region have a rare glimpse of the inimitable San paintings embossed in some rocks.

The region also holds rich historical sentiments centered around the monument of the late Mozambican President, Samora Machel, constructed in the village of **Mbuzini**. Due to their proximity to this region, visitors have the opportunity to visit Swaziland and Mozambique in a short space of time.

Grass and Wetlands

Grass and Wetlands is indeed a paradise, with its variety of bird species. This region stretches across the deep valleys and mountains of the east where thermal springs bubble to the surface.

There are 270 pans and lakes within a 20 km radius of Lake Chrissie. In this region, visitors can take part in the unusual 'frogging expedition' or simply gaze at the stars during 'star-gazing weekends'.

Gauteng

Gauteng, the Place of Gold, is the economic powerhouse of South Africa. It is characterised by a cosmopolitan, multicultural mix of people from all walks of life. The province's unique cultural and social legacy is evident from the many excellent museums, theatres, cultural precincts and craft markets.

The Vaal Dam, which supplies water to most of Gauteng's residents, covers some 300 km² and is a popular venue for watersport. Numerous resorts line the shore. The dam also attracts a great diversity of birds.

Vanderbijlpark was built during the late 1940s by the then Iron and Steel Corporation to accommodate its employees.

The Sterkfontein caves near **Krugersdorp** are the site of the discovery of the skull of the famous

Mr Ples (previously known as Mrs Ples), an estimated 2,5 million-year-old hominid fossil, and Little Foot, an almost complete hominid skeleton some 3,3 million years old.

The broader Cradle of Humankind site consists of 47 000 ha, with numerous caves, the most famous of which is the Sterkfontein caves.

In 1999, Sterkfontein and its environs were declared a World Heritage Site.

Forty percent of all the world's human ancestor fossils have been found here, including several of the world's most famous and important fossils.

A further 500 hominid fossils and more than 9 000 stone tools have been excavated in the area, and work is ongoing.

The Krugersdorp Game Reserve provides sanctuary for several game species, including four of the Big Five. The African Fauna and Bird Park houses various species of wildlife and birds.

The South African National Railway and Steam Museum at Randfontein Estates Gold Mine outside Krugersdorp houses some of the country's old steam locomotives, a diesel-electric locomotive, and more than 50 vintage passenger coaches. Train rides are offered once a month.

A team of Lippizaner stallions performs every Sunday at the South African National Horsemanship Centre, in **Kyalami**, near Johannesburg.

Visitors to **Roodepoort** can go on walks and trails through the Kloofendal Nature Reserve, or enjoy a picnic or a show at the popular Kloofendal Amphitheatre. The Walter Sisulu National Botanical Garden (formerly known as the Witwatersrand National Botanical Garden) boasts a 70 m-high waterfall.

Forty kilometres north of Pretoria lies a ring of hills a kilometre in diameter and 100 m high. These are the walls of an impact crater left by an asteroid that hit the area some 200 000 years ago. The Tswaing Meteorite Crater is similar in size to the well-known Barringer Meteor Crater in Arizona, USA. The crater walls at Tswaing were originally about twice as high as they are today.

There is a museum adjacent to the crater. A path leads from the museum to the crater, along the rim, and down to the central lake. The crater is covered with indigenous trees and bushes which attract a variety of bird life.

The old mining town of **Cullinan** developed around the Premier Diamond Mine and many turn-of-the-century houses still stand. The mine has produced some of the world's most famous diamonds, including the Cullinan diamond, the world's largest at 3 106 carats.

Johannesburg

The Adler Museum of the History of Medicine depicts the history of medicine, dentistry and pharmacy in South Africa. The Pharmacy Museum in Melrose houses a large variety of medicines, including more than 670 traditional medicines that have been collected throughout southern Africa.

There is also a display of old prescription books and dictionaries used by pharmacists.

The Nelson Mandela Bridge is a landmark gateway into Newtown, also known as the arts precinct of Johannesburg. It is the largest cable-stayed bridge in southern Africa.

Museum Africa in Newtown tells the story of life in South Africa from the Stone Age to the Nuclear Age and beyond. The museum is located in the old fruit-and-vegetable building next to the Market Theatre.

The Market Theatre Complex comprises three theatres, an art gallery, restaurants and pubs.

A bronze statue of the champion of passive resistance, Mahatma Gandhi, can be seen in the city centre.

Lesedi Cultural Village in the Swartkops Hills north of Johannesburg gives visitors the opportunity to meet families of different cultural groupings. It features four traditional homesteads where visitors can spend the night with a family of their choice.

The Phumanegna Zulu Kraal is home to traditional Zulu people living and working there.

The Melville Koppies in Johannesburg was once the site of a Stone Age African village and iron-smelting works. Flora includes 80% of the species recorded on the Witwatersrand. It is open to the public from September to April.

Gold Reef City is a theme park based on Johannesburg during the gold-rush era.

The Apartheid Museum tells the story of the legacy of apartheid through exhibitions consisting of film footage, photographs, text panels and artefacts.

Constitution Hill opened to the public in March 2004. It features the impressive building housing South Africa's Constitutional Court, and offers visitors the chance to view the fort, the so-called native gaol, the women's gaol and the awaiting-trial block. Inmates imprisoned at these facilities include Mahatma Gandhi and Albert Luthuli, as well as the only woman to be executed in South Africa's history, Daisy de Melker.

At Santarama Miniland and Entertainment World visitors can explore models of South Africa's most popular beacons, such as Robben Island, Johannesburg International Airport, East London Harbour, and the Union Buildings in Pretoria.

The South African Museum of Military History houses an impressive collection of weaponry and uniforms from the two world wars.

The South African Transport Museum (**Heidelberg**) represents all aspects of South Africa's transport services.

A large, well-established park surrounds Zoo Lake, which is frequented by breeding bird colonies. Other attractions include jazz concerts, rowing boats for hire, a tea garden and a restaurant.

Soweto is a popular tourist destination. It is estimated that some 1 000 foreign tourists visit Soweto every day. Its tourism industry contributes about R143 million to Gauteng's GDP.

The two-bedroom house where former President Mandela lived before his incarceration has been declared a national monument and converted into a museum.

The Walter Sisulu Square in Kliptown (Soweto) is the place where the Freedom Charter was signed in 1955.

No tour of Soweto would be complete without a visit to the Hector Petersen Museum, which commemorates the people who died following the student uprising of 16 June 1976. The museum was named after the young boy who was the first person to be shot dead by police on that day.

Guest-houses and bed-and-breakfast establishments are a fast-growing phenomenon in Soweto.

Pretoria

A variety of historical buildings are found in the city, which is known as the Jacaranda City because of the many jacaranda trees that line its streets. When these are in full bloom in October, they cover the city in a lilac haze, providing spectacular views from the surrounding hills.

Church Square is centred around a statue of Paul Kruger, president of the former *Zuid-Afrikaansche Republiek*, and includes buildings such as the *Old Raadsaal* and the Palace of Justice.

Ten minutes away from Church Square is Freedom Park which is being built to commemorate the country's political history.

Once completed in 2007, the 35-ha site will comprise a garden of remembrance, a museum, and statues and sculptures to honour South Africans who contributed to the country's freedom and development.

The Kruger House Museum contains the personal belongings of President Kruger. Melrose House is a beautiful example of Victorian architecture. The Peace Treaty of Vereeniging, which ended the Anglo-Boer/South African War, was signed here in 1902.

Demonstrations at the Pioneer Open-Air Museum include milking cows, making butter and candles, baking bread and grinding coffee beans.

Other museums include the Police Museum, the Coert Steynberg Museum and the Transvaal Museum of Natural History.

The Voortrekker Monument also houses a museum and commemorates the Great Trek. Some 260 steps lead to the dome, where spectacular views of the city can be enjoyed. The monument receives about 200 000 visitors a year.

Fort Schanskop has been refurbished and boasts a 375-seat amphitheatre.

The Union Buildings were designed by Sir Herbert Baker and completed in 1913. They were the setting for the presidential inauguration of Nelson Mandela in 1994, and those of Thabo Mbeki on 16 June 1999 and 27 April 2004.

The Sammy Marks Museum just outside Pretoria dates from 1885. Rooms in the house are filled with Victorian paintings, furniture, silver and porcelain.

Visitors can relax at the tea garden and restaurant on the premises.

The General Smuts House Museum in Irene, south-east of Pretoria, contains the original furnishings of the Smuts family. A popular arts and craft market is held here on certain Saturdays.

The Rietvlei Nature Reserve is notable for its grass types, herbs, a large number of game and many bird species.

The Mapoch Ndebele Village, north of Pretoria, is being restored by its residents and the National Cultural History Museum. To develop the project into a viable, living tourist village, the 50 families staying there have undergone tourist-guide and business training. It is the first living cultural village in South Africa owned and managed by its residents.

Mamelodi is situated approximately 20 km from the city centre and features the Solomon Mahlangu Square, which is dedicated to this freedom fighter.

The Willem Prinsloo Agricultural Museum outside Pretoria centres around a farmstead dating from 1880. Traditional farming activities are demonstrated, and annual events include a prickly-pear festival, a mampoer festival and the Agricultural Museum Show.

KwaZulu-Natal

Also known as the Zulu Kingdom, KwaZulu-Natal is a many-splendoured interaction of natural wonders, ultra-modern facilities, fascinating cultural imprints and reminders of a dynamic history in a breathtakingly beautiful and varied setting.

Durban and surroundings

Tourist Junction, in Durban's historical station building, provides access to tourist information and accommodation bookings for Ezemvelo KwaZulu-Natal Wildlife and South African National Parks.

The Golden Mile skirts the main beaches of the Indian Ocean. Attractions include an amusement centre, paddling pools, paved walkways and fountains.

The uShaka Island marine theme park, oceanarium, dolphinarium and oceanographic research institute on Durban's Point opened in May 2004. This is the new home of a wide variety of sea life, including sharks, dolphins and seals.

There is a snorkelling trail and a tubing river around the park.

Durban's most popular fishing spot is situated at Blue Lagoon Beach at the wide Umgeni River mouth. Beyond the river, the La Lucia and Beachwood Mangroves nature reserves offer long, tranquil walks along empty sands.

The Durban area has more than 50 reserves, developed parks and specialised gardens, the most renowned being the Municipal Botanical Garden.

The Fitzsimons Snake Park offers lectures and venom-milking demonstrations. MiniTown is a model city depicting Durban's best-known buildings. Museums include the Natural History Museum, the Natural Science Museum, the Old House Museum and the Old Fort.

The Shree Ambalavaanar Alayam Temple (The Second River Temple) in **Cato Manor** was the first Hindu temple in Africa. It is a national monument.

The Juma Musjid Mosque is the largest mosque in the southern hemisphere. Daily tours are available.

Annual events in and around the city include the popular Comrades Marathon between Durban and Pietermaritzburg, an international surfing competition, the Duzi canoe marathon, the Midmar Mile swimming event, and the July Handicap horse-race.

Umhlanga Rocks, just north of Durban, is notable for its ski-boating facilities. The annual Ski

Widely regarded as the continent's premier travel trade exhibition, Indaba has grown in status, quality and diversity to become one of the industry's top three 'must visit' travel trade shows of its kind on the global calendar.

Indaba 2005, regarded as the most successful and productive ever, saw a record number of 10 700 participants. Tourism products and services from over 1 500 companies came together to showcase the best the southern African region has to offer the international tourism trade. Visitor numbers were up by 5%, reflecting the increased interest to do business with southern Africa. Almost 600 media, both local and international, provided extensive coverage through radio, television, newspaper and dedicated travel publications worldwide.

Boat Festival takes place in April. The Natal Sharks Board offers shark dissections and interesting displays. Guided tours of the Hawaan Forest are on offer. Hawaan is the last relic of coastal forest in the region and contains rare indigenous trees.

The Umgeni River Bird Park overlooks the Umgeni River and ranks among the world's best. Many varieties of birds, indigenous and exotic, inhabit walk-in aviaries.

The Millennium Town at the end of the Bluff houses the maritime offices, which control the entry of ships into and out of the busiest port in Africa.

East Griqualand

East Griqualand is an area of great beauty featuring colourful, living history. **Kokstad** lies in the Umzimhlava River basin between Mount Currie and the Ngele mountains.

The original town hall – built in 1910 – is a national monument, now serving as the local library. The former library – built in 1907 – is also a national monument, and houses the Kokstad Museum.

The Weza State Forest runs through indigenous forests and commercial plantations. The forest is home to several antelope species and a huge variety of birds.

East Griqualand is home to the southernmost portion of the Drakensberg World Heritage Site, plus the impressive Swartberg, Bokkiesberg, Cedarberg and Ngele mountain ranges.

The Mountain Lake Nature Reserve is a National Heritage Site comprising rolling grasslands and pristine wetlands. When full, the lake offers 30 ha of deep, trout-filled waters. It also boats 80 bird species and panoramic views of the Drakensberg mountain range.

Between **Kokstad** and **Matatiele**, the hamlet of **Cedarville** provides tranquil canoe-borne excursions on its surrounding, water-filled hollows. Also nearby, the carp-abundant Umzimvubu River is an ever-popular recreation ground for locals and visitors alike.

Steam-train journeys can be undertaken between **Swartberg** and **Creighton**.

Dolphin Coast (North Coast)

The coastline between the Umdloti and the Tugela rivers is aptly called the Dolphin Coast, as Indian Ocean bottlenose dolphins can be seen here all year round. The larger humpback dolphins are also found here, but are rarely seen.

Many of the first Indian immigrants settled here, and the area's markets, mosques and temples bring an authentic eastern flavour to the region.

Tongaat is an area where sugar was first planted in 1854. The town's Indian ambience is accentuated by two prominent Hindu temples – the Juggernath Puri and Vishwaroop temples.

Other coastal towns on the Dolphin Coast include **Shaka's Rock**, **Salt Rock**, **Ballito**, **Verulam**, **Stanger**, **Darnall** and **Umdloti**.

Zululand and the Elephant Coast

Cultural tourism is inextricably linked to economic upliftment in Zululand, and historically disadvantaged communities are applying their traditional skills to meet visitors' interests.

Zululand's north-east quadrant – between Mozambique, Swaziland and the warm Indian Ocean – has its own unique tale to tell. This is the Elephant Coast or Maputaland, named after the mid-17th century king who established dominion here some 200 years before Shaka consolidated his Zulu empire to the south. The Tembe Elephant Park in the far north is home to herds of the massive African elephant.

The Hluhluwe-Umfolozi Park is one of the largest game parks in South Africa and hosts the Big Five as well as the elusive cheetah and wild dog.

The eMakhosini Valley, birthplace of King Shaka, is the venue for a new tourism- and economic-development project. Known as eMakhosini, The Valley of Zulu Kings, the joint public-private sector project aims to preserve the culture and history of the Zulu people.

The eMakhosini Memorial Site, where seven Zulu kings are buried, was unveiled in May 2003.

Ulundi lies at the hub of the old Zulu Kingdom. The KwaZulu Cultural Museum houses interesting displays relating to Zulu history and archaeology. The beehive huts and the layout of the original Zulu village have been reproduced.

Umgungundlovu used to be the royal capital of King Dingaan and is being reconstructed. A tour provides the opportunity to observe Zulu building techniques and experience the social life of the Zulu people.

Authentic Zulu villages such as Shakaland, Kwabhekithunga Kraal, Damazulu and Stewart's Farm offer accommodation and the opportunity to experience traditional Zulu culture.

The Greater St Lucia Wetland Park, the province's second World Heritage Site, has some of the highest forested dunes in the world. **St Lucia** and its surroundings comprise a wetland of global importance and boast five separate ecosystems. It is a fishing and birdwatching paradise, and boat trips on the lake offer opportunities for crocodile and hippo sightings.

The Kosi Bay Nature Reserve is part of the Coastal Forest Reserve between Mozambique and **Sodwana Bay**. The adjacent Indian Ocean provides exciting snorkelling and fishing opportunities. On offer is a four-day guided walking trail around the estuarine system.

Mkuze is a small trade and transport centre. The Mkuze River cuts through the Ubombo mountains before serving as a boundary for Zululand's popular Mkuzi Game Reserve.

Lake Sibaya is South Africa's largest natural freshwater lake, covering some 77 km^2. Birdwatching and walks through the coastal forest are popular pastimes.

Sibaya Lake Lodge, the first South African eco-tourism development jointly owned by private enterprise and the local community, was officially launched in September 1999.

The coral reef in the Sodwana Bay National Park attracts hundreds of scuba-divers throughout the year, and in summer, power-boaters arrive for some of the best marlin-fishing in the world.

South Coast

The Banana Express is a narrow-gauge steam train running between **Port Shepstone** and **Paddock** and back (39 km) twice a week. A shorter route is also offered.

Amanzimtoti is popular for its safe swimming beaches and various other activities and attractions.

The Hibiscus Coast stretches between Umkomaas and the Wild Coast. **Margate** is the largest resort town along this coast, and is very popular during the holidays. The Hibiscus Festival is held in July.

The Oribi Gorge Nature Reserve encompasses forest, rivers, rapids and ravines. Prolific bird life, including five kingfisher species and seven eagle species, inhabits the reserve, along with a variety of mammals. There is also a 140-m abseil and gorge swing for adrenalin junkies.

Port Edward is known for its safe swimming and good fishing opportunities. Nearby, the Umthamvuna Nature Reserve is noted for its beautiful scenery, bird life and many rare plant species.

The Shell Museum at **Shelly Beach** is well worth a visit.

Other popular coastal towns include **Port Shepstone**, **Ramsgate**, **St Michael's-on-Sea**, **Uvongo** and **Scottburgh**.

Sardine fever strikes the South Coast around the end of June every year, when people flock to the beaches and anglers wait for the game fish to arrive.

Pietermaritzburg and the Midlands

Pietermaritzburg boasts various museums, including the Voortrekker Museum, the Natal Museum and the Natal Steam Railway Museum, which offers steam-train rides on the second Sunday of every month. The Tatham Art Gallery is also extremely popular.

The Albert Falls Public Resort Nature Reserve and the Albert Falls Dam provide opportunities for sailing, canoeing and fishing.

Birdwatching, horse-riding and hiking are also popular activities.

The Howick falls are situated in the Nature Valley Reserve, where the river tumbles down 100 m in a single fall. Several climbing routes are on offer.

The Midlands Meander is a scenic drive between **Hilton** and **Mooi River** with about 70 ports of call *en route*, ranging from art studios, potters and painters, to herb gardens and cheese-makers.

Midmar Dam is zoned for yachting and power-boating. The 1 000-ha Midmar Game Park is inhabitated by rhino, zebra, a wide variety of antelope species, and waterfowl. The popular Midmar Mile event attracts thousands of swimmers every year.

Drakensberg

The Drakensberg mountain range forms the northwestern border of KwaZulu-Natal. The entire area is a bird sanctuary, featuring among other species, the endangered lammergeier (or bearded vulture). The highest concentration of walks and trails in South Africa is found here.

The Ukhahlamba-Drakensberg Park was declared a World Heritage Site in 2001 and consists of almost the entire range of the Drakensberg mountain range from Bushman's Neck in the south to the Royal Natal National Park in the north. Peaks soar to over 3 000 m and are often snow-covered in winter. The park is administered by Ezemvelo KwaZulu-Natal Wildlife. Their trout hatcheries are located in the Kamberg Reserve area.

The Lotheni Nature Reserve is notable for its trout-fishing facilities (angling permits are required). Relics of the area's history have been preserved in the Settler Museum.

The Himeville Nature Reserve has two lakes stocked with trout. The Swamp Nature Reserve close by attracts a variety of waterfowl, including the rare wattled crane.

The Ndema Gorge is located in the Mdedelelo Wilderness Area near Cathedral Peak and contains examples of Khoi and San art.

Sani Pass is the only road across the high escarpment between KwaZulu-Natal and the Kingdom of Lesotho. The Giant's Cup hiking trail, starting at the foot of the pass, is described as one of South Africa's finest. Giant's Castle Game Reserve is especially known for its more than 5 000 San paintings. The Bushman Site Museum is well worth a visit.

The Royal Natal National Park offers many scenic highlights, including the Amphitheatre, Mont-aux-Sources and the Tugela Falls.

Battlefields

The KwaZulu-Natal Battlefields Route has the highest concentration of battlefields and related military sites in South Africa. The Battlefields Route starts at Estcourt and winds north through Colenso and Ladysmith to Newcastle and Volksrust, and eastwards to Utrecht, Glencoe, Dundee, Nqutu, Paulpietersburg, Vryheid, Babanango and Ulundi.

All the towns along the route have their unique charm and range of attractions: arts and crafts, scenic hiking trails, farm resorts, Zulu culture and roadside stalls. Game viewing, natural hot springs, horse trails and watersport can also be enjoyed.

The Chelmsford Nature Reserve near **Newcastle** is a birdwatcher's paradise. Powerboating and carp-fishing are added attractions. Game includes springbok, zebra, rhino and blesbok. Other interesting places to visit are Majuba Hill and O'Neill's Cottage.

The Ladysmith Siege Museum provides insight into the battles of Colenso, Spioenkop, Vaalkrans and Tugela Heights. Guided tours to nearby battlefields such as Wagon Hill are arranged by museum staff. Other attractions in **Ladysmith** include the Statue of Gandhi, the All Saints Church, the Soofi Mosque and the Spioenkop Dam and Nature Reserve.

Near **Dundee**, tourists can visit various battlefields, including Ncome-Blood River, Isandlwana, Rorke's Drift and Talana. The Talana Museum depicts various facets of the coal industry, as well as local Zulu, Boer and British history.

Rorke's Drift was the setting for one of the most famous battles of the war. The main attrraction is the Rorke's Drift Battle Museum.

Acknowledgements

BuaNews

Business Day

Business Report

Department of Environmental Affairs and Tourism

South African National Parks

South African Tourism

South African Tourism Institute

Tourism Business Council of South Africa (TBCSA)

Western Cape Provincial Government

www.capetourism.org

www.cape-town.net

www.doorway.co.za

www.ectourism.co.za

www.freestateprovince.co.za

www.gauteng.net

www.gov.za

www.indaba-southafrica.co.za

www.joburg.org.za

www.kzn.org.za

www.mpumalanga.com

www.northerncape.org.za

www.sasdi.co.za

www.sati-web.za

www.southafrica.info

www.southafrica.net

www.soweto.co.za

www.travel.iafrica.com

www.tourismboard.org.za

www.tourismgrading.co.za

www.tourismnorthwest.co.za

www.wheretostay.co.za

Suggested reading

Ballard, S. *South African Handbook.* 2nd ed. Bath, United Kingdom (UK): Footprint Handbooks, 1997.

Barbour, A. *Fodor's South Africa.* New York: Fodor, 1996.

Beckett, D. *Madibaland.* Johannesburg: Penguin Books South Africa, 1998.

Bell, G. *Somewhere Over the Rainbow: Travels in South Africa.* London: ABACUS, 2001.

Bennet, A., Jooste, C. and Strydom, L. eds. *Managing Tourism Services: A Southern African Perspective.* Pretoria: Van Schaik, 2005.

Braak, L.E.O. *Kruger National Park: A Visitor's Guide.* Revised edition. Cape Town: Struik, 1998.

Brett, M. and Mountain, A. *Touring Atlas of Southern Africa.* Cape Town: Struik, 1997.

Brett, M. *et al. South Africa.* London: Dorling Kindersley, 1999.

Bulpin, T. V. *Discovering Southern Africa.* 6th ed. Cape Town: Tafelberg, 2001.

Butchart, D. *Wild About Johannesburg: All-in-One Guide to Common Animals, and Plants of Gardens, Parks and Nature Reserves.* Halfway House: Southern Book Publishers, 1995.

Connolly, D. *Connolly's Guide to Southern Africa*. 5th ed. Scottburgh: Connolly Publishers, 1992.

Crewe-Brown, M. *Traveller's Companion to South Africa*. 2nd ed. Johannesburg: CBM Publishing, 1994.

Deacon, H. *The Essential Robben Island*. Cape Town: Mayibuye Books and David Philip, 1997.

Dennis, N. and Scholes, B. *The Kruger National Park: Wonders of an African Eden*. London, Cape Town: New Holland, 1994.

Derwent, S. *Guide to Cultural Tourism in South Africa*. Cape Town: Struik, 1999.

Detert, L. ed. *Automobile Association (AA) Hotels, Lodges, Guest-Houses, B&Bs, 2002/03 edition*. Johannesburg: Automobile Association, 2002.

Du Plessis, H. *Tourism Destinations: Southern Africa*. Cape Town: Juta, 2000.

Duncan, P. *Thomas Cook Traveller's South Africa*. Basingstoke, Hampshire (UK): AA Publishing, 1996.

Erasmus, B.P.J. *On Route in South Africa:* 2nd ed. Johannesburg: Jonathan Ball, 2004.

Federated Hotel Association of Southern Africa. Hotelier and Caterer Buyers' Guide. 1996 – 1997. Cape Town: Ramsay Son and Parker, 1997.

George, R. *Marketing South African Tourism*. Cape Town: Oxford University Press, 2004.

Greenwood Guide to South Africa: Hand-Picked Accommodation. 4th ed. London: Greenwood Guides, 2005.

Haw, S., Unsworth, A. and Robertson, H. *Rediscovering South Africa*. Cape Town: Spearhead, 2001.

Isaacson, R. *The Healing Land: A Kalahari Journey*. London: Fourth Estate, 2001.

Jordaan, M.J.S. *Tourism in South Africa*. 2nd ed. Bloemfontein: The Author, 2001.

Joyce, P. *South Africa*. 2nd ed. London: New Holland Publishers, 1996. (Globetrotter Travel Guide.)

Kellett, F. and Williams, L. *Footprint South Africa*. 7th ed. Bath, England: Footprint Travel Guides, 2004.

Keyser, H. *Tourism Development*. Cape Town: Oxford University Press, 2002.

Kok, P. and Pietersen, J. *Tourism*. Pretoria: Human Sciences Research Council, 2000.

Koornhof, A. *Dive Guide: South Africa*. London: New Holland Publishers, 2000.

Leigh, M. *Touring in South Africa*. 2nd ed. Revised and updated by B.J. Burker. Cape Town: Struik, 1993.

Levy, J. *Complete Guide to Walks and Trails in Southern Africa*. 3rd ed. Cape Town: Struik, 1993.

Loubser, J. ed. *Tourist and Leisure Destinations 2002/03*. Cape Town: Comparex Africa, 2001.

Loubser, J. ed. *Western Cape Tourist and Leisure Road Atlas*. Cape Town: Lapa Publishers, 2000.

Magubane, P. *Soweto*. text by C. Smith. Cape Town: Struik, 2001.

Maylam, P. and Edwards, I. eds. *The People's City: African Life in the Twentieth Century*. Pietermaritzburg: University of Natal Press, 1996.

Meintjies, M. *Remarkable Flyfishing Destinations of Southern Africa*. Cape Town: Struik, 2005.

New South African Book of the Road. 2nd ed. Cape Town: AA Motorist Publications, 1995.

O'Hagan, T. *Wild Places of Southern Africa*. 3rd edition. Cape Town: Struik, 2001.

Olivier, W. *Guide to Backpacking and Wilderness Trails*. Halfway House: Southern Book Publishers, 1991.

Olivier, W. and Olivier, S. *Overland Through Southern Africa*. Cape Town: Struik, 1998.

Paynter, D. and Nussey, W. *Kruger: Portrait of a National Park*. Halfway House: Southern Book Publishers, 1992.

Places to Visit in Southern Africa. Cape Town: AA Motorist Publications, 1995.

Reader's Digest Illustrated Guide to the Game Parks and Nature Reserves of Southern Africa. 3rd ed. Cape Town: Reader's Digest Association, 1997.

Ryan, B. (text) and Bannister, A. (photography). *National Parks of South Africa*. Cape Town: Struik, 1993.

Saayman, M. *Tourism Marketing in South Africa*. Potchefstroom: Leisure Consultants and Publications, 1997.

South Africa: The Rough Guide. 2nd ed. London: Rough Guides, 1999.

South Africa Focus: South African Tourism Directory. Johannesburg: Africa Focus, 1997.

Southern African Travel Guide. 31st edition. Rosebank, Cape: Promeo, 2001.

Stern, J. *Engen Guide to Adventure Travel in Southern Africa*. Halfway House: Southern Book Publishers, 1997.

Stuart, C. and Stuart, T. *Guide to Southern African Game and Nature Reserves*. 4th ed. Cape Town: Struik, 1997.

Sycholt, A. *A Guide to the Drakensberg*. Cape Town: Struik, 2002.

Van der Merwe, P. and Saayman, M. *Managing Game Farms from a Tourism Perspective*. Potchefstroom: Leisure Consultants and Publications, 2002.

Van der Walt, B. *The Enchanting World of the Drakensberg Mountains*. Potchefstroom: Institute for Contemporary Christianity in Africa, 2003.

Weinberg, P. *Once We Were Hunters: A Journey with Africa's Indigenous People*. Cape Town: David Philip, 2000.

Transport

The Department of Transport aims to establish a national transport system that enables national, provincial and local provision of efficient, affordable and fully integrated infrastructure and services. The transport system seeks to best meet the needs of transport users and promote economic and social development, while being environmentally and economically sustainable.

The department's other key objectives include:
- facilitating access and affordability of public transport to the commuting public
- planning, developing and maintaining transport infrastructure to improve mobility and quality of life and contribute to economic development
- promoting sector and enterprise reforms to create a reliable, safe and competitive transport system.

Policy

The department is working to improve and expand infrastructure and, through subsidies, reduce the costs of public transport.

Transport policy is built on the framework set out by the Moving South Africa Strategy (1999) and the National Land Transport Transition Act, 2000 (Act 22 of 2000).

These established the vision of an efficient public transport system through the use of targeted subsidies, and the provision of a high-quality, comprehensive transport infrastructure.

In 2005/06, the department was allocated R3 billion to improve the public transport system and roads.

During 2004, the Department of Transport was restructured and refocused its strategic approach. As a result, the number of programmes has been reduced from eight to six. The main changes are the introduction of the Programme: Freight Logistics and Corridor Development; the consolidation of all of the regulatory functions into the Programme: Transport Regulation and Public Entity Oversight; and the consolidation of the planning and infrastructure functions into the Programme: Integrated Planning and Inter-Sphere Co-ordination. Key elements of the new strategic approach include:
- restructuring public transport subsidies to better target poorer commuters, irrespective of the mode of transport, and to align subsidised transport services to support municipal integrated transport plans

- streamlining the freight logistics network along key freight movement corridors by promoting infrastructure investment and improved operational efficiency
- increasing investment in transport infrastructure, both through increased public investment in road and rail infrastructure, and through public-private partnerships (PPPs)
- building capacity to monitor and oversee the public entities that report to the Minister of Transport
- developing the regulatory systems and capacity required to ensure that operators in the transport sector meet the required safety and security standards, and to establish a single economic regulator for the transport sector
- ensuring that the transport sector contributes to government's broad priorities of creating jobs and promoting Black Economic Empowerment (BEE).

A seamless logistics system

A critical area of focus is a seamless logistics system, characterised by an efficient flow of freight that promotes the economy's competitiveness. It is expected that the transport system will be restructured to prevent logistics from acting as a restraint on economic growth, employment and sustainable development. The removal of blockages within the ports and rail systems is regarded as a priority.

An integrated approach will be adopted to use the transport system as a catalyst to stimulate new development corridors in various regions of the nine provinces.

The development of strategic corridors will serve as a guide as to where transport infrastructure will be located in future. The development of these corridors will be interlinked with nodal and spatial development initiatives (SDIs) to prevent areas outside of the corridors from being delinked from the rest of the economy.

An example is the Kei Rail Project, which involves the upgrading and development of new facilities along the Umtata-Amabele railway line in the Eastern Cape. In 2004/05, the Department of Public Enterprises contributed R28 million to the Kei rail infrastructure upgrade.

Collaboration with other government departments saw commitments of about R44 million for the upgrade of the Belmont-Douglas railway line in the Northern Cape and Nkwaleni railway line in KwaZulu-Natal.

These projects are collaborative efforts between the Department of Transport, Spoornet and the respective provinces to increase the producers' access to freight transport and to reduce the cost of doing business in South Africa's rural areas.

Public-transport subsidies

The chief objectives of a sustainable public transport system are to improve the public transport system, broaden access to affordable transport, and stimulate economic activities.

Transport subsidies are potentially important tools for improving efficiency, access and equity. In the past, they have been targeted loosely and implemented selectively. The Department of Transport is channelling subsidies to those with the greatest need to maximise economic and social gains.

By mid-2005, there were 34 interim bus contracts in the whole country that accounted for 67% of the total subsidy allocation of R2,28 billion. There was R2,5 billion in subsidies a year for train commuters.

The transformation of bus contracts is part of initiatives to implement government's existing policy of regulated competition.

Tendered contracts will be the norm while negotiated contracts will be approved only as an exception. The tendered bus contracts will cover a period of seven years to provide certainty to the industry and enable bus operators to purchase new buses to provide commuters with safe, reliable and improved services. Negotiated contracts will cover a period of five years.

Black Economic Empowerment

By August 2005, the development of the Transport Sector BEE Charter was in the final stages of negotiations in eight subsector working groups. These are aviation, maritime, road freight, buses, freight forwarding, rail, the public sector and the taxi industry.

The charter sets targets for small, medium and micro enterprises (SMMEs), women, and people with disabilities.

The aim is to transfer ownership of enterprises throughout the industry value chain to black people and to increase their participation at all levels – employment, management, procurement and the development of new enterprises.

Non-motorised transport (NMT)

The promotion of NMT primarily aims to increase transport mobility and accessibility, mainly in rural areas. These include the donkey carts of the Northern Cape and the Shova Kalula Bicycle Programme.

The NMT Programme in the Kgalagadi and Botlhabela Presidential rural nodes has four sub-components:

- Promoting ownership and usage of various rural-transport operations (e.g. human/animal-drawn carts) in low-income rural areas and at local project level.
- Creating and/or improving appropriate, safe on- and off-the-road rural-transport infrastructure.
- Alleviating rural poverty by promoting the economic, as well as the strong industrial dimension, of NMT project operations and infrastructure (e.g. SMMEs). This will be achieved by exploiting local expertise to the maximum in running and sustaining the programme.
- Impact assessment and programme evaluation. The main objective of this component is to make meaningful contributions to the Rural Transport Strategy.

Transport safety

Increased emphasis is placed on safety issues in all transport modes. The Road to Safety Strategy, the transportation of dangerous goods by road, the establishment of the Maritime Rescue Centre, the setting-up of the Railway Safety Regulator, and the Road-Traffic Management Corporation (RTMC) are examples.

New Partnership for Africa's Development (NEPAD)

From a transport point of view, key issues in creating an effectively co-ordinated African response to global market challenges are market access, mobility and systems integration.

The Department of Transport is contributing actively to the practical realisation of NEPAD and the Southern African Development Community (SADC) development goals in several major areas, by promoting:

- efficient and effective maritime transport services
- rail-systems integration
- road-systems development and infrastructure maintenance.

Agencies

The Department of Transport has established four bodies to move certain elements of government's operational activities to commercial agencies. They are the South African National Roads Agency Ltd (SANRAL), the South African Maritime Safety Authority (SAMSA), the Cross-Border Road Transport Agency (CBRTA) and the South African Civil Aviation Authority (CAA).

South African National Roads Agency Ltd

The SANRAL is an independent, statutory company responsible for the design, construction, management and maintenance of South Africa's national road network, including toll and non-toll roads.

The SANRAL's responsibilities are to:

- strategically plan, design, construct, operate, rehabilitate and maintain South Africa's national roads
- deliver and maintain a world-class primary road network
- generate revenue from the development and management of its assets
- undertake research and development to enhance the quality of the country's roads
- upon request of the Minister of Transport and in agreement with a foreign country, provide, operate and maintain roads in that country.

South African Maritime Safety Authority

The SAMSA is a statutory body that reports to the Minister of Transport. Its responsibilities include the promotion of safety of life and property at sea, the prevention of marine pollution by pollutants emanating from ships, and the co-ordination of overall technical operations. It also develops policy on legal issues, foreign relations, marine pollution and certain specific safety matters.

The SAMSA's main functions are to:
- provide shipping competence and pollution services in a regional context
- manage marine incidents, casualties and wrecks, and participate in search-and-rescue missions
- control standby tugs and pollution stores
- maintain seafarers according to standards of training and staffing criteria
- provide a shipping-administration support service
- manage the registration of ships
- manage a coastal patrol service
- manage vessel traffic, including navigation aids
- provide lighthouse services.

Funding comes from, among other sources, levies on ships calling at South African ports, direct user charges and government service fees.

Cross-Border Road Transport Agency

The CBRTA regulates and controls cross-border passenger, freight and road transport. It also facilitates the establishment of co-operative and consultative relationships and structures between public and private-sector institutions, with an interest in cross-border road transport.

The CBRTA is also involved in collecting, processing and disseminating relevant information; providing training and capacity-building; and promoting entrepreneurship, with the focus on SMMEs with an interest in cross-border road transport.

The functions of the agency include:
- advising the Minister of Transport on cross-border transport matters and assisting in the process of negotiating and renegotiating cross-border road-transport agreements on request

- regulating the road-transport industry's access to the cross-border road-transport market
- facilitating ongoing co-operative and consultative relationships and structures between the public and private sectors in support of cross-border road-transport operations
- undertaking road-transport law enforcement.

The main source of income for the CBRTA is fees charged for cross-border permits.

South African Civil Aviation Authority

The CAA is charged with promoting, regulating and enforcing civil-aviation safety and security.

The CAA has proved to be a leader in the aviation regulatory sector in the SADC region. It has hosted several regional meetings and conferences since 1994, and is the driving seat of efforts to harmonise aviation regulations in the region and improve the level of aviation surveillance.

In 2003, South Africa was elected as a member of the International Civil Aviation Organisation (ICAO) Council and was requested to establish a South African office at the ICAO headquarters in Montreal, Canada.

The CAA is funded by a combination of direct and indirect fees and government funding for the investigation of aircraft accidents. User fees are based on the recovery of the agency's costs to provide the relevant direct services. This approach creates a more efficient and cost-effective regulatory regime and a safer civil aviation system.

Indirect fees are recovered through a R7 aircraft and passenger safety charge payable by all scheduled passengers.

Transnet Limited

Transnet Limited, a public company of which the South African Government is the sole shareholder, was established on 1 April 1990.

The company is recognised as a dominant player in the southern African transport infrastructure. Its activities are not restricted to southern Africa but extend beyond its borders into Africa and the rest of the world.

Government is embarking on a major investment drive of some R40,8 billion in Transnet over the next five years.

Transnet handles 176 million tons (mt) of rail freight per year, 2,8 mt road freight and 194 mt of freight through the harbours, while 13,8 million litres (ML) are pumped through its petrol pipelines annually.

By February 2005, the Department of Public Enterprises, in conjunction with Transnet and South African Airways (SAA), was working on the separation of SAA, which was expected to be finalised by 2006.

This will allow Transnet to focus on its rail, port and petro-pipeline core business. SAA will be a stand-alone entity reporting to the Department of Public Enterprises. The airline is now focusing on opening new routes around the globe and forging strong partnerships with other African airlines.

Transnet investment plans are focused on key operating divisions such as ports, rail and pipelines. The challenge facing Transnet is to expand the capacity of the freight system and ensure significant improvements in efficiency.

The key investments are:
- expanding and redesigning Pier 1 and widening the entrance of Durban harbour at a cost of R2,9 billion
- constructing the container terminal at Ngqura, at a cost of R2,6 billion
- expanding the Cape Town container terminal, at a cost of R2,6 billion
- constructing the multi-purpose pipeline from Durban to Gauteng, at a cost of R3 billion
- the purchasing by Spoornet of locomotives, wagons and equipment worth R8 billion.

Transnet Limited consists of eight main divisions, a number of subsidiaries, and their related businesses:
- Spoornet focuses on transporting freight, containers and mainline passengers by rail
- the National Ports Authority (NPA) focuses on providing total port infrastructure and marine-related services, managing port activities in a landlord capacity, and regulating port systems
- South African Port Operations (SAPO) focuses on port-terminal and cargo operations in commercially viable business units

- Petronet focuses on transporting petroleum products and gas through a high-pressure long-distance pipeline network
- Propnet manages a profitable property-development portfolio, and handles the management and investment function of Transnet's vast property portfolio
- Metrorail is a commuter rail transport business
- Transtel is the telecommunications unit of Transnet
- Transwerk is involved in engineering activities and is one of South Africa's leading manufacturers and refurbishers of railway rolling stock.

Road transport

National roads

In terms of the National Roads Act, 1998 (Act 7 of 1998), government is responsible for overall policy, while road-building and maintenance is the responsibility of the SANRAL.

The Department of Transport continues to improve the road network, ensuring that it is well-maintained and safe. A new national roads plan is being developed, indicating the importance of roads to the economy.

The South African road network comprises some 754 600 km of roads and streets.

Responsibility for the network is carried by the department with the SANRAL, the nine provinces, and local authorities.

A new proposed road-classification system has been developed to integrate the 29% of unclassified roads into the road system. Unclassified roads are predominantly access roads in rural communities and roads in settlements on the urban periphery.

The various categories include:
- 9 600 km of surfaced national toll and non-toll roads
- 56 000 km of surfaced provincial roads
- 300 000 km of gravel provincial roads
- 168 000 km of surfaced and unsurfaced urban roads
- 221 000 km of unclassified roads.

Cabinet approved a five-year road-infrastructure strategy to prevent the further deterioration of the country's road network.

The Minister of Finance, Mr Trevor Manuel, announced at the tabling of the Medium Term Budget Policy Statement in October 2005, that R31,5 billion would be allocated for infrastructure projects, including significant increases in spending on national and provincial roads over the Medium Term Expenditure Framework period.

Provincial roads

The planning, construction and maintenance of roads and bridges, other than those falling under the SANRAL or local governments, is the responsibility of provincial governments. The Department of Transport is always ready to assist provincial and local governments to improve and develop the state of their roads.

Spatial development initiatives

SDIs are recognised as effective means of stimulating economic growth by exploiting the existing economic potential within an area. The department's involvement in this project is focused on infrastructure provision, BEE, skills transfer and the creation of sustainable jobs.

The SDI programme uses public resources – particularly project planning, scoping and logistical coordination skills – to leverage private-sector involvement.

The SDI areas are Lubombo, West Coast, Fish River, Maputo Development Corridor, Wild Coast, Platinum, Phalaborwa and Richards Bay. (See Chapter 7: *Economy*.)

Municipal roads

The construction and maintenance of most roads and streets within the municipal boundaries of cities and towns is the responsibility of the municipality concerned.

Toll roads

Toll roads cover some 2 400 km and are serviced by 32 toll plazas, including concessioned roads.

The viability of every toll road is determined over a 30-year period to assess the private-sector funding.

The performance of all toll roads is within the forecast, and in many cases roads perform better than forecast. It is envisaged that all new major toll-road projects will be financed through the Build, Operate and Transfer principle. This allows greater private-sector involvement in the financing, building, operation and maintenance of toll projects. When the concession period expires, the facility is transferred back to the State at no cost.

Road-traffic signs

A revised road-traffic-sign system, which closely conforms to international standards, has been phased in since November 1993.

The revised system involves changes to the colours of some of the regulatory and all of the warning signs, changes in design parameters, the modernisation of text and symbols, and the addition of new signs, signals and markings. Many of the new signs make use of symbols rather than text to eliminate language problems and reduce observation time.

Credit-card format (CCF) licences

CCF licences are valid for a period of five years, whereafter licence holders have to apply for a replacement.

The CCF licence contains more than 20 different security features, one of which is the encrypted two-dimensional bar code which complies with international standards.

Public transport

In terms of the Constitution of the Republic of South Africa, 1996 (Act 108 of 1996), legislative and executive powers in respect of public transport are a provincial competency. National government, however, is responsible for policy-formulation, monitoring and strategic implementation. The Department of Transport continues to administer subsidies for buses and other subsidised forms of public transport.

According to the *National Household Travel Survey, 2003*, there are about 3,9 million public transport commuters. The 2,5 million taxi commuters account for over 63% of public transport work trips. Bus services account for another 22% of public transport commuters and the balance are carried to work by train. In addition to the 2,5 million commuters who use minibus-taxis as the main mode of travel, there are another 325 000 commuters who use taxis either as a feeder mode to other public transport services, or as a distribution service from the main mode to their places of work.

National Transport Register

The establishment of the National Transport Register is a requirement of the National Land Transport Transition Act, 2000.

The purpose of the register is to integrate the land-transport systems, i.e. the Subsidy Management System (SUMS), the Land-Transport Permit System (LTPS) and the Registration Administration System (RAS).

The LTPS facilitates the issuing of public road-carrier permits, to regulate entry into the road-carrier markets.

The objective is to facilitate the processing of permit applications and enable the local road transportation boards (provincial permit boards) to provide an efficient service to the industry. In achieving this goal, the LTPS supports the boards with:
- registering applications
- generating and verifying advertisements
- capturing objections and appeals
- generating agendas
- verifying vehicle information
- generating permits and permit transfers.

The RAS facilitates the registration of minibus-taxi associations with the Provincial Registrar to formalise the industry. They support the registrar with:
- registering members and associations
- registering vehicle particulars of members
- registering corridor particulars of associations
- management reporting.

The SUMS manages claims from provincial departments and payments thereof for bus contracts.

Urban transport

Metropolitan transport advisory boards govern urban areas which have been declared metropolitan transport areas. Both short- and long-term programmes for adequate transportation development are drawn up by the core city of each area and are revised and adjusted annually.

Nine such core areas exist, namely Johannesburg, Cape Town, Pretoria, Durban, Pietermaritzburg, Port Elizabeth, the East Rand, Bloemfontein and East London.

The planning of transport for metropolitan and major urban areas must be done in accordance with a growth-management plan, and travel modes should not compete with one another. In urban areas, passenger road-transport services are provided by local governments, private bus companies, which operate scheduled bus services between peripheral areas and city centres, and minibus taxis.

The Department of Transport supports provincial departments of transport and of public works in the construction of intermodal facilities and in their efforts to achieve integration between bus and taxi operations.

The minibus-taxi industry has shown phenomenal growth during the last few years, leading to a decrease in the market share of buses and trains as modes of transport.

Motor vehicles

According to the *National Household Travel Survey, 2003*, about 26% of households in South Africa have access to a motor car. In households where income exceeds R6 000 per month, 82% have access to one or more cars. Gauteng and the Western Cape have the highest car-ownership levels.

At 108 cars per 1 000 of the population for the country as a whole, car ownership in South Africa remains in its infancy.

Minibus taxis

The South African National Taxi Council (SANTACO) is the umbrella body for all provincial taxi organisations and strives to regulate, formalise and stabilise the industry. The council acts as a mediator in disputes between taxi organisations and plays a role in eliminating the causes of conflict within the industry.

In May 1999, government signed a memorandum of understanding (MoU) with SANTACO, paving the way for the replacement of the industry's ageing fleet and its absorption into South Africa's formal economy.

The MoU commits SANTACO to act against violent elements in the industry, participate in the regulation of the industry by ensuring its members have legal operations, and implement a programme of acceptable labour practices. Government, in turn, is bound by the MoU to find an acceptable solution to the industry's recapitalisation issues, legalise illegal operations within agreed parameters, and provide taxi operators with extensive training.

Taxi Recapitalisation Programme (TRP)

The TRP aims to replace the current ageing taxi fleet with new, safer and purpose-built minibus taxis.

Government announced in October 2004 that it would roll out its revised TRP at a cost of about R7,7 billion over seven years, starting at the beginning of the 2005/06 financial year.

In February 2005, the TRP was allocated R885 million over the next three years.

By July 2005, government had approved the detailed strategy for the roll-out of the TRP.

It comprises the introduction of safety requirements for the new taxi vehicles, scrapping of existing vehicles, effective regulation of the taxi industry, effective law enforcement in respect of public transport and empowerment of the taxi industry.

The new safety requirements, which are effective from 1 January 2006, involve:

In October 2005, the Minister of Transport, Mr Jeff Radebe, issued 20 operating licences to Free State taxi operators who had converted their radius permits.
The conversion is part of the roll-out plan of the Taxi Recapitalisation Programme that is aimed at ridding the country of the current unsafe taxi fleet and replacing them with new, safer and more reliable vehicles.

- seatbelts
- roll-over bars
- type-two braking systems
- commercially rated tyres: size 185 R or 195 R
- warning markings
- wheel bands
- tamper-proof speed governors (100 km per hour will be set as the maximum)
- diesel-fuelled vehicles.

Any new vehicle entering the taxi industry without meeting these safety requirements will not be licensed to operate as a taxi.

Government intends to remove 10 000 old and unroadworthy vehicles from the roads by December 2006. With effect from August 2005, taxi operators who wish to exit the industry are invited to voluntarily hand in their vehicles and permits/operating licences.

The payment of a scrapping allowance of R50 000 to operators handing in their vehicles will only take place after operating licensing boards have registered applications, evaluated them and verified the validity of the permit/operating licences linked to the taxi vehicle.

Taxi operators failing to register their old vehicles will face impoundment of their vehicles and risk forfeiting the scrapping allowance.

In 2006, the Minister of Transport, Mr Jeff Radebe, is expected to introduce amendments to the National Land Transport Transition Act, 2000 to strengthen the regulation of the taxi industry. Among key amendments to be introduced is ensuring that municipalities take control of taxi ranks and their management.

Taxi ranks and routes will no longer be under the control of taxi associations or other bodies.

The Department of Transport, in consultation with the taxi industry, is considering the need for a regulatory body to facilitate the integration of the industry into the formal public transport system.

Bus transport

A network of public and privately owned passenger bus services links the major centres of South Africa and also serves commuters in the deep rural areas. Cabinet has approved measures intended to improve public-transport safety. These include the intensification of law enforcement, lowering the maximum speed limit for buses and minibus taxis to 100 km/h, and a fitness-testing programme for buses.

International models being explored emphasise the need for a formal safety fitness-rating methodology. A vehicle operator will receive a safety rating when an accredited or authorised safety specialist conducts an on-site review of the operator's compliance with applicable safety and hazardous material regulations.

In terms of the formal compliance review, the operator will be awarded one of three ratings: satisfactory, conditional or unsatisfactory.

To meet safety-fitness standards, the carrier will have to demonstrate that it has adequate safety-management controls in place to reduce the risks associated with:

- inadequate levels of financial responsibility
- inadequate inspection, repair and maintenance of vehicles
- professional driver's permit standard violations
- the use of unqualified and fatigued drivers
- improper use of motor vehicles
- unsafe vehicles operating on highways
- failure to maintain collision registers and copies of collision reports
- motor-vehicle crashes
- driving and parking violations
- the violation of hazardous material regulations.

The operator of a vehicle that has received an unsatisfactory safety rating will have a specified period of time from the effective date of rating notice to improve the safety rating to conditional or satisfactory.

Should the operator fail to do so, the carrier will be prohibited from operating commercial motor vehicles or transporting passengers for reward.

The Department of Transport has been working closely with the South African Bureau of Standards (SABS) to ensure that the emergency exits of buses and taxis meet required standards and allow passengers to escape without difficulty in emergencies.

The department has requested the SABS to pay specific attention to the relevant safety standards.

This includes the ability of young children and the aged to break through emergency windows.

The SABS has also been requested to look at the locations of all emergency exits and the education of passengers on how to use them.

The department has intensified its education campaign on how to use emergency exits and is engaging manufacturers in ensuring that more visible and reflective material is used to identify emergency exits.

Cross-border transport

Multilateral

The SADC Protocol on Transport, Communications and Meteorology provides a comprehensive framework for regional integration across the entire spectrum of the transport, communications and meteorology sectors. The general objective is to promote the provision of efficient, cost-effective and fully integrated infrastructure and operations in these fields.

The protocol also specifically addresses road transport, and aims to facilitate the unimpeded flow of goods and passengers between and across the territories of SADC member states. It aims to promote the adoption of a harmonised policy, which lays down general operational conditions for carriers.

Cross-border transport within the Southern African Customs Union (SACU) is undertaken in terms of the SACU MoU. The memorandum facilitates transport between member countries through the use of the single-permit system.

In April 2005, the Minister of Labour, Mr Membathisi Mdladlana, launched the Taxi Sectoral Determination. The regulation sets minimum wages and establishes basic conditions of employment for the taxi sector, with effect from July 2005.

This includes registration with the Unemployment Insurance Fund (UIF) of taxi drivers, administrative staff, rank queue marshals, fare collectors and cleaners.

The monthly contribution to the UIF is 2% – 1% is deducted from the driver's salary by the employer and the other 1% is contributed by the employer.

The MoU provides the framework for co-operation between the signatory countries, which has resulted in the establishment of technical working groups for traffic standards, road-user charges and passenger transport.

The activities of the passenger-transport working group led to the establishment of joint route management committees (JRMCs) for certain cross-border passenger routes within the SACU. The JRMCs comprise representatives from the public and private sectors of the countries concerned, and are aimed at jointly managing the routes in consultation with all stakeholders.

Bilateral

Bilateral agreements facilitate and encourage cross-border road transport in support of regional trade.

The Maputo Development Corridor between South Africa and Mozambique is a good example.

The two governments also signed agreements dealing with road freight and passenger transport between the two countries, which will facilitate the movement of goods and people by road, and eliminate bureaucratic proceedings at border posts.

The project also includes the upgrading and modernisation of the railway line between the two countries and of Maputo harbour, at a cost of about R150 million.

On 29 September 2003, South Africa, Namibia and Botswana signed an MoU on the development and management of the Trans-Kalahari Corridor (TKC).

The TKC was formally established in 1998 following the completion of the Trans-Kgalagadi Highway in Botswana. The TKC links the three southern African countries by road.

One of the benefits of the TKC is that it links the hinterlands of Botswana, Namibia and South Africa (especially Gauteng) with the Port of Walvis Bay. This port is the western seabord port in southern Africa and is closest to shipping routes to and from markets in the Americas and Europe.

The development of the TKC has the potential of significantly reducing transaction costs for SADC exporters and importers. This is expected to enable economic operators to become increasingly internationally competitive by enhancing their ability to exploit the benefits of preferential trade agreements with the United States of America (USA) and the European Union.

Domestic

The CBRTA fosters investment in the cross-border road-transport industry and provides high-quality cross-border freight and passenger road-transport services at reasonable prices. The agency works on a cost-recovery basis and any profits from cross-border permit fees are ploughed back into the system through a price reduction on permits in the following financial year. It also encourages small-business development in the industry.

Goods transport

In South Africa alone, road transport accounts for the movement of some 650 mt of freight traffic per year, compared with about 180 mt by rail.

The total throughput, inclusive of local production and imports, in the whole of the South African economy that requires logistics interventions amounted to 745 mt in 2003.

This was divided between 49% for mining, 45% for manufacturing and 6% for agriculture. It is estimated that it cost R135 billion in 2003 in transport costs to move that quantity, where 62% of the total cost was attributable to long-haul road transport, 22% to road distribution, 8% each to rail and air, and 1% to pipeline and water modes. It is estimated that logistical costs to the South African economy are in the region of 14,7% of gross domestic product, with transport representing some 75% of that cost.

The department is working with provincial counterparts and major stakeholders on the Overload-Control Infrastructure Programme, which deals with reckless overloading. The programme is based on the construction of a strategic network of traffic-control centres and fixed weigh stations on major roads, supported by mobile weigh stations on alternative roads in the main freight corridors.

In September 2005, Minister Radebe launched the National Freight Logistics Strategy (NFLS) in Pretoria. The NFLS aims to:

- regulate the freight system to ensure economic efficiency
- exercise effective oversight of the environmental and security elements of the freight system
- promote better physical and operational integration of seaports, airports and land-transport networks.

Road-traffic safety

Greater road-safety awareness has been generated through the activities of the *Arrive Alive* Campaign, which is part of the Road to Safety Strategy.

The RTMC Act, 1999 (Act 20 of 1999), provides for the establishment of the RTMC to:

- enhance the overall quality of road-traffic management and service provision
- strengthen co-operation and co-ordination between the national, provincial and local spheres of government in the management of road traffic
- maximise the effectiveness of provincial and local government efforts, particularly in road-traffic law enforcement
- create business opportunities, particularly for the historically disadvantaged sectors, to supplement public-sector capacity
- guide and sustain the expansion of private-sector investment in road-traffic management.

The RMTC is a partnership between the three spheres of government to strengthen its collective capacity for road-traffic management. The process for adjudicating road-traffic offences has been reformed and is now administrative, rather than judicial.

The Road Traffic Infringement Agency will serve as the collection agency for outstanding traffic fines and adjudicate contested traffic offences. This is a more efficient and effective system for administering traffic offences.

In mid-2005, the RTMC was tasked to finalise a detailed business plan, which aims to strengthen the State's law-enforcement capacity. Government has committed R2,5 billion over the next five years to increase its law-enforcement capacity relating to public transport.

The law-enforcement strategy includes strengthening the capacity of existing public transport law-enforcement units in the various provinces by June 2006, and establishing such units where necessary.

The Constitution authorises provinces to exercise legislative and executive powers pertaining to road-traffic safety, while the promotion thereof is primarily the responsibility of the Department of Transport.

The Road Traffic Safety Board (RTSB) endorses and acts as guardian of the Road Traffic Management Strategy (RTMS); assists in the identification, formulation and prioritisation of projects; monitors progress; and gives direction in the implementation of the RTMS.

The RTSB is made up of members of all three spheres of government, as well as traffic stakeholders in the private sector. The ministers of education, of health, of justice and constitutional development, of provincial and local government, of safety and security and of transport serve on the board.

Three Acts provide for the national co-ordination of regulation and law enforcement, the registration and licensing of motor vehicles, and the training and appointment of traffic officers. These are the RTMC Act, 1999; the National Road-Traffic Amendment Act, 1999 (Act 21 of 1999); and the Administrative Adjudication of Road-Traffic Offences Amendment Act, 1999 (Act 22 of 1999).

The Administrative Adjudication of Road-Traffic Offences Amendment Act, 1999 provides for a more efficient system of collecting traffic fines and for the introduction of a points demerit system, linked to the CCF driver's licence.

In February 2005, total new vehicle sales rose to 42 832, which is a 32,5% increase compared with the same month in 2004.

National Association of Automobile Manufacturers of South Africa figures showed that in February 2005, new car sales increased by 34,4%, light commercial vehicle sales rose by 28,5%, medium commercial vehicle sales by 49,5% and heavy truck and bus sales by 19%.

In March 2005, Statistics South Africa reported that the total motor trade sales in 2004 rose by 17,4% to R175,3 billion.

In terms of the Act, motorists' driver's licences will be suspended when they have 12 penalty points against their names. For every point over and above 12, the motorist's licence will be suspended for three months.

Points can easily be accumulated, for example, four penalty points each for exceeding the speed limit by 50%, driving an unregistered vehicle, refusing to undergo a blood or breathalyser test, or driving a vehicle without registration plates. The use of hand-held cellphones in vehicles is not allowed and non-compliance could cost a motorist two points.

When a driver's licence is suspended for a third time, it will be cancelled and the motorist will again have to undergo a driver's test. In more serious cases, a court may forbid a motorist to drive on a public road ever again. However, the system in no way detracts from the accused's constitutional right to a fair trial. The points demerit system is to be implemented in phases.

Arrive Alive

Government's *Arrive Alive* Road-Safety Campaign aims to:

- reduce the number of road-traffic accidents in general, and fatalities in particular, by 5%, compared with the same period the previous year
- improve road-user compliance with traffic laws
- forge an improved working relationship between traffic authorities in the various spheres of government.

South Africa's rate of pedestrian fatalities is unacceptably high. Factors that have exaggerated the problem in South Africa include lack of infrastructure, such as adequate pavements or road-crossing facilities, lack of education in road usage, a traffic mix with vehicles and pedestrians sharing the road, poor town and transport planning of facilities, such as schools and community halls, and an absence of law enforcement.

The department launched the *Niyabonwa* (You are Seen) Campaign in November 2004.

The campaign aims to reduce pedestrian deaths by encouraging pedestrians to ensure that they are visible to motorists.

Road-safety awareness education is being gradually integrated into the mainstream school curriculum as a set of basic life skills that can be continuously expanded and deepened over time.

Pupils at pre-school level through to grade nine are being exposed to systematic, practical road-safety education within the framework of the 'life-skills' component of their curriculum.

By March 2005, about R9 million was being spent on a multimedia road-safety project involving the training of 116 000 primary school educators in 2 300 workshops throughout the country.

Patrol Car Project

On 17 March 2005, Minister Radebe launched the Arrive Alive Patrol Car Project, which aims to provide provincial and metropolitan/local traffic authorities with additional patrol vehicles.

During this first phase, 60 vehicles worth R6,29 million were distributed.

The vehicles were allocated to provinces as follows: Eastern Cape eight; Free State four; Gauteng nine; KwaZulu-Natal nine; Limpopo six; Mpumalanga six; North West six; Northern Cape four; and Western Cape eight.

The project aims to:

- increase the visibility of traffic authorities and the level of patrolling on identified top hazardous sections of national and major provincial roads
- improve personal interaction between traffic officials and the road-using public
- promote enforcement of selected traffic offences and contraventions
- change the behaviour of drivers
- promote traffic-law compliance in general, to reduce the number of road accidents.

Road-traffic control

The Department of Transport is responsible for co-ordinating and harmonising traffic control (law enforcement) in South Africa. This is done in conjunction with the provinces, which have legislative and executive powers in this regard.

The aim is to enhance traffic quality, promote voluntary compliance of road users with rules and regulations, reduce the incidence of traffic offences, prevent accidents, ensure effective adjudication and implement improved management.

An important facet of the department's work is the development of a standardised management system for traffic control at micro level, to assist traffic authorities in managing their internal and external environments optimally, and to achieve the highest levels of traffic quality.

About 100 provincial and local traffic authorities have implemented the traffic-management model.

Roadblocks are held on a continuous basis by provincial and local traffic authorities. They take many forms, ranging from formal joint roadblocks with the South African Police Service (SAPS), the South African National Defence Force (SANDF) and other role-players, to standard driver and vehicle roadside checks, run by traffic officers to check on driving licences, alcohol usage by drivers, vehicle licences, tyres, lights, brakes, outstanding fines, etc.

Road Accident Fund (RAF)

The RAF is a public entity that compensates victims of motor-vehicle accidents for bodily injuries and/or loss of financial support caused by the death of a breadwinner. The rights for compensation are prescribed by the RAF Act, 1996 (Act 56 of 1996).

The RAF derives its income from a tax levied on petrol and diesel sold in South Africa.

The RAF pays out numerous claims each year due to accidents caused by recklessness; inconsiderate, negligent and aggressive driver behaviour, as well as drunken driving. In 2004/05, 164 346 claims totalling R11,7 billion were lodged. Some 13 441 claims totalling R82 million were finalised and paid out.

Legislation

In September 2005, Minister Radebe introduced the second reading of the RAF Amendment Bill.

The Amendment Bill seeks to ensure the progressive realisation of the right to social security and healthcare and to provide appropriate relief without the introduction of unfair discrimination.

It introduces an equitable, fair and transparent system of compensation and also provides for good

corporate governance, while addressing the financial position of the fund.

The Bill removes unreasonable limitations on passengers in favour of reasonable and transparent limitations for all road users. For the first time, users of public transport will now be able to claim from the fund.

The Bill ensures that more compensation reaches the primary victims of road accidents by reducing the settlement costs. The Bill further protects those seriously injured who will be able to receive compensation to help them adjust their lives accordingly.

The Bill introduces measures of transparency in providing healthcare according to public healthcare tariffs to ensure that current inequalities are not perpetuated through fuel levy monies.

Fraud and corruption

Due to the prevalence of fraud and corruption, claims have to go through a verification process to fully investigate and assess their authenticity and legitimacy. During 2004/05, the RAF identified and reported fraudulent claims to the value of R27,2 million countrywide. Arrests made came as a result of a joint effort with the National Prosecuting Authority (NPA) and the SAPS.

By May 2005, the NPA had reached plea bargaining agreements with the accused in 78 matters where they were ordered to refund the RAF. The agreements made included provision for an accused to refund the RAF in monthly instalments. The total amount received in 2004/05 in respect of the 78 cases was R430 136 and the closing balance (still to be recovered) was R817 398.

Road-safety initiatives

Although the core business of the RAF involves providing compensation to people who have wrongfully suffered loss or damage caused by motor-vehicle accidents, it also promotes a road-safety culture among road users. The RAF contributes to and supports Arrive Alive initiatives and has established partnerships with road safety and law-enforcement agencies to create awareness of road safety and crime prevention.

Patient Outreach Programme

The RAF initiated the Patient Outreach Programme to educate claimants on how to administer and manage the undertaking certificate, and also trace downtrodden patients in need of ongoing medical treatment. The offices are managed by professional nurses and occupational therapists appointed as case managers.

Upon identification of these patients, case managers then come up with a comprehensive treatment plan, taking into account the social, physical and psychological aspects of the person. In 2004/05, case managers managed to make a difference in the lives of 2 016 patients.

Rail transport

The Department of Transport embarked on a comprehensive recapitalisation programme to improve rail safety and revive rail transport as a viable public-transport alternative.

The National Railway Safety Regulator Act, 2002 (Act 16 of 2002), is the enabling legislation for the setting up of the independent Railway Safety Regulator, reporting and accountable to the Minister of Transport.

The regulator oversees safety by means of conducting audits and inspections; undertaking occurrence investigations; analysing occurrence statistics, operator-safety plans and accident reports; and issuing notices to operators to cease an activity or to improve an unsafe activity. Failure to respond to a notice could result in the operator, including the top management and even the board, being prosecuted.

In June 2005, the regulator launched the South African National Standard 3000-1, the first in a series of national safety standards to assist rail operators to understand and comply with new safety management regulations.

The development of industrial and local standards, which will cover certain geographical locations and circumstances, is expected to be completed in 2008.

Spoornet

Spoornet is the largest railroad and heavy haulier in Africa with an annual turnover in excess of US$1 billion. Spoornet's core competency is rail freight, which comprises 95% of turnover with the remaining turnover being derived from long-distance passenger services. Spoornet's core business is the transportation of mining or raw material along dense strategic corridors to ports.

Spoornet is being transformed as a competitive company that:

- provides an efficient and sustainable transport and logistics service
- contributes to the world competitiveness of its customers, the country and the continent
- operates in a manner that contributes to the reduced cost of doing business with the nation
- takes up its rightful place, relative to other transport modes, in the total surface freight transport industry and the economy of the country.

At the core of Spoornet's strategy is an emphasis on the basic imperatives of safety, customer service, operational efficiency, profitability, and attracting and retaining a skilled workforce.

Spoornet intends to spend about R14 billion on capital investment over the next five years to address technological challenges. About 90% of the investment will be spent on the rehabilitation and renewal of infrastructure, locomotives and wagons.

Capital programmes are underway in a number of areas:

Infrastructure

Investment in network infrastructure focuses on the rehabilitation of signalling and overhead power supply systems, which will result in more reliable train services. Focus is also placed on increasing network availability through reductions in line occupation time on the heavy haul and high-density corridors by 50%.

Locomotives

Much of the investment in locomotives will be directed towards upgrades for general freight locomotives and the acquisition of new locomotives for the heavy haul and high-density lines. This will have a 25% and 75% increase in tractive effort respectively, giving Spoornet the leverage to run longer and more reliable trains.

The reliability of an upgraded locomotive will improve by 40% and reduce maintenance costs by 55%. Spoornet has the skills within the business to carry out loco upgrade design and execution. As Spoornet commissions additional locomotives, improvements will also be experienced in other critical corridors.

Wagons

Investment in the wagon fleet will increase carrying capacity (from 45 to 60 tons per wagon) and address unsafe incidents (e.g. derailments) that negatively affect services to customers. Spoornet is embarking on a change in technology from friction to roller bearings, giving it the leverage to increase train speeds from an average of 60 km/h to 80 km/h. This change will also provide Spoornet with the leverage of running heavier loads and longer trains that will benefit customers.

Spoornet is a world leader in heavy-haul bulk railway operations. Spoornet also has general freight operations that are operated below standard. Plans are deployed to tap into the heavy-haul expertise and migrate some of the general freight lines and traffic to heavy haul. In this regard, Spoornet's Engineering and Technology Department aims to stay abreast of the latest global technological developments as the company strives to cater for customers' ever-changing transport needs.

Business units

Spoornet has seven transport divisions providing transport services in all transport modes.

Spoornet's special focus businesses include Shosholoza Meyl, LuxRail (Blue Train and Premier Class), LinkRail and Spoornet International Rail.

The revision of the public-transport subsidy system is expected to underpin the merger of Metrorail, Shosholoza Meyl and the South African Rail Commuter Corporation (SARCC) to report to the Department of Transport, and allow Spoornet to concentrate on freight.

Spoornet represents the group's rail transport interests and is the largest of the Transnet divisions

in revenue, size and employee numbers.

Planned investment expenditure for the next 15 years is about R1 billion a year to address the estimated backlog of R15 billion.

Spoornet consists of the following business units, each with its own core business focus, namely:

GFB Commercial

Known previously as General Freight Business, GFB Commercial is the largest of Spoonet's business units, accounting for some 70% of its income and handling some 52% of its freight tonnage.

GFB Commerical manages the flow of material and information between suppliers and customers along sections of their supply chains. It strives to integrate the rail component of the supply chain with adjoining components to increase supply-chain efficiency and reliability at the lowest-possible cost.

COALlink

COALlink provides world-class transport for South Africa's export coal from the Mpumalanga coalfields to the Richards Bay Coal Terminal. It is one of the world's most efficient bulk export logistic supply chains, and its steam-coal export tonnage is second only to Australia's.

Orex

Orex deals with the transport of iron ore over the

Sub-Saharan Africa boasts about 83% of all Africa's railways. South Africa's share of the African total is some 35% and 42% of sub-Saharan Africa.

South Africa accounts for about 47% of the total number of locomotives of all types in sub-Saharan Africa and 32% of the African total. South Africa's dominance of electric locomotives is nearly complete, with about 96% of sub-Saharan locomotives and 92% of the continent's total number of electric locomotives.

South Africa's dominance of the African freight wagon fleet is 62% of the total African fleet and 74% of the sub-Saharan total. The amount of rail freight tonnes moved occurs mostly in the South African system, with about 71% of the African total and some 91% of sub-Saharan traffic.

861-km railway line from Sishen to Saldanha. Following the high demand for ore in the export markets, improvements to the line are underway to increase the capacity of the Orex line from 18 mt a year to more than 22 mt a year.

In a recent benchmark study, Orex was rated as 38% better than the next best-practice operator in its field.

Luxrail

Luxrail's primary focus is the operation of the Blue Train, which caters for a growing international tourist market. It has won several World Travel Awards for the world's leading luxury train. Crossing South Africa's varied landscape along four routes, the train combines the comfort and luxury of a five-star hotel with unparalleled journeys.

Luxrail also manages contracts with other luxury train operators using Spoornet's infrastructure. These include Rovos Rail, which travels throughout southern Africa, and the Spier, which travels on the Western Cape wine routes.

Shosholoza Meyl

Previously known as Main Line Passenger Services, Shosholoza Meyl provides affordable intercity passenger rail services to and from South African destinations. These include Johannesburg, Durban, Makhado, Polokwane, Komatipoort, East London,

In October 2005, Spoornet hosted the 15th International Railway Safety Conference in Cape Town.

The conference, under the theme *Innovative Safety Solutions for Tomorrow's Railway*, was officially opened by the Minister of Public Enterprises, Mr Alec Erwin.

The conference was hosted in conjunction with various role-players in the South African railway industry, including the South African Railway Commuter Association and the Rail Safety Regulator.

Participants included safety experts, consultants and representatives of various railway companies from around the world, as well as from railway-safety regulators, railway associations, labour organisations, and departments of transport.

Port Elizabeth, Bloemfontein, Kimberley and Cape Town. Services also connect with destinations in Zimbabwe, Mozambique and Swaziland.

About four million passengers use Shosholoza Meyl's services a year.

Spoornet International Joint Ventures (IJV)

IJV is responsible for all Spoornet activities outside South Africa, as well as for all non-core activities and joint ventures within the country.

Spoornet aims to be a global leader in operations on the 1 000-mm and 1 067-mm (narrow gauge) rail networks of the world, especially in Africa. The IJV is Spoornet's vehicle for achieving this and other objectives outside the company's normal areas of activity.

Metrorail

Metrorail, a division of Transnet, is South Africa's only commuter rail service and has been operating in five metropolitan areas in the Western Cape, Eastern Cape, KwaZulu-Natal and Gauteng since 1990. The SARCC, a government agency, owns all commuter rail assets (property, infrastructure and rolling stock) to the value of R69 million. Metrorail provides the commuter services under a contract with the SARCC.

By February 2005, the Department of Public Enterprises was working with Transnet, Metrorail and the SARCC to consolidate the executive functions of Metrorail and the SARCC.

The transitional executive team's tasks include halting the continuing deterioration of the commuter rail service and putting together a stabilisation strategy. They will also need to accelerate the implementation of the rolling stock refurbishment programme, improve service levels on priority corridors in the Western Cape and Gauteng, reduce fare evasion, and improve the levels of safety and security on the commuter rail service.

The new entity was expected to be in place by December 2005. These initiatives were being undertaken in parallel with the development of the Interim National Rail Passenger Plan, which will provide a comprehensive vision and model and investment requirements for passenger rail.

Metrorail trains carry some 1,5 million passengers a day in 352 train-sets over 2 400 km of railway track nationally and serve 473 stations.

Metrorail regularly conducts safety campaigns to heighten the public's awareness of safety and security matters relating to the railway environment.

Some of the mini-themes that have been explored include the:

- *Close-the-Door* Campaign, which urges commuters to ensure that doors are closed before and while the train is in motion
- *Empty-Coach* Campaign, which advises commuters to be aware of activity around them inside trains.

South African Rail Commuter Corporation

The SARCC was established in 1990 to provide commuter rail services in South Africa.

The SARCC operates two major businesses – Rail Commuter Services and Property Management.

Rail Commuter Services is operated as a social responsibility programme requiring considerable government subsidisation. The assets that were transferred to the SARCC included property with a net potential of R2 billion in the main metropolitan areas.

The corporation's role as concessionaire is to establish and monitor service standards, safety and security levels, and operating efficiencies. More than two million people use the commuter rail service daily.

In 2004/05, the SARCC infrastructure and assets comprised 380 stations, some 2 240 km of electrified single-rail track and 4 564 coaches.

Intersite

Commuter rail stations and properties are managed and developed by Intersite Property Management Services (Pty) Ltd. Intersite is a wholly-owned subsidiary of SARCC that was formed in 1992.

The commuter rail portfolio comprises 478 stations, 4 200 hectares (ha) of land, and property in the major metropolitan areas of Johannesburg, Pretoria, Durban and Cape Town. Apart from building new stations and upgrading and maintaining

stations, Intersite is commercialising them and generating income for commuter rail.

Since 1992, Intersite has completed a number of station upgrades at a cost of R542 million while a further R196 million has been invested in Metrorail operational assets. Several new stations/intermodal transport facilities were also completed totalling some R94 million.

In 2003/04, Intersite generated some R179 million for the SARCC.

The SARCC is implementing an active programme to improve the state of commuter rail rolling stock.

This is accomplished by increasing the number of coaches in the refurbishment process, at the same time improving repair standards. The new standard includes the upgrade of a modular body train set that shares the same aesthetics as the 10M3 and 10M4 coaches currently running in the Johannesburg and Cape Town regions.

During the 2004/05 financial year, 413 coaches were overhauled at a cost of R715 million.

Civil aviation

During 2004, a total of 567 074 arrivals and departures were handled at the 19 air-traffic service units, compared with 558 743 during 2001 and 543 627 in 2000.

By mid-2005, there were 9 063 aircraft on the South African register.

The number of airlines operating in South African airspace increased from nine in 1994 to more than 50 in 2004. Some 21 air-traffic control centres support operations covering some 145 licensed airports with paved runways and over 580 aerodromes with unpaved runways.

Airports

The Airports Company of South Africa (ACSA), which was officially established on 23 July 1993, owns and operates South Africa's 10 principal airports, including the three major international airports in Johannesburg, Cape Town and Durban. ACSA also has a 35-year concession to operate the Pilanesberg Airport near Sun City in North West. The other six airports are: Bloemfontein, Port Elizabeth, East London,

George, Kimberley, Upington and Pilaneberg.

By June 2005, South Africa had 136 licensed airports/aerodromes categorised as either public or private, as well as 56 approved heli-stops.

ACSA's three core activities are:

- airport services, including the development of airport infrastructure such as providing and maintaining runways, taxiways and aprons; terminal facilities; and aviation security, fire and rescue services
- retail and advertising activities, including the provision of space within terminals to appropriate retailers, and other sites to operations such as car-hire firms, banks and space for advertisers
- property activities, retail and office premises, and car-parking facilities, as well as functioning as commercial landlords.

ACSA recorded a 7,4% rise in total departing passenger traffic during the financial year ended 31 March 2004, to 11,9 million. This was mainly attributable to an increase of 7,9% in domestic passenger volumes and 6,4% in international passenger volumes.

During the same period, revenue increased by 17% to R1,86 billion and operating profit rose by 19% to R902,3 million. Despite poor trading conditions, retail revenue increased by 15%, while advertising revenue increased significantly by 39% to R67,9 million and revenue from property increased by 6% to R138,4 million.

Despite a difficult market aggravated by a stronger rand, passenger volumes increased by 7,4% to 11,9 million. This was mainly attributable to an increase of 7,9% in domestic passenger volumes and 6,4% in international passenger volumes. Aircraft landings declined moderately by 2%. Domestic and international landings increased by 6,4% and 2,3% respectively, with regional landings decreasing by 2,1%.

During 2004, ACSA came closer to achieving its mission of managing world-class airports by completing projects to the value of more than R471 million at its airports. These included the upgrade of the terminal at Port Elizabeth, which was officially opened by the Minister of Transport in May 2004. At the company's flagship gateway, Johannesburg

International Airport (JIA), new security gates and landside access roads were completed.

The completion of these projects marked the conclusion of a five-year expansion and upgrading programme, which started in 1998. Some R3 billion was invested in new or significantly upgraded airport infrastructure intended to bring facilities at ACSA airports in line with the world's best.

The board approved a sum of R3,58 billion over the next five years to increase capacity and efficiency at all airports, including the domestic airports in Kimberley, Bloemfontein and East London.

Major plans include a multistorey parkade at Cape Town International Airport (CTIA) with inhouse check-in counters, and an international passenger transfer facility in the JIA terminal. This will be integrated with the Gautrain Rapid Rail Link between JIA, Sandton and Johannesburg, to be constructed by the Gauteng Provincial Government.

Echo Apron, in conjunction with the Northern Pier development, will increase JIA's capacity to accommodate the new wide-body long-haul aircraft such as the A380 at connecting stands.

Furthermore, the Johannesburg International Trade Bureau (JITB), a joint venture between ACSA, the International Trade Bureau, and the National African Federated Chamber of Commerce, was expected to be completed in 2005.

The JITB will offer 2 200 m^2 of permanent exhibition space to over 120 of South Africa's premier exporters, with unparalleled access to international business visitors. The bureau will also feature a business information library, an exhibitor information desk, meeting rooms and consultation areas.

CTIA now boasts a world-class international terminal with capacity for up to five million passengers a year.

The Port Elizabeth Airport's new R30-million terminal building was officially opened in May 2004. The number of arriving and departing passengers moving through Port Elizabeth has increased over the past few years, with just under a million people moving through the airport during 2003/04.

ACSA will spend about R14 million at Bloemfontein Airport on a terminal revamp, the upgrade of fire-fighting equipment, and runway rehabilitation.

Some R23 million was allocated to East London Airport for a new instrument-landing system (ILS) and fire-fighting equipment.

Kimberley and George airports will each receive R6 million for terminal refurbishment, replacement and upgrade of equipment, and R17 million for terminal upgrade, ILS and equipment replacement.

Given its strong, although seasonal freight traffic, about R14 million was budgeted for cargo-apron extension, fire fighting and general equipment replacement, while R21 million was set aside for strengthening the runway, terminal extension and equipment improvement at Pilanesberg International Airport.

Air-Traffic Navigation Service (ATNS)

The ATNS is responsible for the efficient running of South Africa's air-traffic control systems and the maintenance of navigation equipment, which includes the deployment of air-traffic controllers and aviation technical staff.

The company college is a well-established facility that is used by several African countries for air-traffic services training and for technical training for equipment support.

The ATNS does not receive government transfers and derives its funding from its operations.

Air-traffic service fees contributed 90% to total revenue earned in 2003/04. Revenue from the air-traffic satellite communication system in the SADC region contributed 5% during the same period.

The balance of revenue is earned from technical maintenance services, aeronautical information services and the provision of training in air-traffic control.

Having started in 2004, the ATNS aims to achieve a return on capital employed of 11,1% over a five-year period, with medium-term targets of 6,1%, 6,9% and 8,2%.

The company expects to improve service-delivery targets, reduce pilot and controller workloads, and enhance the efficiency of the system by implementing the South African Advanced Air Traffic System (SAAATS).

The benefits of SAAATS to airlines include a reduction of delays due to improved approach sequencing, significant fuel savings, improved coverage and optimised routings in oceanic sectors.

A joint operations centre at the JIA is the nerve centre of all airport communications and operations. From here, all activities related to maintenance and building management are co-ordinated. The centre serves as a control office, crisis control centre for emergencies, and an Information Technology (IT) centre.

The ATNS was expected to increase the number of air-traffic controllers at JIA by 30%, from 69 to 96, by 2006. By June 2005, air-traffic control services were provided at 19 aerodromes in the country.

Airlines

SAA is by far the largest air carrier in Africa, with the JIA being the busiest airport in Africa. Nearly 75% of air traffic activity in Africa takes place in the region.

SAA, British Airways (BA)/Comair, SA Express, SA Airlink and Interair operate scheduled air services within South Africa and the Indian Ocean islands. In addition to serving Africa, SAA operates services to Europe, Latin America and the Far East.

Scheduled international air services are also provided by Air Afrique, Air Austral, Air Botswana, Air France, Air Gabon, Air Madagascar, Air Malawi, Air Mauritius, Air Namibia, Air Portugal, Air Seychelles, Air Tanzania, Air Zimbabwe, Airlink Swaziland, Alliance Express, BA, Cameroon Airlines, Delta Airlines, El Al, Egyptair, Emirates, Ethiopian Airlines, Ghana Airways, Iberia, KLM, Kenya Airways, LAM, LTU, Lufthansa, MK Airlines, Malaysia Airlines, Martinair Holland, North-West Airlines, Olympic Airways, Quantas, Royal Air Maroc, Saudi Arabian Airlines, Singapore Airlines, Swissair, Taag, Thai International, Turkish Airlines, Uganda Airlines, United Airlines, Varig, Virgin Atlantic, Yemenia, Zambian Air Services and Zambian Skyways.

Aviation safety and security

South Africa complies with the ICAO-recommended practices on aviation security.

South Africa is also participating in the development and establishment of an upper airspace control centre for the SADC. This initiative proposes that a single centre hosted by an SADC country will provide air-navigation services to all aircraft flying above 24 500 feet.

Emphasis is being placed on improved international access to and from South Africa by air, the

Interesting facts and figures about South African Airways (SAA):
- SAA serves more than 700 destinations throughout the world.
- It carries more than 6,5 million passengers each year and serves 34 cities in 26 countries on six continents.
- It employs close to 12 000 people worldwide, including 3 600 at SAA Technical. Staff include about 2 800 flight attendants and more than 800 pilots.
- SAA has a development programme known as Women in Aviation to develop high-calibre female managers to feed SAA's executive leadership.
- Some 77% of SAA leadership is black with a 56:44 male to female ratio. At senior management level, 44% are black; and 41% of middle management and 55% non-management staff are black.
- SAA Technical at Johannesburg International Airport (JIA) is the largest maintenance facility in Africa.
- SAA undertakes maintenance for more than 40 major airlines, including British Airways (BA), Singapore Airlines, Air France and Lufthansa.
- Some 20% of SAA's domestic travellers are 'regular' i.e. they fly more than one trip per month on average.
- SAA flies more than 20 domestic routes; there are 20 flights between Cape Town and Johannesburg per day.
- The Airbus has 15 movie channels in addition to video games, short features, actuality programmes and travel information.
- Airbus aircraft have 12 audio channels and a jukebox feature, allowing passengers to select and play their choice of music.
- SAA's business class flat-bed seat is the best in the world, according to Skytrax, which surveyed competitors, including BA and Virgin Atlantic.
- Voyager, SAA's loyalty programme, has 1,4 million members.
- Each year, wine experts sample 800 wines to select 70 for on-board aircraft.
- The Cycad Premium Lounge at JIA was ranked number three in the world by Skytrax World First-Class Survey in 2002.
- The Baobab Lounge for business class international travellers at JIA has 33 workstations offering ergonomic business modules, computers, printers and faxes.

Source: South African Airways

expansion of the bilateral air-services framework, the implementation of the Yamoussoukro Declaration, effective monitoring of airline activities, and the efficient licensing and regulation of domestic and international air services. Other aims include promoting:

- safer skies: this involves ensuring that adequate safety and upper-air space-control regimes are in place across the continent, supported by efficient air-traffic and navigational services and systematic human resource development programmes
- efficient and effective aviation networks: this involves regulating as necessary to make air transport more affordable, creating regional hubs and air-carrier alliances, and supporting one another to establish a high-quality African airports network.

Ports

Commercial ports play a crucial role in South Africa's transport, logistics and socio-economic development. About 98% of South Africa's exports are conveyed by sea.

South Africa's eight commercial seaports are managed and controlled by the NPA, a division of Transnet Limited. The NPA was established in August 2001 from the restructuring of Portnet to enhance the efficiency of South Africa's seaports in the evolving maritime climate of the 21st century, a vital function in sustaining the growth of the national economy.

The new structure, comprising the NPA and the SAPO as separate entities, is specifically designed to separate operational and landlord functions to optimise the benefits and potential of public/private-sector partnerships, while at the same time retaining state ownership of this essential part of the national infrastructure.

The NPA is responsible for the maintenance and development of port infrastructure and is the biggest port authority in southern Africa, controlling eight of the 17 major ports in this region, namely Richards Bay, Durban, East London, Port Elizabeth, Mossel Bay, Cape Town, Saldanha and Ngqura.

The eighth commercial port, the Port of Ngqura, was set to become operational in 2005. The port is situated at the Coega River mouth about 20 km from Port Elizabeth. It boasts state-of-the-art facilities that complement the other seven national ports regarding additional volumes of commercial traffic, providing a variety of different cargo applications from breakbulk and liquid bulk to container and conveyer services. As the deepest container terminal in Africa, the port is one of the biggest government-sponsored infrastructure developments in South Africa.

With the conclusion of the NPA Bill, the South African port system is at the threshold of an exciting era. The NPA Bill, a product of government's National Commercial Ports Policy, provides South African ports with insight into government's vision for ports and a clear direction of how ports are to be managed and operated under the NPA.

Based on the National Commercial Ports Policy, the vision for South African ports is to become a system of ports, seamlessly integrated in the logistics network that is jointly and individually self-sustainable.

This will be achieved through the delivery of high levels of service and increasing efficiency for a growing customer base, and will result in the enhancement of South Africa's global competitiveness and facilitate the expansion of the economy through socially and environmentally sustainable port development.

The NPA is responsible for:
- port facilities to handle all types of cargo and ships through an extensive port network
- efficient transfer of goods between ship, road and rail through the provision of efficient port services
- efficient transportation of goods within and beyond the borders of South Africa through extensive and modern road, rail and sea links.

The NPA's business consists of the following divisions:

Trade and Logistics
This division is the strategic business arm of the NPA. It is responsible for customer relationship marketing along with a combination of technology and human resources.

Landlord Services
Landlord Services ensures the planning, develop-

ment and optimal use of port property and infrastructure, as well as a safe, secure and healthy port environment.

The division consists of property, engineering and planning and development. Landlord Services has traditionally been the NPA's major revenue earner, initially through wharfage, and currently through cargo dues.

Maritime Services
Maritime Services includes improving efficiency in shipping services, the dredging of navigational waterways, and ensuring a safe shipping environment through vessel-tracing services, pilotage and lighthouse services.

The ports provide:
- pilotage, tug and berthing services
- bulk-handling installations to handle dry and liquid bulk, complemented by storage facilities
- container-handling facilities
- multi-purpose terminals for the handling of breakbulk and containers
- access to rail and road links
- ship-repair facilities
- feeder services.

Lighthouse Services
Lighthouse Services operates 45 lighthouses along the South African coastline.

The NPA has vessel-traffic systems in all ports, which ensure improved safety of navigation within the port and port limits, and enhance the service provided to the port user.

Marine Services
Marine Services operates 24 large tugs, eight work boats, four pilot boats and 14 launches in South Africa's eight commercial ports. Twenty-four hour services are provided at the ports of Durban and Richards Bay.

Portcon International
This division provides a consultancy and training service appropriate to ports operating within the African context.

Port and Corporate Affairs

This division is responsible for the efficient and profitable running of the ports as service-delivery platforms.

Deepwater ports

The Port of Richards Bay is a relatively young port, having opened on 1 April 1976. It is South Africa's leading port in terms of cargo volumes and handles in excess of 80 mt per year, representing about 57% of South Africa's seaborne cargo trade.

The port covers a surface area of 2 157 ha on land and 1 443 ha on water, making it the biggest port in South Africa in terms of size. It offers easy access to South Africa's national rail network with substantial growth capacity in the rail network link.

One of the port's inherent strengths is its deepwater infrastructure, with a maximum permissible draught of 17,5 m. This, coupled with the high-tech state-of-the-art terminal infrastructures, allows for high-speed, high-volume cargo handling and a fast turnaround of vessels.

Feasibility studies for the R2-billion ship-repair facility at the Port of Richards Bay are almost complete and construction was expected to start early in 2005. The facility will refurbish an estimated 40 ships per year, including bulk carriers and oil tankers. The design includes a 260-m long dry dock, 760 m of ship-repair outfitting quay, and 300 m for material and workboats. The facility is expected to be completed by mid-2007.

For industrial investors, the port offers an abundance of prime industrial land, both immediately adjacent to the port and further inland. About 1 644 commercial ocean-going vessels call at the port's five terminals annually, of which three are privately operated and two are operated by SAPO. The privately operated terminals are the Richards Bay Coal Terminal; Island View Storage, which handles bulk liquids and liquified gases; and Fedmis, which exports phosphoric acid.

Saldanha Port, situated on the West Coast, is the deepest and the largest natural port in southern Africa. The port is unique in that it has a purpose-built railroad serving a bulk-handling facility, which is connected to a dedicated jetty for the shipment of iron ore.

Saldanha also serves as a major crude-oil importation and transhipment port.

As the only iron-ore handling port in South Africa, a R930-million upgrade aimed at maintaining and increasing the carrying capacity of the iron-ore export plant was undertaken. This includes acquiring new equipment and increasing workspace efficiency. The project was expected to be completed in 2005/06.

Hub ports

The Port of Durban is a full-service general cargo and container port. It is the most conveniently situated port for the industrialised Durban/Pinetown and Gauteng areas and cross-border traffic.

As South Africa's premier cargo and container port, the Port of Durban handles over 55 mt of cargo per year and is a catalyst in the development of trade throughout the region. Durban has abundant shipping opportunities, both in terms of frequency and destinations served.

This is the busiest port in Africa, as well as the biggest in terms of container capacity due to its strategic location. It has a surface land area of 1 854 ha. The Durban Container Terminal is the largest such facility in the southern hemisphere and is geared to expand in terms of cargo handling.

It is especially effective as a hub port for cargo to and from the Far East, Europe and the Americas, serving South Africa, as well as west and east African countries. The port is also the premier port for a wide range of commodities, including coal, mineral ores, granite, chemicals, petrochemicals, steel, forest products, citrus products, sugar and grain.

The Port of Cape Town is one of two hubs in South Africa. It offers multi-purpose dry and liquid and dry terminals, as well as fully serviced dry docks. The port is renowned for its deciduous fruit and frozen-product exports. A major fishing industry is also based here.

The Port of Cape Town is strategically positioned and ideally situated to serve as a hub for cargoes between Europe, the Americas, Africa, Asia and Oceania. The port provides a complex network of services to its clients and a favourable environment for all stakeholders, to maximise benefits to the local and national economy.

Integrated intermodal cargo systems, ship repair, bunkering facilities and the reefer trade are examples of these services.

In 2005/06, Transnet approved investment of R2,075 billion to upgrade Durban and Cape Town container terminals. The aim is to improve the capacity within the ports and upgrade and develop the facilities to meet the economy's growing demands.

An amount of R1,437 billion was expected to be invested in the Port of Durban to develop the container-handling facility. This will be jointly funded by SAPO and NPA. An amount of R600 million was approved to upgrade the Cape Town Container Terminal.

In addition, R10 million was invested in 2005/06 to increase reefer infrastructure at the Cape Town Container Terminal.

These projects formed part of the five-year R37-billion infrastructure plan that was approved by Cabinet in 2004. They will strengthen Transnet's position to provide a seamless intermodal freight transport service that is consistent with the company's strategic vision of reducing the cost of doing business in South Africa.

The Port of East London is situated at the mouth of the Buffalo River on South Africa's east coast, and is the country's only commercial river port.

It boasts a large container terminal and grain elevator as it is the largest exporter of maize.

With a world-class R80-million car terminal, the port has become one of the major motor-vehicle export and import terminals in South Africa.

Multi-purpose ports

The Port of Port Elizabeth, with its proximity to heavily industrialised and intensively farmed areas, has facilities for the handling of all commodities – bulk, general and container cargo.

Being situated at the centre of the country's motor-vehicle-manufacturing industry, the port imports large volumes of containerised components and raw material for this industry. The bulk of

exports comprises agricultural products. Apart from agricultural produce, manganese ore, motor-vehicle-industry-related products and steel are exported.

The container terminal has maintained the highest handling rates in Africa in recent years and is accredited to International Standards Organisation (ISO) 9002.

Located mid-way between Cape Town and Port Elizabeth, the Port of Mossel Bay has in the past specialised in serving the local inshore and deep-sea fishing industry, as well as limited commercial cargo. However, it now serves the oil industry as well as other client-orientated marine cargo handling.

This port is the only South African port that operates two offshore mooring points within port limits. Both mooring points are used for the transport of refined petroleum products.

Pipelines

Petronet owns, maintains and operates a network of 3 000 km of high-pressure petroleum and gas pipelines.

Transnet has approved R3 billion for the design, construction and commissioning of a new multi-products pipeline between Durban and Gauteng. The new pipeline will enhance Petronet's capacity to service the transport needs of refined petroleum products such as petrol, diesel and jet fuel along the Durban-Gauteng corridor.

Apart from doubling the current pipeline capacity to accommodate growing need, there is also the imperative to have this pipeline completed to coincide with South Africa's hosting of the 2010 Soccer World Cup. As the safest mode of bulk petroleum product transportation, this pipeline project will, in the long term, ensure optimal use of the fuel transport infrastructure in the country.

The Petroleum Pipelines Act, 2003 (Act 60 of 2003), has been promulgated and the appointment of a regulator was expected towards the end of 2005. The Gas Act, 2001 (Act 48 of 2001), was passed by Parliament in August 2001. Regulators for both gas and liquid fuels were expected to be in place by the end of 2005. This Act will result in commercial regulation of petroleum pipelines and will have a profound influence on Petronet. In 2006, Petronet will prepare for regulation and also focus on expanding the non-regulated side of the business with a specific focus on terminal management.

Maritime affairs

Maritime administration, legislation and shipping

Marine transport encompasses all forms of transport by sea, intermodal links and inland ports. It caters to a large degree for the freight market, and in the South African context offers no significant passenger-carrying ability.

South Africa's maritime administration and legislation is the responsibility of the Department of Transport, and is controlled on its behalf by the SAMSA in terms of the SAMSA Act, 1998 (Act 5 of 1998).

The broad aim of the SAMSA is to maintain the safety of life and property at sea within South Africa's area of maritime jurisdiction, and to ensure the prevention of marine pollution by oil and other substances emanating from ships.

The Department of Environmental Affairs and Tourism is responsible for combating pollution and has specific means at its disposal, such as the *Kuswag* coast-watch vessels, with which to perform this function.

Some of the South African Maritime Safety Authority's (SAMSA) recent achievements include:
• 1 011 ships with a gross tonnage of 238 196 tons were registered under the South African flag
• 219 foreign flagged ships were inspected and four detained
• 19 oil-pollution incidents were investigated
• 277 candidates passed various examinations conducted by SAMSA
• 3 082 safety certificates were issued out of 3 530 ship surveys
• 930 dry-dock certificates were issued out of 1 023 surveys.

The SAMSA is responsible for the introduction and maintenance of international standards set by the International Maritime Organisation in London, with respect to:
• ship construction
• maritime training and training curricula
• watch-keeping
• certification of seafarers
• manning and operation of local and foreign ships
• maritime search-and-rescue
• marine communications and radio navigation aids
• pollution prevention.

The SAMSA has an operations unit, a policy unit and a corporate support division to handle all financial, human resource and IT issues.

Other functions include the registration of ships, the establishment of a coastal patrol service, and the management of marine casualties and wrecks.

The SAMSA is steadily improving its capacity to monitor safety standards on foreign vessels. A considerable number of ships calling at South Africa's major ports were inspected and those not in compliance with international safety standards were detained until the deficiencies were corrected.

In February 2004, the department released the Proposed Maritime Agenda 2010 Strategy, which, among other objectives, seeks to promote and facilitate safe, secure, environmentally sound, efficient and sustainable maritime transport.

The South African Marine Corporation (Safmarine), Unicorn Lines and Griffin Shipping are South Africa's predominant shipping lines. Their fleets of container, oil tanker, general cargo and bulk cargo vessels operate not only between South African ports, but also as cross-traders to other parts of the world.

Training

The South African Maritime Training Academy at Simonstown in the Western Cape provides advanced training to the broader maritime sector, including the merchant navy, harbour-craft operations, the fishing industry and the South African Navy.

The South African Merchant Navy Academy, General Botha, established at Granger Bay, is integrated with the Cape Peninsula University of

Technology, with a similar training facility at the Durban Institute of Technology. Deck and engineering students and officers complete their academic training at the Cape Peninsula University of Technology and the Durban Institute of Technology, while lower classes of certificates are offered at the Training Centre for Seamen, situated in the Duncan Dock area in Cape Town.

This training institution also caters for deck, engine-room and catering department ratings.

The SAMSA is responsible for setting all standards of training certification and watch-keeping on behalf of the Department of Transport, while the Maritime Education and Training Board is responsible for the accreditation of all maritime courses.

Other maritime training organisations offer a wide range of courses that have been developed within the South African maritime industry. These are situated mainly in the ports of Cape Town and Durban and, to a lesser degree, Port Elizabeth.

Search-and-rescue services

The Department of Transport is responsible for the provision of a search-and-rescue function in South Africa. The search-and-rescue programme has been in existence since 1948.

The South African Search-and-Rescue Organisation (SASAR) provides South Africa with a world-class search-and-rescue capability.

The SASAR is a voluntary organisation functioning under the auspices of the Department of Transport.

Its main function is to search for, assist, and, if necessary, rescue survivors of aircraft accidents or forced landings, vessels in distress, and accidents at sea. It is also charged with co-ordinating the resources made available to the department by various government departments, voluntary organisations, and private aircraft and shipping companies for search-and-rescue purposes. The executive committee of the SASAR, in conjunction with the relevant officials of the department, is responsible for formulating policy and procedures.

The Department of Transport, the SANDF, Telkom, Portnet, SAMSA, CAA, ATNS, SAPS, the Independent Communications Authority of South Africa, SAA and the Department of Provincial and Local Government are members of the SASAR and contribute their services and/or facilities.

Voluntary organisations such as the 4x4 Rescue Club, the Mountain Club of South Africa, Hamnet and the National Sea Rescue Institute are also members of the SASAR.

Maritime safety

South Africa has been identified as a focal point for a regional search-and-rescue centre. During 2003/04, the Department of Transport set aside R3,5 million for the establishment of a dedicated maritime rescue co-ordination centre. The process is at an advanced stage.

Acknowledgements

Air Traffic and Navigation Services

Airports Company South Africa

BuaNews

South African Civil Aviation Authority

Department of Transport

Estimates of National Expenditure 2005, published by National Treasury

National Household Travel Survey, 2003

National Ports Authority of South Africa

South African Rail Commuter Corporation

Spoornet Ltd

Transnet Ltd

Road Accident Fund

www.gov.za

www.transnet.co.za

www.southafrica.info

www.spoornet.co.za

www.saa.co.za

Suggested reading

Burkett, D. *Jetlag: South African Airways in the Andrews Era*. Sandton: Penguin, 2001.

Byrom, J. *Fields of Air: Triumphs, Tragedies and Mysteries of Civil Aviation in Southern Africa*. Rivonia, Sandton: Ashanti, 1993.

Development Bank of Southern Africa. *Infrastructure: A Foundation for Development. Development Report 1998*. Midrand: Development Bank of Southern Africa, 1998.

Du Toit, A. *South Africa's Fighting Ships, Past and Present*. Rivonia, Sandton: Ashanti, 1992.

Harris, C.J. and Ingpen, B.D. *Mailships of the Union-Castle Line*. Cape Town: Fernwood, 1994.

Illsley, J. *In Southern Skies: A Pictorial History of Early Aviation in Southern Africa*. Cape Town: Jonathan Ball, 2003.

Infrastructure Mandates for Change: 1994 – 1999. Pretoria: Human Sciences Research Council (HSRC), 2000.

Ingpen, B.D. *South African Merchant Ships: An Illustrated Recent History of Coasters, Colliers, Containerships, Tugs and Other Vessels*. Cape Town: Balkema, 1979.

Khosa, M. ed. *Empowerment Through Service Delivery*. Pretoria: HSRC, 2000.

Moore, D. *Sunset of Steam: A Tribute in Colour to the Golden Years of Steam Locomotives in South Africa*. Johannesburg: Chris van Rensburg, 1990.

Nöthling, C.J. and Becker, D. *Pride of the Nation: A Short History of the South African Air Force*. Pretoria: South African Air Force, 1995.

Robbins, D. *Blue Train*. Johannesburg: Penguin, 1993.

Schnettler, F. *A Century of Cars*. Cape Town: Tafelberg, 1997.

Stirling, W.G.M. and House J.A. *They Served Africa With Wings: 60 Years of Aviation in Central Africa*. Saanichton BC Canada: Bookmark Publishing, 2004.

631

23. Water affairs and forestry

The Department of Water Affairs and Forestry's core function is to ensure that all South Africans have equitable access to water and sanitation, and that the country's water resources and forests are managed in a sustainable manner.

Hydrological conditions

South Africa is located in a predominantly semi-arid part of the world. The climate varies from desert and semi-desert in the west to sub-humid along the eastern coastal area, with an average rainfall for the country of about 450 mm per year. This is well below the world average of about 860 mm per year, while evaporation is comparatively high.

The country's water resources are, in global terms, scarce and extremely limited. The total flow of all the rivers in the country combined amounts to about 49 200 million cubic metres (m³) per year. This is less than half of that of the Zambezi River, the closest large river to South Africa. Groundwater plays a pivotal role, especially in rural water supplies. However, due to the predominantly hard-rock nature of South Africa's geology, there are few major groundwater aquifers that can be utilised on a large scale.

Owing to the poor spatial distribution of rainfall, the natural availability of water across the country is also highly uneven. This is compounded by the strong seasonality of rainfall over virtually the entire country, as well as the high within-season variability of rainfall, and consequently of run-off.

As a result, stream flow in South Africa's rivers is at relatively low levels for most of the time, with sporadic high flows occurring – characteristics which limit the proportion of stream flow that can be relied upon to be available for use, and which also have implications for water-related disasters such as floods and droughts.

To aggravate the situation, most urban and industrial development, as well as some dense rural settlements have been established in remote locations away from large watercourses. As a result, the requirements for water already far exceed its natural availability in several river basins. Widely spread and often large-scale transfers of water across catchments have, therefore, been implemented in South Africa.

To facilitate the management of water resources, the country has been divided into 19 catchment-based water-management areas. Eleven water-management areas share international rivers.

Water-resource development and management in South Africa have, over the years, continuously evolved to meet the needs of a growing population and a vibrant economy, within the constraints imposed by nature. These developments have largely been made possible by recognising water as a national asset, thereby allowing its transportation from where it is available to where the greatest overall benefits for the nation can be achieved.

Sufficient water resources have been developed and are available to ensure that all current requirements for water can reasonably be met, without impairing the socio-economic development of the country.

Where feasible, special management techniques may be applied to improve water quality to appropri-ate standards for particular uses. The quality of groundwater varies according to the hydrogeological conditions and anthropogenic impact. However, most major aquifer systems contain potable quality water.

Measures will be introduced to ensure the most beneficial and efficient use of water in the country from a social and economic perspective.

Provided that the water resources of South Africa are judiciously managed and wisely allocated and utilised, sufficient water of appropriate quality will be available to sustain a strong economy, high social standards and healthy aquatic ecosystems for many generations.

South Africa is mainly dependent on surface water resources for most of the urban, industrial and irriga-tion water supplies in the country. In general, the sur-face water resources are highly developed over most of South Africa. Groundwater, while also extensively utilised, particularly in the rural and more arid areas, is limited due to the geology of the country, much of which is hard rock. Large porous aquifers occur only in a few areas.

In the northern parts of the country, both surface and groundwater resources are nearly fully developed and utilised. Some overexploitation occurs in localised areas, with little undeveloped resource potential remaining. The reverse applies to the well-watered south-eastern region of the country where there are still significant undeveloped and little-used resources.

The total mean annual run-off of water in South Africa under natural (undeveloped) conditions is estimated at a little over 49 200 million m^3 per year, which includes about 4 800 million m^3 per year of water originating from Lesotho, and about 700 million m^3 per year originating from Swaziland, which naturally drain into South Africa. Agricultural irrigation represents close to 60% of the total water requirements of the country, while urban requirements constitute about 25% as the second-largest user sector. The remaining 15% is shared by the other four sectors (all standardised to 98% assurance of supply).

The total net abstraction of water from surface water resources amounts to about 10 200 million m^3 per year for the whole of South Africa, after allowing for the re-use of return flows. This repre-

Major dams of South Africa		
Dam	Full supply capacity (10^6 m^3)	River
Gariep	5 341	Orange
Vanderkloof	3 171	Orange
Sterkfontein	2 616	Nuwejaarspruit
Nuwejaarspruit Vaal	2 603	Vaal
Pongolapoort	2 445	Pongolo
Bloemhof	1 264	Vaal
Theewaterskloof	480	Sonderend
Heyshope	451	Assegaai
Woodstock	380	Tugela
Loskop	361	Olifants
Grootdraai	354	Vaal
Kalkfontein	318	Riet
Goedertrouw	304	Mhlatuze
Albert Falls	288	Mgeni
Brandvlei	284	Brandvlei
Spioenkop	277	Tugela
Umtata	253	Mtata
Driekoppies	250	Lomati
Inanda	241	Mgeni
Hartbeespoort	212	Crocodile
Erfenis	207	Groot Vet
Rhenosterkop	204	Elands
Molatedi	200	Groot Marico
Ntshingwayo	198	Ngagane
Zaaihoek	192	Slang
Midmar	175	Mgeni
Vaal	2 603	Vaal

Source: Department of Water Affairs and Forestry

sents about 20% of the total mean annual run-off of 49 200 million m³ per year (all standardised to 98% assurance of supply). A further 8% is estimated to be lost through evaporation from storage and conveyance along rivers, and 6% through land-use activities. As a national average, about 66% of the natural river flow (mean annual run-off) therefore still remains in the country's rivers.

Water-resource management, development and water services

The Department of Water Affairs and Forestry facilitates the provision of access to basic water and sanitation to every South African household.

By the end of March 2005:
• Some 44,5 million people had access to an improved water supply.
• Basic water infrastructure had been supplied to 15 million people (over 10 million of this by the Department of Water Affairs and Forestry).
• Some 31,9 million South Africans (66,3%) had access to Free Basic Water (FBW).
• Basic sanitation infrastructure had been provided to over 8,2 million people.
• It was estimated that by 2008, the entire water supply backlog, and by 2010 that of sanitation will have been eradicated.
• The Strategic Framework for Water Services (SFWS) had been drafted through a consultative process to update sector policy.
• Local government had been established throughout South Africa and the division of powers and functions outlined. Local government had been capacitated to take on their rightful, constitutional water-services provision function.
The department was in the process of substantial restructuring, which is expected to be completed in eight to 10 years' time. The restructuring process includes:
• establishing catchment-management agencies (CMAs) to perform water-resource management

functions currently performed by the department's regional offices
• transferring the management of commercial plantations and indigenous forests to appropriate agencies and institutions
• transferring water-service delivery and operations to water-services authorities (WSAs).
WSAs are now responsible for water-services provision. The role of the department is to:
• act as custodian of the country's water resources
• provide water-services policy and guidelines
• provide ongoing support to the water sector
• act as water-sector regulator.
The department remains focused on the phased implementation of the National Water Act, 1998, (Act 36 of 1998), with a particular emphasis on implementing a new organisational structure, which includes:
• establishing the National Water Resource Strategy (NWRS), which will set out the procedures, guidelines and overall strategy for managing water resources
• developing and testing a strategy for compulsory water-use licensing to facilitate equitable access to water resources for historically disadvantaged individuals
• enhancing water-use efficiency
• ensuring compliance with dam-safety regulations and enhancing public safety at water-resource installations

In October 2005, the Minister of Water Affairs and Forestry, Ms Buyelwa Sonjica, Sasol, Eskom and the Trans Caledon Tunnel Authority signed project agreements for the R2,5-billion Vaal Pipeline Project, a high-priority project designed to support the industrial needs of Sasol and Eskom in Mpumalanga, through the transfer of water from the Vaal River system.

The 115-km Vaal pipeline, which will transfer 160 million cubic meters of water per year through to a distribution structure at Knoppiesfontein, near Secunda, is expected to be completed by 2007.

- investigating and implementing appropriate institutional arrangements for the optimal management of the Working for Water (WfW) Programme
- building national capacity to monitor the state of water resources, so that accurate information is used in decision-making about the use and management thereof
- creating the National Water Resource Infrastructure Agency (NWRIA) to manage and develop national infrastructure.

Monitoring water resources

The oldest flow-gauging station still in operation in South Africa is on the Mooi River near Potchefstroom in North West. It celebrated a century of monitoring in August 2004.

River flow is being monitored at 1 200 flow-gauging stations. In addition, some 260 major reservoirs are being monitored. The evaporation and rainfall station network consists of 360 stations.

A new initiative to monitor precipitation in mountainous areas has been launched. Twenty-one rainfall stations are operational in the mountains of the Western Cape and five stations are operational in the Mpumalanga escarpment. Observations are relayed through the cellular short message system. The data is updated daily on the Department of Water Affairs and Forestry's website at *www.dwaf.gov.za.*

Water levels are being monitored at about 1 000 observation boreholes across South Africa. Particular attention is given to monitoring in dolomitic areas. In addition, a small network of rain gauges is in operation to monitor rainwater quality.

In June 2005, the Department of Water Affairs and Forestry and the Department of Education signed a memorandum of collaboration in Pretoria.

This was in line with the water-education programme Vision 2020, which aims to educate learners about water and sanitation issues.

Vision 2020 promotes water-use efficiency, water-quality management, and awareness of alien invasive plants, health and hygiene.

The importance of qualitative information on South Africa's water resources led to an increasing drive towards the creation of a national water-quality monitoring network.

One of the current water-quality monitoring programmes is the National Aquatic Ecosystem Biomonitoring Programme or, in short, the River Health Programme (RHP).

A key objective of the RHP is to generate and disseminate information on river health to ensure the ecologically sound management of the country's rivers, and to inform and educate South Africans about the health status of rivers. The RHP primarily uses biological indicators (e.g. fish communities, riparian vegetation and aquatic invertebrate fauna) to assess the health of river systems.

This programme is operational in all water-management areas focusing on rivers, but will be linked to wetlands/estuaries within the next five years to provide a holistic picture of the resources' condition.

Preliminary findings of the RHP indicate that 39% of South Africa's rivers (based on biological indices) are in a very good natural state, while 33% are fair and 28% are in a poor state. The main driving forces (stressors) on river health are water abstractions not based on reserve studies, the destruction of riparian vegetation, and invasion by alien species.

The National Chemical Monitoring Programme assesses and reports on the chemical status of water resources in South Africa. Based on the report produced in 2002, the main water-quality challenges for domestic water users are high total dissolved salts and in some places, high fluoride concentration. The other challenge facing irrigated agriculture is the high sodium adsorption ratio, electrical conductivity, pH and chloride.

Another challenge, not only in South Africa, but globally, is eutrophication or excessive plant (including algae) growth in dams. This is due to high levels of nutrient input from point sources of pollution and diffuse sources of pollution from catchments. Annual reports indicate that 50% of dams in South Africa are seriously impacted (hypertrophic), while the rest ranges from good (oligotrophic) to poor (mesotrophic).

Another problem facing South Africa is the sporadic outbreak of cholera and other water-borne diseases, which are mainly due to poor sanitation and hygiene at household level. The Eastern Cape and KwaZulu-Natal are generally prone to cholera outbreaks.

The Department of Water Affairs and Forestry is designing water-resource monitoring programmes to assess and report on the radiological (radioactivity) and toxicological quality status of South African water resources. The National Toxicity Monitoring Programme will also report on the status of DDT (Dichloro-Diphenyl-Trichloroethane) and other persistent organic pollutants in South Africa. This information will be reported internationally to the Stockholm Convention through the Department of Environmental Affairs and Tourism.

Another international obligation includes reporting on chemical water quality through the Global Environmental Monitoring Systems-Water Programme.

Funding

The department's budget grew rapidly between 2000/01 and 2003/04, increasing from R3 billion to R4,6 billion. This is an annual average increase of 15,1%. The increase in 2003/04 was due to costs related to the transfer of the water-services schemes to local authorities, with additional transitory costs being incurred related to the preparation, planning and implementation of the transfer; an increase in expenditure on the sanitation programme; and the writing off of water-user association (WUA) debt.

The expenditure declined from R4,6 billion in 2003/04 to R3,3 billion in 2004/05 due to the removal of capital and operating costs for the water-services schemes from the department's vote, as reflected in the reduced allocations to the water-services programme. These funds were transferred to the Municipal Infrastructure Grant (MIG), which is administered by the Department of Provincial and Local Government.

Water and sanitation for all

According to the Constitution of the Republic of South Africa, 1996 (Act 108 of 1996), everyone has a right to clean and safe drinking water and an appropriate and dignified sanitation service.

Water supply and sanitation programmes

Since 1994, there has been a dedicated programme to provide water and sanitation services to the previously unserved population, located mostly in the rural areas. In 1994, there were 15,9 million people without clean, safe water while 20,4 million people did not have access to adequate sanitation facilities.

The water and sanitation programme, initially the responsibility of the Department of Water Affairs and Forestry, began in 1994 as part of the Reconstruction and Development Programme. In 2002, the responsibility to implement the programme was transferred to the Department of Provincial and Local Government. The department now regulates, monitors and supports the programme.

National Water Week 2005 was celebrated from 21 to 27 March under the theme *Water for Life*. The Department of Water Affairs and Forestry used this opportunity to encourage South Africans to use water responsibly and wisely in their everyday lives.

As part of a national information and awareness campaign targeting schools, shopping centres and taxi ranks, the department distributed a series of useful hints on how to save water.

Other events that took place during the week included the Women in Water Awards; the handover of the Ngqushwa Sanitation Project in Peddie, Eastern Cape; the Western Cape Water Summit in Cape Town; the *Baswa le Meetse* (Youth in Water) Awards; the launch of the water-use efficiency strategies for the agricultural, water services, industry, mining and power-generation sectors; and the launch of the Nzelele Water User Association in Limpopo.

By March 2005, 3,6 million people still lacked access to clean safe water, while 16 million were without adequate sanitation facilities. Government remains on track to eradicate the backlogs by 2008 (water) and 2010 (sanitation) respectively. It has already exceeded the millennium development goals set by the United Nations in 2000 to reduce the population without access to basic water and sanitation by 50% in 2015.

The focus of water services broadened in 2001 to include the provision of free basic services to all indigent South Africans. By March 2005, 162 of the 170 WSAs provided FBW. The 2004/05 target of FBW being accessible to 75% of the population was achieved with 31,9 million people receiving FBW.

The department is actively eradicating all bucket systems and continues to collaborate with the departments of health and of education to improve sanitation in schools and clinics. Some R40 million will be spent on clinic-sanitation programmes and R150 million on schools.

Municipal Infrastructure Grant

MIG, a conditional grant from national government to local government to support investment in basic municipal infrastructure to eradicate backlogs, was implemented in April 2004.

The purpose of MIG is to facilitate and ensure more effective and integrated service delivery by local government and the Department of Water Affairs and Forestry, working with the Department of Provincial and Local Government in seeking to ensure that funds are made available. (See chapter 12: *Government system.*)

Policy and legislation

South Africa's Constitution and the Bill of Rights enshrine the basic human right to have access to sufficient water and a safe and healthy environment. The two Acts that enable government to fulfil these rights through the Department Water Affairs and Forestry are:

- The National Water Act, 1998, which aims to ensure that water resources are protected, used, developed, conserved, managed and controlled

in a sustainable manner, for the benefit of everyone in South Africa.
- The Water Services Act, 1997 (Act 108 of 1997), which created a regulatory framework within which water services could be provided. Schedule 4 of the Constitution vests the responsibility for water and sanitation services in local government. National government, however, is responsible for the regulatory function.

National Water Resource Strategy

Cabinet approved the first edition of the NWRS in September 2004. The NWRS describes how the water resources of South Africa will be protected, used, developed, conserved, managed and controlled in accordance with the requirements of the National Water Policy and the National Water Act, 1998.

Through the NWRS, South Africa reached one of the first recommendations of the Johannesburg Plan of Action, adopted at the 2002 World Summit on Sustainable Development, to develop national water-resource management plans.

The strategy contains estimates of present and future water availability and water requirements. It also proposes actions to be taken to achieve a sustainable balance between water availability and requirements. This is necessary to provide sufficient water, which is essential for human life, for participation in economic activity and for the progressive reallocation of water to sectors of society that were previously excluded.

A vital element of the NWRS is the progressive decentralisation of the responsibility and authority for water-resources management to CMAs and, at a local level, WUAs. These institutions, representative of water users and other stakeholders, will facilitate effective participation in the management of water resources in their areas. It will also enable the Department of Water Affairs and Forestry to move from its present multiple roles as operator, developer and regulator to become the sector leader, policy-maker, regulator and monitor.

The department will lead the creation of new institutions over a number of years and support and guide them in the execution of their tasks.

While the actions include the construction of new infrastructure such as dams, pumping stations and pipelines to meet increasing water demands, attention is mainly given to arrangements for the careful management, use and protection of water resources.

Water Services Act, 1997

The Act aims to:

- set out the rights of consumers and the rights and duties of those responsible for providing water services
- provide for the right of access to basic water supply and the right to basic sanitation necessary to secure sufficient water and an environment not harmful to human health or well-being
- allow the Minister of Water Affairs and Forestry to set national standards (including norms and standards for tariffs) to ensure efficient, equitable and sustainable water services
- promote the effective and sustainable use of financial and natural resources
- establish effective and financially viable statutory institutions to assist local government to fulfil its obligations
- ensure the production by WSAs of water-service development plans, within the framework of integrated development plans, required by municipal legislation
- provide a comprehensive framework for the oversight and regulation of water boards under the authority of the Minister of Water Affairs and Forestry
- provide a framework for the collection and publication of information about water services.

National Water Act, 1998

The Act provides for:

- integrated management and sustainable use of surface water and groundwater
- devolution of surface and groundwater to catchment and local level
- government to play a support role through functions such as promoting awareness, information provision and capacity-building.

The Act aims to control the use of water resources, protect them from being impacted on or exploited and polluted, and ensure that every person has equitable access to them.

The Act gives the Department of Water Affairs and Forestry the tools to gather the information that it needs to optimally manage the country's water resources. The registration of water-use is one of these tools.

All water users instructed to register have the statutory obligation to do so. There are strict penalties, prescribed in the Act, for those who do not comply.

All water users who do not receive their water from a service-provider, local authority, water board, irrigation board, government water scheme or other bulk supplier, and who are using water for irrigation, mining purposes, industrial use, feedlots or in terms of a general authorisation, must register.

This includes the use of surface and groundwater.

Other uses of water that must be registered include:

- Diversion of rivers and streams.
- Discharge of waste or water containing waste.
- Storage. This includes any person or body storing water for any purpose (including irrigation, domestic supply, industrial use, mining, aquaculture, fishing, water sport, aesthetic value, gardening, landscaping, golfing, etc.) from surface run-off, groundwater or fountain flow in excess of 10 000 m³ or where the water area at full supply level exceeds one hectare (ha) in total on land owned or occupied by that person or body, and is not in possession of a permit or permission.
- Stream-flow reduction activities (afforestation). All afforestation for commercial purposes, including communal forestry for commercial gain, that took place prior to 1972, must be registered. Forest owners who have permits issued under forestry legislation need not register.
- Local authorities and other bulk suppliers with their own water sources and purification works.
- Controlled activities such as irrigating with waste, power generation with water, atmospheric modification or recharging an aquifer.

An assessment of the environmental requirements of the rivers and streams concerned is conducted before a licence can be issued.

The implementation of the National Pricing Strategy for Raw Water began in 2002 to ensure that, as far as possible, the costs of the management of water resources and water-supply infrastructure are borne by water users.

The majority of water users are paying the water-resource charge or cost for which they are accordingly billed. However, there is still a considerable underrecovery of costs.

Action has been taken against a number of illegal water users across South Africa in response to growing concern about an apparent increase in the rate of illegal water-use in some catchment areas.

Strategic Framework for Water Services

In 1994, the *White Paper on Community Water Supply and Sanitation* played a key part in creating an enabling policy framework for the delivery of water and sanitation services. However, since 1999, local government's responsibilities have changed significantly and the Department of Water Affairs and Forestry has had to transform from being an implementer to a regulator. This necessitated the revision of the policy, which culminated in the SFWS. The framework was approved by Cabinet on 17 September 2003 after extensive consultation with the relevant stakeholders.

The framework provides a comprehensive policy summary regarding the total water-services sector in South Africa and sets out the vision, targets and policy for the next 10 years. The key challenges are to address inequality where it still persists and to provide basic services, higher levels of service and sustainable service provision (including institutional sustainability).

In October 2003, following the approval of the SFWS, the department and the South African Local Government Association signed a joint declaration committing both parties to give effect to the SFWS.

The key policy themes of the SFWS are:
• eliminating the backlog in basic services provision

• providing higher levels of service
• free basic services (water supply and sanitation)
• credit control
• institutional reform of water-services providers
• a decentralised fiscal framework
• a long-term vision for regulation.

Existing policies on free basic services, the provision of basic household sanitation and the transfers of infrastructure from national to local government aim to ensure that:
• everyone in South Africa who has access to a functioning basic water supply should have been provided with FBW by 2005
• everyone who has access to a functioning basic sanitation facility should be provided with free basic sanitation by 2010
• everyone has access to a functioning basic sanitation facility supply by 2010
• all assets of water-services schemes are transferred from the department to WSAs by 2008.

More detailed strategies to give effect to the implementation of the SFWS are the:
• Institutional Reform Strategy
• Regulatory Strategy
• legislative review (amendments to the Water Services Act, 1997)
• Sanitation Strategy
• Free Basic Services Strategy
• Transfer Strategy (of infrastructure assets to local government).

Water-resource management

Water-resource management in South Africa has undergone major revision along with the reform of water policy and legislation. The National Water Act, 1998 provides the principles for water-resource management. This policy aims to manage water resources in an integrated manner to ensure a healthy and stable water-resource base to meet the current and future needs of South Africa.

National Water Resource Infrastructure Agency

In August 2005, Cabinet approved the establishment of the NWRIA to ensure long-term water security for South Africa.

The agency is the result of studies that began with the recommendations of the *1998 White Paper on a National Water Policy.*

The NWRIA will develop and operate South Africa's major national dams and water-transfer schemes, which are currently managed directly by the Department of Water Affairs and Forestry. These include the Vaal Dam, the Tugela-Vaal transfer system, the Orange River scheme and the Western Cape system.

The organisations' assets are valued at nearly R40 billion and bulk water sales bring in more than R2 billion annually.

The agency will also integrate the Trans Caledon Tunneling Authority (TCTA), the parastatal organisation responsible for funding the Lesotho Highlands Water Project. It will not be responsible for domestic water supplies, which remain the responsibility of municipalities and regional water boards.

The Minister of Water Affairs and Forestry will still be responsible for deciding what projects need to be built, in terms of the NWRS. The agency will be required to make funding arrangements and ensure that projects are designed and built according to appropriate technical, social and environmental standards, and operated effectively and efficiently.

To establish the NWRIA by the target date of April 2008, the following milestones will have to be achieved:

- promulgating the National Water Agency Act during 2006
- restructuring the Infrastructure Branch of the Department of Water Affairs and Forestry to facilitate transfer to the new agency
- preparing a detailed agency establishment plan
- establishing an effective utilities governance component in the department to maintain oversight of the new agency
- working with the TCTA, it will also be necessary to implement:
  - effective financial and organisational management systems
  - a transformation plan to address change management, employment equity and service delivery.

Water-management institutions

The National Water Act, 1998 sets out the framework for the management of South Africa's water resources. This framework provides for the establishment of water-management institutions, which include CMAs and WUAs.

Natural mean annual run-off and ecological reserve (million m/a)

Water-management area	Natural mean annual run-off [1]	Ecological reserve [1,2]
Limpopo	985	156
Luvuvhu/Letaba	1 185	224
Crocodile West and Marico	855	165
Olifants	2 042	460
Inkomati [3]	3 539	1 008
Usutu to Mhlatuze [4]	4 780	1 192
Thukela	3 799	859
Upper Vaal	2 423	299
Middle Vaal	888	109
Lower Vaal	368	48
Mvoti to Umzimkulu	4 798	1 160
Mzimvubu to Keiskamma	7 241	1 122
Upper Orange	6 981	1 349
Lower Orange [5]	502	69
Fish to Tsitsikamma	2 154	243
Gouritz	1 679	325
Olifants/Doring	1 108	156
Breede	2 472	384
Berg	1 429	217
Total	**49 228**	**9 544**

1) Quantities refer to the water-management area under consideration only (water that originates or is required in that water-management area).
2) Total volume given, based on preliminary estimates, impact on yield being a portion of this.
3) Includes Komati catchment in Swaziland (mean annual run-off = 517 million m/a).
4) Includes Pongola catchment in Swaziland (mean annual run-off = 213 million m/a).
5) Includes contributions from Sengu and Caledon rivers in Lesotho (mean annual run-off = 4,765 billion m/a).

Source: Department of Water Affairs and Forestry

Catchment management agencies

CMAs aim to ensure equitable, efficient and sustainable water-resource management. They are required to establish governing boards, which are responsible for integrated water-resource management and the development of a catchment management strategy.

The boards have to represent the various sectors of society within that specific water-management area and will consist of water users, potential water users, local and provincial government, and environmental interest groups.

The department aims to establish CMAs in all 19 water-management areas across South Africa, as required by the National Water Act, 1998.

The first CMA at Umkomati in Mpumalanga was established on 30 March 2004 and became operational in September 2005. Another five CMAs were awaiting financial feasibility studies. It will cost up to R3 million to establish each CMA.

The department will devolve administration to the local water users and communities, accompanied by vigorous capacity-building, so that historically excluded communities can participate in water management.

Internal strategic perspectives have been developed for all 19 water-management areas.

These are the forerunners of the catchment management strategies that will be prepared by the

A team of South African youngsters from the Free State won the first prize in the annual Stockholm Junior Water Prize. The prize, which forms part of the World Water Week activities, aims to encourage and interest young people in issues related to water and the environment.

South Africa has won the competition twice in the last three years, with a second place in 2004. In 2005, South Africa was among 27 countries entered into the competition.

The winning group from Setshaba Se Botshabelo High School developed the 'Nocturnal Hydro Minimiser', which is regarded as a revolutionary solution to problems of very low annual rainfall and high evaporation levels characteristic of dry countries like South Africa. The device is an electrically operated watering system designed to use water efficiently for irrigation.

CMAs when they are established. They describe the water availability and water requirements in each area, and outline the approaches to be adopted for managing water resources. In particular, they provide general principles for the CMAs to authorise water use.

Water boards

Water boards have been established as service-providers that report to the Minister of Water Affairs and Forestry. These boards manage water services within their supply areas and provide potable water at cost-effective prices.

Irrigation boards and water-user associations

In 2003/04, subsidies worth R28,4 million were awarded to water irrigation boards and WUAs. These were increased to R30 million in the 2004/05 financial year.

The Department of Water Affairs and Forestry, in partnership with the Department of Agriculture, has developed a strategy to create opportunities for poor farmers on irrigation schemes, by providing them with access to water for high-value crops.

In 2005/06, the department was expected to extend financial support to resource-poor farmers, particularly women, for rainwater-harvesting tanks and other appropriate technologies. The department has secured the co-operation of the departments of land affairs and of agriculture, as well as the relevant provincial departments of agriculture to test the feasibility of developmental projects proposed for resource-poor farmers that will utilise the Orange River water reserved for them.

At least three projects were expected to start in 2005/06, namely the Karoo Irrigation Project near Hopetown, the Blocuso Trust Project between Upington and Keimoes, and the Tella Community Project near Pofadder. These projects will involve funding for infrastructure, as well as the training of participants.

Working for Water Programme

Alien plants have invaded over 10 million ha of South Africa – or 8% of the land – and their number is projected to double in as little as 15 years. These plants threaten the country's rich biodiversity by competing for water, light, space and nutrients – to the detriment of indigenous flora and water reserves.

The WfW Programme is a labour-intensive project to clear invasive alien plants. It is a multidepartmental initiative led by the departments of water affairs and forestry, of environmental affairs and tourism, and of agriculture. It started in 1995 with a budget of R25 million and has grown into one of government's key poverty-relief-fund initiatives.

During 2004, R440 million was spent and the programme employed about 32 000 people.

As an alien-clearing programme, WfW has made significant achievements in meeting its goals:

- it is estimated that over one million ha of invasive alien plants have been cleared over the past eight years
- this clearing yields an estimated release of between 48 m^3 and 56 million m^3 meters of additional water for alternative uses annually.
- more than 20 000 beneficiaries receive gainful employment and training through the programme annually
- over 15 million person-days of employment have been generated by WfW since its inception
- the cost-per-person day was assessed to be the most efficient of all the poverty-relief programmes of national government
- it provided 55% of wages to women, 20% to youth and 1% to the disabled, which is still slightly below its targets
- it has spearheaded a massive catchment-rehabilitation programme comprising 303 clearing sites, in addition to work on aquatic weeds and the use of biological control agents.
- it has established fire programmes in eight fire-prone regions of South Africa
- it is recognised and acknowledged as a global leader in the field, and has received 38 national and international awards
- it has established the fully fledged and successful Working for Wetlands Programme in all nine provinces
- WfW is aligned with the Global Invasive Species

Programme, which has chosen to locate its secretariat in South Africa.

Flood and drought management

The latest South African Disaster Management Policy and ensuing legislation brought about a major shift in focus from reactive to preventative and mitigative disaster management.

From a flood management perspective, the South African focus has shifted from primarily structural to non-structural, accentuating the value of, for example, floodplain zoning and flood warnings. During 2004/05, a number of localised flooding events occurred throughout the country. These mainly affected smaller river basins in the Western and Eastern Cape and KwaZulu-Natal, as well as a limited number of local authorities and farming communities, although no large area floods were registered.

In response to drought conditions seriously affecting many parts of the country since 2003, government allocated additional funds for emergency water supplies on three occasions. During 2003/04, R295 million was made available through two allocations. About R203 million of this amount went to municipalities for emergency water provision at local authority level, while around R92 million was used by the Department of Water Affairs and Forestry to supplement regional water supplies. During 2004/05, an additional R280 million was made available to municipalities for emergency water provision through the Department of Provincial and Local Government, while an additional R50 million was allocated to strengthen national and regional water supplies.

Although many of the larger dams and surface-water resources were substantially replenished during the 2004/05 summer rainy season, the overall water situation was a matter for concern. Dam levels in the Western Cape were at their lowest in many years, while the dam levels in the Free State, Limpopo and North West did not even reach their already low levels of the same time in the previous year. Water use was accordingly restricted in many areas in these provinces. As far as groundwater was concerned, levels were generally very low and in many cases the situation was critical. Groundwater is an important source of water to many local authorities, communities and farms. The largest proportion of the funds earmarked for emergency water supplies to municipalities is to support problematic groundwater situations.

Dams and water schemes

The first edition of the NWRS describes how the water resources of South Africa will be protected, used, developed, conserved, managed and controlled in accordance with policy and legislation. The central objective of managing water resources is to ensure that water is used to support equitable and sustainable social and economic transformation and development.

Dams and water schemes form an integral component of the strategy to meet these objectives. The NWRS provides details on possible major water schemes to be developed in the next 25 years, amounting to about R21 billion at 2004 price levels.

The Department of Water Affairs and Forestry follows an integrated approach to the management of South Africa's water resources. Proposed new water schemes need to comply with the NWRS, requiring that water-demand management programmes be implemented before embarking on new infrastructure development.

Strict environmental impact assessments must also be performed in accordance with laws and regulations administered by the Department of Environmental Affairs and Tourism. The guidelines issued by the World Commission on Dams must be followed.

The following major schemes are under construction or reaching the implementation stage:
- Berg River Project: The Minister of Water Affairs and Forestry has directed the TCTA to implement the R1,55-billion privately funded scheme comprising the Berg River Dam near Franschhoek in the Western Cape and the associated supplement scheme comprising a weir, pumping stations and pipelines to augment the water supply to the Western Cape. Construction of the dam by a private contractor started in June 2004 and is

due for completion in 2007. Construction of the supplement scheme, utilising government and private resources, was expected to commence in 2005 for commissioning during 2007. At 70 m, the 990-m long dam wall will be the highest concrete-faced, rock-filled dam in South Africa.
- Luvuvhu Government Waterworks: This scheme, worth more than R900 million, funded by National Treasury and implemented by the Department of Water Affairs and Forestry, comprises the Nandoni Dam, pumping station and water treatment works (WTW), and the Xikundu weir, pumping station and WTW. The scheme will provide potable water to more than a million people in Limpopo. It will stabilise the water flow in the Luvuvhu River for irrigation and ecological flow requirements, and alleviate the water shortages in the Kruger National Park. The Nandoni pumping station and WTW will be completed during 2007 while the dam and other components were expected to become fully operational in 2005.
- Vaal River Eastern Subsystem Augmentation Project: The Minister of Water Affairs and Forestry directed the TCTA to augment the water supply to Sasol and Eskom by implementing abstraction and desilting works alongside the Vaal Dam shoreline, and a pumping station and a 120-km long steel pipeline of 1 900-mm diametre to Bosjesspruit and Trichardsfontein dams in Mpumalanga. Construction of the privately funded project was expected to commence during the second half of 2005 for completion in 2007 at an estimated cost of more than R2 billion.
- Olifants River Water Resources Development Project: This development in Limpopo and Mpumalanga will enable considerable mining expansion (mainly platinum) and sustained water supply to local authorities and communities.
The project is to be developed in two phases. Phase one comprises the five-metre raising of the Flag Boshielo Dam on the Olifants River near Marble Hall by the Department of Water Affairs and Forestry at an estimated cost of R234 million in a public-private partnership arrangement

with the Lebalelo WUA. Construction started during 2004 and is expected to be completed in 2006.

The proposed second phase of the project will comprise the 70-m high De Hoop Dam located 40 km south of Steelpoort on the Steelpoort River and a substantial primary bulk distribution system from the De Hoop and Flag Boshielo dams. It is envisaged that the project, costing in excess of R3 billion, will be implemented by the department and the private sector in phases, starting during 2006.

- Mooi-Mgeni River Transfer Scheme: Phase one of the water-transfer project comprising the new Mearns weir on the Mooi River near the town of Mooi River and the raised Midmar Dam near Howick on the Mgeni River was commissioned during 2003 to augment the water supply to the Umgeni area in KwaZulu-Natal. Phase 2A, to be completed towards the end of the decade, will include the construction of the Spring Grove Dam on the Mooi River near the town of Rosetta. The Spring Grove pumping station (Phase 2B) will follow at a later stage to suit the demand requirements of Umgeni Water.

Groundwater resources

Groundwater, despite its relatively small contribution to bulk water supply (13%), represents an important and strategic water resource in South Africa.

Owing to the lack of perennial streams in the semi-desert to desert parts, two-thirds of South Africa's surface area is largely dependent on groundwater. Although irrigation is the largest user, the supply to more than 300 towns and smaller settlements is also extremely important. Through government's commitment to meeting the basic water needs of communities, groundwater has become a strategic resource for village water supply in the wetter parts of the country, because of its cost-effectiveness in a widely scattered small-scale-user situation.

Underground water sources also contribute to river flow. This requires reserving a significant part of groundwater resources for the protection of aquatic ecosystems in terms of the National Water Act, 1998. The maximum quantity of groundwater that can be developed economically is estimated at about 6 000 million m³ a year.

Regional and international co-operation and initiatives

South Africa has signed co-operative agreements with a number of countries in the southern African region with which it shares water resources, such as:

- Mozambique and Swaziland on the Incomati and Maputo rivers
- Botswana, Lesotho and Namibia on the establishment of the Orange Senqu River Commission
- Botswana, Zimbabwe and Mozambique on the establishment of the Limpopo Watercourse Commission
- Botswana
- Lesotho on the Lesotho Highlands Water Project
- Swaziland on the Komati River Development Project.

These co-operative agreements improve South Africa's bilateral and multilateral relations in the

A feasibility study for the second phase of the multi-billion Rand Lesotho Highlands Water Project (LHWP) started at the end of April 2005. The study – funded by the Lesotho and South African governments – is expected to take two years, after which a decision will be made on the future of the project by the two governments. The LHWP sells water to Gauteng.

Phase one of the project consists of the Katse Dam that supplies water to the Mohale Dam through a 32-km tunnel. In turn, Mohale Dam supplies water to the Muela Dam through an 82-km tunnel. From Muela, the water is delivered to South Africa.

Phase two of the project entails the construction of the Mashai Dam high up in the highlands of Lesotho. It will supply water to the Katse Dam through a 30-m tunnel.

African Union. All the countries involved benefit, while sharing development costs.

The African Ministers' Council for Water was established in December 2003. It has become a platform to share experiences on all water-related matters.

Forestry

Indigenous forests are indispensable to the country's heritage, beauty, wildlife and environment, while commercial forests provide jobs and economic opportunities for many people, especially in rural areas. Forestry represents a substantial investment in the country and plays an important role in the Integrated Rural Development Programme.

South Africa has developed one of the largest planted forests in the world. Production from these plantations amounted to more than 19,2 million m³, valued at almost R4,1 billion in 2003. Together with the processed products, the total industry turnover was about R14,6 billion in 2003, including R8,4 billion worth of wood-pulp.

More than 10,9 million tons (mt) of pulpwood, mining timber, matchwood and charcoal, and almost six million cubic metres of sawlogs, veneer and poles, were sold in this period.

Collectively, the forestry and forestry products sector employs about 151 000 people.

An equivalent of about 60 000 full-time staff are employed in the primary sector (growing and harvesting), while the remainder are employed in the processing industries (sawmilling, pulp and paper, mining timber and poles, and board products).

The organised forest industry claims that each job created within the sector results in four others in supporting industries, through the multiplier effect. The sector thus contributes about 600 000 jobs to the economy.

About half of the more than 1 700 indigenous tree and shrub species found in South Africa grow along the south and east coasts and on the southern and south-eastern slopes of inland mountains. The other half are spread over the interior plateaux.

The yellowwood tree (*Podacarpus*) is South Africa's national tree. Yellowwood trees can grow to a height of more than 40 m with a girth of 8 m, and can live up to 800 years. The Big Tree near the Storms River Bridge (46 m), the King Edward VII in the Knysna Forest (46 m) and the Eastern Monarch in the Amatola mountains (44 m) are the best-known giants.

National Arbour Week is celebrated annually at the beginning of September to encourage the greening of South Africa. Two different trees of the year are nominated annually: a common variety and a scarcer, possibly endangered, species. The 2005 trees of the year were the false cabbage tree (*Schefflera umbellifera*) and the baobab (*Adansonia digitata*).

The aim of Arbour Week is to promote awareness of the need for planting and preserving indigenous trees throughout South Africa. It highlights the opportunities for sustainable economic development, community participation, poverty alleviation and job creation in forestry to create a better life for all. The theme for 2005 was *Plant a Tree – Grow our Future*.

Contributing to socio-economic reform and growth

In January 2005, the Minister of Water Affairs and Forestry, Ms Buyelwa Sonjica, signed agreements which transferred the management of 140 000 ha of state forest land to new operators. This is part of government's ongoing restructuring of state-owned forests. One agreement relates to 25 000 ha in the Hogsback and Stutterheim areas of the Eastern Cape where Amathole Forest Holdings, and its Black Economic Empowerment (BEE) partner, Wildbreak Investment Holdings, will take over the running of the forests. The other covers forests in the southern and Western Cape, where the management of about 115 015 ha of state forest land will be taken over by the BEE company, Cape Timber Resources.

These agreements follow two others concluded in 2001 with Singisi Forests in the Eastern Cape and the Siyaqhubeka consortium in KwaZulu-Natal.

The restructuring process also has further benefits for government and the people of South Africa. This includes the annual lease rental payments of about R20 million, which is generated from land leases, as well as various socio-economic undertakings that the successful bidders for the various packages have committed to as part of the restructuring transactions. The shareholding of each of the successful bidders includes significant black ownership, varying between 10% and 50% of the bidding vehicles.

The forest land is not sold as part of the packages, but leased to the successful bidders for 70 years with an option to renew for a further 35 years. The new owners will pay substantial lease rentals to the department, which will be used to compensate any successful land claimants or revert to the State.

These transactions are in line with government's policy of exiting from direct forest management activities while promoting BEE in the forestry industry. At the same time, land which is less suitable for forestry will be converted to other uses or reserved for conservation.

In the southern and Western Cape, 44 000 ha of marginal state forest land will be clear felled and handed over for other uses. These include 29 000 ha for conservation, 9 000 ha for agriculture, 6 000 ha for community forestry and 200 ha for settlement.

The minister also assigned management responsibility for the Tokai Cecilia state forests in Cape Town to South African National Parks. This follows Cabinet's decision in 1996 to develop the Cape Peninsula Protected Natural Environment. The Tokai and Cecilia forests are located in the protected environment area and contain important lowland and mountain fynbos, as well as pockets of Afro-montane forest, which need to be maintained. Eventually, the two forests will be incorporated into the Table Mountain National Park.

South African Forestry Company Limited (SAFCOL)

SAFCOL, a wholly-owned state enterprise, was formed in 1992 and acquired the Department of Water Affairs and Forestry's commercial forestry assets and related business with effect from 1 April 1993.

SAFCOL's objectives are to enhance the development of the local forestry industry and to optimise the State's forestry assets. This will be achieved through running the business according to accepted commercial management practices and sustainable forestry management (SFM) principles.

In 2001/02, SAFCOL's commercial forestry operations were transferred into five special-purpose vehicles to facilitate privatisation transactions.

A special restructuring dividend is payable to government as the sole shareholder of SAFCOL upon successful completion of each transaction. On 30 June 2004, R85 million was paid over in respect of transactions completed prior to that date.

Government's decision to restructure its commercial forestry assets, not only those managed by the Department of Water Affairs and Forestry, but also those managed by SAFCOL, has had a marked impact on the company and the local industry.

By April 2005, the disposal of state forests was in its final stages. The remaining key transaction was the sale of Komatiland forests, which was expected to go before the Competition Tribunal.

SAFCOL's remaining responsibilities included aftercare of the transactions, residual shareholding and various management obligations in certain areas.

SAFCOL also had to sell up to a 9% shareholding interest to the employees in the five forestry entities created after the restructuring. It was expected to be concluded by the end of 2005.

WeedBuster Week 2005 took place from 10 to 16 October under the theme *Stop the Invasion: Plant Indigenous*.

WeedBuster Week represents the annual culmination of the ongoing campaign aimed at managing and containing invasive alien plants. The campaign is a multidepartmental initiative led by the Department of Water Affairs and Forestry through the Working for Water Programme and supported by various partners and stakeholders.

The South African campaign is linked bilaterally to invasive-plant control initiatives by countries such as Australia and New Zealand and multilaterally to the broader Global Invasive Species Programme and other structures and frameworks.

Industry and exports

The industry was a net exporter to the value of over R3,9 billion in 2004, more than 98% of which was in the form of converted value-added products. Had it not been for this trade surplus in forest products, the country's trade deficit in 2004 of R13 billion would have been 30% higher.

The forest-product industry ranks among the top exporting industries in the country, having contributed 3,09% to the total exports and 1,68% of total imports in 2004. Capital investment in the industry amounted to some R24 billion in 2004.

The value of forest-product exports has grown significantly over the past decade, from R2,3 billion in 1992 to R9 billion in 2004, a growth of 286%. In real terms (taking inflation into account), this growth was 73,6% or a compounded real growth of 4,7% per year over that period. As imports did not increase to the same extent as exports, the net trade balance in foreign trade in forest products increased even more, by 323% in nominal terms (90% in real terms) to R3,9 billion in 2004.

In 2004, paper exports were the most important (R3,204 billion or 35% of the total), followed by solid wood products (R3,032 billion or 34%), pulp (R2,460 billion or 27%), and other products (R326 million or 4%). Woodchip exports, which are exported mainly to Japan, accounted for 58% (R1,764 billion) of the total solid wood products exports.

As with other export-based industries, the strength of the Rand had a negative effect on the Rand-value of forest-product exports during 2004, with the total value being R898 million or 9% less than in 2003.

Stringent environmental codes of practice are implemented in all plantation and processing activities. The Chief Directorate: Forestry of the Department of Water Affairs and Forestry promotes optimal development of forestry and arboriculture in South Africa.

The National Forests Advisory Council (NFAC) was established in terms of the National Forests Act, 1998 (Act 84 of 1998). It advises the Minister of Water Affairs and Forestry on all aspects of forestry in the country. The NFAC is actively involved in developing local criteria, indicators and standards for SFM and makes recommendations on how public access to state-owned forests can be improved.

Sustainable forest management

Apart from the ecological considerations in determining where it is appropriate to grow trees, there are other ecological, social and economic considerations, which must be addressed during the growing of trees.

A comprehensive set of criteria indicators and measures, which addresses these considerations, has been developed. These criteria indicators will form the basis for monitoring sustainability of forestry operations both in commercial and natural forests. Managers/owners will be required to report against these criteria. They also form useful guidelines for new entrants into the sector.

The commercial forestry industry in South Africa is committed to practising SFM and is a world leader in forest certification. This is demonstrated by the fact that over one million ha, or over 80% of the entire planted area of commercial forestry plantations in South Africa, is certified by the Forest Stewardship Council (FSC) and the ISO 14001 certification schemes as being sustainably managed. By March 2005, nearly 1,7 million ha of forestry land in South Africa was certified by the FSC, the second-largest area in the southern hemisphere after Brazil.

This is a remarkable achievement considering that there were no certified plantations in 1996. Although not all these forests are owned by the large forestry companies, the rapid expansion in this certified area has been facilitated by the fact that all the large companies have their own specialist environmental departments. These ensure that their land is managed according to their own stringent environmental codes of practice. To promote transparency, members of the public are invited to join company staff when the regular audits are done.

There has also been a large increase in the number of non-corporate growers who have become certified. This can be attributed to various factors, such as the acceptance by the FSC of 'group-certification schemes' and the availability of local FSC auditors, both of which have reduced the cost of certification considerably.

Another development has been the introduction of small low-intensity managed forest audits which enable small and community forestry schemes to be FSC-certified. As part of its commitment to the practice of SFM, the forestry industry is also involved in the NFAC's Committee for SFM, which develops criteria, indicators and standards for SFM, tailored to meet South Africa's specific conditions.

The Institute of Natural Resources, which was contracted by the Committee for SFM to develop these criteria has, after an extensive consultative process, developed a draft set which was being tested in mid-2004. This process of in-field testing was expected to be completed in 2005.

Through the Forestry Industry Environmental Committee, a set of environmental guidelines was published in 1995 to encourage and facilitate timber growers to practise SFM through the implementation of best environmental practices.

These guidelines were not only highly acclaimed, but widely used both within South Africa and abroad. A second updated, and far more comprehensive and user-friendly edition of the guidelines was published in July 2002. These are being used by the certification agents for the auditing of the physical environment component of their FSC audits.

The indigenous forests of the southern Cape, previously managed by the Department of Water Affairs and Forestry, received FSC certification, which is a first on the continent for high forests. It is a major step towards the sustainable management of the country's natural forests.

Legislation

The National Forests Act, 1998 reflects the vision for the future of forestry in South Africa, which emphasises SFM. It explains how people and communities can use forests without destroying them and sets out rules for the protection of indigenous forests. The Act ensures that the public has reasonable access to state forest land for recreational, cultural, spiritual and educational purposes.

South Africa is richly endowed with more than 1 700 tree species. Some species are threatened and a list of 47 species is now protected under the Act. Protected trees may not be cut, damaged or sold without a licence. The listing of protected trees is not primarily aimed at preventing the use of such trees, but to ensure sustainable use through licensing control measures.

A list of protected tree species is available on the Department of Water Affairs and Forestry's website at *www.dwaf.gov.za*.

The National Veld and Forest Fire Act, 1998 (Act 101 of 1998), bans open-air fires when the risk of veld blazes in an area is high. It also introduces the concept of voluntary fire-protection associations formed by landowners. It furthermore obliges the Minister of Water Affairs and Forestry to operate a national fire-rating system in consultation with the South African Weather Service and fire associations. The Act also allows the minister to impose minimum fire-fighting requirements on landowners.

Indigenous forest

There are around 530 000 ha of indigenous or natural forests in the country, which occur mainly along the southern and eastern escarpment, the coastal belt and in sheltered kloofs or ravines.

The low natural forest cover led to the development of the commercial forest sector in South Africa over the last 100 years. Nonetheless, natural forests have continued to play a major role in the livelihoods and well-being of many rural communities.

The first steering committee meeting of the Forestry Broad-Based Black Economic Empowerment (BBBEE) Committee took place in June 2005.

Set up by the Minister of Water Affairs and Forestry, Ms Buyelwa Sonjica, the steering committee aims to drive the BBBEE process in the forestry sector. The committee was expected to complete the first draft of the charter before the end of 2005. The meeting also determined and agreed on the powers and mandate of the steering committee.

There has been an increase in the use of natural forests as sources of medicine, building material, fuel wood and food. It is estimated that around 80% of South Africa's population still use medicinal plants, most of which are sourced from natural forests.

For the first time, South Africa now has a detailed inventory of all its natural forests, which will be used to accurately monitor changes in forest areas. The Department of Water Affairs and Forestry also completed a forest-type classification for natural forests, which are represented by 24 broad forest types. The Natural Forests Protected Areas System, completed for all forests in 2004, guides the setting aside and demarcation of natural forests into protected areas.

Systematic timber harvesting occurs in areas of the production management class. Harvesting is concentrated on overmature trees, with logs being sold by tender and/or on public auction. On average, 3 750 m³ of round logs are harvested annually (150 m³ of stinkwood, 750 m³ of yellowwood, 2 500 m³ of Australian blackwood and 350 m³ of other species). Timber harvesting in Knysna amounts to 2 600 m³. Another valuable product of the indigenous forests of South Africa is the seven-week fern (*Rumohra adiantiformis*), which is harvested in the Knysna and Tsitsikamma forests.

In September 2005, the Minister of Water Affairs and Forestry, Ms Buyelwa Sonjica, launched the National Fire Danger Rating System for South Africa (NFDRSA) in Cape Town.

The NFDRSA, which is run in partnership with the South African Weather Service, is an early-warning system for predicting conditions conducive to veldfires.

The system will:
- help veldfire managers and decision-makers to decide on precautionary measures to take when managing veldfires
- identify conditions that could lead to high fire danger probability
- identify activities which are prohibited under prevailing conditions
- increase the state of veldfire readiness
- raise awareness among the general public.

Woodlands

Woodlands can be defined as vegetation formation dominated by trees, but not to the extent that the canopies are continuous and overlapping. Woodlands cover 29 million ha, making up 21% of land cover. This vegetation covers extensive areas in the low-lying, drier areas of Limpopo, KwaZulu-Natal and Mpumalanga.

Woodlands are the most extensive vegetation type in southern Africa and dominate Africa as a whole. Globally, woodlands cover between an eighth and a sixth of the Earth's land surface.

The woodlands are, however, a valuable source of fuel, building material, craft timber and a variety of non-timber products. These include fruit, fodder, medicinal compounds, honey, meat and mushrooms, and form the backbone of the livelihoods of millions of people.

Commercial forests

During the 1930s, government started to establish extensive plantations to make South Africa self-sufficient in its timber requirements, and to provide more job opportunities in a diversified economy during the depression years. Commercial plantations of exotic species proved to be a sound investment and the private sector established large plantations of pine, eucalyptus and wattle trees.

By mid-2005, the private sector owned 1 028 877 ha (or 76%) of the total plantation area of 1 351 402 ha, as well as virtually all the processing plants in the country. The remaining 24% (322 525 ha) was under public ownership. The extent of public ownership will decrease significantly once the restructuring process is complete.

In 2004, capital investment in these plantations stood at R16 billion, 55% of which was attributable to investment in trees. A further 23,3% was tied up in land, 13% in roads, 7,2% in fixed assets and 1,4% in machinery and equipment.

Plantation yields

Of the 1 371 625 ha of plantations in 2003, 52% were softwood species and 48% hardwood species. Some 36% of the plantation area were managed mainly for saw-log production, 57% for pulpwood and 4% for mining timber, while the balance of 3% was grown for the production of poles, matchwood (poplar) and other minor products. Plantation yields vary from an average of 16 m³ per ha per year for softwood, to 21 m³ per ha per year for eucalyptus and 10 m³ per ha per year for wattle (timber and bark).

Likewise, the rotation ages vary from a maximum of 30 years in the case of pine saw-logs, to six to 10 years in the case of eucalyptus pulp and mining timber.

The production from plantations amounted to some 19,2 million m³ or 16,9 mt in 2003.

Primary wood-processing

South Africa has 194 primary wood-processing plants, 189 of which are owned by the private sector and only five of which are owned by local and state authorities. Of these, some 109 are sawmills; 15 mining-timber sawmills; 42 pole-treating plants; 22 pulp, paper and board mills; one match factory; and five charcoal plants. The total roundwood intake in 2003 was 20,4 million m³ valued at R3,3 billion. The value of sales of timber products produced by these primary processing plants totalled R14,591 billion. Some R18,96 billion was invested in primary round-wood-processing plants (at book value). At market value, this increased to an estimated R30 billion.

The pulp industry in South Africa is dominated by two main pulp-and-paper manufacturing companies, namely Sappi and Mondi. They rank among the largest in the southern hemisphere, own assets in many parts of the world, and are internationally listed.

The saw-milling industry produces sawn timber, which is used in the production of solid wood products, such as lumber for roof trusses, flooring etc. and consumer products such as furniture. A large number of companies operate in this sector, with the five biggest companies contributing 51% of total production. Some 52% of total sawn timber is produced in Mpumalanga.

Research and training

South Africa has world-class forestry-research infrastructure and personnel, with almost 2% of the forestry industry turnover (private and public sec-

tors) devoted to research. The priority fields of research include tree-breeding through applied silviculture, climate and soils, environmental impact and management solutions, forest biology, hydrology and forest protection.

The major institutes servicing the research needs of the industry are the Institute of Commercial Forestry Research in Pietermaritzburg, and the Forestry and Agriculture Biotechnology Institute and the Council for Scientific and Industrial Research in Pretoria.

Degrees in forestry are offered by the Faculty of Agricultural and Forestry Sciences at the University of Stellenbosch, the University of KwaZulu-Natal and the University of Venda. Diplomas and limited degree courses in forestry disciplines are also offered at the Nelson Mandela Metropolitan University, George (Saasveld Campus). The Natal University of Technology offers a diploma in Pulp and Paper Technology, and the Fort Cox College of Agriculture and Forestry offers a diploma in social forestry.

Skills training is provided by a number of industry-sponsored and in-house training centres. Industry-sponsored bursaries are available, as are company-sponsored bursaries for study at these institutions.

Community forestry

The *White Paper on Sustainable Forest Development in South Africa* states that community forestry is designed and applied to meet local social, household and environmental needs and to favour local economic development.

The forestry industry is promoting rural development and economic empowerment through a small-grower afforestation programme. By mid-2004, there were more than 24 000 small emerging timber growers belonging to formal schemes and a further 5 000 to 10 000 independent growers. The schemes run under the auspices of Sappi Forests (Project Grow), Mondi Forests (Khulanathi) and the Wattle Growers' Association. Combined, these growers, most of whom are women, cultivated 48 000 hectares of plantations.

Community forestry is implemented by communities or with the participation of communities, and includes tree-centered projects in urban and rural areas, woodlots and woodland management by communities and individuals. Community forestry has gained impetus through more focused core functions, particularly in urban greening and forest enterprise development.

Participatory Forest Management (PFM) of the Department of Water Affairs and Forestry is an integrated approach that contributes to achieving the SFM of South African forests.

Elements of PFM were initially developed for indigenous state forests. However, the aim is to use PFM as an approach to the management of all forest types where feasible (indigenous forests, plantations, woodlots and woodlands) and where different types of ownership and management (state, provincial, communal, private and community) exist.

Food and Trees for Africa (FTFA)

FTFA is the sub-Saharan African partner of Global Releaf, an international greening organisation.

FTFA's mission is to contribute to a healthy and sustainable quality of life for all, through environmental awareness and greening programmes.

Since its inception in 1990, FTFA has developed, managed and promoted numerous sustainable greening programmes, including land-use management and food security through permaculture.

FTFA works in partnership with government, the private and public sectors, and civil society.

FTFA attempts to provide trees to as many underserved communities as possible through the help of sponsors and certificate programmes. Over 2,2 million trees have been distributed to schools, clinics, old-age homes, hospices, police stations, streets and parks.

The Urban Greening Fund is managed by the FTFA, the departments of water affairs and forestry and of agriculture, and the Institute of Environment and Recreation Management. It was set up with donor funds, which included R1,2 million from the Department of Water Affairs and Forestry.

It is a collective fund that supports partnerships aimed at sustainable development through tree planting, parks, food-gardening projects and environmental education.

Organisations, companies and individuals can contribute to the fund to help disadvantaged South Africans to create a greener, healthier and more secure life.

Eduplant

Improving food security in impoverished communities is at the core of the Woolworths Trust EduPlant's activities. It is managed by FTFA in partnership with the Department of Water Affairs and Forestry, SABC Education and Landcare SA.

EduPlant is a schools food-gardening and greening programme that promotes and supports schools in the growing of food in a sustainable and natural way. It is aligned with the aims of government's National School Nutrition Programme.

Over the past 10 years, EduPlant has helped thousands of schools to enhance food security in their communities and to improve the nutrition of their learners.

In 2005, many EduPlant workshops were held in all provinces, providing instruction and resources to assist educators in developing food gardens at schools.

The Eduplant 2005 Awards ceremony took place on 30 September 2005. More than 400 schools with permaculture food-gardening projects entered the competition. This annual event recognises the achievements of all educators and learners who participate in the EduPlant Programme.

Acknowledgements

Department of Water Affairs and Forestry
Estimates of National Expenditure, 2005, published by National Treasury
Forestry South Africa
South African Forestry Company Limited
Water Research Commission
www.csir.co.za
www.dwaf.gov.za
www. forestry.co.za
www.gov.za
www.trees.org.za
www.southafrica.info

Suggested reading

Bate, R. and Tren, T. *The Cost of Free Water*. Johannesburg: Free Market Foundation, 2002.
Davies, B.R. and Day, J. *Vanishing Waters*. Cape Town: University of Cape Town Press, 1998.
Keith, P. and Coates Palgrave, M. *Everyone's Guide to Trees of South Africa*. 4th revised ed. Cape Town: Struik, 2002.
Lawes, M.J. *et al.* eds. *Indigenous Forests and Woodlands in South Africa*. Scottsville: University of KwaZulu-Natal Press, 2004.
McCullum, H. ed. *Biodiversity of Indigenous Forests and Woodlands in South Africa*. Maseru: Southern African Development Community/International Union for the Conservation of Nature and Natural Resources/Southern African Research and Documentation Centre, 2000.
Van Wyk, B. and Van Wyk, P. *Field Guide to the Trees of Southern Africa*. Cape Town: Struik, 1997.
Venter, F. and Venter, J. *Making the Most of Indigenous Trees*. Pretoria: Briza Publications, 1999.

Addendum

Abbreviations

A

AADP –	African Agricultural Development Programme
AAIICT –	African Advanced Institute for Information and Communication Technology
ABC –	Agricultural Business Chamber
ABET –	Adult Basic Education and Training
Absa –	Amalgamated Banks of South Africa
ACAP –	Agreement on the Conservation of Albatrosses and Petrels
ACEP –	African Coelacanth Ecosystems Programme
ACE –	Advanced Certificate in Education
ACP –	African-Caribbean-Pacific
ACR –	Army Conventional Reserve
ACS –	Agricultural Credit Scheme
ACSA –	Airports Company of South Africa
ACT –	Arts and Culture Trust
ADEA –	Association for the Development of Education In Africa
ADS –	Approved Destination Status
AEC –	African Economic Community
AFIS –	Automated Fingerprint Information System
AFU –	Asset Forfeiture Unit
AHPCSA –	Allied Health Professions Council of South Africa
AGOA –	African Growth and Opportunity Act
AICs –	African independent churches
AIICT –	Advanced Institute for Information and Communications Technology
AIP –	Association of Independent Publishers
AISA –	African Institute of International Affairs
AIsi –	all-share index
ALTX –	Alternative Exchange
AMCOST –	African Ministers' Council on Science and Technology
AMIB –	African Peace Mission in Burundi
AMP –	African Mining Partnership
AMPS –	All Media Products Survey
ANC –	African National Congress
APRM –	African Peer Review Mechanism
AP –	Associated Press
ARC –	Agricultural Research Council
Armscor –	Armaments Corporation of South Africa
ARV –	antiretroviral
ASA –	Advertising Standards Authority
ASATA –	Association of Southern African Travel Agents

ASEAN –	Association of South-East Asian Nations
ASOM –	Association of Marketers
ATD –	awaiting-trial detainees
ATEE –	Assessment, Technology and Education Evaluation
ATNS –	Air-Traffic Navigation Service
ATR –	Army Territorial Reserve
ATU –	African Telecoms Union
AU –	African Union

B

BA –	British Airways
BASA –	Business Arts South Africa
BBBEE –	Broad-Based Black Economic Empowerment
bbls –	barrels
BBSP –	Black Business Supplier Programme
BCI –	Business Confidence Index
BCLME –	Benguela Current Large Marine Ecosystem
BED –	Business and Entrepreneurial Development
BEE –	Black Economic Empowerment
BENEFIT –	Benguela Fisheries Interaction and Training
BESA –	Bond Exchange of South Africa
BFI –	Bridges to the Future Initiative
Biopad –	Biotechnology Partnership for Africa's Development
BlindSA –	formerly known as the South African Blind Workers Organisation
Blindbib –	South African Library for the Blind
BLNS –	Botswana, Lesotho, Namibia and Swaziland
BMCC –	Broadcasting Monitoring Complaints Committee
BNC –	Binational Commission
BoM –	Buddyz on the Move
BRAIN –	Business Referral and Information Network
BRICs –	biotechnology regional innovation centres
BSRP –	Building for Sport and Recreation Project
BTec –	Bachelor's Degree in Technology
BTT –	Board of Tariffs and Trade

C

CAADP –	Comprehensive African Agricultural Development Programme
Caricom –	Caribbean Community
CBE –	Council for the Built Environment
CaBEERE –	Capacity-Building Programme for Renewable Energy and Energy Efficiency
CBNRM –	Community-Based Natural Resource Management

CBD – Convention on Biological Diversity
CBOs – community-based organisations
CBPWP – Community-Based Public Works Programme
CBRTA – Cross-Border Road Transport Agency
CC – Constitutional Court
CCD – Convention to Combat Desertification
CCF – credit-card format
CCF – Comprehensive Country Co-operation Framework
CCMA – Commission for Conciliation, Mediation and Arbitration
CCP – Cape Conversion Process
CDA – Central Drug Authority
CDI – Co-operative Development Initiative
CDM – Clean Development Mechanism
CDWs – community development workers
CEE – Commission for Employment Equity
CEED – Chairs of Entrepreneurship and Enterprise Development
CEF – Central Energy Fund
CEIRD – centres of excellence in industrial research and development
CEM – Council of Education Ministers
CEO – Chief Executive Officer
CETA – Construction Education and Training Authority
CFCs – chlorofluorocarbons
CGE – Commission on Gender Equality
CGS – Council for Geoscience
CHE – Council on Higher Education
CIDB – Construction Industry Development Board
CIDP – Construction Industry Development Programme
CIP – Critical Infrastructure Programme
CIPRO – Companies and Intellectual Property Registration Office
CIS – Cadastral Information System
CITES – Convention on International Trade in Endangered Species
CJS – criminal justice system
ClaRA – Communal Land Rights Act
CMAs – catchment management agencies
CoEs – centres of excellence
COP – Conference of the Parties
COSAB – Council of South African Banks
COSSE – SADC Committee of Stock Exchanges
CPA – comprehensive peace agreement
CPA – Cotonou Partnership Agreement
CPA – Community Press Association
CPD – Continuing Professional Development
CPF – Community Policing Forum
CPI – Consumer Price Index
CPIDP – Construction and Industry Development Programme
CPIX – consumer price index excluding mortgage costs

CPOs – citizens post offices
CPP – Court Process Project
CPSI – Centre for Public Service Innovation
CRC – Criminal Record Centre
CREATE SA – Creative Education and Training Enterprise South Africa
CSD – Commission on Sustainable Development
CSDP – South African central securities depository participants
CSG – Child Support Grant
CSIR – Council for Scientific and Industrial Research
CSN – Community Services Network
CSP – customised sector programmes
CSPBs – correctional supervision and parole boards
CSSDCA – Conference on Security, Stability, Development and Co-operation in Africa
CTIA – Cape Town International Airport
CVDs – card-verification devices
CWSS – Community Water Supply and Sanitation
CYFD – Child, Youth and Family Development

D

D&G – Democracy and Governance
DA – Democratic Alliance
DBSA – Development Bank of Southern Africa
DCOs – doping control officers
DCT – Durban Container Terminal
DDT – dichloro-diphenyl-trichloroethane
DFID – Department for International Development
DIA – Durban International Airport
DISSA – Disability Sport South Africa
DIU – Departmental Investigation Unit
DMO – Destination Marketing Organisation
DNR – Direct Normal Radiation
DNS – Digital Nervous System
DOTS – document-tracking system
DOTS – Directly Observed Treatment Short Course
DPP – Director of Public Prosecutions
DRC – Democratic Republic of Congo
DRS – Deeds Registration System
DSO – Directorate: Special Operations

E

EAP – Employee Assistance Programme
EC – European Commission
ECC – Employment Conditions Commission
ECD – Early Childhood Development
ECDP – Emerging Contractor Development Programme
ECOSOCC – Economic, Social and Cultural Council
ECOWAS – Economic Community of West African States
EDI – electricity distribution industry
EDL – Essential Drug List
EE – Eskom Enterprises

EEPR – Employment and Economic Policy Research
EEZ – Exclusive Economic Zone
EFA – Education For All
EIAs – environmental impact assessments
EIB – European Investment Bank
EIDD – Enterprise and Industry Development Division
EIPs – environmental implementation plans
ELRC – Education Labour Relations Council
EMEM – Excellence in Mining Environmental Management
ENPAT – National Environmental Potential Atlas
EPA – economic partnership agreements
EPRD – European Programme for Reconstruction and Development
EPWP – Expanded Public Works Programme
ESF – Equitable Shares Formula
ESI – Electricity Supply Industry
ETD – Education, Training and Development
EU – European Union

F

FAIS – financial advisory and intermediary services
FAO – Food and Agricultural Organisation
FAS – Financial Administration System
FAS – Foetal Alcohol Syndrome
FATF – Financial Action Task Force
FBOs – faith-based organisations
FBW – Free Basic Water
FCJ – Forum of Community Journalists
FCTC – Framework Convention on Tobacco Control
FDI – Foreign Direct Investment
FET – Further Education and Training
FETC – Further Education and Training Certificate
FFC – Financial and Fiscal Commission
FIC – Financial Intelligence Centre
FIG – Foreign Investment Grant
FM – Frequency Modulation
FMD – foot-and-mouth disease
FNB – First National Bank
FOSAD – Forum of South African Directors-General
FPMC – National Food Pricing Monitoring Committee
FSB – Financial Services Board
FSC – Forest Stewardship Council
FTA – free trade agreement
FTFA – Food and Trees for Africa
FXI – Freedom of Expression Institute

G

G&A – Governance and Administration
GAAP – Generally Accepted Accounting Practice
GAW – Global Atmosphere Watch
GBADS – ground-based air defence systems
GBIF – Global Biodiversity Information Facility

GCIS – Government Communication and Information System
GDP – Gross Domestic Product
GDPR – Gross Domestic Product per Region
GDS – Growth and Development Summit
GEF – Global Environment Facility
GEPF – Government Employees Pension Fund
GEOSS – Global Earth Observation System of Systems
GET – General Education and Training
GGP – Gross Geographical Product
GHG – greenhouse gas
GIS – Agricultural Georeferenced Information System
GITO – government information technology officers
GLTP – Great Limpopo Transfrontier Park
GM – Genetically Modified
GMOs – genetically modified organisms
GPS – Global Positioning System
GPT – General Preferential Tariff
GRAP – Generally Recognised Accounting Practice
GSP – General System of Preferences
GSLWP – Greater St Lucia Wetlands Park
GWh – gigawatt-hour

H

ha – hectare
HartRAO – Hartebeesthoek Radio Astronomy Observatory
HCE – Housing Consumer Education Programme
HDIs – historically disadvantaged individuals
HE – Higher Education
HEAIDS – Higher Education HIV and AIDS Programme
HEDCOM – Heads of Education Departments Committee
HEQC – Higher Education Quality Committee
HESS – High-Energy Stereoscopic System
HEU – high enriched uranium
HG – Higher Grade
HMO – Hermanus Magnetic Observatory
HPCSA – Health Professions Council of South Africa
HPP – High-Performance Programme
HRD – human resource development
HRM – human resource management
HSIC – Heads of State and Government Implementation Committee
HSRC – Human Sciences Research Council

I

IAAF – International Association of Athletics Federations
IBA – Independent Broadcasting Authority
IBSA – India-Brazil-South Africa
ICAO – International Civil Aviation Organisation
ICASA – Independent Communications Authority of South Africa

ICC – International Criminal Court
ICD – Independent Complaints Directorate
ICGEB – Centre for Genetic Engineering and Biotechnology
ICN – International Congress of Nutrition
ICSSPE – International Council of Sport Science and Physical Education
ICSU – International Council for Science
ICT – Information and Communications Technology
ID – Identity Document
IDASA – Institute for Democracy in South Africa
IDC – Industrial Development Corporation
IDMT – Interdepartmental Management Team
IDP – Integrated Development Plan
IDZ – Industrial Development Zone
IEC – Independent Electoral Commission
IECs – integrated energy centres
IEP – Integrated Energy Planning
IF – Innovation Fund
IFCC – International Fellowship of Christian Churches
IFP – Inkatha Freedom Party
IFSNP – Integrated Food Security and Nutrition Programme
IHERI-AB – Institut Des Hautes et de la Recherche Islamique
IHSA – Institute of Housing of South Africa
IJS – integrated justice system
IKS – indigenous knowledge systems
ILS – instrument landing system
IMC – International Marketing Council
IMCI – Integrated Management of Childhood Illnesses
IMDP – Integrated Management Development Programme
IMF – International Monetary Fund
IMS – Integrated Manufacturing Strategy
INP – Integrated Nutrition Programme
INEP – Integrated National Electrification Programme
IOC – International Olympic Committee
IOR-ARC – Indian Ocean Rim Association for Regional Co-operation
IPC – International Paralympic Committee
IPCA – International Prison Chaplaincy Association
IPP – Independent Power Producer
IPPC – International Plant Protection Convention
IPSP – Integrated Provincial Support Programme
IRRD – Integrated Rural and Regional Development
ISL – International Science Liaison
ISO – International Organisation for Standardisation
ISPs – internal strategic perspectives
ISPs – Internet service-providers

ISRDP – Integrated Sustainable Rural Development Programme
ISRDS – Integrated Sustainable Rural Development Strategy
ISSA – Institute for Satellite and Software Applications
ISSET-SETA – Information Systems Electronic and Telecom Technologies Sector Education and Training Authority
IT – Information Technology
IST – Innovation, Science and Technology
ITAC – International Trade Administration Commission
ITEC – Intergovernmental Committee on Trade and Economic Co-operation
ITED – International Trade and Economic Development
ITU – International Telecommunications Union
IUCN – World Conservation Union

J

JBC – Joint Bilateral Commission (for Co-operation)
JCC – Joint Commission of Co-operation
JCPS – Justice, Crime Prevention and Security
JET – Joint Education Trust
JIA – Johannesburg International Airport
JITB – Johannesburg International Trade Bureau
JMC – Joint Ministerial Commission
JPA – joint parliamentary activities
JPC – Joint Permanent Commission
JPCC – Joint Permanent Commission for Co-operation
JPOI – Johannesburg Plan of Implementation
JRMCs – joint route management committees
JSC – Judicial Service Commission
JSCD – Joint Standing Committee on Defence
JSE – JSE Limited

K

km – kilometre
KM – Knowledge Management
kWh – kilowatt-hours

L

l – litre
LABS – Laboratory for Accelerator-Based Sciences
LBC – Large Business Centre
LED – local economic development
LHWP – Lesotho Highlands Water Project
LIASA – Library Association of South Africa
LIS – Library and Information Services
LPG – liquid petroleum gas

LRAD –	Land Redistribution for Agricultural Development
LREF –	Land Reform Empowerment Facility
LTPS –	Land Transport Permit System

M

M³ –	million cubic metres
m –	metre
M&E –	monitoring and evaluation
MAFISA –	micro-agricultural financial institutions of South Africa
MAPPP-SETA –	Media, Advertising, Publishing, Printing and Packaging Sector Education and Training Authority
MBA –	Master of Business Administration
MCA –	MultiChoice Africa
MCC –	Medicines Control Council
MCLI –	Maputo Corridor Logistics Initiative
MDDA –	Media Development and Diversity Agency
MDGs –	millennium development goals
MDIs –	Network of African Management Development Institutes
MEC –	Member of the Executive Council
MERCOSUR –	South American Common Market
MERS –	Micro-Economic Reform Strategy
MFMA –	Municipal Finance Management Act
MFRC –	Micro-Finance Regulatory Council
MFSA –	Marketing Federation of South Africa
MHIC –	Mental Health Information Centre
MHSA –	Mine Health and Safety Act
MHSC –	Mine Health and Safety Council
MHSI –	Mine Health and Safety Inspectorate
MICE –	meetings, incentives, conferences and exhibitions
MIDP –	Motor Industry Development Programme
MIG –	Municipal Infrastructure Grant
MinMecs –	ministerial fora
MiningTek –	Mining Technology Division
M*l* –	million litres
MLA –	Micro-Lenders Association
MMM –	MultiMarket Model
MMSD –	Mineral and Mining for Sustainable Development
MoU –	Memorandum of Understanding
MPAs –	marine protected areas
MPC –	Monetary Policy Committee
MPCCs –	multipurpose community centres
MPRDA –	Minerals and Petroleum Resources Development Act
MQA –	Mining Qualifications Authority
MRC –	Medical Research Council
MRLs –	maximum residue limits
MRMC –	Major Radiation Medicine Centre
MRS –	Micro-Economic Reform Strategy
MST –	Marketable Securities Tax

mt –	metric ton
MTech –	Master's Degree in Technology
Mt –	million tons
MTN –	Mobile Telephone Network
MTO –	Mountain-to-Ocean
MTR –	mid-term review
MW –	medium wave
MW –	megawatts
MTEF –	Medium Term Expenditure Framework
MYIP –	Multi-Year Implementation Plan

N

NAASP –	New Asian-African Strategic Partnership
NAC –	National Arts Council of South Africa
NACF –	National Anti-Corruption Forum
NACHRET –	National Centre for Human-Rights Education and Training
NACI –	National Advisory Council on Innovation
NACOC –	National Co-ordinating Committee
NACTT –	National AIDS Children's Task Team
NAFU –	National African Farmers' Union
NAFVSA –	National Film, Video and Sound Archives
NAIL –	New Africa Investments Limited
NAM –	Non-Aligned Movement
NAMAC –	National Manufacturing Advisory Centres
NAMC –	National Agricultural Marketing Council
NAMF –	New Africa Mining Fund
NARF –	National Agricultural Research Forum
NBFET –	National Board for Further Education and Training
NBI –	National Botanical Institute
NBS –	National Biotechnology Strategy
NCACC –	National Conventional Arms Control Committee
NCCS –	National Crime Combating Strategy
NCHM –	National Cultural History Museum
NCLIS –	National Council for Library and Information Services
NCOH –	National Centre for Occupational Health
NCOP –	National Council of Provinces
NCS –	National Curriculum Statement
NCSP –	National Crime Prevention Strategy
NDA –	National Development Agency
NDMP –	South African National Drug Master Plan
NDPP –	National Director of Public Prosecutions
NECSA –	South African Nuclear Energy Corporation
NEDLAC –	National Economic Development and Labour Council
NEAF –	National Environmental Advisory Forum
NEF –	National Empowerment Fund
NEMISA –	National Electronic Media Institute of South Africa
NEPAD –	New Partnership for Africa's Development
NER –	National Electricity Regulator
NERI –	National Energy Research Institute

NFAC –	National Forests Advisory Council
NFDRSA –	National Fire Danger Rating System for South Africa
NFLS –	National Freight Logistics Strategy
NFVF –	National Film and Video Foundation
NG –	Nederduitse Gereformeerde (kerk)
NGOs –	non-governmental organisations
NHBRC –	National Home-Builders Registration Council
NHC –	National Heritage Council
NHS –	National Health System
NHFC –	National Housing Finance Corporation
NHLS –	National Health Laboratory Service
NIA –	National Intelligence Agency
NIB –	National Immigration Branch
NICD –	National Institute for Communicable Diseases
NIPP –	National Industrial Participation Programme
NIRP –	National Integrated Resource Plan
NIU –	National Intervention Unit
NIV –	National Institute for Virology
NLP –	National LandCare Programme
NLPF –	National Language Policy Framework
NLR –	National Loans Register
NLS –	National Language Service
NLSA –	National Library of South Africa
NLUs –	National Lexicography Units
NMPS –	National Mining Promotion System
NMT –	non-motorised transport
NNP –	New National Party
NNR –	National Nuclear Regulator
NOCSA –	National Olympic Committee of South Africa
NPA –	National Prosecuting Authority
NPA –	National Ports Authority
NPLs –	non-performing loans
NPOs –	non-profit organisations
NPS –	National Prosecuting Services
NPWP –	National Public Works Programme
NQF –	National Qualifications Framework
NRF –	National Research Foundation
NSA –	National Skills Authority
NSDF –	National Spatial Development Framework
NSDS –	National Skills Development Strategy
NSIF –	National Spatial Information Framework
NSF –	National Skills Fund
NSFAS –	National Student Financial Aid Scheme
NSI –	National System of Innovation
NSNP –	National School Nutrition Programme
NSSD –	National Strategy for Sustainable Development
NTGL –	National Transitional Government of Liberia
NSW –	National Science Week
NUFCOR –	Nuclear Fuels Corporation
NURCHA –	National Urban Reconstruction and Housing Agency
NWRIA –	National Water Resource Infrastructure Agency

NWRS –	National Water Research Strategy
NYC –	National Youth Commission
NZG –	National Zoological Gardens

O

OAG –	Office of the Auditor-General
OAU –	Organisation of African Unity
OBE –	outcomes-based education
OBP –	Onderstepoort Biological Products
ODA –	Overseas Development Assistance
ODS –	ozone-depleting substances
OHS –	occupational health and safety
OIE –	Office International des Épizooties
ONUB –	United Nations Operation in Burundi
OPA –	Online Publishers' Association
OPSC –	Office of the Public Service Commission
OSI –	Open Society Institute

P

PAC –	Pan Africanist Congress
PanSALB –	Pan South African Language Board
PAP –	Pan-African Parliament
PAPU –	Pan African Postal Union
PAS –	Provincial Academies of Sport
PASA –	Petroleum Agency SA
PBMR –	Pebble Bed Modular Reactor
PC –	Project Consolidate
PCC –	President's Co-ordinating Council
PCS –	Public Service Commission
PetroSA –	Petroleum, Gas and Oil Corporation of South Africa
PFM –	Participatory Forest Management
PFMA –	Public Finance Management Act
PGDS –	Provincial Growth and Development Strategies
PGMs –	platinum-group metals
PHC –	primary healthcare
PHP –	People's Housing Process
PHPT –	People's Housing Partnership Trust
PIC –	Public Investment Commissioner
PIC –	Public Investment Corporation
PILIR –	Management Policy and Procedure on Incapacity Leave and Ill-Health
PIMS –	Planning and Implementation Management Support
PIPs –	properties in possession
PITs –	public internet terminals
PlantBio –	Plant Biotechnology Innovation Centre
PLROs –	provincial land reform offices
PMSA –	Print Media South Africa
PMTCT –	preventing mother-to-child transmission
PPPs –	public private partnerships
PRC –	People's Republic of China
PSC –	Peace and Security Council

PSC –   Public Service Commission
PSCBC –   Public Service Co-ordinating Bargaining Council
PSM&ES –   Public Service Monitoring and Evaluation System
PTA –   preferential trade agreement
PTDs –   person-training days
PUB –   Public Understanding of Biotechnology
PUSET –   Public Understanding of Science, Engineering and Technology
PV –   photovoltaic

R

R&D –   research and development
RAC –   Regional Advisory Committee
RAF –   Road Accident Fund
RAS –   Registration Administration System
RCD –   research capacity development
RDP –   Reconstruction and Development Programme
RECs –   regional economic communities
REDs –   regional electricity distributors
RERA –   Regional Electricity Regulators' Association
RFSTP –   Regional Food Security Training Programme
RHLF –   Rural Housing Loan Fund
RHP –   River Health Programme
RISA –   Research and Innovation Support Agency
RNCS –   Revised National Curriculum Statement
RSC –   Regional Services Council
RTMC –   Road Traffic Management Corporation
RTMS –   Road Traffic Management Strategy
RTSB –   Road Traffic Safety Board

S

S&T –   science and technology
SAA –   South African Airways
SAAF –   South African Air Force
SAAFQIS –   South African Agricultural Food and Quarantine Inspection Services
SAAO –   South African Astronomical Observatory
SAASTA –   South African Agency for Science and Technology
SAAVI –   South African Aids Vaccine Initiative
SAATS –   South African Air Traffic System
SAB –   South African Breweries
SABC –   South African Broadcasting Corporation
SABI –   South African Biodiversity Initiative
SABIF –   South African Bioinformatics Facility
SABS –   South African Bureau of Standards
SACC –   South African Council of Churches
SACCA –   South African Civil Aviation Authority
SACE –   South African Council for Educators
SACOB –   South African Chamber of Business
SACU –   Southern African Customs Union

SADC –   Southern African Development Community
SAEON –   South African Environmental Observation Network
SAFCERT –   South African Certifications Council
SAFCOL –   South African Forestry Company Limited
SAFEX –   South African Futures Exchange
SAGBVHI –   South African Gender-Based Violence and Health Initiative
SAGNC –   South African Geographical Names Council
SAHA –   Social Aspects of HIV and AIDS and Health
SAHARA –   Social Aspects of AIDS Research Alliance
SAHRA –   South African Heritage Resources Agency
SAHRC –   South African Human Rights Commission
SAIAB –   South African Institute for Aquatic Biodiversity
SAIDS –   South African Institute for Drug-Free Sport
SAIMR –   South African Institute for Medical Research
SALGA –   South African Local Government Association
SALRC –   South African Law Reform Commission
SALT –   South African Large Telescope
SAMAF –   South African Micro-Finance Apex Fund
SAMDI –   South African Management Development Institute
SAMHS –   South African Military Health Service
SAMM –   Surveys, Analysis, Mapping and Modelling
SAMOS –   South African Multiple Option Settlement
SAMSA –   South African Maritime Safety Authority
SANAC –   South African National AIDS Council
SANAI –   South African Academy of Intelligence
SANAP –   South African National Antarctic Programme
SANBI –   South African National Biodiversity Institute
SANC –   South African Nursing Council
SANCOR –   South African Network for Coastal and Oceanic Research
SANDF –   South African National Defence Force
SANEF –   South African National Editors' Forum
SANGALA –   South African National Games and Leisure Activities
SANLI –   South African National Literacy Initiative
SANParks –   South African National Parks
SANRAL –   South African National Roads Agency Ltd
SAPA –   South African Press Association
SAPIP –   South African Pesticide Initiative Programme
SAPP –   Southern African Power Pool
SAPS –   South African Police Service
SANTACO –   South African National Taxi Council
SAPA –   South African Press Association
SAPCA –   South African Pest Control Association
SAPO –   South African Port Operations
SAPO –   South African Post Office
SAPP –   Southern African Power Pool
SAQA –   South African Qualifications Authority
SARCC –   South African Rail Commuter Corporation
SARS –   South African Revenue Service
SASAR –   South African Search-and-Rescue Organisation

SASC – South African Sports Commission
SASS – South African Secret Service
SASSA – South African Social Security Agency
SASSMC – South African Small-Scale Mining Chamber
SATI – South African Tourism Institute
SAUJ – South African Union of Journalists
SAURA – South African Utility Regulators' Association
SAWEN – South African Women Entrepreneurs Network
SAWIMA – South African Women in Mining Association
SAWS – South African Weather Service
SCI – Social Cohesion and Integration
SCOPA – Standing Committee on Public Accounts
SDF – service-delivery facilitator
SDF – Spacial Development Framework
SDI – Spatial Development Initiative
SDIP – Service-Delivery Improvement Programme
SDP – Strategic Defence Procurement
SEDA – Small Enterprise Development Agency
SET – science, engineering and technology
SETAs – sector education and training authorities
SFF – Strategic Fuel Fund
SFM – sustainable forest management
SFWS – Strategic Framework for Water Services
SGB – Housing Standard Generation Body
SHF – Social Housing Foundation
SHI – Social Health Insurance
SHIs – social housing institutions
SIP – Strategic Investment Programme
SISA – Sports Information and Science Agency
SITA – State Information Technology Agency
SIU – Special Investigating Unit
SKA – South African Square Kilometre Array
SMEs – small and medium-sized enterprises
SMEDP – Small Medium Enterprise Development Programme
SMMEs – small, medium and micro enterprises
SMS – Senior Management Service
SNO – Second National Operator
SOCA – Sexual Offences and Community Affairs
SOEs – state-owned enterprises
SPAs – strategic partnership agreements
SPF – Sector Partnership Fund
SPI – Spatial planning and information
SPLM – Sudanese People's Liberation Movement
SQF – SiyaQhubeka Forests
SRI Index – Socially Responsible Investment Index
SRSA – Sport and Recreation South Africa
SSM – small-scale mining
SSP – Skills Support Programme
SSPD – Sasol Slurry Phase Distillate
STAC – Science and Technology Agreements Committee
STIs – sexually transmitted infections
StanSA – Standards South Africa
Stats SA – Statistics South Africa

Strips – Separate Trading of Registered Interest and Principal Securities
SUMS – Subsidy-Management System

T

t – ton
TAC – Total Allowable Catch
TAE – Total Applied Effort
TAU – Transvaal Agricultural Union
TB – tuberculosis
TBCSA – Tourism Business Council of South Africa
TCTA – Trans Caledon Tunnel Authority
TDCA – Trade Development and Co-operation Agreement
TEBA – Employment Bureau of Africa
TEP – Tourism Enterprise Programme
TFCAs – transfrontier conservation areas
TGCSA – Tourism Grading Council of South Africa
THETA – Tourism and Hospitality Education and Training Authority
THRIP – Technology and Human Resource for Industry Programme
TICAD – International Conference on African Development
TISA – Trade and Investment South Africa
TISSA – Telephone Interpreting Service of South Africa
TKC – Trans-Kalahari Corridor
TLP – Tourism Learnership Project
TMNP – Table Mountain National Park
TNO – Third Licence Operator
TRC – Truth and Reconciliation Commission
TRP – Taxi Recapitalisation Programme
TTC – Technology Transfer Centre
TURF – Territorial User Rights Fishery
TWIB – Technology for Women in Business

U

UAE – United Arab Emirates
UAVs – unmanned aerial vehicles
UIF – Unemployment Insurance Fund
UK – United Kingdom
UN – United Nations
UNAMSIL – United Nations Mission in Sierra Leone
UNCCD – United Nations Convention to Combat Desertification
UNCED – United Nations Conference on Environment and Development
UNCTAD – United Nations Conference on Trade and Development
UNDP – United Nations Development Programme
UNEP – United Nations Environment Programme
UNFCCC – United Nations Framework Convention on Climate Change

UNGA – United Nations General Assembly
UNICEF – United Nations Children's Fund
UNISA – University of South Africa
UNESCO – United Nations Educational, Scientific and Cultural Organisation
UNMIL – United Nations Mission In Liberia
UNMIS – United Nations Mission in Sudan
UNSG – United Nations Secretary-General
UPU – Universal Postal Union
URP – Urban Renewal Programme
USA – United States of America
USA – Universal Service Agency
USALS – under-serviced area licences
USOs – universal service obligations
USSASA – United School Sport Association of South Africa
USSR – Union of Soviet Socialist Republics
UST – uncertified securities tax
UUDP – Urban Upgrading and Development

V

VAT – value-added tax
VCT – voluntary counselling and testing
VEP – Victim-Empowerment Programme
VLBI – very long baseline interferometry
VOC – Dutch East India Company

W

WADA – World Doping Agency
WEF – World Economic Forum
WEPS – Wholesale Electricity Pricing System
WESTCO – Western Power Corridor Project
WfW – Working for Water
WGC – World Golf Championships
WHO – World Health Organisation
WPC – World Petroleum Congress
WIO-LAB – West Indian Ocean Land-Based Activities Project
WRC – Water Research Commission
WSAs – water service authorities
WSSD – World Summit on Sustainable Development
WTO – World Trade Organisation
WTO-SPS – World Trade Organisation Agreement on the Application of Sanitary and Phytosanitary Measures
WTW – Water Treatment Works
WUAs – water-user associations
WWF – World Wildlife Fund

Z

ZAPU – Zimbabwe African People's Union
ZCC – Zion Christian Church
ZIPRA – Zimbabwean People's Revolutionary Army
ZPCSA – Zone of Peace and Co-operation in the South Atlantic

Contact information as at 15 November 2005

National government departments and organisational components

Agriculture
Website: *www.nda.agric.za*
Private Bag X250
Pretoria 0001
Tel: (012) 319-6000
Fax: (012) 321-8558

Arts and Culture
Website: *www.dac.gov.za*
Private Bag X897
Pretoria 0001
Tel: (012) 337-8000
Fax: (012) 323-2720

Communications
Website: *www.doc.gov.za*
Private Bag X860
Pretoria 0001
Tel: (012) 427-8000
Fax: (012) 427-8016

Correctional Services
Website: *www.dcs.gov.za*
Private Bag X136
Pretoria 0001
Tel: (012) 307-2000
Fax: (012) 328-6149

Defence
Website: *www.dod.mil.za*
Private Bag X161
Pretoria 0001
Tel: (012) 355-6321
Fax: (012) 355-6398

Education
Website: *www.education.gov.za*
Private Bag X895
Pretoria 0001
Tel: (012) 312-5911
Fax: (012) 325-6260

Environmental Affairs and Tourism
Website: *www.environment.gov.za*
Private Bag X447
Pretoria 0001
Tel: (012) 310-3911
Fax: (012) 322-2682

Foreign Affairs
Website: *www.dfa.gov.za*
Private Bag X152
Pretoria 0001
Tel: (012) 351-1000
Fax: (012) 351-0165

Government Communications (GCIS)
Website: *www.gcis.gov.za*
Private Bag X745
Pretoria 0001
Tel: (012) 314-2911
Fax: (012) 325-2030

Health
Website: *www.doh.gov.za*
Private Bag X828
Pretoria 0001
Tel: (012) 312-0000
Fax: (012) 326-4395

Home Affairs
Website: *www.home-affairs.gov.za*
Private Bag X114
Pretoria 0001
Tel: (012) 810-8911
Fax: (012) 810-7307

Housing
Website: *www.housing.gov.za*
Private Bag X644
Pretoria 0001
Tel: (012) 421-1311
Fax: (012) 341-8513

Independent Complaints Directorate
Website: *www.icd.gov.za*
Private Bag X941
Pretoria 0001
Tel: (012) 392-0400
Fax: (012) 320-3116

Justice and Constitutional Development
Website: *www.doj.gov.za*
Private Bag X81
Pretoria 0001
Tel: (012) 315-1111
Fax: (012) 315-1112

Labour
Website: *www.labour.gov.za*
Private Bag X117
Pretoria 0001
Tel: (012) 309-4000
Fax: (012) 309-4082/320-2059

Land Affairs
Website: http://land.pwv.gov.za
Private Bag X833
Pretoria 0001
Tel: (012) 312-8911
Fax: (012) 323-7124

Minerals and Energy
Website: *www.dme.gov.za*
Private Bag X59
Pretoria 0001
Tel: (012) 317-8000
Fax: (012) 322-3416

National Intelligence Agency
Website: *www.nia.org.za*
Private Bag X87
Pretoria 0001
Tel: (012) 427-4000
Fax: (012) 427-4651

National Treasury
Website: *www.treasury.gov.za*
Private Bag X115
Pretoria 0001
Tel: (012) 315-5111
Fax: (012) 315-8416

The Presidency
Private Bag X1000
Pretoria 0001
Tel: (012) 300-5200
Fax: (012) 323-8246
and
Private Bag X1000
Cape Town 8000
Tel: (021) 464-2100
Fax: (021) 461-6456

Provincial and Local Government
Website: *www.dplg.gov.za*
Private Bag X804
Pretoria 0001
Tel: (012) 334-0600
Fax: (012) 334-0603

Public Enterprises
Website: www.dpe.gov.za
Private Bag X15
Hatfield 0028
Tel: (012) 431-1000
Fax: (012) 432-1039

Public Service and Administration
Website: www.dpsa.gov.za
Private Bag X916
Pretoria 0001
Tel: (012) 314-7911
Fax: (012) 323-2386/324-5616

Public Service Commission
Website: www.psc.gov.za
Private Bag X121
Pretoria 0001
Tel: (012) 328-7690
Fax: (012) 325-8382

Public Works
Website: www.publicworks.gov.za
Private Bag X65
Pretoria 0001
Tel: (012) 337-2000
Fax: (012) 328-4217

Science and Technology
Website: www.dst.gov.za
Private Bag X894
Pretoria 0001
Tel: (012) 317-4300
Fax: (012) 317-4636

Secretariat for Safety and Security
Website: www.info.gov.za/sss/
Private Bag X922
Pretoria 0001
Tel: (012) 393-2500
Fax: (012) 393-2536/2557

Social Development
Website: www.socdev.gov.za
Private Bag X901
Pretoria 0001
Tel: (012) 312-7500
Fax: (012) 312-7943

South African Management Development Institute
Website: www.samdi.gov.za
Private Bag X759
Pretoria 0001
Tel: (012) 314-7911
Fax: (012) 321-1810

South African Police Service
Website: www.saps.gov.za
Private Bag X94
Pretoria 0001
Tel: (012) 393-5488/9
Fax: (012) 393-5520

South African Revenue Service
Website: www.sars.gov.za
Private Bag X923
Pretoria 0001
Tel: (012) 422-4000
Fax: (012) 422-6848

South African Secret Service
Website: www.sass.gov.za
Private Bag X5
Elarduspark 0047
Tel: (012) 427-6110
Fax: (012) 427-6428

Sport and Recreation
Website: www.srsa.gov.za
Private Bag X896
Pretoria 0001
Tel: (012) 334-3100
Fax: (012) 326-4026

Statistics South Africa
Website: www.statssa.gov.za
Private Bag X44
Pretoria 0001
Tel: (012) 310-8911
Fax: (012) 310-8500/8495

Trade and Industry
Website: www.thedti.gov.za
Private Bag X84
Pretoria 0001
Tel: 0861 843 384 (local)
Tel: +27(12) 394-9500 (international)

Transport
Website: www.transport.gov.za
Private Bag X193
Pretoria 0001
Tel: (012) 309-3000
Fax: (012) 328-5926

Water Affairs and Forestry
Website: www.dwaf.gov.za
Private Bag X313
Pretoria 0001
Tel: (012) 336-7500
Fax: (012) 336-8850

Parliamentary information

National Assembly
Website: www.parliament.gov.za
PO Box 15
Cape Town 8000
Tel: (021) 403-2549
Fax: (021) 461-9462

National Council of Provinces
Website: www.parliament.gov.za
PO Box 15
Cape Town 8000
Tel: (021) 403-2110/5/3221
Fax: (021) 461-9460

Provincial governments

Eastern Cape
Website: www.ecprov.gov.za
Private Bag X0047
Bisho 5605
Tel: (040) 609-6379
Fax: (040) 635-1166

Free State
Website: www.fs.gov.za
PO Box 20538
Bloemfontein 9301
Tel: (051) 405-5799
Fax: (051) 405-4803

Gauteng
Website: www.gpg.gov.za
Private Bag X61
Marshalltown 2107
Tel: (011) 355-6000
Fax: (011) 836-9334

KwaZulu-Natal
Website: www.kwazulunatal.gov.za
PO Box 412
Pietermaritzburg 3200
Tel: (033) 395-2978/9
Fax: (033) 342-7368

Limpopo
Website: www.limpopo.gov.za
Private Bag X9483
Polokwane 0700
Tel: (015) 287-6000
Fax: (015) 295-5831

Mpumalanga
Website:
www.mpumalanga.gov.za
Private Bag X11291
Nelspruit 1200
Tel: (013) 766-2641
Fax: (013) 766-2494

Northern Cape
Website: *www.northern-cape.gov.za*
Private Bag X5042
Kimberley 8300
Tel: (053) 830-8600
Fax: (053) 831-1023

North West
Website: *www.nwpg.gov.za*
Private Bag X65
Mafikeng 2735
Tel: (018) 387-4445
Fax: (018) 387-3008

Western Cape
Website:
www.capegateway.gov.za
PO Box 659
Cape Town 8000
Tel: (021) 483-4705/6
Fax: (021) 483-3421

Government structures and organisational components

Agricultural Research Council
Website: *www.arc.agric.za*
PO Box 8783
Pretoria 0001
Tel: (012) 427-9700
Fax: (012) 342-3948

Airports Company South Africa
Website: *www.airports.co.za*
PO Box 75480
Gardenview 2047
Tel: (011) 453-9116
Fax: (011) 453-9353/4

Armaments Corporation of South Africa
Website: *www.armscor.co.za*
Private Bag X337
Pretoria 0001
Tel: (012) 428-1911
Fax: (012) 428-5635

Central Energy Fund
Website: *www.cef.org.za*
PO Box 786141
Sandton 2199
Tel: (011) 280-0300
Fax: (011) 880-9803

Commission for Conciliation, Mediation and Arbitration
Website: *www.ccma.org.za*
Private Bag X096
Marshalltown 2107
Tel: (011) 377-6600
Fax: (011) 377-6658/78/80

Commission on Gender Equality
Website: *www.cge.org.za*
PO Box 32175
Braamfontein 2017
Tel: (011) 403-7182
Fax: (011) 403-7188

Commission on the Restitution of Land Rights
Website:
http://land.pwv.gov.za/restitution
Private Bag X833
Pretoria 0001
Tel: (012) 312-9244
Fax: (012) 321-0428

Commission on the Promotion and Protection of the Rights of Cultural, Religious and Linguistic Communities
c/o Department of Provincial and Local Government
Private Bag X804
Pretoria 0001
Tel: (012) 334-0600
Fax: (012) 334-0603

Competition Commission
Website: *www.compcom.co.za*
Private Bag X23
Lynnwood Ridge 0040
Tel: (012) 394-3200
Fax: (012) 394-4332

Constitutional Court
Website:
www.constitutionalcourt.org.za
Private Bag X1
Braamfontein 2017
Tel: (011) 359-7400
Fax: (011) 403-6524

Council for Geoscience
Website: *www.geoscience.org.za*
Private Bag X112
Pretoria 0001
Tel: (012) 841-1911
Fax: (012) 841-1203/21

Council for Scientific and Industrial Research
Website: *www.csir.co.za*
PO Box 395
Pretoria 0001
Tel: (012) 841-2911
Fax: (012) 349-1153

Council on Higher Education
Website: *www.che.org.za*
PO Box 13354
The Tramshed 0126
Tel: (012) 392-9100
Fax: (012) 392-9110

Denel (Pty) Ltd
Website: *www.denel.co.za*
PO Box 8322
Centurion 0046
Tel: (012) 428-0658
Fax: (012) 428-0651

Development Bank of Southern Africa
Website: *www.dbsa.org*
PO Box 1234
Halfway House 1685
Tel: (011) 313-3911
Fax: (011) 313-3086

Directorate: Special Operations and Serious Economic Offences
Private Bag X752
Pretoria 0001
Tel: (012) 845-6000
Fax: (012) 845-7130

Eskom
Website: *www.eskom.co.za*
PO Box 1091
Johannesburg 2001
Tel: (011) 800-8111
Fax: (011) 800-4299

Film and Publication Board
Website: *www.fpb.gov.za*
Private Bag X2205
Houghton 2041
Tel: (011) 483-0971
Fax: (011) 483-1084

Financial Intelligence Centre
Website: www.fic.gov.za
Private Bag X115
Pretoria 0001
Tel: (012) 309-9200
Fax: (012) 315-5828

Financial and Fiscal Commission
Website:
www.financialandfiscal.co.za
Private Bag X69
Halfway House 1685
Tel: (011) 0861 315 710
Fax: (011) 207-2344

Financial Services Board
Website: www.fsb.co.za
PO Box 35655
Menlo Park 0102
Tel: (012) 428-8000
Toll-free: 0800 110443/202087
Fax: (012) 347-0221

Government Printing Works
Private Bag X85
Pretoria 0001
Tel: (012) 334-4500
Fax: (012) 323-0009

Human Sciences Research Council
Website: www.hsrc.ac.za
Private Bag X41
Pretoria 0001
Tel: (012) 302-2000
Fax: (012) 302-2001

Independent Communications Authority of South Africa
Website: www.icasa.org.za
Private Bag X10002
Sandton 2146
Tel: (011) 321-8200
Fax: (011) 444 1919

Independent Development Trust
Website: www.idt.org.za
PO Box 73000
Lynnwood Ridge 0043
Tel: (012) 845-2000
Fax: (012) 348-0894

Independent Electoral Commission
Website: www.elections.org.za
PO Box 7943
Pretoria 0001
Tel: (012) 428-5700
Fax: (012) 428-5863

Industrial Development Corporation
Website: www.idc.co.za
PO Box 784055
Sandton 2146
Tel: (011) 269-3000
Fax: (011) 269-3116

International Marketing Council
Website: www.imc.org.za
PO Box 3207
Houghton 2198
Tel: (011) 483-0122
Fax: (011) 483-0124

Judicial Service Commission
Private Bag X258
Bloemfontein 9300
Tel: (051) 447-2769
Fax: (051) 447-0836

Khula Enterprise Finance Ltd
Website: www.khula.org.za
PO Box 28423
Sunnyside 0132
Tel: (012) 394-5560/5900
Fax: (012) 394-6560

Land Bank and Agricultural Bank of South Africa (Land Bank)
Website: www.landbank.co.za
PO Box 375
Pretoria 0001
Tel: (012) 312-3999
Fax: (012) 328-4055

Land Claims Court
Website:
wwwserver.law.wits.ac.za/lcc/
index.php
Private Bag X10060
Randburg 2125
Tel: (011) 781-2291
Fax: (011) 781-2217/8

Media Development and Diversity Agency
Website: www.mdda.org.za
PO Box 42846
Fordsburg 2033
Tel: (011) 492-2003
Fax: (011) 492-1198

Mintek
Website: www.mintek.co.za
Private Bag X3015
Randburg 2125
Tel: (011) 709-4111
Fax: (011) 793-2413

Municipal Demarcation Board
Website: www.demarcation.org.za
Private Bag X28
Hatfield 0028
Tel: (012) 342-2481/2
Fax: (012) 342-2480

National Advisory Council on Innovation
Website: www.naci.org.za
PO Box 1758
Pretoria 0001
Tel: (012) 392-9352
Fax: (012) 392-9353

National Agricultural Marketing Council
Website: www.namc.co.za
Private Bag X935
Pretoria 0001
Tel: (012) 341-1115
Fax: (012) 341-1811/1911

National Archives of South Africa
Website:
www.national.archives.gov.za
Private Bag X236
Pretoria 0001
Tel: (012) 323-5300
Fax: (012) 323-5287

National Arts Council of South Africa
Website: www.nac.org.za
PO Box 500
Newtown 2113
Tel: (011) 838-1383
Fax: (011) 838-6363

National Crime Prevention Strategy
Private Bag X922
Pretoria 0001
Tel: (012) 393-2550
Fax: (012) 393-2538

National Development Agency
Website: www.nda.org.za
PO Box 31959
Braamfontein 2017
Tel: (011) 403-6650
Fax: (011) 403-2514/5

National Director of Public Prosecutions
Website: www.ndpp.gov.za
PO Box 752
Pretoria 0001
Tel: (012) 317-5000
Fax: (012) 321-0968

National Economic Development and Labour Council
Website: www.nedlac.org.za
PO Box 1775
Saxonwold 2132
Tel: (011) 328-4200
Fax: (011) 447-2089/6053

National Electricity Regulator
Website: www.ner.org.za
PO Box 40343
Arcadia 0007
Tel: (012) 401-4600
Fax: (012) 401-4700

National Empowerment Fund
Website: www.nefcorp.co.za
PO Box 31
Melrose Arch
Melrose North 2076
Tel: (011) 731-9000
Fax: (011) 447-4859

National Gambling Board
Website: www.ngb.org.za
Private Bag X27
Hatfield 0028
Tel: (012) 394-3800
Fax: (012) 394-0831

National Homebuilders' Registration Council
Website: www.nhbrc.org.za
PO Box 461
Randburg 2125
Tel: (011) 348-5700
Fax: (011) 789-2902

National House of Traditional Leaders
Private Bag X804
Pretoria 0001
Tel: (012) 301-1054
Fax: (012) 326-1019

National Housing Finance Corporation
Website: www.nhfc.co.za
PO Box 31376
Braamfontein 2017
Tel: (011) 644-9800
Fax: (011) 484-0076

National Lotteries Board
Website: www.nlb.org.za
PO Box 1556
Brooklyn Square 0075
Tel: (012) 394-3440
Fax: (012) 394-0452

National Nuclear Regulator
Website: www.nnr.co.za
PO Box 7106
Centurion 0046
Tel: (012) 674-7100
Fax: (012) 663-5513

National Programme of Action for Children in South Africa
Website: www.children.gov.za
The Presidency
Private Bag X1000
Pretoria 0001
Tel: (012) 300-5200
Fax: (012) 321-4566

National Prosecuting Authority
Website: www.npa.gov.za
Private Bag X752
Pretoria 0001
Tel: (012) 845-6000
Fax: (012) 843-3111

National Research Foundation
Website: www.nrf.ac.za
PO Box 2600
Pretoria 0001
Tel: (012) 481-4000
Fax: (012) 349-1179

National Youth Commission
Website: www.nyc.gov.za
Private Bag X938
Pretoria 0001
Tel: (012) 309-7800
Fax: (012) 324-4759

Office of the Auditor-General
Website: www.agsa.co.za
PO Box 446
Pretoria 0001
Tel: (012) 426-8000
Fax: (012) 426-8371

Pan South African Language Board
Website: www.pansalb.org.za
Private Bag X08
Arcadia 0007
Tel: (012) 341-9638
Fax: (012) 341-5938

Public Investment Corporation
Website: www.pic.gov.za
Private Bag X187
Pretoria 0001
Tel: (012) 369-3300
Fax: (012) 348-6106

Office of the Public Protector
Private Bag X677
Pretoria 0001
Tel: (012) 366-7000
Fax: (012) 366-7105

Petroleum Oil and Gas Corporation of South Africa (Pty) Ltd
Website: www.petrosa.co.za
Private Bag X1
Waterfront, Cape Town 8002
Tel: (021) 417-3000
Fax: (021) 417-3144

Rand Water
Website: www.randwater.co.za
PO Box 1127
Johannesburg 2000
Tel: (011) 682-0911
Fax: (011) 682-0663

Small Enterprise Development Agency
Website: *www.seda.org.za*
PO Box 56714
Arcadia 0007
Tel: (012) 483-2000
Fax: (012) 428-5142

South African Airways
Website: *www.saa.co.za* or
www.flysaa.com
Private Bag X13
Johannesburg International Airport
1627
Tel: (011) 978-1000/2500
Fax: (011) 978-3507

South African Bureau of Standards
Website: *www.sabs.co.za*
Private Bag X191
Pretoria 0001
Tel: (012) 428-7911
Fax: (012) 344-1568

South African Civil Aviation Authority
Website: *www.caa.co.za*
Private Bag X73
Halfway House 1685
Tel: (011) 545-1000
Fax: (011) 545-1465

South African Diamond Board
Website: *www.sadb.co.za*
PO Box 16001
Doornfontein 2023
Tel: (011) 334-8980
Fax: (011) 334-8898

South African Council for Educators
Website: *www.sace.org.za*
Private Bag X127
Centurion 0046
Tel: (012) 663-9517
Fax: (012) 663-9238

South African Forestry Company Ltd
PO Box 1771
Silverton 0127
Tel: (012) 481-3500
Fax: (012) 804-3716

South African Human Rights Commission
Website: *www.sahrc.org.za*
Private Bag X2700
Houghton 2041
Tel: (011) 484-8300
Fax: (011) 484-7147

South African Law Reform Commission
Website: *www.law.wits.ac.za/salc/salc.htm*
Private Bag X668
Pretoria 0001
Tel: (012) 322-6440
Fax: (012) 320-0936

South African Local Government Association
Website: *www.salga.net*
PO Box 2094
Pretoria 0001
Tel: (012) 369-8000
Fax: (012) 369-8001

South African National Parks
Website: *www.sanparks.org*
PO Box 787
Pretoria 0001
Tel: (012) 426-5000
Fax: (012) 343-9959

South African National Roads Agency
Website: *www.nra.co.za*
PO Box 415
Pretoria 0001
Tel: (012) 426-6000
Fax: (012) 362-2116/2101/2117

South African Nuclear Energy Corporation
Website: *www.necsa.co.za*
PO Box X582
Pretoria 0001
Tel: (012) 305-4911
Fax: (012) 305-3111

South African Post Office Ltd
Website: *www.sapo.co.za*
PO Box 10000
Pretoria 0001
Tel: (012) 401-7000/7700
Fax: (012) 401-7707

South African Qualifications Authority
Website: *www.saqa.org.za*
Private Bag X06
Waterkloof 0145
Tel: (012) 431-5000
Fax: (012) 431-5039

South African Rail Commuter Corporation
Website: *www.sarcc.co.za*
Private Bag X02
Sunninghill 2157
Tel: (011) 804-2900
Fax: (011) 804-3852/3

South African Reserve Bank
Website: *www.resbank.co.za*
PO Box 427
Pretoria 0001
Tel: (012) 313-3911
Fax: (012) 313-3929

South African Sports Commission
Website: *www.sasc.org.za*
PO Box 11239
Centurion 0046
Tel: (012) 677-9700
Fax: (012) 677-9856/7

South African Tourism
Website: *www.southafrica.net*
Private Bag X10012
Sandton 2146
Tel: (011) 895-3000
Fax: (011) 895-3001

Special Investigating Unit
Website: *www.siu.org.za*
PO Box 893
East London 5200
Tel: (043) 704-6000
Fax: (043) 704-6116

State Information Technology Agency (Pty) Ltd
Website: *www.sita.co.za*
PO Box 26100
Monument Park 0105
Tel: (012) 482-3000
Fax: (012) 482-2100

State Tender Board
Website: *www.treasury.gov.za*
Private Bag X115
Pretoria 0001
Tel: (012) 315-5111
Fax: (012) 315-5234

Technology for Women in
Business
Website: *www.twib.co.za*
PO Box 395
Pretoria 0001
Tel: (012) 841-4983
Fax: (012) 841-4954

Telkom SA Ltd
Website: *www.telkom.co.za*
Private Bag X74
Pretoria 0001
Tel: (012) 311-3911
Fax: (012) 323-6733

Trade and Investment
South Africa
Website: *www.thedti.gov.za/
thedti/organisation/f.htm*
Private Bag X84
Pretoria 0001
Tel: (012) 394-1014
Customer care centre:
0861 843 384

Transnet Ltd
Website: *www.transnet.co.za*
PO Box 72501
Parkview 2122
Tel: (011) 308-2524
Fax: (011) 308-2312

Truth and Reconciliation
Commission
Website: *www.doj.gov.za/trc/
index.html*
Private Bag X81
Pretoria 0001
Tel: (012) 315-1293/1672
Fax: (012) 357-8835/8004

Water Research Commission
Website: *www.wrc.org.za*
Private Bag X03
Gezina 0031
Tel: (012) 330-0340
Fax: (012) 331-2565

Government Communication and Information Centres

Eastern Cape
Eastern Cape Provincial Office
Private Bag X608
East London 5200
Tel: (043) 722-2602
Fax: (043) 722-2615
E-mail: jeanine@gcispe.ecape.
gov.za

Free State
Free State Regional Office
PO Box 995
Bloemfontein 9300
Tel: (051) 448-4504
Fax: (051) 430-7032
E-mail: tshenolo@gcis.ofs.gov.za

Kroonstad Satellite Regional
Office
PO Box 995
Bloemfontein 9300
Tel: (056) 213-2795
E-mail: kroonstad@intekom.co.za

Gauteng
Gauteng Regional Office
Private Bag X16
Johannesburg 2000
Tel: (011) 834-3560
Fax: (011) 834-3621
E-mail: peterj@gcisjhb.pwv.gov.za

KwaZulu-Natal
KwaZulu-Natal Regional Office
Private Bag X54332
Durban 4000
Tel: (031) 301-6787/8
Fax: (031) 305-9431
E-mail:
malcolm@gcisdbn.kzntl.gov.za

Limpopo
Limpopo Regional Office
PO Box 2452
Polokwane 0700
Tel: (015) 291-4689
Fax: (015) 295-6982
E-mail:
neels@gcisptb.norprov.gov.za

Mpumalanga
Mpumalanga Regional Office
PO Box X2856
Nelspruit 1200
Tel: (013) 753-2397
Fax: (013) 753-2531
E-mail:
sydwel@gcisnls.mpu.gov.za

Northern Cape
Northern Cape Regional Office
Private Bag X5038
Kimberley 8300
Tel: (053) 832-1378/9
Fax: (053) 832-1377
E-mail:
mariusn@gcis.ncape.gov.za

Upington Satellite Regional Office
PO Box 2872
Upington 8800
Tel: (054) 332-6206
Fax: (054) 332-6218
E-mail:
upingtongic@intekom.co.za

North West
North West Regional Office
Private Bag X2120
Mafikeng 2745
Tel: (018) 381-7068/71
Fax: (018) 381-7066
E-mail:
mareka@gcismmb.nwp.gov.za

Western Cape
Western Cape Regional Office
Private Bag X9007
Cape Town 8000
Tel: (021) 421-5070
Fax: (021) 419-8846
E-mail:
brent@gcisct.wcape.gov.za

Multipurpose community centres

Eastern Cape
Centane MPCC
GCIS Office
Bell Street
Centane 4980
Tel: (047) 498-1207
Fax: (047) 498-1011

Cofimvaba MPCC
PO Box 456
Comfimvaba 5380
Tel: (047) 874-0444
Fax: (047) 874-0388

Sandrift MPCC
Urban Dondges Building
Hancock Street
North End
Port Elizabeth 6000
Tel: (041) 484-2022
Fax: (041) 484-2020

Sterkspruit MPCC
PO Box 18
Lady Grey 9755
Tel: (051) 611-0042
Fax: (051) 611-0042

Tombo MPCC
PO Box 182608
Port St Johns 5120
Tel: (047) 564-1131
Fax: (047) 564-2529

Free State
Botshabelo MPCC
1230 Section E
Botshabelo 9781
Telefax: (051) 532-6791

Namahadi MPCC
PO Box 17942
Witsieshoek 9870
Telefax: (058) 789-1147

Onalerona MPCC
PO Box 4627
Sediba Village
Thaba Nchu 9784
Tel: 082 550 8512

Gauteng
Alexandra MPCC
Cnr 8th Avenue & Roosevelt Str
Alexandra 2090
Tel: (011) 531-5599
Fax: (011) 531-5657

Atteridgeville
Mini-Munitoria Building
1770 Komane Street
Atteridgeville
Tel: (012) 358-7326

Brandvlei MPCC
Stand 64 off Randfontein-
Ventersdorp Rd
Brandvlei 1759
Telefax: (011) 414-1888
Tel: (011) 414-1072

Daveyton MPCC
Daveyton Mall
Eiselen Street
Daveyton
Benoni 1520
Tel: (011) 741-6188

Diepsloot MPCC
Stand 381 Diepsloot West
Diepsloot 2189
Tel: (011) 982-1200

Dobsonville MPCC
2332 Luthuli Street
Dobsonville
Tel: (011) 986-0036
Fax: (011) 932-1440

Faranani MPCC
PO Box 70021
Tsakane 1550
Tel: (011) 738-8753
Fax: (011) 753-8182

Ipelegeng MPCC
1238 White City Jabavu
Soweto 1809
Tel: (011) 982-5810
Fax: (011) 982-6400

Khutsong
Portion 1 of Stand 1
Khutsong South
Khutsong
Carletonville
Tel: (018) 783-9000/9075
Fax: (018) 783-9033

Mamelodi MPCC
9864 Makhubela Street
Mamelodi West 0122
Tel: (012) 805-9085

Mohlakeng MPCC
262 Ralerata Street
Mohlakeng
Randfontein 1759
Telefax: (011) 414-1888
Cell: 083 792 3575

Orlando East MPC
1425a Sofasonke Street
Orlando East 1804
Tel: (011) 935-8432
Fax: (011) 935-6492

Ratanda MPCC
Cnr. Heidelberg & Boshoek Str
Ratanda

Soshanguve MPCC
Shop 49
Nafcoc Shopping Centre
Section F
Soshanguve 0152
Telefax: (012) 799-5005

Tembisa MPCC
238 Igqagqa Section
Tembisa 1632
Tel: (011) 920-1120

Thokoza MPCC
8015 Khumalo Street
Thokoza
Tel: (011) 905-1404

Vaal/Sebokeng MPCC
Private Bag X029
Vanderbijlpark 1900
Tel: (016) 988-1502
Fax: (016) 988-1082
E-mail: sebokeng@intekom.co.za

Zithobeni MPCC
2237 Mothibe Drive
Zithobeni 1024
Tel: (013) 937-0133

KwaZulu-Natal
Bamshela MPCC
PO Box 131
Ozwathini 3242
Tel: (032) 294-9076
Fax: (032) 294-9075

Dududu MPCC
Private Bag X54332
Durban 4000
Telefax: (039) 974-0989

Dukuza MPCC
Private Bag X1620
Bergville 3350
Tel: (036) 438-6103
Fax: (036) 438-6136

Mbazwana MPCC
PO Box 231
Mbazwana 3974
Tel: (035) 571-0970
Fax: (035) 571-0971
E-mail: mbazwana@intekom.co.za

Mtshezi/Mbabazane MPCC
PO Box 750
Estcourt 3310
Telefax: (036) 353-3212

Tugela Ferry MPCC
Private Bag X461
Tugela Ferry 3010
Tel: (033) 493-0895
Fax: (033) 493-0724

Limpopo
Atok MPCC
PO Box 154
Atok 0749
Tel: (015) 622-8000

Botlokwa (Ramokgopa) MPCC
Botlokwa Village
Makhado
Tel: (015) 231-8027

Kgautswane MPCC
PO Box 9
Ohrigstad 1122
Tel: (013) 231-7515
Fax: (013) 238-0122

Leboeng MPCC
Leboeng Village
Safety Centre
Burgersfort
Tel: (013) 769-9026

Makhuva MPCC
PO Box 30
Phangweni 0816
Telefax: (015) 812-5602
E-mail: makhuva@intekom.co.za

Mapela MPCC
Private Bag X35
Mokopane 0600
Tel: (015) 413-0000/02

Vaalwater MPCC
268 Paul Kruger Street
Vaalwater
Tel: (015) 413-0000/2

Mpumalanga
Kgolomodumo MPCC
Maklerekeng Village
Moutse West
Telefax: (013) 980-0017
Cell: 072 3240965

Marapyane MPCC
Marapyane Shopping Centre
Cell: 073 2383365

Matsamo MPCC
PO Box 601
Shongwe Mission 1341
Tel: (013) 781-0659
E-mail: matsamo@intekom.co.za

Mpuluzi MPCC
PO Box 1408
Fernie 2339
Cell:082 9612143

Tholulwazi MPCC
Norda Street
Govan Mbeki Building, Leandra
Tel: (017) 683-3000
Fax: (017) 683-1031/0385

Northern Cape
Augrabies MPPC
199 Tin Crescent
Augrabies 8874
Tel: (054) 332-6206

Colesberg MPCC
PO Box 101
Colesberg 9795
Tel: (051) 753-2170
Fax: (051) 753-1154

Rethusaneng MPCC
Private Bag X5016
Kimberley 8300
Tel: (053) 872-1197
Fax: (053) 872-2647

Pescodia MPCC
62 Sparrow Street
Pescodia
Kimberley 8309
Tel: (053) 873-1072
Fax: (053) 873-1298

North West
Leretlhabetse MPCC
PO Box 223
Lebotlwane 0411
Telefax: (012) 701-5330

Tshedimosetso MPCC
PO Box 15
Boikhutso Village
Ventersdorp 2710
Cell: 073 165 8084

Tshidilamolomo
Taung Forum
1st Floor, Office No 3
Taung 8580
Tel: (018) 683-0010
Fax: (018) 683-0445

Victor Tong MPCC
PO Box 522
Ganyisa 8613
Tel: (053) 761-1028
Fax: (053) 761-1002

Western Cape
Bonteheuwel MPCC
Cnr Jakkalsvlei and Elder Street
Bonteheuwel
Cape Town 8000
Telefax: (021) 695-5425

Beaufort West MPPC
51 Devries Street, Rustdene
Beaufort West 6979
Telefax: (023) 415-3144

George/Tembalethu MPCC
PO Box 9669
George Central 6530
Cell: 082 592 1493

Guga Sithembe MPCC
PO Box 6
Langa 7455

Hartebeeskraal/Atlantis MPCC
1 Nottingham Street
Atlantis
Cape Town 7349
Tel: (021) 572-1872

Langebaan MPCC
PO Box 11
Langebaan 7537
Tel: (022) 772-2622
Fax: (022) 772-2271

Laingsburg MPCC
Cnr Main Street & 3rd Avenue
Laingsburg 6900
Telefax: (023) 415-3144

Masibambane/Vanrhynsdorp
MPCC
1 Mandela Street
Vanrhynsdorp 8170
Tel: (027) 219-1917
Fax: (027) 219-1754

Plettenberg Bay MPCC
Southern Life Centre
Lower Burg Street
Cape Town
Tel: (044) 501-3134
Fax: (044) 533-2691

Waboomskraal MPCC
PO Box 10610
George 6530
Tel: (044) 886-0040
Fax: (044) 886-0052

Worcester MPCC
Cnr Mtwazi & Nkenta Street
Zweletemba
Worcester 6854
Tel: (023) 348-2600
Fax: (023) 345-1031

Zolane MPCC
6th Avenue
Nyanga East 7755
Tel: (021) 386-8656
Fax: (021) 386-1032

Foreign representatives in South Africa

Albania (Republic of)
[Honorary Consulate]
PO Box 87393
Houghton 2041
Tel: (011) 884-1617
Fax: (011) 884-2510
E-mail: nrose@icon.co.za

Algeria (Democratic People's Republic of) [Embassy]
PO Box 57480
Arcadia 0007
Tel: (012) 342-5074/5
Fax: (012) 342-6479

Angola (Republic of)
[Embassy]
PO Box 8685
Pretoria 0001
Tel: (012) 342-4404
Fax: (012) 342-7039

Argentina (Republic of)
[Embassy]
PO Box 11125
Hatfield 0028
Tel: (012) 430-3513/6
Fax: (012) 430-3521
E-mail: argembas@global.co.za

Australia
[High Commission]
Private Bag X150
Pretoria 0001
Tel: (012) 342-3740
Fax: (012) 342-8442
E-mail: ian.wilcock@dfat.gov.au

Austria (Republic of)
[Embassy]
PO Box 95572
Waterkloof 0145
Tel: (012) 452-9155/9121
Fax: (012) 460-1151
E-mail: pretoria-ob@bmaa.gv.at

Bangladesh (People's Republic of) [High Commission]
410 Farenden Street
Sunnyside
Pretoria 0002
Tel: (012) 343-2105/7
Fax: (012) 343-5222
E-mail: bdoot@mweb.co.za

Belarus (Republic of)
[Embassy]
PO Box 4107
Pretoria 0001
Tel: (012) 430-7664
Fax: (012) 342-6280
E-mail: sa@belembassy.org

Belgium (Kingdom of)
[Embassy]
625 Leyds Street
Muckleneuk
Pretoria 0002
Tel: (012) 440-3201/2
Fax: (012) 440-3216
E-mail: pretoria@diplobel.org

Benin (Republic of)
[Embassy]
PO Box 26484
Arcadia 0007
Tel: (012) 342-6978
Fax: (012) 342-1823
E-mail: bih@mweb.co.za

Bosnia and Herzegovina
[Embassy]
PO Box 11464
Hatfield 0028
Tel: (012) 346-5547/7366
Fax: (012) 346-2295
E-mail: bih@mweb.co.za

Botswana (Republic of)
[High Commission]
PO Box 57035
Arcadia 0007
Tel: (012) 430-9640
Fax: (012) 342-1845

Brazil (Federative Republic of)
[Embassy]
PO Box 3269
Pretoria 0001
Tel: (012) 426-9400
Fax: (012) 426-9494
E-mail:
pretoria@brazilianembassy.org.za

Bulgaria (Republic of)
[Embassy]
PO Box 26296
Arcadia 0007
Tel: (012) 342-3720
Fax: (012) 342-3721
E-mail: embulgsa@iafrica.com

Burundi (Republic of)
[Embassy]
PO Box 12914
Hatfield 0028
Tel: (012) 342-4881/3
Fax: (012) 342-4885
E-mail: ambabusa@mweb.co.za

Cameroon (Republic of)
[High Commission]
PO Box 13790
Hatfield 0028
Tel: (012) 362-4731
Fax: (012) 362-4732
E-mail: hicocam@cameroon.co.za

Canada
[High Commission]
Private Bag X13
Hatfield 0028
Tel: (012) 422-3000
Fax: (012) 422-3052

Central African Republic
[Honorary Consulate-General]
PO Box 2774
Kempton Park 1620
Tel: (011) 970-1355
Fax: (011) 970-1352
E-mail: johan@eriksons.co.za

Chile (Republic of)
[Embassy]
PO Box 2449
Brooklyn Square 0075
Tel: (012) 460-8090/4482
Fax: (012) 460-8093
E-mail: chile@iafrica.com

China (People's Republic of)
[Embassy]
PO Box 95764
Waterkloof 0145
Tel: (012) 342-4194/5560/431-6500
Fax: (012) 342-4244/431-6590
E-mail: reception@chinese-embassy.org.za

Colombia (Republic of)
[Embassy]
PO Box 12791
Hatfield 0028
Tel: (012) 342-0211/4
Fax: (012) 342-0216
E-mail: concol@mweb.co.za

Comores (Federal Islamic Republic of the)
[Embassy]
200 Beckett Street
Arcadia 0083
Telefax: (012) 343-9483

Congo (Democratic Republic of)
[Embassy]
PO Box 28795
Sunnyside 0132
Tel: (012) 343-2455
Fax: (012) 344-4054
E-mail: rdcongo@lantic.co.za

Congo (Republic of)
[Embassy]
PO Box 40427
Arcadia 0007
Tel: (012) 342-5507
Fax: (012) 342-5510
E-mail: congo@telkomsa.net

Costa Rica (Republic of)
[Honorary Consulate]
PO Box 68140
Bryanston 2021
Tel: (011) 705-3434
Fax: (011) 705-1222
E-mail: ricacost@netactive.co.za

Cote d'Ivoire (Republic of)
[Embassy]
PO Box 13510
Hatfield 0028
Tel: (012) 342-6913
Fax: (012) 342-6713
E-mail: ambacr.pret@frenchdoor.co.za

Croatia (Republic of)
[Embassy]
PO Box 11335
Hatfield 0028
Tel: (012) 342-1206/1598
Fax: (012) 342-1819
E-mail: vrhjar@iafrica.com

Cuba (Republic of)
[Embassy]
PO Box 11605
Hatfield 0028
Tel: (012) 346-2215
Fax: (012) 346-2216
E-mail: embacuba@cubanembassy.co.za

Cyprus (Republic of)
[High Commission]
PO Box 14554
Hatfield 0028
Tel: (012) 342-5258
Fax: (012) 342-5596
E-mail: cyprusjb@mweb.co.za

Czech Republic
[Embassy]
PO Box 13671
Hatfield 0028
Tel: (012) 431-2380
Fax: (012) 342-2033
E-mail: pretoria@embassy.mzv.ca

Denmark (Kingdom of)
[Embassy]
PO Box 11439
Hatfield 0028
Tel: (012) 430-9340
Fax: (012) 342-7620
E-mail: pryamb@um.dk

Egypt (Arab Republic of)
[Embassy]
PO Box 30025
Sunnyside 0132
Tel: (012) 343-1590/1
Fax: (012) 343-1082
E-mail: egyptemb@global.co.za

Eritrea (State of)
[Embassy]
PO Box 11371
Queenswood 0121
Tel: (012) 333-1302
Fax: (012) 333-2330
E-mail: eremb@lantic.net

Estonia (Republic of)
[Honorary Consulate]
16 Hofmeyer Street
Welgemoed
Belville 7530
Tel: (021) 913-3850
Fax: (021) 913-2579

Ethiopia (Federal Republic of)
[Embassy]
PO Box 11469
Hatfield 0028
Tel: (012) 346-3542
Fax: (012) 346-3867
E-mail: ethiopia@sentechsa.com

Finland (Republic of)
[Embassy]
PO Box 443
Pretoria 0001
Tel: (012) 343-0275
Fax: (012) 343-3095
Fax: (visas) (012) 343-4369
E-mail: sanomat.pre@formin.fi

France (Republic of)
[Embassy]
250 Melk Street
Cnr Middle Street
New Muckleneuk 0181
Tel: (012) 425-1600
Fax: (012) 425-1609
E-mail: france@ambafrance-rsa.org

Gabon (Republic of)
[Embassy]
PO Box 9222
Pretoria 0001
Tel: (012) 342-4376/7
Fax: (012) 342-4375

Germany (Federal Republic of)
[Embassy]
PO Box 2023
Pretoria 0001
Tel: (012) 427-8900
Fax (visas): (012) 427-8984
Fax: (012) 343-9401
E-mail: germanembassypretoria-
@gonet.co.za

Ghana (Republic of)
[High Commission]
1038 Arcadia Street
Hatfield 0038
Tel: (012) 342-5847/9
Fax: (012) 342-5863
E-mail: ghcom27@icon.co.za

Greece (Hellenic Republic)
[Embassy]
1003 Church Street
Arcadia 0083
Tel: (012) 430-7351
Fax: (012) 430-4313
E-mail: embgrsaf@global.co.za

Grenada (Republic of)
[Honorary Consulate]
3rd Floor Digital House
Park Lane 2196
Tel: 083 461 6559
Fax: (011) 787-6407

Guatemala (Republic of)
[Honorary Consulate]
PO Box 222
Sunninghill 2157
Tel: (011) 804-5080
Fax: (011) 804-4844
E-mail: marcelr@exatrade.co.za

Guinea (Republic of)
[Embassy]
PO Box 13523
Hatfield 0028
Telefax: (012) 342-734
Tel: (012) 342-0893
E-mail: ambaguinea@iafrica.com

Guinea-Bissau (Republic of)
[Honorary Consulate]
P O Box 9689
Edenglen 1613
Tel: (011) 622-688
Fax: (011) 622-5351

Holy See (The Vatican)
[Apostolic Nunciature of the]
PO Box 26017
Arcadia 0007
Tel: (012) 344-3815/6
Fax: (012) 344-3595
E-mail: nunziosa@iafrica.com

Hungary (Republic of)
[Embassy]
PO Box 13843
Hatfield 0028
Tel: (012) 430-3020/30
Fax: (012) 430-3029
E-mail: huembprt@mweb.co.za

India (Republic of)
[High Commission]
PO Box 40216
Arcadia 0007
Tel: (012) 342-5392
Fax: (012) 342-5310
E-mail: hcipta@iafrica.com

Indonesia (Republic of)
[Embassy]
PO Box 13155
Hatfield 0028
Tel: (012) 342-3350/4
Fax: (012) 342-3369
E-mail: indonemb@lantic.co.za

Iran (Islamic Republic of)
[Embassy]
PO Box 12546
Hatfield 0028
Tel: (012) 342-5880/1
Fax: (012) 342-1878
E-mail:
office@iranembassy.org.za

Iraq (Republic of)
[Embassy]
PO Box 11089
Hatfield 0028
Tel: (012) 362-2012/2048
Fax: (012) 362-2027/4662

Ireland
[Embassy]
PO Box 4174
Pretoria 0001
Tel: (012) 342-5062
Fax: (012) 342-4752
E-mail: pretoria@dfa.ie

Israel (State of)
[Embassy]
PO Box 3726
Pretoria 0001
Tel: (012) 348-0470/470-3500
Fax: (012) 348-8594/0256
E-mail: operator@pretoria.mfa.gov.il

Italy (Republic of)
[Embassy]
796 George Avenue
Arcadia 0083
Tel: (012) 423-0000
Fax: (012) 430-5547
E-mail: ambital@iafrica.com

Ivory Coast (see: Côte d'Ivoire)

Japan
[Embassy]
Private Bag X999
Pretoria 0001
Tel: (012) 452-1500
Fax: (012) 460-3800/1
E-mail:
enquiries@embjapan.org.za

Jordan (Hashemite Kingdom of)
[Embassy]
Website: *www.embjord.co.za*
PO Box 14730
Hatfield 0028
Tel: (012) 342-8026/7
Fax: (012) 342-7847
E-mail: embjordpta@telkomsa.net

Kenya (Republic of)
[High Commission]
PO Box 35954
Menlo Park 0102
Tel: (012) 362-2249/50/1
Fax: (012) 362-2252
E-mail: kenrep@mweb.co.za

Korea (Democratic People's Republic)
[Embassy]
PO Box 1238
Garsfontein 0042
Tel: (012) 991-8661
Fax: (012) 991-8662
E-mail: dprkembassy@lantic.net

Korea (Republic of)
[Embassy]
PO Box 939
Groenkloof 0027
Tel: (012) 460-2508/9
Fax: (012) 460-1158
E-mail: korrsa@mweb.co.za

Kuwait (State of)
[Embassy]
Private Bag X920
Pretoria 0001
Tel: (012) 342-0877
Fax: (012) 342-0876
E-mail: safarku@global.co.za

Latvia (Republic of)
[Honorary Consulate]
24 Impala Rd
Chiselhurston
Sandton 2196
Tel: (011) 505-9100
Fax: (011) 505-9147
E-mail: neishlos@icon.co.za

Lebanon (Lebanese Republic of) [Embassy]
PO Box 941
Groenkloof 0027
Tel: (012) 346-7020
Fax: (012) 346-7022
E-mail: stelebsa@iafrica.com

Lesotho (Kingdom of)
[High Commission]
PO Box 55817
Arcadia 0007
Tel: (012) 460-7648
Fax: (012) 460-7649
E-mail:
lesothopretoria@metroweb.co.za

Liberia (Republic of)
[Embassy]
PO Box 14082
Hatfield 0028
Telefax: (012) 342-5671
E-mail: libempta@pta.lia.net

Libya (Socialist People's Libyan Arab Jamahiriya)
[Embassy]
PO Box 40388
Arcadia 0007
Tel: (012) 342-3902
Fax: (012) 342-3904
E-mail: libyansaf@yebo.co.za

Lithuania (Republic of)
[Honorary Consulate]
PO Box 1737
Houghton 2041
Tel: (011) 486-3660
Fax: (011) 486-3650
E-mail: heidi@garbjoffe.co.za

Luxembourg (Grand Duchy of)
[Honorary Consulate]
PO Box 78922
Sandton 2146
Tel: (011) 463-1744
Fax: (011) 463-3269
E-mail: motlana@iafrica.com

Madagascar (Republic of)
[Consulate-General]
PO Box 786098
Sandton 2146
Tel: (011) 442-3322
Fax: (011) 442-6660
E-mail: consul@infodoor.co.za

Malawi (Republic of)
[High Commission]
PO Box 11172
Hatfield 0028
Tel: (012) 342-0146/1759
Fax: (012) 342-0147
E-mail:
highcommalai@telkomsa.net

Malaysia
[High Commission]
PO Box 11673
Hatfield 0028
Tel: (012) 342-5990/3
Fax: (012) 430-7773
E-mail:
mwpretoria@ishoppe.co.za

Maldives (Republic of)
[Honorary Consulate]
PO Box 398
Plumstead 7801
Tel: (021) 761-5038/797-9940
Fax: (021) 761-5039

Mali (Republic of)
[Embassy]
PO Box12978
Hatfield 0028
Tel: (012) 342-7464/0676
Fax: (012) 342-0670
E-mail: malipta@iafrica.com

Malta (Republic of)
[Honorary Consulate]
PO Box 1351
Morningside 2057
Tel: (011) 706-3052
Fax: (011) 706-0301
E-mail:
maltaconsulate@intekom.co.za

Mauritius (Republic of)
[High Commission]
1163 Pretorius Street
Hatfield 0083
Tel: (012) 342-1283/4
Fax: (012) 342-1286
E-mail: mhcpta@mweb.co.za

Mexico (United Mexican State)
[Embassy]
PO Box 9077
Pretoria 0001
Tel: (012) 362-2822/9
Fax: (012) 362-1380
E-mail: embamexza@mweb.co.za

Monaco (Principality of)
[Honorary Consulate]
Unit No. 1 Milton's Way
11 Bell Crescent Close
Westlake Business Park,
Westlake, Cape Town 7945
Tel: (021) 702-0991
Fax: (021) 702-0993
E-mail: consulmonaco@telkomsa.net

Morocco (Kingdom of)
[Embassy]
PO Box 12382
Hatfield 0028
Tel: (012) 343-0230/49
Fax: (012) 342-0613
E-mail: sifmapre@telkomsa.net

Mozambique (Republic of)
[High Commission]
PO Box 40750
Arcadia 0007
Tel: (012) 401-0300
Fax: (012) 326-6388
E-mail: highcomm@iafrica.com

Myanmar (Union of)
[Embassy]
PO Box 12121
Queenswood 0121
Tel: (012) 341-2556/7
Fax: (012) 341-2553
E-mail: euompta@global.co.za

Namibia (Republic of)
[High Commission]
PO Box 29806
Sunnyside 0132
Tel: (012) 481-9100
Fax: (012) 343-7294
E-mail: secretary@namibia.org.za

Netherlands (Kingdom of the)
[Embassy]
PO Box 117
Pretoria 0001
Tel: (012) 425-4500
Fax: (012) 425-4511
E-mail: nlgovpre@cis.co.za

New Zealand
[High Commission]
Private Bag X17
Hatfield 0028
Tel: (012) 342-8656
Fax: (012) 342-8640
E-mail: nzhc@global.co.za

Nigeria (Federal Republic of)
[High Commission]
PO Box 27332
Sunnyside 0132
Tel: (012) 342-0642
Fax: (012) 342-0718
E-mail: nhcp@iafrica.com

Norway (Kingdom of)
[Royal Norwegian Embassy]
PO Box 11612
Hatfield 0028
Tel: (012) 342-6100
Fax: (012) 342-6099
E-mail: emb.pretoria@mfa.no

Oman (Sultanate of)
[Embassy]
PO Box 2650
Brooklyn 0075
Tel: (012) 346-4429
Fax: (012) 346-1660
E-mail: sult-oman@telkomsa.net

Pakistan (Islamic Republic of)
[High Commission]
PO Box 11803
Hatfield 0028
Tel: (012) 362-4073
Fax: (012) 362-3967

Palestine (State of)
[Embassy]
PO Box 56021
Arcadia 0007
Tel: (012) 342-6411
Fax: (012) 342-6412
E-mail: palembsa@intekom.co.za

Panama (Republic of)
[Honorary Consulate]
Old Mutual Centre
26th Floor, 303 West Street
Durban 4001
Tel: (031) 336-2682
Fax: (031) 336-2511
E-mail: ino644@aol.com

Paraguay (Republic of)
[Embassy]
189 Strelitzia Road
Waterkloof Heights 0181
Tel: (012) 347-1047/8
Fax: (012) 347-0403
E-mail: embapar@hotmail.com

Peru (Republic of)
[Embassy]
PO Box 907
Groenkloof 0027
Tel: (012) 346-8744/1
Fax: (012) 346-8886
E-mail: embaperu6@telkomsa.net

Philippines (Republic of the)
[Embassy]
PO Box 2562
Brooklyn 0075
Tel: (012) 346-0451/2
Fax: (012) 346-0454
E-mail:
101663.1537@compuserve.com

Poland (Republic of)
[Embassy]
PO Box 12277
Queenswood 0121
Tel: (012) 430-2631/2
Fax: (012) 430-2608
E-mail: amb.pol@pixie.co.za

Portugal (Republic of)
[Embassy]
PO Box 27102
Sunnyside 0132
Tel: (012) 341-2340/1/2
Fax: (012) 341-3975
E-mail: portemb@satis.co.za

Qatar (State of)
[Embassy]
Private Bag X13
Brooklyn Square 0075
Tel: (012) 452-1700
Fax: (012) 346-6732
E-mail: qatar-emb@lantic.net

Romania (Republic of)
[Embassy]
PO Box 11295
Hatfield 0028
Tel: (012) 460-6940
Fax: (012) 460-6947
E-mail: romembsa@global.co.za

Russian Federation (The)
[Embassy]
PO Box 6743
Pretoria 0001
Tel: (012) 362-1337/8
Fax: (012) 362-0116
E-mail: ruspospa@mweb.co.za

Rwanda (Republic of)
[Embassy]
PO Box 55224
Arcadia 0007
Tel: (012) 342-6536
Fax: (012) 342-7106
E-mail:
ambapretoria@minaffet.gov.rw

San Marino (Republic of)
[Honorary Consulate-General]
PO Box 2013
Brooklyn Square 0075
Telefax: (012) 460-5826

**Sao Tome & Principe
(Democratic Republic of)**
[Honorary Consulate]
PO Box 28
Franschoek 7690
Tel: (021) 876-2494
Fax: (021) 876-3237
E-mail: office@chamonix.co.za

**Saharawi (Arab Democratic
Republic of)**
[Embassy]
PO Box 11352
Hatfield
0028
Tel: (012) 342-5532
Fax: (012) 430-7428
E-mail: samoba19@yahoo.com

Saudi Arabia (Kingdom of)
[Embassy]
PO Box 13930
Hatfield 0028
Tel: (012) 362-4230
Fax: (012) 362-4239
E-mail: rosa@lantic.net

Senegal (Republic of)
[Embassy]
PO Box 2948
Brooklyn Square 0075
Tel: (012) 460-5263
Fax: (012) 346-5550
E-mail: rosenhos@mweb.co.za

Seychelles (Republic of)
[Consulate General]
PO Box 1548
Ferndale 2160
Tel: (011) 462-1607
Fax: (011) 462-1609

Singapore (Republic of)
[High Commission]
PO Box 11809
Hatfield 0028
Tel: (012) 430-6035
Fax: (012) 342-4425
E-mail: sporehc@cis.co.za

Slovakia (Slovak Republic of)
[Embassy]
PO Box 12736
Hatfield 0028
Tel: (012) 342-2051/2
Fax: (012) 342-3688
E-mail: slovakemb@telkomsa.net

Spain (Kingdom of)
[Embassy]
PO Box 1633
Pretoria 0001
Tel: (012) 344-3875/7
Fax: (012) 343-4891
E-mail: embespza@mail.mae.es

Sri Lanka (Democratic Socialist Republic of)
[High Commission]
410 Alexander Street
Brooklyn 0181
Tel: (012) 460-7690
Fax: (012) 460-7702
E-mail: srilanka@global.co.za

Sudan (Republic of)
[Embassy]
PO Box 25513
Monument Park 0105
Tel: (012) 342-4538
Fax: (012) 342-4539
E-mail: sudanrsa@pop.co.za

Swaziland (Kingdom of)
[High Commission]
PO Box 14294
Hatfield 0028
Tel: (012) 344-1910
Fax: (012) 343-0455
E-mail:
p.mswane@swazhighcom.co.za

Sweden (Kingdom of)
[Embassy]
PO Box 13477
Hatfield 0028
Tel: (012) 426-6400
Fax: (012) 426-6464
E-mail: sweden@iafrica.com

Switzerland (Swiss Confederation of)
[Embassy]
PO Box 2508
Brooklyn Square 0075
Tel: (012) 452-0660
Fax: (012) 346-6605
E-mail:
vertretung@pre.rep.admin.ch

Syrian Arab Republic
[Embassy]
PO Box 12830
Hatfield 0028
Tel: (012) 342-4701
Fax: (012) 342-4702
E-mail: syriaemb@telkomsa.net

Taipei
[Liaison Office in South Africa]
PO Box 649
Pretoria 0001
Tel: (012) 430-6071
Fax: (012) 430-5816
E-mail: taipeisa@telkomsa.net

Tanzania (United Republic of)
[High Commission]
PO Box 56572
Arcadia 0007
Tel: (012) 342-4393/71
Fax: (012) 430-4383
E-mail: tanzania@cis.co.za

Thailand (Kingdom of)
[Embassy]
PO Box 12080
Hatfield 0028
Tel: (012) 342-4600
Fax: (012) 342-4805
E-mail:
thailand@thaiembpta.co.za

Tunisia (Republic of)
[Embassy]
PO Box 56535
Arcadia 0007
Tel: (012) 342-6282/3
Fax: (012) 342-6284
E-mail: asdrubal@mweb.co.za

Turkey (Republic of)
[Embassy]
PO Box 56014
Arcadia 0007
Tel: (012) 342-6053/7
Fax: (012) 342-6052
E-mail: pretbe@global.co.za

Uganda (Republic of)
[High Commission]
PO Box 12442
Hatfield 0028
Tel: (012) 342-6031
Fax: (012) 342-6206
E-mail: ugacomer@mweb.co.za

Ukraine
[Embassy]
PO Box 36463
Menlo Park 0102
Tel: (012) 460-1946
Fax: (012) 460-1944
E-mail: dniepr@mweb.co.za

United Arab Emirates
[Embassy]
PO Box 57090
Arcadia 0007
Tel: (012) 342-7736
Fax: (012) 342-7738
E-mail: uae@mweb.co.za

United Kingdom of Great Britain and Northern Ireland
[Her Britannic Majesty's High Commission]
Website: *www.britain.org.za*
255 Hill Street
Arcadia 0083
Tel: (012) 421-7500
Fax: (012) 421-7555
E-mail: media.pretoria@fco.gov.uk

United Kingdom of Great Britain and Northern Ireland
[Her Britannic Majesty's High Commission]
– during parliamentary session
Website: *www.britain.org.za*
91 Parliament Street
Cape Town 8001
Tel: (021) 461-7220
Fax: (021) 461-0017
E-mail: britain@icon.co.za

United States of America
[Embassy]
Website: *www.usembassy.state. gov/southafrica*
PO Box 9536
Pretoria 0001
Tel: (012) 431-4000
Fax: (012) 342-2299

Uruguay (Oriental Republic of)
[Embassy]
PO Box 14818
Hatfield 0028
Tel: (012) 362-6521
Fax: (012) 362-6523
E-mail: urusud@pixie.co.za

Venezuela (Republic of)
[Embassy]
PO Box 11821
Hatfield 0028
Tel: (012) 362-6593
Fax: (012) 362-6591
E-mail: embasudaf@icon.co.za

Vietnam (Socialist Republic of)
[Embassy]
Website: *www.vietnam.co.za*
PO Box 13692
Hatfield 0028
Tel: (012) 362-8119
Fax: (012) 362-8115
E-mail: vnto@worldonline.co.za

Yemen (Republic of)
[Embassy]
PO Box 13343
Hatfield 0028
Tel: (012) 425-0760
Fax: (012) 425-0762
E-mail:
info@yemenembassy.org.za

Zambia (Republic of)
[High Commission]
PO Box 12234
Hatfield 0028
Tel: (012) 326-1854
Fax: (012) 326-2140
E-mail: zahpta@mweb.co.za

Zimbabwe (Republic of)
[High Commission]
PO Box 55140
Arcadia 0007
Tel: (012) 342-5125
Fax: (012) 342-5126
E-mail: zimpret@lantic.net

Representatives of the Republic of South Africa abroad

African Union and United Nations Economic Commission for Africa
[South African Mission]
PO Box 1091
Addis Ababa
Ethiopia
Tel: 0925 111 3713034
Fax: 0925111 371 1330
E-mail:
sa.embassy.addis@telecom.net.et

Algeria (Democratic People's Republic of)
[South African Embassy]
30 Rue Capitan Hocine Slimane
El Biar
Algiers 16000
Tel: 09 2132 123 0384
Fax: 09 213 2132 123 0827
E-mail: sae@medianet.dz

Angola (Republic of)
[South African Embassy]
Website: *www.sambangola.info*
Caixa Postal 6212
Luanda
Tel: 09 2442 22 33 0593/4189/ 9126
Fax: 09 2442 22 39 8730/ 09 2442 22 39 8725
E-mail:
saemb.ang@netangola.com

Argentina (Republic of)
[South African Embassy]
Website: *www.sudafrica.org.ar*
www.southafrica.org.ar
Avenida Marcelo T de Alvaear 590
C1058AAF
Buenos Aires 1050
Tel: 0954 11 4317 2900
Fax: 0954 11 4317 2951
E-mail: info@sudafrica.org.ar

Australia (Commonwealth of)
[South African High Commission]
Website: *www.rsa.emb.gov.au*
Rhodes Place State Circle
Yarralumla
Canberra ACT 2600
Tel: 0961 26273 2424/7
Fax: 0961 26273 3543
E-mail:
info@highcom@sahc.org.au

Austria (Republic of)
[South African Embassy]
Website: *www.saembvie.at*
Sandgasse 33
A-1190 Vienna
Tel: 09 431 320 6493
Fax: 09 431 320 649351
E-mail: ambassador@saembvie.at

Belgium (Kingdom of)
[South African Embassy]
Website: *www.southafrica.be*
Rue de la Loi b-7/8
Brussels 1040
Tel: 09 32 2285 4400
Fax: 09 32 2285 4402
E-mail: embassy@southafrica.be

Botswana (Republic of)
[South African High Commission]
Private Bag 00402
Gaborone
Tel: 09 267 390 4800/1/2
Fax: 09 267 390 5501
E-mail: sahcgabs@botsnet.bw

Brazil (Federative Republic of)
[South African Embassy]
Website:
www.africadosulemb.org.br
Avenida das Nacoes, Lote 6
Brasilia-CEP 70406-900
Tel: 09 55 6133 12 9500
Fax: 09 55 6133 22 8491
E-mail: saemb@solar.com.br

Bulgaria (Republic of)
[South African Embassy]
26 Bacho Kiro Street
2nd Floor
Sofia 1000
Tel: 09 359 2 981 6682
Fax: 09 359 2 981 5770
E-mail: saembsof@techno-
link.com

Burundi
[South African Liaison Office]
B.P. 185 Bujumbura
Burundi
Tel: 09 257 244 650
Fax: 09 257 987 779
E-mail: saebujfin@usan-bu.net

Cameroon (Republic of)
[South African High Commission]
Boite Postal 1636
Yaounde
Cameroon
Tel: 09 237 220 0438/9
Fax: 09 237 220 0995
E-mail: yaounde@foreign.gov.za

Canada
[South African High Commission]
Website: *www.southafrica-
canada.ca*
15 Sussex Drive
Ontario KIM 1M8
Ottawa
Tel: 091 613 744 0330
Fax: 091 613 741 1639
E-mail: rsafrica@southafrica-
canada.ca

Chile (Republic of)
[South African Embassy]
*Website: www.embajada-
sudafrica.cl*
Torre San Ramon Piso 6
Avenida 11 de Septiembre
2353
Santiago, Providencia
Tel: 0956 2 231 2860/3
Fax: 0956 2 231 3185
E-mail: embsachi@interaccess.cl

China (People's Republic of)
[South African Embassy]
5 Dongzhimenwai Dajie
Beijing 100600 PRC
Tel: 0986 10 6532 0171
Fax: 0986 10 6532 7139
E-mail: safrican@163bj.com

Comores (The Union of)
[South African High Commission]
Room 12 Itsandra Royal Hotel
Moroni
Tel: 09 269 321 947

Congo (Republic of)
[South African Embassy]
Le Meriden Hotel
Room 704
Brazzaville
Tel: 09 242 530 1388

Costa Rica (Republic of)
[South African Consulate-General]
PO Box 2816-1000
San Jose
Tel: 09 506 222 1470
Fax: 09 506 223 8223
E-mail: gicaltd@racsa.co.cr

Côte D'Ivoire (Republic of)
[South African Embassy]
Ambassade D'Afrique du Sud
08 BP 1806
Abidjan 08
Tel: 09 225 2244 5963
Fax:L 09 225 2244 7450
E-mail: ambafsudpol@aviso.ci

Croatia (Republic of)
[South African Honorary
Consulate]
Agrokor d.d Trg D. Petrovica 3
10 000 Zagreb
Croatia
Tel: 091 385 1 4894 111
Fax: 091 385 1 4844 363
E-mail: branko.milksa@agrokor.hr

Cuba (Republic of)
[South African Embassy]
Website: *www.sudafrica.cu*
Ave 5ta no 4201 esq 42 Miramar
Playa
Havanna
Tel: 09 53 7 204 9671/6
Fax: 09 53 7 204 1101
E-mail: rsacuba@cenial.inf.cu

Cyprus (Republic of)
[South African Honorary
Consulate-General]
PO Box 21312
Nicosia 1506
Tel: 09357 237 4411
Fax: 09357 237 7011

Czech Republic
[South African Embassy]
PO Box 133
100 00 Prague 10
Tel: 0942 26731 1114/26731
Fax: 0942 26731 1395
E-mail: saprague@terminal/.cz

Denmark (Kingdom of)
[South African Embassy]
Website: *www.southafrica.dk*
PO Box 128
DK-2900 Hellerup
Denmark
Tel: 0945 3918 0155
Fax: 0945 3918 4006
E-mail:
sa.embassy@southafrica.dk

**DRC (Democratic Republic of
the Congo)**
[South African Embassy]
Boite Postale 7829
Kinshasa
DRC
Tel: 09 243 88 48287
Fax: 09 243 880 4152
E-mail: ambasud@ckt.cd

Egypt (Arab Republic of)
[South African Embassy]
55 Road 18
Maadi
Cairo
Tel: 09202 359 4365/4950
Fax: 09202 359 5015
E-mail: saembcai@tedata.net.eg

Equatorial Guinea (Republic of)
[South African Embassy]
PO Box 5
Malabo
Tel: 09 240 207737
Fax: 09 240 092746
E-mail: malabo@foreign.gov.za

**Ethiopia (Federal Democratic
Republic of)**
[South African Embassy]
PO Box 1091
Addis Ababa
Ethiopia
Tel: 09 25 111 371 3034
Fax: 09 25 111 371 1330
E-mail:
sa.embassy.addis@telecom.net.et
econ.saemb@telecom.net.et

European Union
[South African Mission]
Website:
http://ambassade.net/southafrica/
index.html
26 Rue de la Loi B7/8
Brussels 1040
Tel: 0932 2285 4400
Fax: 0932 2285 4402
E-mail: embassy.southafrica@
belgium.online.be

Finland (Republic of)
[South African Embassy]
Website:
www.southafricanembassy.fi
Rahapajankatu 1A 5
00160 Helsinki
Tel: 09 358 9 6860 3100
Fax: 09 358 9 6860 3160
E-mail: saeinfo@welho.com

France (Republic of)
[South African Embassy]
Website: www.afriquesud.net
50 Quai d'Orsay
75343 Paris Cedex 07
Tel: 0933 15359 2323
Fax: 0933 15359 2333
E-mail: info@afriquesud.net

Gabon (Republic of)
[South African Embassy]
BP 4063
Libreville, Gabon
Tel: 09241 77 4530/1
Fax: 09241 77 4536
E-mail:
saegabon@internetgabon.com

Germany (Federal Republic of)
[South African Embassy]
Website: www.suedafrika.org
Tiergartenstrasse 18
10785 Berlin
Germany
Tel: 0949 30 220 730
Fax: 0949 30 220 73190
E-mail: botschaft@suedafrika.org

Ghana (Republic of)
[South African High Commission]
PO Box 298
Trade Fair, Accra
Ghana
Tel: 09 233 2176 2380/4480/
3880
Fax: 09 233 2176/2381
E-mail:
sahcgh@africaonline.com.gh

Greece (Hellenic Republic of)
[South African Embassy]
Website: www.southafrica.gr
PO Box 61152
GR 151-10
Athens
Tel: 0930 210 610 6645
Fax: 0930 210 610 6640
E-mail: embassy@southafrica.gr

Guatemala (Republic of)
[South African Honorary
Consulate]
10 A Avenida 30-57, Zona 5
Ciudad de Guatemala
Guatemala
Tel: 09 502 2332 6953/2385
0482
Fax: 09 502 2331 5734
E-mail: fmonterroso@ufm.edu.gt

Honduras (Republic of)
[South African Honorary
Consulate]
2 Ave. 12 Calle
Barrio Las Acacias, Casa 104
San Pedro Sula
Honduras
Tel: 09 504 552 4702
E-mail: bmemb@globalnet.hn

Hong Kong
[South African Consulate-General]
2706-10 Great Eagle Centre
23 Harbour Road
Wanchai
Hong Kong
Tel: 09852 2577 3279
Fax: 09852 2890 1975
E-mail: sacghgk@netvigator.com

Hungary (Republic of)
[South African Embassy]
Website: www.sa-embassy.hu
H-1026 Budapest
Gardonyi Geza ut 17
Hungary
Tel: 0936 1392 0999
Fax: 0936 1200 7277
E-mail: saemb@sa-embassy.hu

Iceland (Republic of)
[South African Honorary
Consulate-General]
Borgatun 35
105 Reykjavik, Iceland
Tel: 09354 591 0355
Fax: 09354 591 0358
E-mail: jr@fif.is

India (Republic of)
[South African High Commission]
Website: www.sahc-india.com
B18 Vasant Marg, Vasant Vihar
New Delhi 110 057
Tel: 099111 2 614 9411/19
Fax: 099111 2 614 3605
E-mail: highcommissioner@sahc-
india.com

Indonesia (Republic of)
[South African Embassy]
Website: www.saembassy-
jakarta.or.id
PO Box 1329
Jakarta
Indonesia
Tel: 0962 21 574 0660
Fax: 0962 21 574 0661
E-mail: saembassy@centrin.net.id

**International Monetary Fund
and World Bank – Washington
DC**
[South African Permanent
Mission]
Suite 380 3201
New Mexico Avenue NW
Washington DC 20016
Tel: 091 202 364 8320
Fax: 091 202 354 6008

Iran (Islamic Republic of)
[South African Embassy]
PO Box 11365-7476
Tehran
Iran
Tel: 0998 21270 2866/9
Fax: 0998 21271 9516
E-mail: saemb@neda.net

Ireland
[South African Embassy]
2nd Floor, Alexandra House
Earlsfort Centre, Earlsfort Terrace
Dublin 2
Tel: 09353 1661 5553
Fax: 09353 1661 5590
E-mail:
information@saedublin.com

Israel (State of)
[South African Embassy]
Website: www.safis.co.il
PO Box 7138
Tel Aviv 61071
Tel: 09972 3525 2566
Fax: 09972 3525 3230
E-mail: amb@saemb.org.il

Italy (Italian Republic)
[South African Embassy]
Website: *www.sudafrica.it*
Via Tanaro 14
Rome 0019
Tel: 0939 0685 2541
Fax: 0939 0685 254300/4301
E-mail: sae@flashnet.it

Jamaica
[South African High Commission]
15 Hillcrest Avenue
Kingston 6
Jamaica, WI
Tel: 09 876 978 3160/4457
Fax: 09 876 978 0339
E-mail: sahc@kasnet.com

Japan
[South African Embassy]
Website: *www.rsatk.com*
414 Zenkyoren Building
2-7-9 Hirakawa-cho
Chiyoda-ku
Tokyo
Tel: 0981 03 3265 2131
Fax: 0981 03 3261 6445
E-mail: visa@rsatk.com

Jordan (Hashemite Kingdom of)
[South African Embassy]
Website: *www.saembjor.com*
PO Box 851508
Sweifieh 11185
Jordan
Tel: 099626 592 1194
Fax: 099626 592 0080
E-mail: saembjor@index.com.jo

Kazakhstan (Republic of)
[South African Embassy]
48 A Ivanilov Street
Gorny Gigant Suburb
Almaty 050059
Kazakhstan
Tel: 09 7 3272 598 260/1
Fax: 09 7 3272 598 259
E-mail: almaty@foreign.gov.za

Kenya (Republic of)
[South African High Commission]
PO Box 42441
Nairobi
Kenya
Tel: 09254 20 282 7100
Fax: 09254 20 282 7236
E-mail: sahc@africaonline.co.ke

Korea (Republic of South)
[South African Embassy]
Website: *www.southafrica-embassy.or.kr*
1-37 Hannam-dong
Yongsan-gu
Seoul 140-885
Tel: 0982 2792 4855
Fax: 0982 2792 4856
E-mail: general@southafrica-embassy.or.kr

Kuwait (The State of)
[South African Embassy]
Website: *www.southafricaq8.com*
PO Box 2262
40173 Mishref
Kuwait
Tel: 09965 561 7988/8456
Fax: 09965 561 7917
E-mail:
saemb@southafricaq8.com

Lesotho (Kingdom of)
[South African High Commission]
Private Bag A266
Maseru 0100
Kingdom of Lesotho
Tel: 09266 2231 5758
Fax: 09266 2231 0128
E-mail: sahcmas@leo.co.ls

Libya (Great Socialist People's Libyan Arab Jamahiriya)
[South African Embassy]
PO Box 1230
Tripoli
Tel: 09218 21333 7006
Fax: 09218 21 334 0432
E-mail: satripoli@hotmail.com

Madagascar (Republic of)
[South African Embassy]
BP 12101-05
Zoom
101 Antananarivo
Tel: 09 261 20 224 3350
Fax: 09 261 20 224 3386
E-mail:
antananarivo@foreign.gov.za

Malawi (Republic of)
[South African High Commission]
PO Box 30043
Lilongwe 3
Tel: 09265 1773 722/597/036
Fax: 09265 1772 571
E-mail: sahc@malawi.net

Malaysia (Federation of)
[South African High Commission]
Suite 22,01 Level 22
No. 3 Jalan Kia Peng
50450 Kuala Lumpur
Tel: 09 603 2170 2412
Fax: 09 603 2164 3742
E-mail: azmansth@tim.net.my

Mali (Republic of)
[South African Embassy]
Website: *www.saemali.info*
Boite Postal 2015
Bamako
Mali
Tel: 09223 229 2925/27
Fax: 09223 229 2926
E-mail: bamako@foreign.gov.za

Mauritius (Republic of)
[South African High Commission]
PO Box 908
Port Louis
Tel: 09230 212 6925/6/8/9
Fax: 09230 212 6936/9346
E-mail: sahc@intnet.mu

Mexico (United Mexican States)
[South African Embassy]
Aportado Postal 105-219
Colonia Polanco
C.P 11560
Mexico DF
Tel: 09525 55282 9260/65
Fax: 09525 55282 9259
E-mail:
admin@embajadasudafrica.com.mx

Morocco (Kingdom of)
[South African Embassy]
34 Rue des Saadiens
Rabat
Tel: 09212 37 706760
Tel: 09212 37 724550
E-mail: sudaf@menara.ma

Mozambique (Republic of)
[South African High Commission]
Caixa Postal 1120
Maputo
Tel: 09258 2149 1614/0059
Fax: 09258 2149 3029/4402
E-mail:
sahc_admin@tropical.co.mz

Namibia (Republic of)
[South African High Commission]
PO Box 23100
Windhoek
Tel: 09264 61205 7111
Fax: 09264 6122 4140
E-mail: sahcwin@iafrica.com.na

Netherlands (Kingdom of the)
[South African Embassy]
Website: www.southafrica.nl
Wassenaarseweg 40
2596 CJ, The Hague
Tel: 0931 70 392 4501
Fax: 0931 70 346 0669
E-mail: info@zuidafrika.nl

Nigeria (Federal Republic of)
[South African High Commission]
71 Usuma Street
Maitama
Abuja
Tel: 09234 9413 3862/3246
Fax: 09234 9413 3829
E-mail: sahcniga@rosecom.net

Nigeria (Federal Republic of)
[South African High Commission]
10B Club Road
Ikoyi
Lagos
Tel: 09234 1 269 2709/3842
Fax: 09234 1 269 0448/1324
E-mail: sahc_abuja@yahoo.com

Norway (Kingdom of)
[South African Embassy]
Drammensveien 88 c
0271 Oslo
Tel: 0947 2327 3220
Fax: 0947 2244 3975
E-mail: info@saemboslo.no

Oman (Sultanate of)
[South African Embassy]
PO Box 231 PC 118
Al Harthy Complex
Muscat
Tel: 09 968 694 791
Fax: 09 968 694 792

Pakistan (Islamic Republic of)
[South African High Commission]
Website: www.southafrica.org.pk
48 Khayaban-e-Iqbal Sector
F-8/2, Islamabad
Tel: 09 9251 226 2354/5/6
Fax: 09 9251 225 0114
E-mail: xhosa@isb.comsats.net.pk

Palestine (State of)
[South African Representative
Office]
Website: www.sarep.org
PO Box 567
Ramallah
West Bank
Tel: 09 972 2298/7355/7929
Fax: 09 972 2298 7356
E-mail: info@sarep.org

Palestine (State of)
[South African Representative
Office]
PO Box 1258
Gaza City
Tel: 09 972 8284 1313/23
Fax: 09 972 8284 1333
E-mail: info@sarep.org

Peru (Republic of)
[South African Embassy]
PO Box 27-013
L27, Lima
Peru
Tel: 09511 440 9996
Fax: 09511 422 3881
E-mail: saemb@terra.com.pe

Peru (Republic of)
[South African Honorary
Consulate]
PO Box 27-013
L27, Lima, Peru
Tel: 09511 422 2280
Fax: 09511 442 7154

Philippines (Republic of the)
[South African Embassy]
29th Floor Yuchengco Tower
RCBC Plaza
Ayala Avenue
Makati City,
Metro Manila
Tel: 0963 2 889 9383
Fax: 0963 2 889 9337
E-mail: manila@foreign.gov.za

Poland (Republic of)
[South African Embassy]
IPC Business Centre
6th Floor U1
Koszykowa 54
Warsaw 00-675
Tel: 0948 22625 6228/6233
Fax: 0948 22625 6270/6284
E-mail:
saembassy@supermedia.pl

Portugal (Republic of)
[South African Embassy]
Website: www.embaixada-
africadosul.pt
Avenida Luis Bvar 10
1069-024 Lisbon
Tel: 09351 21 319 2200
Fax: 09351 21 353 5713
E-mail: embsa@embaixada-
africadosul.pt

Portugal (Republic of)
[South African Honorary
Consulate]
Av. da Voavusta 2674
4100-119 Porto
Tel: 09351 226 165 3330
Fax: 09351 226 165 339
E-mail: consulado@kqnet.pt

Portugal (Republic of)
[South African Honorary
Consulate]
Praca Antonio Nobre
9004-531 Funchal
Madeira
Tel: 09351 291 223 521
Fax: 09351 291 227 314

Qatar (State of)
[South African Embassy]
PO Box 24744
Doha
Tel: 09 974 485 7111
Fax: 09 974 483 5961
E-mail: saembdoha@qatar.net.qa

Russian Federation
[South African Embassy]
Website: www.saembassy.ru
Granatny Pereulok 1
Building 9
103102 Moscow
Tel: 097 095 540 1177
Fax: 097 095 540 1178
E-mail: southafrica@embassy-
moscow.ru

Rwanda (Republic of)
[South African Embassy]
Website: www.saembassy-
kigali.org.rw
PO Box 6563
Kacyiru-Sud
Kigali
Tel: 09 250 583 185/6/7/8
Fax: 09 250 511 578
E-mail: saemkgl@rwanda1.com

Saudi Arabia (Kingdom of)
[South African Embassy]
Website: *www.southafrica.com.sa*
PO Box 94006
Riyadh 11693
Tel: 09 966 1422 9716/19/20
Fax: 09 966 1422 9712
E-mail: embriyad@cyberia.net.sa

Saudi Arabia (Kingdom of)
[South African Consulate-General]
Website: *www.southafrica.com.sa*
PO Box 12737
Jeddah 21483
Tel: 09 9662 661 0452/0459
Fax: 09 9662 663 1034
E-mail: info@southafrica.com.sa

Senegal (Republic of)
[South African Embassy]
Website: *www.saesenegal.info*
PO Box 21010
Dakar-Ponty
Dakar
Tel: 09 221 865 1959
Fax: 09 221 864 2359
E-mail: ambafsud@sentoo.sn

Singapore (Republic of)
[South African High Commission]
Website:
http://web.singnet.com.sg
15th Floor Odeon Towers
331 North Bridge Road
Singapore 188720
Tel: 0965 6339 3319
Fax: 0965 6339 6658
E-mail: sinsahc@sahc.iep.net.sg

Slovak Republic
[South African Honorary
Consulate]
Revova 27
811 02 Bratislava
Slovak Republic
Tel: 09 421 2 544 17 841
Fax: 09 421 2 544 17 853

Spain (Kingdom of)
[South African Embassy]
Website: *www.sudafrica.com*
Edificio Lista
Calle de Claudio Coello 91-6
Cor of J Ortega Y Gasset
Madrid 28006
Tel: 0934 91436 3780
Fax: 0934 91577 7414
E-mail: embassy@sudafrica.com

Spain (Kingdom of)
[South African Honorary
Consulate-General]
c/o Albareda 54,2
35008 Las Palmas de G.C.
Canary Islands
Tel: 0934 928 265 452
Fax: 0934 928 224 975
E-mail: istier@idecnet.com

Spain (Kingdom of)
[South African Honorary
Consulate-General]
Las Mercedes No 31-4
48930 Las Arenas
Viscaya
Bilbao
Tel: 0934 94 464 1124
Fax: 0934 94 464 1124
E-mail: clerchundi@cgac.es

Spain (Kingdom of)
[South African Honorary
Consulate-General]
c/o Teodora Lamadrid 7-11
08022 Barcelona
Tel: 0934 93 418 6445
Fax: 0934 93 418 0538

Sudan (Republic of the)
[South African Embassy]
Grand Holidy Villa Hotel
Nile Road
Khartoum
Tel: 09 249 183 77 0055
Fax: 09 249 183 77 0115
E-mail: khartoum@foreign.gov.za

Swaziland (Kingdom of)
[South African High Commission]
PO Box 2507
Mbabane H100
Tel: 09268 404 4651/4
Fax: 09268 404 4335
E-mail: sahc@iafricaonline.co.sz

Sweden (Kingdom of)
[South African Embassy]
Website:
www.southafricanemb.se/
Linnegatan 76
115 23 Stockholm
Tel: 0946 824 3950
Fax: 0946 8660 7136
E-mail: saemb.swe@telia.com

**Switzerland (Swiss
Confederation)**
[South African Embassy]
Website: *www.southafrica.ch*
29 Alpenstrasse
3006 Berne 6
Tel: 0941 31 350 1313
Fax: 0941 31 350 1310/1311
E-mail:
ambassador@southafrica.ch

Syria (Arab Republic of)
[South African Embassy]
PO Box 33972
Damascus
Tel: 09 963 11 322 2650
Fax: 09 963 11 222 9200
E-mail: saembdam@scs-net.org

Taiwan
[Liaison Office of South Africa]
PO Box 18-140
Taipei
Tel: 09886 22715 3251/4
Fax: 09886 22712 5109
E-mail: saemail@gcn.net.tw

Tanzania (United Republic of)
[South African High Commission]
PO Box 10723 Msaki
Dar-es-Salaam
Tel: 092 5522 260 1800
Fax: 092 5522 260 0684
E-mail: highcomm@sah-tz.com

Thailand (Kingdom of)
[South African Embassy]
6th Floor
The Park Place Building
231 Soi Sarasin
Lumpini
Bangkok 10330
Tel: 0966 2253 8473/4/5/6
Fax: 0966 2253 8477
E-mail: saembbkk@loxinfo.co.th

Thailand (Kingdom of)
[South African Honorary
Consulate]
32 Hueaykeaw Road
Tambon Changpuek
Amphur Muang
Chiang Mai 50300
Tel: 0966 53 711 800
Fax: 0966 53 712 972
E-mail: sawaeng@loxinfo.co.th

Tunisia (Republic of)
[South African Embassy]
Website: *www.southafrica.intl.tn*
7 Rue Achtart
Nord-Hilton
Tunis
Tel: 09216 7179 8449
Fax: 09216 7180 1918/1170
E-mail: sa@emb-safrica.intl.tn

Turkey (Republic of)
[South African Embassy]
Website: *www.southafrica.org.tr*
PO Box 30
Kucukesat
06662 Ankara
Tel: 0990 312 446 4056
Fax: 0990 313 446 6434
E-mail: saemb@ada.net.tr

Turkey (Republic of)
[South African Honorary
Consulate]
Alarko Holding Building
Muallim Naci Cad. 113-115
Ortakoy
Istanbul
Tel: 0990 212 227 5200
Fax: 0990 212 260 2378

Turkey (Republic of)
[South African Honorary
Consulate-General]
Ocartur Tourism and Travel
Agency
Ataturk Cad
A-Blok, No 82
Mersin 33010
Tel: 0990 324 237 1075
Fax: 0990 324 237 1079
E-mail:
sa.consulate@olcartour.com

Turkey (Republic of)
[South African Honorary
Consulate-General]
Ataturk Organize Sanayi
Bolgesi
10008 Sokak No 1
35620 Cigli, Izmir
Tel: 0990 232 376 8445
Fax: 0990 232 376 7942
E-mail:
tamertaskin@petrofer.com.tr

Uganda (Republic of)
[South African High Commission]
PO Box 22667
Kampala
Tel: 09256 4134 3543/4/5
Fax: 09256 4134 8216
E-mail: sahc@utlonline.co.ug

Ukraine
[South African Embassy]
PO Box 7
Central Post Office
22 Kreschchatik Street
01001 Kyiv
Tel: 0938044 227
7172/4451/34789
Fax: 0938 044 220 7206
E-mail: saemb@utel.net.ua

Ukraine
[South African Honorary
Consulate]
2 Marazlievskaya Street
App.8, Odessa
Tel: 09380 48 224 2059
E-mail:
saconsulate@blacksea.net.ua

United Arab Emirates
[South African Embassy]
Website: *www.southafrica.ae*
PO Box 29446
Abu Dhabi
Tel: 099712 633 7565
Fax: 099712 633 3909
E-mail: saemb@emirates.net.ae

United Arab Emirates
[South African Consulate-General]
Website: *www.southafrica.co.ae*
PO Box 3488, Dubai
Tel: 0997 14397 5222
Fax: 0997 14397 9602
E-mail: sacons@emirates.net.ae

**United Kingdom of Great Britain
and Northern Ireland**
[South African High Commission]
Website:
www.southafricahouse.com
South Africa House
Trafalgar Square
London WC2N 5DP
Tel: 0944 207 451 7299
Fax: 0944 207 451 7284
E-mail:
general@southafricahouse.com

United Nations – New York
[South African Permanent
Mission]
333 East 38th Street
9th Floor, New York
NY 10016
Tel: 091212 213 5583
Fax: 091212 692 2498
E-mail: soafun@worldnet.att.net

United Nations – Geneva
[South African Permanent
Mission]
65 Rue du Rhone
Geneva 1204
Tel: 0941 22 849 5454
Fax: 0941 22 849 5432
E-mail: mission@south-
africa@ties.itu.int

**United Nations (International
Atomic Energy Agency)**
[South African Permanent
Mission]
Sandgasse 33
Vienna, A-1190
Tel: 0943 222 320 6493
Fax: 0943 222 320 7584

United States of America
[South African Embassy]
Website: *www.saembassy.org/*
3051 Massachusetts Avenue NW
Washington DC 20008
Tel: 091 202 232 4400
Fax: 091 202 265 1607
E-mail: info@saembassy.org

United States of America
[South African Consulate-General]
Website: *www.southafrica-
newyork.net*
333 East 38th Street
9th Floor, New York
NY 10016
Tel: 091 212 213 4880
Fax: 091 212 883 0653
E-mail:sacg@southafrica-
newyork.net

United States of America
[South African Consulate-General]
200 South Michigan Avenue
6th Floor
Chicago IL 60604
Tel: 091 312 939 7929
Fax: 091 312 939 2588
E-mail:
sacongenchicago@worldnet.att.net

United States of America
[South African Consulate-General]
Website:
www.link2southafrica.com
Suite 600,
6300 Wilshire Boulevard
Los Angeles
California 90048
Tel: 091 323 651 0902
Fax: 091 323 651 5969
E-mail: sacgla@link2sa.com

United States of America
[South African Honorary
Consulate]
2308 First National Bank Building
Mobile
Alabama 36602
Tel: 091 205 438 2145

United States of America
[South African Honorary
Consulate]
2272 Ridgewood Way
Bountiful
Salt Lake City
Utah 84010
Tel: 091 801 266 7867

Uruguay (Oriental Republic of)
[South African Embassy]
PO Box 498
Montevideo 11000
Tel: 09598 2623 0161
Fax: 09598 2623 0066
E-mail: safem@netgate.com.uy

Uzbekistan (Republic of)
[South African Embassy]
30-A Asaka Street
Taskent
Tel: 0999 871 137 0170/1
Fax: 0999 871 137 2546
E-mail: mtimcke@bbc.com.uz

**Venezuela (Bolivarian Republic
of)** [South African Embassy]
PO Box 2613 Carmelitas
1010 Caracas
Tel: 0958 212 991
4622/6822/0412
Fax: 0958 2991 5555
E-mail: rsaven@ifxnw.com.ve

Vietnam
[South African Embassy]
Central Building 3F
31 Hai Ba Trung Street
Hanoi

Tel: 0984 4936 2000/1/2/3
Fax: 0984 4936/1991
E-mail: hanoi@foreign.gov.za

Yemen (Republic of)
[South African Honorary
Consulate]
PO Box 353
Sana'a
Tel: 0967 122 4051
Fax: 0967 122 1611
E-mail: zubieri@ynet.ye

Zambia (Republic of)
[South African High Commission]
Private Bag W369
Lusaka
Tel: 09260 126 0999
Fax: 09260 126 3001
E-mail: sahc@zamnet.zm

Zimbabwe (Republic of)
[South African High Commission]
PO Box A1654
Avondale
Harare
Tel: 09263 475 3147/8/9
Fax: 09263 475 9657
E-mail: sahcomm@ecoweb.co.za

Legislation

2005 (as at 15 November 2005)

Defence Special Account Amendment Act, 2005 (Act 18 of 2005)
South African Abattoir Corporation Act Repeal Act, 2005 (Act 17 of 2005)
Constitutional Matters Amendment Act, 2005 (Act 15 of 2005)
Co-operatives Act, 2005 (Act 14 of 2005)
Intergovernmental Relations Framework Act, 2005 (Act 13 of 2005)
National Ports Act, 2005 (Act 12 of 2005)
Minerals and Energy Laws Amendment Act, 2005 (Act 11 of 2005)
Taxation Laws Second Amendment Act, 2005 (Act 10 of 2005)
Taxation Laws Amendment Act, 2005 (Act 9 of 2005)
South African Sports Commission Act Repeal Act, 2005 (Act 8 of 2005)
Sectional Titles Amendment Act, 2005 (Act 7 of 2005)
Re-determination of the Boundaries of Cross-boundary Municipalities Act, 2005 (Act 6 of 2005)
Citation of Constitutional Laws Act, 2005 (Act 5 of 2005)
Appropriation Act, 2005 (Act 4 of 2005)
Sterilisation Amendment Act, 2005 (Act 3 of 2005)
Petroleum Products Amendment Act, 2005 (Act 2 of 2005)
Division of Revenue Act, 2005 (Act 1 of 2005)

Index

Blyderiviersrspoort Nature Reserve
595
Boer goat farming 83
Bohlabela district, Limpopo 593
Boksburg 20
Bond Exchange of South Africa
(BESA) 301-302
Bonnievale 581
Bontebok National Park 242, 584
Bophirima district, North West 594
Borakalalo Game Reserve 593
Bosbult Monument 593
botanical gardens 246-247
Botanical Society Conservatory
246
Botanical Society of South Africa
265
Bothaville 589
Botsalano Game Reserve 593
Botshabelo 588
Botshabelo Historical Village,
Middelburg 595
Botswana
co-operation, water 646
foreign relations with 310
national parks 243
boxing, highlights of 2005 561-
562
Boxing South Africa 560
Brakpan 20
Brandvlei 587
Dam 635
River 635
Brazil, relations with 326
Bredasdorp 11, 584
Breede River Valley region 580
breeding centres 248-249
Bridges to the Future Initiative (BFI)
223
British colonial period 32-34
Brits 19
Broad-Based BEE
see BBBEE
broadcasting 146-149
commercial radio stations 147-
148
community radio stations 148
control 146
editorial policy 146
languages 146
Low Power Sound Broadcasting
Licences 148
policy and legislation 146

radio 147
role-players 147-149
Satellite Communications
Network 148
South African content 146
television 148-149
Broadcasting Act, 1999 (Act 4 of
1999) 146, 148
Broadcasting Amendment Act,
2002 (Act 64 of 2002) 146
Broadcasting Complaints
Commission of South Africa 157
Broadcasting Monitoring
Complaints Committee (BMCC)
157-158
Bronkhorstspruit 20
Buddyz on the Move (BoMO) 386
budget highlights, 2005/2006
270-271
Budget Council 278
Building for Sport and Recreation
Project (BSRP) 556, 557
Bulgaria, relations with 333
Bureau of Heraldry 129
Burger, Die
circulation figures, Jul-Dec 2004
155
contact information 155
Burgersdorp 591
Burkina Faso, foreign relations with
320
Burundi
foreign relations with 316
peace support by SANDF 501
Bushbuck Ridge 592
Bushmen
see San people
Bushveld Complex 461, 479
Business Arts South Africa (BASA)
113-114
Business Day 150, 151
circulation figures, Jul-Dec 2004
155
contact information 155
business confidence, 2005 170
Business Confidence Index
(SACOB) 2005 170
Business Development Unit
agriculture 90
Business Partners Ltd 190
Business Trust of South Africa 194
bus transport 613-614
Buyisa-e-Bag 259

C

cabbages production 81
Cabinet 343-345
as on 1 October 2005 345
committees 52
cadastral surveys 99-100
Chief Directorate: Cadastral
Surveys 99
Cairns Group 183, 326
Caledon 585
onions production 81
Calitzdorp 579
Call of South Africa
see national anthem
Calvinia
Abraham Esau Hospital 385
Camden power station 463
Camperdown 81
Canada, foreign relations with
329-330
Canal Walk Century City 578
Cancer Association of South Africa
549
Cango Caves 10, 579
canned hunting 263
Cape Action Plan for People and
the Environment Project 246-
247
Cape Agulhas 584
Cape Argus, The
circulation figures, Jul-Dec 2004
155
contact information 155
Cape Craft and Design Institute
122
Cape Floral Kingdom 10, 244, 247
Cape Floristic Region World
Heritage Site 10
Cape Metropole, Western Cape
tourist attractions 577-578
Cape Metropolitan Area
tourist attractions 577-578
Cape Peninsula 480, 648
Cape Peninsula National Park 242
see also Table Mountain National
Park (TMNP)
Cape Peninsula University of
Technology 10, 222, 629-630
Cape Philharmonic Orchestra 113
Cape Point 577

King William's Town 12, 591
Kirstenbosch National Botanical
    Garden, Cape Town 10, 246
Kirstenbosch Research Centre
    246, 247
Klawer 583
Klein Karoo Nasionale Kunstefees,
    Oudtshoorn 117, 579
Kleinmond 584
Kleinmond Coastal Nature Reserve
    584
Kleinplasie Open Air Museum 128,
    581
Klerksdorp 19, 594
Kliptown 19
Kloofendal Amphitheatre 596
Kloofendal Nature Reserve 596
Knowledge Management (KM)
    HSRC research programme 530
Knysna National Lakes Area 10,
    242, 244
    tourist attractions 579
Koffiefontein 588
Kogelberg Biosphere Reserve 243,
    584
Koeberg Nuclear Power Station
    465
Koekenaap 583
Kokstad 599
Komati Power Station 463
Kosi Bay Lake System 245
Koringberg 582
Kortkloof Cultural Village 593
Kosi Bay 14
Kosi Bay Lakes 14
Kosi Bay Nature Reserve 600
Kromdraal hominid site 20, 244
Kruger Mpumalanga International
    Airport 22
Kruger National Park 24, 25, 241,
    243, 575, 592
    bird species 238
    savanna biome 237
    signing of memorandum of
    understanding (MoU) 242
    tourist attractions 592, 593
Kruger, Pres Paul 35, 598
Kruger House Museum, Pretoria
    126, 128, 598
Krugersdorp 20, 596
Krugersdorp Game Reserve 596
Kruger-to-Canyons Biosphere
    Reserve 244

Kuruman 15, 585
KwaZulu-Natal 13-15
    agriculture 14-15, 78-81, 83
    Blue Flag beaches 256
    coastline 13
    communications 137
    conservation activities 14
    Cultural Museum 600
    drought relief 85
    Durban Institute of Technology 14
    fishing 253
    forests 14, 651
    game farming 84
    GDPR 14
    industry 14-15
    KwaZulu-Natal Botanical Garden,
    Pietermaritzburg 246
    Kyoto Protocol 257, 263-264
    languages 14
    Midlands region 15
    museums 600, 601
    people/population 2, 14
    Philharmonic Orchestra 113
    provincial government as on 15
    Sep 2005 347
    tourist attractions 598-602
    unemployment 14
    UNFPA Second Country Support
    Programme for South Africa 552
    University of KwaZulu-Natal 14,
    222
Kyalami 596

L

labour legislation 62
Labour Court 420
labour relations 199-201
    Directorate: Collective Bargaining
    201
    Directorate: Employment
    Standards 199-200
    registration of 201
Labour Relations Act, 1995 (Act
    66 of 1995) 199, 201, 449
Ladismith/Ladysmith 14, 35
    tourist attractions 602
Ladybrand 17, 589
L'Agulhas 584
Lake Chrissie 23, 596
Lake Sibaya 245, 600
Lambert's Bay 257, 583
    see also Bird Island Group

La Mercy 15
land, asset poverty alleviation 56
land affairs
    see Department of Land Affairs
Land and Agricultural Development
    Bank of South Africa
    see Land Bank
Land and Agricultural Development
    Bank Act, 2002 (Act 15 of
    2002) 92, 291
land and its people 2-25
    land 7-9
    people 2-7
    provinces 9-25
Land and Tenure Reform
    Programme
Land Bank 291-292
LandCare Programme 74, 90-92,
    653
Land Claims Court 420
land redistribution
    claims as at June 2005 56, 103
    Extension of Tenure Programme
    56
    Land Reform for Agricultural
    Development programme 56
    rural claims 103
    urban claims 103
Land Redistribution for Agricultural
    Development (LRAD) 92
land reform 102-103
    Chief Directorate: Land Reform
    Implementation Management
    and Co-ordination 102
    Chief Directorate: Land-Reform
    Systems and Support Services
    102
Land Reform Empowerment
    Facility (LREF) 102
Land Reform for Agricultural
    Development programme 56
Langebaan 245, 582
Langebaan Lagoon 582
Langkloof 12
Langkloof Valley 12, 579
languages 2-5
    according to Census 2001 3
    indigenous 3, 4
    national language bodies 5
    national lexicography units 4
    official 3
    policy 3
    rights, protection of 2-3

communications 137
hospitals 385
manufacturing 19
mining 18-19
people/population 18, 19
provincial government as on 15
  Sep 2005 348
reserves 18
statistics 19
tourist attractions 593, 594
unemployment 18
universities 221-222
North West University 221-222
Nourivier 586
Ntshingwayo Dam 635
Ntsika Enterprise Promotion
  Agency 62, 63
Nuclear Energy Act, 1999 (Act 46
  of 1999) 465-466
Nuclear Energy Corporation of
  South Africa 515
Nuclear Fuels Corporation
  (NUFCOR) 460
nuclear power 465-466
nurses 384
  see also health personnel/teams
  registered and enrolled, 2003-
  2004 385
  statistics per province, 2004 384
Nursing Bill 380
Nursing Council
  see South African Nursing Council
  (SANC)
Nutrition Society of South Africa
  398
Nuwejaarspruit Vaal Dam 635
Nylsvlei Nature Reserve 246, 592
Nylsvlei Ramsar Site 243
Nylstroom
  see Modimolle

O

Occupational Diseases in Mines
  and Works Act, 1973 (Act 78 of
  1973) 397
Occupational Diseases in Mines
  and Works Act, 1993 (Act 208
  of 1993) 198
occupational health 397
occupational health and safety
  (OHS) 198-199
Occupational Health and Safety

Act, 1993 (Act 181 of 1993)
  397
Occupational Health and Safety
  Act, 1993 (Act 85 of 1993) 198
Occupational Injuries and Diseases
  Act, 1993 (Act 130 of 1993)
  198, 199
Occupational Injuries and Diseases
  Amendment Act, 1997 (Act 61
  of 1997) 199
oceans 8
  World Oceans Day 233
ocean energy 476-477
Office of the Family Advocate 435
official languages
  see languages
Okavango Upper Zambezi
  International Tourism SDI 572
Old-Age Grants 543
Old-Age Pension Grants 543
Older Persons Bill 541
Olifants River 635
Olifants River Valley 583
Olifants River Water Resources
  Development Project 645
Omnibus Outreach Programme
  437
Onderstepoort Biological Products
  (OBP) 85
Onderstepoort Veterinary Institute
  21, 95
onions production /industry 81
Oostenberg 578
open-air museums 128
Operation Isidima 542
Operation Rachel 65
OPM Prozesky Bird Sanctuary,
  Potchefstroom 594
oral health professionals 383
Oral History Project 129
Orange River 8, 15, 16, 586, 635
Orange River Mouth Wetland 245
Orange River Valley 9, 16, 238,
  583
Orange River Water Scheme 588
Orange River Wine Cellar Co-op
  586
Order of Baobab 109-110
Order of Companions of OR
  Thambo 109-110
Order of Ikhamanga 109-110, 559
Order of Luthuli 109-110
Order of Mapungubwe 109-110

Order of the Mendi Decoration for
  Bravery 109-110
Orex 620-621
Organisation for African Unity
  (OAU) 69
organised crime 66
  see also corruption
  statistics 66
Organised Local Government Act,
  1997 (Act 52 of 1997) 348
Oribi Gorge Nature Reserve 601
Orkney 594
ornamental plants production 82
ostrich farming/industry 10, 11,
  13, 84
  gross value 84
Otter Trail 592
Oudtshoorn 10, 11, 579
  Cango Caves 10
  lucerne seed production 78
Outcomes-Based Education 214,
  229
Outeniqua Choo-Tjoe 578
Outeniqua Pass 578
Overberg, Western Cape
  tourist attractions 584-585
ozone-depleting substances
  (ODSs) 264-265

P

Paarl 581
Paarl Post 151
Pacific islands, relations with 327
paddling, highlights of 2005 564
Paddock 600
Pakistan, relations with 325
Pan-Africanist Congress (PAC) 355
  history 40
Pan-African Parliament (PAP) 44,
  69, 271, 306-307
Pan-African Postal Union (PAPU)
  145
Panorama, Mpumalanga 594-595
Pan South African Language Board
  (PanSALB) 4, 5, 108, 123, 219
Pan South African Language Board
  (PanSALB) Act, 1995 (Act 59 of
  1995) 4
Pan South African Language Board
  (PanSALB) Amendment Act
  1999 (Act 10 of 1999) 4
Parliament 343

SA-EU Trade, Development and
Co-operation Agreement (SA-EU
TDCA) 69, 96
SAFCOL
  see South African Forestry
  Company Limited
safety, security and defence 484-
508
  armaments 503-506
  defence 493-502
  intelligence services 506-508
  safety and security 484-486
  South African Police Service 486-
  493
Safety in Mines Research Advisory
  Committee 459
SA Host 571
Sahrawi Arab Democratic Republic
  (SADR), foreign relations with
  319
Saldanha 582-583
Saldanha Bay
  fishing 255
  mussel-farming 84
  port/harbour 9, 10, 625, 627
Saldanha IDZ 185
Saldanha Steel Project 11
Salt Rock 595, 600
Sammy Marks Museum, Pretoria
  126, 128, 598
Samora Machel Project 115
San people
  language protection 4, 5, 219
  rock engravings 16, 17, 121,
  585, 589, 601
Sani Pass 601
sanitation 59
  see also water
  asset poverty alleviation 56
  basic infrastructure, as at March
  2005 56
  backlog 56
SanParks TFCAs 244
Sao Tome and Principe, foreign
  relations with 317
SAPS Victim Empowerment
  Programme (VEP)
  see Victim Empowerment
  Programme
Sasol 466, 534
Sasolburg 589
Sasol Slurry Phase Distillate
  Process 466

satellite broadcasting 149
Satellite Communications Network
  148
Saturday courts 66-67
Saturday Dispatch 150
  circulation figures, Jul-Dec 2004
  156
  contact information 156
Saturday Star, The
  circulation figures, Jul-Dec 2004
  156
  contact information 156
Savanna biome 23, 24, 236-237
Save the Children Fund 547
Scarce Skills Development Fund
  521
Scaw Metals Group 391
Schoemanskloof 595
school admission policy 218
school fees 216-217
School Register of Needs 59, 225-
  226
schools 225-226
Science and Technology
  see also Department of Science
  and Technology
  international co-operation 517
  internationalisation 520
  knowledge management 520
  policy and funding 512-517
  private sector involvement 537-
  538
  research areas 535-537
  research organisations 534-535
  science councils 518-533
  student support 519-520
Science and Technology
  Agreements Committee (STAC)
  Fund 520-521
Scottburgh 601
Second Decade of Freedom 45
  challenges and opportunities 72
Second National Operator (SNO)
  137
Second Revenue Laws
  Amendment Act, 2004 (Act 34
  of 2004) 273
Second Revenue Laws
  Amendment Bill 273
Secretariat for Safety and Security
  484, 485

Sector Education and Training
  Authorities (SETAs) 195-197,
  226
  Co-ordination Programme 196-
  197
  Co-ordination Programme
  Performance Management 197
sector policing 491
Secunda 23
Securities Services Act, 2004 (Act
  36 of 2004) 273, 276, 287,
  302
Sedgefield 579
Seekoeivlei 245
Seekoeivlei Nature Reserve 589
segregation 37-38
Senegal, foreign relations with
  321-322
Sentech 136
  signal distribution 149-150
SepCo 137
Servcon Housing Solutions 410,
  411
Sesotho, official language 3, 4
Sesotho sa Leboa 3, 4
Setlogelo Dam 588
Setswana, official language 3, 4
Sexual Assault Policy and Clinical
  Management Guidelines 395
sexual offences 65
  courts 65
  legislation 65
  Thuthuzela care centres 65
Sexual Offences Amendment Bill
  65
Sexual Offences and Community
  Affairs Unit 550
Shaka's Rock 600
Sharpeville anti-pass
  demonstration, 1960
Shelly Beach 601
sheep-farming 83
shipping, marine pollution 260
Shosholoza Meyl 621
Sho't Left Campaign 571-572
Sierra Leone, relations with 322
signal distribution 149-150
sign language 4, 5
silicosis
  Compensation Fund 199
  elimination of 198-199
  National Programme for the
  Elimination of Silicosis 198-199

White River 594
Wild Coast, Eastern Cape 12
    SDI 13, 185
    tourist attractions 590, 601
Wilderness 579
Wilderness National Park 242, 579
Wilderness Lakes 245, 579
Wild Frontier, Mpumalanga 596
Wildlife and Environment Society
    265
Willem Prinsloo Agricultural
    Museum, Pretoria 126, 128,
    598
William Fehr Collection 127
William Humphreys Art Gallery,
    Kimberley 126, 127
Wills Act, 1953 (Act 7 of 1953)
Winburg 589
wind energy 475-476
Windybrow Theatre, Johannesburg
    113
Winelands region 10
Wine and Spirits Agreement 80
wine and spirits
    production/industry 11, 80
Witbank 22
Witness, The 151
    circulation figures, Jul-Dec 2004
    155
    contact information 155
Witness Protection Programme
    427
Witness Protection Programme
    Act, 1998 (Act 112 of 1998)
    427
Witsand 578
Witsand Nature Reserve 586
Witwatersrand
    geology of 480-481
Witwatersrand National Botanical
    Garden, Roodepoort/Mogale City
    246
women
    economic empowerment 63,
    547-548

entrepreneurs 189
    magazines 152-153
    researchers 513
    SAPS Women's Network 492
    social services 548-549
    Subdirectorate: Women's Health
    393
    violence against 395
    Women in Science Awards 518
Women's Monument Project,
    Pretoria 115
Wonderdraai 587
Wonderwerk Cave, Kuruman, rock
    art 121, 586
woodlands 651
Woody Cape Nature Reserve 242
Worcester 10
Working for Water Programme
    (WfW Programme) 643-644
Working for Wetlands Programme
    245, 247
Worcester 81
Workplace Challenge Programme
    186
World Anti-Doping Agency (WADA)
    561
World Economic Forum (WEF) 183
World Fund for Nature South Africa
    265
World Heritage Convention 244
World Heritage Convention Act,
    1999 (Act 49 of 1999) 234,
    244
World Heritage Sites 10, 14, 20,
    24, 244, 245
World Summit on Sustainable
    Development (WSSD) 234-236
World Trade Organisation (WTO)
    176, 182-183
    Agreement on Sanitary and
    Phytosanitary Measures (WTO-
    SPS) 88
    Doha Round participation 61, 69,
    182-183

Worldwide Fund for Nature South
    Africa 265
Woza Campaign 572
Wupperthal 583
WWF South Africa

X

Xhariep, Free State 588
Xitsonga, official language 3, 4

Y

yachting, highlights in 2005 565
Young Champions Project 558
youth
    see also children, juveniles
    abuse/neglect 548
    magazines 153
    protection against crime 547-
    548
    protection of rights 547-548
    social services 547-548
Youth Best Practice Treatment
    Model 551
Yzerfontein 582

Z

Zastron 589
Zambia, foreign relations with
    312-313
Zimbabwe
    co-operation, water 646
    foreign relations with 312-313
Zion Christian Church (ZCC) 6,
    592
zirconium 461
Zoar 579
zoological gardens 247-248
Zululand, KwaZulu-Natal
    tourist attractions 599-600
    University of Zululand 221
Zulu villages 600